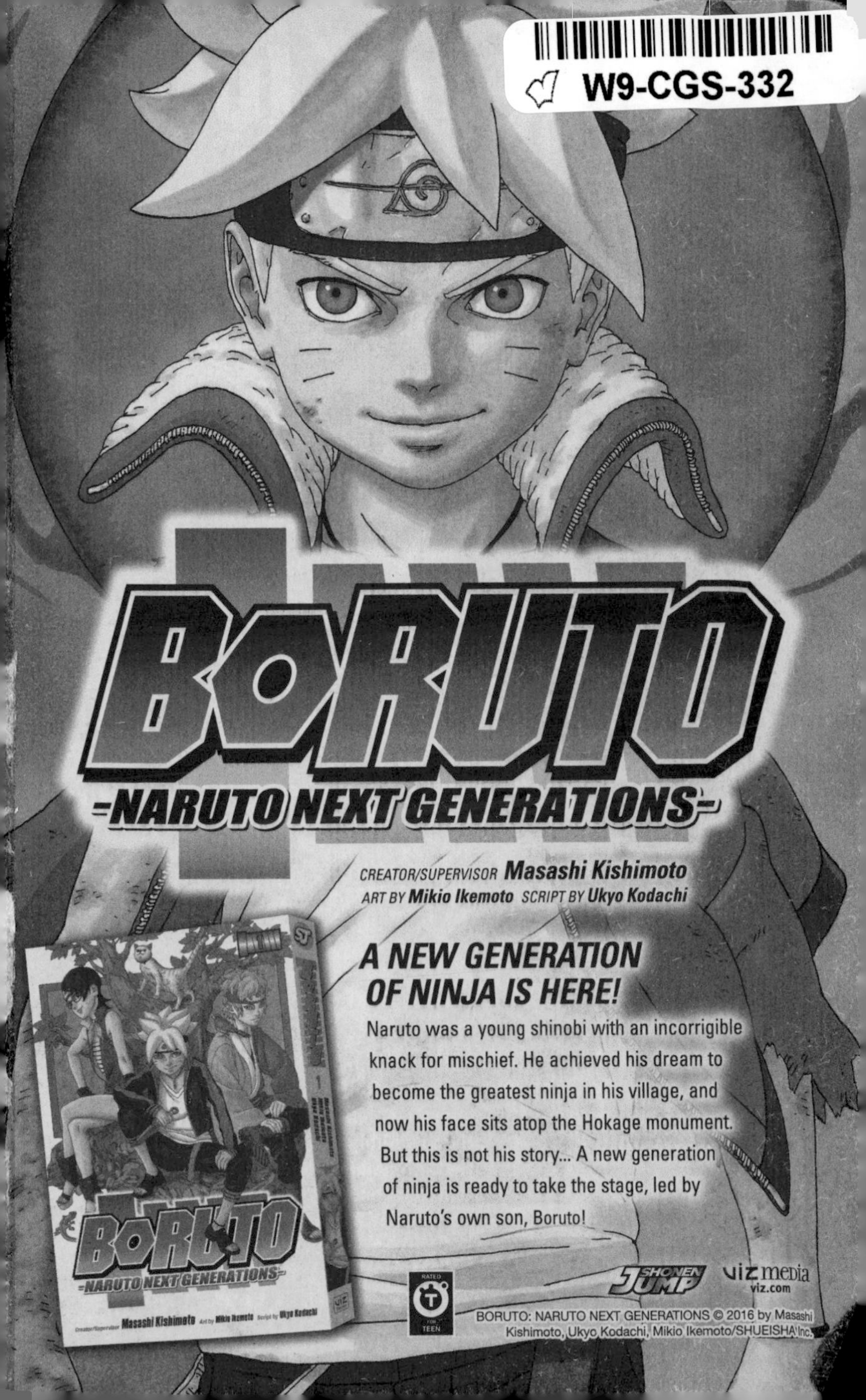
W9-CGS-332
BORUTO
-NARUTO NEXT GENERATIONS-
CREATOR/SUPERVISOR Masashi Kishimoto
ART BY Mikio Ikemoto SCRIPT BY Ukyo Kodachi
A NEW GENERATION OF NINJA IS HERE!
Naruto was a young shinobi with an incorrigible knack for mischief. He achieved his dream to become the greatest ninja in his village, and now his face sits atop the Hokage monument. But this is not his story... A new generation of ninja is ready to take the stage, led by Naruto's own son, Boruto!
BORUTO
-NARUTO NEXT GENERATIONS-
Masashi Kishimoto
RATED T TEEN
SHONEN JUMP
VIZ media
viz.com
BORUTO: NARUTO NEXT GENERATIONS © 2016 by Masashi Kishimoto, Ukyo Kodachi, Mikio Ikemoto/SHUEISHA Inc.

Black ✤ Clover

STORY & ART BY YŪKI TABATA

Asta is a young boy who dreams of becoming the greatest mage in the kingdom. Only one problem—he can't use any magic! Luckily for Asta, he receives the incredibly rare five-leaf clover grimoire that gives him the power of anti-magic. Can someone who can't use magic really become the Wizard King? One thing's for sure—Asta will never give up!

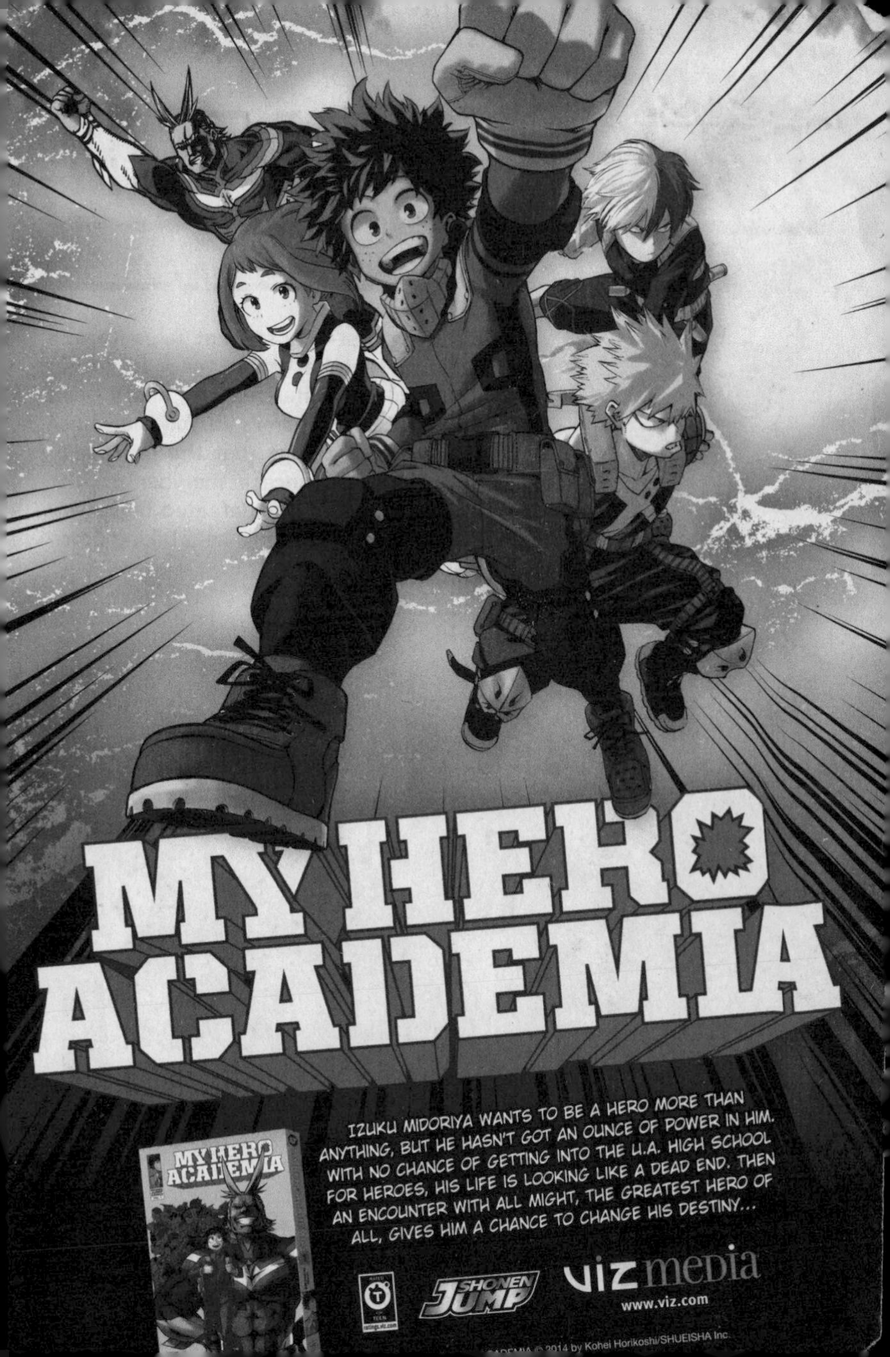
MY HERO ACADEMIA
IZUKU MIDORIYA WANTS TO BE A HERO MORE THAN ANYTHING, BUT HE HASN'T GOT AN OUNCE OF POWER IN HIM. WITH NO CHANCE OF GETTING INTO THE U.A. HIGH SCHOOL FOR HEROES, HIS LIFE IS LOOKING LIKE A DEAD END. THEN AN ENCOUNTER WITH ALL MIGHT, THE GREATEST HERO OF ALL, GIVES HIM A CHANCE TO CHANGE HIS DESTINY...
SHONEN JUMP
VIZ MEDIA
www.viz.com
ADEMIA © 2014 by Kohei Horikoshi/SHUEISHA Inc.

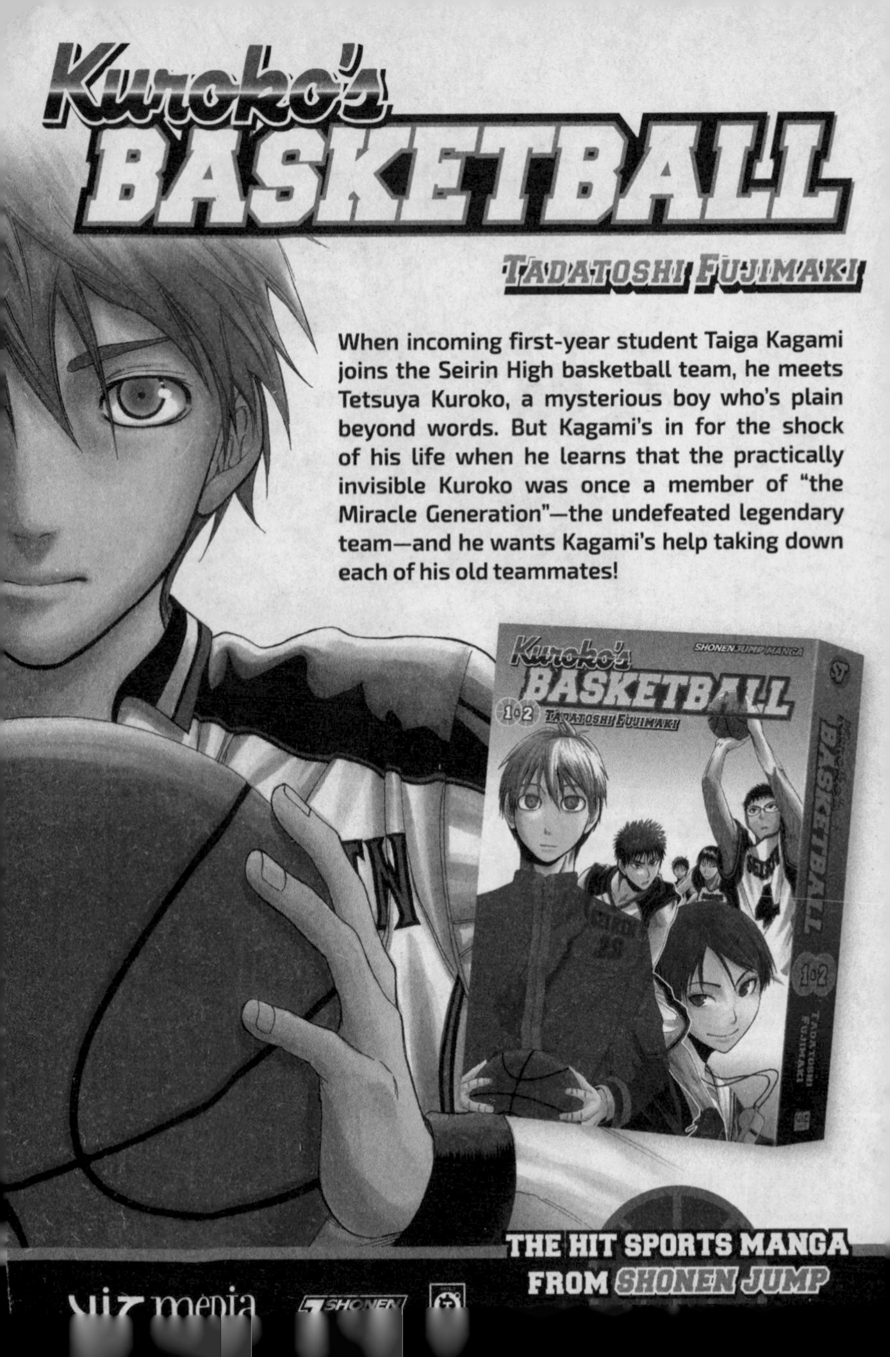
Kuroko's
BASKETBALL
TADATOSHI FUJIMAKI
When incoming first-year student Taiga Kagami joins the Seirin High basketball team, he meets Tetsuya Kuroko, a mysterious boy who's plain beyond words. But Kagami's in for the shock of his life when he learns that the practically invisible Kuroko was once a member of "the Miracle Generation"—the undefeated legendary team—and he wants Kagami's help taking down each of his old teammates!
Kuroko's
BASKETBALL
1•2
TADATOSHI FUJIMAKI
SHONEN JUMP MANGA
THE HIT SPORTS MANGA
FROM SHONEN JUMP
viz media

SHOYO HINATA IS OUT TO PROVE THAT IN VOLLEYBALL YOU DON'T NEED TO BE TALL TO FLY!

HAIKYU!!

Story and Art by **HARUICHI FURUDATE**

Ever since he saw the legendary player known as the "Little Giant" compete at the national volleyball finals, Shoyo Hinata has been aiming to be the best volleyball player ever! He decides to join the team at the high school the Little Giant went to—and then surpass him. Who says you need to be tall to play volleyball when you can jump higher than anyone else?

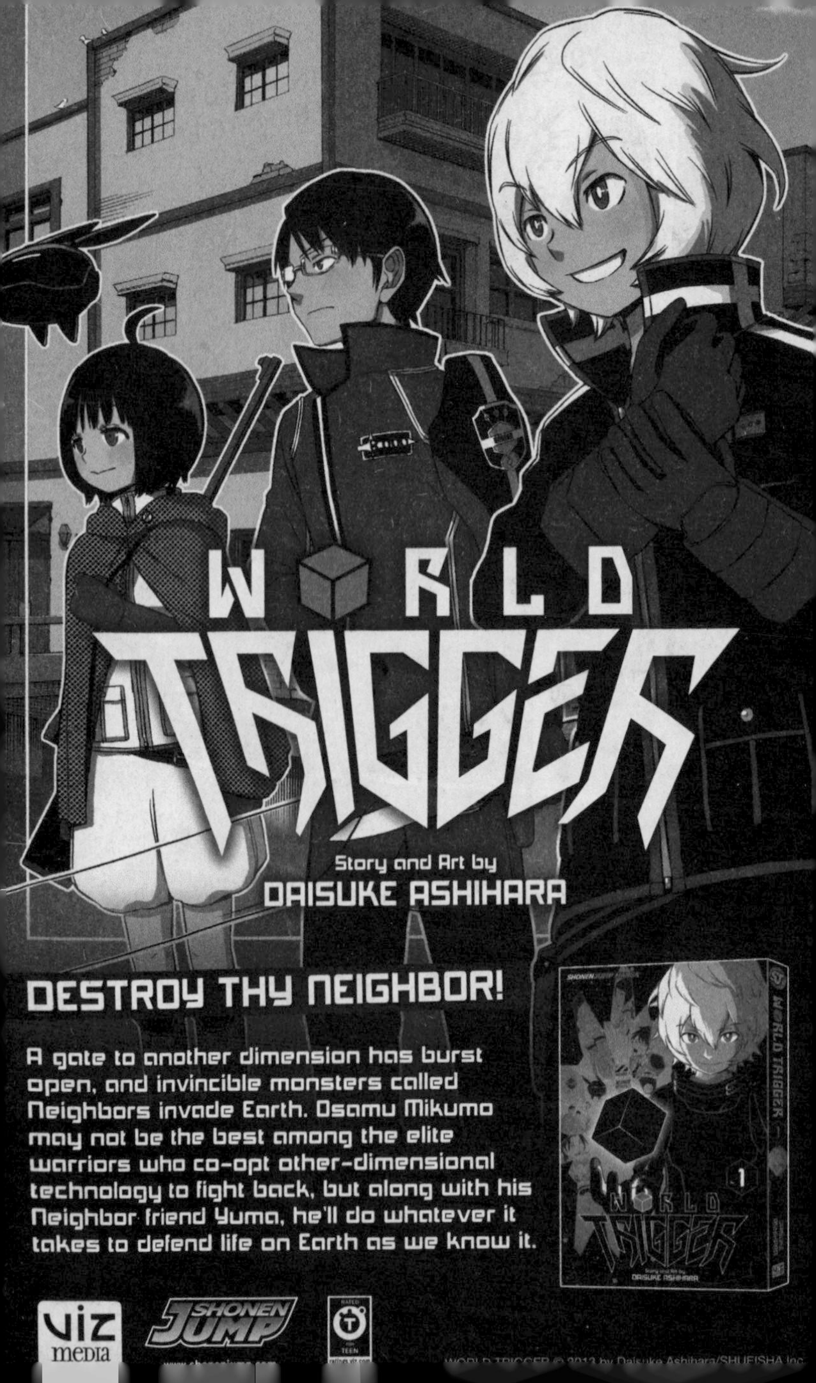
WORLD TRIGGER
Story and Art by
DAISUKE ASHIHARA
DESTROY THY NEIGHBOR!
A gate to another dimension has burst open, and invincible monsters called Neighbors invade Earth. Osamu Mikumo may not be the best among the elite warriors who co-opt other-dimensional technology to fight back, but along with his Neighbor friend Yuma, he'll do whatever it takes to defend life on Earth as we know it.
SHONEN JUMP MANGA
WORLD TRIGGER
1
DAISUKE ASHIHARA
viz media
SHONEN JUMP
RATED T FOR TEEN
ratings.viz.com
WORLD TRIGGER © 2013 by Daisuke Ashihara/SHUEISHA Inc.

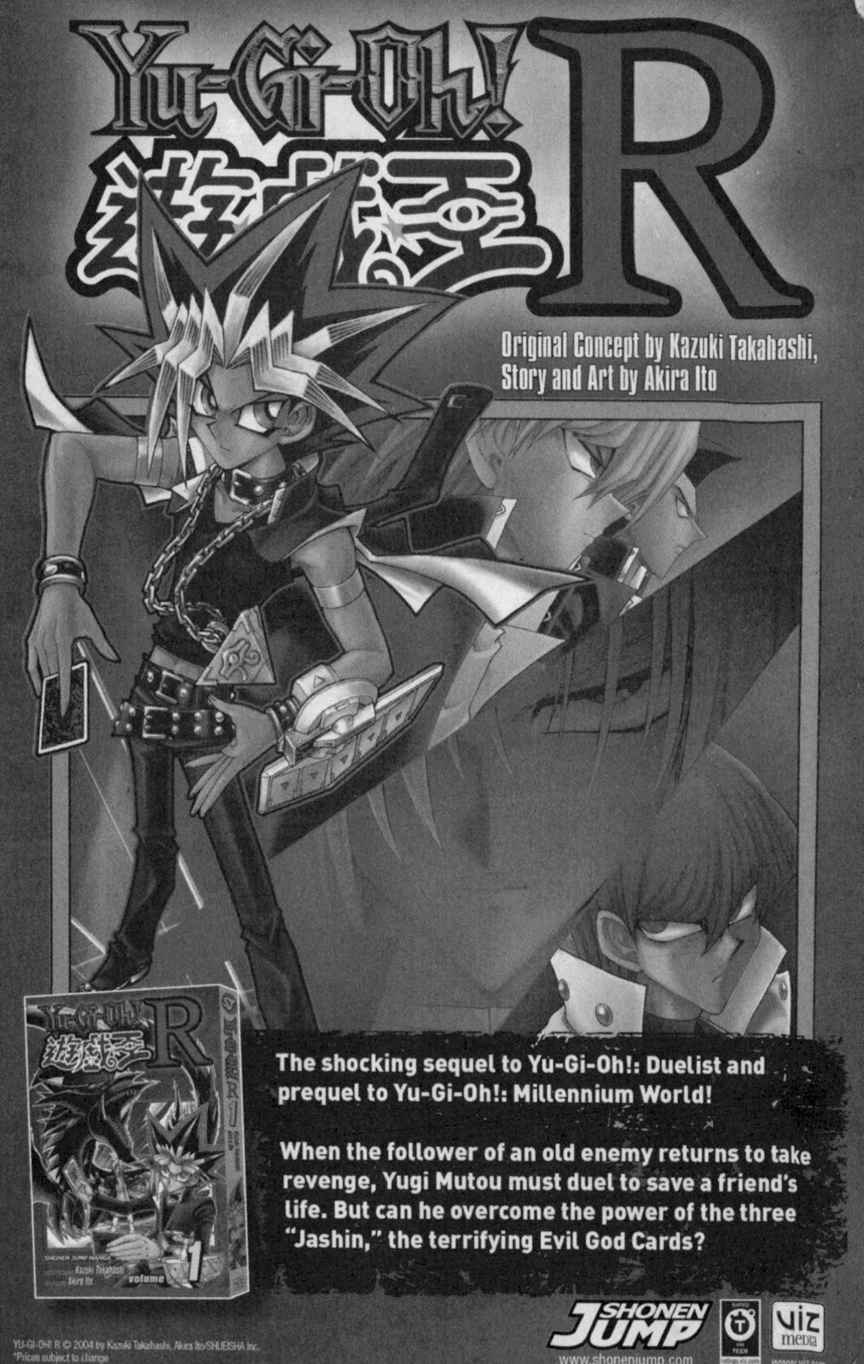
YU-GI-OH! R
Original Concept by Kazuki Takahashi, Story and Art by Akira Ito
The shocking sequel to Yu-Gi-Oh!: Duelist and prequel to Yu-Gi-Oh!: Millennium World!
When the follower of an old enemy returns to take revenge, Yugi Mutou must duel to save a friend's life. But can he overcome the power of the three "Jashin," the terrifying Evil God Cards?
SHONEN JUMP
www.shonenjump.com
VIZ media
www.viz.com
YU-GI-OH! R © 2004 by Kazuki Takahashi, Akira Ito/SHUEISHA Inc.
*Prices subject to change

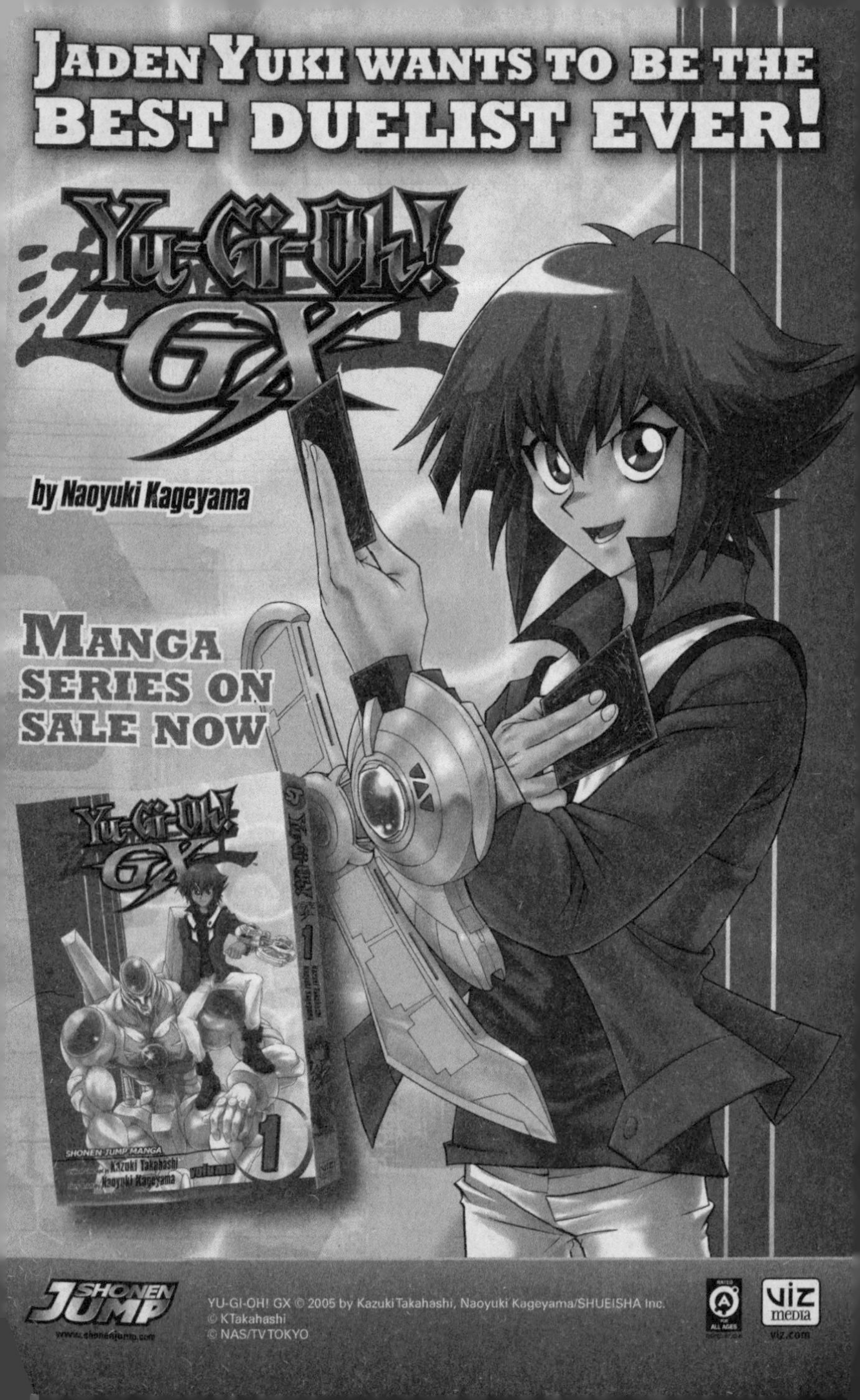

JADEN YUKI WANTS TO BE THE
BEST DUELIST EVER!
YU-GI-OH! GX
by Naoyuki Kageyama
MANGA
SERIES ON
SALE NOW
SHONEN JUMP MANGA
Kazuki Takahashi
Naoyuki Kageyama
SHONEN JUMP
www.shonenjump.com
YU-GI-OH! GX © 2005 by Kazuki Takahashi, Naoyuki Kageyama/SHUEISHA Inc.
© KTakahashi
© NAS/TV TOKYO
RATED A FOR ALL AGES
VIZ media
viz.com

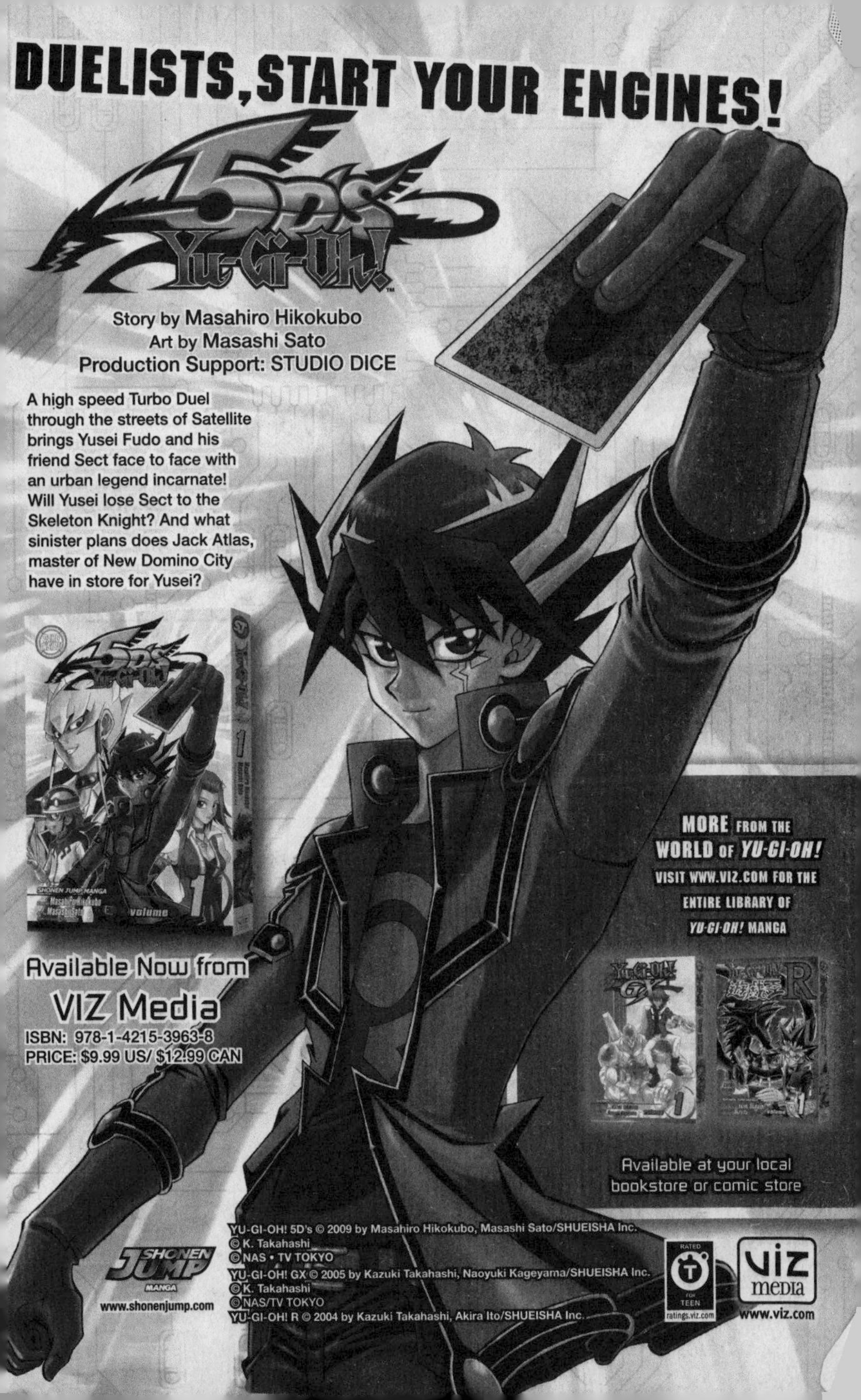
DUELISTS, START YOUR ENGINES!
5D's
YU-GI-OH!
Story by Masahiro Hikokubo
Art by Masashi Sato
Production Support: STUDIO DICE
A high speed Turbo Duel through the streets of Satellite brings Yusei Fudo and his friend Sect face to face with an urban legend incarnate! Will Yusei lose Sect to the Skeleton Knight? And what sinister plans does Jack Atlas, master of New Domino City have in store for Yusei?
Available Now from
VIZ Media
ISBN: 978-1-4215-3963-8
PRICE: $9.99 US/ $12.99 CAN
MORE FROM THE WORLD OF YU-GI-OH!
VISIT WWW.VIZ.COM FOR THE ENTIRE LIBRARY OF YU-GI-OH! MANGA
Available at your local bookstore or comic store
SHONEN JUMP MANGA
www.shonenjump.com
YU-GI-OH! 5D's © 2009 by Masahiro Hikokubo, Masashi Sato/SHUEISHA Inc.
© K. Takahashi
© NAS • TV TOKYO
YU-GI-OH! GX © 2005 by Kazuki Takahashi, Naoyuki Kageyama/SHUEISHA Inc.
© K. Takahashi
© NAS/TV TOKYO
YU-GI-OH! R © 2004 by Kazuki Takahashi, Akira Ito/SHUEISHA Inc.
RATED T FOR TEEN
ratings.viz.com
viz media
www.viz.com

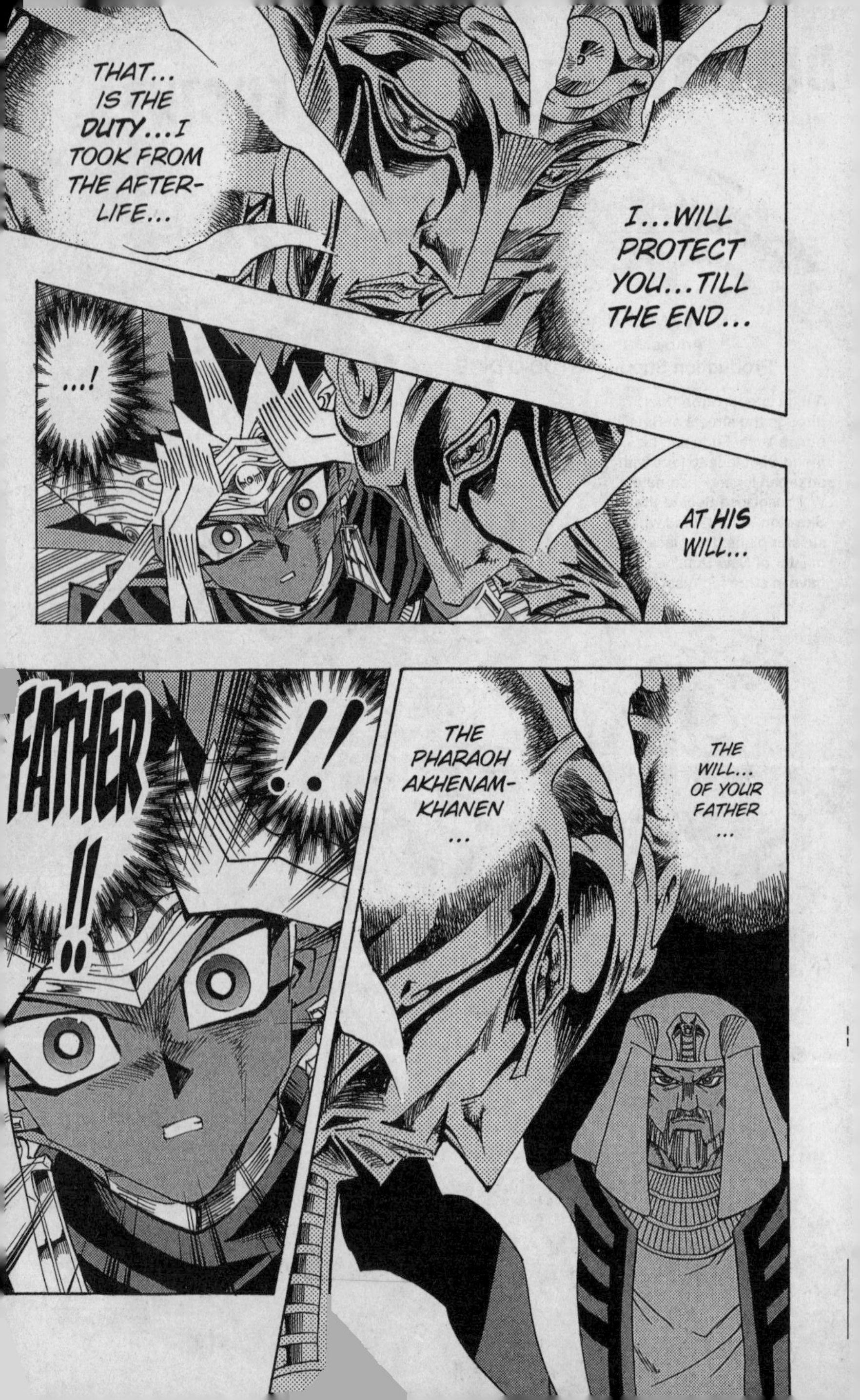
THAT... IS THE DUTY...I TOOK FROM THE AFTER-LIFE...
I...WILL PROTECT YOU...TILL THE END...
AT HIS WILL...
...!
THE WILL... OF YOUR FATHER ...
THE PHARAOH AKHENAM-KHANEN ...
!!
FATHER !!

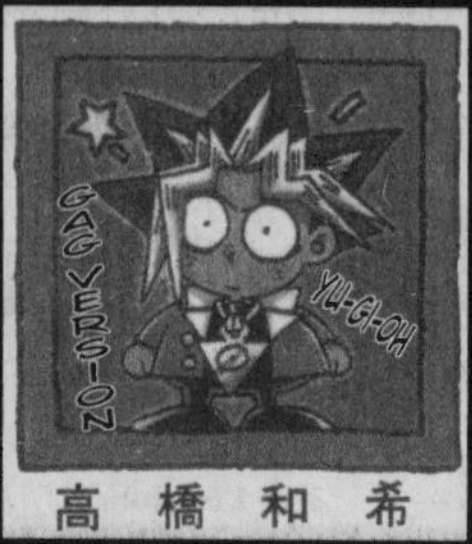
GAG VERSION
YU-GI-OH
高橋和希

THE OTHER DAY AT A SHONEN JUMP PARTY, I GOT TO TALK TO THE GAG COMIC ARTISTS, YOSHIO SAWAI (BOBOBO-BO BO-BOBO) AND KYOSUKE USUTA (SUGOI YO! MASARU-SAN). FOR ARTISTS WHO CREATE SUCH AMUSING GAGS, THEY WERE UNUSUALLY STRAIGHTFORWARD PEOPLE.

BUT WHEN YOU THINK ABOUT IT, GAG COMIC ARTISTS HAVE TO BREAK DOWN COMMON SENSE TO TURN EVERYDAY LIFE INTO SOMETHING BIZARRE. YOU CAN'T CREATE THIS KIND OF IRRATIONAL WORLD UNLESS YOU HAVE COMMON SENSE AND A GOOD GRASP ON REALITY TO BEGIN WITH.

GAG COMIC ARTISTS ARE AMAZING! AS FOR MYSELF, I DON'T HAVE ANY COMMON SENSE. (HA HA HA!)

—KAZUKI TAKAHASHI, 2003

Artist/author Kazuki Takahashi first tried to break into the manga business in 1982, but success eluded him until **Yu-Gi-Oh!** debuted in the Japanese **Weekly Shonen Jump** magazine in 1996. **Yu-Gi-Oh!**'s themes of friendship and fighting, together with Takahashi's weird and wonderful art, soon became enormously successful, spawning a real-world card game, video games, and two anime series. A lifelong gamer, Takahashi enjoys Shogi (Japanese chess), Mahjong, card games, and tabletop RPGs, among other games.

Yu-Gi-Oh!
3-in-1 Edition
Volume 12

SHONEN JUMP Manga Omnibus Edition
A compilation of the graphic novel volumes 34-35-36

STORY AND ART BY Kazuki Takahashi

Translation & English Adaptation/Anita Sengupta
Touch-up Art & Lettering/Kelle Han
Design/Sean Lee (Manga Edition)
Design/Sam Elzway (Omnibus Edition)
Editor/Jason Thompson (Manga Edition)
Editor/Erica Yee (Omnibus Edition)

Printed in the U.S.A.

Published by VIZ Media, LLC
P.O. Box 77010
San Francisco, CA 94107

10 9 8 7 6 5 4 3 2 1
Omnibus edition first printing, November 2017

www.viz.com

PARENTAL ADVISORY
YU-GI-OH! is rated T for Teen and is recommended for ages 13 and up. This volume contains fantasy violence, alcohol and tobacco use, and suggestive situations.
ratings.viz.com

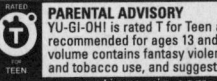

SHONEN JUMP MANGA

YU-GI-OH! Millennium World

Vol. 34

THE RETURN OF BAKURA

STORY AND ART BY

KAZUKI TAKAHASHI

THE MAIN CHARACTERS

KATSUYA JONOUCHI

BOBASA   **ANZU MAZAKI**   **HIROTO HONDA**

YUGI MUTOU

THE STORY SO FAR…

Shy 10th grader Yugi spent most of his time alone playing games…until he solved the Millennium Puzzle, a mysterious Egyptian artifact. Possessed by the puzzle, Yugi developed an alter ego: Yu-Gi-Oh, the King of Games, the soul of a pharaoh from ancient Egypt!

Discovering that the collectible card game "Duel Monsters" was of Ancient Egyptian origin, Yu-Gi-Oh collected the three Egyptian God Cards—Slifer the Sky Dragon, the God of the Obelisk, and the Sun Dragon Ra—and used them to travel into the "world of memories" of his own life 3,000 years ago. There, he found that he was the pharaoh, served by six priests who used the Millennium Items to summon *ka*—spirits and monsters—from people's souls.

But all was not well in Ancient Egypt. Bakura, a fiendish tomb-robber, attacked the palace. With his powerful spirit Diabound, Bakura was undefeatable, until Yugi summoned the God of the Obelisk. But Bakura escaped, and then ambushed and killed the priest Mahado, stealing the Millennium Ring.

Meanwhile, with the help of the Egyptian mystic Bobasa, Yugi and his friends followed Yu-Gi-Oh into the "world of memories" in order to find the pharaoh's forgotten name. But a sinister hitchhiker has gone with them into the past…

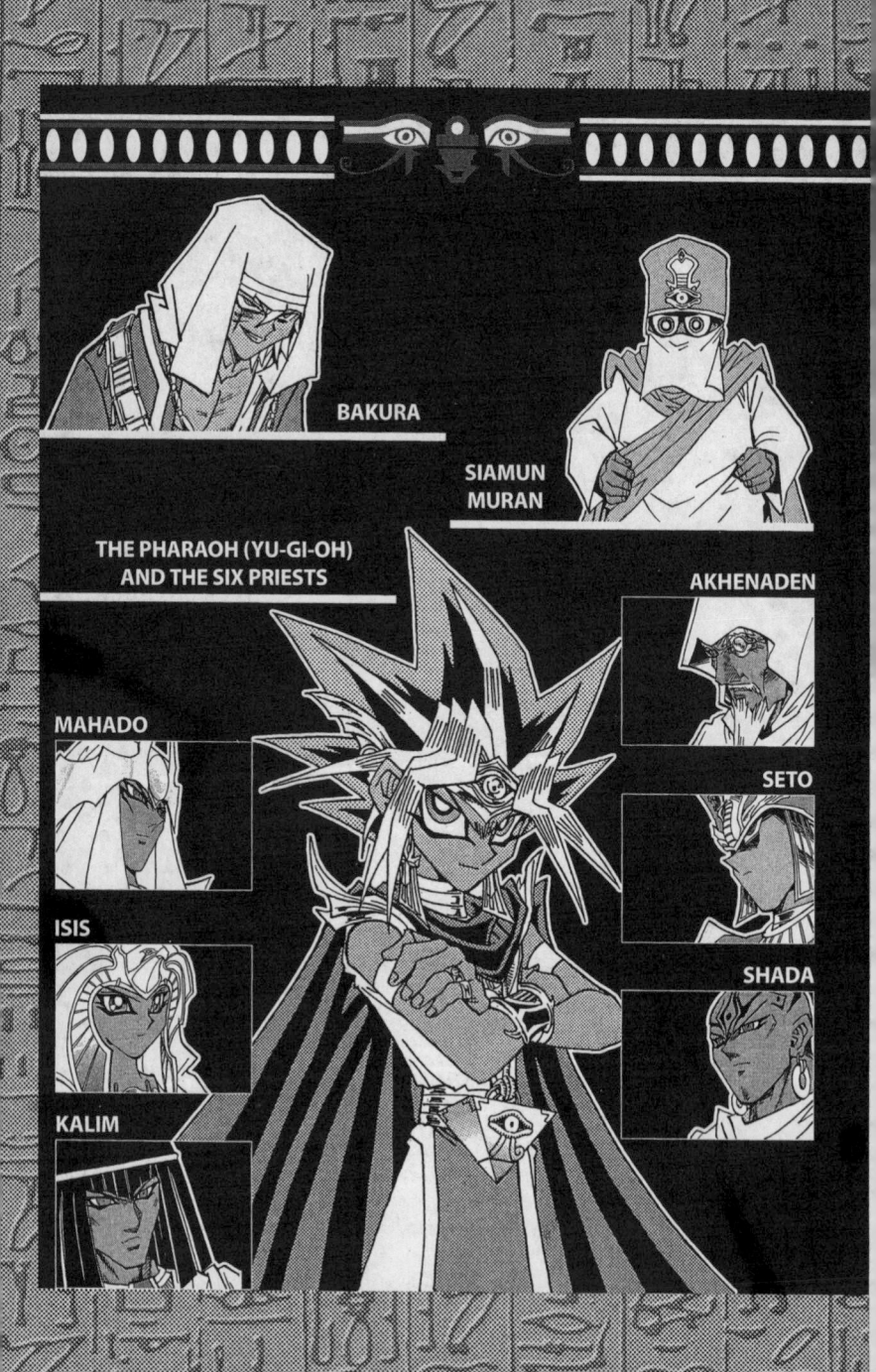

BAKURA

SIAMUN
MURAN

THE PHARAOH (YU-GI-OH)
AND THE SIX PRIESTS

AKHENADEN

MAHADO

SETO

ISIS

SHADA

KALIM

Yu-Gi-Oh! Millennium World

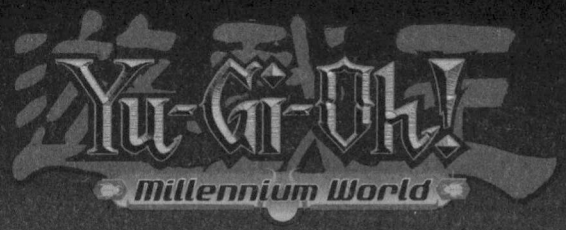

Vol. 34

CONTENTS

Duel 297: Bakura Lives!

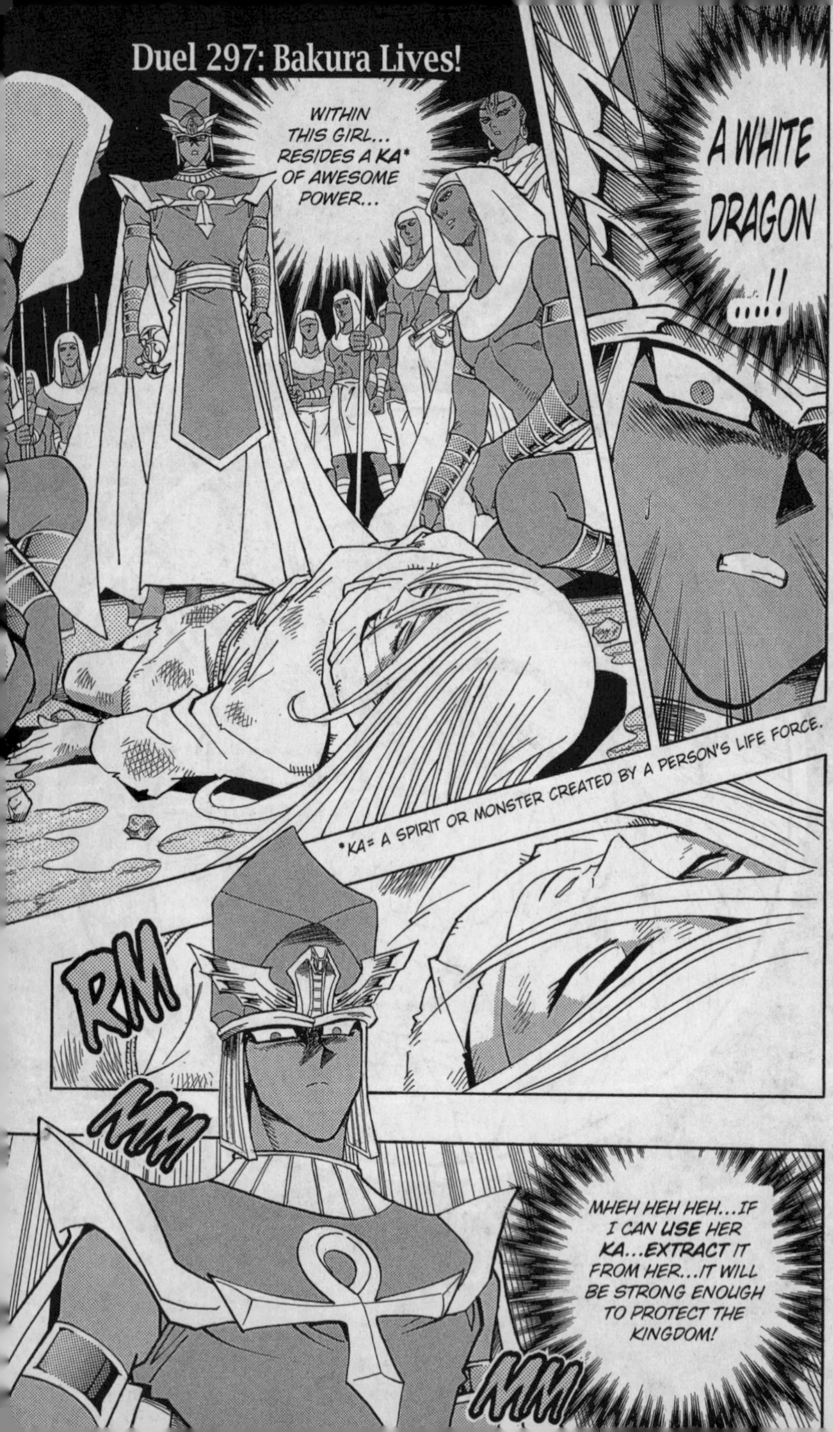
A WHITE DRAGON .....!!
WITHIN THIS GIRL... RESIDES A KA* OF AWESOME POWER...
*KA= A SPIRIT OR MONSTER CREATED BY A PERSON'S LIFE FORCE.
RM
MM
MHEH HEH HEH...IF I CAN USE HER KA...EXTRACT IT FROM HER...IT WILL BE STRONG ENOUGH TO PROTECT THE KINGDOM!
MM

Duel 297: Bakura Lives!

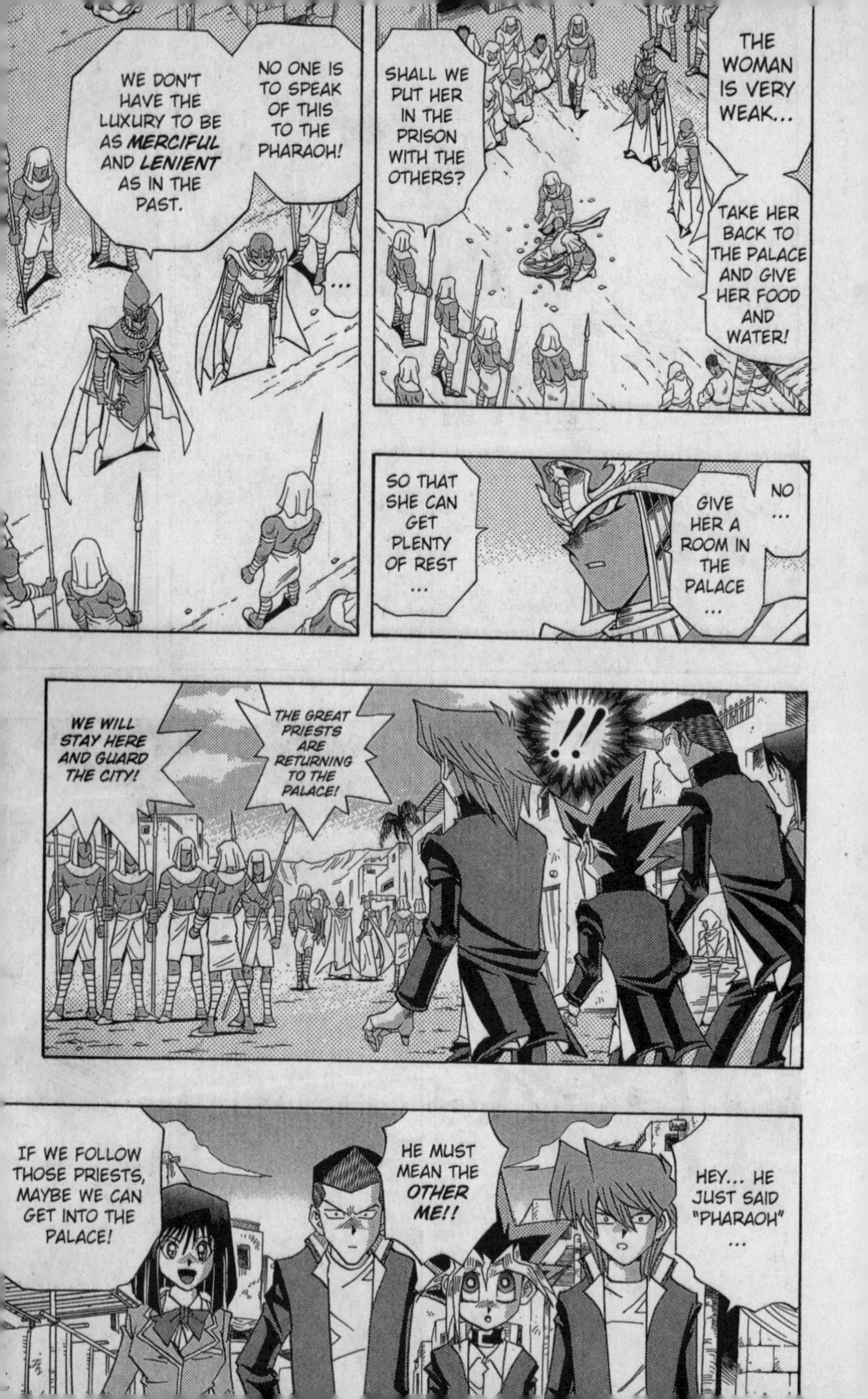
THE WOMAN IS VERY WEAK...
TAKE HER BACK TO THE PALACE AND GIVE HER FOOD AND WATER!
SHALL WE PUT HER IN THE PRISON WITH THE OTHERS?
NO...
GIVE HER A ROOM IN THE PALACE...
SO THAT SHE CAN GET PLENTY OF REST...
NO ONE IS TO SPEAK OF THIS TO THE PHARAOH!
WE DON'T HAVE THE LUXURY TO BE AS *MERCIFUL* AND *LENIENT* AS IN THE PAST.
...
!!
THE GREAT PRIESTS ARE RETURNING TO THE PALACE!
WE WILL STAY HERE AND GUARD THE CITY!
HEY... HE JUST SAID "PHARAOH"...
HE MUST MEAN THE *OTHER ME!!*
IF WE FOLLOW THOSE PRIESTS, MAYBE WE CAN GET INTO THE PALACE!

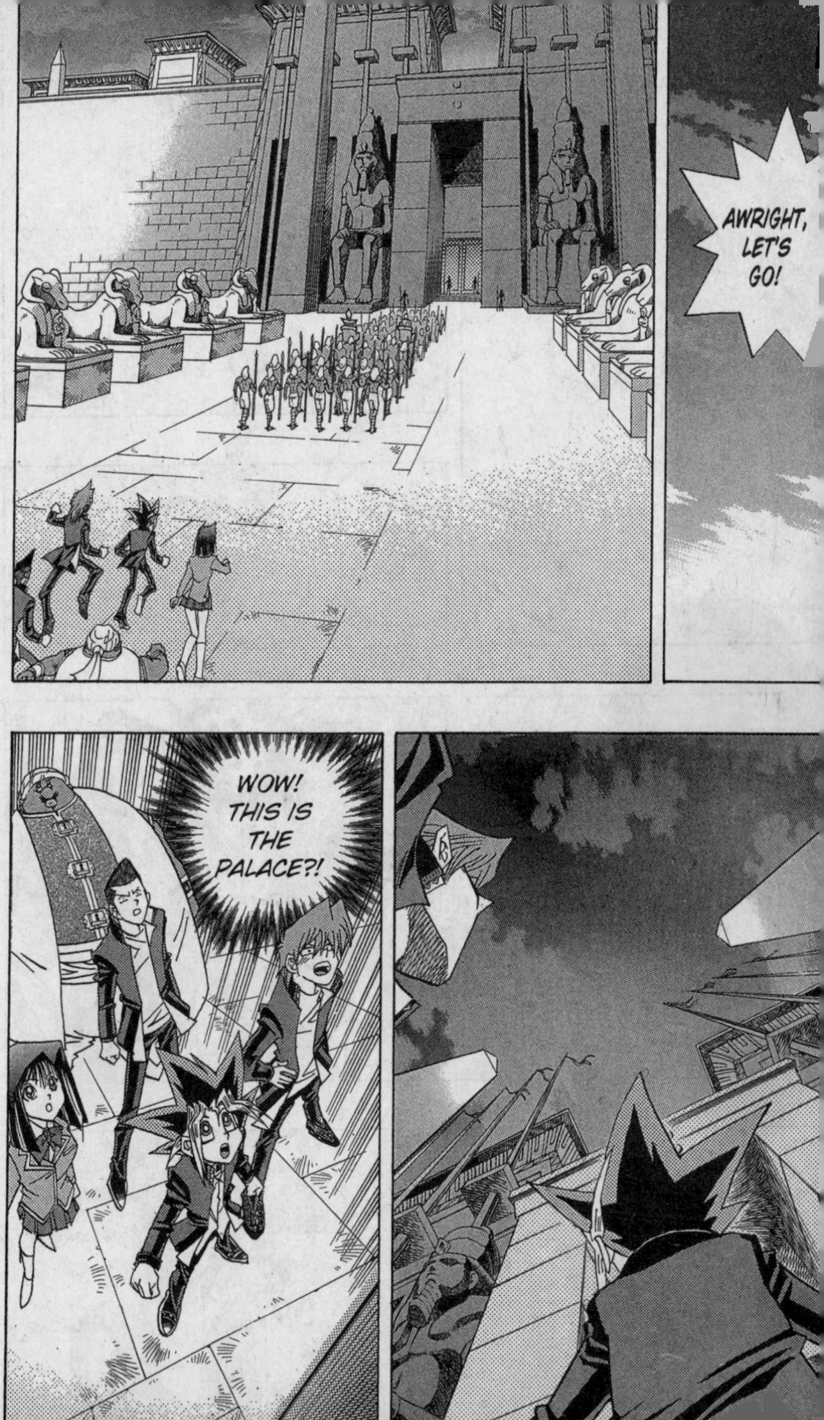
AWRIGHT, LET'S GO!
WOW! THIS IS THE PALACE?!

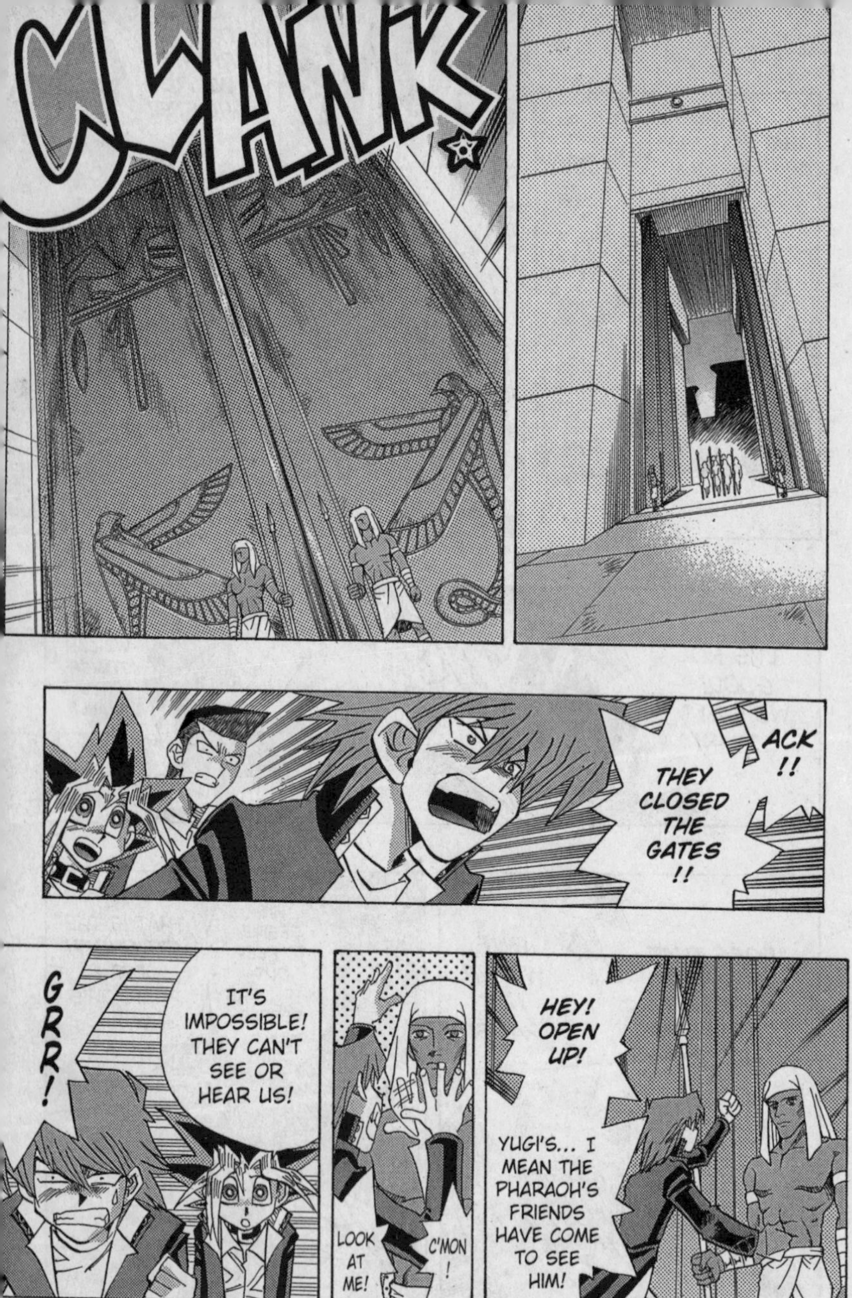
CLANK
ACK!!
THEY CLOSED THE GATES!!
HEY! OPEN UP!
YUGI'S... I MEAN THE PHARAOH'S FRIENDS HAVE COME TO SEE HIM!
C'MON!
LOOK AT ME!
IT'S IMPOSSIBLE! THEY CAN'T SEE OR HEAR US!
GRR!

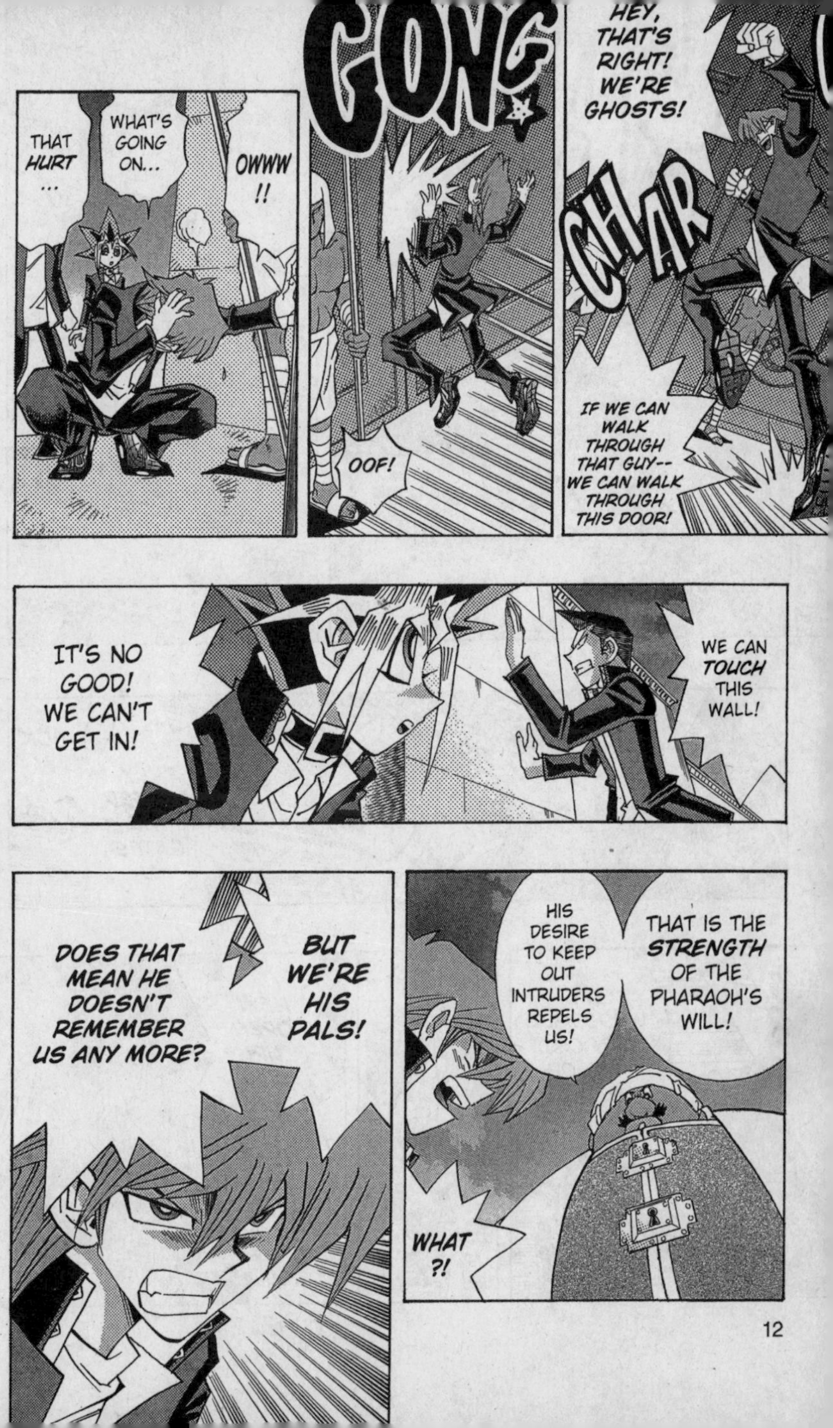
HEY, THAT'S RIGHT! WE'RE GHOSTS!
CHAR
IF WE CAN WALK THROUGH THAT GUY-- WE CAN WALK THROUGH THIS DOOR!
GONG
OOF!
OWWW !!
WHAT'S GOING ON...
THAT HURT ...
WE CAN TOUCH THIS WALL!
IT'S NO GOOD! WE CAN'T GET IN!
DOES THAT MEAN HE DOESN'T REMEMBER US ANY MORE?
BUT WE'RE HIS PALS!
THAT IS THE STRENGTH OF THE PHARAOH'S WILL!
HIS DESIRE TO KEEP OUT INTRUDERS REPELS US!
WHAT ?!

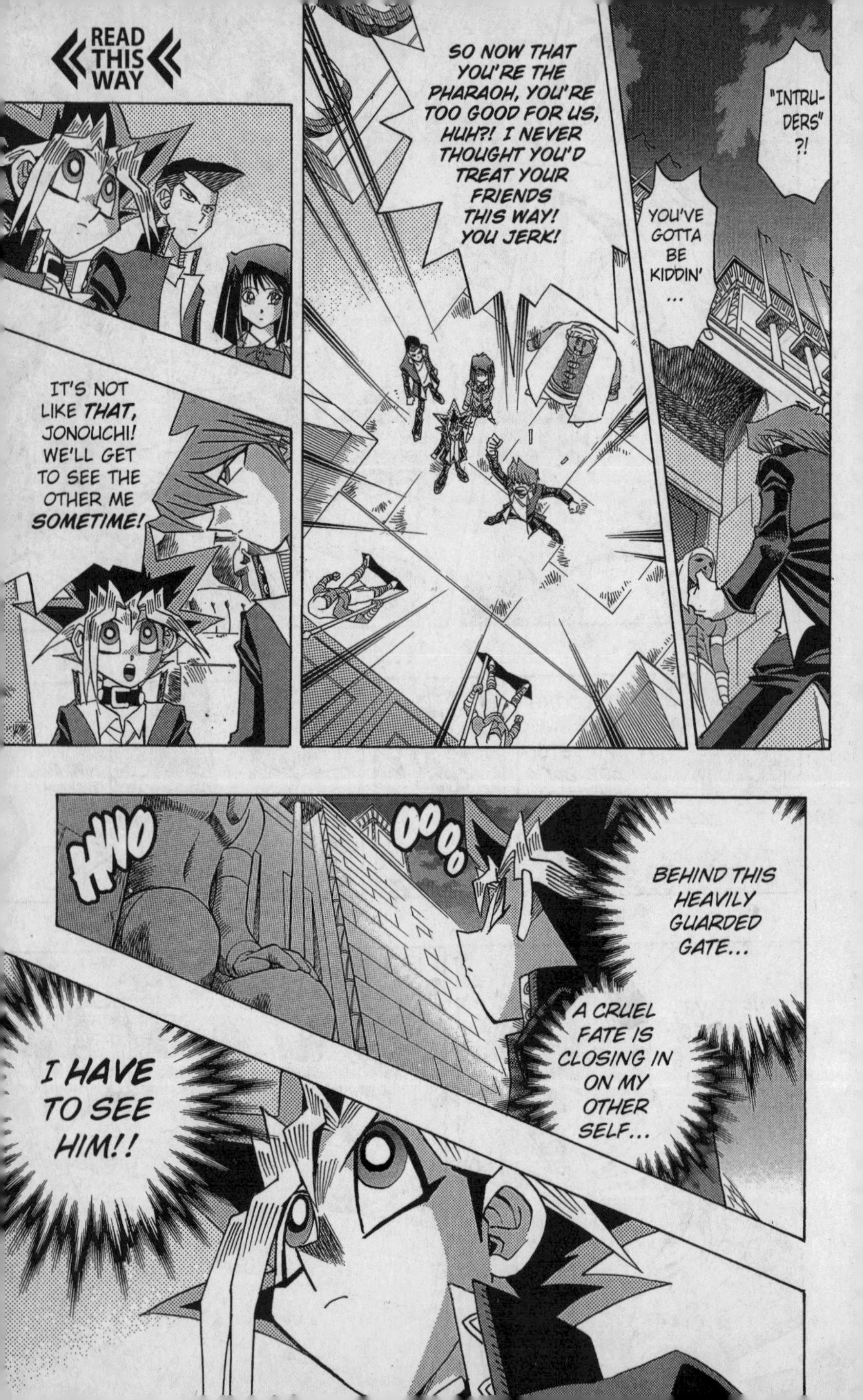
READ THIS WAY
"INTRU-DERS"?!
YOU'VE GOTTA BE KIDDIN'...
SO NOW THAT YOU'RE THE PHARAOH, YOU'RE TOO GOOD FOR US, HUH?! I NEVER THOUGHT YOU'D TREAT YOUR FRIENDS THIS WAY! YOU JERK!
IT'S NOT LIKE THAT, JONOUCHI! WE'LL GET TO SEE THE OTHER ME SOMETIME!
HWOOOO
BEHIND THIS HEAVILY GUARDED GATE...
A CRUEL FATE IS CLOSING IN ON MY OTHER SELF...
I HAVE TO SEE HIM!!

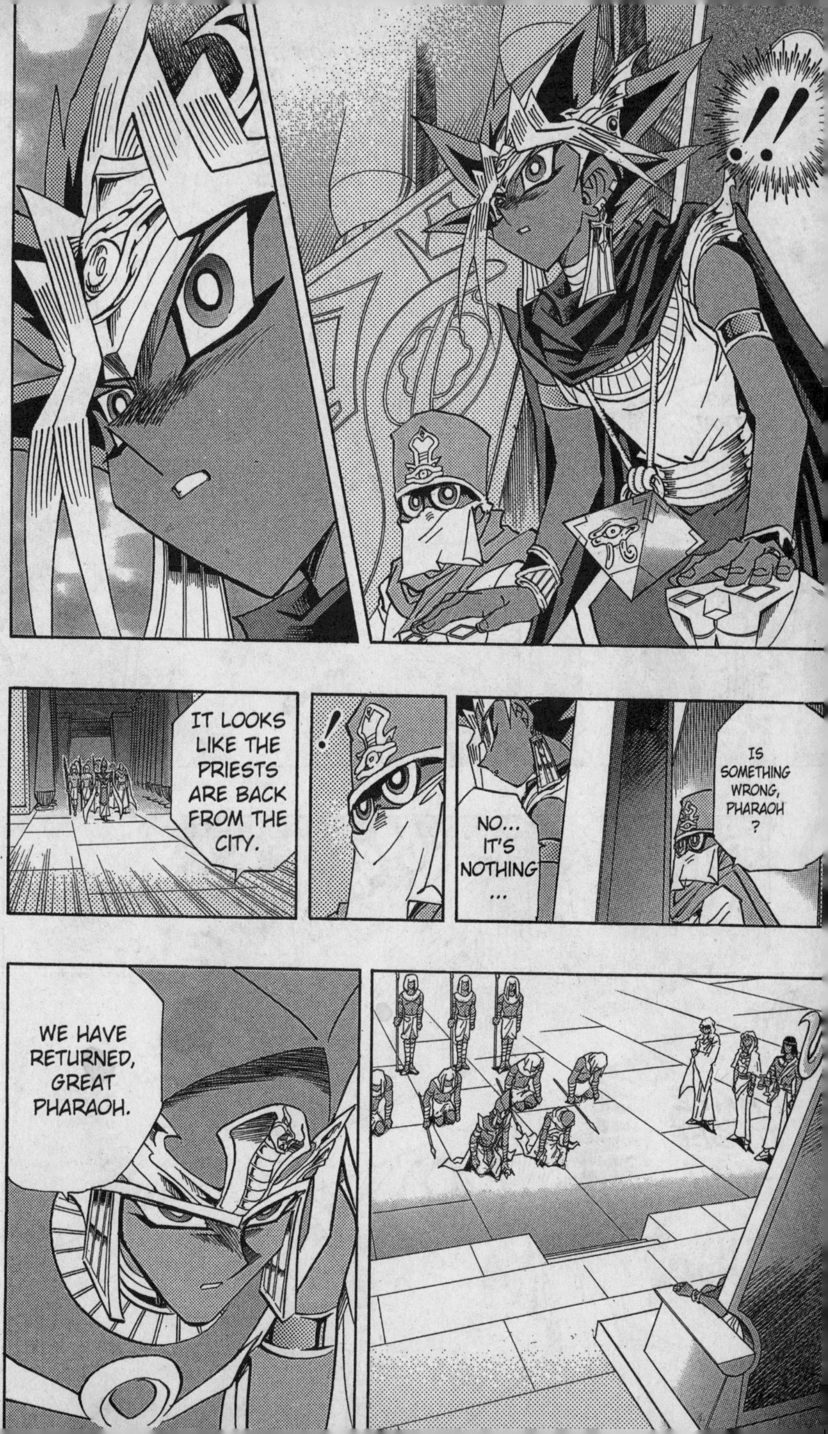
!!
IT LOOKS LIKE THE PRIESTS ARE BACK FROM THE CITY.
!
IS SOMETHING WRONG, PHARAOH ?
NO... IT'S NOTHING ...
WE HAVE RETURNED, GREAT PHARAOH.

WE WERE UNABLE TO CONFIRM BAKURA'S DEATH...
BUT WE HAVE STRENGTHENED THE GUARD. NOT EVEN A MOUSE COULD GET INTO THE CITY. ITS PEACE IS SECURE.
YOU SAY THAT...
BUT I HAVE A BAD FEELING ABOUT THIS...
I HEARD A VOICE...
...TRYING TO TELL ME SOMETHING...
...FROM MY MILLENNIUM PENDANT...

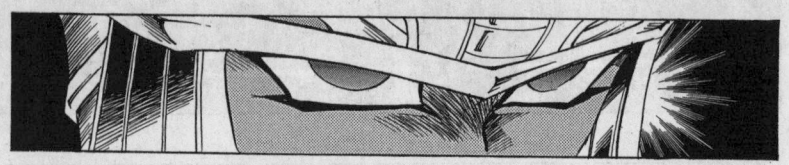

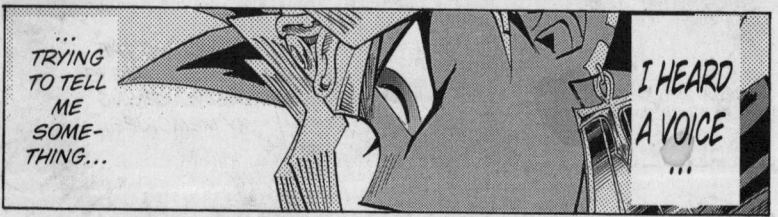

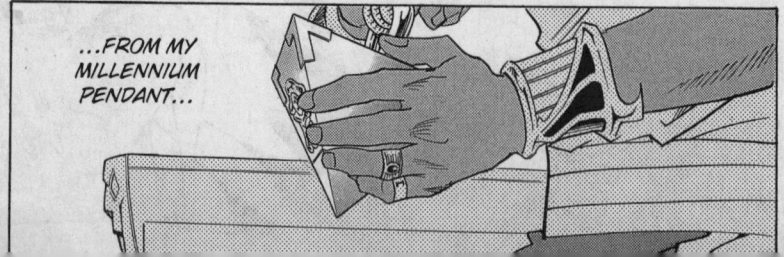

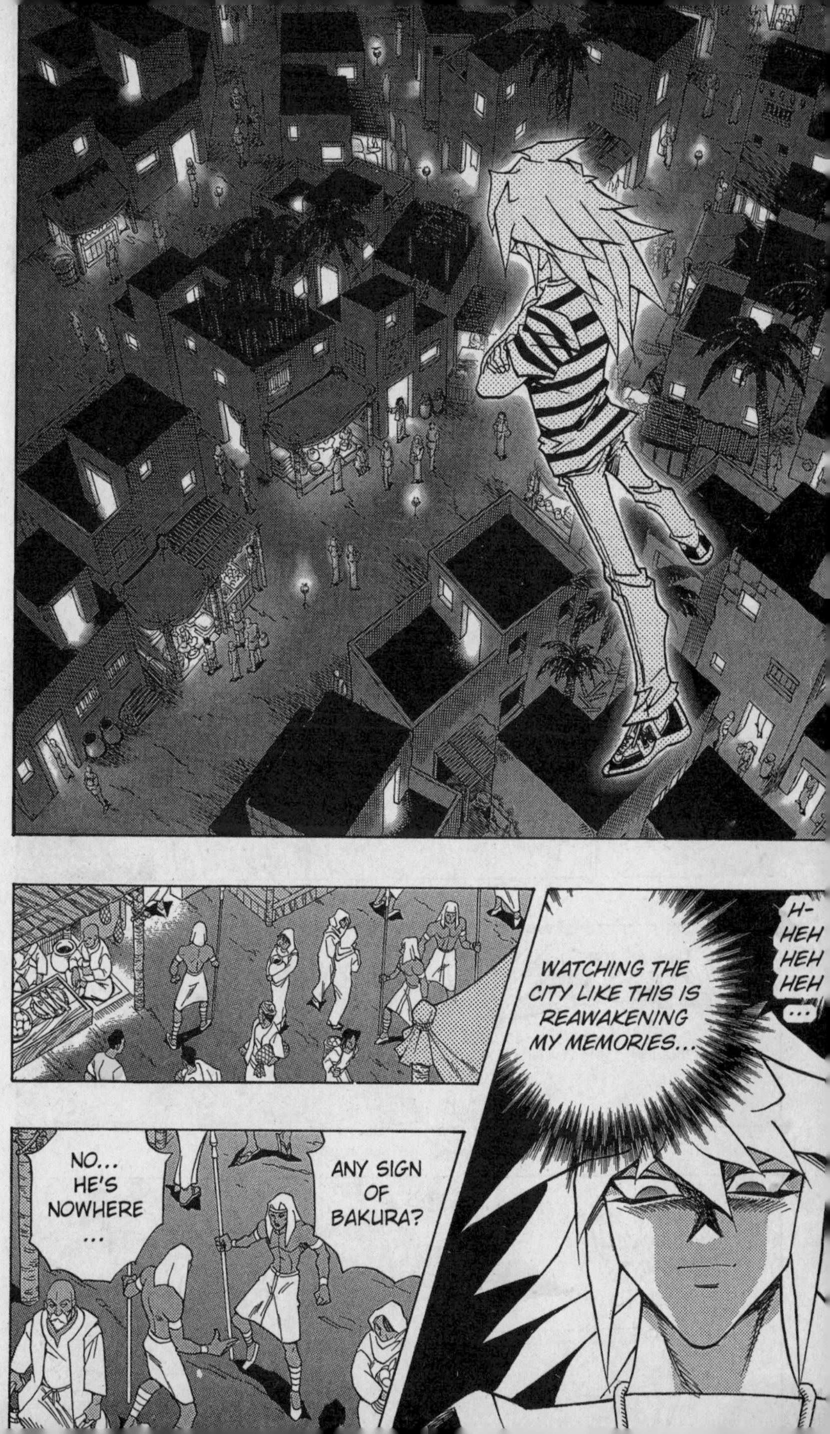
H-HEH HEH HEH...
WATCHING THE CITY LIKE THIS IS REAWAKENING MY MEMORIES...
ANY SIGN OF BAKURA?
NO... HE'S NOWHERE...

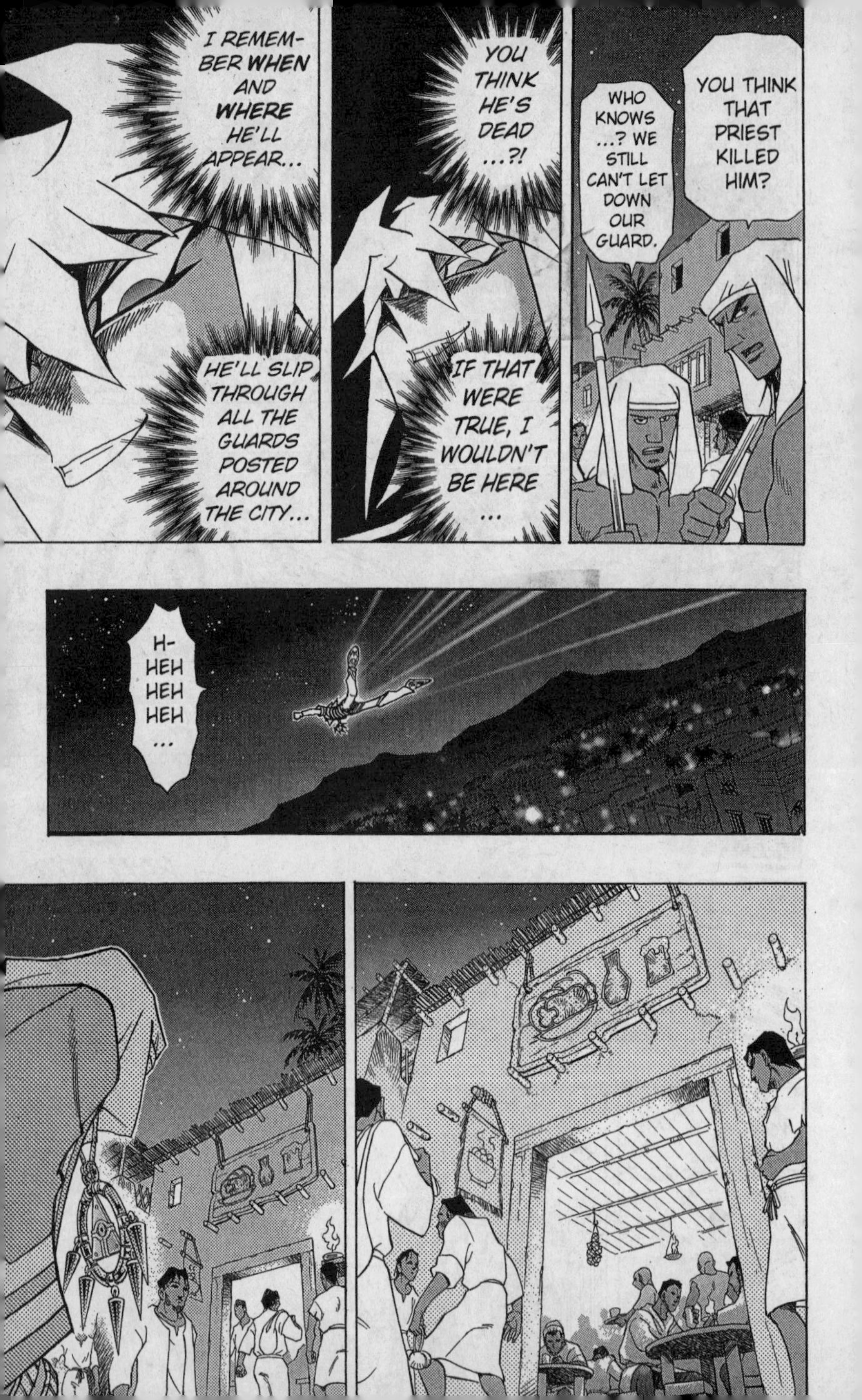
YOU THINK THAT PRIEST KILLED HIM?
WHO KNOWS ...? WE STILL CAN'T LET DOWN OUR GUARD.
YOU THINK HE'S DEAD ...?!
IF THAT WERE TRUE, I WOULDN'T BE HERE ...
I REMEMBER WHEN AND WHERE HE'LL APPEAR...
HE'LL SLIP THROUGH ALL THE GUARDS POSTED AROUND THE CITY...
H-HEH HEH HEH ...

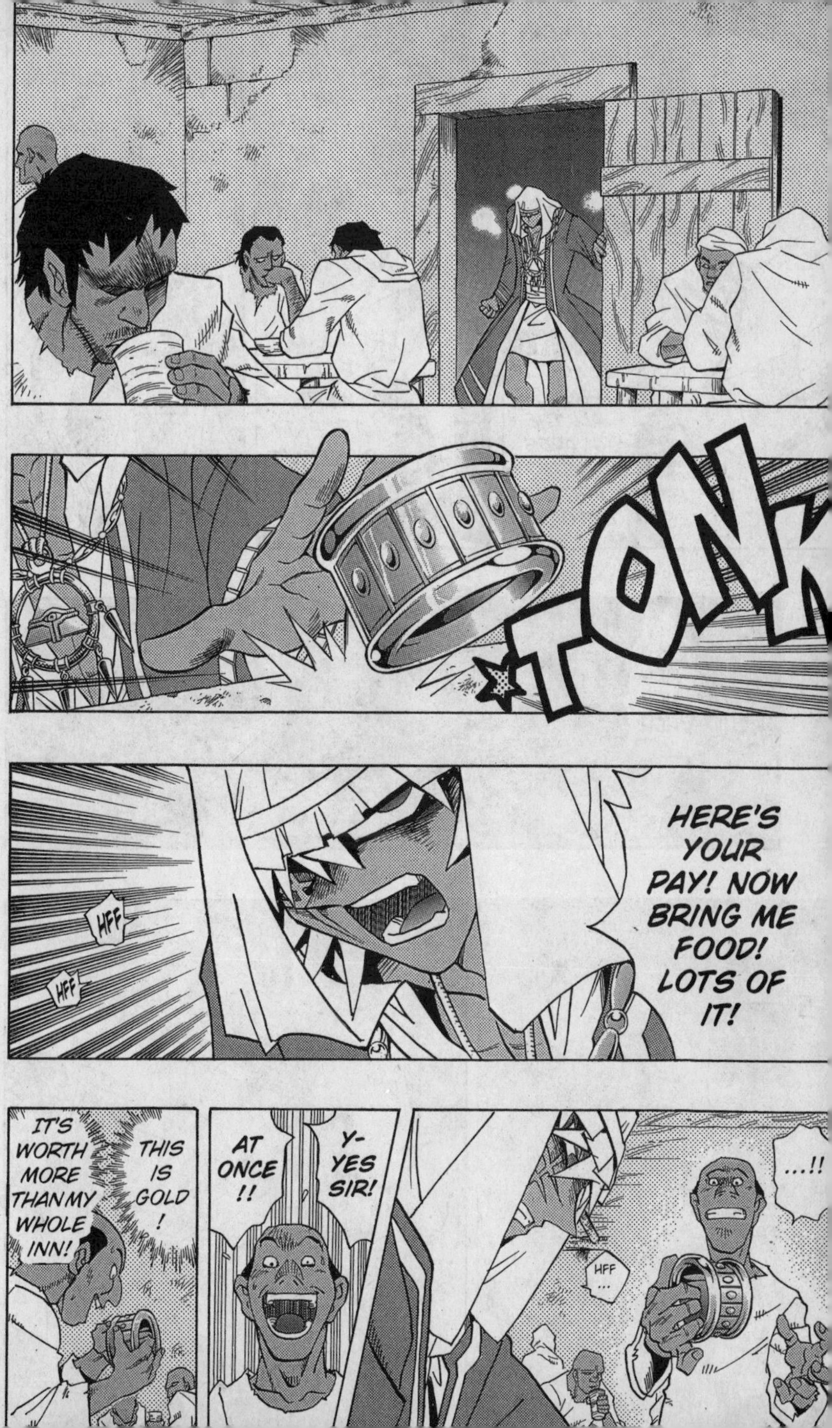
TONK
HERE'S YOUR PAY! NOW BRING ME FOOD! LOTS OF IT!
HFF
HFF
...!!
HFF ...
Y-YES SIR!
AT ONCE!!
THIS IS GOLD!
IT'S WORTH MORE THAN MY WHOLE INN!

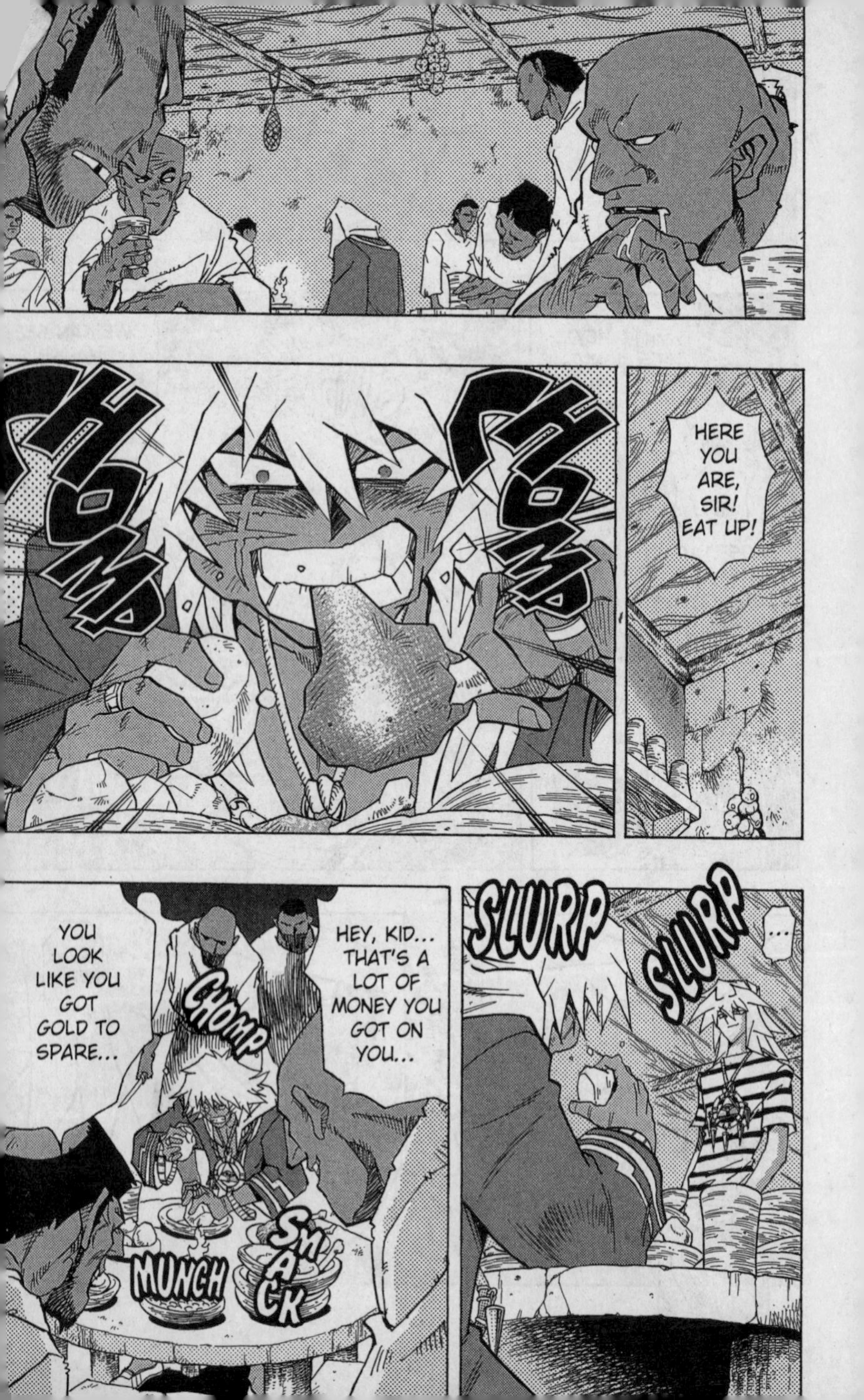
HERE YOU ARE, SIR! EAT UP!
CHOMP
CHOMP
SLURP
SLURP
...
HEY, KID... THAT'S A LOT OF MONEY YOU GOT ON YOU...
YOU LOOK LIKE YOU GOT GOLD TO SPARE...
CHOMP
SMACK
MUNCH

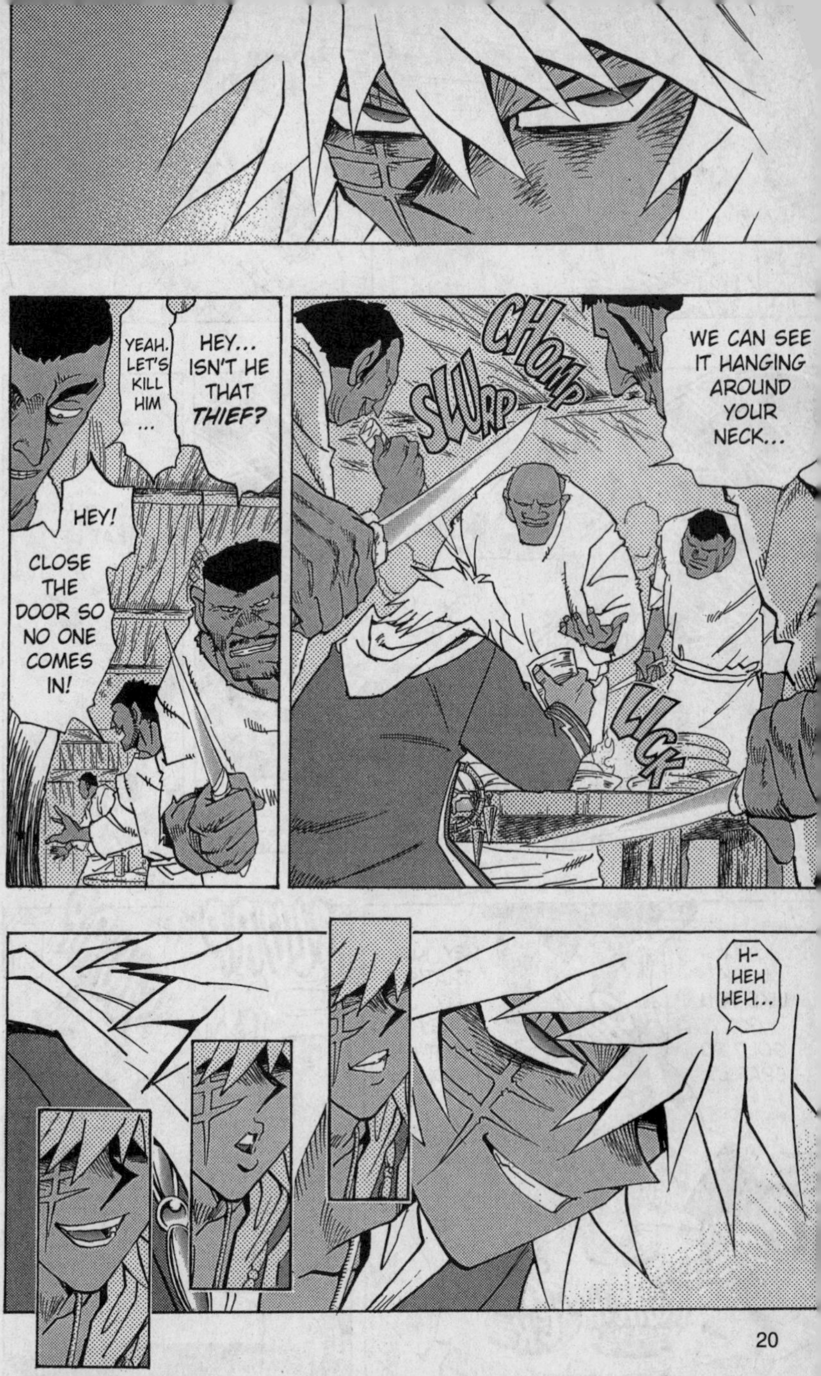

HEY… ISN'T HE THAT *THIEF?*
YEAH. LET'S KILL HIM…
HEY!
CLOSE THE DOOR SO NO ONE COMES IN!
CHOMP
SLURP
LICK
WE CAN SEE IT HANGING AROUND YOUR NECK…
H-HEH HEH…

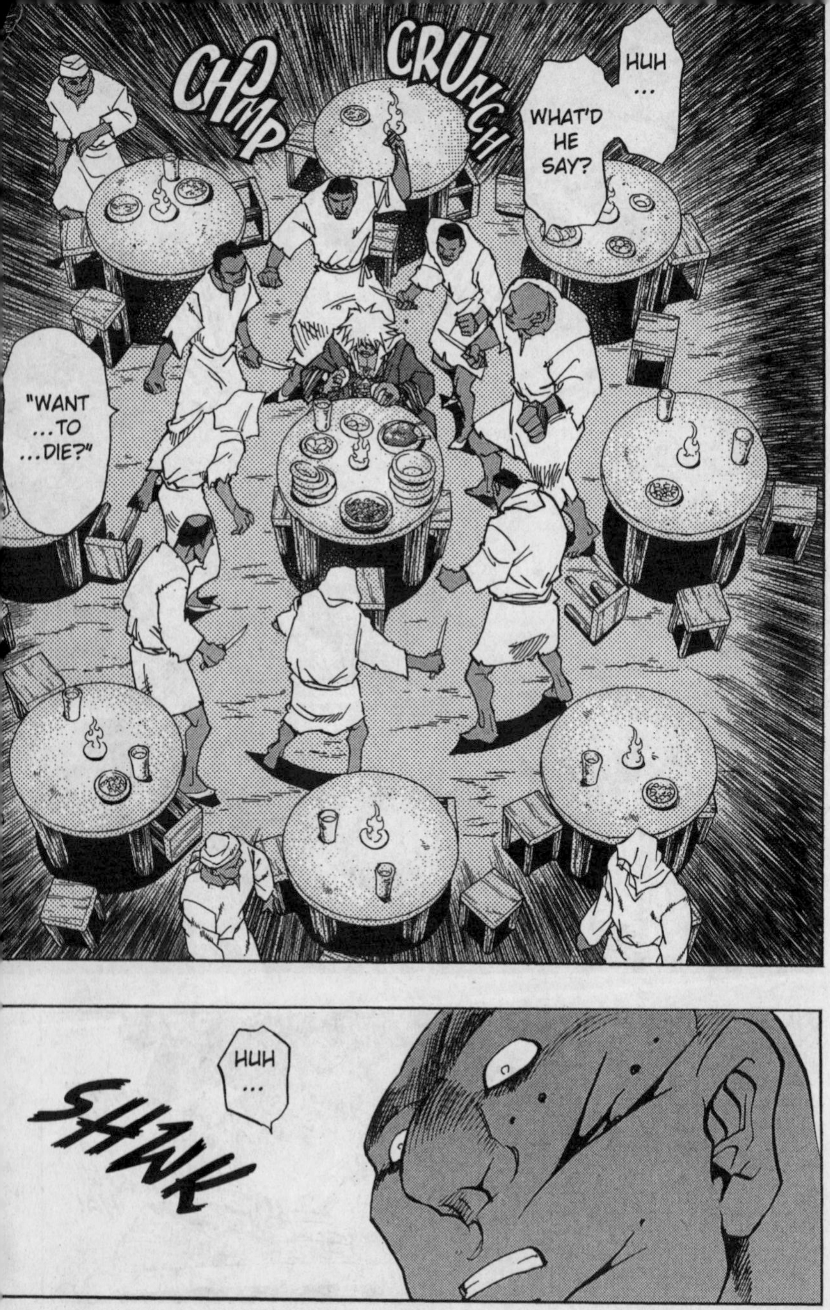
CRUNCH
CHOMP
HUH ...
WHAT'D HE SAY?
"WANT ...TO ...DIE?"
HUH ...
SHNK

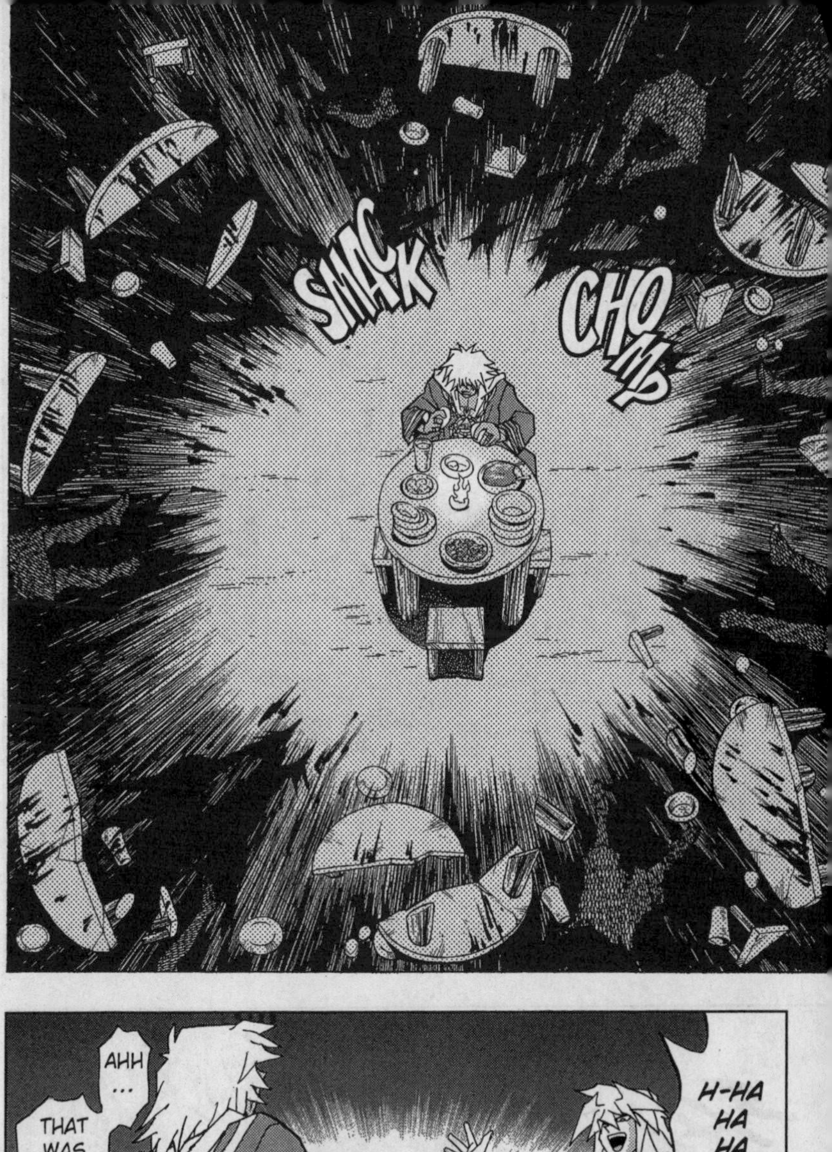
SMACK
CHOMP

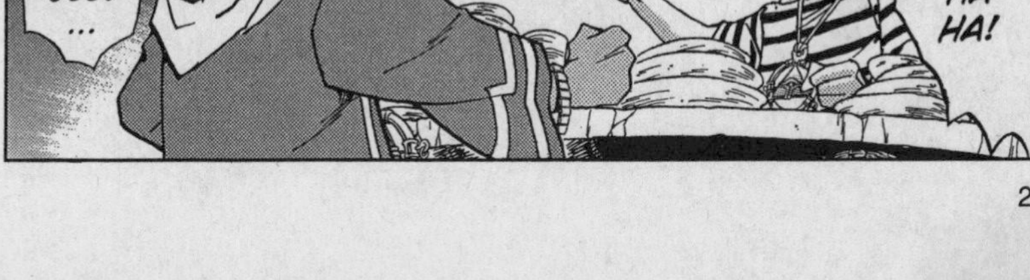
H-HA HA HA HA HA!
AHH ... THAT WAS GOOD ...

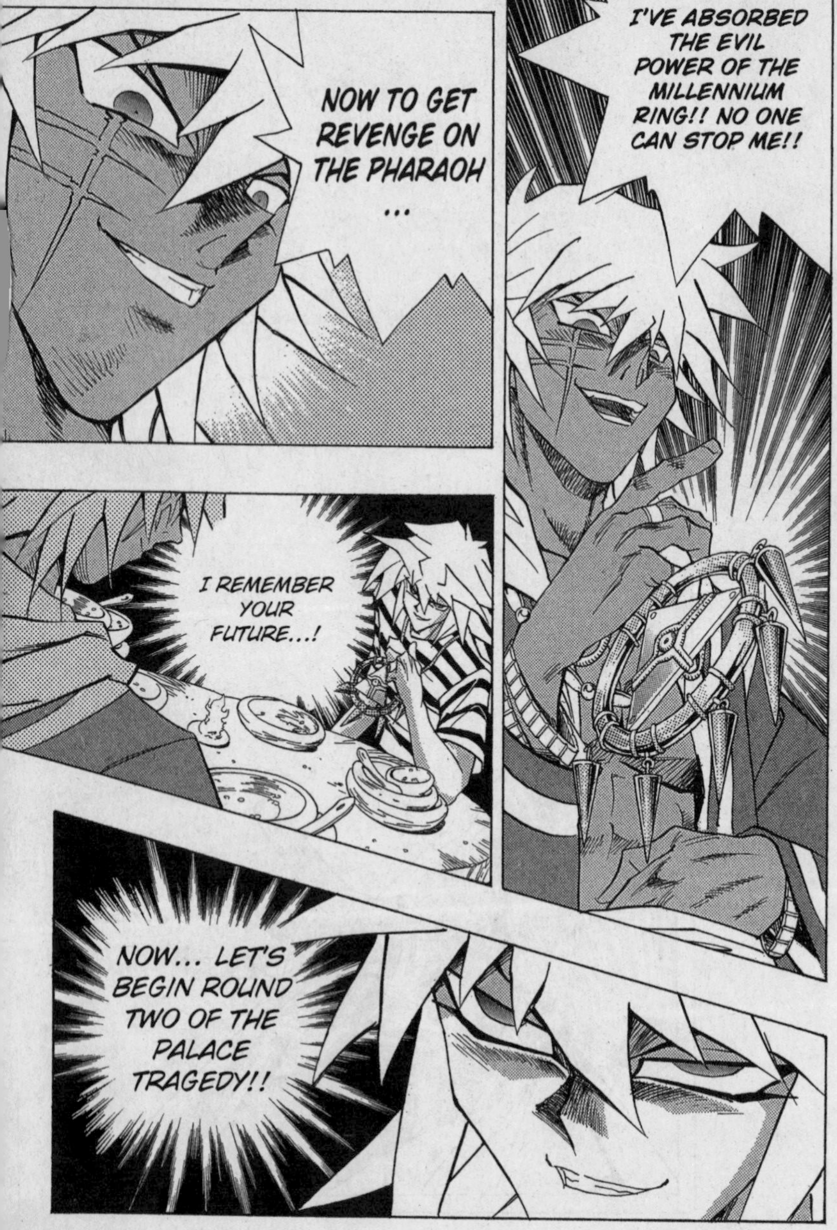
READ THIS WAY
I'VE ABSORBED THE EVIL POWER OF THE MILLENNIUM RING!! NO ONE CAN STOP ME!!
NOW TO GET REVENGE ON THE PHARAOH ...
I REMEMBER YOUR FUTURE...!
NOW... LET'S BEGIN ROUND TWO OF THE PALACE TRAGEDY!!

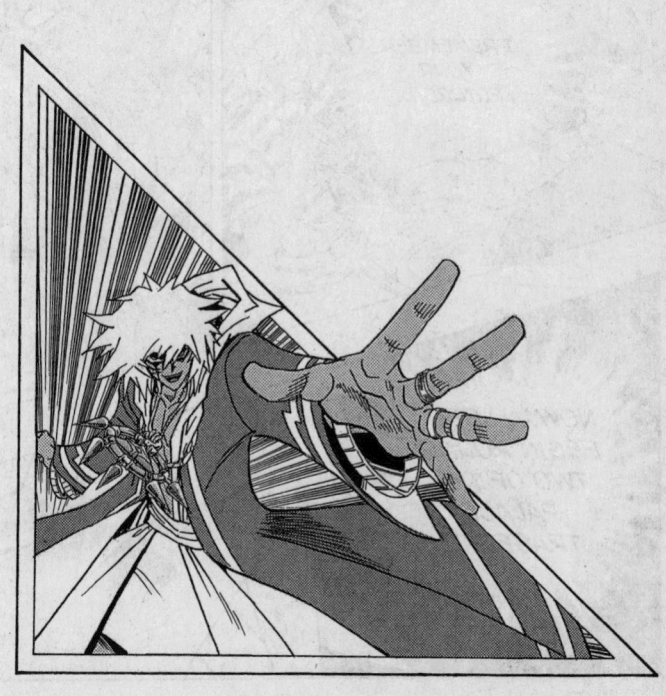

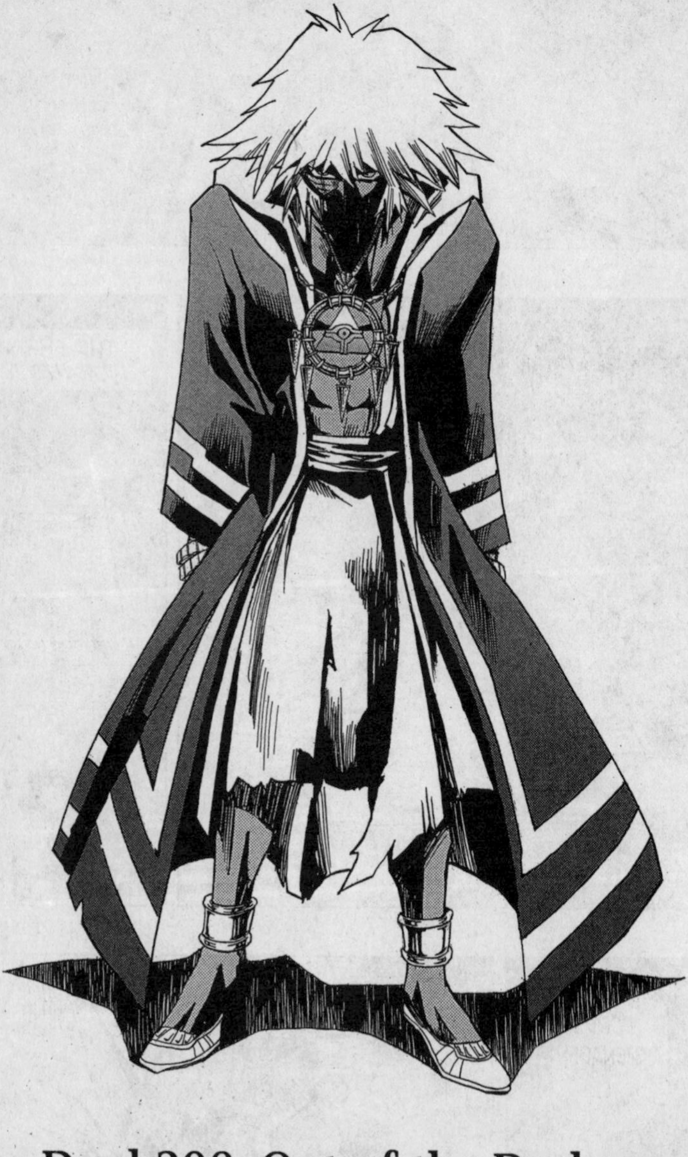

Duel 298: Out of the Darkness

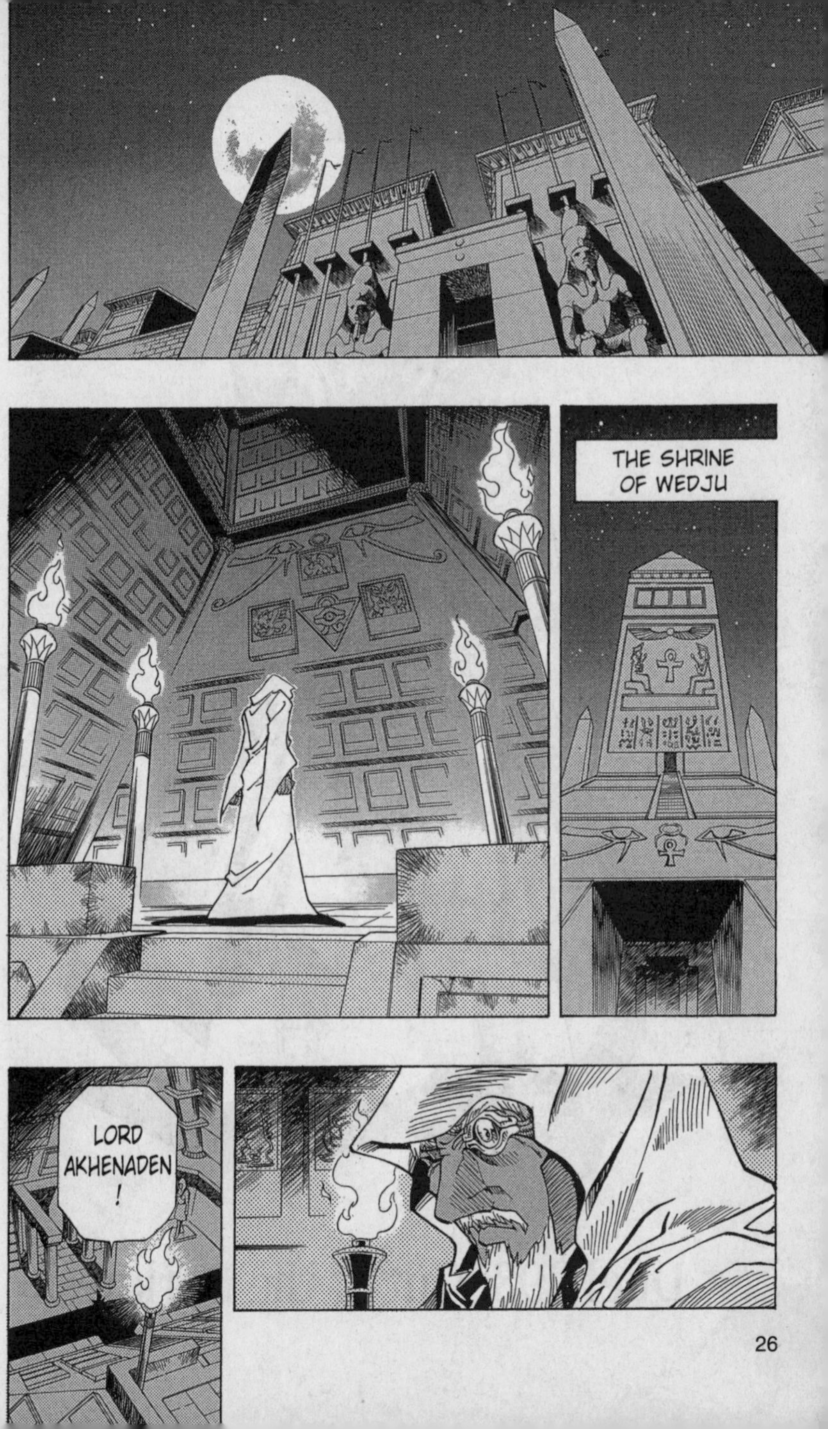
THE SHRINE OF WEDJU
LORD AKHENADEN!

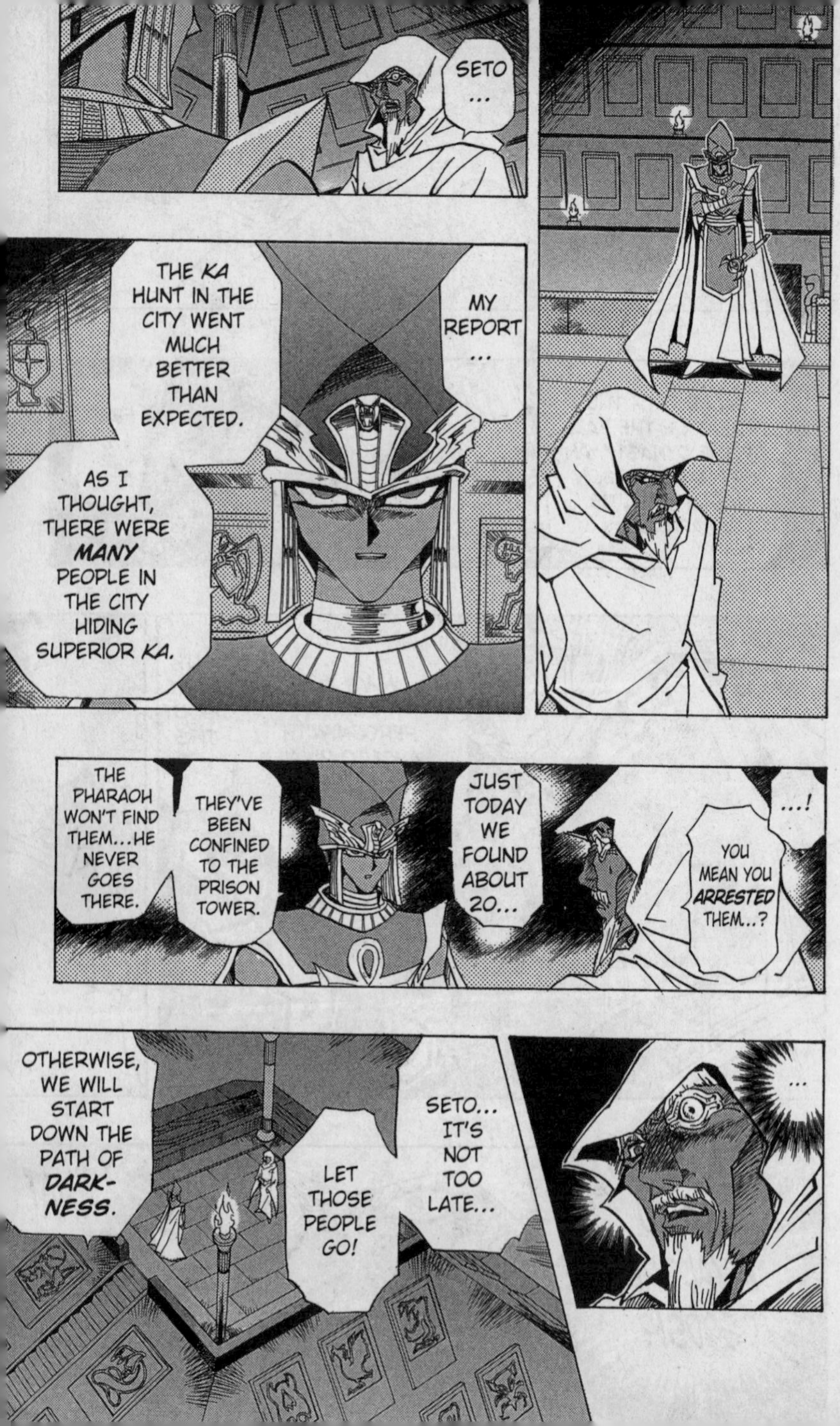
SETO ...
MY REPORT ...
THE KA HUNT IN THE CITY WENT MUCH BETTER THAN EXPECTED.
AS I THOUGHT, THERE WERE MANY PEOPLE IN THE CITY HIDING SUPERIOR KA.
...!
YOU MEAN YOU ARRESTED THEM...?
JUST TODAY WE FOUND ABOUT 20...
THEY'VE BEEN CONFINED TO THE PRISON TOWER.
THE PHARAOH WON'T FIND THEM...HE NEVER GOES THERE.
...
SETO... IT'S NOT TOO LATE...
LET THOSE PEOPLE GO!
OTHERWISE, WE WILL START DOWN THE PATH OF DARK-NESS.

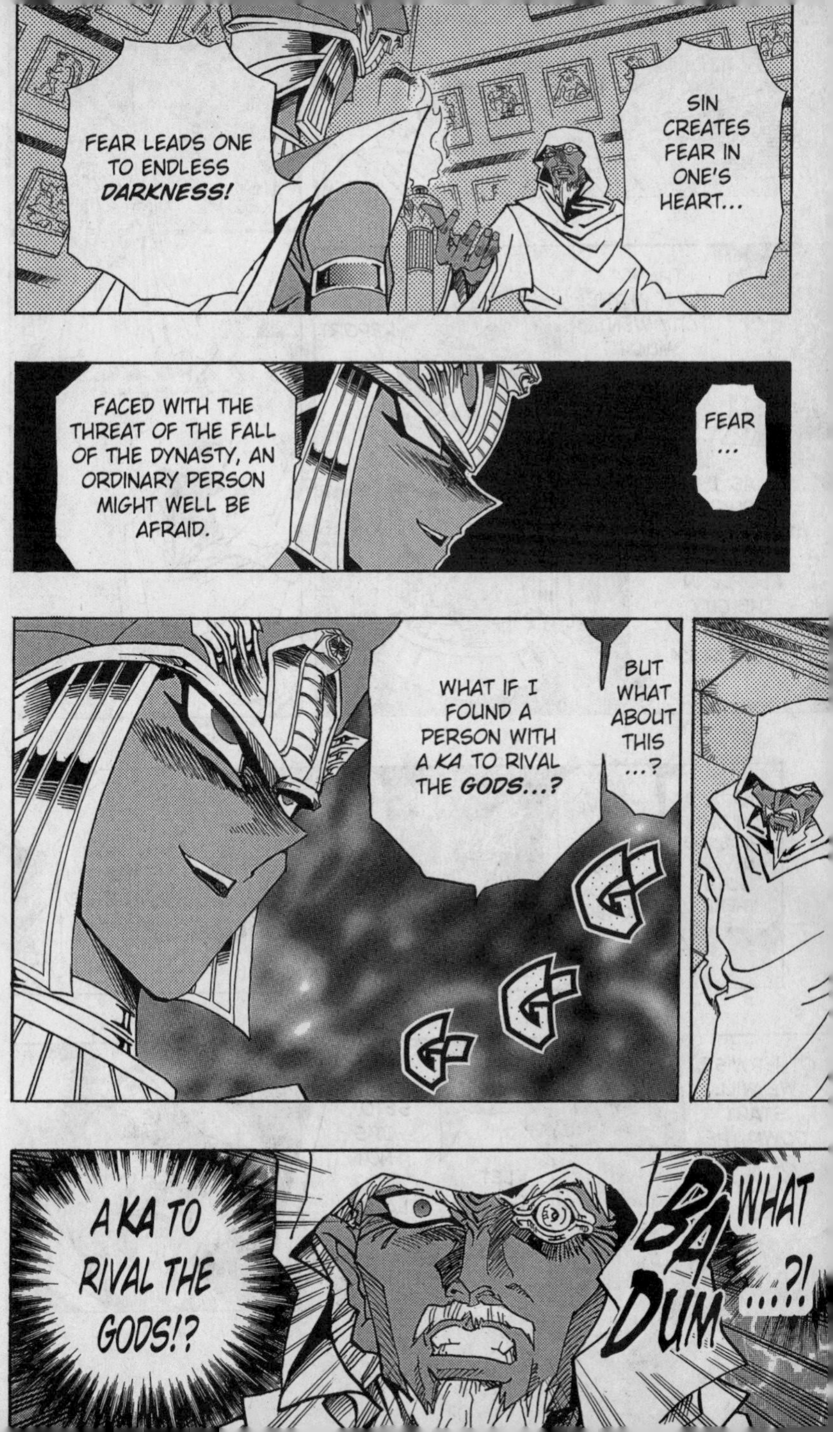
SIN CREATES FEAR IN ONE'S HEART...
FEAR LEADS ONE TO ENDLESS **DARKNESS!**
FEAR...
FACED WITH THE THREAT OF THE FALL OF THE DYNASTY, AN ORDINARY PERSON MIGHT WELL BE AFRAID.
BUT WHAT ABOUT THIS...?
WHAT IF I FOUND A PERSON WITH A *KA* TO RIVAL THE **GODS...?**
G G G
WHAT ...?!
BA DUM
A KA TO RIVAL THE GODS!?

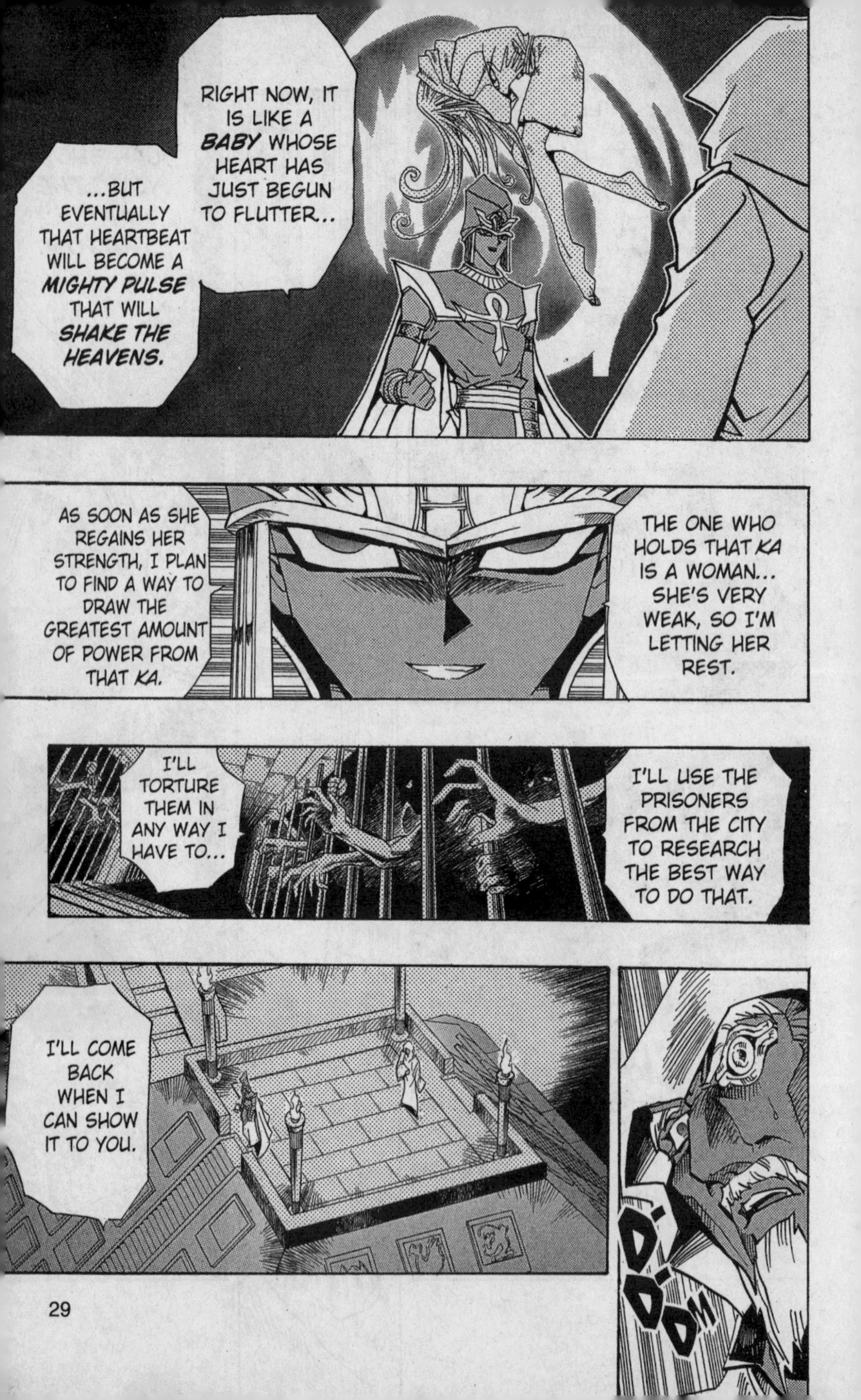
RIGHT NOW, IT IS LIKE A BABY WHOSE HEART HAS JUST BEGUN TO FLUTTER...
...BUT EVENTUALLY THAT HEARTBEAT WILL BECOME A MIGHTY PULSE THAT WILL SHAKE THE HEAVENS.
THE ONE WHO HOLDS THAT KA IS A WOMAN... SHE'S VERY WEAK, SO I'M LETTING HER REST.
AS SOON AS SHE REGAINS HER STRENGTH, I PLAN TO FIND A WAY TO DRAW THE GREATEST AMOUNT OF POWER FROM THAT KA.
I'LL USE THE PRISONERS FROM THE CITY TO RESEARCH THE BEST WAY TO DO THAT.
I'LL TORTURE THEM IN ANY WAY I HAVE TO...
D-D-DOM
I'LL COME BACK WHEN I CAN SHOW IT TO YOU.

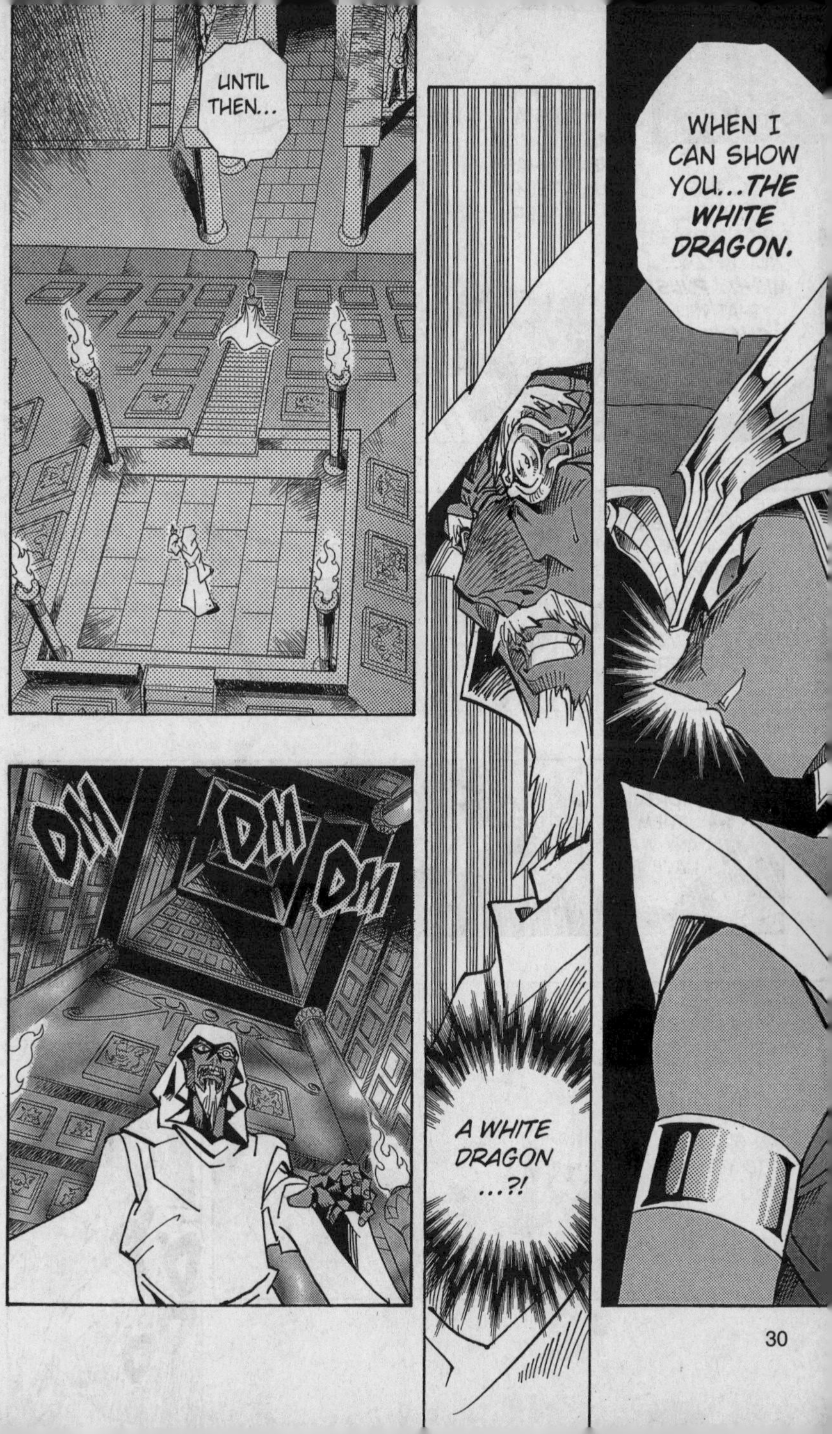
UNTIL THEN...
WHEN I CAN SHOW YOU...THE WHITE DRAGON.
A WHITE DRAGON ...?!
DM DM DM

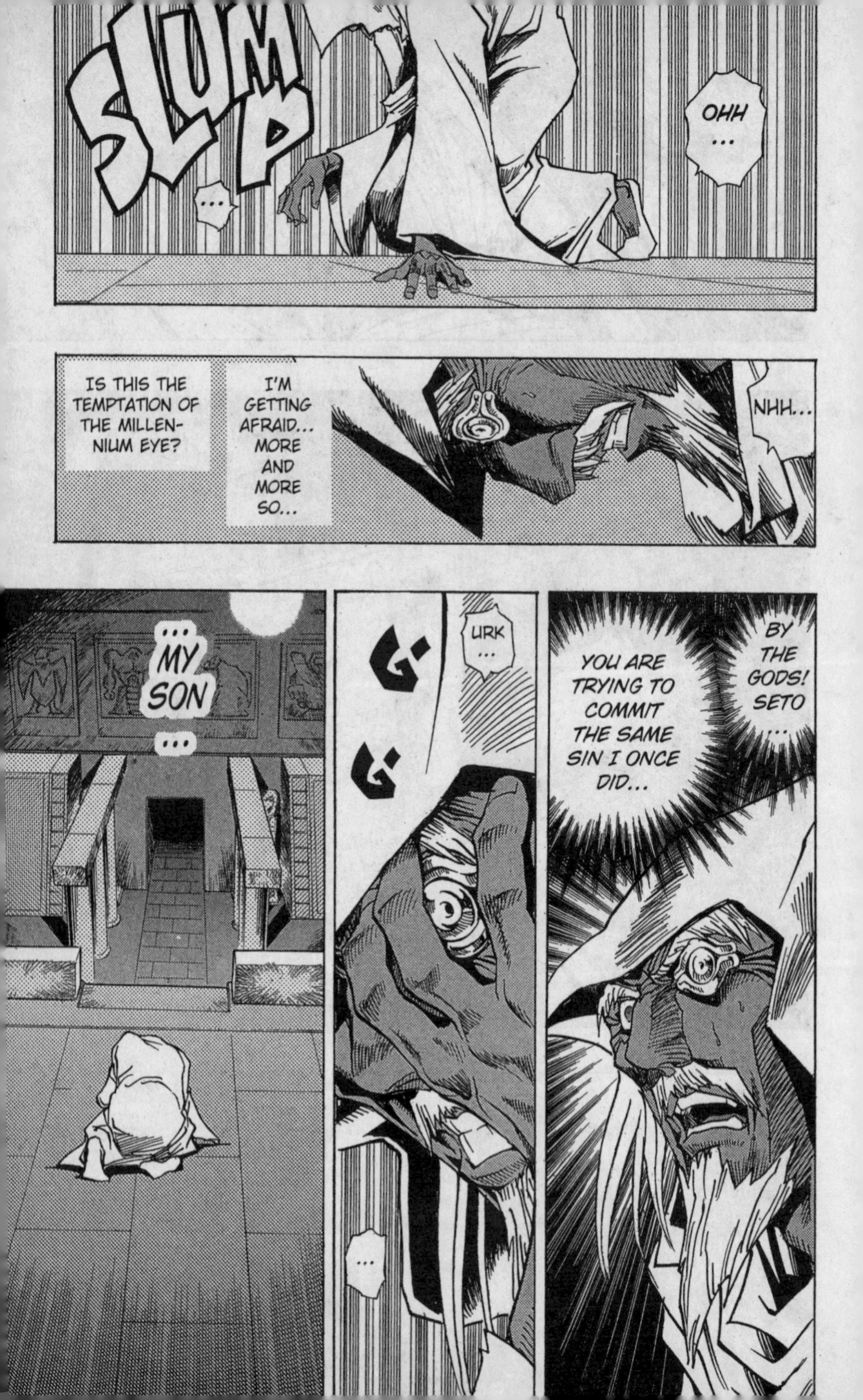
OHH ...
SLUMP
...
NHH...
I'M GETTING AFRAID... MORE AND MORE SO...
IS THIS THE TEMPTATION OF THE MILLEN-NIUM EYE?
BY THE GODS! SETO ...
YOU ARE TRYING TO COMMIT THE SAME SIN I ONCE DID...
URK ...
G
G
...
... MY SON ...

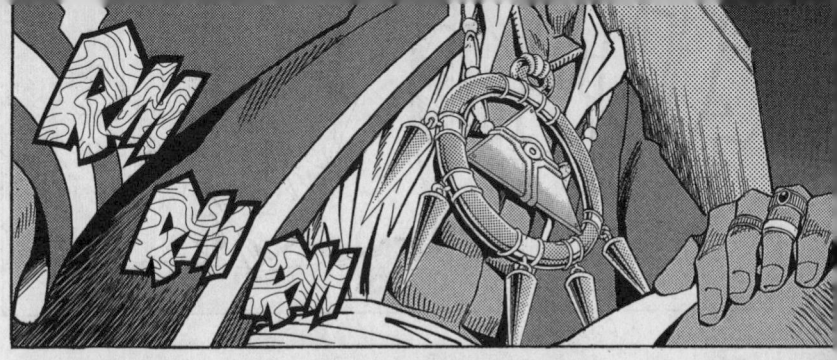

THIS TIME
I ATTACK
AT
NIGHT...

LIKE A
THIEF
SHOULD
...

READ THIS WAY

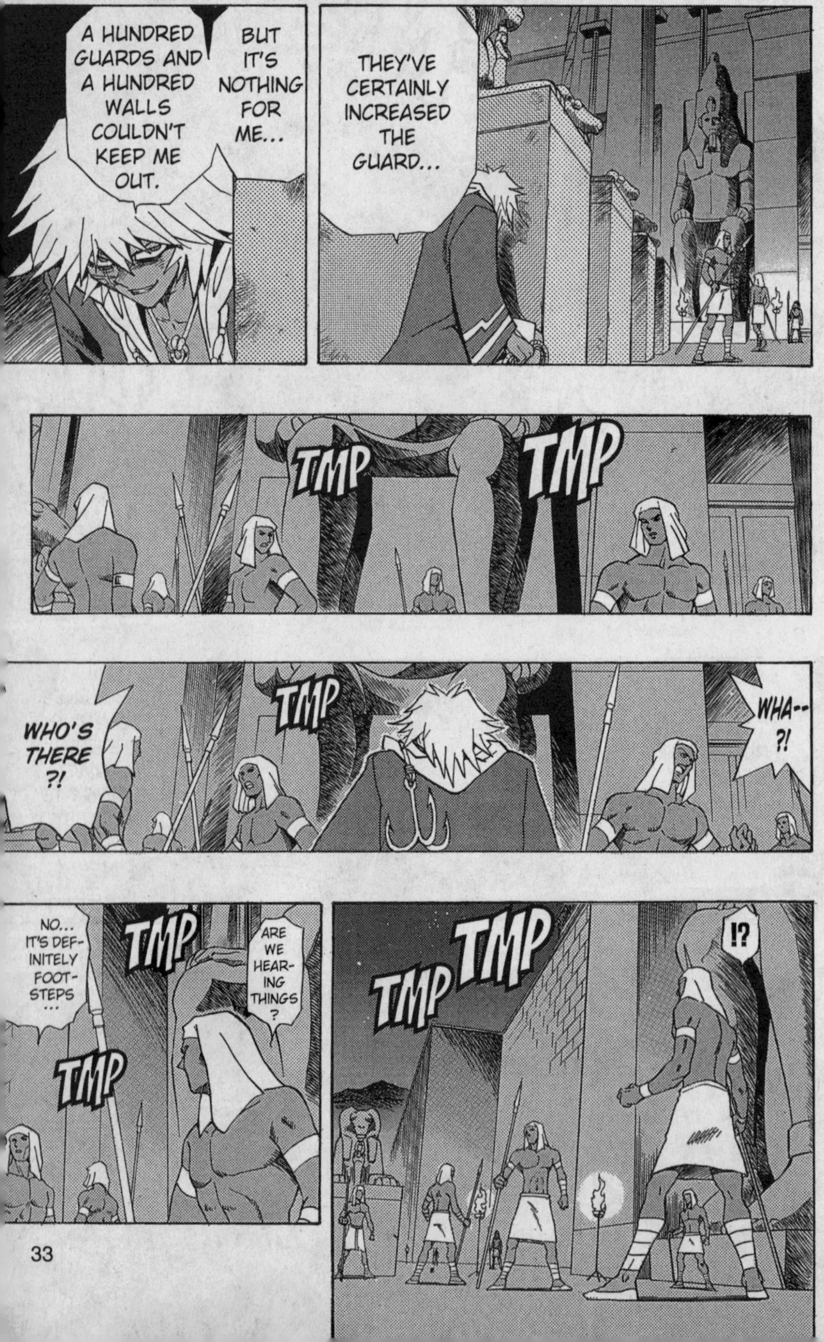
THEY'VE CERTAINLY INCREASED THE GUARD...
BUT IT'S NOTHING FOR ME...
A HUNDRED GUARDS AND A HUNDRED WALLS COULDN'T KEEP ME OUT.
TMP
TMP
WHA-- ?!
TMP
WHO'S THERE ?!
!?
TMP
TMP
ARE WE HEARING THINGS ?
TMP
NO... IT'S DEFINITELY FOOTSTEPS...
TMP

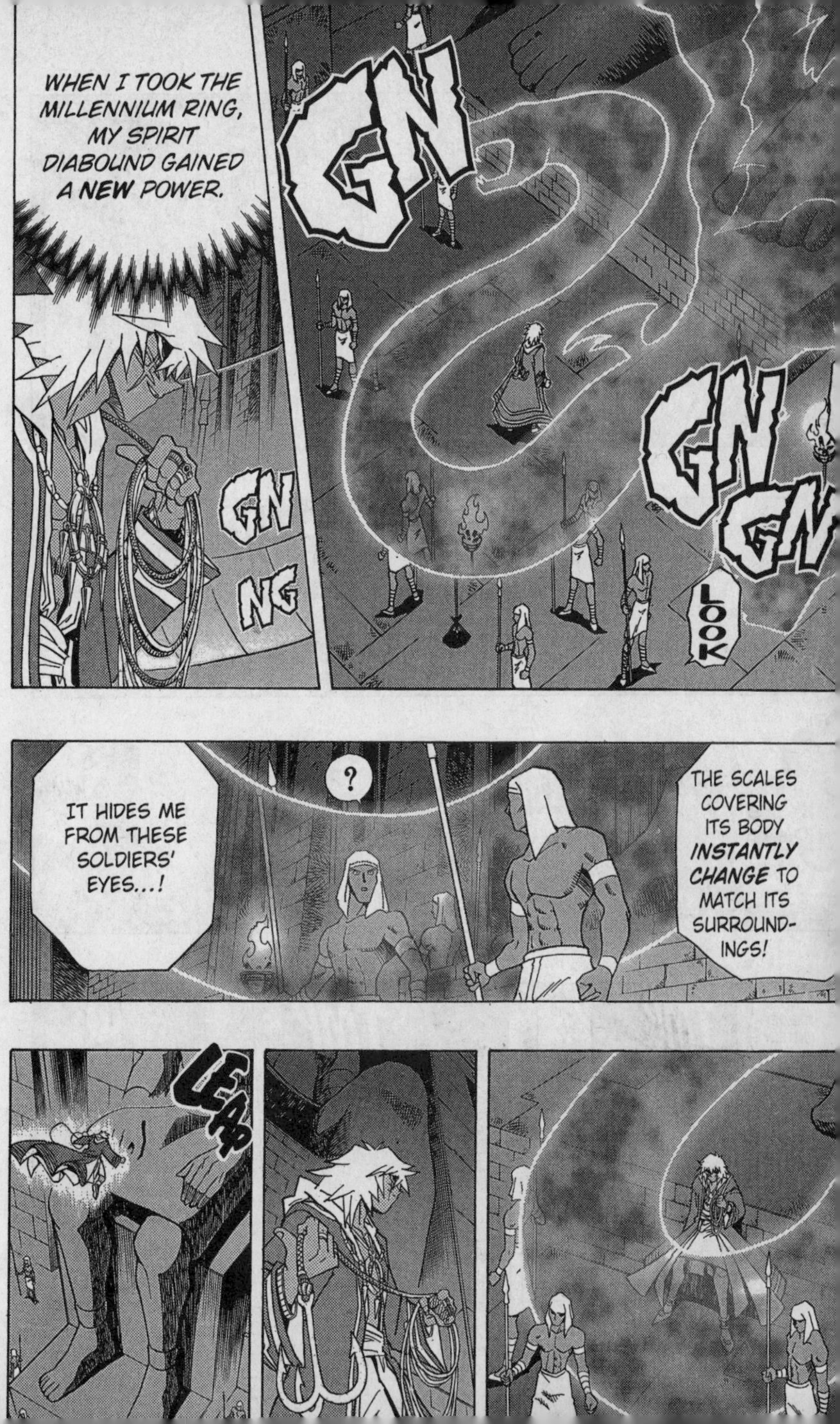
WHEN I TOOK THE MILLENNIUM RING, MY SPIRIT DIABOUND GAINED A **NEW** POWER.
GN
GN
NG
GN GN GN
LOOK
?
IT HIDES ME FROM THESE SOLDIERS' EYES...!
THE SCALES COVERING ITS BODY ***INSTANTLY CHANGE*** TO MATCH ITS SURROUND-INGS!
LEAP

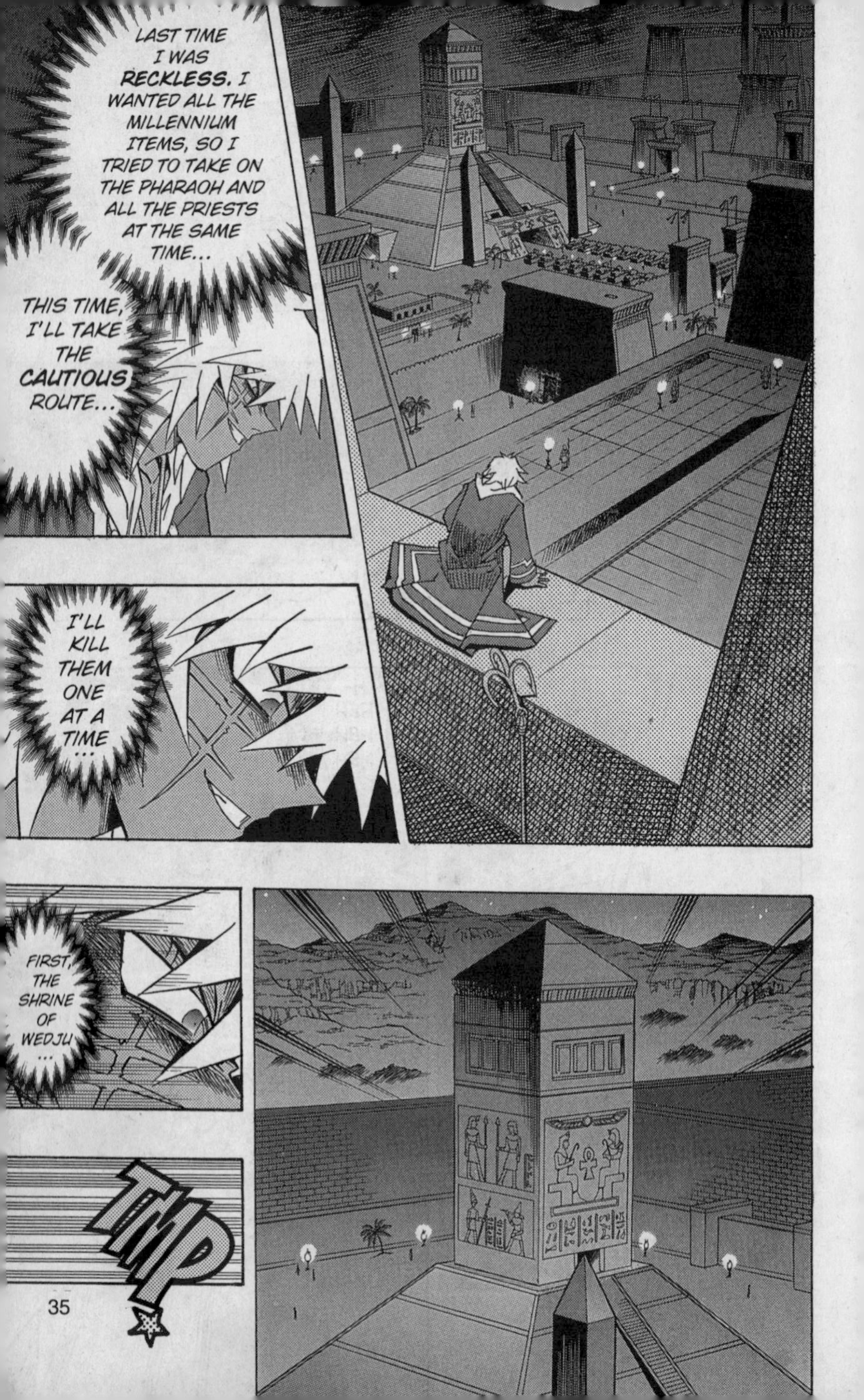
LAST TIME I WAS RECKLESS. I WANTED ALL THE MILLENNIUM ITEMS, SO I TRIED TO TAKE ON THE PHARAOH AND ALL THE PRIESTS AT THE SAME TIME...
THIS TIME, I'LL TAKE THE CAUTIOUS ROUTE...
I'LL KILL THEM ONE AT A TIME...
FIRST, THE SHRINE OF WEDJU...
THP

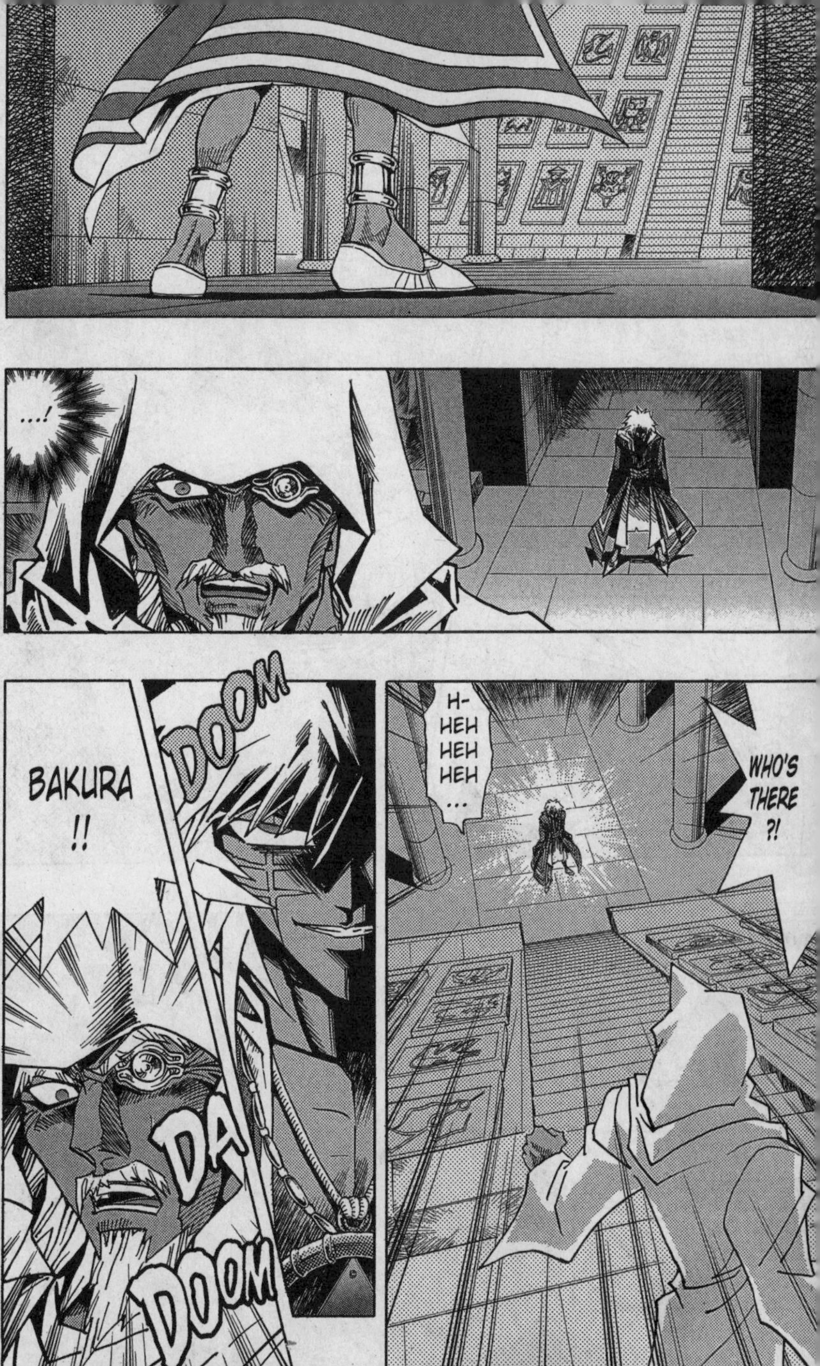
...!
WHO'S THERE ?!
H-HEH HEH HEH ...
DOOM
BAKURA !!
DA
DOOM

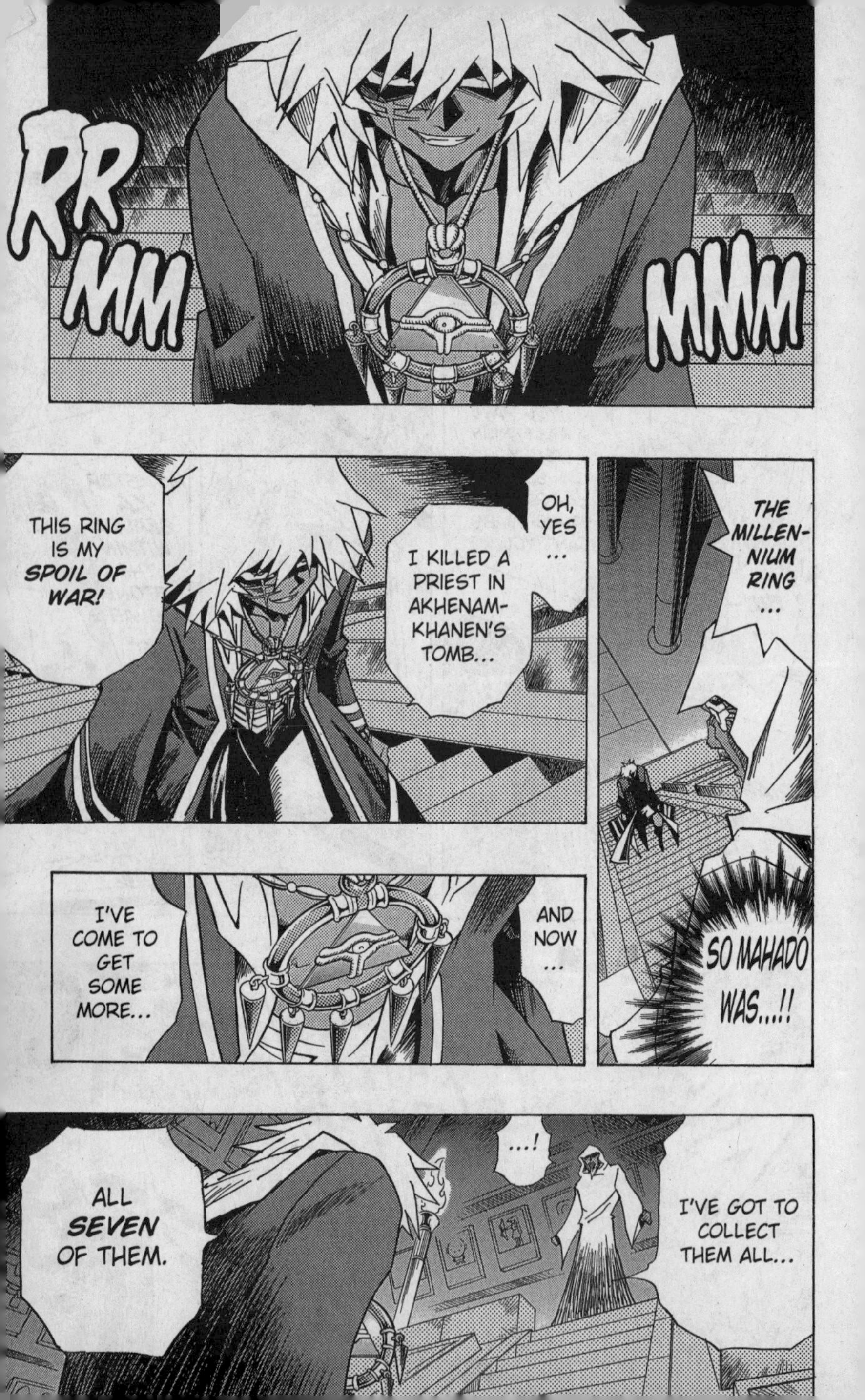
RR
MM
MMM
OH, YES ...
I KILLED A PRIEST IN AKHENAM-KHANEN'S TOMB...
THIS RING IS MY *SPOIL OF WAR!*
THE MILLEN-NIUM RING ...
AND NOW ...
I'VE COME TO GET SOME MORE...
SO MAHADO WAS...!!
...!
I'VE GOT TO COLLECT THEM ALL...
ALL *SEVEN* OF THEM.

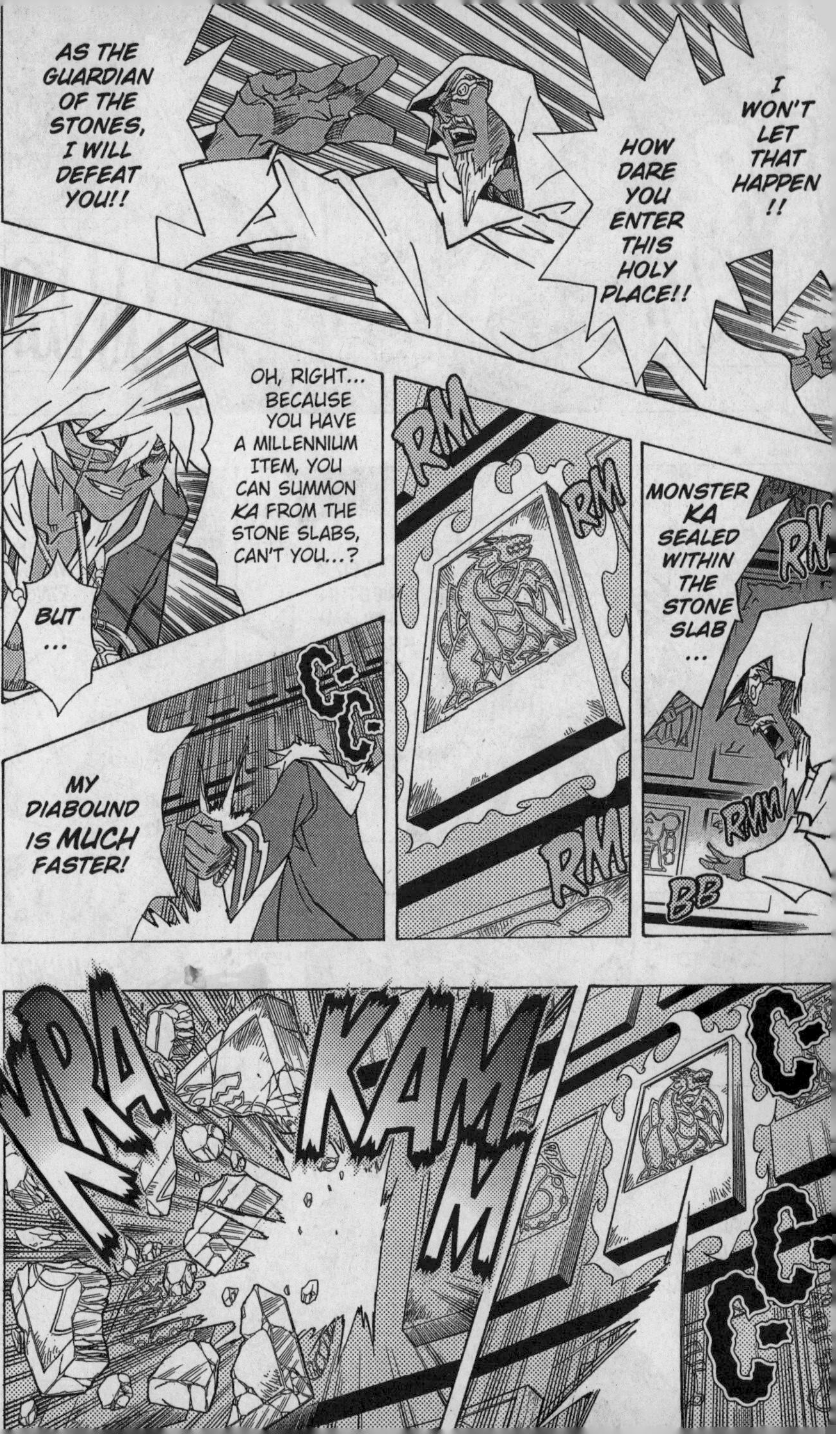
I WON'T LET THAT HAPPEN!!
HOW DARE YOU ENTER THIS HOLY PLACE!!
AS THE GUARDIAN OF THE STONES, I WILL DEFEAT YOU!!
RM
MONSTER KA SEALED WITHIN THE STONE SLAB...
RMM
BB
RM
RM
RM
OH, RIGHT... BECAUSE YOU HAVE A MILLENNIUM ITEM, YOU CAN SUMMON KA FROM THE STONE SLABS, CAN'T YOU...?
BUT...
C-C-
MY DIABOUND IS MUCH FASTER!
C-
C-C-
KAM
M
KRA

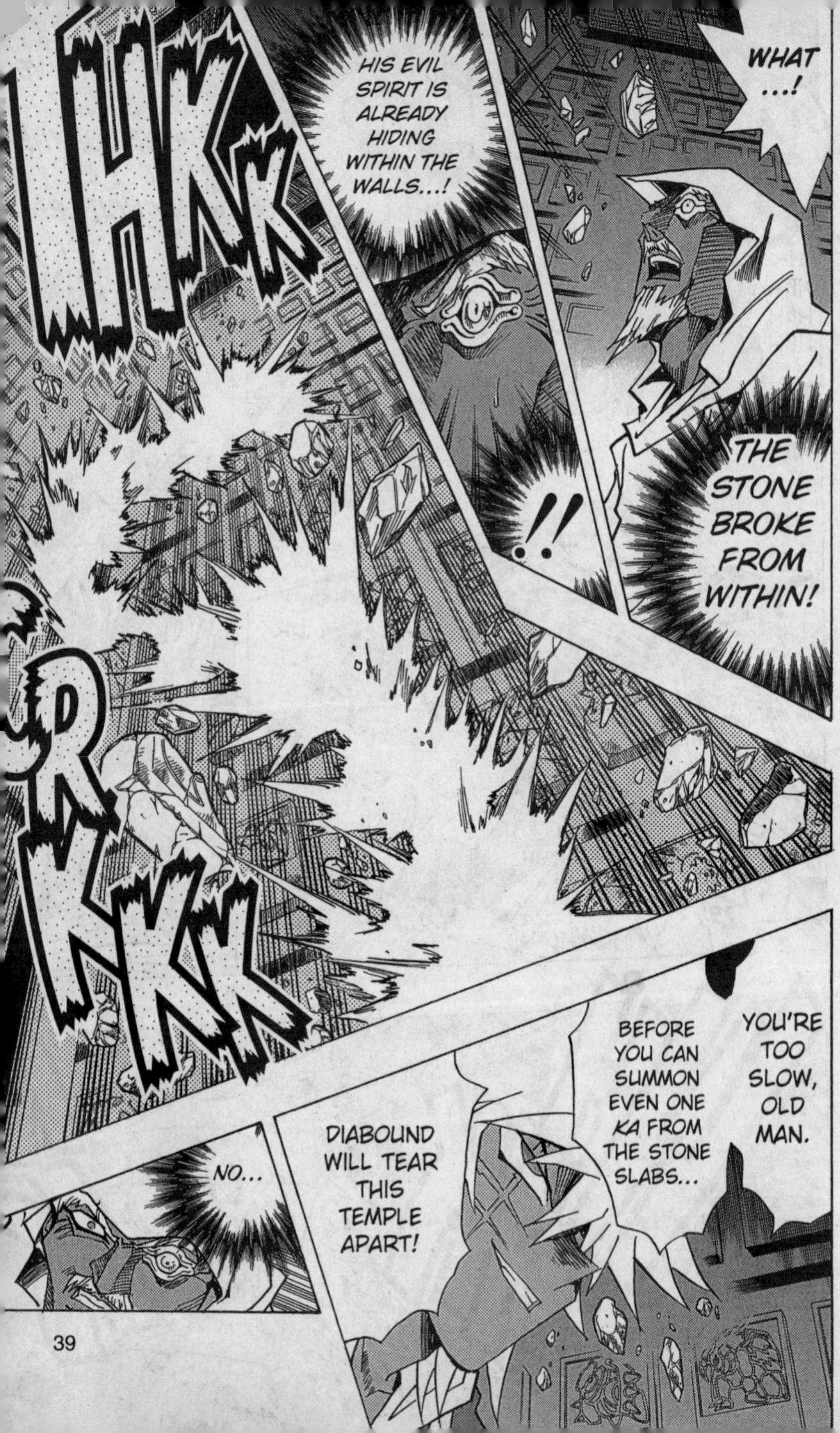
WHAT...!
THE STONE BROKE FROM WITHIN!
!!
HIS EVIL SPIRIT IS ALREADY HIDING WITHIN THE WALLS...!
YOU'RE TOO SLOW, OLD MAN.
BEFORE YOU CAN SUMMON EVEN ONE *KA* FROM THE STONE SLABS...
DIABOUND WILL TEAR THIS TEMPLE APART!
NO...

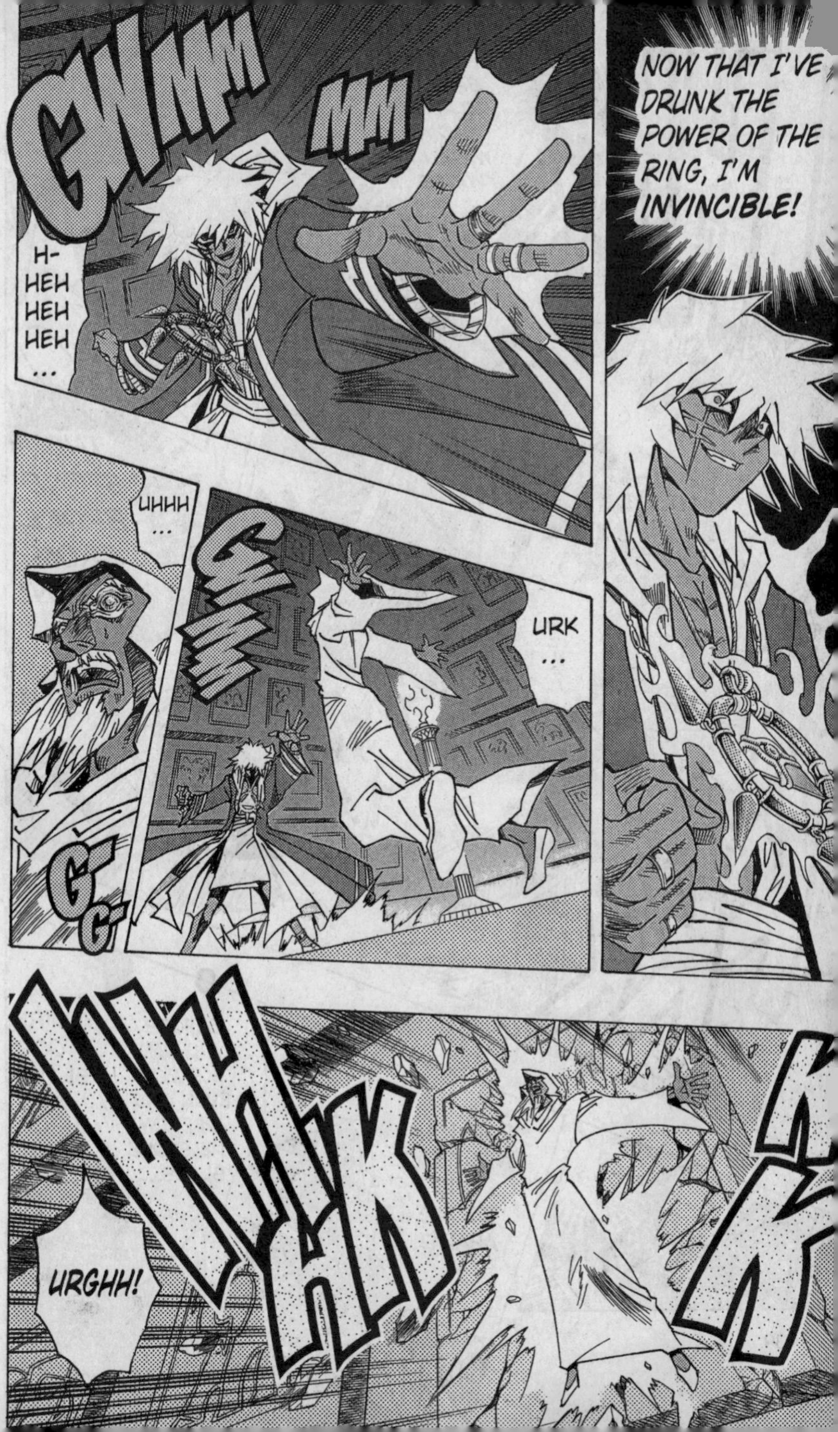

NOW THAT I'VE DRUNK THE POWER OF THE RING, I'M INVINCIBLE!
MM
H-HEH HEH HEH HEH ...
URK ...
UHHH ...
URGHH!

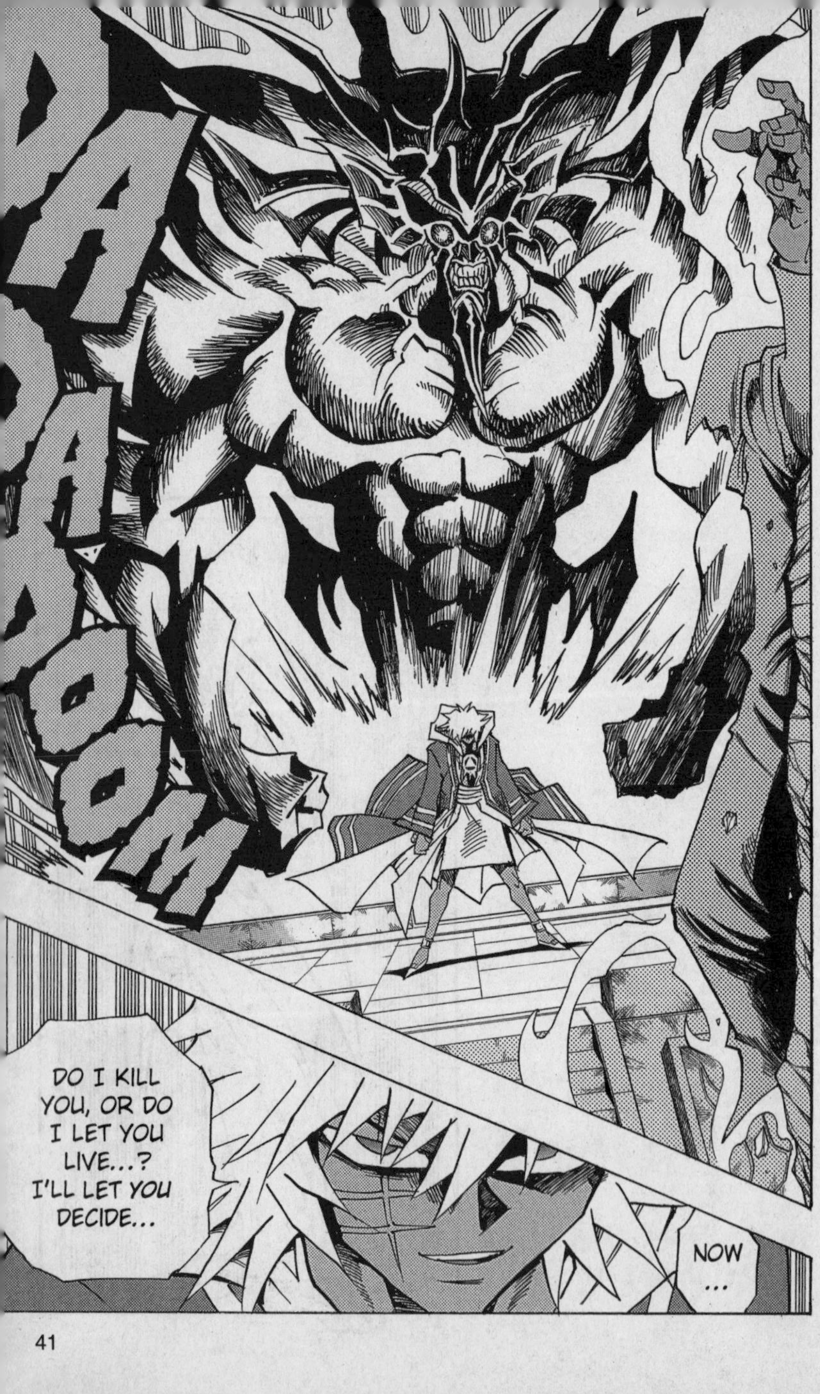
DADOOM
NOW...
DO I KILL YOU, OR DO I LET YOU LIVE...? I'LL LET YOU DECIDE...

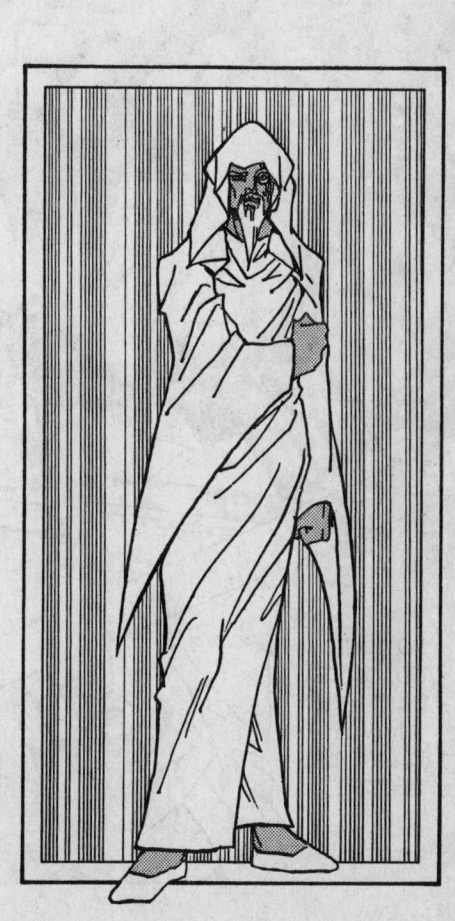

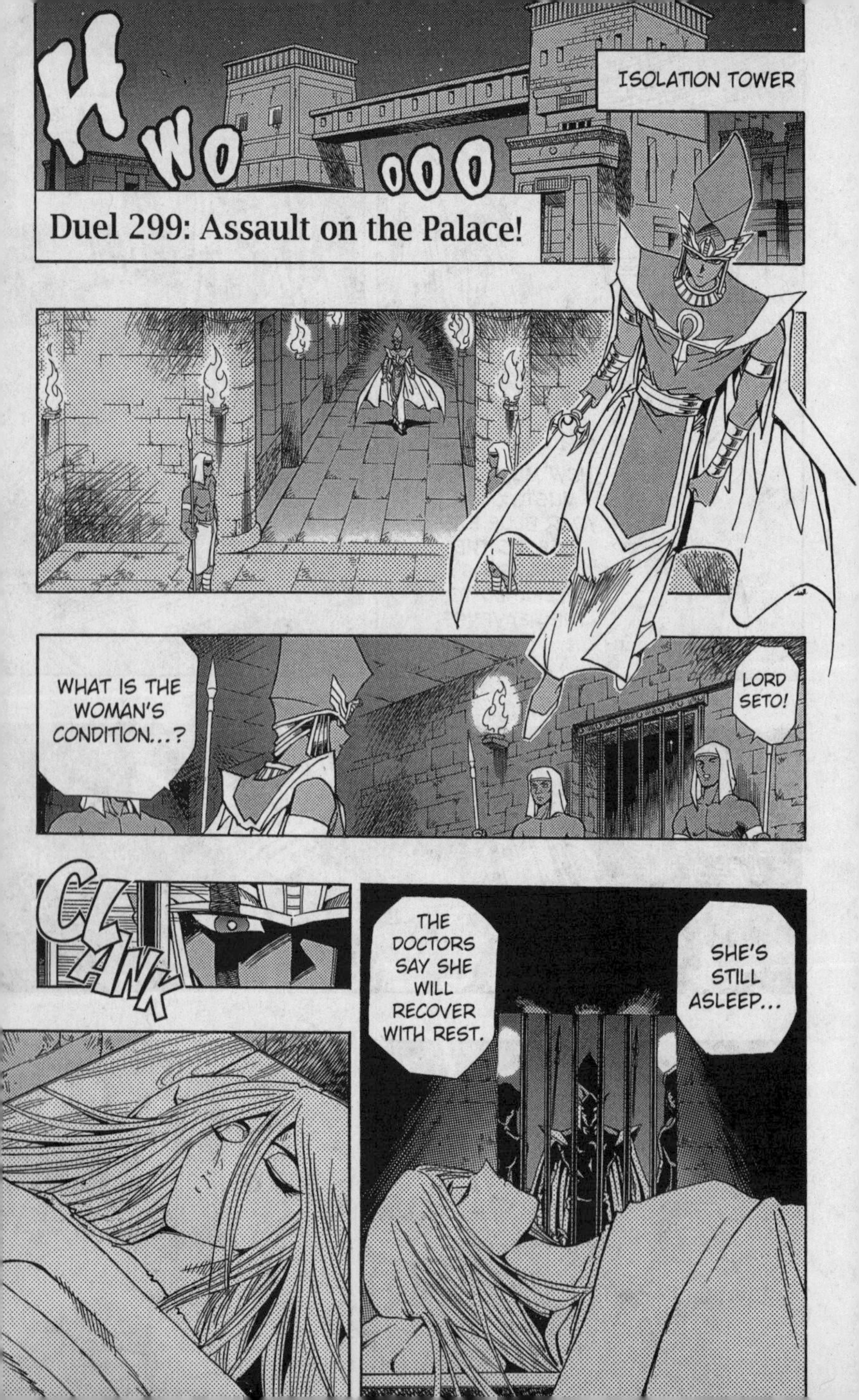
ISOLATION TOWER
HWOOOO
Duel 299: Assault on the Palace!
LORD SETO!
WHAT IS THE WOMAN'S CONDITION...?
SHE'S STILL ASLEEP...
THE DOCTORS SAY SHE WILL RECOVER WITH REST.
CLANK

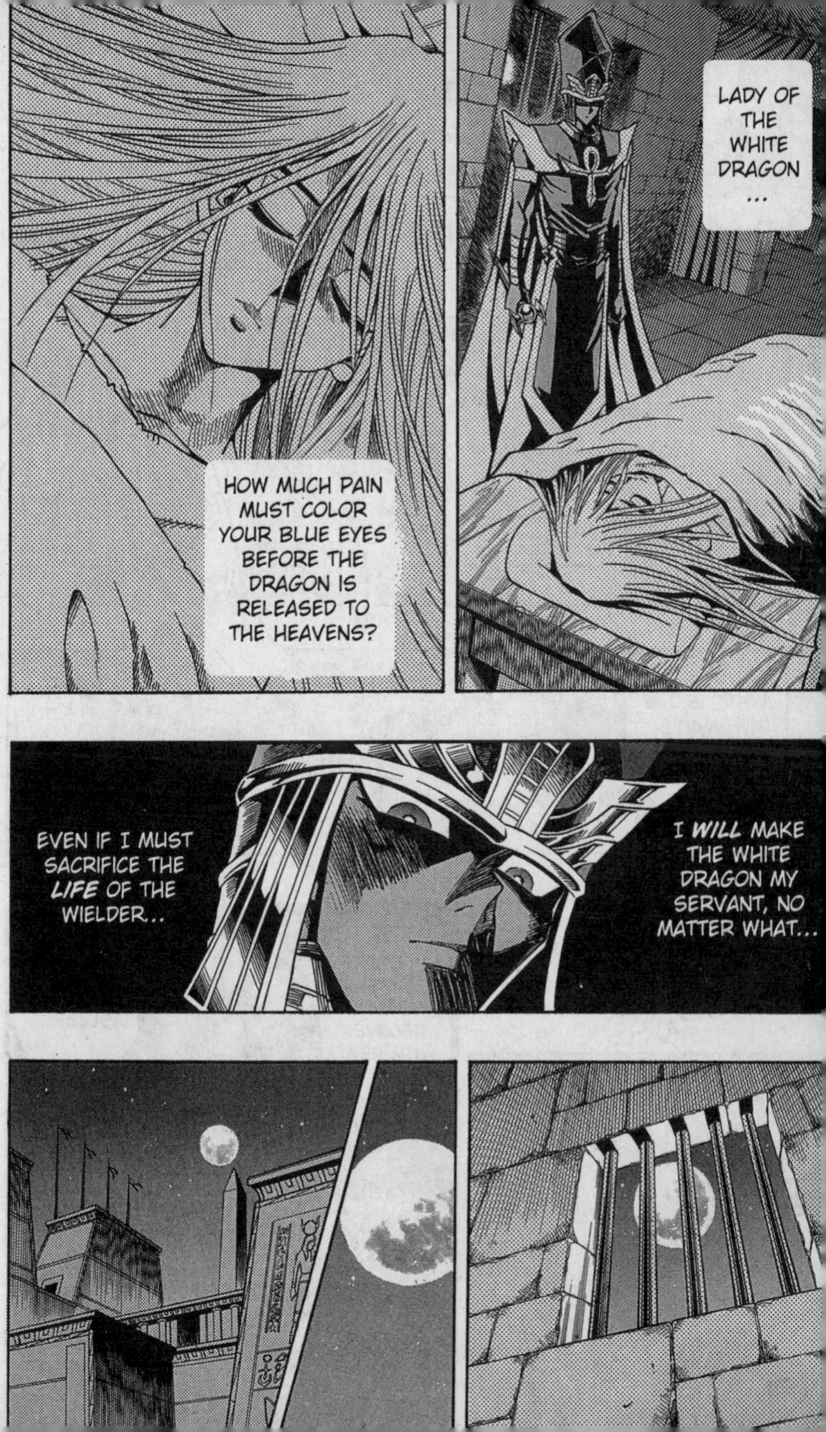
LADY OF THE WHITE DRAGON ...
HOW MUCH PAIN MUST COLOR YOUR BLUE EYES BEFORE THE DRAGON IS RELEASED TO THE HEAVENS?
I *WILL* MAKE THE WHITE DRAGON MY SERVANT, NO MATTER WHAT...
EVEN IF I MUST SACRIFICE THE *LIFE* OF THE WIELDER...

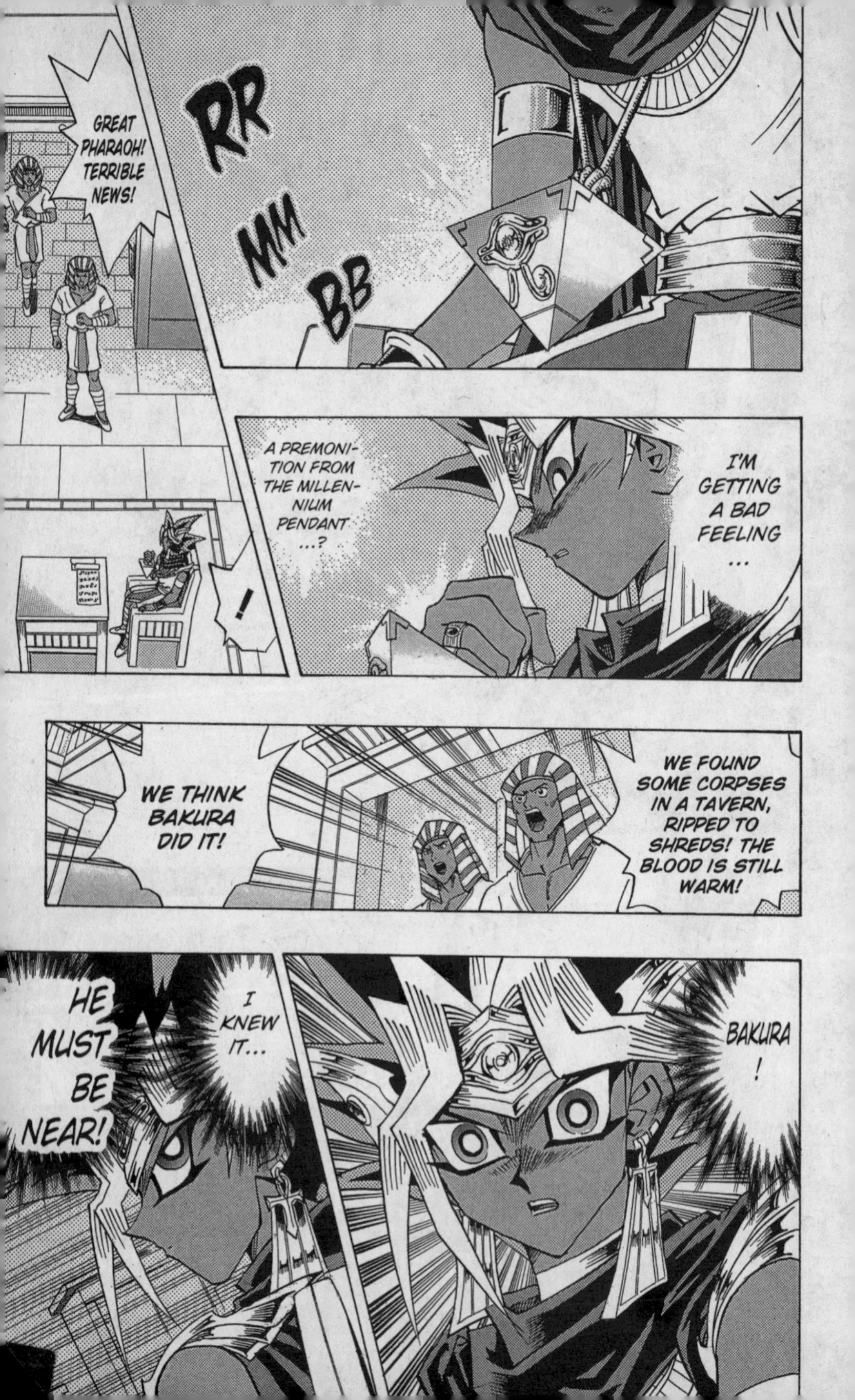
RRMMBB
I'M GETTING A BAD FEELING...
A PREMONITION FROM THE MILLENNIUM PENDANT...?
GREAT PHARAOH! TERRIBLE NEWS!
!
WE FOUND SOME CORPSES IN A TAVERN, RIPPED TO SHREDS! THE BLOOD IS STILL WARM!
WE THINK BAKURA DID IT!
BAKURA!
I KNEW IT...
HE MUST BE NEAR!

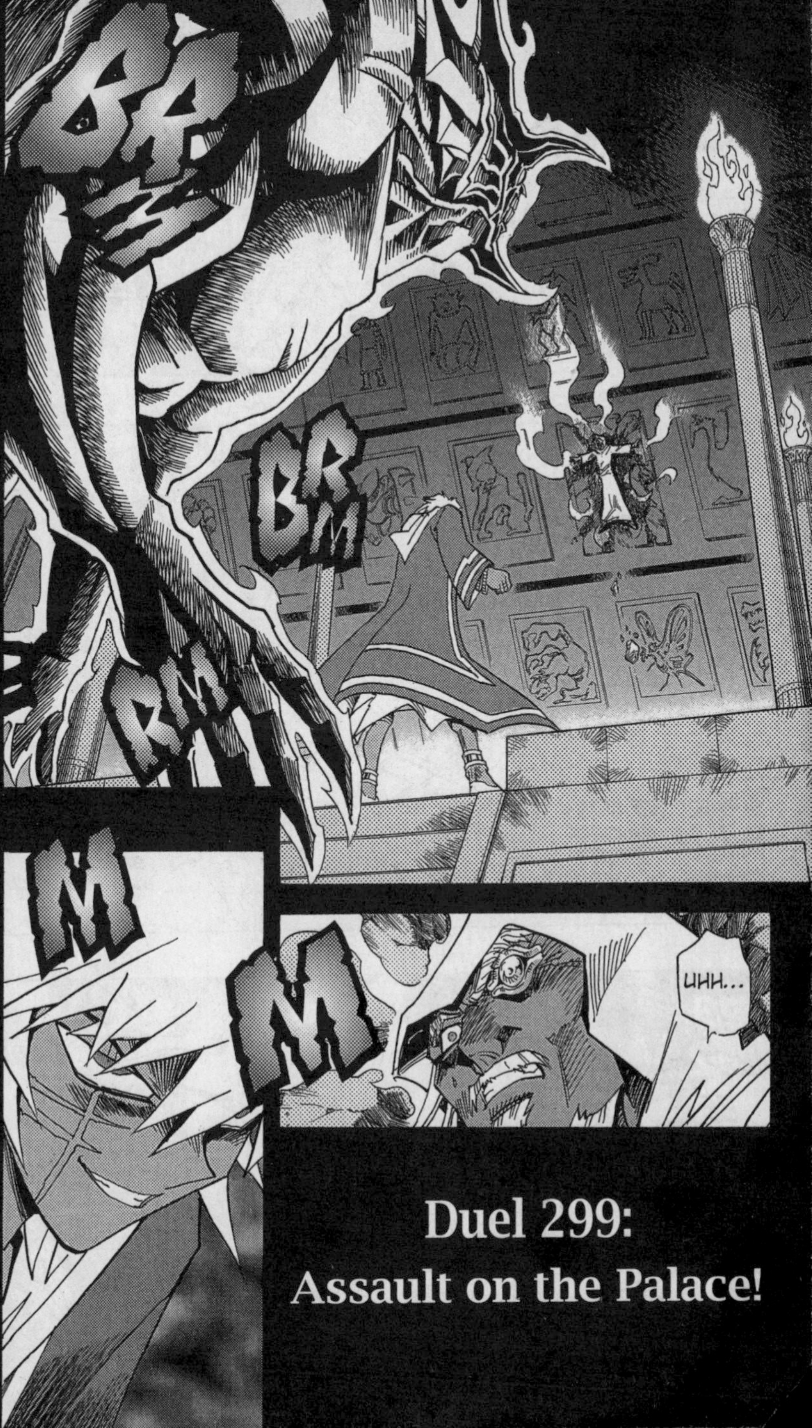
BRA
BR
RM
RM
M
M
UHH...

Duel 299: Assault on the Palace!

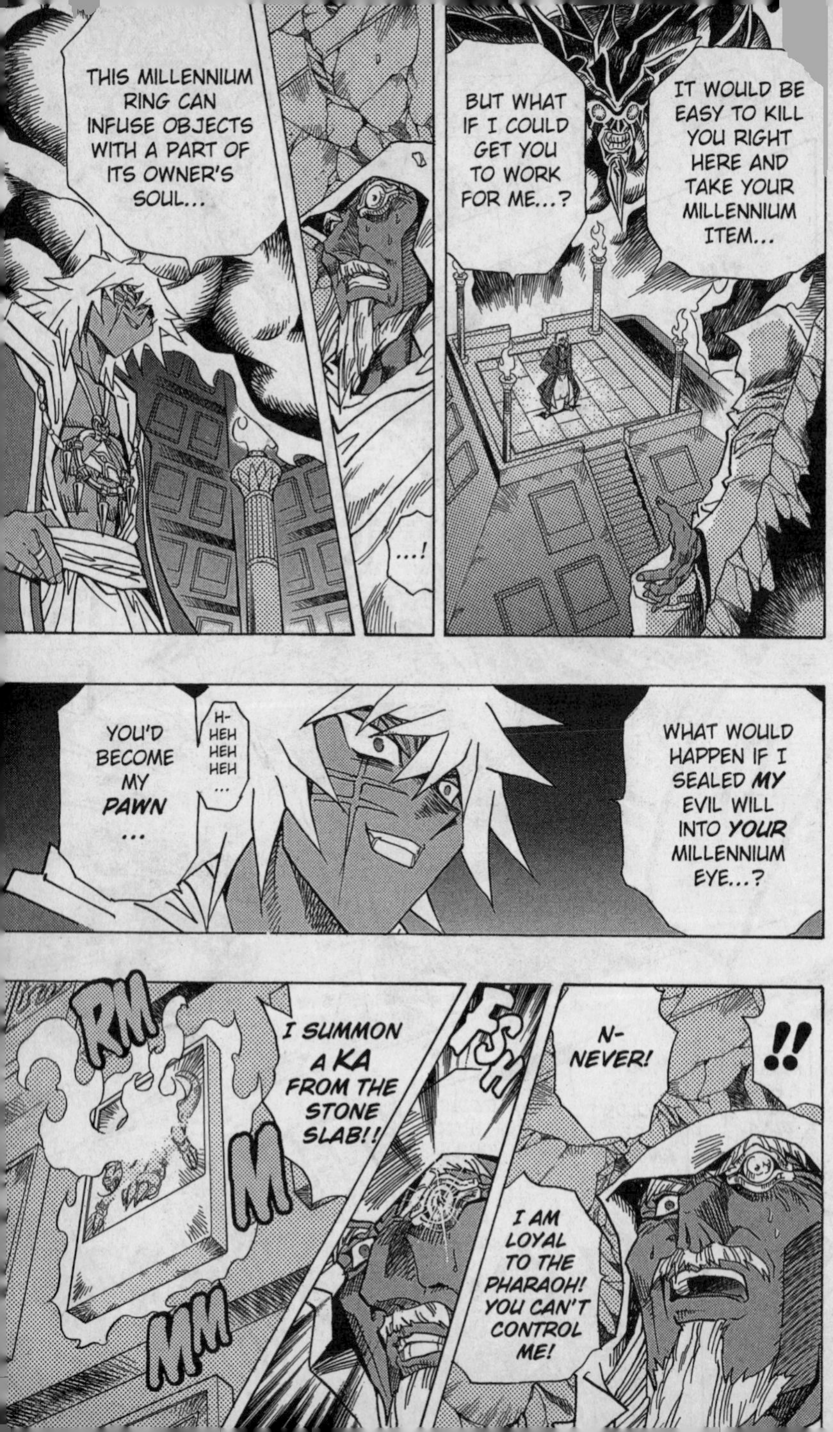
IT WOULD BE EASY TO KILL YOU RIGHT HERE AND TAKE YOUR MILLENNIUM ITEM...
BUT WHAT IF I COULD GET YOU TO WORK FOR ME...?
...!
THIS MILLENNIUM RING CAN INFUSE OBJECTS WITH A PART OF ITS OWNER'S SOUL...
WHAT WOULD HAPPEN IF I SEALED *MY* EVIL WILL INTO *YOUR* MILLENNIUM EYE...?
H-HEH HEH HEH...
YOU'D BECOME MY *PAWN*...
!!
N-NEVER!
I AM LOYAL TO THE PHARAOH! YOU CAN'T CONTROL ME!
FSH
I SUMMON A *KA* FROM THE STONE SLAB!!
RM
M
MM

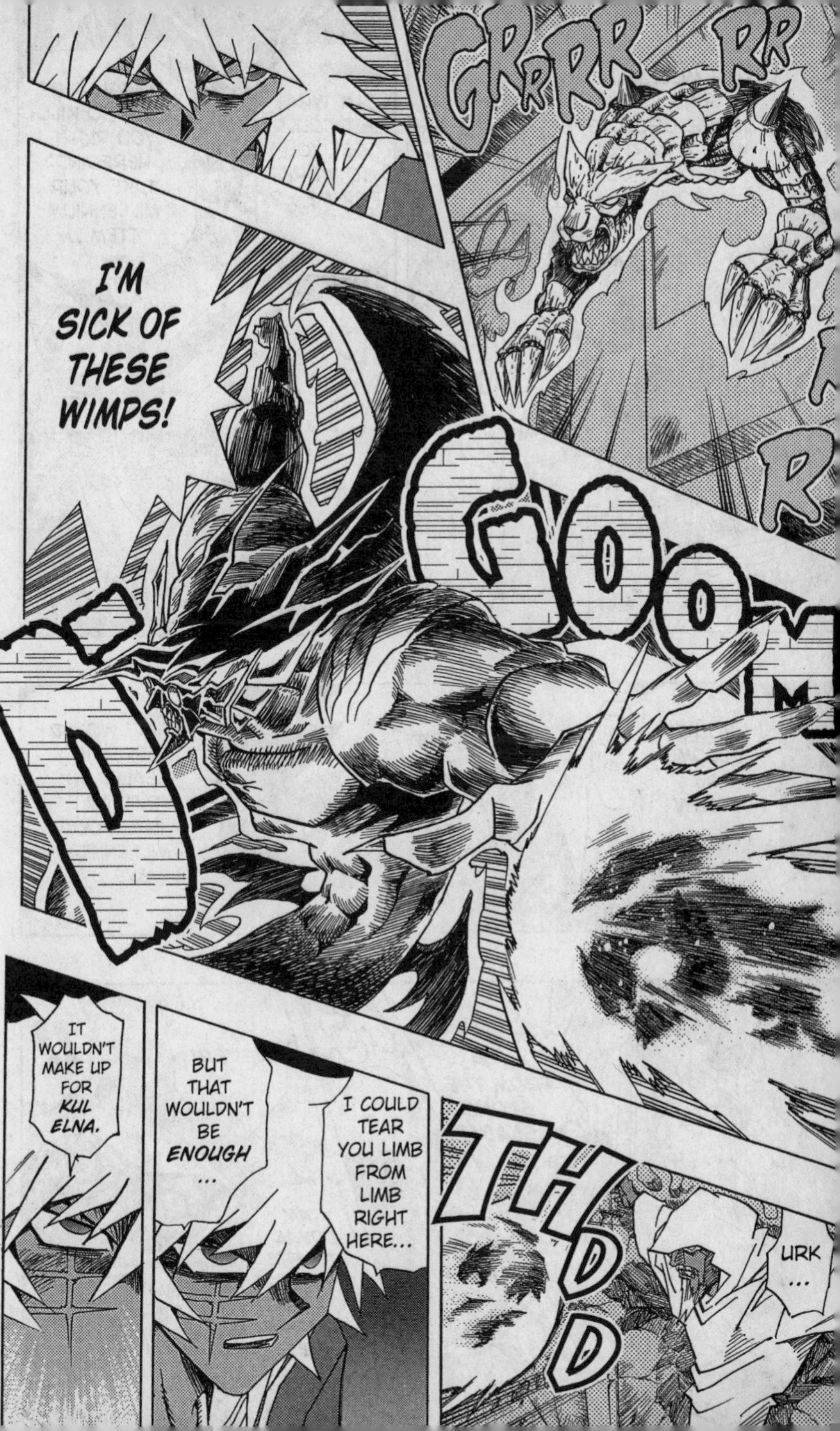

GRRRR RR
I'M SICK OF THESE WIMPS!
URK...
THDDD
I COULD TEAR YOU LIMB FROM LIMB RIGHT HERE...
BUT THAT WOULDN'T BE ENOUGH...
IT WOULDN'T MAKE UP FOR KUL ELNA.

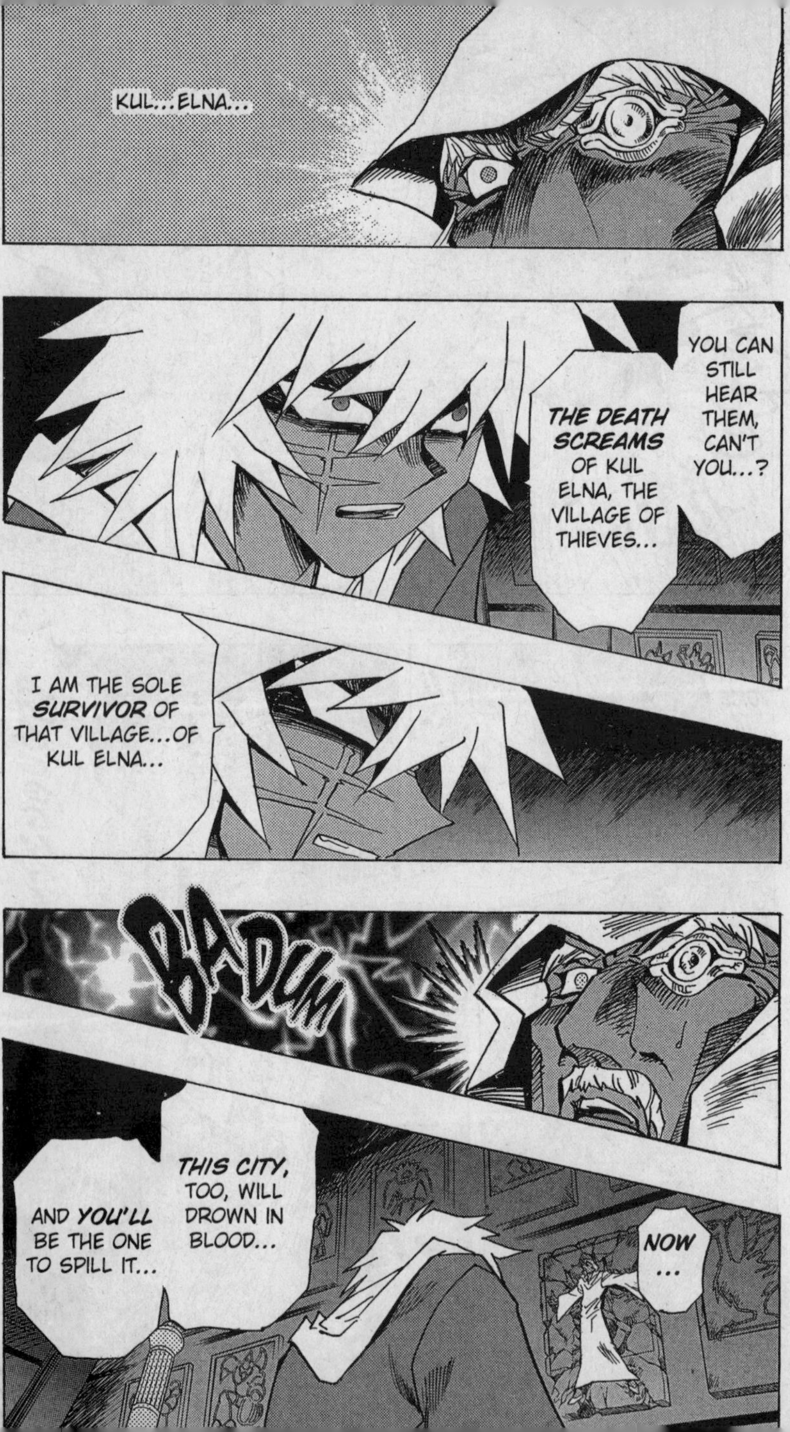
KUL...ELNA...
YOU CAN STILL HEAR THEM, CAN'T YOU...?
THE DEATH SCREAMS OF KUL ELNA, THE VILLAGE OF THIEVES...
I AM THE SOLE *SURVIVOR* OF THAT VILLAGE...OF KUL ELNA...
BA-DUM
NOW...
THIS CITY, TOO, WILL DROWN IN BLOOD...
AND *YOU'LL* BE THE ONE TO SPILL IT...

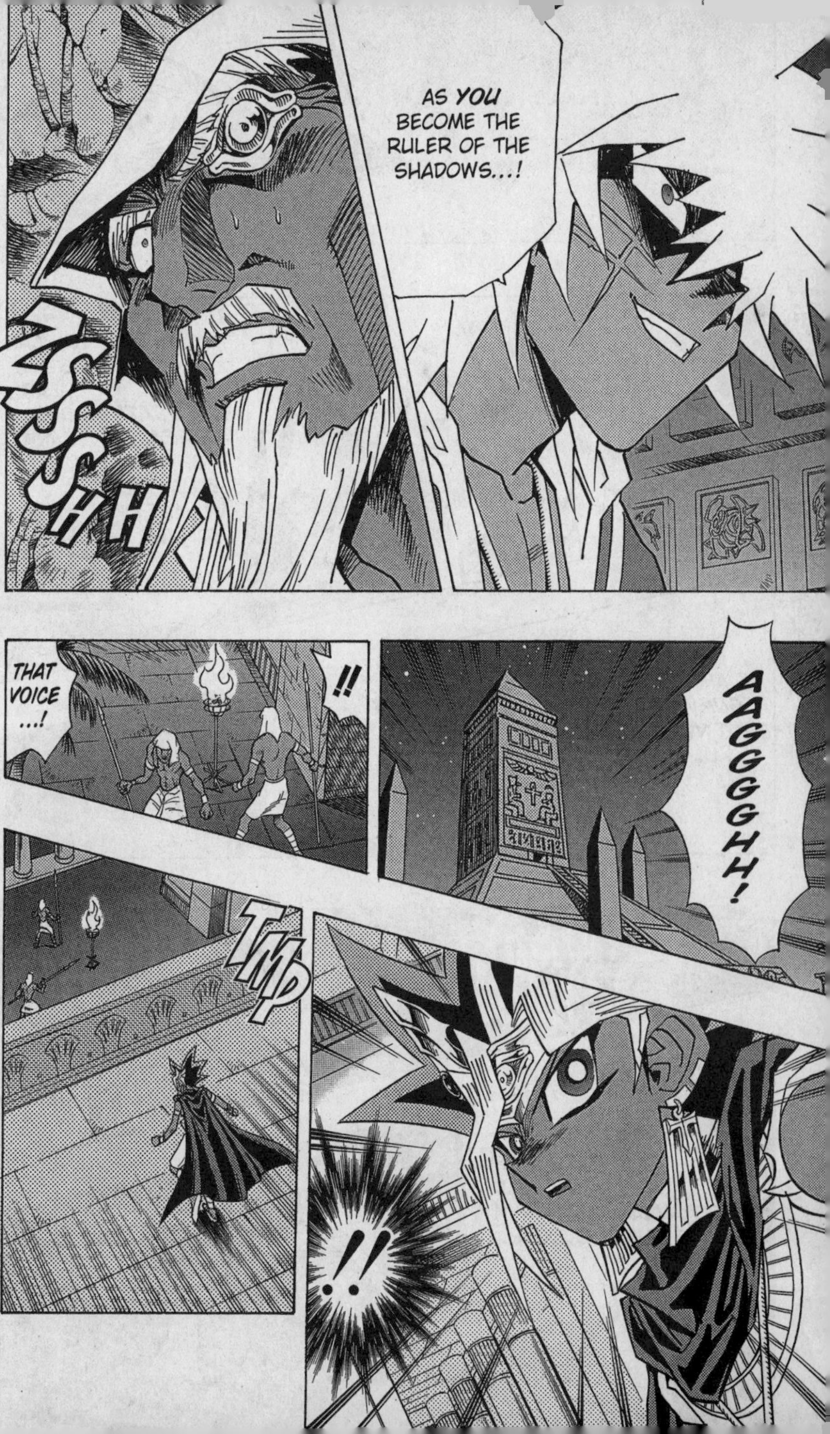
AS YOU BECOME THE RULER OF THE SHADOWS...!
ZSSHH
AAGGGGHH!
!!
THAT VOICE ...!
TMP
!!

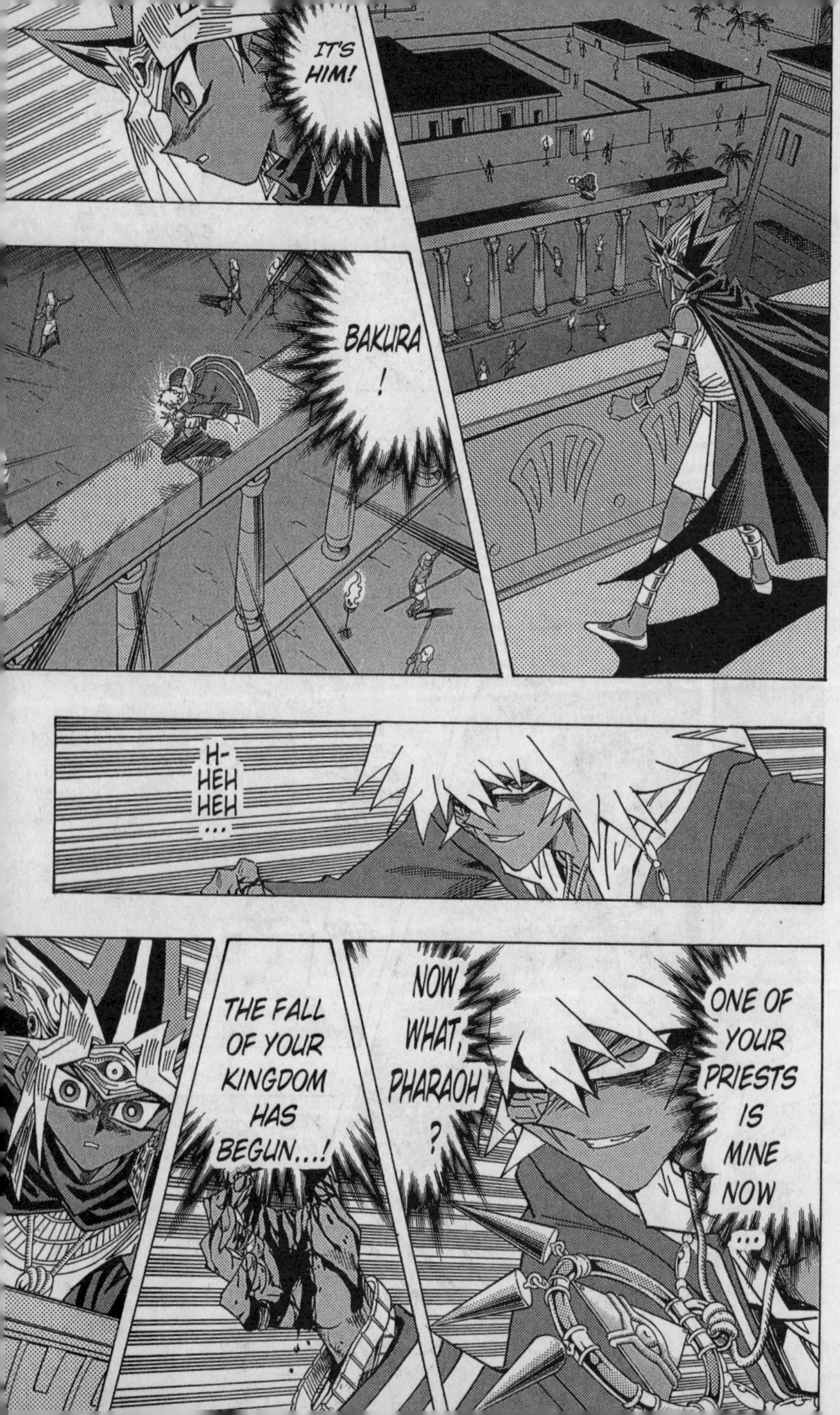
IT'S HIM!
BAKURA!
H-HEH HEH...
ONE OF YOUR PRIESTS IS MINE NOW...
NOW WHAT, PHARAOH?
THE FALL OF YOUR KINGDOM HAS BEGUN...!

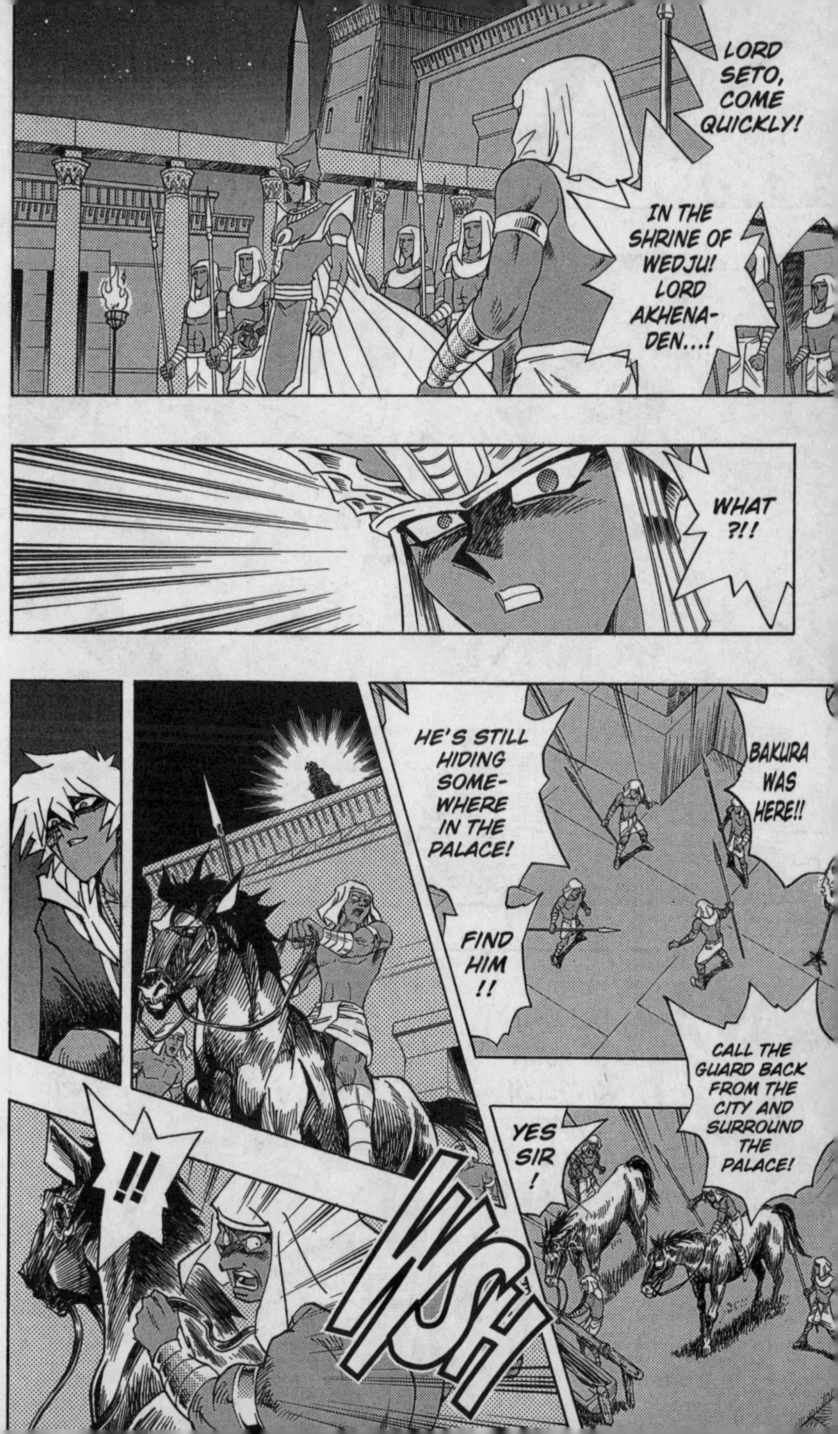
LORD SETO, COME QUICKLY!
IN THE SHRINE OF WEDJU! LORD AKHENA-DEN...!
WHAT ?!!
BAKURA WAS HERE!!
HE'S STILL HIDING SOME-WHERE IN THE PALACE!
FIND HIM !!
CALL THE GUARD BACK FROM THE CITY AND SURROUND THE PALACE!
YES SIR!
!!
WSH

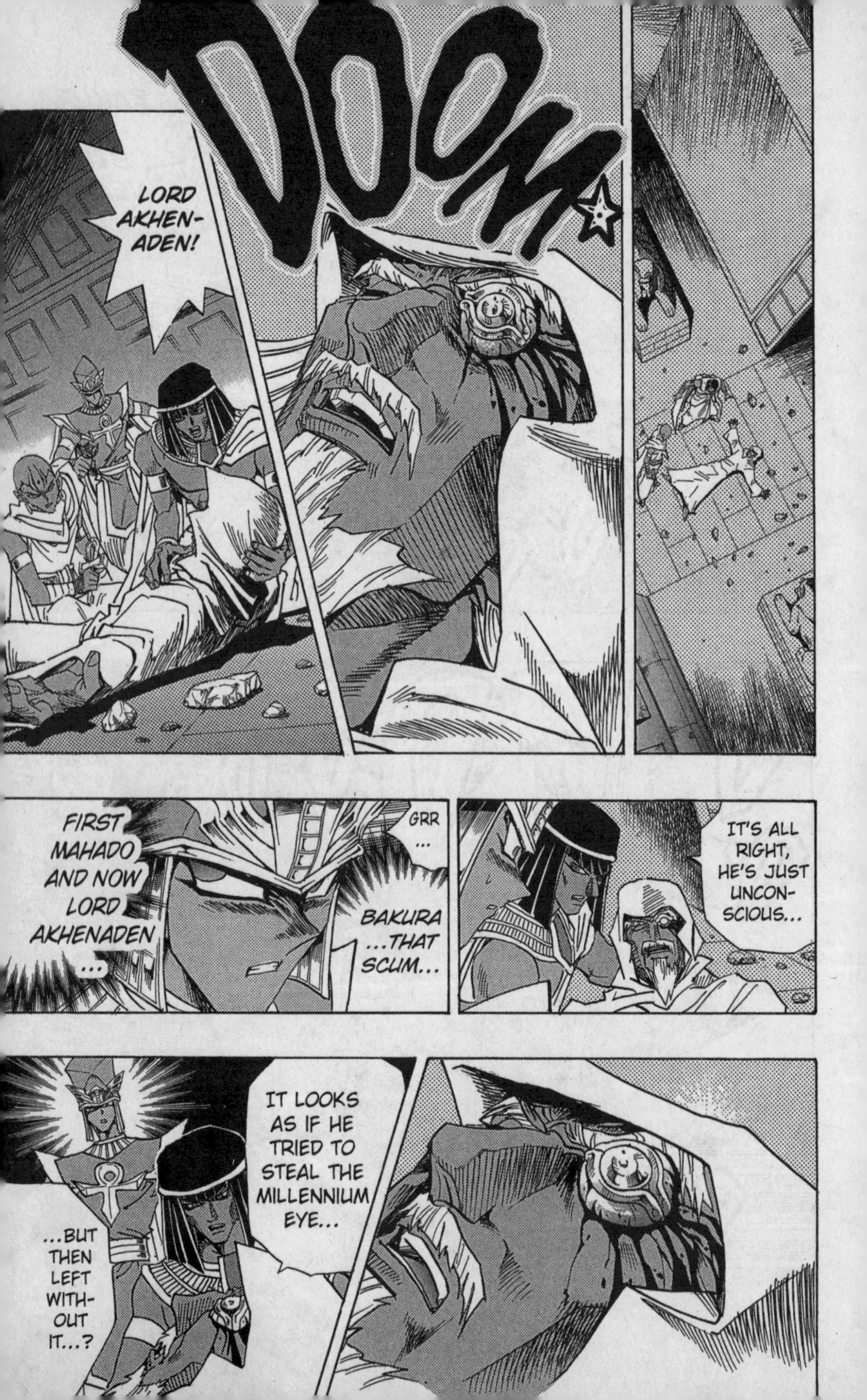
DOOM
LORD AKHENADEN!
IT'S ALL RIGHT, HE'S JUST UNCONSCIOUS...
GRR...
FIRST MAHADO AND NOW LORD AKHENADEN...
BAKURA ...THAT SCUM...
IT LOOKS AS IF HE TRIED TO STEAL THE MILLENNIUM EYE...
...BUT THEN LEFT WITHOUT IT...?

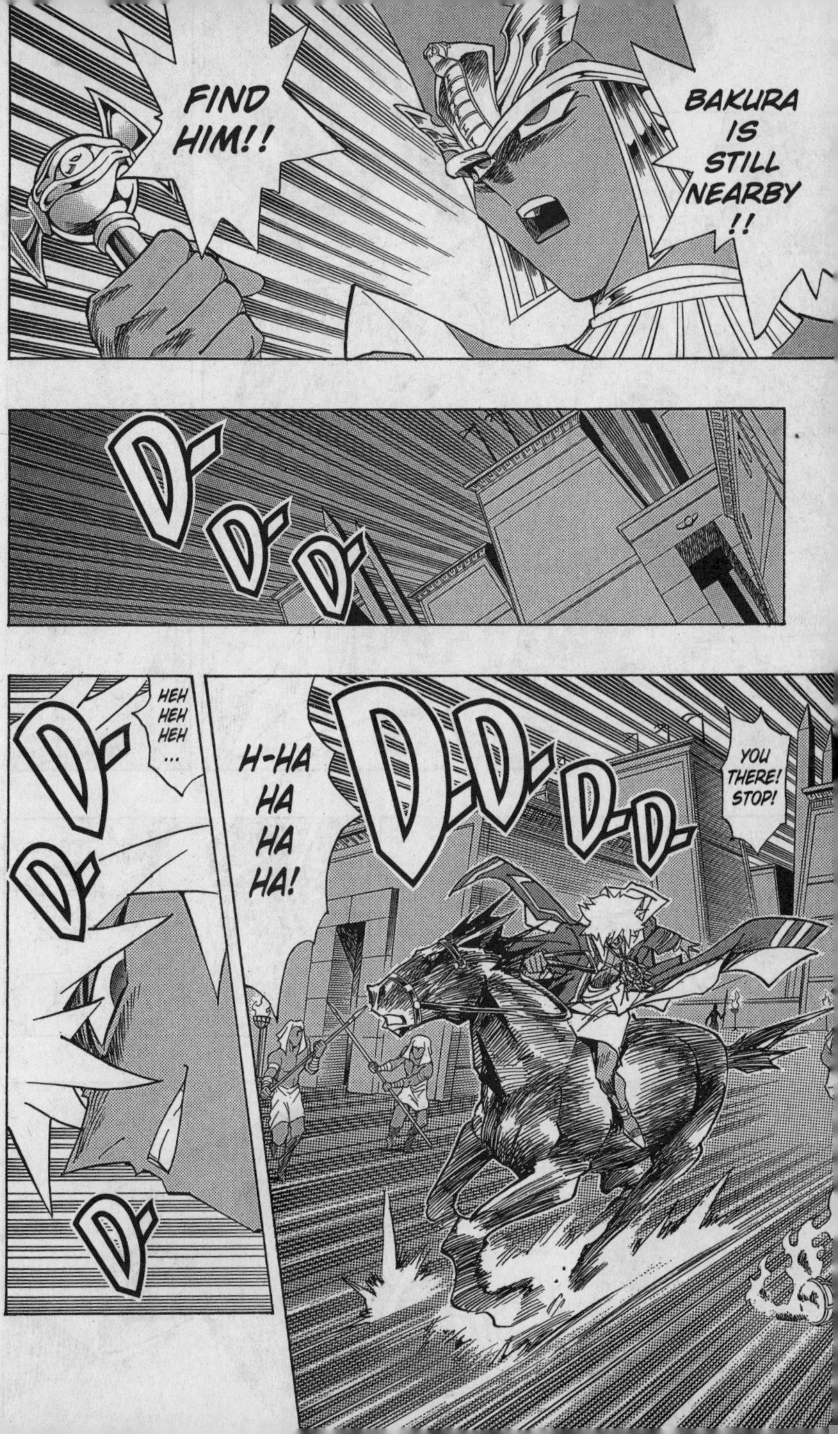
BAKURA IS STILL NEARBY!!
FIND HIM!!
D-D-D
YOU THERE! STOP!
D-D-D-D-D
H-HA HA HA HA!
HEH HEH HEH ...

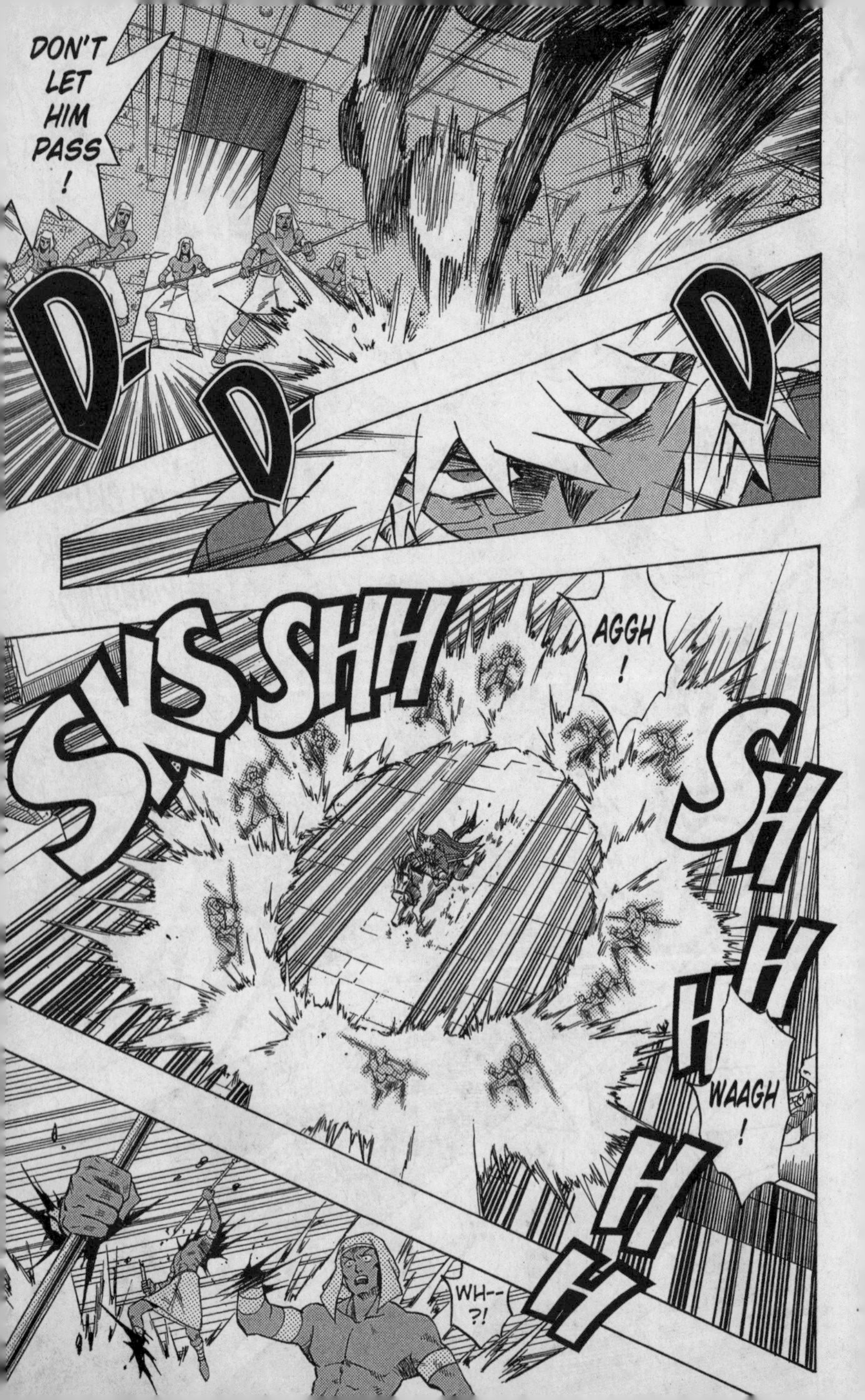
DON'T LET HIM PASS!
D D D
SSSHH
AGGH!
SHHHHHH
WAAGH!
WH--?!

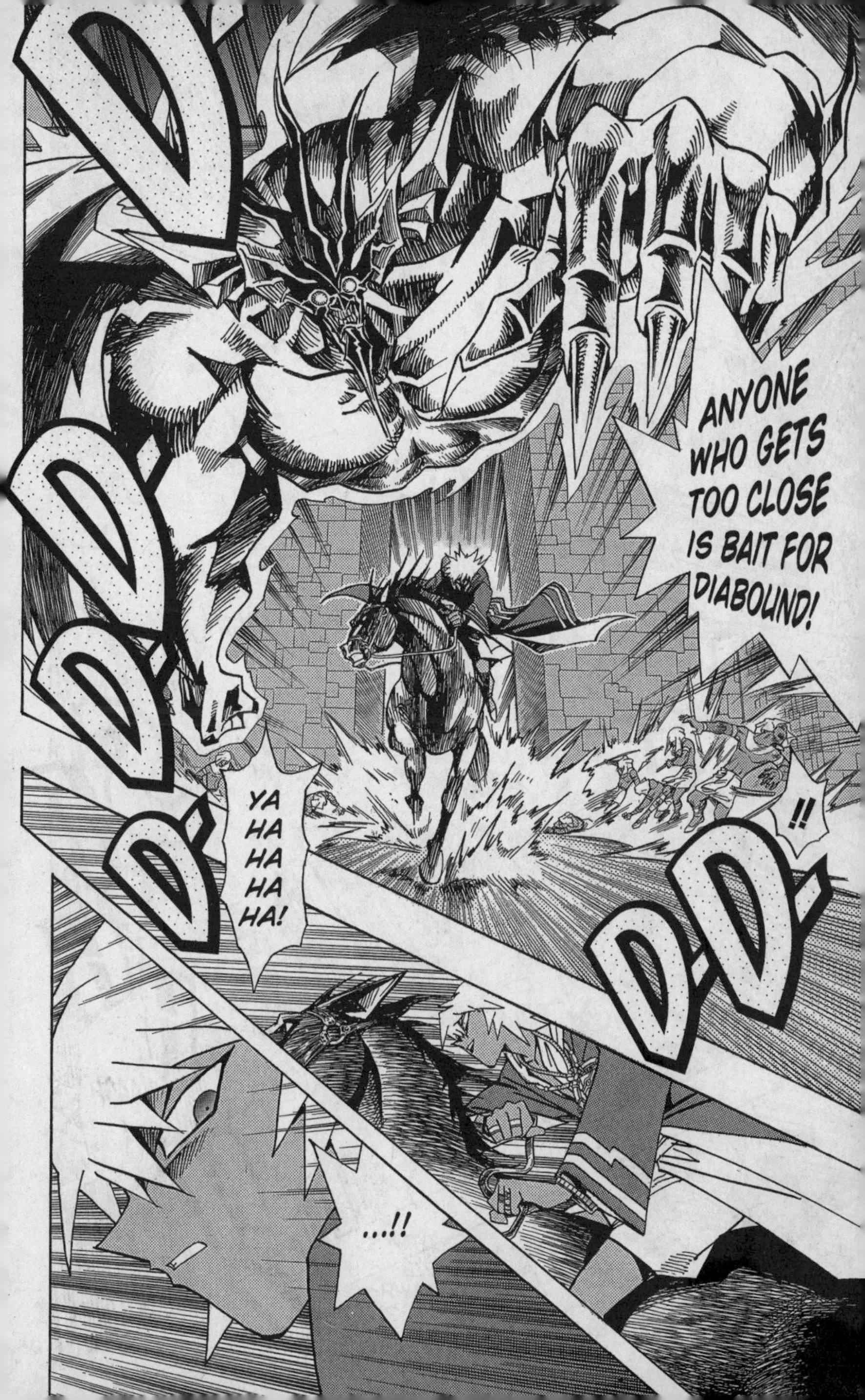
ANYONE WHO GETS TOO CLOSE IS BAIT FOR DIABOUND!
!!
YA HA HA HA HA!
DDDD
DD
...!!

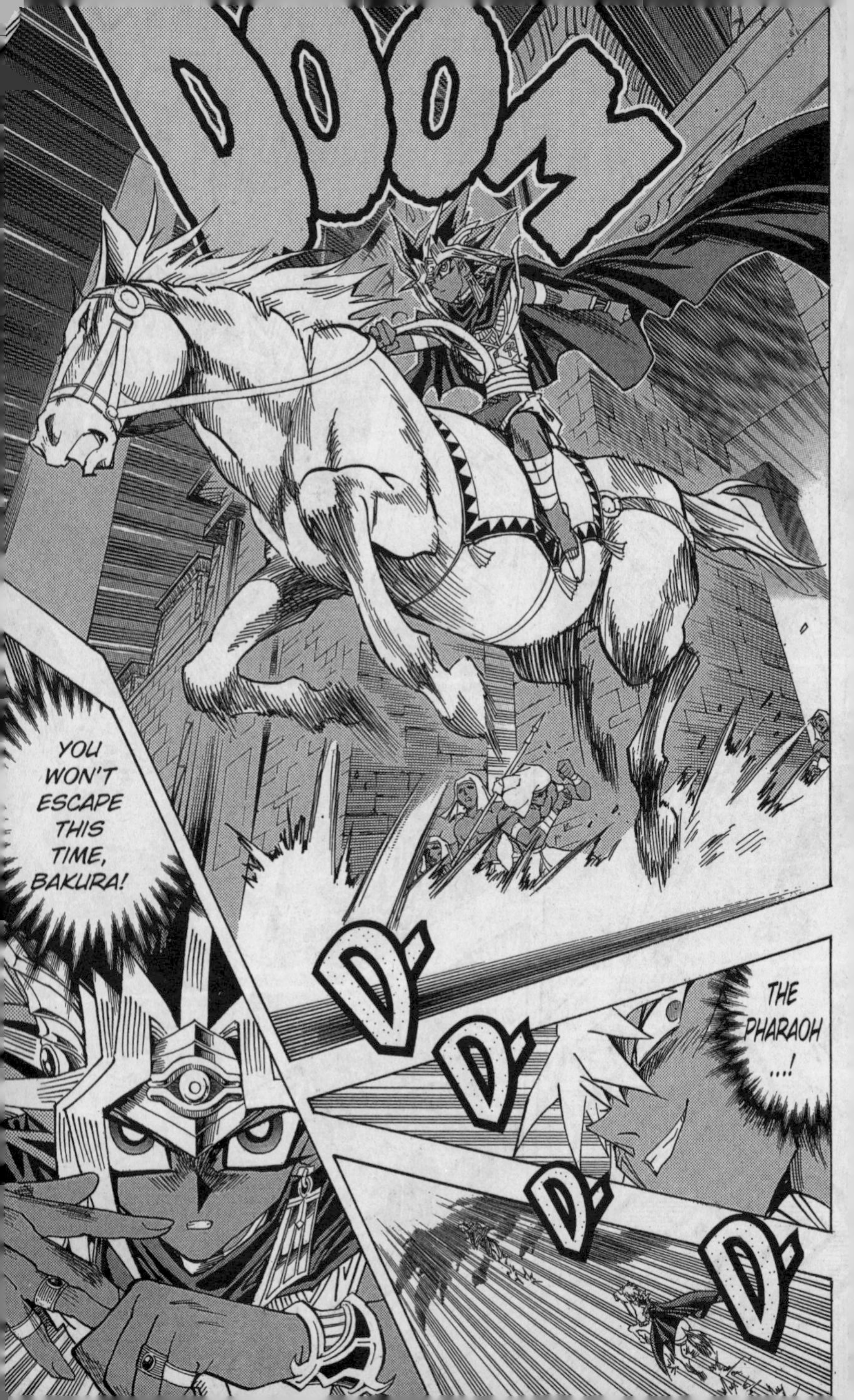
DOOM
YOU WON'T ESCAPE THIS TIME, BAKURA!
THE PHARAOH ...!
D
D
D
D

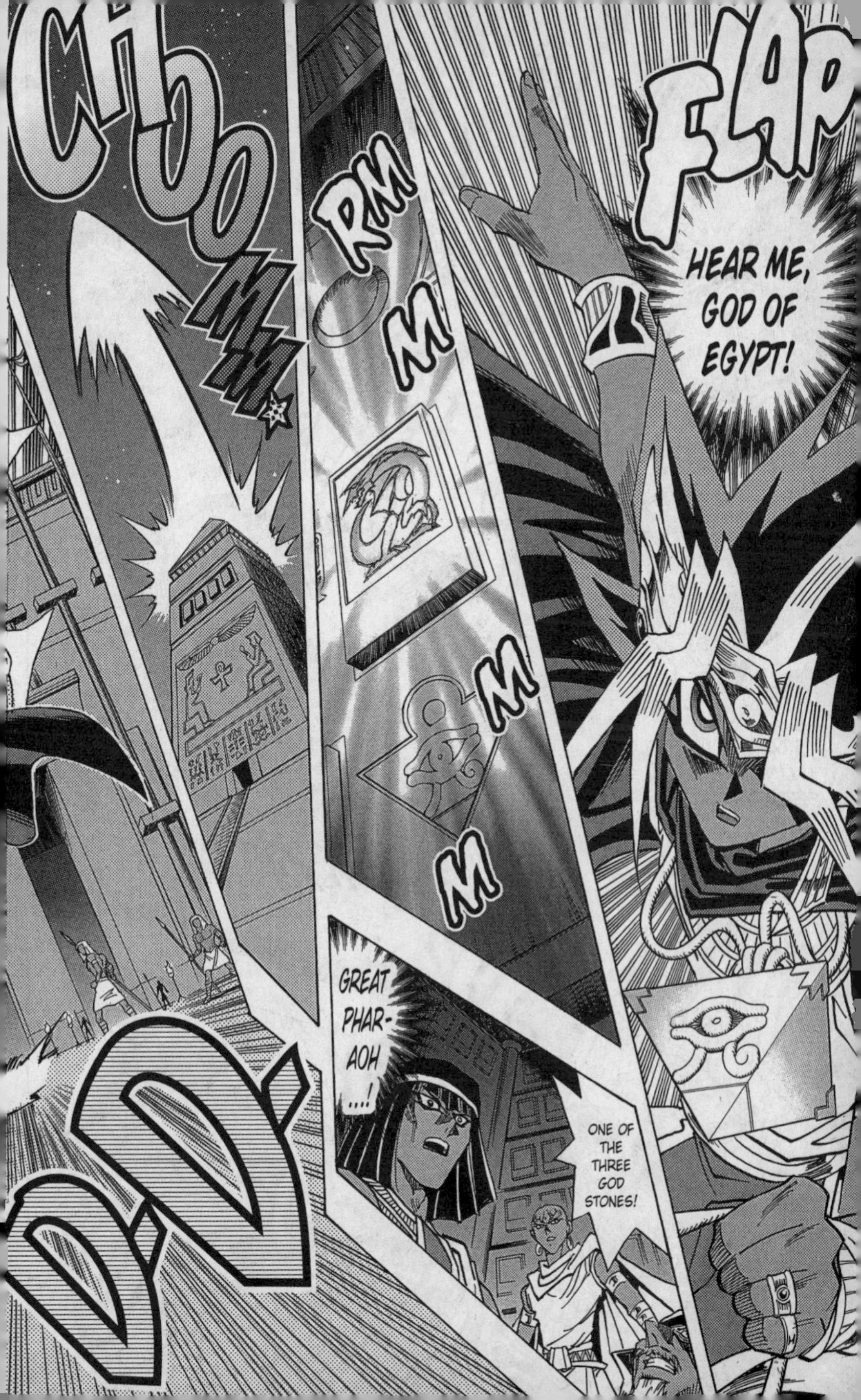
FLAP
HEAR ME, GOD OF EGYPT!
RMMM
GREAT PHARAOH ...!
ONE OF THE THREE GOD STONES!

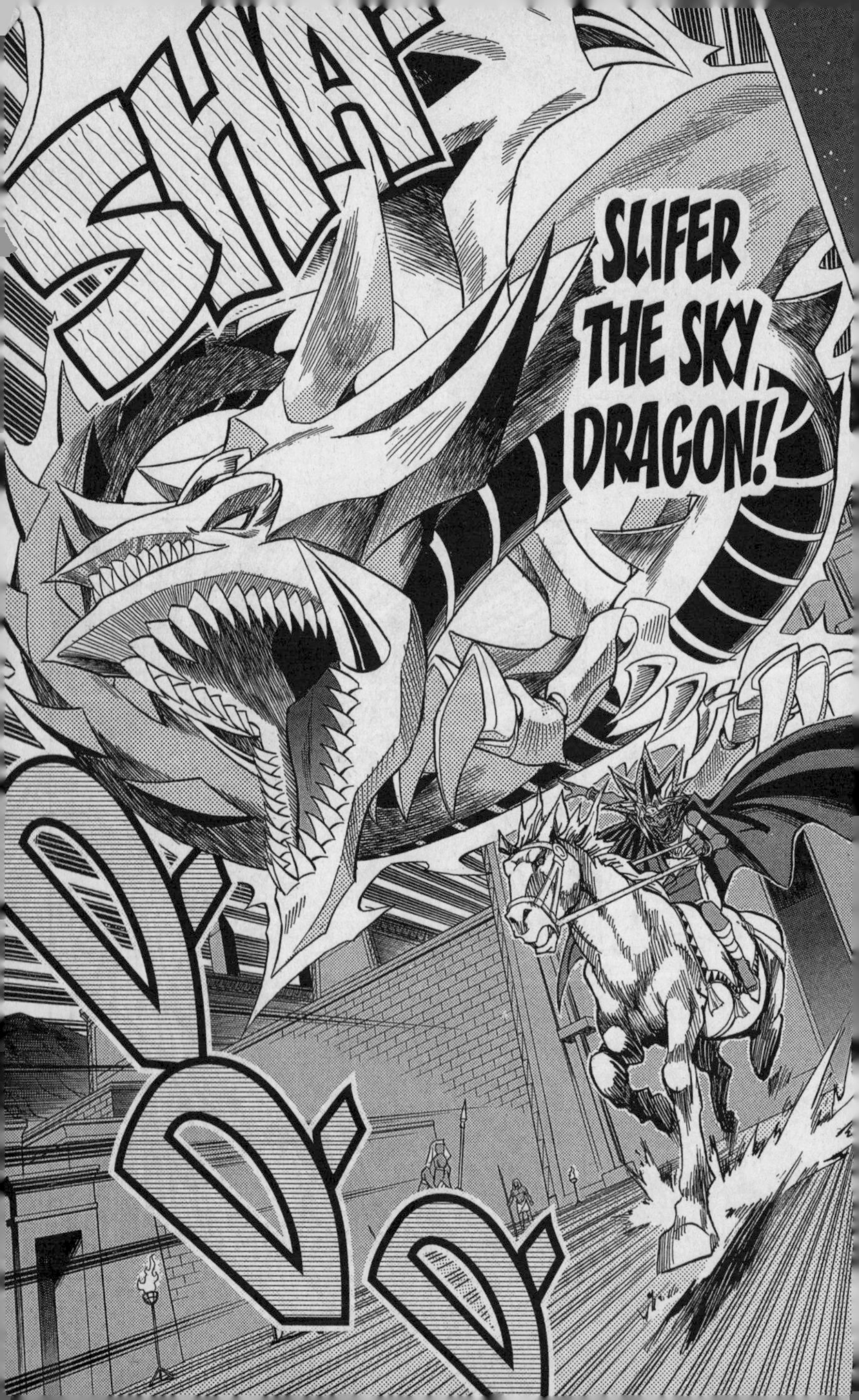
SHAA
SLIFER THE SKY DRAGON!?
DDD

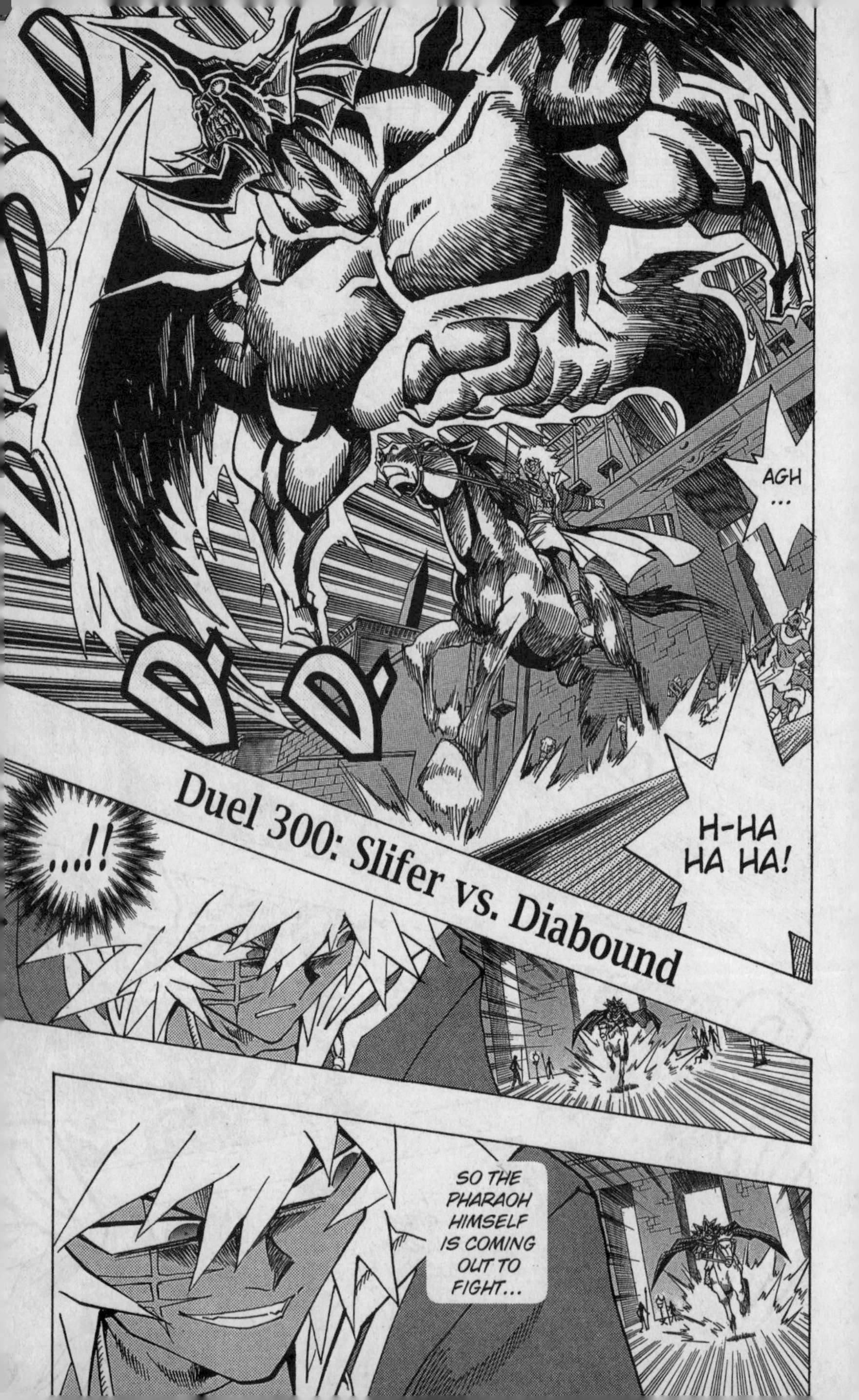
AGH...
H-HA HA HA!
Duel 300: Slifer vs. Diabound
...!!
SO THE PHARAOH HIMSELF IS COMING OUT TO FIGHT...

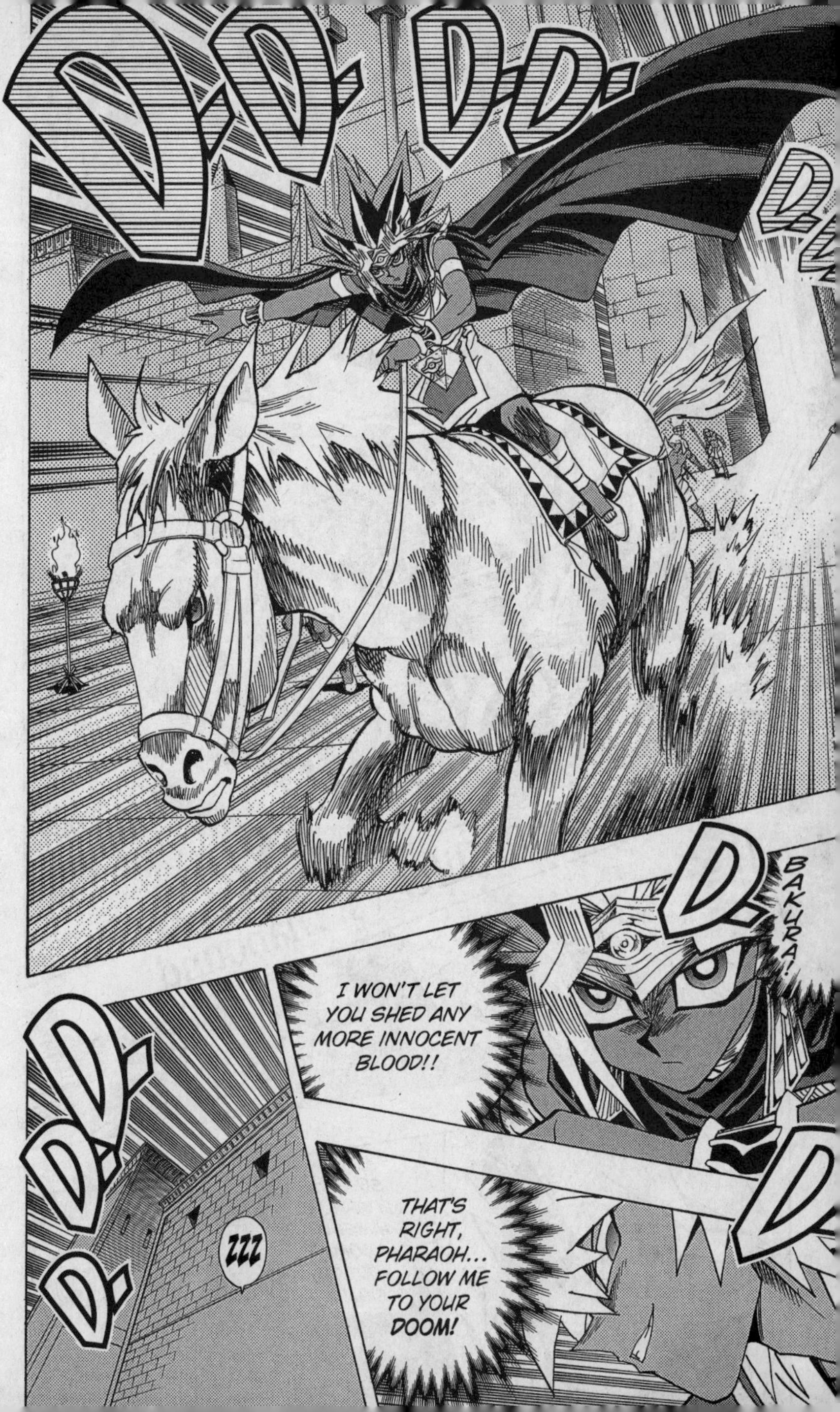
D.D. D.D. D.D.
BAKURA!
D.
I WON'T LET YOU SHED ANY MORE INNOCENT BLOOD!!
D.D. D.D.
ZZZ
D.
THAT'S RIGHT, PHARAOH... FOLLOW ME TO YOUR DOOM!

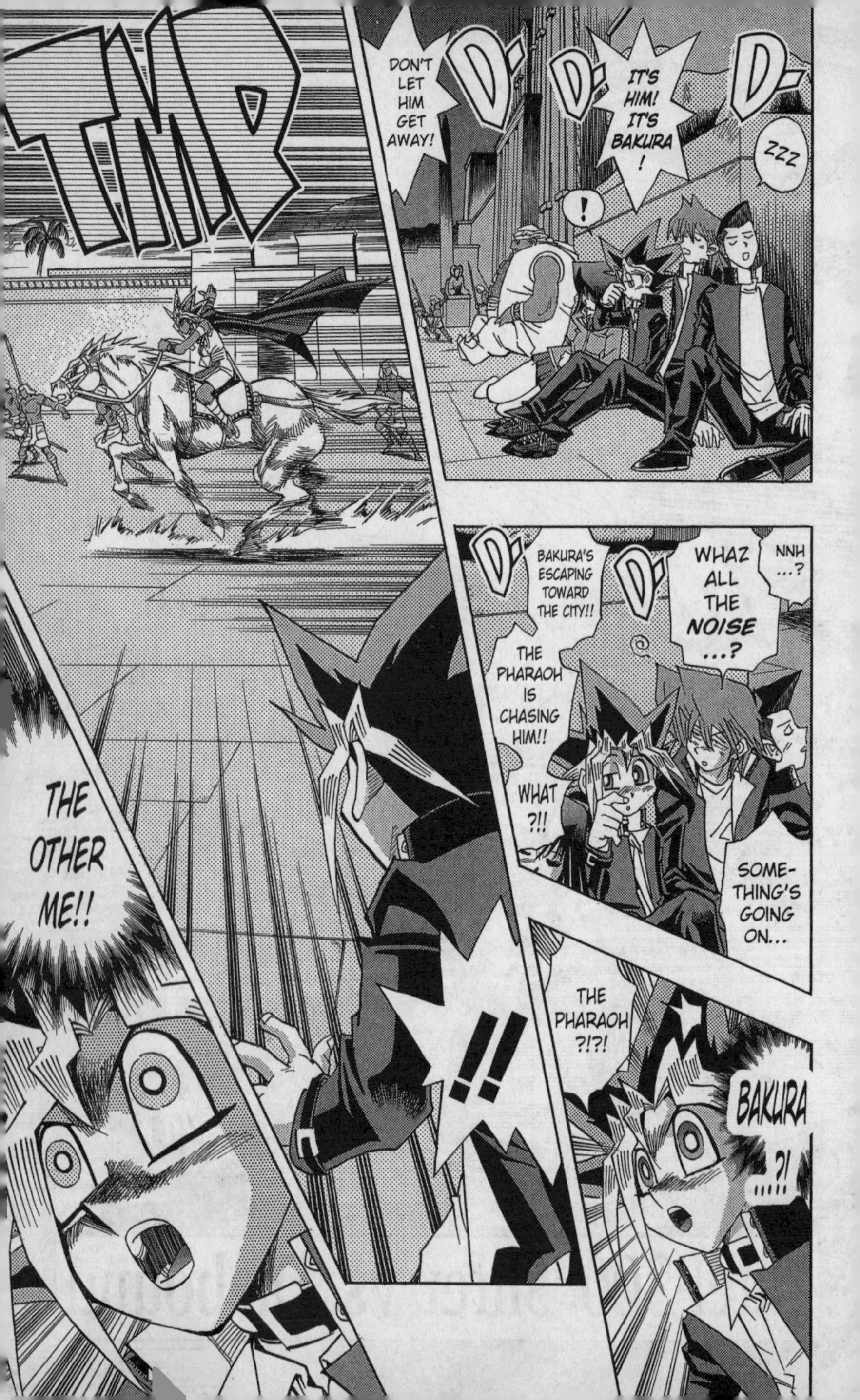
TMP
DON'T LET HIM GET AWAY!
D-
D-
IT'S HIM! IT'S BAKURA!
D-
ZZZ
!
D-
BAKURA'S ESCAPING TOWARD THE CITY!!
D-
WHAZ ALL THE NOISE...?
NNH...?
THE PHARAOH IS CHASING HIM!!
WHAT?!!
SOMETHING'S GOING ON...
THE PHARAOH?!?!
BAKURA...?!
THE OTHER ME!!
!!

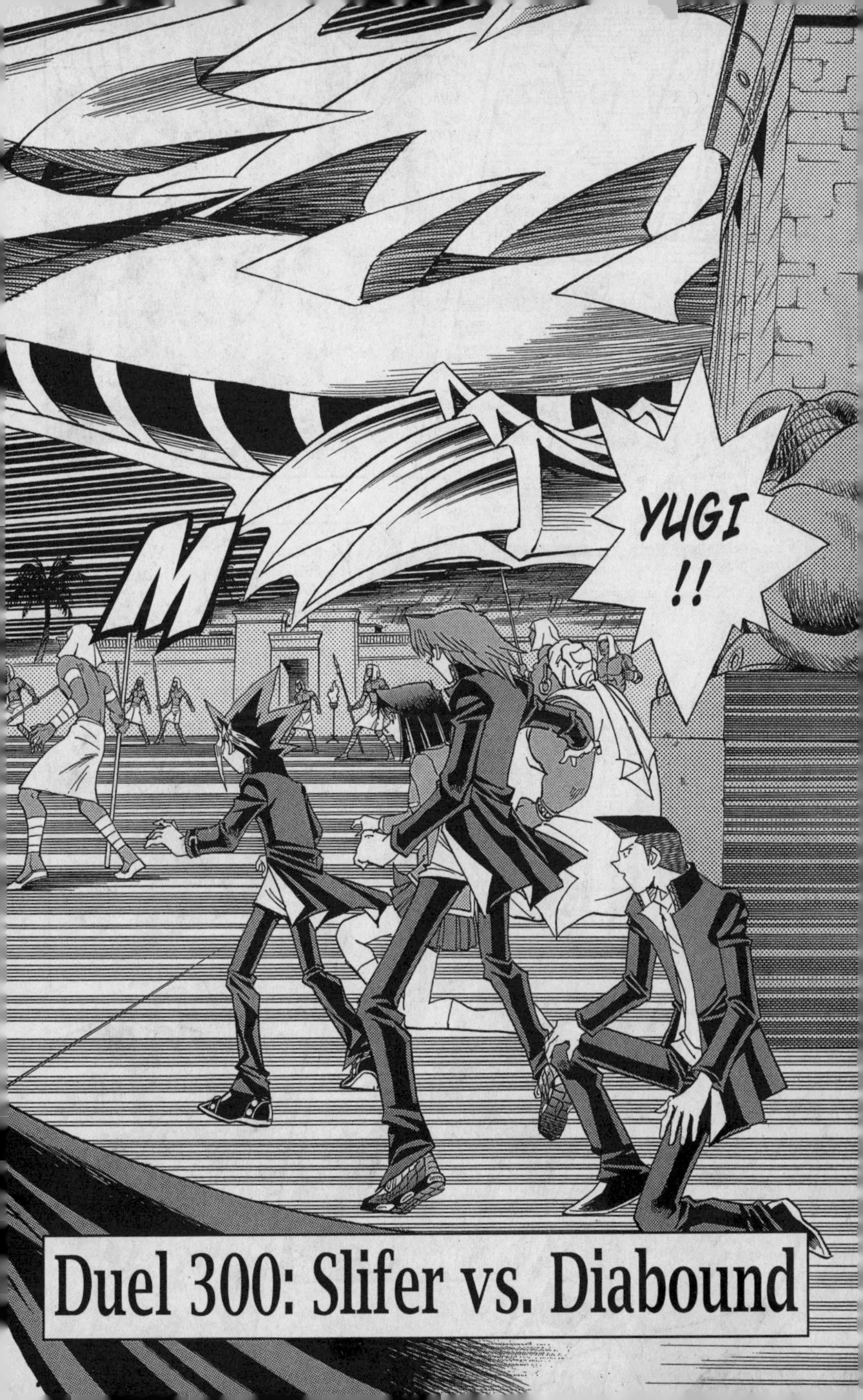
M
YUGI !!

Duel 300: Slifer vs. Diabound

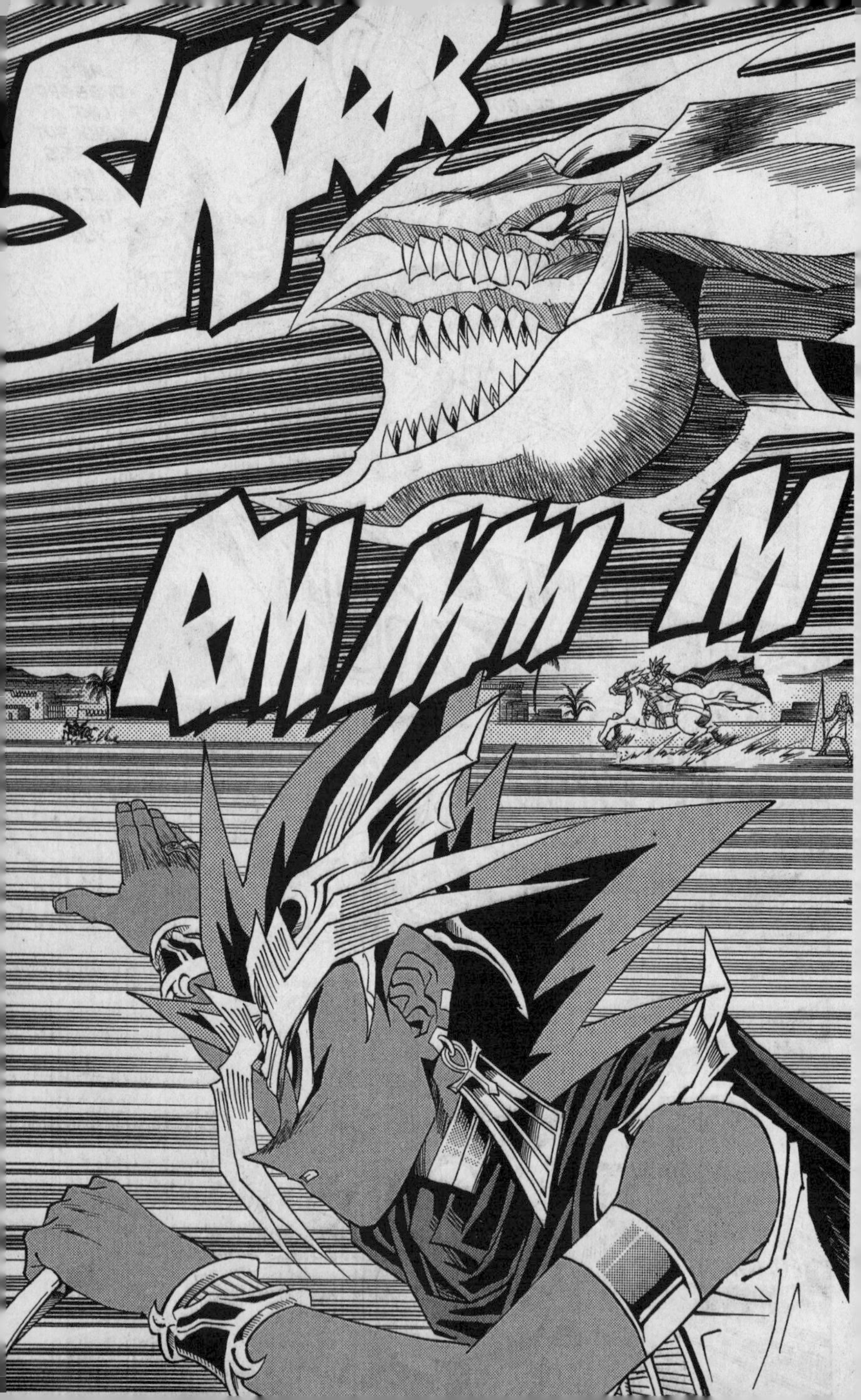

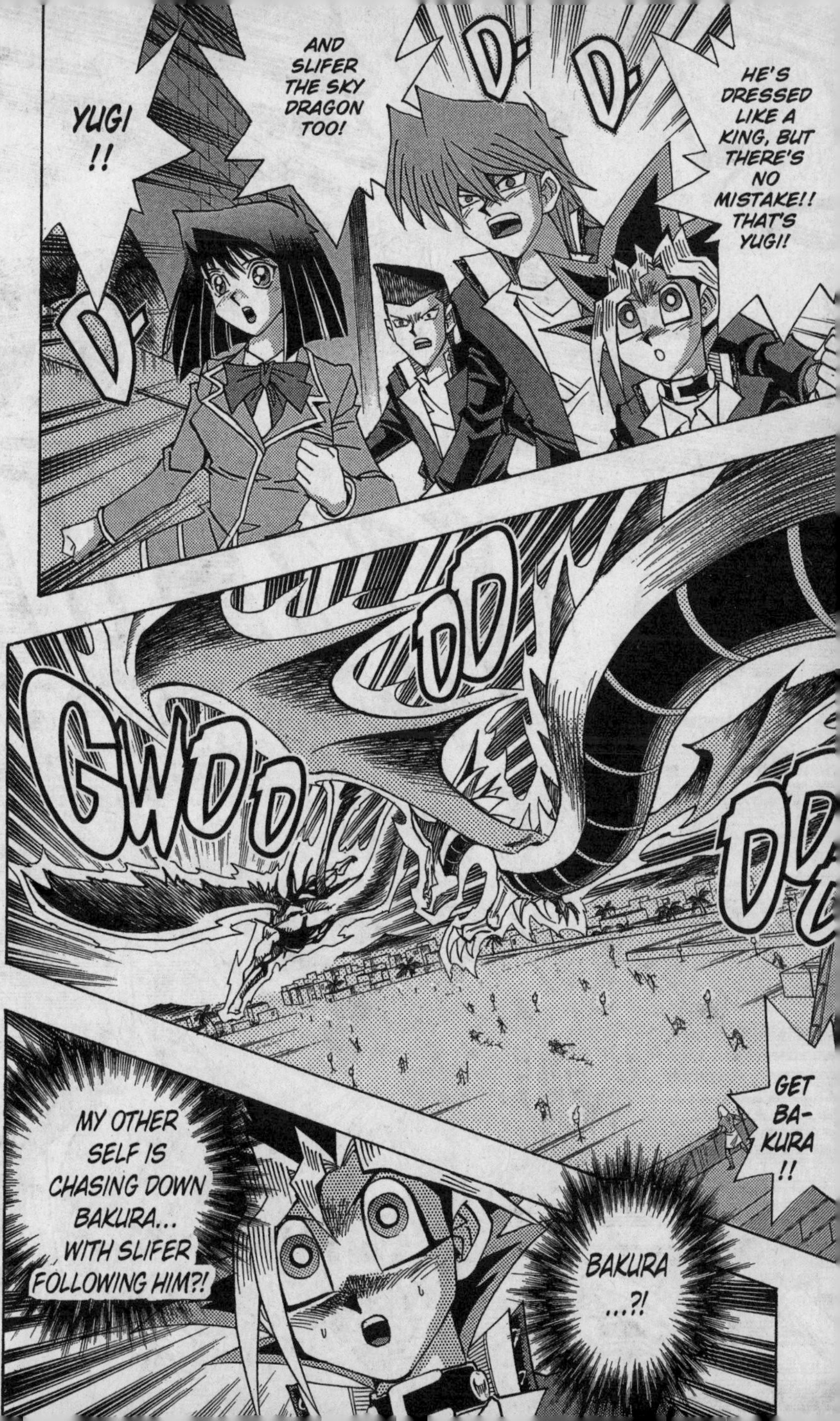
HE'S DRESSED LIKE A KING, BUT THERE'S NO MISTAKE!! THAT'S YUGI!
AND SLIFER THE SKY DRAGON TOO!
YUGI!!
GWDDD
DD
GET BAKURA!!
BAKURA...?!
MY OTHER SELF IS CHASING DOWN BAKURA... WITH SLIFER FOLLOWING HIM?!

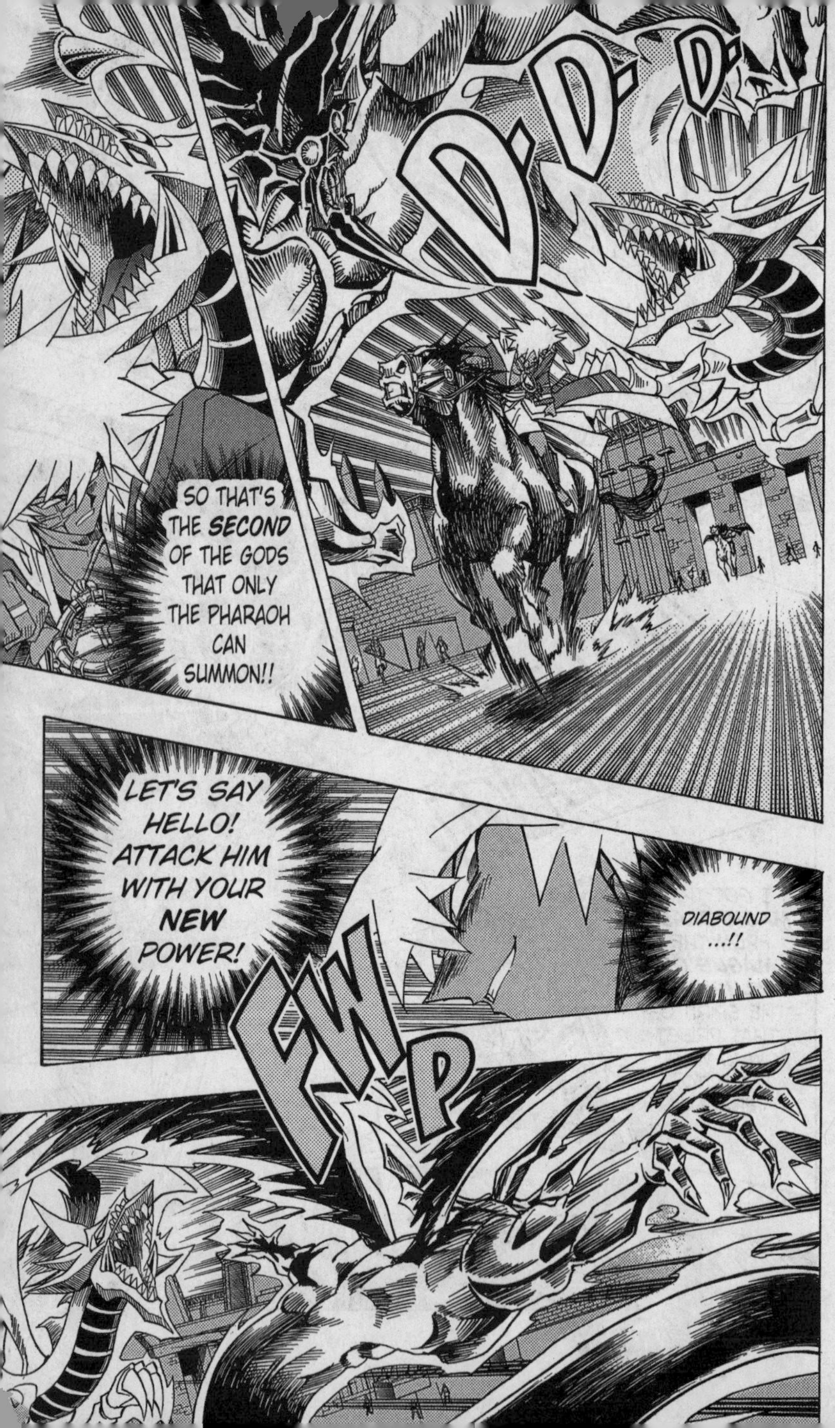
D-D-D
SO THAT'S THE SECOND OF THE GODS THAT ONLY THE PHARAOH CAN SUMMON!!
DIABOUND ...!!
LET'S SAY HELLO! ATTACK HIM WITH YOUR NEW POWER!
FWP

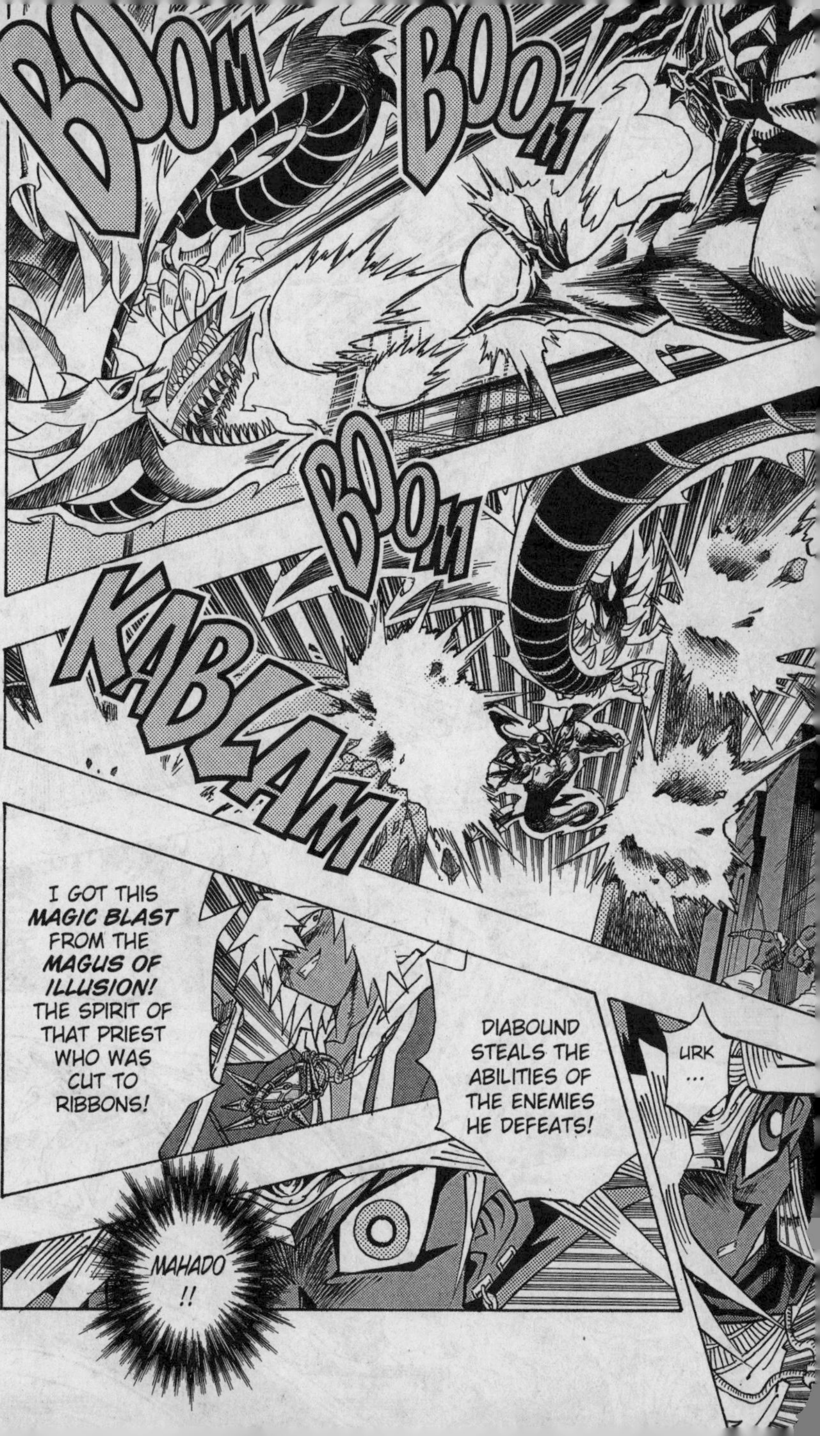
BOOM
BOOM
BOOM
KABLAM
URK ...
DIABOUND STEALS THE ABILITIES OF THE ENEMIES HE DEFEATS!
I GOT THIS *MAGIC BLAST* FROM THE *MAGUS OF ILLUSION!* THE SPIRIT OF THAT PRIEST WHO WAS CUT TO RIBBONS!
MAHADO !!

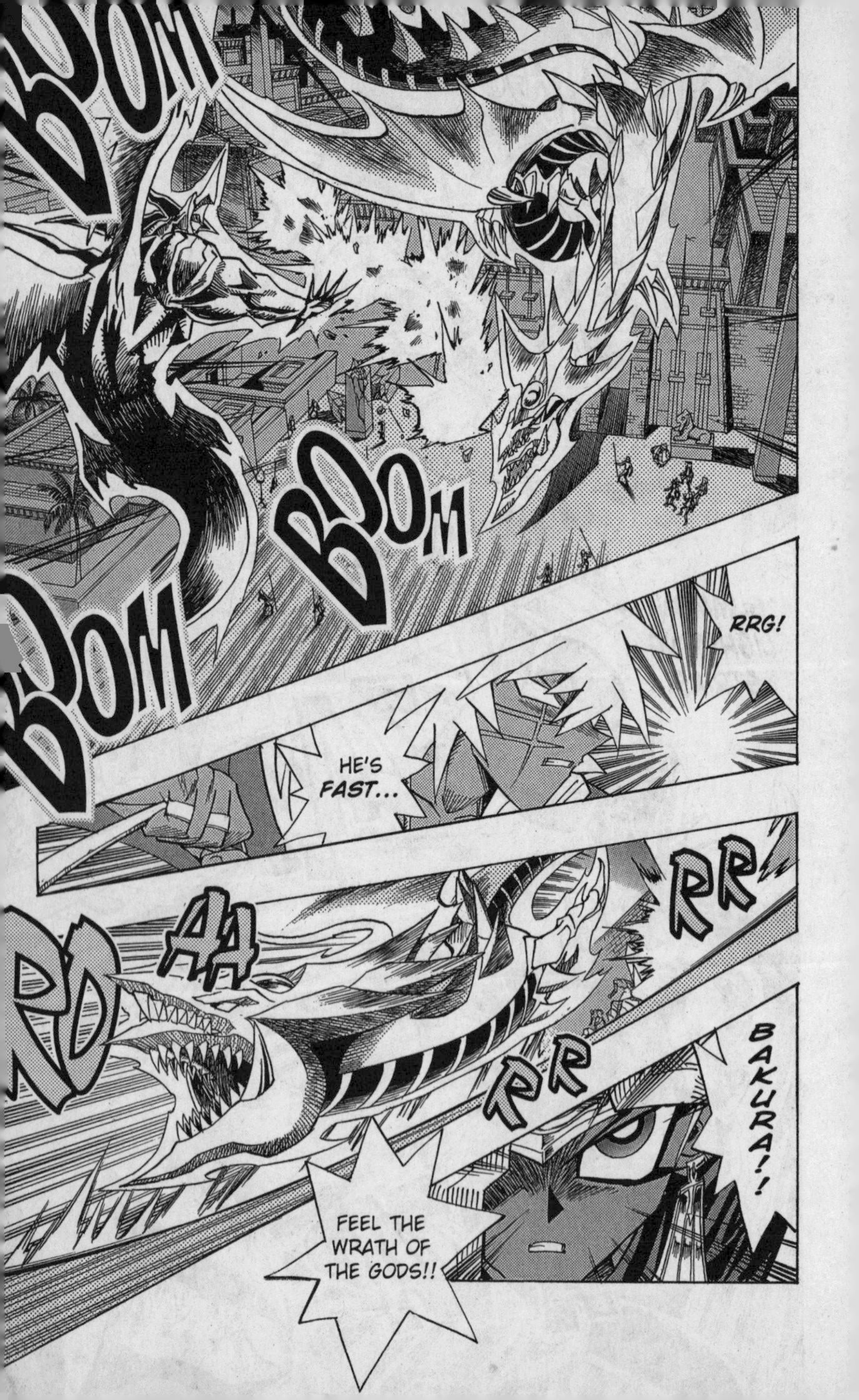

BOOM
BOOM
BOOM
RRG!
HE'S FAST...
RR
AA
RR
BD
BAKURA!!
FEEL THE WRATH OF THE GODS!!

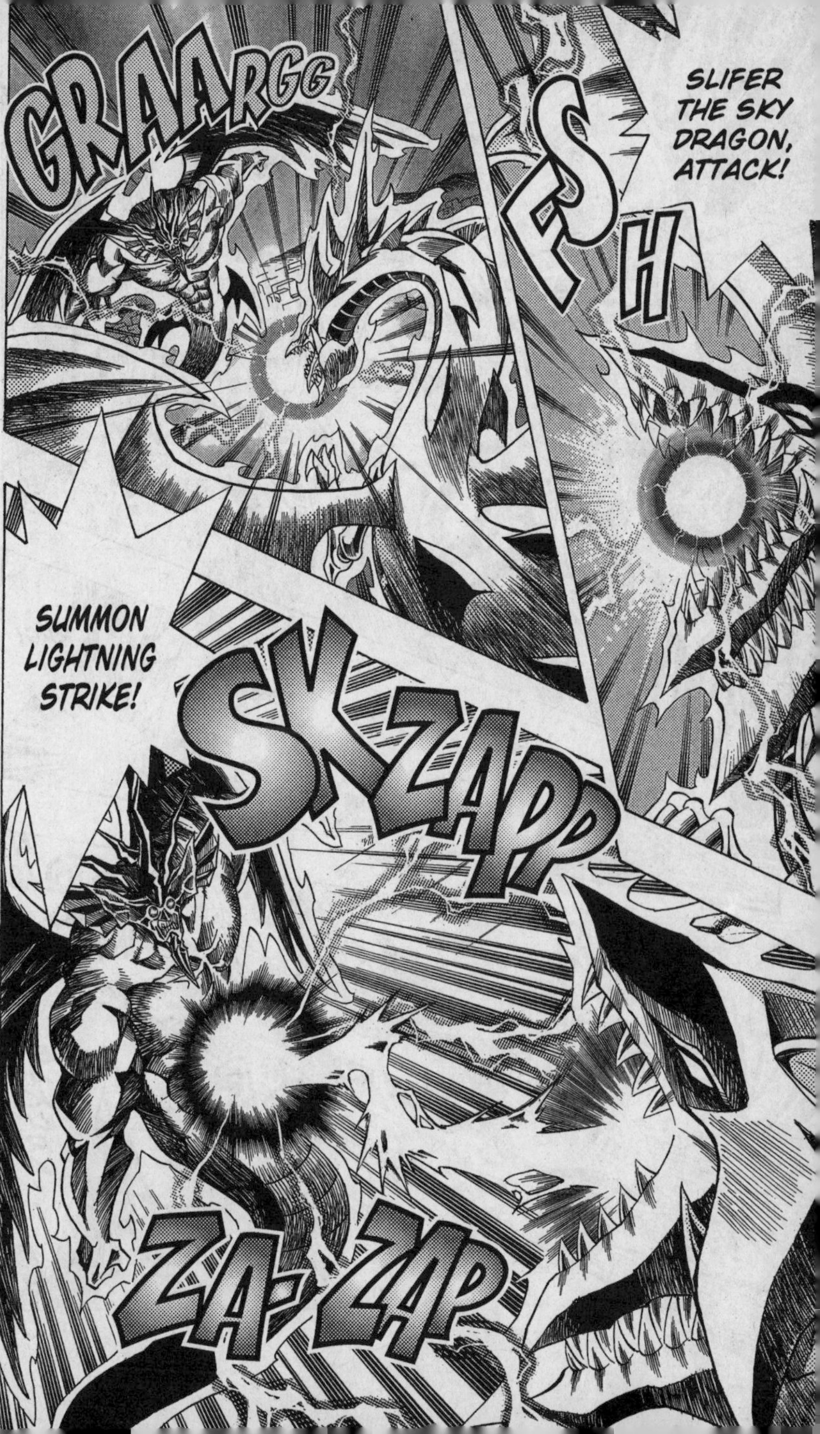
SLIFER THE SKY DRAGON, ATTACK!
FSH
GRAARGG
SUMMON LIGHTNING STRIKE!
SKZAPP
ZA-ZAP

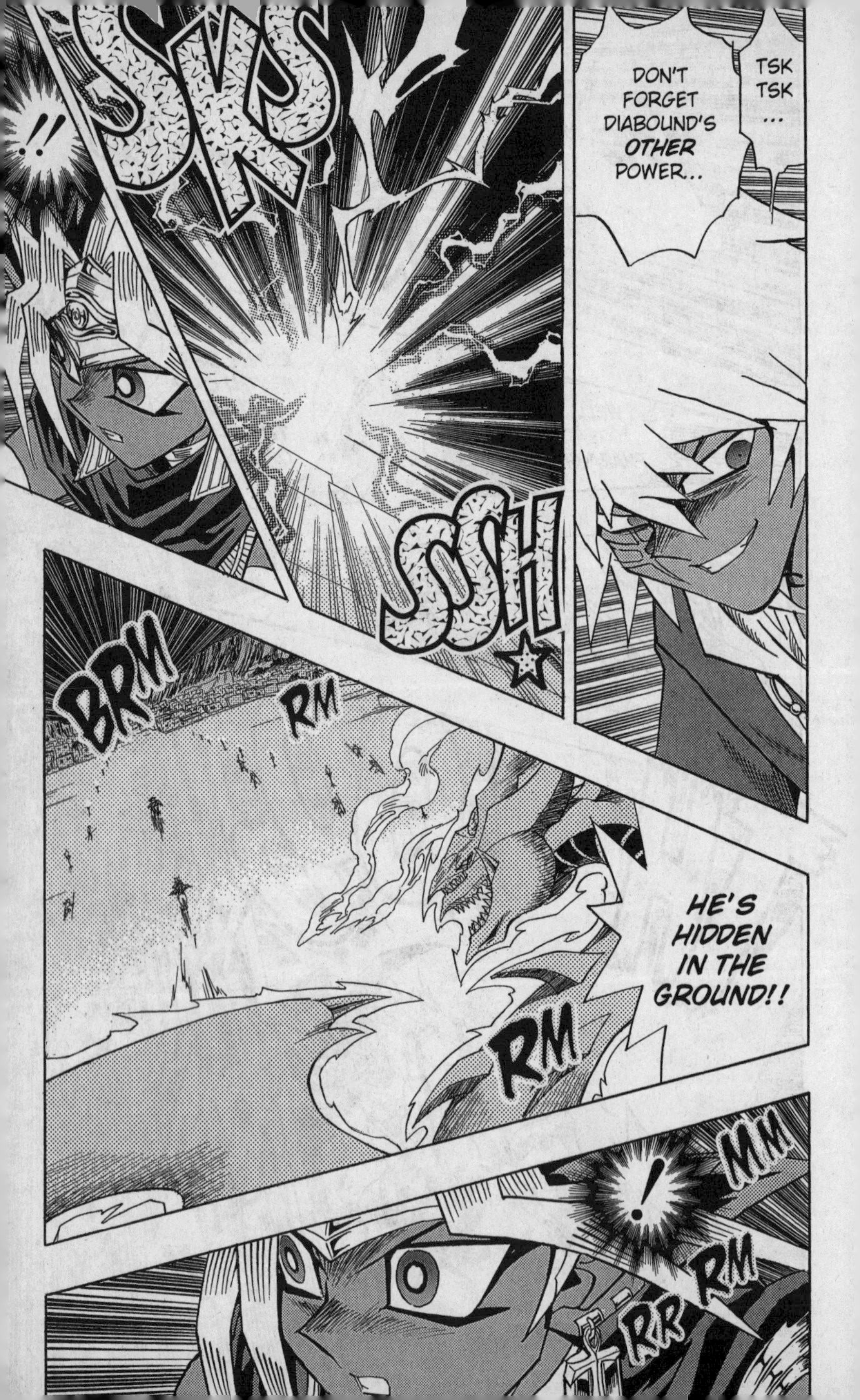
TSK TSK ...
DON'T FORGET DIABOUND'S OTHER POWER...
!!
SSSH
BRM
RM
HE'S HIDDEN IN THE GROUND!!
RM
MM
!
RR RM

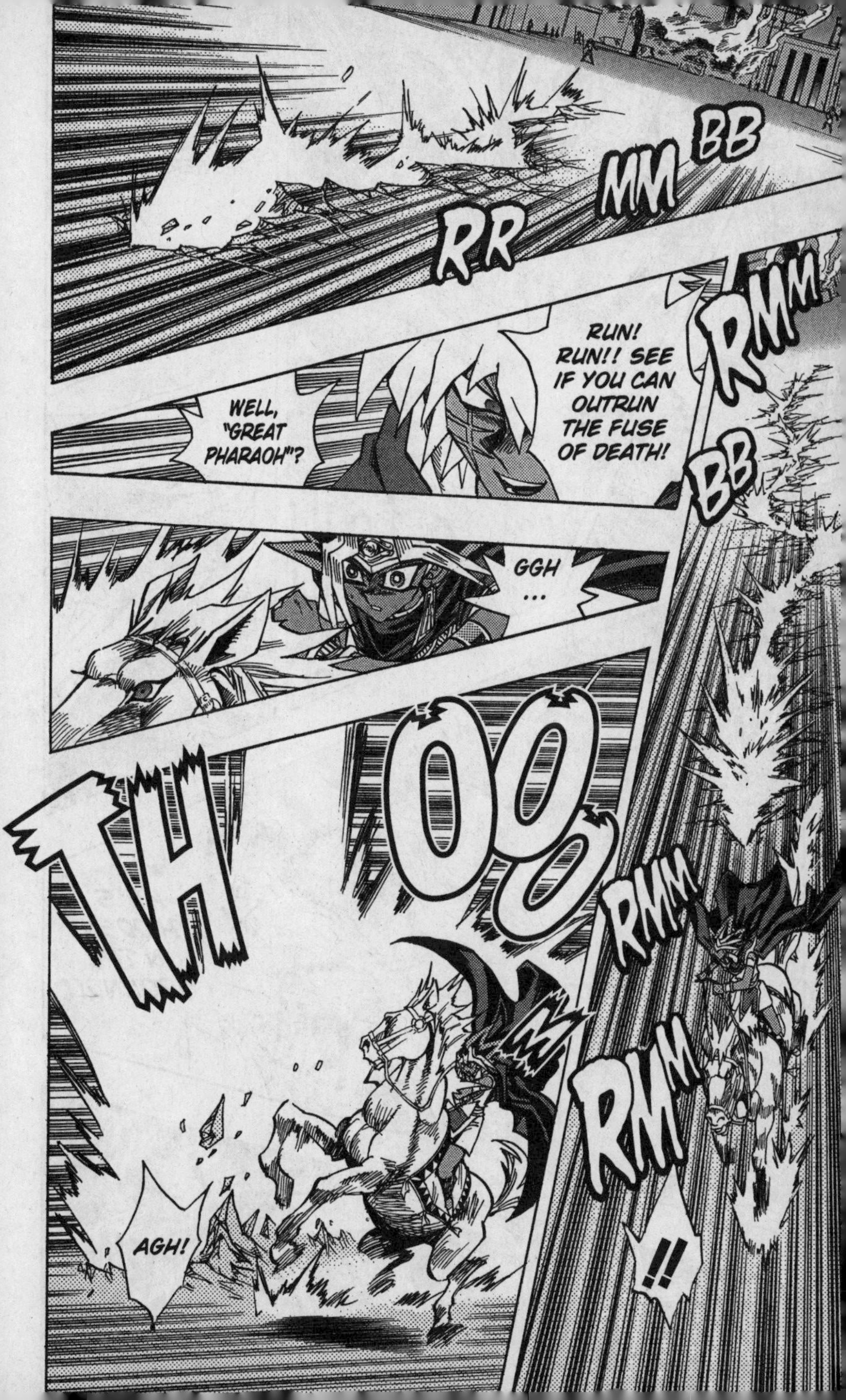

RR
MM
BB
RUN! RUN!! SEE IF YOU CAN OUTRUN THE FUSE OF DEATH!
WELL, "GREAT PHARAOH"?
RMM
BB
GGH ...
THOOO
RMM
RMM
M
!!
AGH!

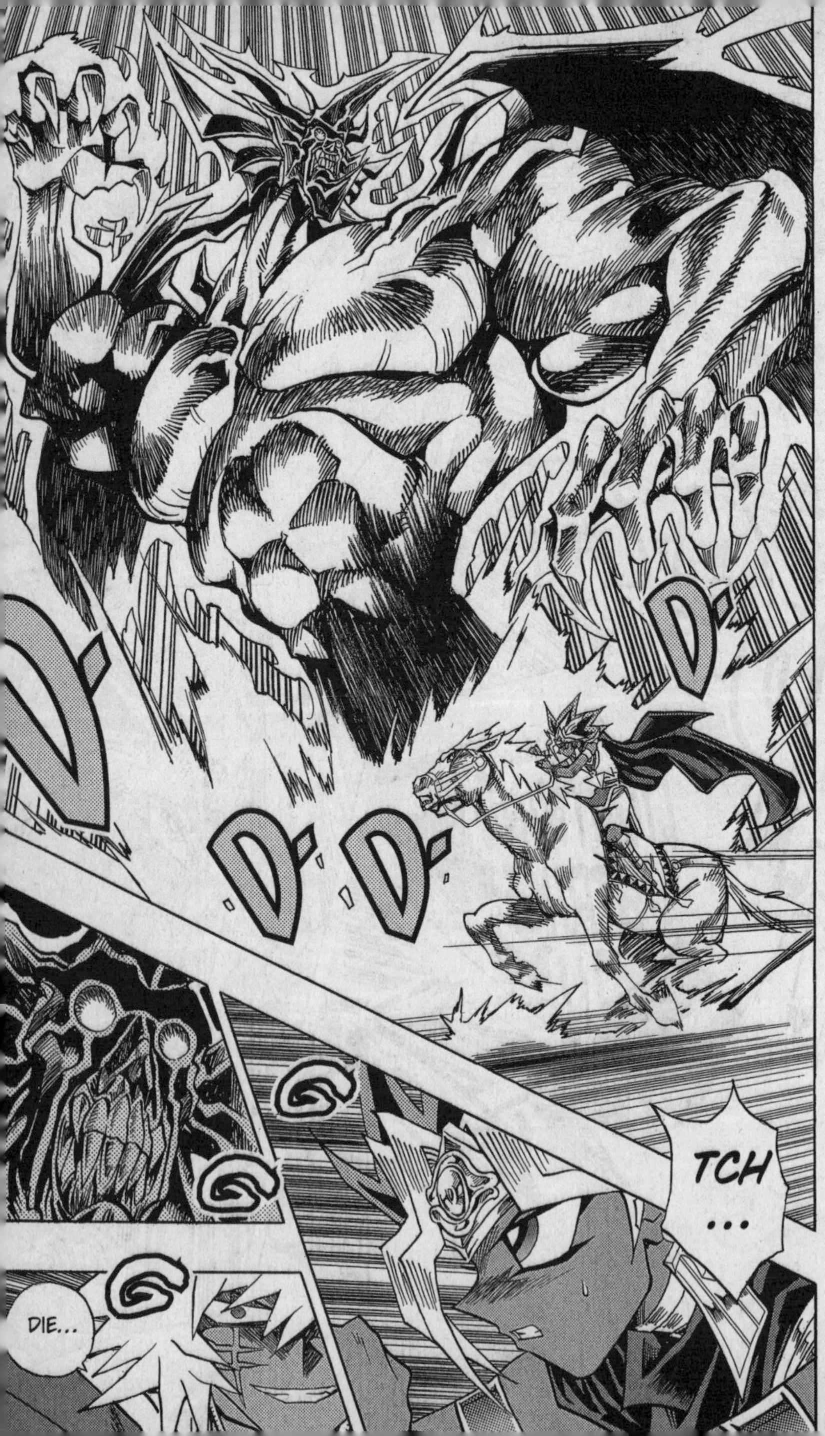
D
D
D
D
TCH ...
DIE...

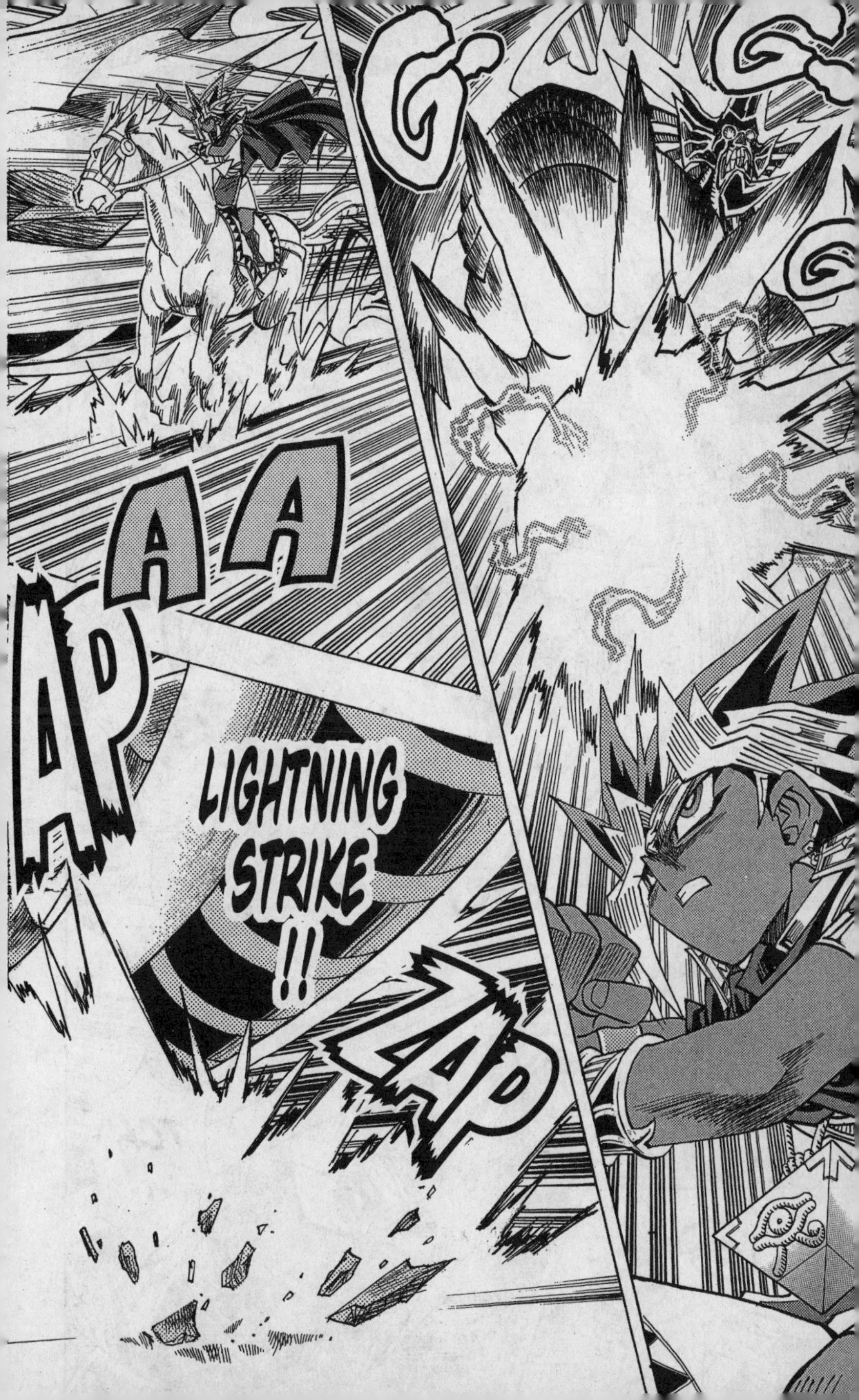
GGG
AAAP
LIGHTNING STRIKE !!
ZAP

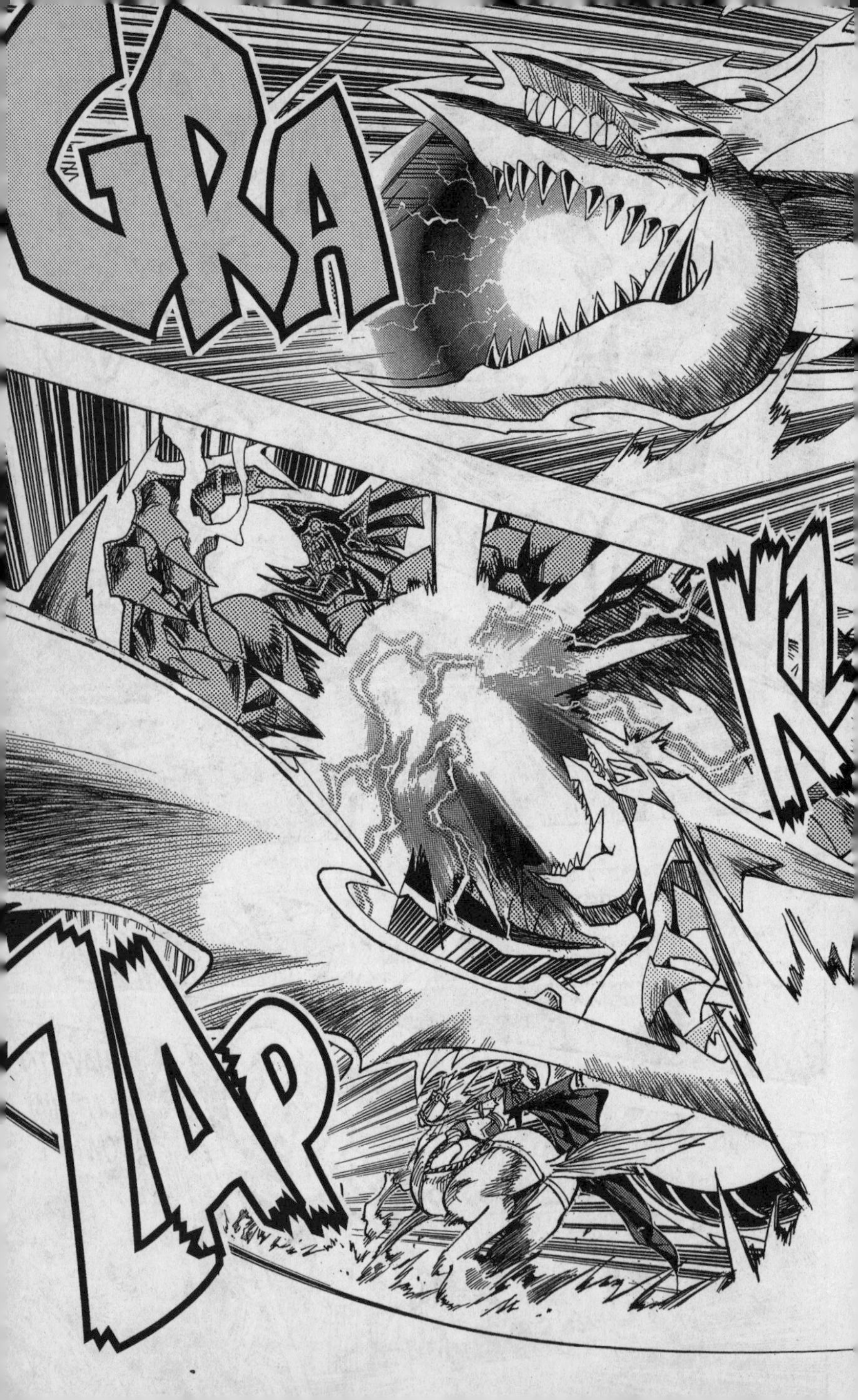
GRA
K
ZAP

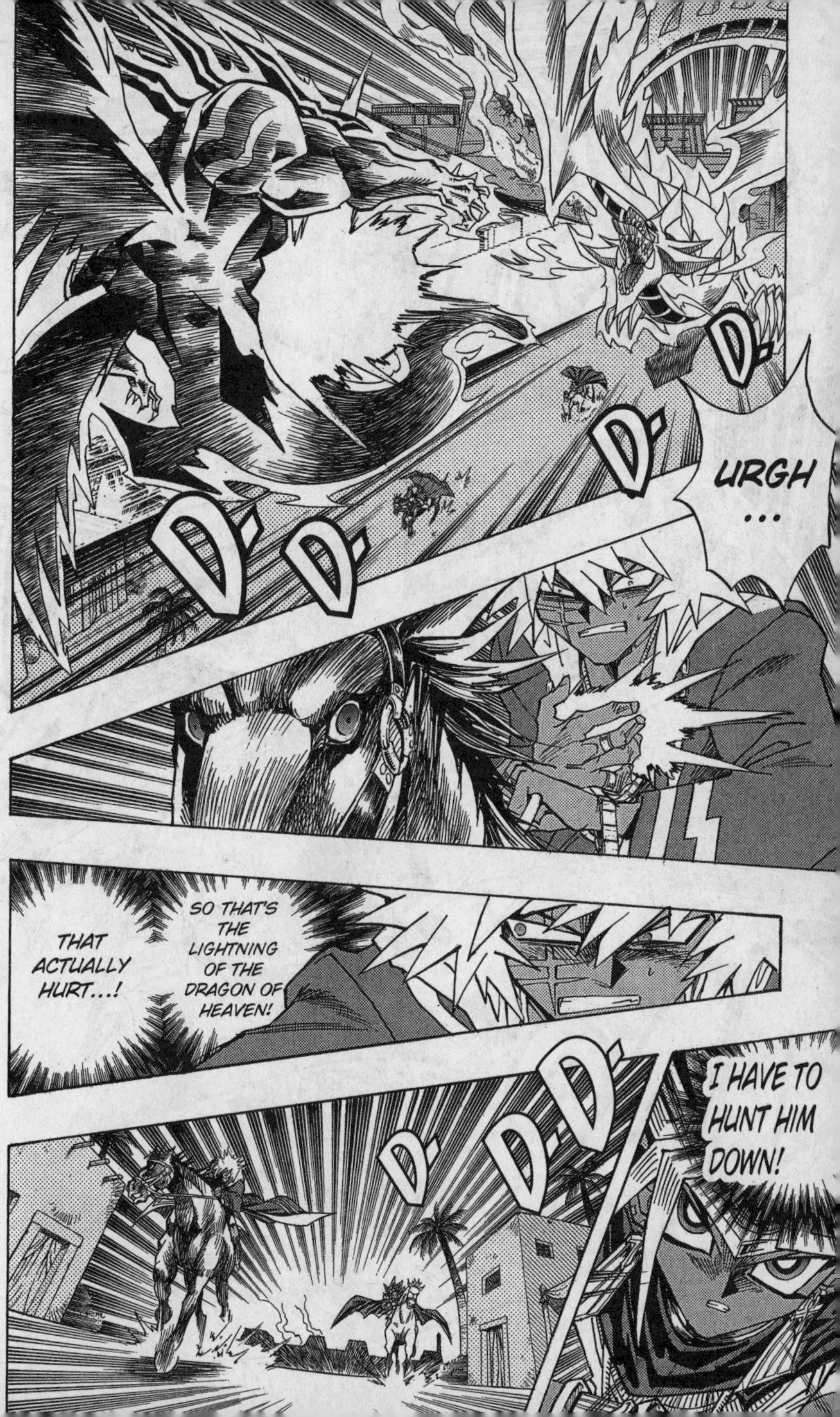
D D D
URGH ...
D D D D
SO THAT'S THE LIGHTNING OF THE DRAGON OF HEAVEN!
THAT ACTUALLY HURT...!
I HAVE TO HUNT HIM DOWN!
D D D

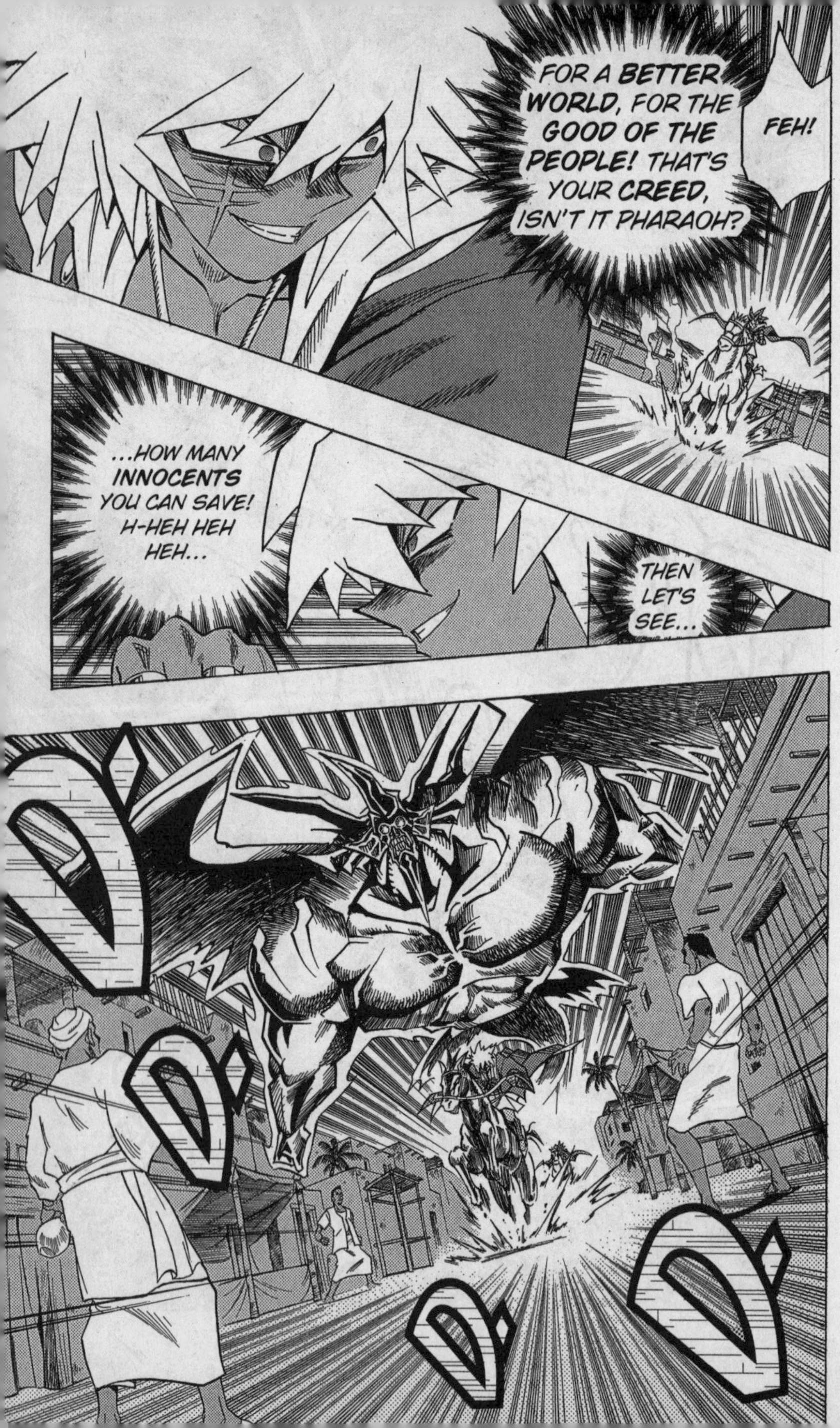

FEH!
FOR A BETTER WORLD, FOR THE GOOD OF THE PEOPLE! THAT'S YOUR CREED, ISN'T IT PHARAOH?
THEN LET'S SEE...
...HOW MANY INNOCENTS YOU CAN SAVE! H-HEH HEH HEH...

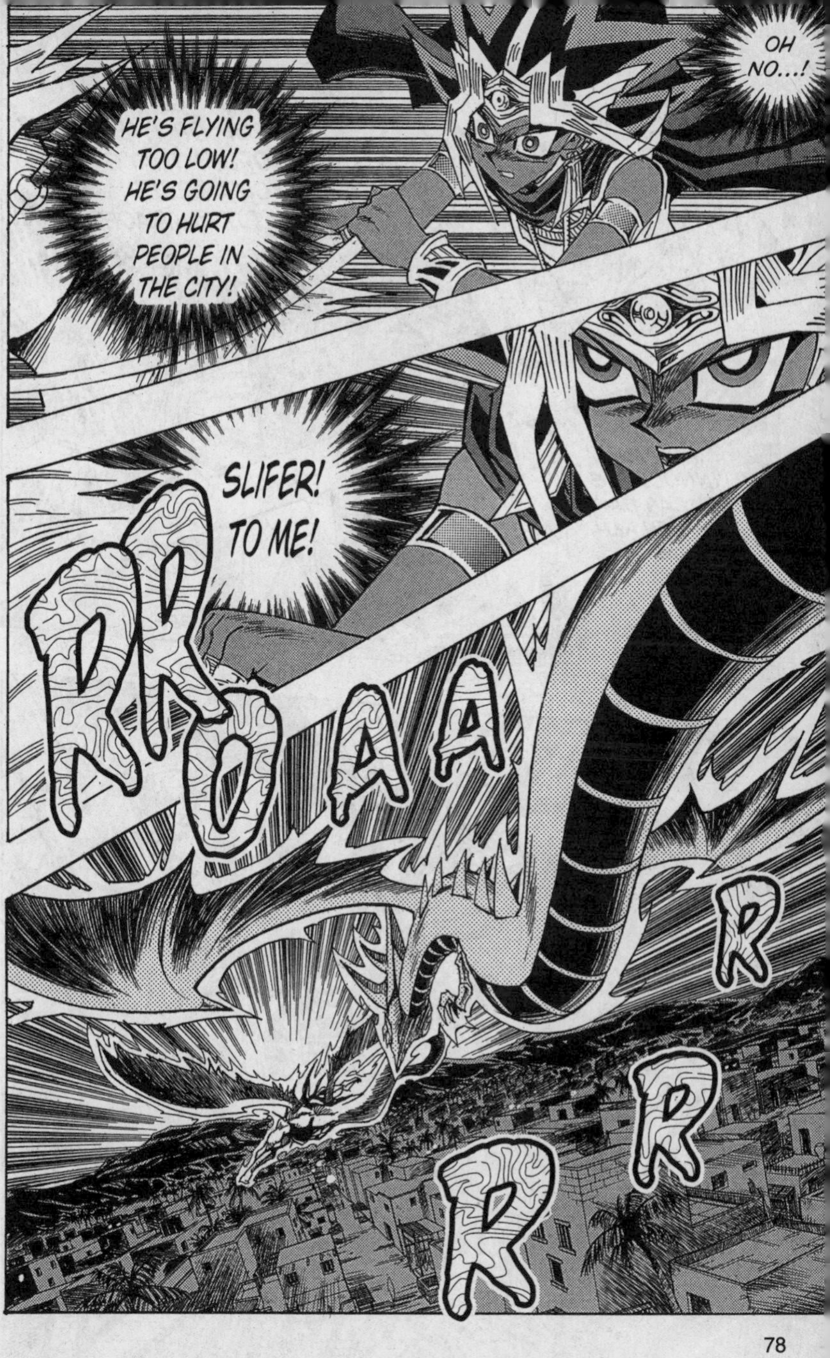
OH NO...!
HE'S FLYING TOO LOW! HE'S GOING TO HURT PEOPLE IN THE CITY!
SLIFER! TO ME!
RROAAARRR

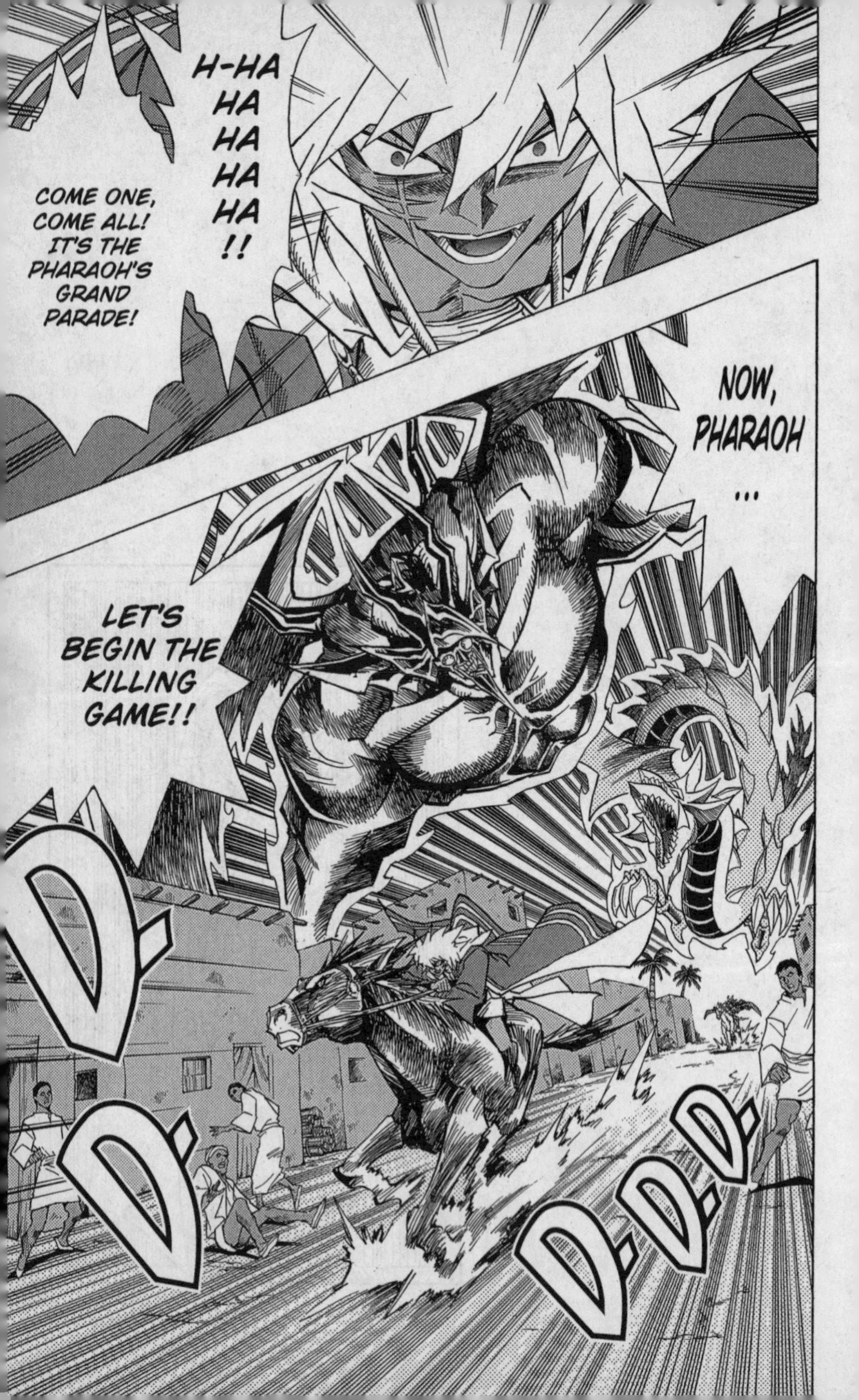
H-HA HA HA HA HA!!
COME ONE, COME ALL! IT'S THE PHARAOH'S GRAND PARADE!
NOW, PHARAOH...
LET'S BEGIN THE KILLING GAME!!
D. D.
D.D.D.

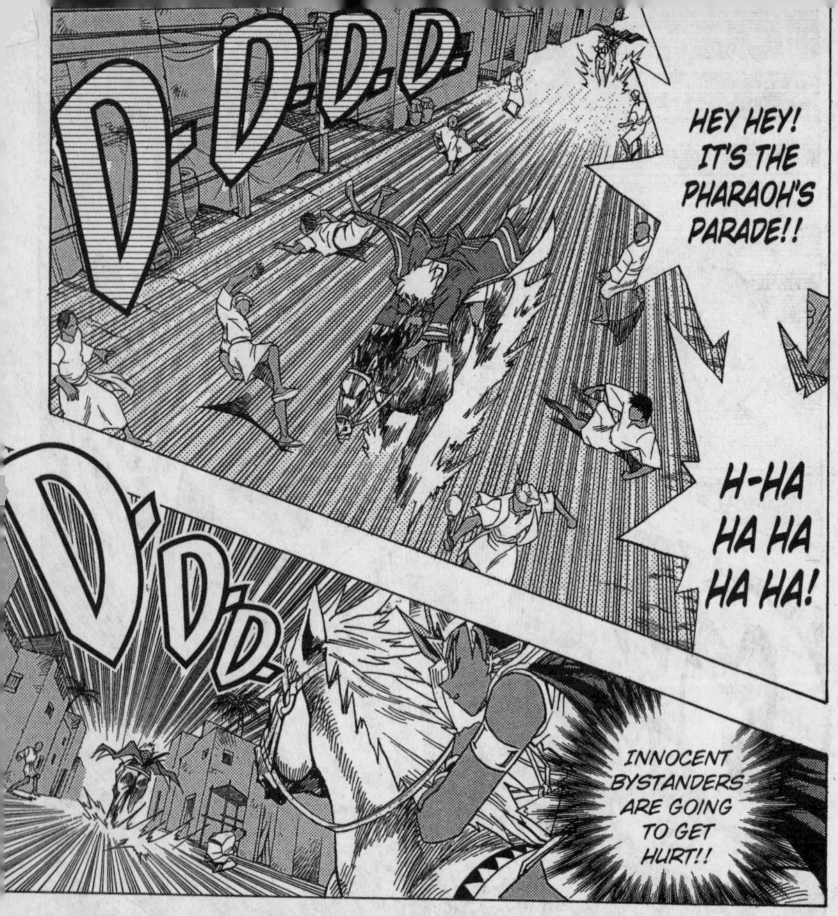
HEY HEY! IT'S THE PHARAOH'S PARADE!!
D-D-D-D
H-HA HA HA HA HA!
D-D-D
INNOCENT BYSTANDERS ARE GOING TO GET HURT!!

Duel 301: Divine Light, Divine Shadow

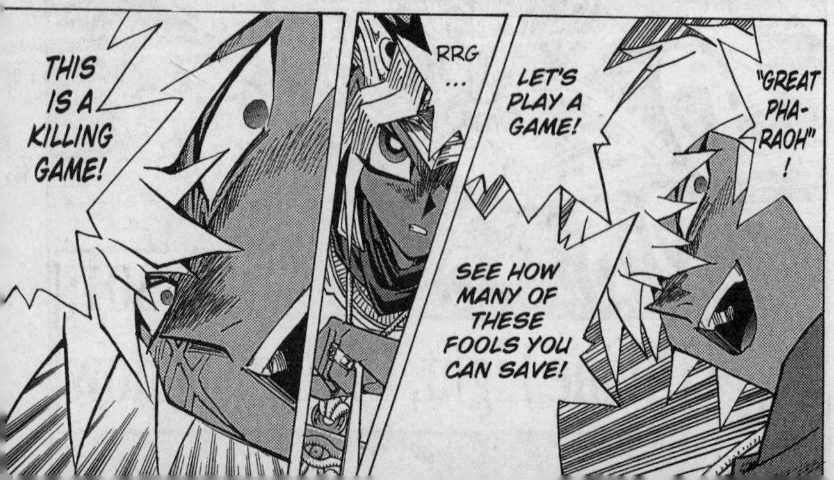
"GREAT PHA-RAOH"!
LET'S PLAY A GAME!
SEE HOW MANY OF THESE FOOLS YOU CAN SAVE!
RRG...
THIS IS A KILLING GAME!

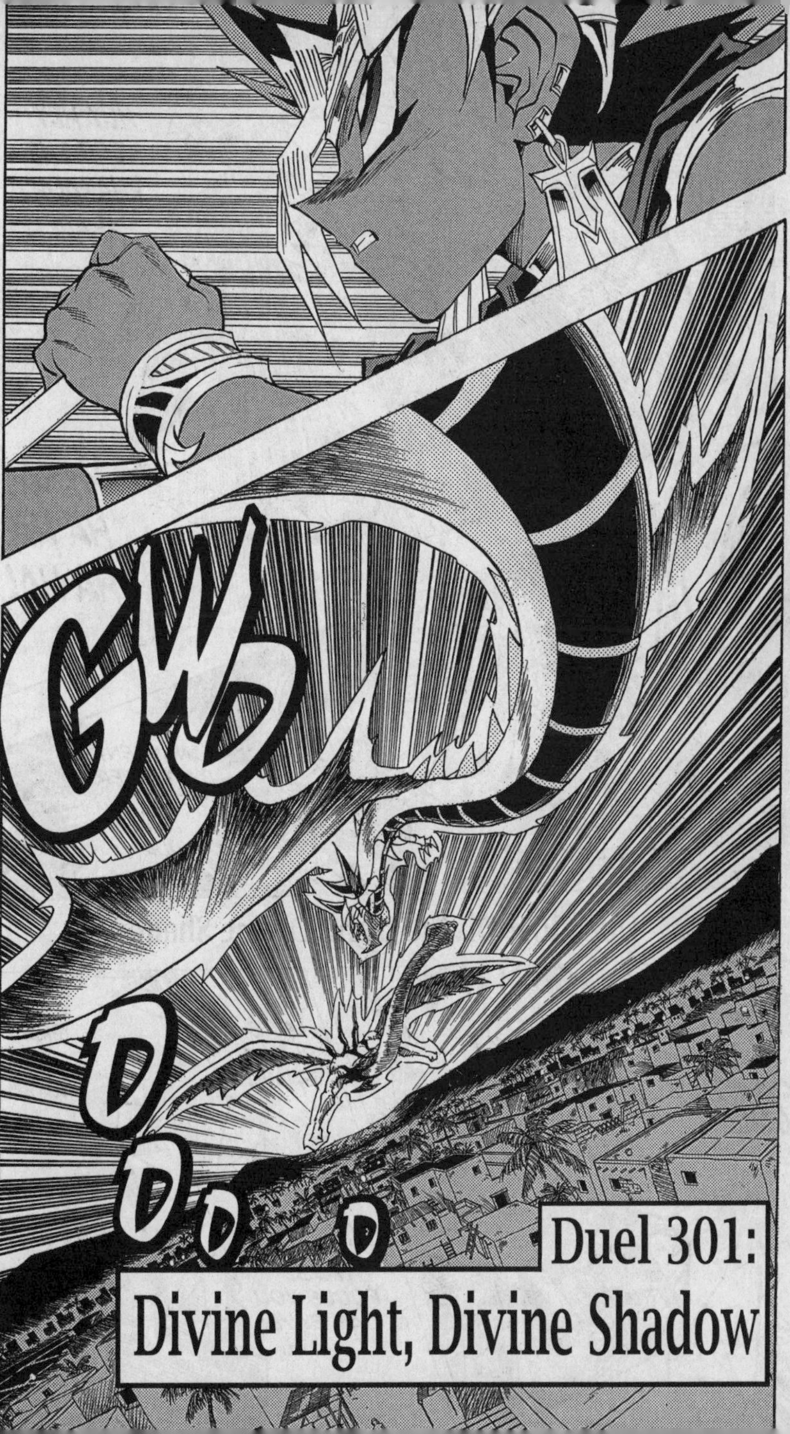
GWO
D D D D

Duel 301: Divine Light, Divine Shadow

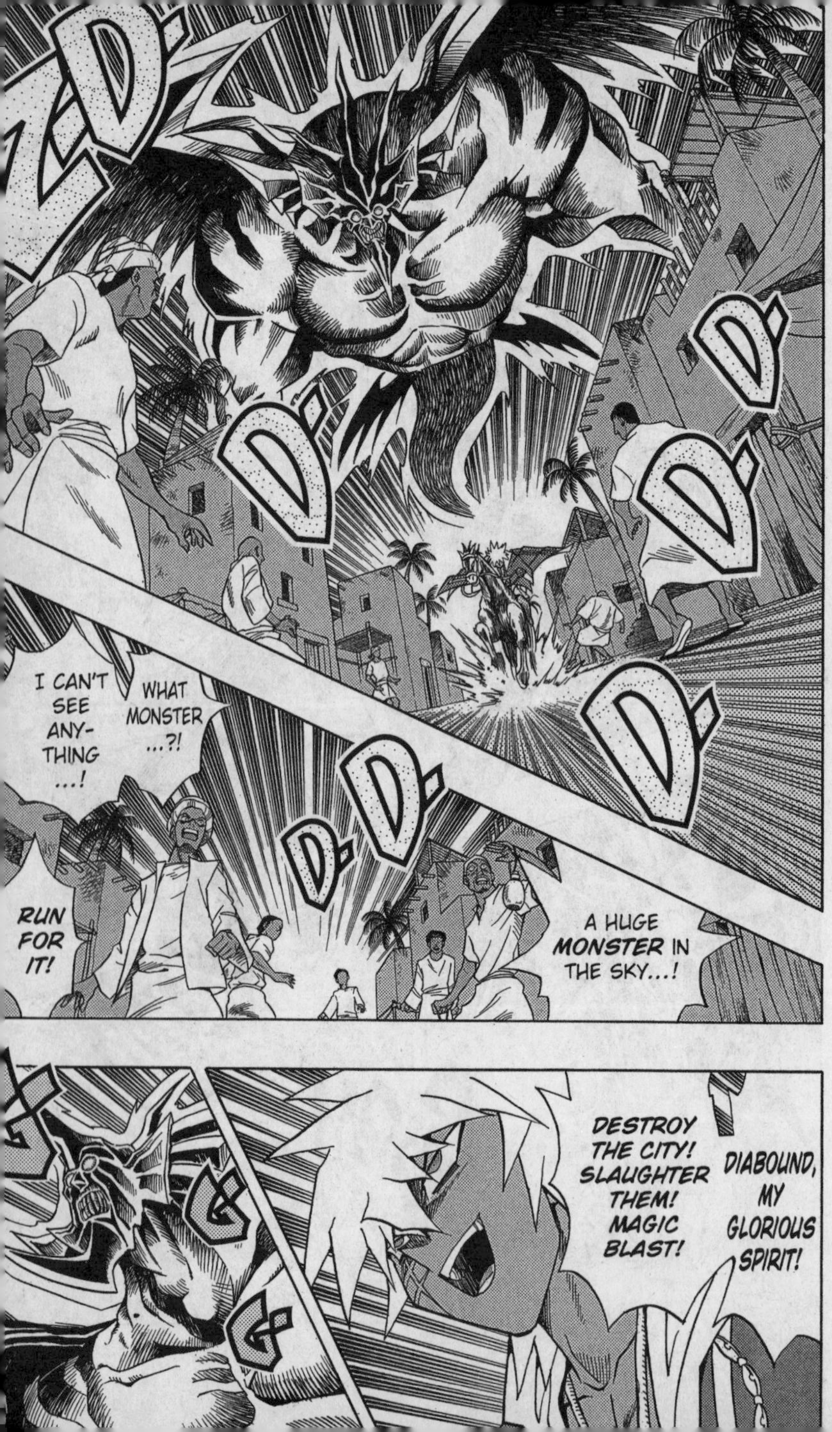
A HUGE *MONSTER* IN THE SKY...!
WHAT MONSTER ...?!
I CAN'T SEE ANYTHING ...!
RUN FOR IT!
DIABOUND, MY GLORIOUS SPIRIT!
DESTROY THE CITY! SLAUGHTER THEM! MAGIC BLAST!

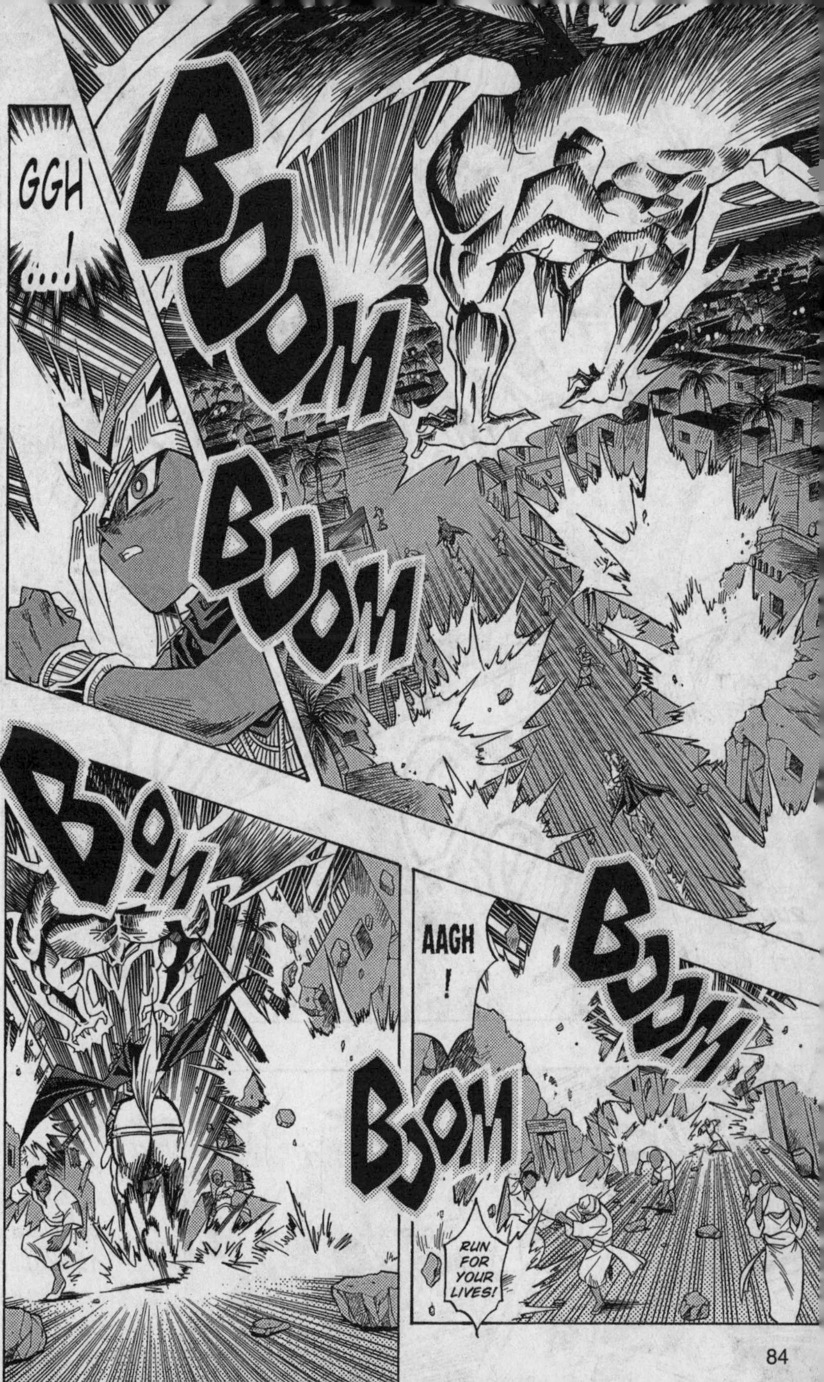
GGH ...!
BOOM
BOOM
BOOM
AAGH!
BOOM
BOOM
RUN FOR YOUR LIVES!

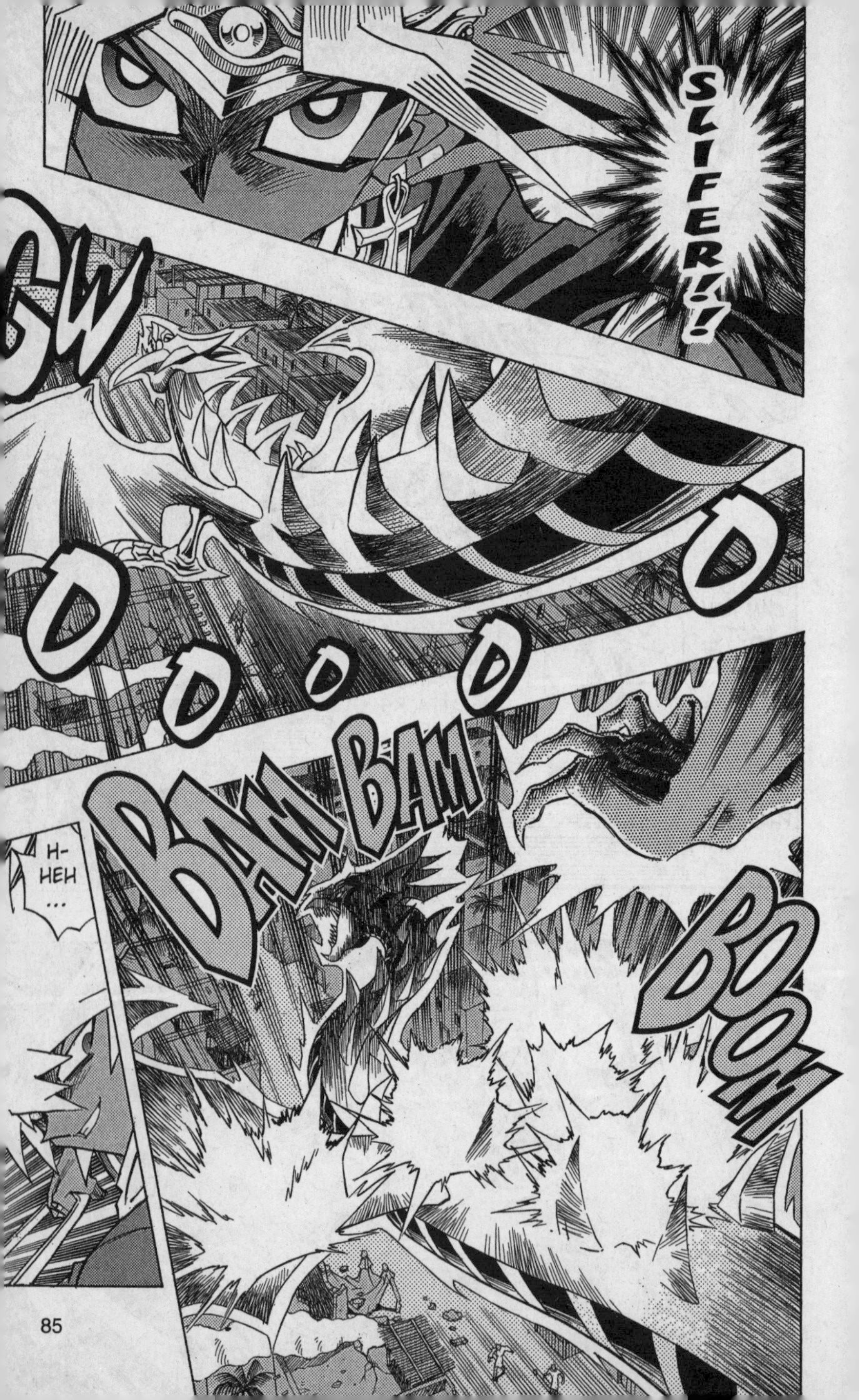
SLIFER!!
GW
D
D
D
D
D
D
BAM
BAM
BOOM
H-HEH...

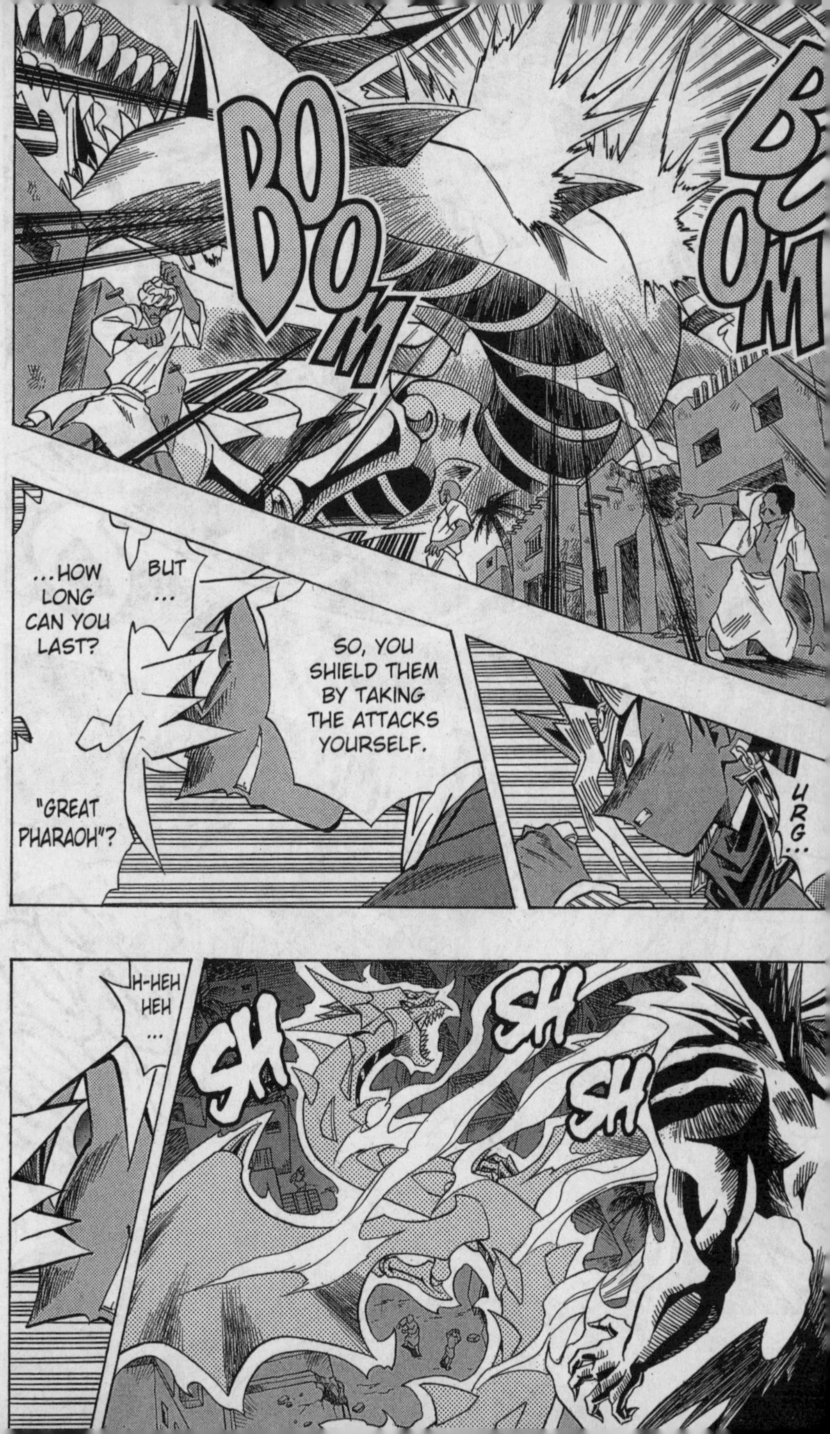
BOOM
BOOM
URG...
SO, YOU SHIELD THEM BY TAKING THE ATTACKS YOURSELF.
BUT...
...HOW LONG CAN YOU LAST?
"GREAT PHARAOH"?
SH
SH
SH
H-HEH HEH...

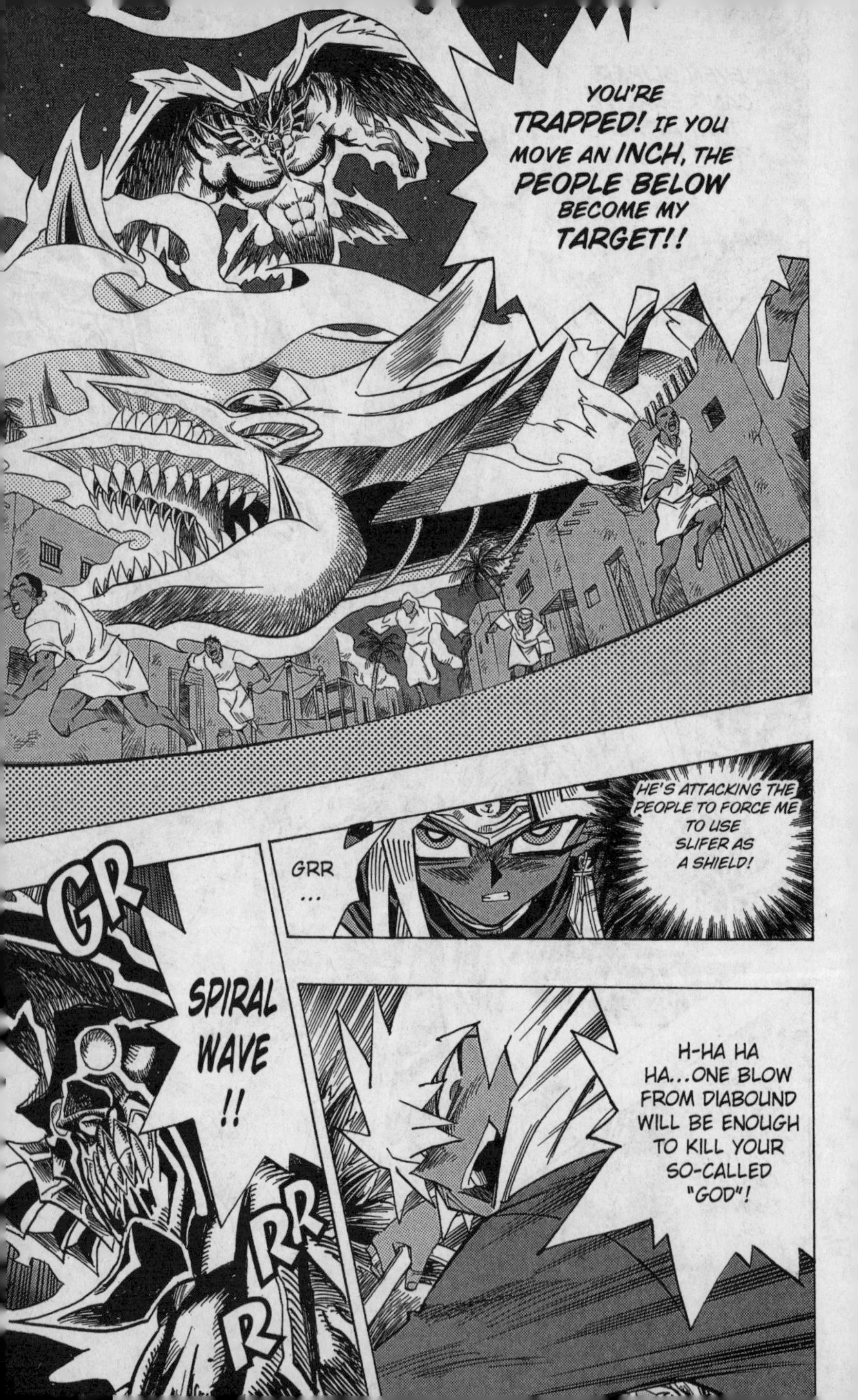
YOU'RE TRAPPED! IF YOU MOVE AN INCH, THE PEOPLE BELOW BECOME MY TARGET!!
HE'S ATTACKING THE PEOPLE TO FORCE ME TO USE SLIFER AS A SHIELD!
GRR ...
GR
SPIRAL WAVE !!
RR
R
H-HA HA HA...ONE BLOW FROM DIABOUND WILL BE ENOUGH TO KILL YOUR SO-CALLED "GOD"!

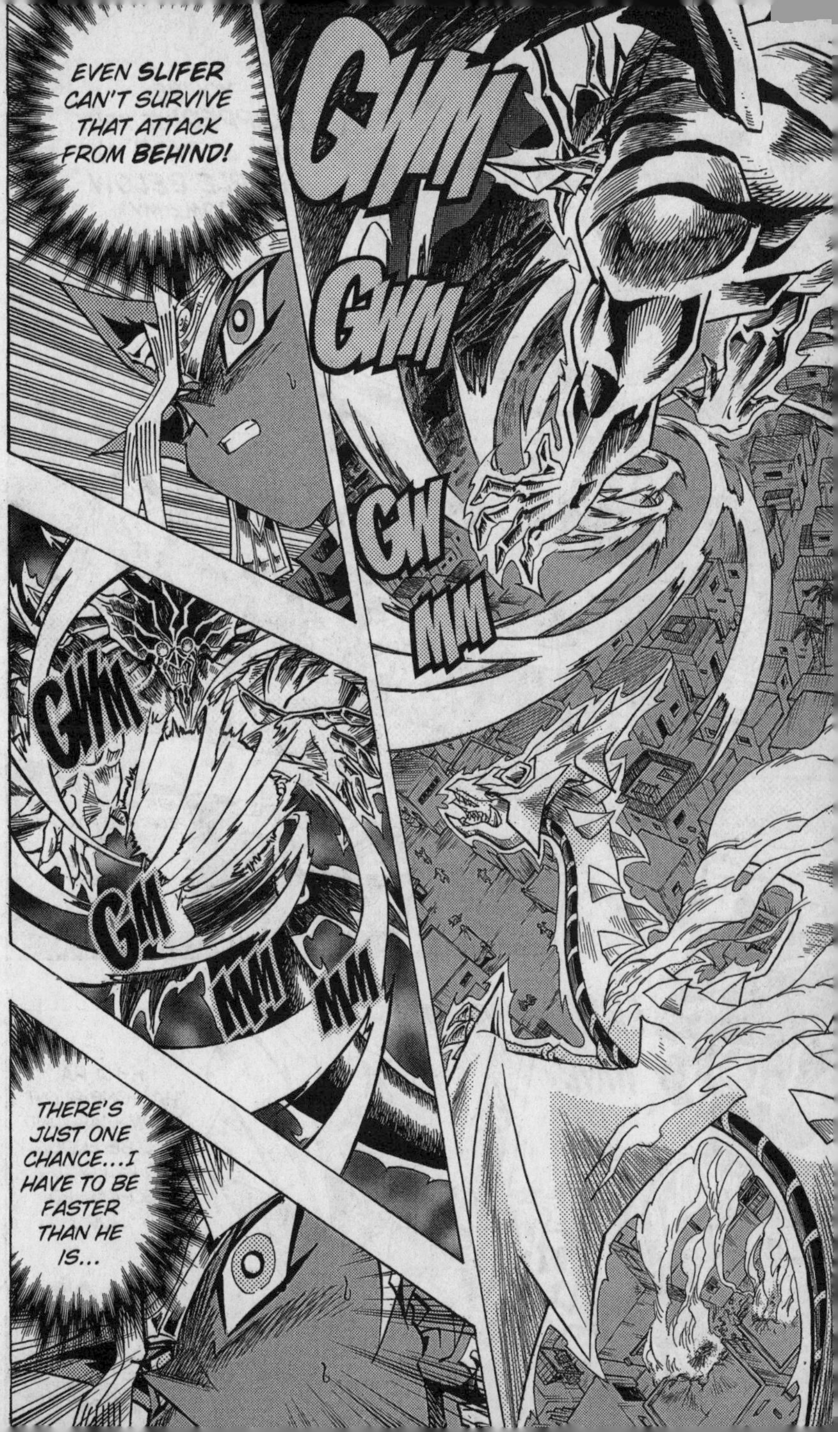
GWM
GWM
GW
MM
EVEN SLIFER CAN'T SURVIVE THAT ATTACK FROM BEHIND!
GWM
GM
MM
MM
THERE'S JUST ONE CHANCE...I HAVE TO BE FASTER THAN HE IS...

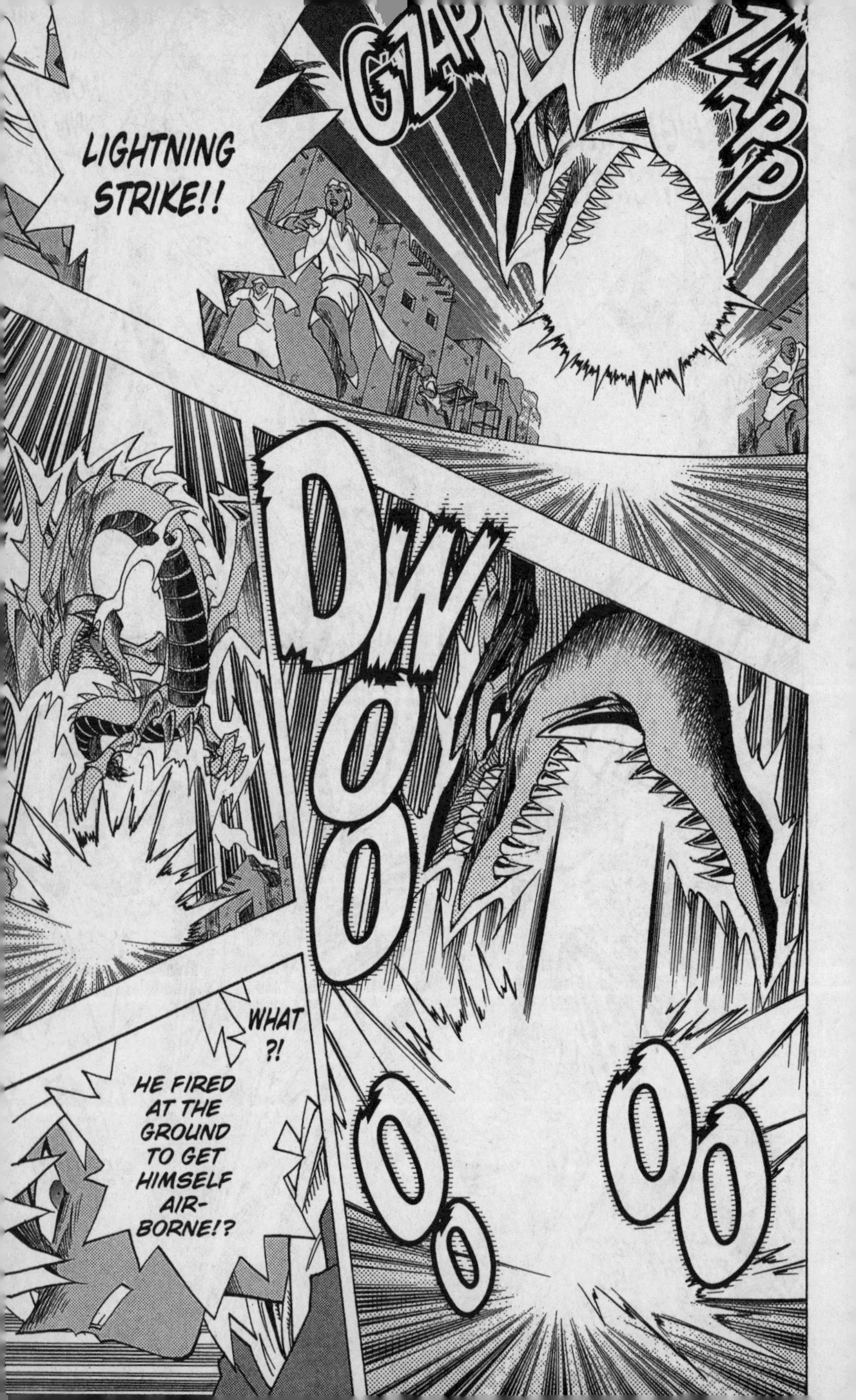
ZAPP
GZAP
LIGHTNING STRIKE!!
DOOOOOO
WHAT ?!
HE FIRED AT THE GROUND TO GET HIMSELF AIR-BORNE!?

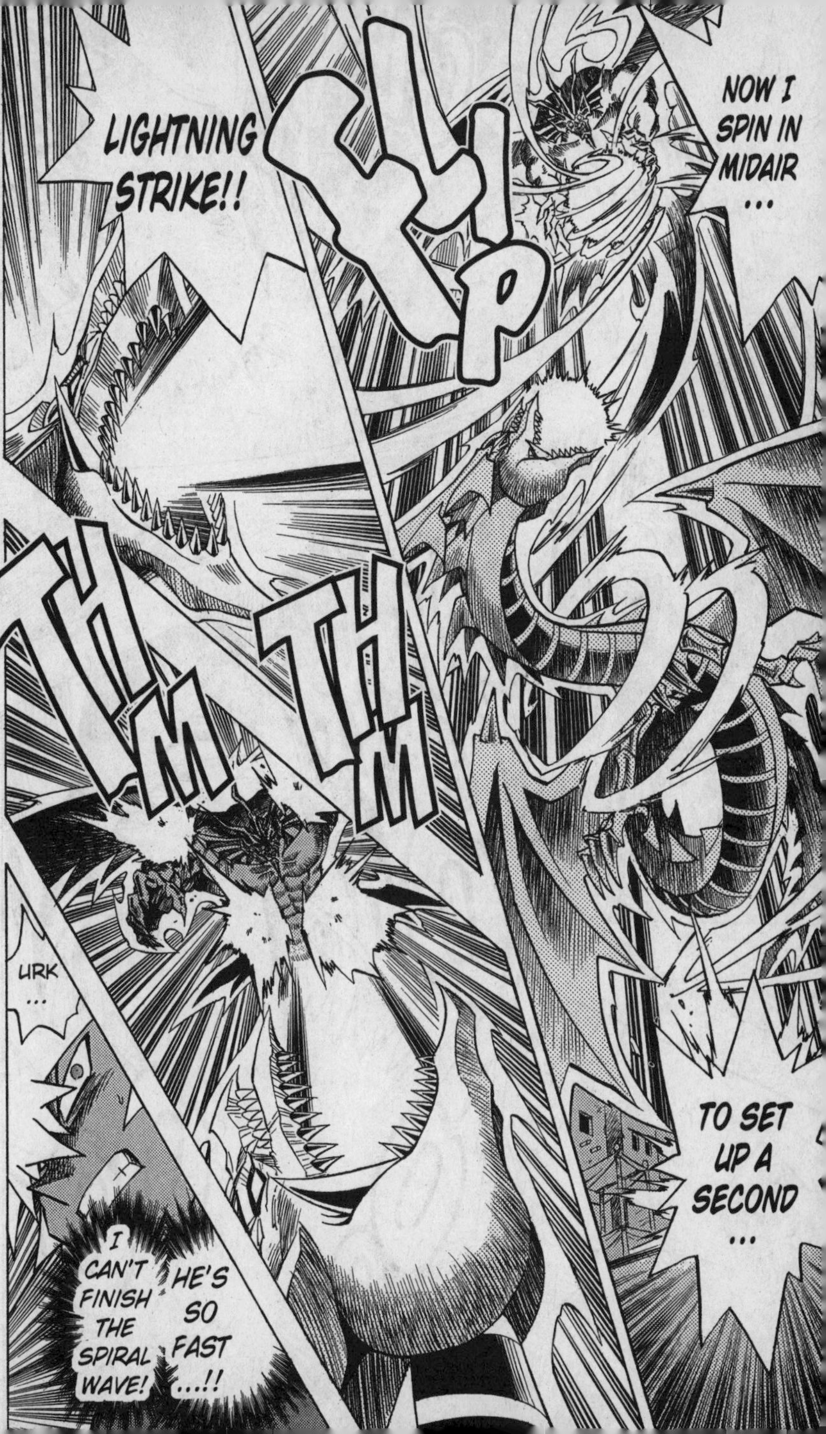
NOW I SPIN IN MIDAIR ...
LIGHTNING STRIKE!!
TO SET UP A SECOND ...
THM
THM
URK ...
HE'S SO FAST ...!!
I CAN'T FINISH THE SPIRAL WAVE!

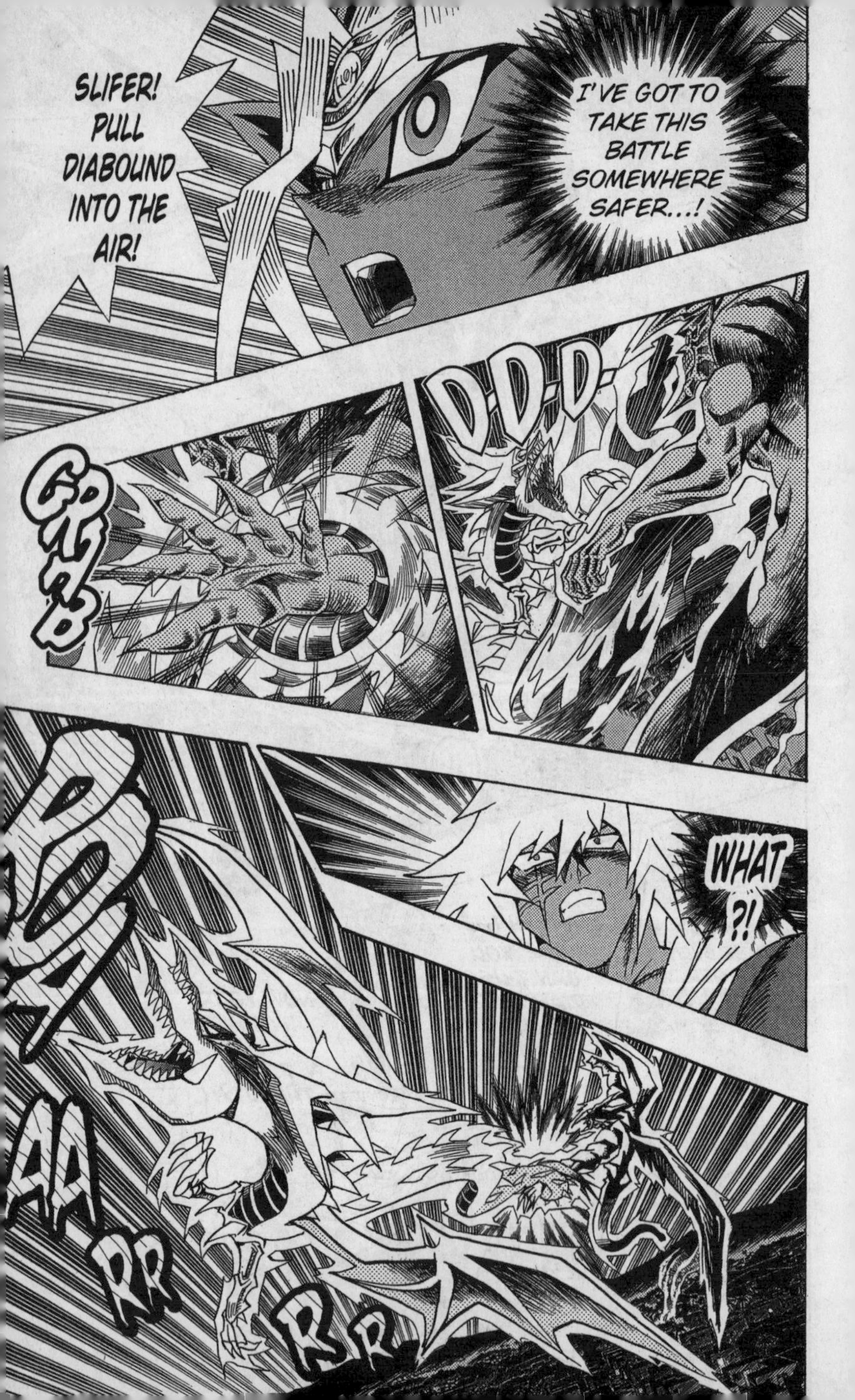

I'VE GOT TO TAKE THIS BATTLE SOMEWHERE SAFER...!
SLIFER! PULL DIABOUND INTO THE AIR!
D-D-D-
GRAB
WHAT ?!
AARRRR

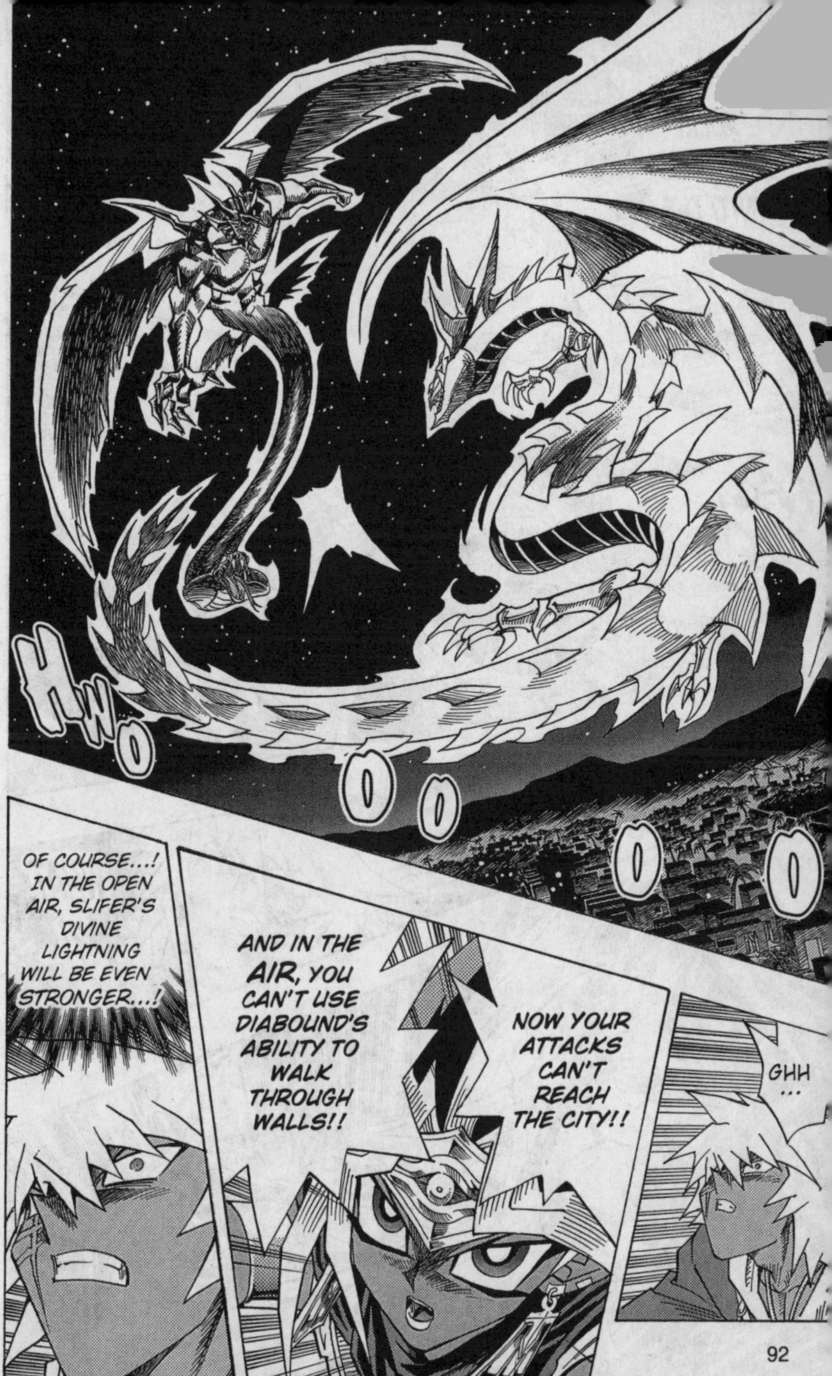
HWO
O
O
O
O
OF COURSE...! IN THE OPEN AIR, SLIFER'S DIVINE LIGHTNING WILL BE EVEN STRONGER...!
AND IN THE AIR, YOU CAN'T USE DIABOUND'S ABILITY TO WALK THROUGH WALLS!!
NOW YOUR ATTACKS CAN'T REACH THE CITY!!
GHH...

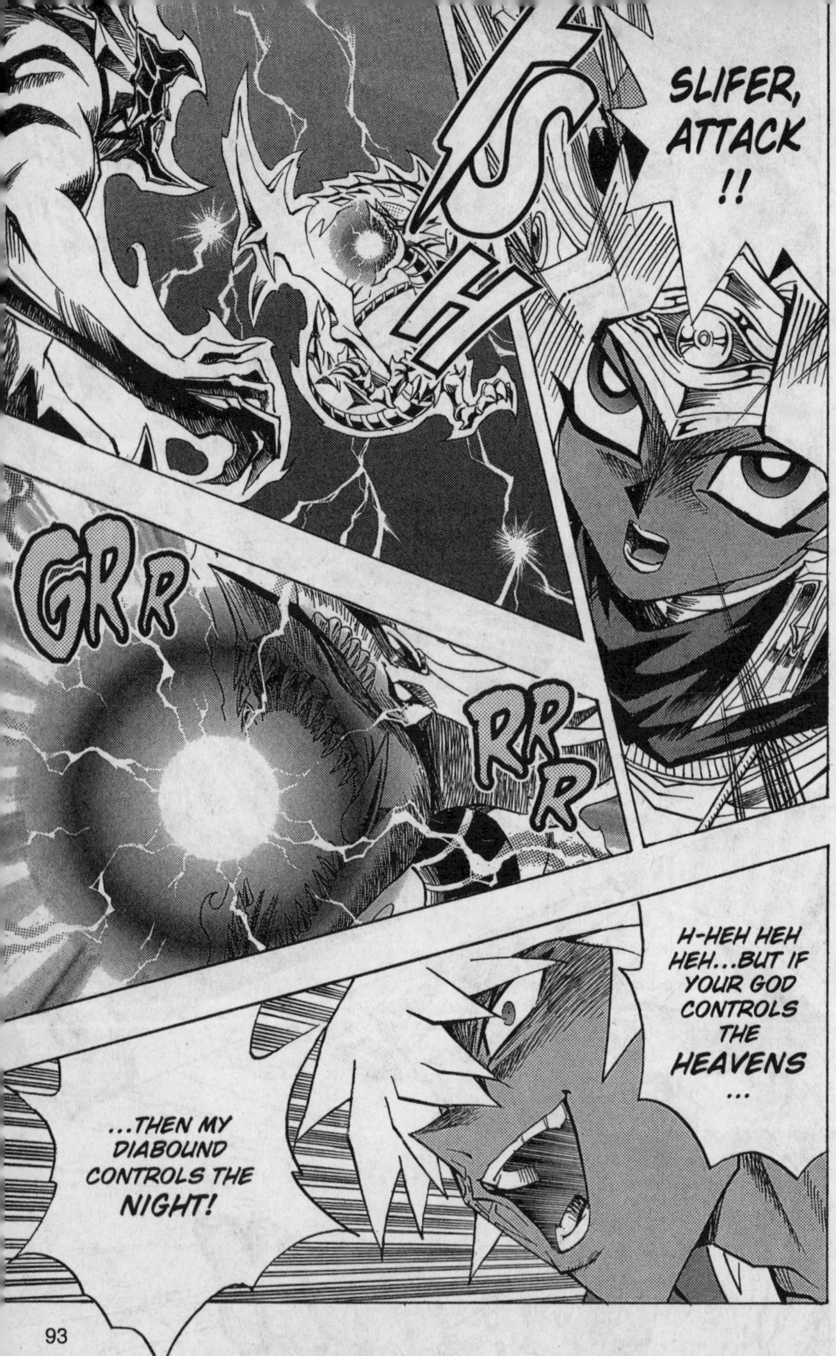
SLIFER, ATTACK !!
GR R
RR R
H-HEH HEH HEH...BUT IF YOUR GOD CONTROLS THE HEAVENS ...
...THEN MY DIABOUND CONTROLS THE NIGHT!

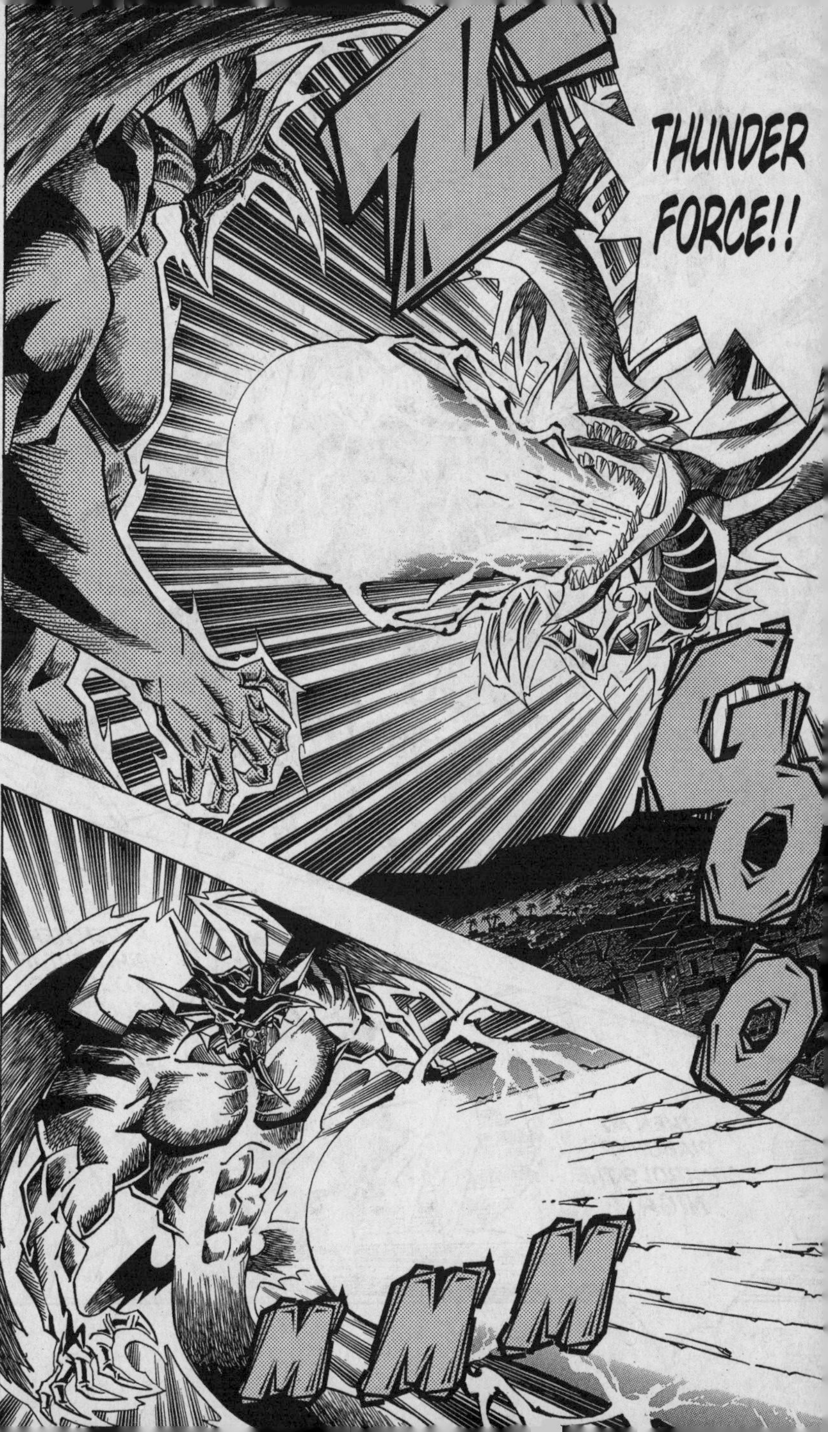
THUNDER FORCE!!

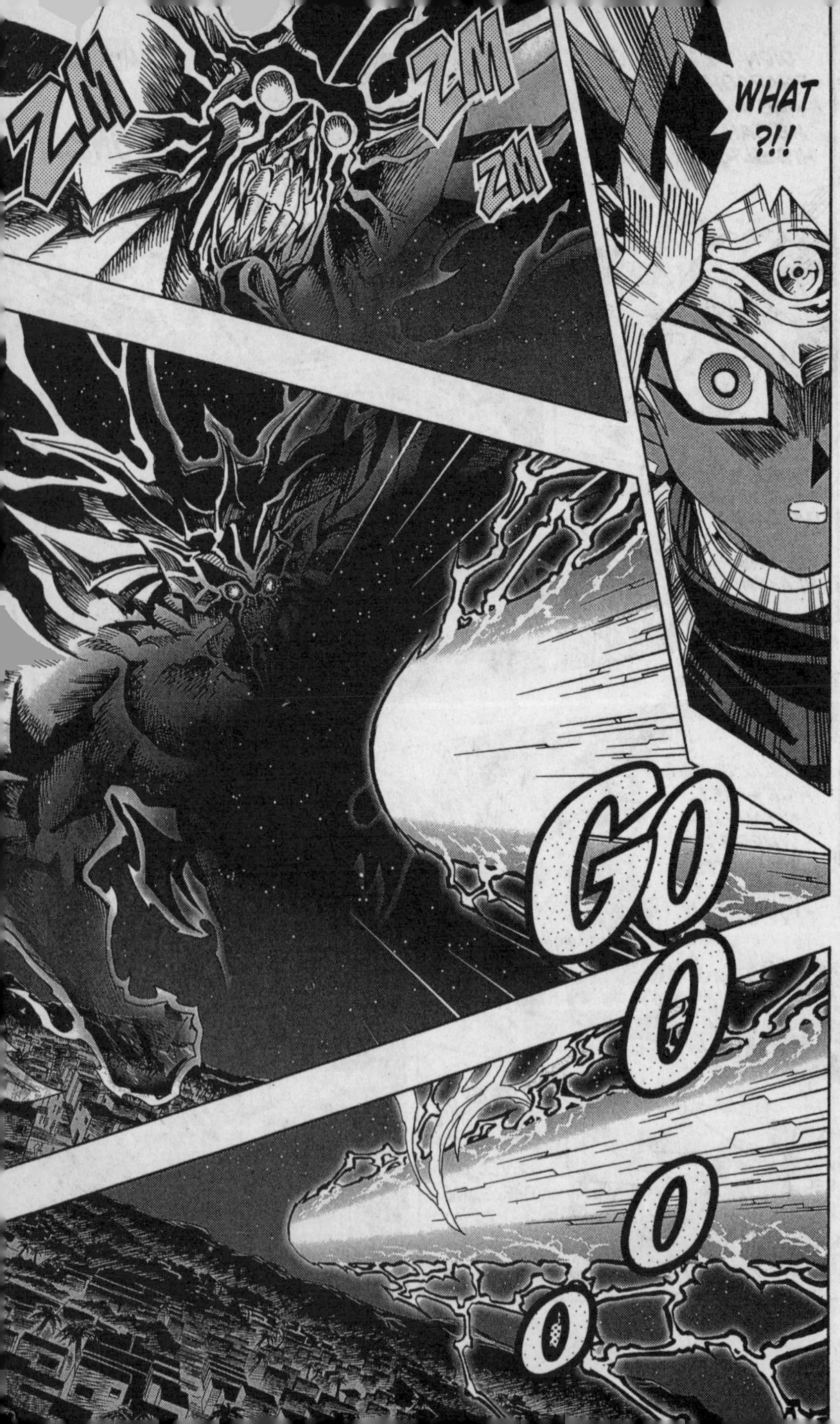
WHAT ?!!
ZM
ZM
ZM
GOOOO

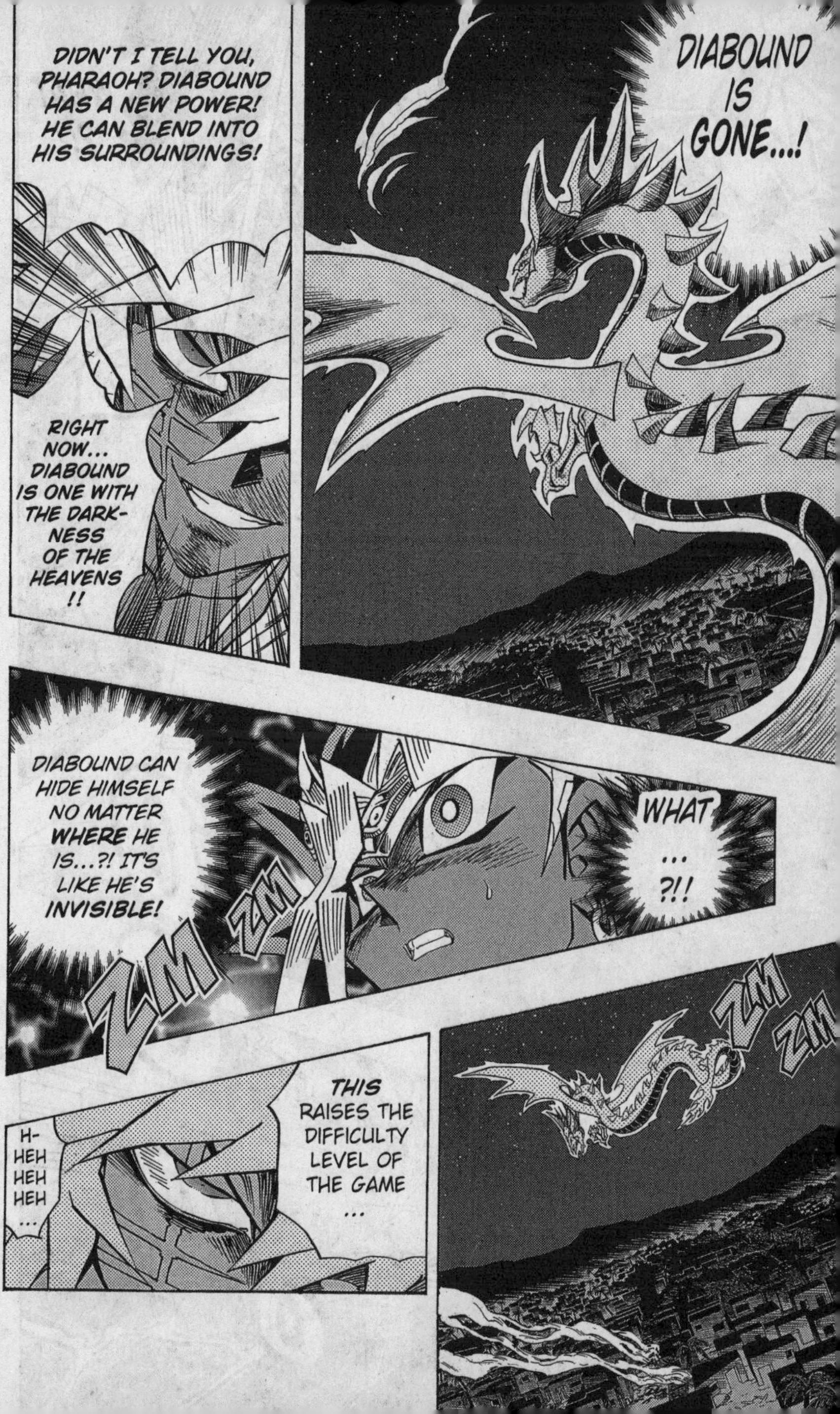
DIABOUND IS GONE...!
DIDN'T I TELL YOU, PHARAOH? DIABOUND HAS A NEW POWER! HE CAN BLEND INTO HIS SURROUNDINGS!
RIGHT NOW... DIABOUND IS ONE WITH THE DARKNESS OF THE HEAVENS!!
WHAT...?!!
DIABOUND CAN HIDE HIMSELF NO MATTER WHERE HE IS...?! IT'S LIKE HE'S INVISIBLE!
ZM ZM
ZM ZM
THIS RAISES THE DIFFICULTY LEVEL OF THE GAME...
H-HEH HEH HEH...

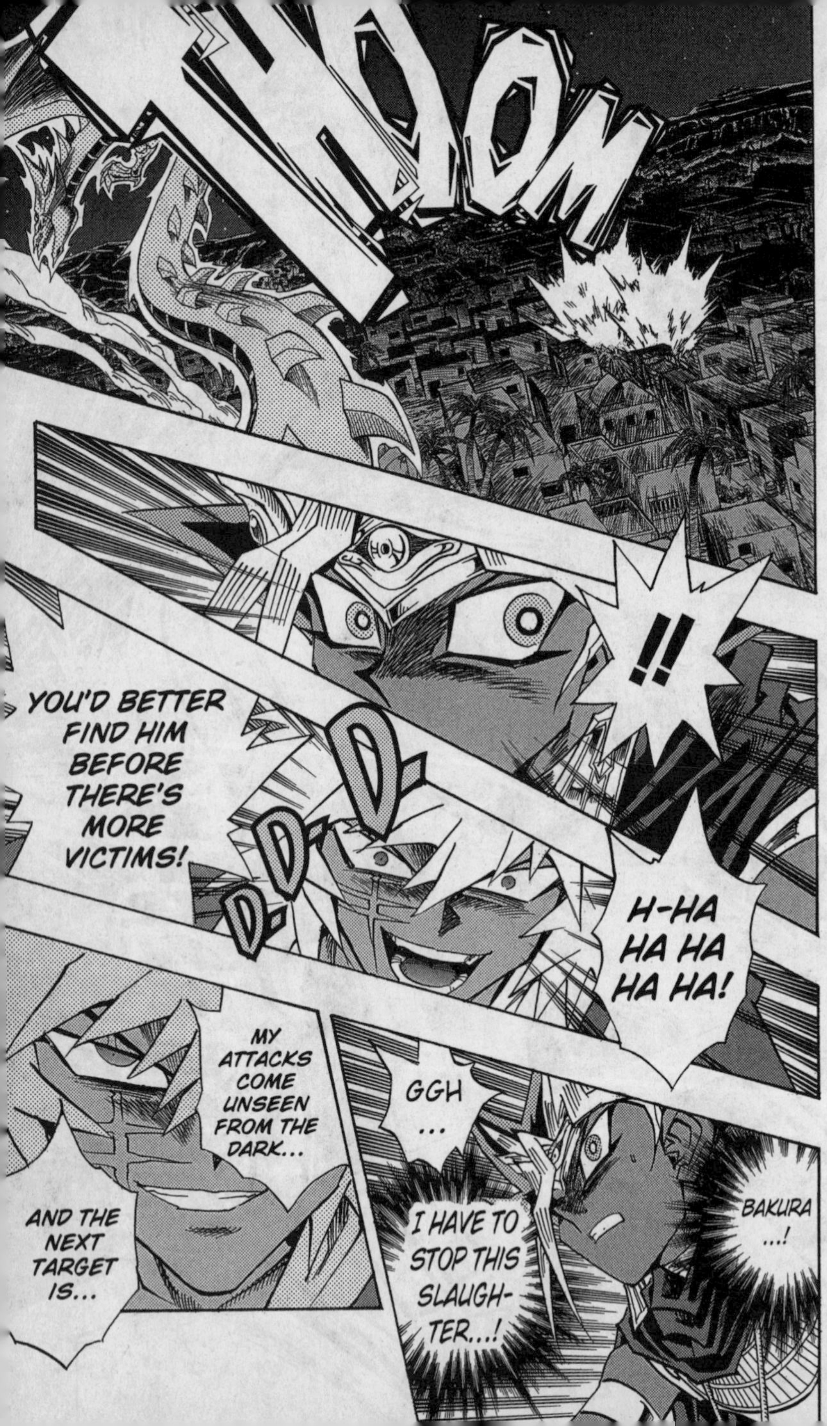
THOOM
!!
YOU'D BETTER FIND HIM BEFORE THERE'S MORE VICTIMS!
H-HA HA HA HA HA!
MY ATTACKS COME UNSEEN FROM THE DARK...
AND THE NEXT TARGET IS...
GGH ...
I HAVE TO STOP THIS SLAUGHTER...!
BAKURA ...!

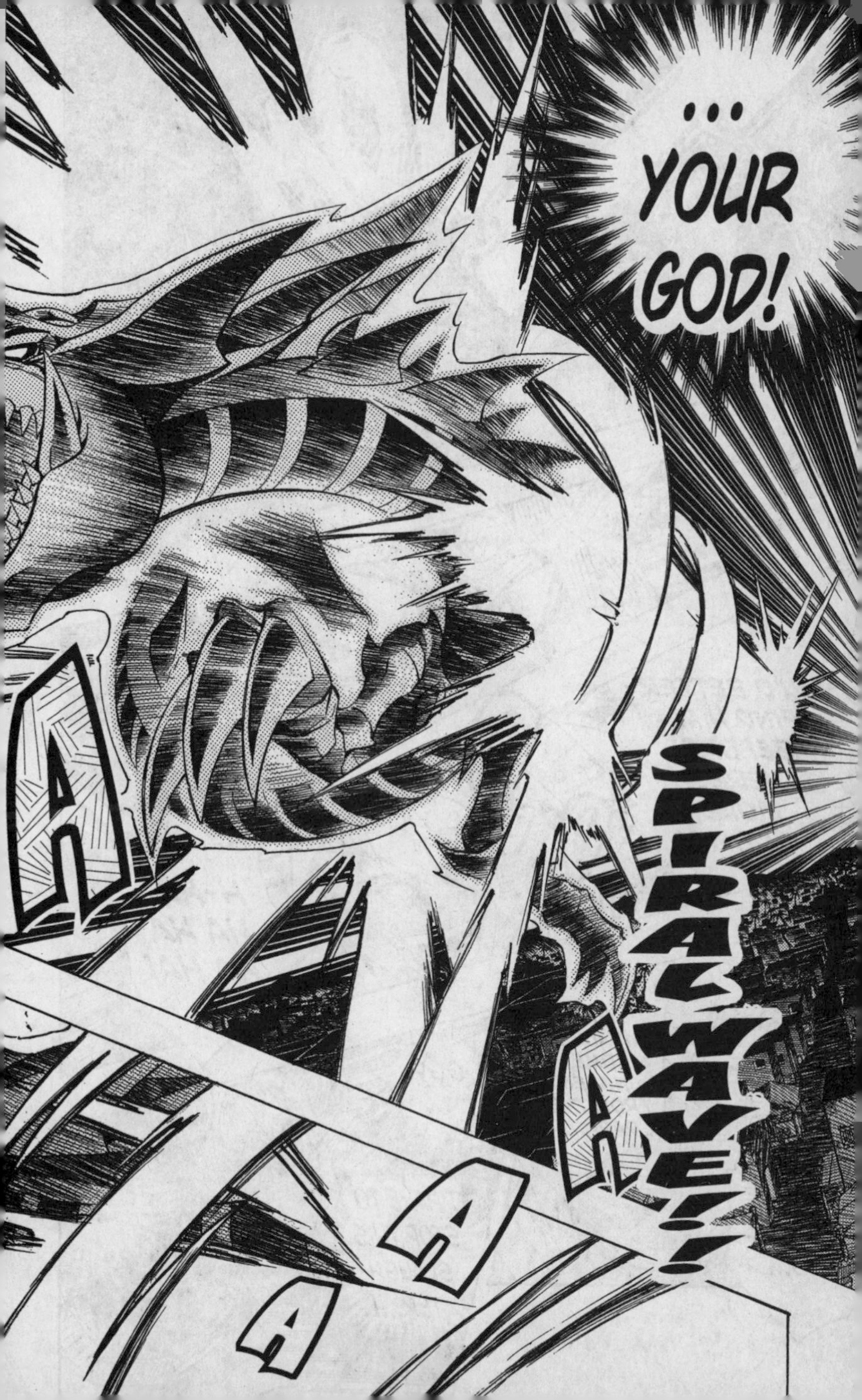
...YOUR GOD!
SPIRAL WAVE!!
AAAAAA

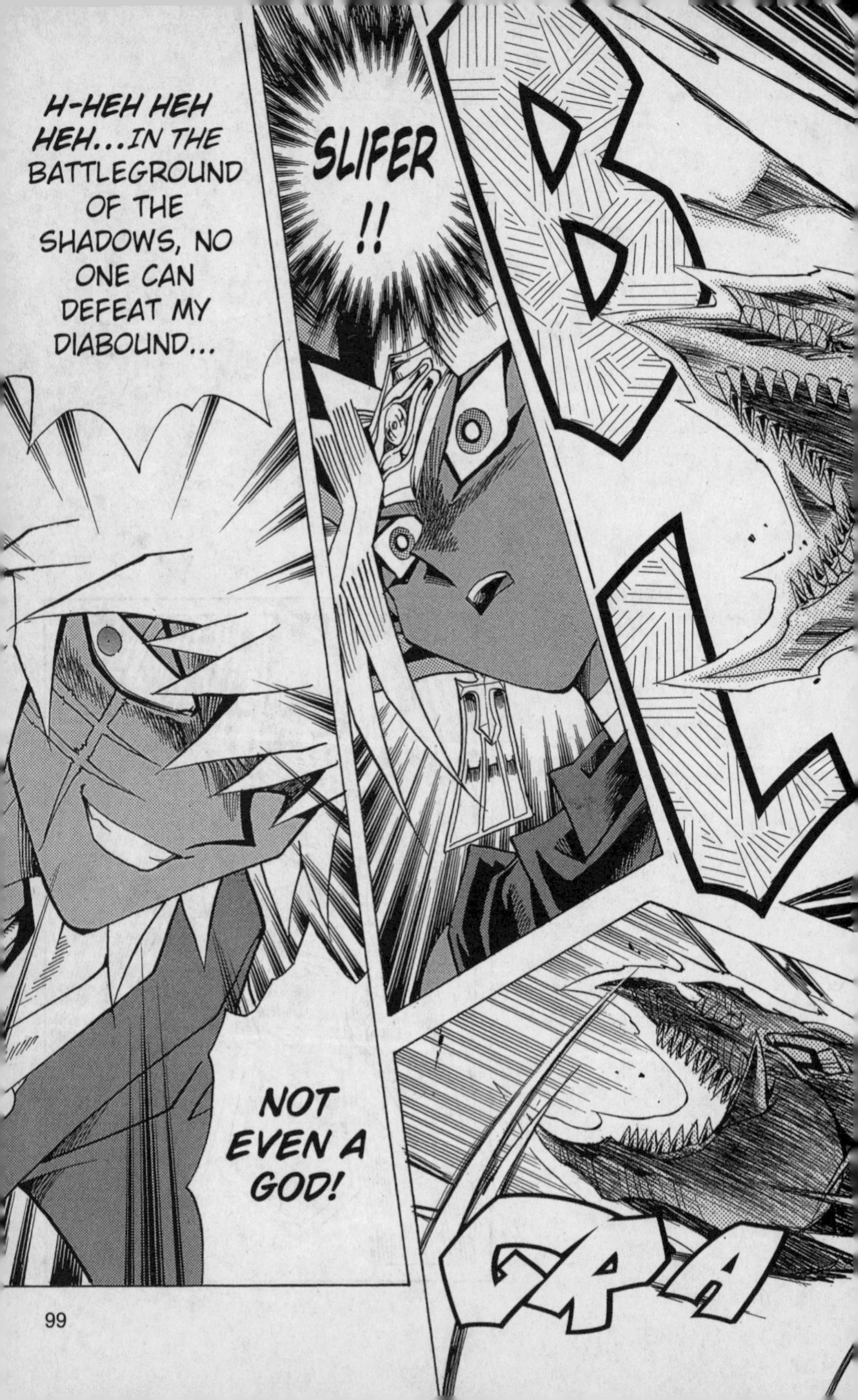
SLIFER !!
H-HEH HEH HEH...IN THE BATTLEGROUND OF THE SHADOWS, NO ONE CAN DEFEAT MY DIABOUND...
NOT EVEN A GOD!
CRA

Duel 302: Surprise Attack! Power Attack!

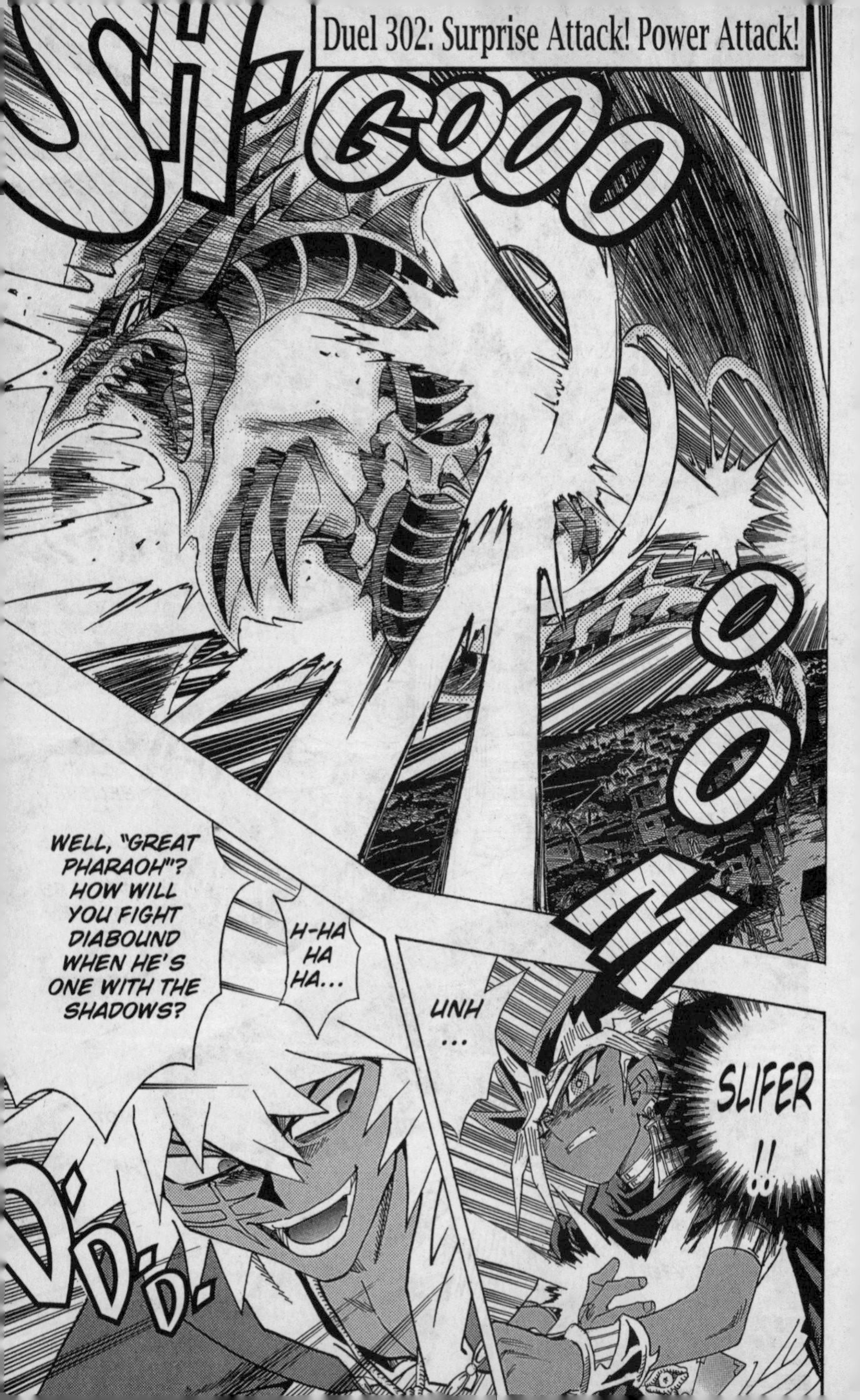
SLIGOOOOOM
WELL, "GREAT PHARAOH"? HOW WILL YOU FIGHT DIABOUND WHEN HE'S ONE WITH THE SHADOWS?
H-HA HA HA...
UNH ...
SLIFER !!
D. D. D. D.

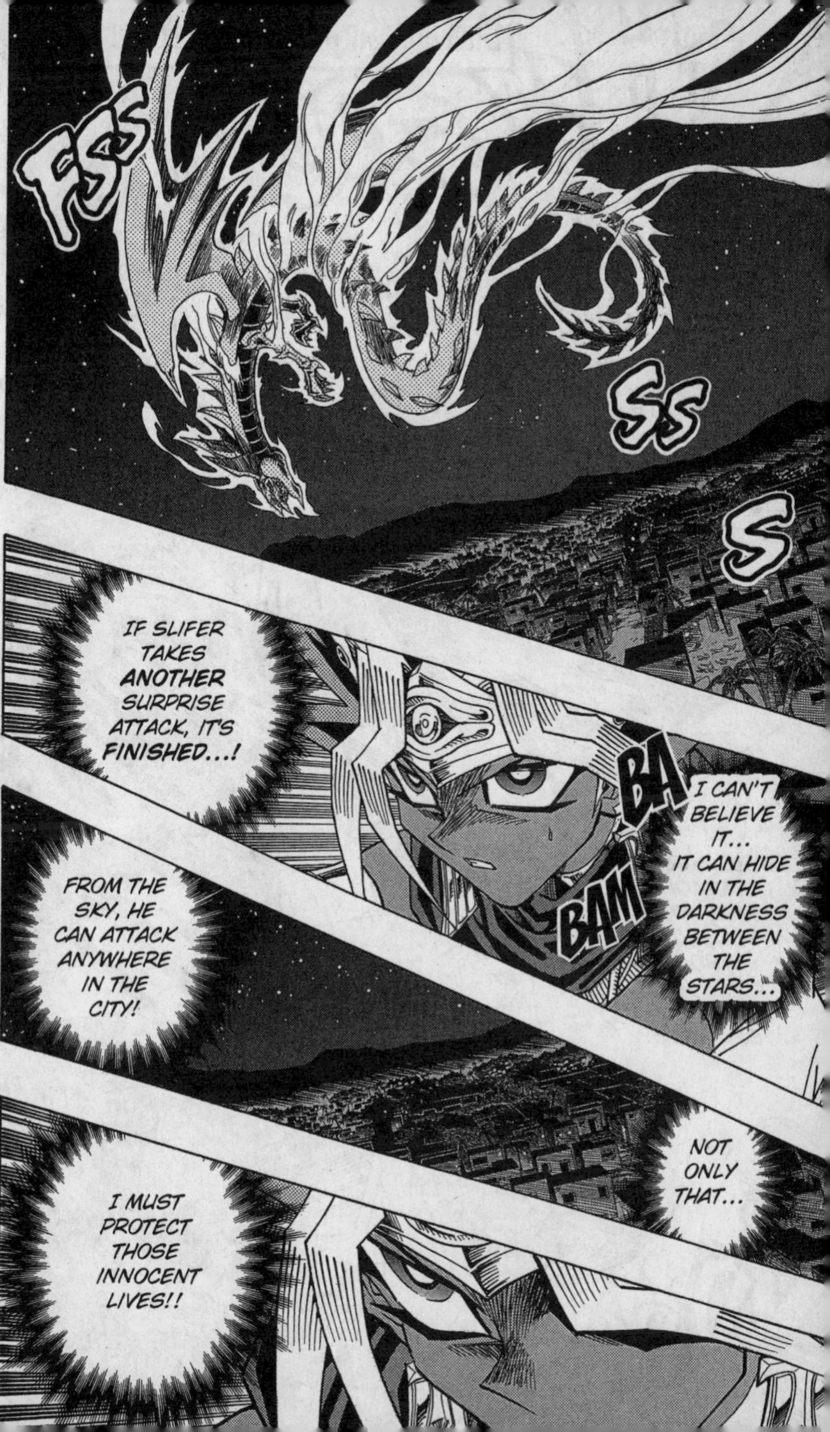
FSS
Ss
S
IF SLIFER TAKES ANOTHER SURPRISE ATTACK, IT'S FINISHED...!
BA
BAM
I CAN'T BELIEVE IT... IT CAN HIDE IN THE DARKNESS BETWEEN THE STARS...
FROM THE SKY, HE CAN ATTACK ANYWHERE IN THE CITY!
NOT ONLY THAT...
I MUST PROTECT THOSE INNOCENT LIVES!!

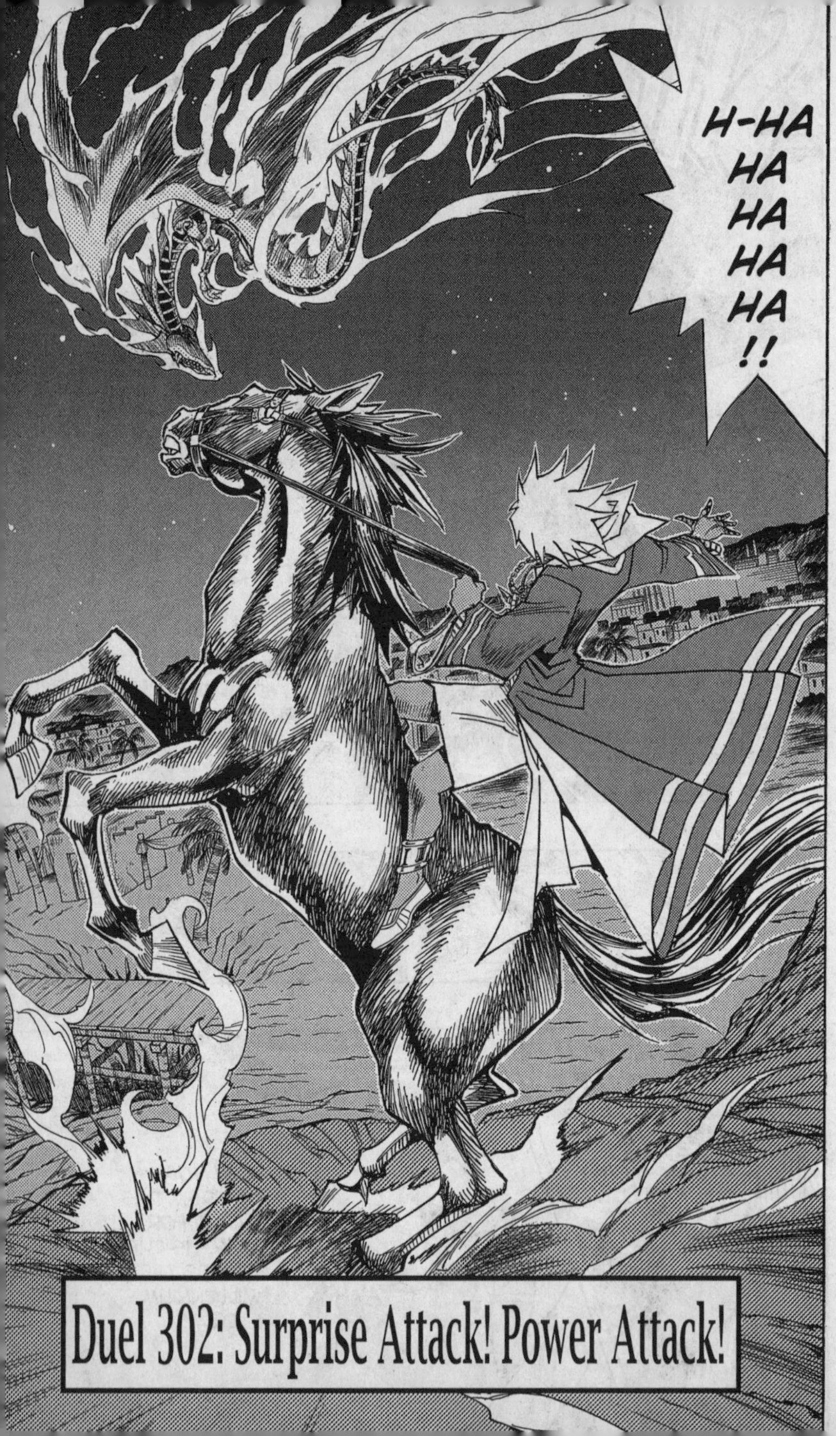
H-HA HA HA HA HA !!

Duel 302: Surprise Attack! Power Attack!

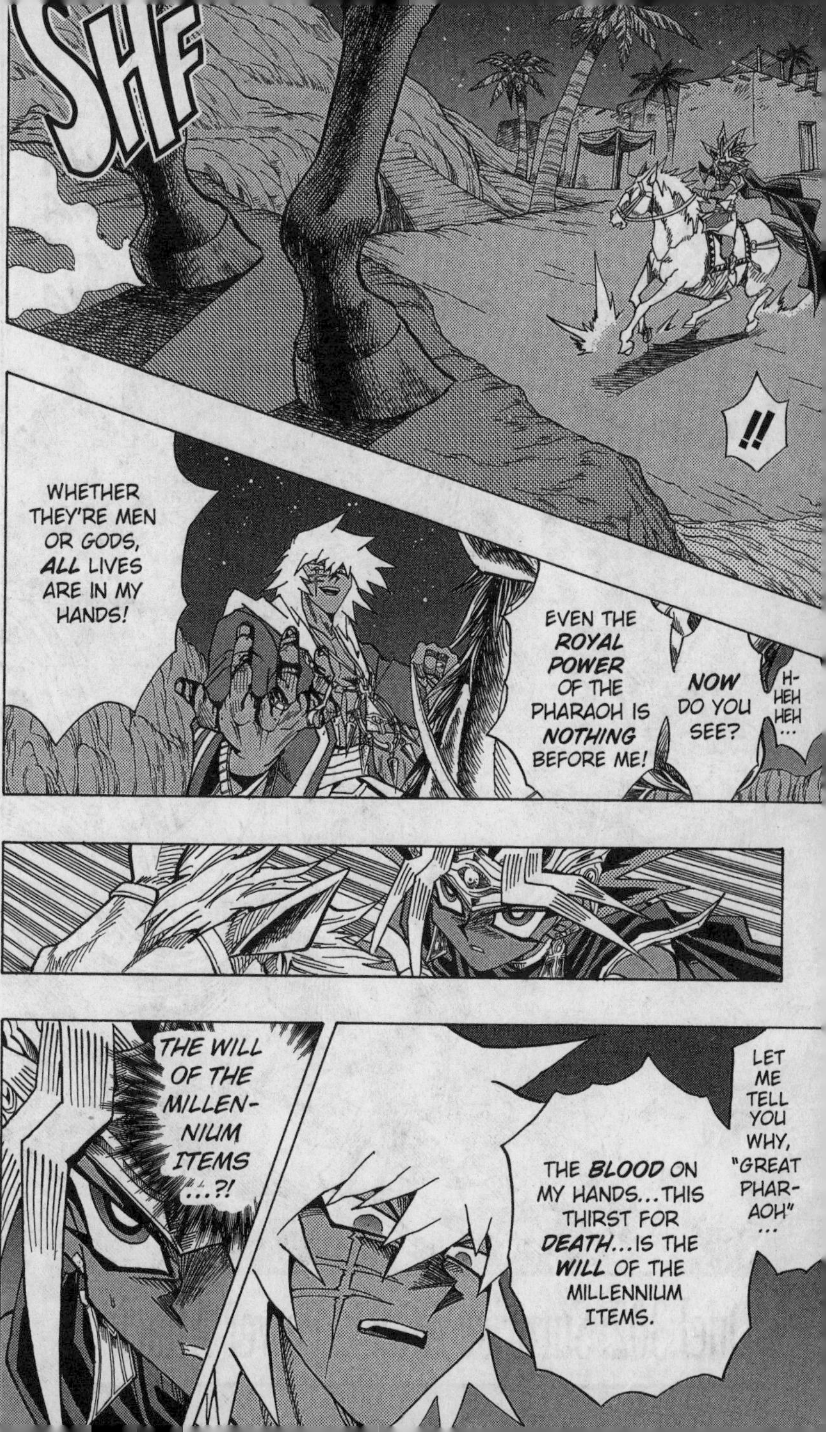
SHF
!!
H-HEH HEH...
NOW DO YOU SEE?
EVEN THE ROYAL POWER OF THE PHARAOH IS NOTHING BEFORE ME!
WHETHER THEY'RE MEN OR GODS, ALL LIVES ARE IN MY HANDS!
LET ME TELL YOU WHY, "GREAT PHARAOH"...
THE BLOOD ON MY HANDS...THIS THIRST FOR DEATH...IS THE WILL OF THE MILLENNIUM ITEMS.
THE WILL OF THE MILLENNIUM ITEMS...?!

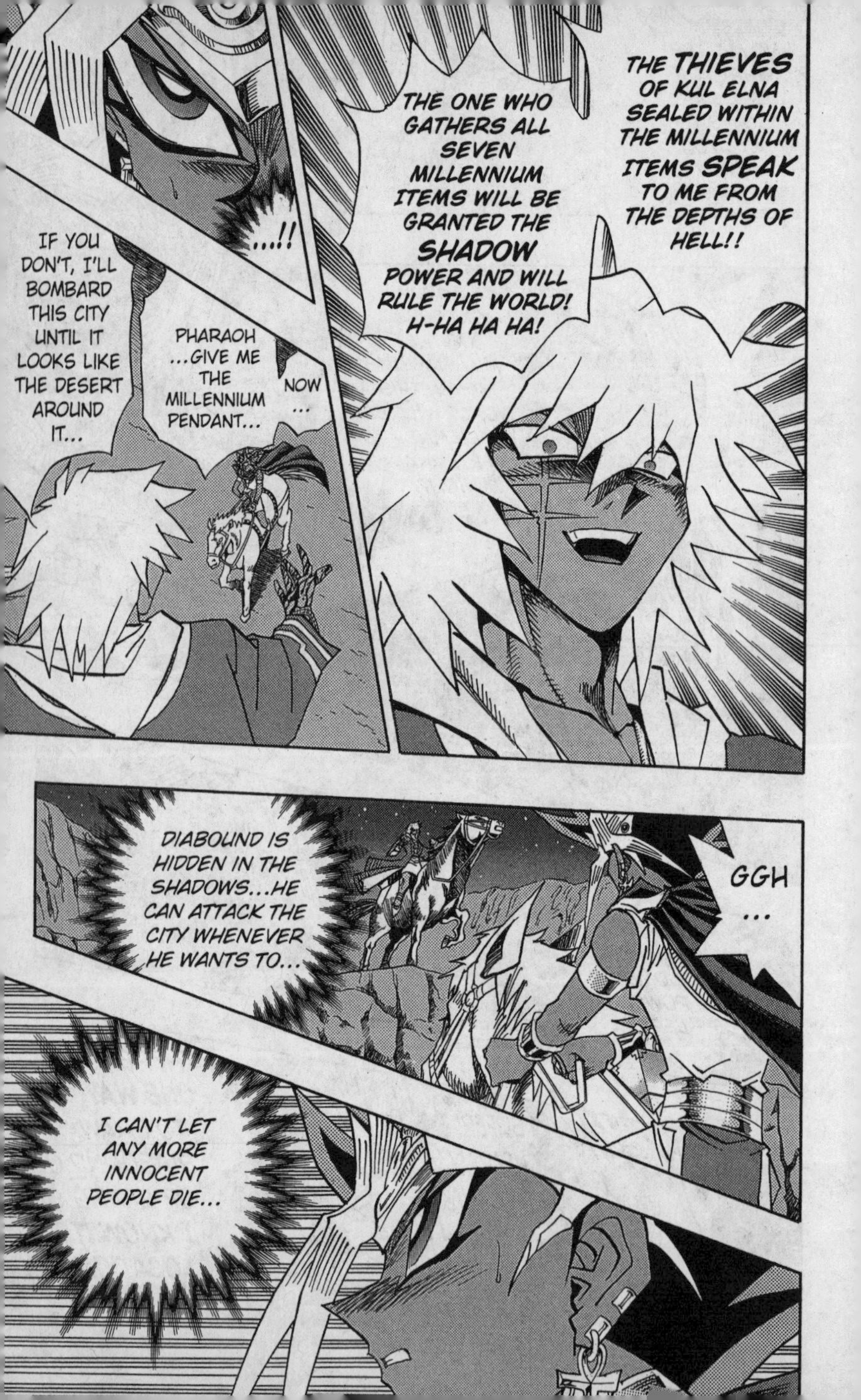
THE THIEVES OF KUL ELNA SEALED WITHIN THE MILLENNIUM ITEMS SPEAK TO ME FROM THE DEPTHS OF HELL!!
THE ONE WHO GATHERS ALL SEVEN MILLENNIUM ITEMS WILL BE GRANTED THE SHADOW POWER AND WILL RULE THE WORLD! H-HA HA HA!
...!!
NOW...
PHARAOH ...GIVE ME THE MILLENNIUM PENDANT...
IF YOU DON'T, I'LL BOMBARD THIS CITY UNTIL IT LOOKS LIKE THE DESERT AROUND IT...
GGH...
DIABOUND IS HIDDEN IN THE SHADOWS...HE CAN ATTACK THE CITY WHENEVER HE WANTS TO...
I CAN'T LET ANY MORE INNOCENT PEOPLE DIE...

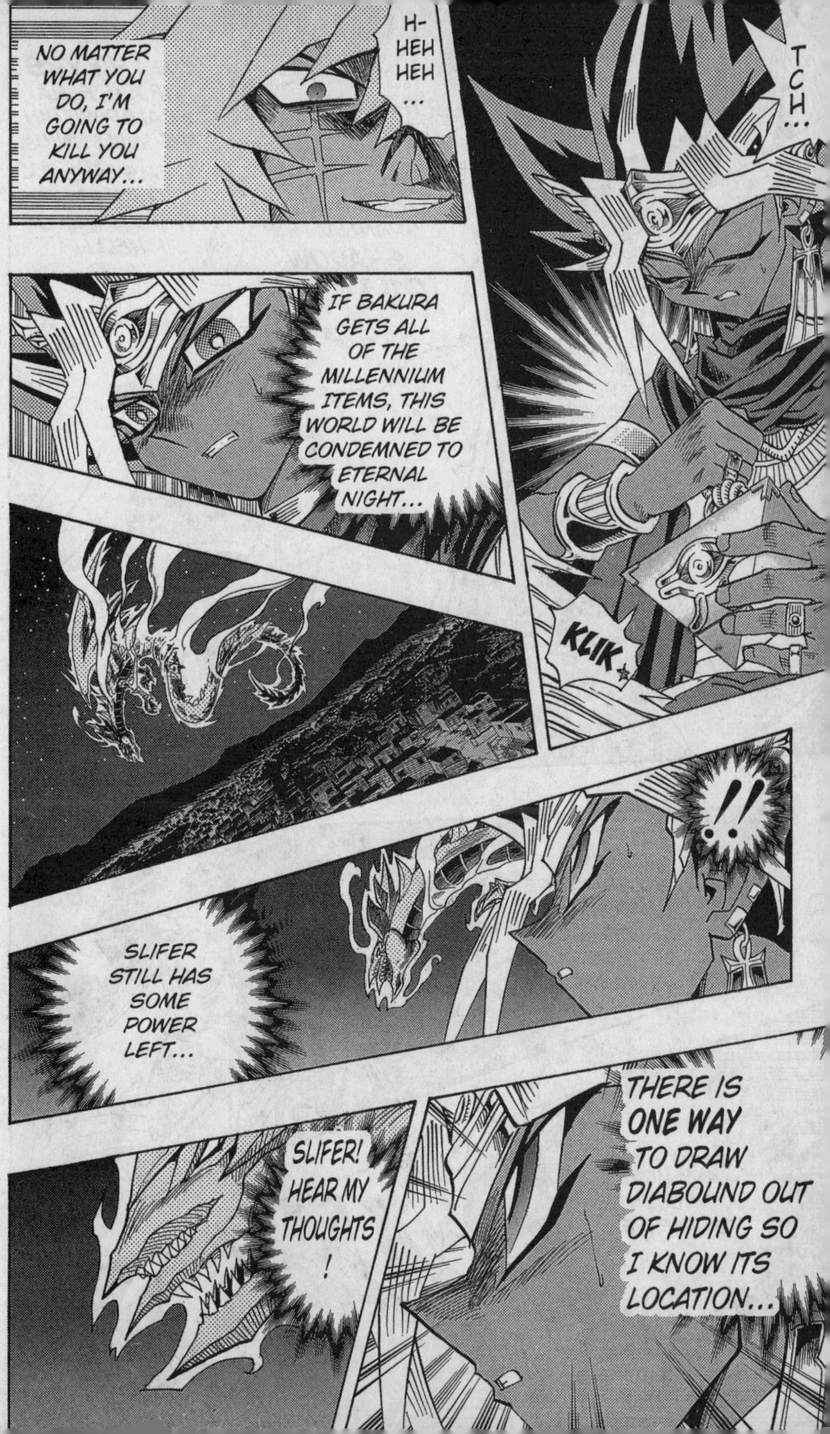

NO MATTER WHAT YOU DO, I'M GOING TO KILL YOU ANYWAY...
H-HEH HEH...
TCH...
IF BAKURA GETS ALL OF THE MILLENNIUM ITEMS, THIS WORLD WILL BE CONDEMNED TO ETERNAL NIGHT...
KLIK
!!
SLIFER STILL HAS SOME POWER LEFT...
THERE IS ONE WAY TO DRAW DIABOUND OUT OF HIDING SO I KNOW ITS LOCATION...
SLIFER! HEAR MY THOUGHTS!

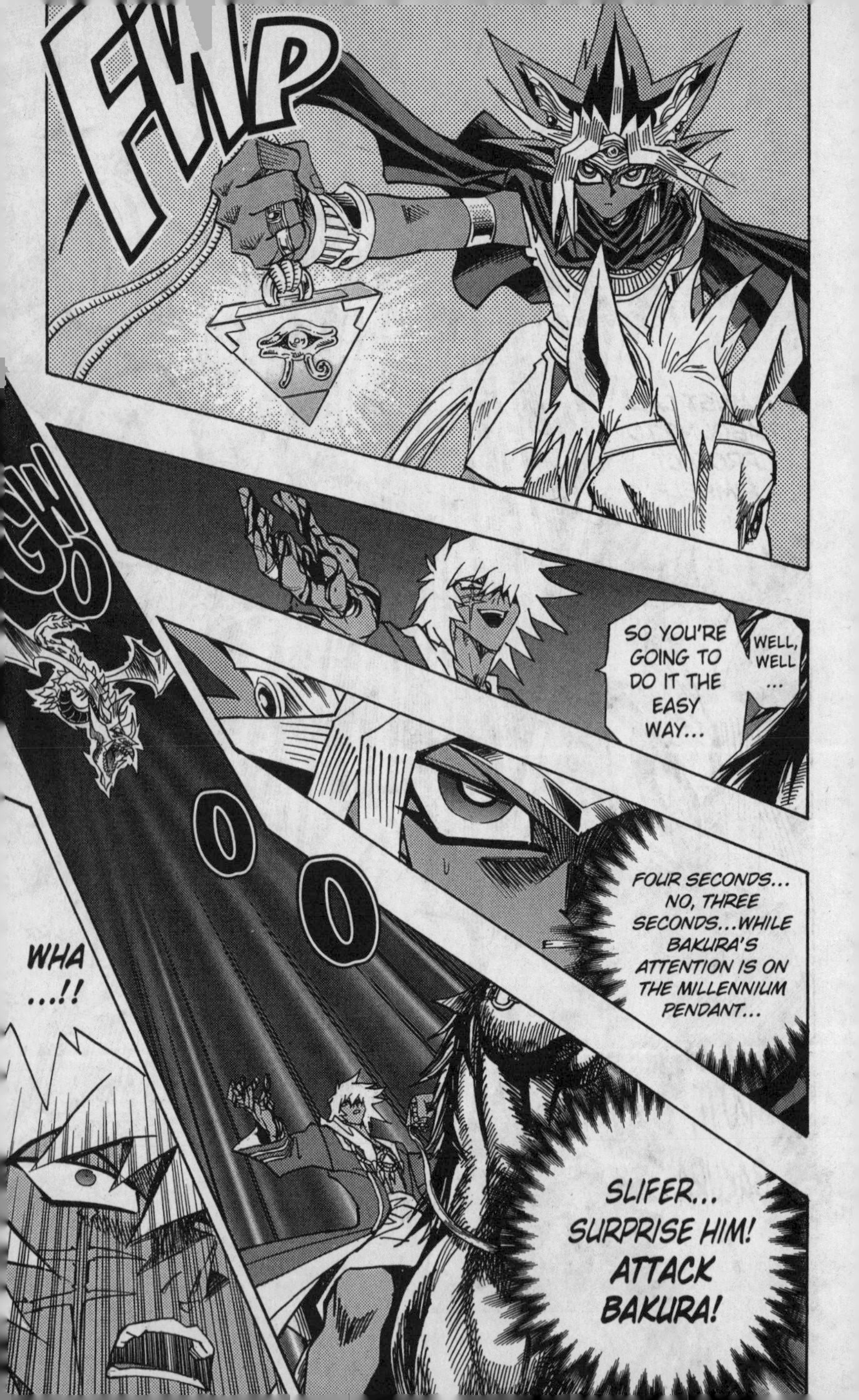
FWIP
WELL, WELL...
SO YOU'RE GOING TO DO IT THE EASY WAY...
GWOOO
FOUR SECONDS... NO, THREE SECONDS...WHILE BAKURA'S ATTENTION IS ON THE MILLENNIUM PENDANT...
SLIFER... SURPRISE HIM! ATTACK BAKURA!
WHA ...!!

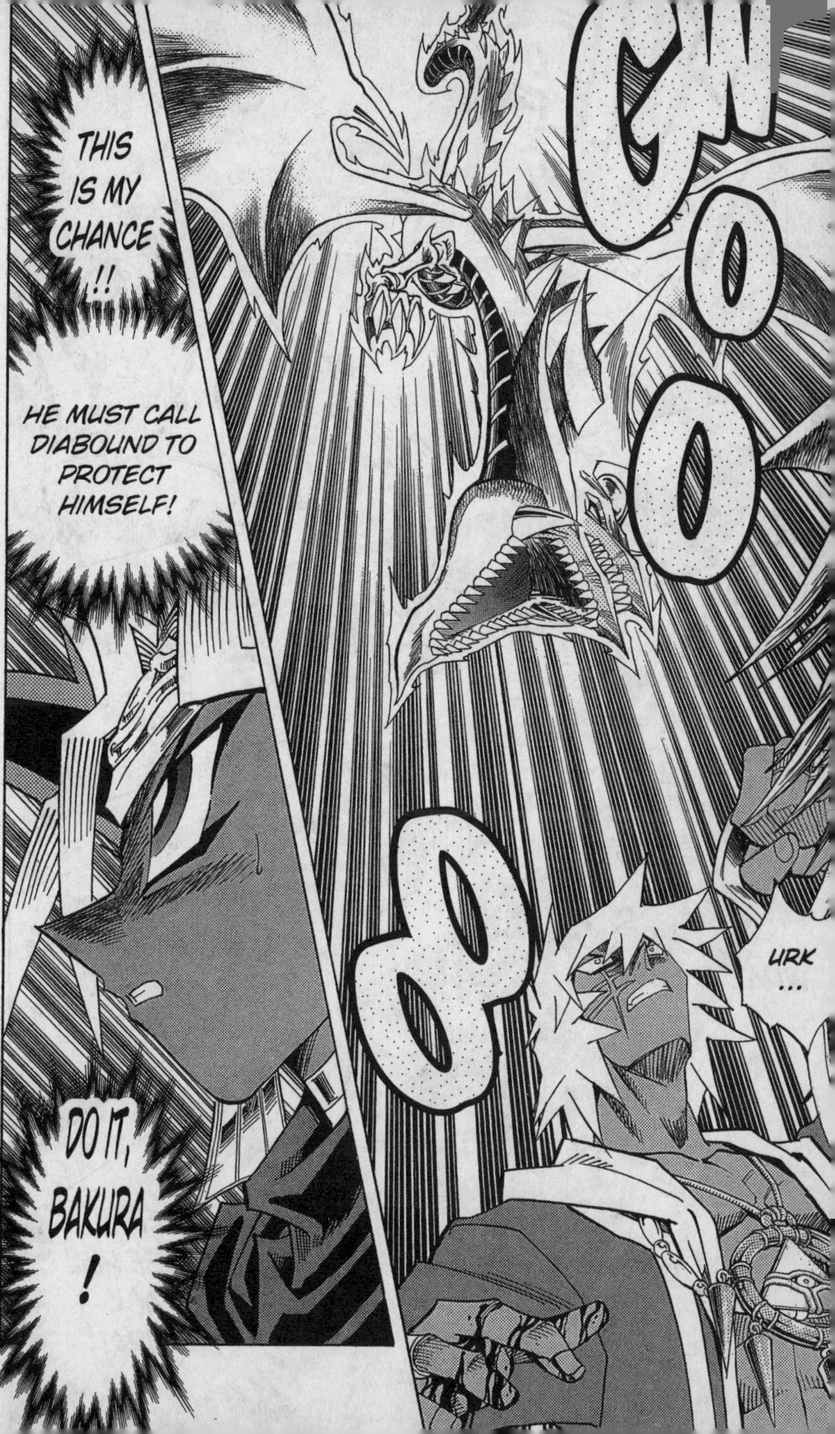
GOOO
URK ...
THIS IS MY CHANCE !!
HE MUST CALL DIABOUND TO PROTECT HIMSELF!
DO IT, BAKURA !

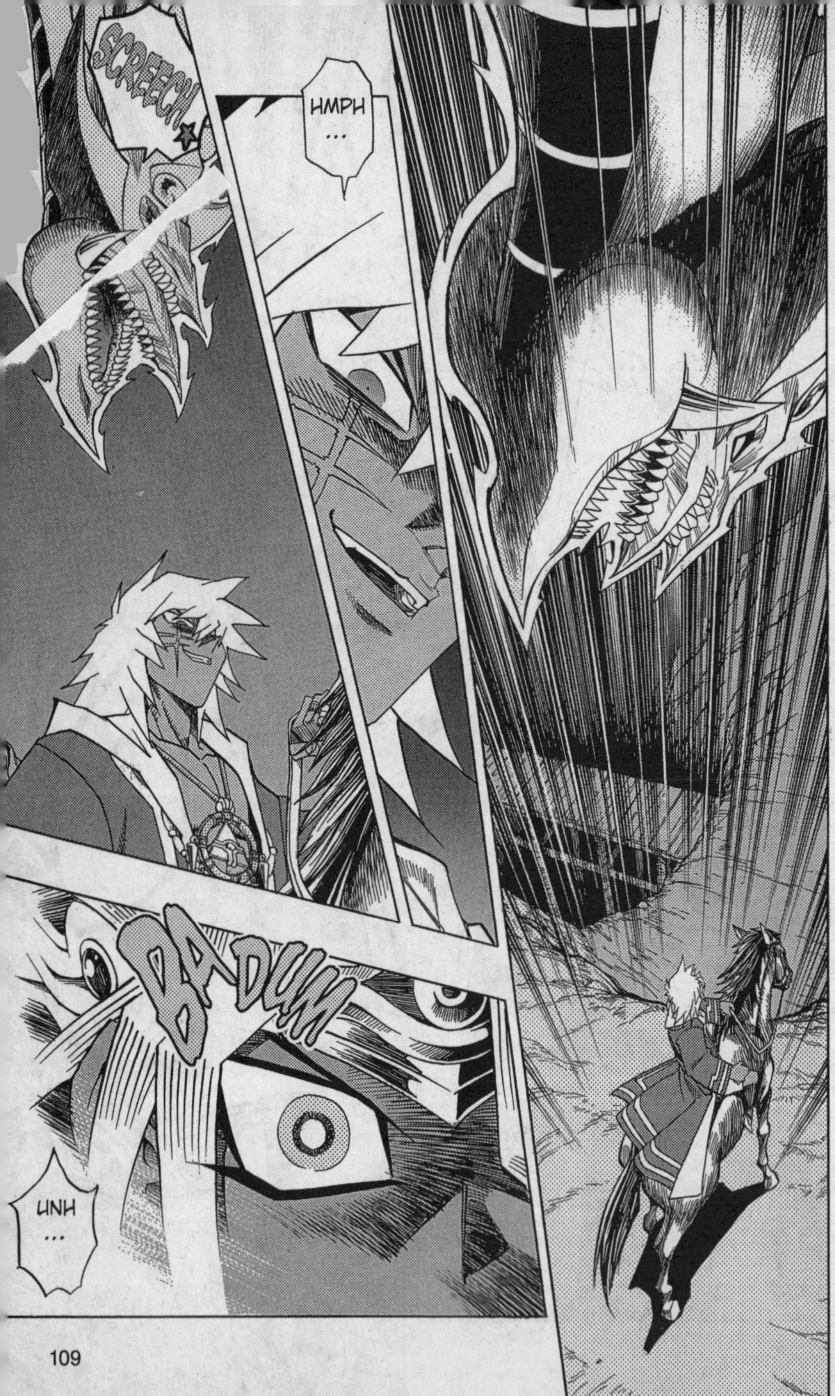
HMPH
...
SCREECH
BA-DUM
UNH
...

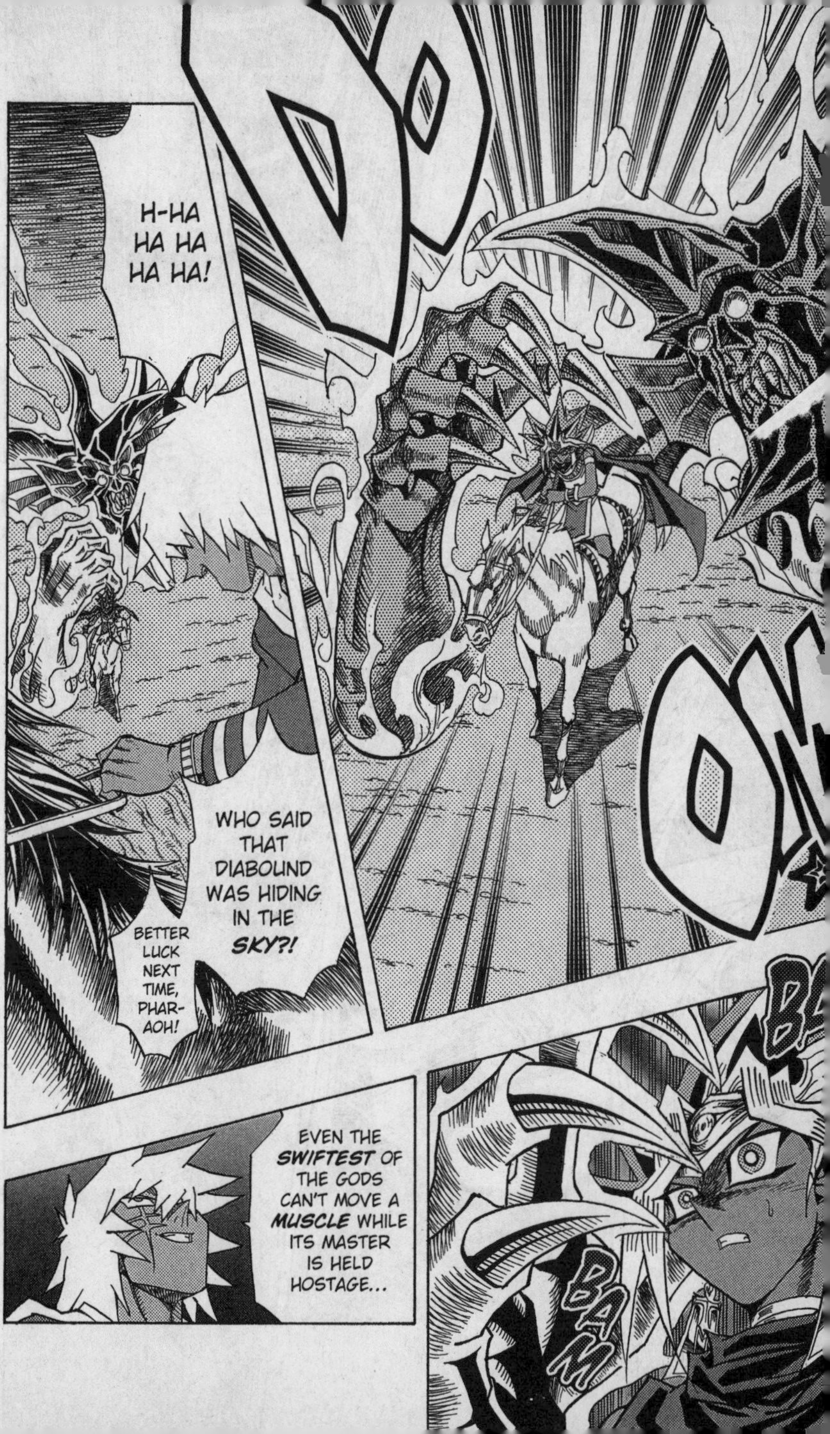
WHO SAID THAT DIABOUND WAS HIDING IN THE SKY?!
BETTER LUCK NEXT TIME, PHARAOH!
H-HA HA HA HA HA!
BAM
EVEN THE SWIFTEST OF THE GODS CAN'T MOVE A MUSCLE WHILE ITS MASTER IS HELD HOSTAGE...

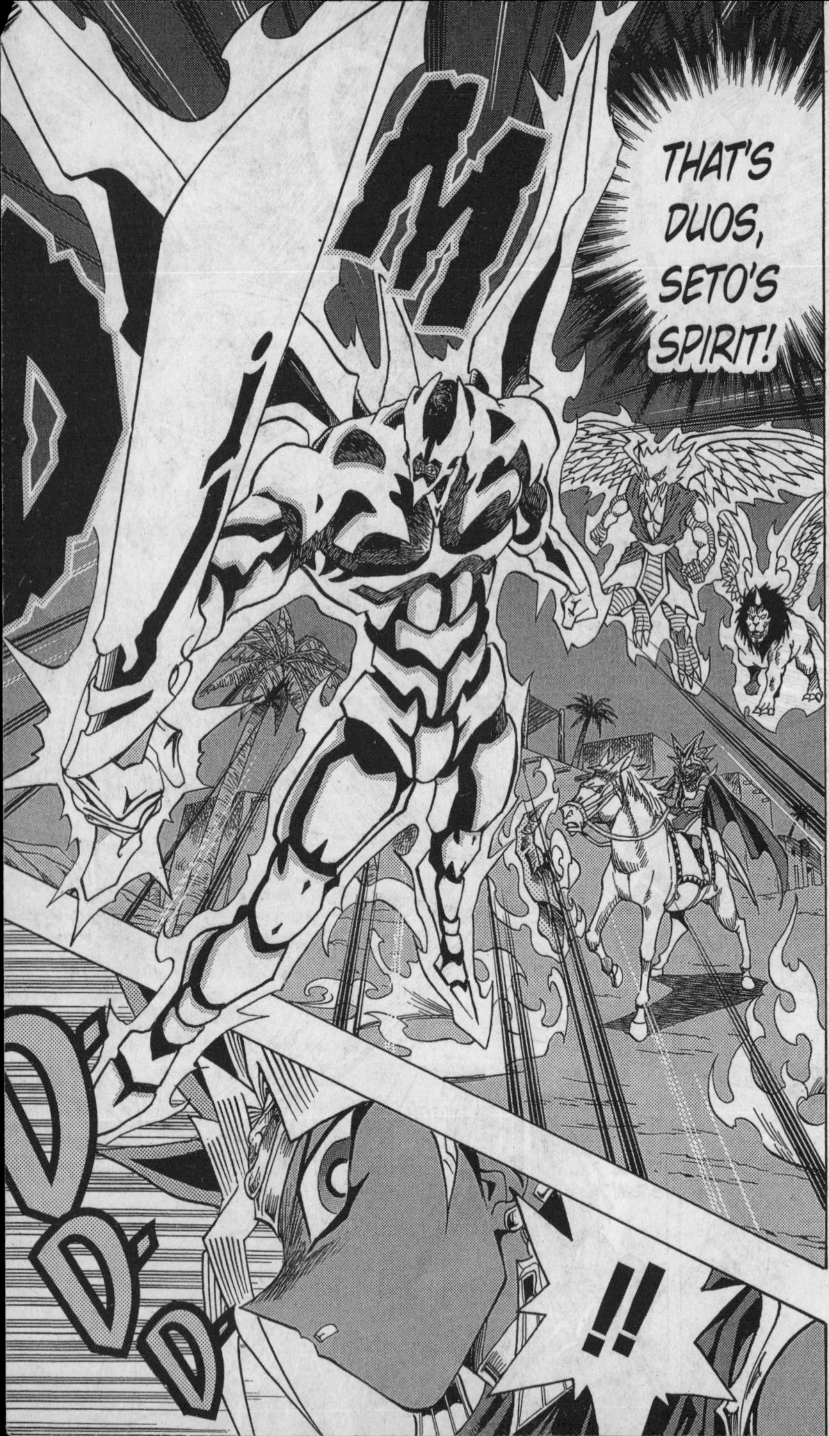
THAT'S DUOS, SETO'S SPIRIT!
!!

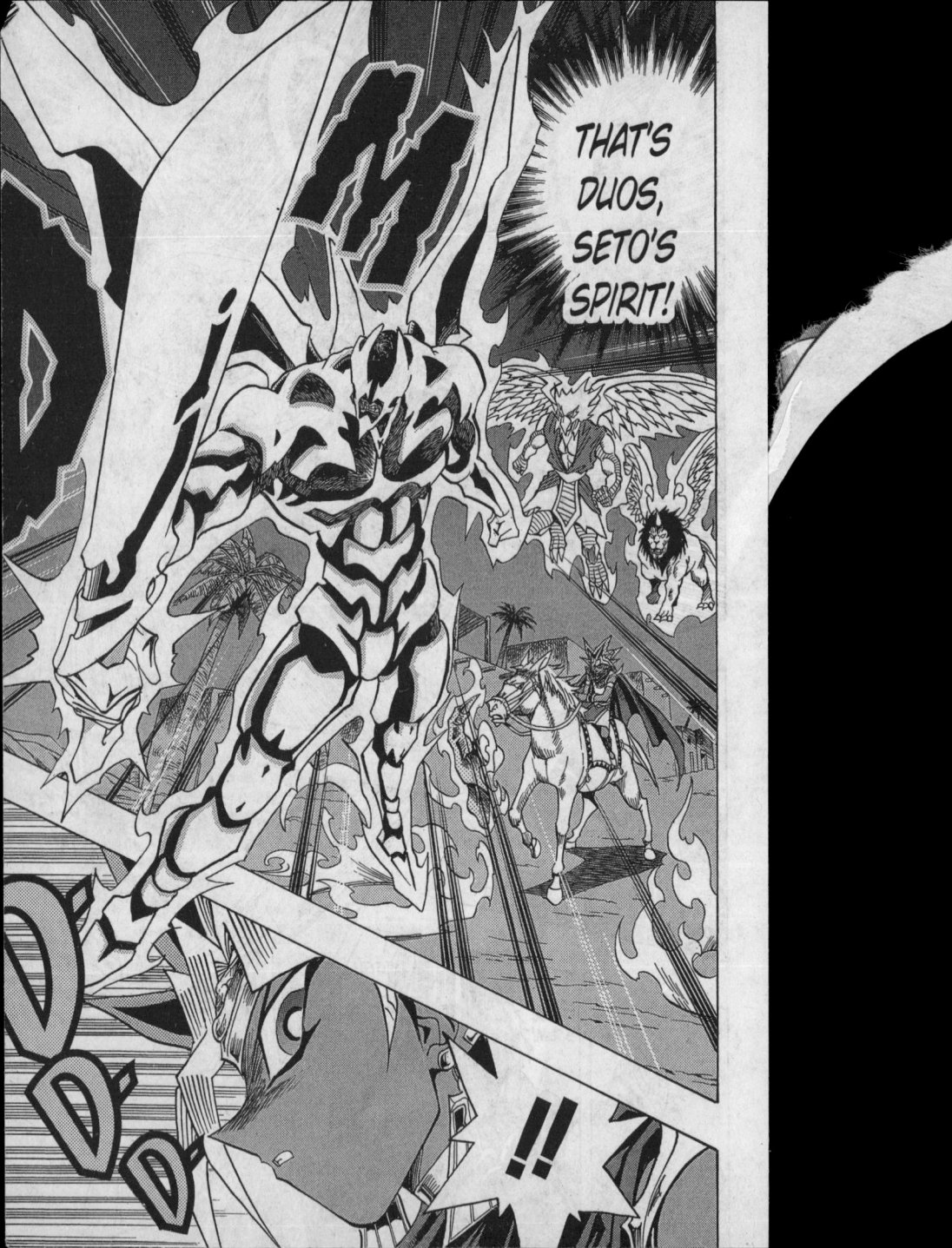

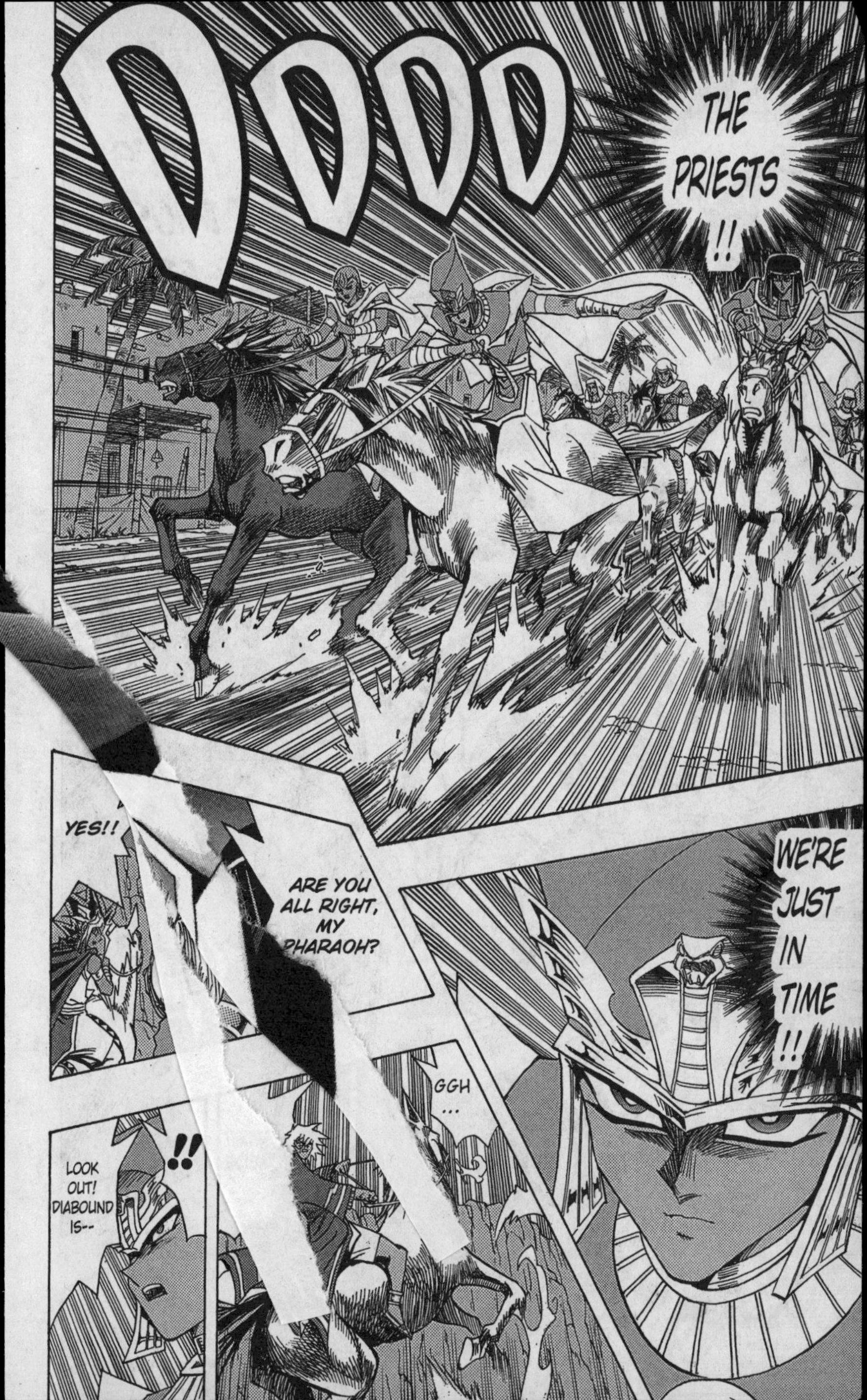
DDDD
THE PRIESTS!!
WE'RE JUST IN TIME!!
ARE YOU ALL RIGHT, MY PHARAOH?
YES!!
GGH...
!!
LOOK OUT! DIABOUND IS--

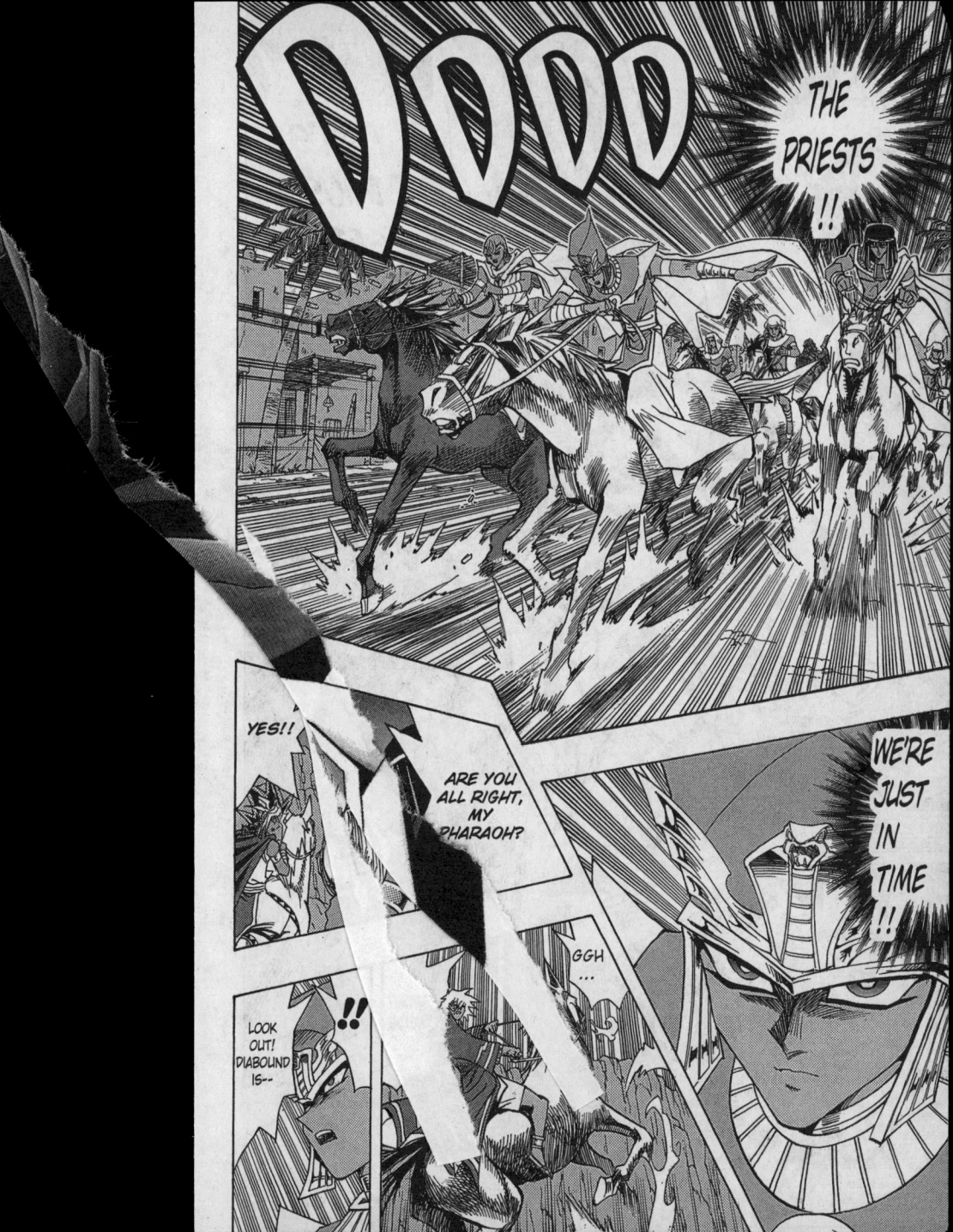

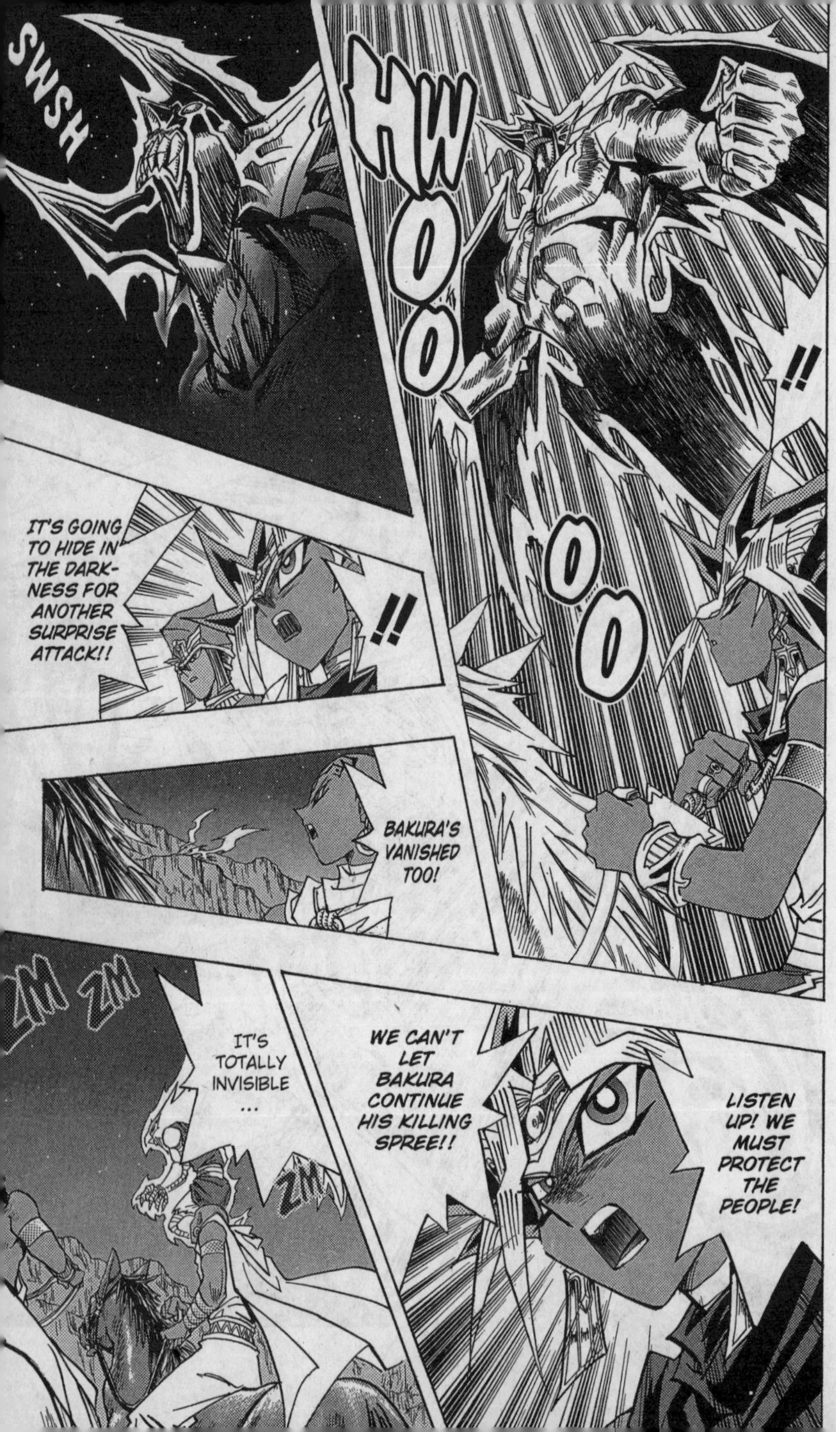
HWOOOOO
!!
SWSH
!!
IT'S GOING TO HIDE IN THE DARKNESS FOR ANOTHER SURPRISE ATTACK!!
BAKURA'S VANISHED TOO!
LISTEN UP! WE MUST PROTECT THE PEOPLE!
WE CAN'T LET BAKURA CONTINUE HIS KILLING SPREE!!
IT'S TOTALLY INVISIBLE ...
ZM ZM
ZM

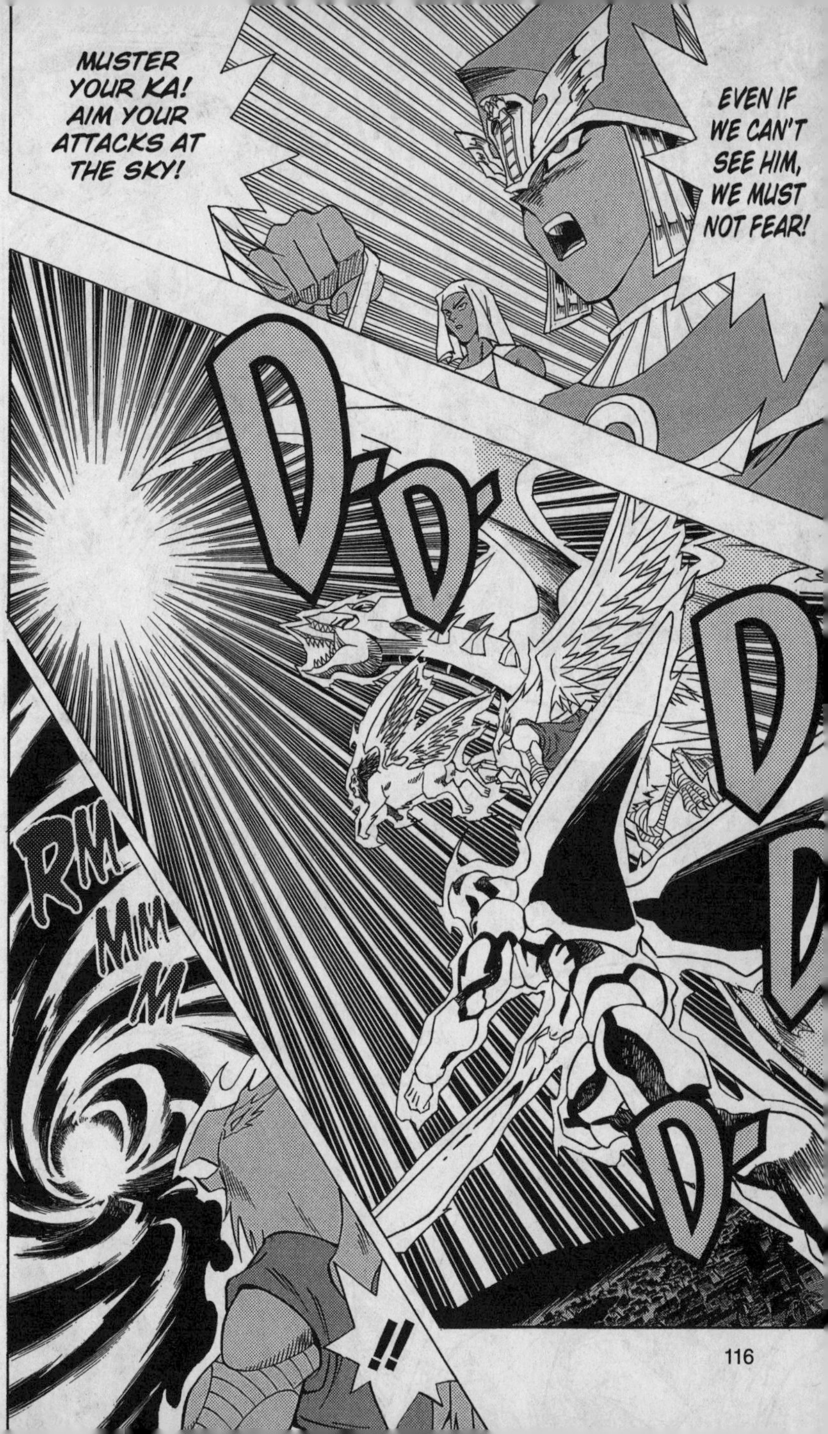

EVEN IF WE CAN'T SEE HIM, WE MUST NOT FEAR!
MUSTER YOUR KA! AIM YOUR ATTACKS AT THE SKY!
DDD
DDD
RMMMM
!!

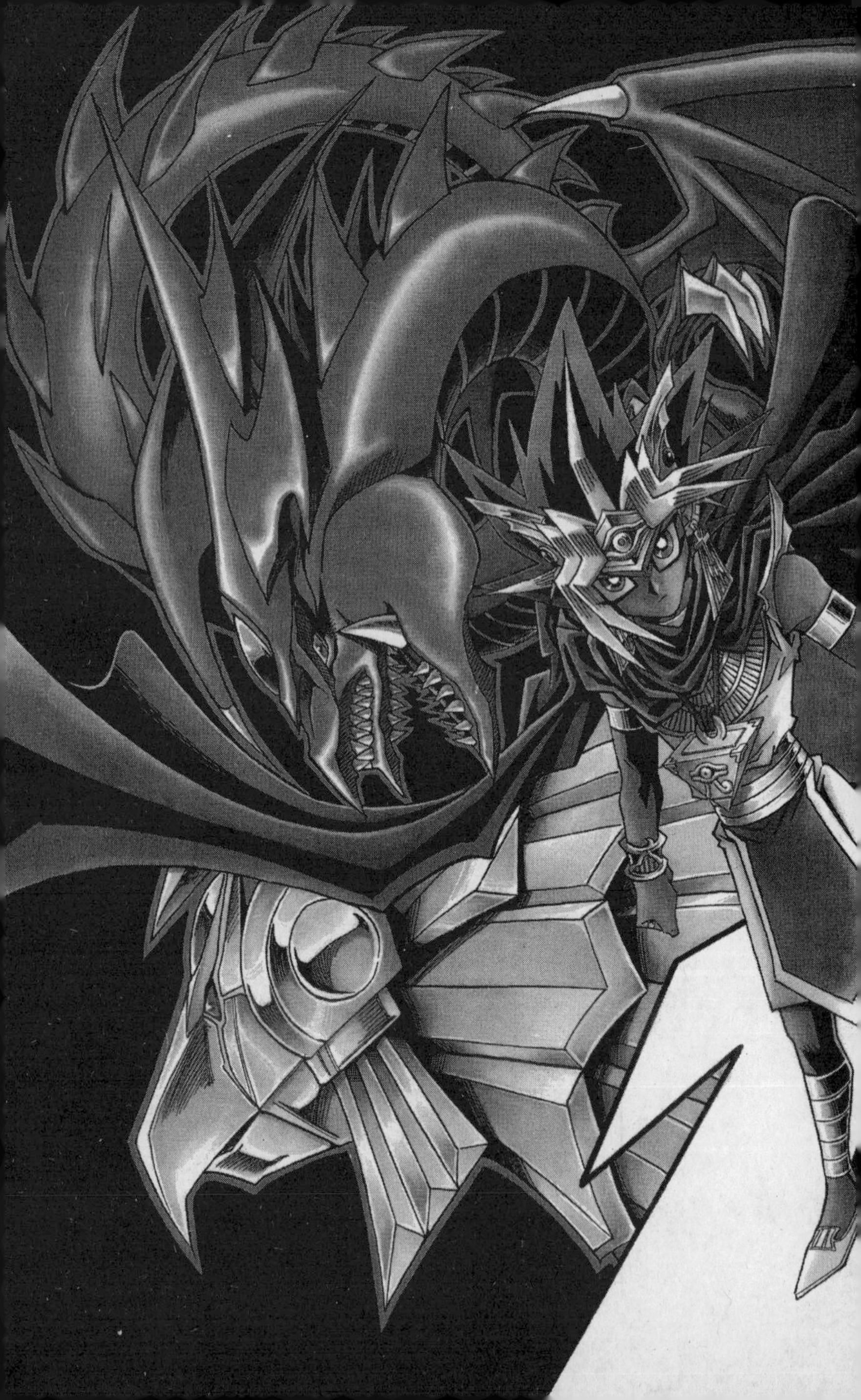

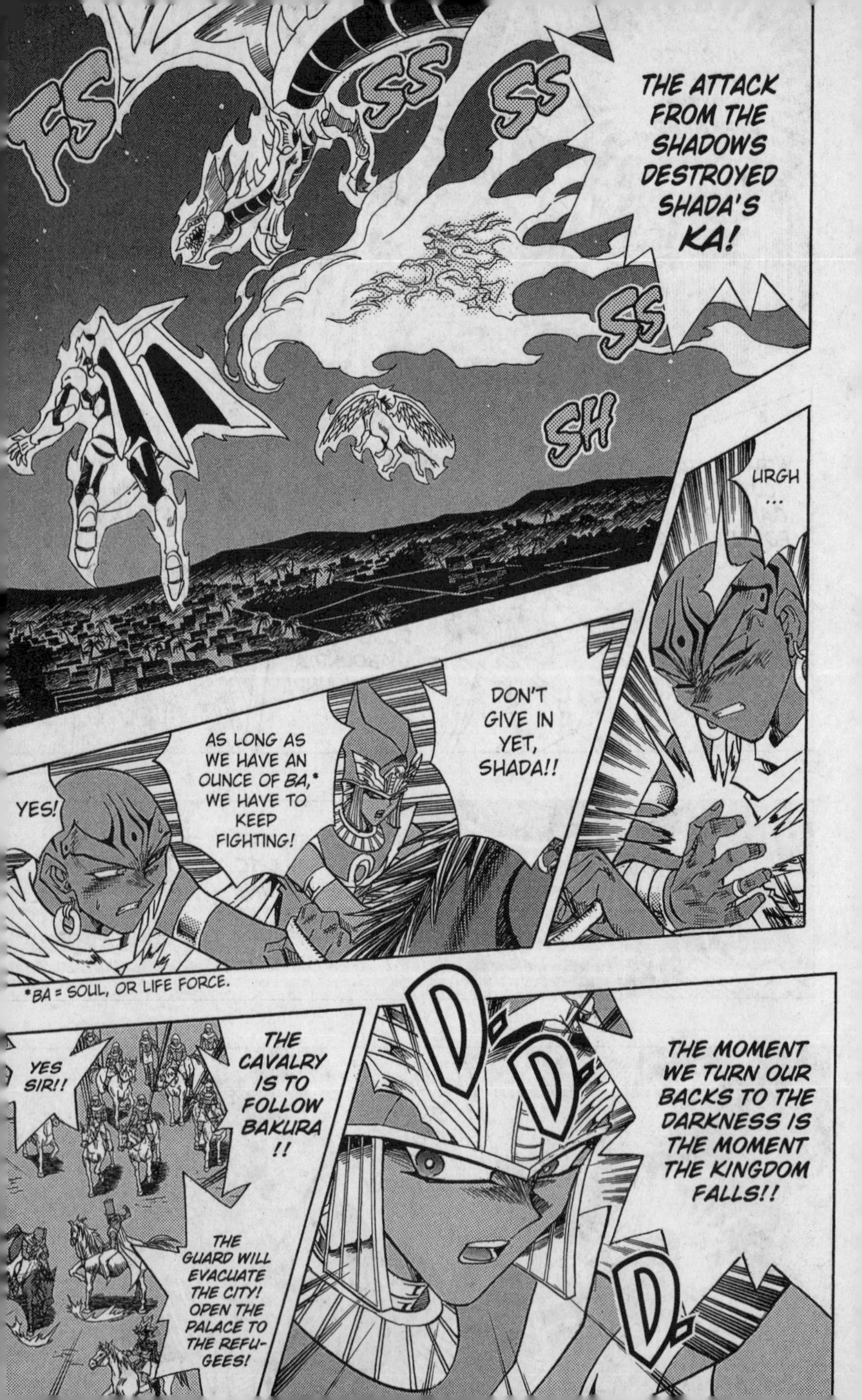
THE ATTACK FROM THE SHADOWS DESTROYED SHADA'S KA!
FS
SS
SS
SS
SH
URGH ...
DON'T GIVE IN YET, SHADA!!
AS LONG AS WE HAVE AN OUNCE OF BA,* WE HAVE TO KEEP FIGHTING!
YES!
THE MOMENT WE TURN OUR BACKS TO THE DARKNESS IS THE MOMENT THE KINGDOM FALLS!!
D
D
D
THE CAVALRY IS TO FOLLOW BAKURA!!
YES SIR!!
THE GUARD WILL EVACUATE THE CITY! OPEN THE PALACE TO THE REFUGEES!

*BA = SOUL, OR LIFE FORCE.

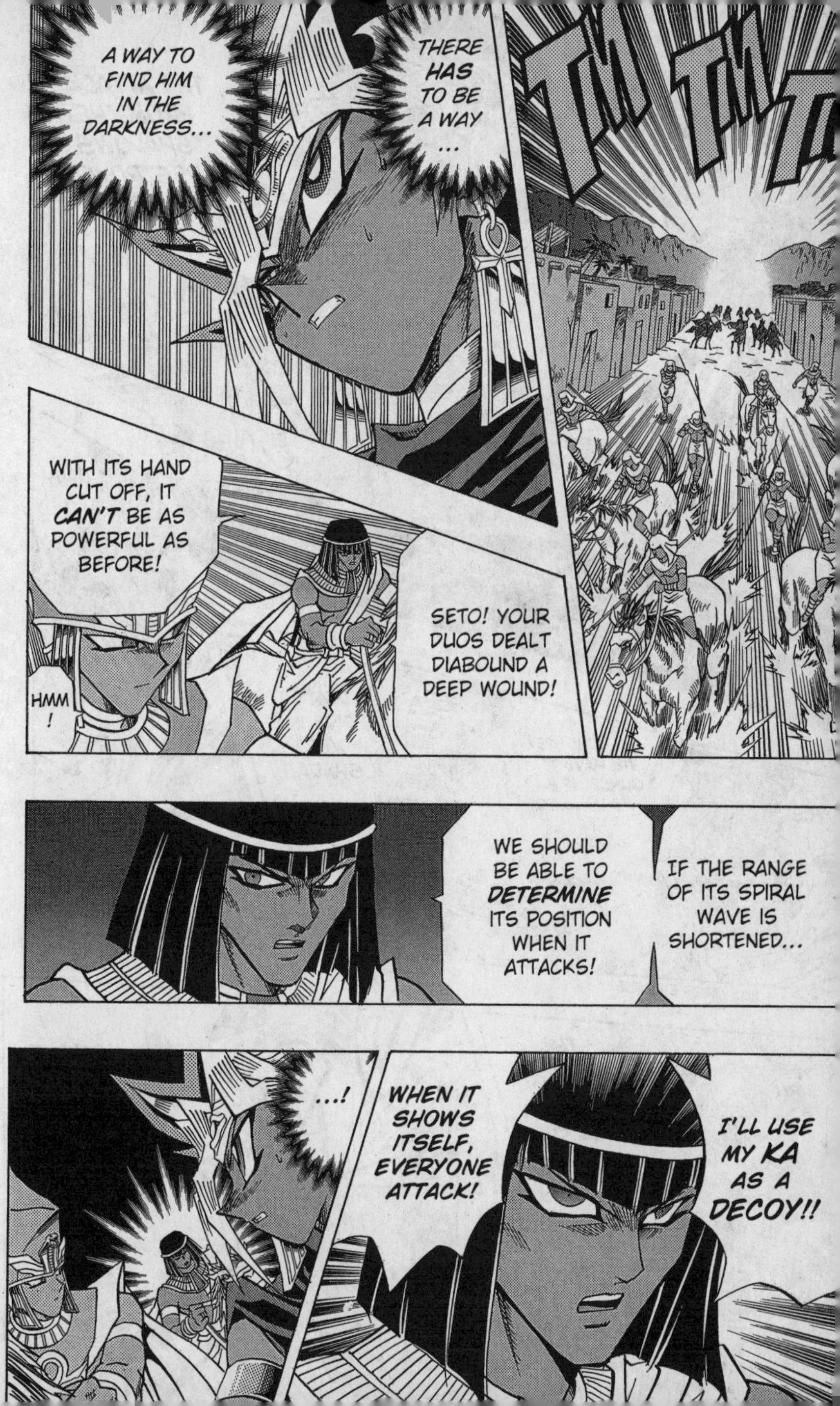
THERE HAS TO BE A WAY...
A WAY TO FIND HIM IN THE DARKNESS...
SETO! YOUR DUOS DEALT DIABOUND A DEEP WOUND!
WITH ITS HAND CUT OFF, IT CAN'T BE AS POWERFUL AS BEFORE!
HMM!
IF THE RANGE OF ITS SPIRAL WAVE IS SHORTENED...
WE SHOULD BE ABLE TO DETERMINE ITS POSITION WHEN IT ATTACKS!
I'LL USE MY KA AS A DECOY!!
WHEN IT SHOWS ITSELF, EVERYONE ATTACK!
...!

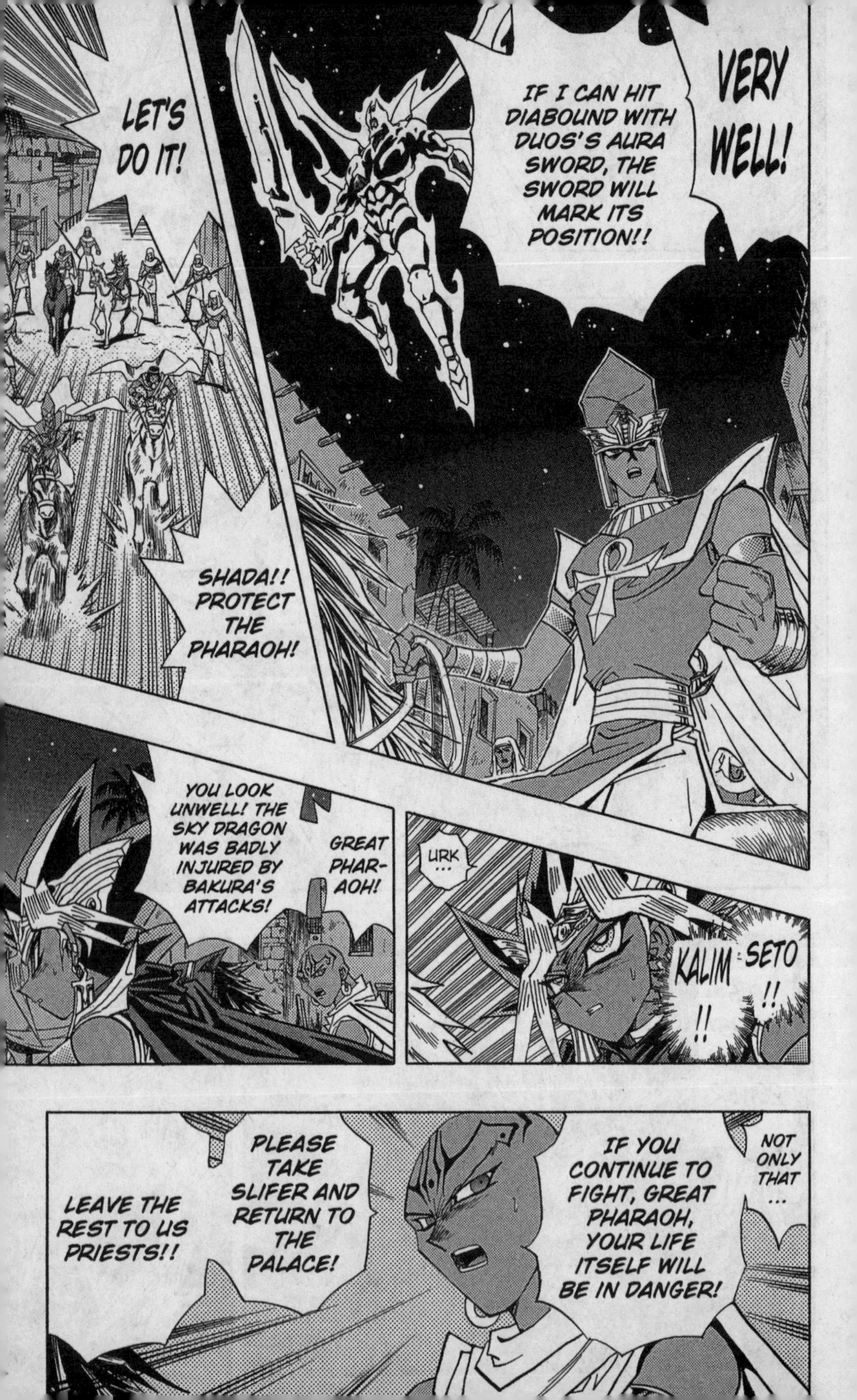
VERY WELL!
IF I CAN HIT DIABOUND WITH DUOS'S AURA SWORD, THE SWORD WILL MARK ITS POSITION!!
LET'S DO IT!
SHADA!! PROTECT THE PHARAOH!
SETO !!
KALIM !!
URK ...
GREAT PHAR-AOH!
YOU LOOK UNWELL! THE SKY DRAGON WAS BADLY INJURED BY BAKURA'S ATTACKS!
NOT ONLY THAT ...
IF YOU CONTINUE TO FIGHT, GREAT PHARAOH, YOUR LIFE ITSELF WILL BE IN DANGER!
PLEASE TAKE SLIFER AND RETURN TO THE PALACE!
LEAVE THE REST TO US PRIESTS!!

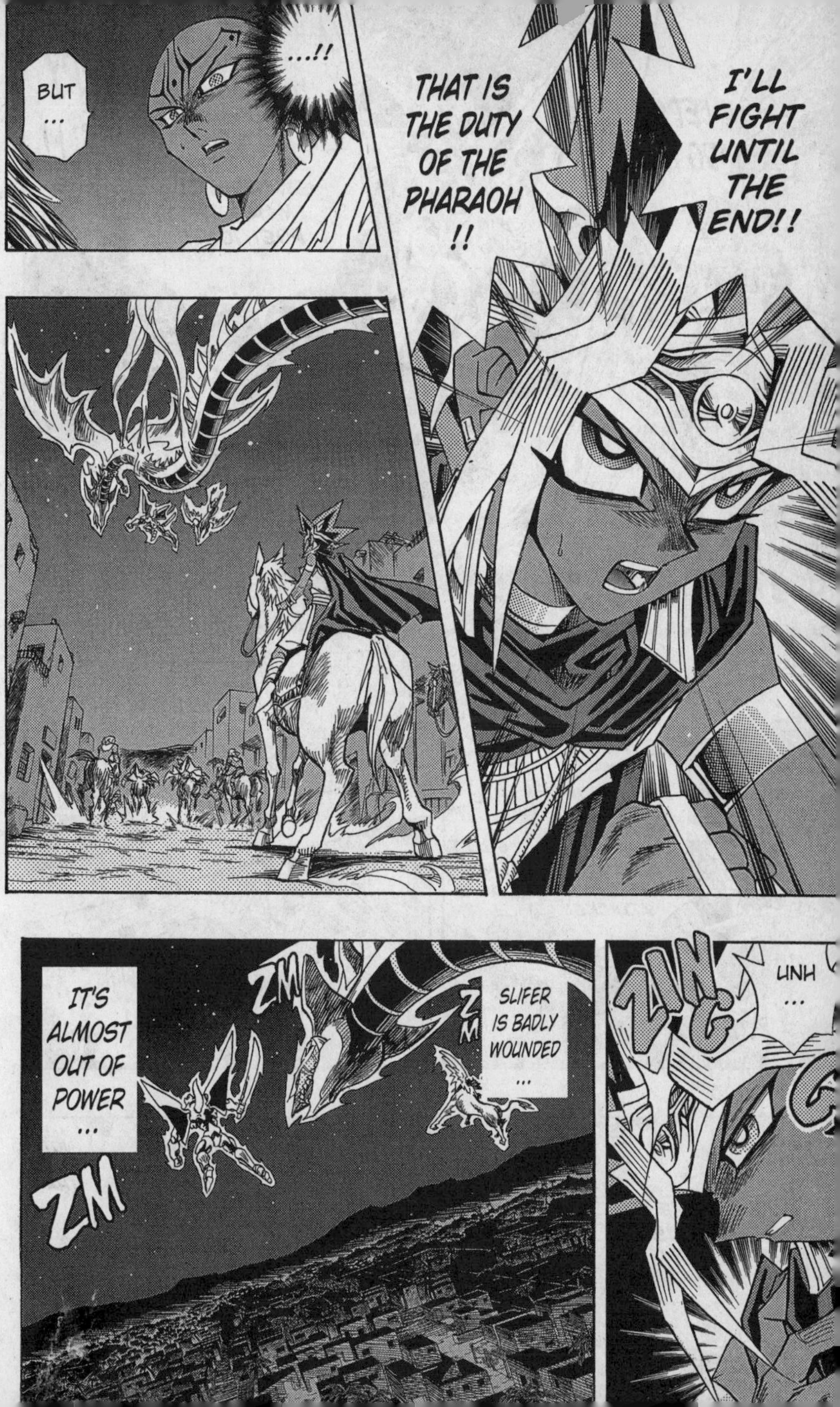
I'LL FIGHT UNTIL THE END!!
THAT IS THE DUTY OF THE PHARAOH !!
...!!
BUT ...
UNH ...
ZING
SLIFER IS BADLY WOUNDED ...
ZM
ZM
IT'S ALMOST OUT OF POWER ...
ZM

MY MASTER...TO THE PEOPLE, THE PHARAOH IS THE *LIVING EMBODIMENT* OF A GOD. HE IS LIKE THE *SUN GOD RA* WHO SHINES WITH THE LIGHT OF HOPE.

YOUR VERY *EXISTENCE* LIGHTS THE SHADOWS OF THIS WORLD!

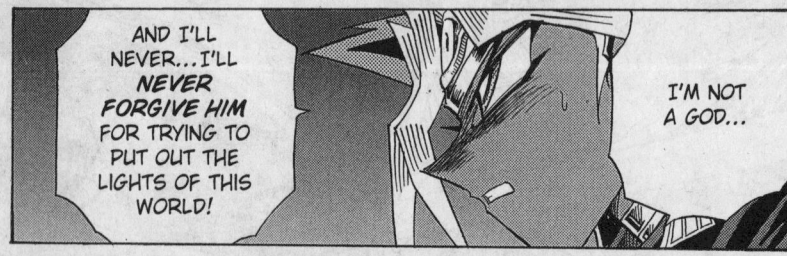

AND I'LL NEVER...I'LL *NEVER FORGIVE HIM* FOR TRYING TO PUT OUT THE LIGHTS OF THIS WORLD!

I'M NOT A GOD...

GRA A AA

IT CAN'T BE...

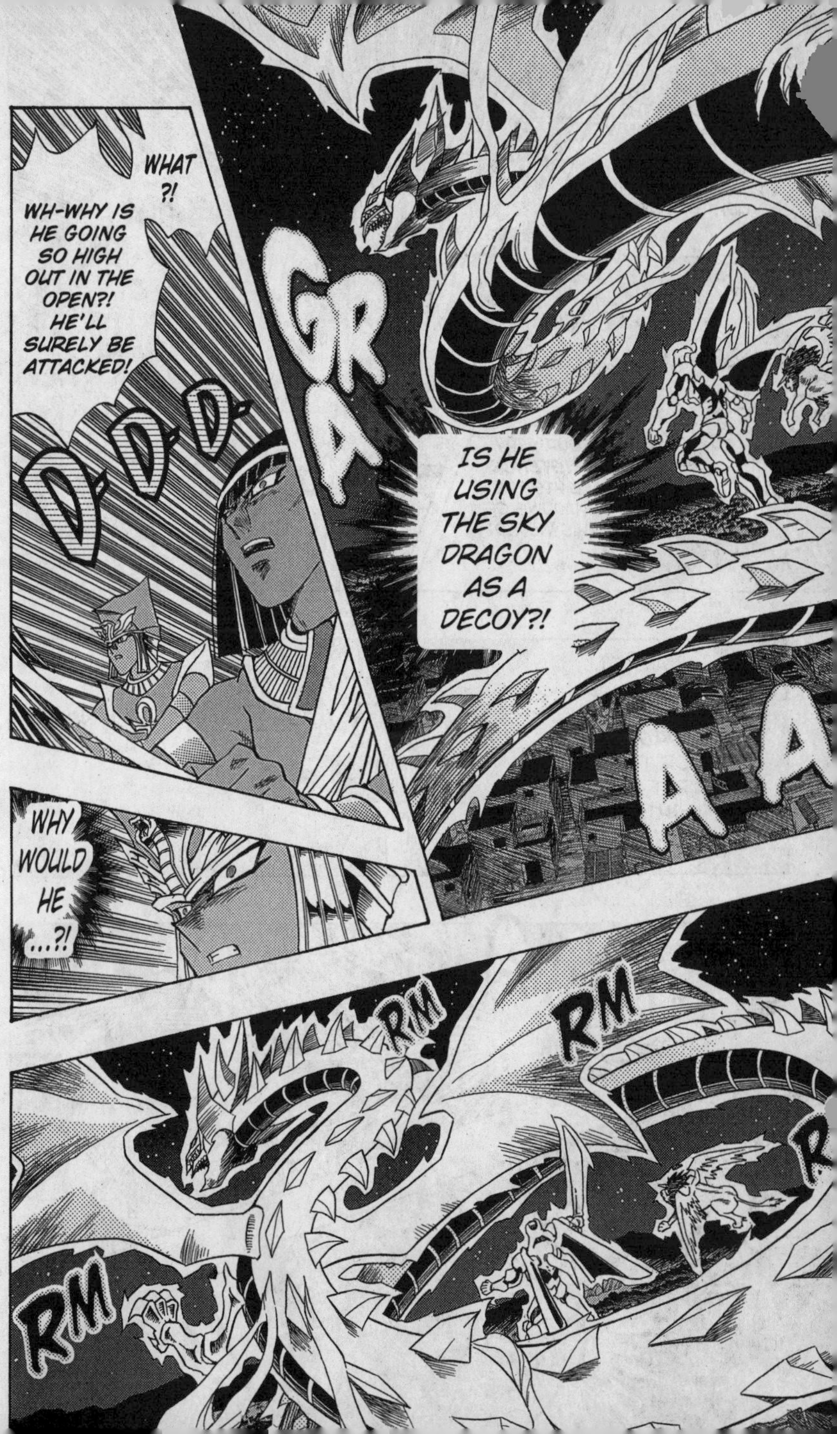
GRA
AA
IS HE USING THE SKY DRAGON AS A DECOY?!
WHAT ?!
WH-WHY IS HE GOING SO HIGH OUT IN THE OPEN?! HE'LL SURELY BE ATTACKED!
D D D
WHY WOULD HE ...?!
RM
RM
R
RM

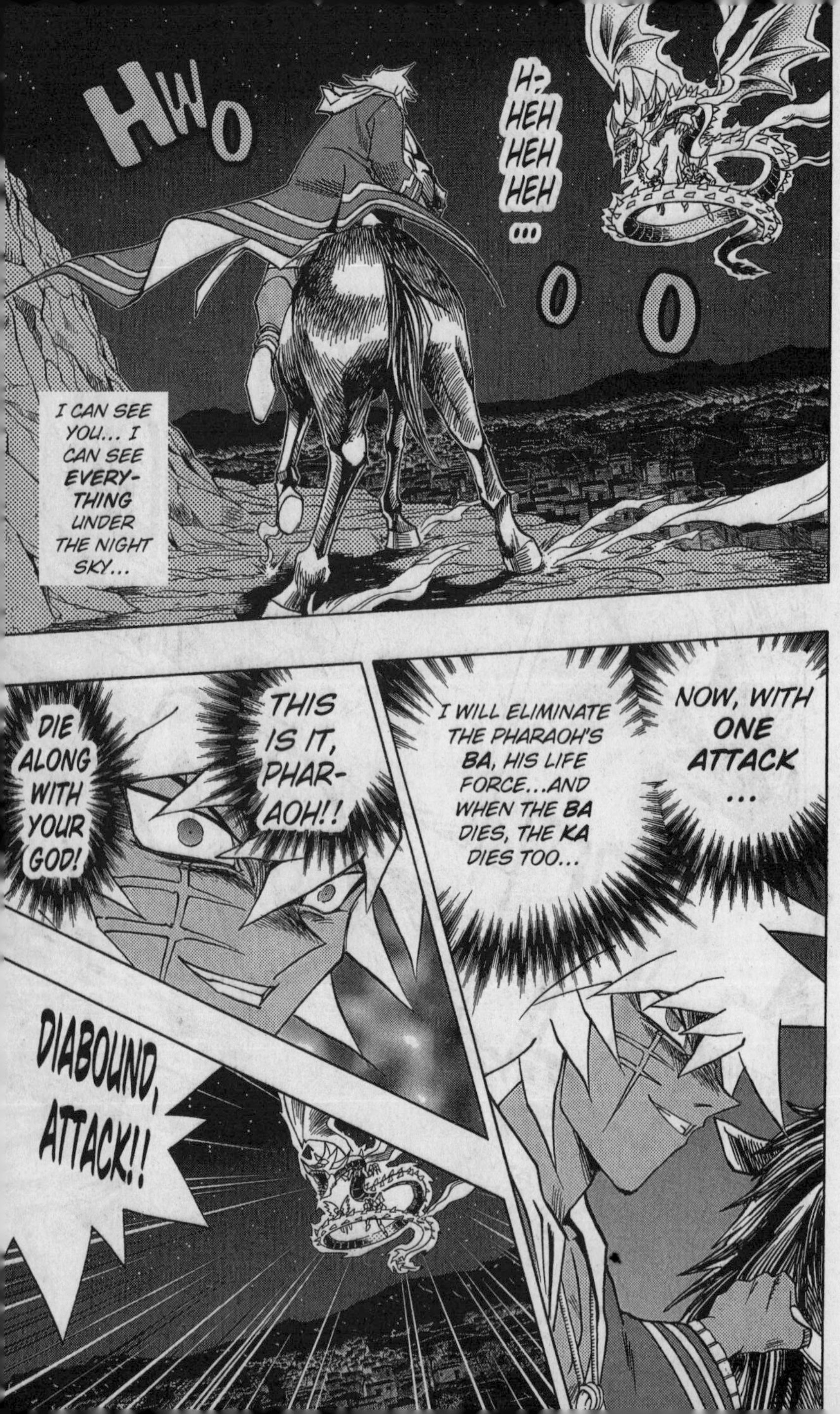
H-HEH HEH HEH...
OO
HWO
I CAN SEE YOU... I CAN SEE EVERYTHING UNDER THE NIGHT SKY...
NOW, WITH ONE ATTACK...
I WILL ELIMINATE THE PHARAOH'S BA, HIS LIFE FORCE...AND WHEN THE BA DIES, THE KA DIES TOO...
THIS IS IT, PHARAOH!!
DIE ALONG WITH YOUR GOD!
DIABOUND, ATTACK!!

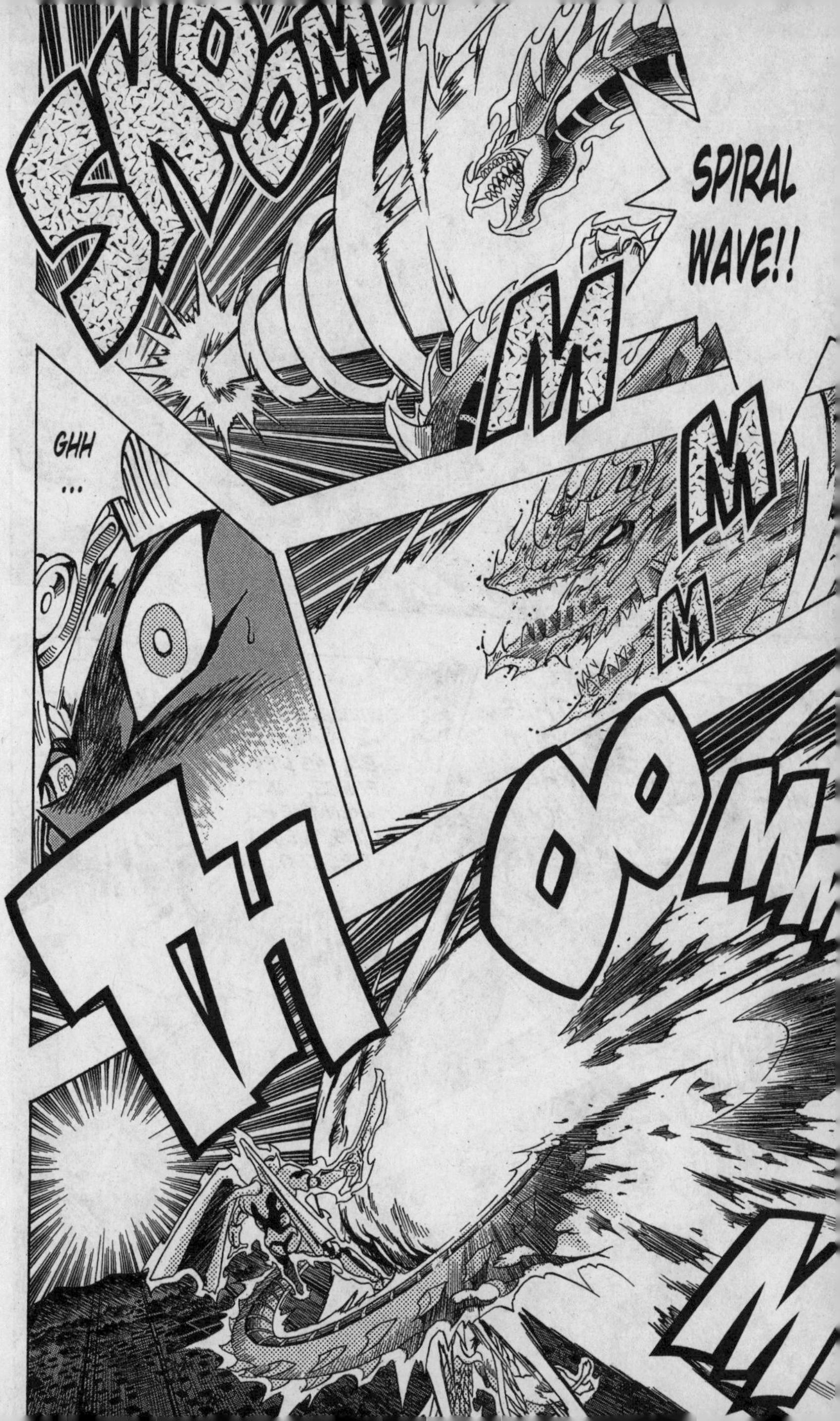
SHOOM
SPIRAL WAVE!!
MMMM
GHH ...
THOOMM

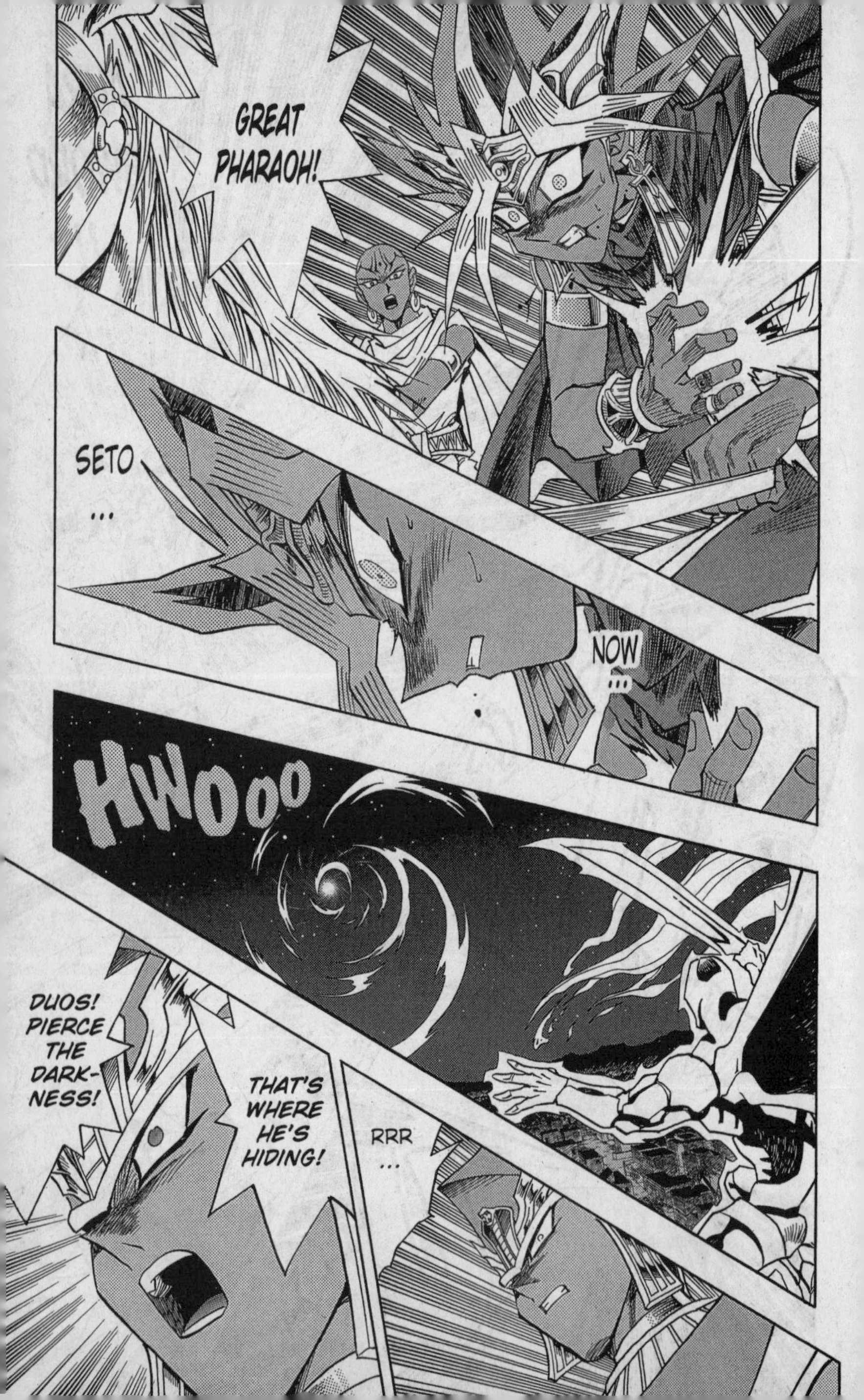
GREAT PHARAOH!
NOW...
SETO...
HWOOO
RRR...
THAT'S WHERE HE'S HIDING!
DUOS! PIERCE THE DARK-NESS!

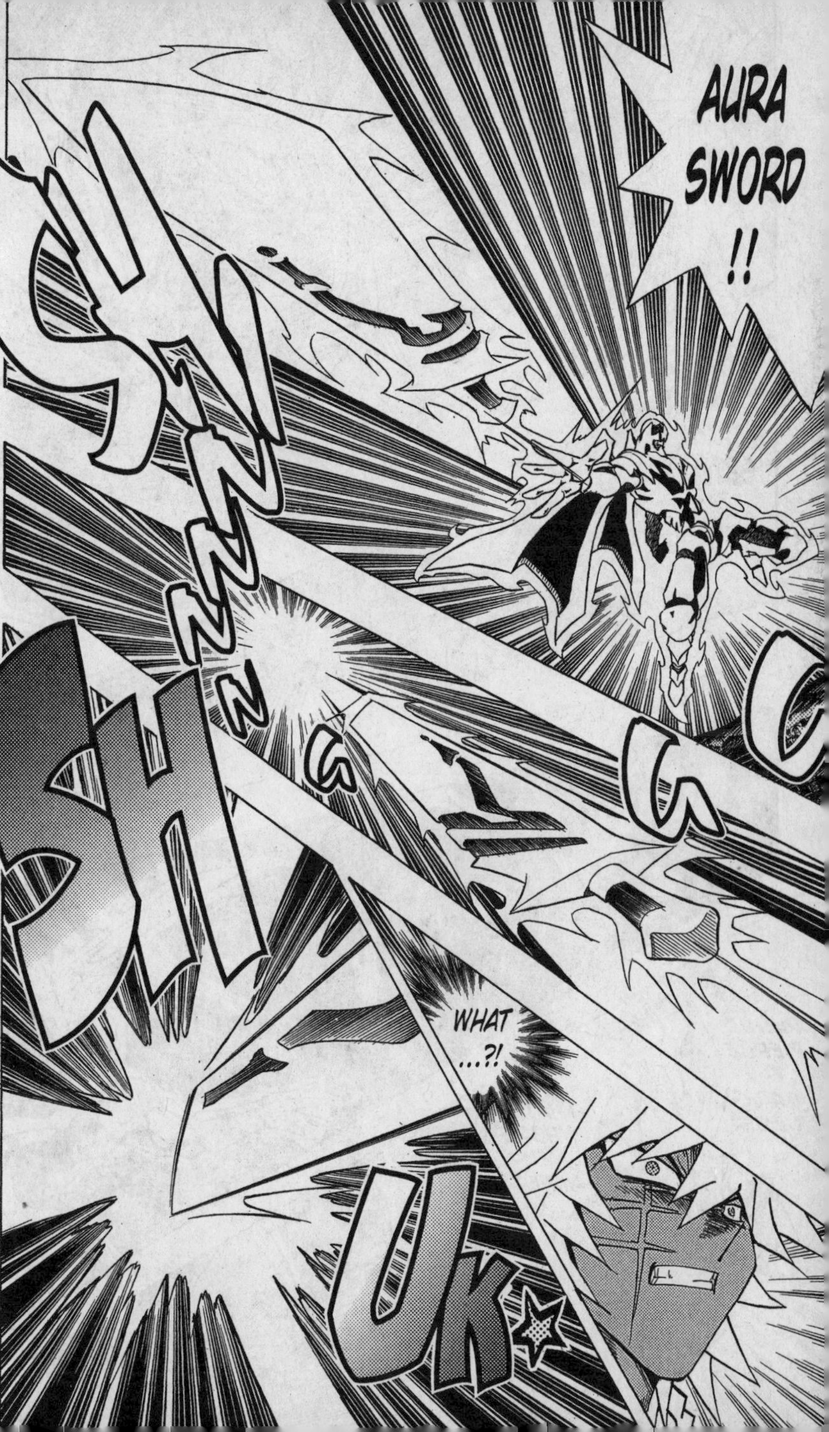
AURA SWORD !!
WHAT ...?!

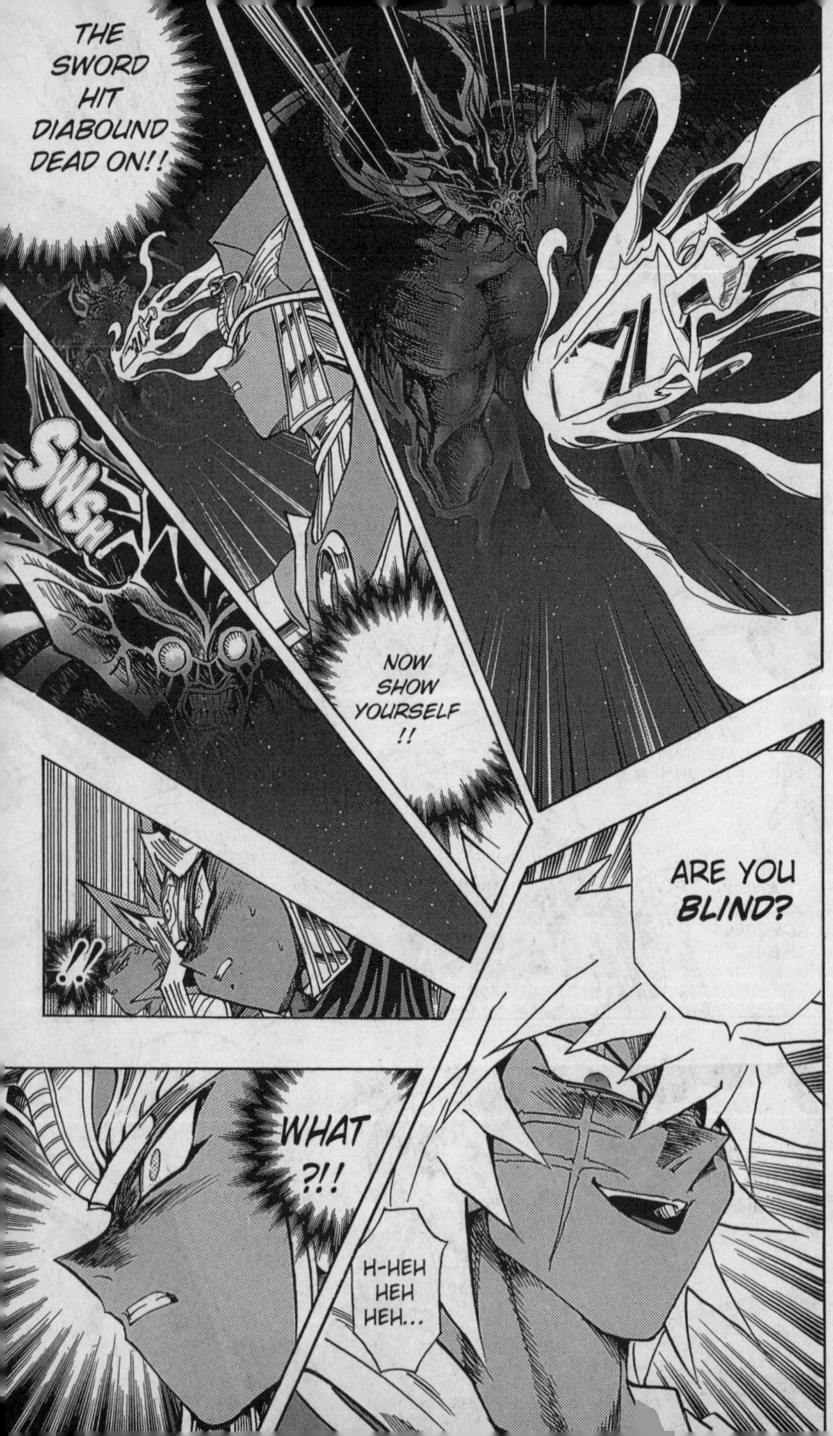
THE SWORD HIT DIABOUND DEAD ON!!
SWSH
NOW SHOW YOURSELF !!
ARE YOU BLIND?
!!
H-HEH HEH HEH...
WHAT ?!!

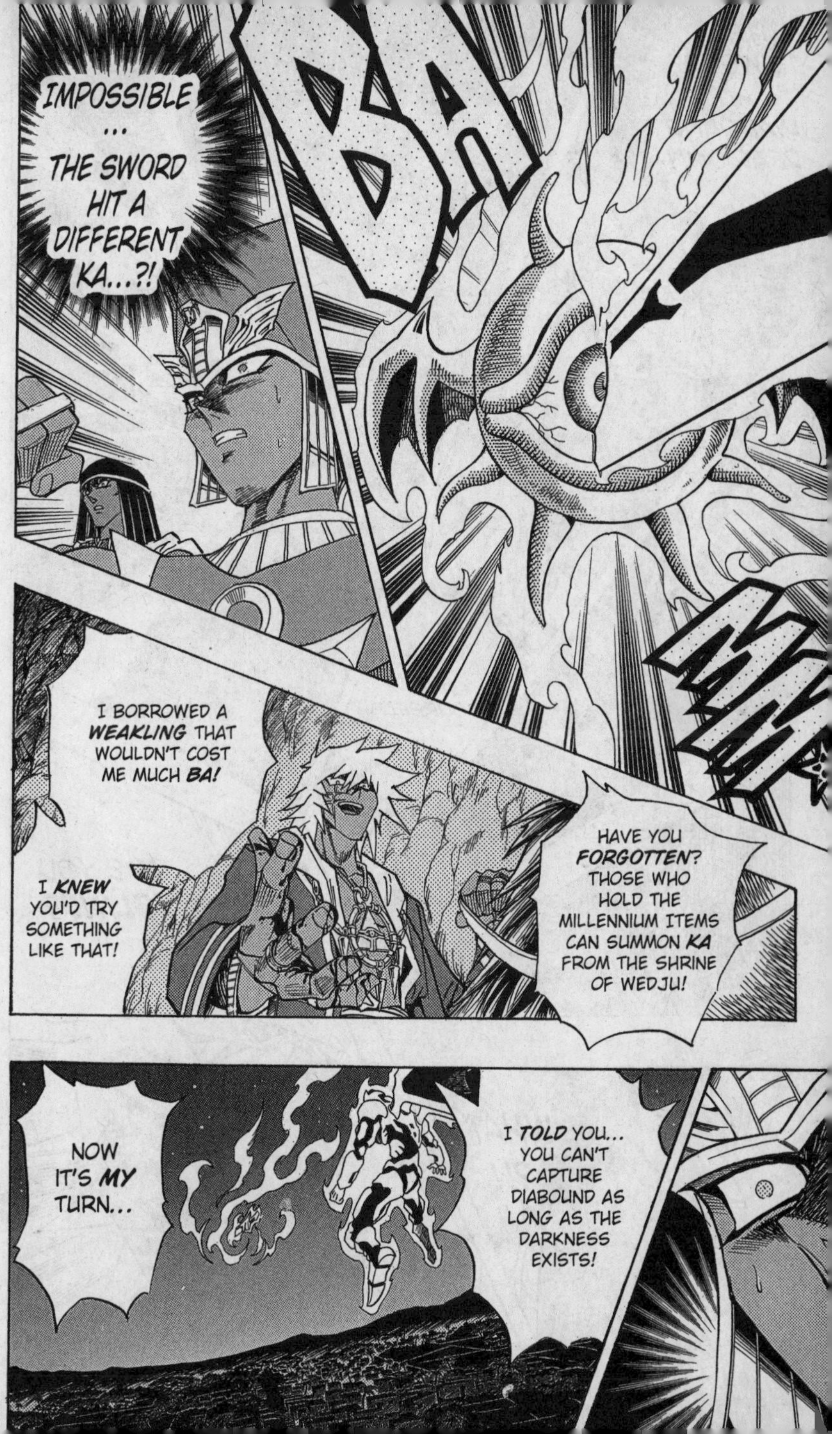
BA
IMPOSSIBLE... THE SWORD HIT A DIFFERENT KA...?!
MMM
HAVE YOU FORGOTTEN? THOSE WHO HOLD THE MILLENNIUM ITEMS CAN SUMMON KA FROM THE SHRINE OF WEDJU!
I BORROWED A WEAKLING THAT WOULDN'T COST ME MUCH BA!
I KNEW YOU'D TRY SOMETHING LIKE THAT!
I TOLD YOU... YOU CAN'T CAPTURE DIABOUND AS LONG AS THE DARKNESS EXISTS!
NOW IT'S MY TURN...

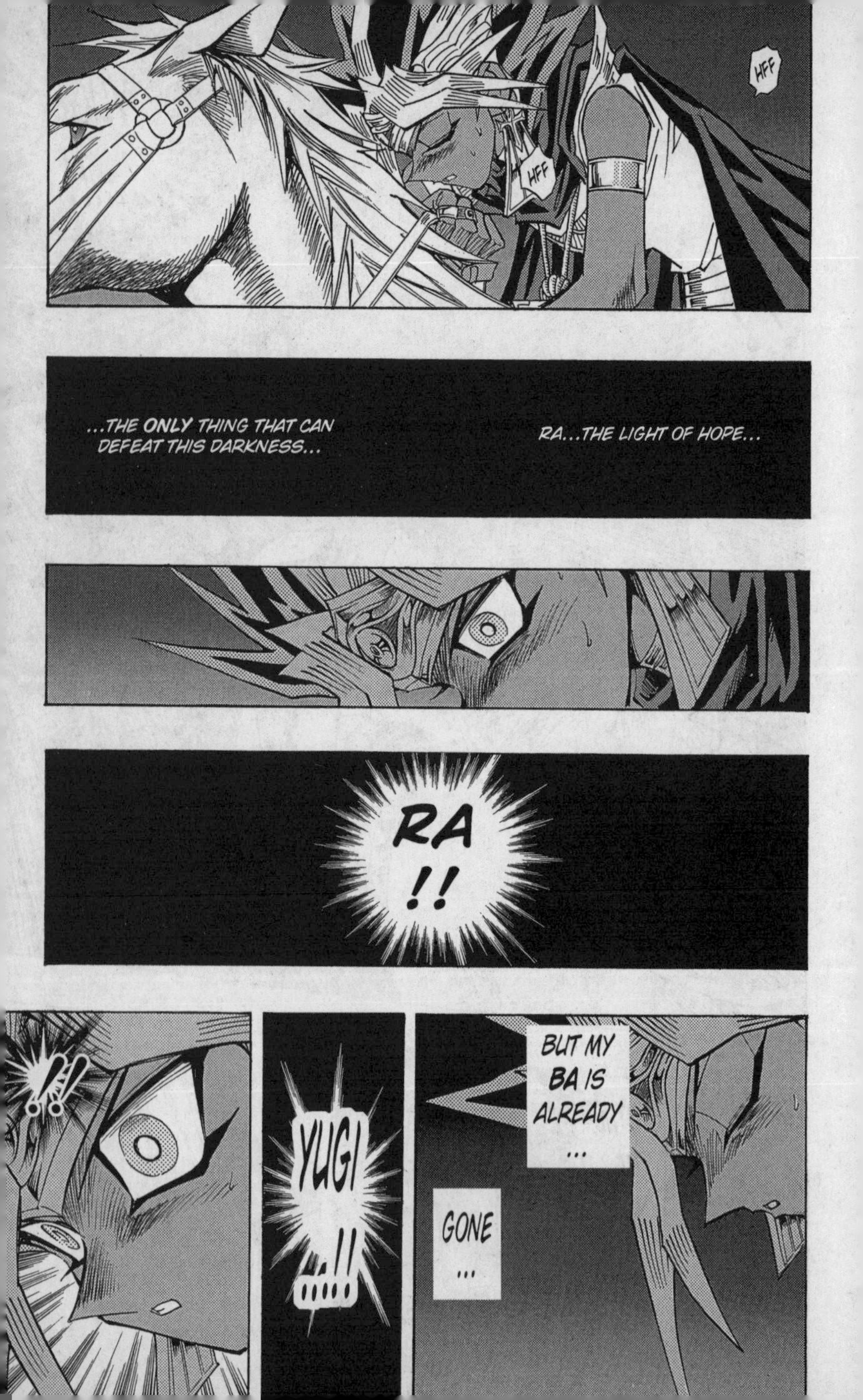
HFF
HFF
RA...THE LIGHT OF HOPE...
...THE ONLY THING THAT CAN DEFEAT THIS DARKNESS...
RA!!
BUT MY BA IS ALREADY ...
GONE ...
YUGI ...!!
!!

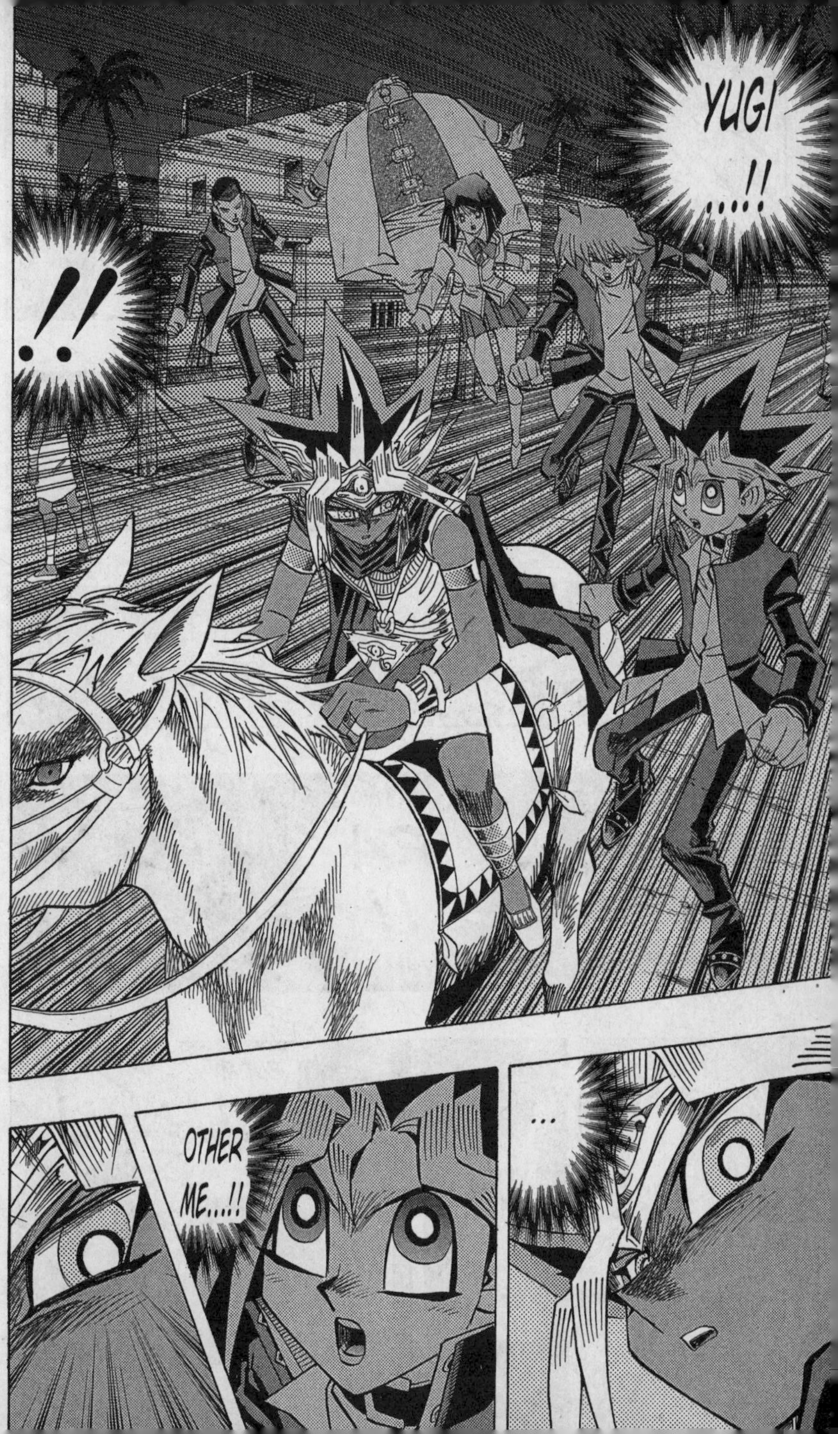
YUGI ....!!
!!
...
OTHER ME...!!

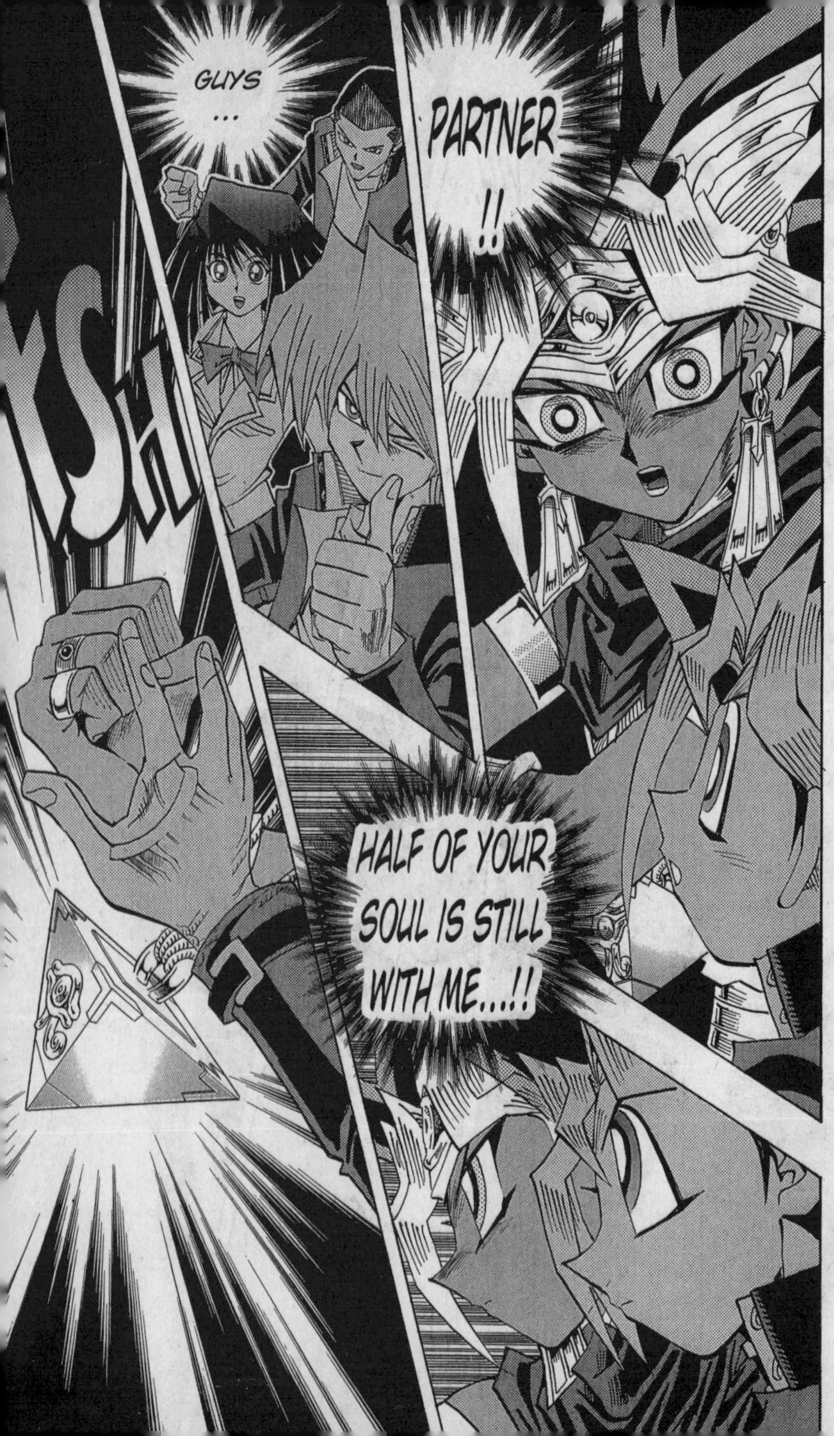
PARTNER!!
GUYS...
HALF OF YOUR SOUL IS STILL WITH ME...!!

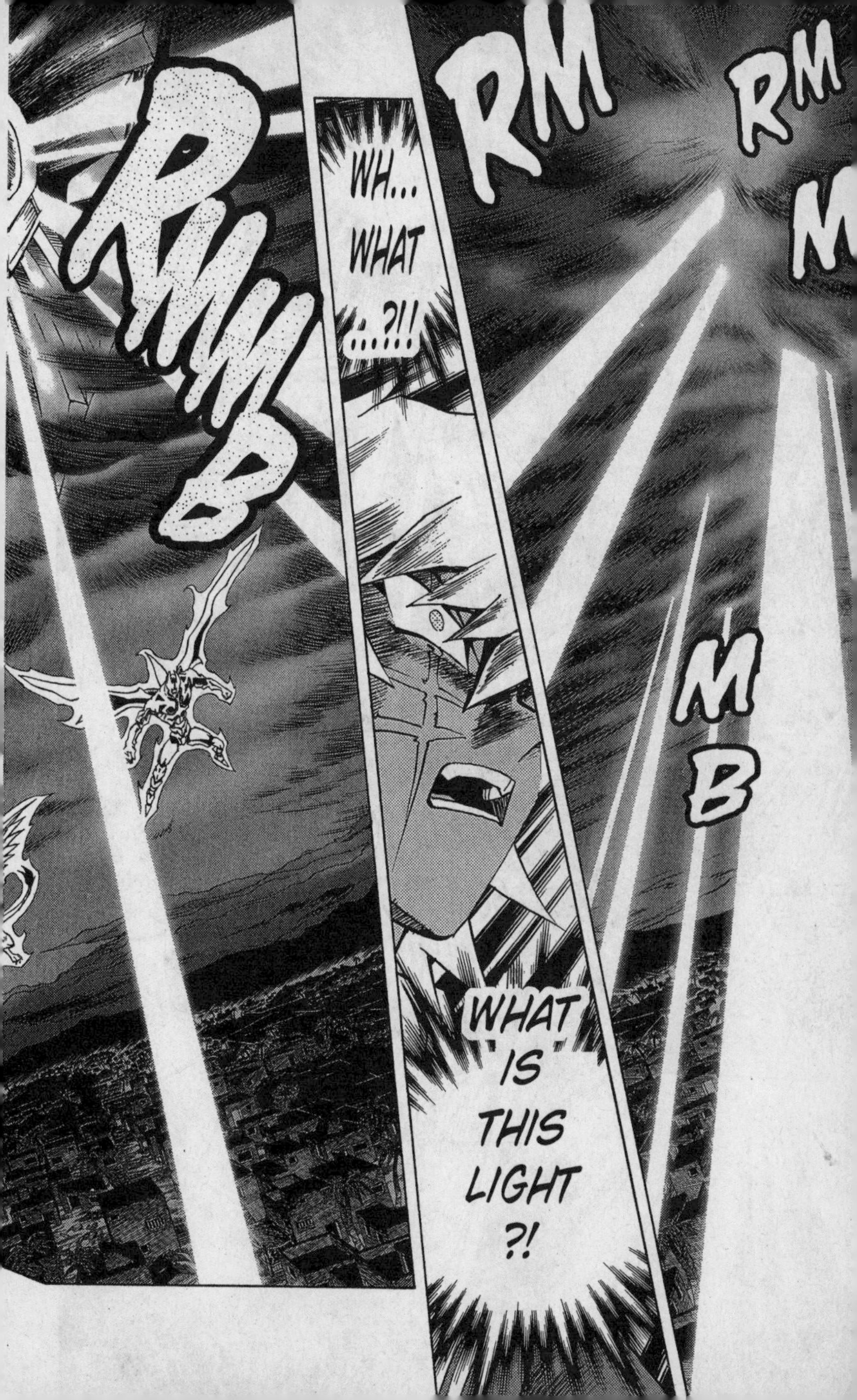
RM
RM
M
M
B
RMMB
WH... WHAT ...?!!
WHAT IS THIS LIGHT ?!

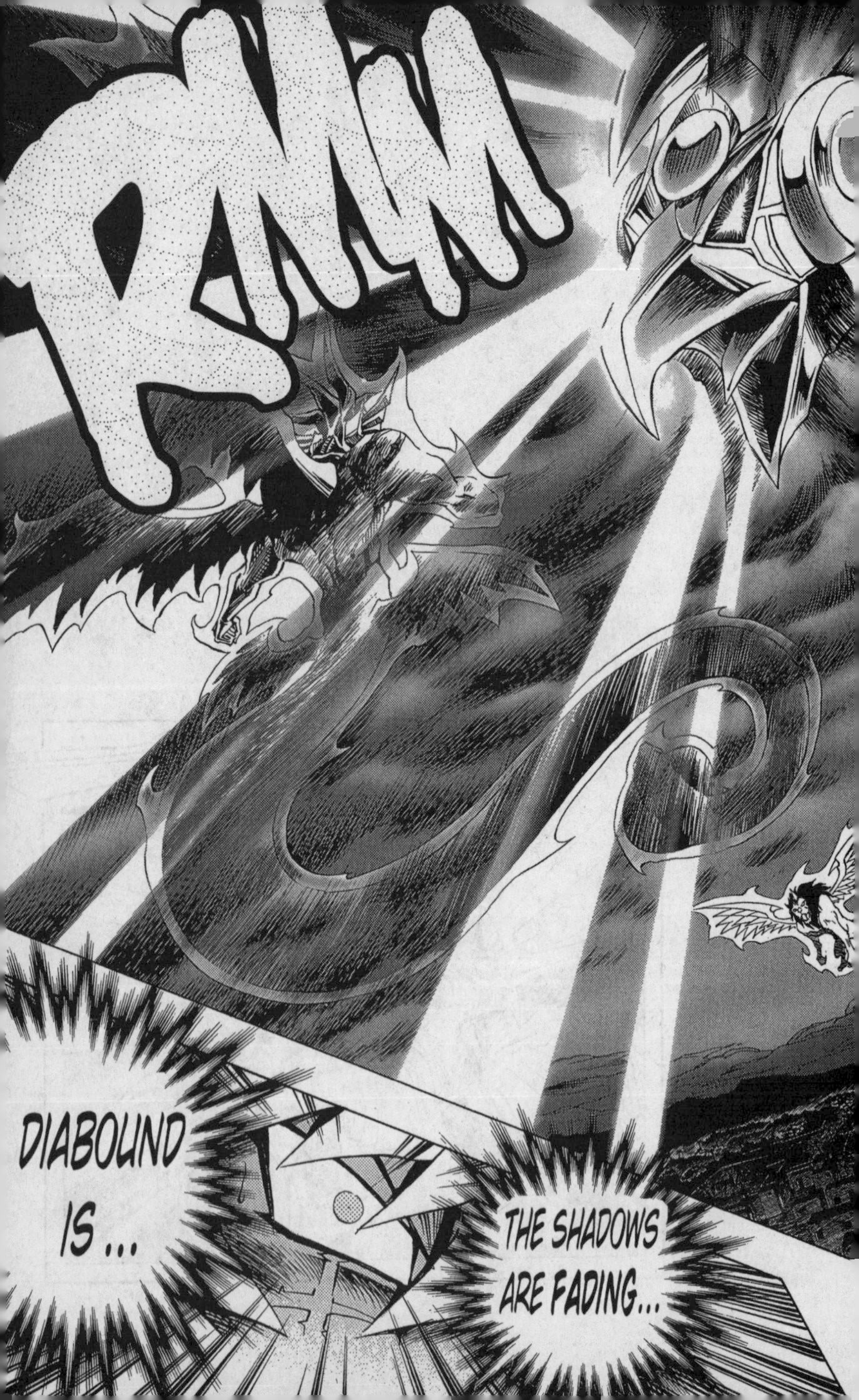
BMMM
DIABOUND IS...
THE SHADOWS ARE FADING...

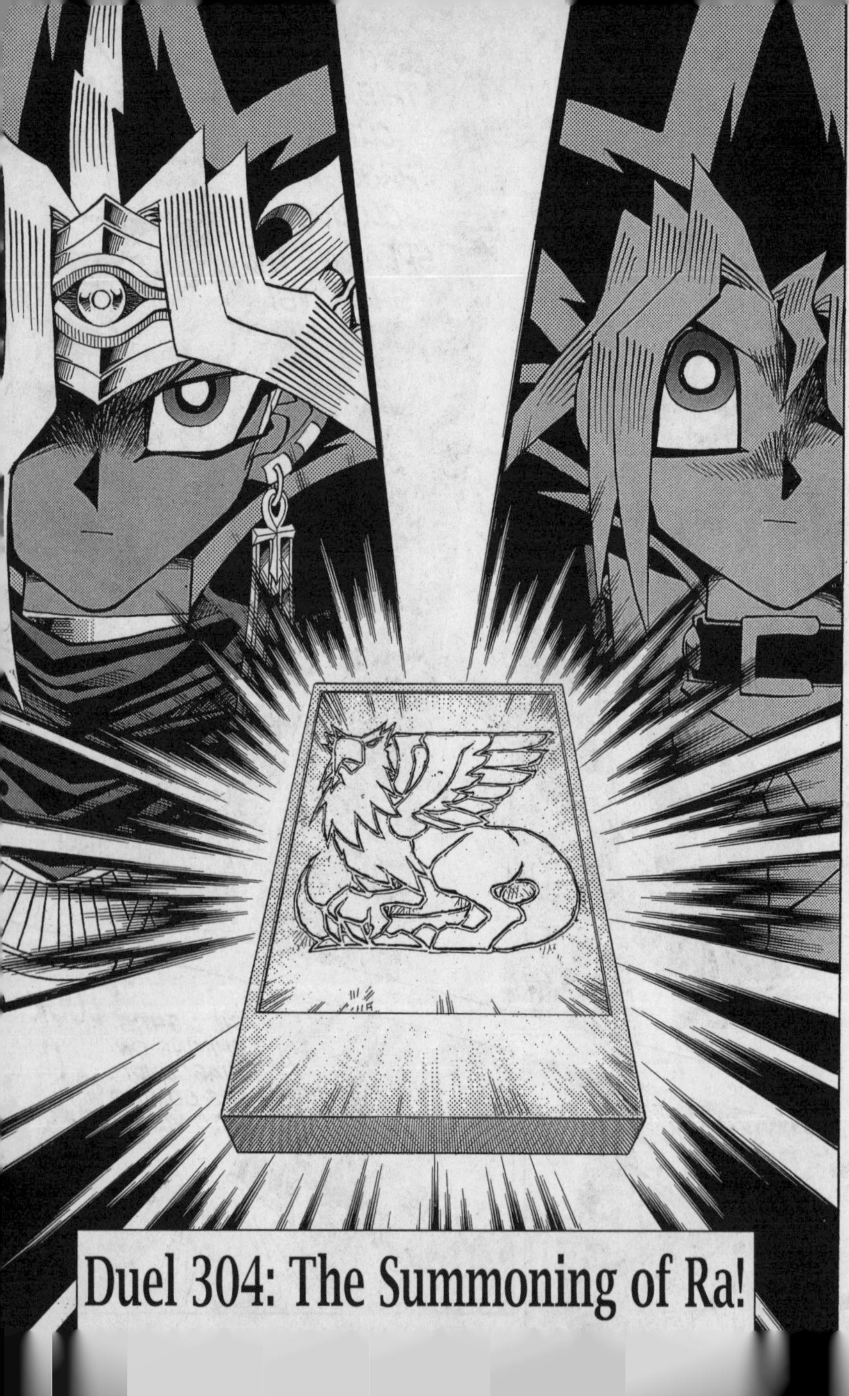

Duel 304: The Summoning of Ra!

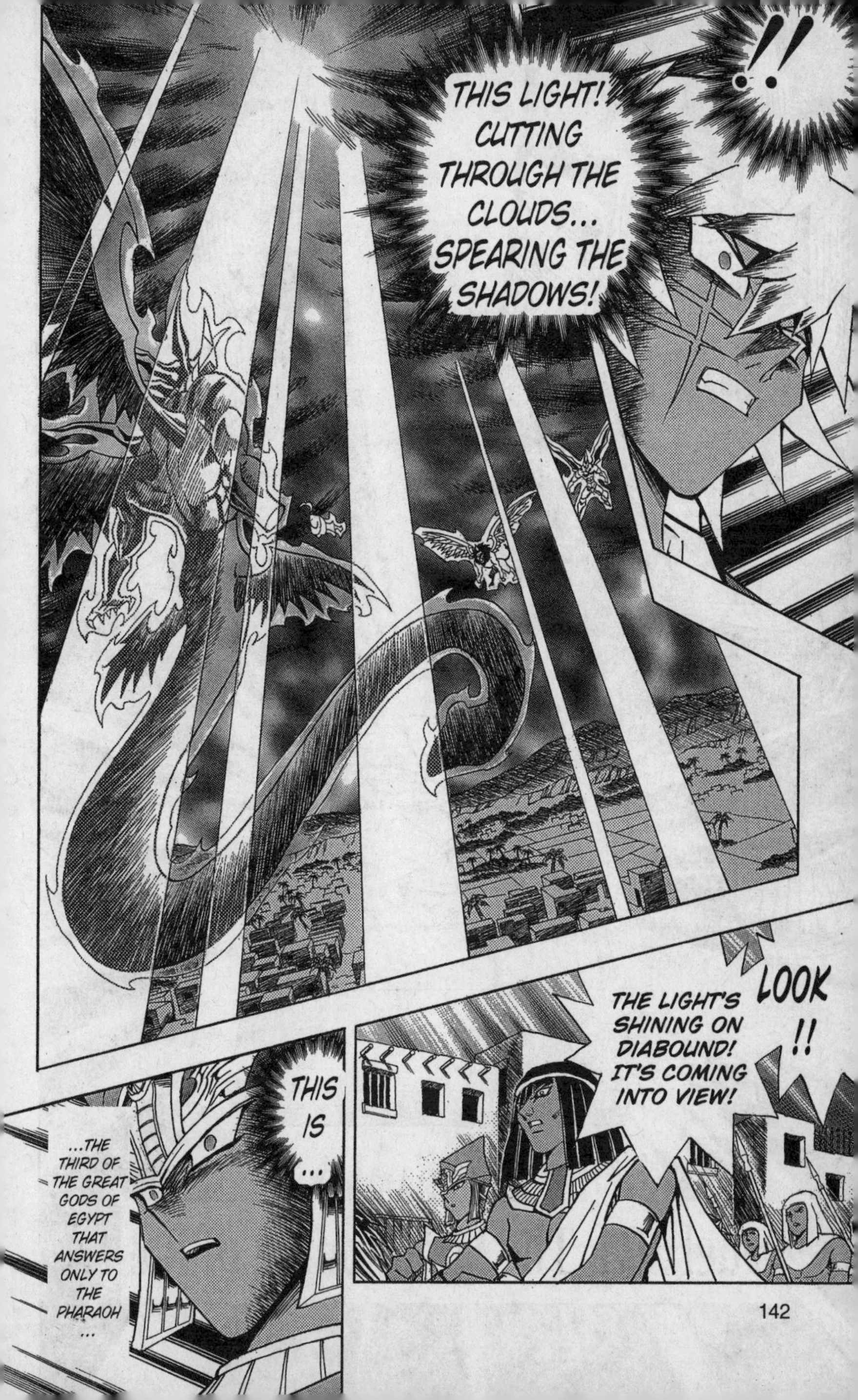
!!
THIS LIGHT! CUTTING THROUGH THE CLOUDS... SPEARING THE SHADOWS!
LOOK !!
THE LIGHT'S SHINING ON DIABOUND! IT'S COMING INTO VIEW!
THIS IS ...
...THE THIRD OF THE GREAT GODS OF EGYPT THAT ANSWERS ONLY TO THE PHARAOH ...

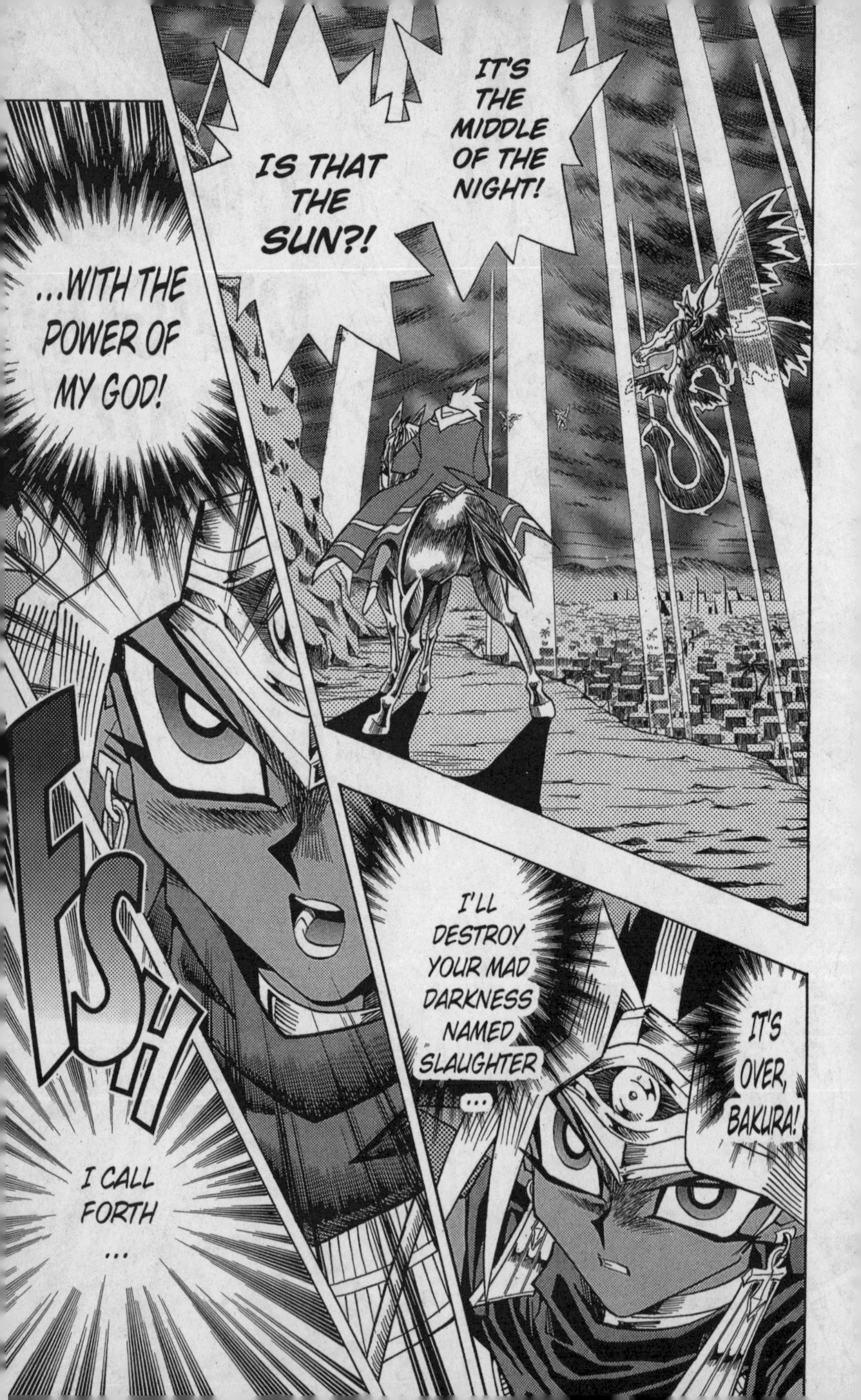
IT'S OVER, BAKURA!
I'LL DESTROY YOUR MAD DARKNESS NAMED SLAUGHTER ...
I CALL FORTH ...
FSSH
...WITH THE POWER OF MY GOD!
IS THAT THE SUN?!
IT'S THE MIDDLE OF THE NIGHT!

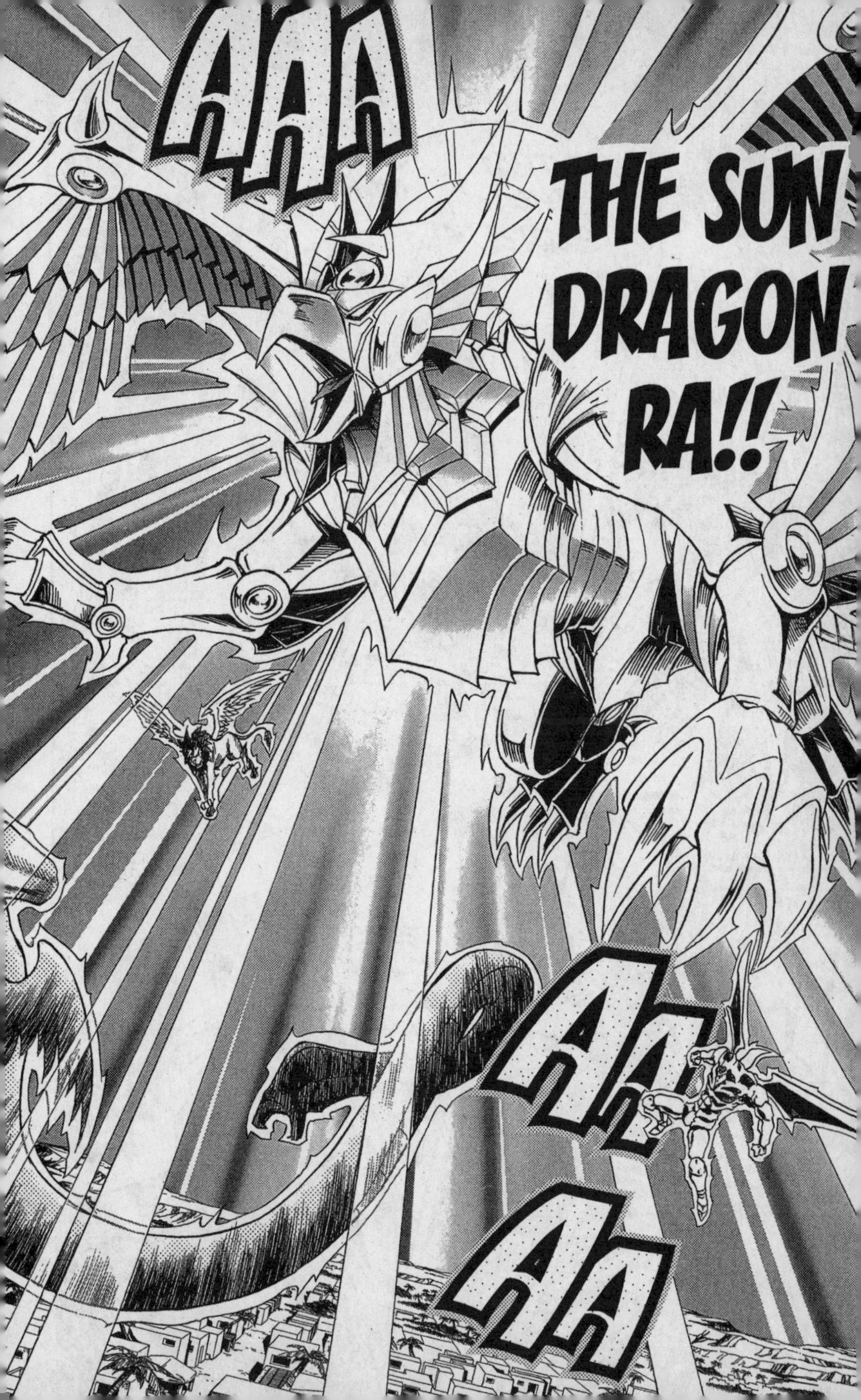
AAA
THE SUN DRAGON RA!!
AA
AA

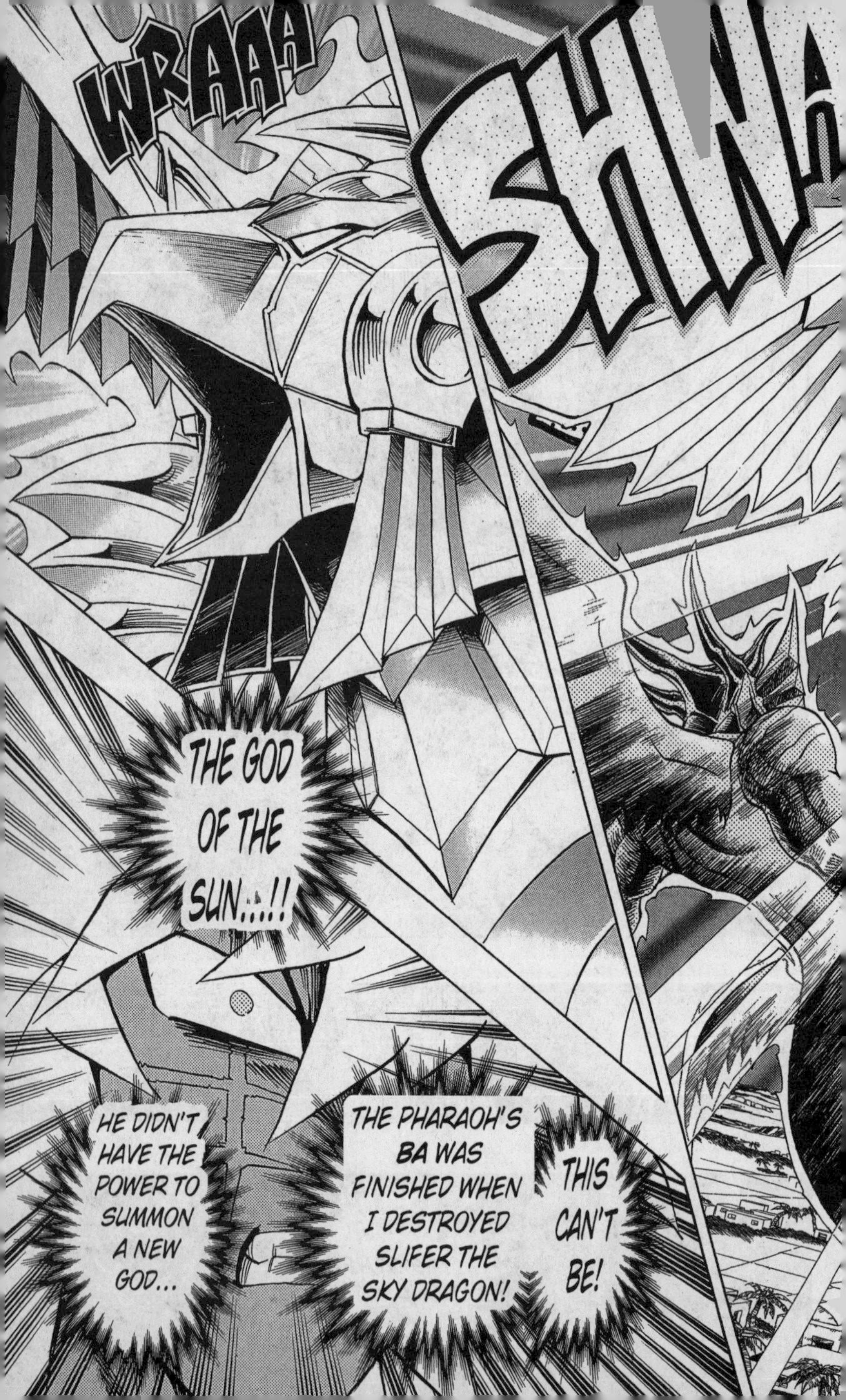
SHWA
WRAAA
THE GOD OF THE SUN...!!
THIS CAN'T BE!
THE PHARAOH'S BA WAS FINISHED WHEN I DESTROYED SLIFER THE SKY DRAGON!
HE DIDN'T HAVE THE POWER TO SUMMON A NEW GOD...

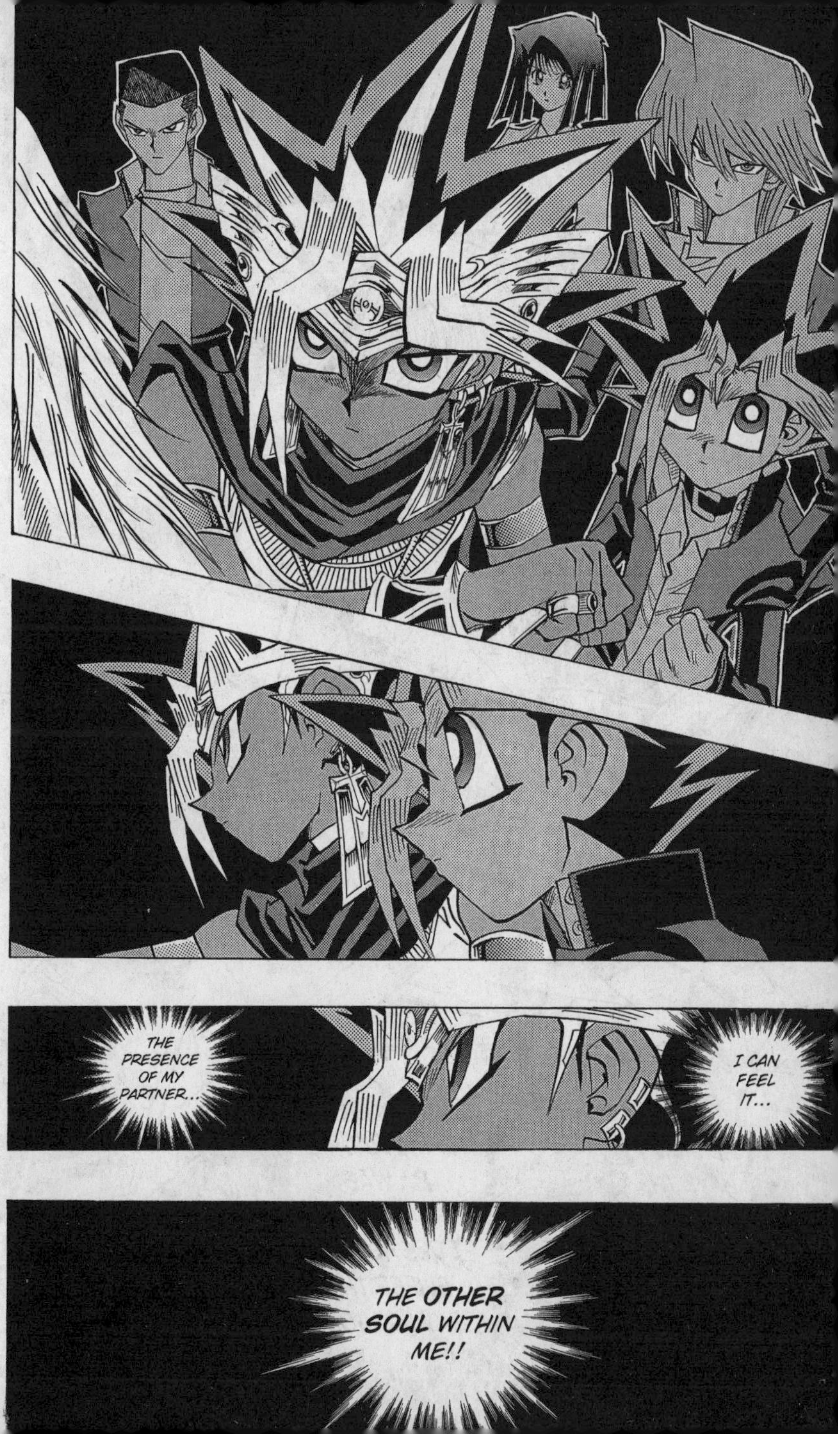
THE PRESENCE OF MY PARTNER...
I CAN FEEL IT...
THE OTHER SOUL WITHIN ME!!

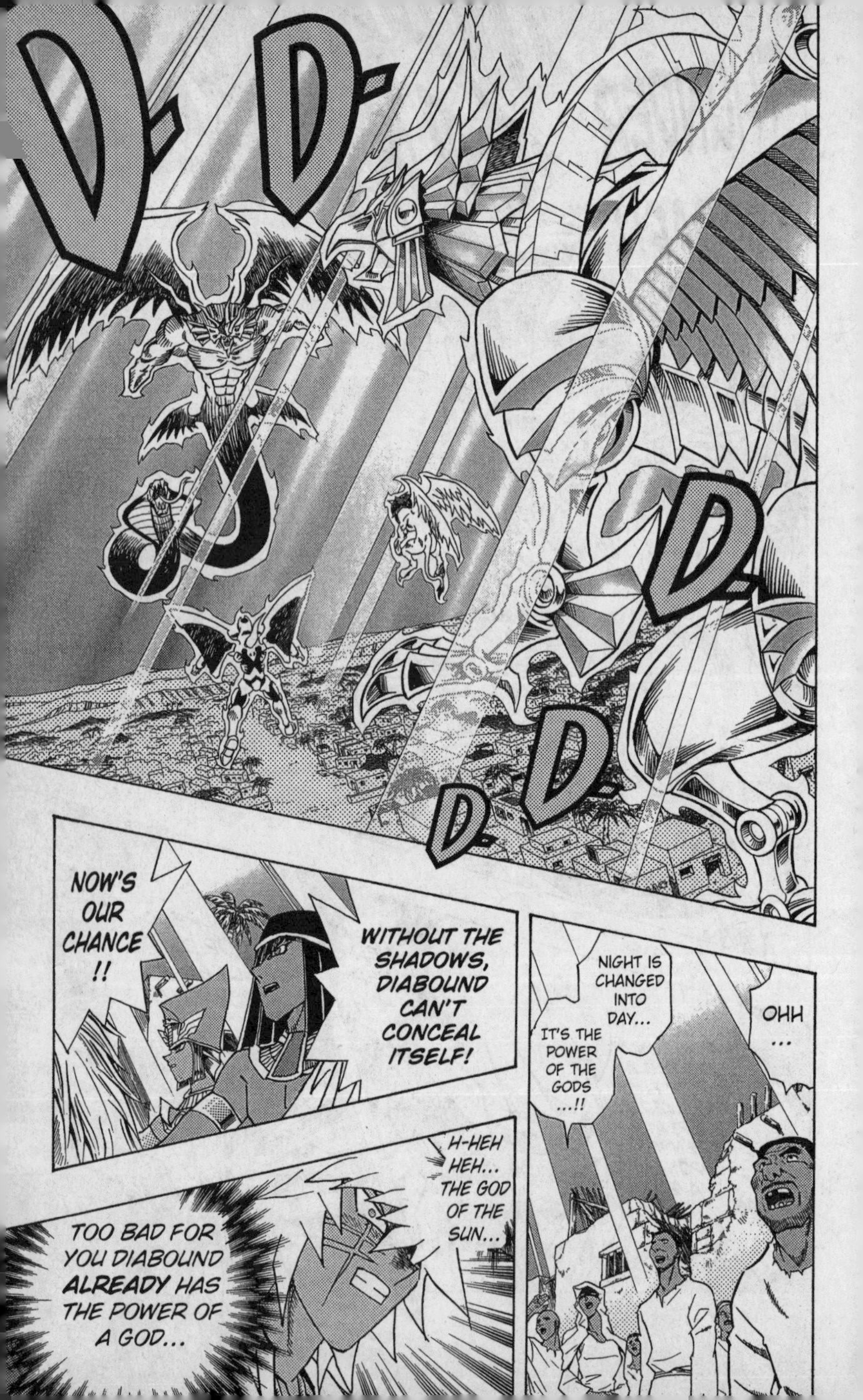
D-
D-
D-
D-
D-
OHH...
NIGHT IS CHANGED INTO DAY...
IT'S THE POWER OF THE GODS ...!!
NOW'S OUR CHANCE !!
WITHOUT THE SHADOWS, DIABOUND CAN'T CONCEAL ITSELF!
H-HEH HEH... THE GOD OF THE SUN...
TOO BAD FOR YOU DIABOUND **ALREADY** HAS THE POWER OF A GOD...

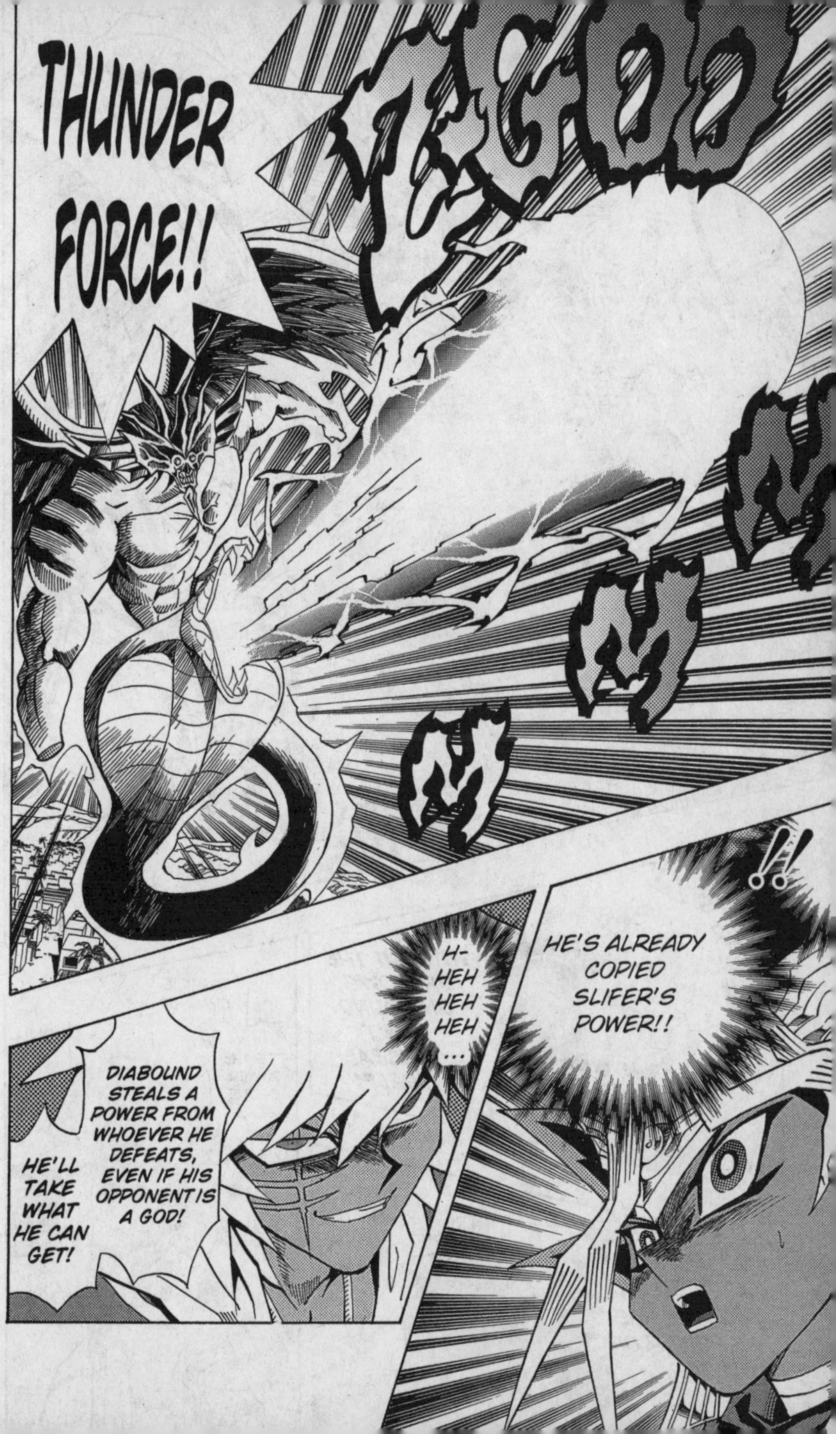
THUNDER FORCE!!
!!
HE'S ALREADY COPIED SLIFER'S POWER!!
H-HEH HEH HEH...
DIABOUND STEALS A POWER FROM WHOEVER HE DEFEATS, EVEN IF HIS OPPONENT IS A GOD!
HE'LL TAKE WHAT HE CAN GET!

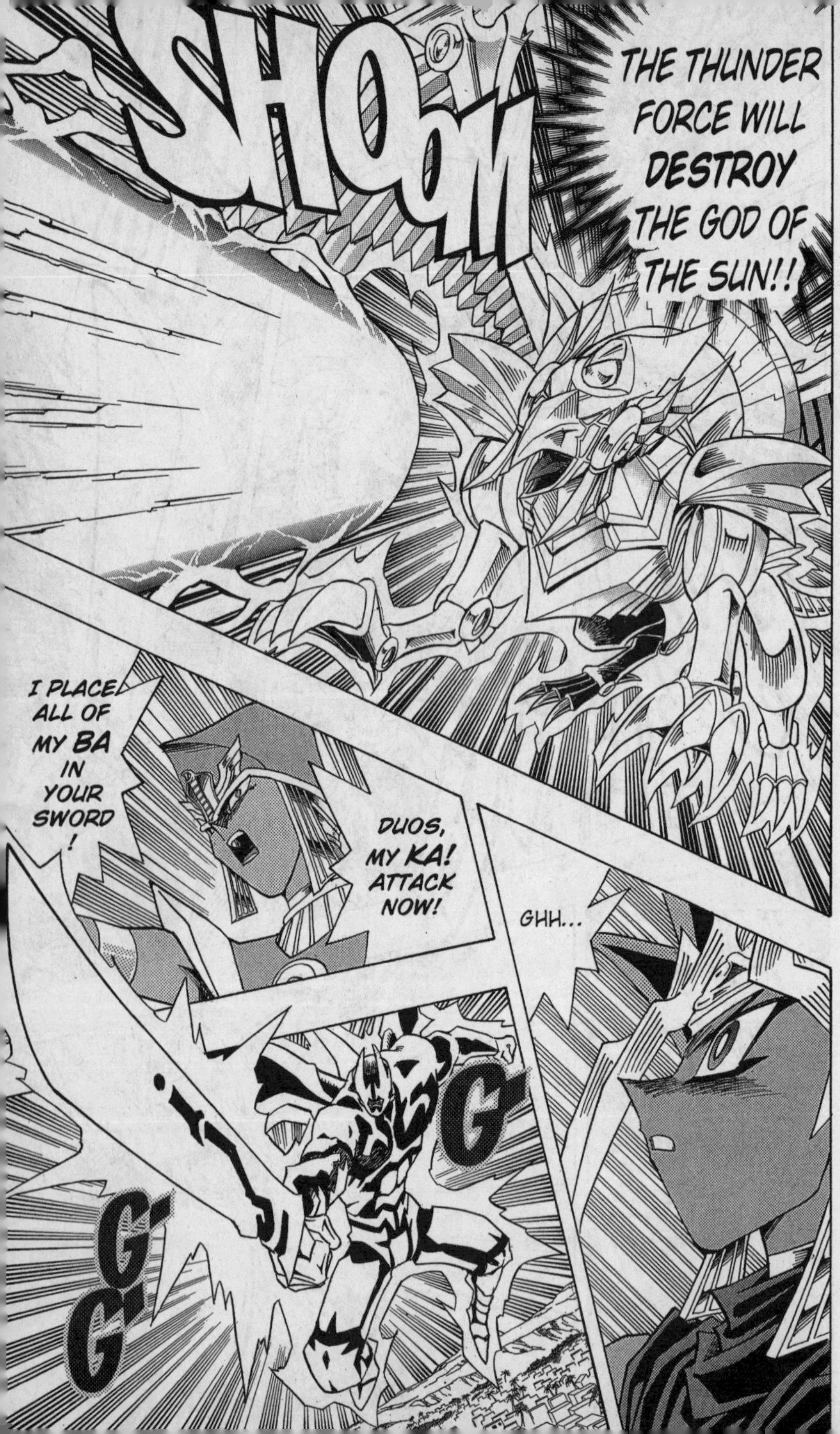
SHOOM
THE THUNDER FORCE WILL DESTROY THE GOD OF THE SUN!!
GHH...
I PLACE ALL OF MY BA IN YOUR SWORD!
DUOS, MY KA! ATTACK NOW!
G
G
G

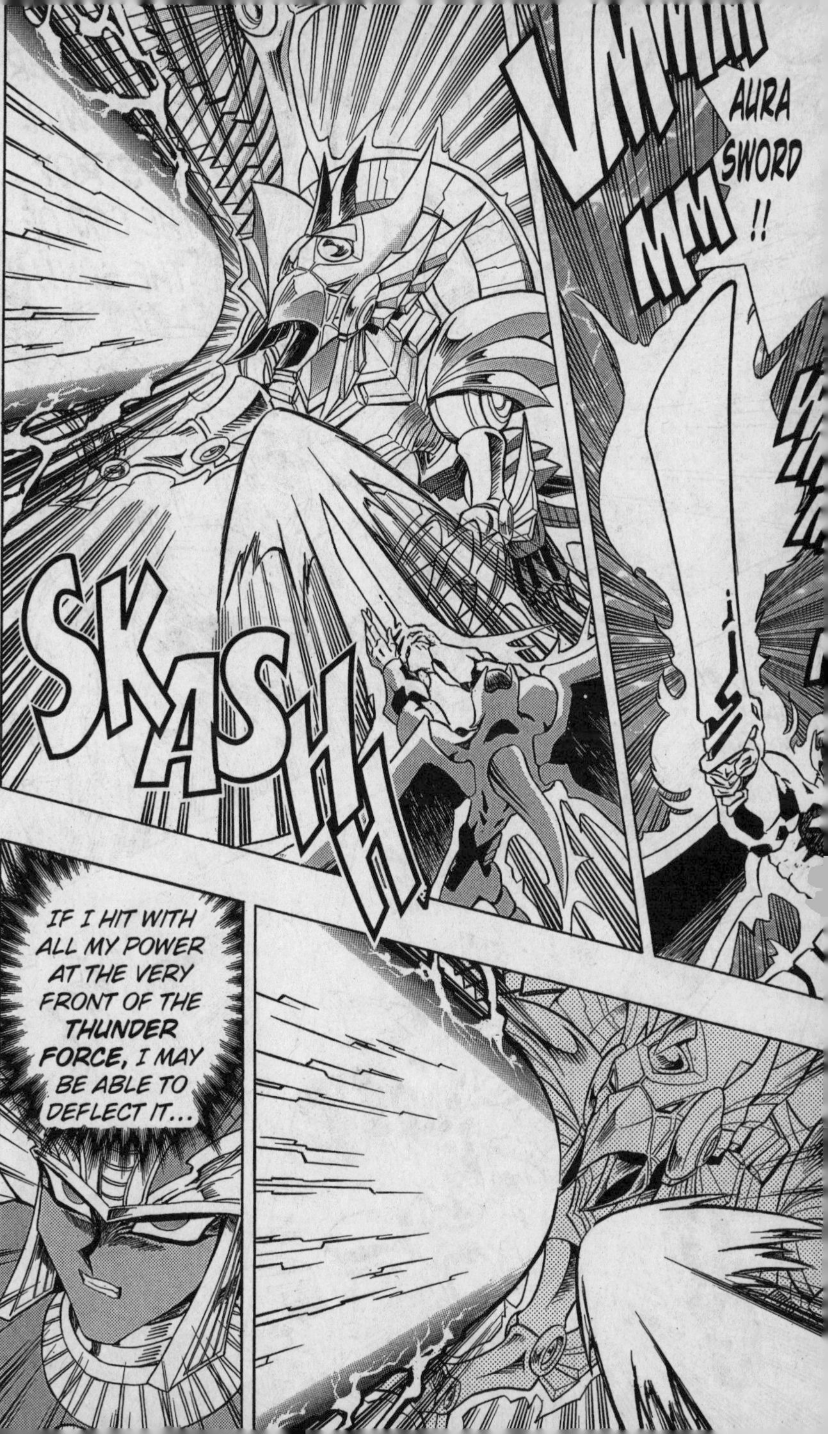
VMMM MM
AURA SWORD !!
SKASH!!
IF I HIT WITH ALL MY POWER AT THE VERY FRONT OF THE THUNDER FORCE, I MAY BE ABLE TO DEFLECT IT...

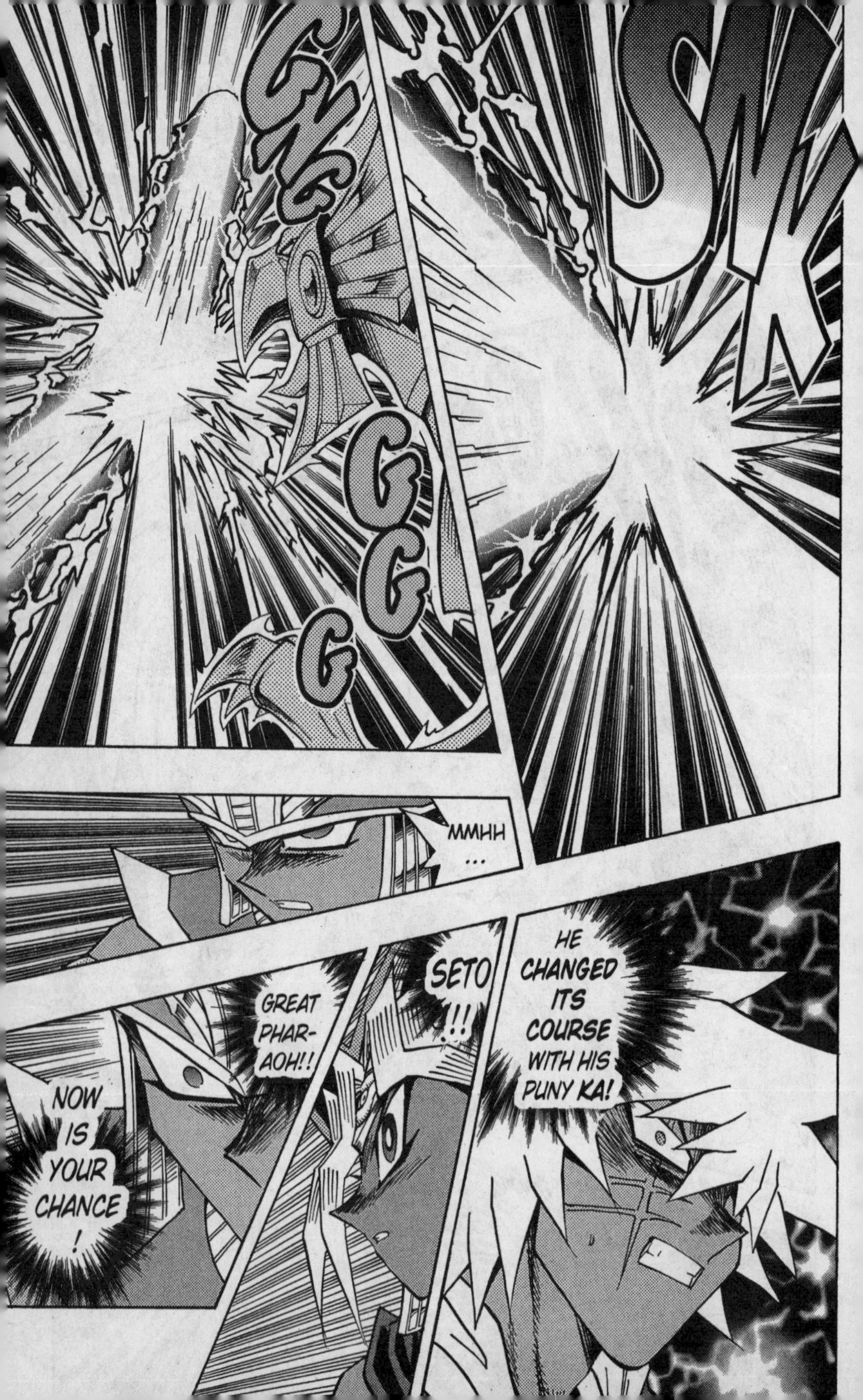
MMHH ...
HE CHANGED ITS COURSE WITH HIS PUNY KA!
SETO!!!
GREAT PHARAOH!!
NOW IS YOUR CHANCE!

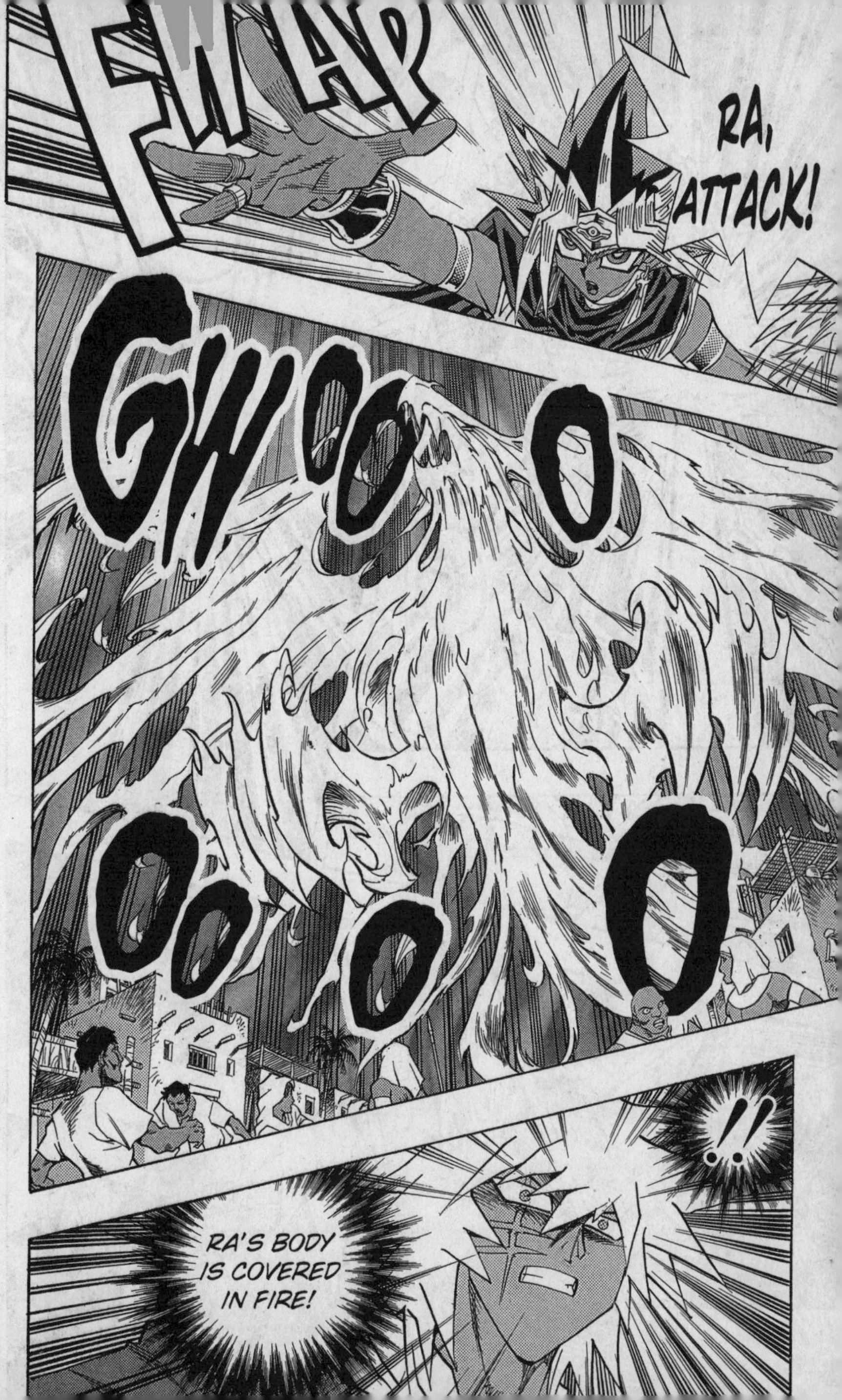
FWAP
RA, ATTACK!
GWOOOOOOOO
!!
RA'S BODY IS COVERED IN FIRE!

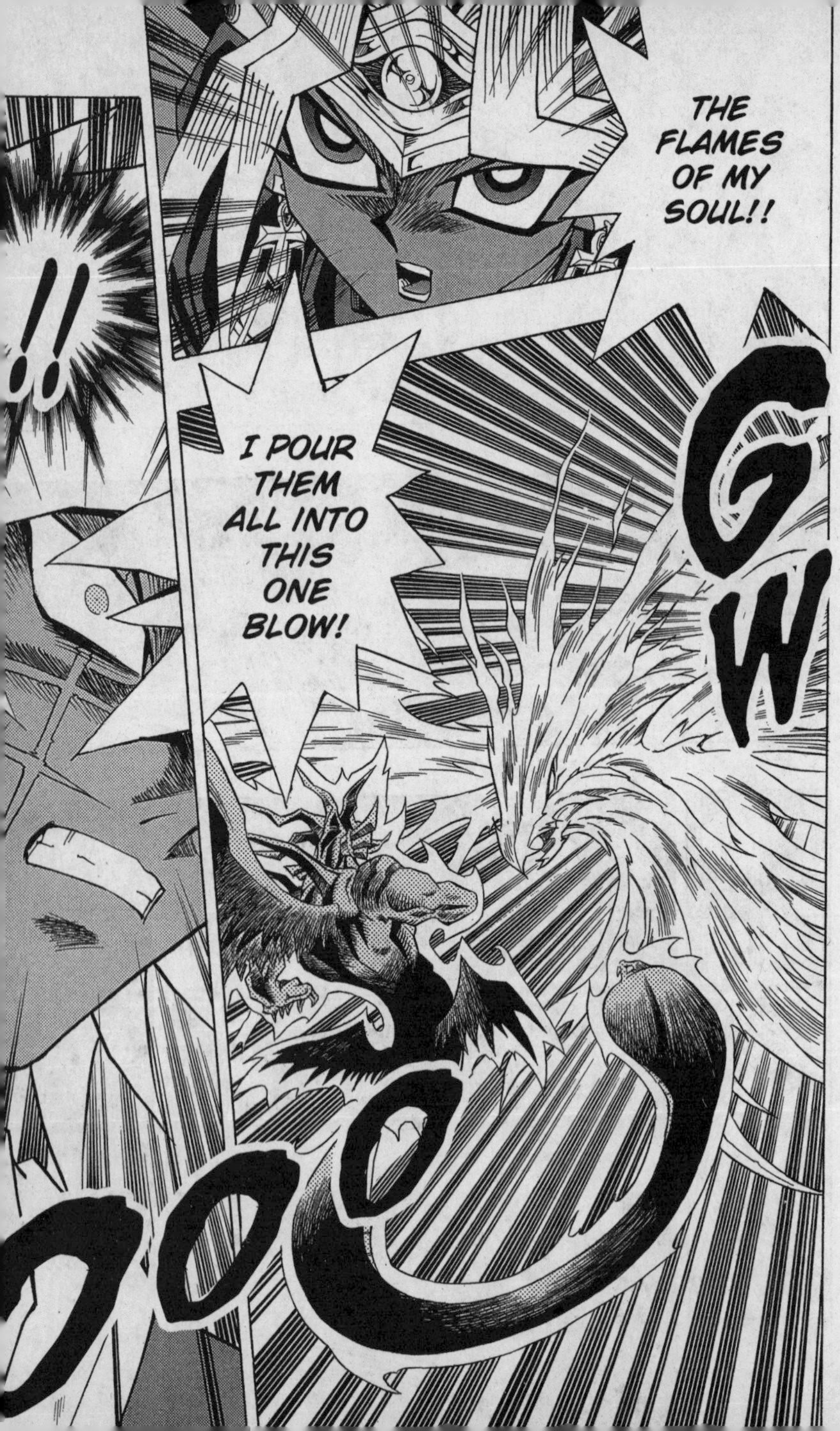
THE FLAMES OF MY SOUL!!
!!
I POUR THEM ALL INTO THIS ONE BLOW!
GWOOO

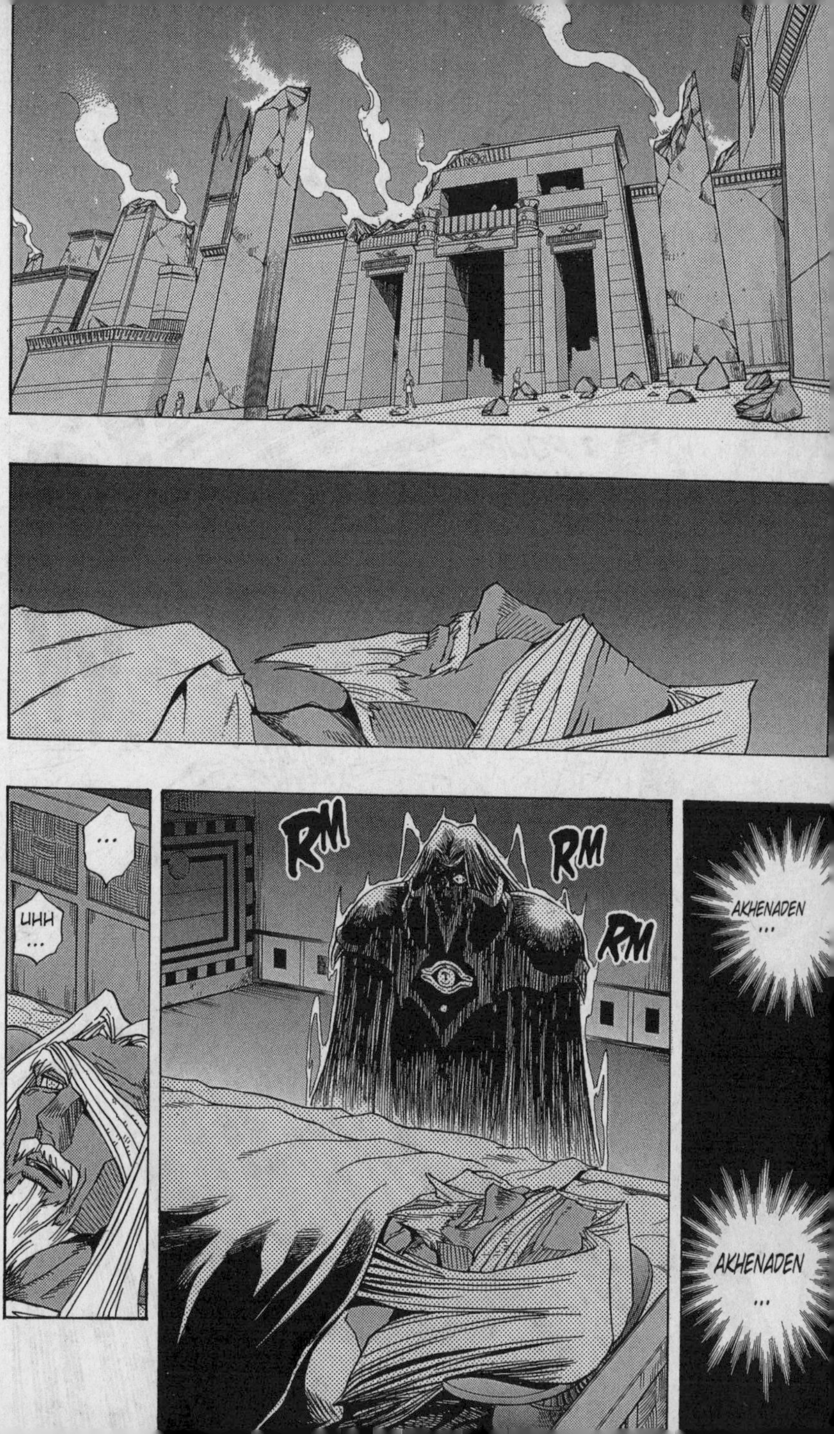
AKHENADEN ...
AKHENADEN ...
RM
RM
RM
...
UHH ...

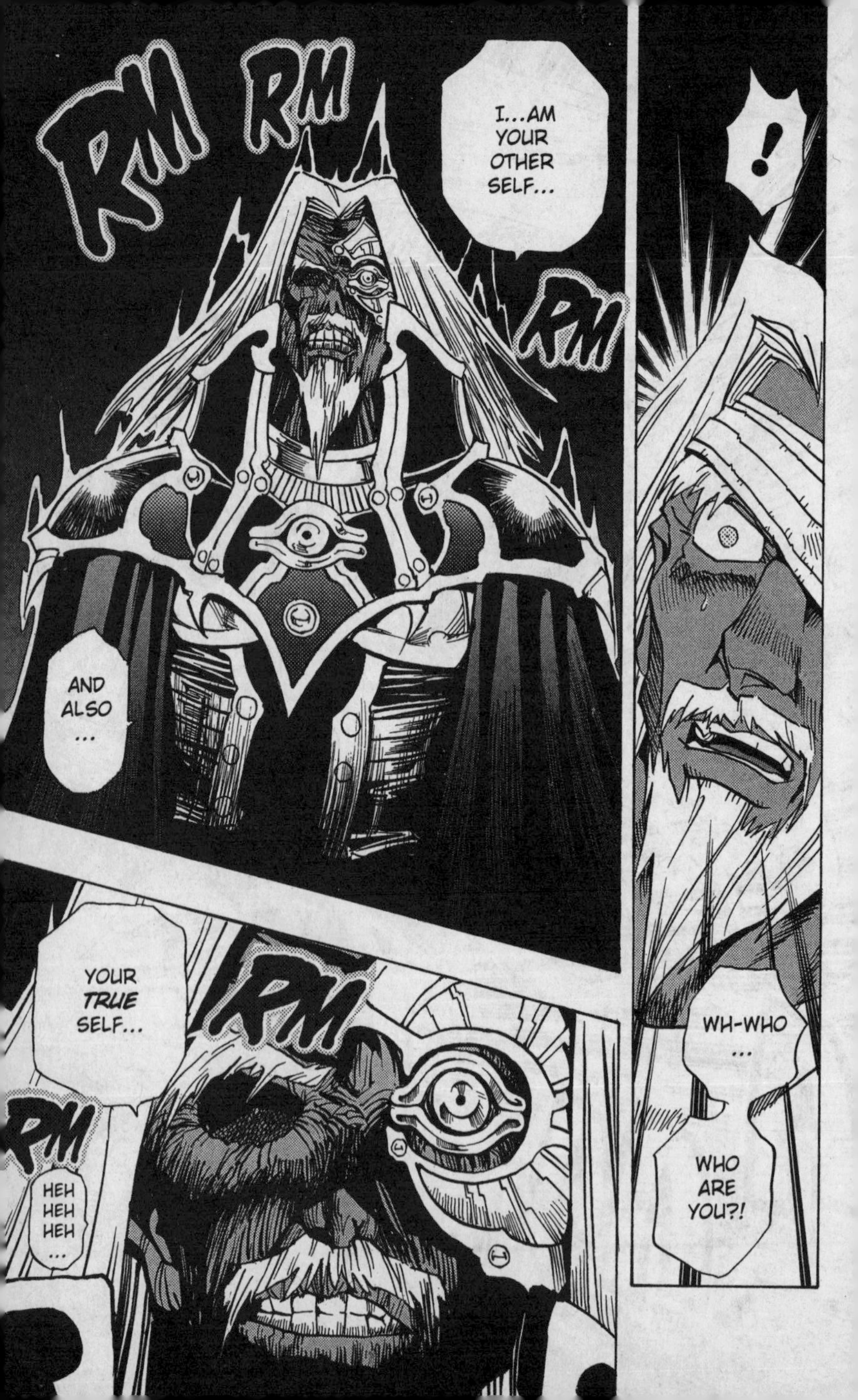
RM RM
I...AM YOUR OTHER SELF...
RM
AND ALSO ...
!
YOUR TRUE SELF...
RM
RM
HEH HEH HEH ...
WH-WHO ...
WHO ARE YOU?!

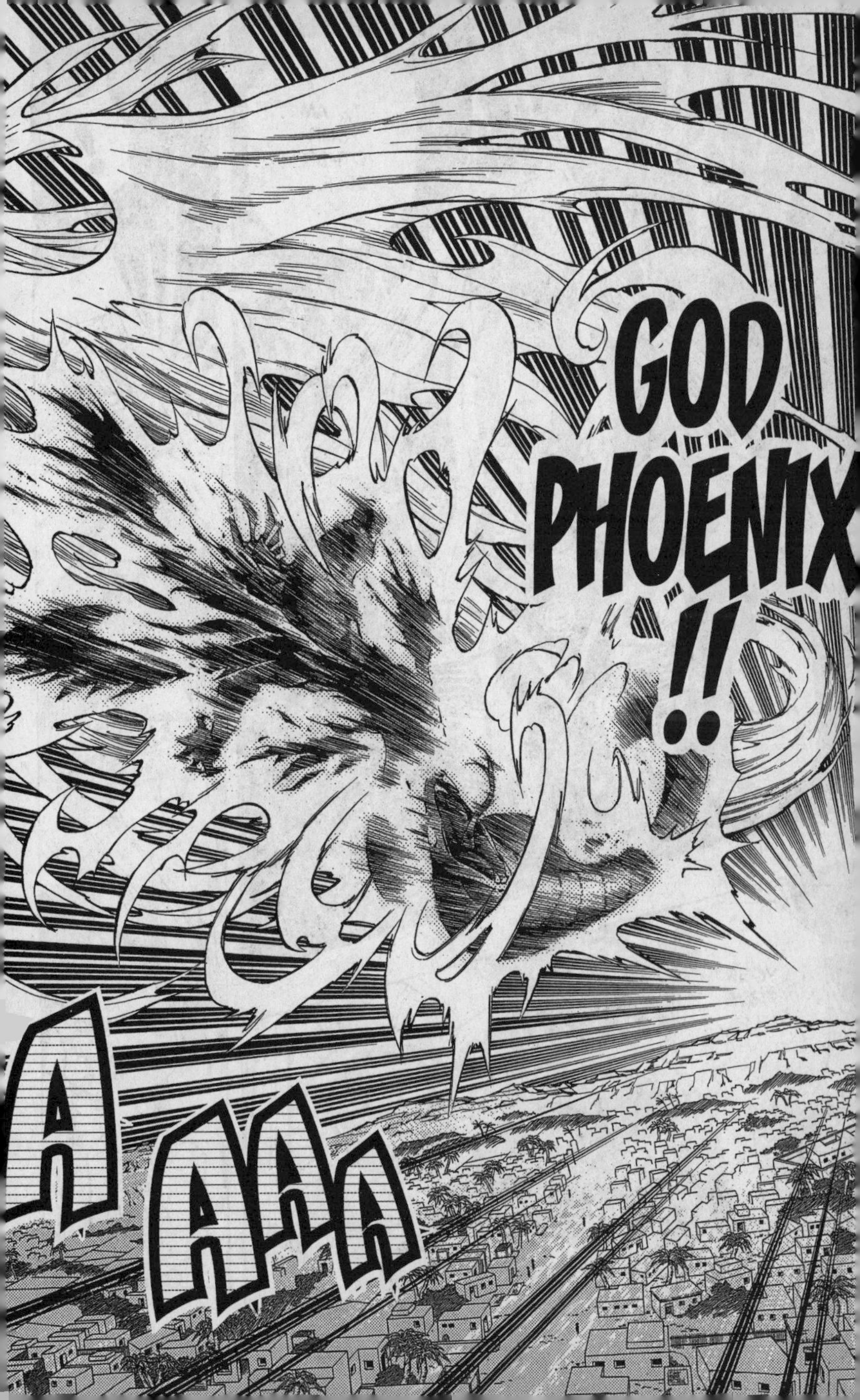
GOD PHOENIX!!
AAAAA

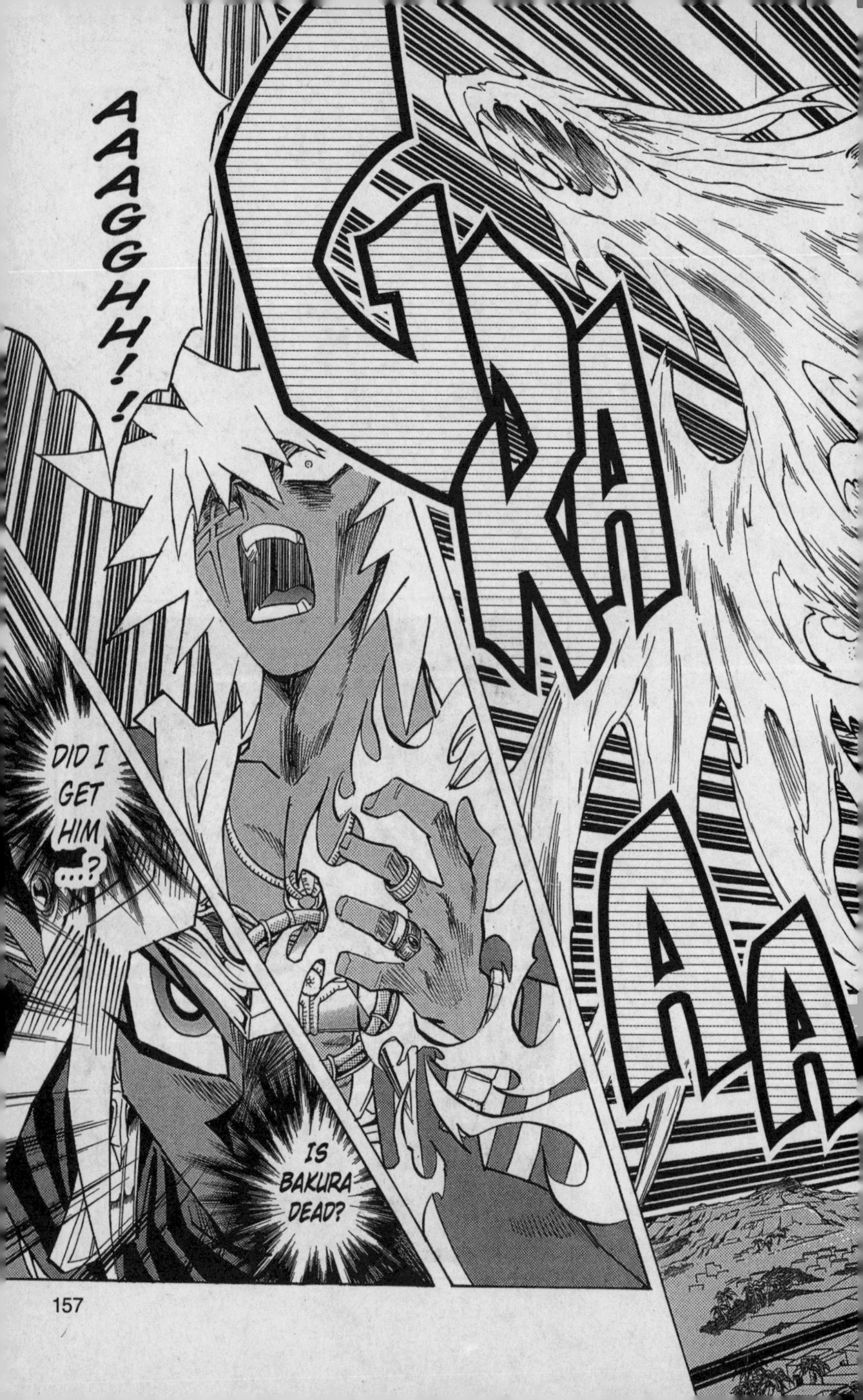
AAAGGHH!!
DID I GET HIM...?
IS BAKURA DEAD?

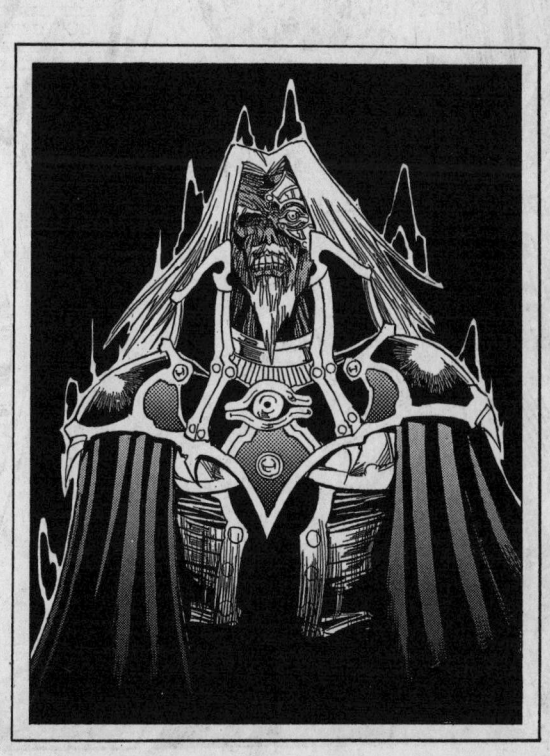

Duel 305: Ruler of Shadows!!

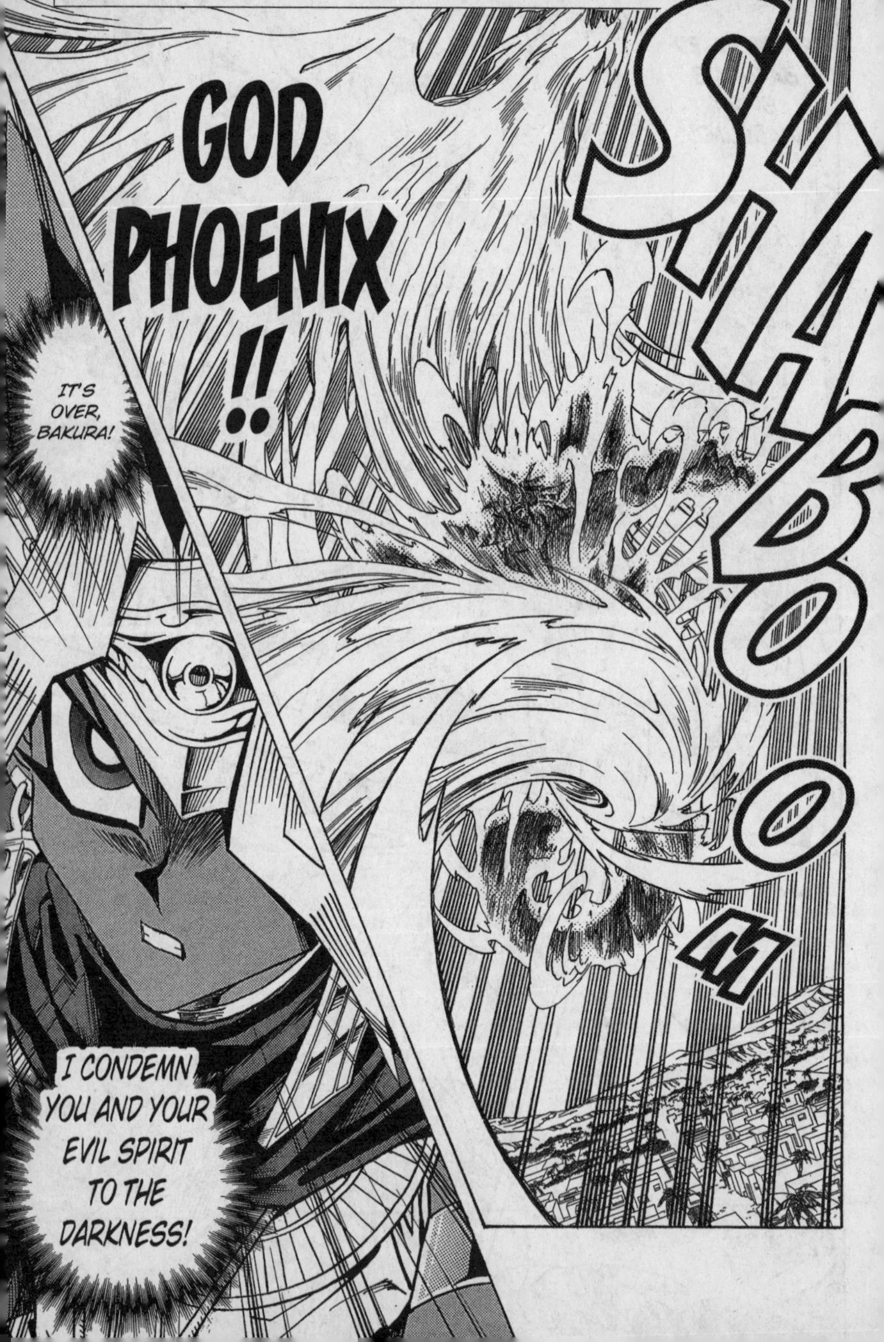
SHA'BOOM
GOD PHOENIX!!
IT'S OVER, BAKURA!
I CONDEMN YOU AND YOUR EVIL SPIRIT TO THE DARKNESS!

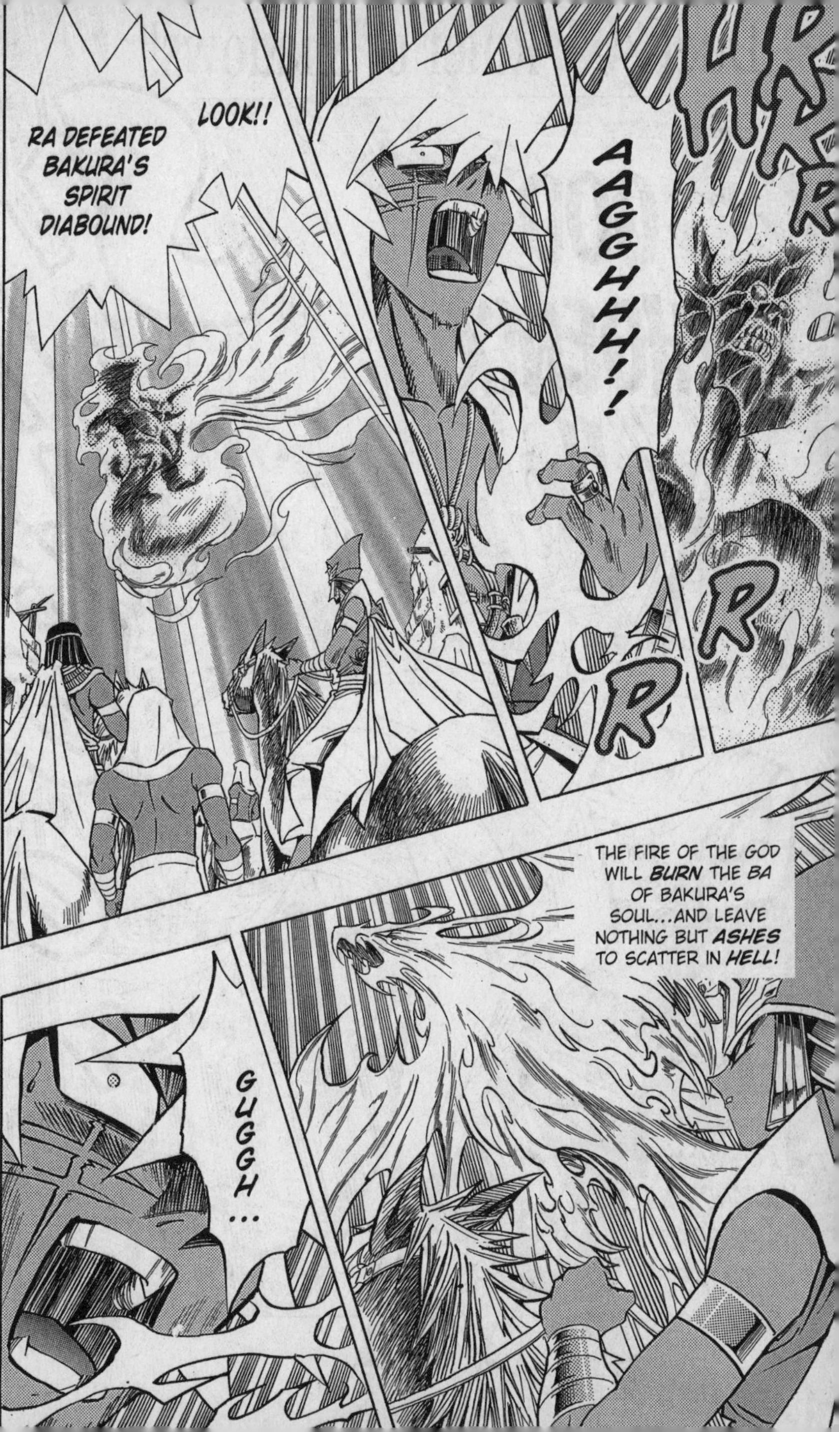
AAGGHHHH!!
URRRRR
LOOK!!
RA DEFEATED BAKURA'S SPIRIT DIABOUND!
THE FIRE OF THE GOD WILL BURN THE BA OF BAKURA'S SOUL...AND LEAVE NOTHING BUT ASHES TO SCATTER IN HELL!
GUGGH...

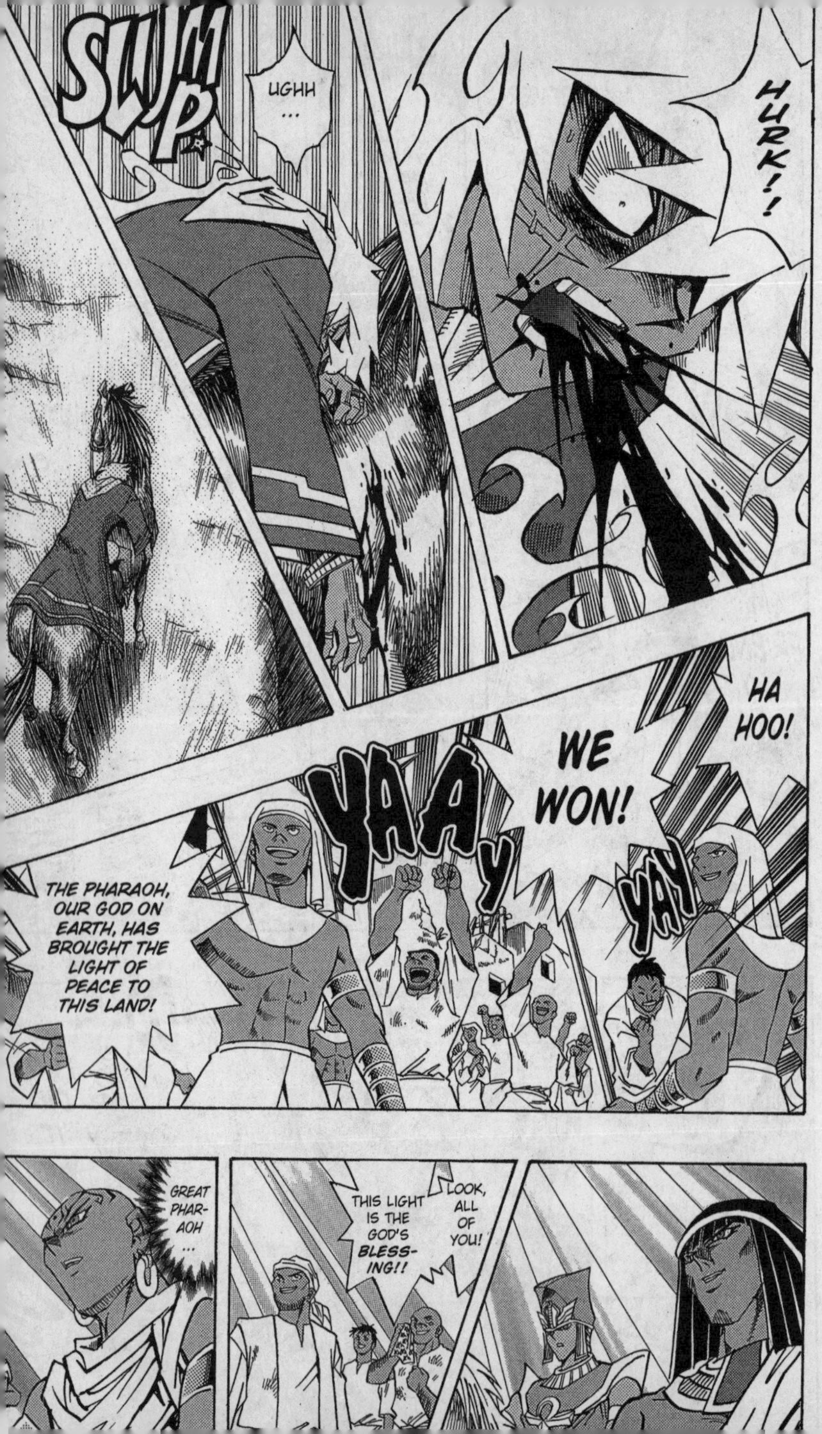

HURK!!
UGHH ...
SLUMP
HA HOO!
WE WON!
YAAAY
YAY
THE PHARAOH, OUR GOD ON EARTH, HAS BROUGHT THE LIGHT OF PEACE TO THIS LAND!
LOOK, ALL OF YOU!
THIS LIGHT IS THE GOD'S BLESSING!!
GREAT PHARAOH ...

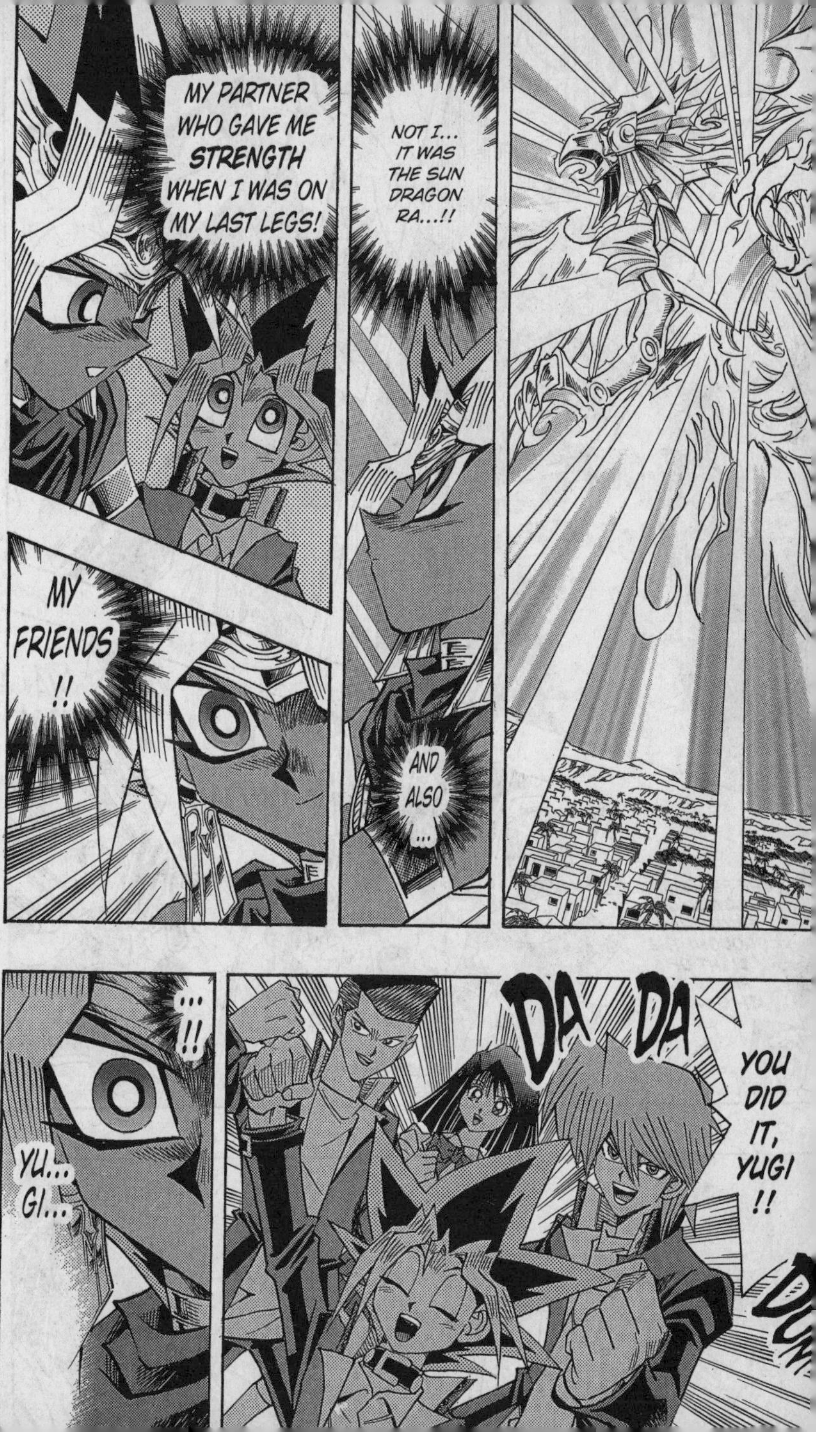
NOT I... IT WAS THE SUN DRAGON RA...!!
MY PARTNER WHO GAVE ME STRENGTH WHEN I WAS ON MY LAST LEGS!
AND ALSO...
MY FRIENDS!!
DA DA
YOU DID IT, YUGI!!
...!!
YU... GI...

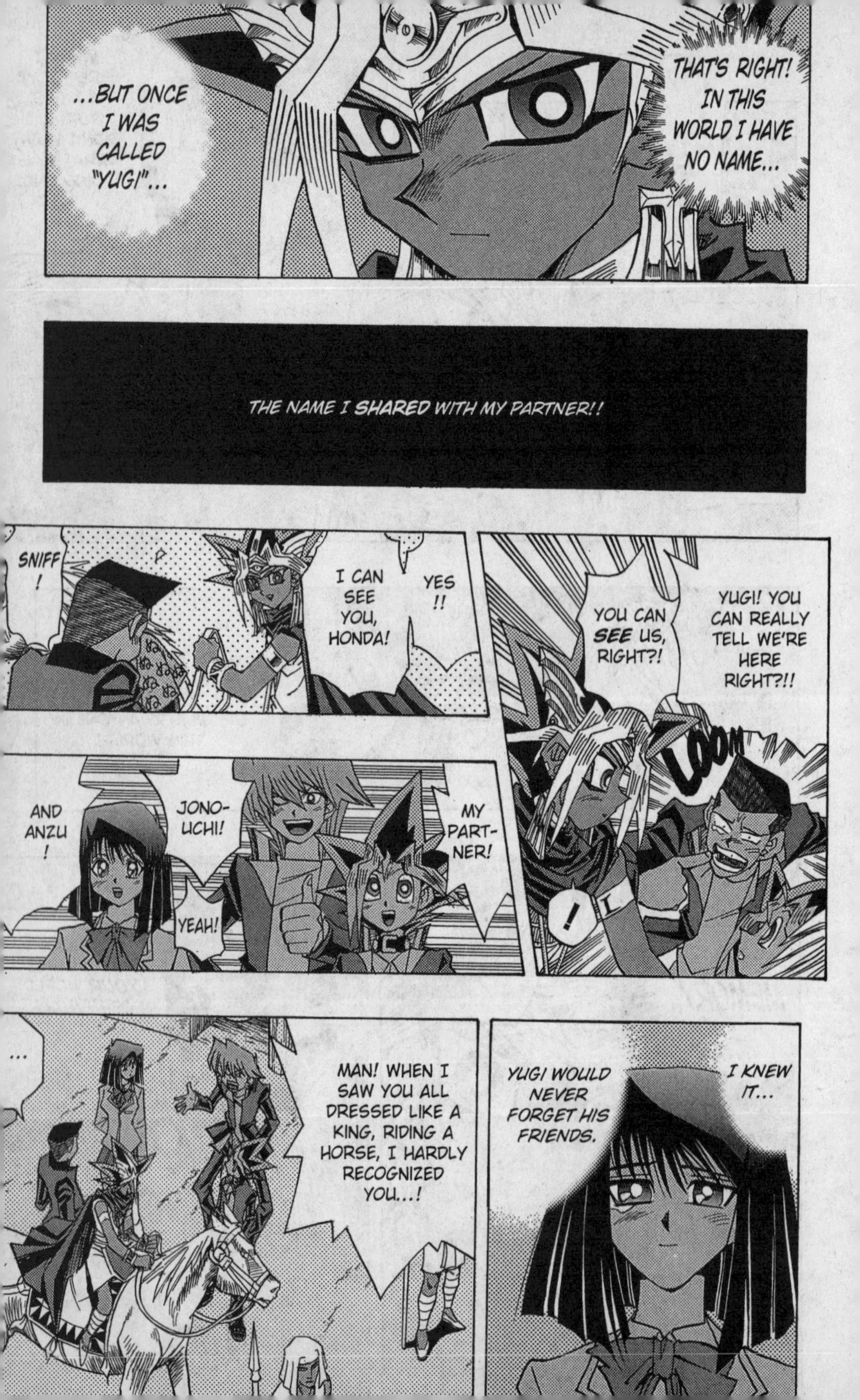
THAT'S RIGHT! IN THIS WORLD I HAVE NO NAME...
...BUT ONCE I WAS CALLED "YUGI"...
THE NAME I SHARED WITH MY PARTNER!!
YUGI! YOU CAN REALLY TELL WE'RE HERE RIGHT?!!
YOU CAN SEE US, RIGHT?!
LOOM
!
YES!!
I CAN SEE YOU, HONDA!
SNIFF!
MY PARTNER!
JONOUCHI!
YEAH!
AND ANZU!
I KNEW IT...
YUGI WOULD NEVER FORGET HIS FRIENDS.
MAN! WHEN I SAW YOU ALL DRESSED LIKE A KING, RIDING A HORSE, I HARDLY RECOGNIZED YOU...!
...

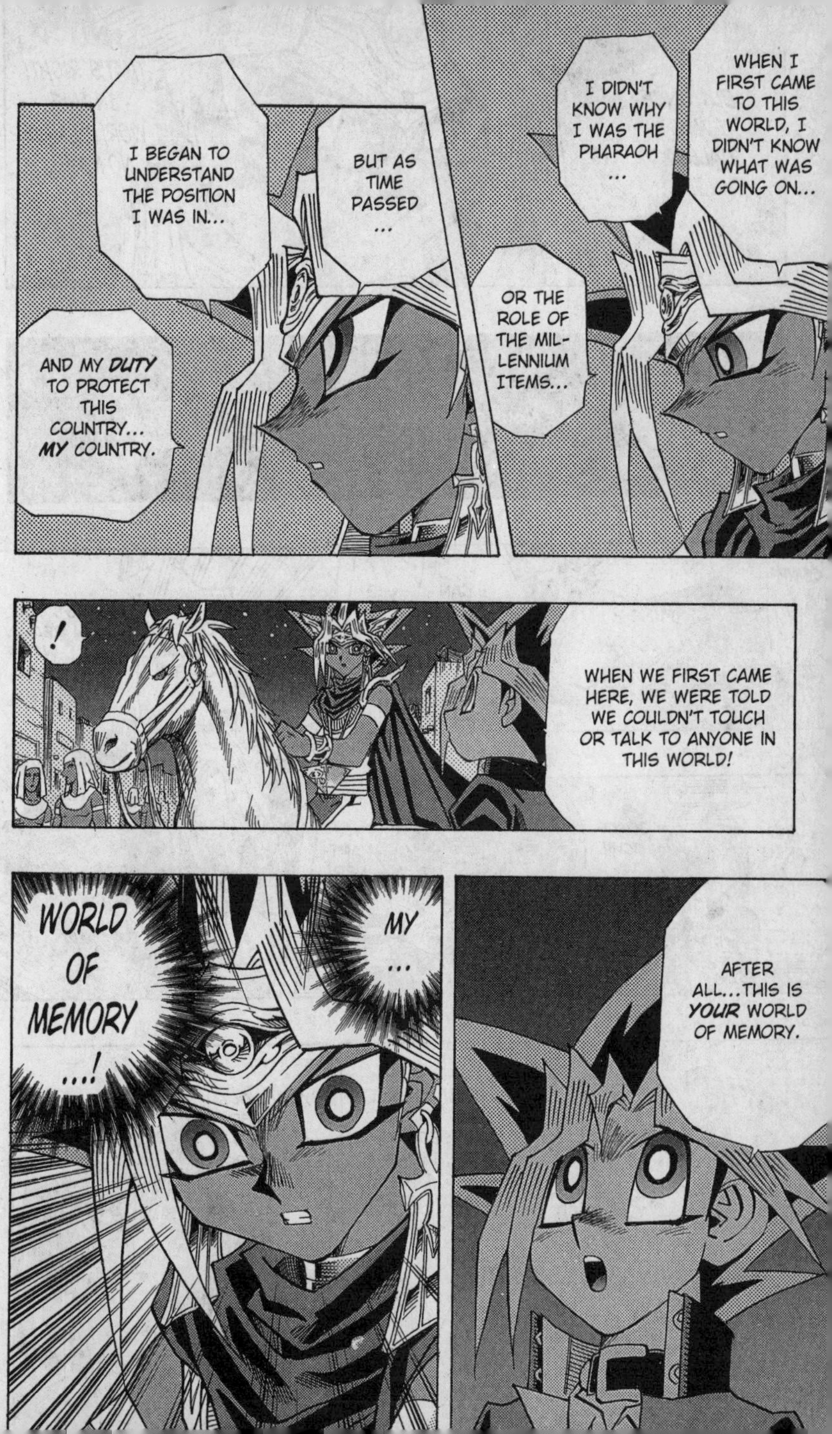
WHEN I FIRST CAME TO THIS WORLD, I DIDN'T KNOW WHAT WAS GOING ON...
I DIDN'T KNOW WHY I WAS THE PHARAOH ...
OR THE ROLE OF THE MIL-LENNIUM ITEMS...
BUT AS TIME PASSED ...
I BEGAN TO UNDERSTAND THE POSITION I WAS IN...
AND MY *DUTY* TO PROTECT THIS COUNTRY... *MY* COUNTRY.
WHEN WE FIRST CAME HERE, WE WERE TOLD WE COULDN'T TOUCH OR TALK TO ANYONE IN THIS WORLD!
!
AFTER ALL...THIS IS *YOUR* WORLD OF MEMORY.
MY ...
WORLD OF MEMORY ...!

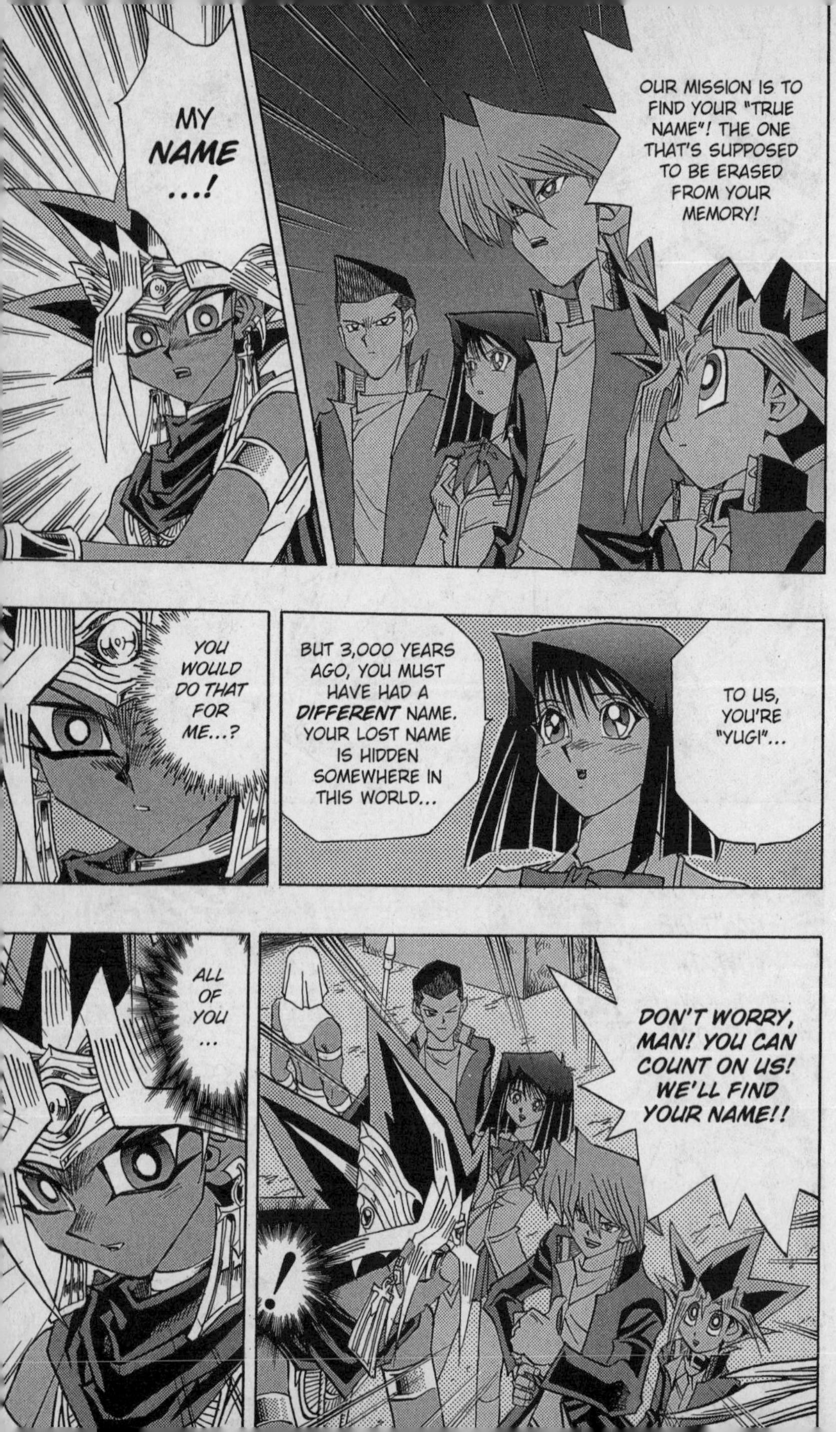

OUR MISSION IS TO FIND YOUR "TRUE NAME"! THE ONE THAT'S SUPPOSED TO BE ERASED FROM YOUR MEMORY!
MY NAME ...!
TO US, YOU'RE "YUGI"...
BUT 3,000 YEARS AGO, YOU MUST HAVE HAD A DIFFERENT NAME. YOUR LOST NAME IS HIDDEN SOMEWHERE IN THIS WORLD...
YOU WOULD DO THAT FOR ME...?
DON'T WORRY, MAN! YOU CAN COUNT ON US! WE'LL FIND YOUR NAME!!
!
ALL OF YOU ...

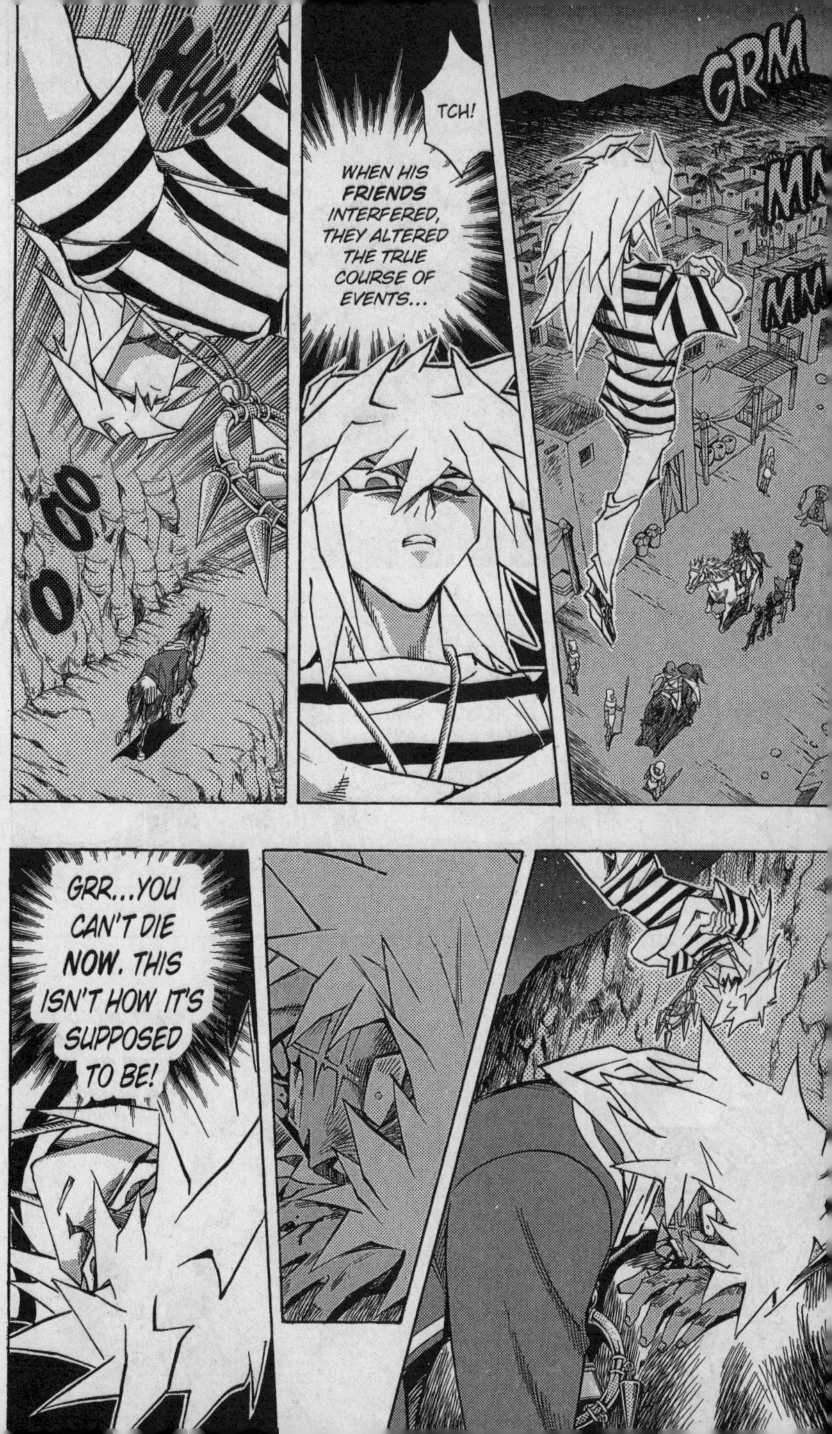
GRM
MMM
MMM
TCH!
WHEN HIS FRIENDS INTERFERED, THEY ALTERED THE TRUE COURSE OF EVENTS...
HOOOO
GRR...YOU CAN'T DIE NOW. THIS ISN'T HOW IT'S SUPPOSED TO BE!

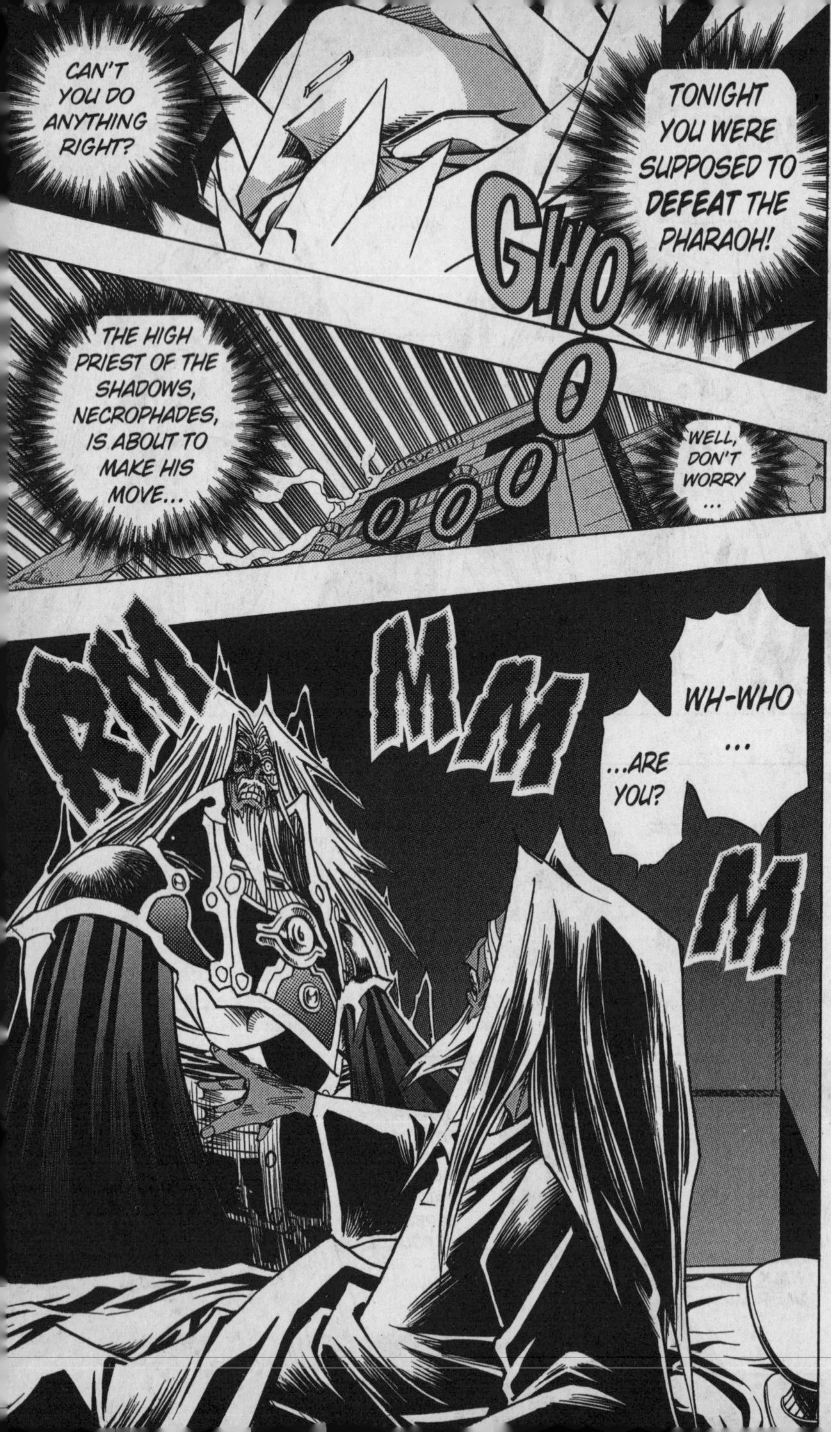
TONIGHT YOU WERE SUPPOSED TO DEFEAT THE PHARAOH!
CAN'T YOU DO ANYTHING RIGHT?
GHOOOOOO
WELL, DON'T WORRY ...
THE HIGH PRIEST OF THE SHADOWS, NECROPHADES, IS ABOUT TO MAKE HIS MOVE...
WH-WHO ...
...ARE YOU?
RMMMM

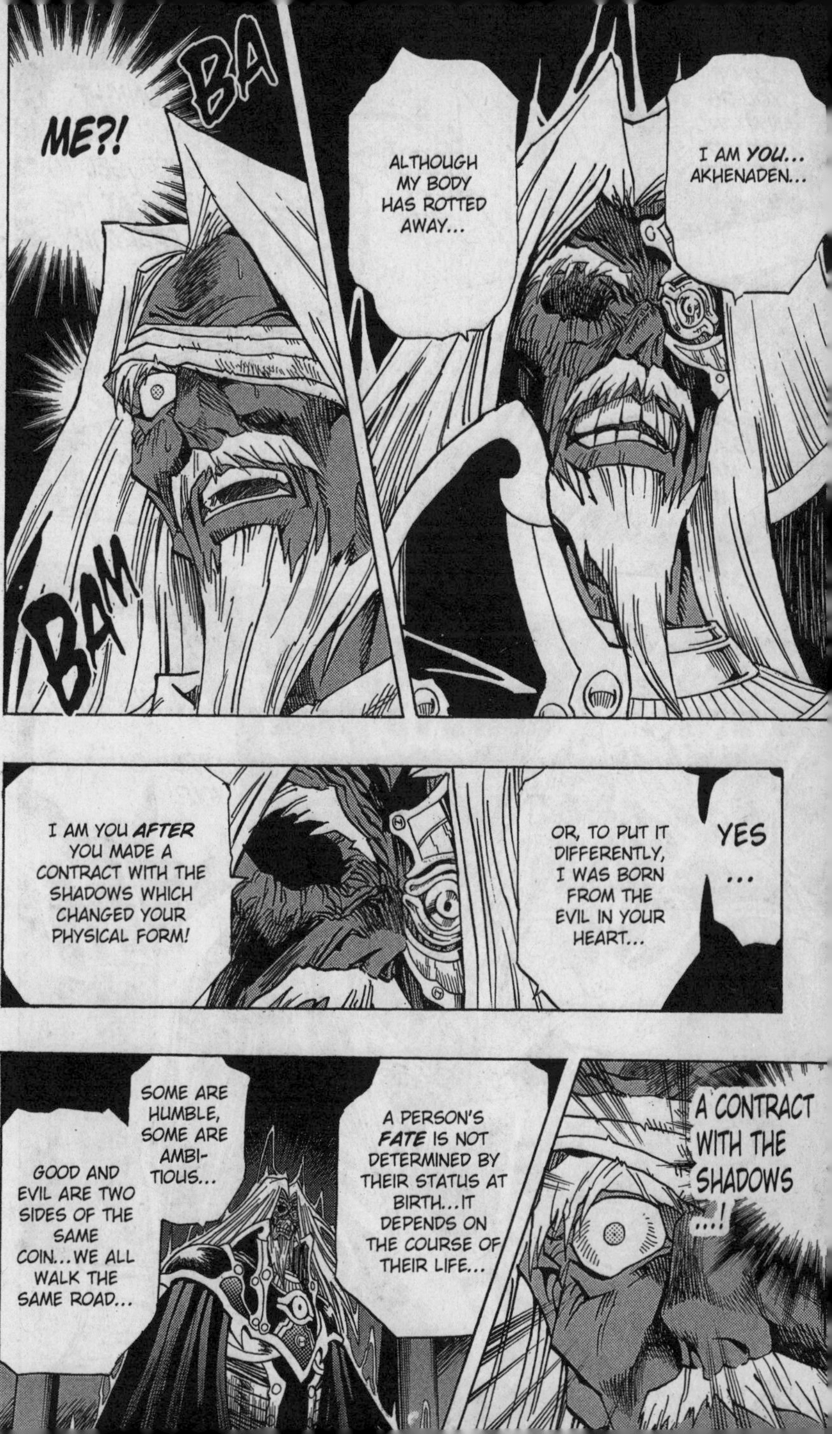
I AM YOU... AKHENADEN...
ALTHOUGH MY BODY HAS ROTTED AWAY...
BA
ME?!
BAM
YES ...
OR, TO PUT IT DIFFERENTLY, I WAS BORN FROM THE EVIL IN YOUR HEART...
I AM YOU AFTER YOU MADE A CONTRACT WITH THE SHADOWS WHICH CHANGED YOUR PHYSICAL FORM!
A CONTRACT WITH THE SHADOWS ...!
A PERSON'S FATE IS NOT DETERMINED BY THEIR STATUS AT BIRTH... IT DEPENDS ON THE COURSE OF THEIR LIFE...
SOME ARE HUMBLE, SOME ARE AMBITIOUS...
GOOD AND EVIL ARE TWO SIDES OF THE SAME COIN... WE ALL WALK THE SAME ROAD...

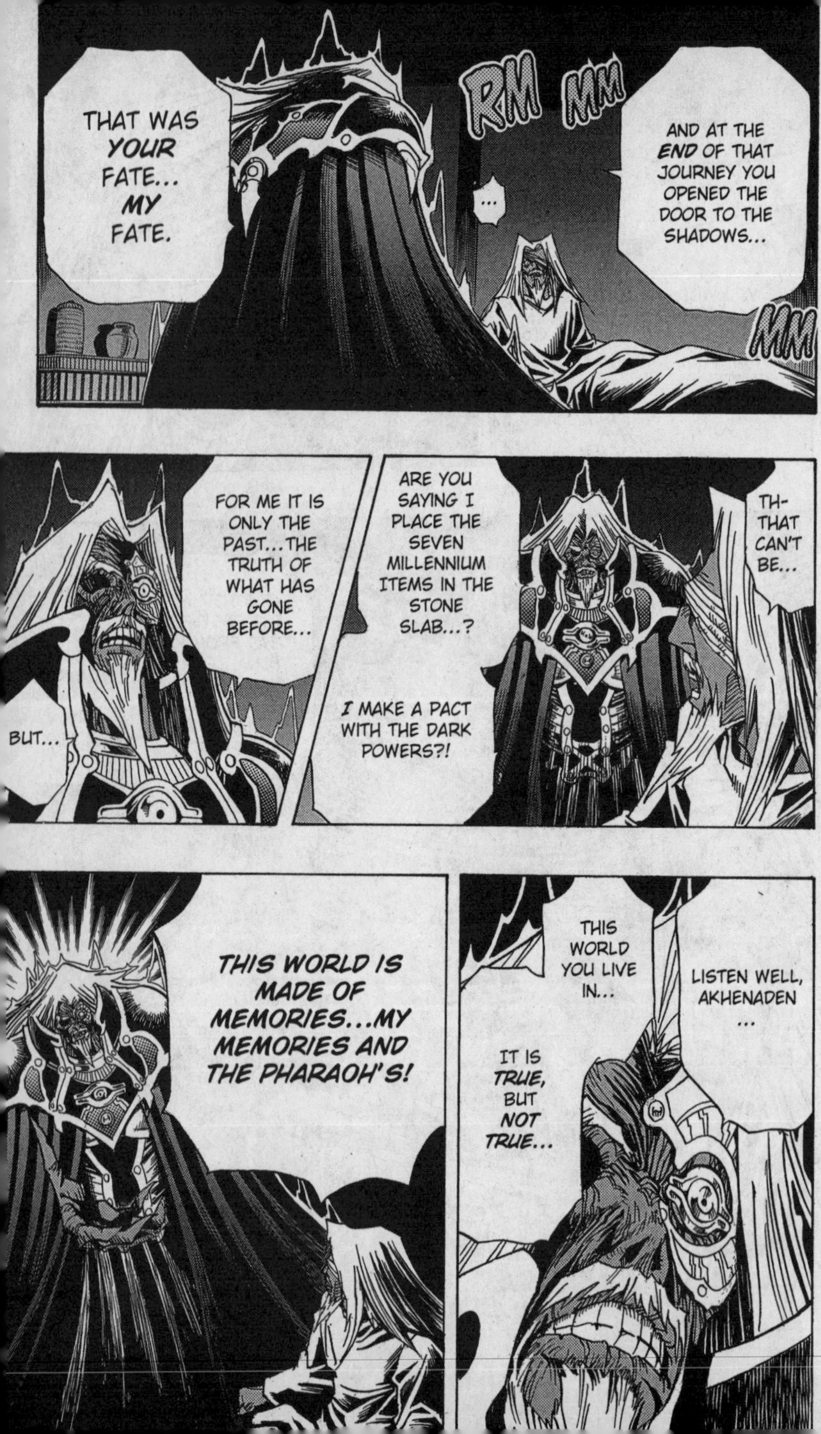
AND AT THE END OF THAT JOURNEY YOU OPENED THE DOOR TO THE SHADOWS...
RM MM MM
...
THAT WAS YOUR FATE... MY FATE.
TH-THAT CAN'T BE...
ARE YOU SAYING I PLACE THE SEVEN MILLENNIUM ITEMS IN THE STONE SLAB...?
I MAKE A PACT WITH THE DARK POWERS?!
FOR ME IT IS ONLY THE PAST...THE TRUTH OF WHAT HAS GONE BEFORE...
BUT...
LISTEN WELL, AKHENADEN...
THIS WORLD YOU LIVE IN...
IT IS TRUE, BUT NOT TRUE...
THIS WORLD IS MADE OF MEMORIES...MY MEMORIES AND THE PHARAOH'S!

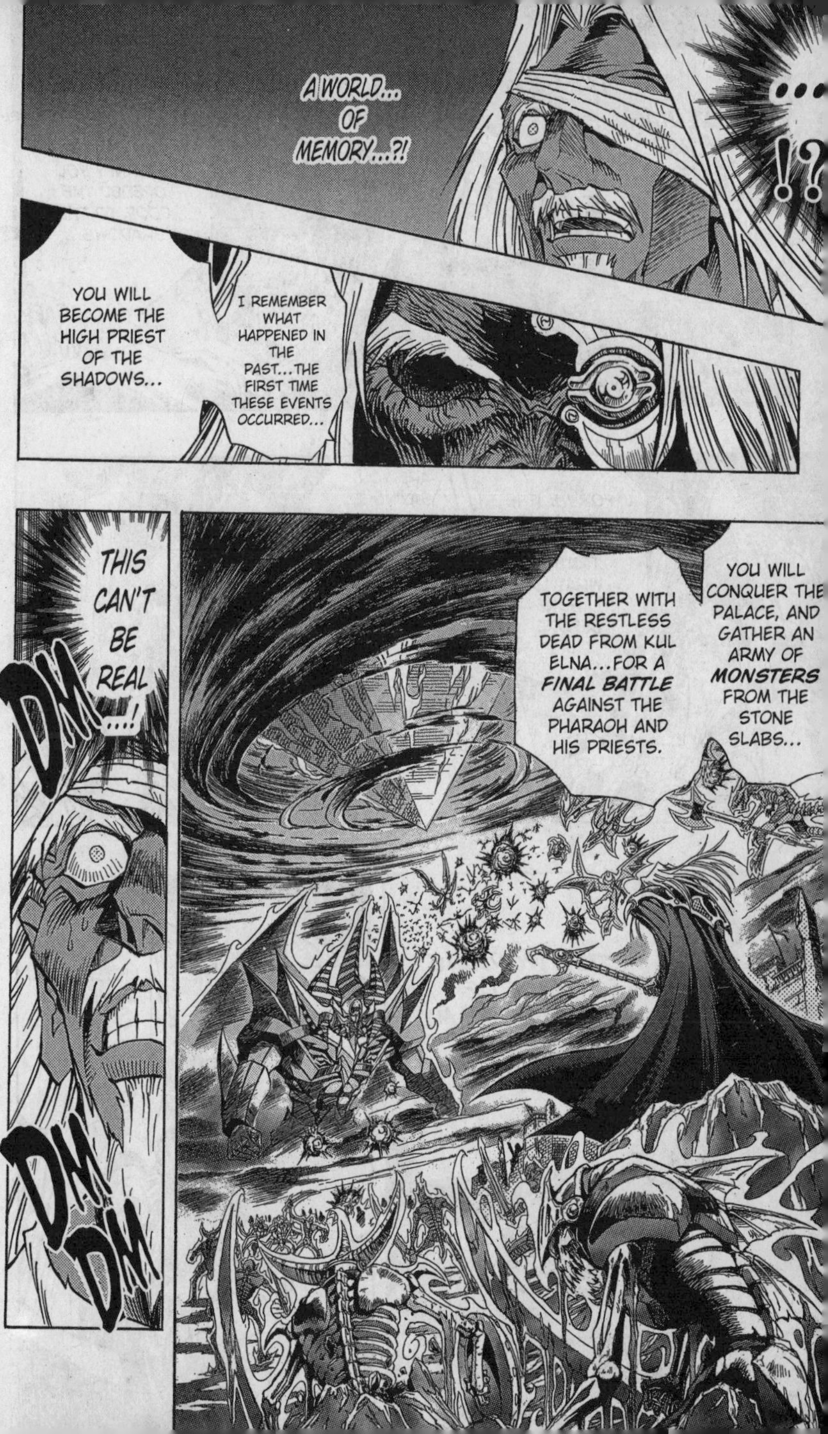

...!?
A WORLD... OF MEMORY...?!
I REMEMBER WHAT HAPPENED IN THE PAST...THE FIRST TIME THESE EVENTS OCCURRED...
YOU WILL BECOME THE HIGH PRIEST OF THE SHADOWS...
YOU WILL CONQUER THE PALACE, AND GATHER AN ARMY OF MONSTERS FROM THE STONE SLABS...
TOGETHER WITH THE RESTLESS DEAD FROM KUL ELNA...FOR A FINAL BATTLE AGAINST THE PHARAOH AND HIS PRIESTS.
THIS CAN'T BE REAL...!!
DM
DM DM

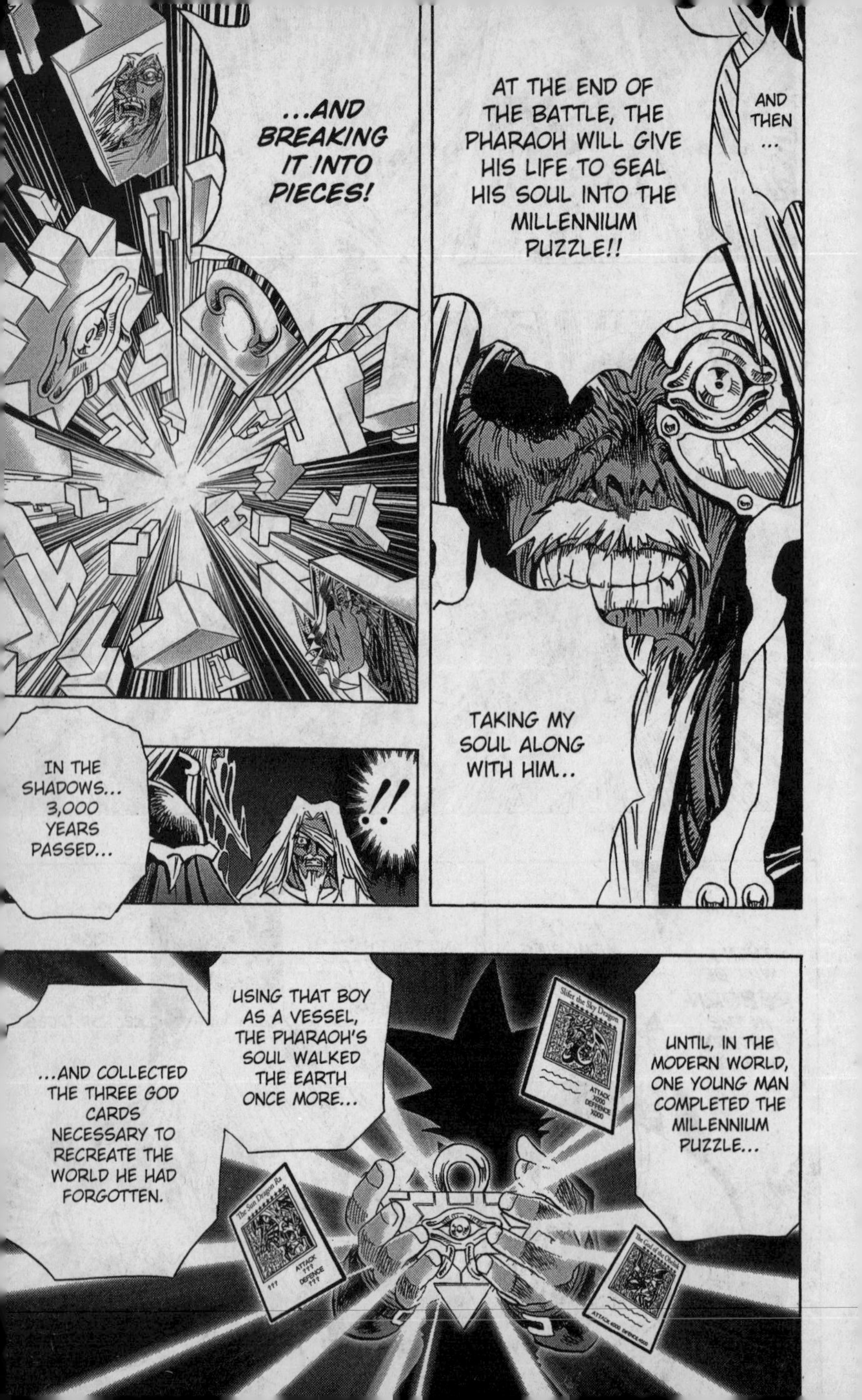
AND THEN ...
AT THE END OF THE BATTLE, THE PHARAOH WILL GIVE HIS LIFE TO SEAL HIS SOUL INTO THE MILLENNIUM PUZZLE!!
...AND BREAKING IT INTO PIECES!
TAKING MY SOUL ALONG WITH HIM...
!!
IN THE SHADOWS... 3,000 YEARS PASSED...
UNTIL, IN THE MODERN WORLD, ONE YOUNG MAN COMPLETED THE MILLENNIUM PUZZLE...
Slifer the Sky Dragon
USING THAT BOY AS A VESSEL, THE PHARAOH'S SOUL WALKED THE EARTH ONCE MORE...
...AND COLLECTED THE THREE GOD CARDS NECESSARY TO RECREATE THE WORLD HE HAD FORGOTTEN.
The Sun Dragon Ra

THIS WORLD EXISTS WITHIN THE MILLENNIUM PUZZLE!!
...
A WORLD... WITHIN THE PUZZLE ...?!
RM
RM
RM
RIGHT NOW...THE MEMORIES OF I, NECROPHADES ...
AND THE PHARAOH ARE MERGED TO CREATE THIS WORLD...
IF MY MEMORIES GAIN CONTROL...
THEN I WILL BE REBORN IN THE MODERN WORLD!

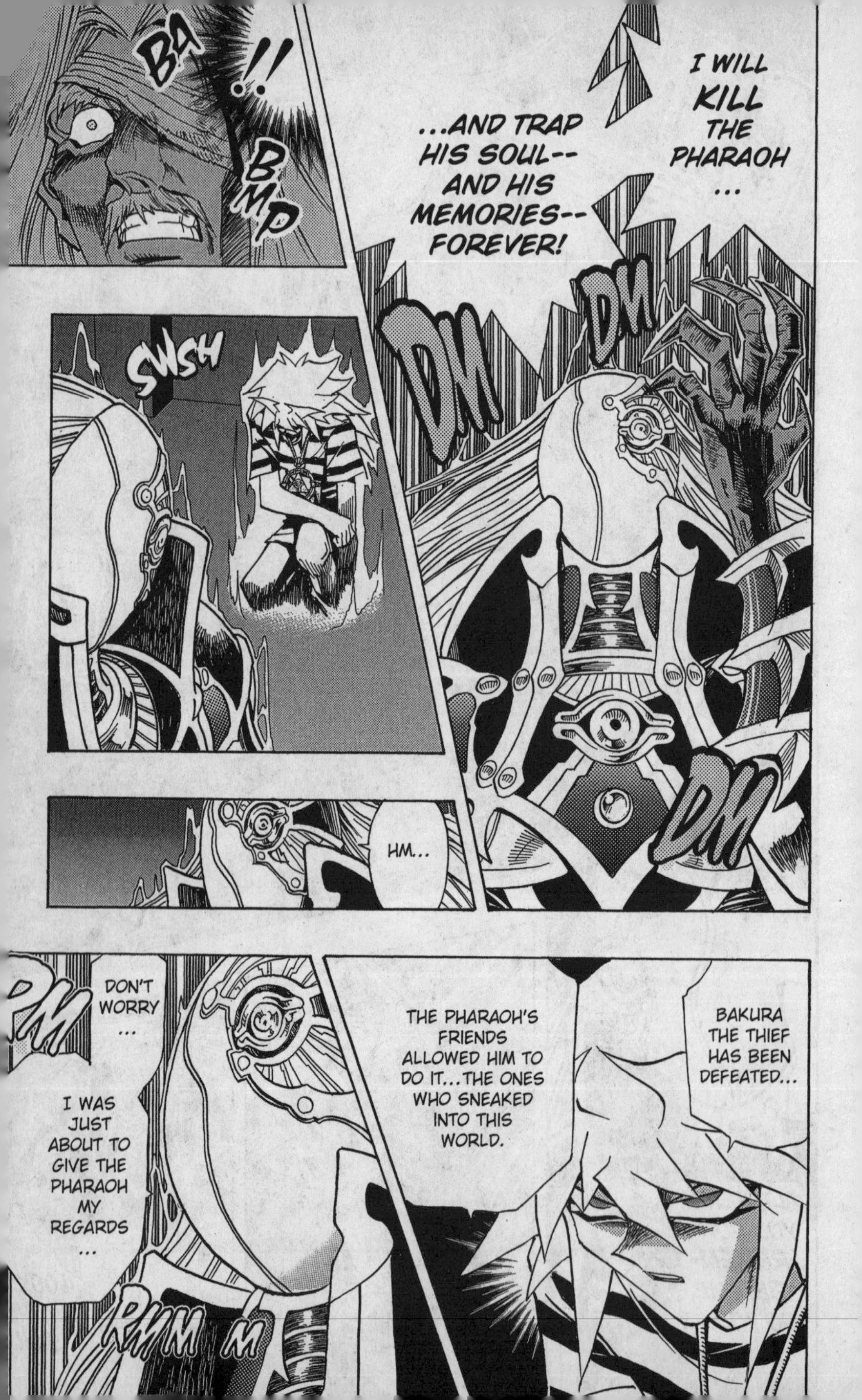
I WILL KILL THE PHARAOH ...
...AND TRAP HIS SOUL-- AND HIS MEMORIES-- FOREVER!
BA !!
BMP
DM
DM
DM
SWSH
HM...
BAKURA THE THIEF HAS BEEN DEFEATED...
THE PHARAOH'S FRIENDS ALLOWED HIM TO DO IT...THE ONES WHO SNEAKED INTO THIS WORLD.
DON'T WORRY ...
I WAS JUST ABOUT TO GIVE THE PHARAOH MY REGARDS ...
RMM M

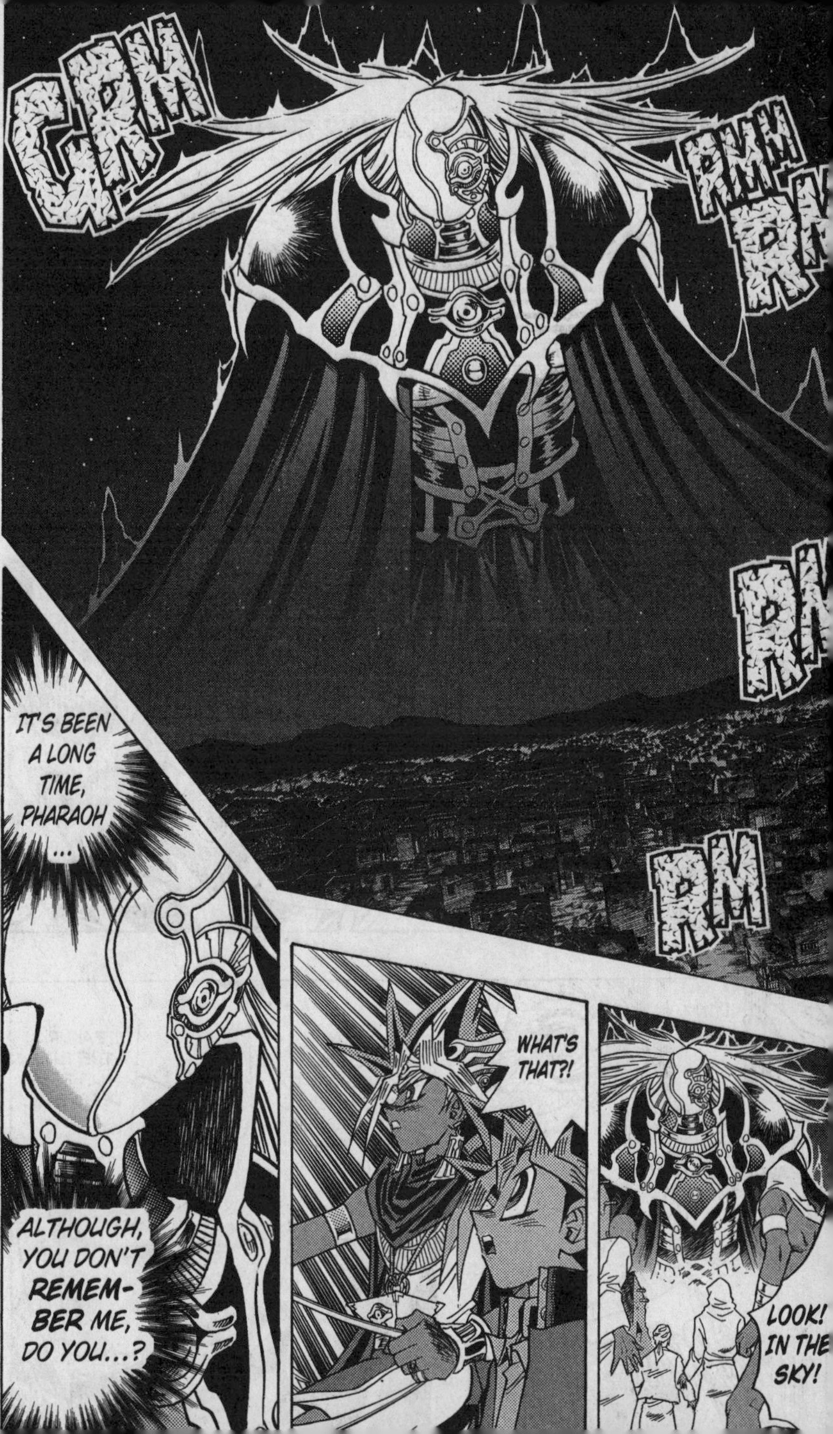

RMM
GRM
RM
LOOK! IN THE SKY!
WHAT'S THAT?!
IT'S BEEN A LONG TIME, PHARAOH ...
ALTHOUGH, YOU DON'T REMEM-BER ME, DO YOU...?

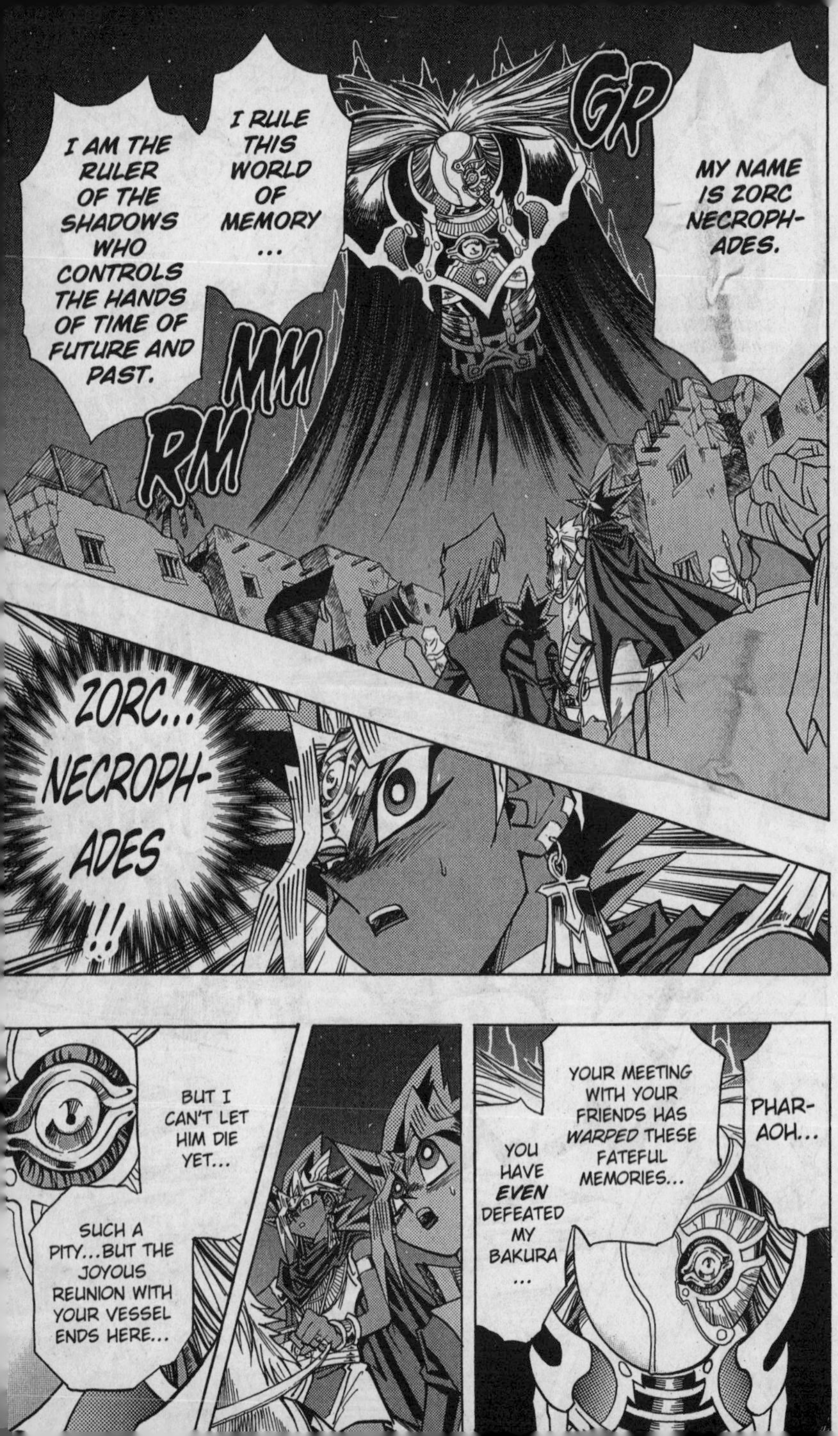
MY NAME IS ZORC NECROPH-ADES.
GR
I RULE THIS WORLD OF MEMORY ...
I AM THE RULER OF THE SHADOWS WHO CONTROLS THE HANDS OF TIME OF FUTURE AND PAST.
MM
RM
ZORC... NECROPH-ADES !!
PHAR-AOH...
YOUR MEETING WITH YOUR FRIENDS HAS WARPED THESE FATEFUL MEMORIES...
YOU HAVE EVEN DEFEATED MY BAKURA ...
BUT I CAN'T LET HIM DIE YET...
SUCH A PITY...BUT THE JOYOUS REUNION WITH YOUR VESSEL ENDS HERE...

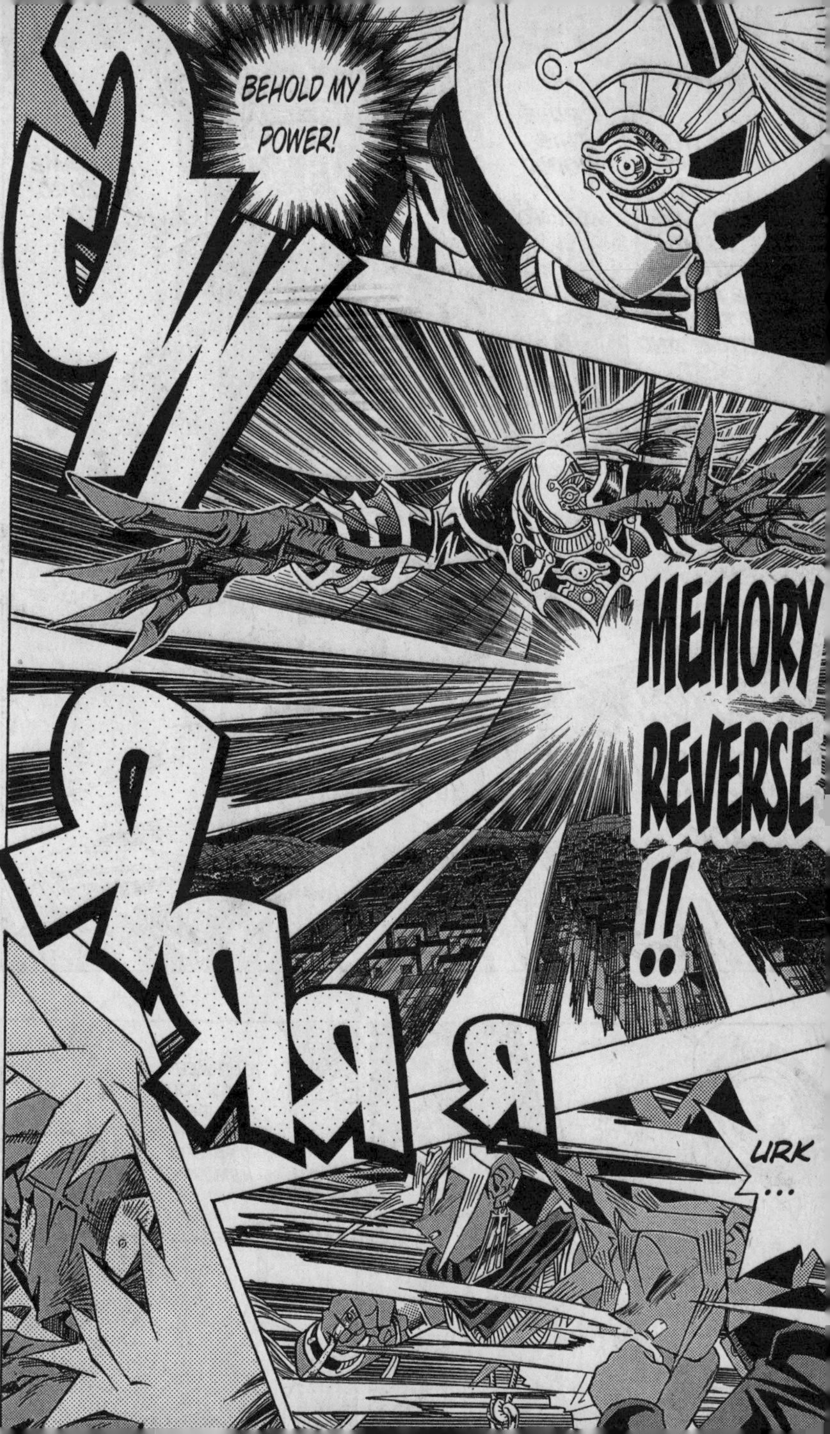
BEHOLD MY POWER!
MEMORY REVERSE!!
URK...

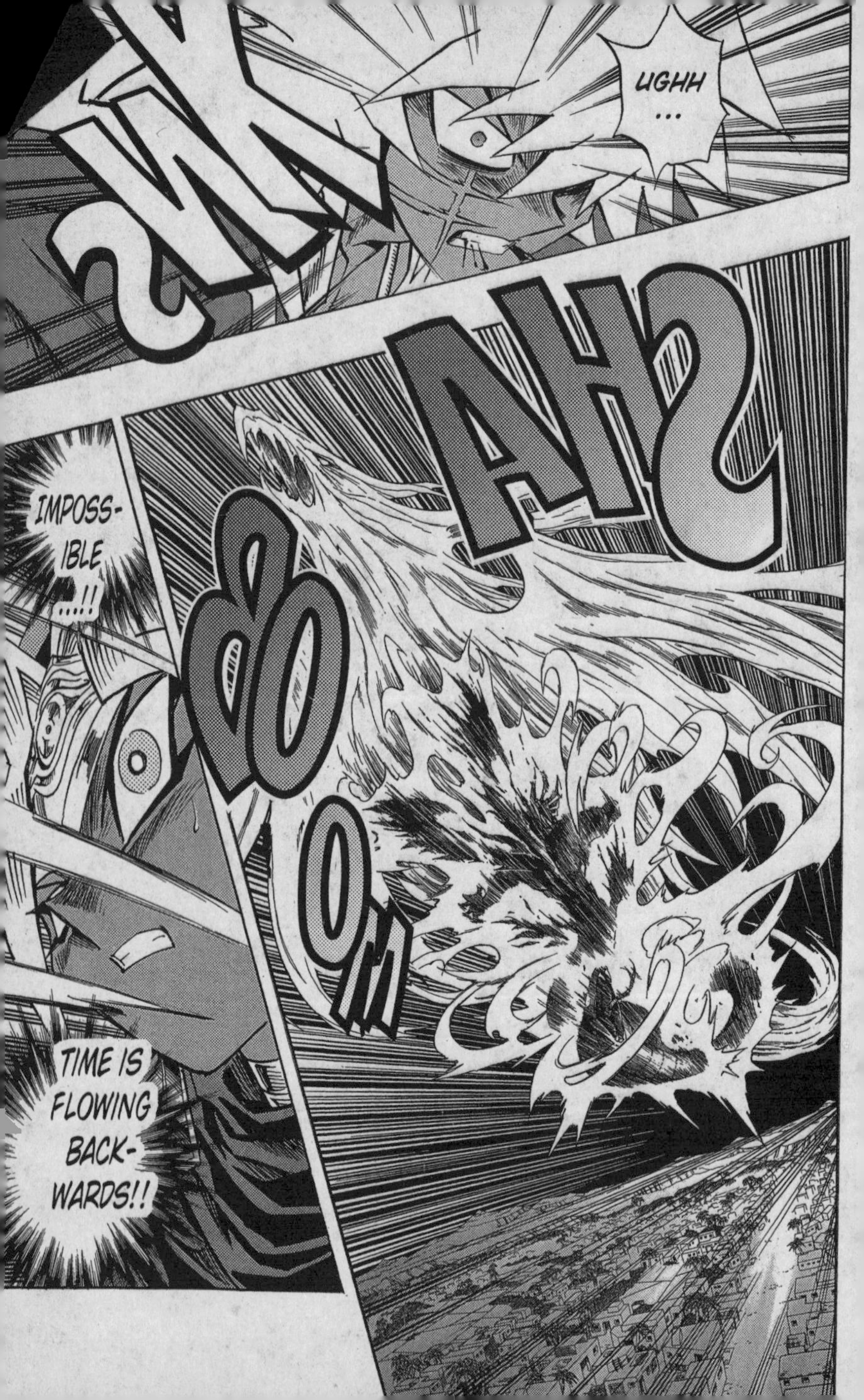
UGHH ...
IMPOSS-IBLE ...!!
TIME IS FLOWING BACK-WARDS!!

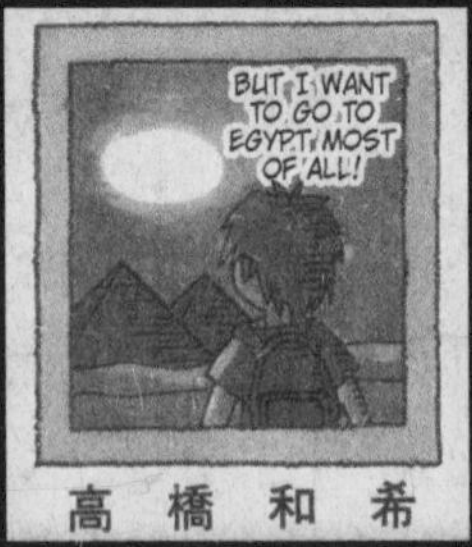
BUT I WANT TO GO TO EGYPT MOST OF ALL!
高橋和希

THIS SUMMER, THE YU-GI-OH! WORLD CHAMPIONSHIP WAS HELD IN NEW YORK CITY. TEN THOUSAND PEOPLE CRAMMED INTO THE AUDITORIUM TO CHEER ON THE DUELISTS' WHITE-HOT BATTLES!

IT'S BEEN SEVEN YEARS SINCE THIS MANGA BEGAN. I SUDDENLY REALIZED THAT YU-GI-OH! HAS SPREAD AROUND THE WORLD TO 30 COUNTRIES, AND HAS BECOME A WORK THAT TRANSCENDS BORDERS. I'M SO GRATEFUL AND MOVED!

NEXT SPRING, I'D LIKE TO TRAVEL AROUND THE WORLD TO SEE YU-GI-OH! IN ALL THE DIFFERENT COUNTRIES WITH MY OWN EYES.

—KAZUKI TAKAHASHI, 2003

SHONEN JUMP MANGA

Yu-Gi-Oh! Millennium World

Vol. 35

BIRTH OF THE DRAGON

STORY AND ART BY

KAZUKI TAKAHASHI

THE MAIN CHARACTERS

KATSUYA JONOUCHI

BOBASA   **ANZU MAZAKI**   **HIROTO HONDA**

YUGI MUTOU

THE STORY SO FAR...

Shy 10th-grader Yugi spent most of his time alone playing games…until he solved the Millennium Puzzle, a mysterious Egyptian artifact. Possessed by the puzzle, Yugi developed an alter ego: Yu-Gi-Oh, the King of Games, the soul of a pharaoh from ancient Egypt!

Discovering that the collectible card game "Duel Monsters" was of Ancient Egyptian origin, Yu-Gi-Oh collected the three Egyptian God Cards—Slifer the Sky Dragon, the God of the Obelisk, and the Sun Dragon Ra—and used them to travel into the "world of memories" of his own life 3,000 years ago. There, he found that he was the pharaoh, served by six priests who used the Millennium Items to summon *ka*—spirits and monsters—from people's souls.

But the pharaoh's court was under attack by Bakura, a fiendish tomb-robber, who possessed the powerful spirit Diabound. Intent on toppling the dynasty, Bakura killed the priest Mahado and stole the Millennium Ring.

Meanwhile, with the help of the Egyptian mystic Bobasa, Yugi and his friends followed Yu-Gi-Oh into the "world of memories" in order to find the pharaoh's forgotten name. They showed up just in time to help Yu-Gi-Oh, giving him the strength to defeat Bakura.

But then, just when they thought it was all over, a terrible vision appeared in the sky. It was Zorc Necrophades…the evil high priest…who possesses the strangest power of all…

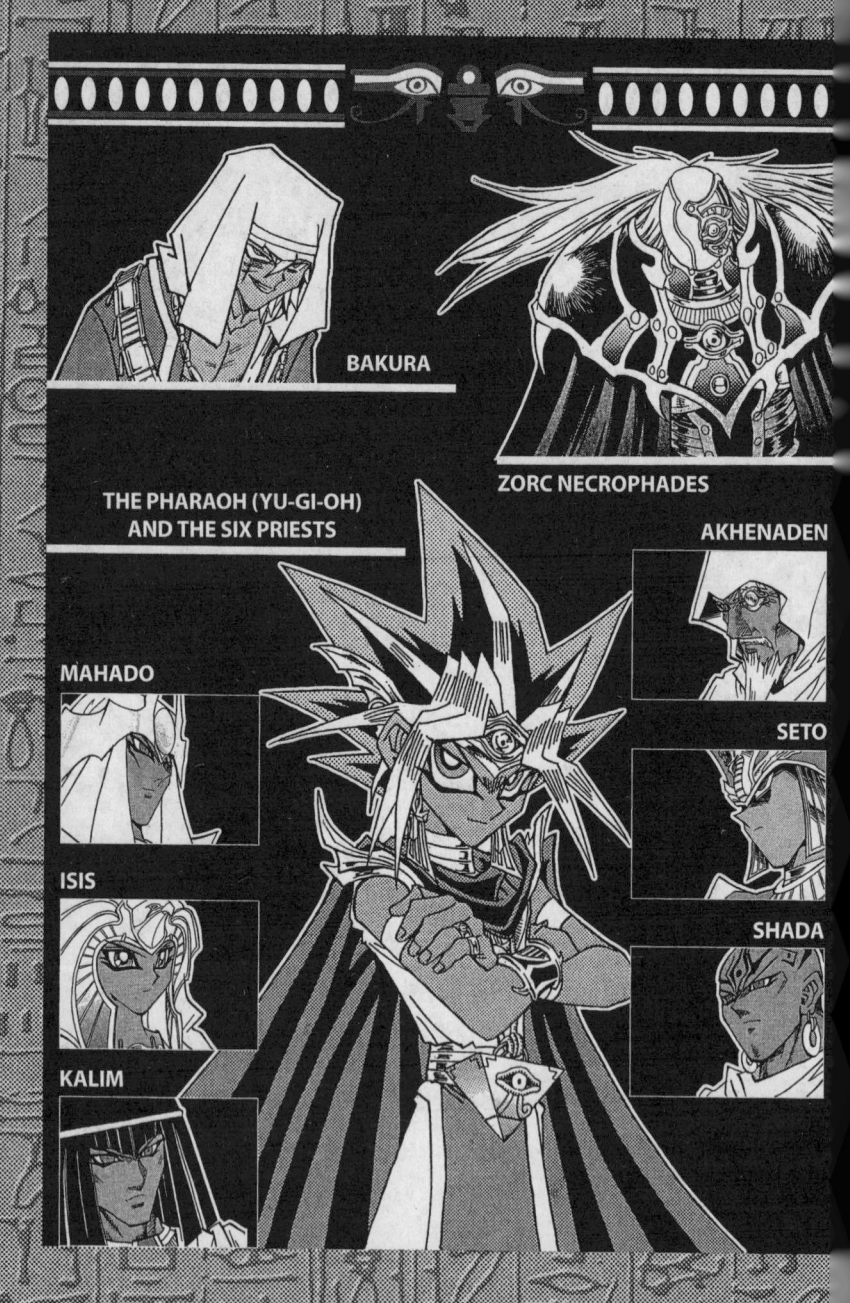

BAKURA

ZORC NECROPHADES

THE PHARAOH (YU-GI-OH)
AND THE SIX PRIESTS

AKHENADEN

MAHADO

SETO

ISIS

SHADA

KALIM

Yu-Gi-Oh! Millennium World

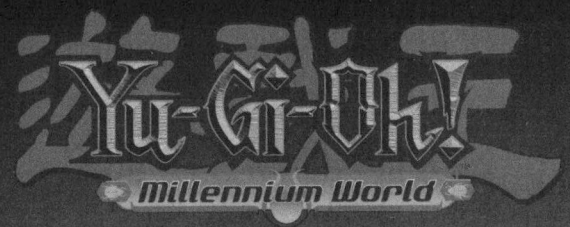

Vol. 35

CONTENTS

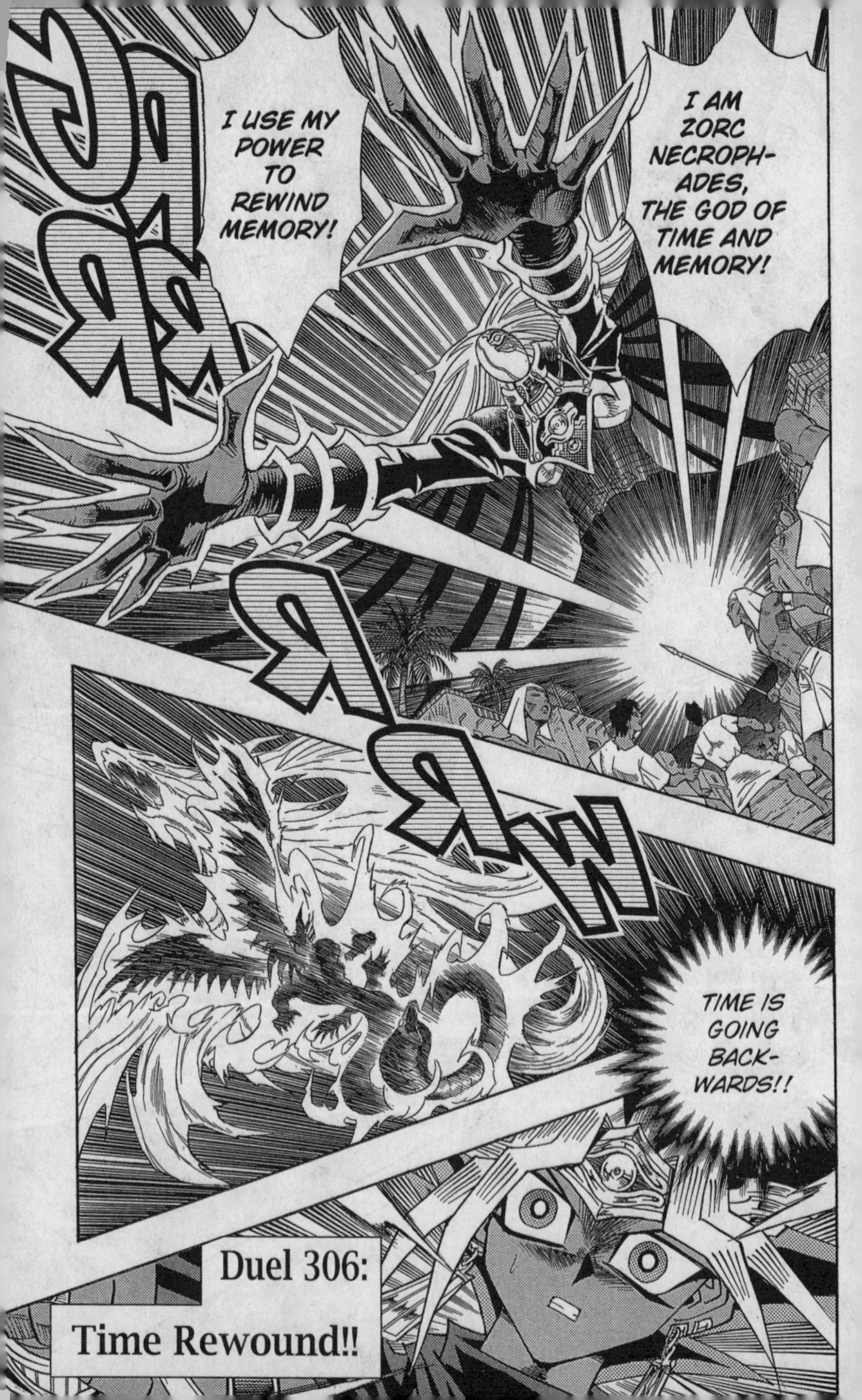
I AM ZORC NECROPH-ADES, THE GOD OF TIME AND MEMORY!
I USE MY POWER TO REWIND MEMORY!
TIME IS GOING BACK-WARDS!!
Duel 306:
Time Rewound!!

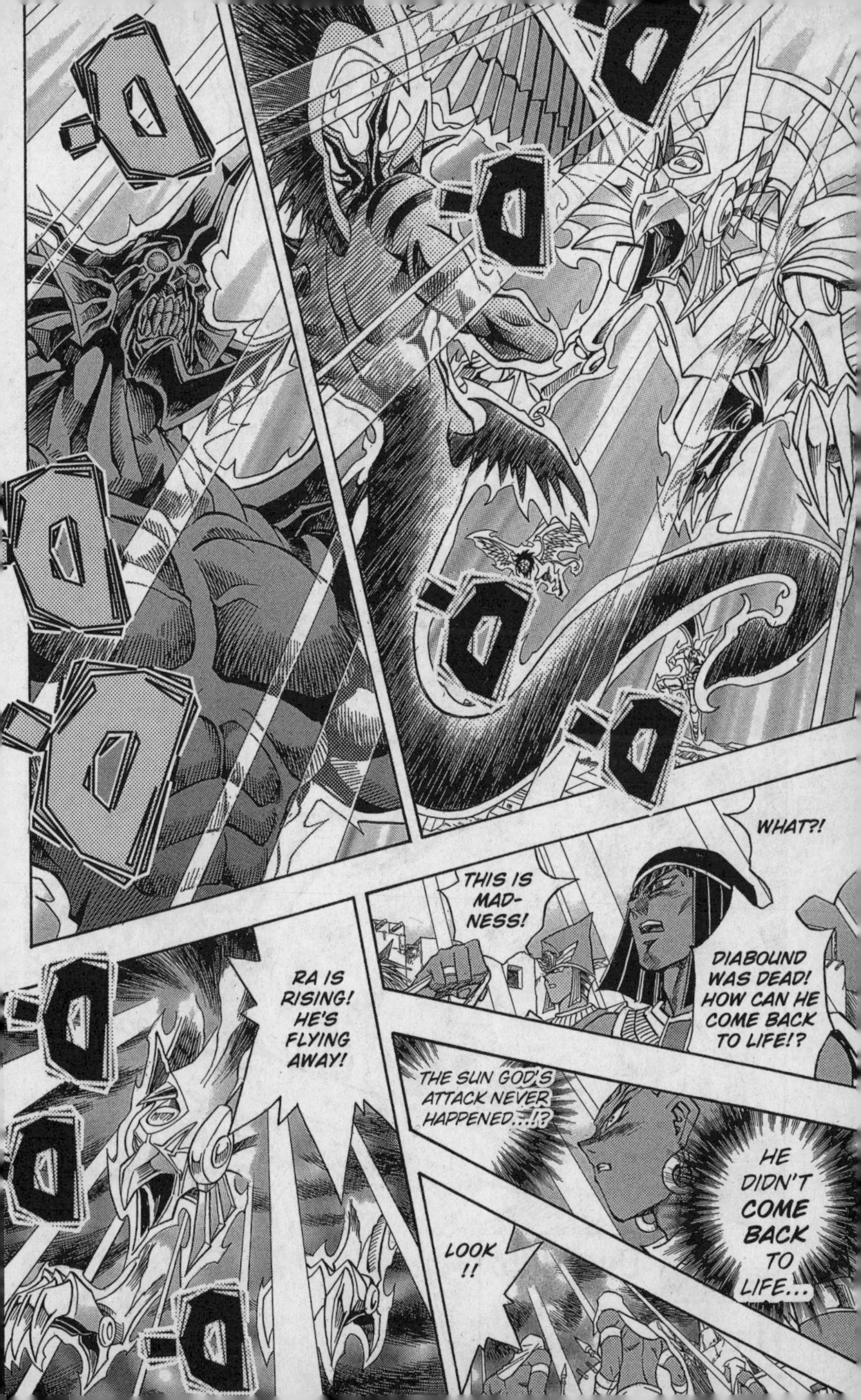
WHAT?!
DIABOUND WAS DEAD! HOW CAN HE COME BACK TO LIFE!?
THIS IS MADNESS!
THE SUN GOD'S ATTACK NEVER HAPPENED...!?
HE DIDN'T COME BACK TO LIFE...
LOOK !!
RA IS RISING! HE'S FLYING AWAY!

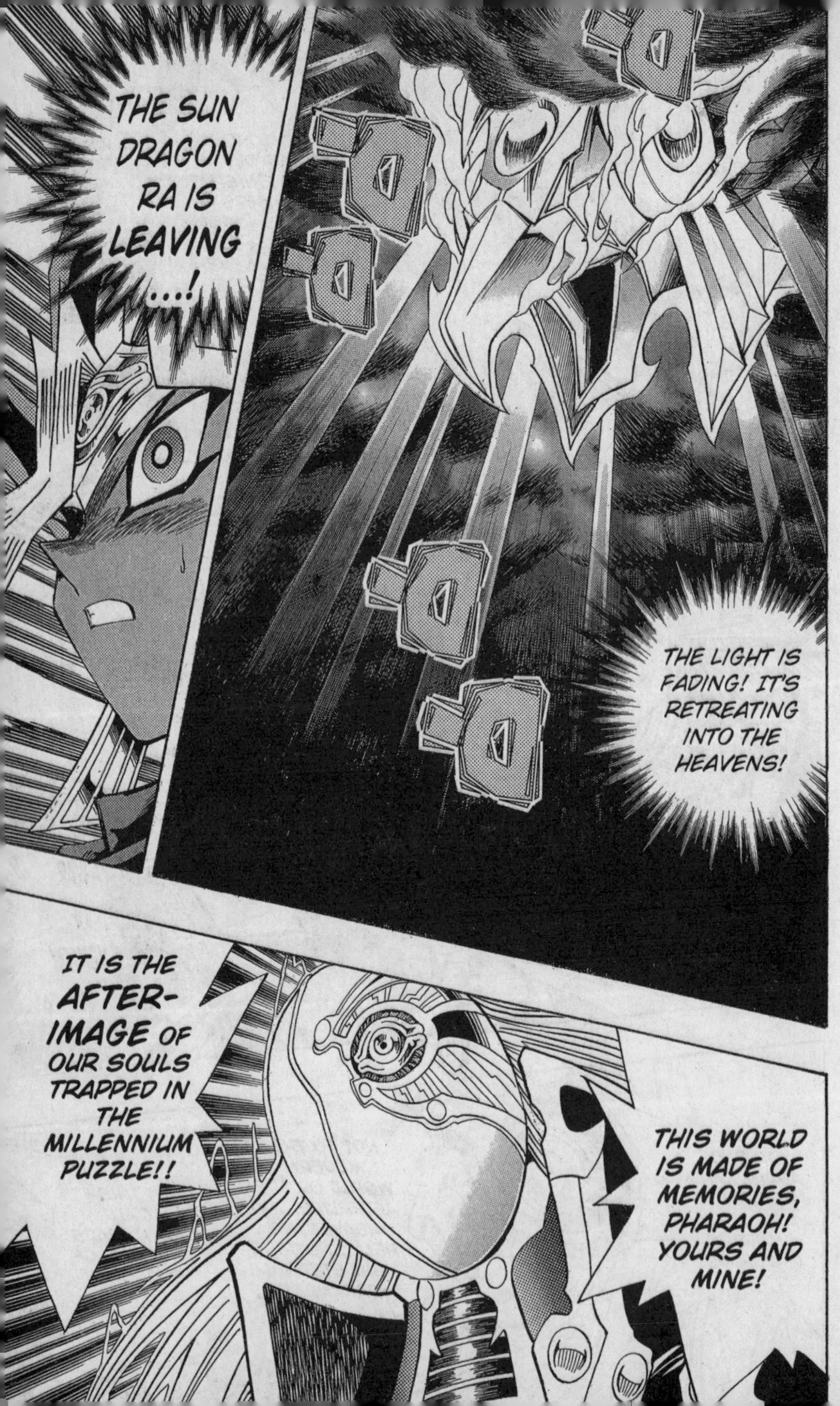
THE SUN DRAGON RA IS LEAVING ...!
THE LIGHT IS FADING! IT'S RETREATING INTO THE HEAVENS!
THIS WORLD IS MADE OF MEMORIES, PHARAOH! YOURS AND MINE!
IT IS THE AFTER-IMAGE OF OUR SOULS TRAPPED IN THE MILLENNIUM PUZZLE!!

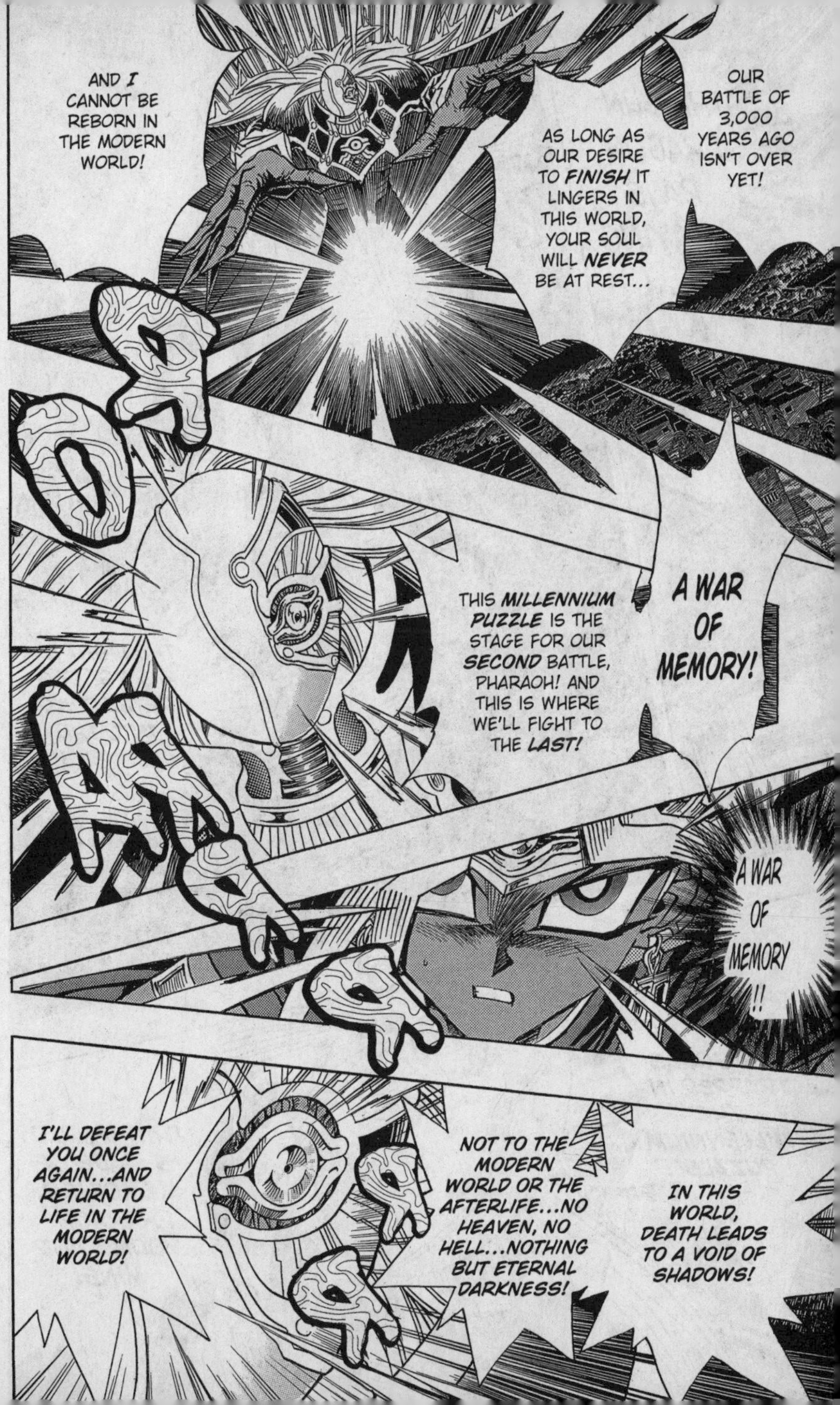
OUR BATTLE OF 3,000 YEARS AGO ISN'T OVER YET!
AS LONG AS OUR DESIRE TO *FINISH* IT LINGERS IN THIS WORLD, YOUR SOUL WILL *NEVER* BE AT REST...
AND *I* CANNOT BE REBORN IN THE MODERN WORLD!
A WAR OF MEMORY!
THIS *MILLENNIUM PUZZLE* IS THE STAGE FOR OUR *SECOND* BATTLE, PHARAOH! AND THIS IS WHERE WE'LL FIGHT TO THE *LAST!*
A WAR OF MEMORY!!
IN THIS WORLD, DEATH LEADS TO A VOID OF SHADOWS!
NOT TO THE MODERN WORLD OR THE AFTERLIFE...NO HEAVEN, NO HELL...NOTHING BUT ETERNAL DARKNESS!
I'LL DEFEAT YOU ONCE AGAIN...AND RETURN TO LIFE IN THE MODERN WORLD!

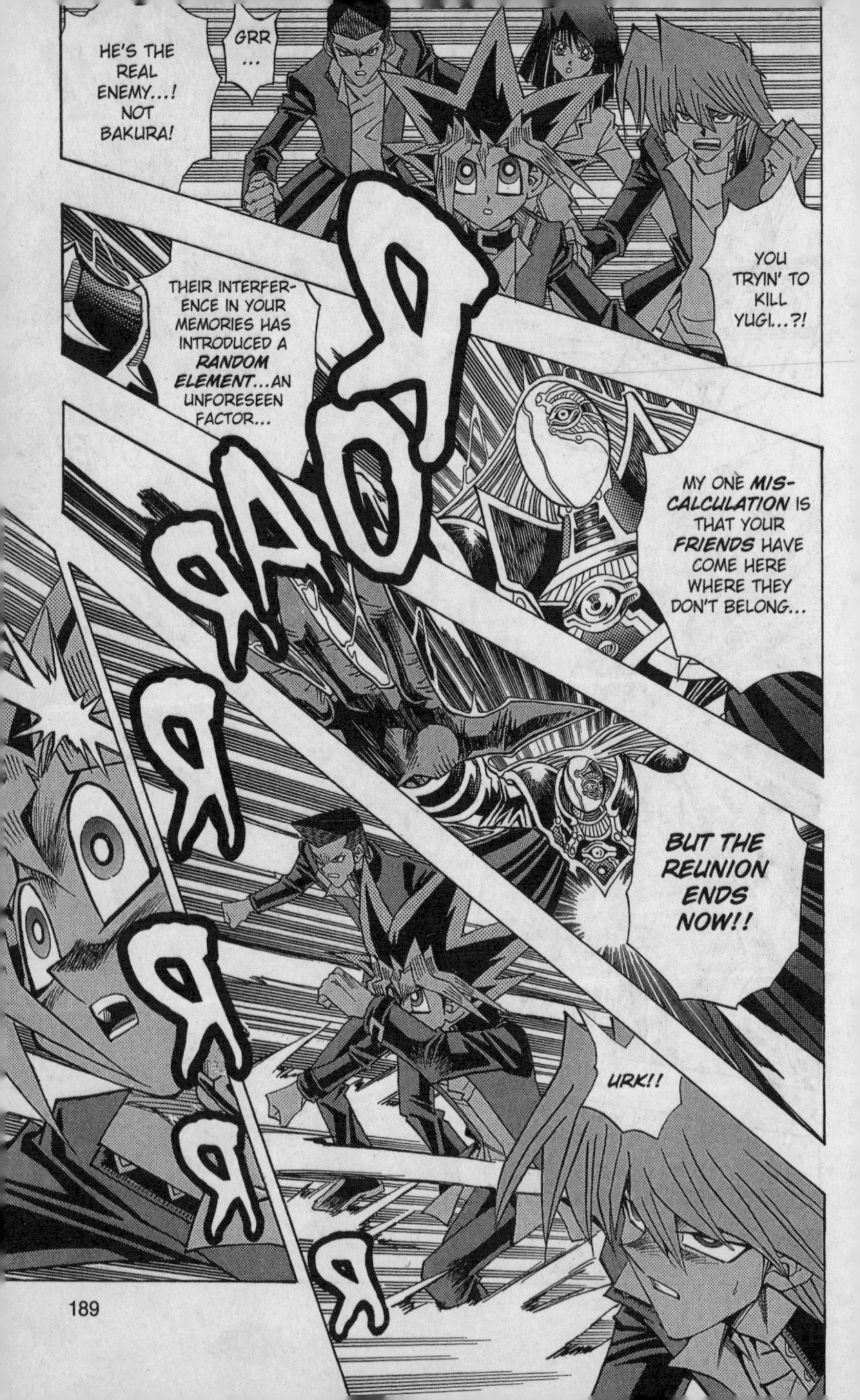
YOU TRYIN' TO KILL YUGI...?!
GRR...
HE'S THE REAL ENEMY...! NOT BAKURA!
THEIR INTERFERENCE IN YOUR MEMORIES HAS INTRODUCED A ***RANDOM ELEMENT***...AN UNFORESEEN FACTOR...
MY ONE ***MIS-CALCULATION*** IS THAT YOUR ***FRIENDS*** HAVE COME HERE WHERE THEY DON'T BELONG...
BUT THE REUNION ENDS NOW!!
URK!!
ROARRRRR

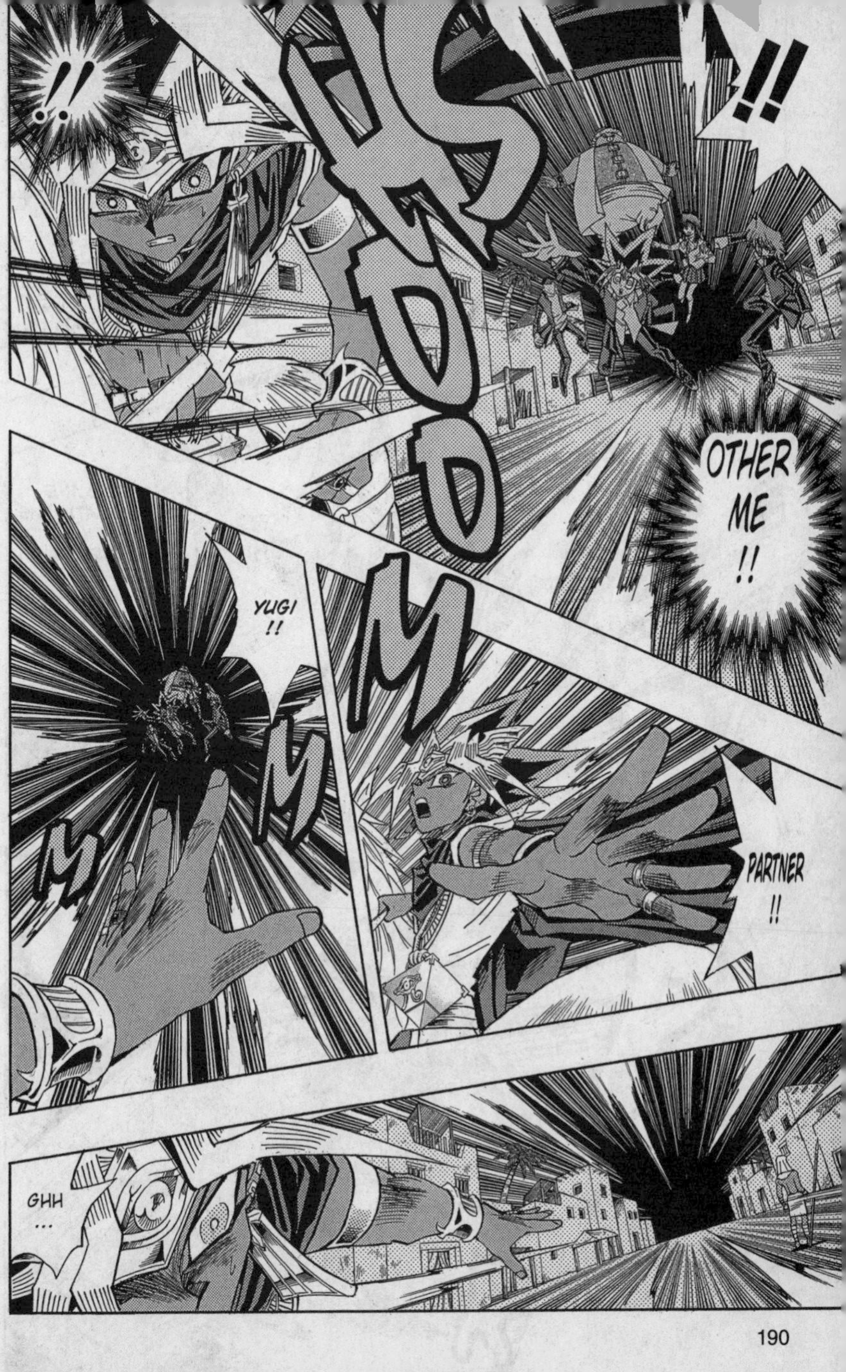
!!
!!
OTHER ME !!
PARTNER !!
YUGI !!
GHH ...

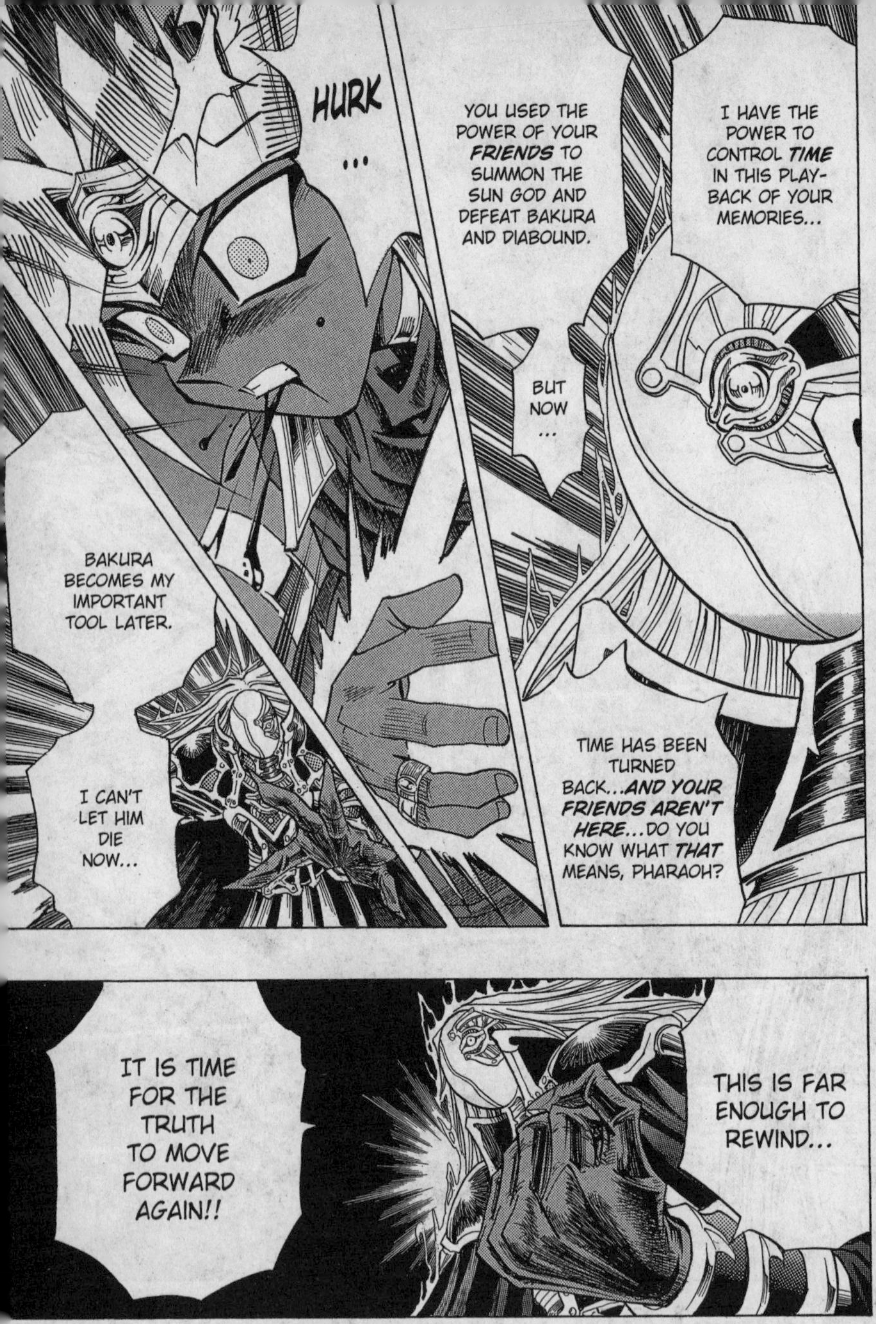
I HAVE THE POWER TO CONTROL TIME IN THIS PLAY-BACK OF YOUR MEMORIES...
YOU USED THE POWER OF YOUR FRIENDS TO SUMMON THE SUN GOD AND DEFEAT BAKURA AND DIABOUND.
BUT NOW ...
TIME HAS BEEN TURNED BACK...AND YOUR FRIENDS AREN'T HERE...DO YOU KNOW WHAT THAT MEANS, PHARAOH?
HURK
...
BAKURA BECOMES MY IMPORTANT TOOL LATER.
I CAN'T LET HIM DIE NOW...
THIS IS FAR ENOUGH TO REWIND...
IT IS TIME FOR THE TRUTH TO MOVE FORWARD AGAIN!!

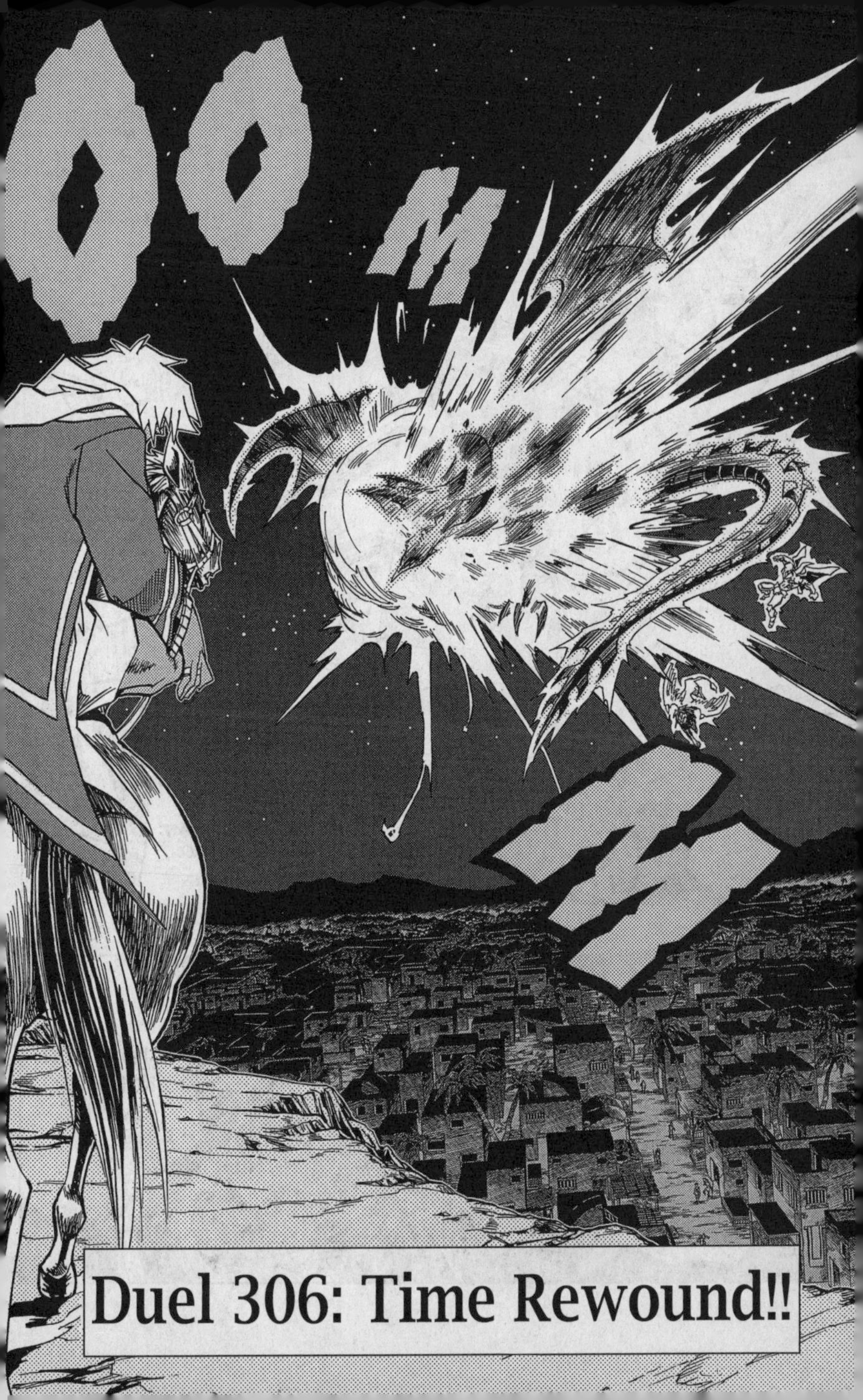
OOM
Duel 306: Time Rewound!!

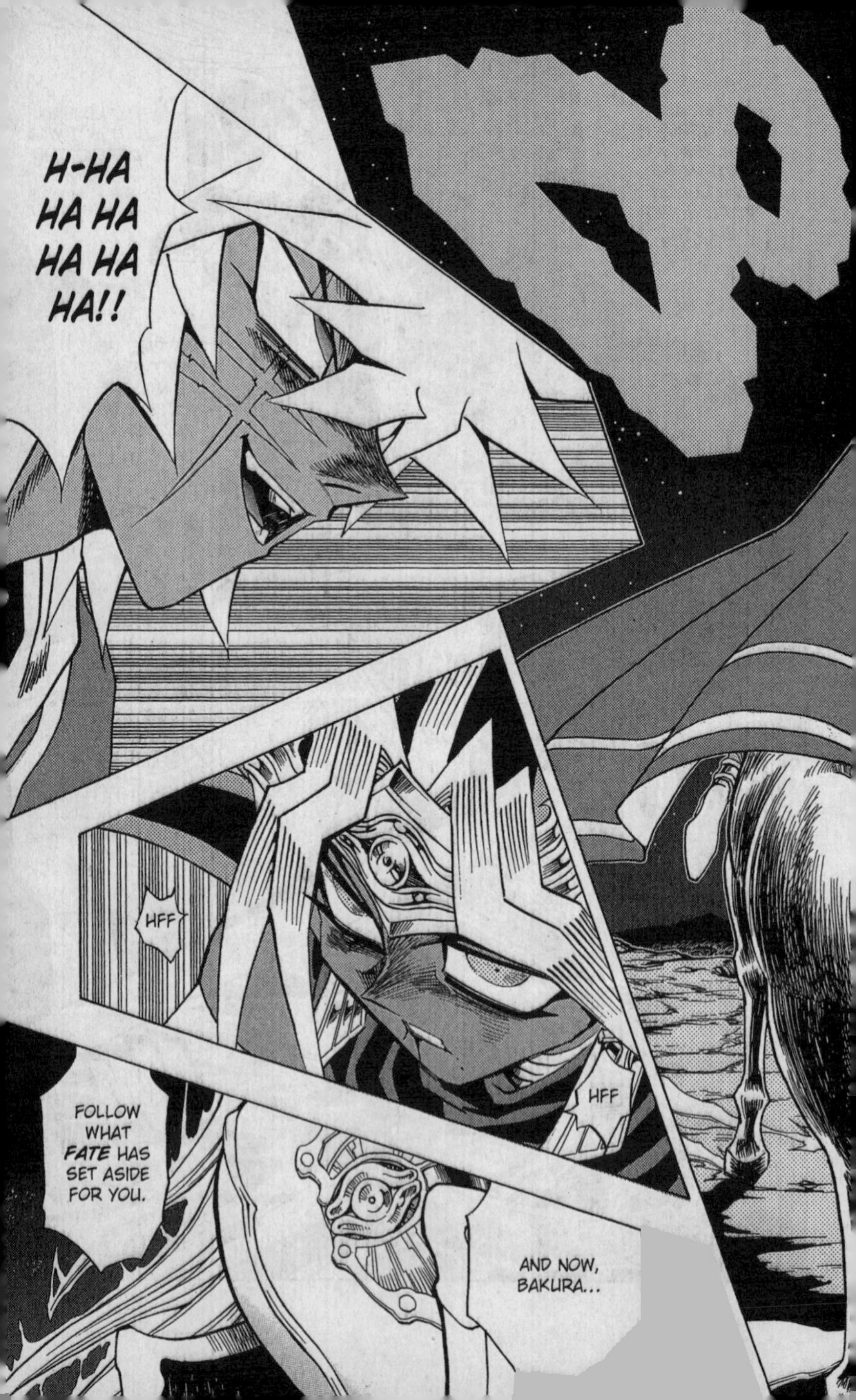
H-HA HA HA HA HA HA!!
HFF
HFF
FOLLOW WHAT FATE HAS SET ASIDE FOR YOU.
AND NOW, BAKURA...

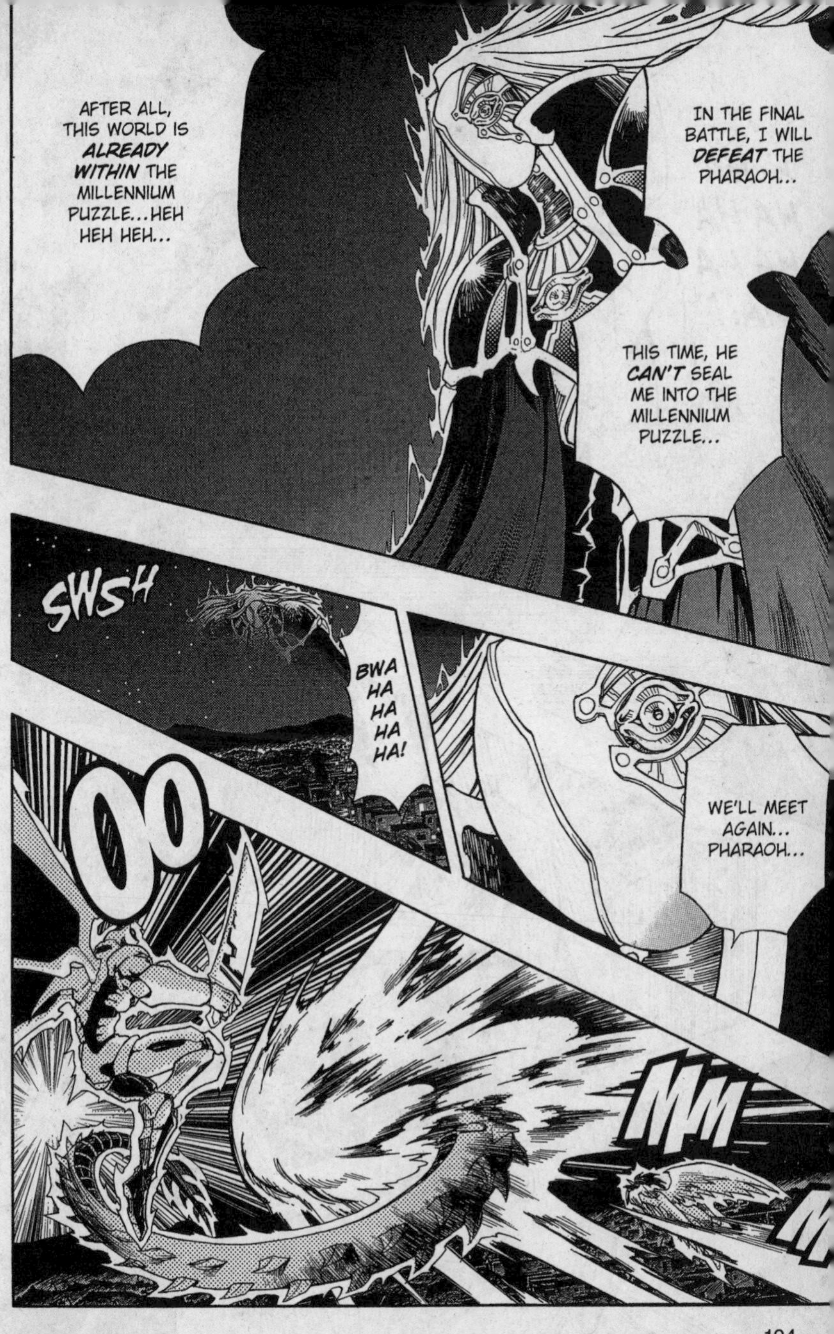

IN THE FINAL BATTLE, I WILL DEFEAT THE PHARAOH...
THIS TIME, HE CAN'T SEAL ME INTO THE MILLENNIUM PUZZLE...
AFTER ALL, THIS WORLD IS ALREADY WITHIN THE MILLENNIUM PUZZLE...HEH HEH HEH...
WE'LL MEET AGAIN... PHARAOH...
BWA HA HA HA HA!
SWSH
OO
MM
M

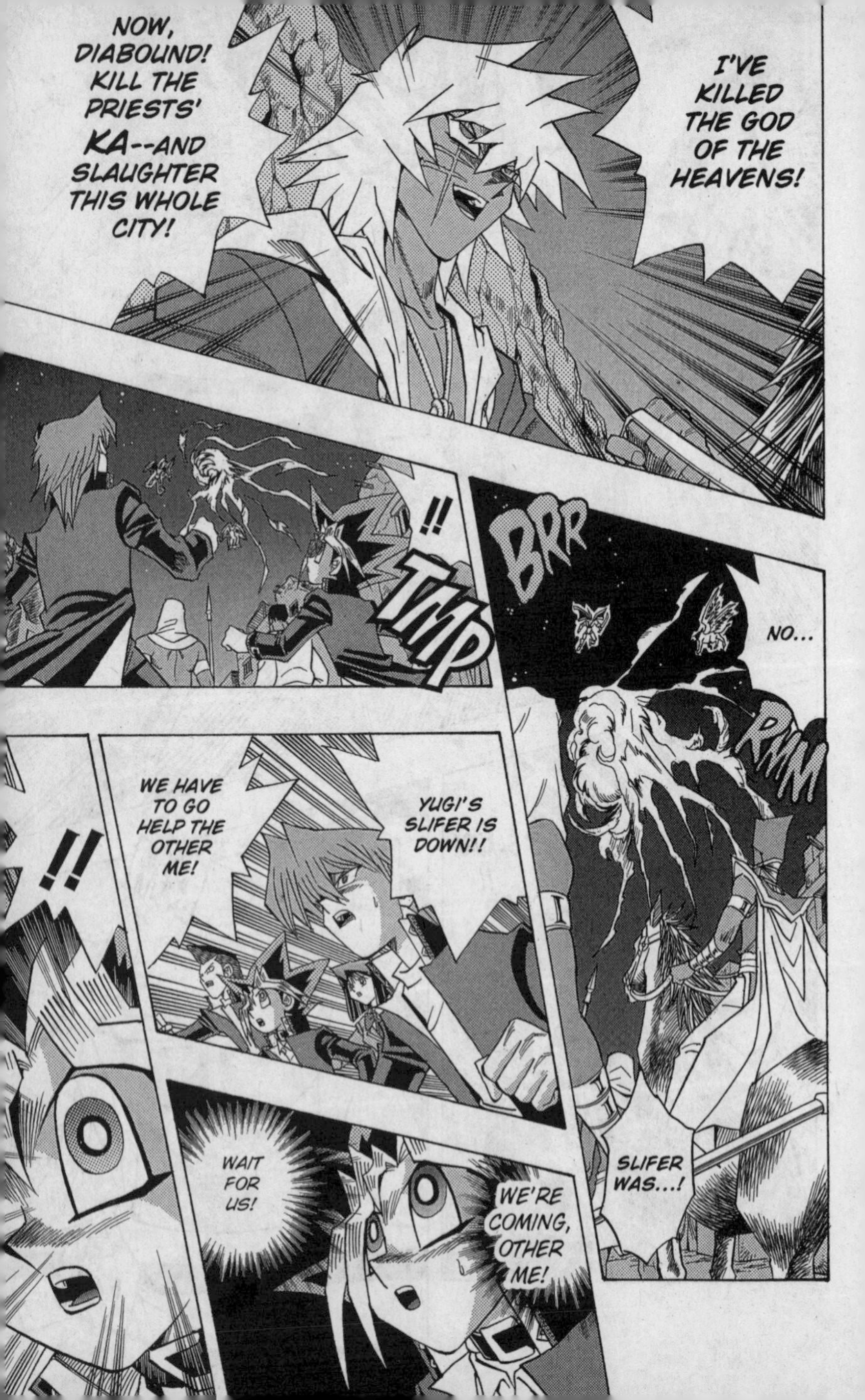
I'VE KILLED THE GOD OF THE HEAVENS!
NOW, DIABOUND! KILL THE PRIESTS' KA--AND SLAUGHTER THIS WHOLE CITY!
BRR
RMM
NO...
SLIFER WAS...!
!!
TMP
YUGI'S SLIFER IS DOWN!!
WE HAVE TO GO HELP THE OTHER ME!
!!
WE'RE COMING, OTHER ME!
WAIT FOR US!

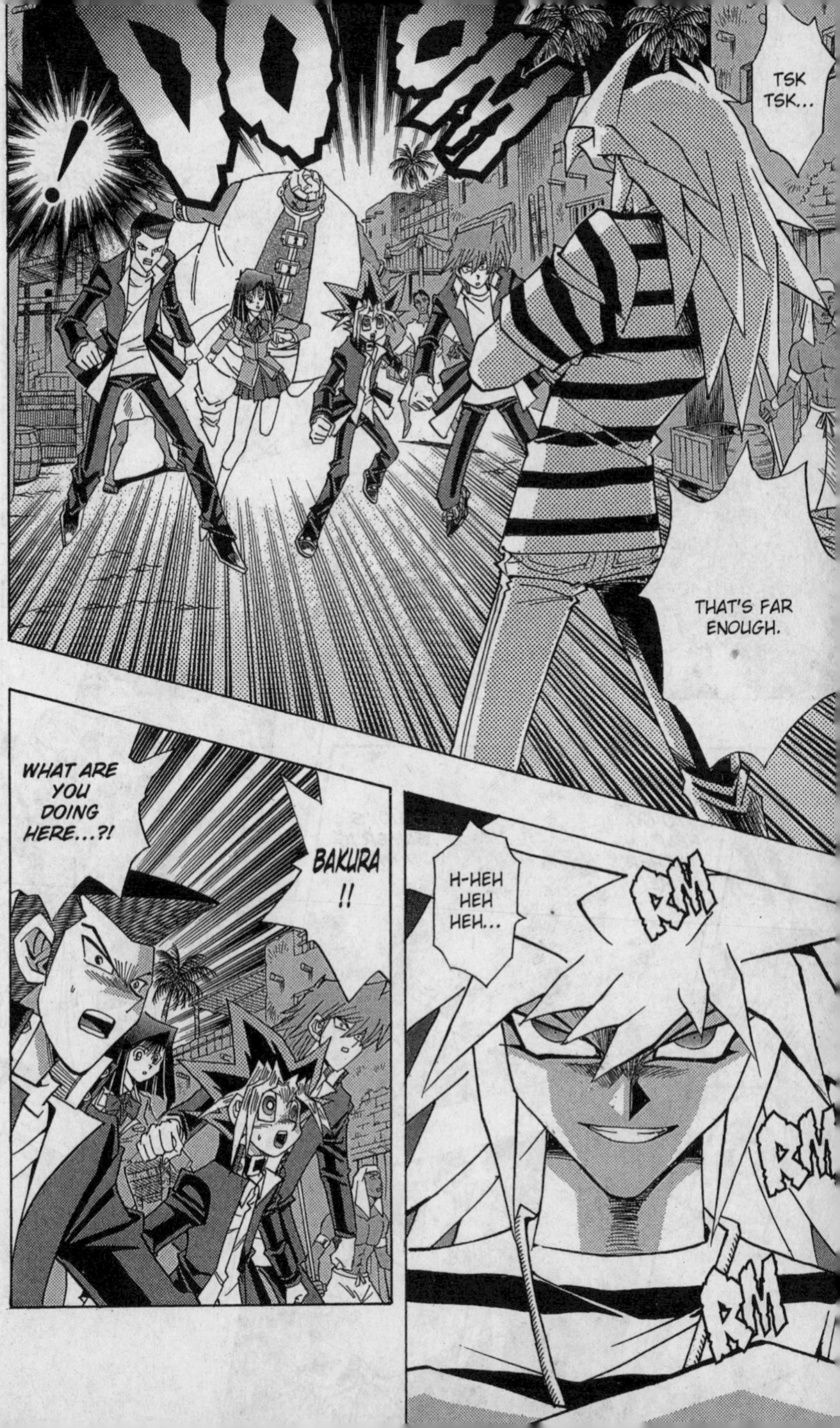
DOOM
!
TSK TSK...
THAT'S FAR ENOUGH.
BAKURA !!
WHAT ARE YOU DOING HERE...?!
H-HEH HEH HEH...
RM
RM
RM

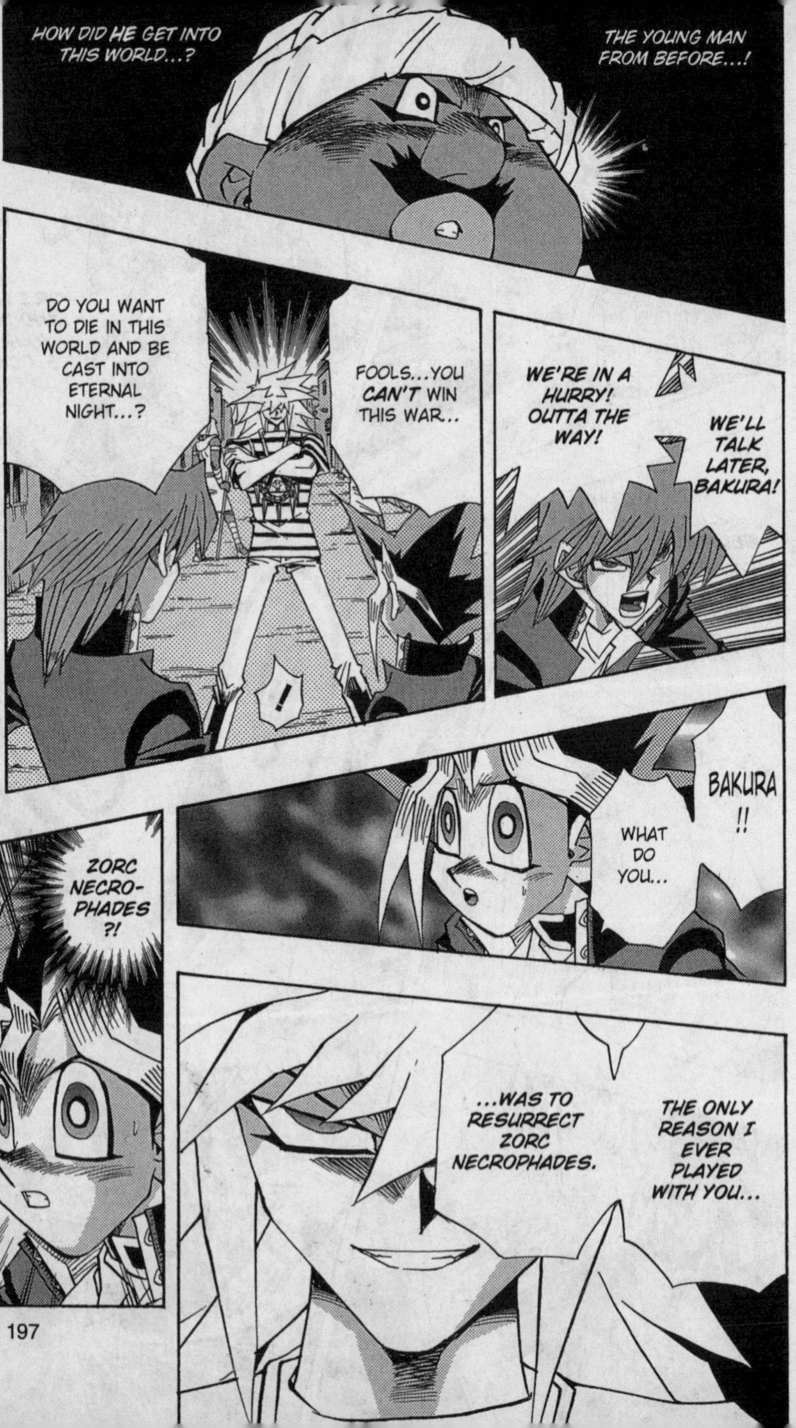
THE YOUNG MAN FROM BEFORE...!
HOW DID HE GET INTO THIS WORLD...?
WE'RE IN A HURRY! OUTTA THE WAY!
WE'LL TALK LATER, BAKURA!
FOOLS...YOU CAN'T WIN THIS WAR..
DO YOU WANT TO DIE IN THIS WORLD AND BE CAST INTO ETERNAL NIGHT...?
!
BAKURA !!
WHAT DO YOU...
THE ONLY REASON I EVER PLAYED WITH YOU...
...WAS TO RESURRECT ZORC NECROPHADES.
ZORC NECRO-PHADES ?!

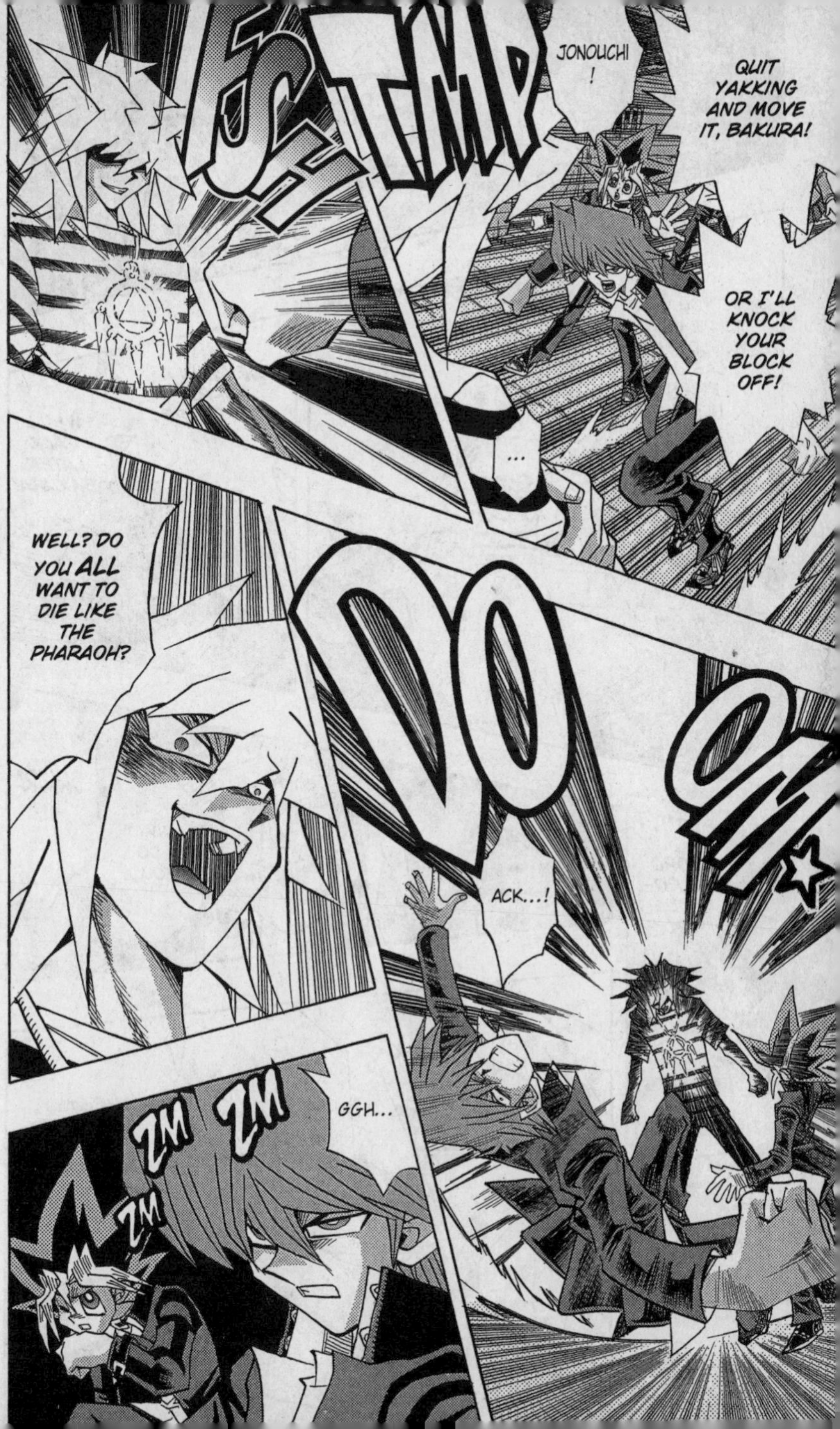
QUIT YAKKING AND MOVE IT, BAKURA!
OR I'LL KNOCK YOUR BLOCK OFF!
JONOUCHI!
...
ACK...!
WELL? DO YOU ALL WANT TO DIE LIKE THE PHARAOH?
GGH...
ZM ZM
ZM

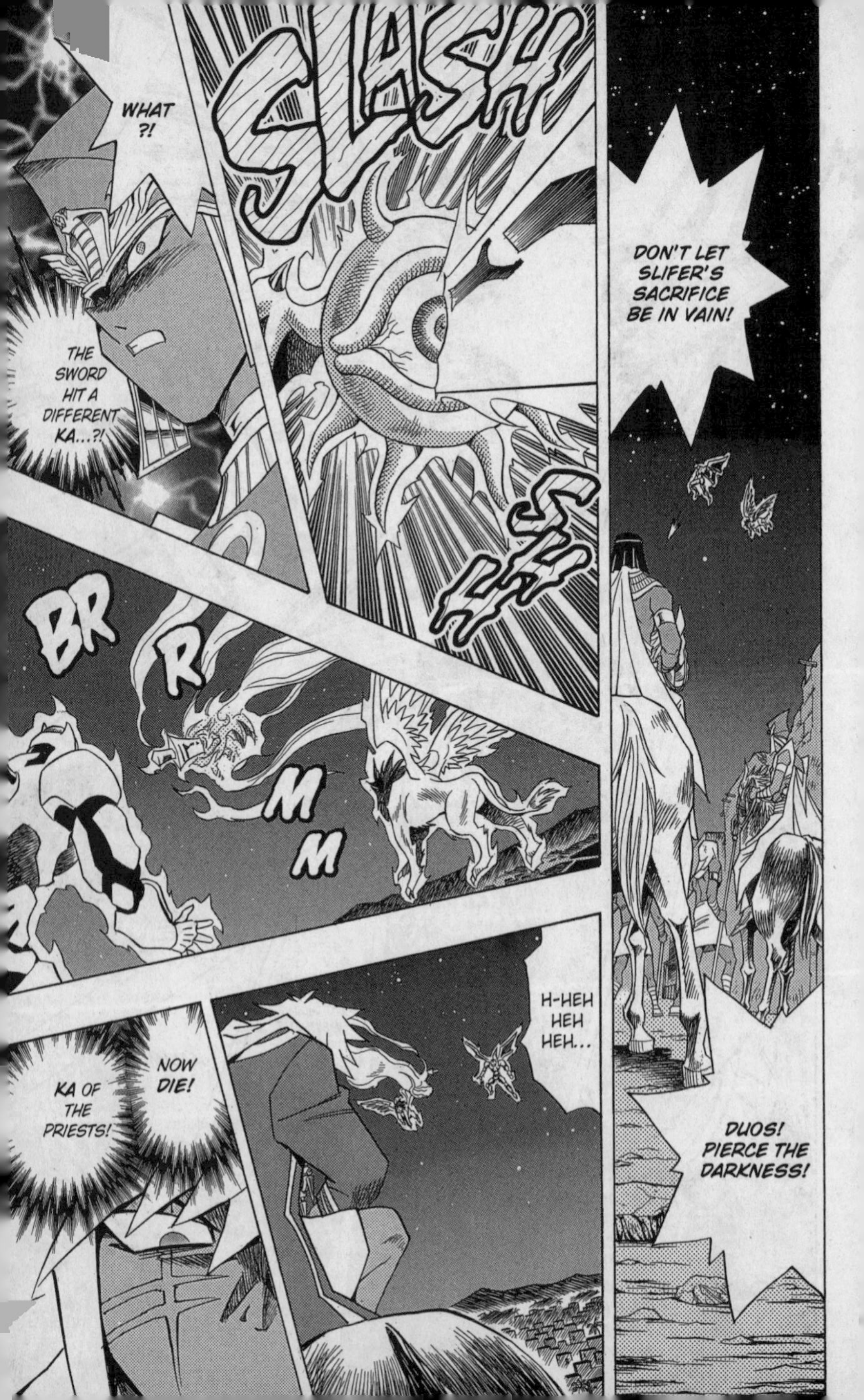
DON'T LET SLIFER'S SACRIFICE BE IN VAIN!
DUOS! PIERCE THE DARKNESS!
SLASH
WHAT ?!
THE SWORD HIT A DIFFERENT KA...?!
BRRMM
H-HEH HEH HEH...
NOW DIE!
KA OF THE PRIESTS!

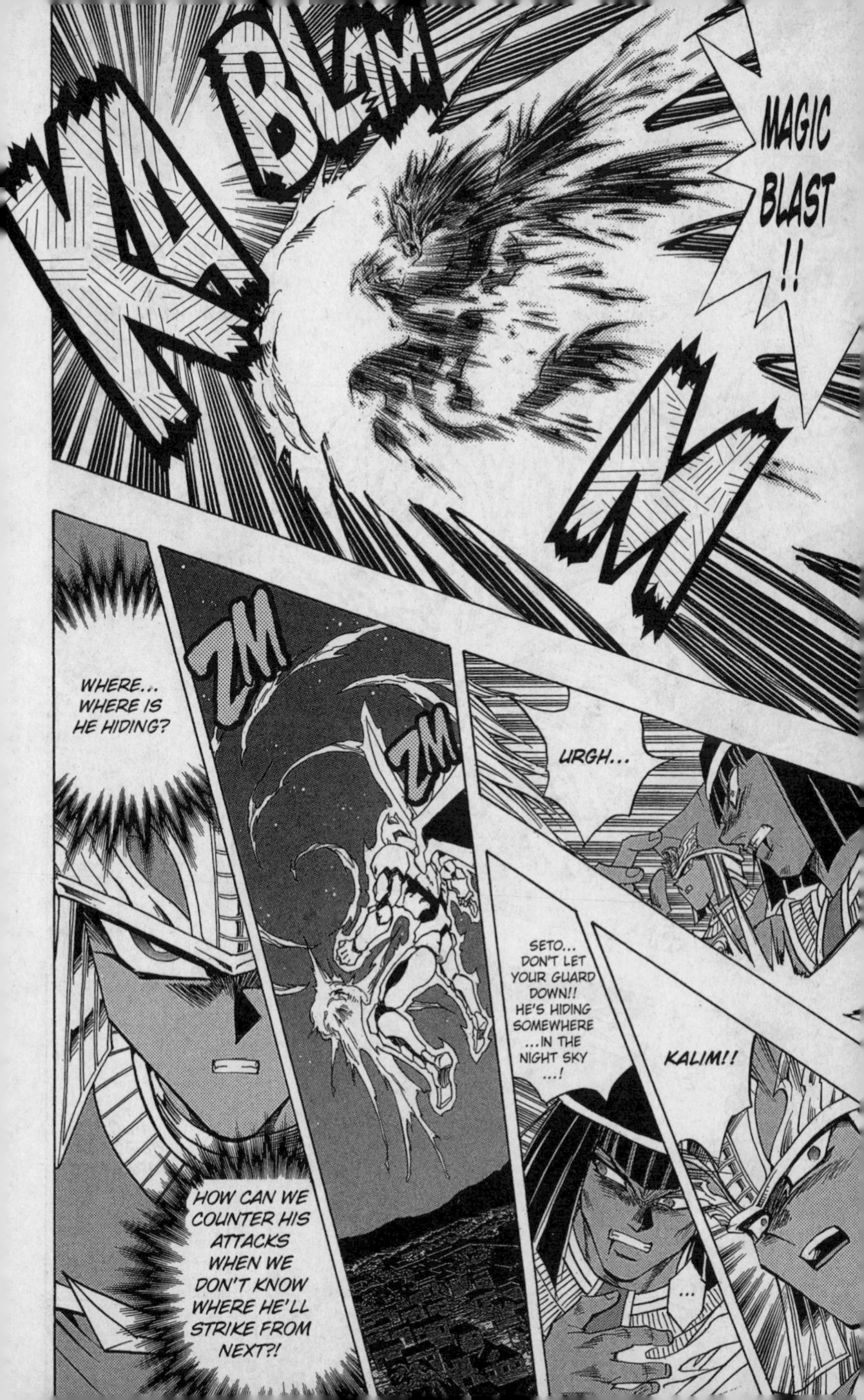

MAGIC BLAST!!
URGH...
KALIM!!
SETO... DON'T LET YOUR GUARD DOWN!! HE'S HIDING SOMEWHERE ...IN THE NIGHT SKY ...!
...
ZM
ZM
WHERE... WHERE IS HE HIDING?
HOW CAN WE COUNTER HIS ATTACKS WHEN WE DON'T KNOW WHERE HE'LL STRIKE FROM NEXT?!

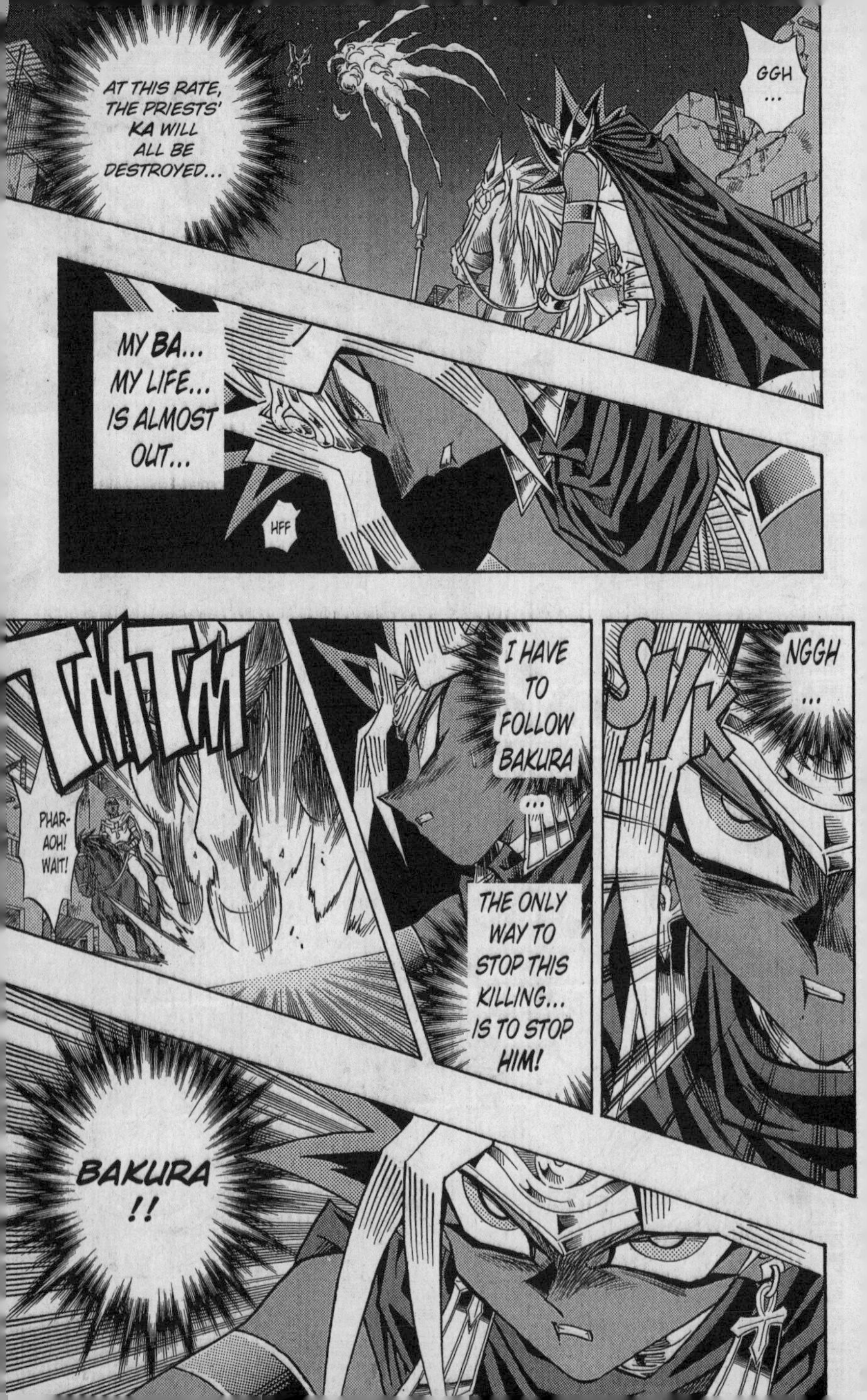
GGH ...
AT THIS RATE, THE PRIESTS' KA WILL ALL BE DESTROYED...
MY BA... MY LIFE... IS ALMOST OUT...
HFF
NGGH ...
SNK
I HAVE TO FOLLOW BAKURA ...
THE ONLY WAY TO STOP THIS KILLING... IS TO STOP HIM!
TMTMTM
PHAR-AOH! WAIT!
BAKURA !!

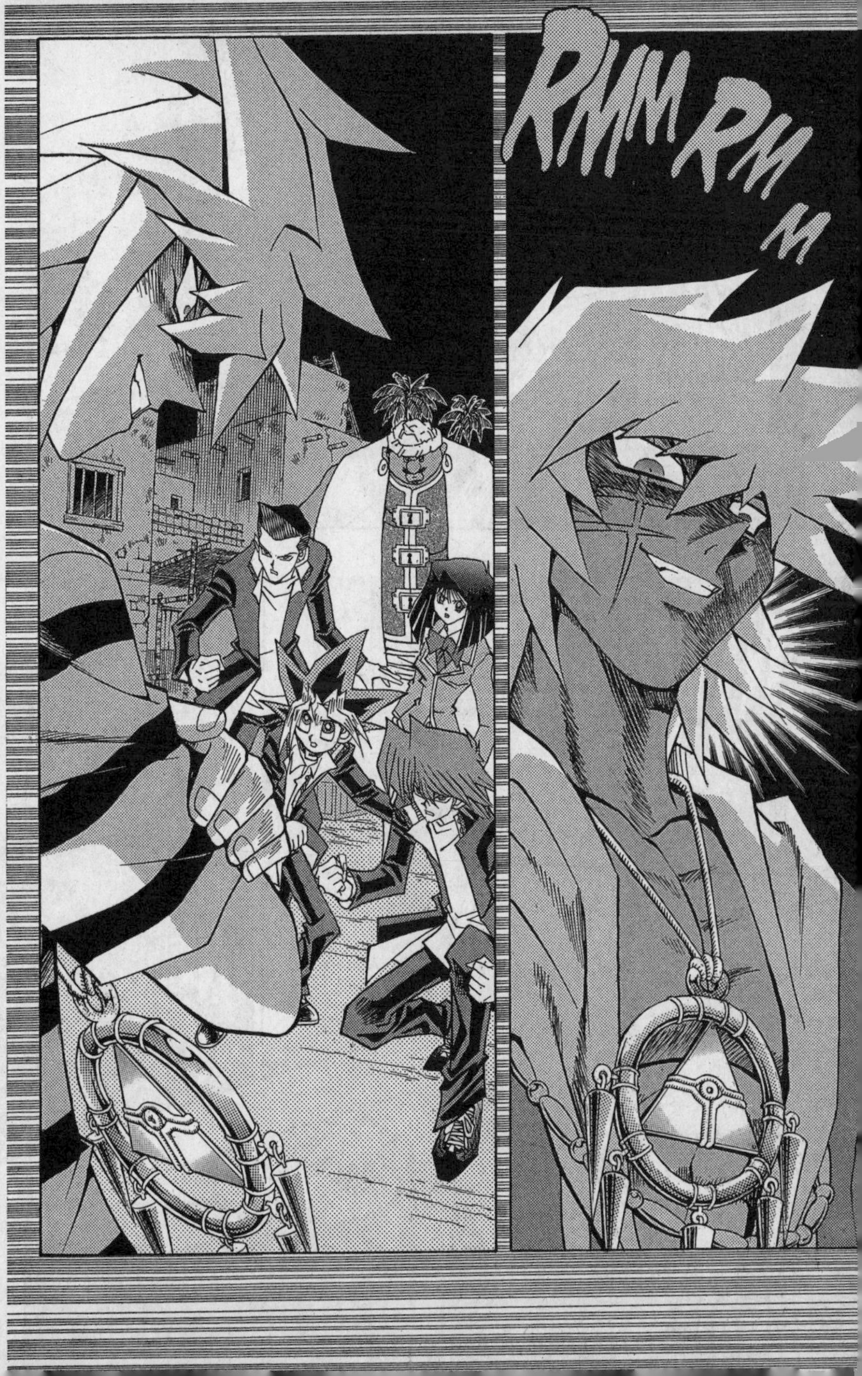
RMM RM M

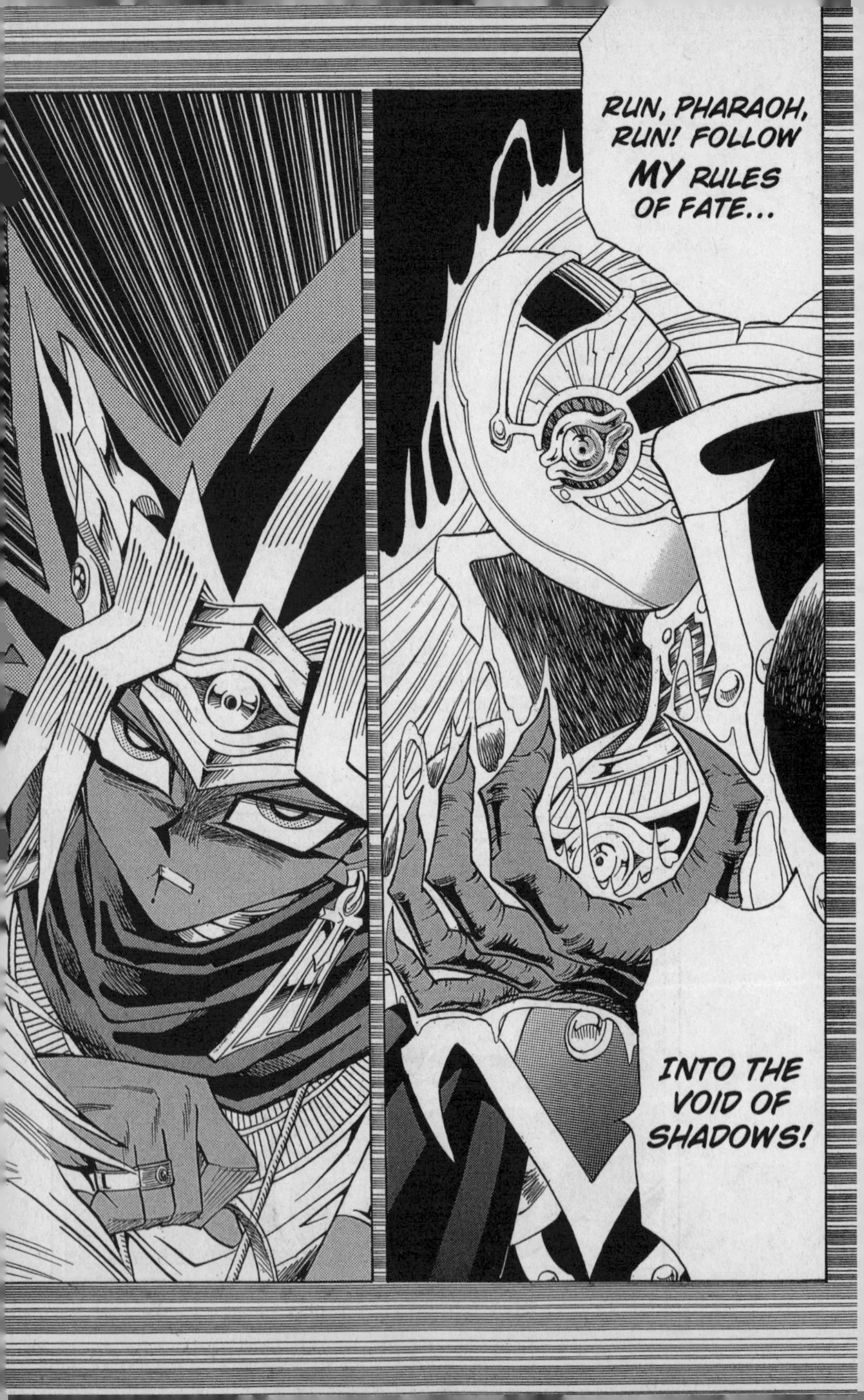
RUN, PHARAOH, RUN! FOLLOW MY RULES OF FATE...
INTO THE VOID OF SHADOWS!

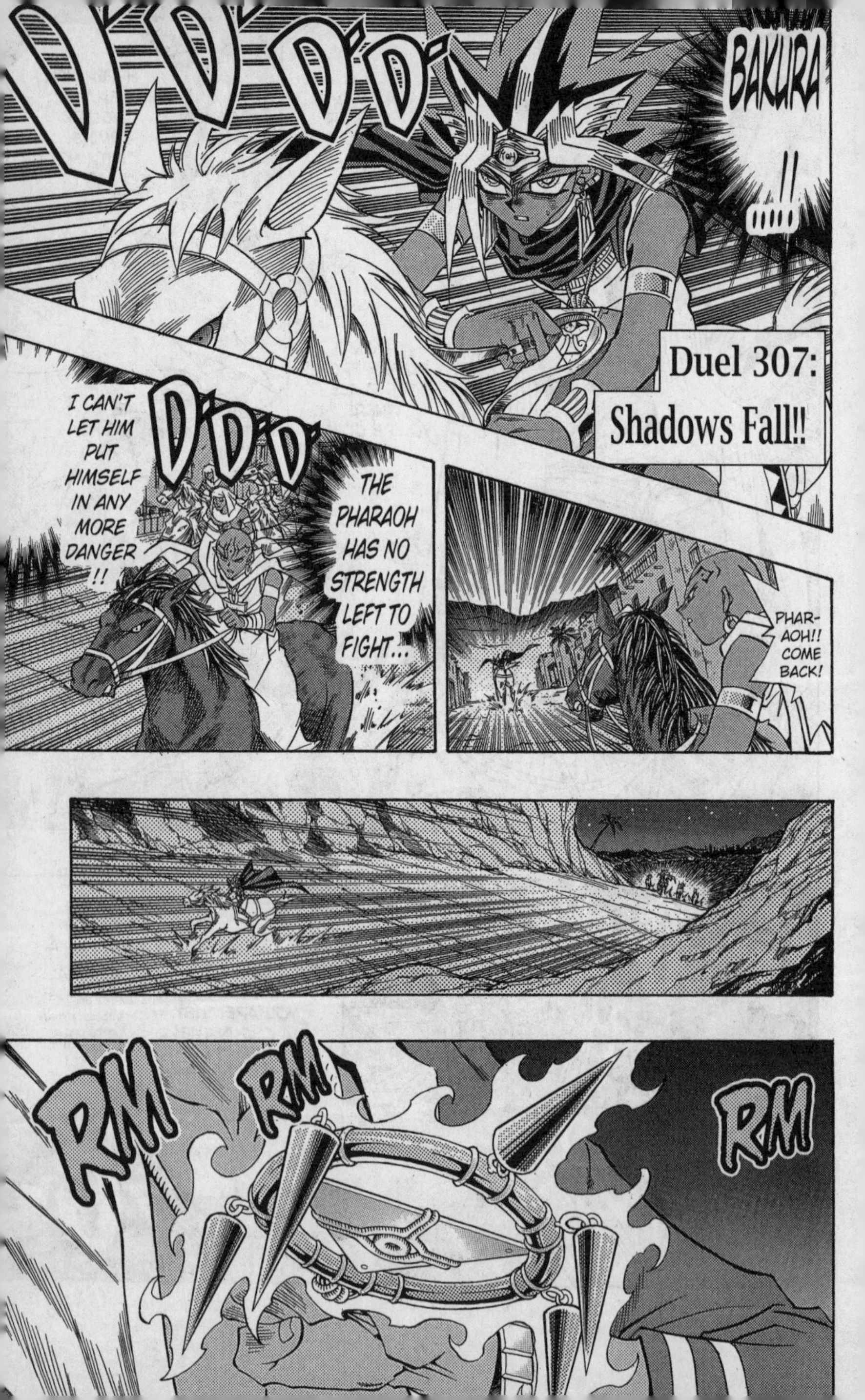

BAKURA ...!!
DDDD
Duel 307:
Shadows Fall!!
PHARAOH!! COME BACK!
THE PHARAOH HAS NO STRENGTH LEFT TO FIGHT...
I CAN'T LET HIM PUT HIMSELF IN ANY MORE DANGER!!
DDD
RM
RM
RM

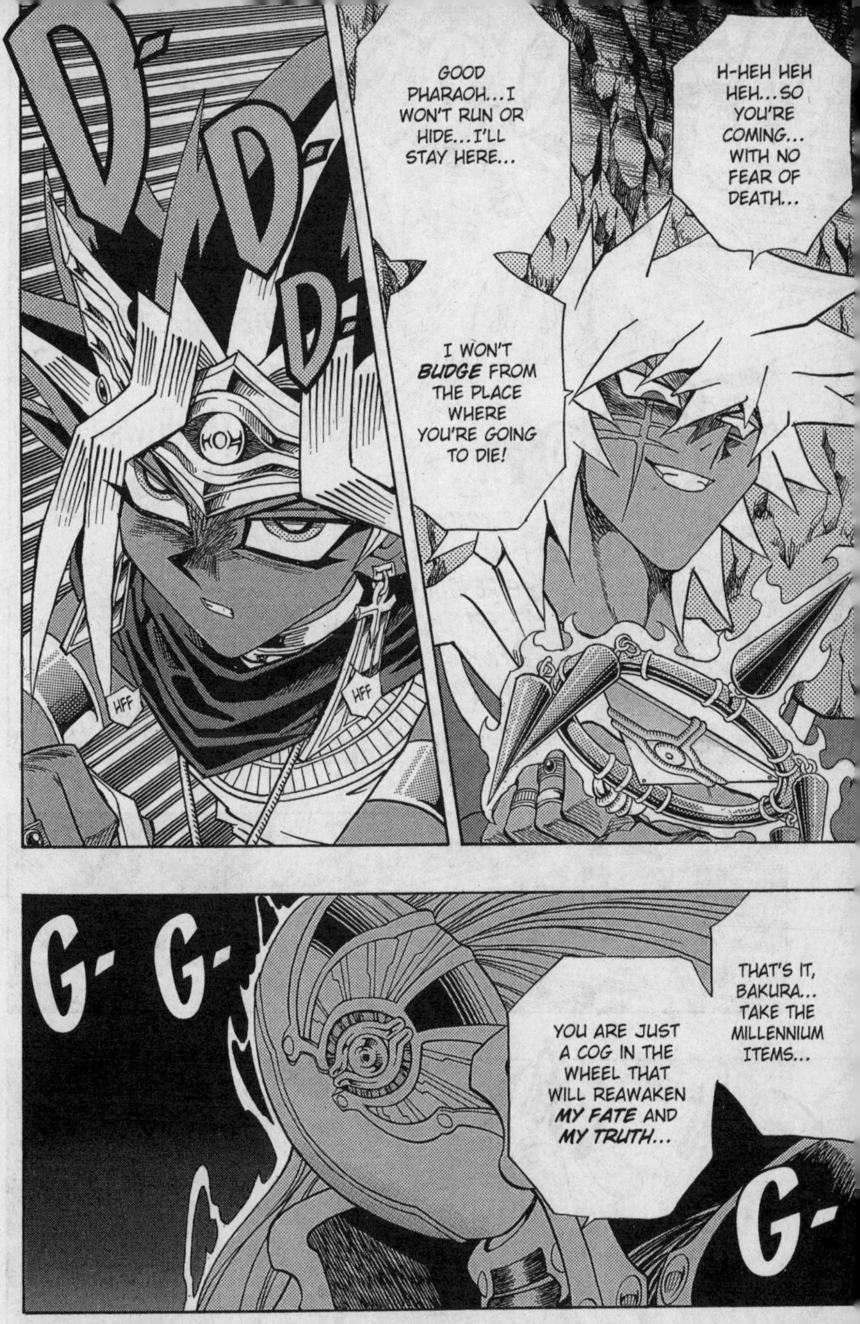

H-HEH HEH HEH...SO YOU'RE COMING... WITH NO FEAR OF DEATH...
GOOD PHARAOH...I WON'T RUN OR HIDE...I'LL STAY HERE...
I WON'T *BUDGE* FROM THE PLACE WHERE YOU'RE GOING TO DIE!
D- D- D-
HFF
HFF
THAT'S IT, BAKURA... TAKE THE MILLENNIUM ITEMS...
YOU ARE JUST A COG IN THE WHEEL THAT WILL REAWAKEN *MY FATE* AND *MY TRUTH*...
G- G-
G-

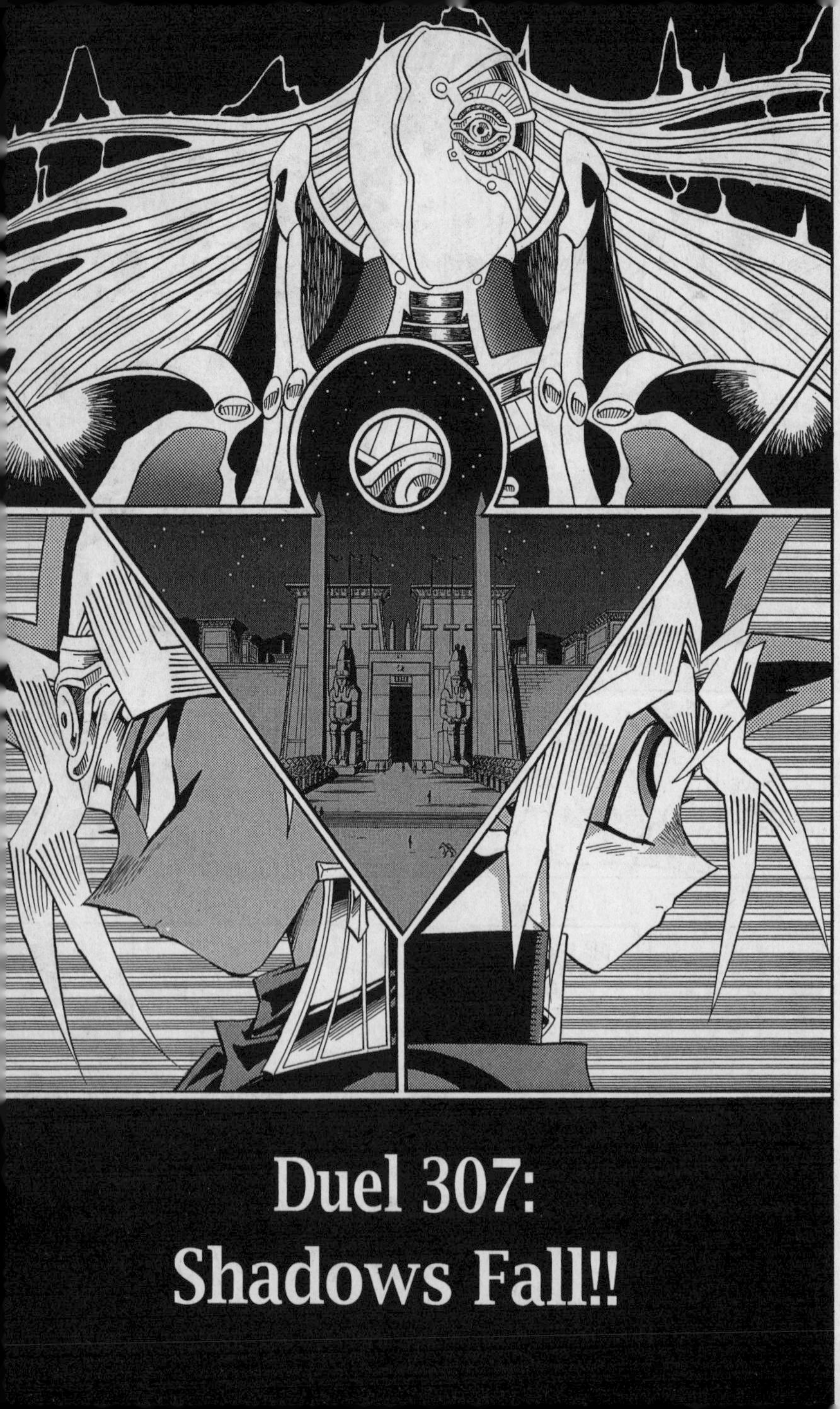

Duel 307:
Shadows Fall!!

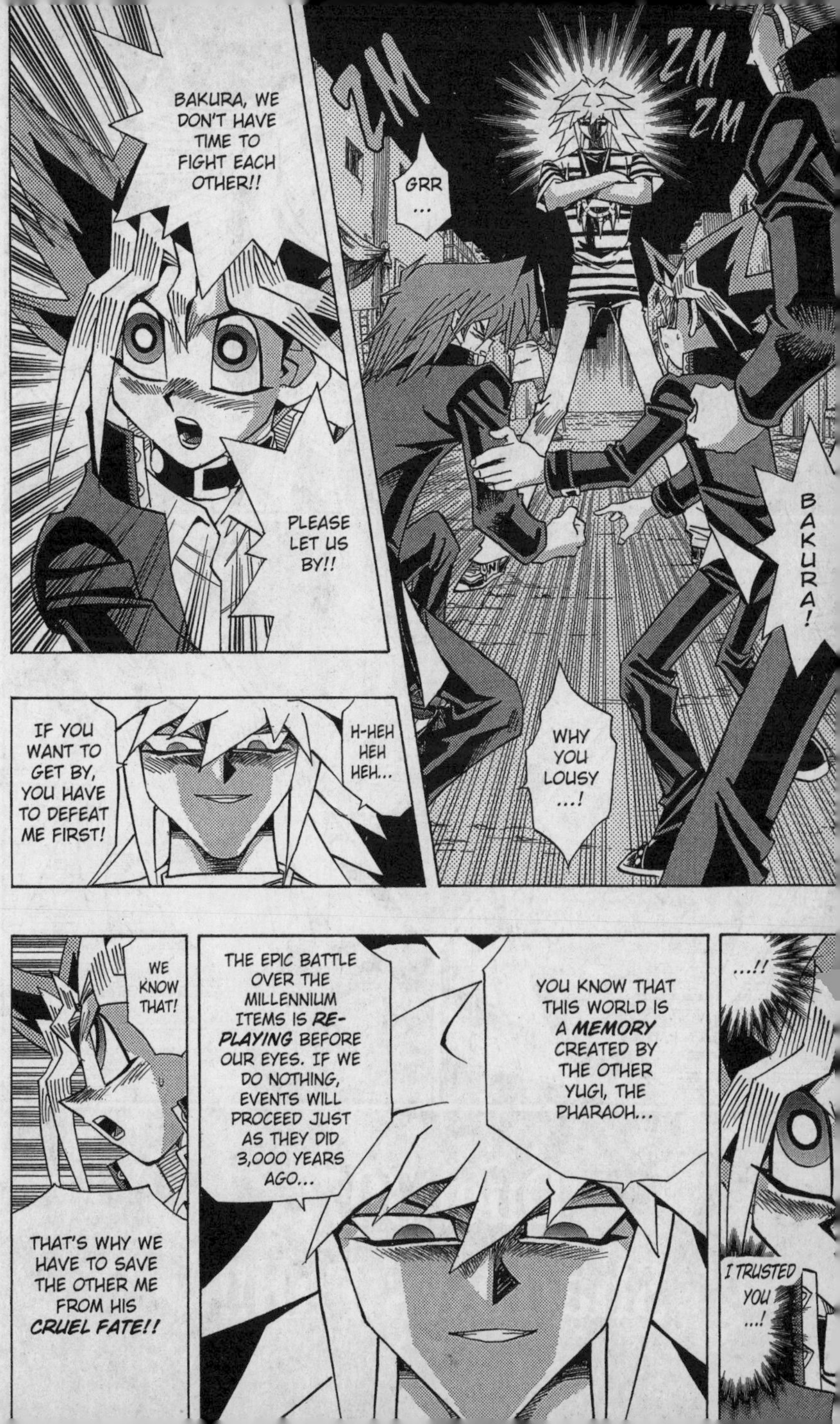
ZM
ZM
ZM
GRR...
BAKURA!
WHY YOU LOUSY...!
BAKURA, WE DON'T HAVE TIME TO FIGHT EACH OTHER!!
PLEASE LET US BY!!
H-HEH HEH HEH...
IF YOU WANT TO GET BY, YOU HAVE TO DEFEAT ME FIRST!
...!!
I TRUSTED YOU...!
YOU KNOW THAT THIS WORLD IS A MEMORY CREATED BY THE OTHER YUGI, THE PHARAOH...
THE EPIC BATTLE OVER THE MILLENNIUM ITEMS IS RE-PLAYING BEFORE OUR EYES. IF WE DO NOTHING, EVENTS WILL PROCEED JUST AS THEY DID 3,000 YEARS AGO...
WE KNOW THAT!
THAT'S WHY WE HAVE TO SAVE THE OTHER ME FROM HIS CRUEL FATE!!

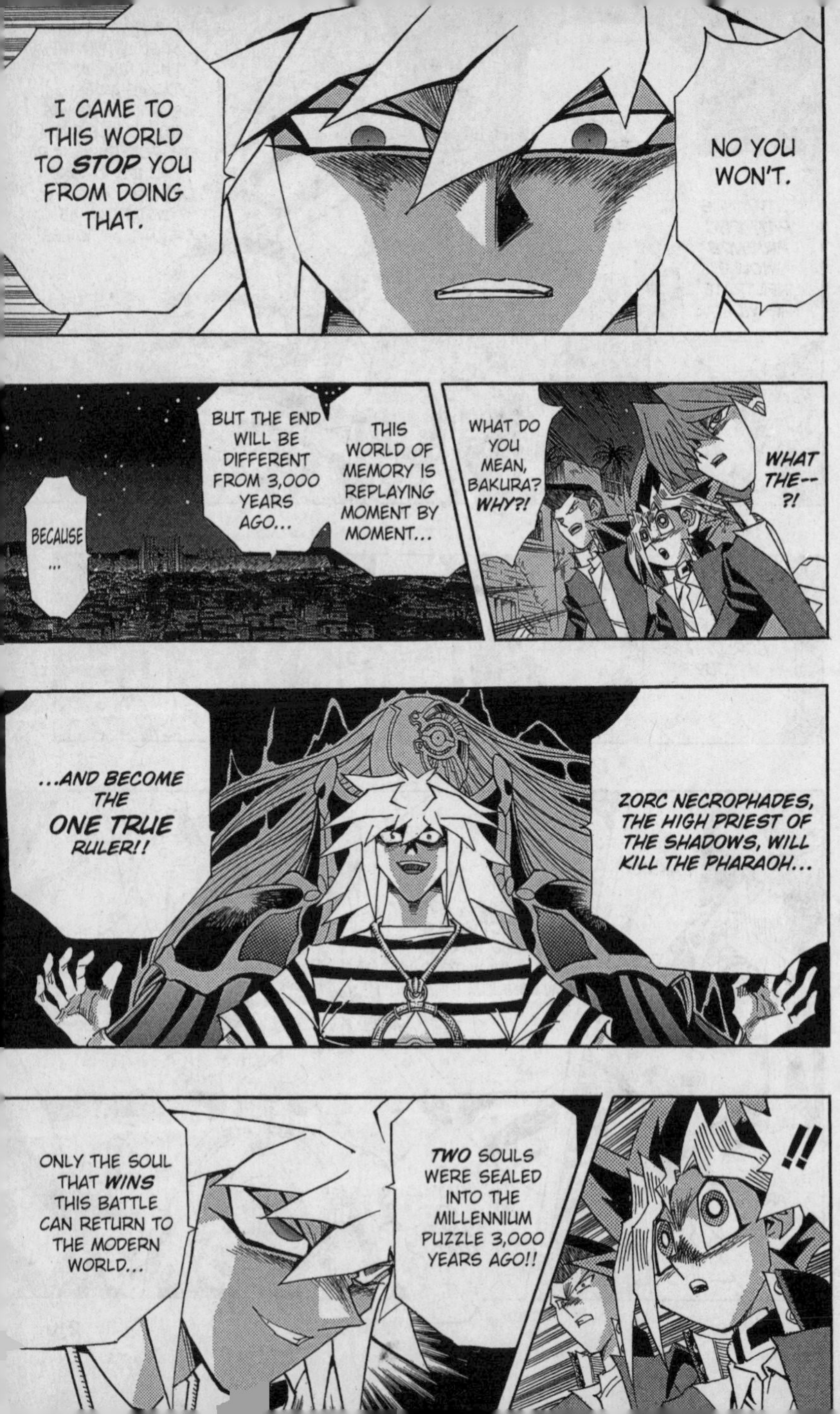
NO YOU WON'T.
I CAME TO THIS WORLD TO STOP YOU FROM DOING THAT.
WHAT THE--?!
WHAT DO YOU MEAN, BAKURA? WHY?!
THIS WORLD OF MEMORY IS REPLAYING MOMENT BY MOMENT...
BUT THE END WILL BE DIFFERENT FROM 3,000 YEARS AGO...
BECAUSE...
ZORC NECROPHADES, THE HIGH PRIEST OF THE SHADOWS, WILL KILL THE PHARAOH...
...AND BECOME THE ONE TRUE RULER!!
!!
TWO SOULS WERE SEALED INTO THE MILLENNIUM PUZZLE 3,000 YEARS AGO!!
ONLY THE SOUL THAT WINS THIS BATTLE CAN RETURN TO THE MODERN WORLD...

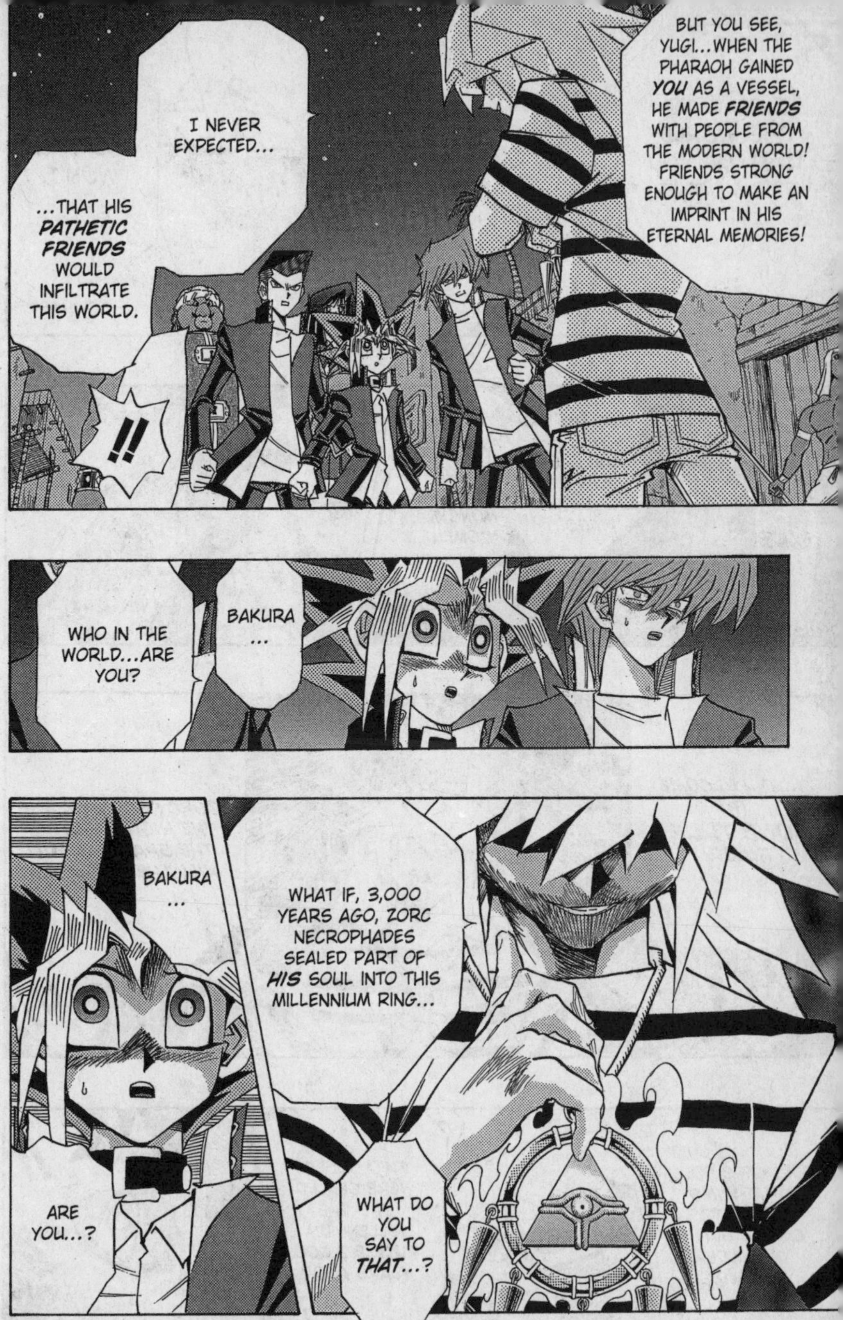
BUT YOU SEE, YUGI...WHEN THE PHARAOH GAINED YOU AS A VESSEL, HE MADE FRIENDS WITH PEOPLE FROM THE MODERN WORLD! FRIENDS STRONG ENOUGH TO MAKE AN IMPRINT IN HIS ETERNAL MEMORIES!
I NEVER EXPECTED...
...THAT HIS PATHETIC FRIENDS WOULD INFILTRATE THIS WORLD.
!!
BAKURA...
WHO IN THE WORLD...ARE YOU?
WHAT IF, 3,000 YEARS AGO, ZORC NECROPHADES SEALED PART OF HIS SOUL INTO THIS MILLENNIUM RING...
WHAT DO YOU SAY TO THAT...?
BAKURA...
ARE YOU...?

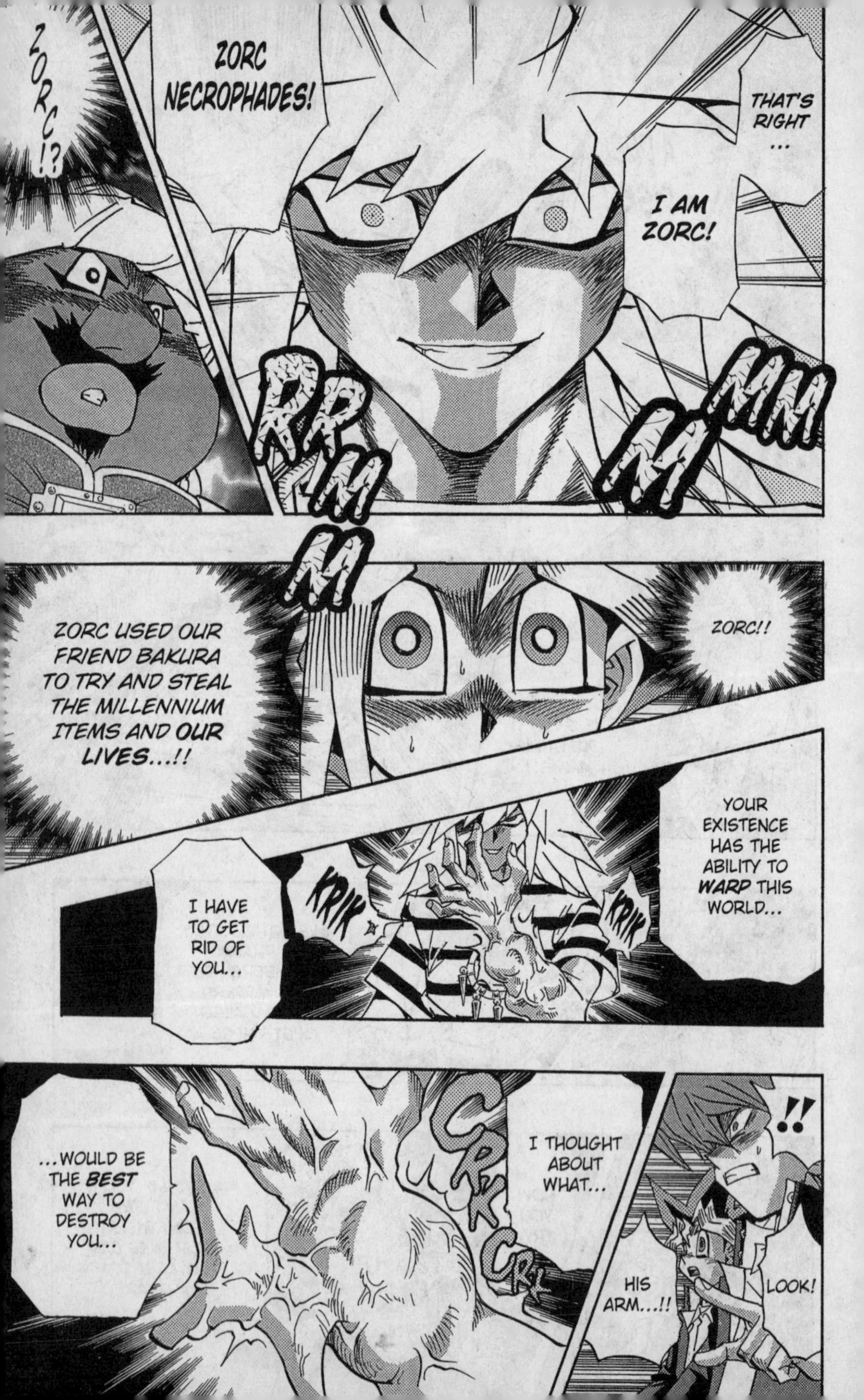
THAT'S RIGHT...
I AM ZORC!
ZORC NECROPHADES!
ZORC!?
ZORC!!
ZORC USED OUR FRIEND BAKURA TO TRY AND STEAL THE MILLENNIUM ITEMS AND OUR LIVES...!!
YOUR EXISTENCE HAS THE ABILITY TO WARP THIS WORLD...
KRIK
KRIK
I HAVE TO GET RID OF YOU...
!!
LOOK!
HIS ARM...!!
I THOUGHT ABOUT WHAT...
...WOULD BE THE BEST WAY TO DESTROY YOU...

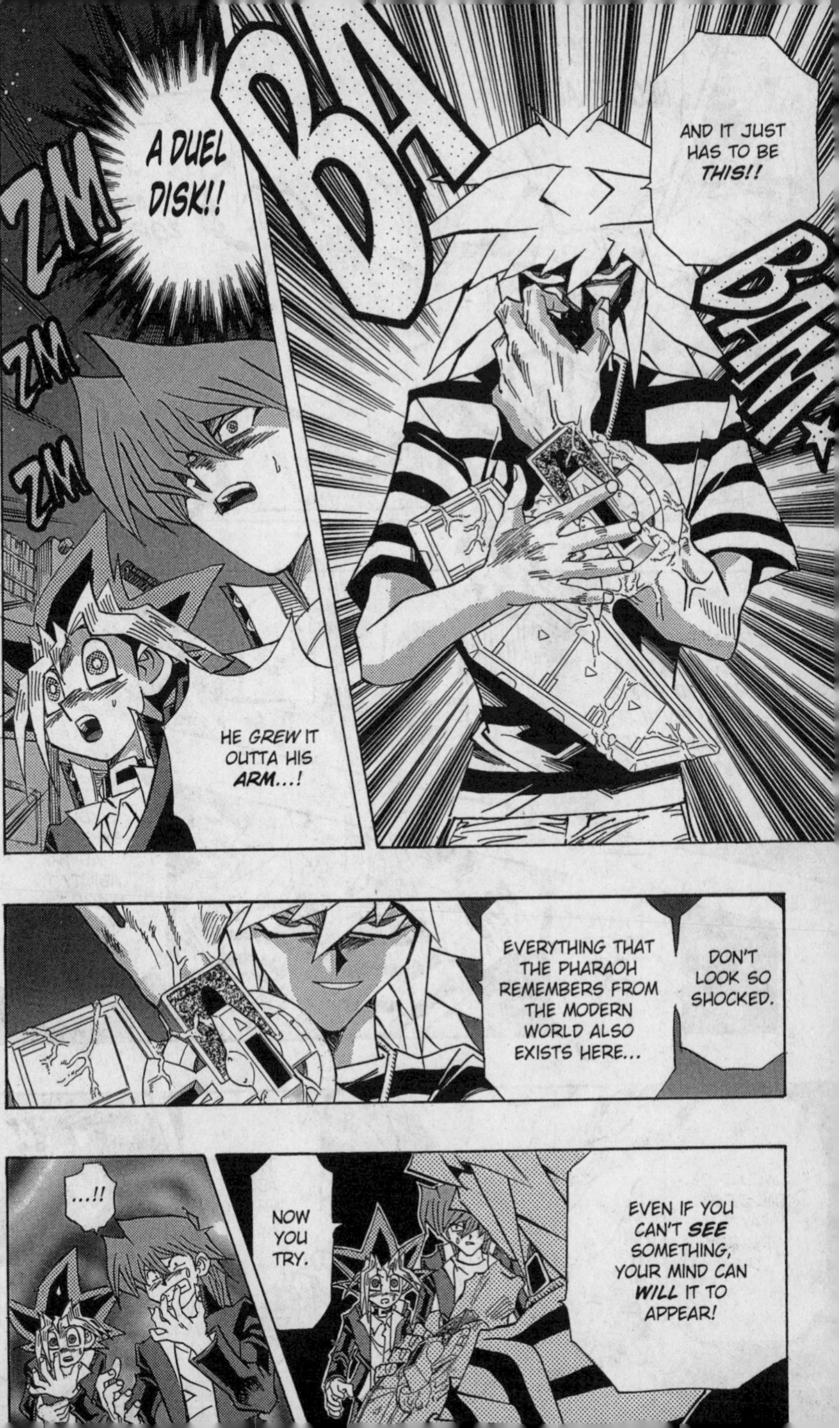

AND IT JUST HAS TO BE *THIS!!*
BA
BAM!
A DUEL DISK!!
ZM
ZM
ZM
HE *GREW* IT OUTTA HIS *ARM*...!
DON'T LOOK SO SHOCKED.
EVERYTHING THAT THE PHARAOH REMEMBERS FROM THE MODERN WORLD ALSO EXISTS HERE...
EVEN IF YOU CAN'T *SEE* SOMETHING, YOUR MIND CAN *WILL* IT TO APPEAR!
NOW YOU TRY.
...!!

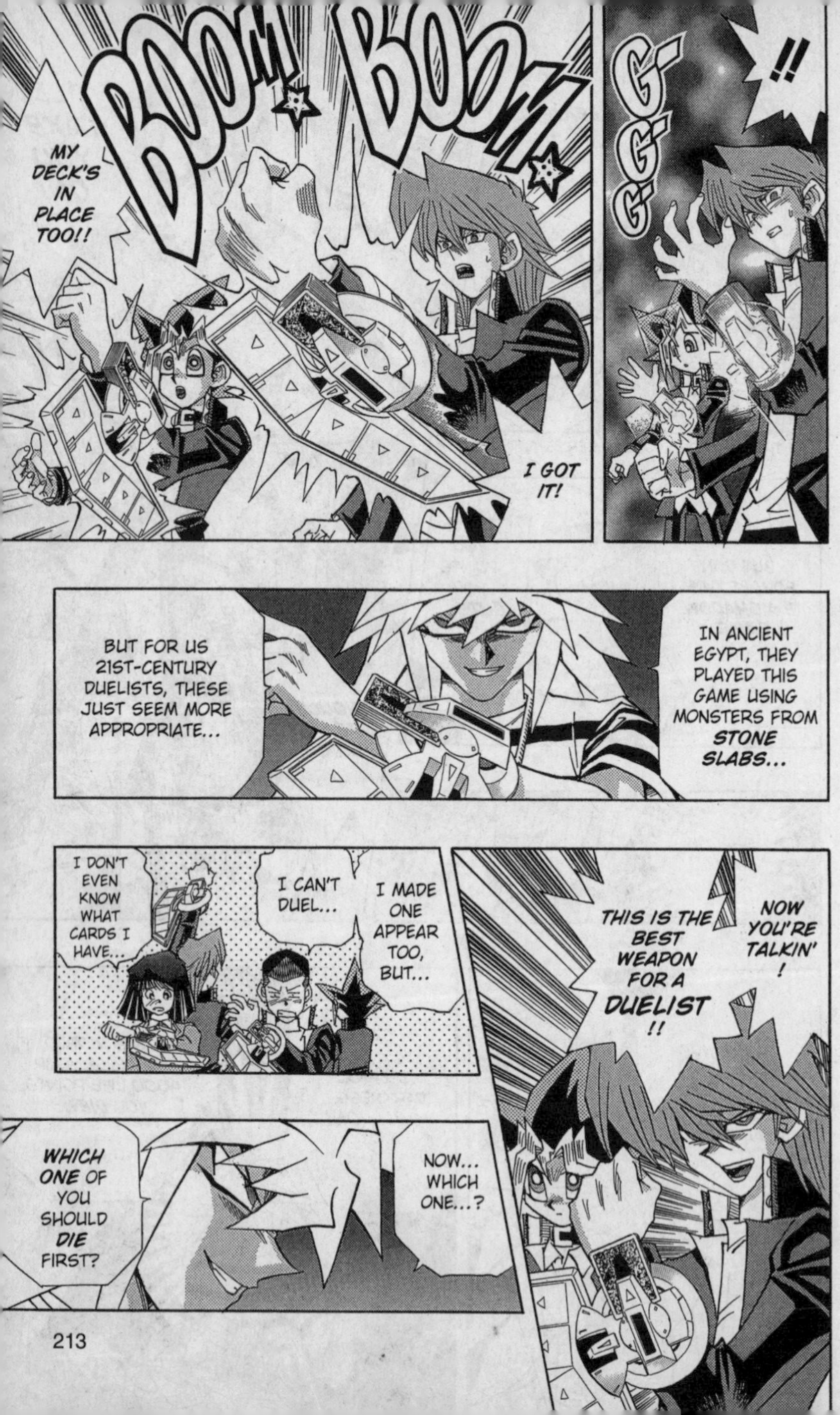
G-G-G-
!!
BOOM BOOM
MY DECK'S IN PLACE TOO!!
I GOT IT!
IN ANCIENT EGYPT, THEY PLAYED THIS GAME USING MONSTERS FROM STONE SLABS...
BUT FOR US 21ST-CENTURY DUELISTS, THESE JUST SEEM MORE APPROPRIATE...
NOW YOU'RE TALKIN'!
THIS IS THE BEST WEAPON FOR A DUELIST!!
I MADE ONE APPEAR TOO, BUT...
I CAN'T DUEL...
I DON'T EVEN KNOW WHAT CARDS I HAVE...
NOW... WHICH ONE...?
WHICH ONE OF YOU SHOULD DIE FIRST?

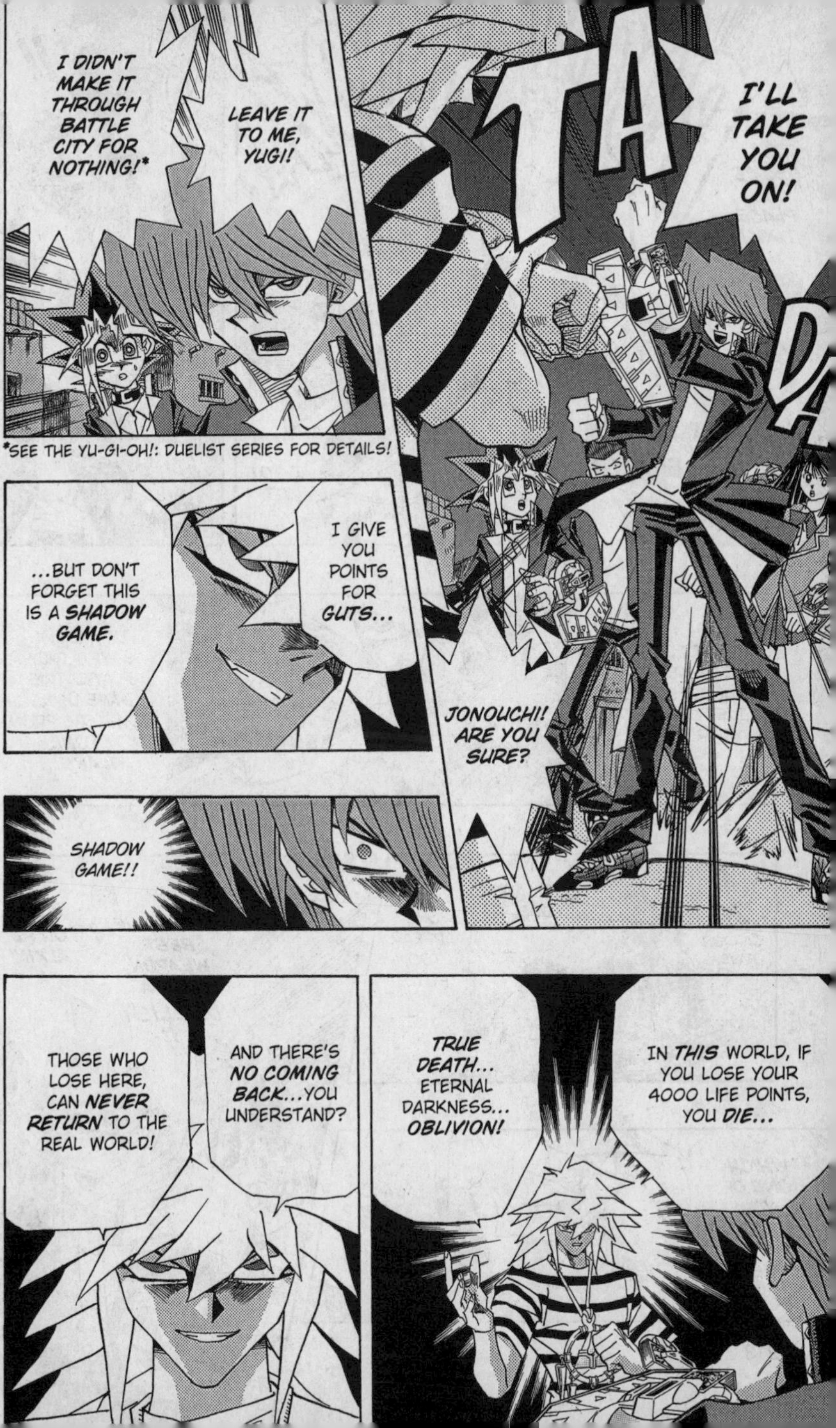
LEAVE IT TO ME, YUGI!
I DIDN'T MAKE IT THROUGH BATTLE CITY FOR NOTHING!*
*SEE THE YU-GI-OH!: DUELIST SERIES FOR DETAILS!
I'LL TAKE YOU ON!
TA
DA
JONOUCHI! ARE YOU SURE?
I GIVE YOU POINTS FOR GUTS...
...BUT DON'T FORGET THIS IS A SHADOW GAME.
SHADOW GAME!!
IN THIS WORLD, IF YOU LOSE YOUR 4000 LIFE POINTS, YOU DIE...
TRUE DEATH... ETERNAL DARKNESS... OBLIVION!
AND THERE'S NO COMING BACK...YOU UNDERSTAND?
THOSE WHO LOSE HERE, CAN NEVER RETURN TO THE REAL WORLD!

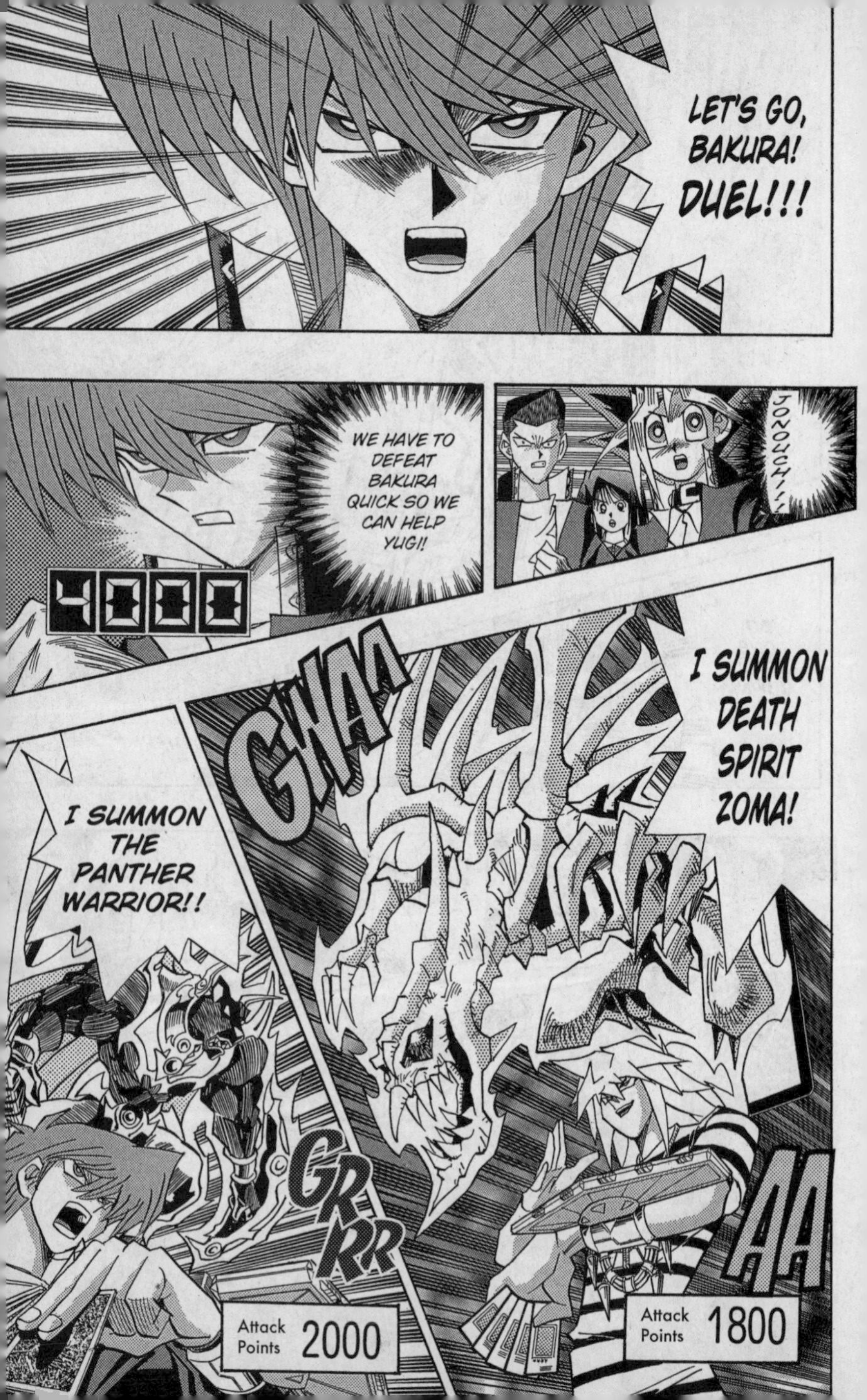
LET'S GO, BAKURA! DUEL!!!
WE HAVE TO DEFEAT BAKURA QUICK SO WE CAN HELP YUGI!!
4000
JONOUCHI!!
GHAA
I SUMMON THE PANTHER WARRIOR!!
I SUMMON DEATH SPIRIT ZOMA!
GRRR
AA
Attack Points 2000
Attack Points 1800

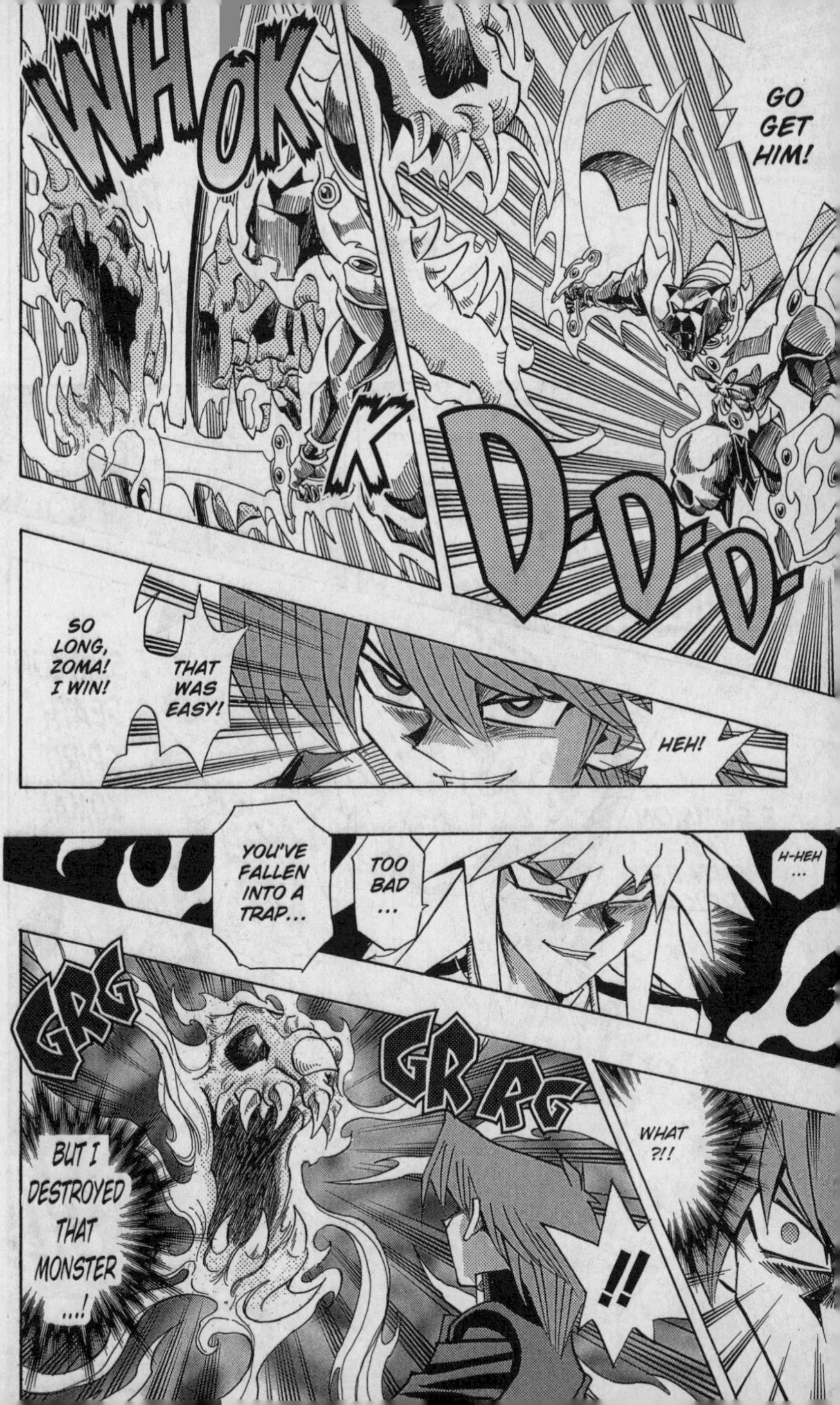
GO GET HIM!
WHOK
K
D-D-D-
HEH!
THAT WAS EASY!
SO LONG, ZOMA! I WIN!
H-HEH...
TOO BAD...
YOU'VE FALLEN INTO A TRAP...
WHAT?!!
GR RG
GRG
!!
BUT I DESTROYED THAT MONSTER...!

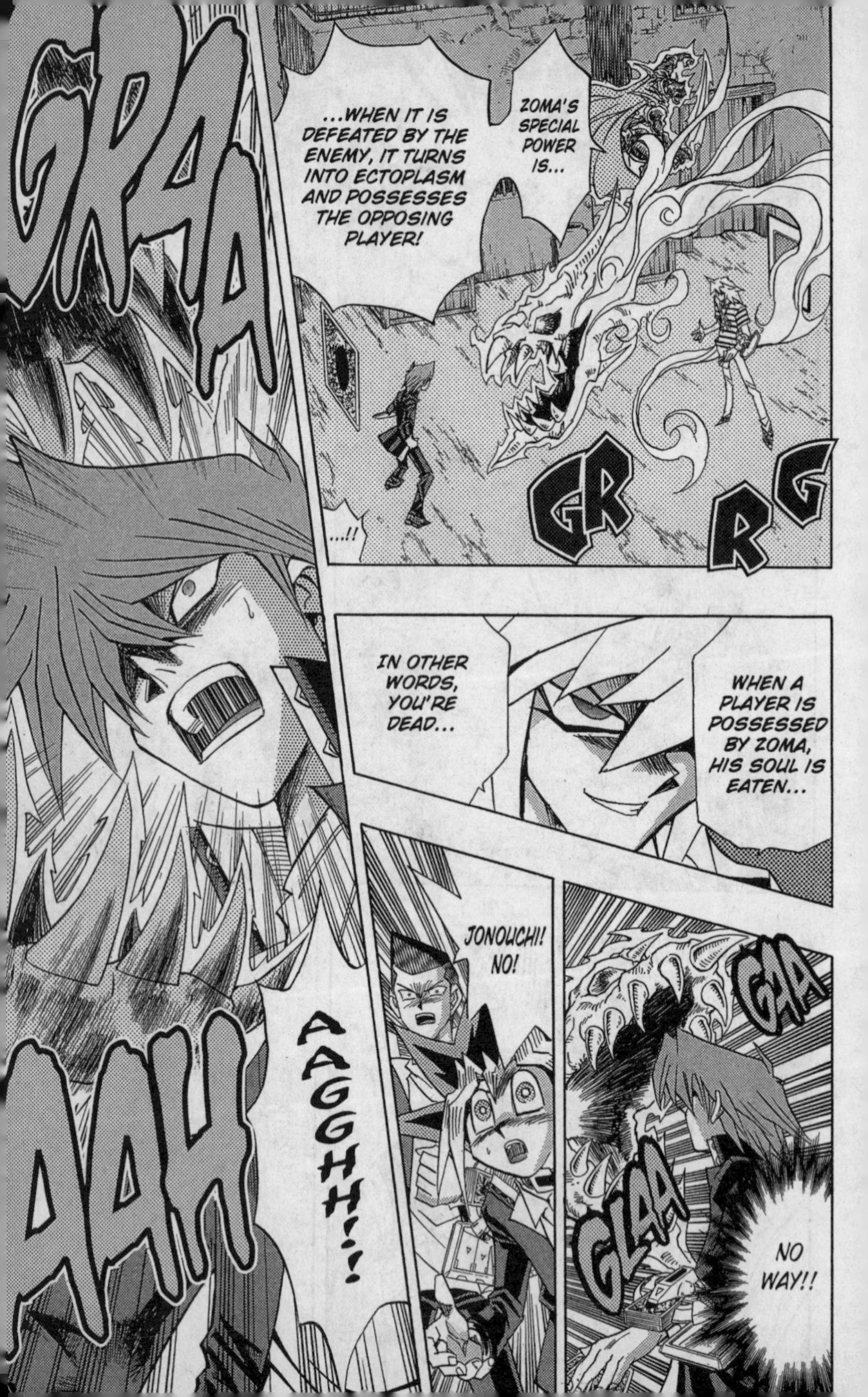
ZOMA'S SPECIAL POWER IS...
...WHEN IT IS DEFEATED BY THE ENEMY, IT TURNS INTO ECTOPLASM AND POSSESSES THE OPPOSING PLAYER!
...!!
GR RG
WHEN A PLAYER IS POSSESSED BY ZOMA, HIS SOUL IS EATEN...
IN OTHER WORDS, YOU'RE DEAD...
GAA
GLAA
NO WAY!!
JONOUCHI! NO!
AAGGHH!!
GRAA

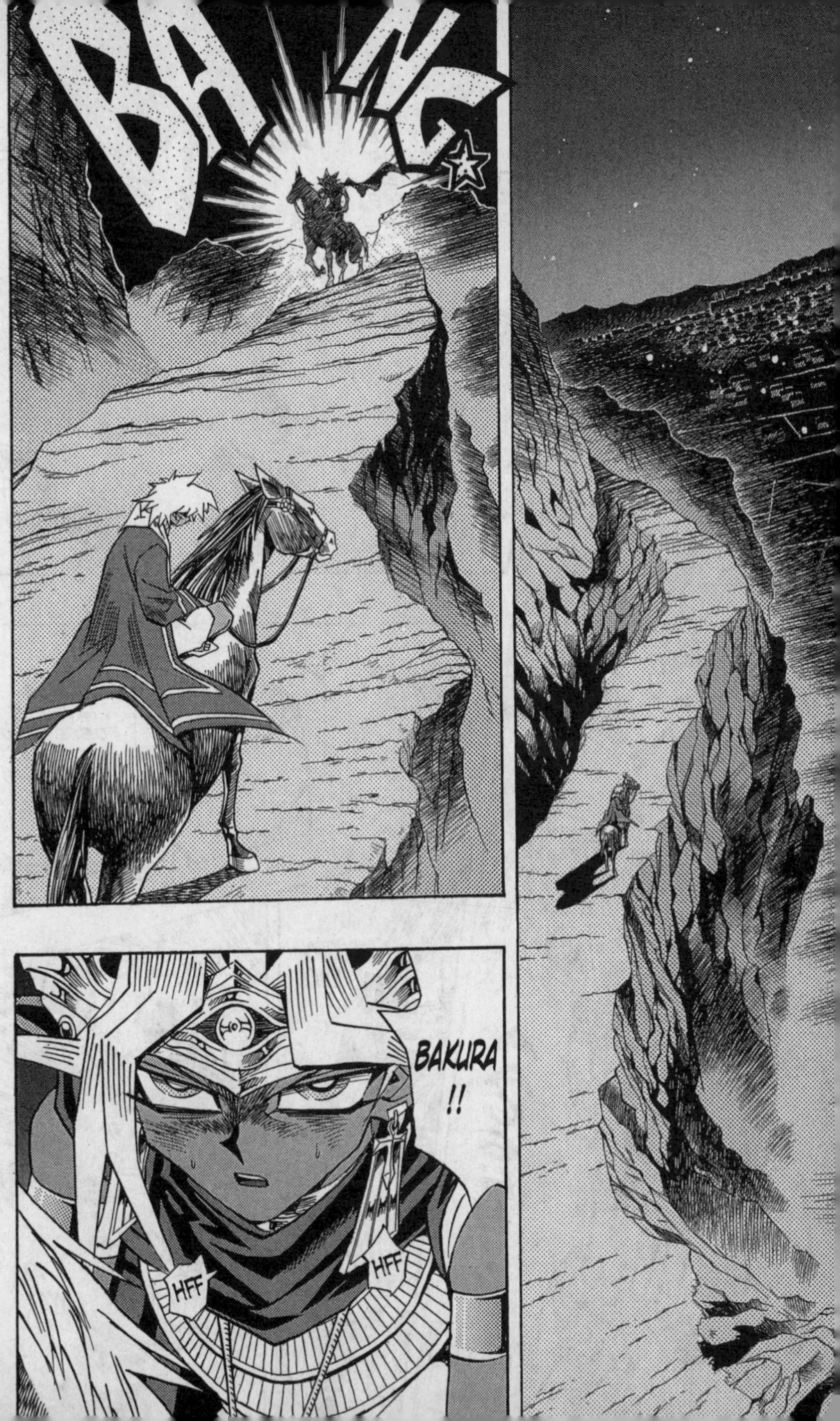
BANG
BAKURA !!
HFF
HFF

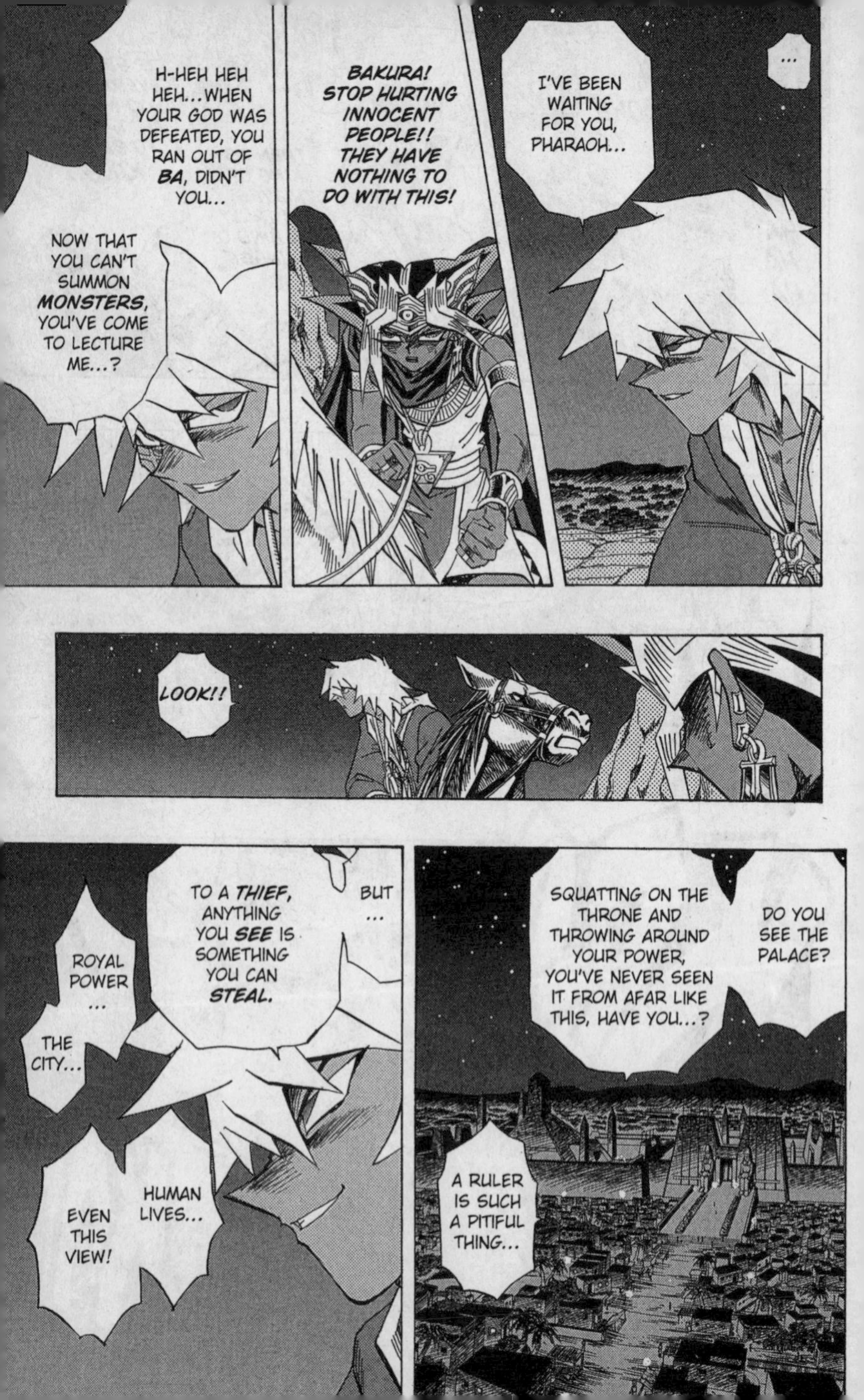
...
I'VE BEEN WAITING FOR YOU, PHARAOH...
BAKURA! STOP HURTING INNOCENT PEOPLE!! THEY HAVE NOTHING TO DO WITH THIS!
H-HEH HEH HEH...WHEN YOUR GOD WAS DEFEATED, YOU RAN OUT OF BA, DIDN'T YOU...
NOW THAT YOU CAN'T SUMMON MONSTERS, YOU'VE COME TO LECTURE ME...?
LOOK!!
DO YOU SEE THE PALACE?
SQUATTING ON THE THRONE AND THROWING AROUND YOUR POWER, YOU'VE NEVER SEEN IT FROM AFAR LIKE THIS, HAVE YOU...?
A RULER IS SUCH A PITIFUL THING...
BUT...
TO A THIEF, ANYTHING YOU SEE IS SOMETHING YOU CAN STEAL.
ROYAL POWER...
THE CITY...
HUMAN LIVES...
EVEN THIS VIEW!

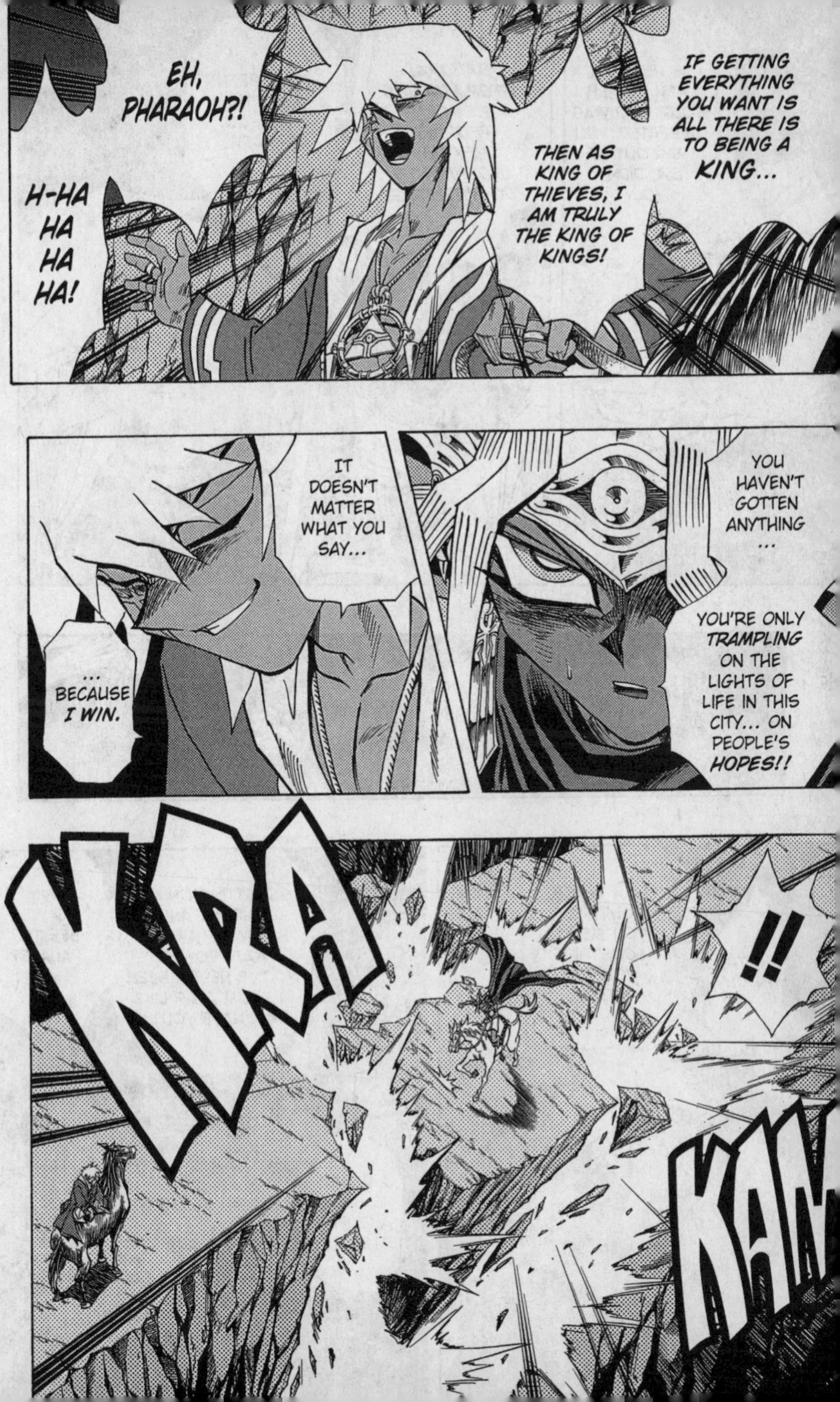

IF GETTING EVERYTHING YOU WANT IS ALL THERE IS TO BEING A KING...
THEN AS KING OF THIEVES, I AM TRULY THE KING OF KINGS!
EH, PHARAOH?!
H-HA HA HA HA!
YOU HAVEN'T GOTTEN ANYTHING...
YOU'RE ONLY TRAMPLING ON THE LIGHTS OF LIFE IN THIS CITY... ON PEOPLE'S HOPES!!
IT DOESN'T MATTER WHAT YOU SAY...
...BECAUSE I WIN.
!!
KRA
KAM

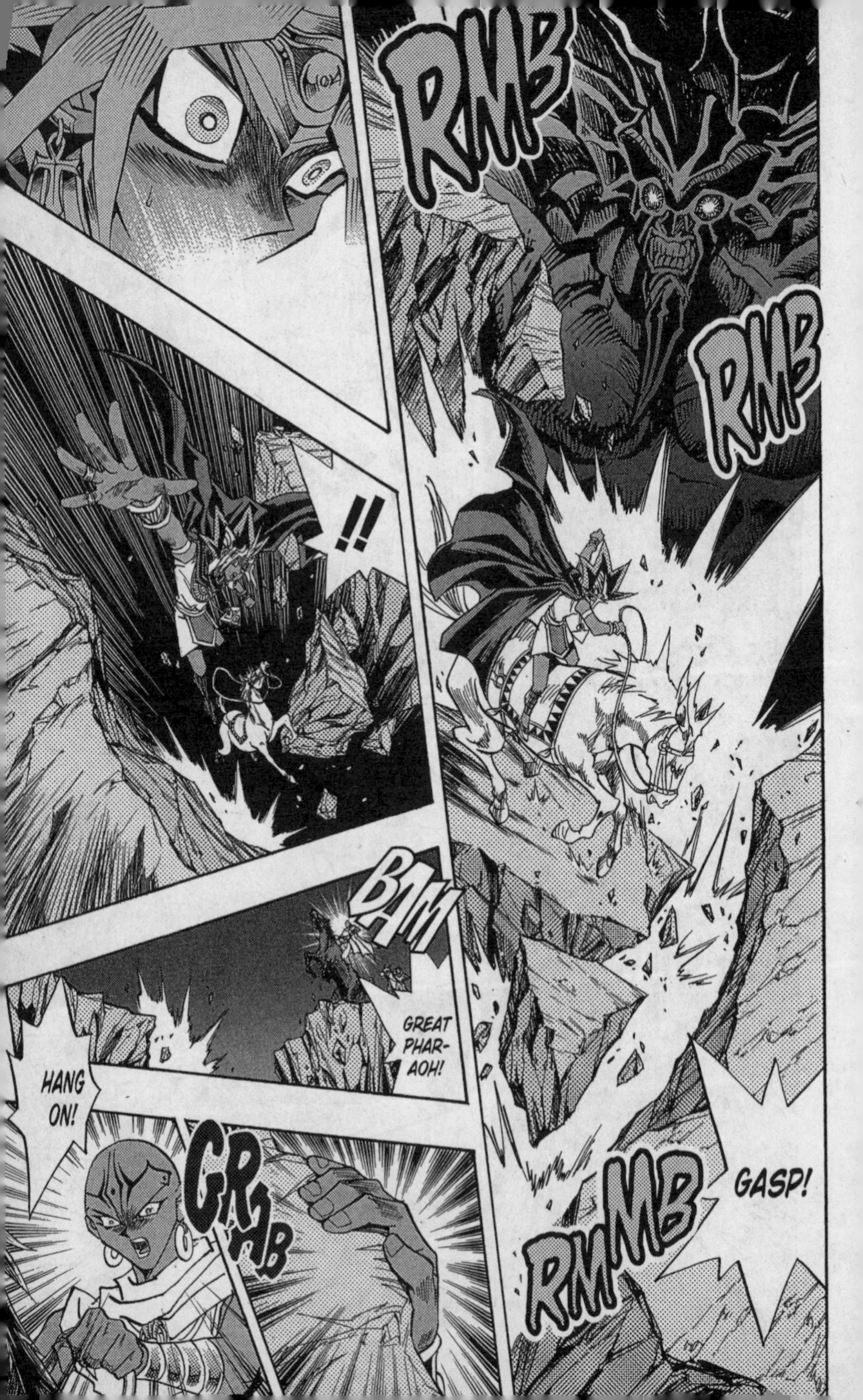

RMB
RMB
!!
BAM
GREAT PHAR-AOH!
HANG ON!
GRAB
RMMB
GASP!

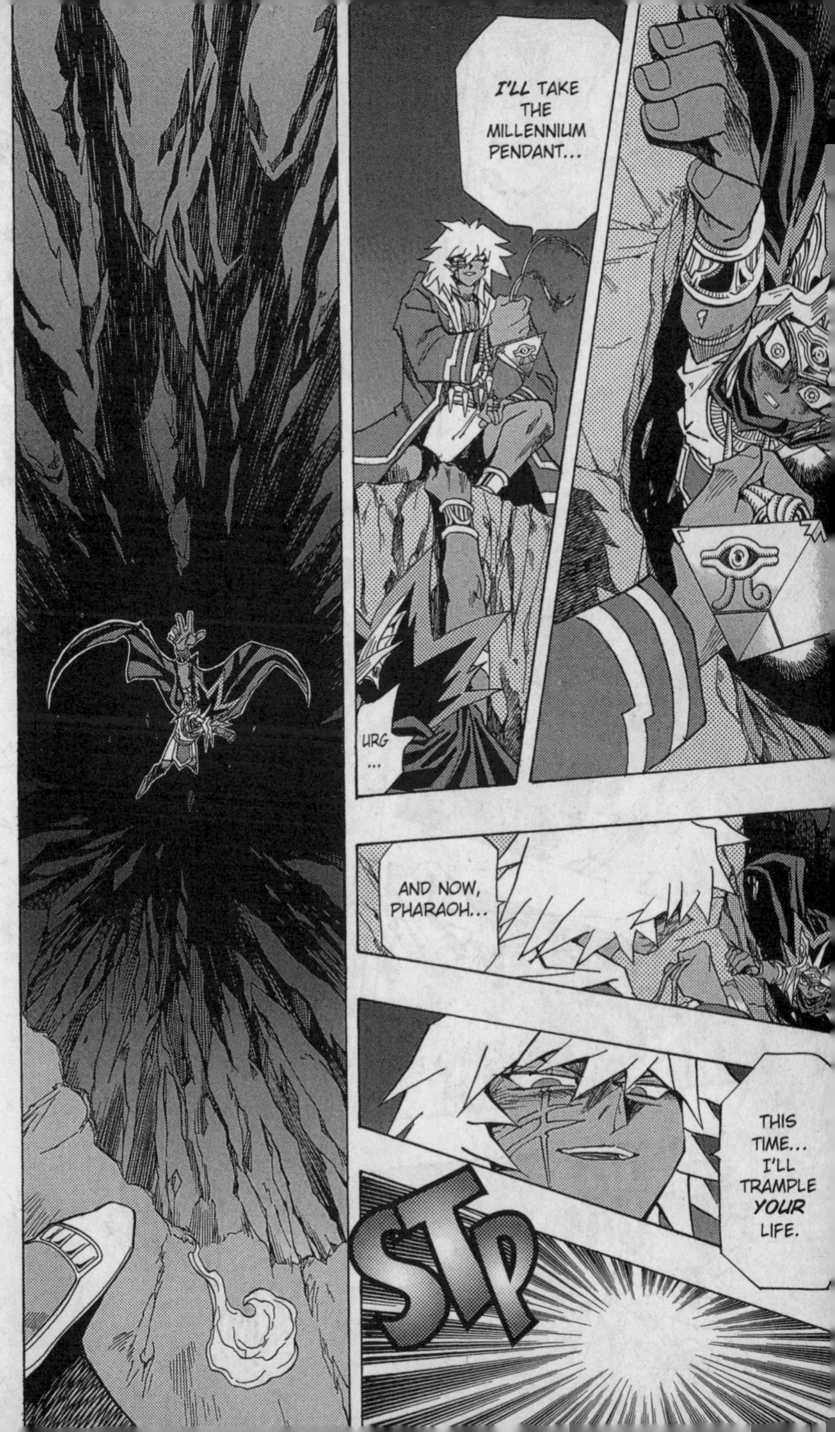
I'LL TAKE THE MILLENNIUM PENDANT...
URG...
AND NOW, PHARAOH...
THIS TIME... I'LL TRAMPLE YOUR LIFE.
STP

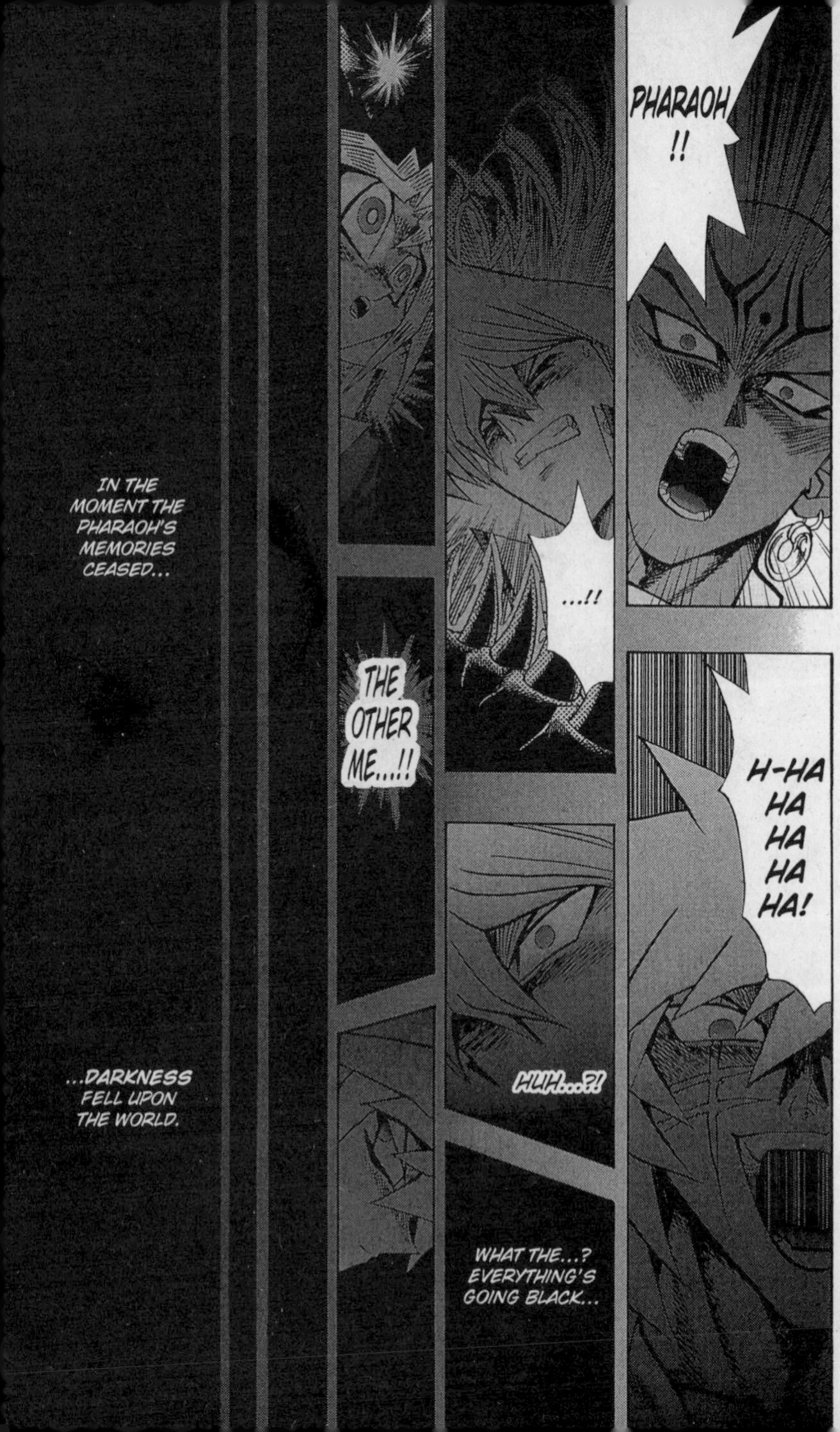
PHARAOH !!
H-HA HA HA HA HA!
...!!
HUH...?!
WHAT THE...? EVERYTHING'S GOING BLACK...
THE OTHER ME...!!
IN THE MOMENT THE PHARAOH'S MEMORIES CEASED...
...DARKNESS FELL UPON THE WORLD.

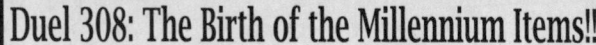

Duel 308: The Birth of the Millennium Items!!

WHEN THE PHARAOH DISAPPEARED, THE WORLD OF MEMORY FELL INTO SHADOW...

EVIL WAS AWAKENING...

MEANWHILE, IN ANOTHER'S MEMORY...

SETO ...

...

...

MY SON...

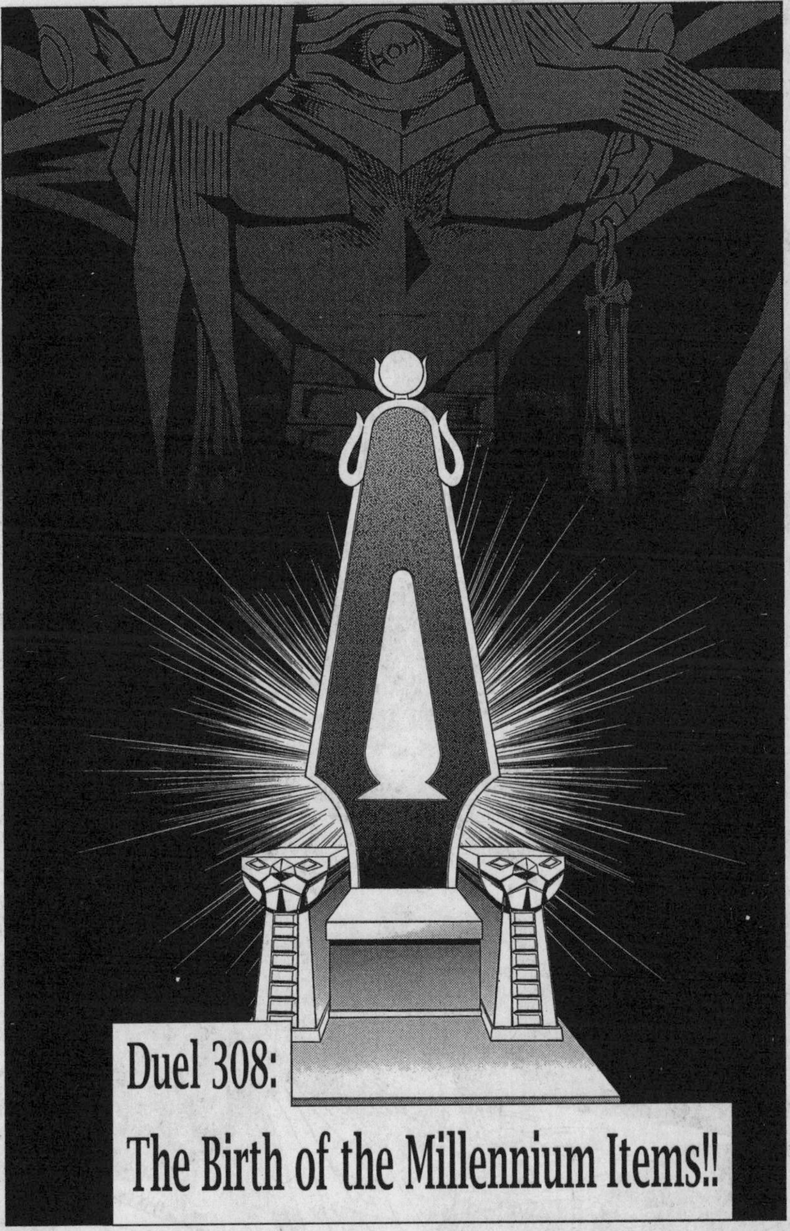
Duel 308:
The Birth of the Millennium Items!!

15 YEARS AGO...

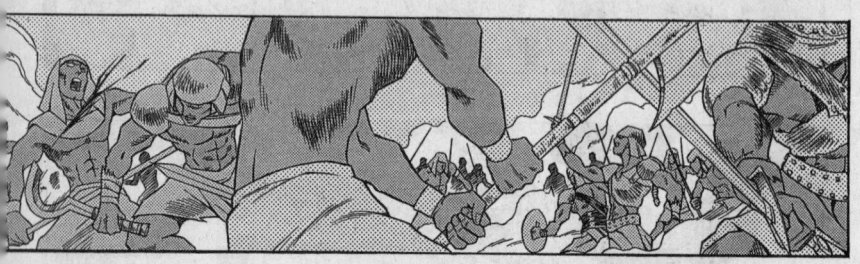

PHARAOH AKHENAMKHANEN!

THE FOREIGN ARMIES HAVE CROSSED INTO OUR LAND!

WE HAVE NO FORCES LEFT TO FIGHT BACK!

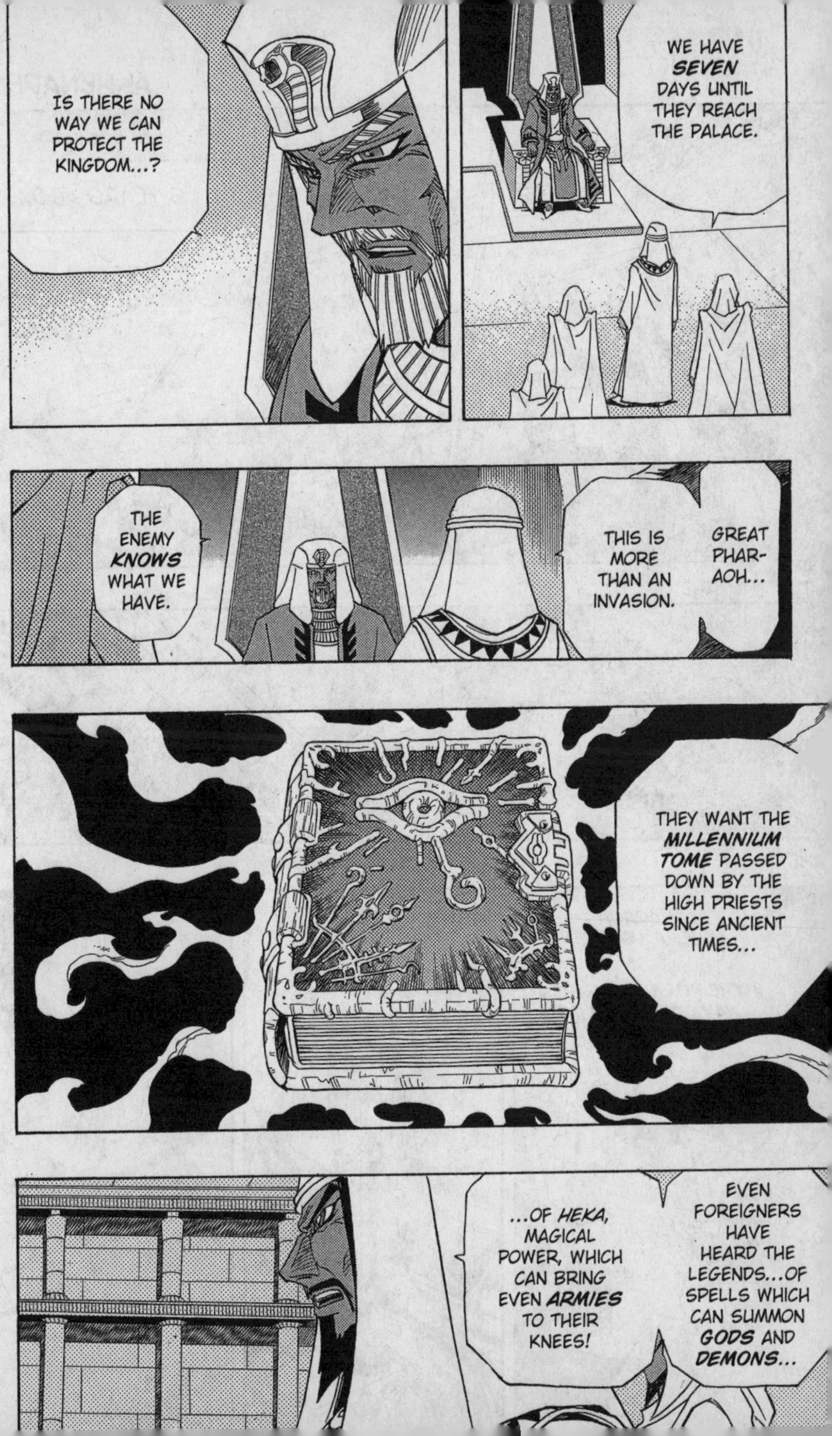
WE HAVE SEVEN DAYS UNTIL THEY REACH THE PALACE.
IS THERE NO WAY WE CAN PROTECT THE KINGDOM...?
GREAT PHARAOH...
THIS IS MORE THAN AN INVASION.
THE ENEMY KNOWS WHAT WE HAVE.
THEY WANT THE MILLENNIUM TOME PASSED DOWN BY THE HIGH PRIESTS SINCE ANCIENT TIMES...
EVEN FOREIGNERS HAVE HEARD THE LEGENDS...OF SPELLS WHICH CAN SUMMON GODS AND DEMONS...
...OF HEKA, MAGICAL POWER, WHICH CAN BRING EVEN ARMIES TO THEIR KNEES!

READ THIS WAY

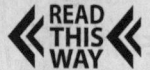

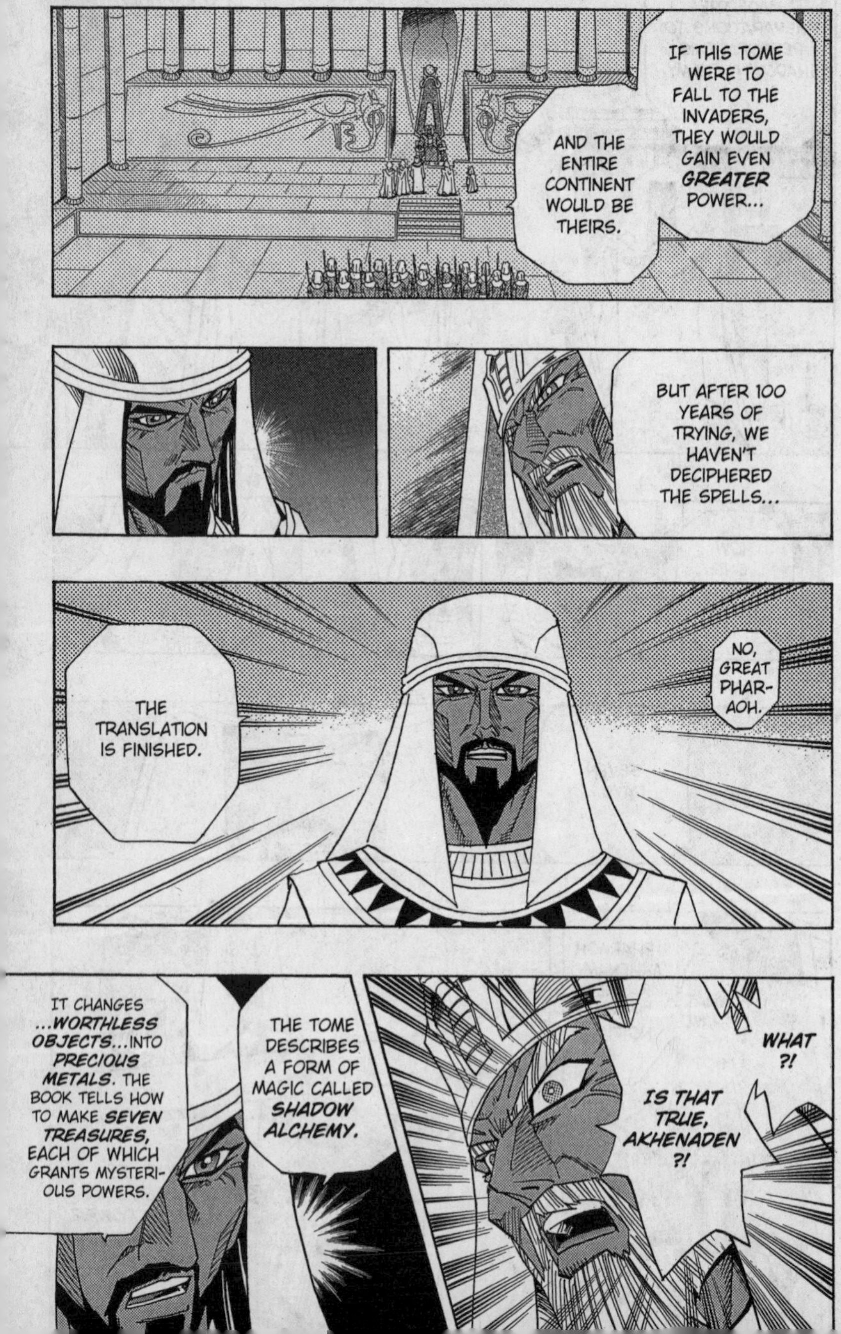
IF THIS TOME WERE TO FALL TO THE INVADERS, THEY WOULD GAIN EVEN GREATER POWER...
AND THE ENTIRE CONTINENT WOULD BE THEIRS.
BUT AFTER 100 YEARS OF TRYING, WE HAVEN'T DECIPHERED THE SPELLS...
NO, GREAT PHAR-AOH.
THE TRANSLATION IS FINISHED.
WHAT ?!
IS THAT TRUE, AKHENADEN ?!
THE TOME DESCRIBES A FORM OF MAGIC CALLED SHADOW ALCHEMY.
IT CHANGES ...WORTHLESS OBJECTS...INTO PRECIOUS METALS. THE BOOK TELLS HOW TO MAKE SEVEN TREASURES, EACH OF WHICH GRANTS MYSTERI-OUS POWERS.

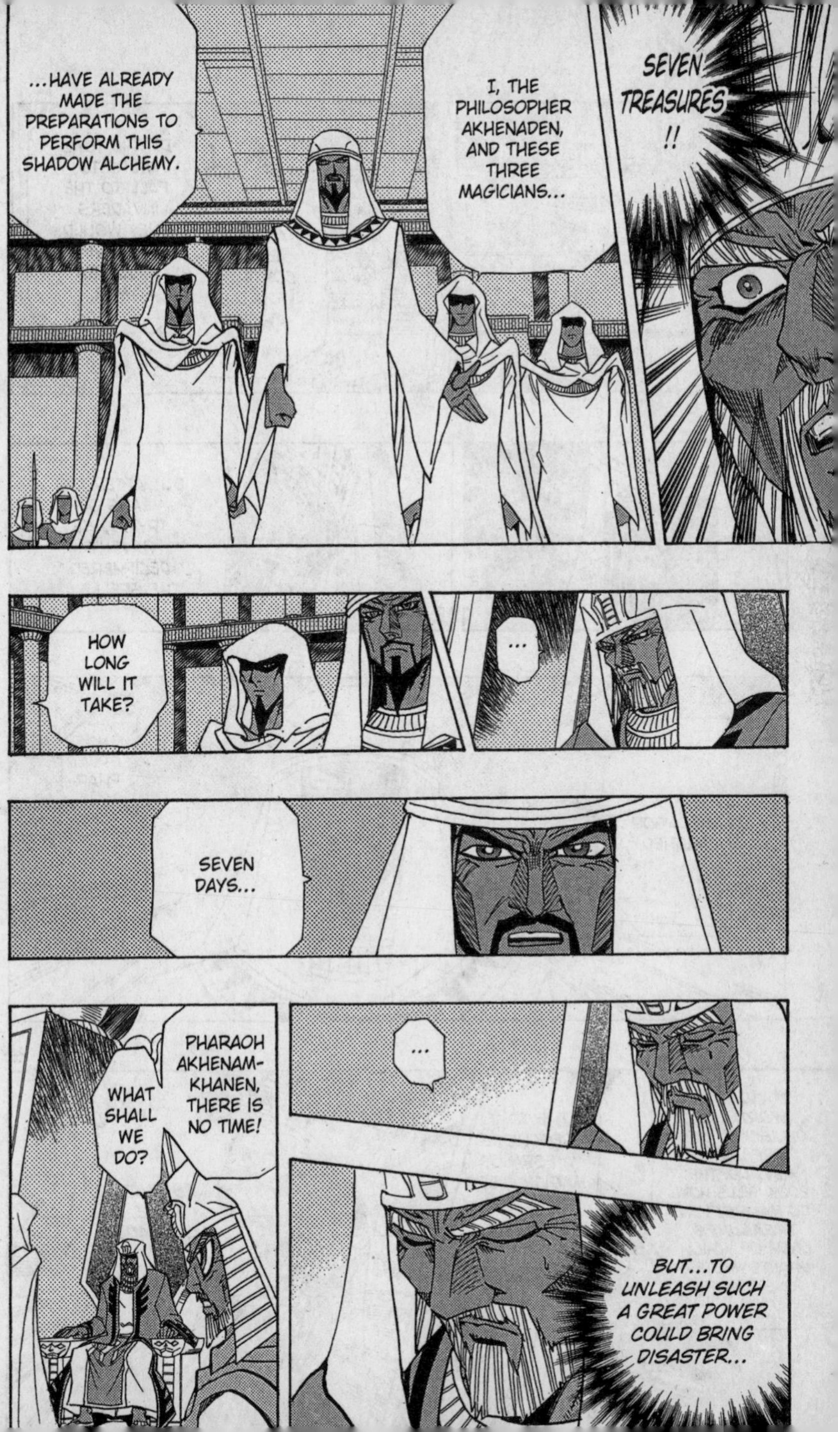
SEVEN TREASURES !!
I, THE PHILOSOPHER AKHENADEN, AND THESE THREE MAGICIANS...
...HAVE ALREADY MADE THE PREPARATIONS TO PERFORM THIS SHADOW ALCHEMY.
...
HOW LONG WILL IT TAKE?
SEVEN DAYS...
...
PHARAOH AKHENAMKHANEN, THERE IS NO TIME!
WHAT SHALL WE DO?
BUT...TO UNLEASH SUCH A GREAT POWER COULD BRING DISASTER...

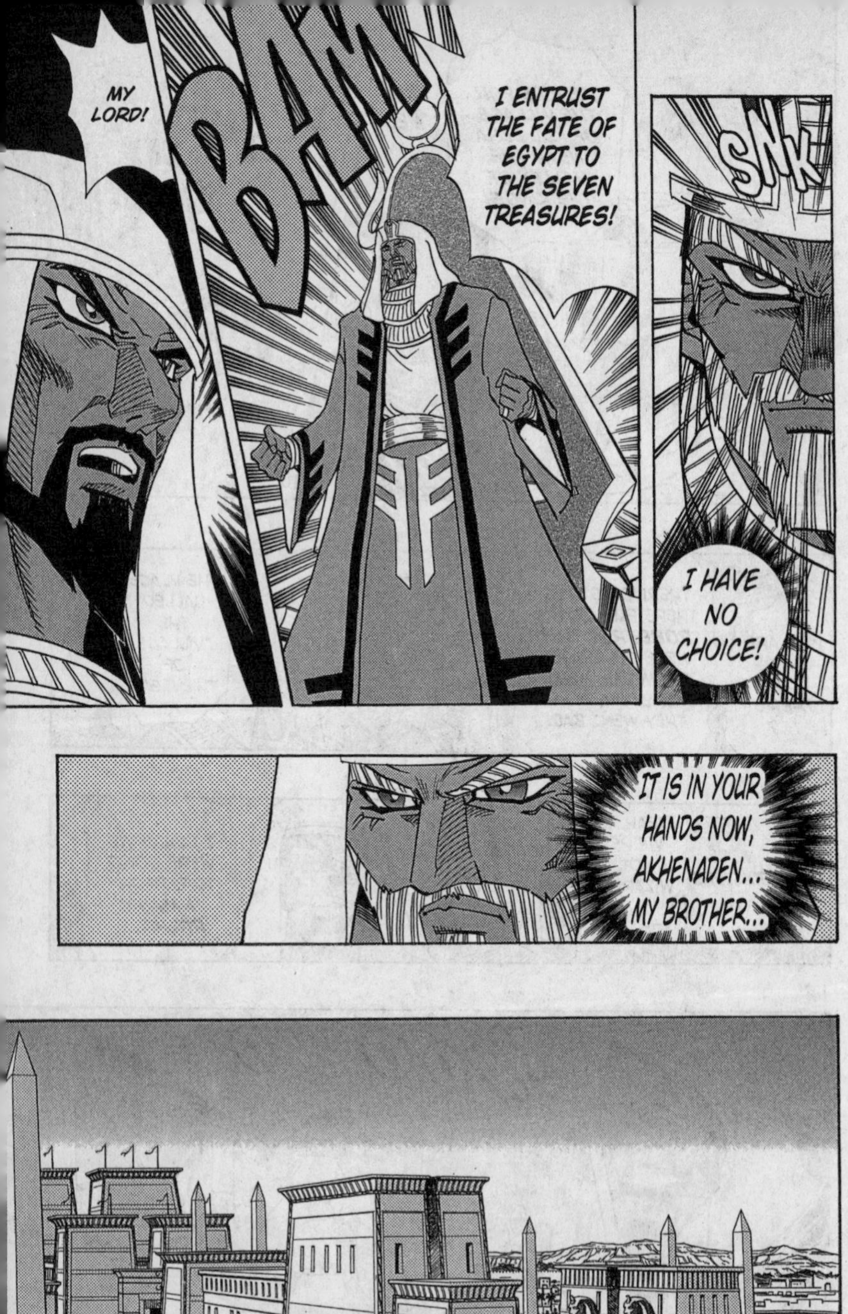
MY LORD!
BAM
I ENTRUST THE FATE OF EGYPT TO THE SEVEN TREASURES!
SNK
I HAVE NO CHOICE!
IT IS IN YOUR HANDS NOW, AKHENADEN... MY BROTHER...

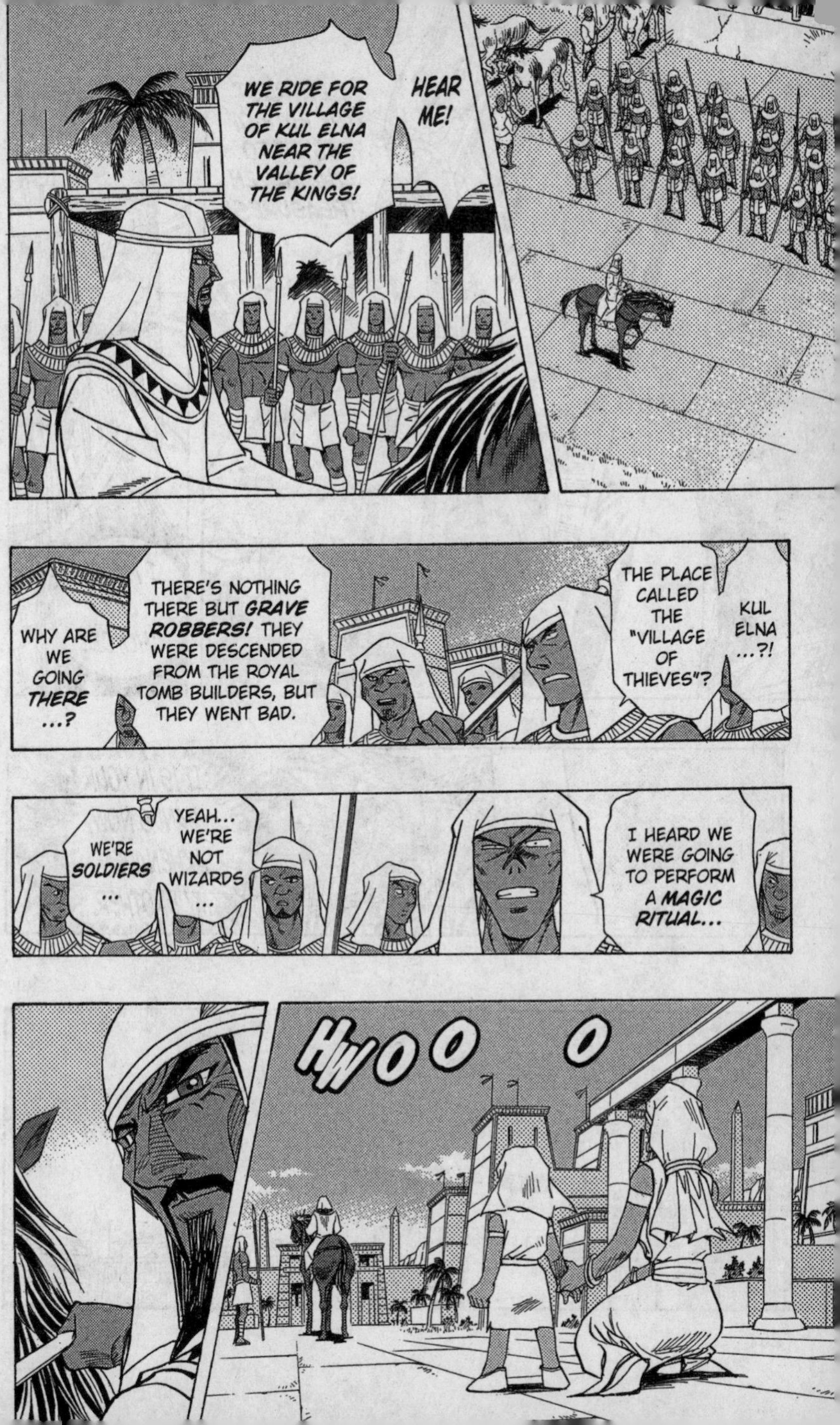
HEAR ME!
WE RIDE FOR THE VILLAGE OF KUL ELNA NEAR THE VALLEY OF THE KINGS!
KUL ELNA ...?!
THE PLACE CALLED THE "VILLAGE OF THIEVES"?
THERE'S NOTHING THERE BUT GRAVE ROBBERS! THEY WERE DESCENDED FROM THE ROYAL TOMB BUILDERS, BUT THEY WENT BAD.
WHY ARE WE GOING THERE ...?
I HEARD WE WERE GOING TO PERFORM A MAGIC RITUAL...
YEAH... WE'RE NOT WIZARDS ...
WE'RE SOLDIERS ...
HWOOO O

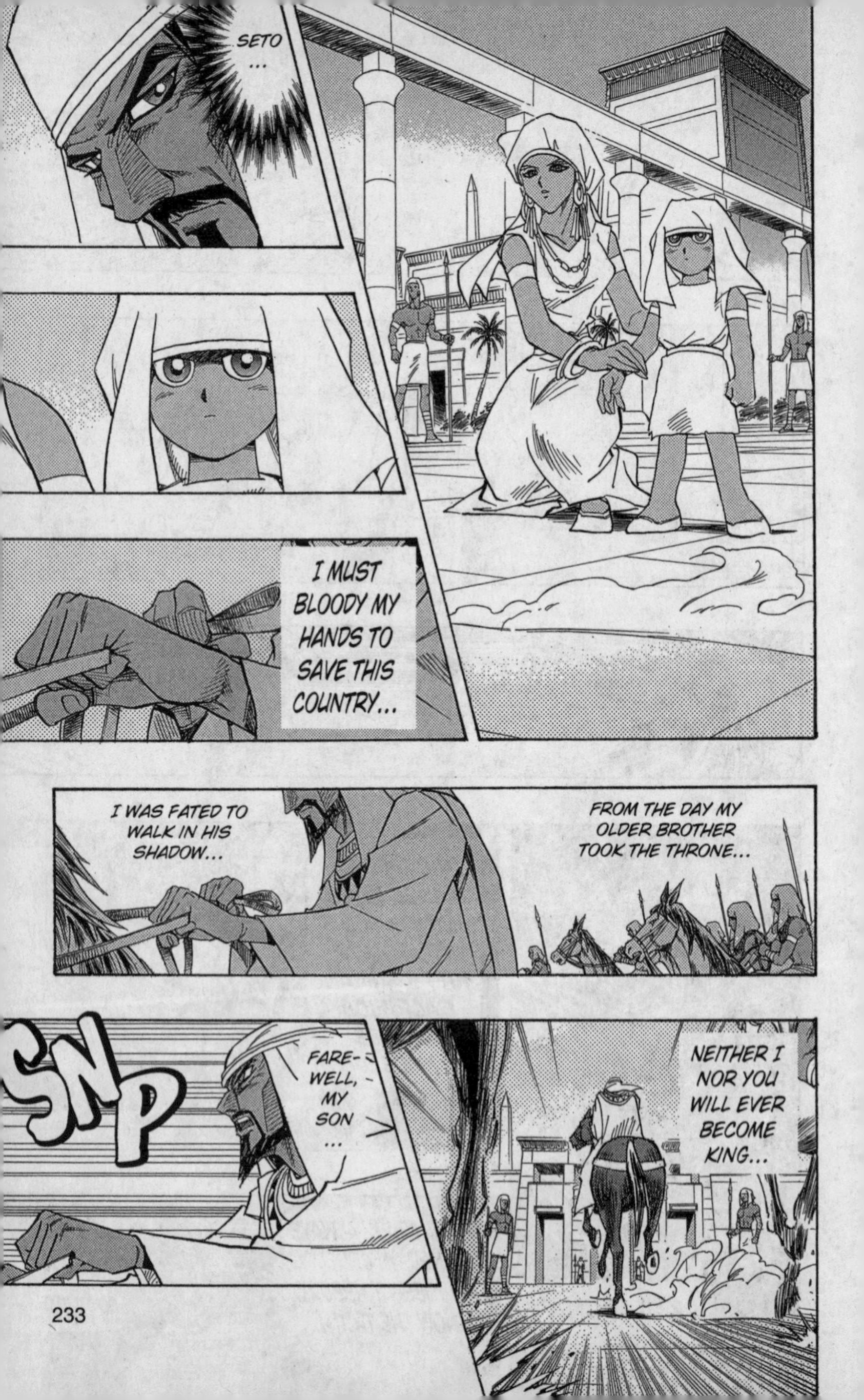
SETO ...
I MUST BLOODY MY HANDS TO SAVE THIS COUNTRY...
I WAS FATED TO WALK IN HIS SHADOW...
FROM THE DAY MY OLDER BROTHER TOOK THE THRONE...
SNP
FARE-WELL, MY SON ...
NEITHER I NOR YOU WILL EVER BECOME KING...

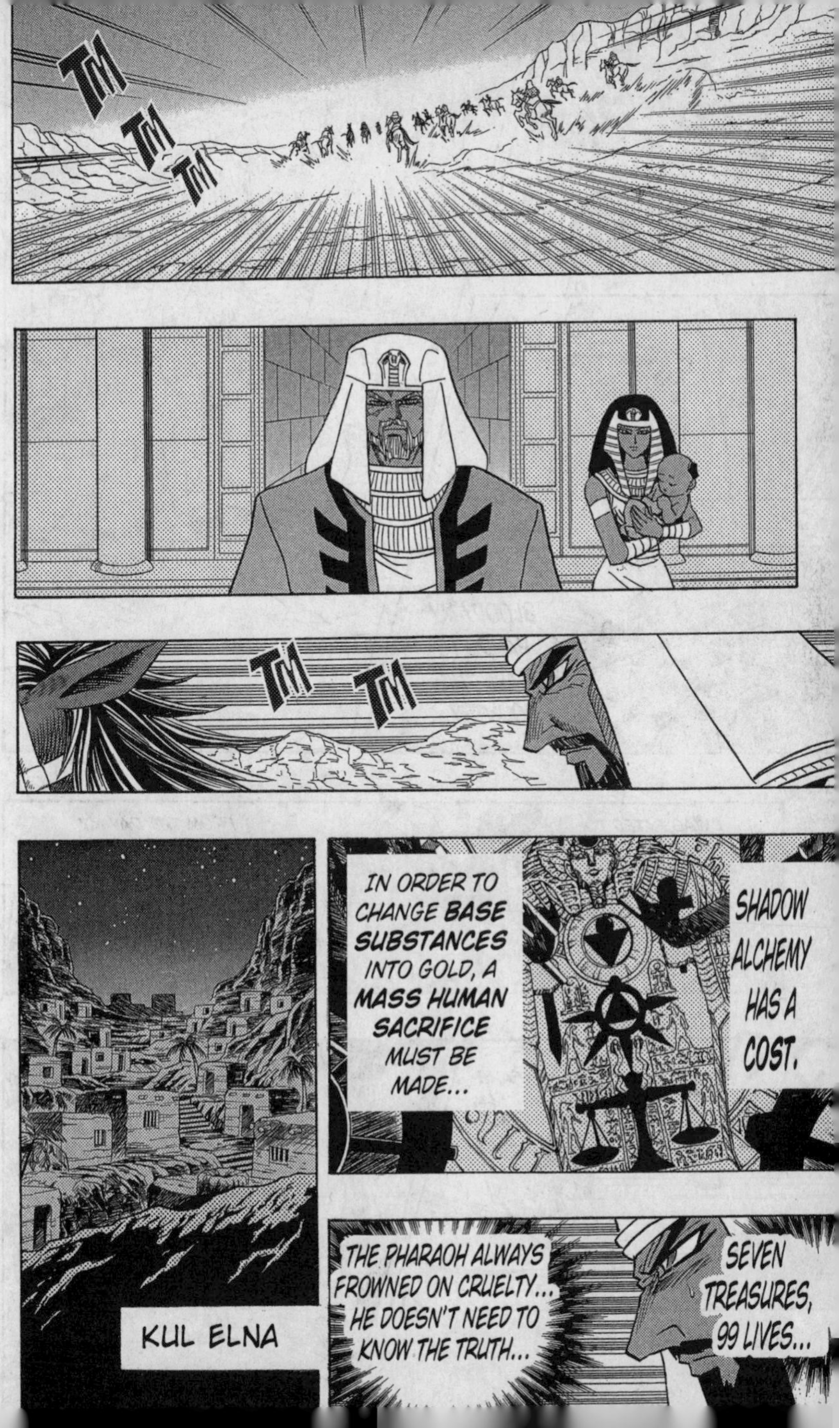
TM
TM
TM
TM
TM
SHADOW ALCHEMY HAS A COST.
IN ORDER TO CHANGE BASE SUBSTANCES INTO GOLD, A MASS HUMAN SACRIFICE MUST BE MADE...
KUL ELNA
SEVEN TREASURES, 99 LIVES...
THE PHARAOH ALWAYS FROWNED ON CRUELTY... HE DOESN'T NEED TO KNOW THE TRUTH...

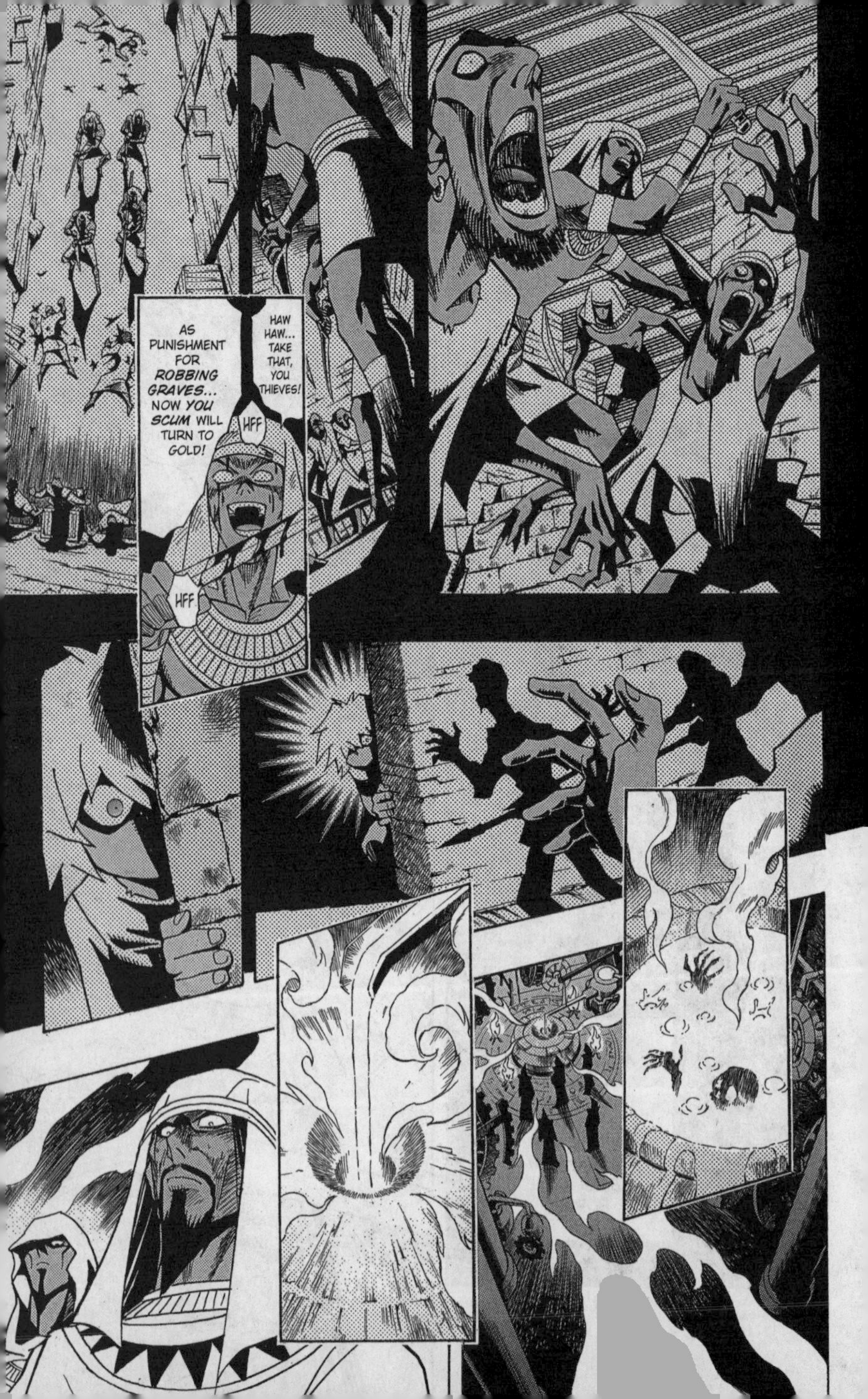
HAW HAW... TAKE THAT, YOU THIEVES!
AS PUNISHMENT FOR ROBBING GRAVES... NOW YOU SCUM WILL TURN TO GOLD!
HFF
HFF

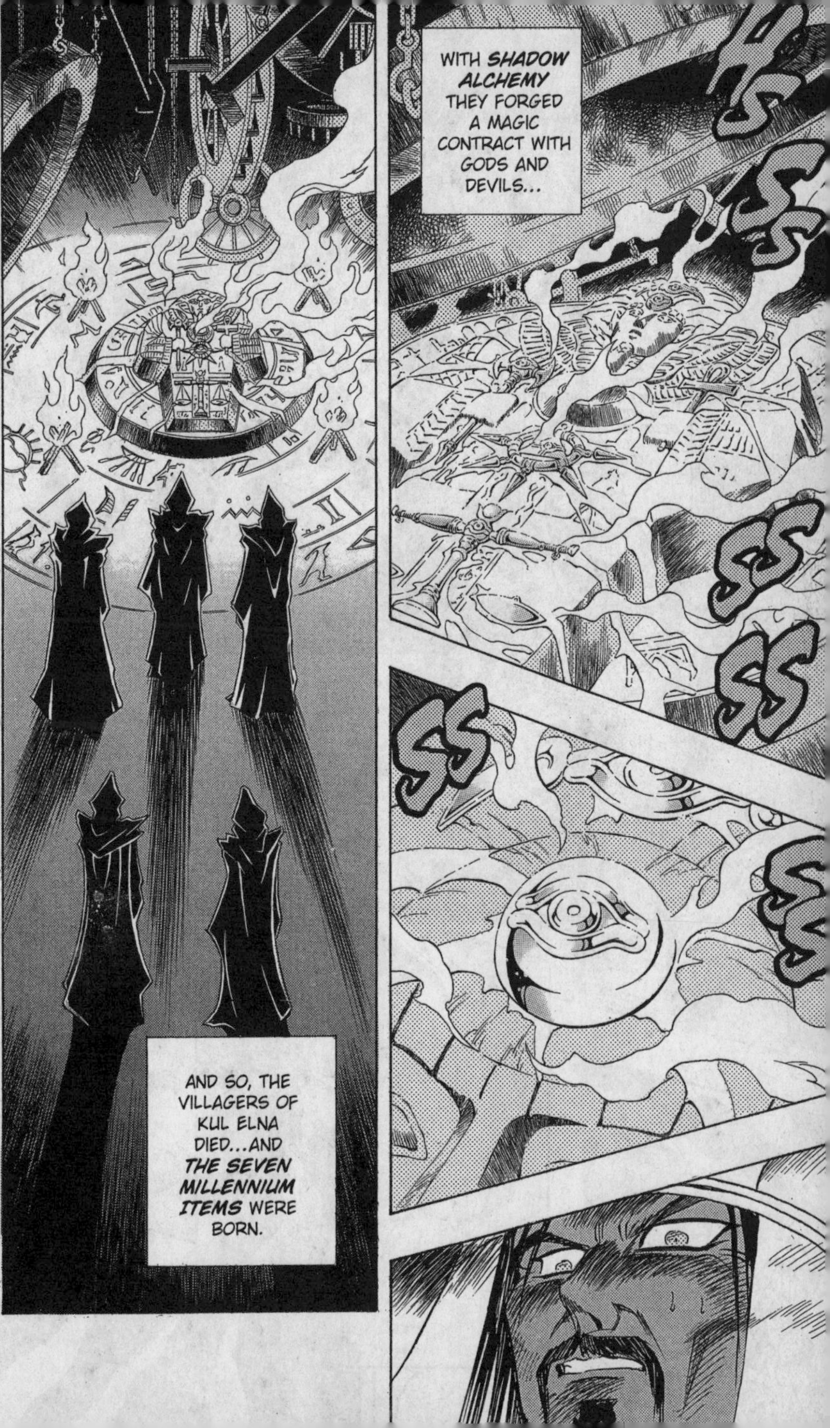
WITH SHADOW ALCHEMY THEY FORGED A MAGIC CONTRACT WITH GODS AND DEVILS...
HSSS
SS
SS
SS
SS
AND SO, THE VILLAGERS OF KUL ELNA DIED...AND THE SEVEN MILLENNIUM ITEMS WERE BORN.

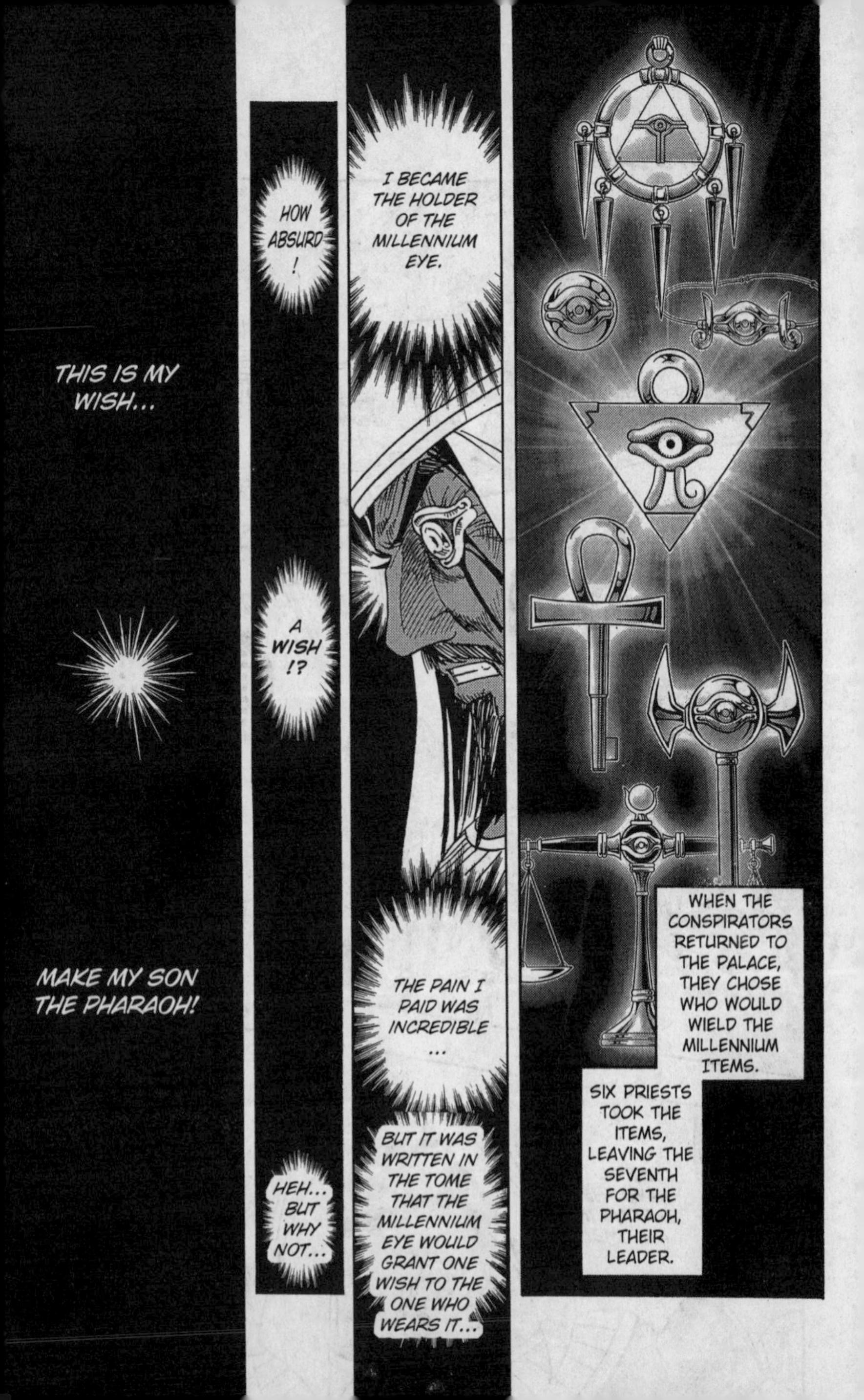
WHEN THE CONSPIRATORS RETURNED TO THE PALACE, THEY CHOSE WHO WOULD WIELD THE MILLENNIUM ITEMS.
SIX PRIESTS TOOK THE ITEMS, LEAVING THE SEVENTH FOR THE PHARAOH, THEIR LEADER.
I BECAME THE HOLDER OF THE MILLENNIUM EYE.
THE PAIN I PAID WAS INCREDIBLE...
BUT IT WAS WRITTEN IN THE TOME THAT THE MILLENNIUM EYE WOULD GRANT ONE WISH TO THE ONE WHO WEARS IT...
HOW ABSURD!
A WISH!?
HEH... BUT WHY NOT...
THIS IS MY WISH...
MAKE MY SON THE PHARAOH!

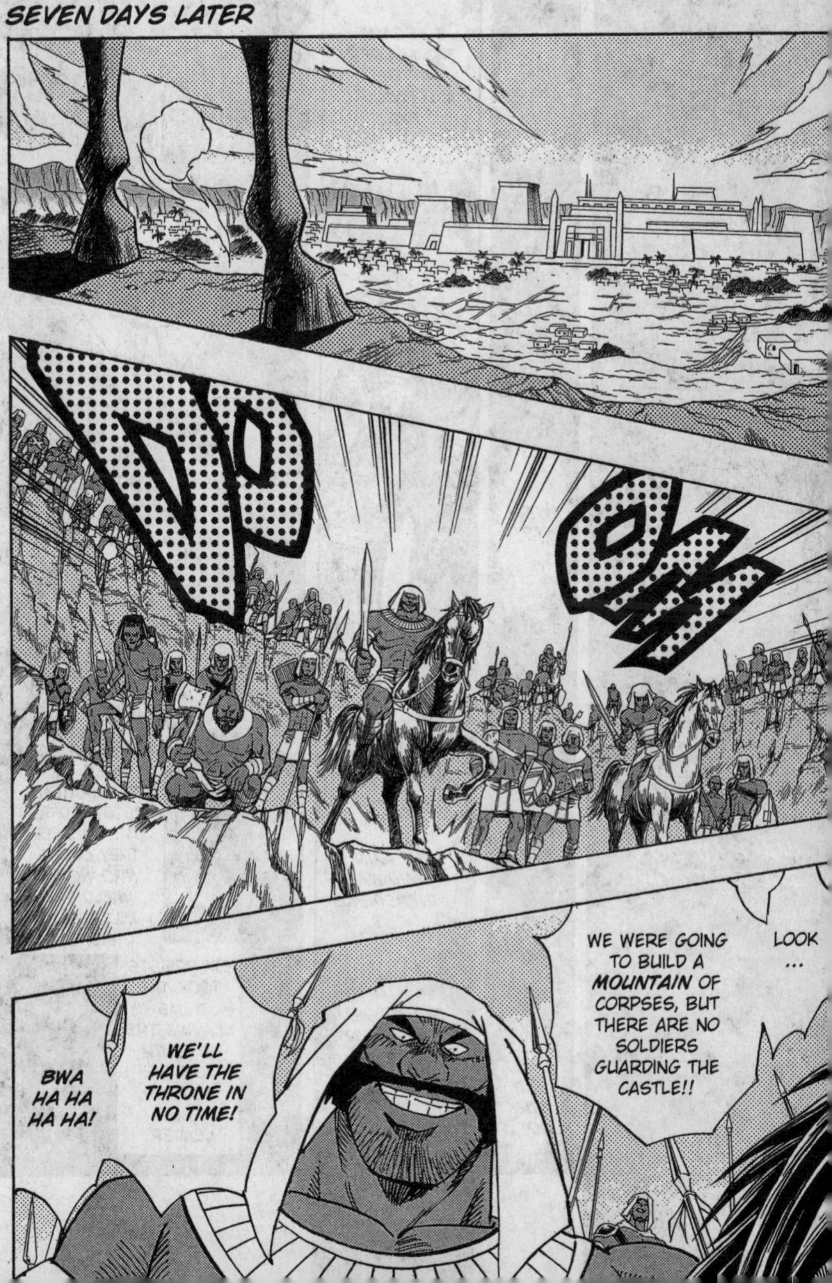
SEVEN DAYS LATER
DOOM
LOOK ...
WE WERE GOING TO BUILD A MOUNTAIN OF CORPSES, BUT THERE ARE NO SOLDIERS GUARDING THE CASTLE!!
WE'LL HAVE THE THRONE IN NO TIME!
BWA HA HA HA HA!

TM
TM
ATTACK !!
THIS LAND IS OURS NOW!
KILL ANYONE YOU FIND ALIVE!
TM
TM
TM
TM
TM
TM
TM
HUH ?!
BAM
BA

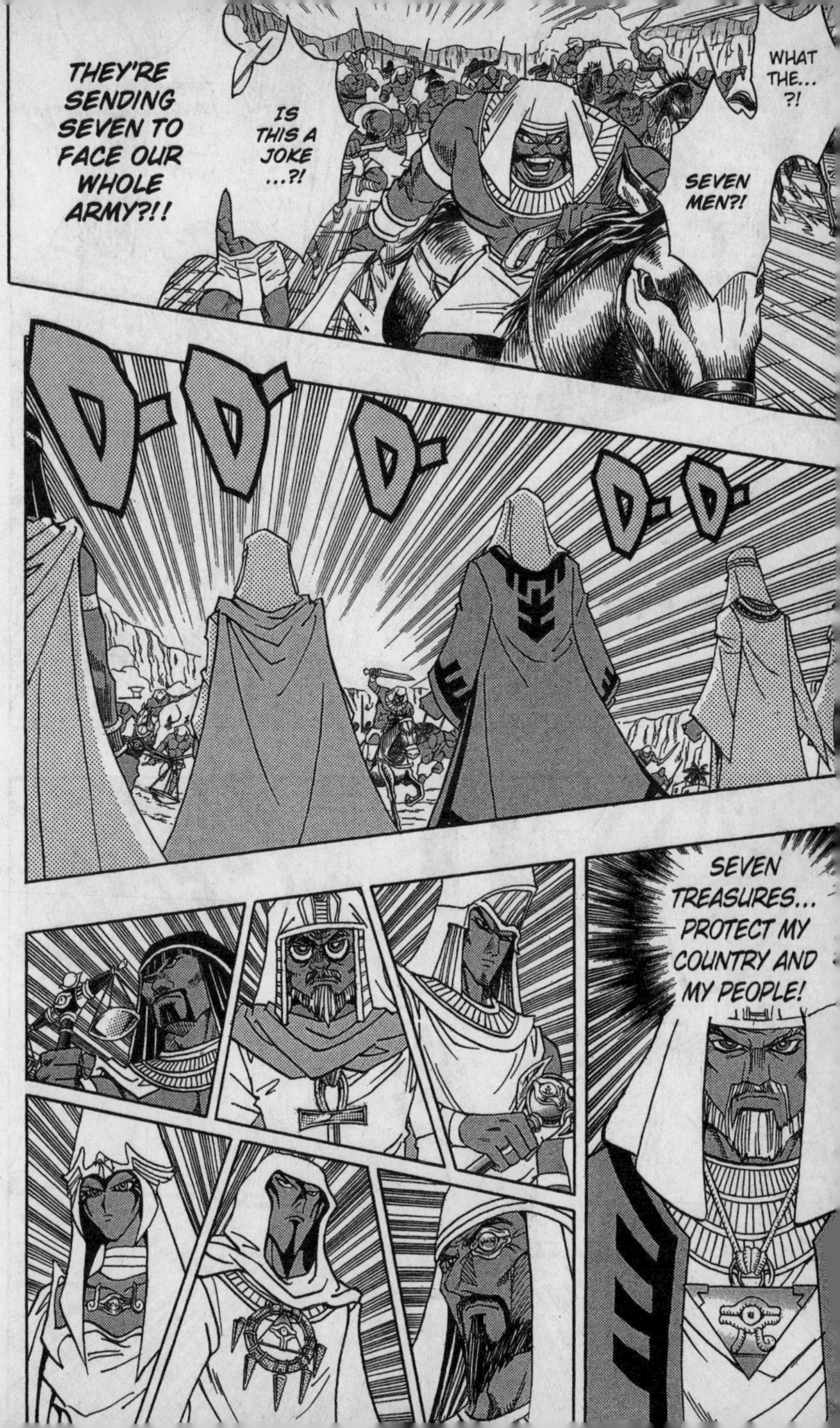
WHAT THE...?!
SEVEN MEN?!
IS THIS A JOKE...?!
THEY'RE SENDING SEVEN TO FACE OUR WHOLE ARMY?!!
D-D-D-D-D-
SEVEN TREASURES... PROTECT MY COUNTRY AND MY PEOPLE!

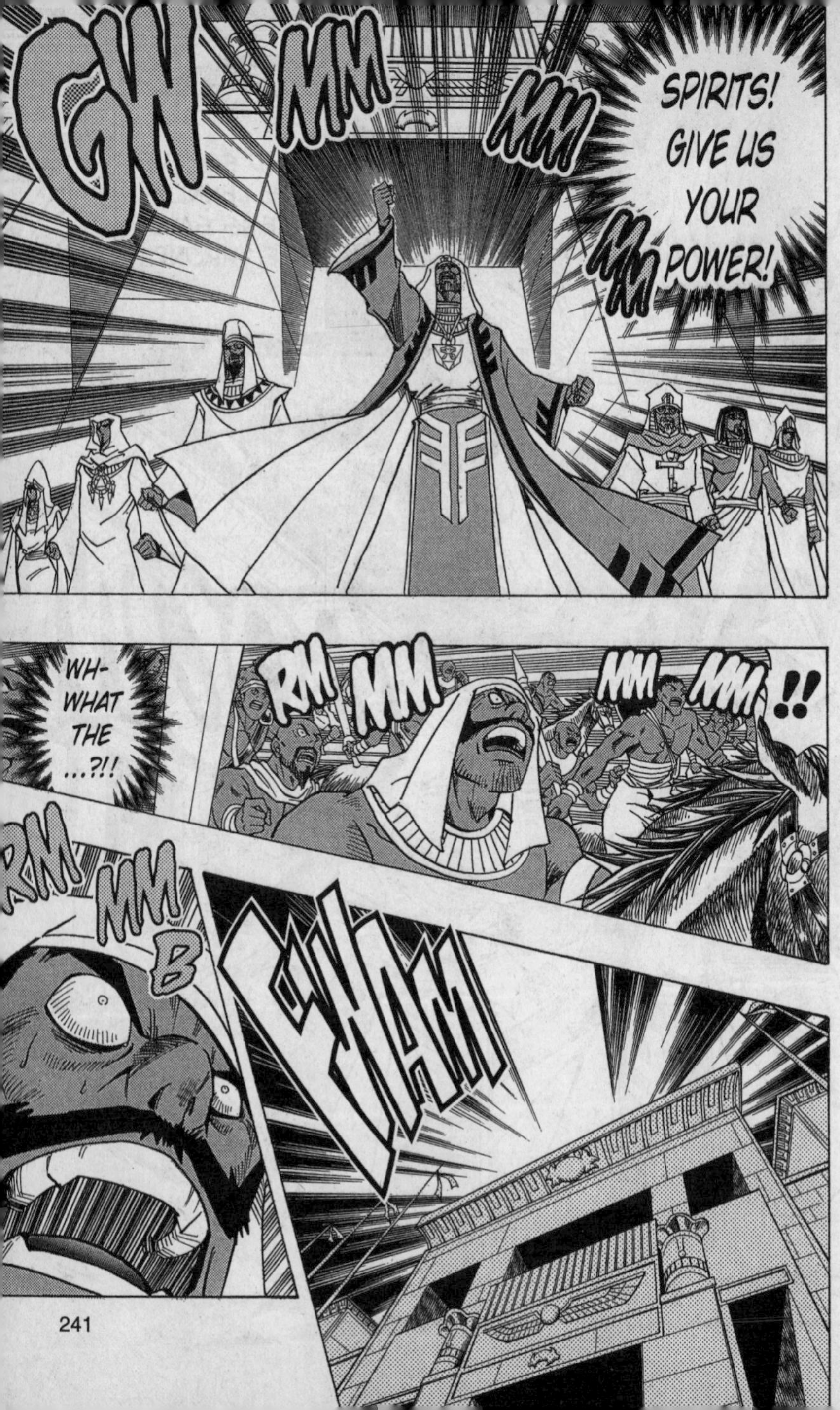
GH
MM
MM
SPIRITS! GIVE US YOUR POWER!
MM
RM MM
MM MM!!
WH-WHAT THE ...?!!
RM
MM
B
WHAM

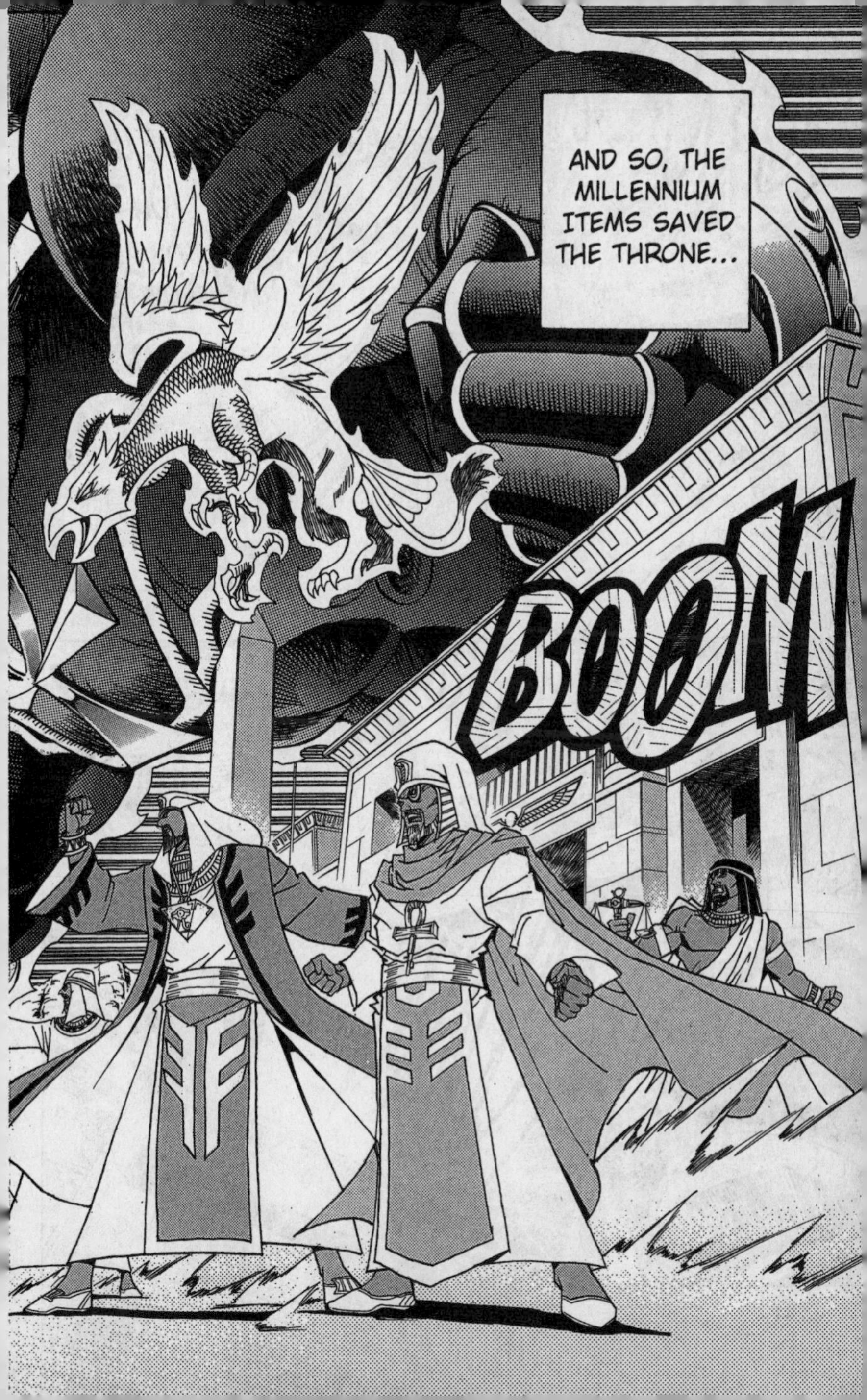
AND SO, THE MILLENNIUM ITEMS SAVED THE THRONE...
BOOM

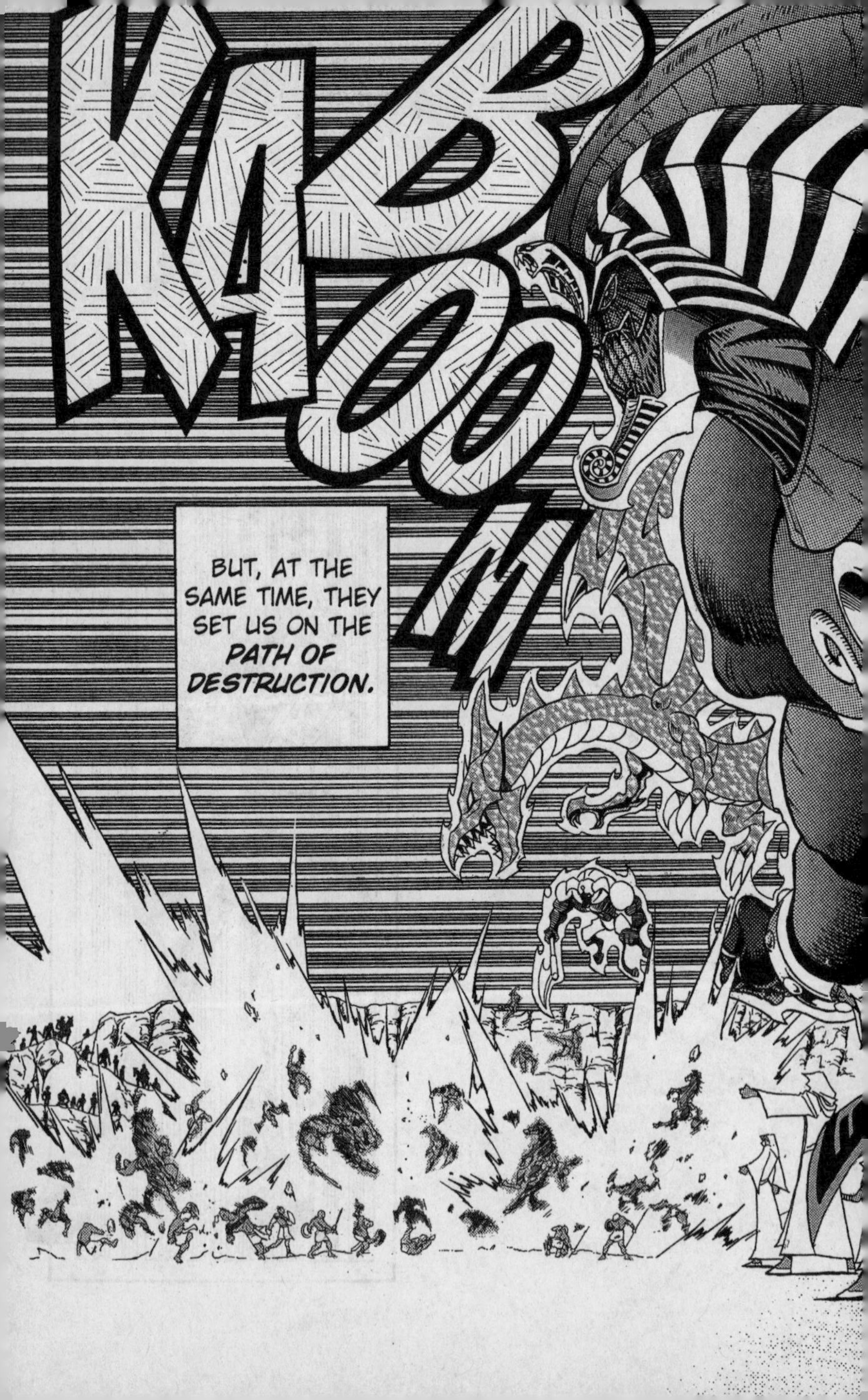
KABOOM
BUT, AT THE SAME TIME, THEY SET US ON THE PATH OF DESTRUCTION.

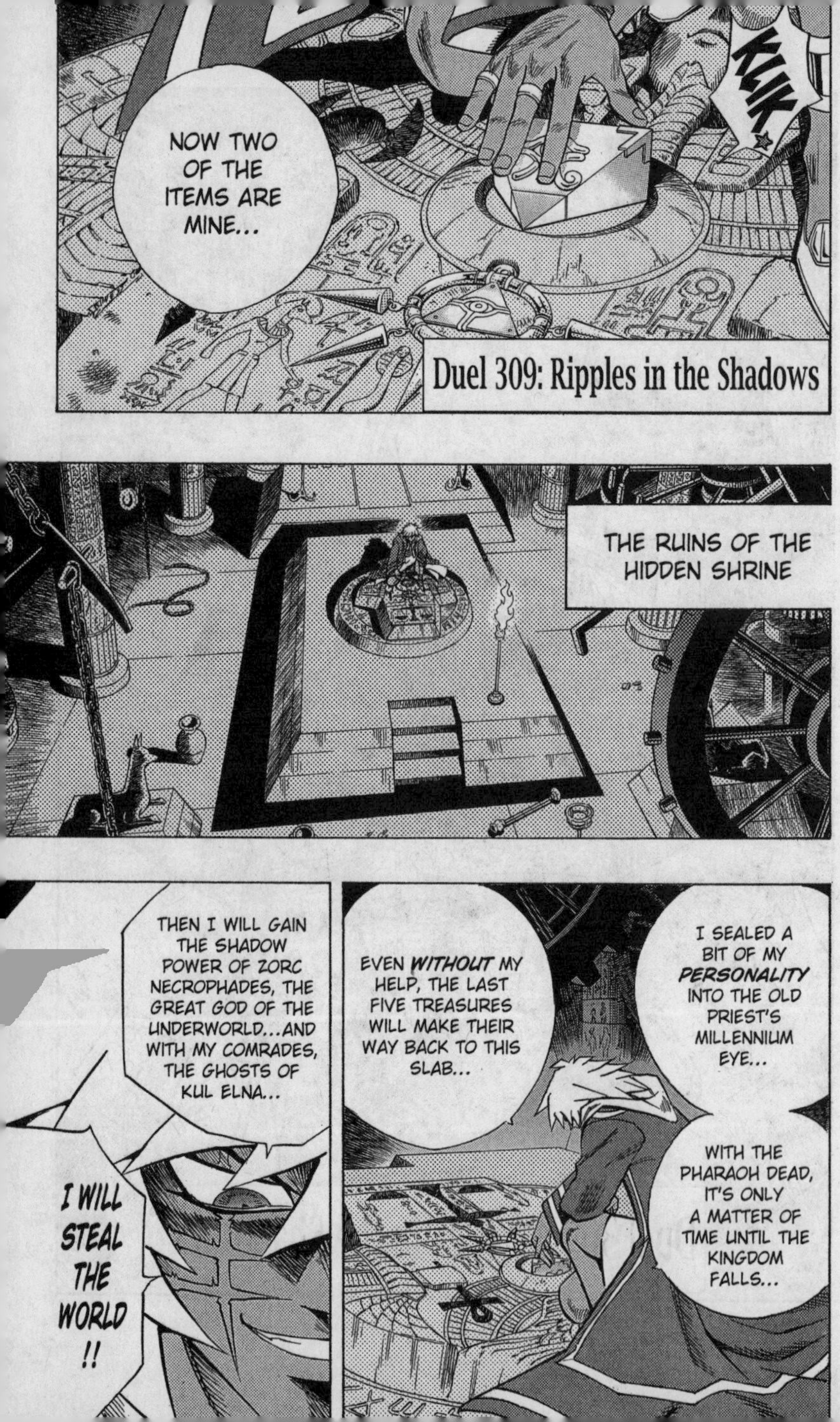
KLIK
NOW TWO OF THE ITEMS ARE MINE...
Duel 309: Ripples in the Shadows
THE RUINS OF THE HIDDEN SHRINE
I SEALED A BIT OF MY *PERSONALITY* INTO THE OLD PRIEST'S MILLENNIUM EYE...
WITH THE PHARAOH DEAD, IT'S ONLY A MATTER OF TIME UNTIL THE KINGDOM FALLS...
EVEN *WITHOUT* MY HELP, THE LAST FIVE TREASURES WILL MAKE THEIR WAY BACK TO THIS SLAB...
THEN I WILL GAIN THE SHADOW POWER OF ZORC NECROPHADES, THE GREAT GOD OF THE UNDERWORLD...AND WITH MY COMRADES, THE GHOSTS OF KUL ELNA...
I WILL STEAL THE WORLD!!

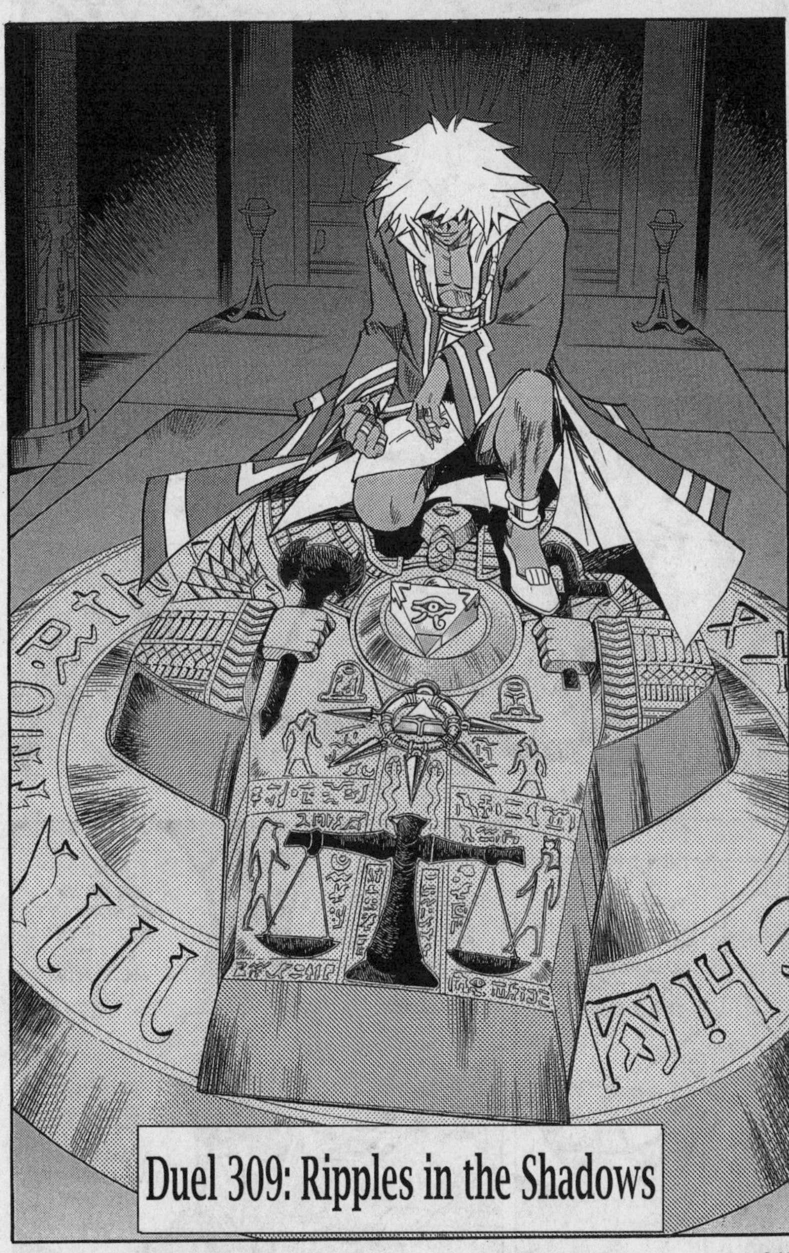
Duel 309: Ripples in the Shadows

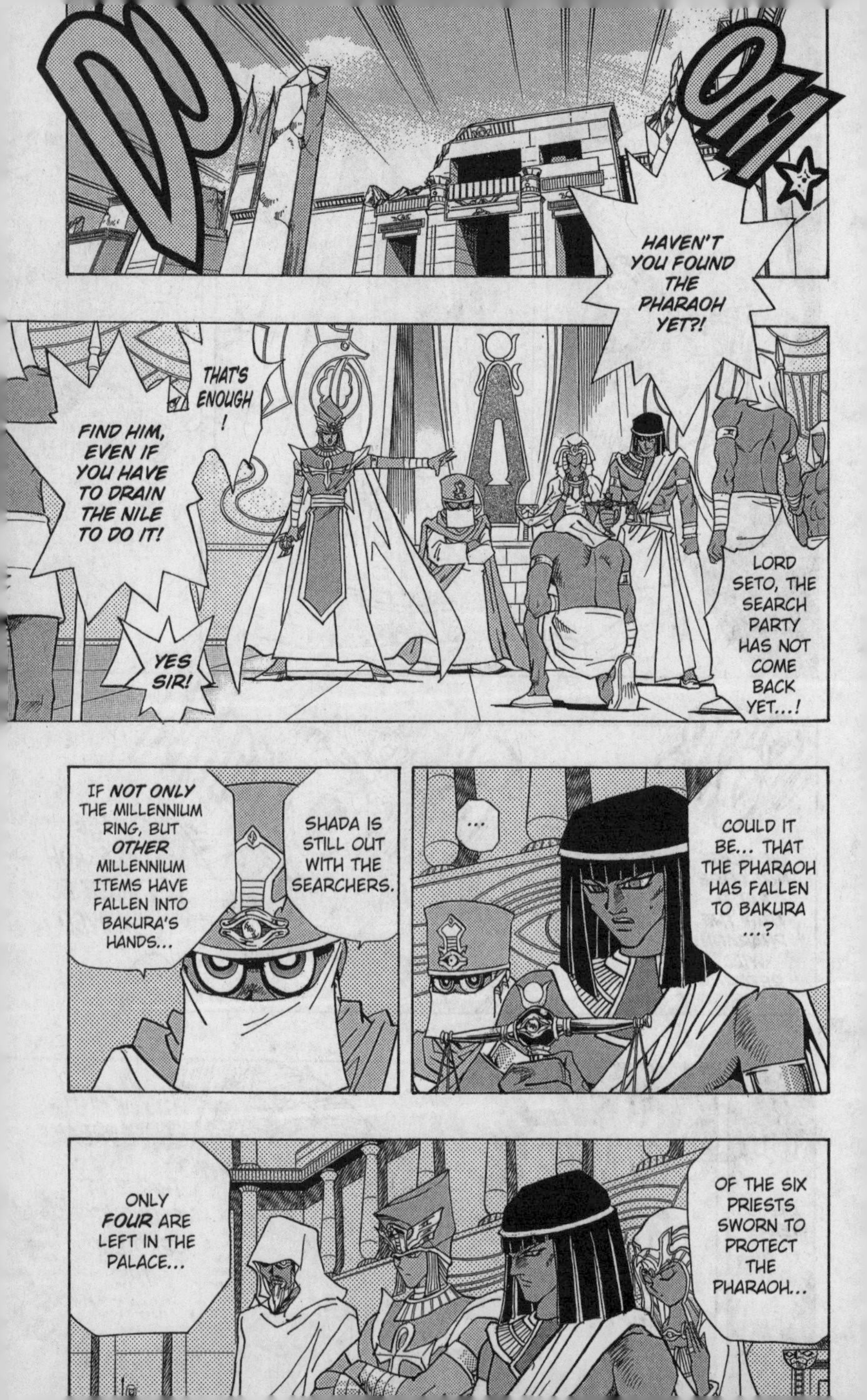
HAVEN'T YOU FOUND THE PHARAOH YET?!
LORD SETO, THE SEARCH PARTY HAS NOT COME BACK YET...!
THAT'S ENOUGH!
FIND HIM, EVEN IF YOU HAVE TO DRAIN THE NILE TO DO IT!
YES SIR!
COULD IT BE... THAT THE PHARAOH HAS FALLEN TO BAKURA...?
...
SHADA IS STILL OUT WITH THE SEARCHERS.
IF NOT ONLY THE MILLENNIUM RING, BUT OTHER MILLENNIUM ITEMS HAVE FALLEN INTO BAKURA'S HANDS...
OF THE SIX PRIESTS SWORN TO PROTECT THE PHARAOH...
ONLY FOUR ARE LEFT IN THE PALACE...

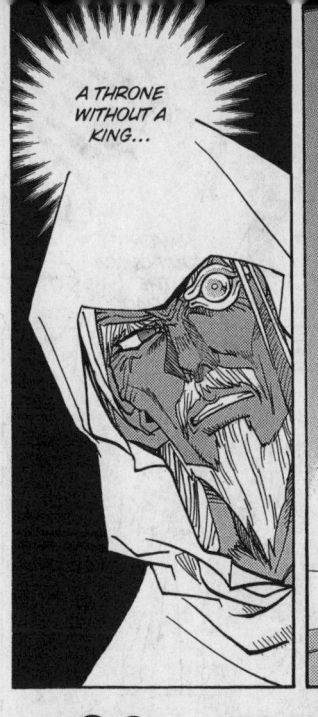

A THRONE WITHOUT A KING...
THE PHARAOH MUST BE ALIVE!!
AND HIS DREAM TO PROTECT HIS COUNTRY IS STILL STRONG!
WE MUST NOT LOSE FAITH THAT THE PHARAOH WILL RETURN!
FAITH... DREAMS...
THAT ISN'T ENOUGH TO PROTECT THIS COUNTRY...
YOU NEED POWER, SETO!
LIKE 15 YEARS AGO...

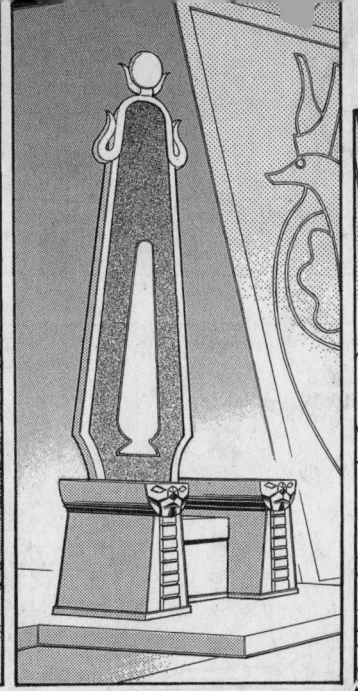

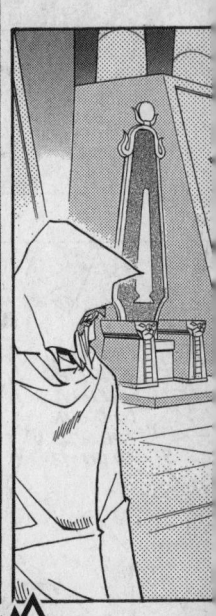

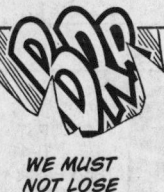

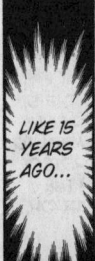

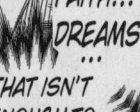

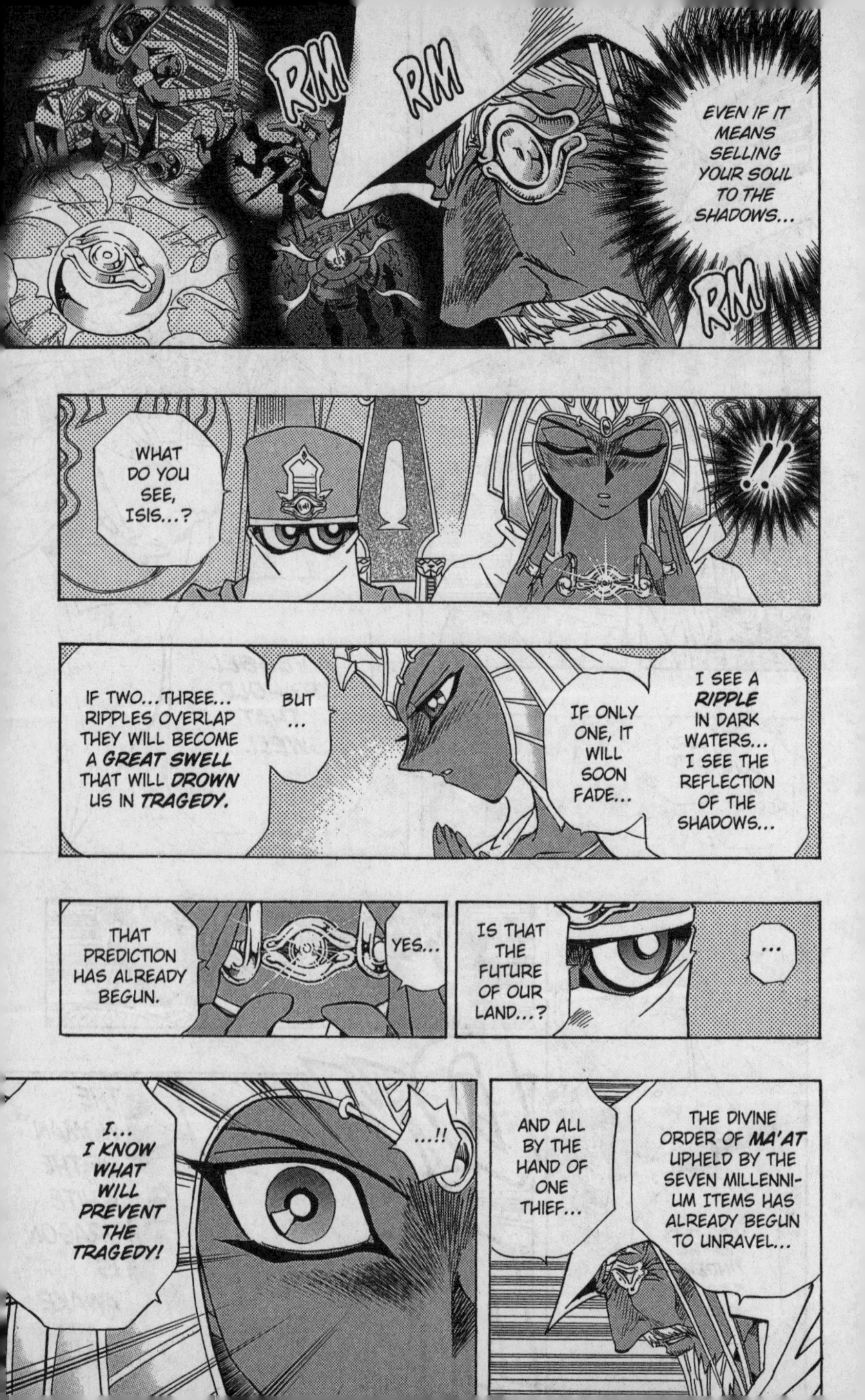
RM
RM
EVEN IF IT MEANS SELLING YOUR SOUL TO THE SHADOWS...
RM
!!
WHAT DO YOU SEE, ISIS...?
I SEE A RIPPLE IN DARK WATERS... I SEE THE REFLECTION OF THE SHADOWS...
IF ONLY ONE, IT WILL SOON FADE...
BUT ...
IF TWO...THREE... RIPPLES OVERLAP THEY WILL BECOME A GREAT SWELL THAT WILL DROWN US IN TRAGEDY.
...
IS THAT THE FUTURE OF OUR LAND...?
YES...
THAT PREDICTION HAS ALREADY BEGUN.
THE DIVINE ORDER OF MA'AT UPHELD BY THE SEVEN MILLENNI-UM ITEMS HAS ALREADY BEGUN TO UNRAVEL...
AND ALL BY THE HAND OF ONE THIEF...
...!!
I... I KNOW WHAT WILL PREVENT THE TRAGEDY!

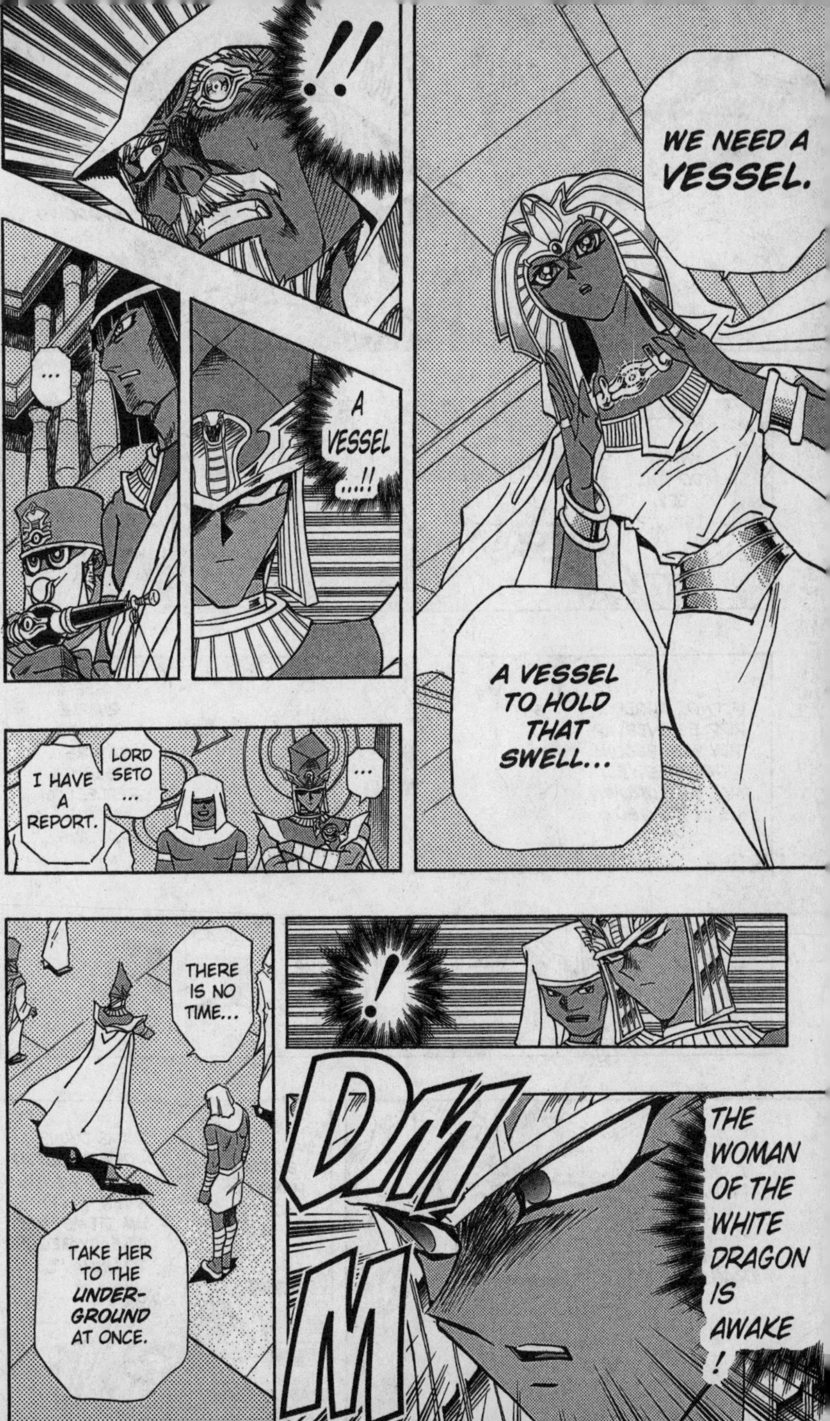
WE NEED A VESSEL.
!!
A VESSEL TO HOLD THAT SWELL...
A VESSEL ...!!
...
LORD SETO ...
I HAVE A REPORT.
...
!
THERE IS NO TIME...
THE WOMAN OF THE WHITE DRAGON IS AWAKE!
DMM
TAKE HER TO THE UNDERGROUND AT ONCE.

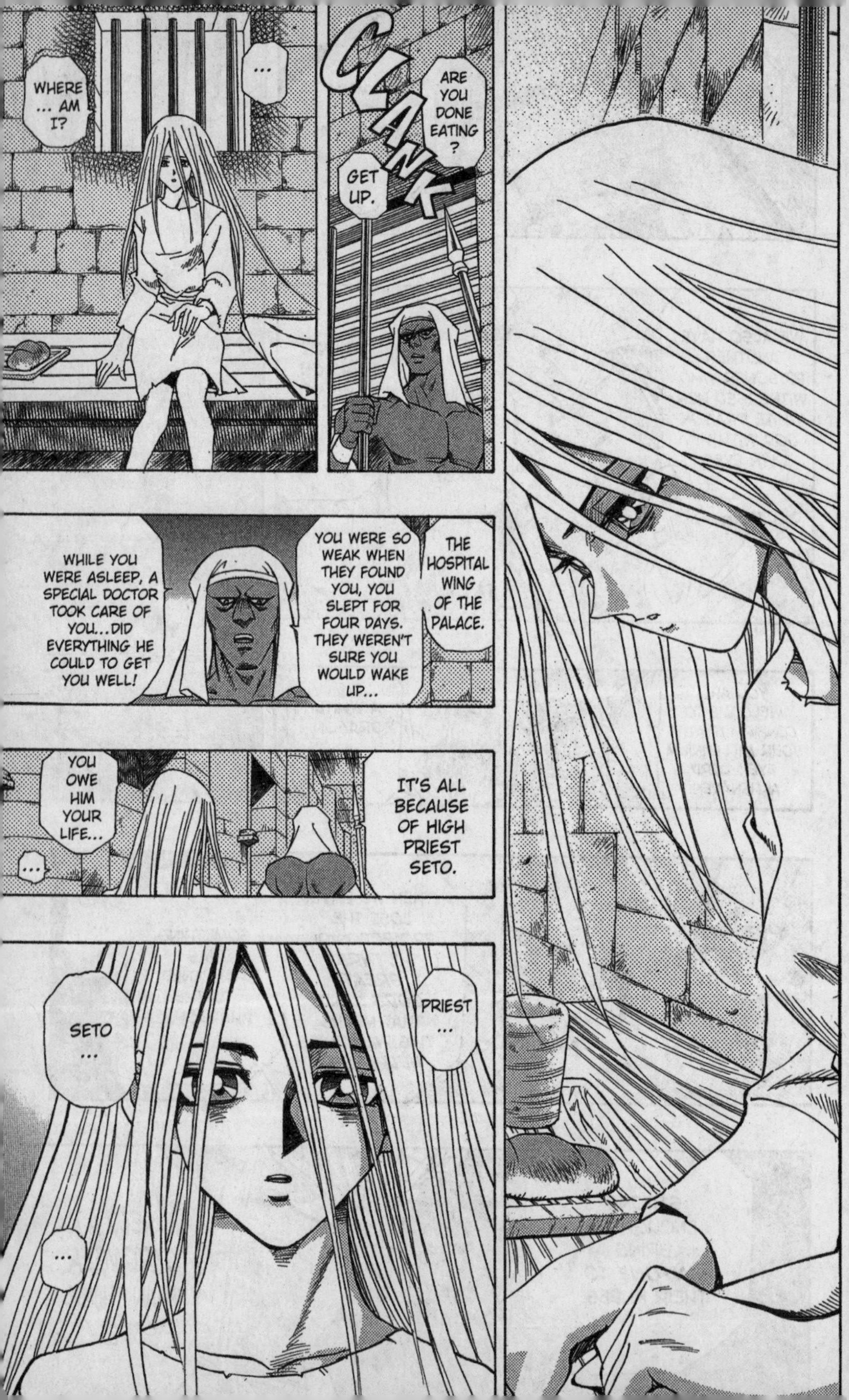
CLANK
ARE YOU DONE EATING?
GET UP.
...
WHERE ... AM I?
THE HOSPITAL WING OF THE PALACE.
YOU WERE SO WEAK WHEN THEY FOUND YOU, YOU SLEPT FOR FOUR DAYS. THEY WEREN'T SURE YOU WOULD WAKE UP...
WHILE YOU WERE ASLEEP, A SPECIAL DOCTOR TOOK CARE OF YOU...DID EVERYTHING HE COULD TO GET YOU WELL!
IT'S ALL BECAUSE OF HIGH PRIEST SETO.
YOU OWE HIM YOUR LIFE...
...
PRIEST ...
SETO ...
...

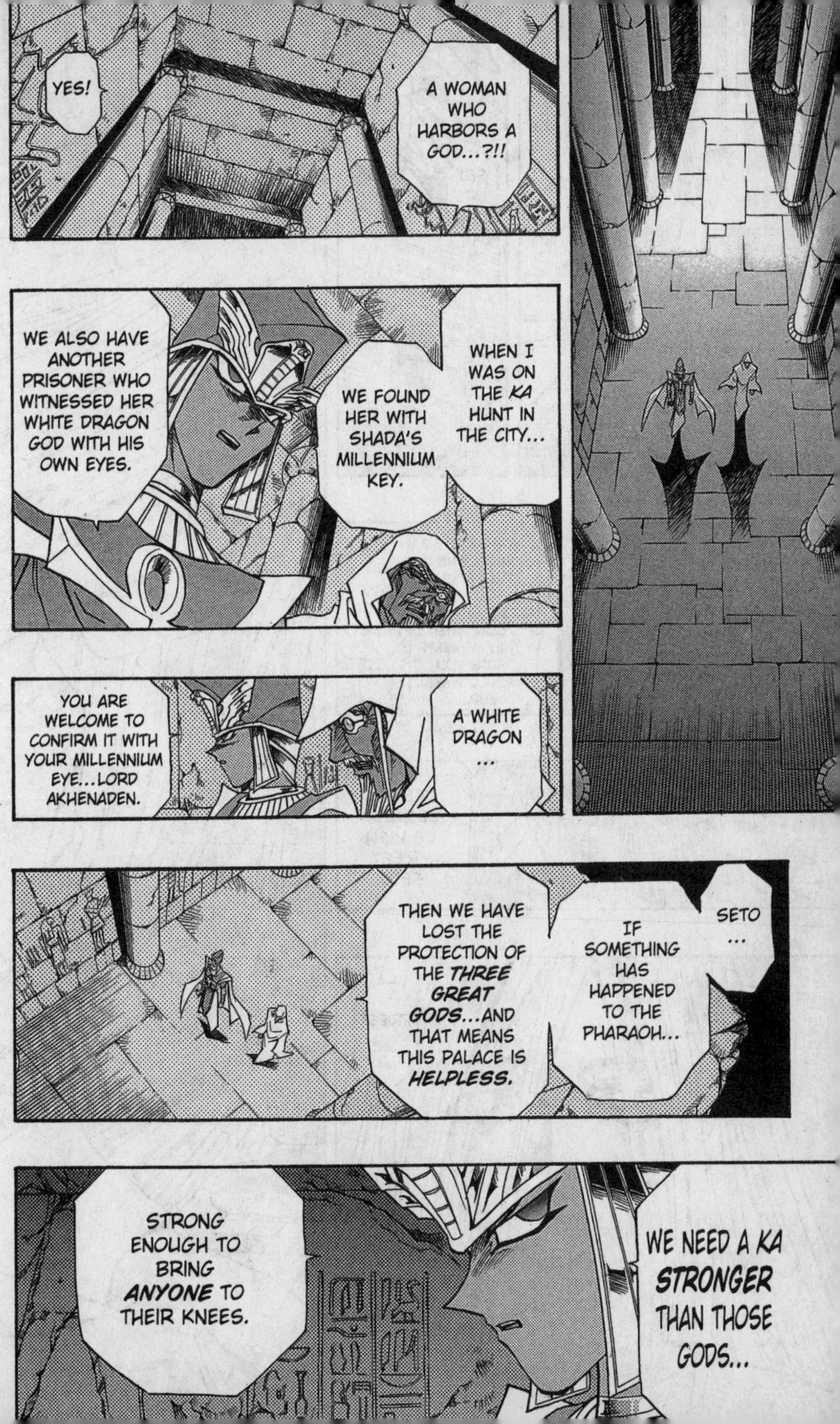
A WOMAN WHO HARBORS A GOD...?!!
YES!
WHEN I WAS ON THE KA HUNT IN THE CITY...
WE FOUND HER WITH SHADA'S MILLENNIUM KEY.
WE ALSO HAVE ANOTHER PRISONER WHO WITNESSED HER WHITE DRAGON GOD WITH HIS OWN EYES.
A WHITE DRAGON...
YOU ARE WELCOME TO CONFIRM IT WITH YOUR MILLENNIUM EYE...LORD AKHENADEN.
SETO...
IF SOMETHING HAS HAPPENED TO THE PHARAOH...
THEN WE HAVE LOST THE PROTECTION OF THE THREE GREAT GODS...AND THAT MEANS THIS PALACE IS HELPLESS.
WE NEED A KA STRONGER THAN THOSE GODS...
STRONG ENOUGH TO BRING ANYONE TO THEIR KNEES.

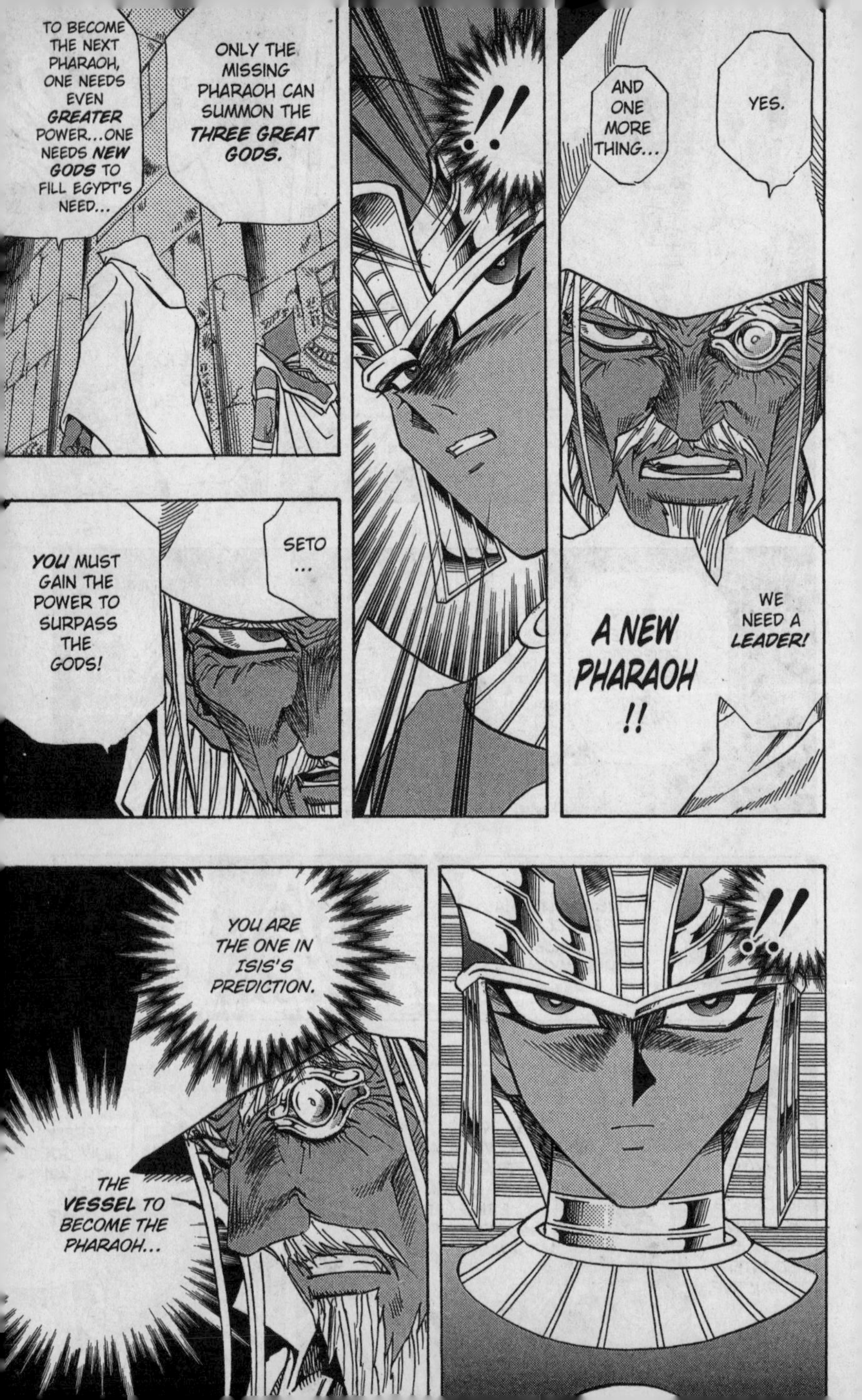

AND ONE MORE THING...
YES.
WE NEED A LEADER!
A NEW PHARAOH !!
!!
ONLY THE MISSING PHARAOH CAN SUMMON THE THREE GREAT GODS.
TO BECOME THE NEXT PHARAOH, ONE NEEDS EVEN GREATER POWER...ONE NEEDS NEW GODS TO FILL EGYPT'S NEED...
SETO ...
YOU MUST GAIN THE POWER TO SURPASS THE GODS!
YOU ARE THE ONE IN ISIS'S PREDICTION.
THE VESSEL TO BECOME THE PHARAOH...
!!

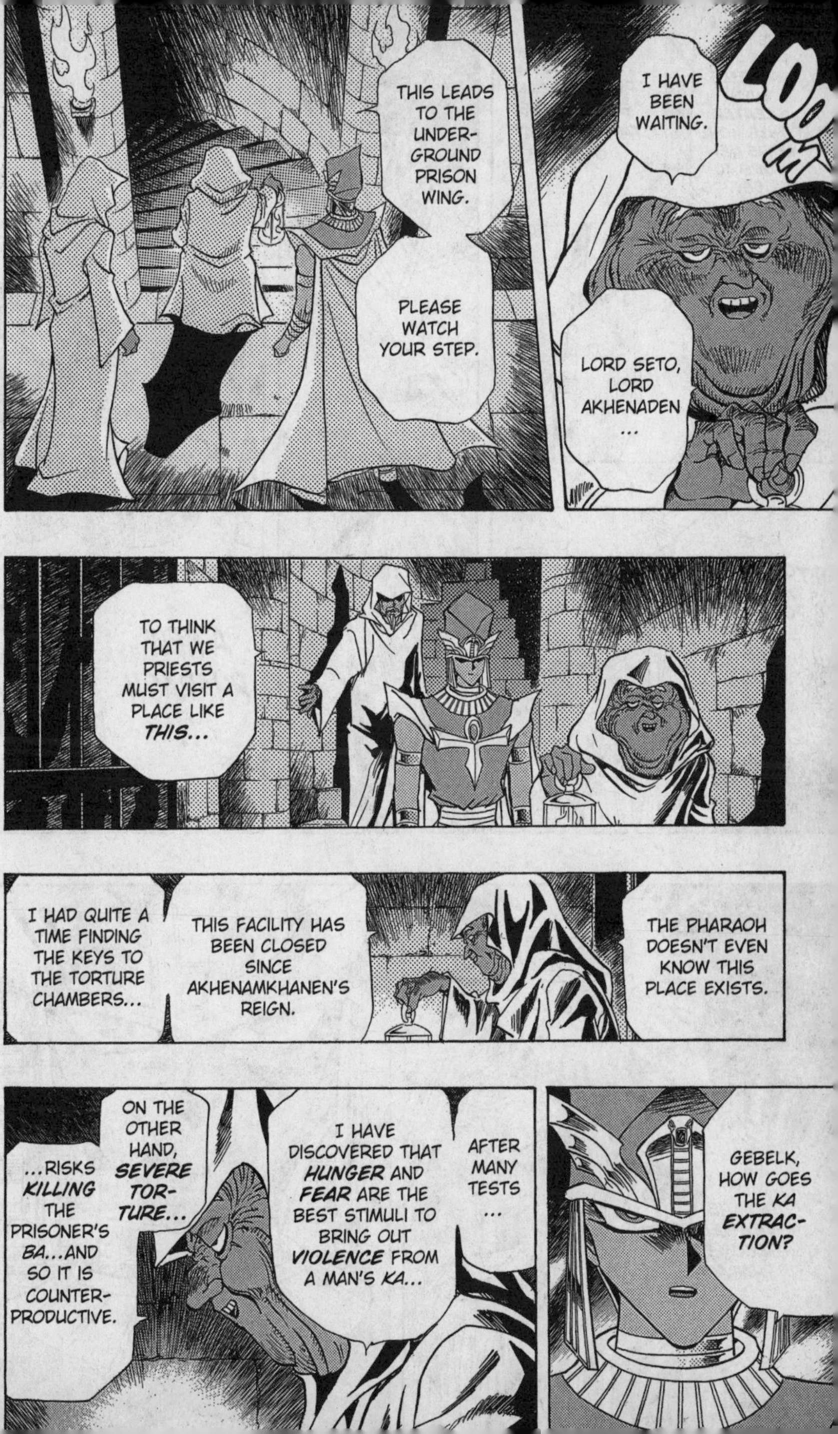
LOOM
I HAVE BEEN WAITING.
LORD SETO, LORD AKHENADEN ...
THIS LEADS TO THE UNDER-GROUND PRISON WING.
PLEASE WATCH YOUR STEP.
TO THINK THAT WE PRIESTS MUST VISIT A PLACE LIKE *THIS...*
THE PHARAOH DOESN'T EVEN KNOW THIS PLACE EXISTS.
THIS FACILITY HAS BEEN CLOSED SINCE AKHENAMKHANEN'S REIGN.
I HAD QUITE A TIME FINDING THE KEYS TO THE TORTURE CHAMBERS...
GEBELK, HOW GOES THE *KA* *EXTRACTION?*
AFTER MANY TESTS ...
I HAVE DISCOVERED THAT ***HUNGER*** AND ***FEAR*** ARE THE BEST STIMULI TO BRING OUT ***VIOLENCE*** FROM A MAN'S *KA*...
ON THE OTHER HAND, ***SEVERE TORTURE...***
...RISKS ***KILLING*** THE PRISONER'S *BA*...AND SO IT IS COUNTER-PRODUCTIVE.

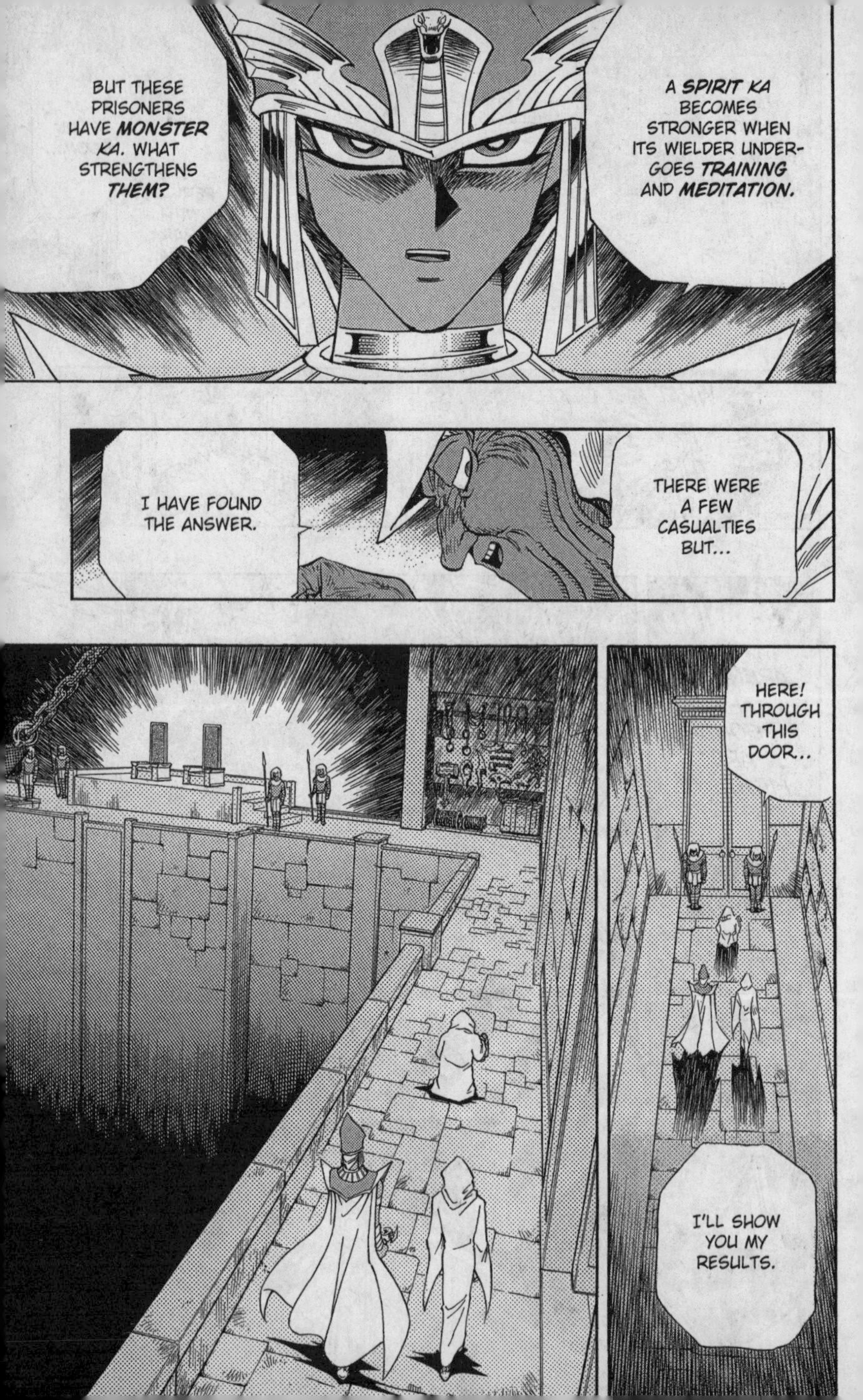
A SPIRIT KA BECOMES STRONGER WHEN ITS WIELDER UNDERGOES TRAINING AND MEDITATION.
BUT THESE PRISONERS HAVE MONSTER KA. WHAT STRENGTHENS THEM?
THERE WERE A FEW CASUALTIES BUT...
I HAVE FOUND THE ANSWER.
HERE! THROUGH THIS DOOR...
I'LL SHOW YOU MY RESULTS.

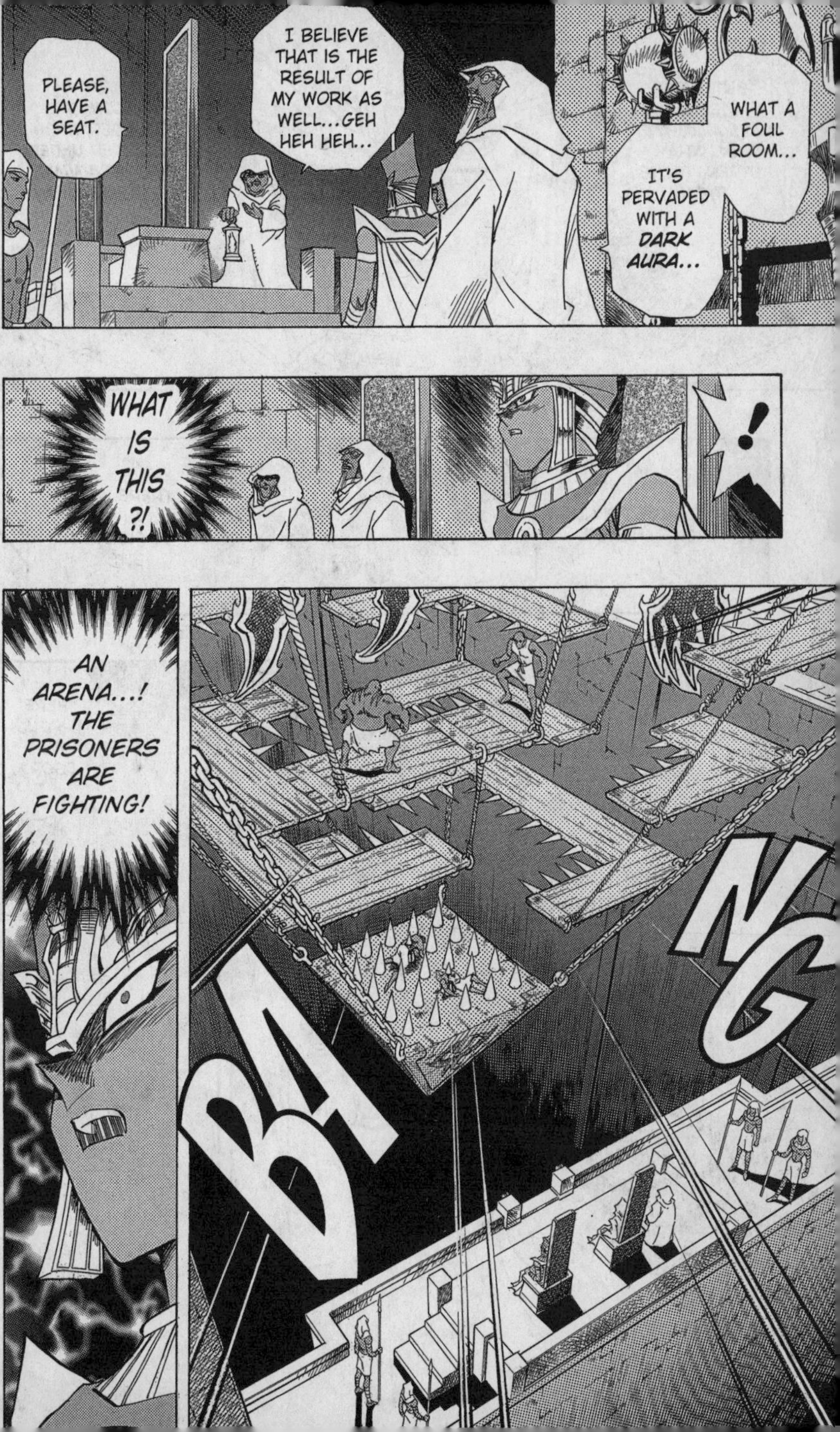
WHAT A FOUL ROOM...
IT'S PERVADED WITH A *DARK AURA*...
I BELIEVE THAT IS THE RESULT OF MY WORK AS WELL...GEH HEH HEH...
PLEASE, HAVE A SEAT.
!
WHAT IS THIS ?!
BA
NG
AN ARENA...! THE PRISONERS ARE FIGHTING!

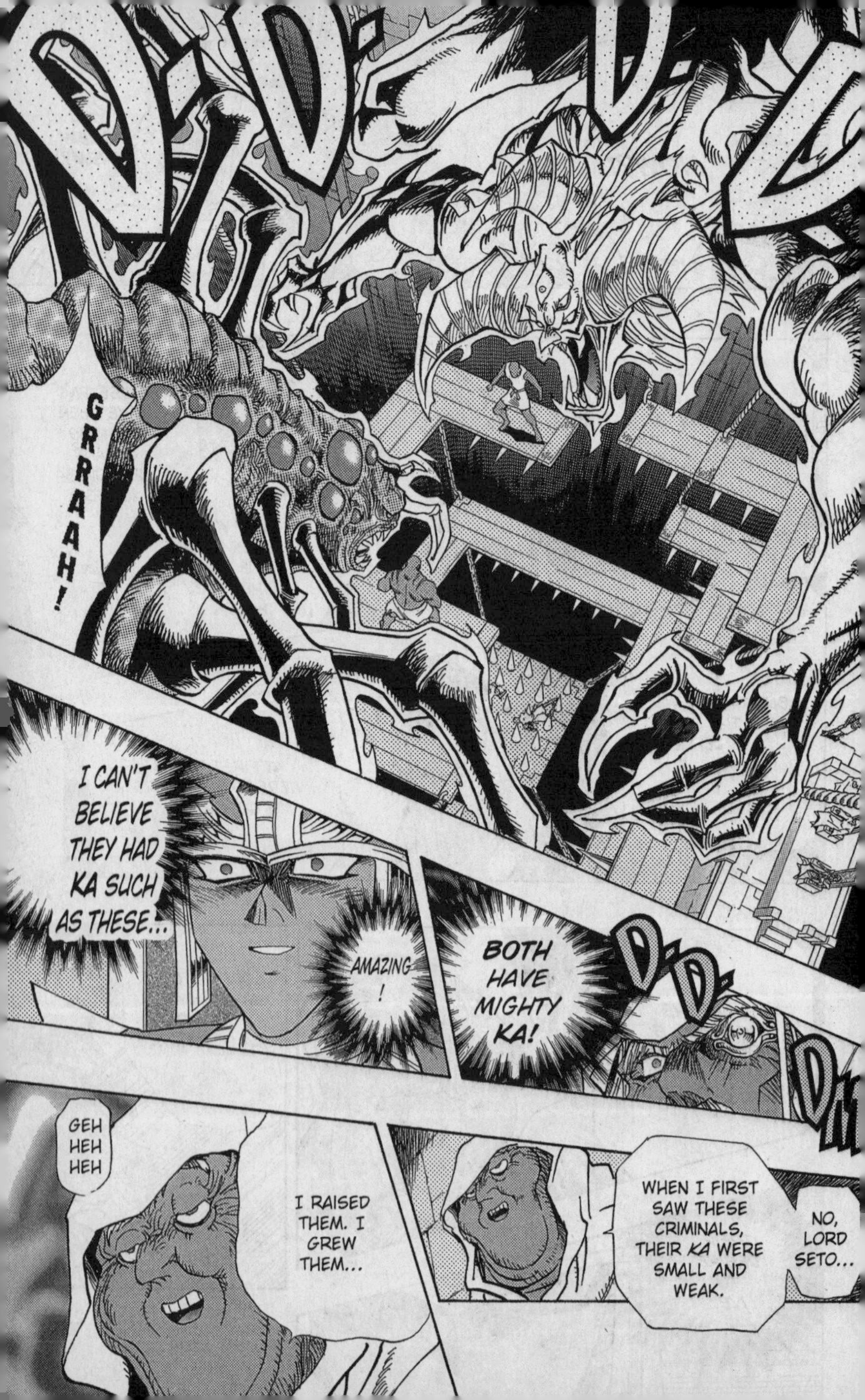
GRRAAH!
BOTH HAVE MIGHTY KA!
AMAZING!
I CAN'T BELIEVE THEY HAD KA SUCH AS THESE...
NO, LORD SETO...
WHEN I FIRST SAW THESE CRIMINALS, THEIR *KA* WERE SMALL AND WEAK.
I RAISED THEM. I GREW THEM...
GEH HEH HEH

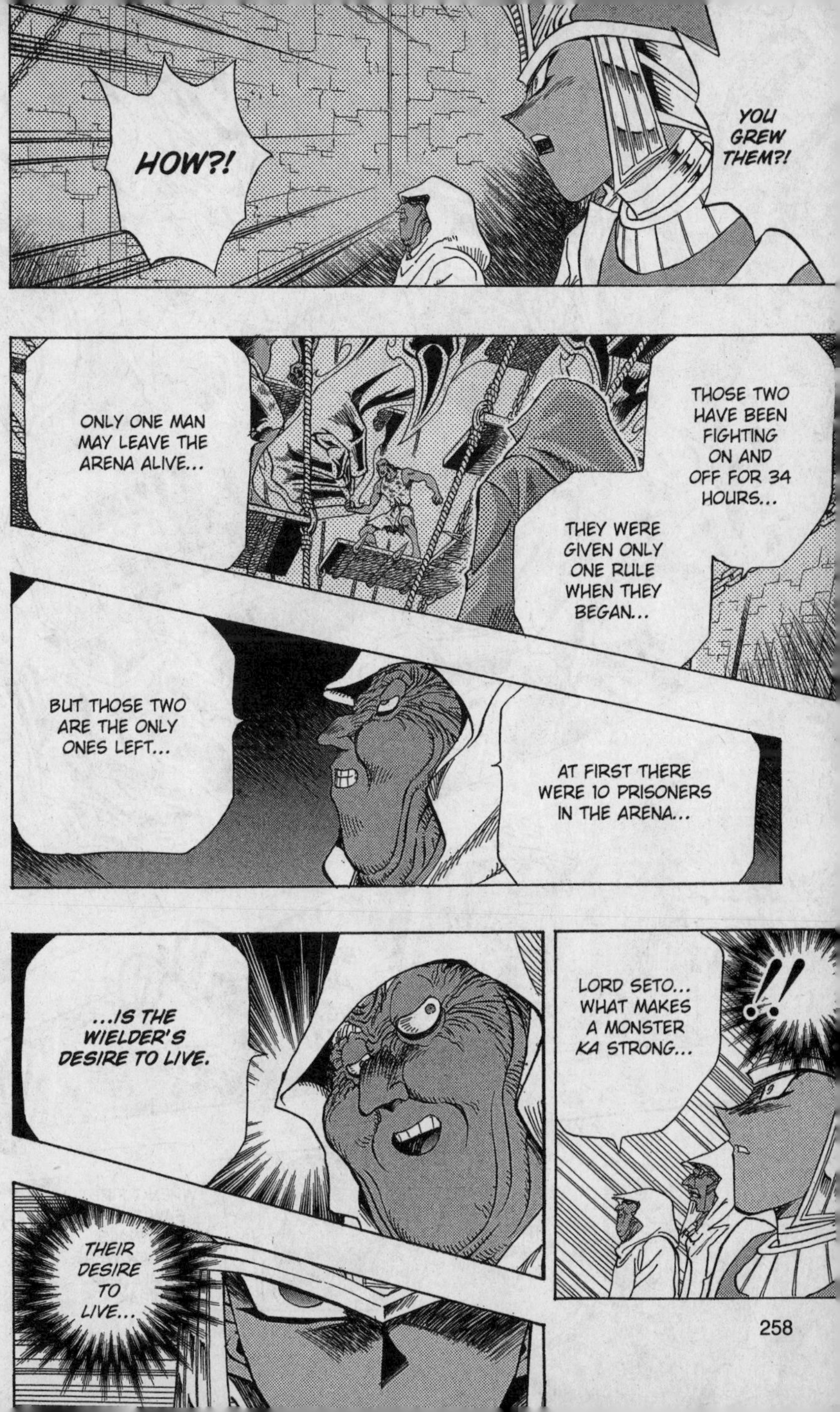
YOU GREW THEM?!
HOW?!
THOSE TWO HAVE BEEN FIGHTING ON AND OFF FOR 34 HOURS...
THEY WERE GIVEN ONLY ONE RULE WHEN THEY BEGAN...
ONLY ONE MAN MAY LEAVE THE ARENA ALIVE...
AT FIRST THERE WERE 10 PRISONERS IN THE ARENA...
BUT THOSE TWO ARE THE ONLY ONES LEFT...
!!
LORD SETO... WHAT MAKES A MONSTER KA STRONG...
...IS THE WIELDER'S DESIRE TO LIVE.
THEIR DESIRE TO LIVE...

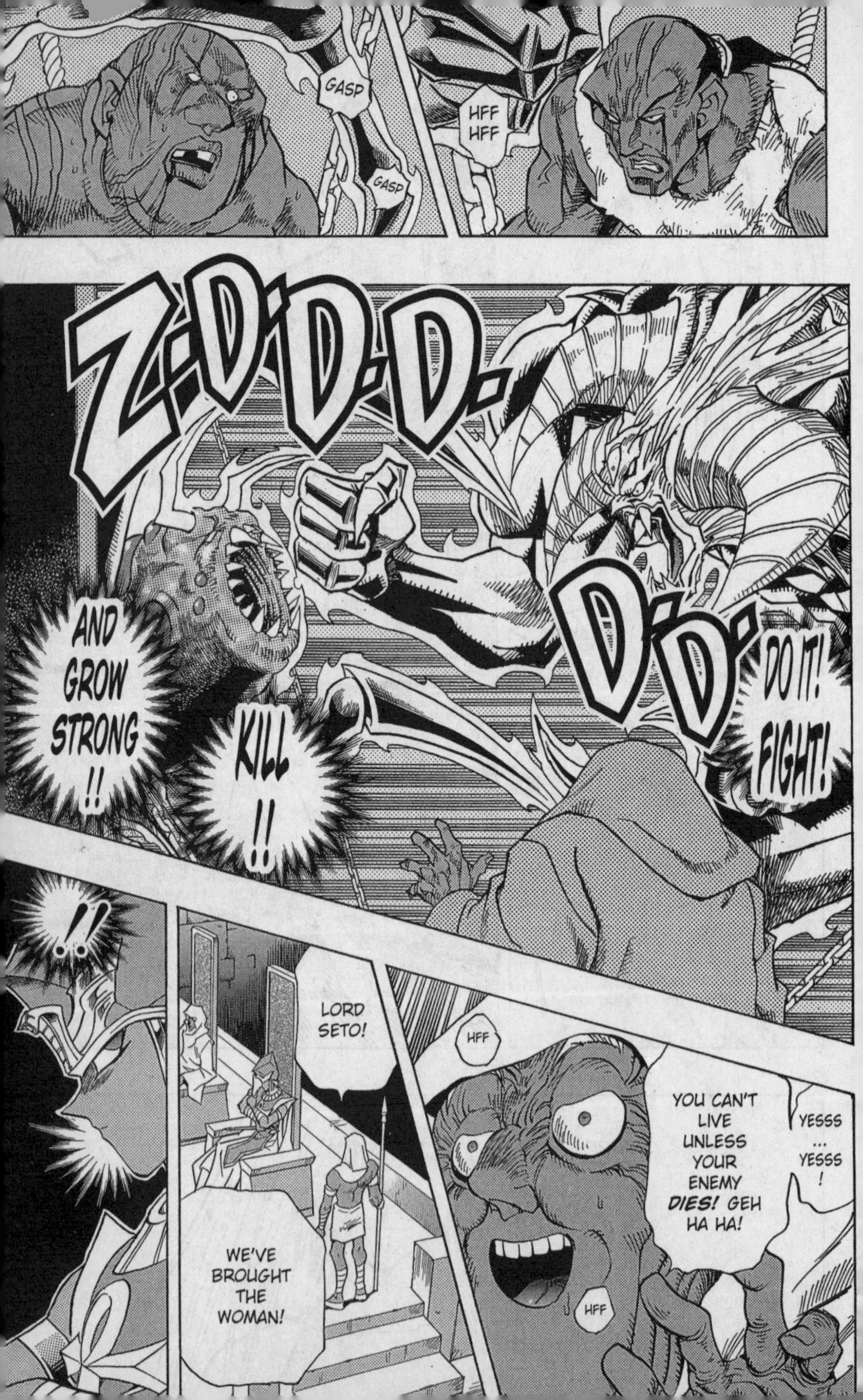
HFF
HFF
GASP
GASP
Z.D.D.D.
D.D.
DO IT! FIGHT!
KILL !!
AND GROW STRONG !!
!!
YESSS ... YESSS !
YOU CAN'T LIVE UNLESS YOUR ENEMY DIES! GEH HA HA!
HFF
HFF
LORD SETO!
WE'VE BROUGHT THE WOMAN!

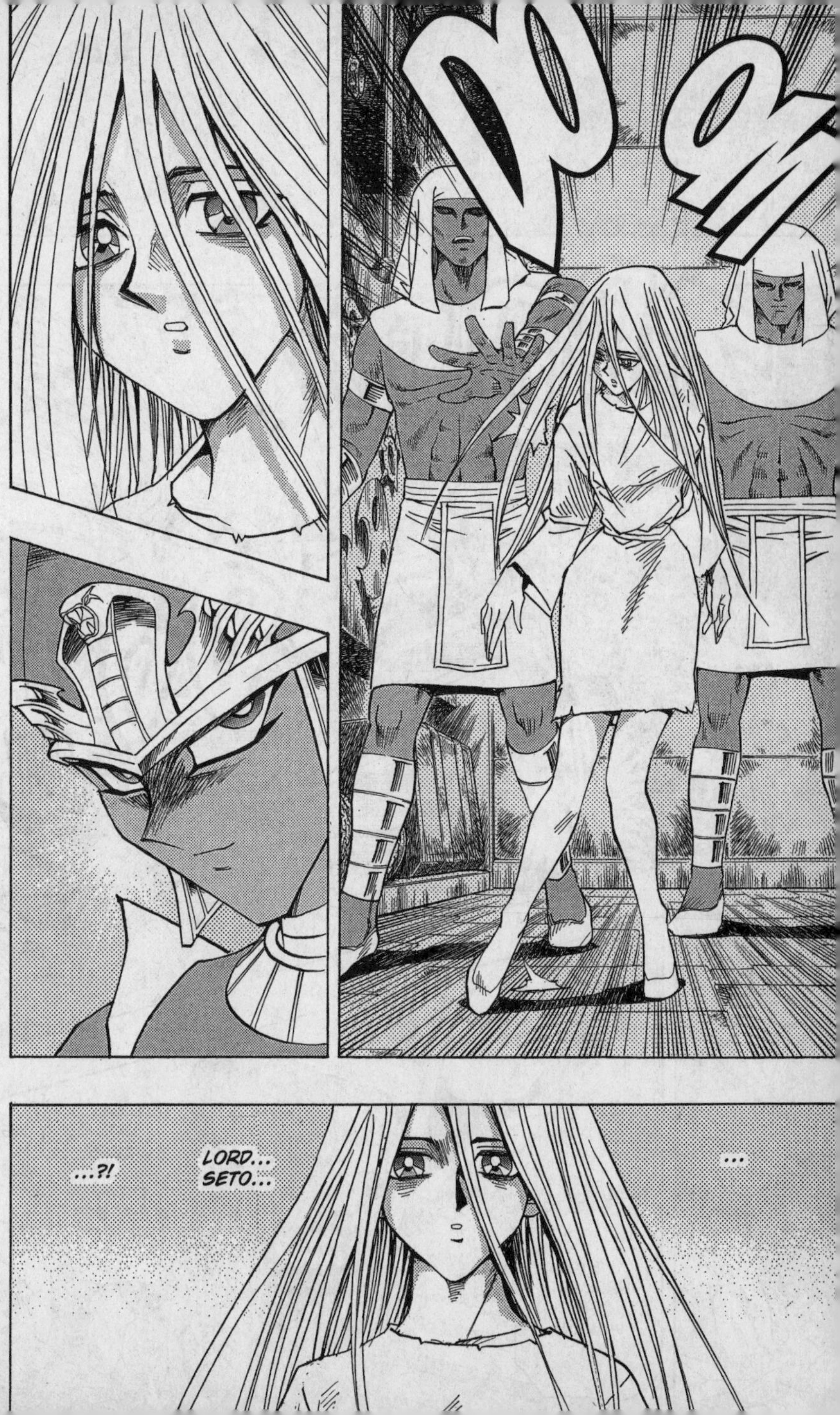
...
LORD... SETO...
...?!

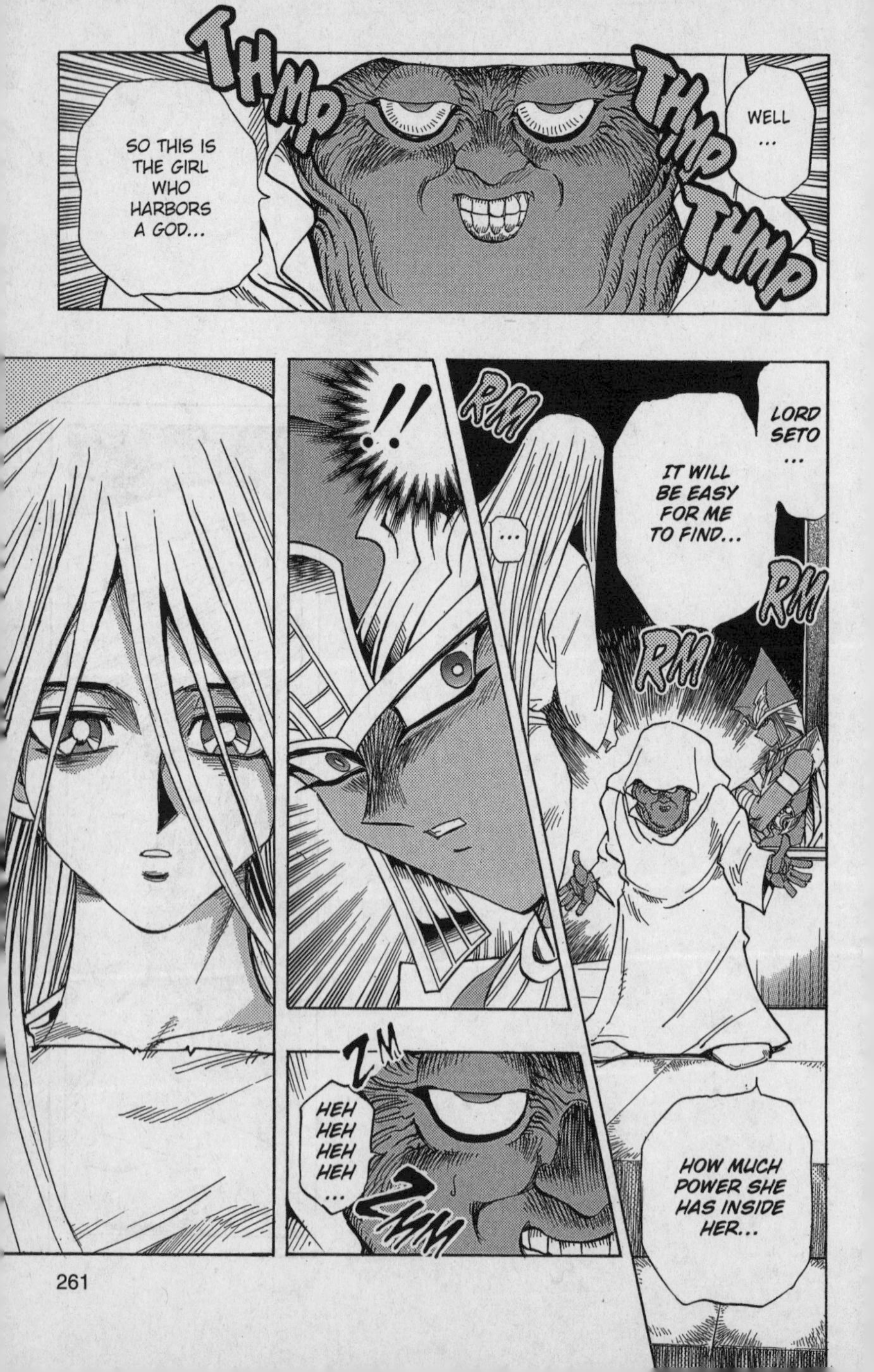
WELL ...
THMP
THMP
THMP
SO THIS IS THE GIRL WHO HARBORS A GOD...
RM
LORD SETO ...
IT WILL BE EASY FOR ME TO FIND...
RM
RM
HOW MUCH POWER SHE HAS INSIDE HER...
!!
...
ZM
HEH HEH HEH HEH ...
ZMM

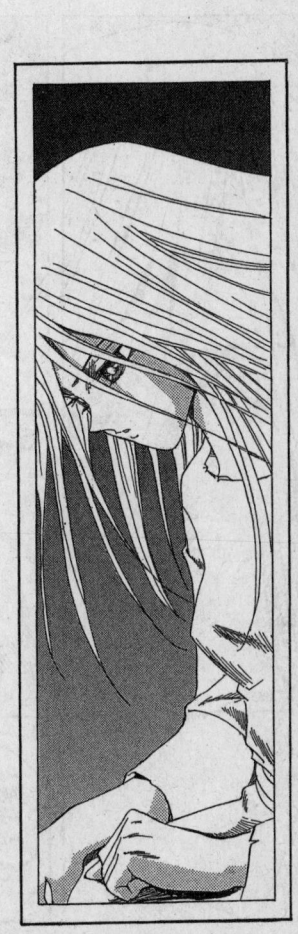

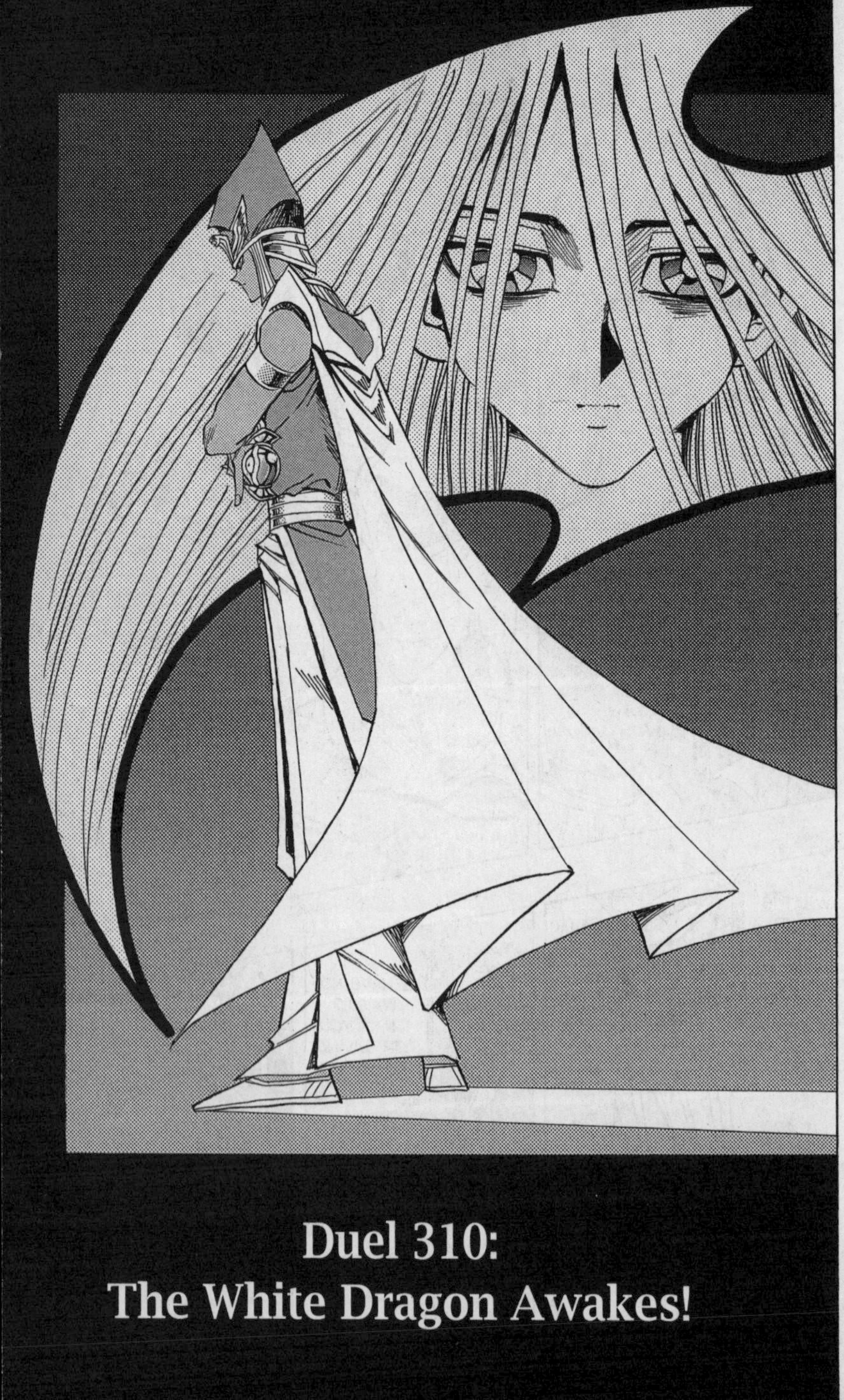

Duel 310:
The White Dragon Awakes!

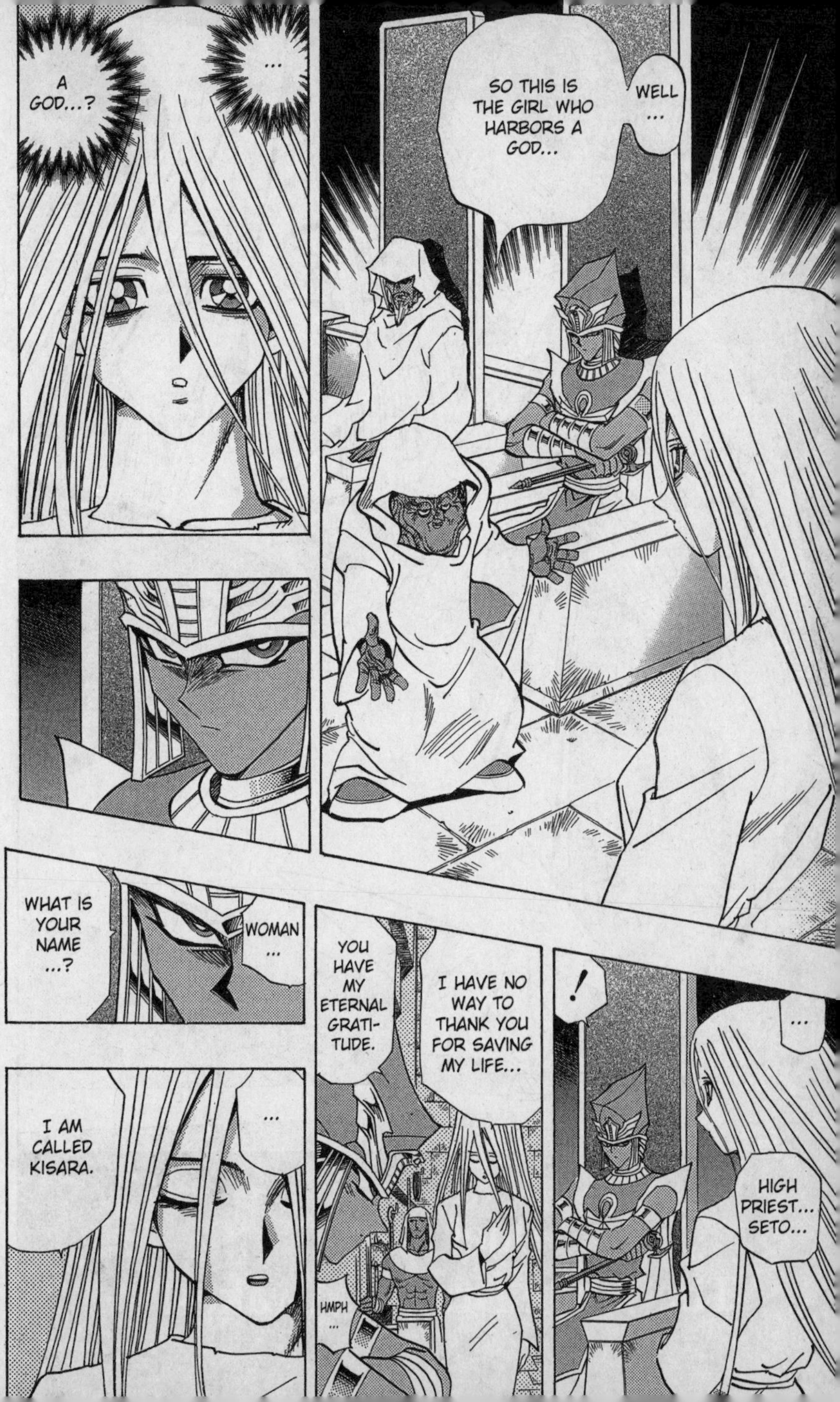
WELL...
SO THIS IS THE GIRL WHO HARBORS A GOD...
...
A GOD...?
!
...
HIGH PRIEST... SETO...
I HAVE NO WAY TO THANK YOU FOR SAVING MY LIFE...
YOU HAVE MY ETERNAL GRATITUDE.
HMPH...
WOMAN...
WHAT IS YOUR NAME...?
...
I AM CALLED KISARA.

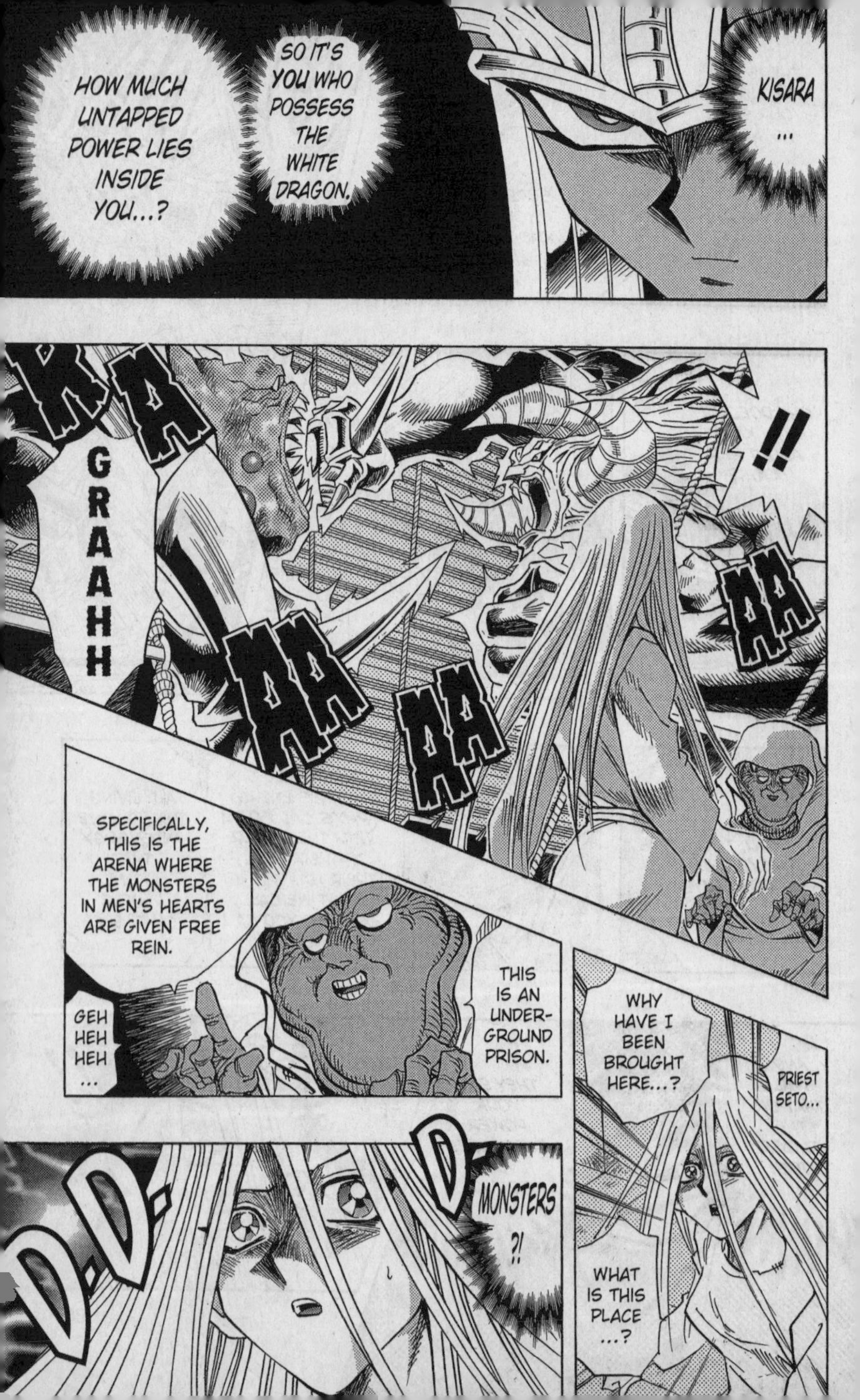
KISARA ...
SO IT'S YOU WHO POSSESS THE WHITE DRAGON.
HOW MUCH UNTAPPED POWER LIES INSIDE YOU...?
!!
GRAAAHH
AA
AA
AA
PRIEST SETO...
WHY HAVE I BEEN BROUGHT HERE...?
THIS IS AN UNDER-GROUND PRISON.
SPECIFICALLY, THIS IS THE ARENA WHERE THE MONSTERS IN MEN'S HEARTS ARE GIVEN FREE REIN.
GEH HEH HEH ...
WHAT IS THIS PLACE ...?
MONSTERS ?!
D-D-D-

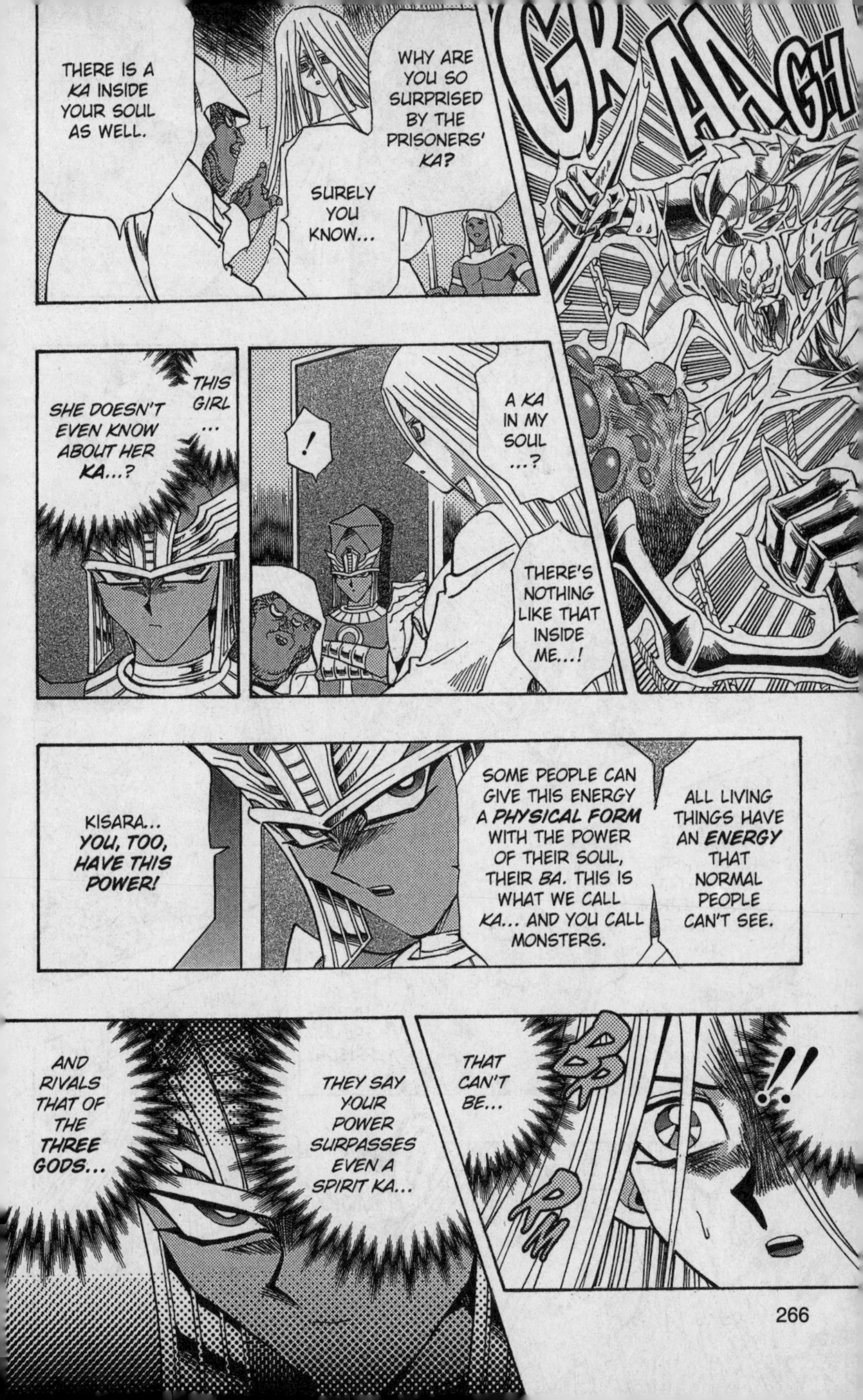
GRAAAGH
WHY ARE YOU SO SURPRISED BY THE PRISONERS' *KA?*
SURELY YOU KNOW...
THERE IS A *KA* INSIDE YOUR SOUL AS WELL.
A *KA* IN MY SOUL ...?
THERE'S NOTHING LIKE THAT INSIDE ME...!
!
THIS GIRL ...
SHE DOESN'T EVEN KNOW ABOUT HER KA...?
ALL LIVING THINGS HAVE AN ***ENERGY*** THAT NORMAL PEOPLE CAN'T SEE.
SOME PEOPLE CAN GIVE THIS ENERGY A ***PHYSICAL FORM*** WITH THE POWER OF THEIR SOUL, THEIR *BA*. THIS IS WHAT WE CALL *KA*... AND YOU CALL MONSTERS.
KISARA... **YOU, TOO, HAVE THIS POWER!**
THAT CAN'T BE...
THEY SAY YOUR POWER SURPASSES EVEN A SPIRIT KA...
AND RIVALS THAT OF THE ***THREE GODS...***

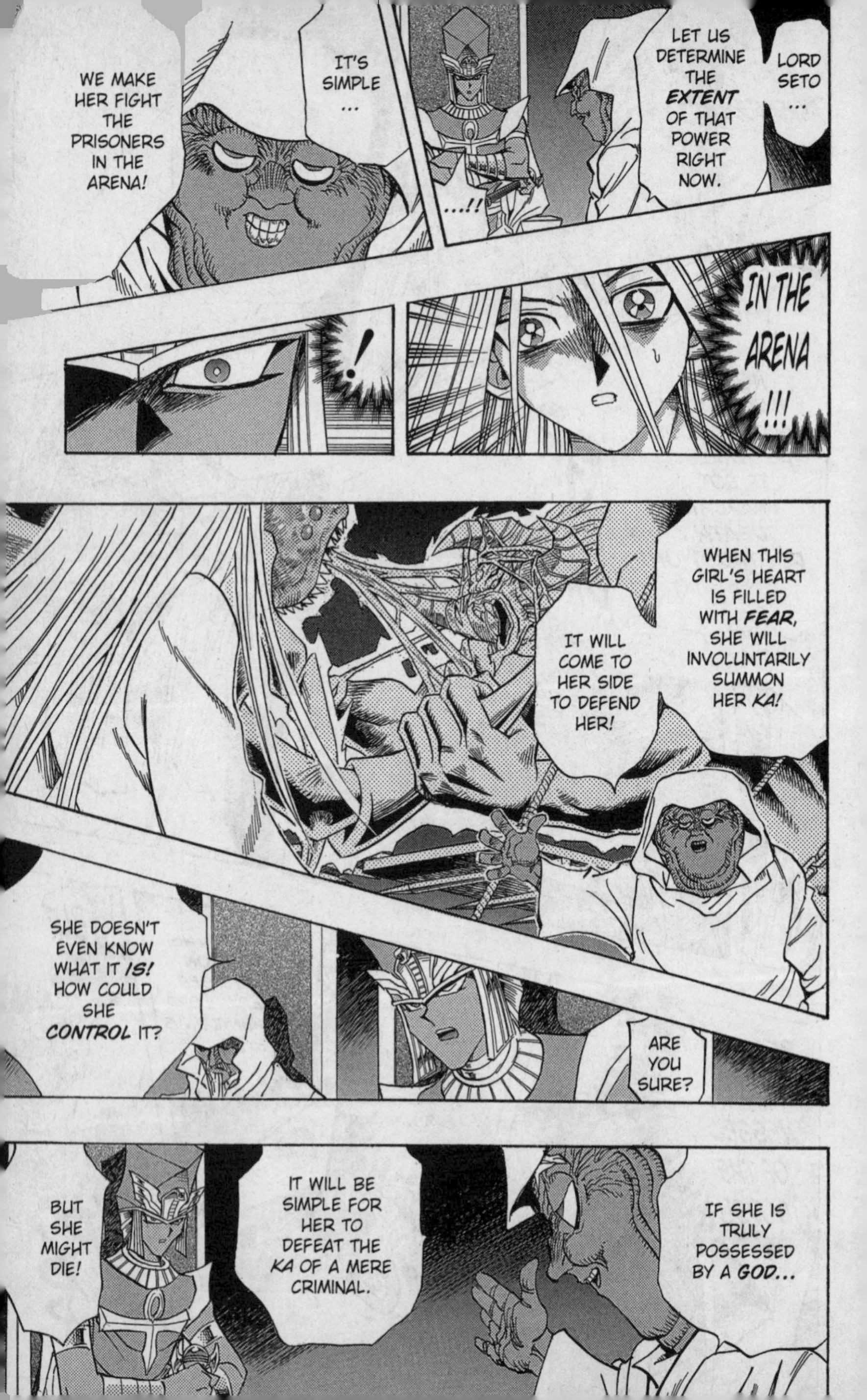

LORD SETO ...
LET US DETERMINE THE EXTENT OF THAT POWER RIGHT NOW.
...!!
IT'S SIMPLE ...
WE MAKE HER FIGHT THE PRISONERS IN THE ARENA!
IN THE ARENA !!!
!
WHEN THIS GIRL'S HEART IS FILLED WITH FEAR, SHE WILL INVOLUNTARILY SUMMON HER KA!
IT WILL COME TO HER SIDE TO DEFEND HER!
ARE YOU SURE?
SHE DOESN'T EVEN KNOW WHAT IT IS! HOW COULD SHE CONTROL IT?
IF SHE IS TRULY POSSESSED BY A GOD...
IT WILL BE SIMPLE FOR HER TO DEFEAT THE KA OF A MERE CRIMINAL.
BUT SHE MIGHT DIE!

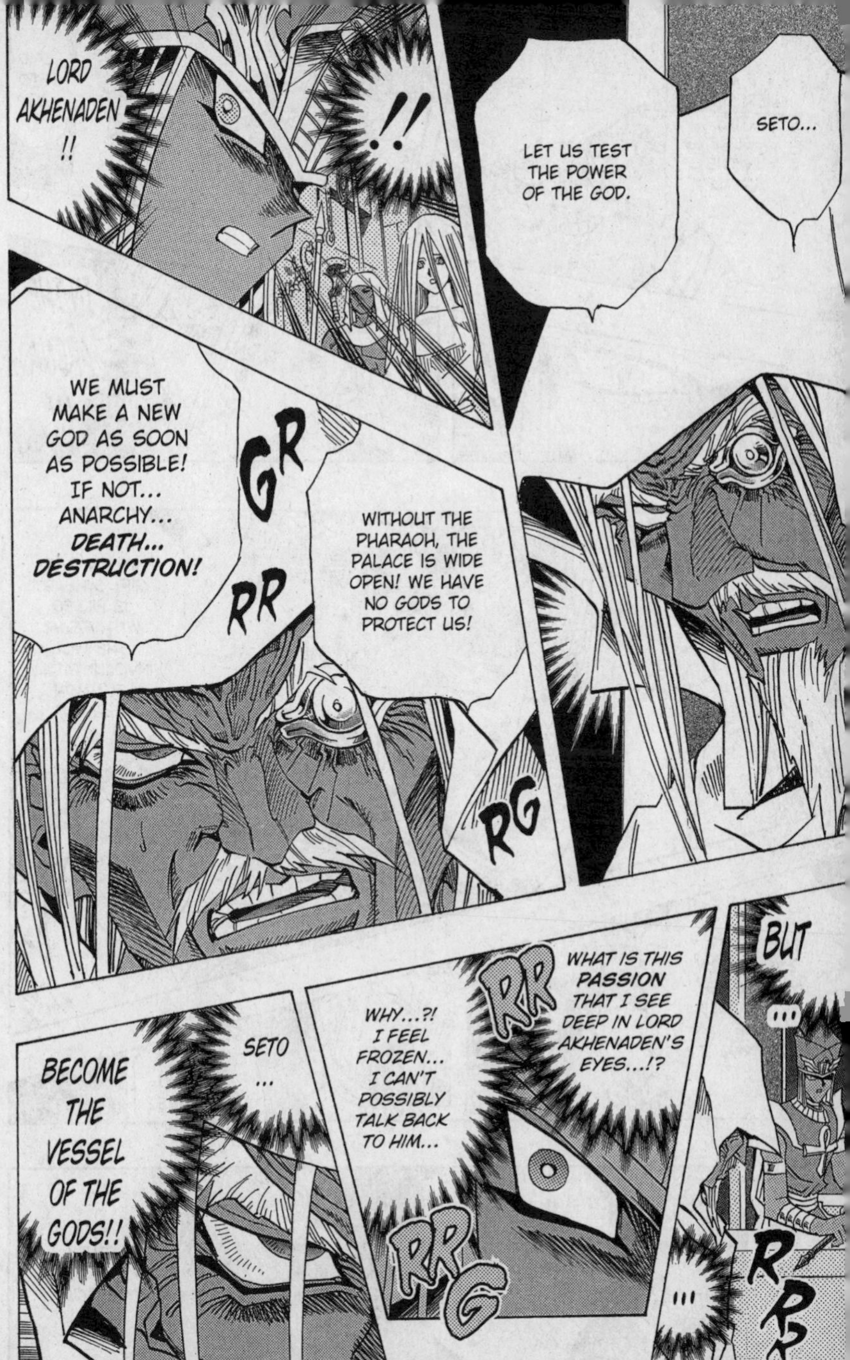
SETO...
LET US TEST THE POWER OF THE GOD.
!!
LORD AKHENADEN !!
WITHOUT THE PHARAOH, THE PALACE IS WIDE OPEN! WE HAVE NO GODS TO PROTECT US!
GRRR
WE MUST MAKE A NEW GOD AS SOON AS POSSIBLE! IF NOT... ANARCHY... DEATH... DESTRUCTION!
RG
BUT ...
RRR
...
WHAT IS THIS PASSION THAT I SEE DEEP IN LORD AKHENADEN'S EYES...!?
RR
WHY...?! I FEEL FROZEN... I CAN'T POSSIBLY TALK BACK TO HIM...
RRG
SETO ...
BECOME THE VESSEL OF THE GODS!!

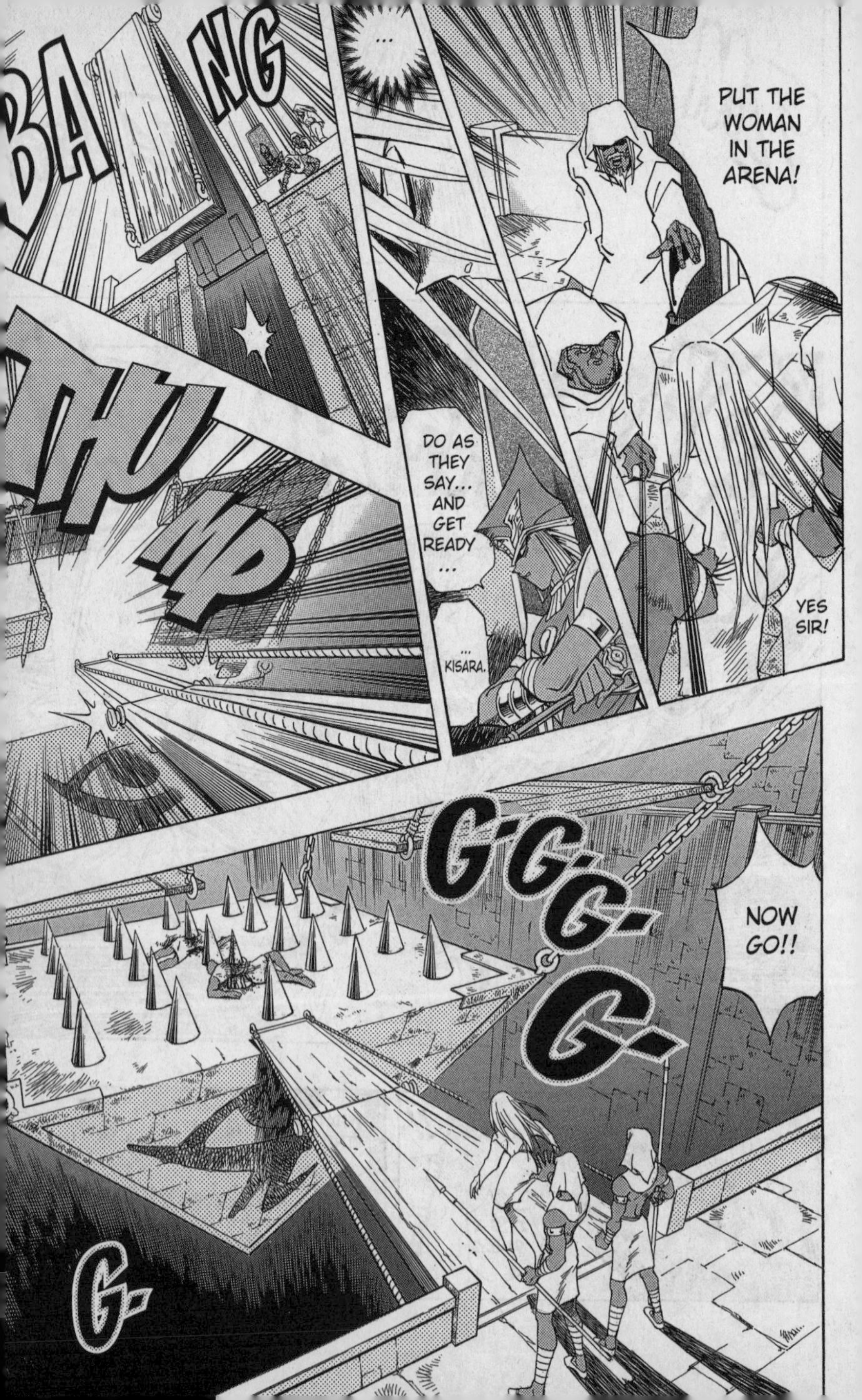
PUT THE WOMAN IN THE ARENA!
YES SIR!
...
DO AS THEY SAY... AND GET READY...
... KISARA.
BANG
THUMP
NOW GO!!
G-G-G-
G-
G-

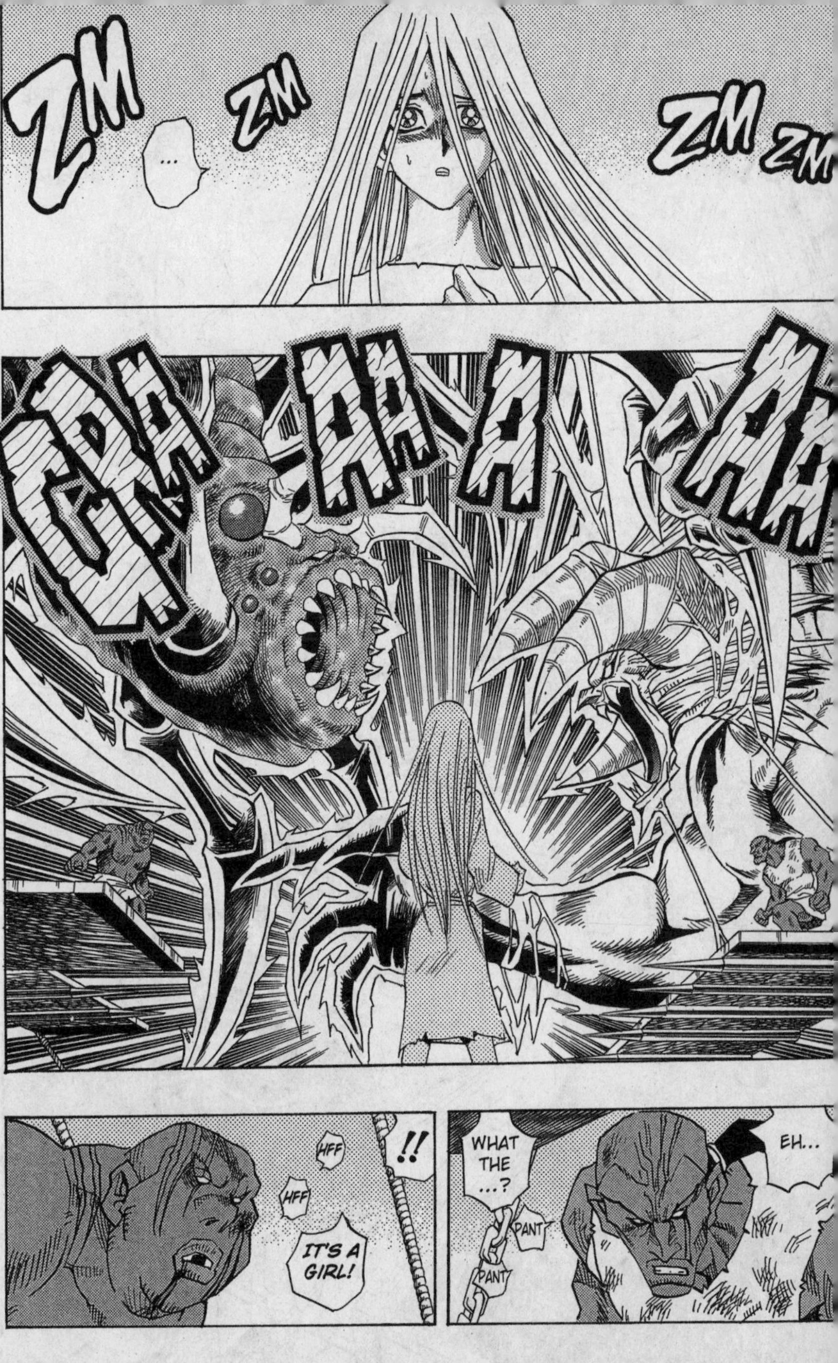
ZM ZM ZM ZM
...
GRA AA A AA
EH...
WHAT THE ...?
PANT
PANT
!!
HFF
HFF
IT'S A GIRL!

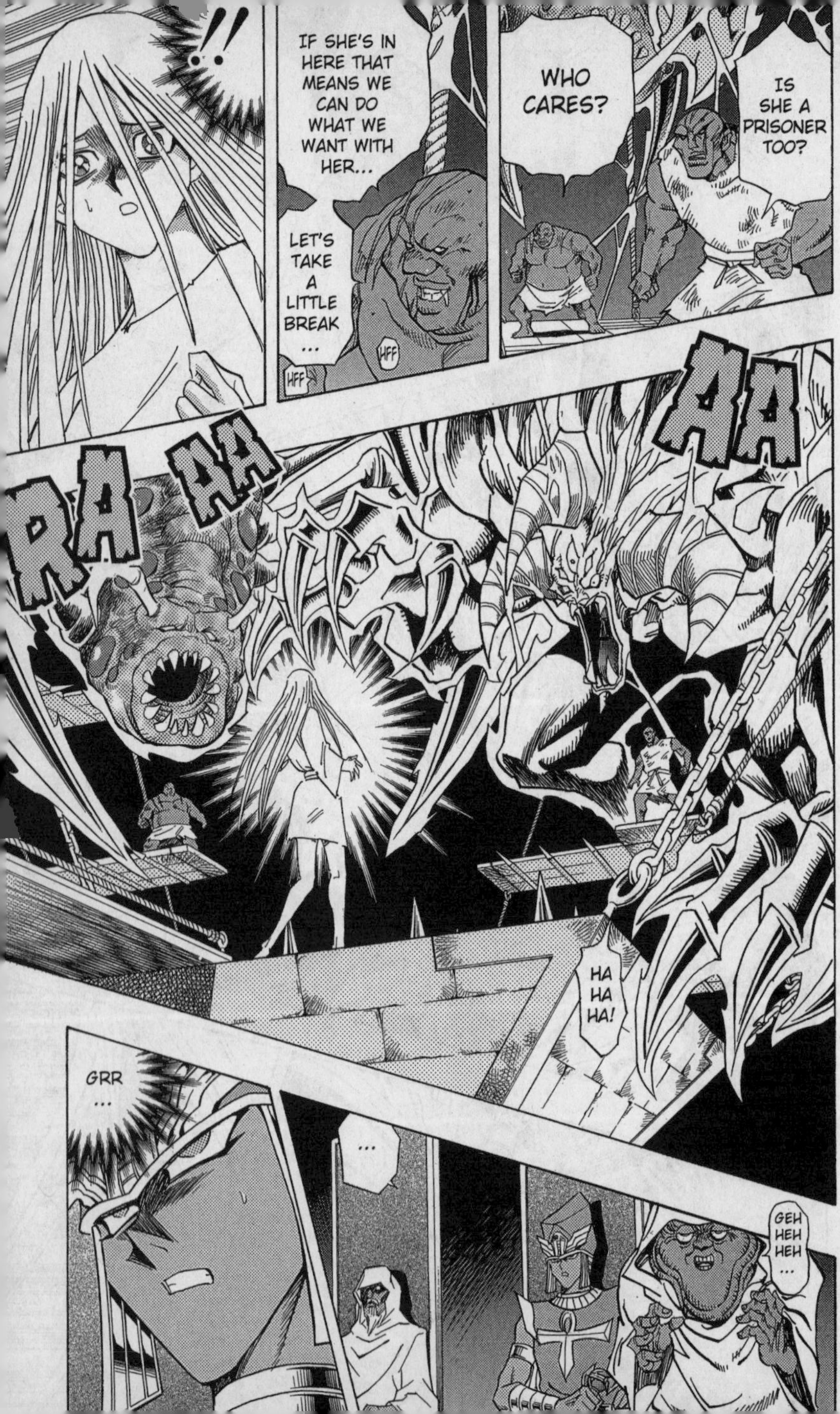
IS SHE A PRISONER TOO?
WHO CARES?
IF SHE'S IN HERE THAT MEANS WE CAN DO WHAT WE WANT WITH HER...
LET'S TAKE A LITTLE BREAK ...
HFF
HFF
!!
RA AA AA
HA HA HA!
GEH HEH HEH ...
...
GRR ...

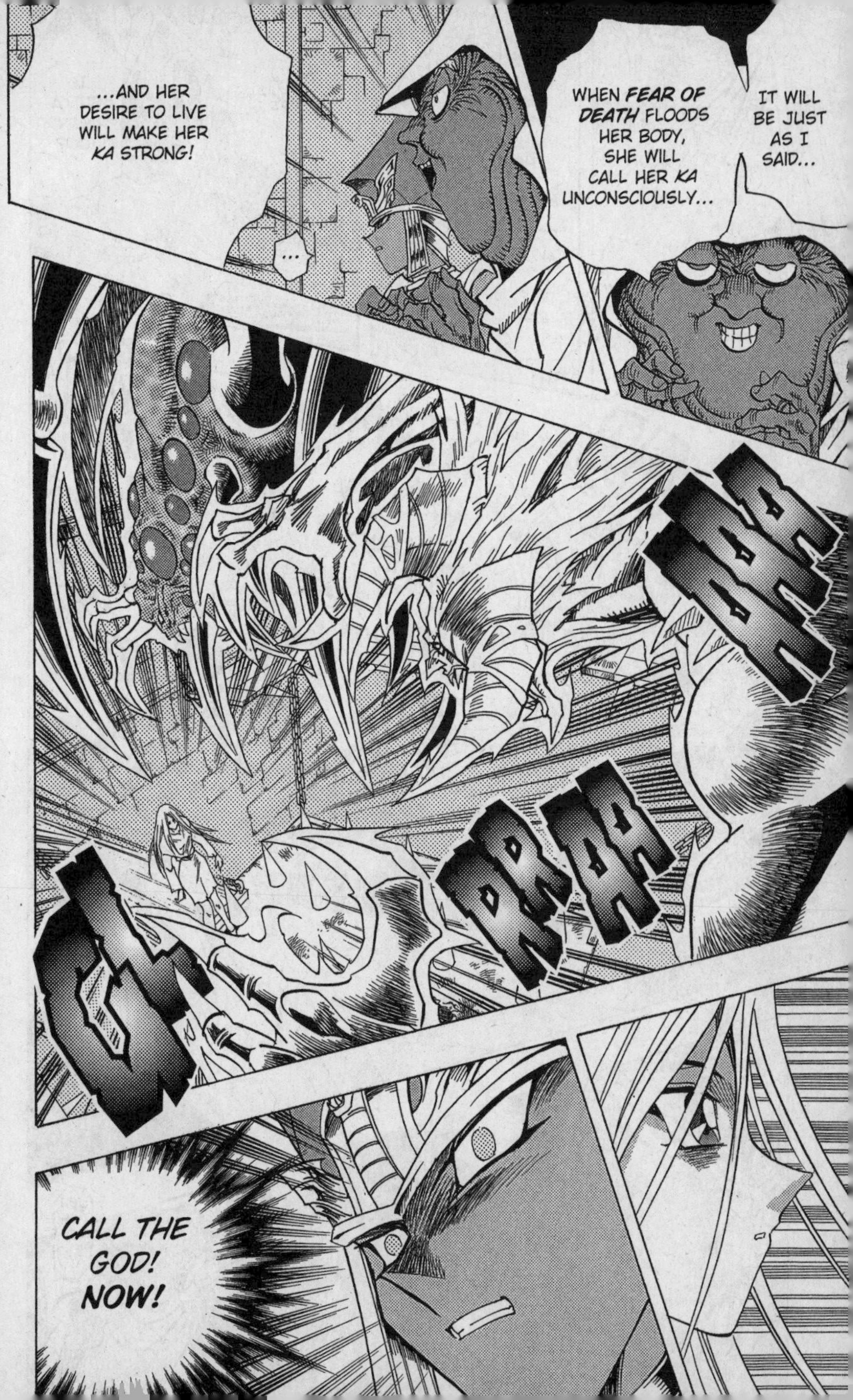

IT WILL BE JUST AS I SAID...
WHEN FEAR OF DEATH FLOODS HER BODY, SHE WILL CALL HER KA UNCONSCIOUSLY...
...AND HER DESIRE TO LIVE WILL MAKE HER KA STRONG!
...
CALL THE GOD! NOW!

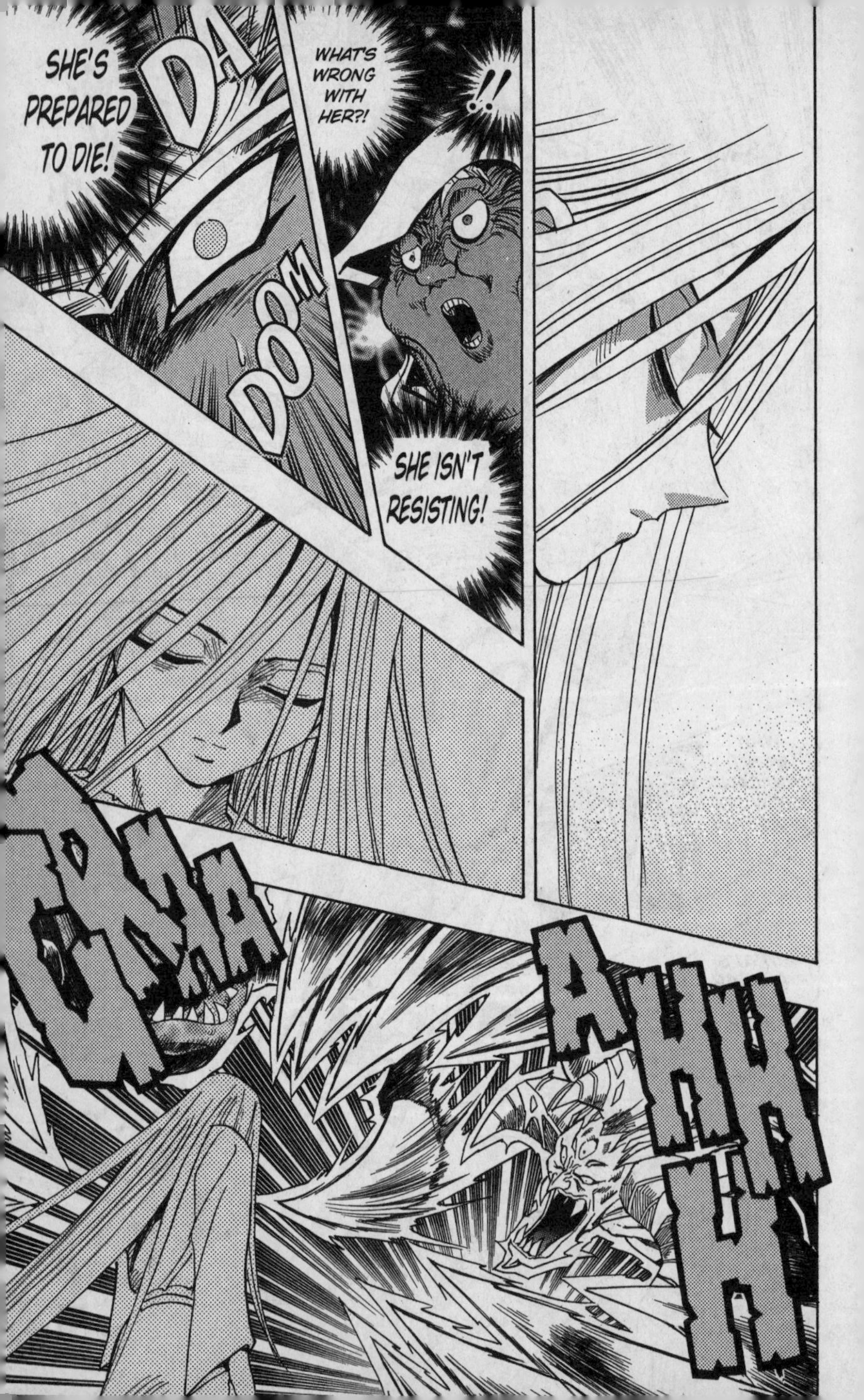
WHAT'S WRONG WITH HER?!
!!
SHE ISN'T RESISTING!
SHE'S PREPARED TO DIE!
DA
DOOM

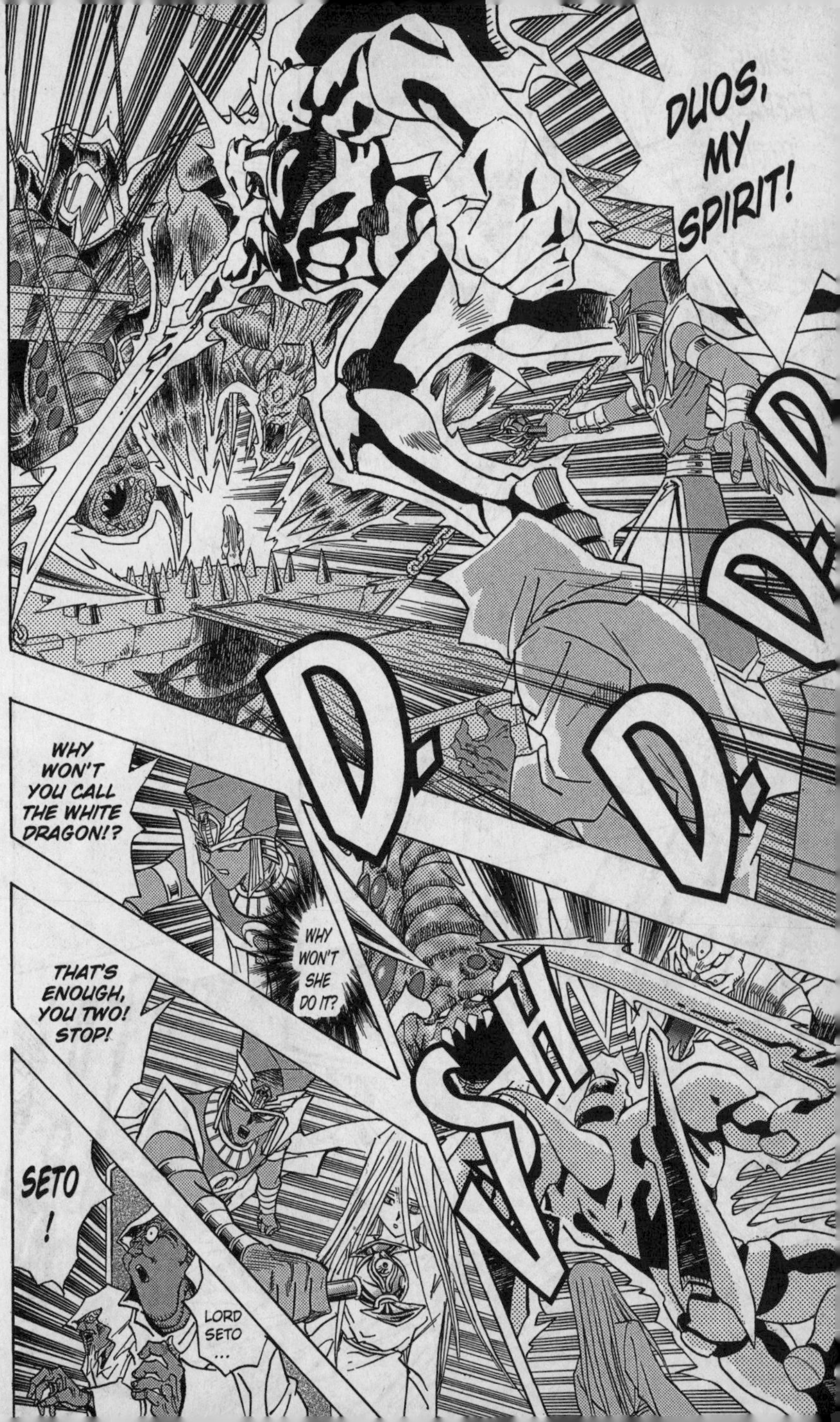
DUOS, MY SPIRIT!
WHY WON'T SHE DO IT?
WHY WON'T YOU CALL THE WHITE DRAGON!?
THAT'S ENOUGH, YOU TWO! STOP!
LORD SETO ...
SETO!

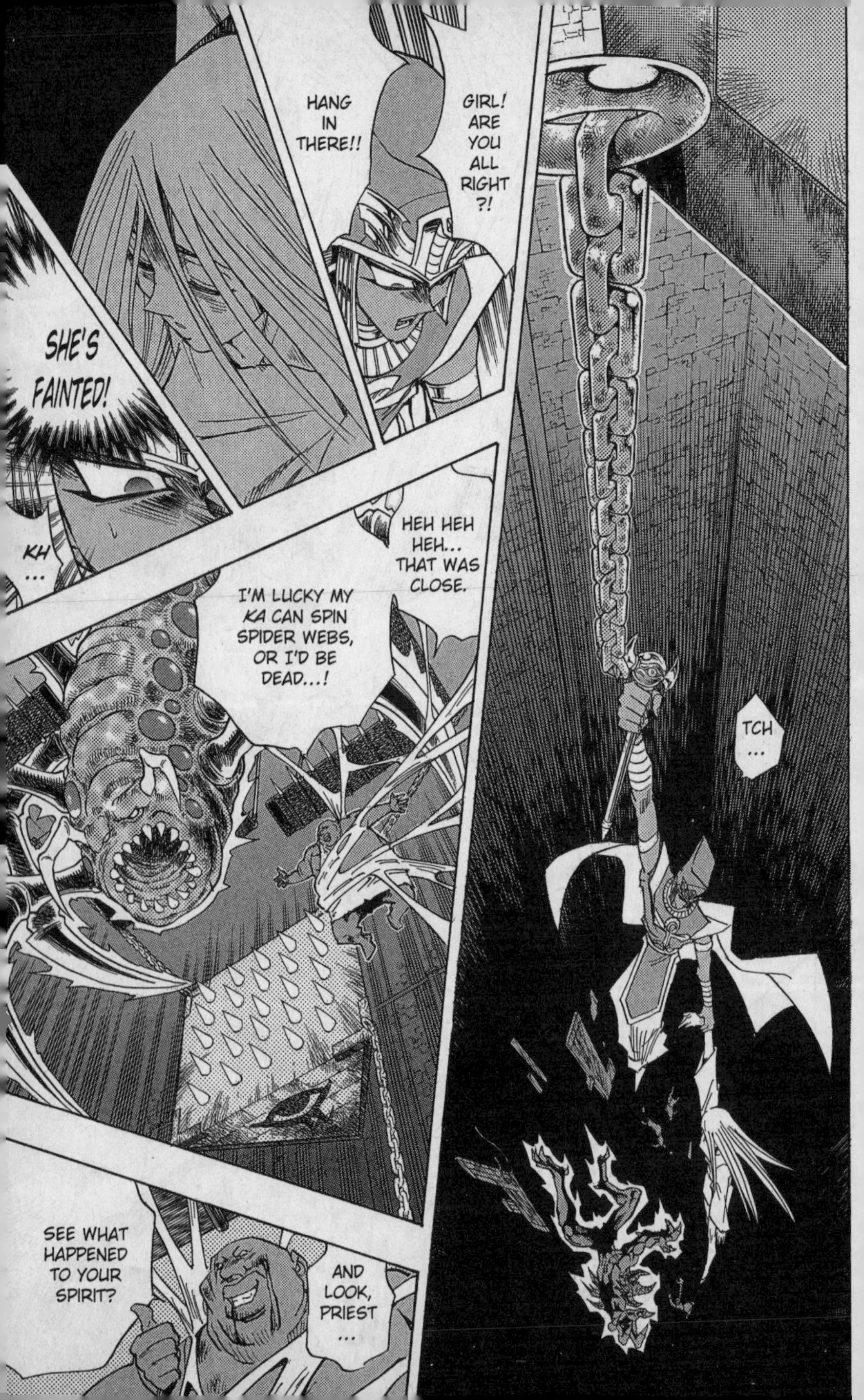
GIRL! ARE YOU ALL RIGHT?!
HANG IN THERE!!
SHE'S FAINTED!
KH...
TCH...
HEH HEH HEH... THAT WAS CLOSE.
I'M LUCKY MY *KA* CAN SPIN SPIDER WEBS, OR I'D BE DEAD...!
AND LOOK, PRIEST...
SEE WHAT HAPPENED TO YOUR SPIRIT?

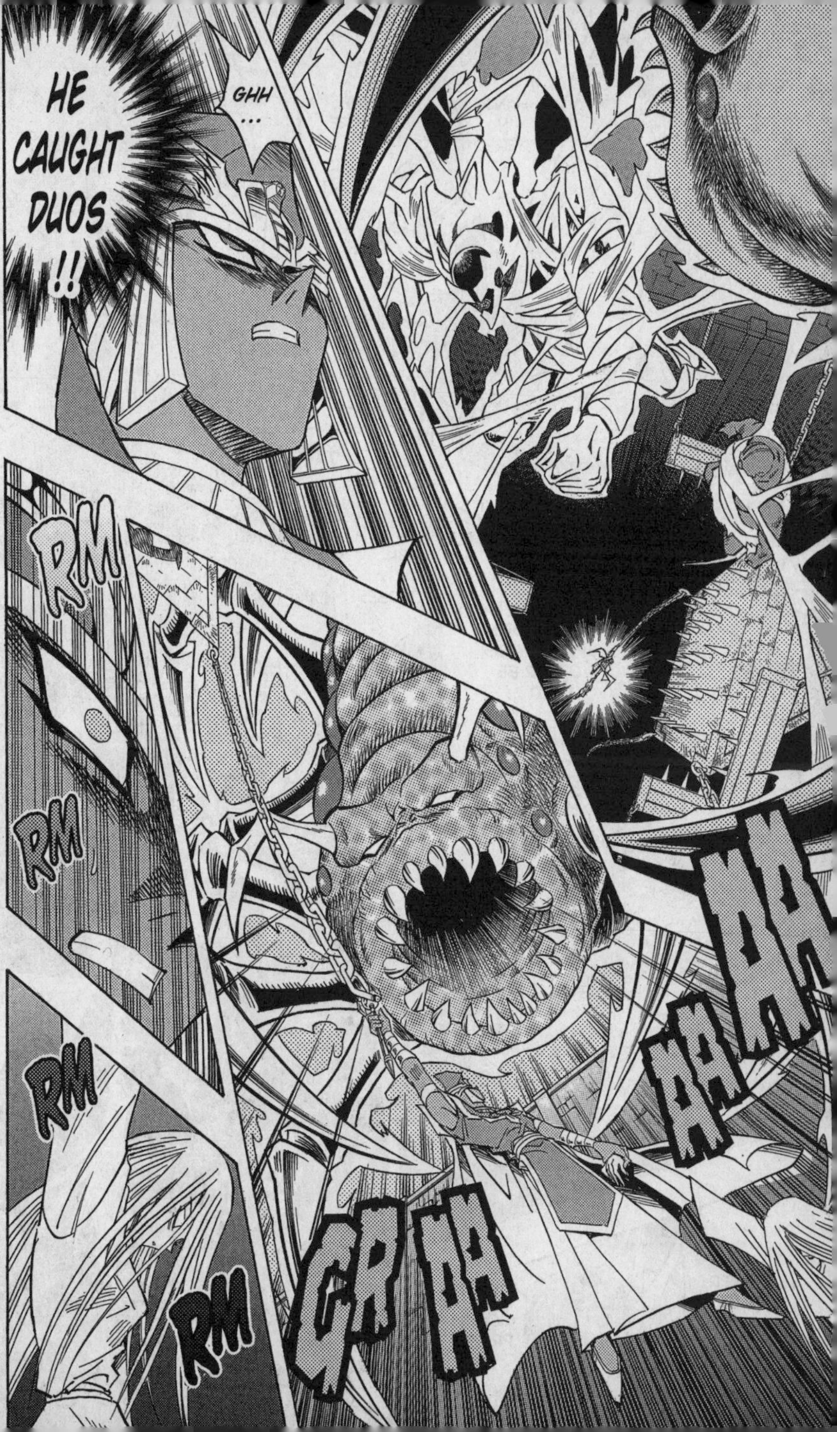
HE CAUGHT DUOS !!
GHH ...
RM
RM
RM
RM
GRAA
AAAAA

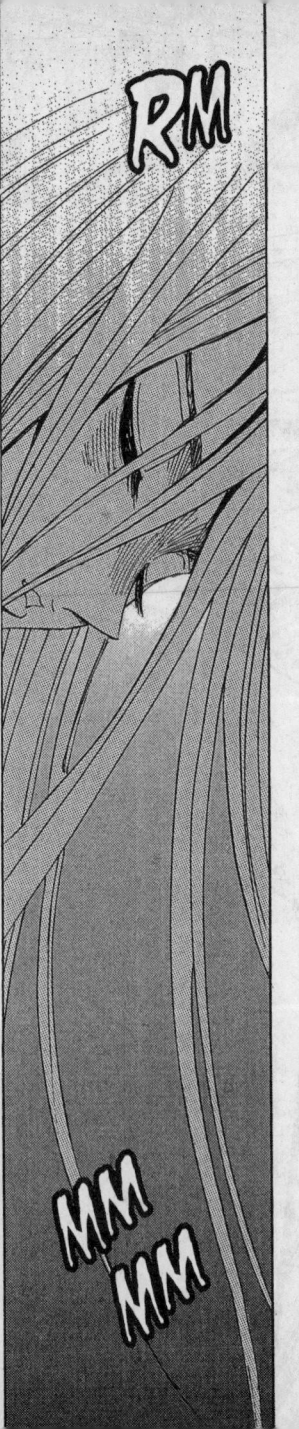

FHA SH

RM

!!

WHAT THE...

IT'S HERE!

WHAT'S THIS LIGHT ?!!

MM MM

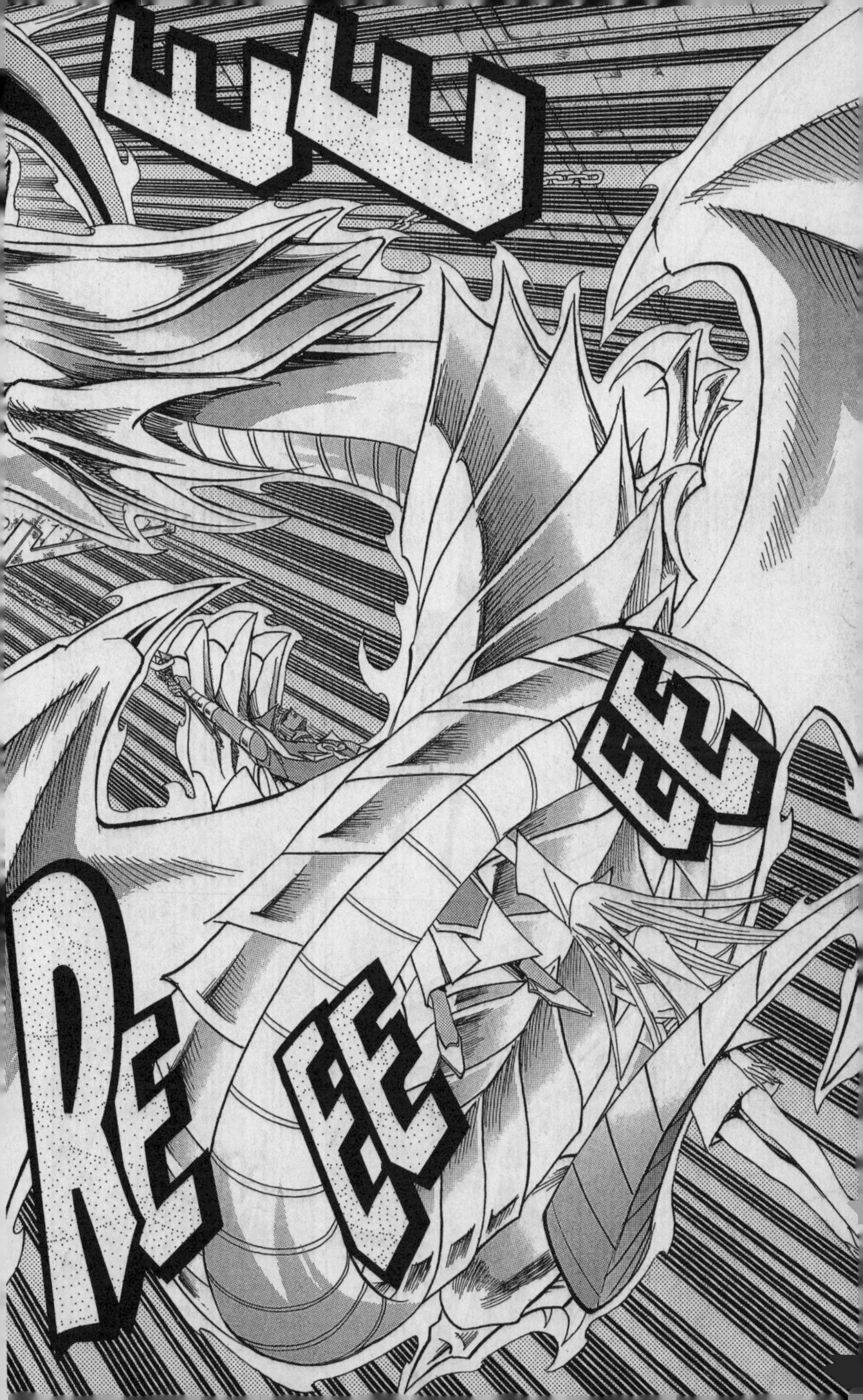
REEE

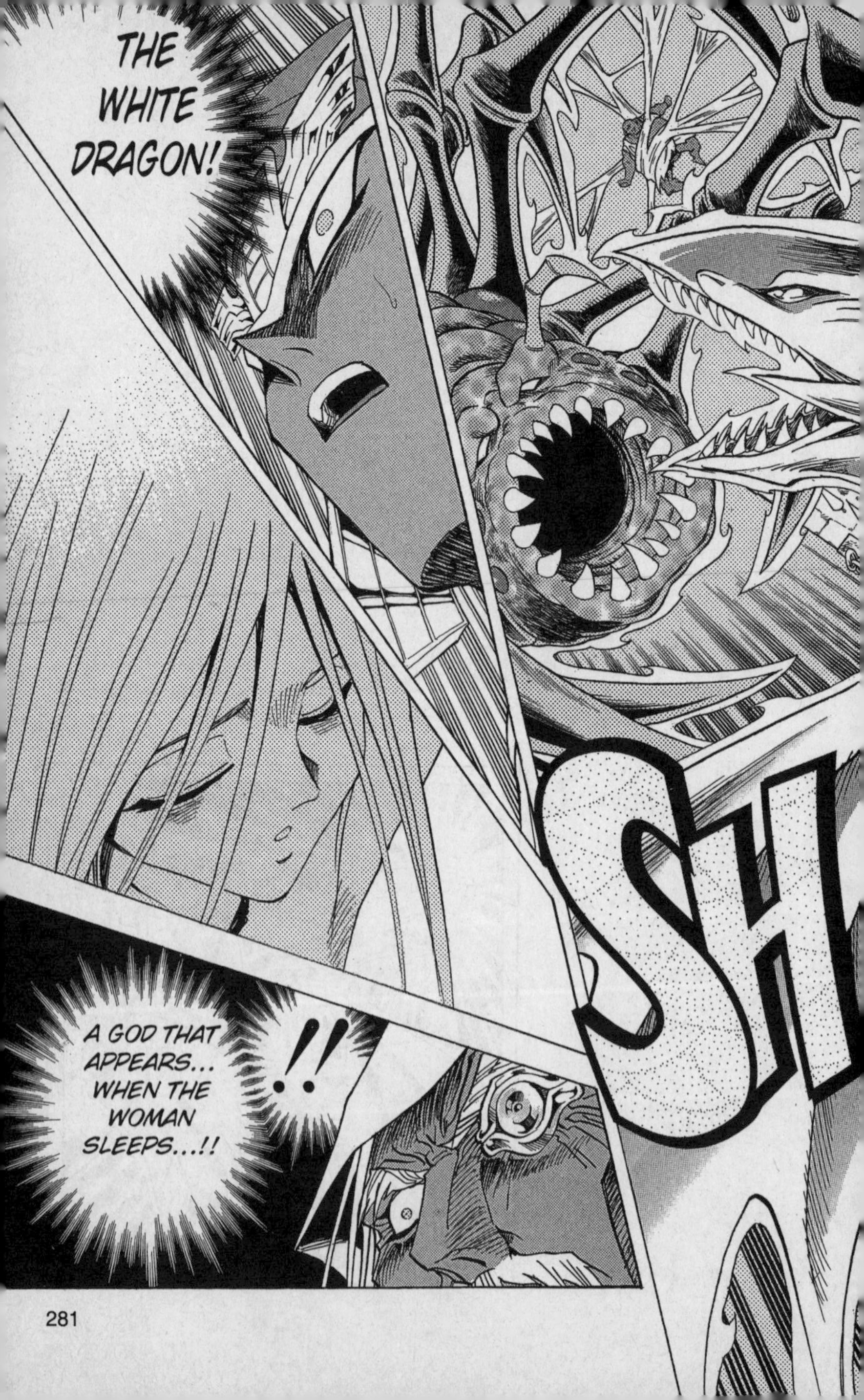
THE WHITE DRAGON!
A GOD THAT APPEARS... WHEN THE WOMAN SLEEPS...!!
!!
SH

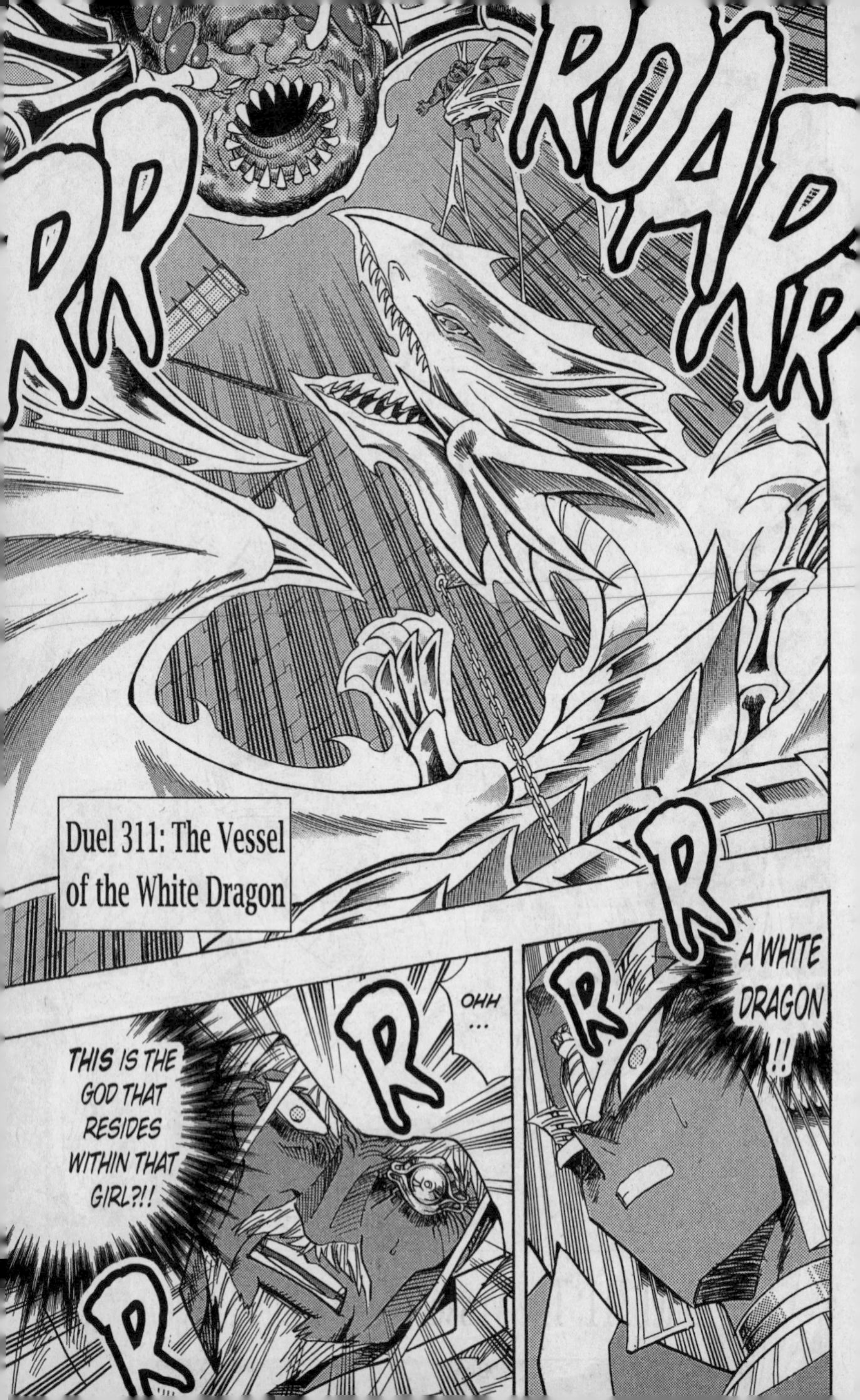
ROAAR
RR
Duel 311: The Vessel of the White Dragon
R
A WHITE DRAGON!!
R
OHH...
R
THIS IS THE GOD THAT RESIDES WITHIN THAT GIRL?!!
R

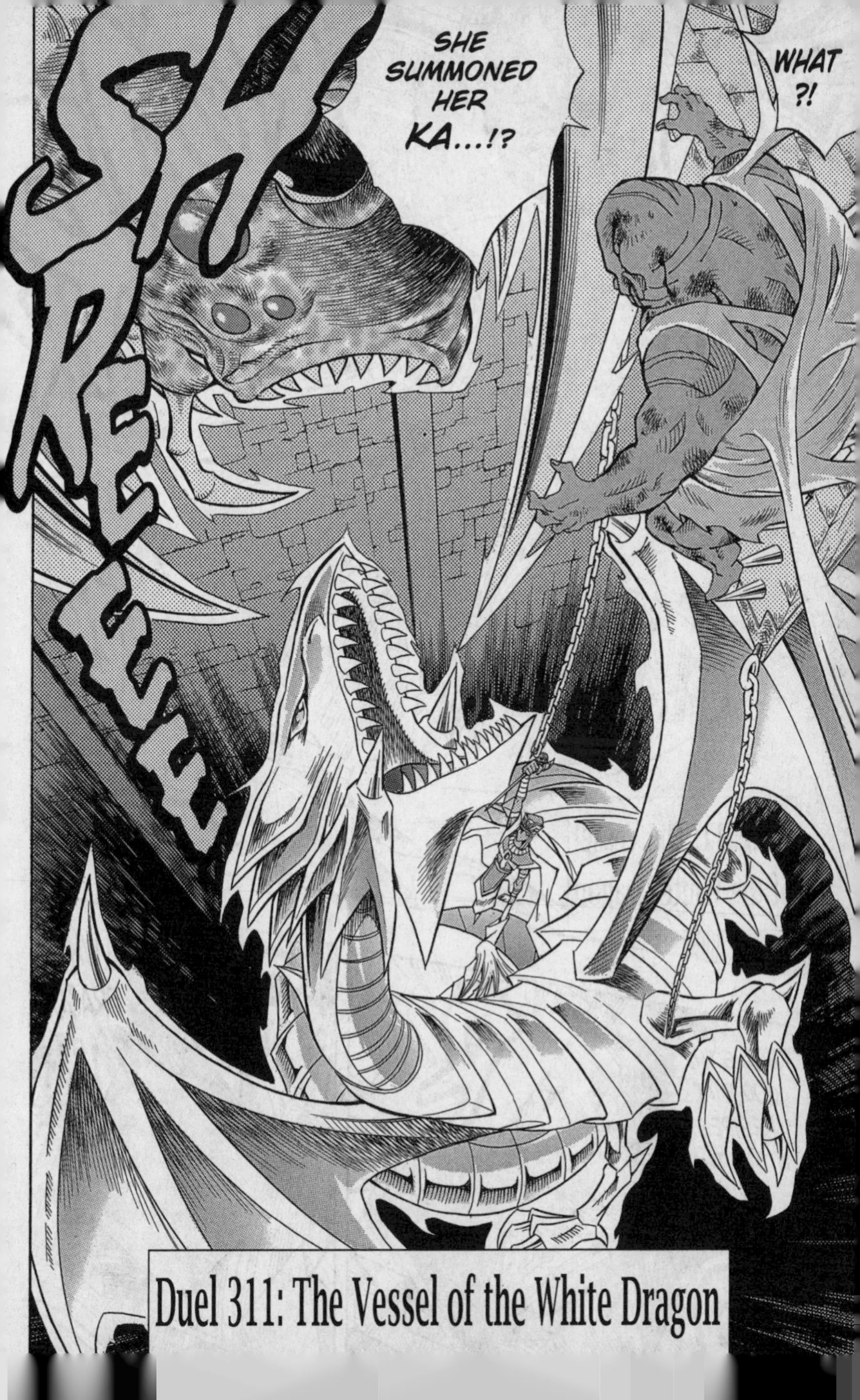
WHAT ?!
SHE SUMMONED HER KA...!?

Duel 311: The Vessel of the White Dragon

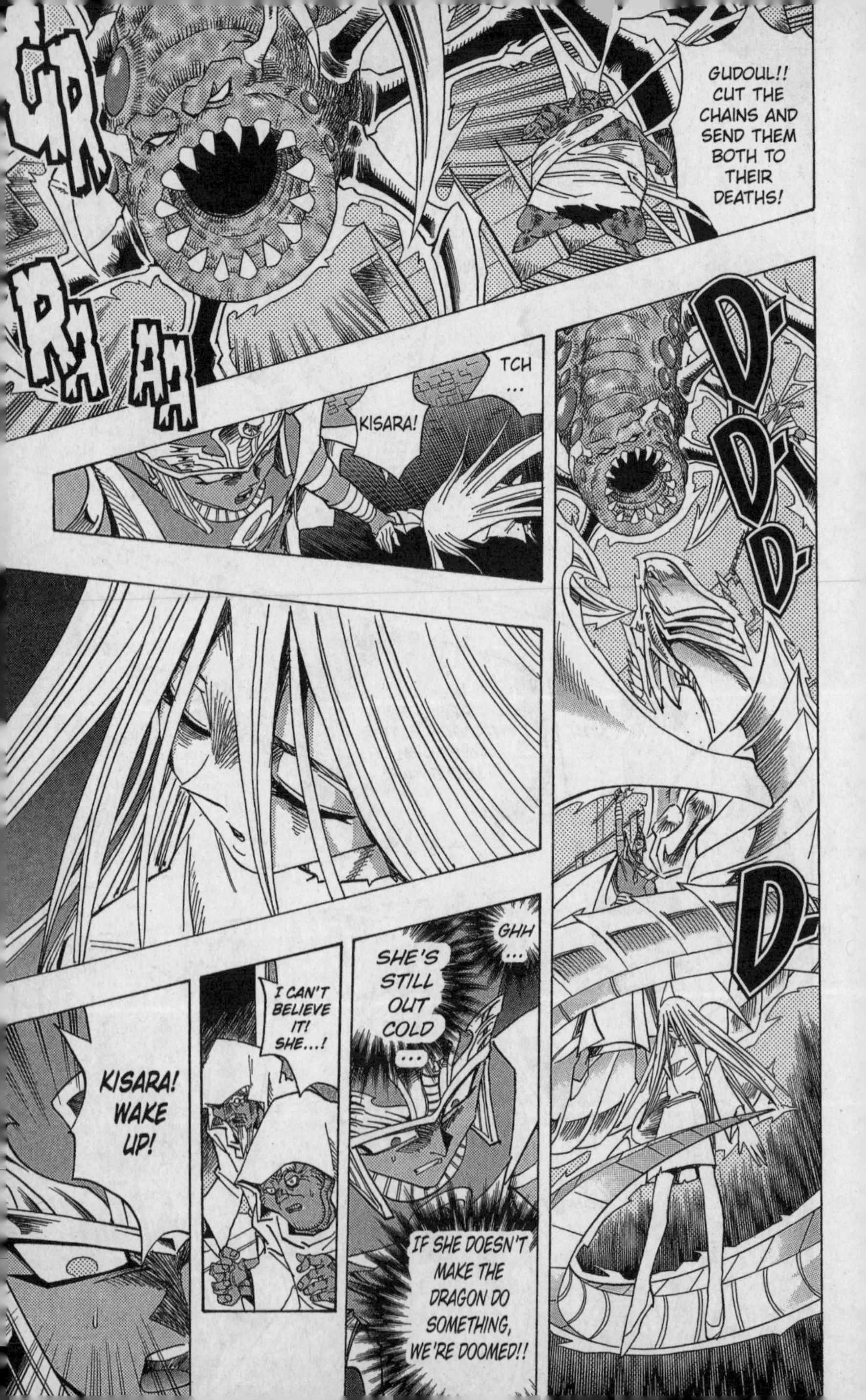
GUDOUL!! CUT THE CHAINS AND SEND THEM BOTH TO THEIR DEATHS!
TCH ...
KISARA!
GHH ...
SHE'S STILL OUT COLD ...
IF SHE DOESN'T MAKE THE DRAGON DO SOMETHING, WE'RE DOOMED!!
I CAN'T BELIEVE IT! SHE...!
KISARA! WAKE UP!

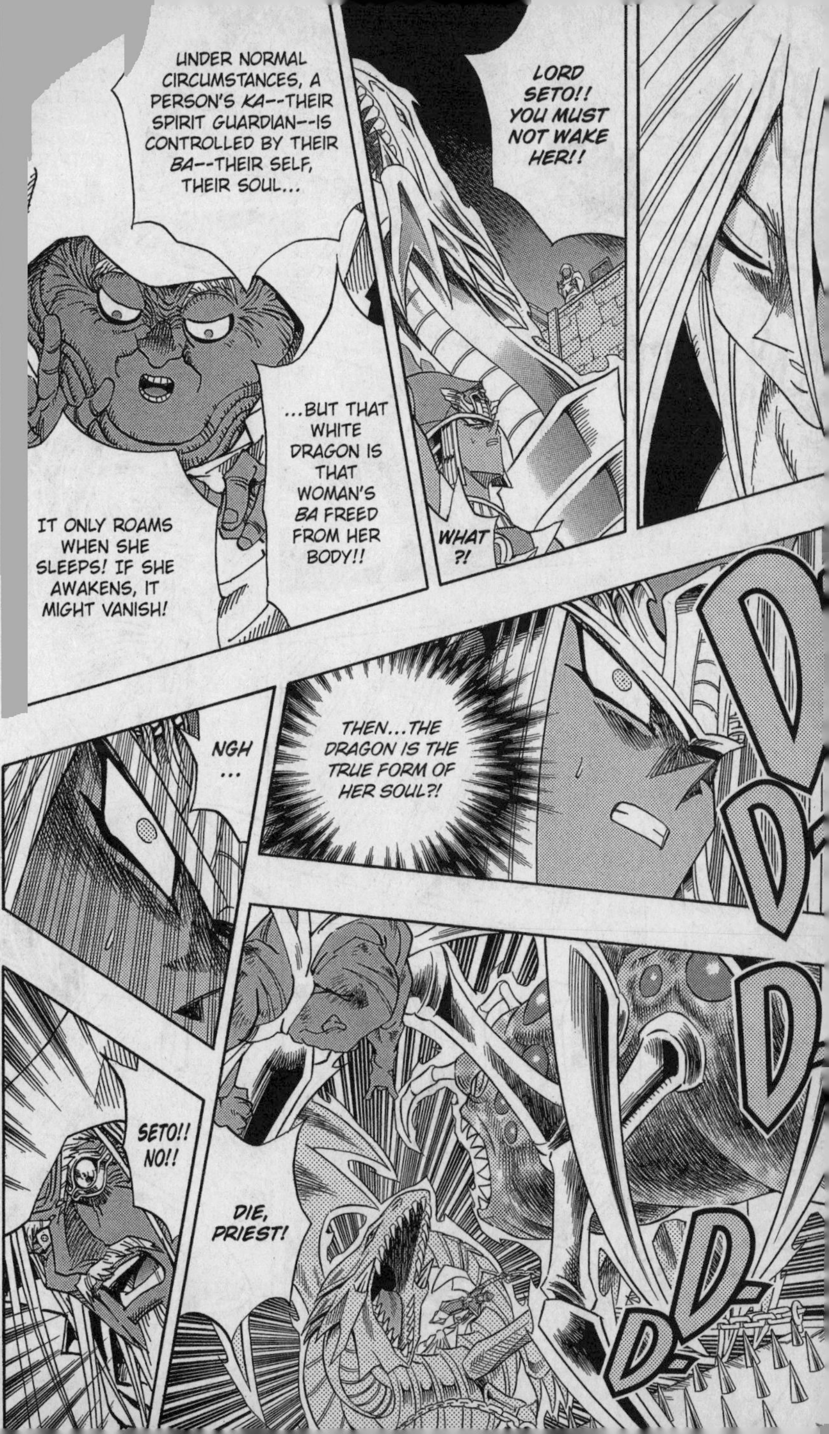
LORD SETO!! YOU MUST NOT WAKE HER!!
WHAT ?!
UNDER NORMAL CIRCUMSTANCES, A PERSON'S KA--THEIR SPIRIT GUARDIAN--IS CONTROLLED BY THEIR BA--THEIR SELF, THEIR SOUL...
...BUT THAT WHITE DRAGON IS THAT WOMAN'S BA FREED FROM HER BODY!!
IT ONLY ROAMS WHEN SHE SLEEPS! IF SHE AWAKENS, IT MIGHT VANISH!
D D-
THEN...THE DRAGON IS THE TRUE FORM OF HER SOUL?!
NGH ...
D D- D- D-
SETO!! NO!!
DIE, PRIEST!

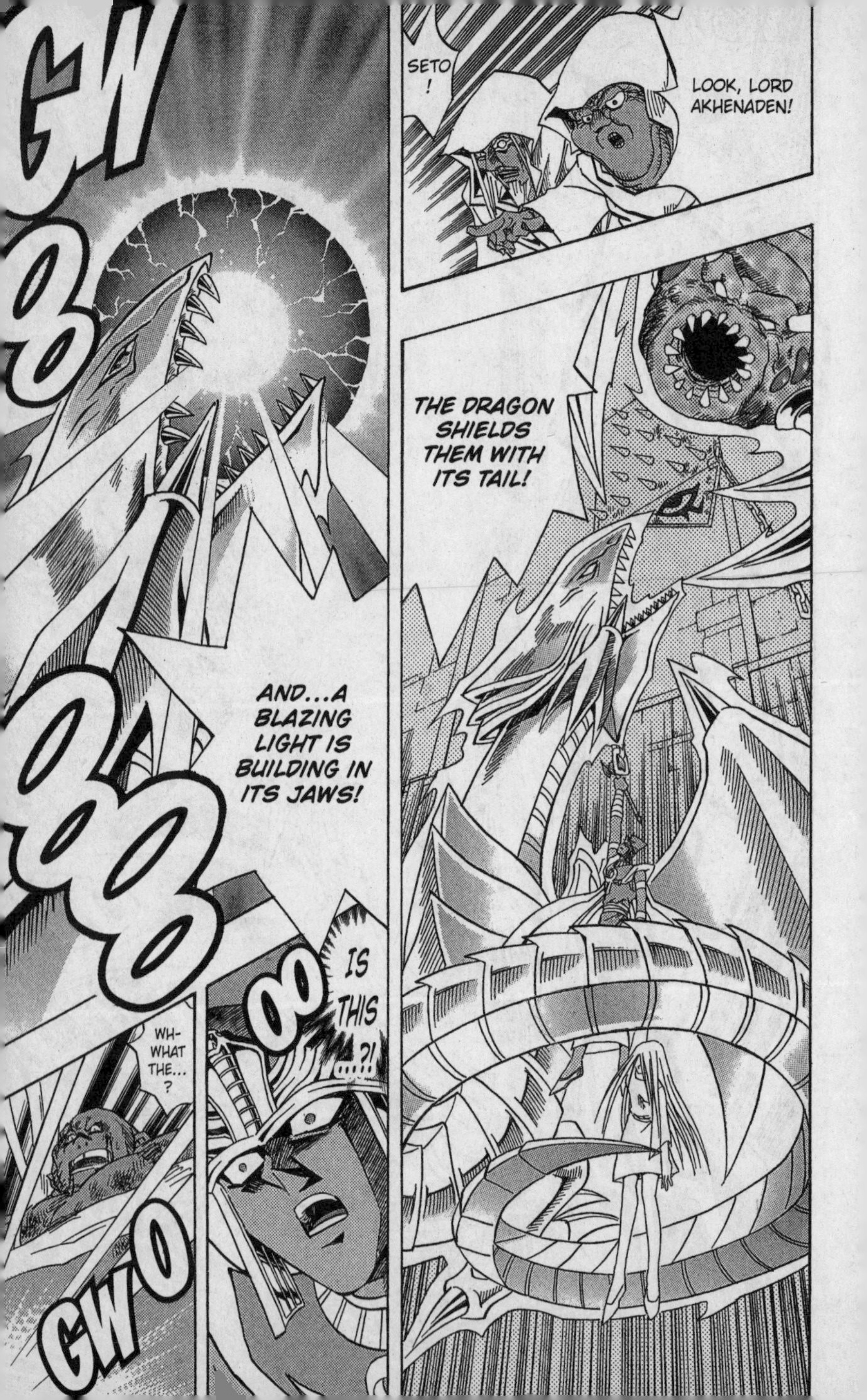
LOOK, LORD AKHENADEN!
SETO!
THE DRAGON SHIELDS THEM WITH ITS TAIL!
GWOOO
AND...A BLAZING LIGHT IS BUILDING IN ITS JAWS!
IS THIS...?!
WH-WHAT THE...?
GWOOO

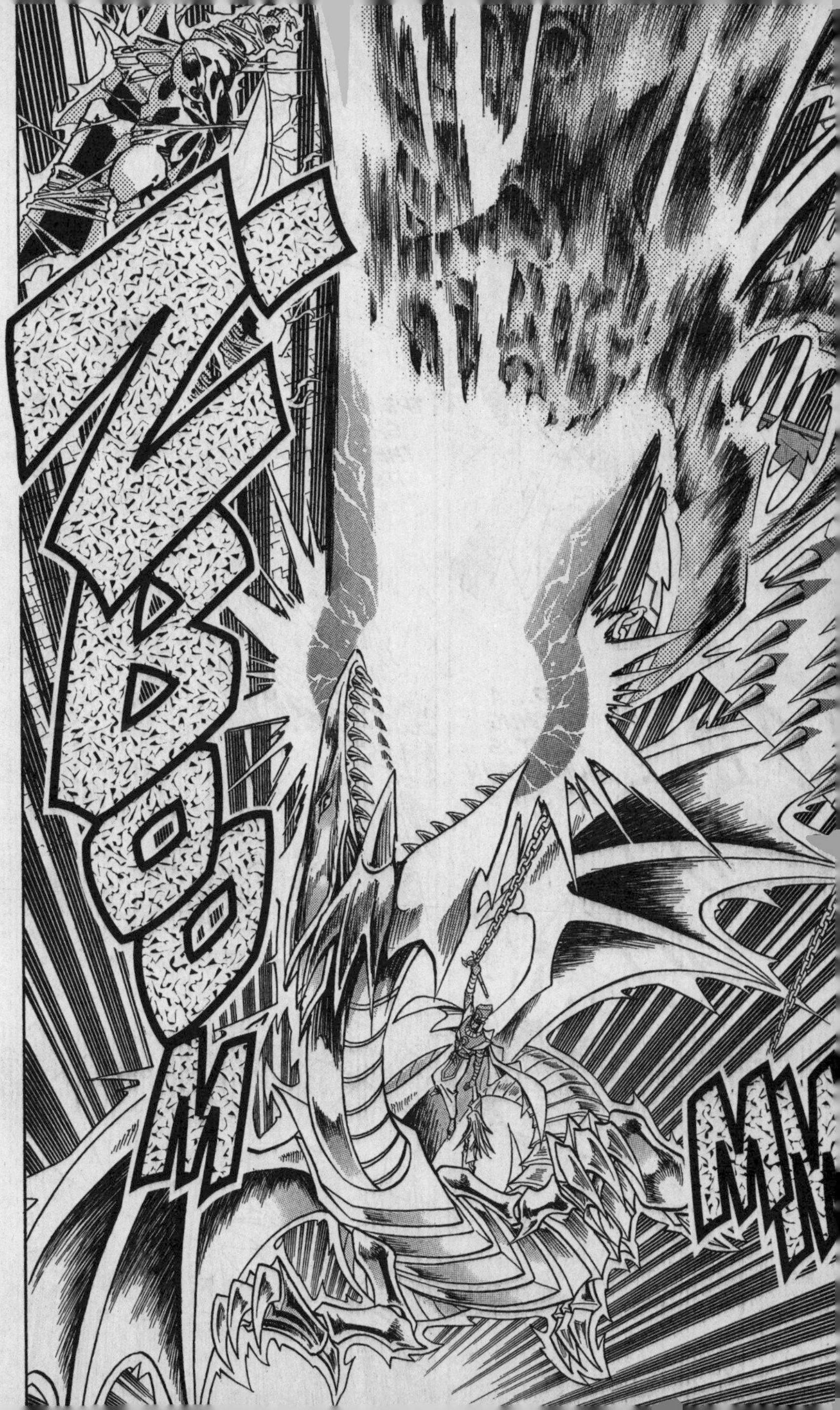
ZBOOM

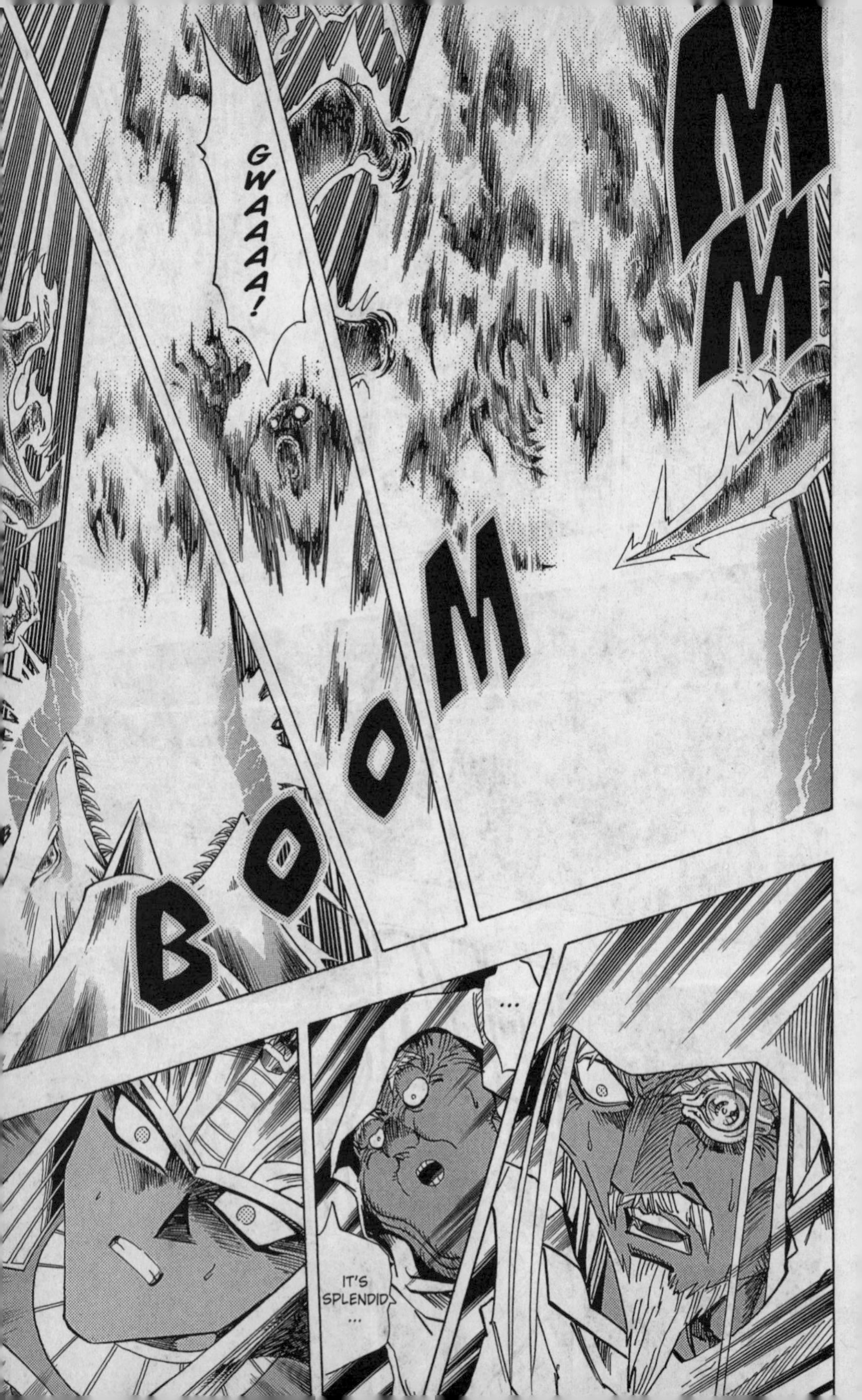
GWAAAAA!
BOOOMMM
...
IT'S SPLENDID ...

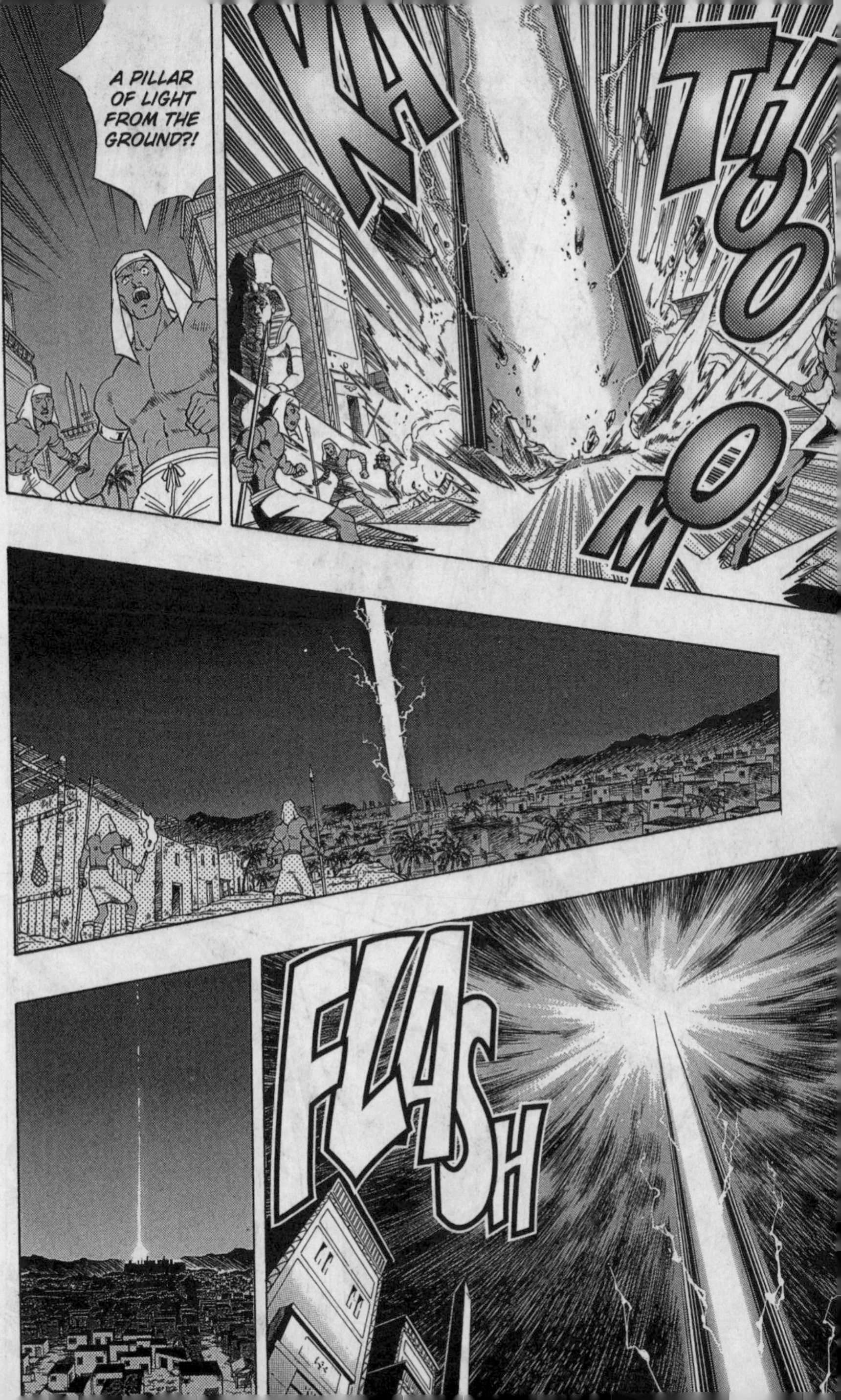
A PILLAR OF LIGHT FROM THE GROUND?!
VA
THOOOM
FLASH

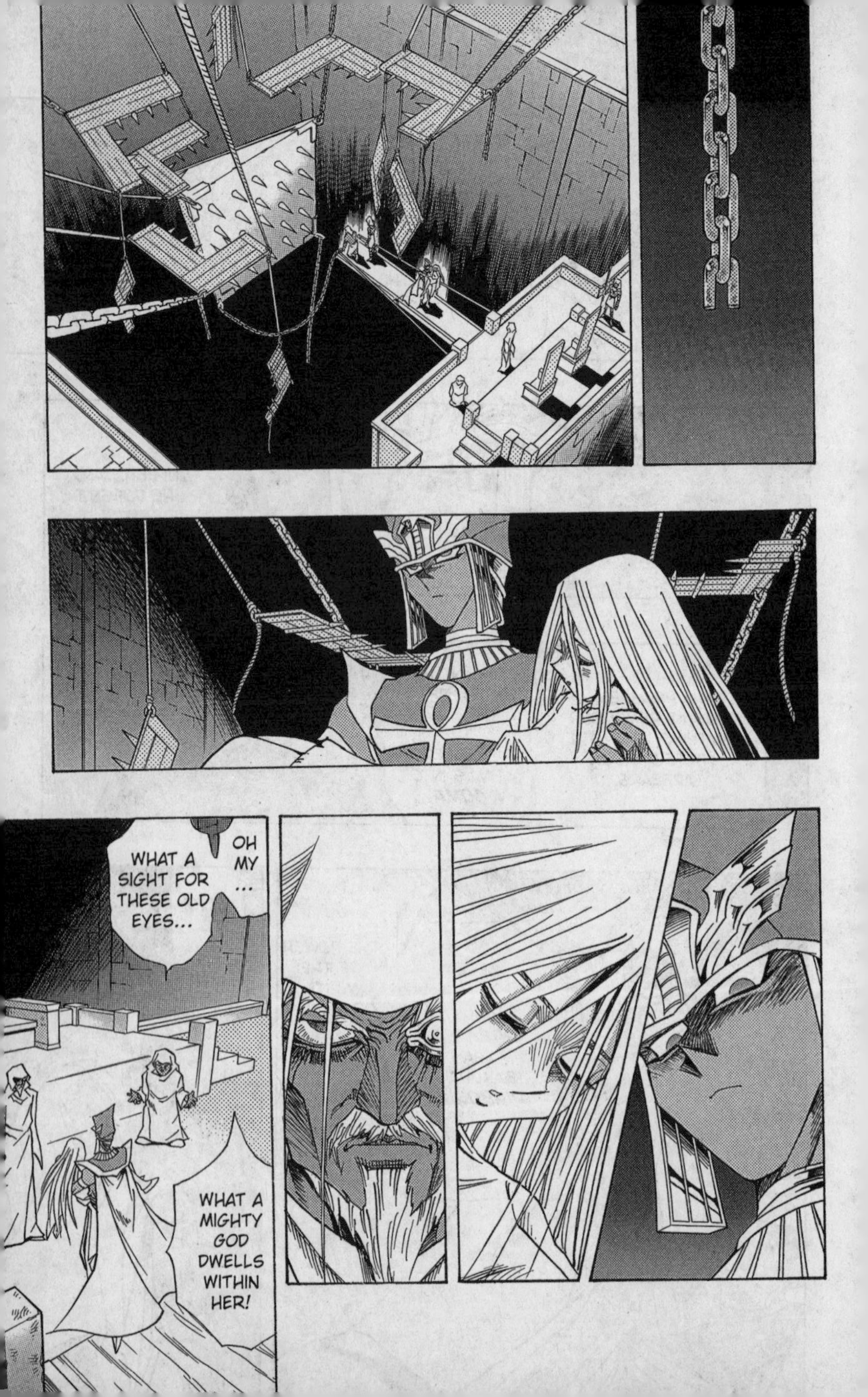

OH MY...
WHAT A SIGHT FOR THESE OLD EYES...
WHAT A MIGHTY GOD DWELLS WITHIN HER!

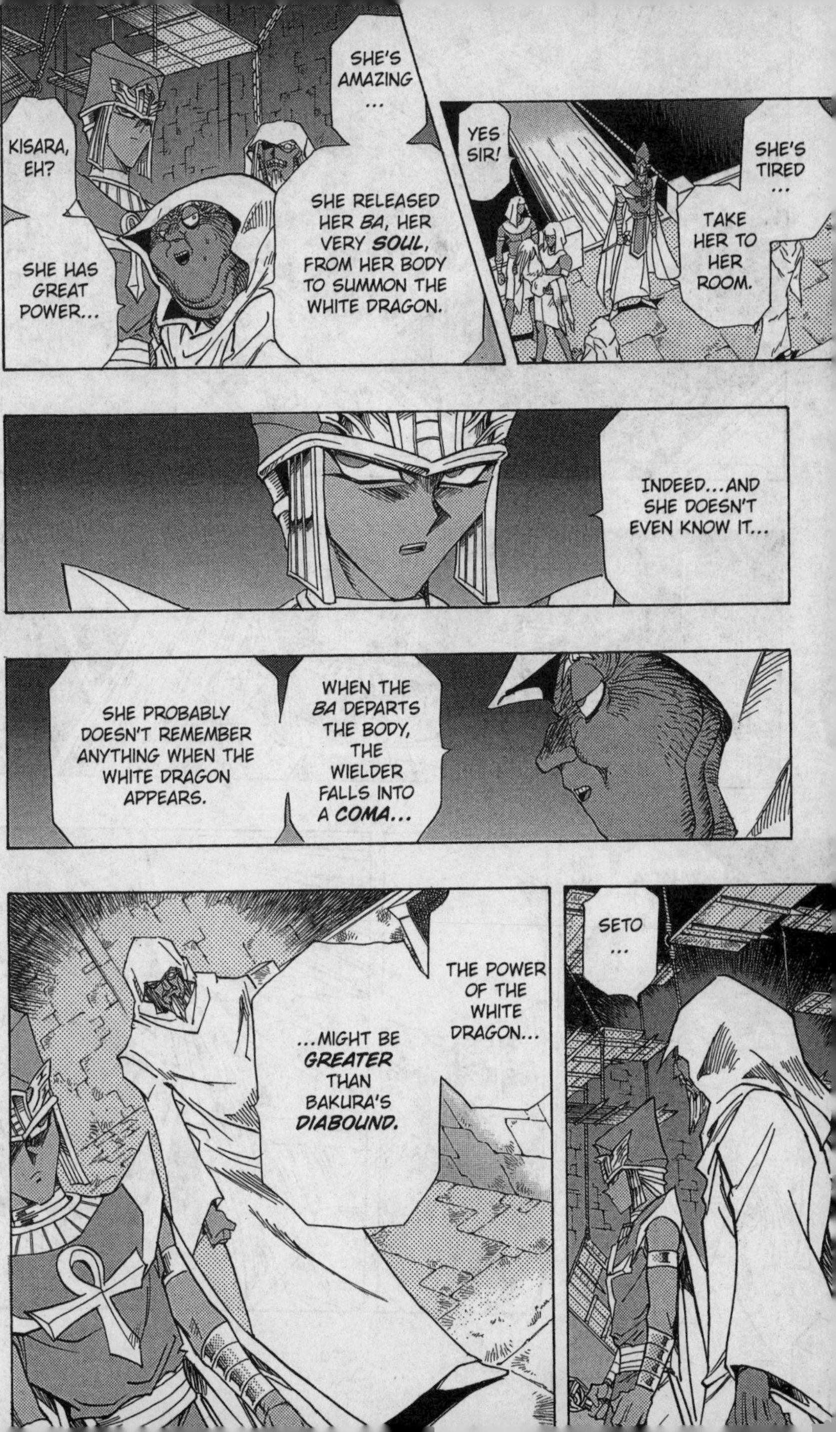
SHE'S TIRED...
TAKE HER TO HER ROOM.
YES SIR!
SHE'S AMAZING...
SHE RELEASED HER BA, HER VERY SOUL, FROM HER BODY TO SUMMON THE WHITE DRAGON.
KISARA, EH?
SHE HAS GREAT POWER...
INDEED...AND SHE DOESN'T EVEN KNOW IT...
WHEN THE BA DEPARTS THE BODY, THE WIELDER FALLS INTO A COMA...
SHE PROBABLY DOESN'T REMEMBER ANYTHING WHEN THE WHITE DRAGON APPEARS.
SETO...
THE POWER OF THE WHITE DRAGON...
...MIGHT BE GREATER THAN BAKURA'S DIABOUND.

READ THIS WAY

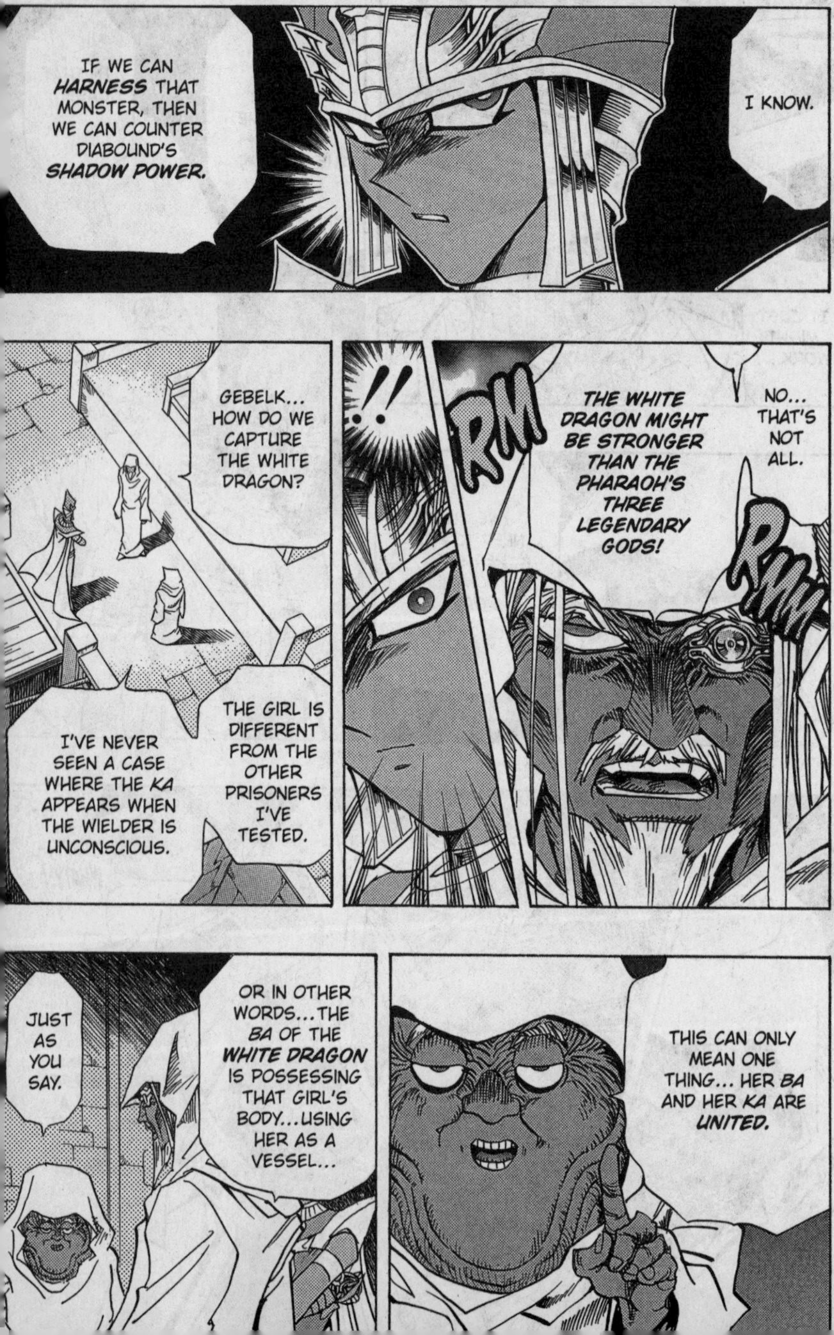
I KNOW.
IF WE CAN HARNESS THAT MONSTER, THEN WE CAN COUNTER DIABOUND'S SHADOW POWER.
NO... THAT'S NOT ALL.
THE WHITE DRAGON MIGHT BE STRONGER THAN THE PHARAOH'S THREE LEGENDARY GODS!
RMM
RM
!!
GEBELK... HOW DO WE CAPTURE THE WHITE DRAGON?
THE GIRL IS DIFFERENT FROM THE OTHER PRISONERS I'VE TESTED.
I'VE NEVER SEEN A CASE WHERE THE KA APPEARS WHEN THE WIELDER IS UNCONSCIOUS.
THIS CAN ONLY MEAN ONE THING... HER BA AND HER KA ARE UNITED.
OR IN OTHER WORDS...THE BA OF THE WHITE DRAGON IS POSSESSING THAT GIRL'S BODY...USING HER AS A VESSEL...
JUST AS YOU SAY.

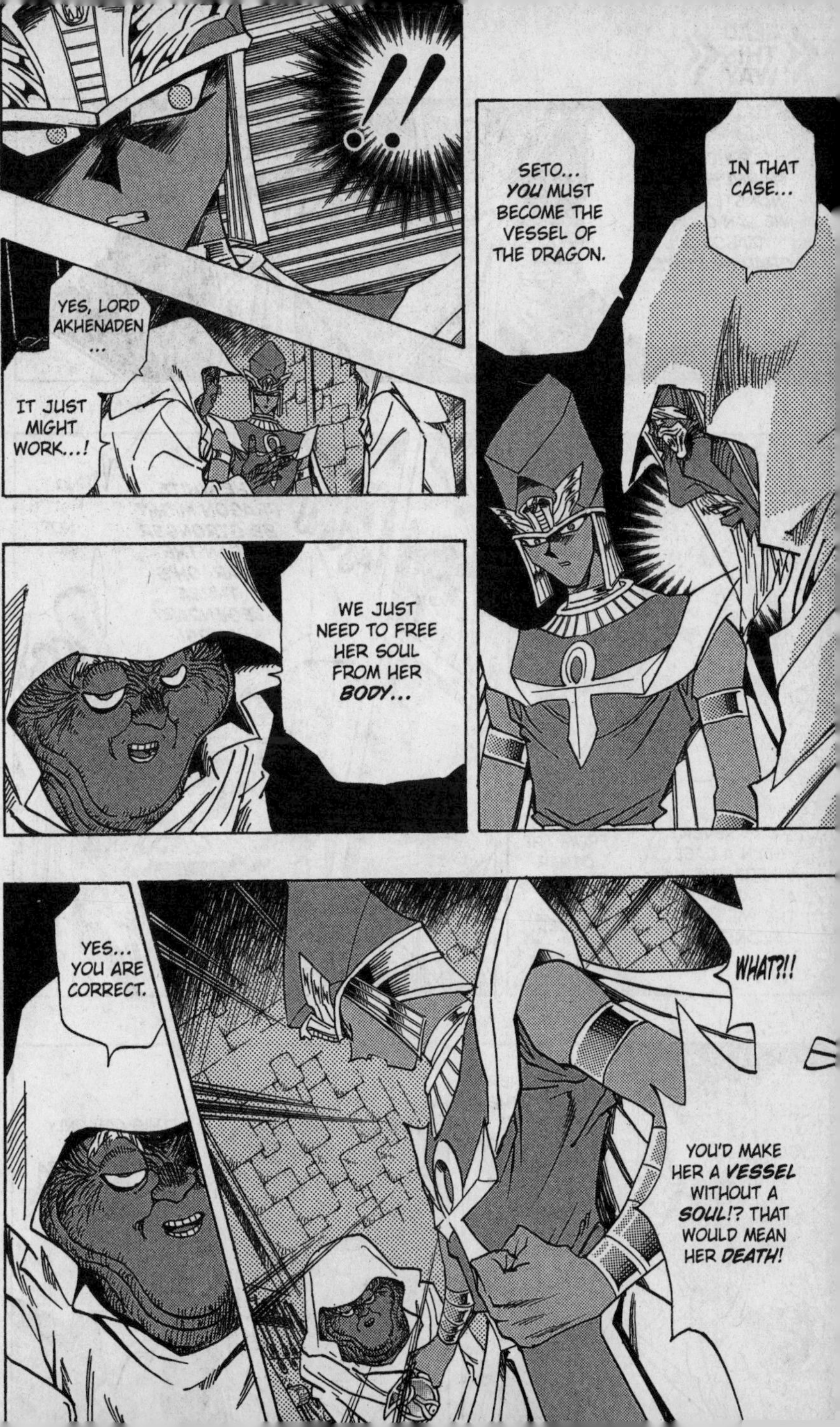
!!
IN THAT CASE...
SETO... YOU MUST BECOME THE VESSEL OF THE DRAGON.
YES, LORD AKHENADEN ...
IT JUST MIGHT WORK...!
WE JUST NEED TO FREE HER SOUL FROM HER BODY...
WHAT?!!
YOU'D MAKE HER A VESSEL WITHOUT A SOUL!? THAT WOULD MEAN HER DEATH!
YES... YOU ARE CORRECT.

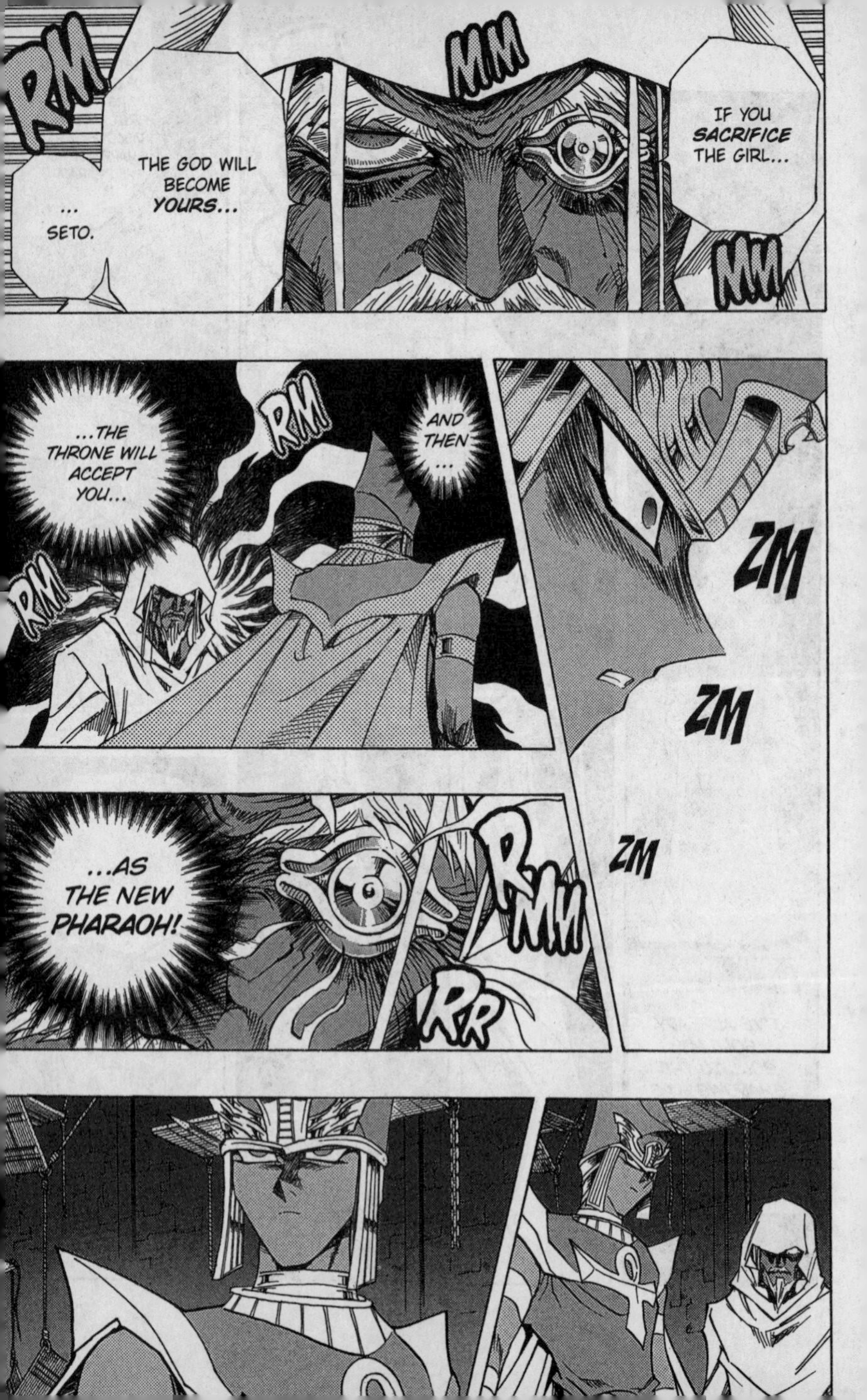
MM
IF YOU SACRIFICE THE GIRL...
THE GOD WILL BECOME YOURS...
... SETO.
RM
MM
ZM
ZM
ZM
AND THEN...
RM
...THE THRONE WILL ACCEPT YOU...
RM
RMM
RR
...AS THE NEW PHARAOH!

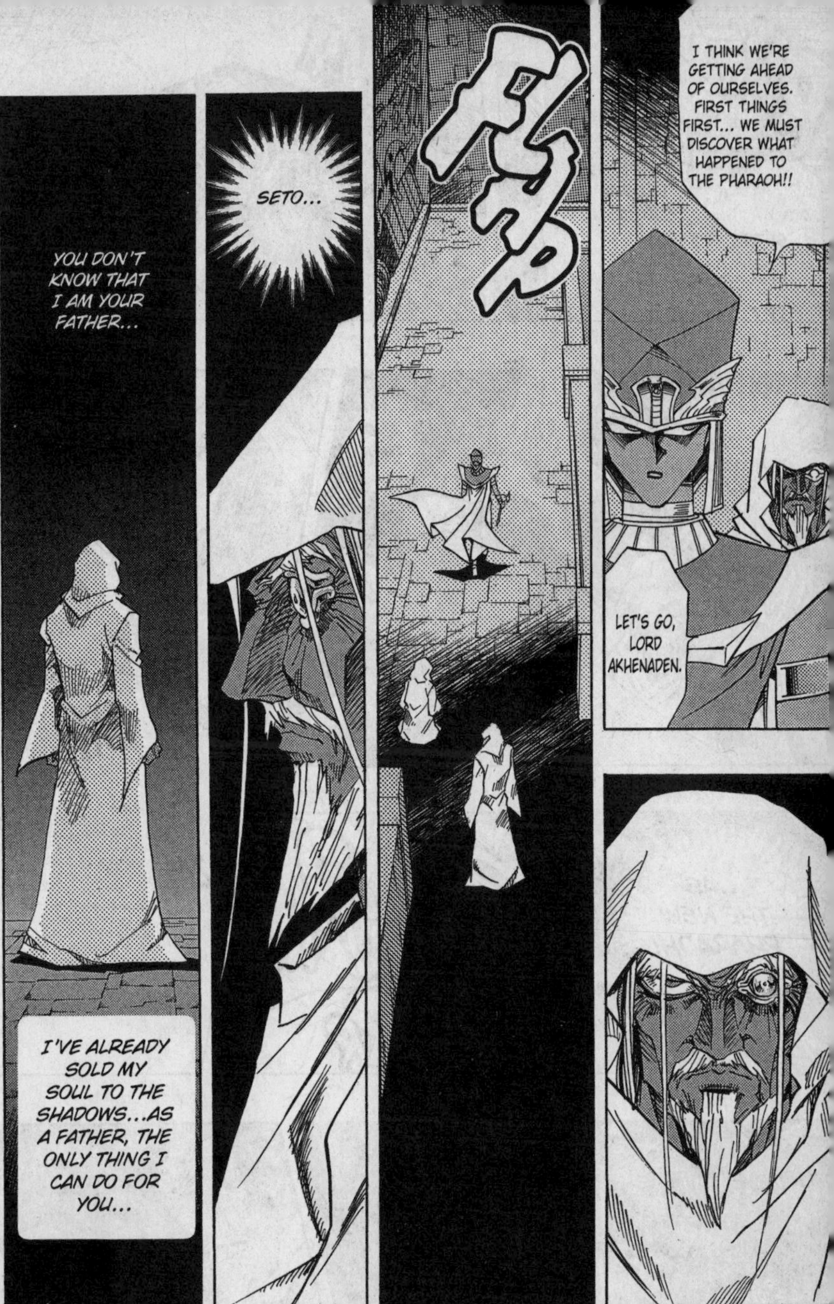
I THINK WE'RE GETTING AHEAD OF OURSELVES. FIRST THINGS FIRST... WE MUST DISCOVER WHAT HAPPENED TO THE PHARAOH!!
LET'S GO, LORD AKHENADEN.
FLAP
SETO...
YOU DON'T KNOW THAT I AM YOUR FATHER...
I'VE ALREADY SOLD MY SOUL TO THE SHADOWS...AS A FATHER, THE ONLY THING I CAN DO FOR YOU...

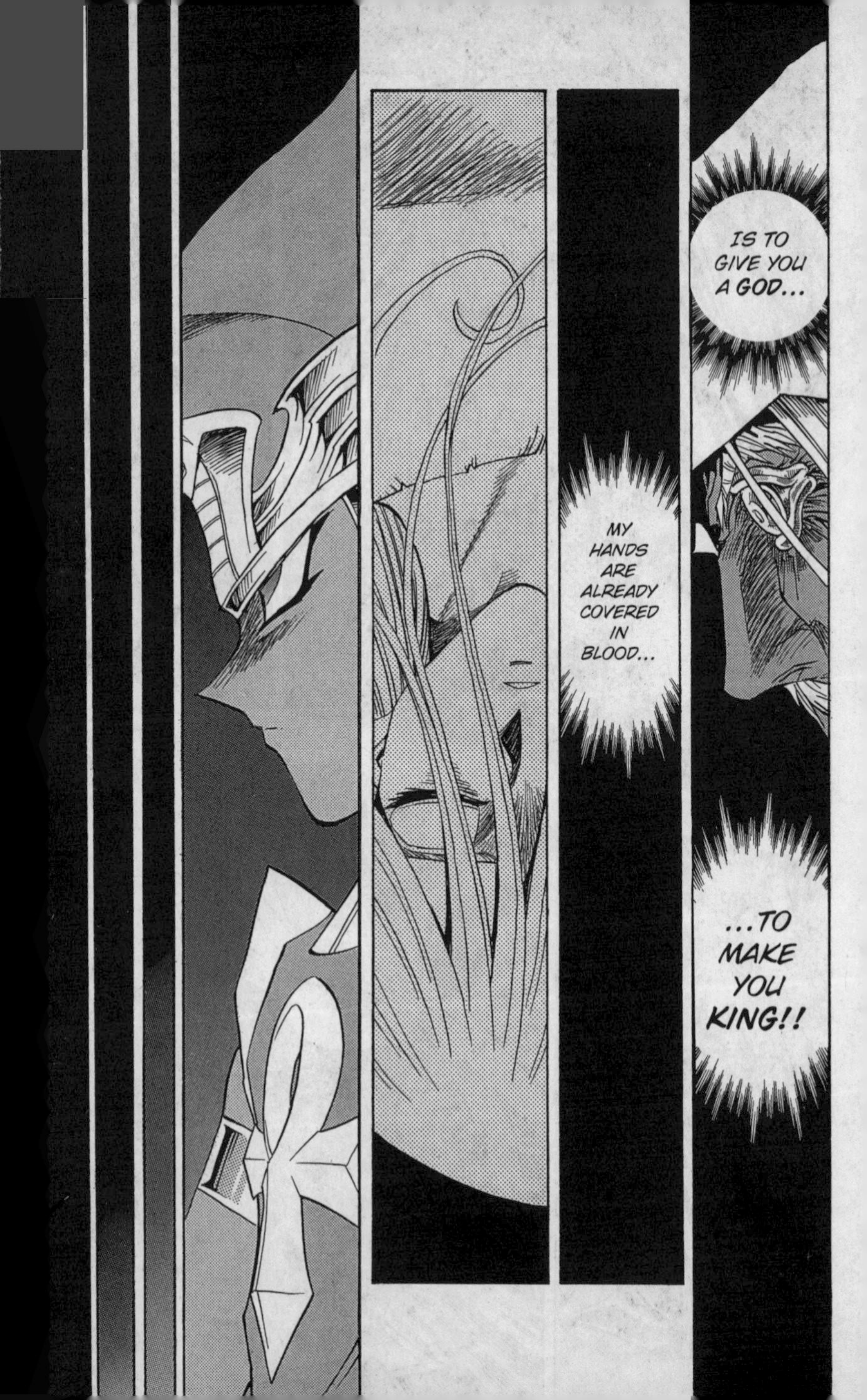
IS TO GIVE YOU A GOD...
...TO MAKE YOU KING!!
MY HANDS ARE ALREADY COVERED IN BLOOD...

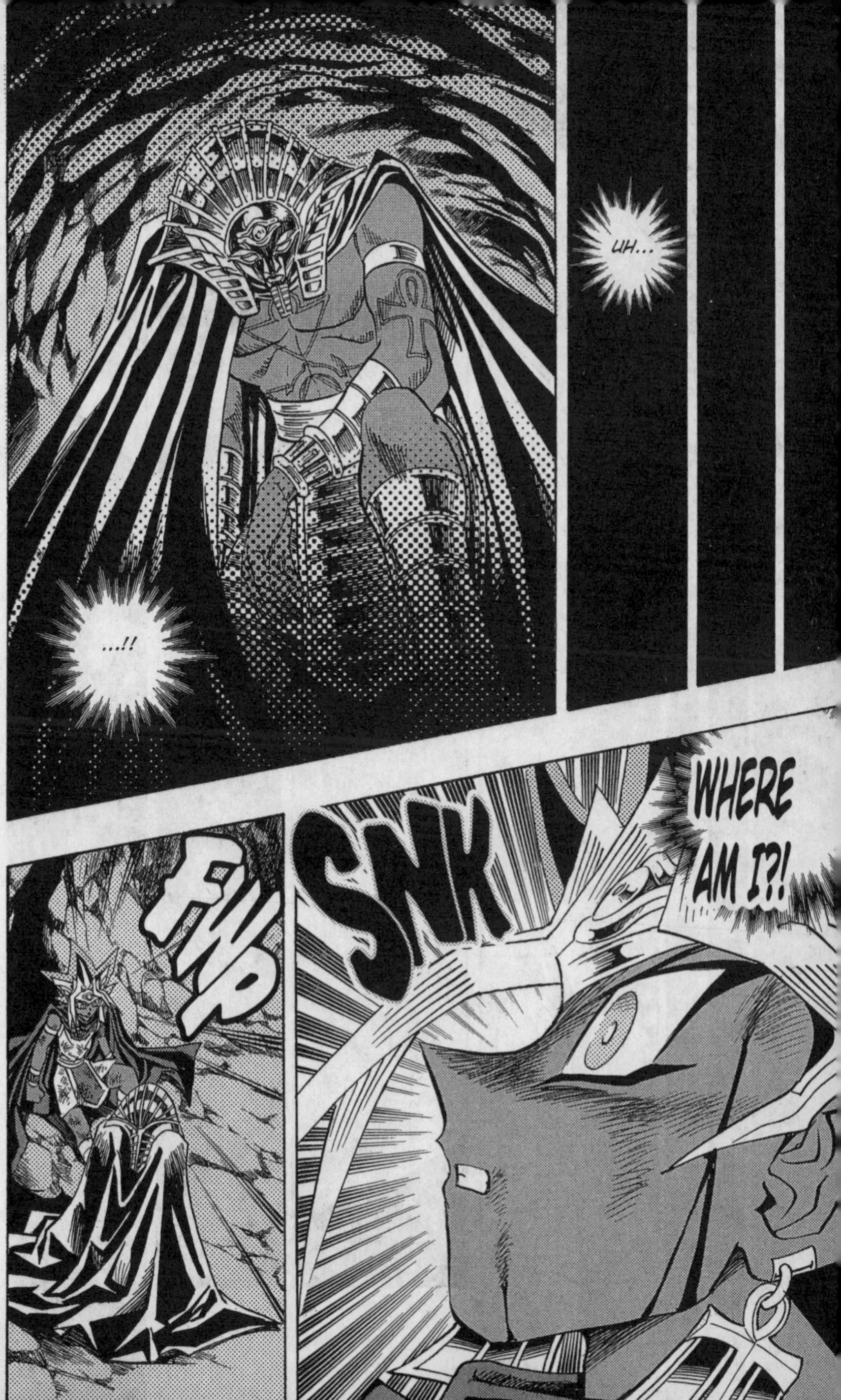

UH...
...!!
WHERE AM I?!
SNK
FWP

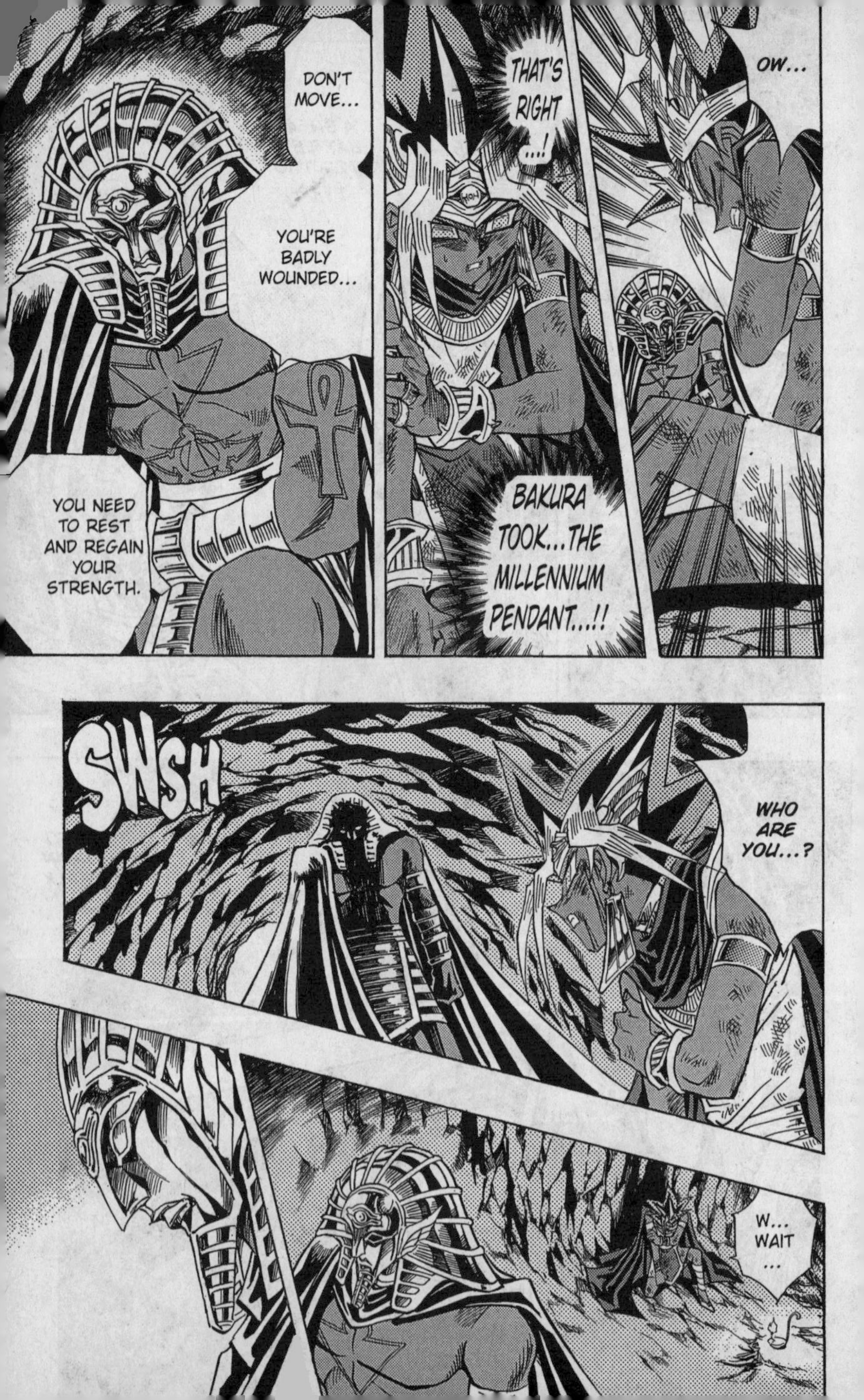
OW...
THAT'S RIGHT ...!
BAKURA TOOK...THE MILLENNIUM PENDANT...!!
DON'T MOVE...
YOU'RE BADLY WOUNDED...
YOU NEED TO REST AND REGAIN YOUR STRENGTH.
WHO ARE YOU...?
SWSH
W... WAIT ...

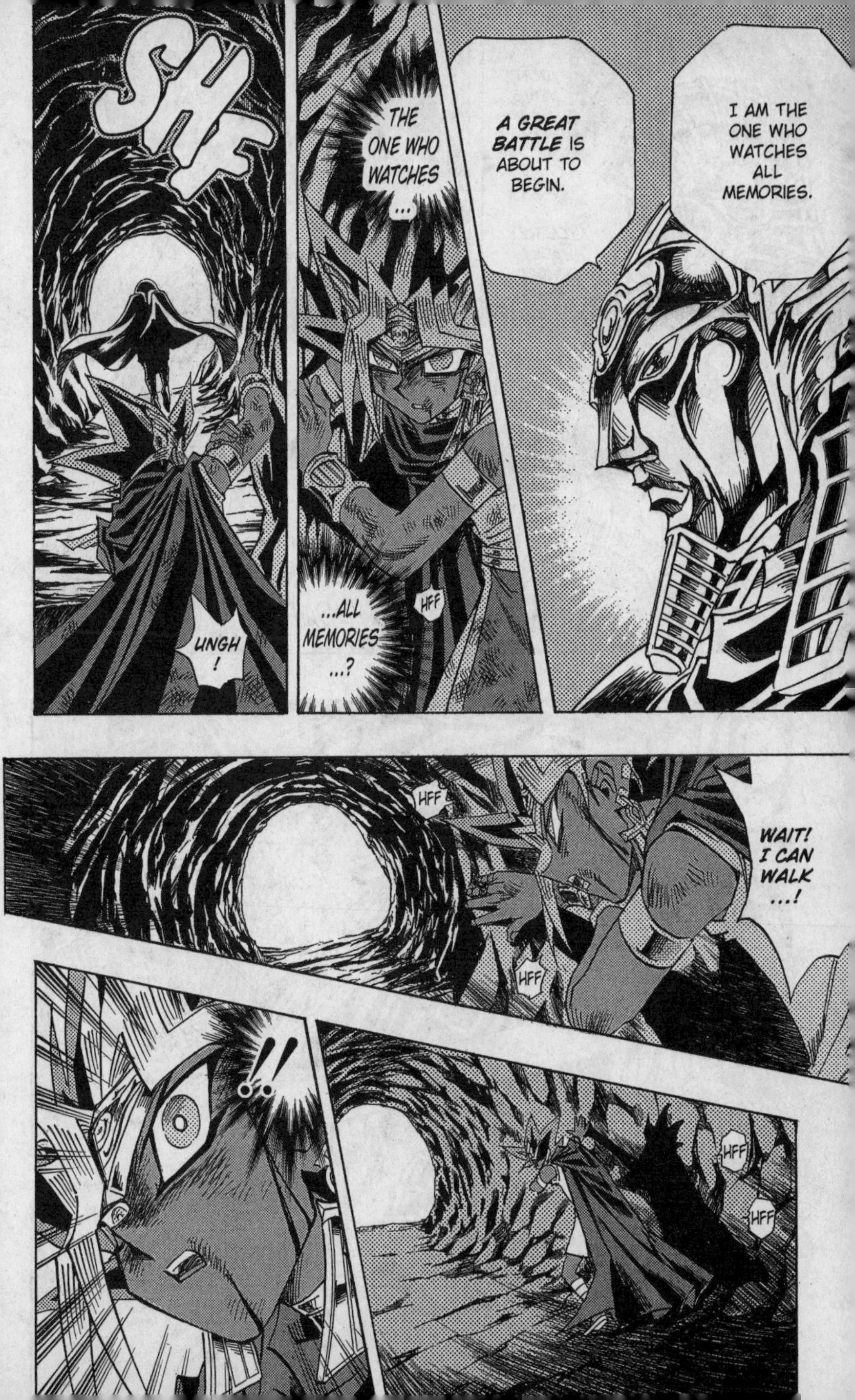
I AM THE ONE WHO WATCHES ALL MEMORIES.
A GREAT BATTLE IS ABOUT TO BEGIN.
THE ONE WHO WATCHES ...
...ALL MEMORIES ...?
HFF
SHF
UNGH !
WAIT! I CAN WALK ...!
HFF
HFF
HFF
HFF
!!

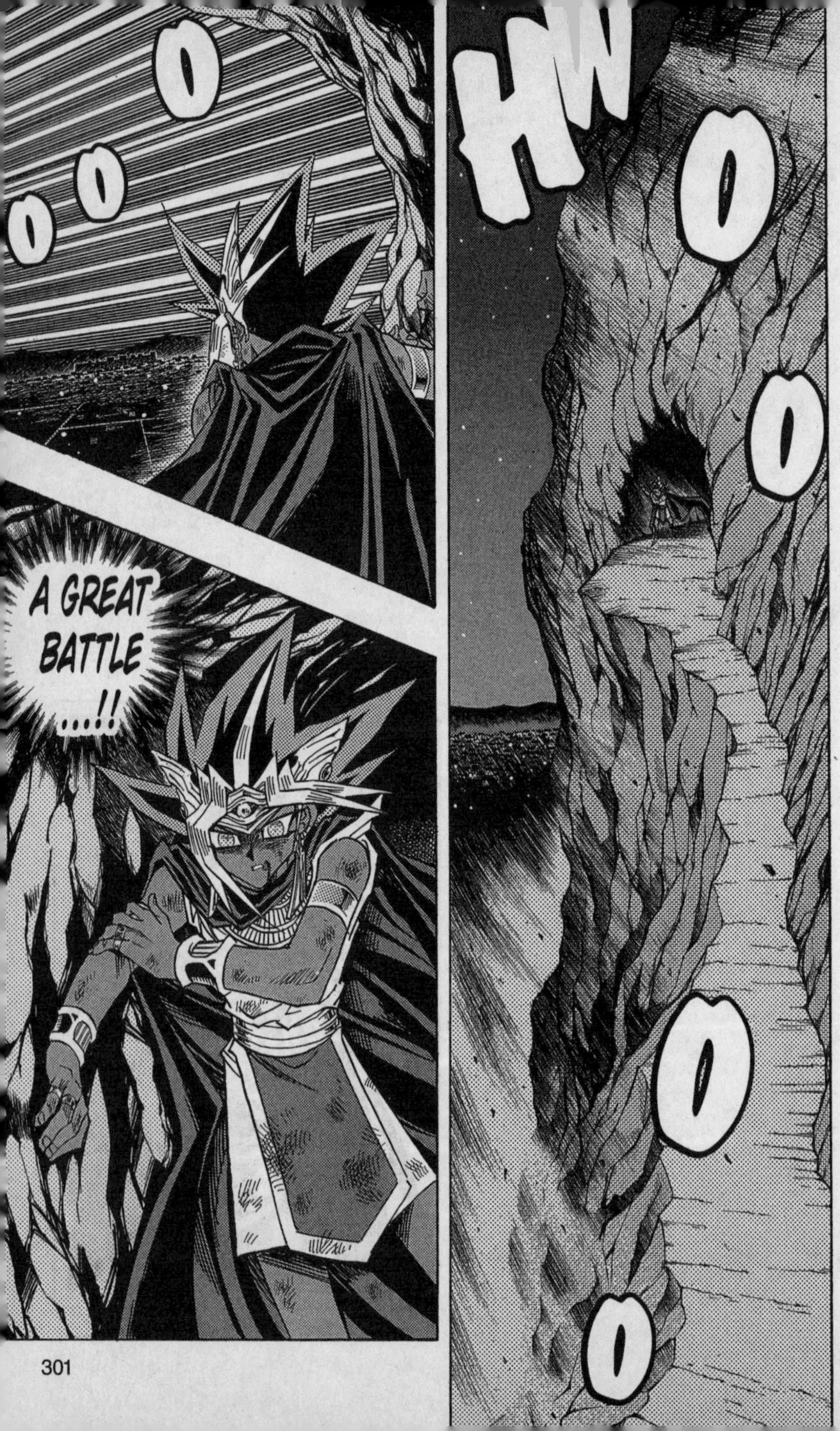
HWOOOO
OOOO
A GREAT BATTLE ...!!

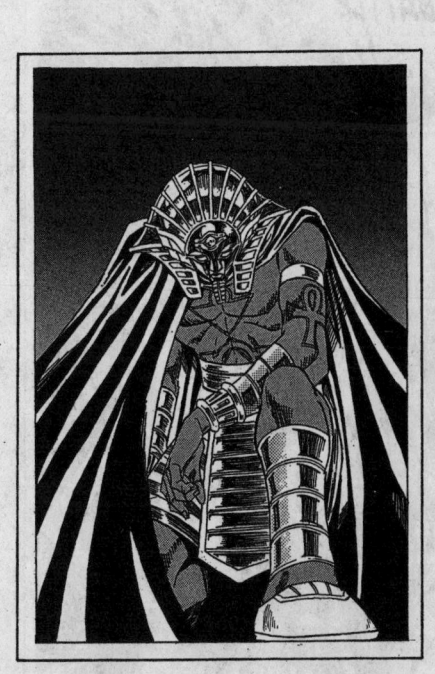

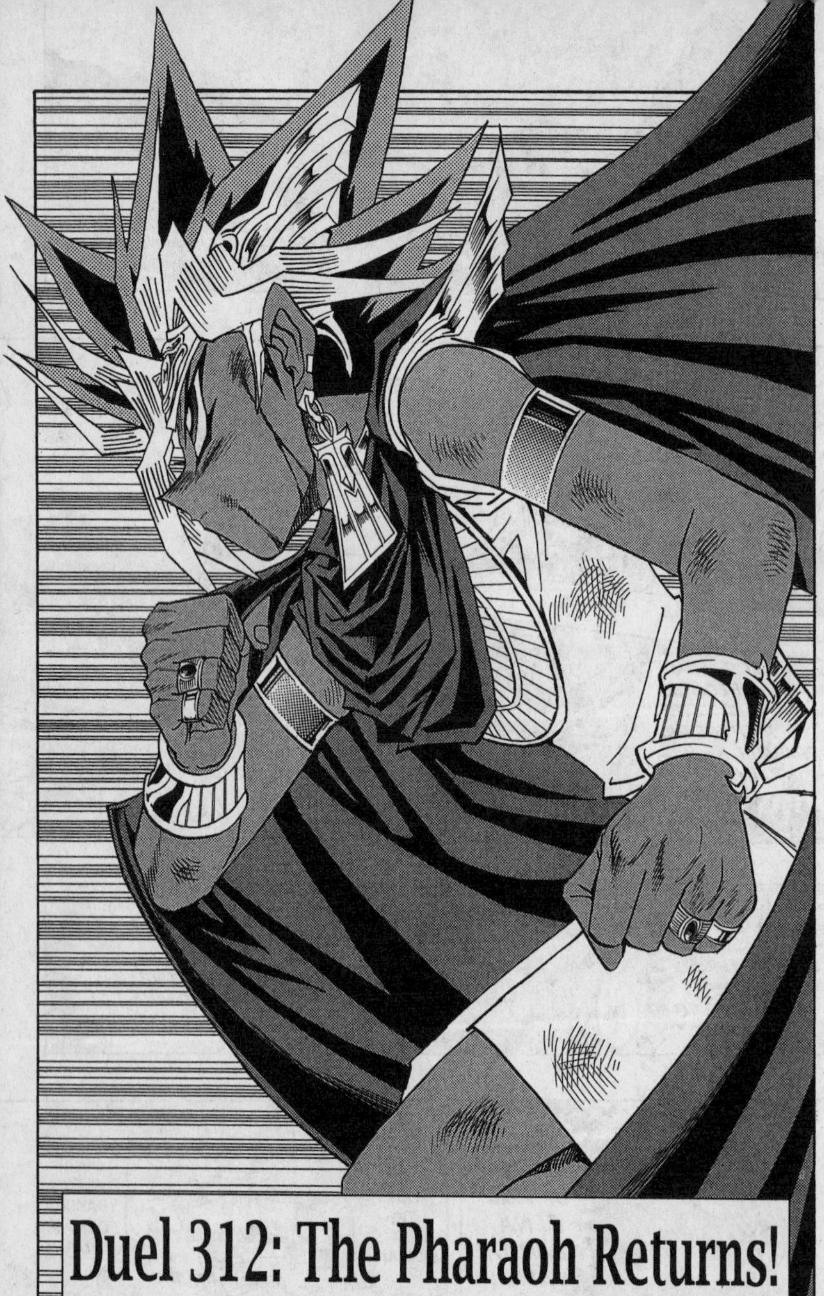

Duel 312: The Pharaoh Returns!

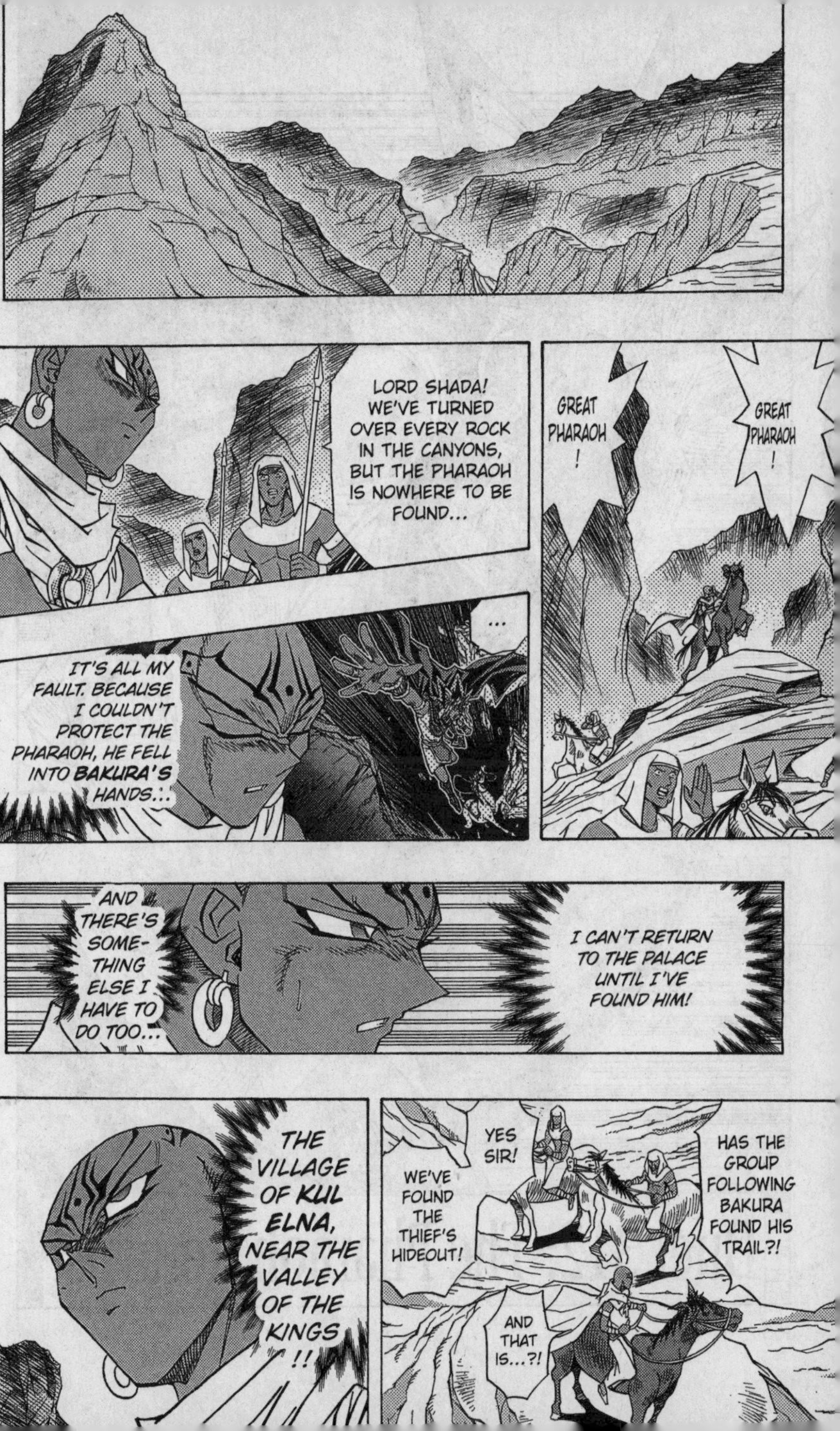
GREAT PHARAOH!
GREAT PHARAOH!
LORD SHADA! WE'VE TURNED OVER EVERY ROCK IN THE CANYONS, BUT THE PHARAOH IS NOWHERE TO BE FOUND...
...
IT'S ALL MY FAULT. BECAUSE I COULDN'T PROTECT THE PHARAOH, HE FELL INTO BAKURA'S HANDS...
I CAN'T RETURN TO THE PALACE UNTIL I'VE FOUND HIM!
AND THERE'S SOMETHING ELSE I HAVE TO DO TOO...
HAS THE GROUP FOLLOWING BAKURA FOUND HIS TRAIL?!
YES SIR!
WE'VE FOUND THE THIEF'S HIDEOUT!
AND THAT IS...?!
THE VILLAGE OF KUL ELNA, NEAR THE VALLEY OF THE KINGS!!

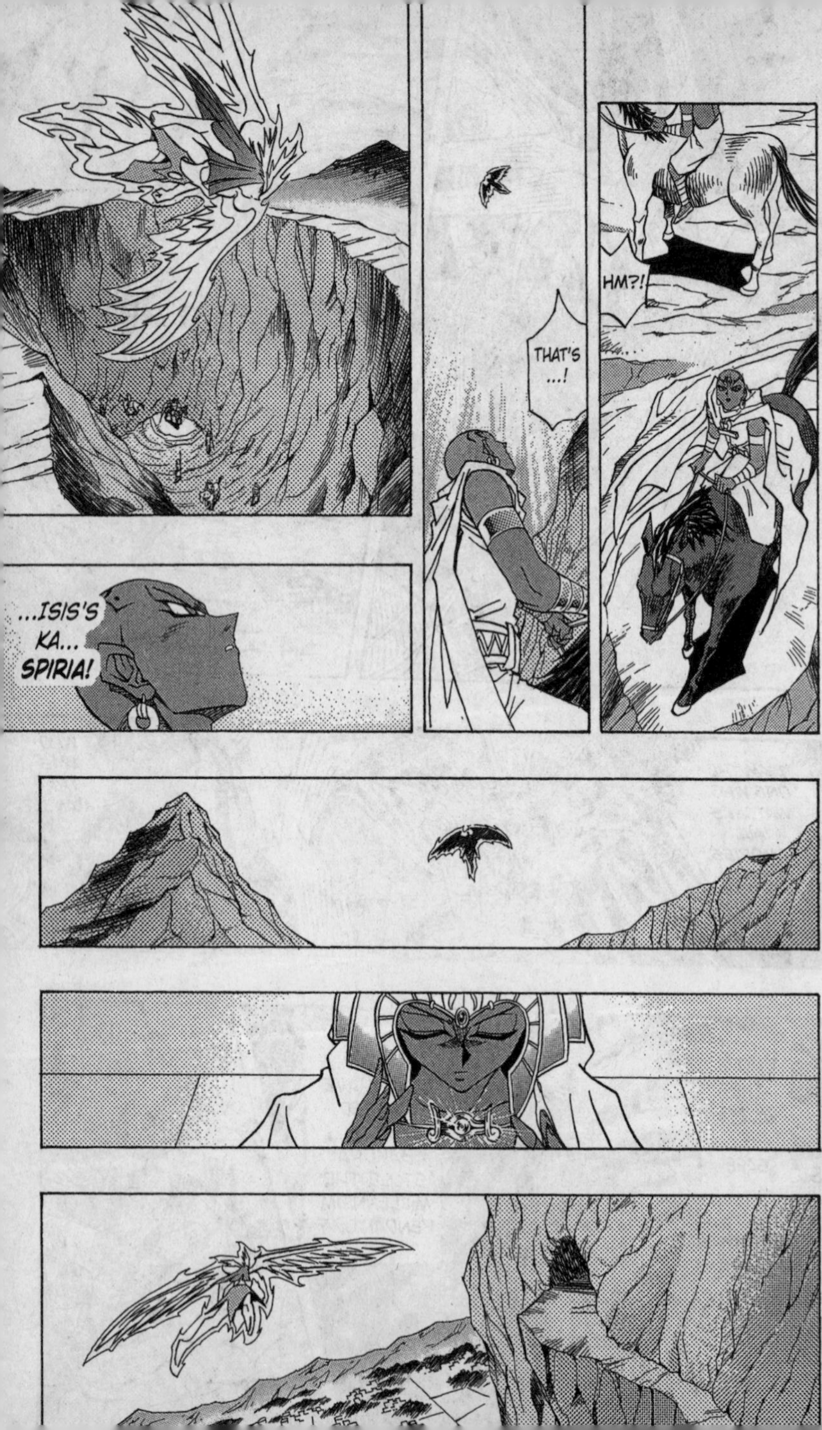
HM?!
THAT'S ...!
...ISIS'S KA... SPIRIA!

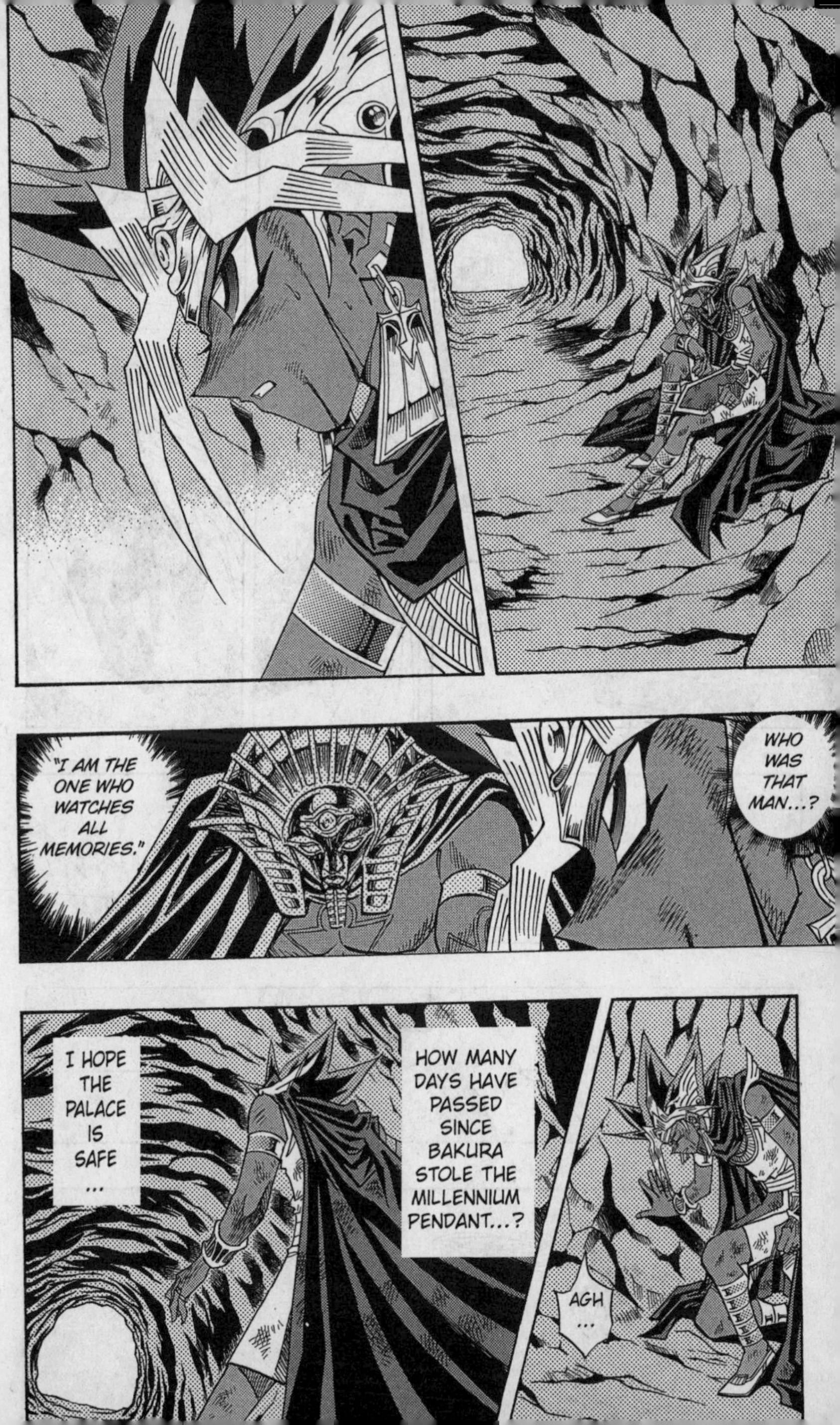
WHO WAS THAT MAN...?
"I AM THE ONE WHO WATCHES ALL MEMORIES."
AGH...
HOW MANY DAYS HAVE PASSED SINCE BAKURA STOLE THE MILLENNIUM PENDANT...?
I HOPE THE PALACE IS SAFE...

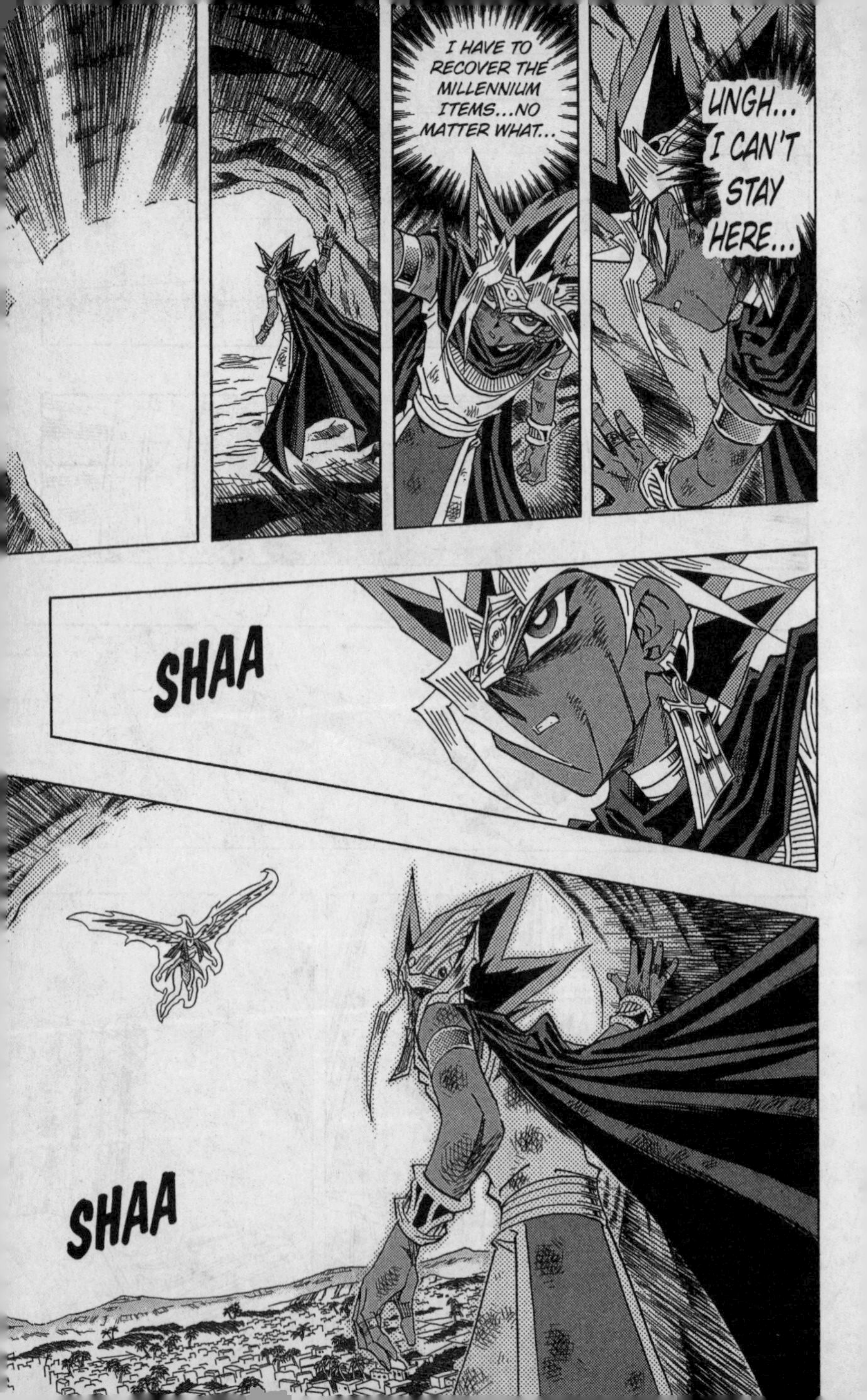
UNGH... I CAN'T STAY HERE...
I HAVE TO RECOVER THE MILLENNIUM ITEMS...NO MATTER WHAT...
SHAA
SHAA

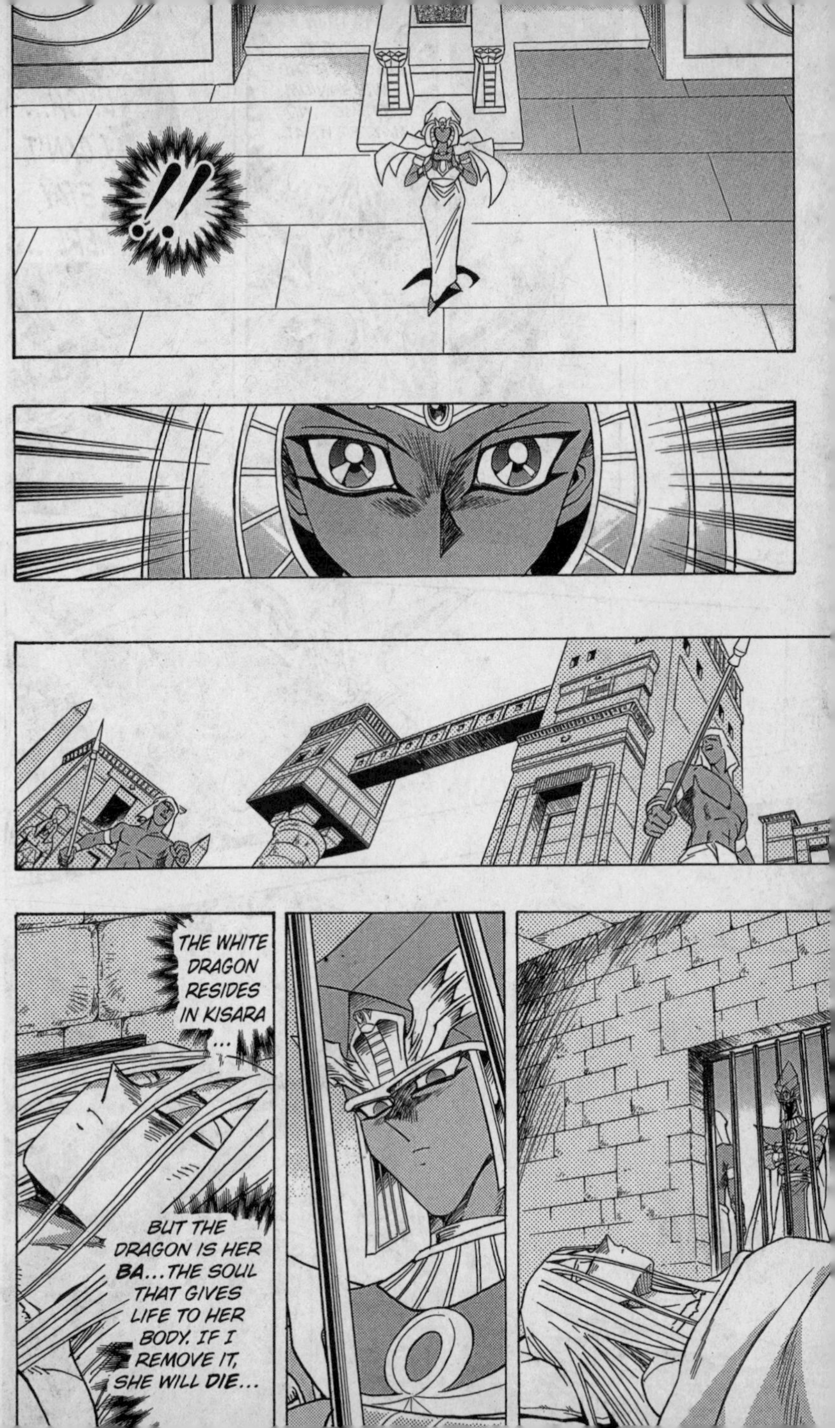

THE WHITE DRAGON RESIDES IN KISARA...

BUT THE DRAGON IS HER **BA**...THE SOUL THAT GIVES LIFE TO HER BODY. IF I REMOVE IT, SHE WILL DIE...

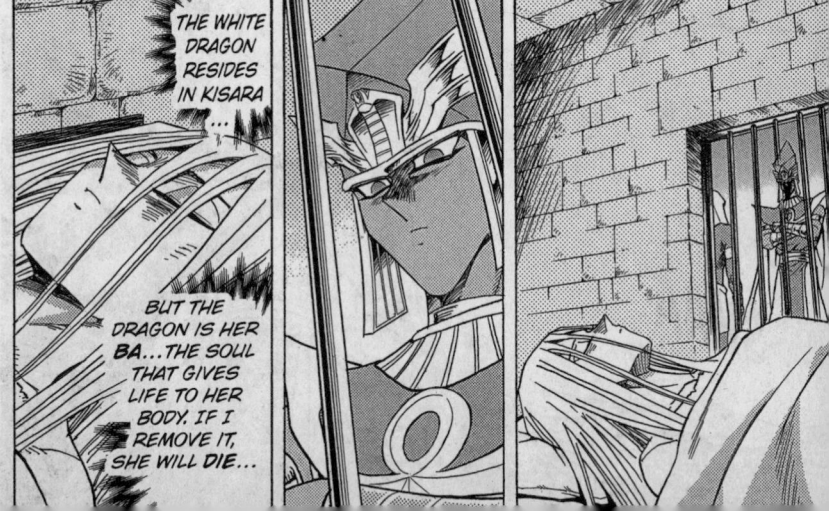

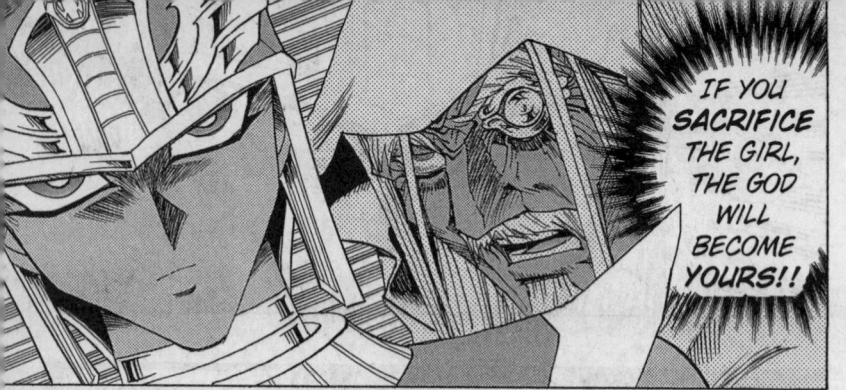

IF YOU SACRIFICE THE GIRL, THE GOD WILL BECOME YOURS!!
LORD AKHENADEN ACTUALLY TOLD ME TO KILL HER SO I COULD TAKE THE GOD...!
I DON'T UNDERSTAND ...
LORD AKHENADEN IS THE HIGHEST OF THE PRIESTS. HE ALWAYS SHOWED MERCY, EVEN TO THE WORST SINNERS...
BUT THEN I SAW ...
THOSE HATE-FILLED EYES...
AND BECOME THE NEXT PHARAOH ...!
WHY ...?
WHEN I ASCENDED TO THE PRIESTHOOD, I WAS JUST A CHILD. YOU WERE THE ONE TO TEACH ME MORALITY...PHILOSOPHY... THE ETERNAL ORDER, THE LAW OF MA'AT...

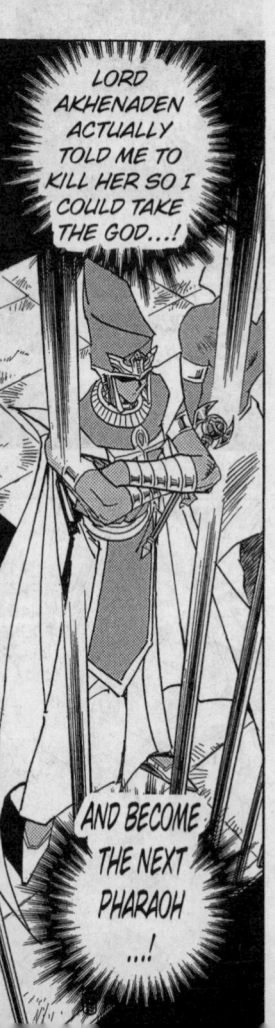

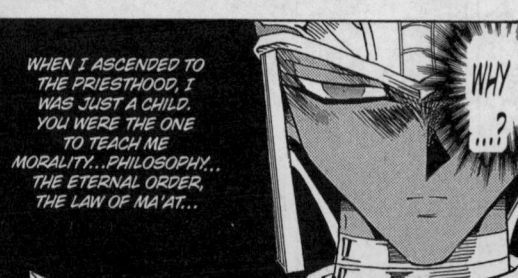

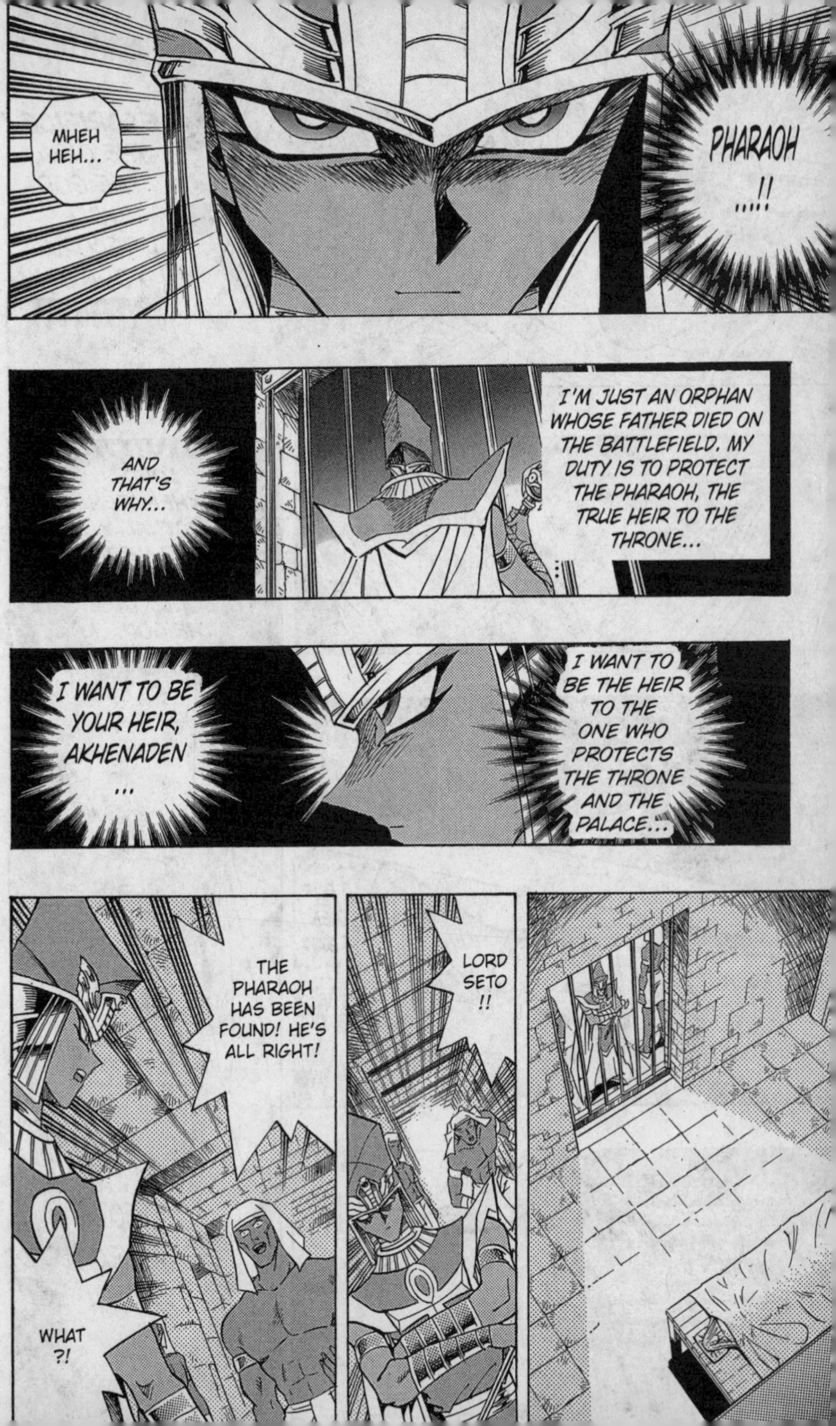
PHARAOH ...!!
MHEH HEH...
I'M JUST AN ORPHAN WHOSE FATHER DIED ON THE BATTLEFIELD. MY DUTY IS TO PROTECT THE PHARAOH, THE TRUE HEIR TO THE THRONE...
AND THAT'S WHY...
I WANT TO BE THE HEIR TO THE ONE WHO PROTECTS THE THRONE AND THE PALACE...
I WANT TO BE YOUR HEIR, AKHENADEN ...
LORD SETO !!
THE PHARAOH HAS BEEN FOUND! HE'S ALL RIGHT!
WHAT ?!

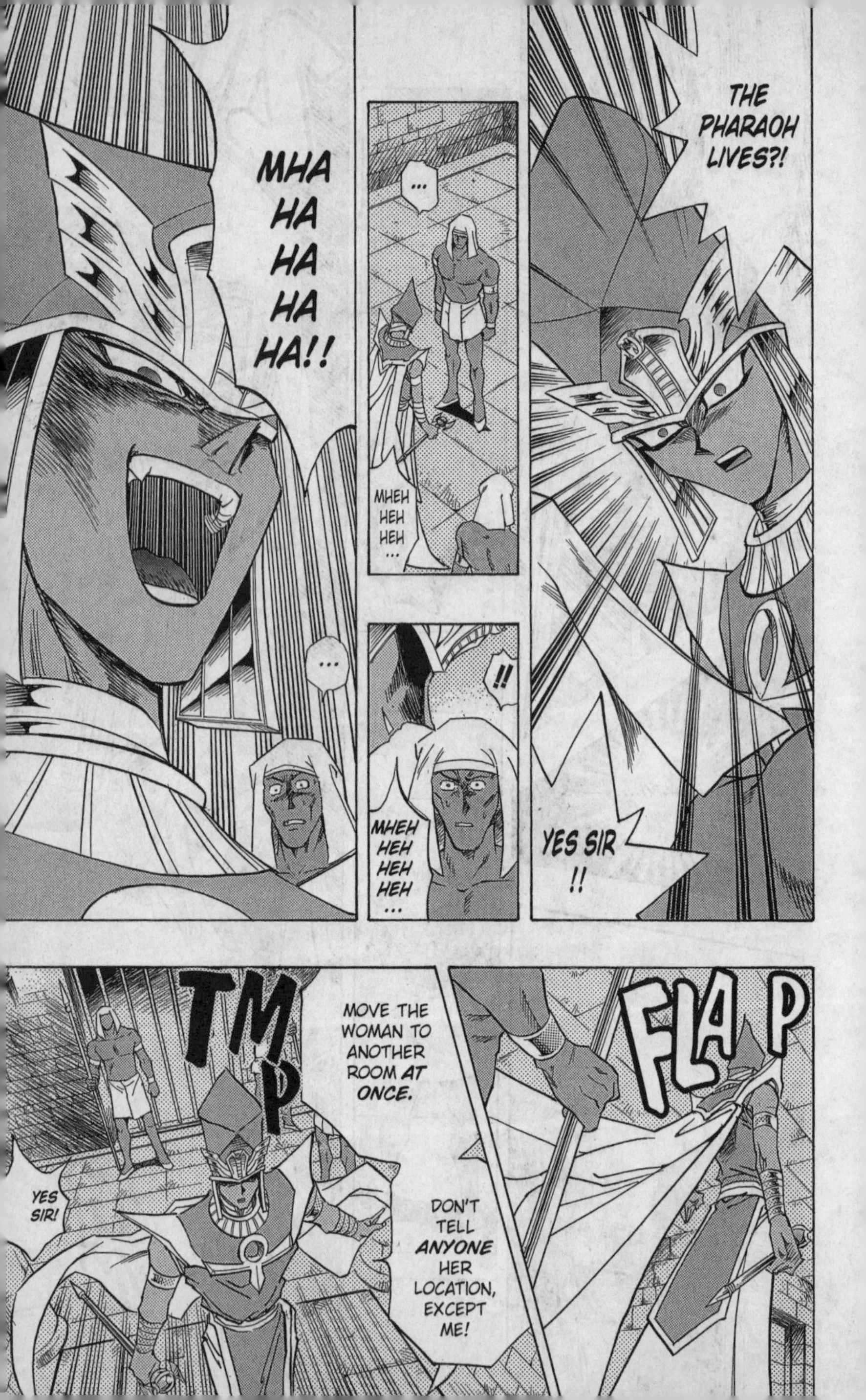
MHA HA HA HA HA!!
...
...
MHEH HEH HEH ...
!!
MHEH HEH HEH HEH ...
THE PHARAOH LIVES?!
YES SIR !!
TMP
MOVE THE WOMAN TO ANOTHER ROOM AT ONCE.
YES SIR!
DON'T TELL ANYONE HER LOCATION, EXCEPT ME!
FLAP

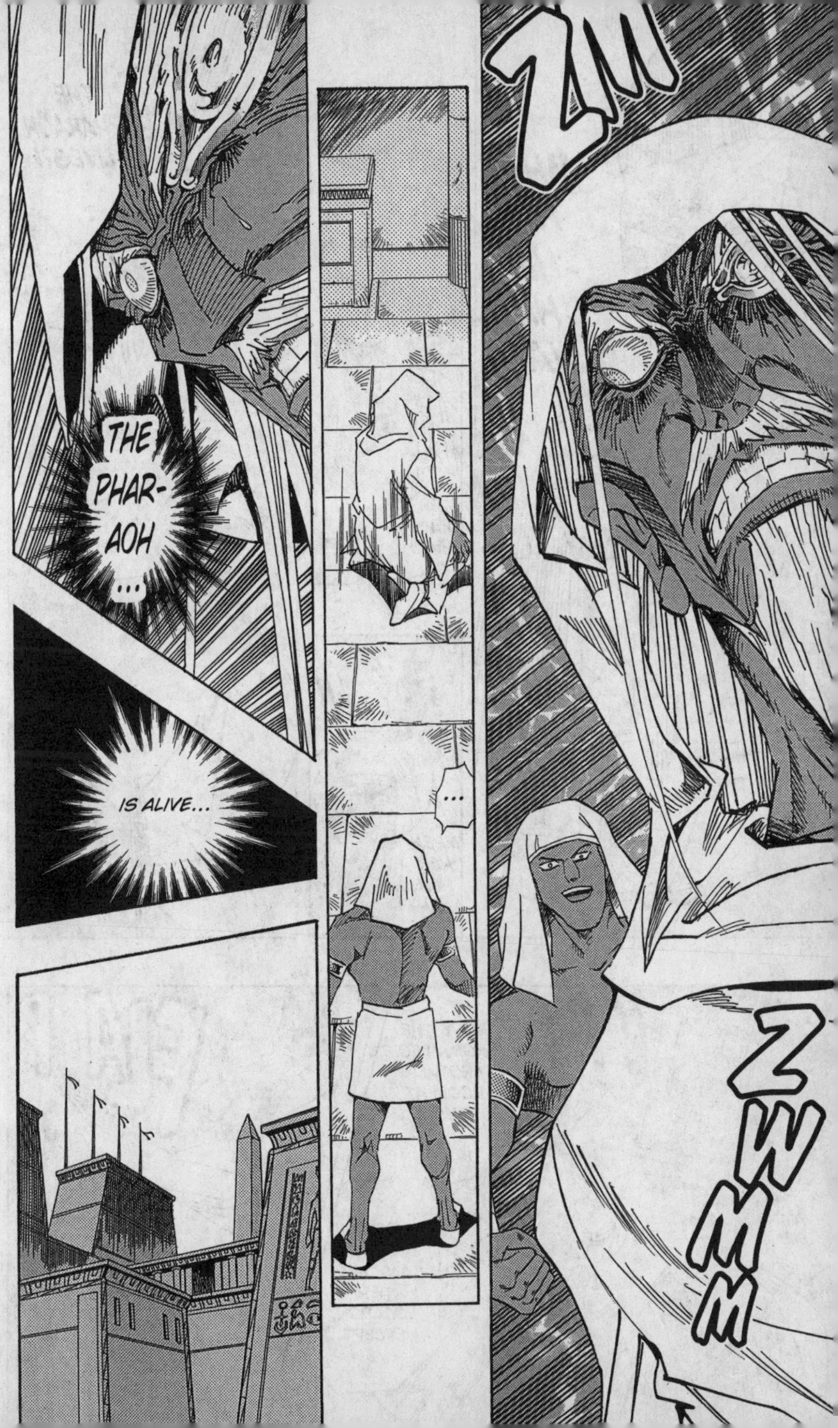
ZM
ZWMM
...
THE PHARAOH...
IS ALIVE...

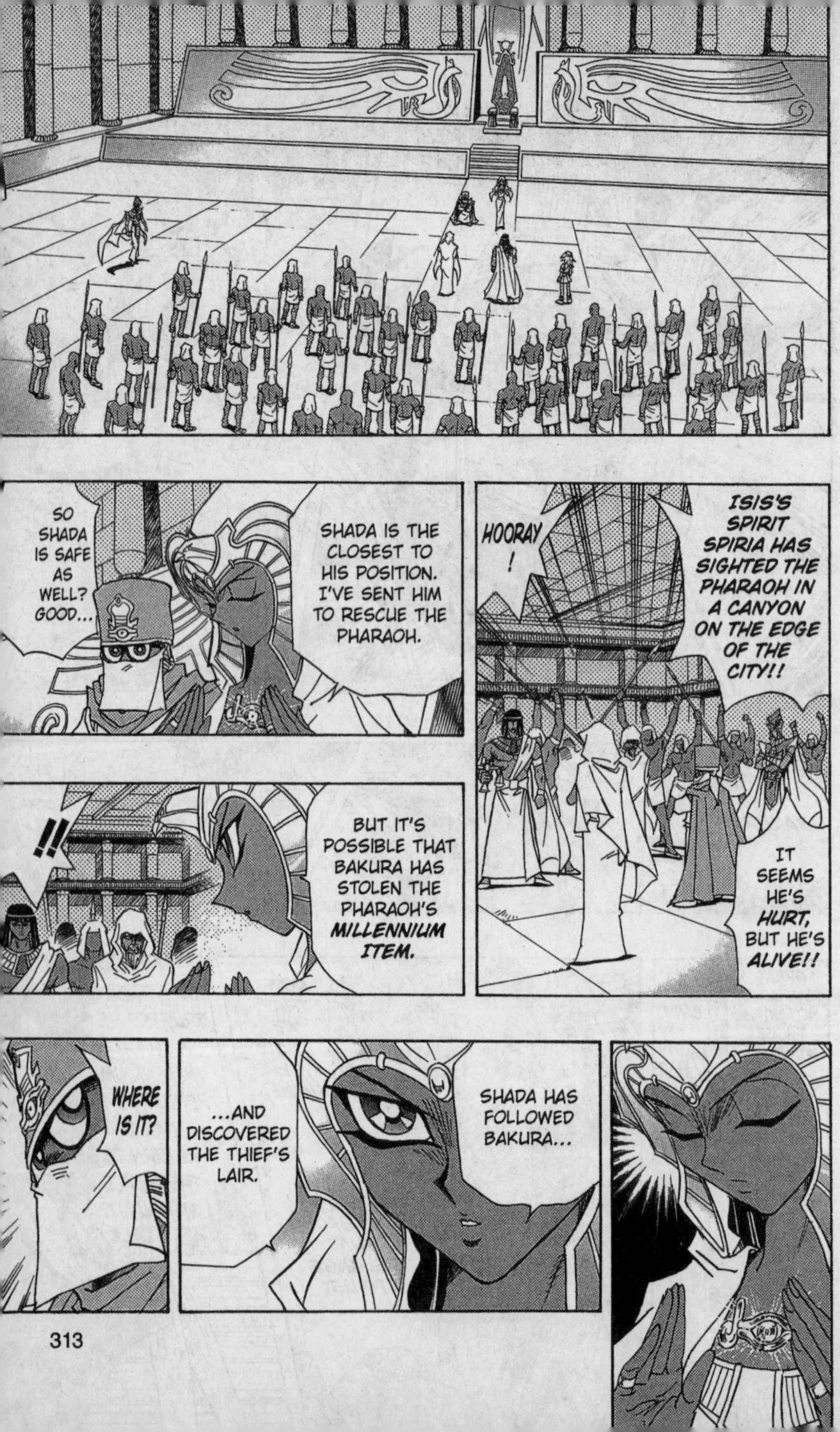
ISIS'S SPIRIT SPIRIA HAS SIGHTED THE PHARAOH IN A CANYON ON THE EDGE OF THE CITY!!
HOORAY!
IT SEEMS HE'S HURT, BUT HE'S ALIVE!!
SHADA IS THE CLOSEST TO HIS POSITION. I'VE SENT HIM TO RESCUE THE PHARAOH.
SO SHADA IS SAFE AS WELL? GOOD...
BUT IT'S POSSIBLE THAT BAKURA HAS STOLEN THE PHARAOH'S MILLENNIUM ITEM.
!!
SHADA HAS FOLLOWED BAKURA...
...AND DISCOVERED THE THIEF'S LAIR.
WHERE IS IT?

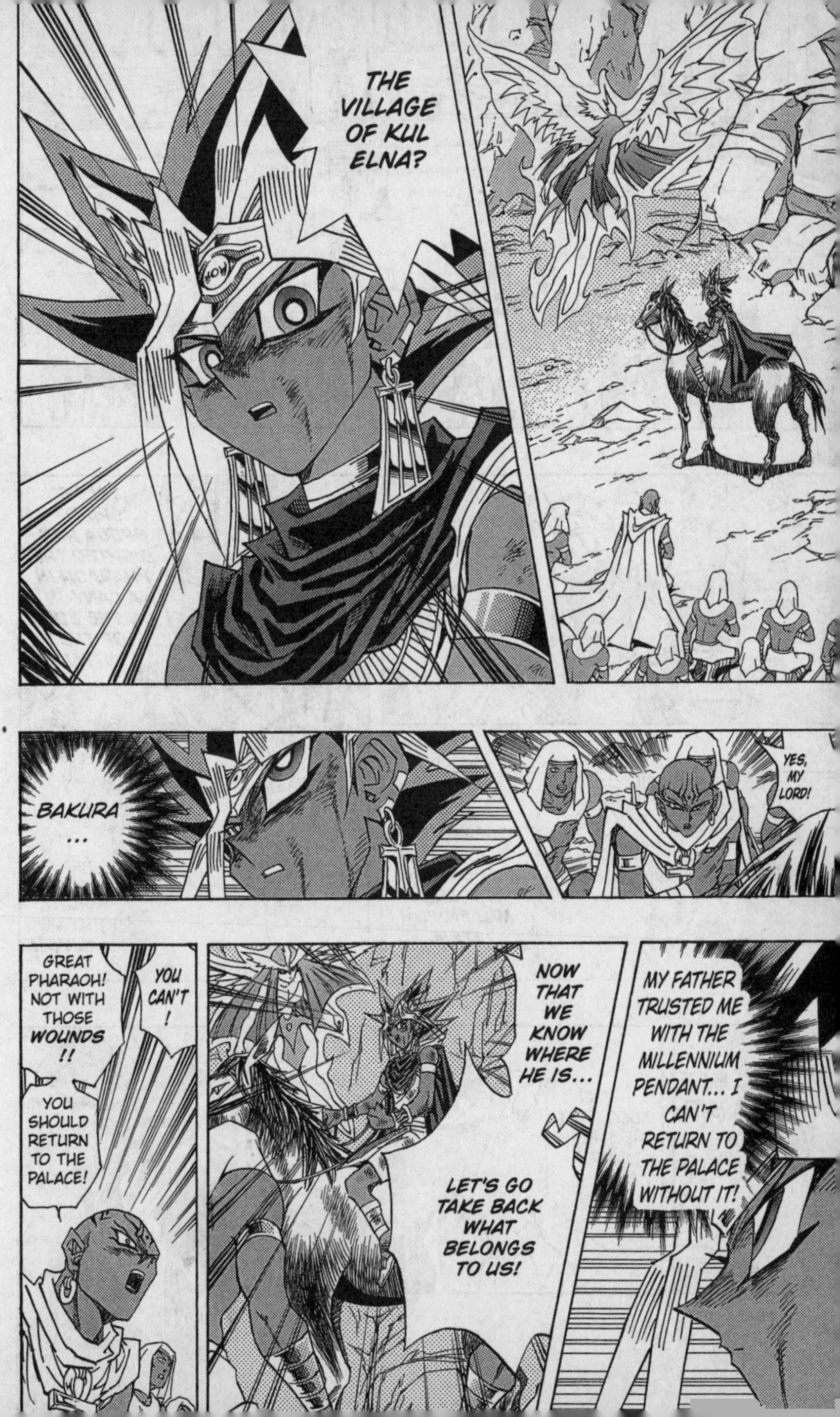
THE VILLAGE OF KUL ELNA?
YES, MY LORD!
BAKURA ...
MY FATHER TRUSTED ME WITH THE MILLENNIUM PENDANT... I CAN'T RETURN TO THE PALACE WITHOUT IT!
NOW THAT WE KNOW WHERE HE IS...
LET'S GO TAKE BACK WHAT BELONGS TO US!
YOU CAN'T !
GREAT PHARAOH! NOT WITH THOSE WOUNDS !!
YOU SHOULD RETURN TO THE PALACE!

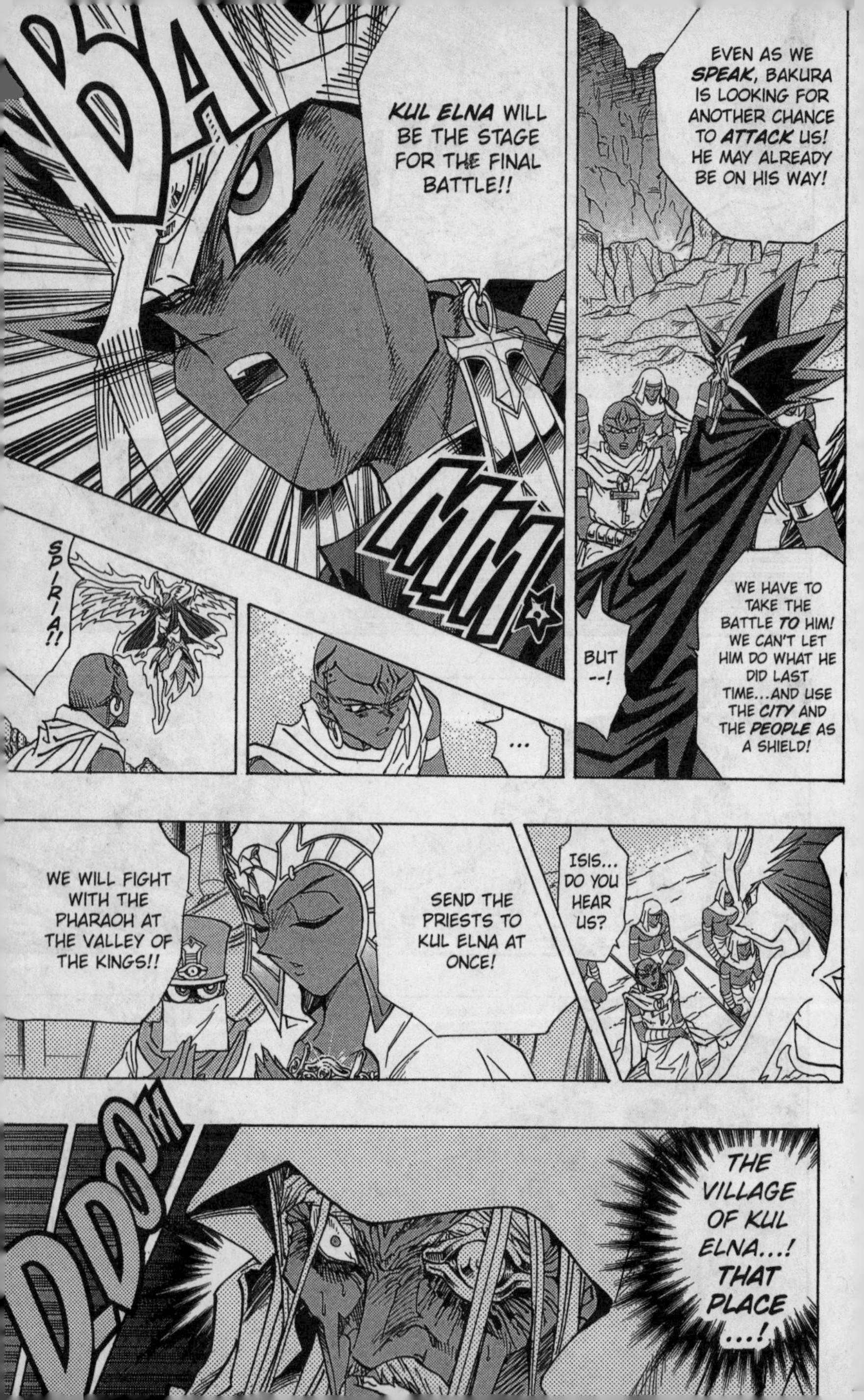

EVEN AS WE SPEAK, BAKURA IS LOOKING FOR ANOTHER CHANCE TO ATTACK US! HE MAY ALREADY BE ON HIS WAY!
KUL ELNA WILL BE THE STAGE FOR THE FINAL BATTLE!!
BADA
MM
WE HAVE TO TAKE THE BATTLE TO HIM! WE CAN'T LET HIM DO WHAT HE DID LAST TIME...AND USE THE CITY AND THE PEOPLE AS A SHIELD!
BUT --!
...
SPIRIA!!
ISIS... DO YOU HEAR US?
SEND THE PRIESTS TO KUL ELNA AT ONCE!
WE WILL FIGHT WITH THE PHARAOH AT THE VALLEY OF THE KINGS!!
THE VILLAGE OF KUL ELNA...! THAT PLACE ...!
DDOOM

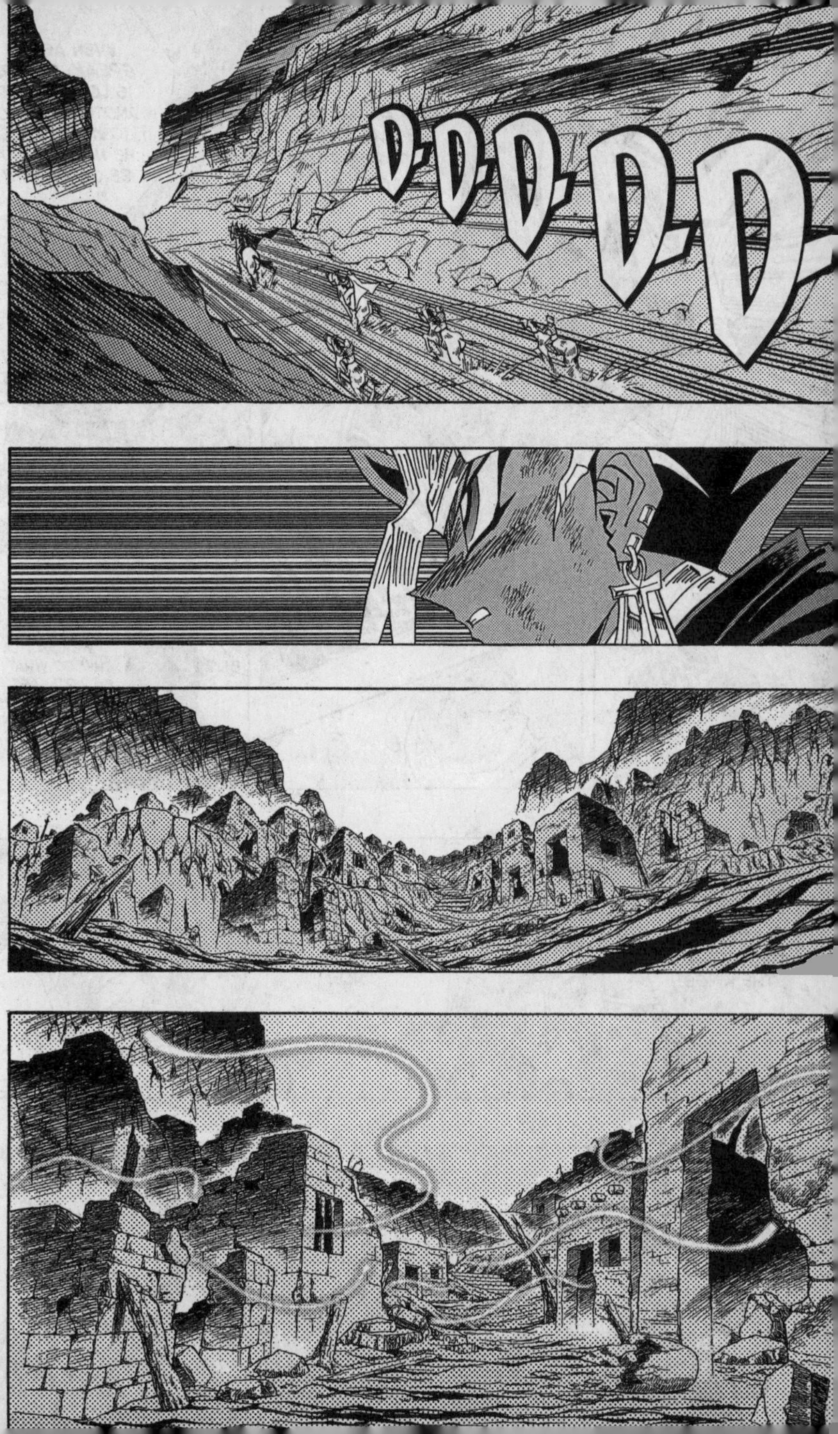
DDDDDD

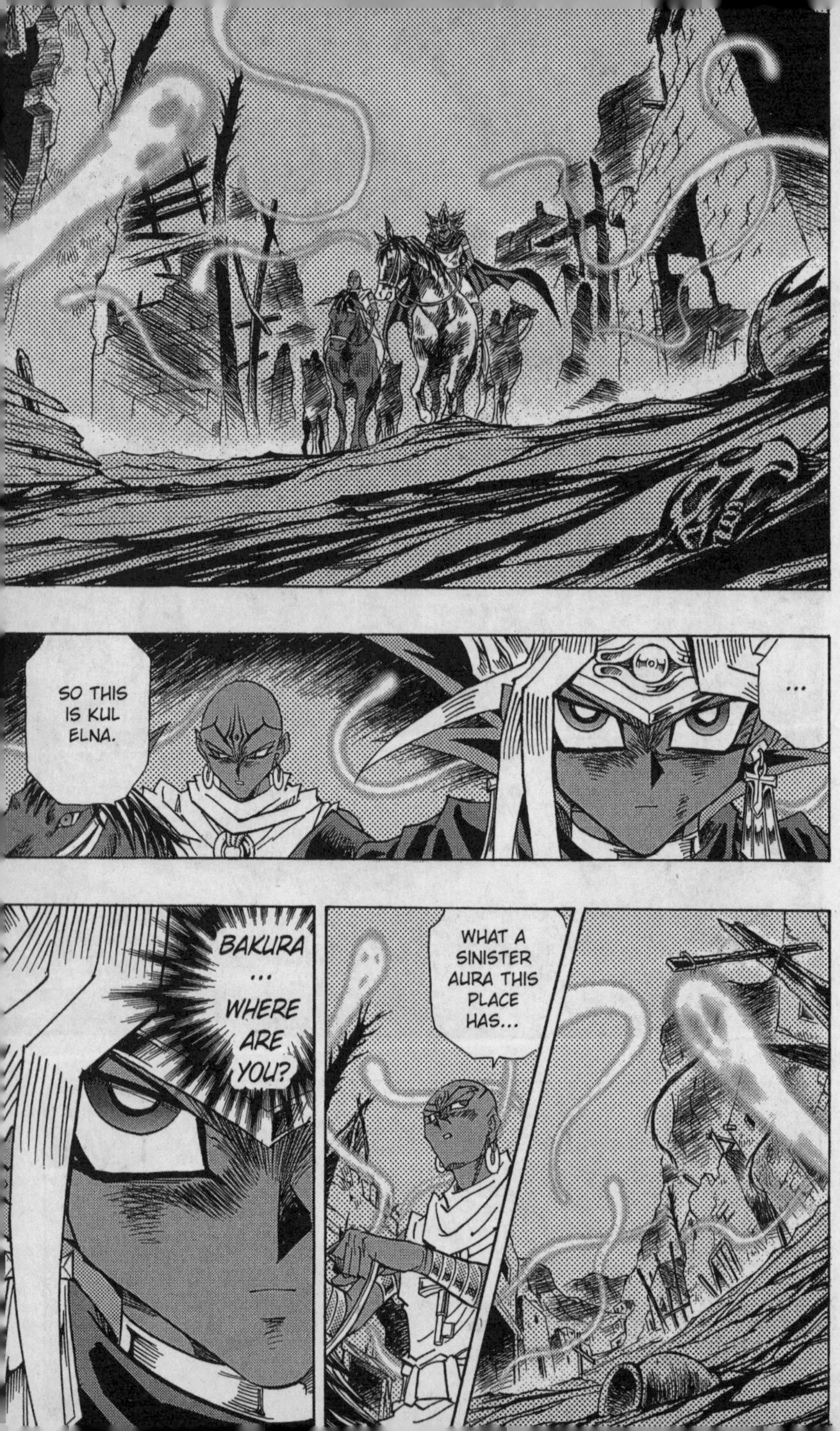
...
SO THIS IS KUL ELNA.
WHAT A SINISTER AURA THIS PLACE HAS...
BAKURA ... WHERE ARE YOU?

GWOOOO
...
RM
RM RM

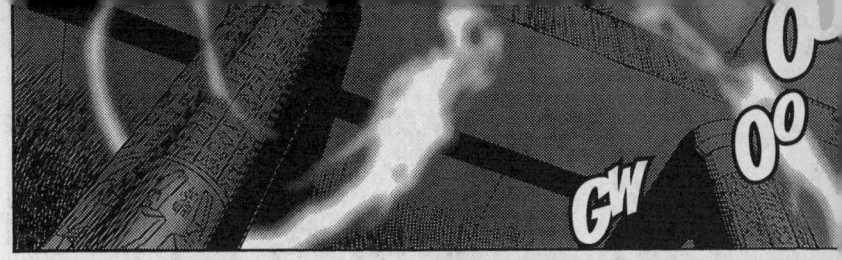

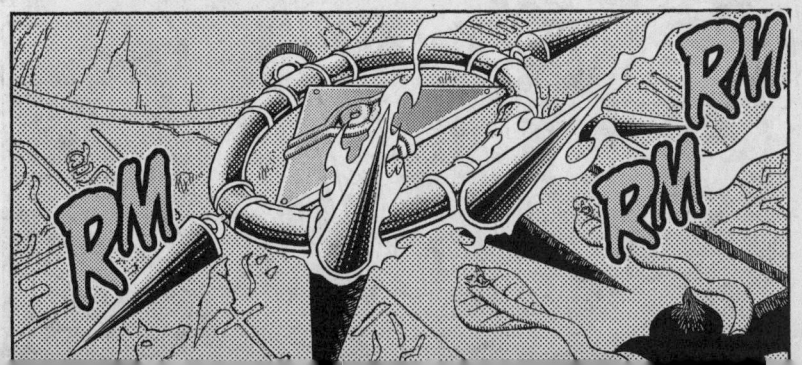

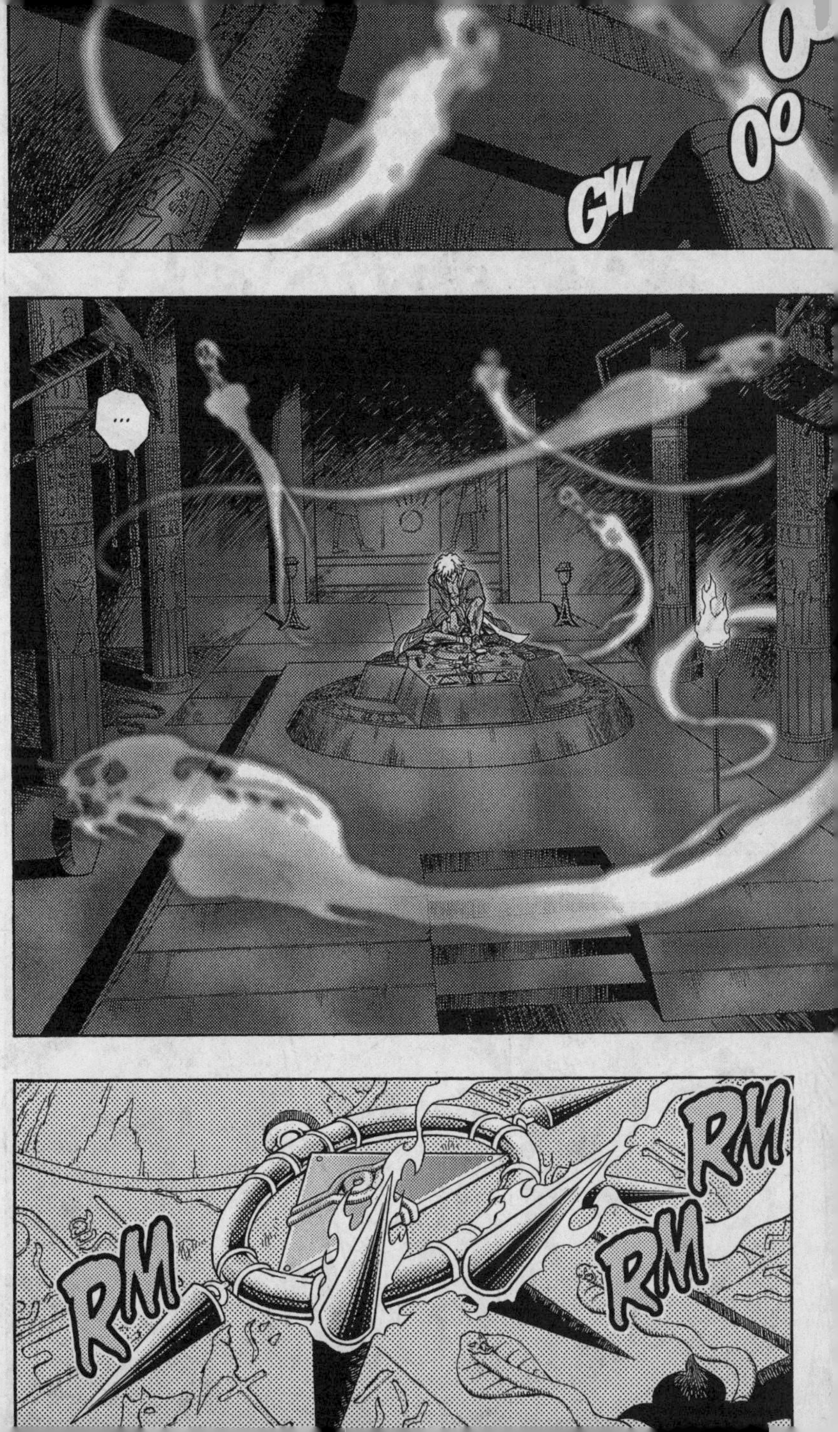

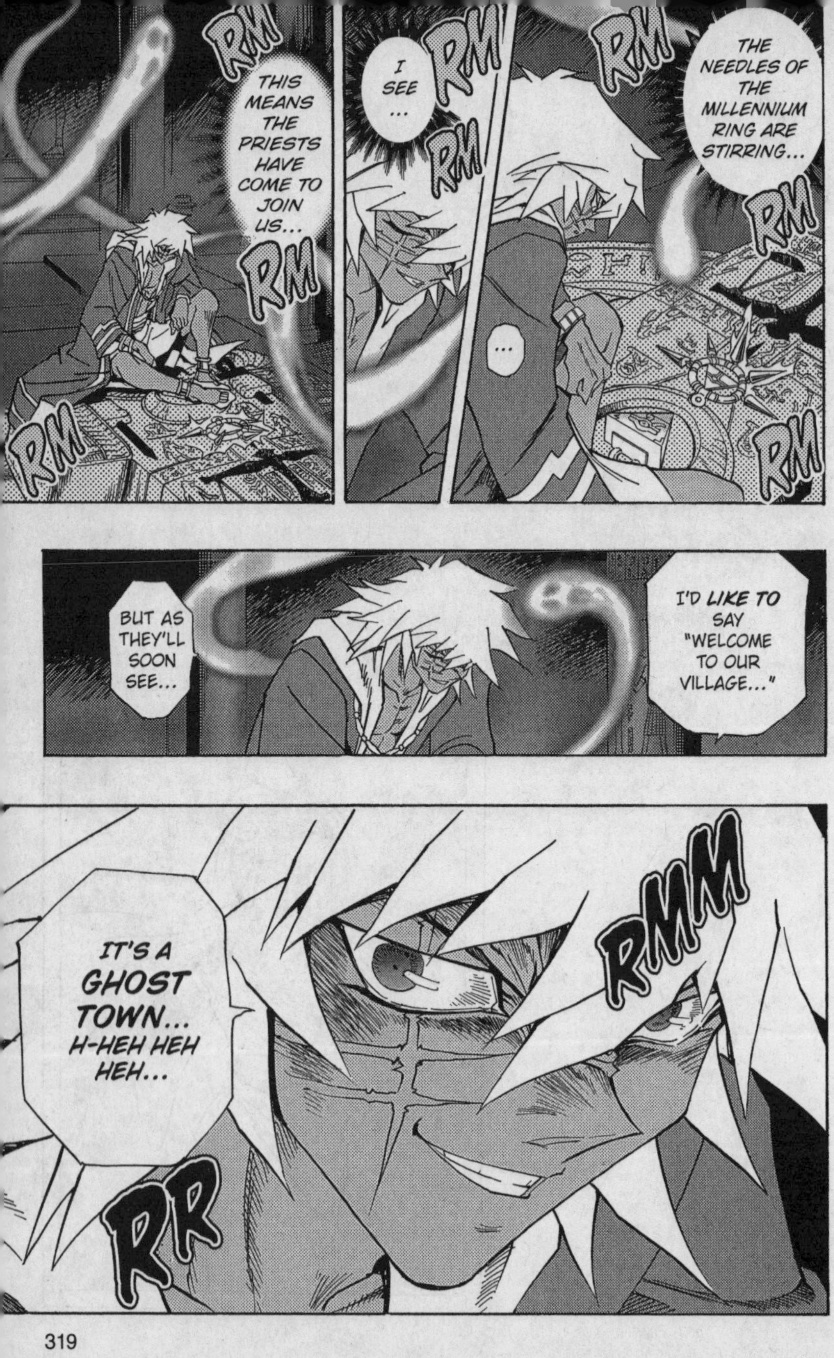
RM
THIS MEANS THE PRIESTS HAVE COME TO JOIN US...
RM
RM
I SEE...
RM
RM
RM
THE NEEDLES OF THE MILLENNIUM RING ARE STIRRING...
RM
...
RM
BUT AS THEY'LL SOON SEE...
I'D LIKE TO SAY "WELCOME TO OUR VILLAGE..."
IT'S A GHOST TOWN... H-HEH HEH HEH...
RMM
RR

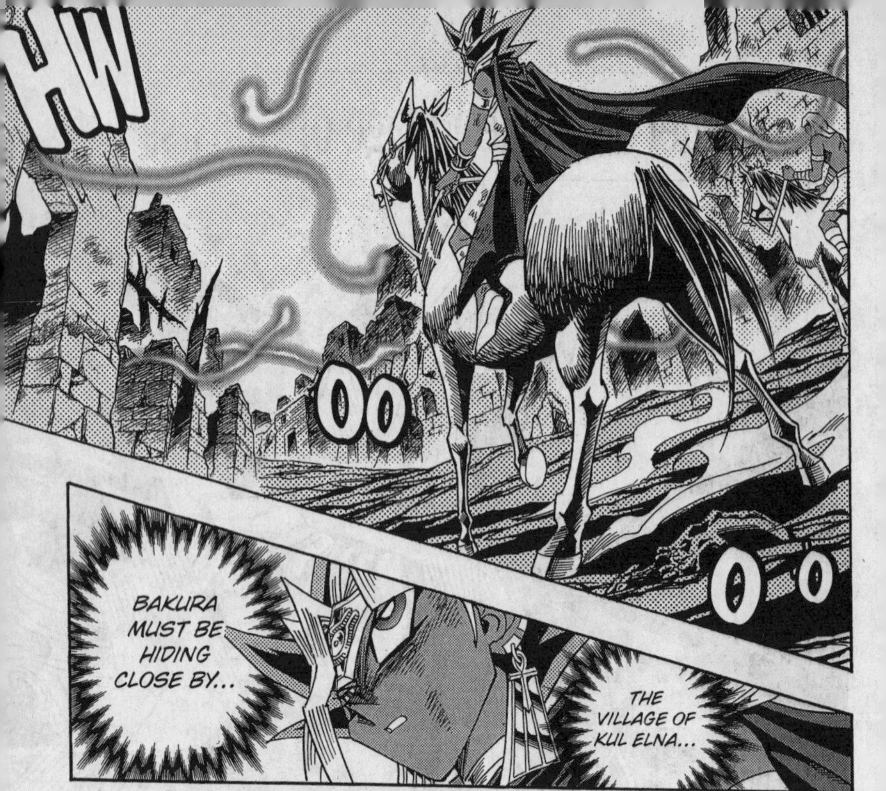
THE VILLAGE OF KUL ELNA...
BAKURA MUST BE HIDING CLOSE BY...

Duel 313: The Village of Ghosts!!

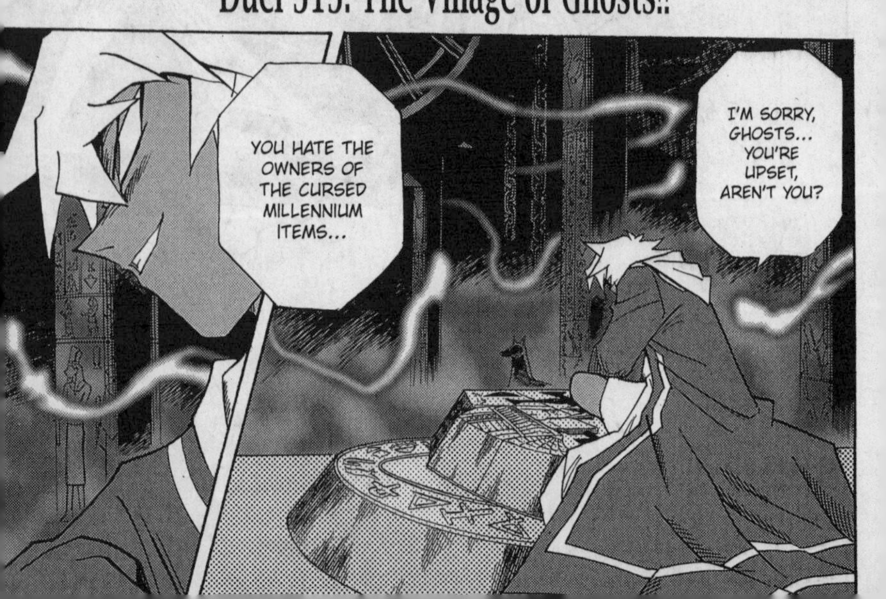
I'M SORRY, GHOSTS... YOU'RE UPSET, AREN'T YOU?
YOU HATE THE OWNERS OF THE CURSED MILLENNIUM ITEMS...

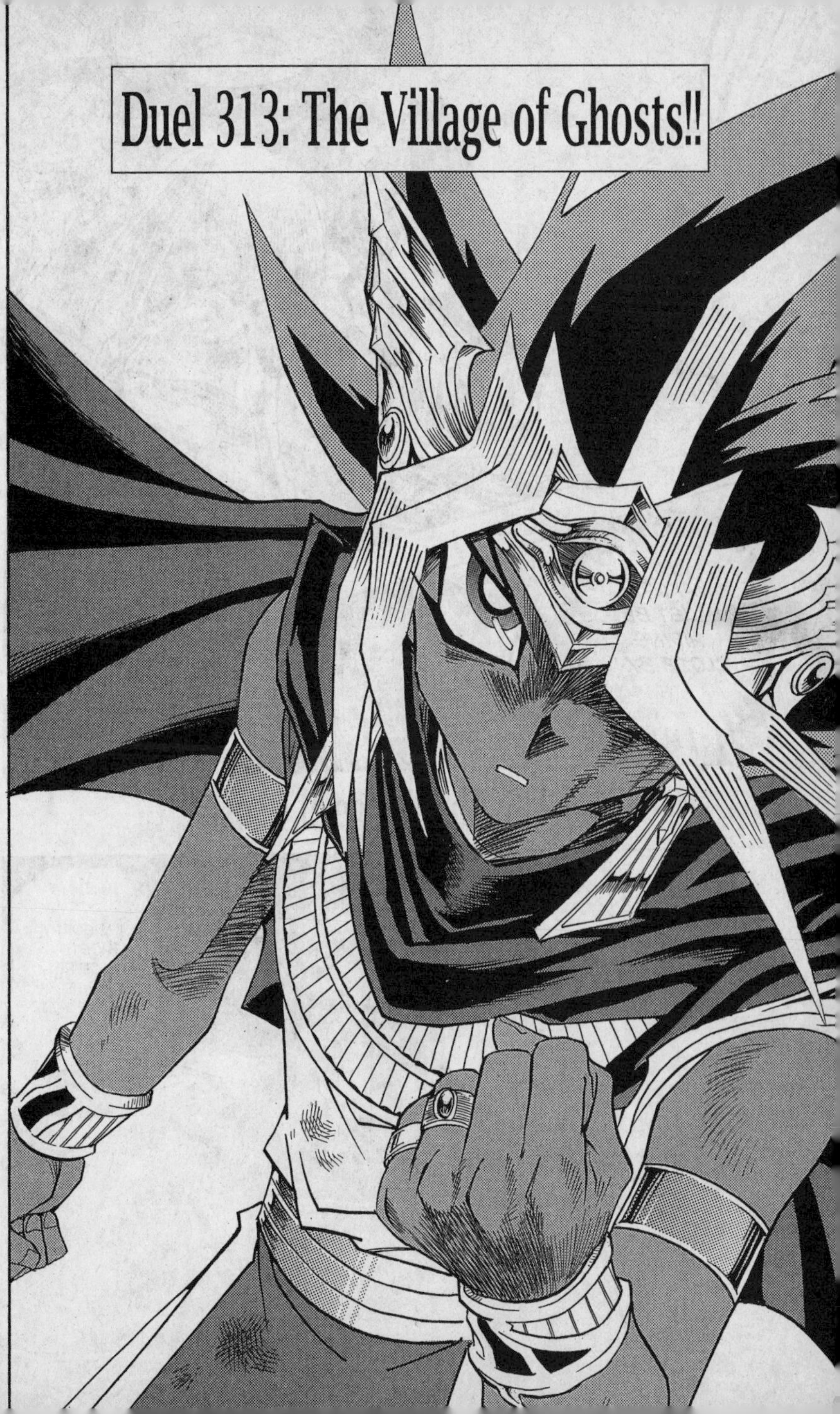
Duel 313: The Village of Ghosts!!

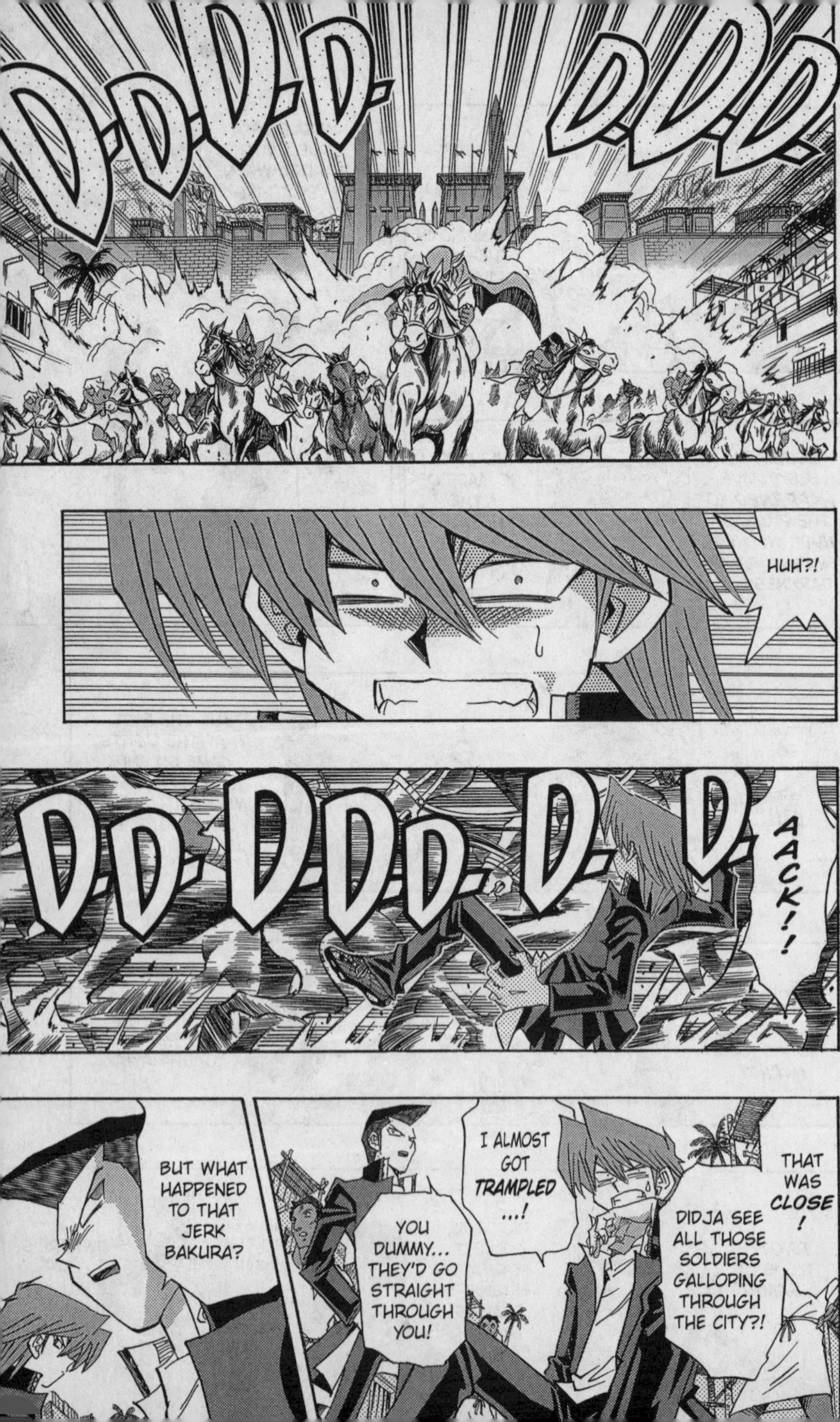

D.D.D.
D.D.D.D.
HUH?!
AACK!!
D.
D.
D.D.D.
D.D.
THAT WAS CLOSE!
DIDJA SEE ALL THOSE SOLDIERS GALLOPING THROUGH THE CITY?!
I ALMOST GOT TRAMPLED ...!
YOU DUMMY... THEY'D GO STRAIGHT THROUGH YOU!
BUT WHAT HAPPENED TO THAT JERK BAKURA?

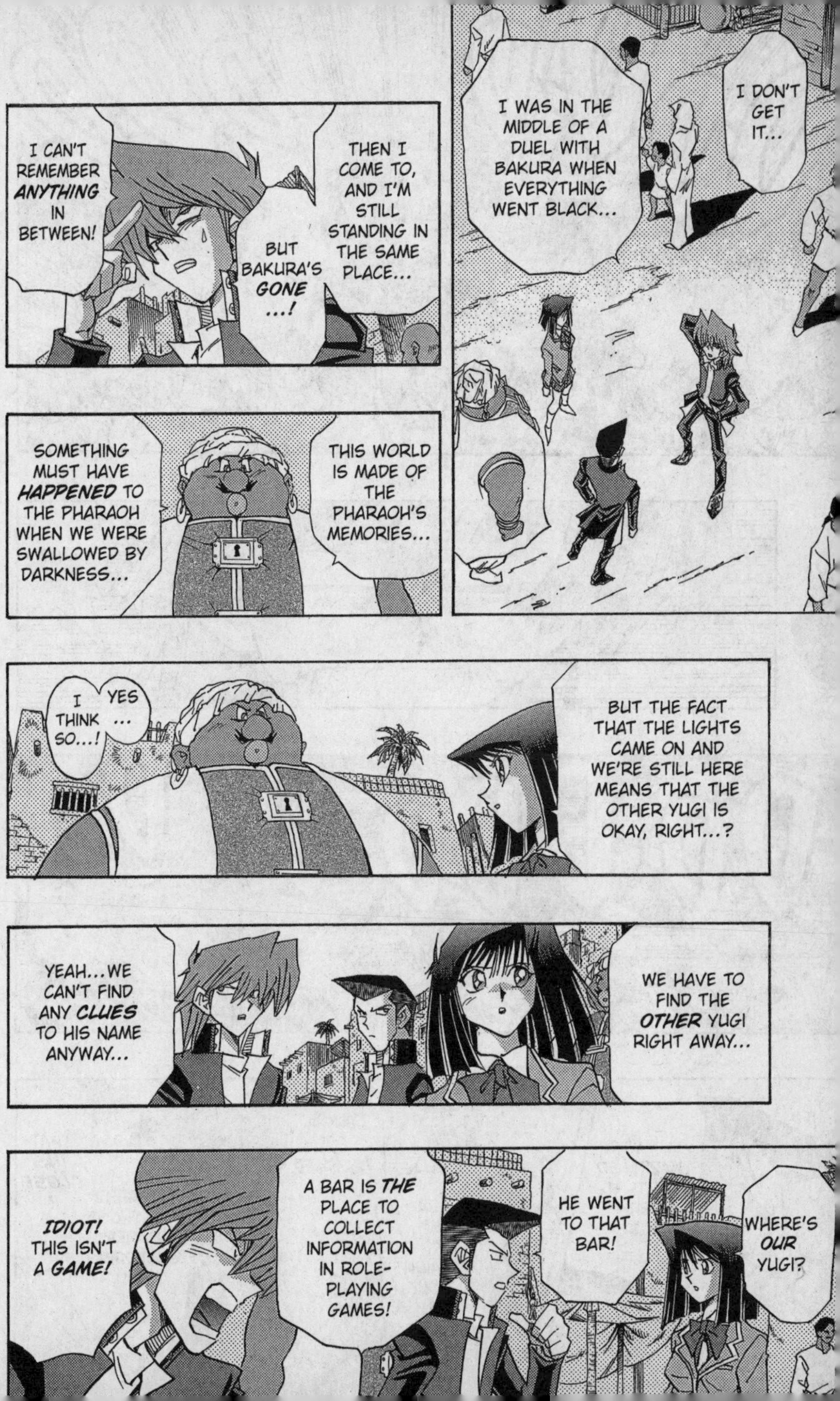

I DON'T GET IT...
I WAS IN THE MIDDLE OF A DUEL WITH BAKURA WHEN EVERYTHING WENT BLACK...
THEN I COME TO, AND I'M STILL STANDING IN THE SAME PLACE...
BUT BAKURA'S *GONE* ...!
I CAN'T REMEMBER *ANYTHING* IN BETWEEN!
THIS WORLD IS MADE OF THE PHARAOH'S MEMORIES...
SOMETHING MUST HAVE *HAPPENED* TO THE PHARAOH WHEN WE WERE SWALLOWED BY DARKNESS...
BUT THE FACT THAT THE LIGHTS CAME ON AND WE'RE STILL HERE MEANS THAT THE OTHER YUGI IS OKAY, RIGHT...?
YES ...
I THINK SO...!
WE HAVE TO FIND THE *OTHER* YUGI RIGHT AWAY...
YEAH...WE CAN'T FIND ANY *CLUES* TO HIS NAME ANYWAY...
WHERE'S *OUR* YUGI?
HE WENT TO THAT BAR!
A BAR IS *THE* PLACE TO COLLECT INFORMATION IN ROLE-PLAYING GAMES!
IDIOT! THIS ISN'T A *GAME!*

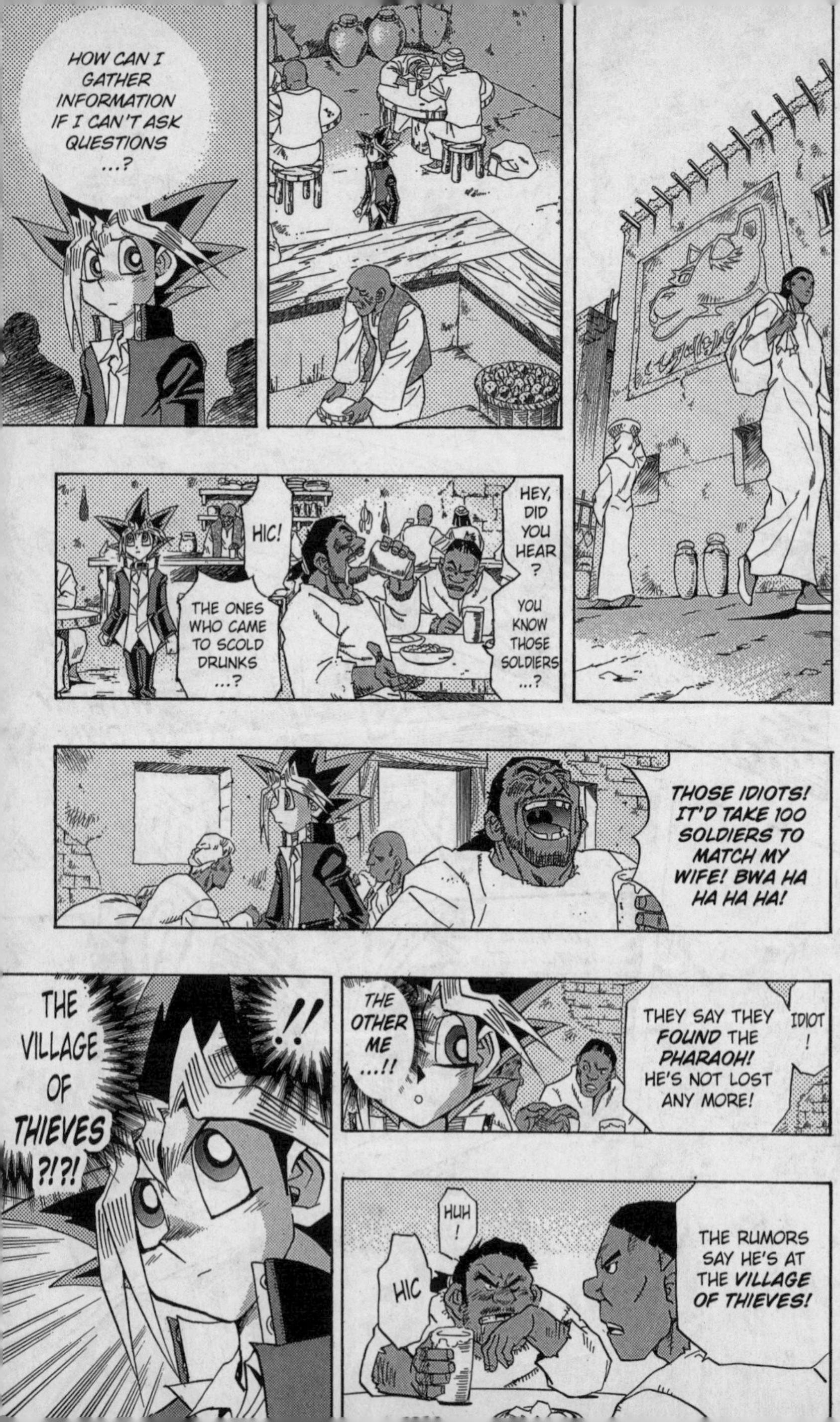
HOW CAN I GATHER INFORMATION IF I CAN'T ASK QUESTIONS ...?
HIC!
HEY, DID YOU HEAR?
YOU KNOW THOSE SOLDIERS ...?
THE ONES WHO CAME TO SCOLD DRUNKS ...?
THOSE IDIOTS! IT'D TAKE 100 SOLDIERS TO MATCH MY WIFE! BWA HA HA HA HA!
THE VILLAGE OF THIEVES ?!?!
!!
THE OTHER ME ...!!
THEY SAY THEY FOUND THE PHARAOH! HE'S NOT LOST ANY MORE!
IDIOT!
HUH!
HIC
THE RUMORS SAY HE'S AT THE VILLAGE OF THIEVES!

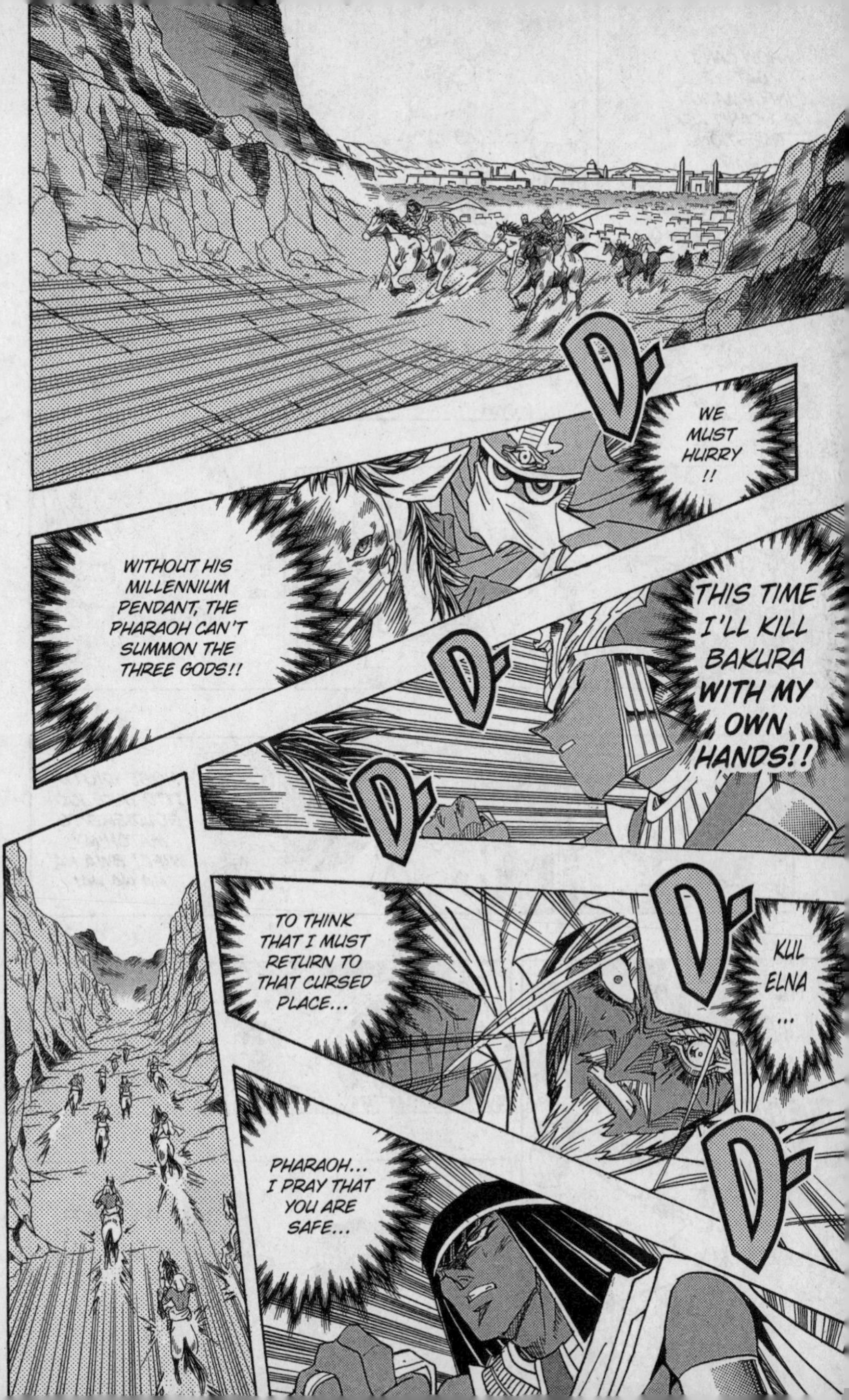
WE MUST HURRY!!
WITHOUT HIS MILLENNIUM PENDANT, THE PHARAOH CAN'T SUMMON THE THREE GODS!!
THIS TIME I'LL KILL BAKURA WITH MY OWN HANDS!!
KUL ELNA...
TO THINK THAT I MUST RETURN TO THAT CURSED PLACE...
PHARAOH... I PRAY THAT YOU ARE SAFE...

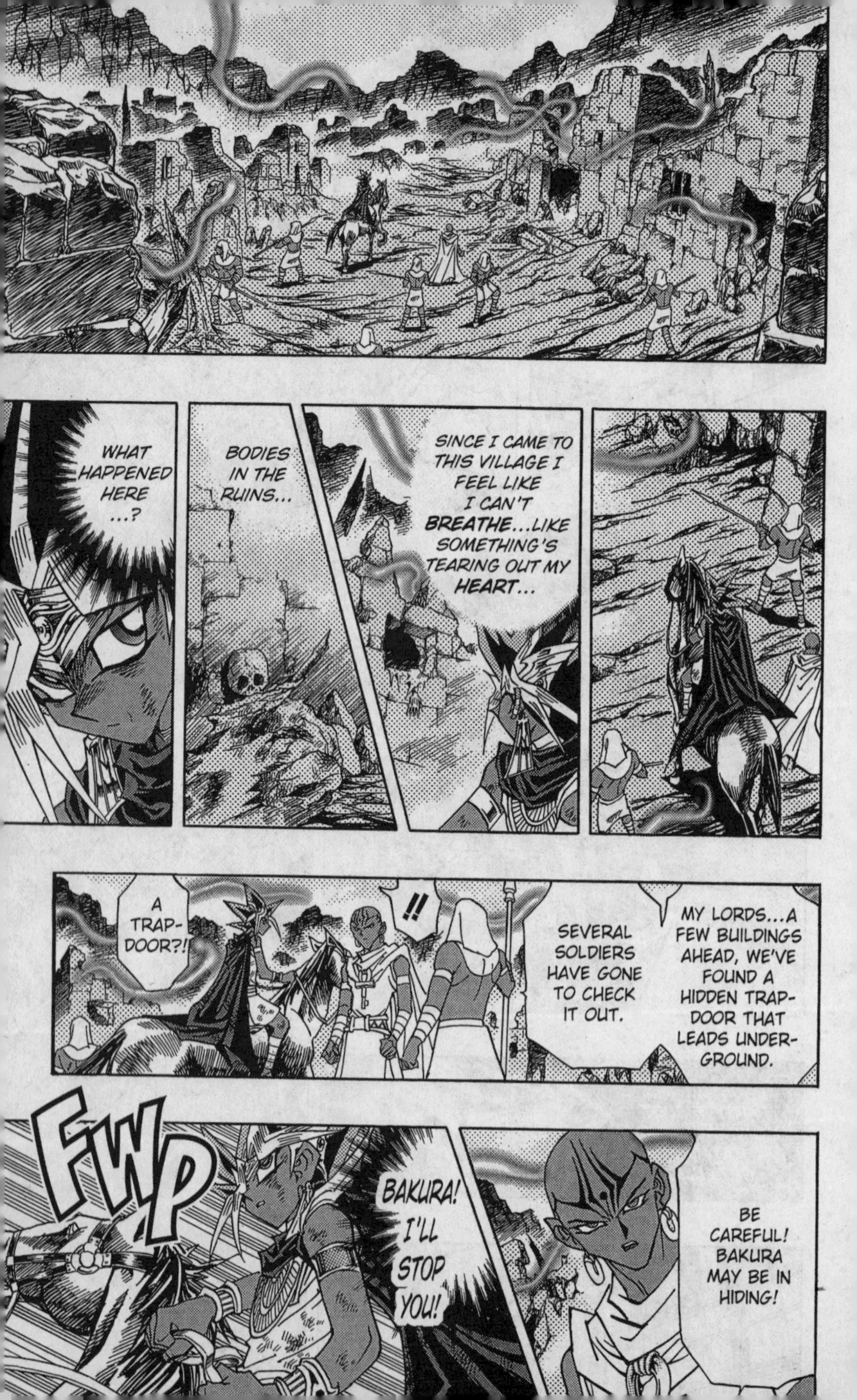
WHAT HAPPENED HERE ...?
BODIES IN THE RUINS...
SINCE I CAME TO THIS VILLAGE I FEEL LIKE I CAN'T BREATHE...LIKE SOMETHING'S TEARING OUT MY HEART...
MY LORDS...A FEW BUILDINGS AHEAD, WE'VE FOUND A HIDDEN TRAP-DOOR THAT LEADS UNDER-GROUND.
SEVERAL SOLDIERS HAVE GONE TO CHECK IT OUT.
!!
A TRAP-DOOR?!
FWP
BAKURA! I'LL STOP YOU!
BE CAREFUL! BAKURA MAY BE IN HIDING!

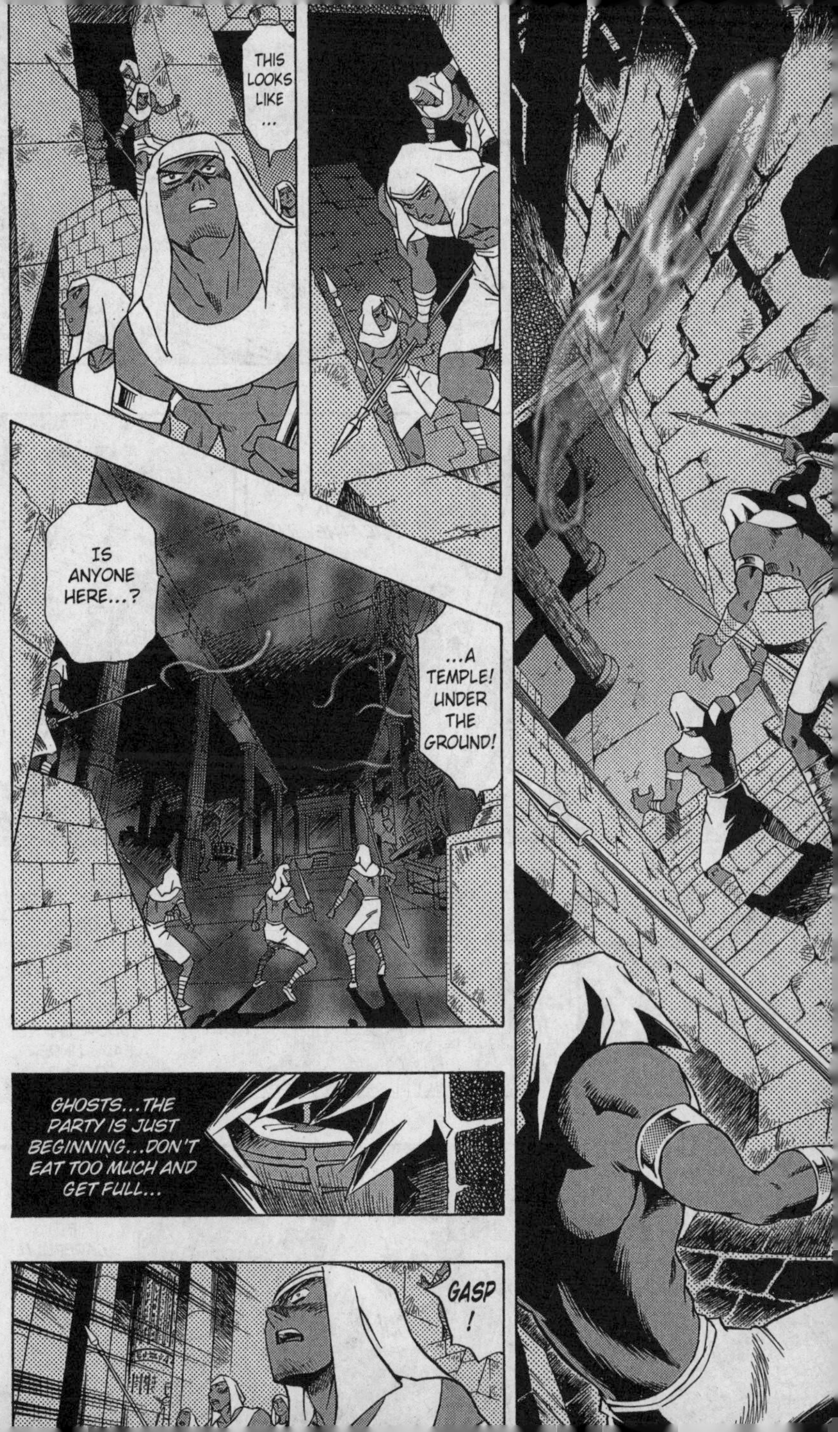
THIS LOOKS LIKE ...
IS ANYONE HERE...?
...A TEMPLE! UNDER THE GROUND!
GHOSTS...THE PARTY IS JUST BEGINNING...DON'T EAT TOO MUCH AND GET FULL...
GASP!

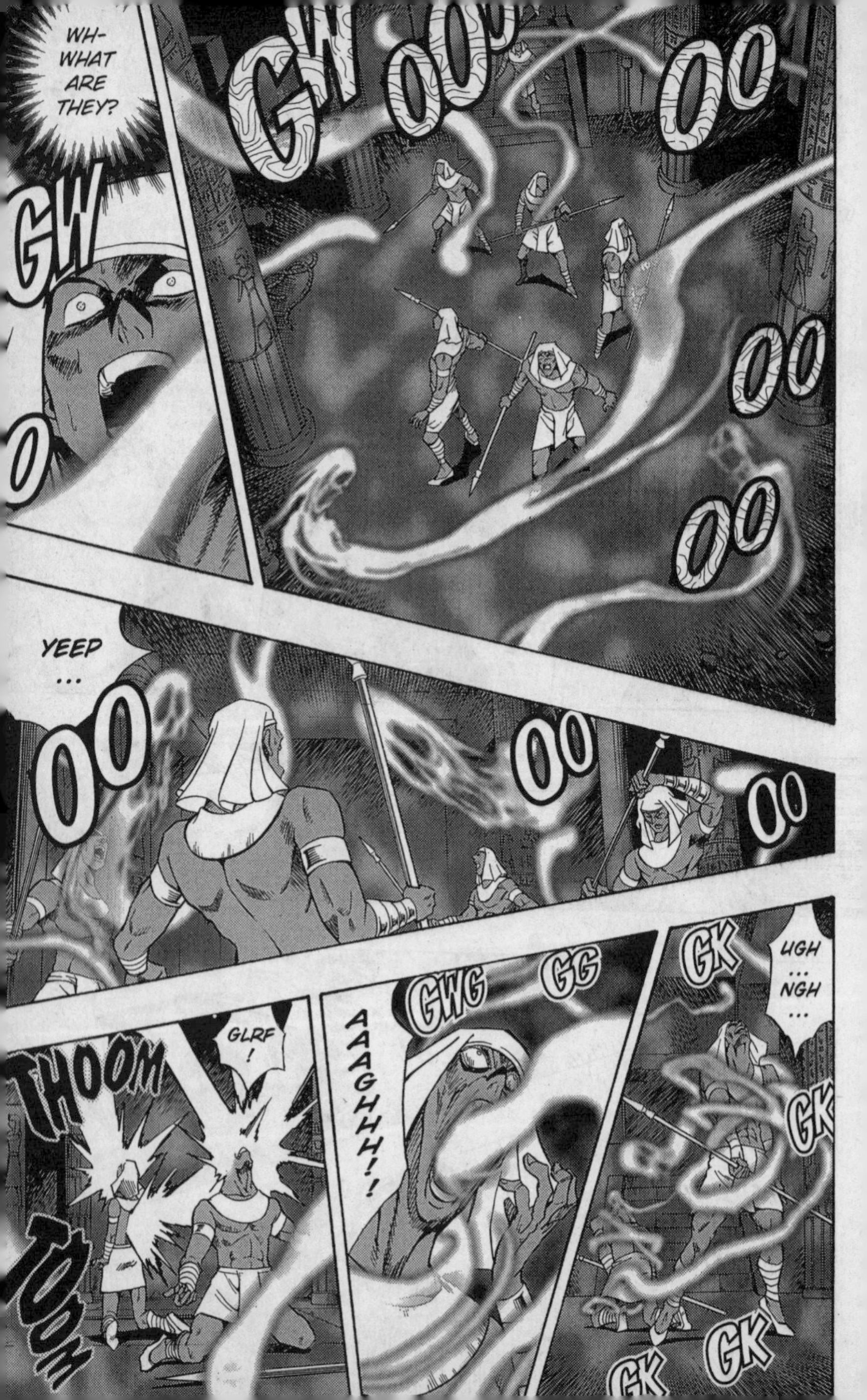
GWOOOOOO
WH- WHAT ARE THEY?
GW
OO
OO
OO
YEEP ...
OO
OO
OO
UGH ... NGH ...
GK
GK
GK
GK
GWG
GG
AAAGHHH!!
GLRF!
THOOM
TUOOM

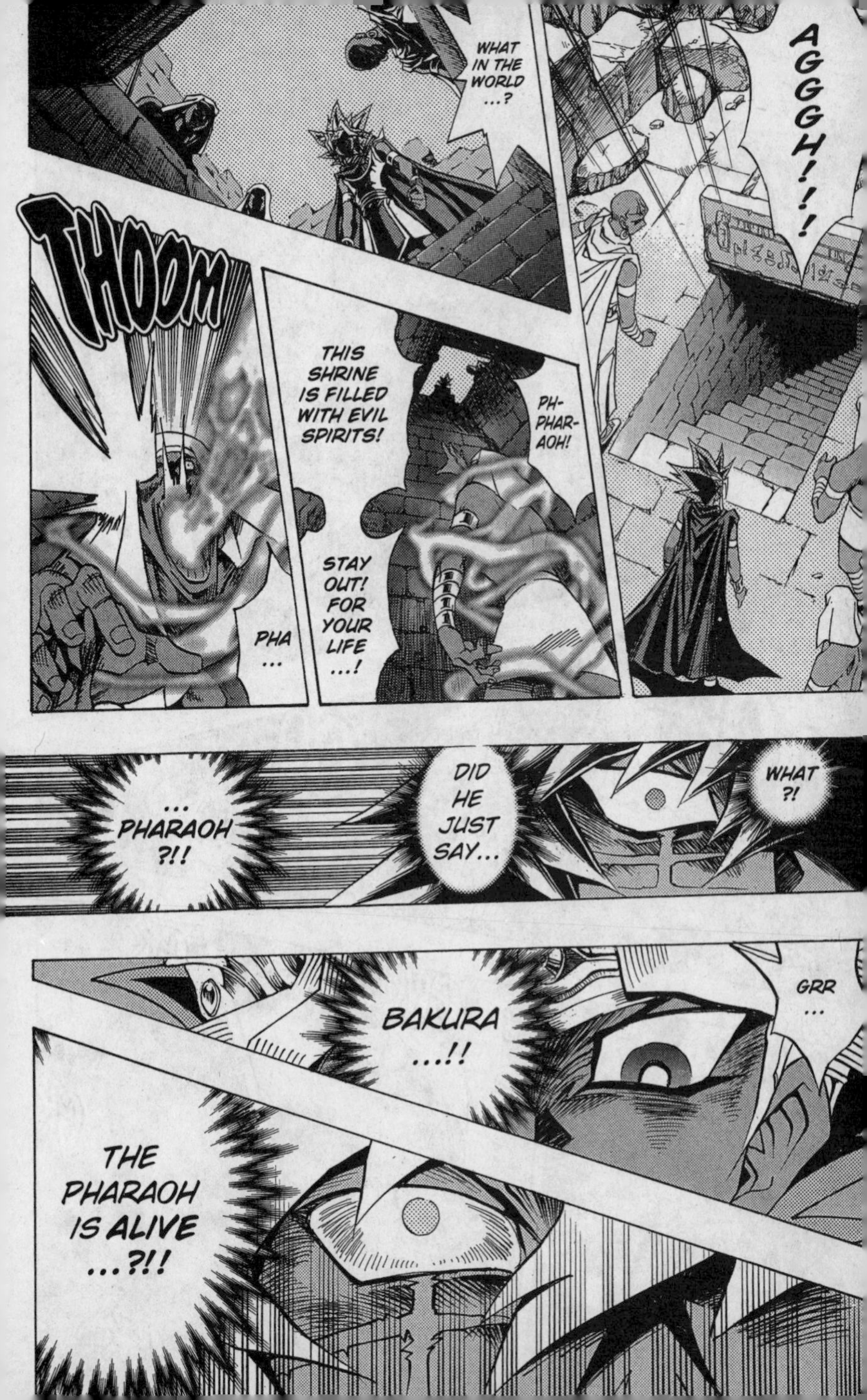
AGGGH!!!
WHAT IN THE WORLD ...?
PH-PHARAOH!
THIS SHRINE IS FILLED WITH EVIL SPIRITS!
STAY OUT! FOR YOUR LIFE ...!
THOOM
PHA ...
WHAT ?!
DID HE JUST SAY...
... PHARAOH ?!!
GRR ...
BAKURA ...!!
THE PHARAOH IS ALIVE ...?!!

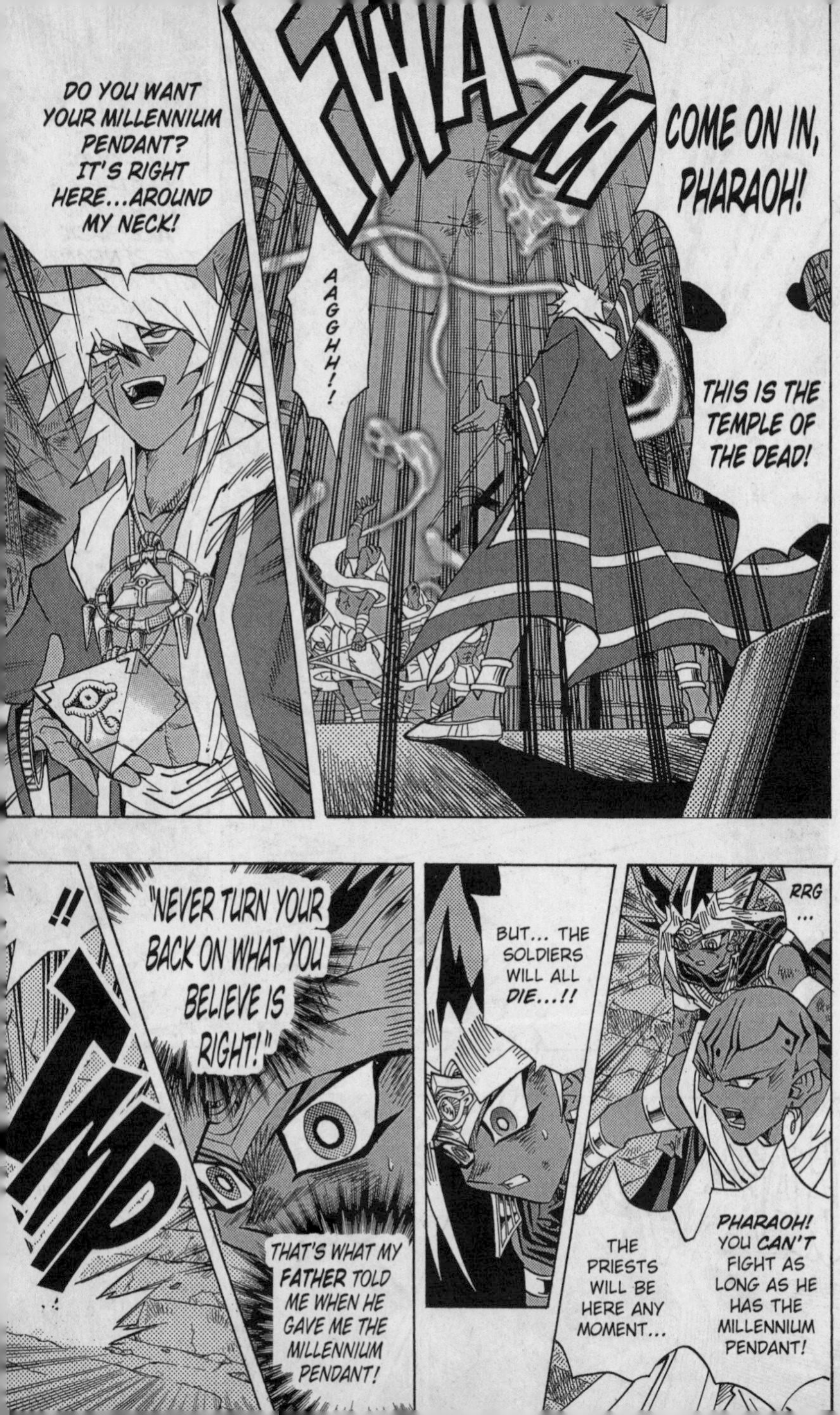
WHAM
COME ON IN, PHARAOH!
THIS IS THE TEMPLE OF THE DEAD!
AAGGHH!!
DO YOU WANT YOUR MILLENNIUM PENDANT? IT'S RIGHT HERE...AROUND MY NECK!
RRG...
PHARAOH! YOU CAN'T FIGHT AS LONG AS HE HAS THE MILLENNIUM PENDANT!
THE PRIESTS WILL BE HERE ANY MOMENT...
BUT... THE SOLDIERS WILL ALL DIE...!!
!!
THMP
"NEVER TURN YOUR BACK ON WHAT YOU BELIEVE IS RIGHT!"
THAT'S WHAT MY FATHER TOLD ME WHEN HE GAVE ME THE MILLENNIUM PENDANT!

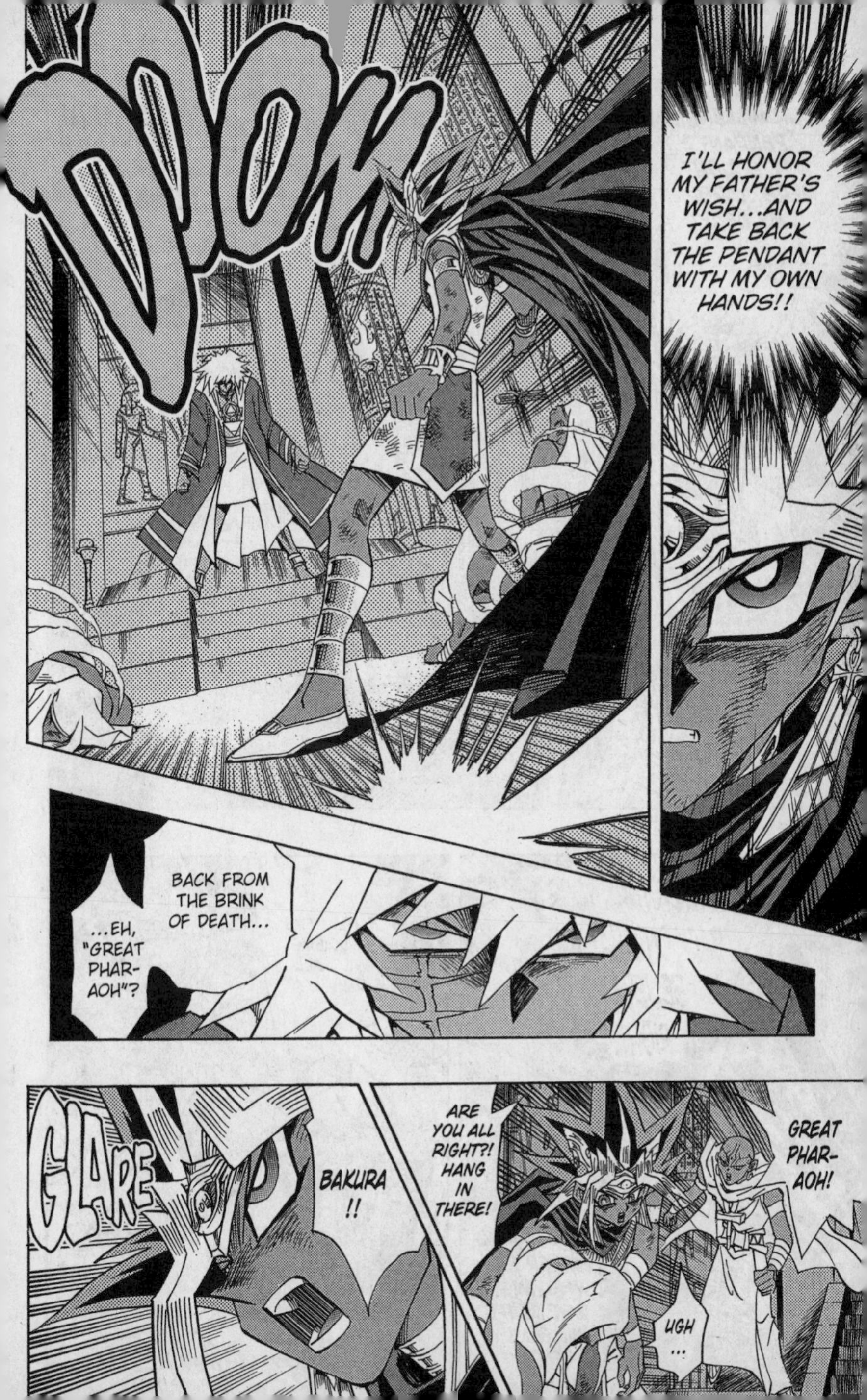

I'LL HONOR MY FATHER'S WISH...AND TAKE BACK THE PENDANT WITH MY OWN HANDS!!
DOOM
BACK FROM THE BRINK OF DEATH...
...EH, "GREAT PHAR-AOH"?
GREAT PHAR-AOH!
ARE YOU ALL RIGHT?! HANG IN THERE!
UGH ...
BAKURA !!
GLARE

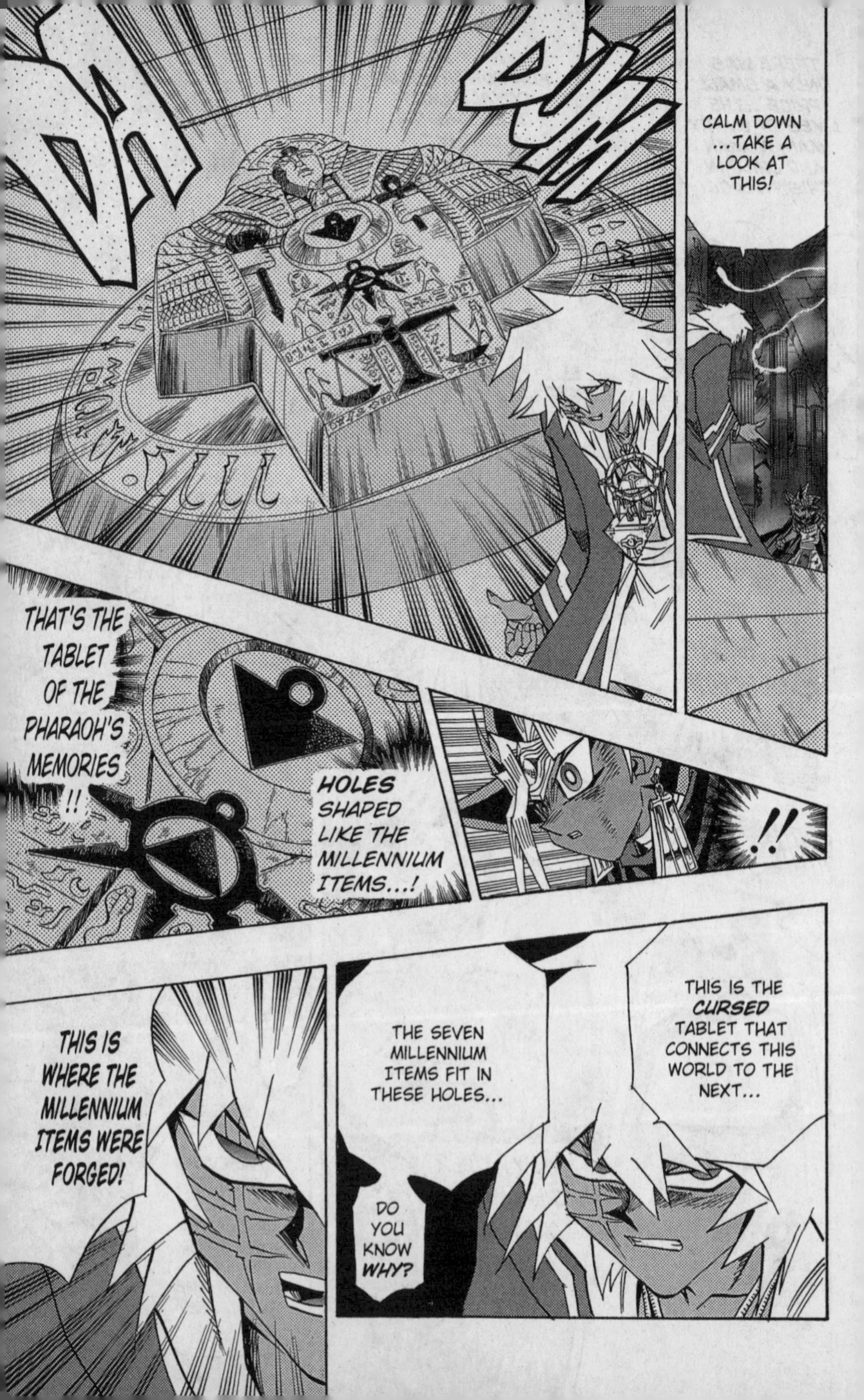
DUM
CALM DOWN ...TAKE A LOOK AT THIS!
!!
HOLES SHAPED LIKE THE MILLENNIUM ITEMS...!
THAT'S THE TABLET OF THE PHARAOH'S MEMORIES !!
THIS IS THE CURSED TABLET THAT CONNECTS THIS WORLD TO THE NEXT...
THE SEVEN MILLENNIUM ITEMS FIT IN THESE HOLES...
DO YOU KNOW WHY?
THIS IS WHERE THE MILLENNIUM ITEMS WERE FORGED!

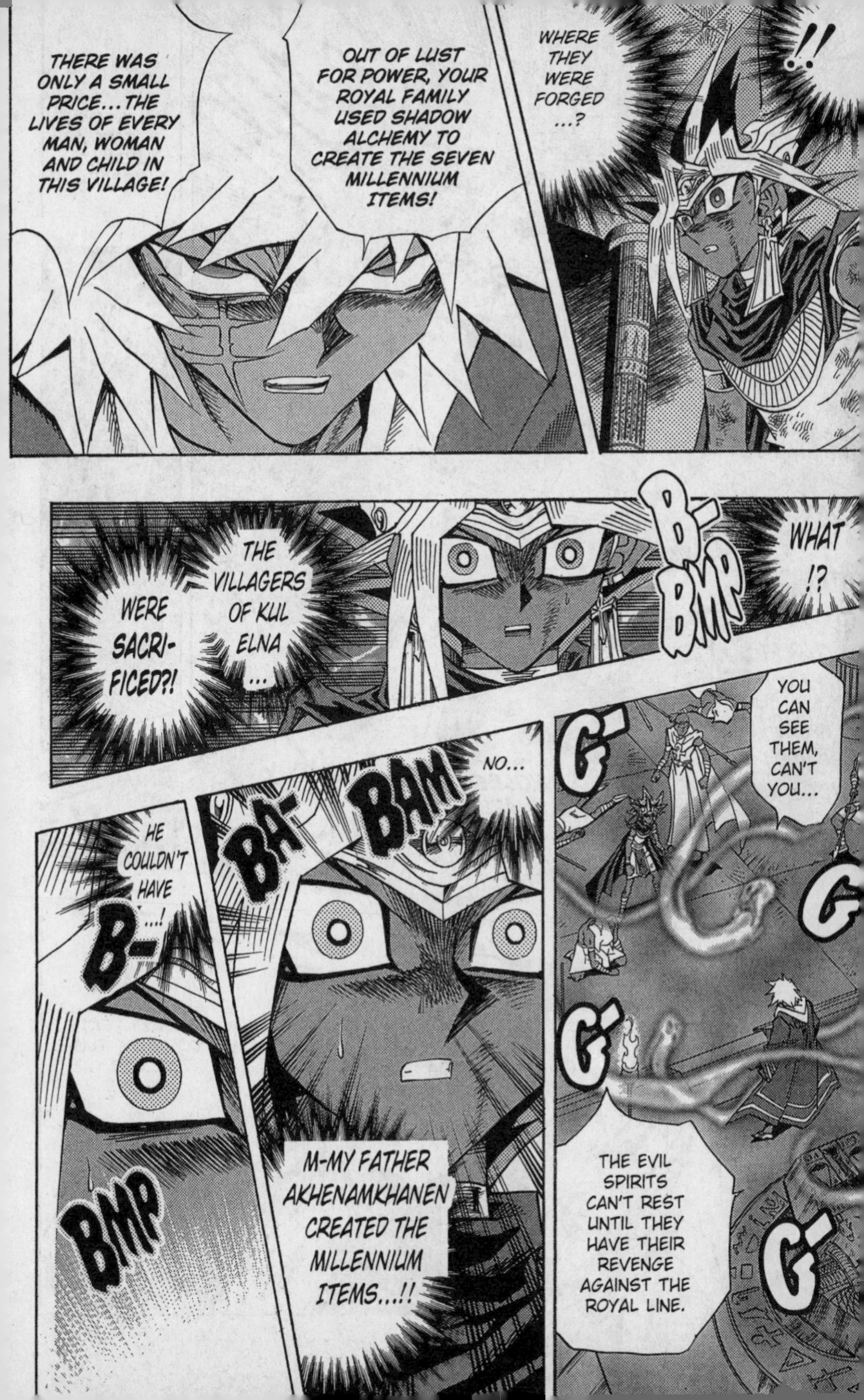
!!
WHERE THEY WERE FORGED ...?
OUT OF LUST FOR POWER, YOUR ROYAL FAMILY USED SHADOW ALCHEMY TO CREATE THE SEVEN MILLENNIUM ITEMS!
THERE WAS ONLY A SMALL PRICE... THE LIVES OF EVERY MAN, WOMAN AND CHILD IN THIS VILLAGE!
WHAT !?
B-BMP
THE VILLAGERS OF KUL ELNA ...
WERE SACRIFICED?!
YOU CAN SEE THEM, CAN'T YOU...
G-
G
G-
THE EVIL SPIRITS CAN'T REST UNTIL THEY HAVE THEIR REVENGE AGAINST THE ROYAL LINE.
G-
NO...
BA-BAM
M-MY FATHER AKHENAMKHANEN CREATED THE MILLENNIUM ITEMS...!!
HE COULDN'T HAVE ...!
B-
BMP

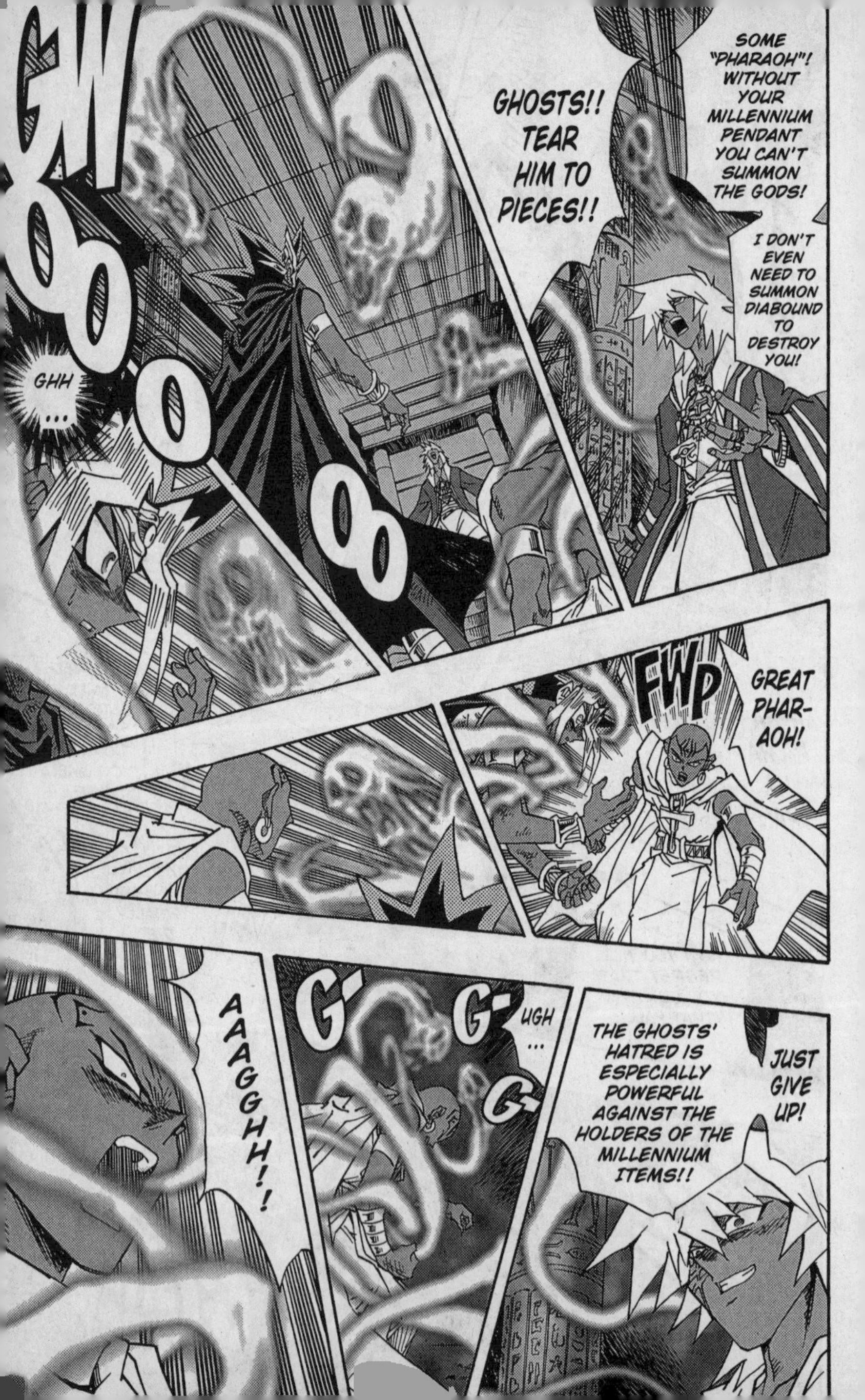

SOME "PHARAOH"! WITHOUT YOUR MILLENNIUM PENDANT YOU CAN'T SUMMON THE GODS!
I DON'T EVEN NEED TO SUMMON DIABOUND TO DESTROY YOU!
GHOSTS!! TEAR HIM TO PIECES!!
GWOOOOOO
GHH ...
FWP
GREAT PHAR-AOH!
JUST GIVE UP!
THE GHOSTS' HATRED IS ESPECIALLY POWERFUL AGAINST THE HOLDERS OF THE MILLENNIUM ITEMS!!
UGH ...
G- G- G-
AAAAGGHH!!

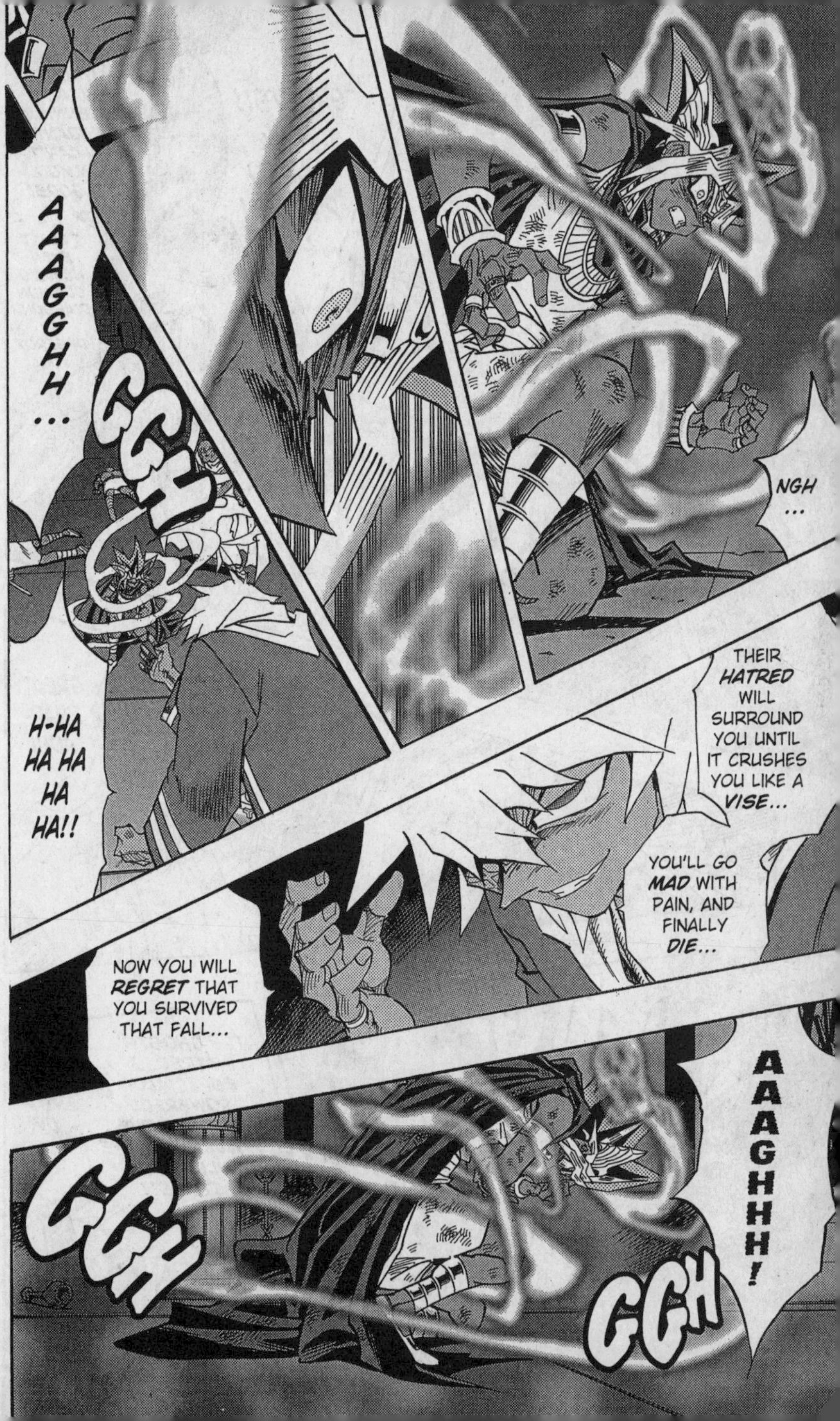
NGH...
AAAAGGHH...
GGH
H-HA HA HA HA HA!!
THEIR HATRED WILL SURROUND YOU UNTIL IT CRUSHES YOU LIKE A VISE...
YOU'LL GO MAD WITH PAIN, AND FINALLY DIE...
NOW YOU WILL REGRET THAT YOU SURVIVED THAT FALL...
AAAGHHH!
GGH
GGH

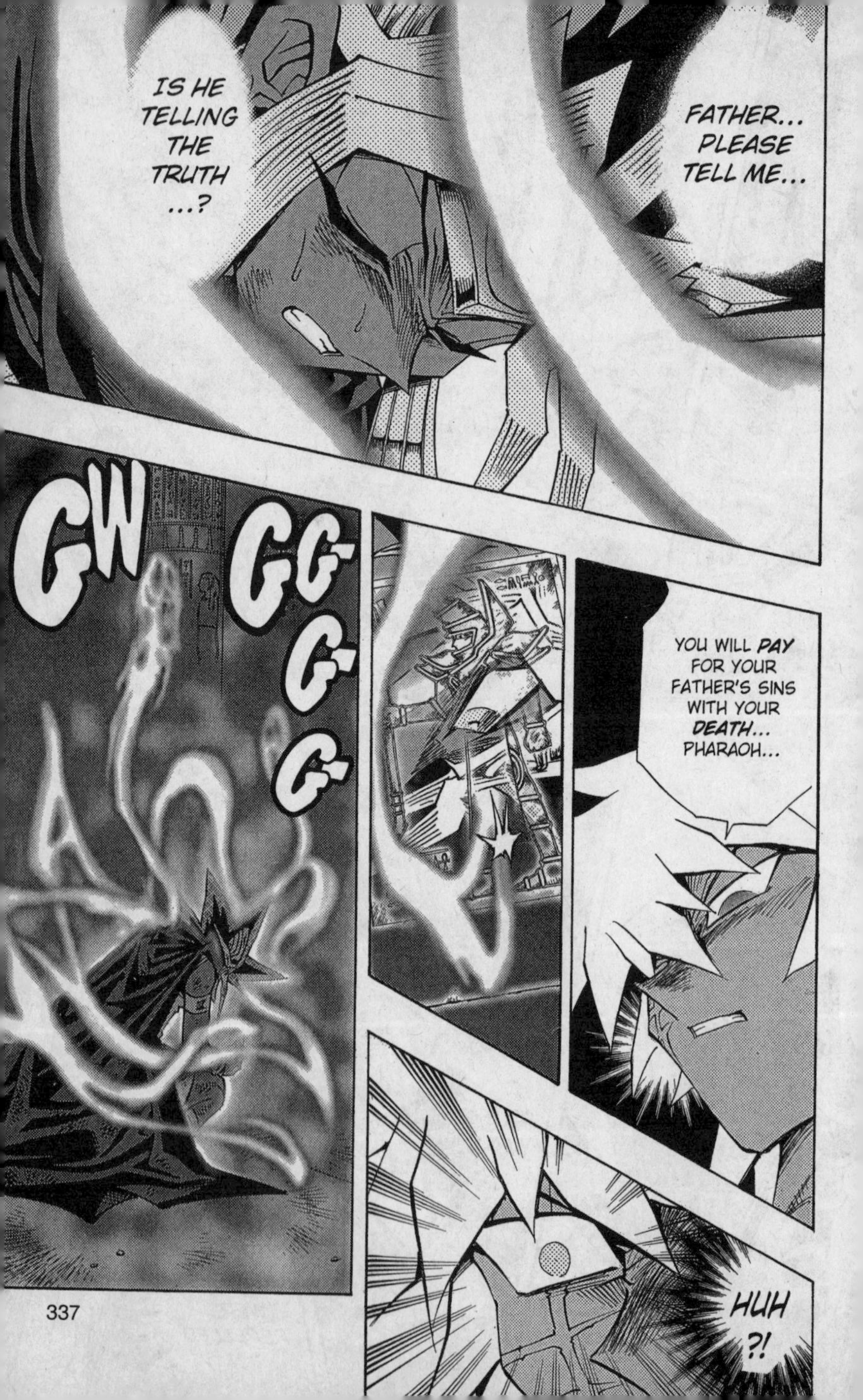
FATHER... PLEASE TELL ME...
IS HE TELLING THE TRUTH ...?
YOU WILL PAY FOR YOUR FATHER'S SINS WITH YOUR DEATH... PHARAOH...
GW GG-G-G-
HUH ?!

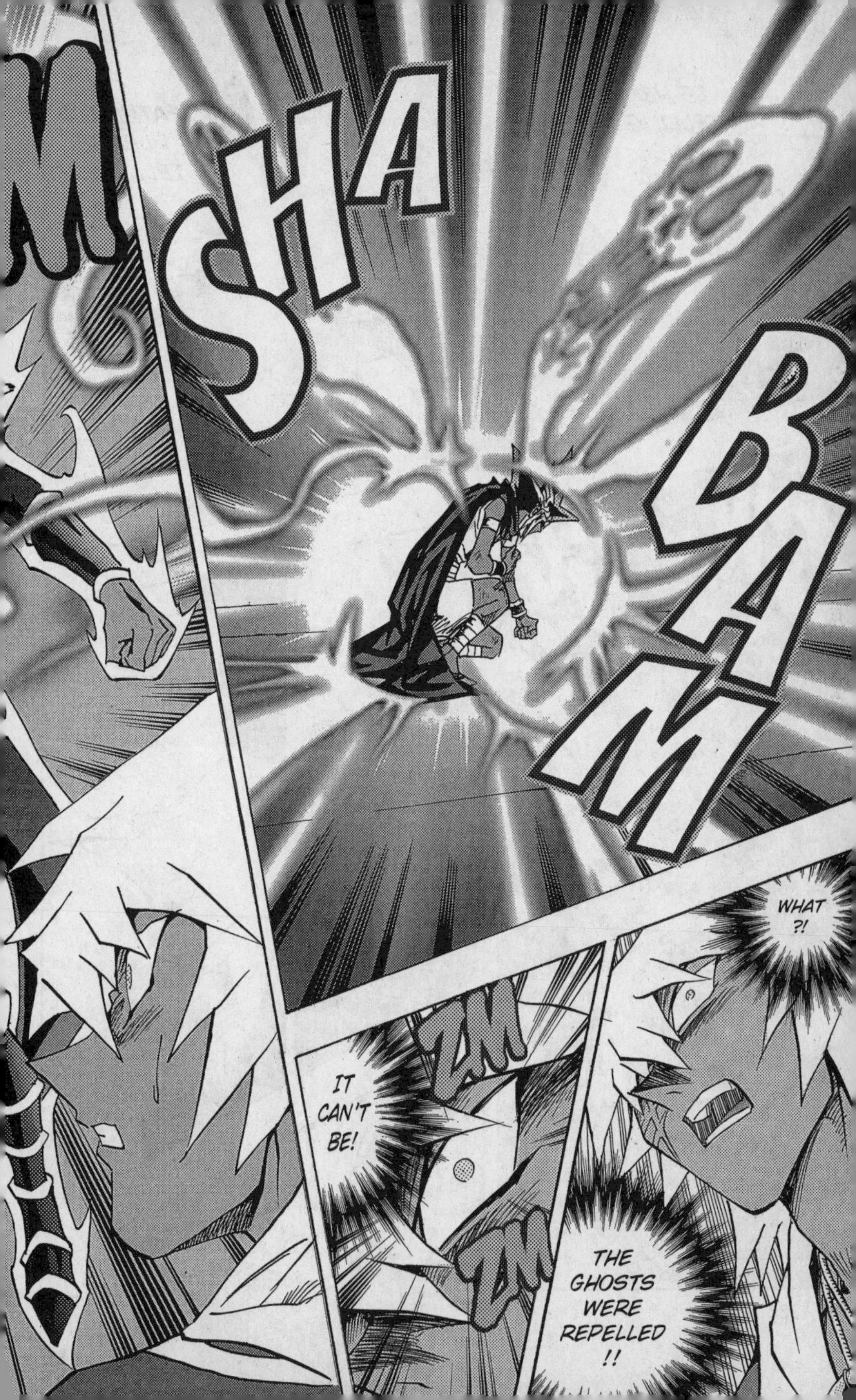
SHA
BAM
M
WHAT ?!
IT CAN'T BE!
THE GHOSTS WERE REPELLED !!

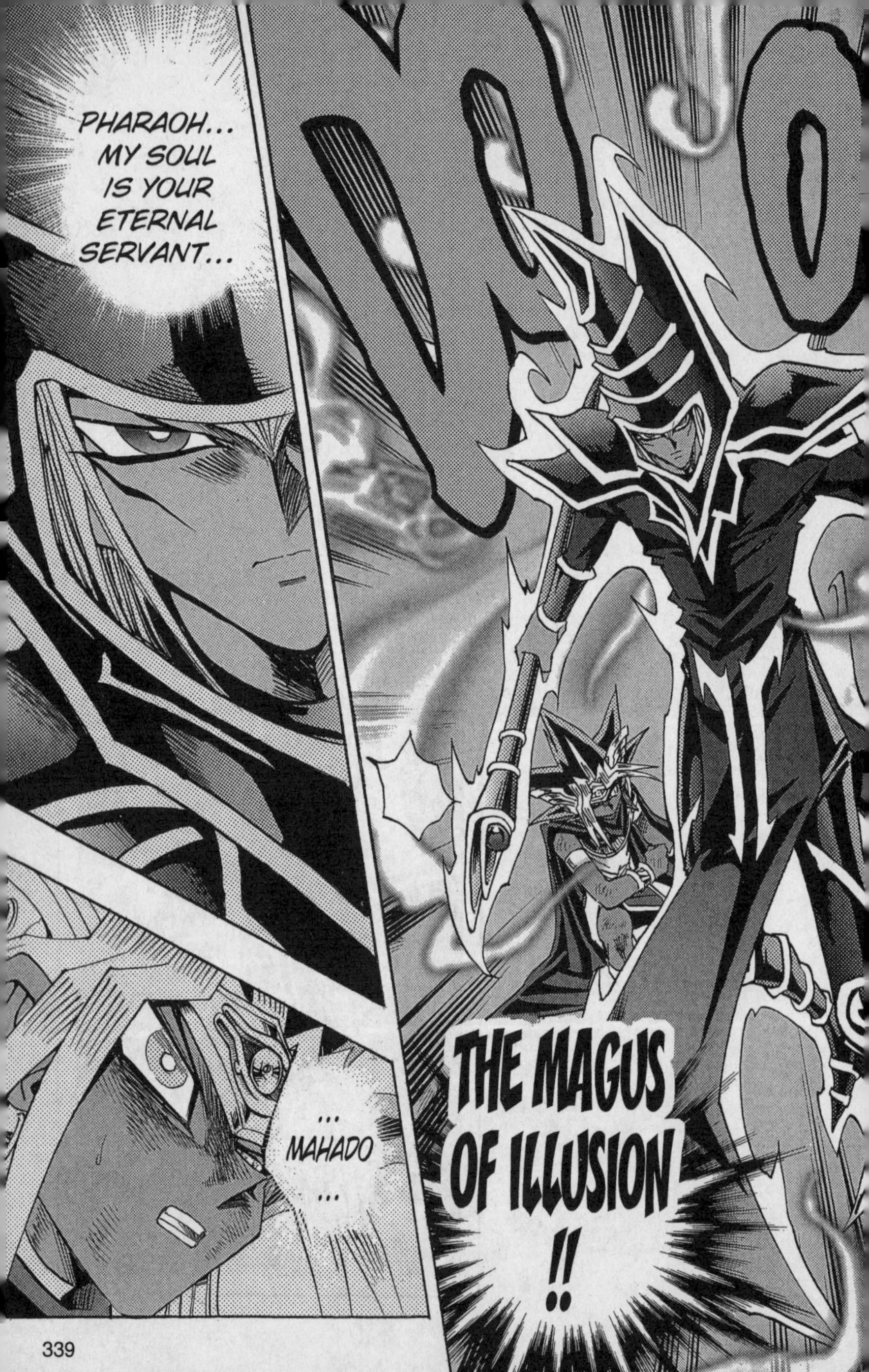
PHARAOH... MY SOUL IS YOUR ETERNAL SERVANT...
... MAHADO ...
THE MAGUS OF ILLUSION !!

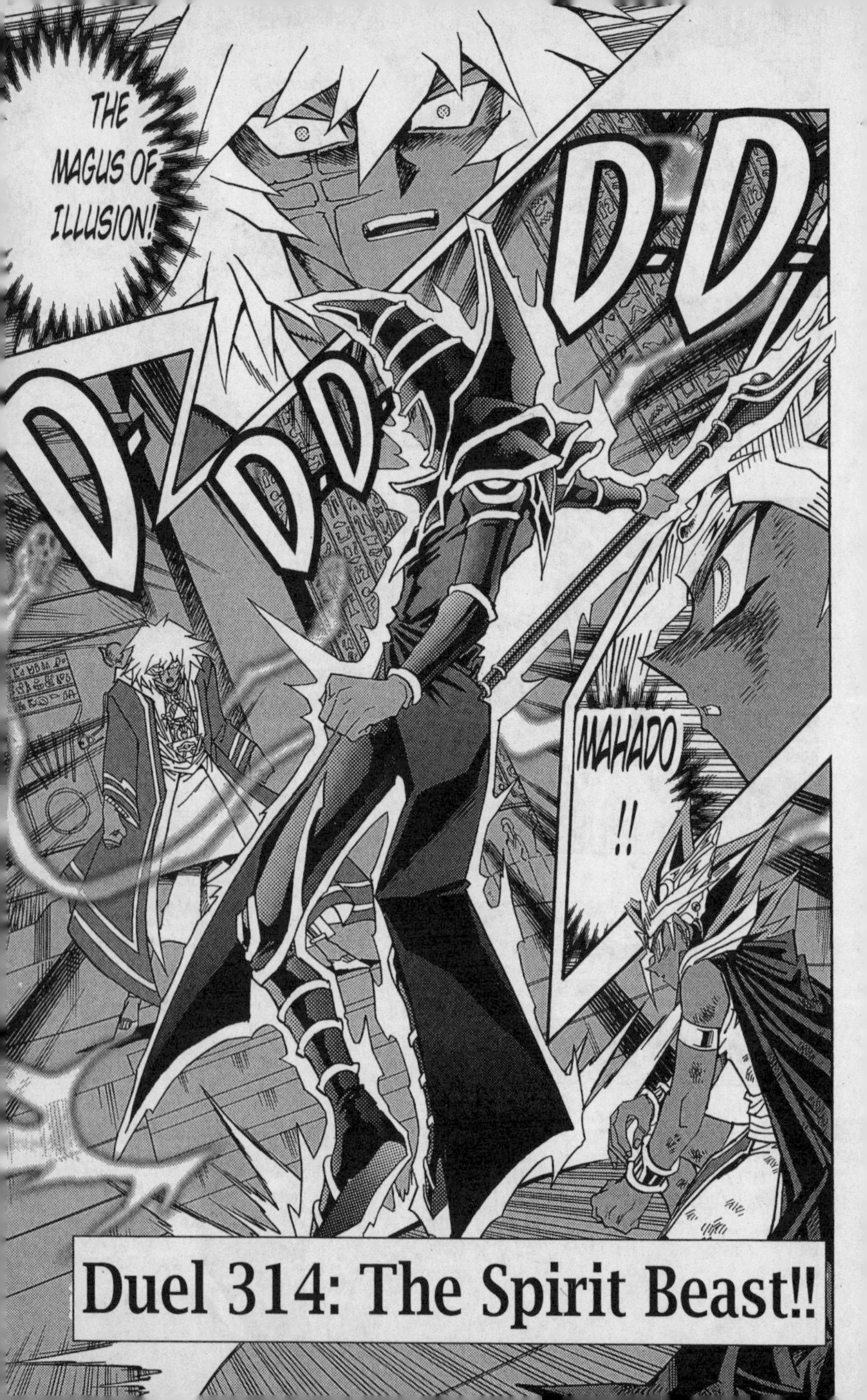
THE MAGUS OF ILLUSION!
D.D.D.
D.D.D.
MAHADO !!

Duel 314: The Spirit Beast!!

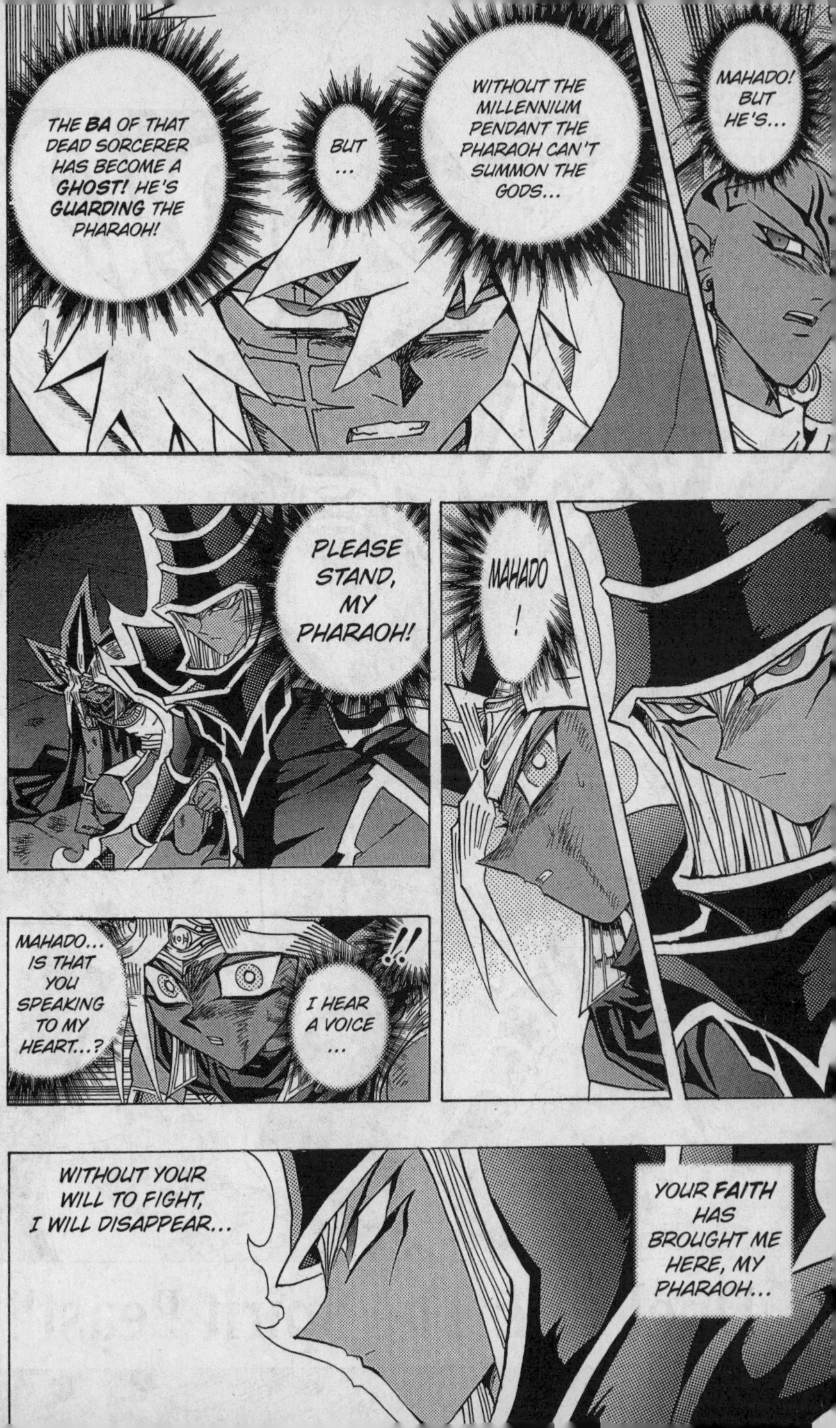
MAHADO! BUT HE'S...
WITHOUT THE MILLENNIUM PENDANT THE PHARAOH CAN'T SUMMON THE GODS...
BUT...
THE BA OF THAT DEAD SORCERER HAS BECOME A GHOST! HE'S GUARDING THE PHARAOH!
PLEASE STAND, MY PHARAOH!
!!
I HEAR A VOICE...
MAHADO... IS THAT YOU SPEAKING TO MY HEART...?
MAHADO!
YOUR FAITH HAS BROUGHT ME HERE, MY PHARAOH...
WITHOUT YOUR WILL TO FIGHT, I WILL DISAPPEAR...

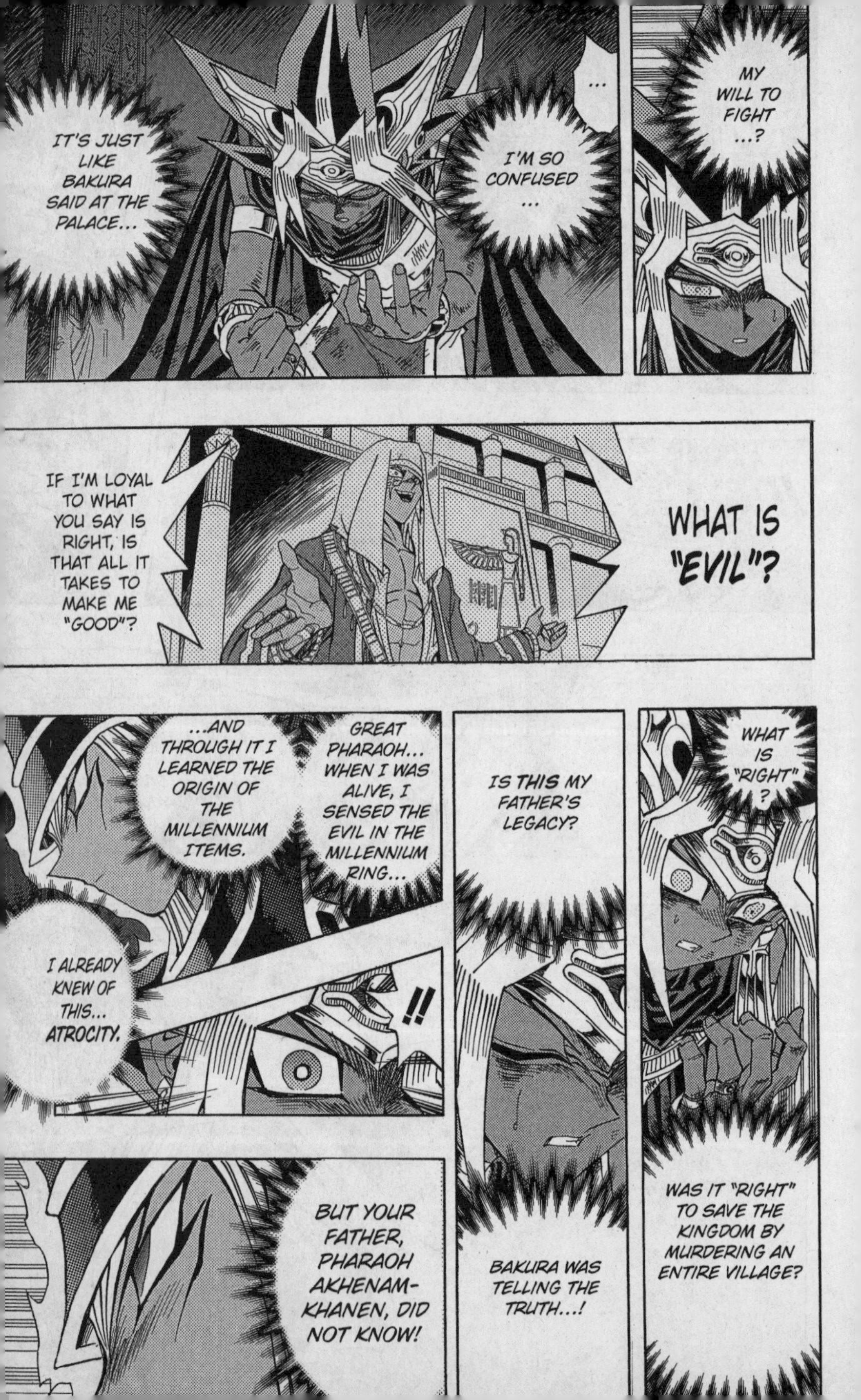
MY WILL TO FIGHT ...?
...
I'M SO CONFUSED ...
IT'S JUST LIKE BAKURA SAID AT THE PALACE...
WHAT IS "EVIL"?
IF I'M LOYAL TO WHAT YOU SAY IS RIGHT, IS THAT ALL IT TAKES TO MAKE ME "GOOD"?
WHAT IS "RIGHT"?
WAS IT "RIGHT" TO SAVE THE KINGDOM BY MURDERING AN ENTIRE VILLAGE?
IS THIS MY FATHER'S LEGACY?
BAKURA WAS TELLING THE TRUTH...!
GREAT PHARAOH... WHEN I WAS ALIVE, I SENSED THE EVIL IN THE MILLENNIUM RING...
...AND THROUGH IT I LEARNED THE ORIGIN OF THE MILLENNIUM ITEMS.
I ALREADY KNEW OF THIS... ATROCITY.
!!
BUT YOUR FATHER, PHARAOH AKHENAM-KHANEN, DID NOT KNOW!

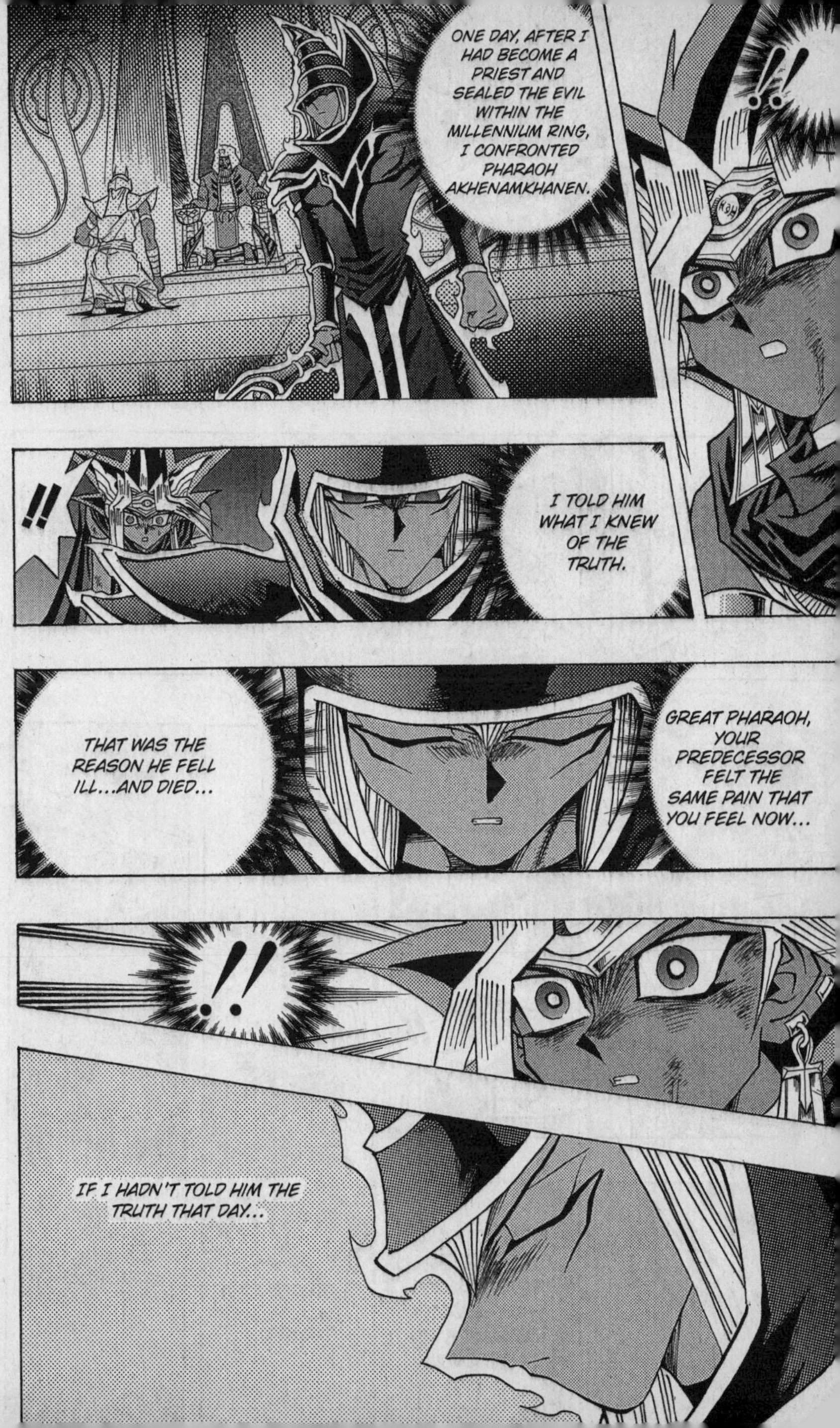
ONE DAY, AFTER I HAD BECOME A PRIEST AND SEALED THE EVIL WITHIN THE MILLENNIUM RING, I CONFRONTED PHARAOH AKHENAMKHANEN.
!!
I TOLD HIM WHAT I KNEW OF THE TRUTH.
!!
GREAT PHARAOH, YOUR PREDECESSOR FELT THE SAME PAIN THAT YOU FEEL NOW...
THAT WAS THE REASON HE FELL ILL...AND DIED...
!!
IF I HADN'T TOLD HIM THE TRUTH THAT DAY...

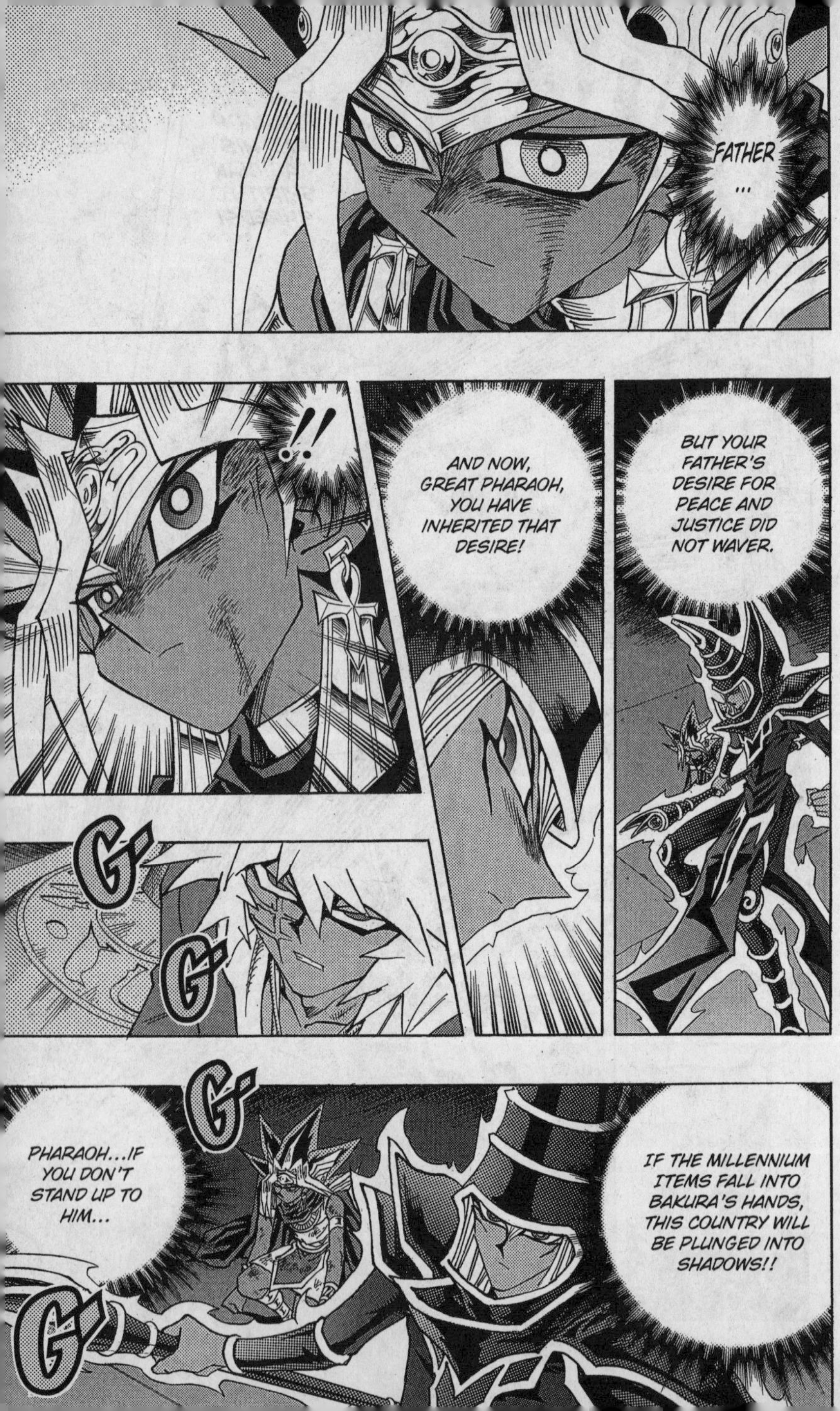
FATHER
...
BUT YOUR FATHER'S DESIRE FOR PEACE AND JUSTICE DID NOT WAVER.
AND NOW, GREAT PHARAOH, YOU HAVE INHERITED THAT DESIRE!
!!
G-
G-
G-
G-
IF THE MILLENNIUM ITEMS FALL INTO BAKURA'S HANDS, THIS COUNTRY WILL BE PLUNGED INTO SHADOWS!!
PHARAOH...IF YOU DON'T STAND UP TO HIM...

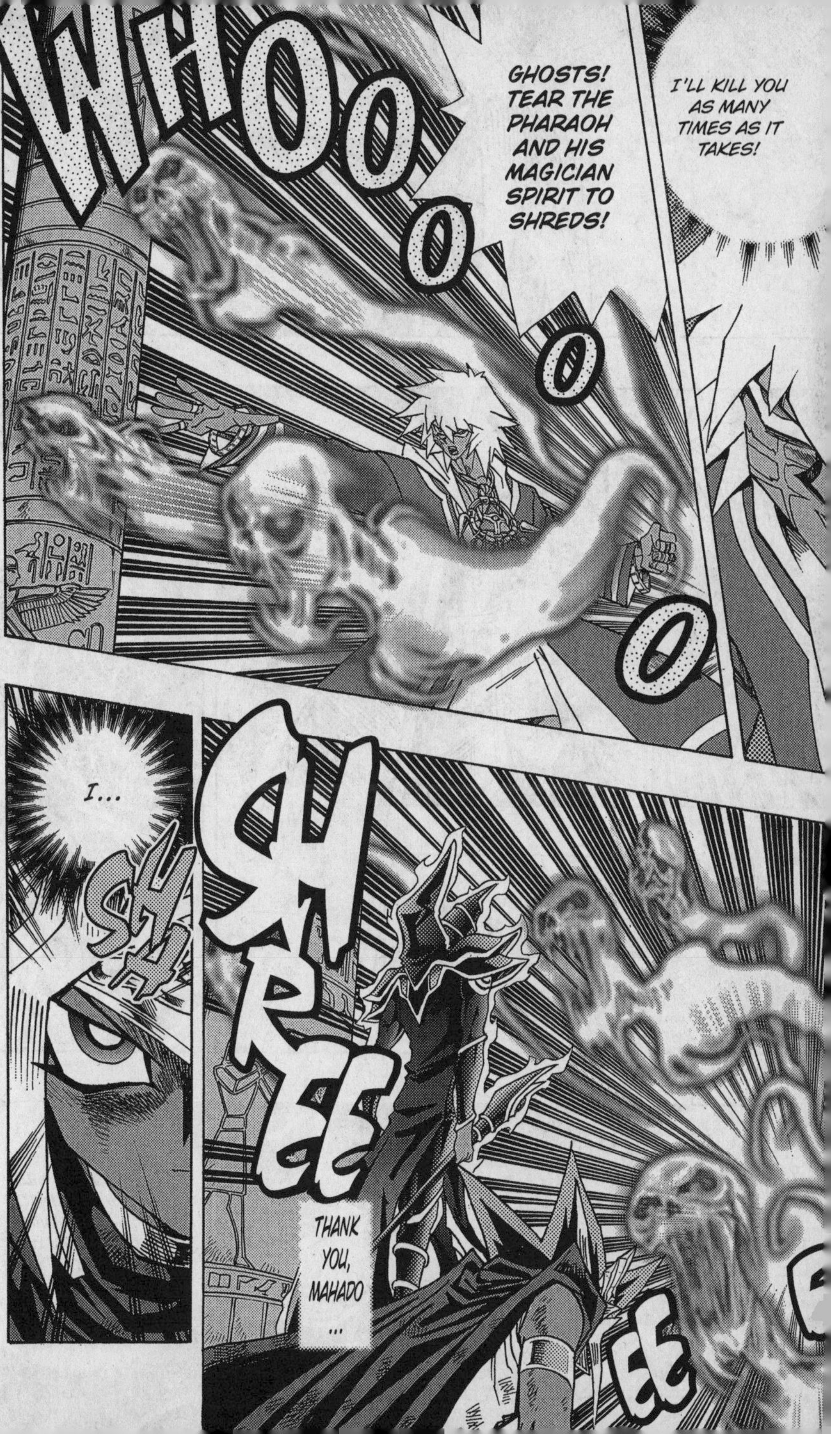
I'LL KILL YOU AS MANY TIMES AS IT TAKES!
GHOSTS! TEAR THE PHARAOH AND HIS MAGICIAN SPIRIT TO SHREDS!
WHOOOOOO
SHREE
THANK YOU, MAHADO ...
I...
SHH

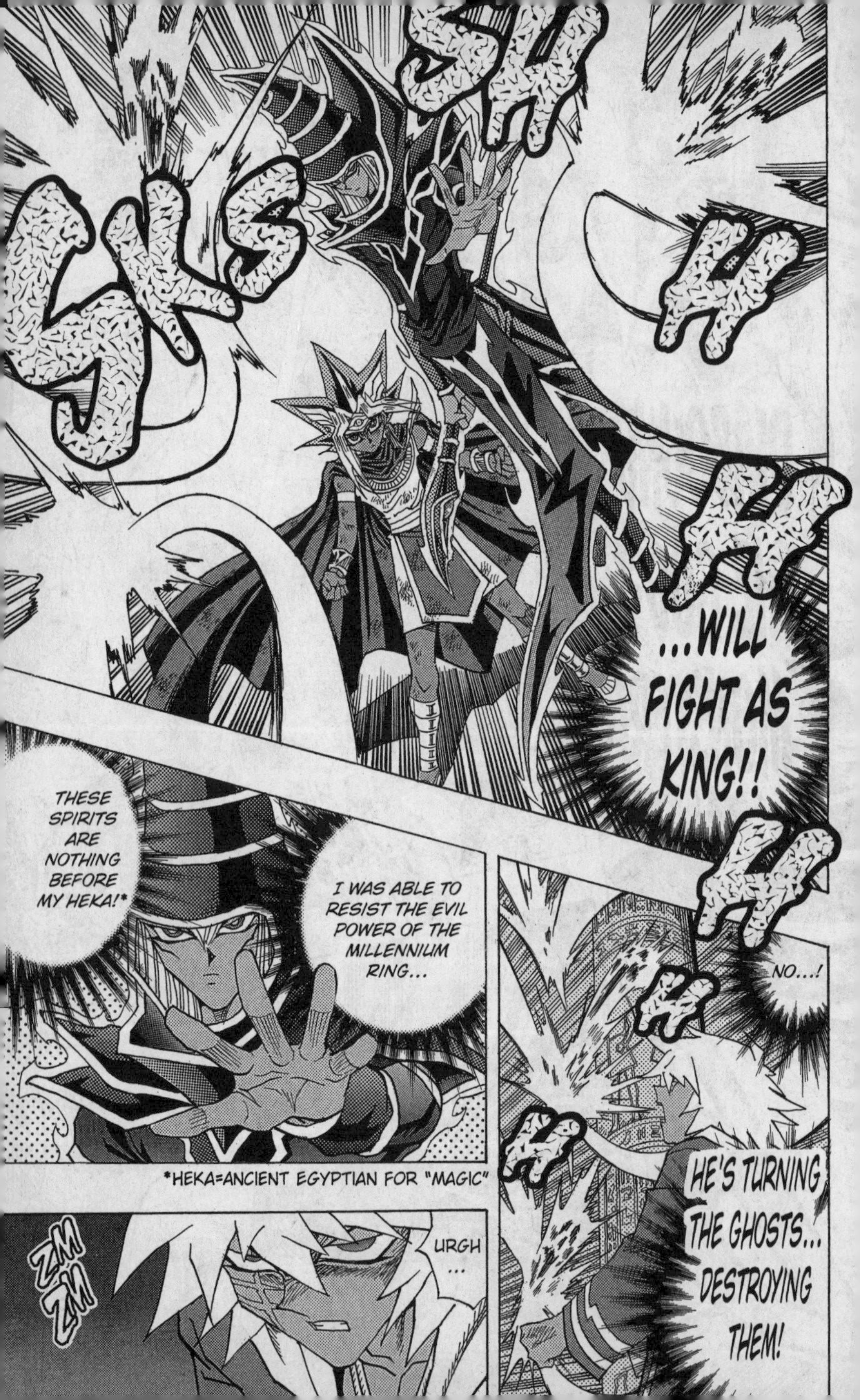
...WILL FIGHT AS KING!!
I WAS ABLE TO RESIST THE EVIL POWER OF THE MILLENNIUM RING...
THESE SPIRITS ARE NOTHING BEFORE MY HEKA!*
*HEKA=ANCIENT EGYPTIAN FOR "MAGIC"
NO...!
HE'S TURNING THE GHOSTS... DESTROYING THEM!
URGH ...

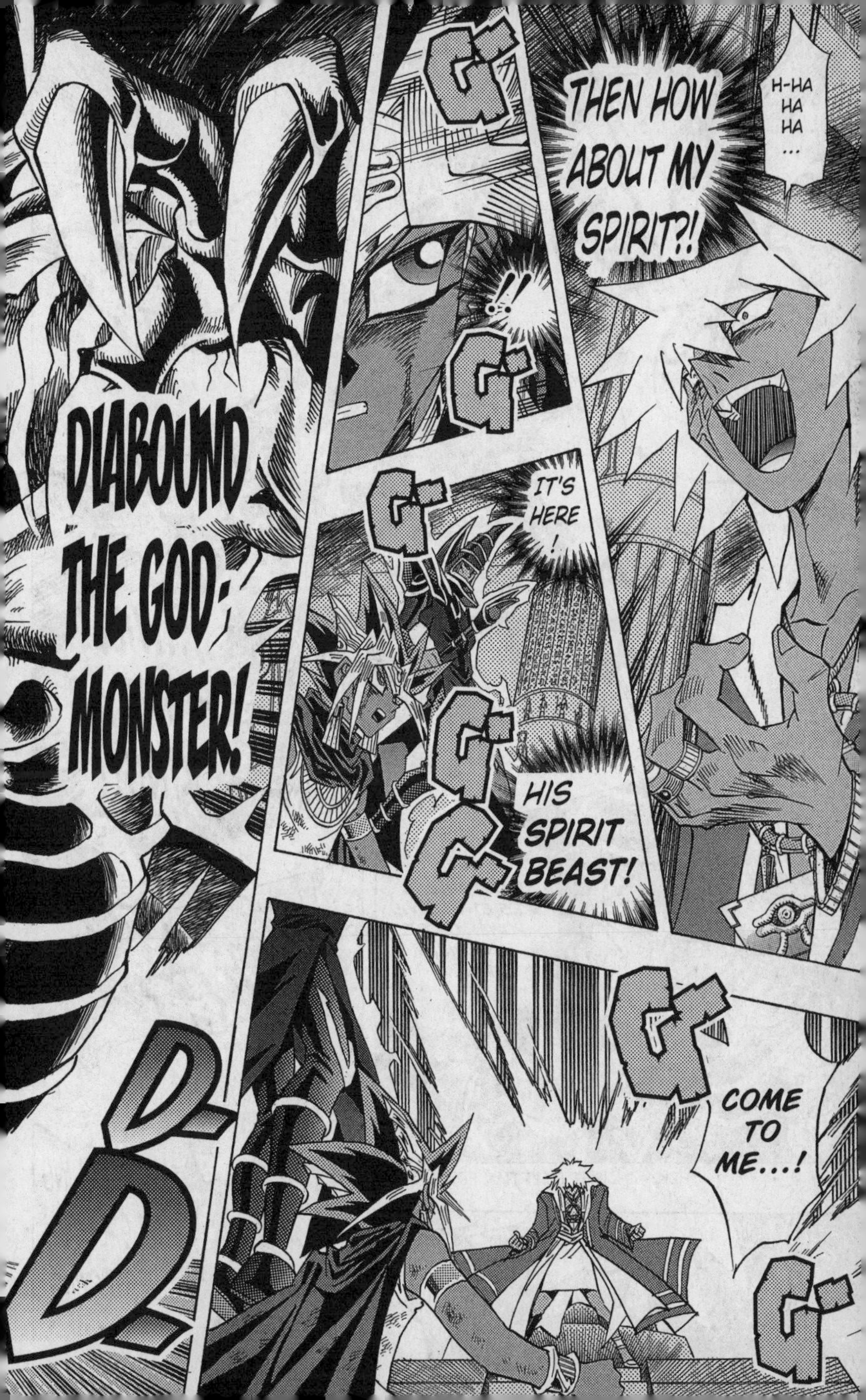
H-HA HA HA ...
THEN HOW ABOUT MY SPIRIT?!
G
!!
G
IT'S HERE!
G
G
HIS SPIRIT BEAST!
G
COME TO ME...!
G
G
DIABOUND THE GOD-MONSTER!
D
D

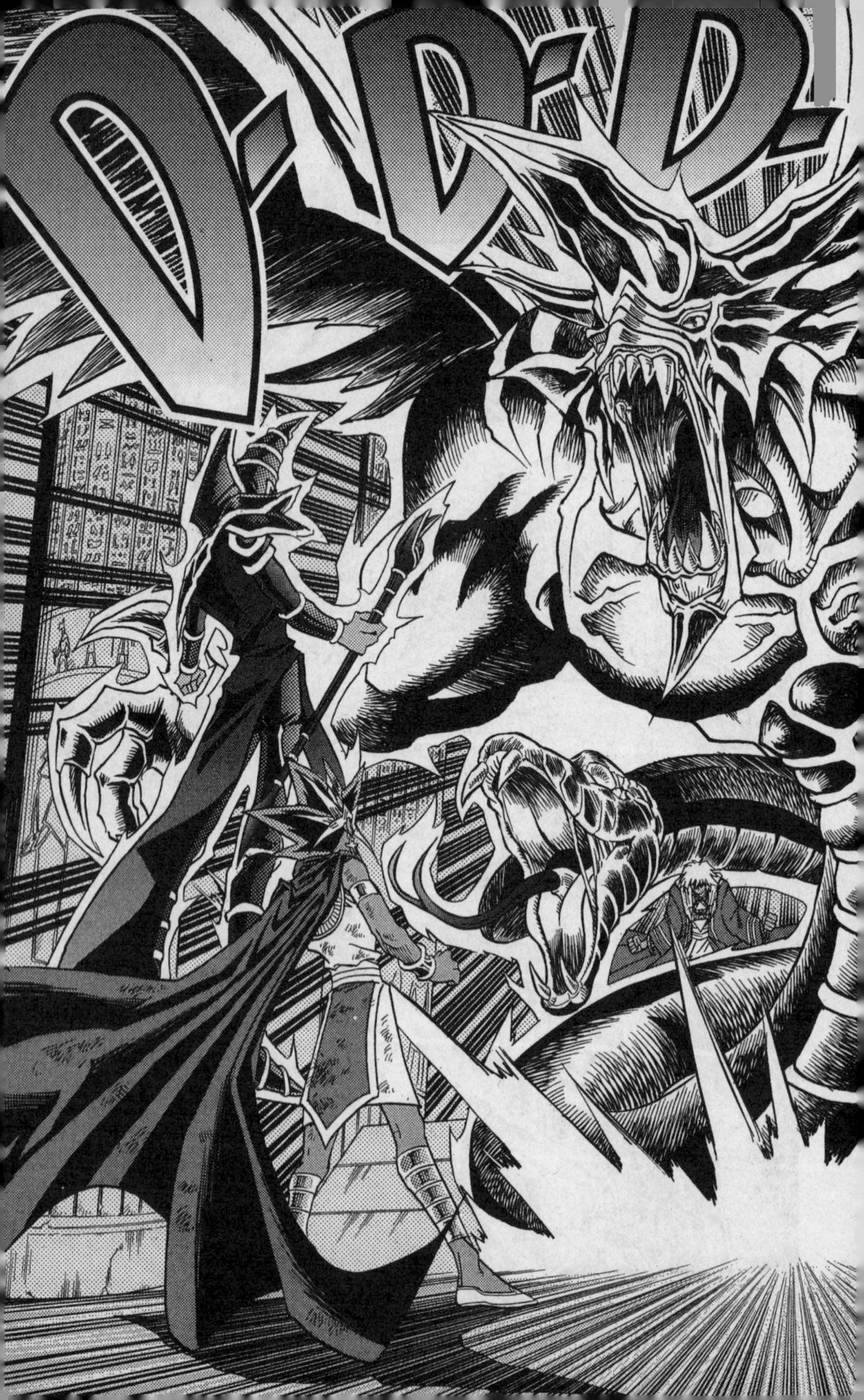
D-D-D

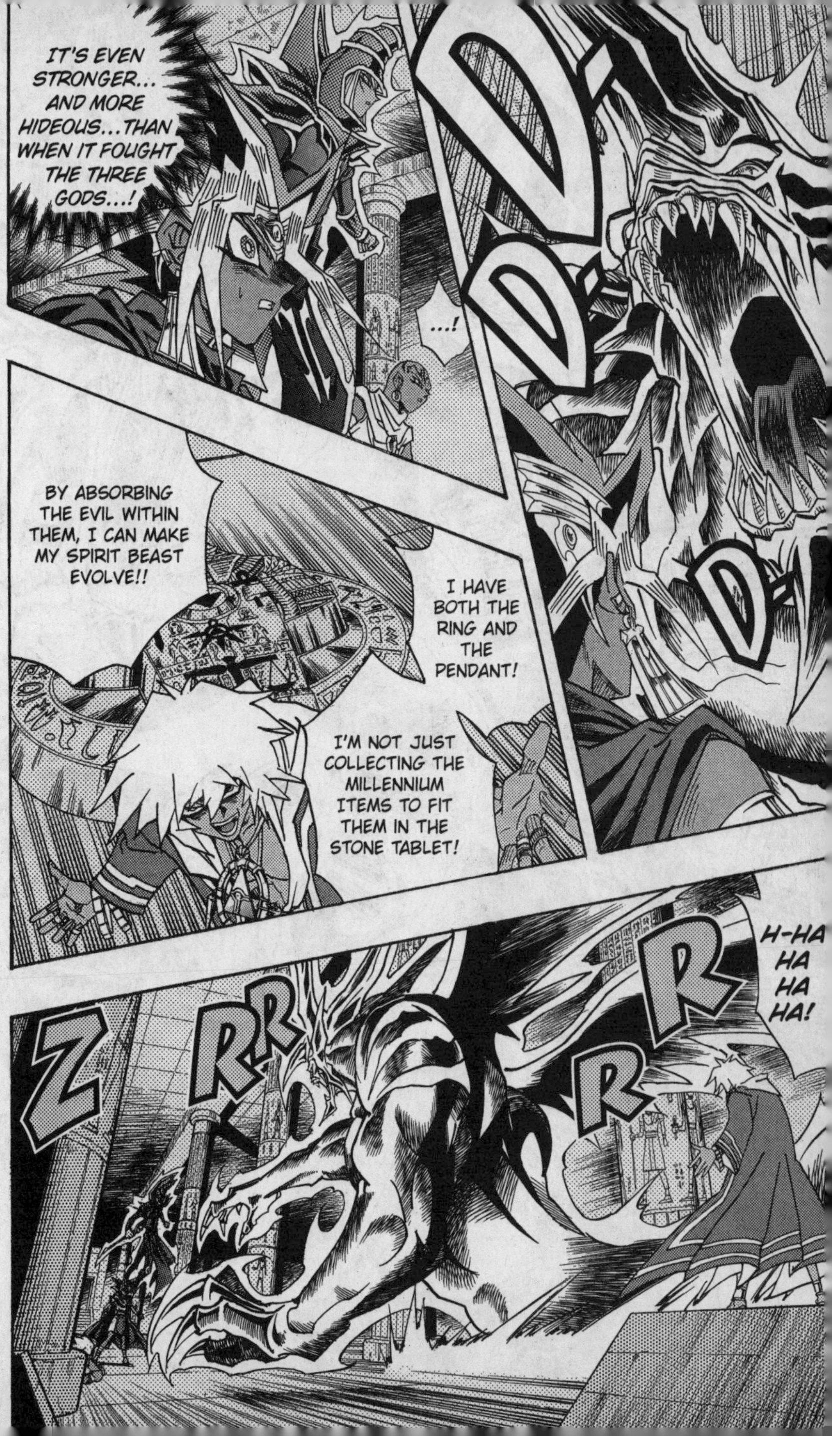
D D D
IT'S EVEN STRONGER... AND MORE HIDEOUS...THAN WHEN IT FOUGHT THE THREE GODS...!
...!
I HAVE BOTH THE RING AND THE PENDANT!
I'M NOT JUST COLLECTING THE MILLENNIUM ITEMS TO FIT THEM IN THE STONE TABLET!
BY ABSORBING THE EVIL WITHIN THEM, I CAN MAKE MY SPIRIT BEAST EVOLVE!!
H-HA HA HA HA!
Z RR R R

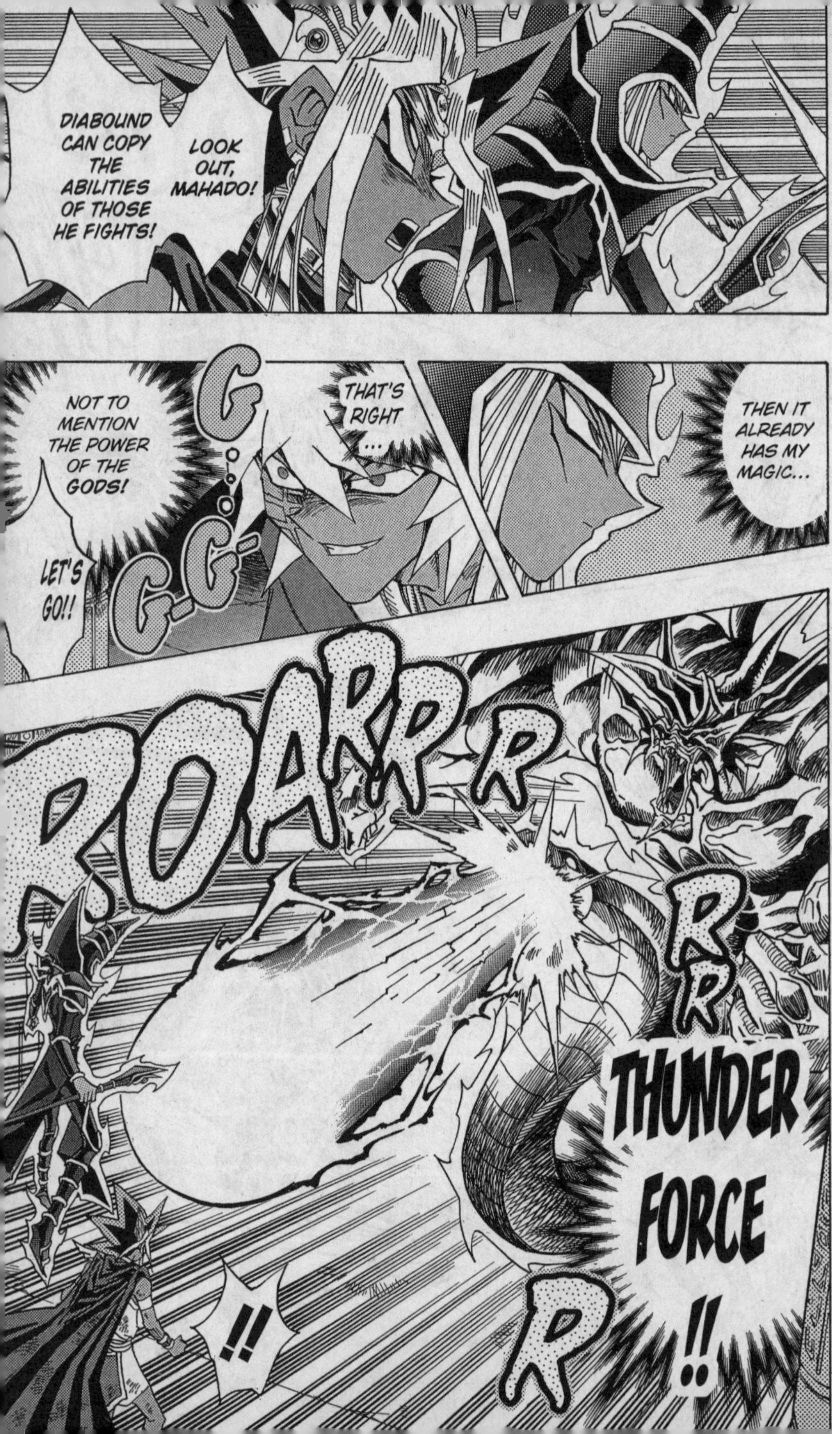
LOOK OUT, MAHADO!
DIABOUND CAN COPY THE ABILITIES OF THOSE HE FIGHTS!
THEN IT ALREADY HAS MY MAGIC...
THAT'S RIGHT...
NOT TO MENTION THE POWER OF THE GODS!
G-G-G
LET'S GO!!
ROARRRRRR
THUNDER FORCE!!
!!

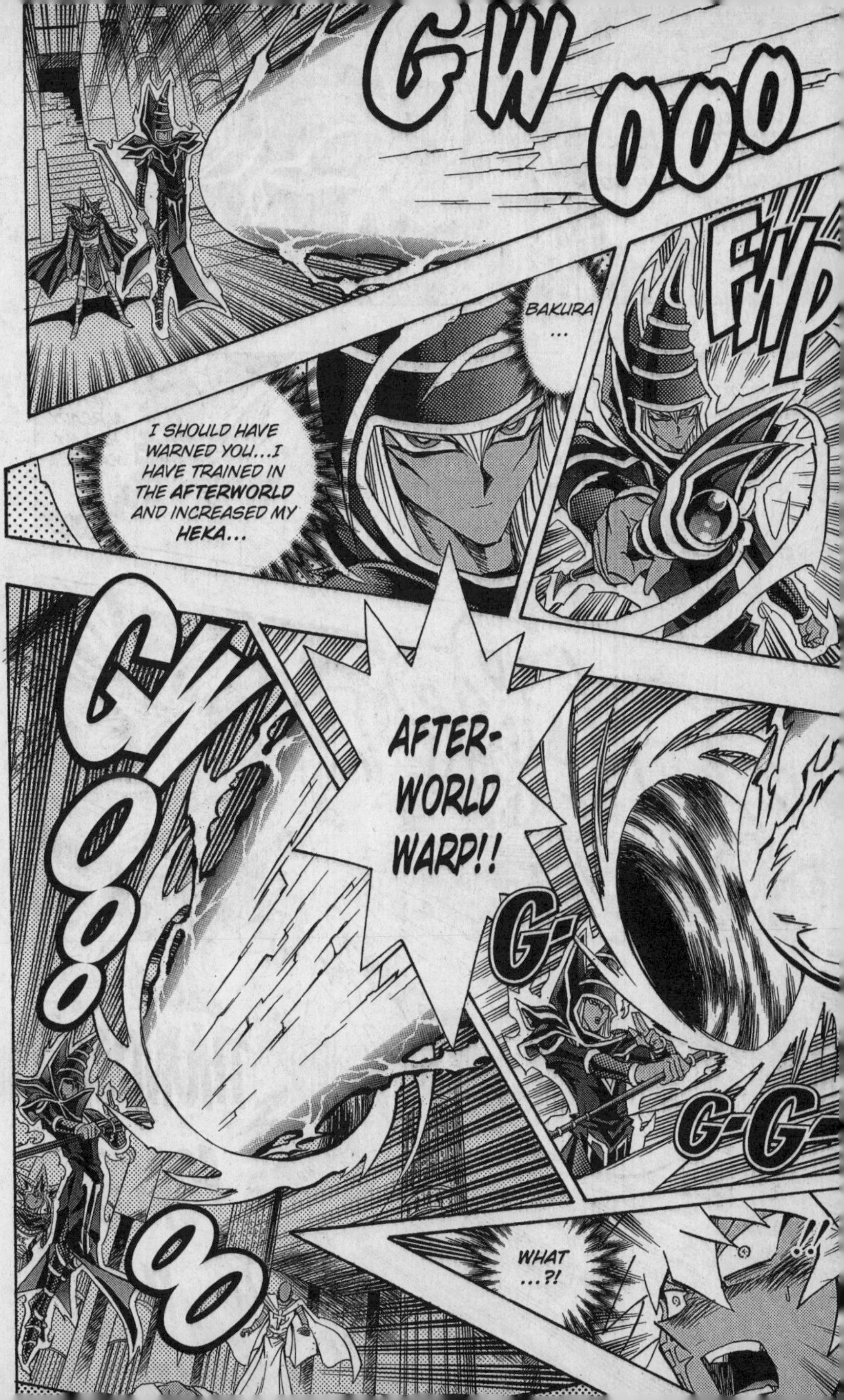
GWOOO
FWP
BAKURA …
I SHOULD HAVE WARNED YOU…I HAVE TRAINED IN THE AFTERWORLD AND INCREASED MY HEKA…
AFTER-WORLD WARP!!
G-
G-G-
GWOOOO
WHAT …?!

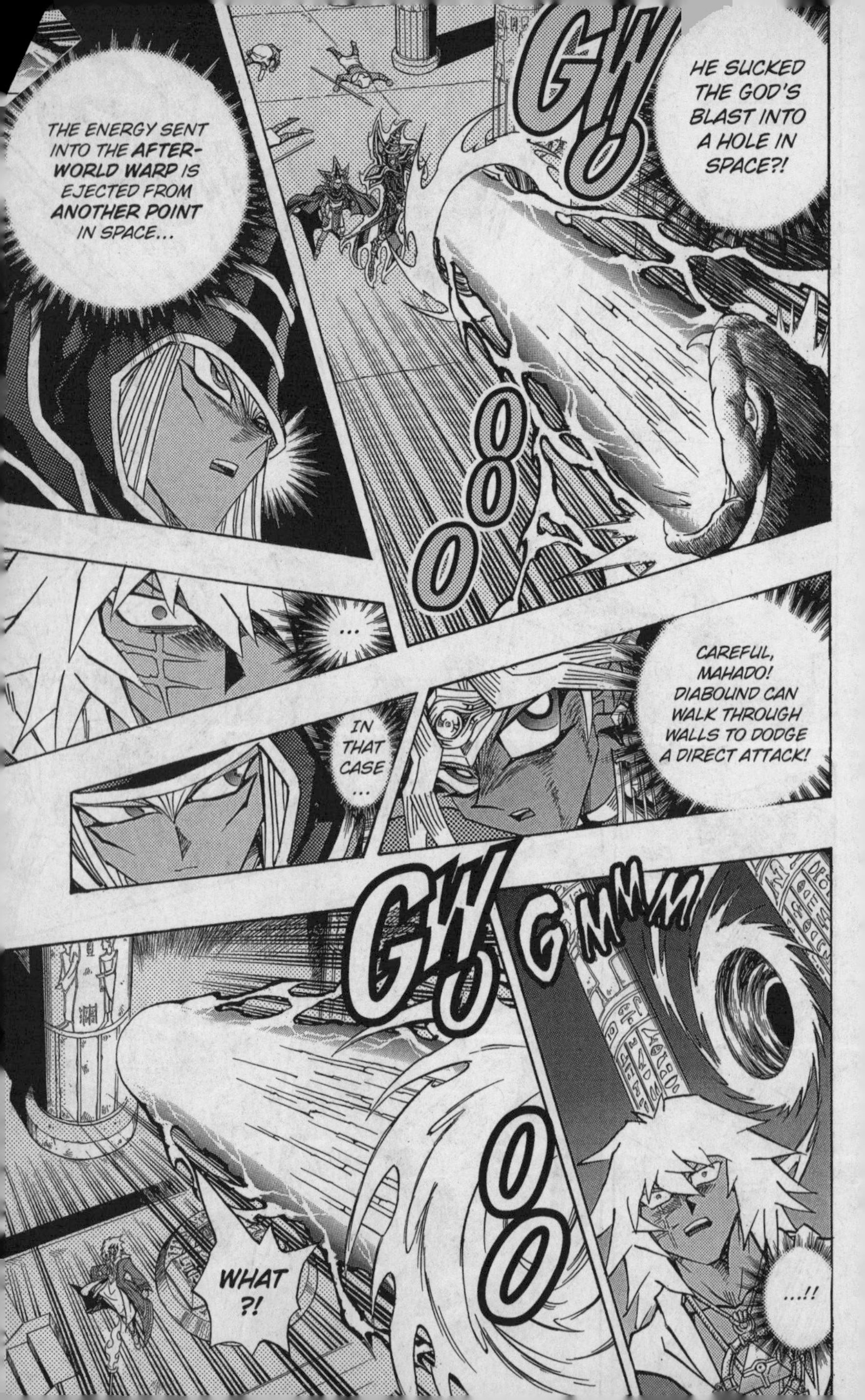
HE SUCKED THE GOD'S BLAST INTO A HOLE IN SPACE?!
GWOOOO
THE ENERGY SENT INTO THE AFTER-WORLD WARP IS EJECTED FROM ANOTHER POINT IN SPACE...
...
CAREFUL, MAHADO! DIABOUND CAN WALK THROUGH WALLS TO DODGE A DIRECT ATTACK!
IN THAT CASE...
GMMMM
GWOOOO
...!!
WHAT?!

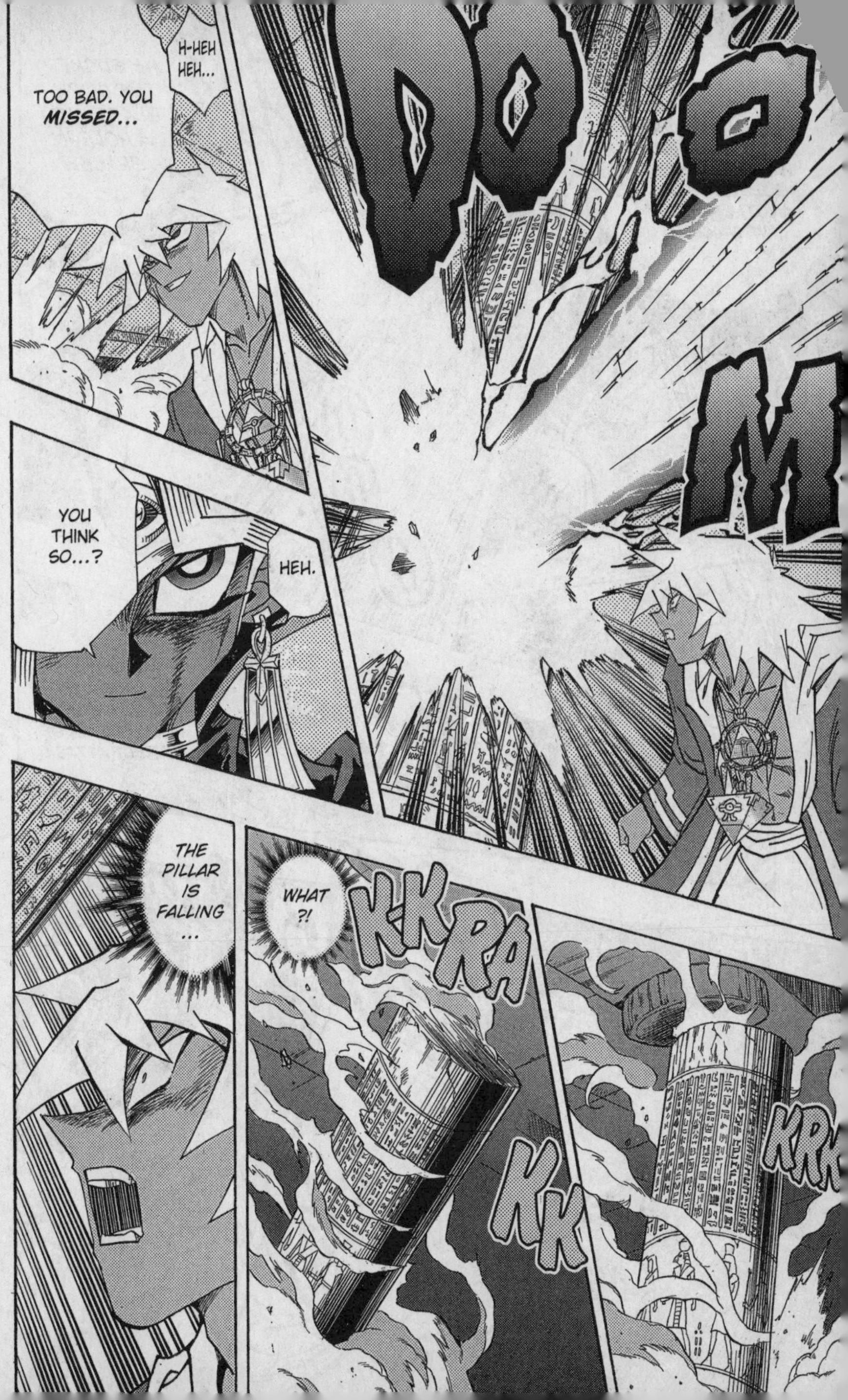
H-HEH HEH...
TOO BAD. YOU MISSED...
HEH.
YOU THINK SO...?
K-KRA
KK
WHAT ?!
THE PILLAR IS FALLING ...

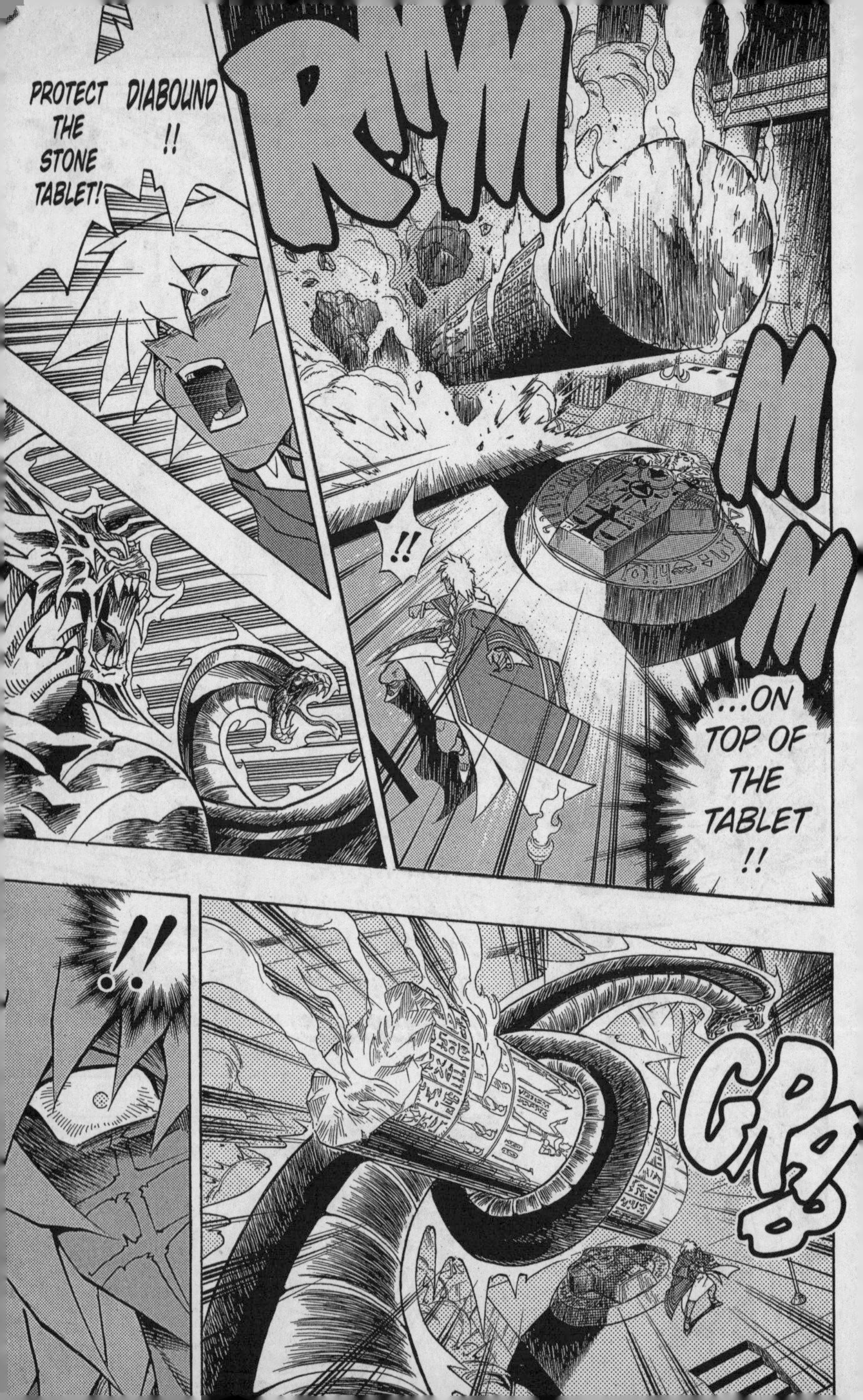
RMM
DIABOUND!!
PROTECT THE STONE TABLET!
!!
MM
...ON TOP OF THE TABLET!!
GRAB
!!

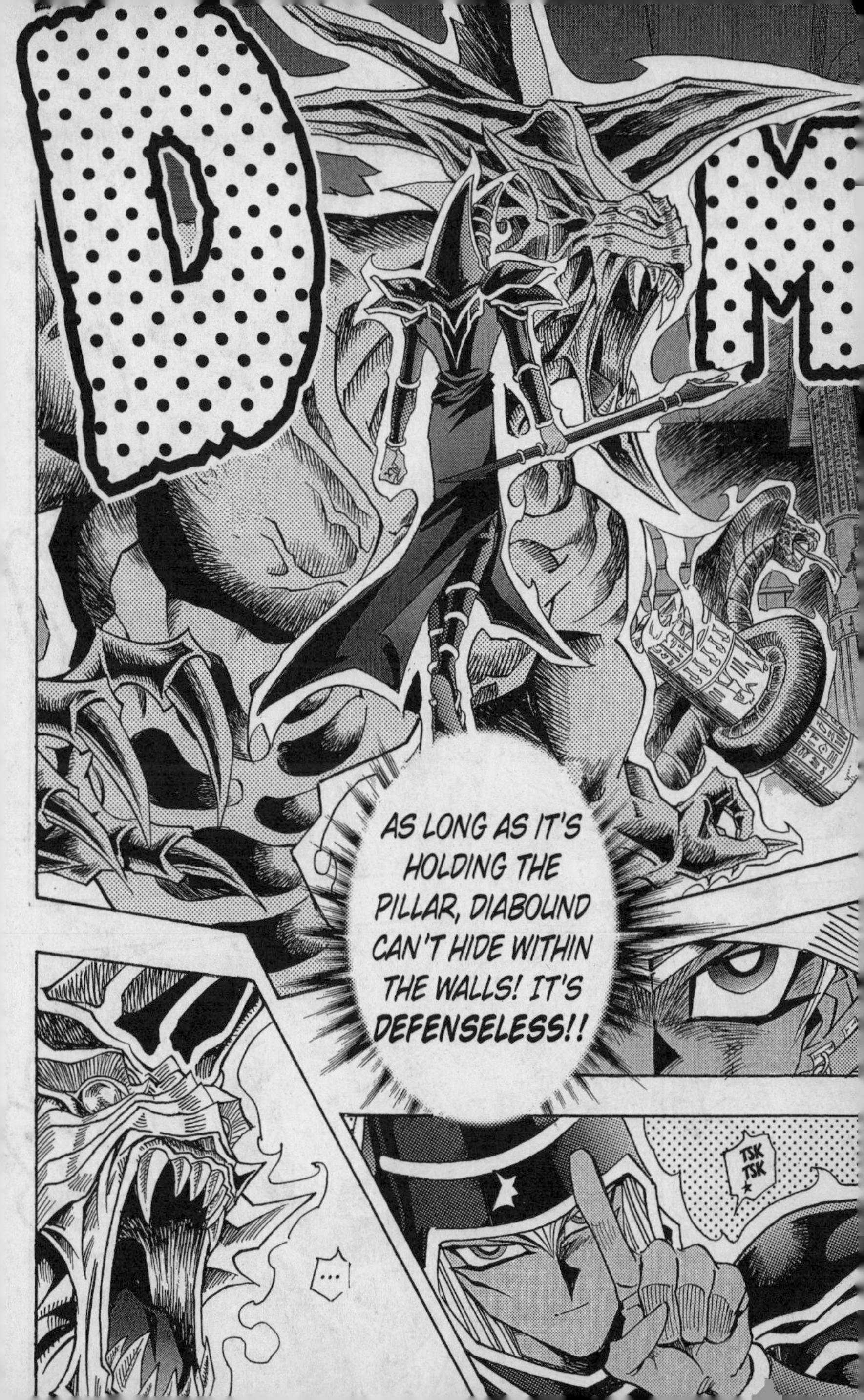
D
M
AS LONG AS IT'S HOLDING THE PILLAR, DIABOUND CAN'T HIDE WITHIN THE WALLS! IT'S DEFENSELESS!!
TSK TSK
...

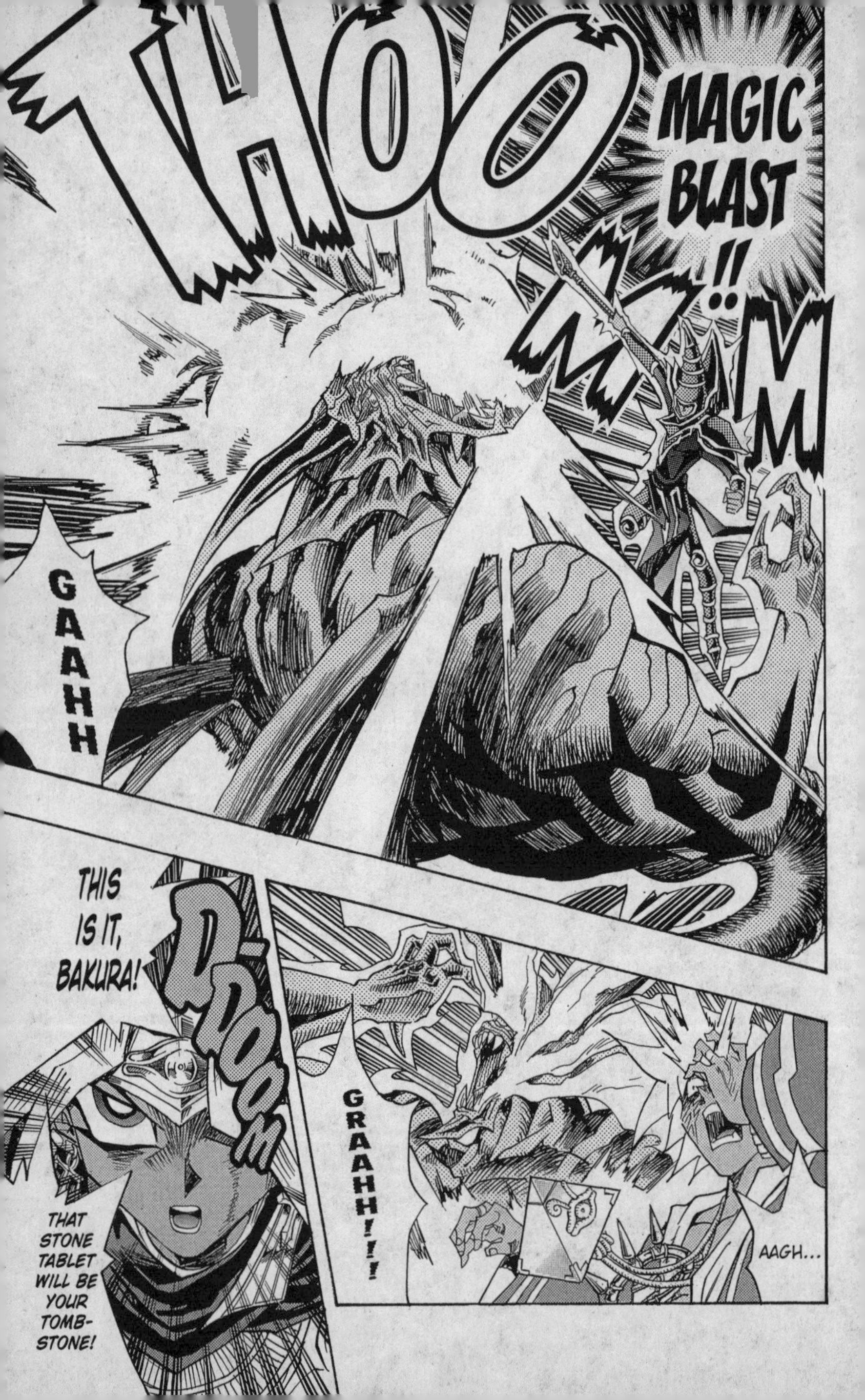
MAGIC BLAST!!
GAAHH
AAGH...
GRAAHH!!!
THIS IS IT, BAKURA!
THAT STONE TABLET WILL BE YOUR TOMB-STONE!

★ Guess what? At first I was planning to draw a horror comic!

IN THE PLANNING PHASE, YUGI LOOKED LIKE THIS!

★ He looks like a monster!

高橋和希

IT'S A BIT LATE, BUT I'D LIKE TO TELL YOU ABOUT MY EXPERIENCES AS A MANGA ARTIST. WHEN I WAS 19, I GOT LUCKY, AND ONE OF MY STORIES WON A CONTEST IN A CERTAIN SHONEN MANGA MAGAZINE. THAT WAS MY DEBUT.

BUT AFTER THAT, IT WAS TERRIBLE! I KEPT WRITING AND WRITING, BUT ALL I MADE WAS A MOUNTAIN OF REJECTED STORIES. I WENT THROUGH SEVERAL PUBLISHERS. TEN YEARS PASSED.

THEN, I STARTED *YU-GI-OH!* IN *WEEKLY SHONEN JUMP*, AND I'VE BEEN DRAWING IT FOR SEVEN YEARS. YOU SEE? IF YOU DON'T GIVE UP, YOU'LL GET THERE SOMEHOW!

—KAZUKI TAKAHASHI, 2004

SHONEN JUMP MANGA

YU-GI-OH! Millennium World

Vol. 36

TOMB OF SHADOWS

STORY AND ART BY

KAZUKI TAKAHASHI

THE MAIN CHARACTERS

KATSUYA JONOUCHI

BOBASA **ANZU MAZAKI** **HIROTO HONDA**

YUGI MUTOU

THE STORY SO FAR...

When he solved the Millennium Puzzle, 10th-grader Yugi developed an alter ego: Yu-Gi-Oh, the King of Games, the soul of a pharaoh from ancient Egypt! Discovering that the collectible card game "Duel Monsters" was of Egyptian origin, Yu-Gi-Oh collected the three Egyptian God Cards—Slifer the Sky Dragon, the God of the Obelisk, and the Sun Dragon Ra—and used them to travel into the "world of memories" of his own life 3,000 years ago. There, he found that he was the pharaoh, served by six priests who used the Millennium Items which had been created to save Egypt from invaders.

But unbeknownst even to the pharaoh, the Millennium Items were stained with blood. Created by the high priest Akhenaden, the Millennium Items were powered by human souls—the souls of the village of Kul Elna, which had been ritually slaughtered by troops under Akhenaden's command! Bakura, the sole survivor of Kul Elna, grew up into a revenge-obsessed madman. His goal: to gather the seven Millennium Items and summon the dark god Zorc Necrophades, so he can rule the world!

Bakura attacked the pharaoh and his priests, stealing the Millennium Ring and the Millennium Puzzle. But instead of stealing Akhenaden's Millennium Eye, he infused part of his own spirit into it, bringing Akhenaden's latent evil back to life. Filled with jealousy, Akhenaden began to plot against the pharaoh, and his dark side took on a life of its own.

Meanwhile, with the help of the Egyptian mystic Bobasa, Yugi and his friends followed Yu-Gi-Oh into the "world of memories." Their goal: to help the pharaoh by finding his forgotten name. But can they save Yu-Gi-Oh from Bakura in a deadly final fight in the Village of Kul Elna itself…?

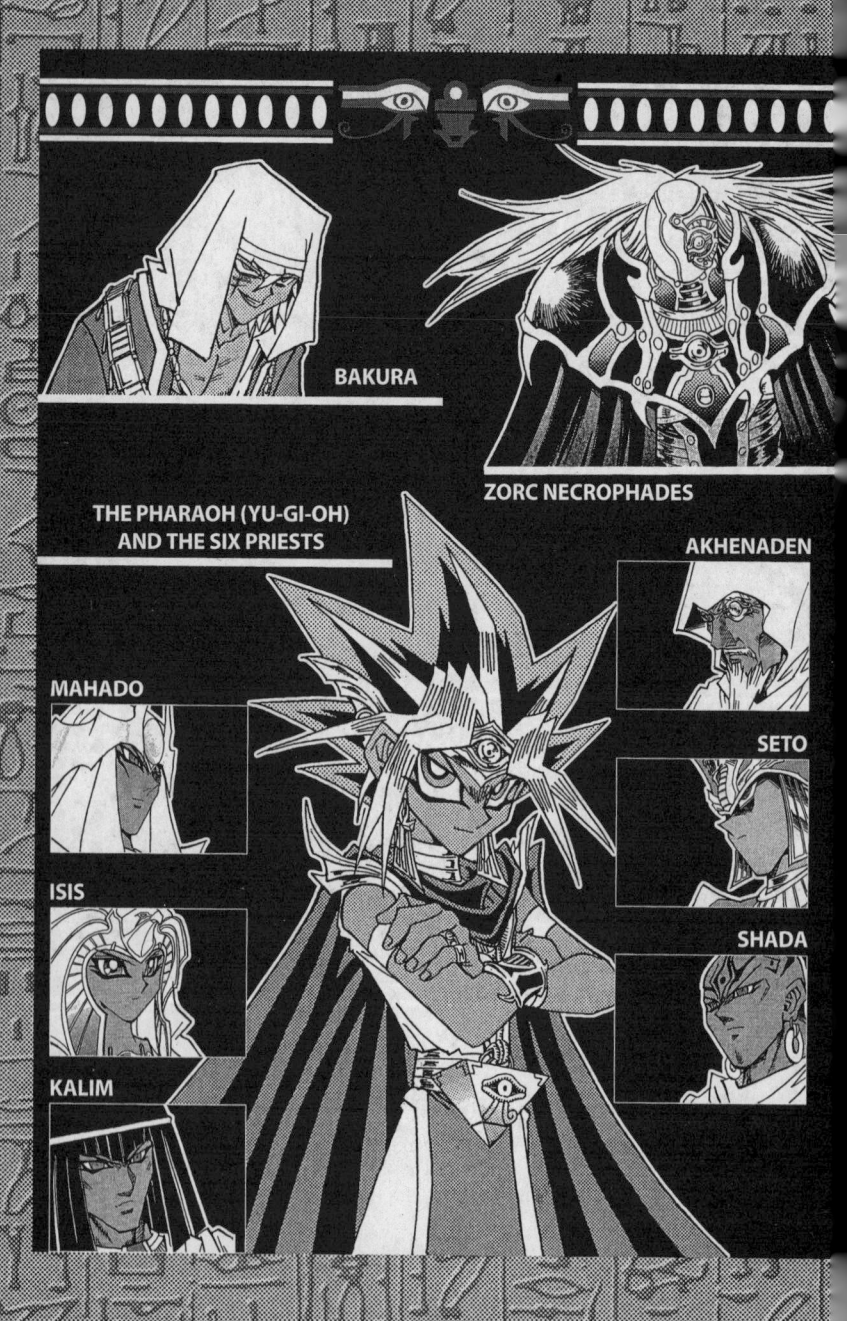

BAKURA

ZORC NECROPHADES

THE PHARAOH (YU-GI-OH)
AND THE SIX PRIESTS

AKHENADEN

MAHADO

SETO

ISIS

SHADA

KALIM

Yu-Gi-Oh! Millennium World

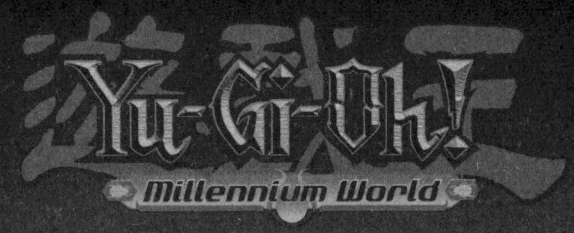

Vol. 36

CONTENTS

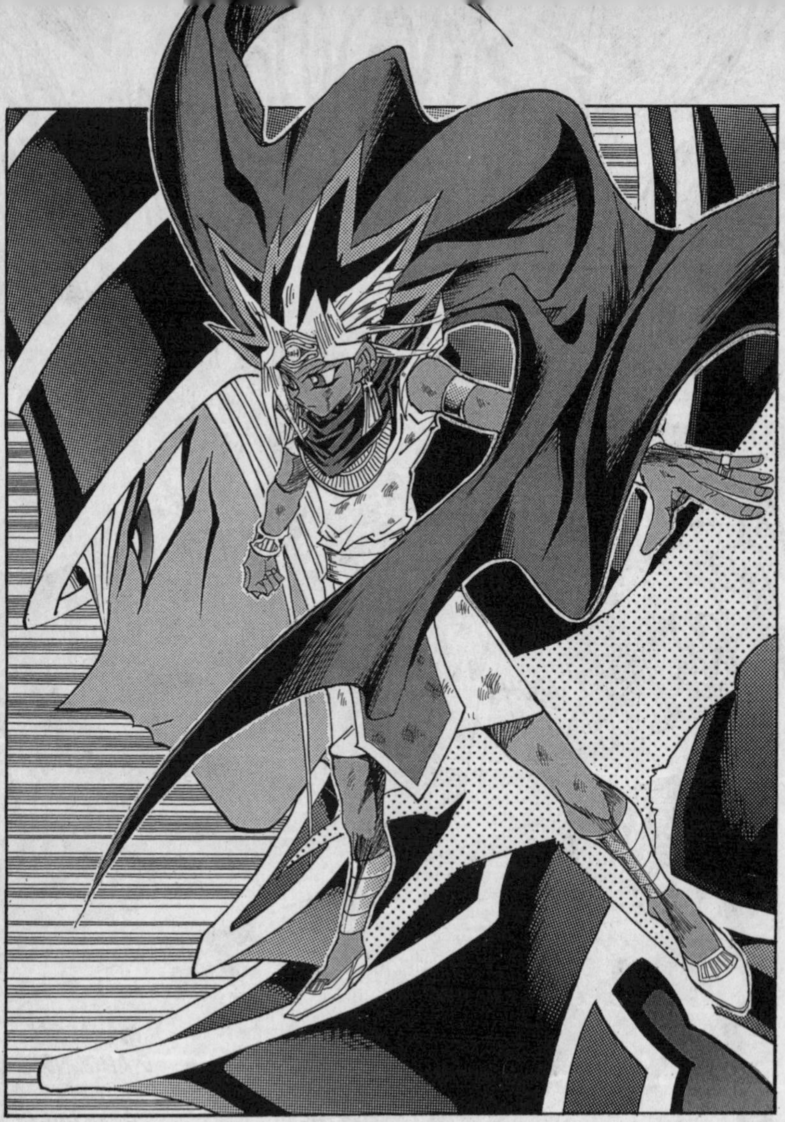

Duel 315:
Shadow Camouflage!!

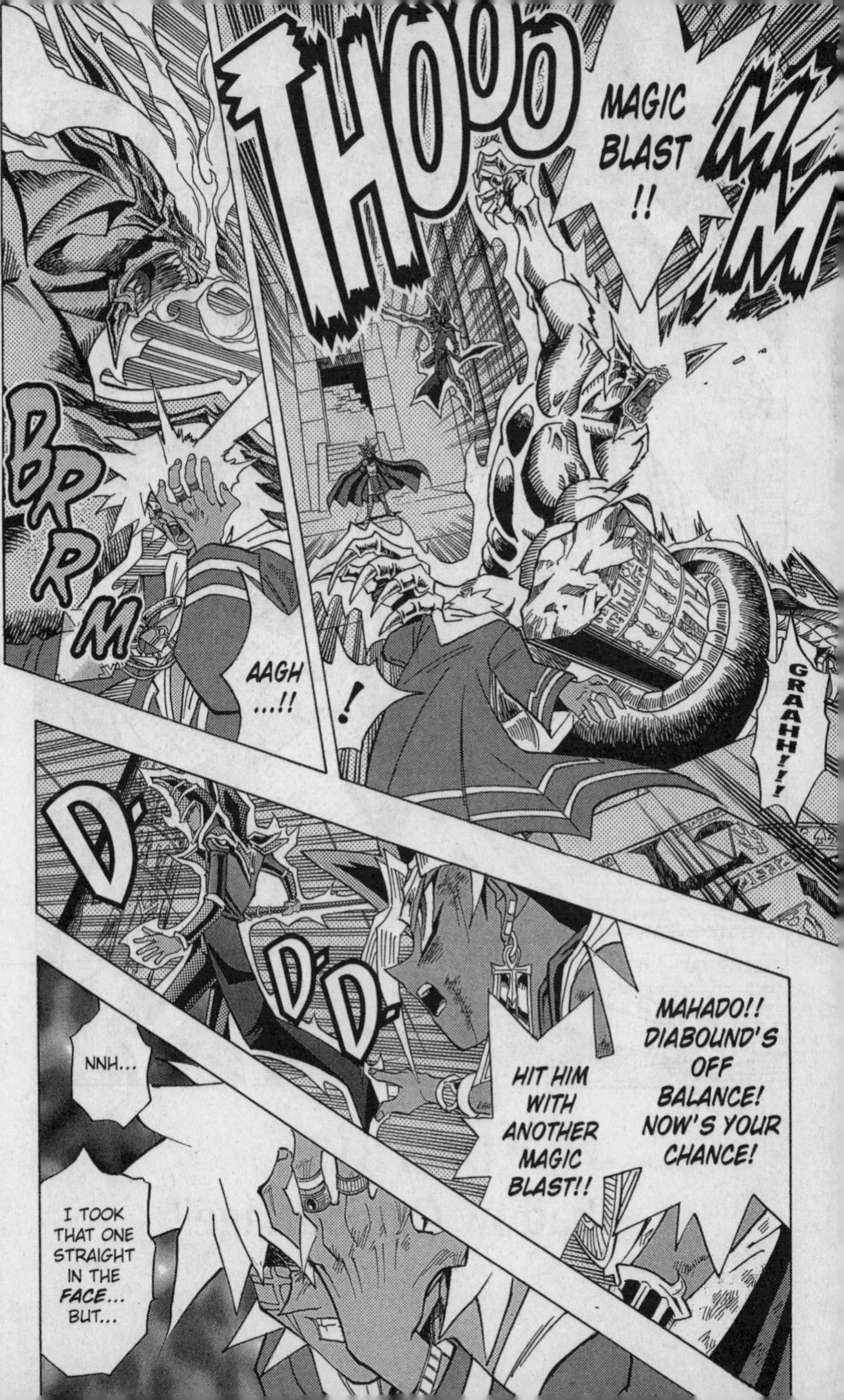
THOOOMMM
MAGIC BLAST !!
GRAAHH!!!
!
AAGH ...!!
BRRM
D
D D
MAHADO!! DIABOUND'S OFF BALANCE! NOW'S YOUR CHANCE!
HIT HIM WITH ANOTHER MAGIC BLAST!!
NNH...
I TOOK THAT ONE STRAIGHT IN THE FACE... BUT...

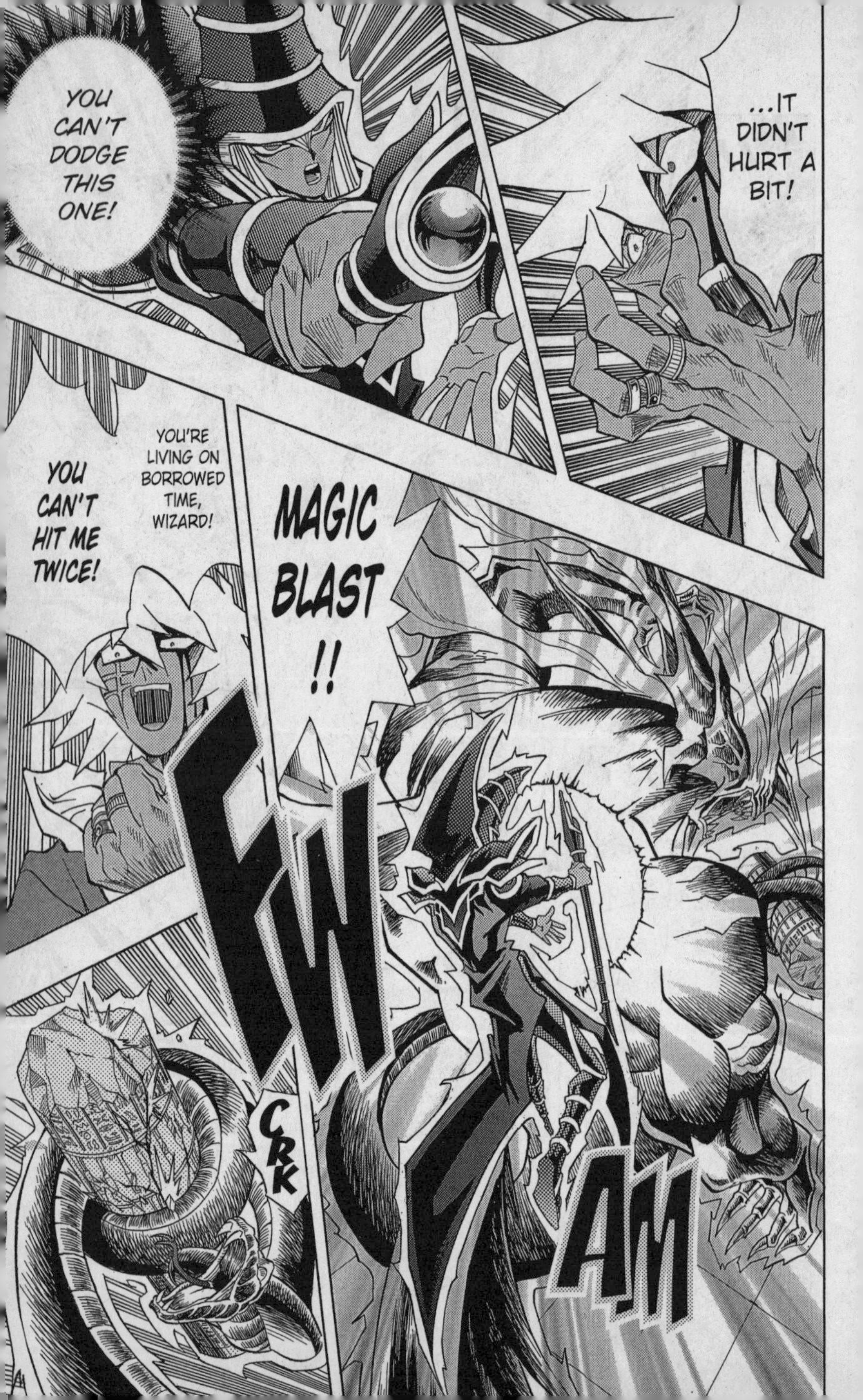
...IT DIDN'T HURT A BIT!
YOU CAN'T DODGE THIS ONE!
MAGIC BLAST!!
YOU'RE LIVING ON BORROWED TIME, WIZARD!
YOU CAN'T HIT ME TWICE!
CRK
AM

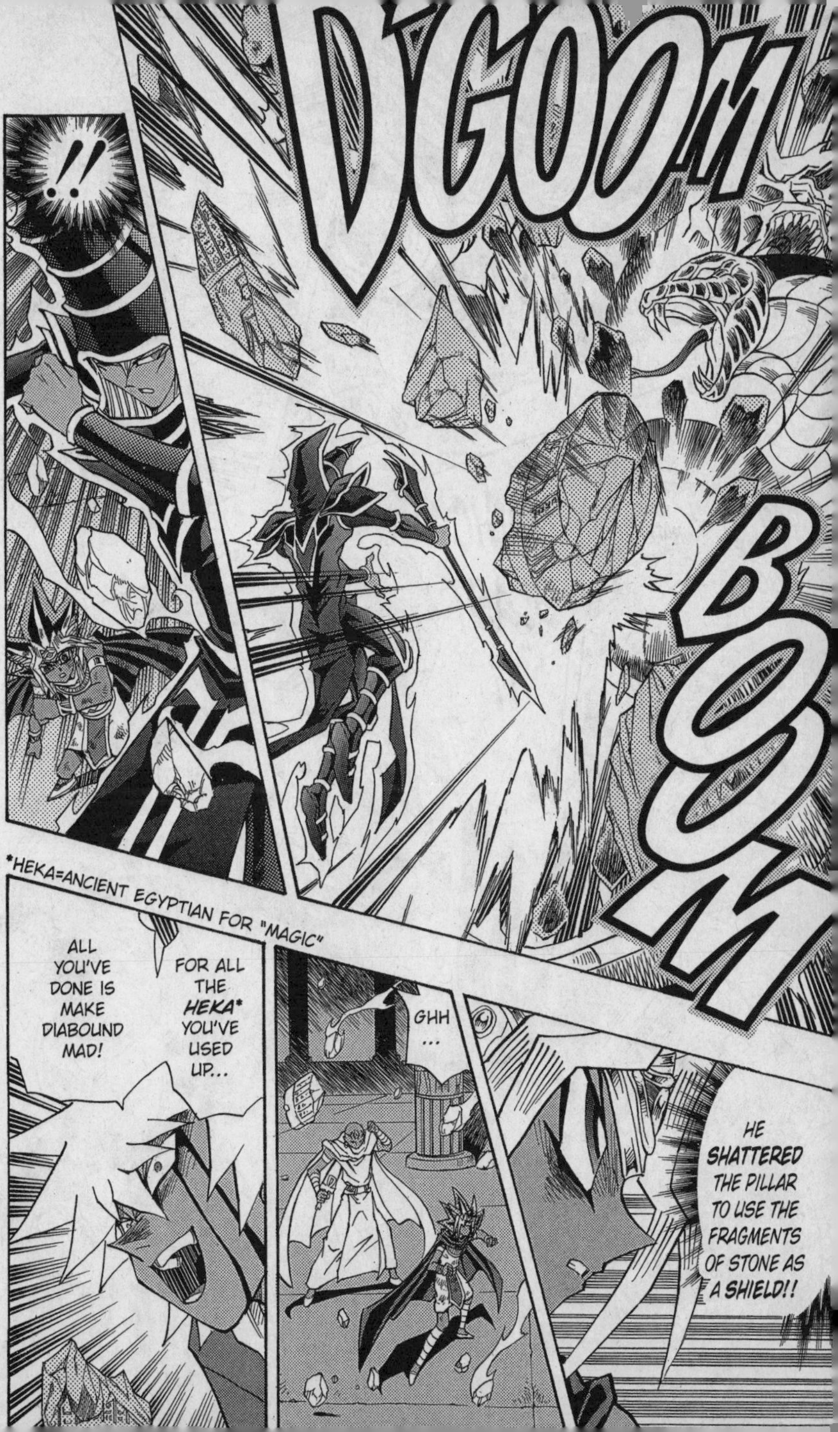

D'GOOM
!!
BOOM
*HEKA=ANCIENT EGYPTIAN FOR "MAGIC"
HE SHATTERED THE PILLAR TO USE THE FRAGMENTS OF STONE AS A SHIELD!!
GHH...
FOR ALL THE HEKA* YOU'VE USED UP...
ALL YOU'VE DONE IS MAKE DIABOUND MAD!

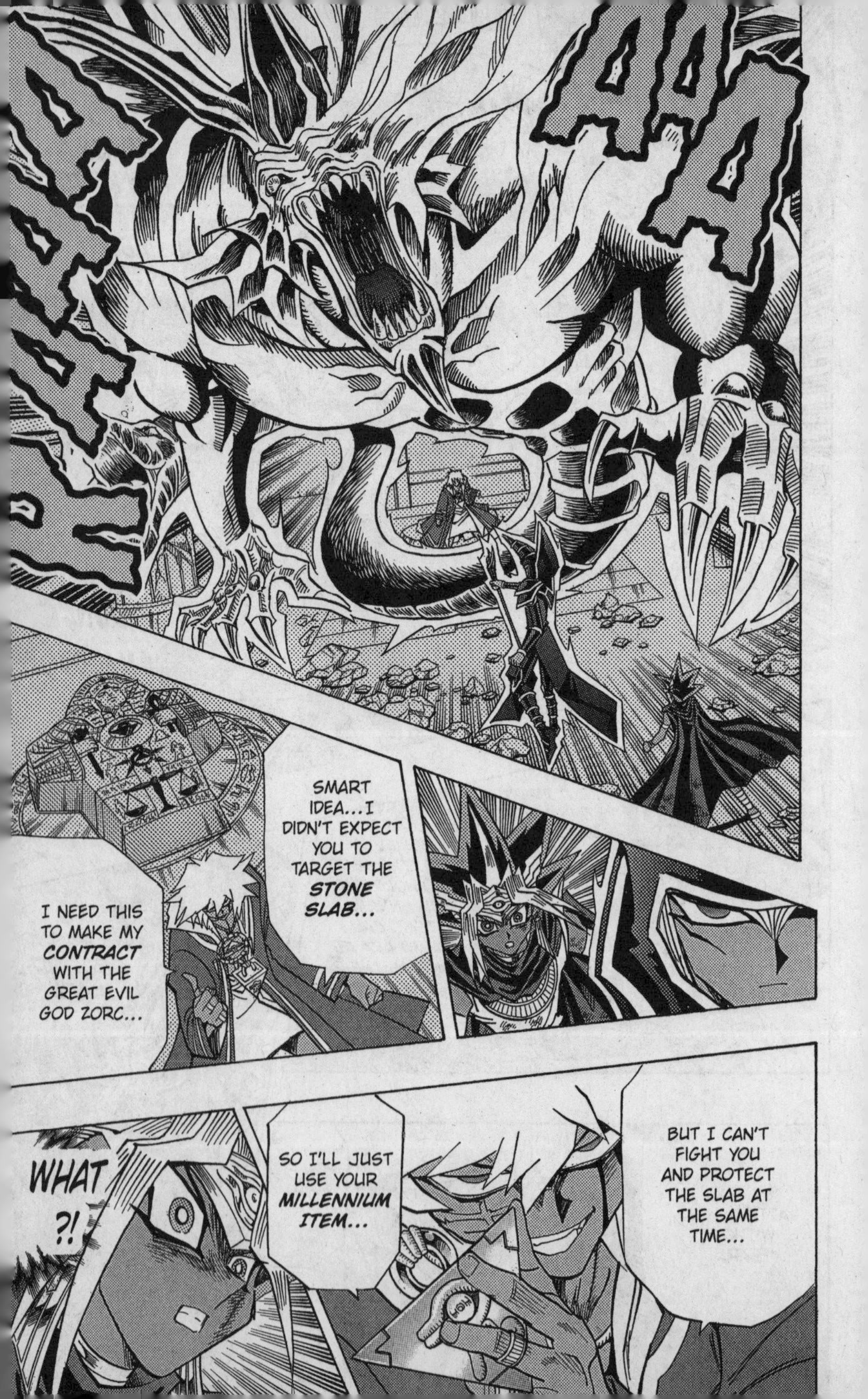
SMART IDEA...I DIDN'T EXPECT YOU TO TARGET THE STONE SLAB...
I NEED THIS TO MAKE MY CONTRACT WITH THE GREAT EVIL GOD ZORC...
BUT I CAN'T FIGHT YOU AND PROTECT THE SLAB AT THE SAME TIME...
SO I'LL JUST USE YOUR MILLENNIUM ITEM...
WHAT ?!

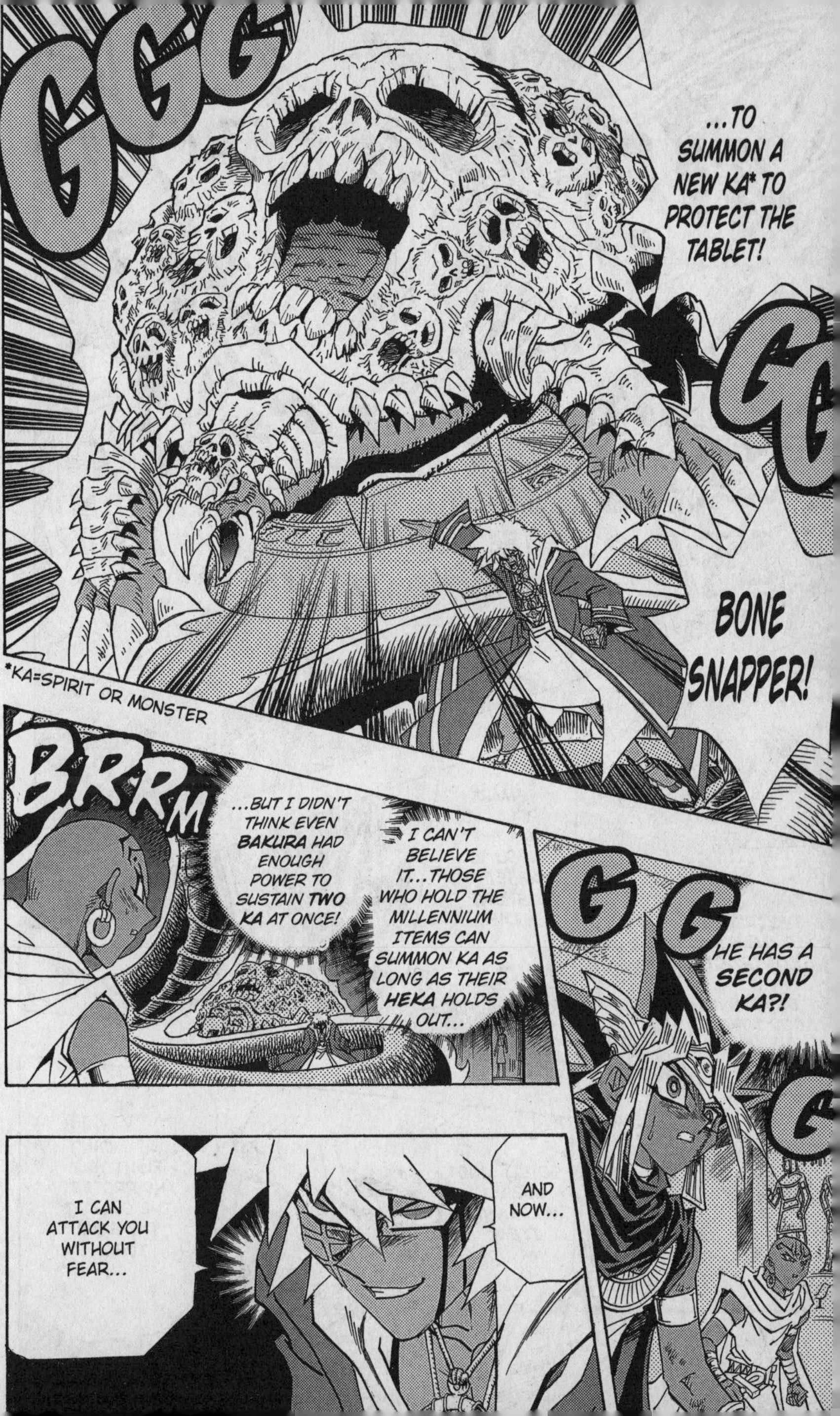
GGG
...TO SUMMON A NEW KA* TO PROTECT THE TABLET!
GG
BONE SNAPPER!
*KA=SPIRIT OR MONSTER
GG
HE HAS A SECOND KA?!
BRRM
I CAN'T BELIEVE IT...THOSE WHO HOLD THE MILLENNIUM ITEMS CAN SUMMON KA AS LONG AS THEIR HEKA HOLDS OUT...
...BUT I DIDN'T THINK EVEN BAKURA HAD ENOUGH POWER TO SUSTAIN TWO KA AT ONCE!
G
AND NOW...
I CAN ATTACK YOU WITHOUT FEAR...

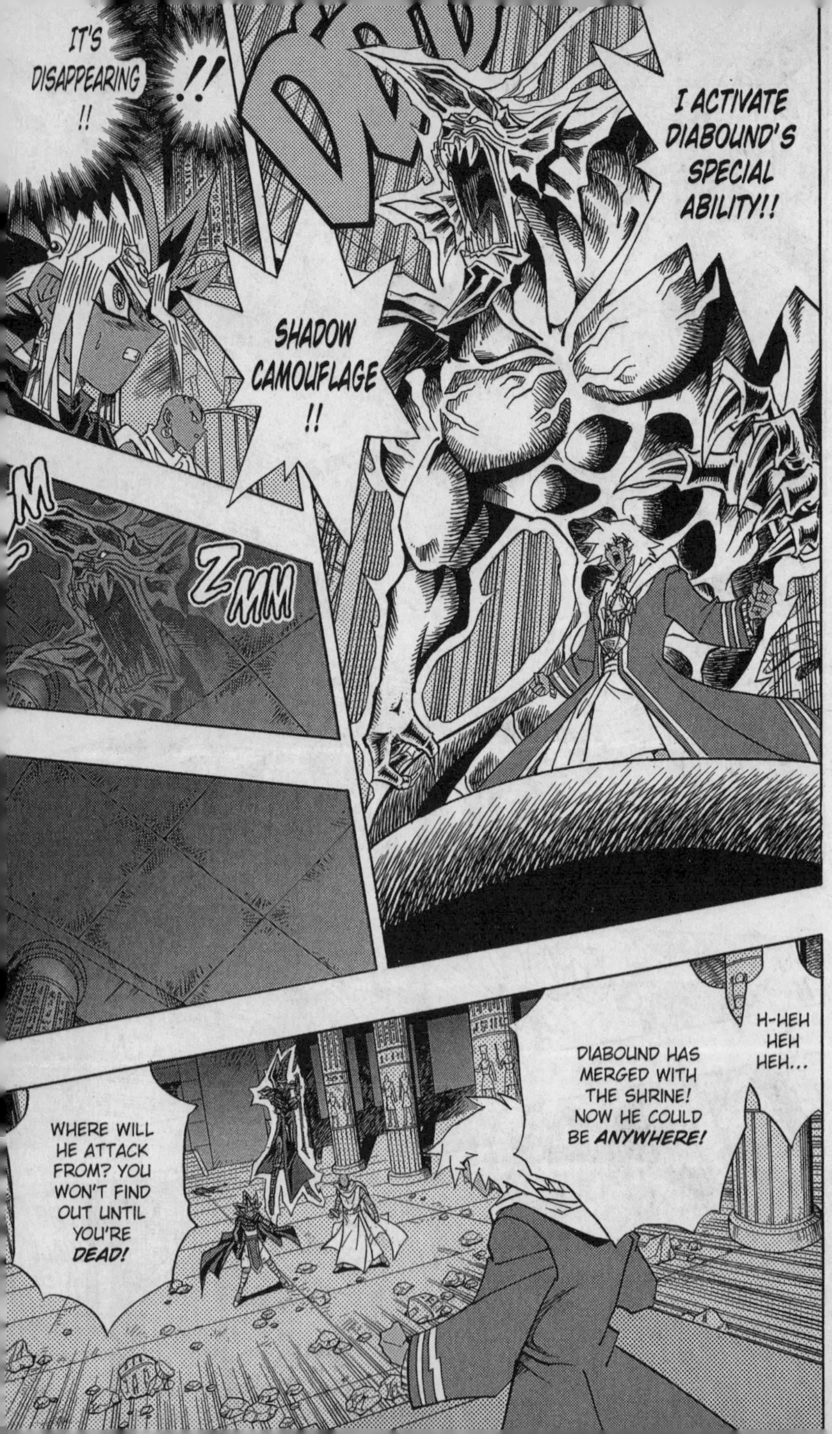
I ACTIVATE DIABOUND'S SPECIAL ABILITY!!
!!
IT'S DISAPPEARING!!
SHADOW CAMOUFLAGE!!
ZMM
H-HEH HEH HEH...
DIABOUND HAS MERGED WITH THE SHRINE! NOW HE COULD BE ANYWHERE!
WHERE WILL HE ATTACK FROM? YOU WON'T FIND OUT UNTIL YOU'RE DEAD!

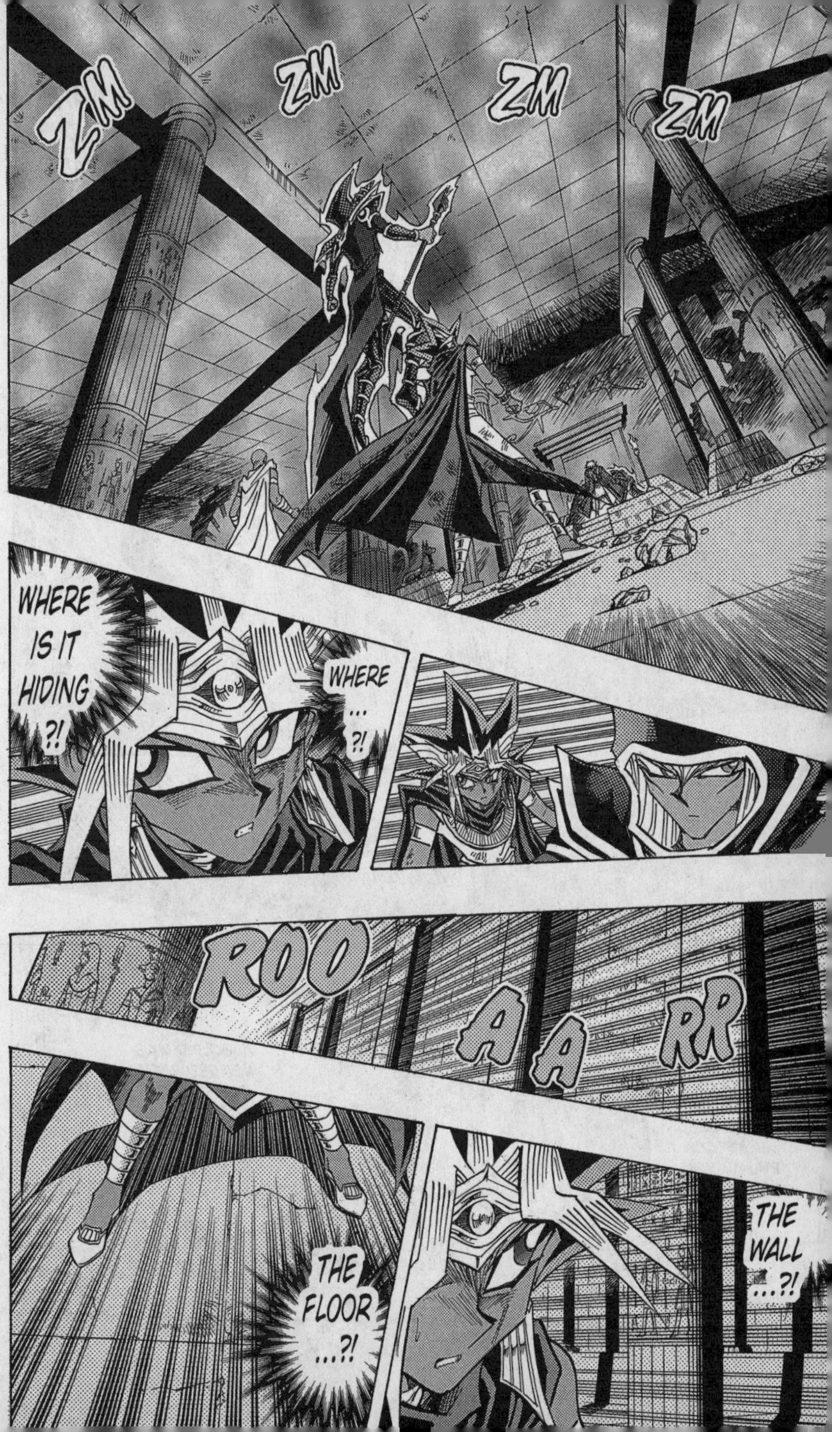

ZM
ZM
ZM
ZM
WHERE ...?!
WHERE IS IT HIDING ?!
ROO A A RR
THE WALL ...?!
THE FLOOR ...?!

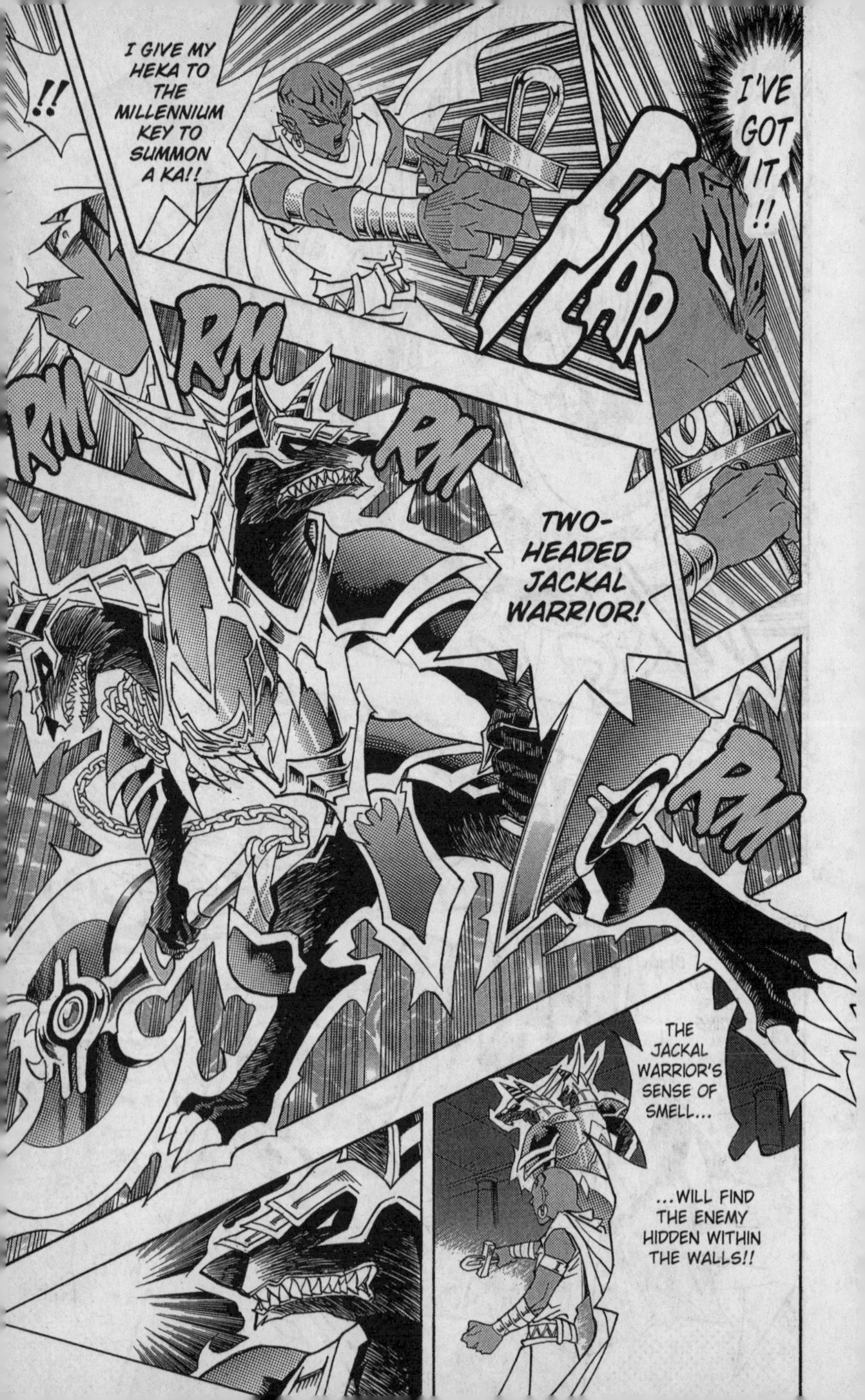
I'VE GOT IT!!
CAP
I GIVE MY HEKA TO THE MILLENNIUM KEY TO SUMMON A KA!!
!!
RM
RM
RM
TWO-HEADED JACKAL WARRIOR!
RM
THE JACKAL WARRIOR'S SENSE OF SMELL...
...WILL FIND THE ENEMY HIDDEN WITHIN THE WALLS!!

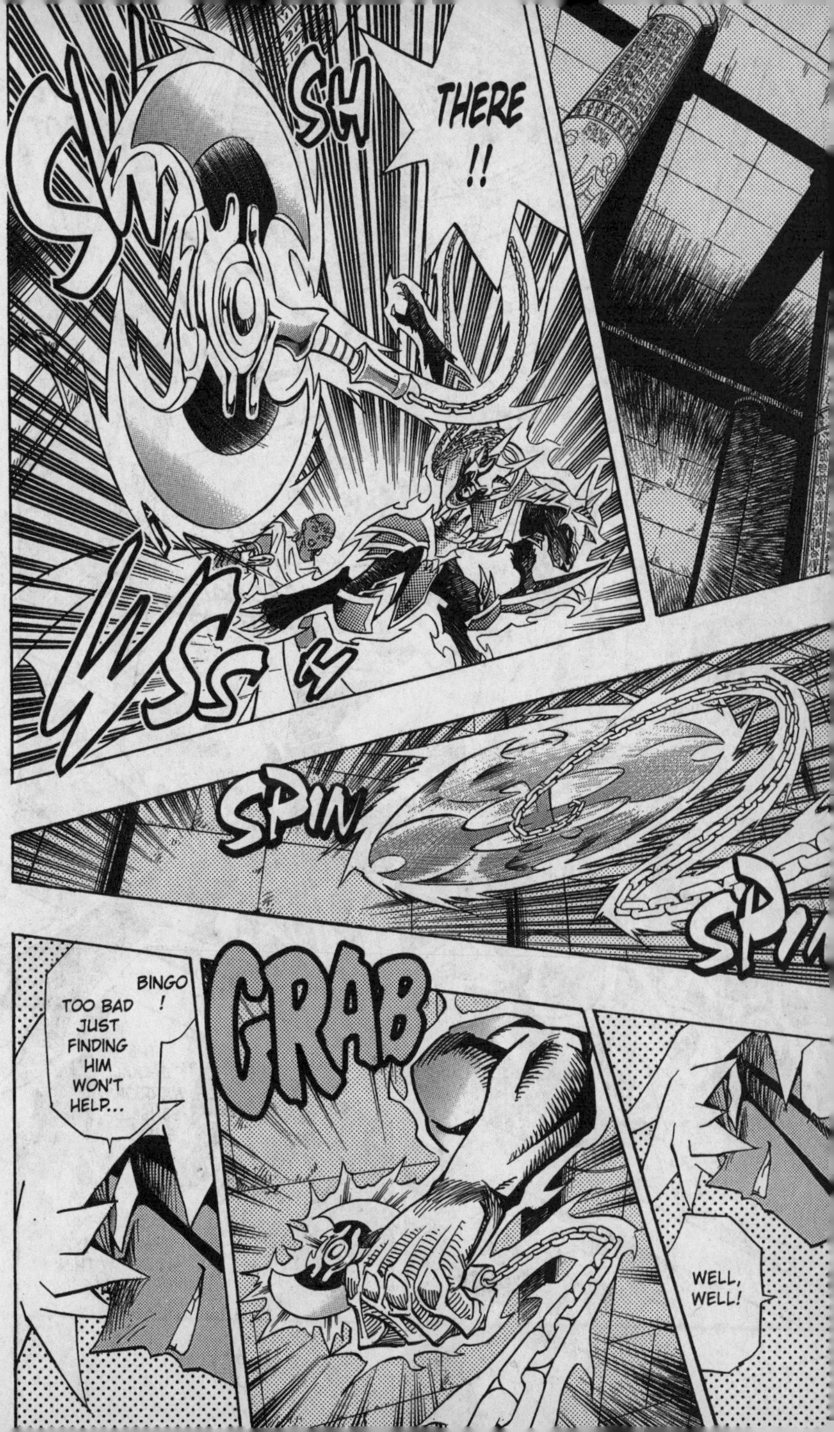
THERE!!
SWOOSH
WSSH
SPIN
SPIN
GRAB
BINGO!
TOO BAD JUST FINDING HIM WON'T HELP...
WELL, WELL!

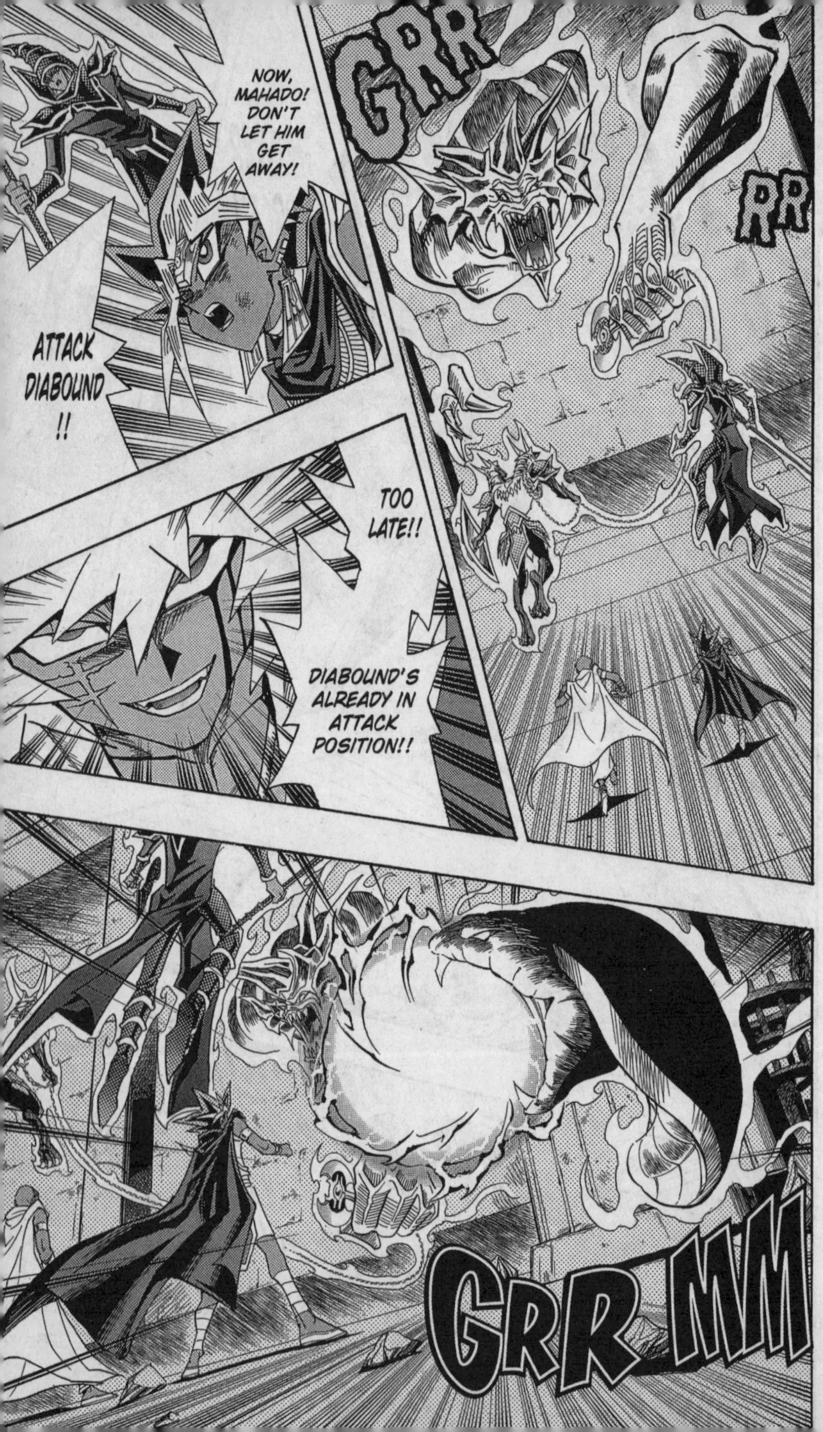
GRR
RR
NOW, MAHADO! DON'T LET HIM GET AWAY!
ATTACK DIABOUND!!
TOO LATE!!
DIABOUND'S ALREADY IN ATTACK POSITION!!
GRR MM

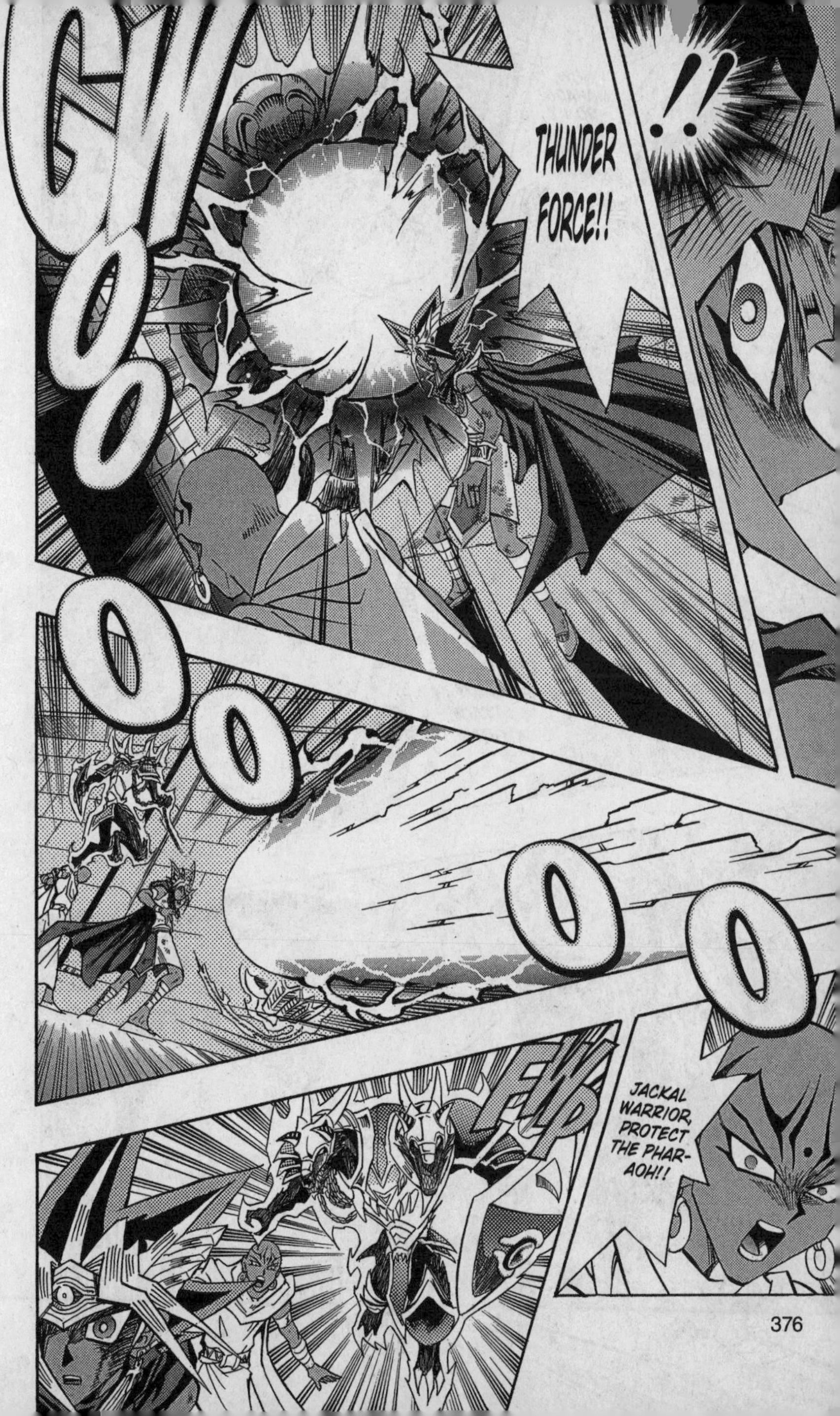
!!
THUNDER FORCE!!
GOOOOOOOO
JACKAL WARRIOR, PROTECT THE PHARAOH!!
FWP

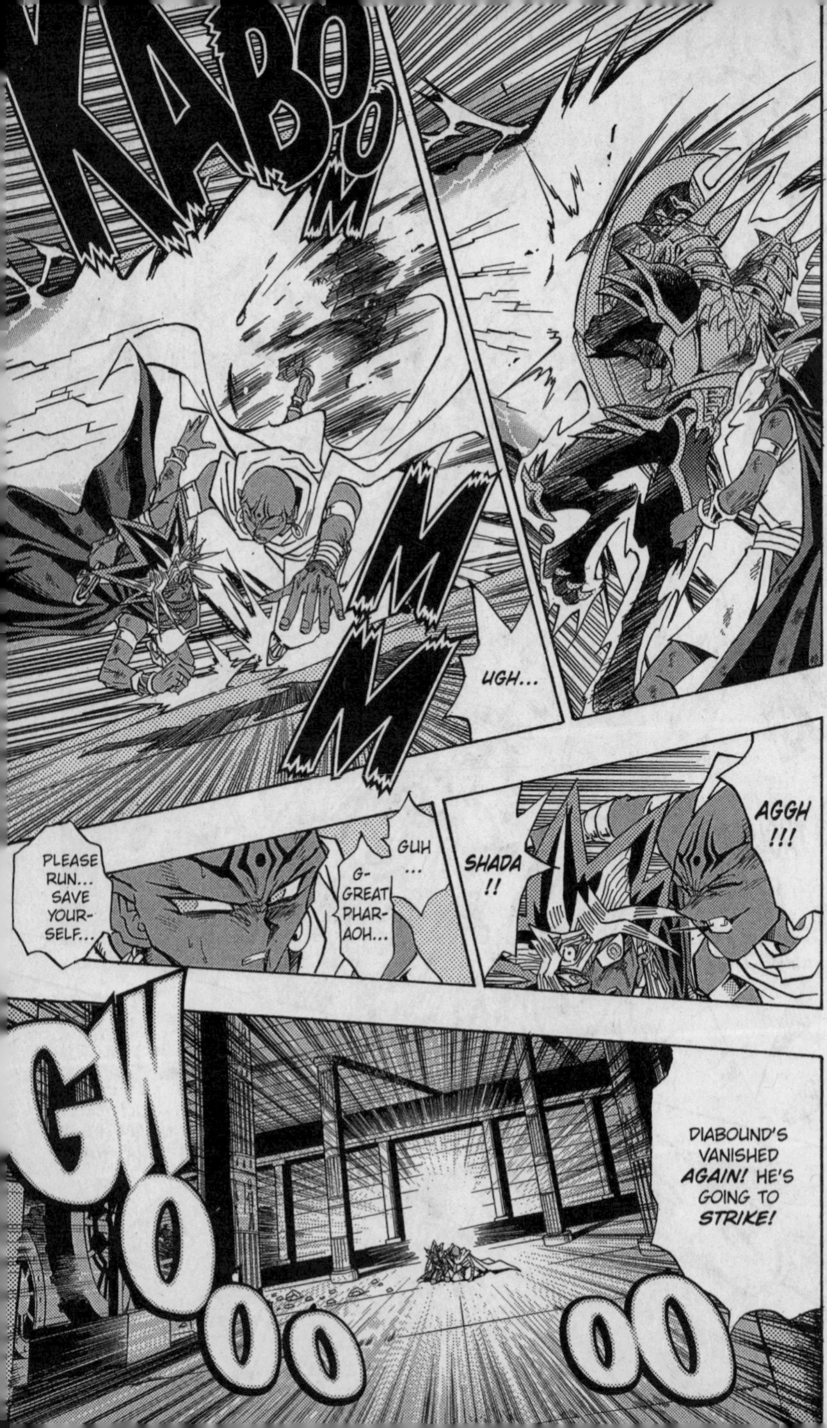
KABOOOM
UGH...
MMM
AGGH!!!
SHADA!!
GUH...
G-GREAT PHARAOH...
PLEASE RUN... SAVE YOURSELF...
DIABOUND'S VANISHED AGAIN! HE'S GOING TO STRIKE!
GWOOOOO

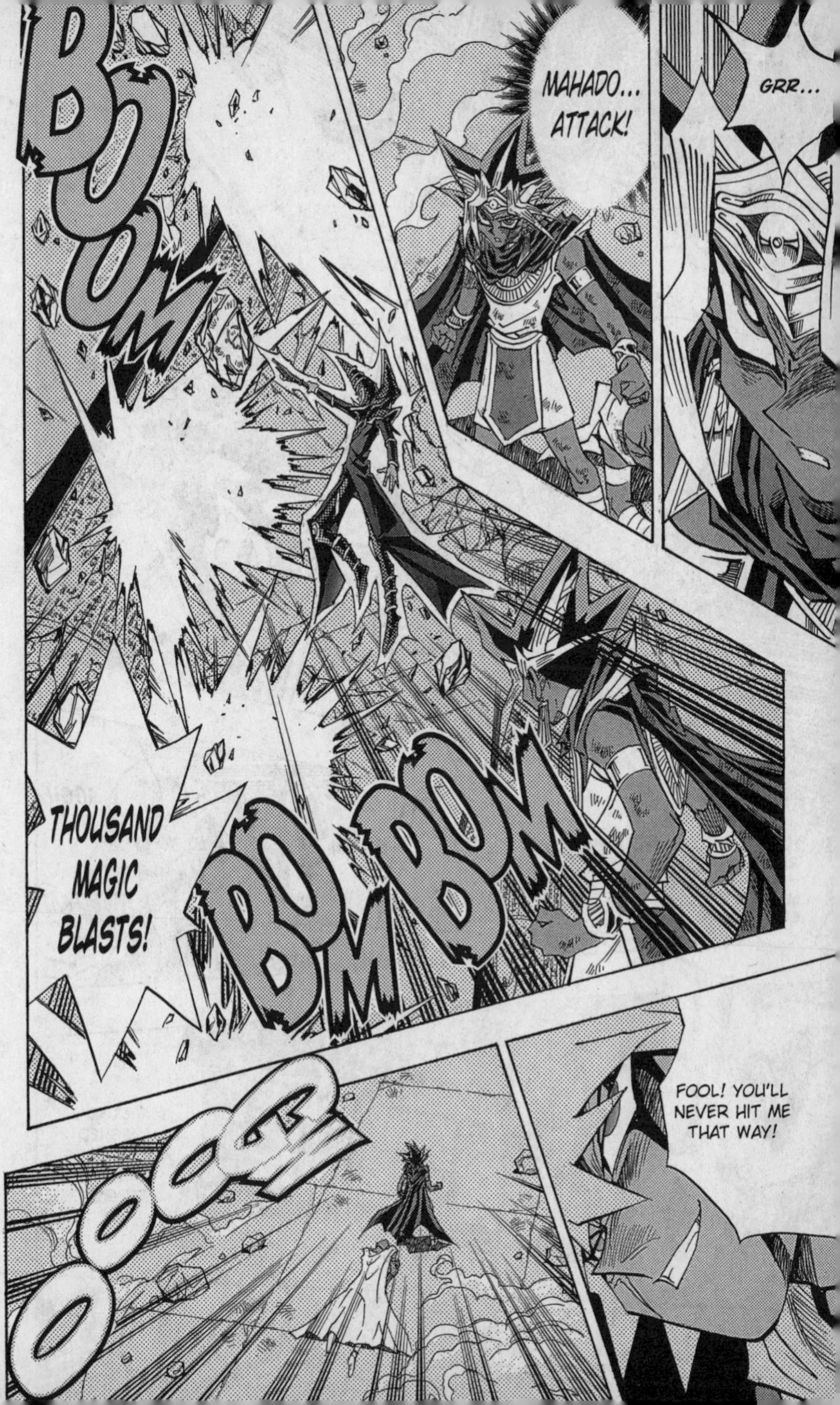
GRR...
MAHADO... ATTACK!
BOOM
THOUSAND MAGIC BLASTS!
BOM BOM
FOOL! YOU'LL NEVER HIT ME THAT WAY!

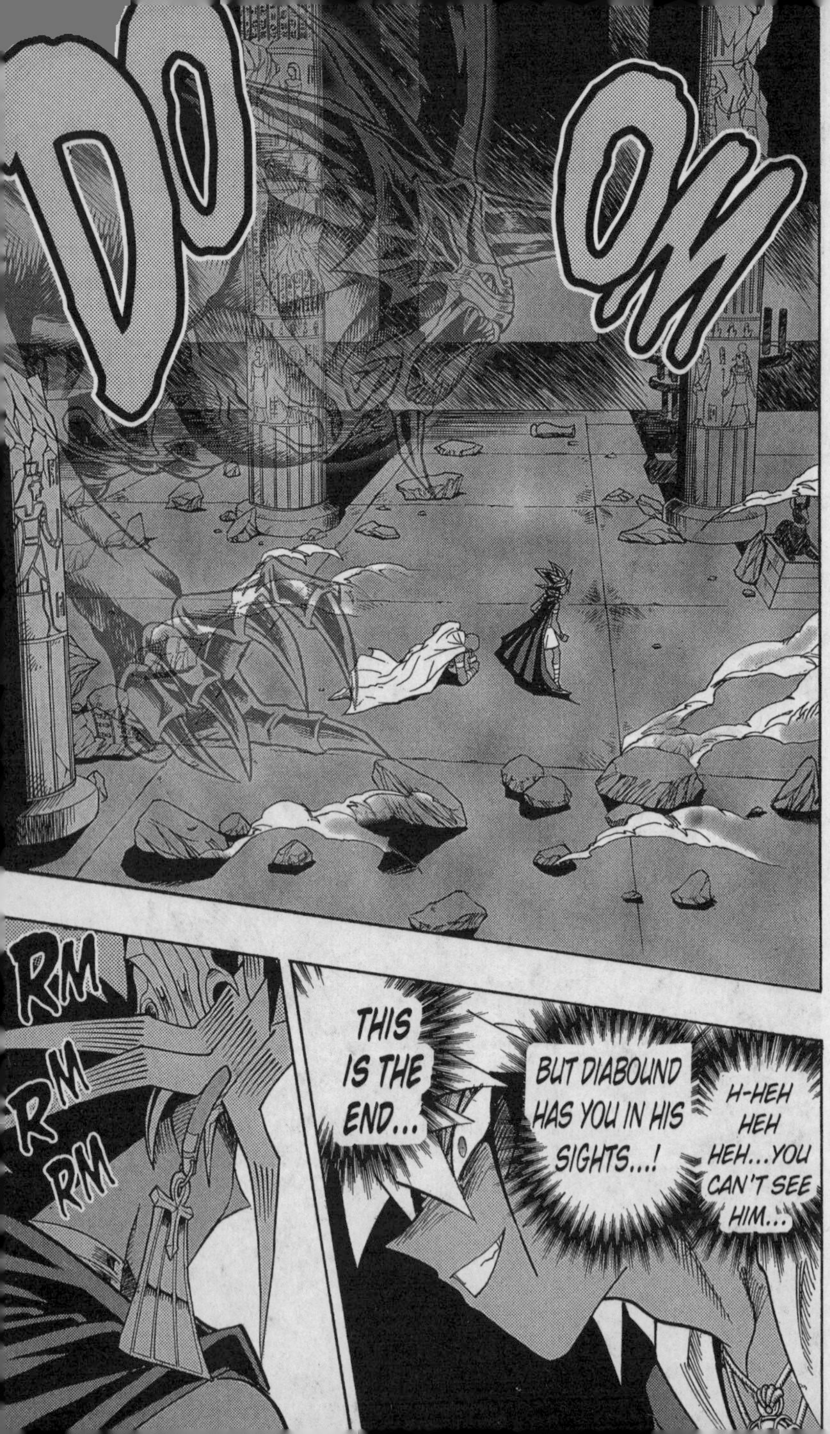
DO
OM
H-HEH HEH HEH...YOU CAN'T SEE HIM...
BUT DIABOUND HAS YOU IN HIS SIGHTS...!
THIS IS THE END...
RM
RM
R
RM

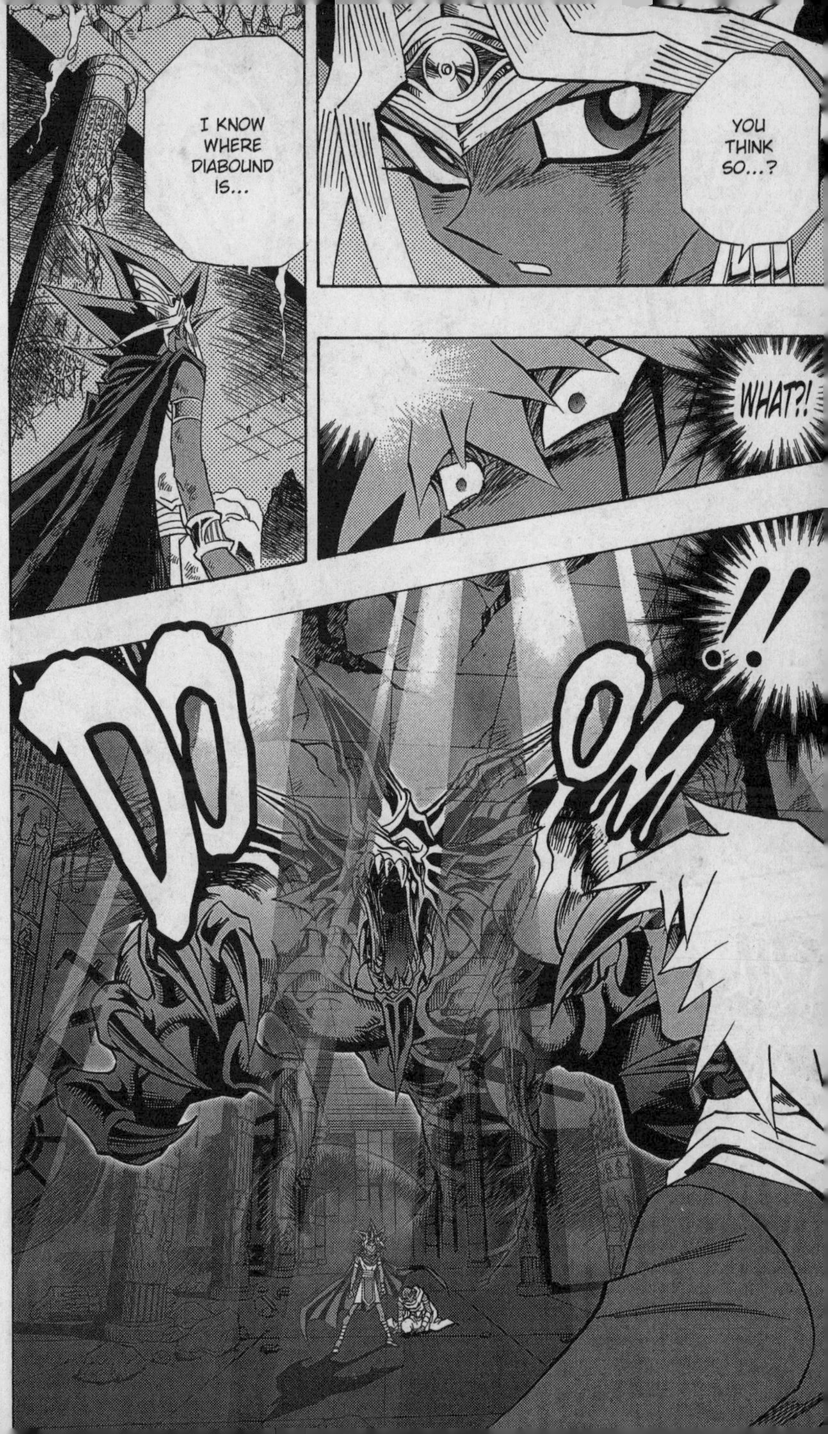
YOU THINK SO...?
I KNOW WHERE DIABOUND IS...
WHAT?!
!!
DOOM

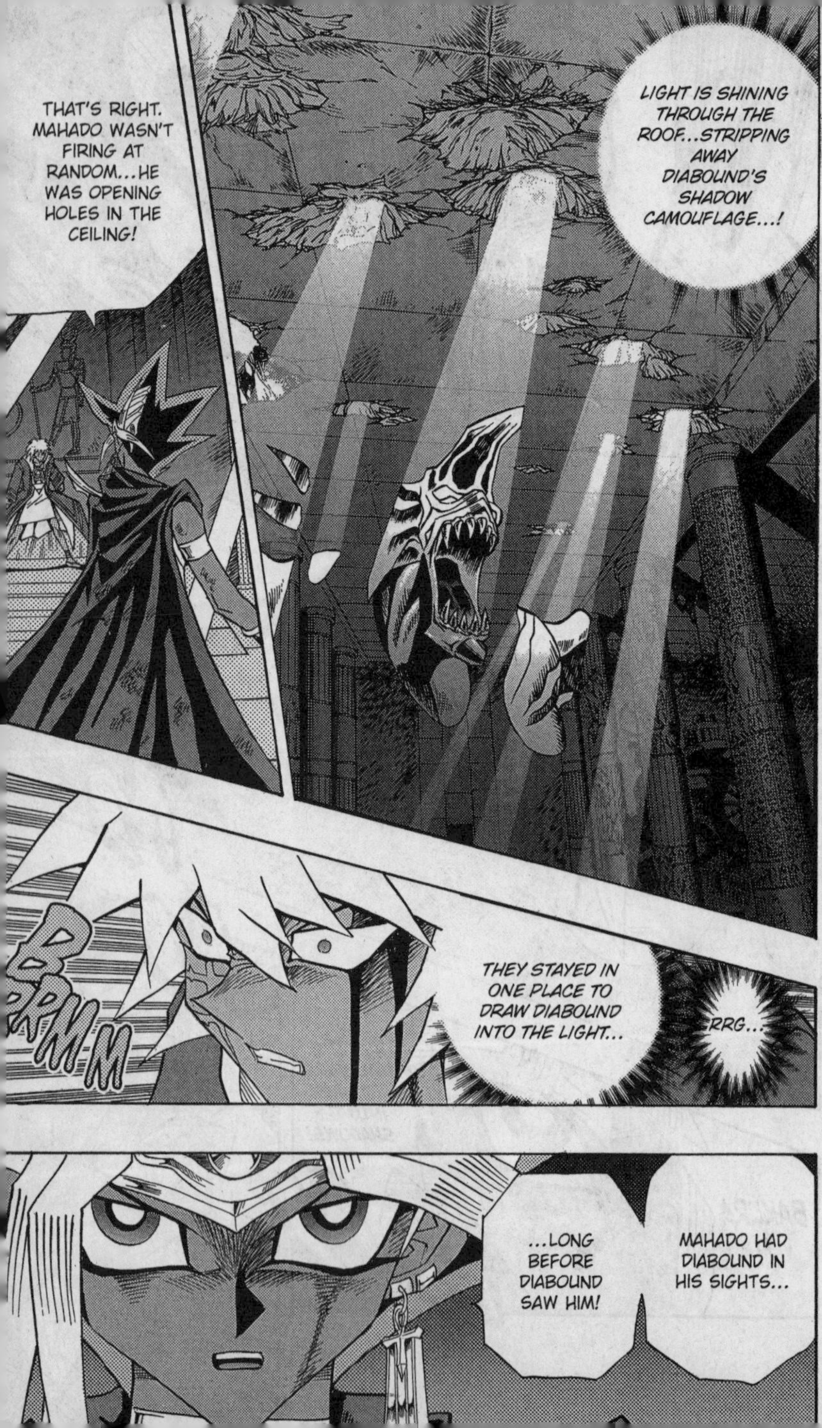
LIGHT IS SHINING THROUGH THE ROOF...STRIPPING AWAY DIABOUND'S SHADOW CAMOUFLAGE...!
THAT'S RIGHT. MAHADO WASN'T FIRING AT RANDOM...HE WAS OPENING HOLES IN THE CEILING!
RRG...
THEY STAYED IN ONE PLACE TO DRAW DIABOUND INTO THE LIGHT...
MAHADO HAD DIABOUND IN HIS SIGHTS...
...LONG BEFORE DIABOUND SAW HIM!

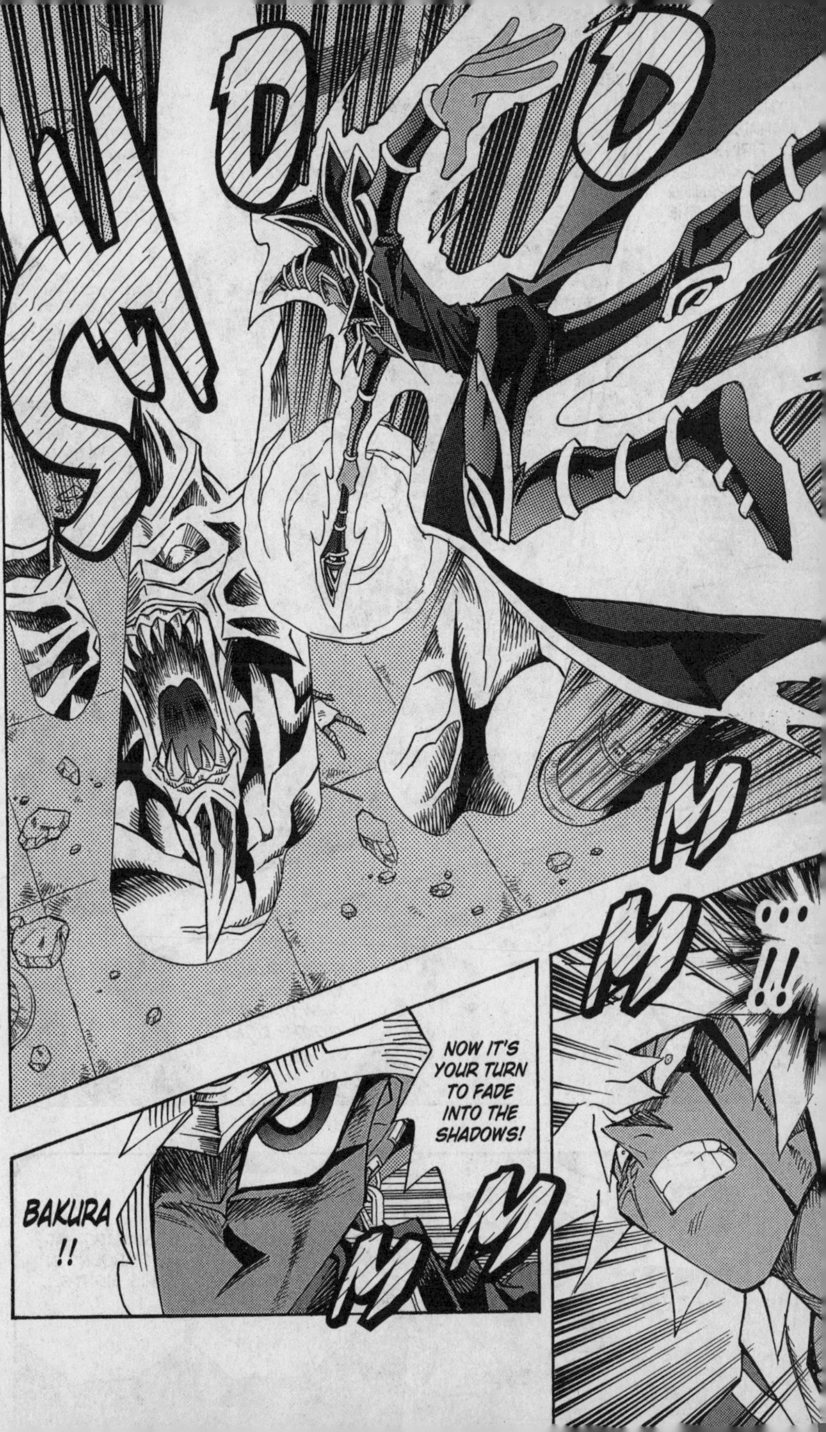

MMM...!!
NOW IT'S YOUR TURN TO FADE INTO THE SHADOWS!
BAKURA !!

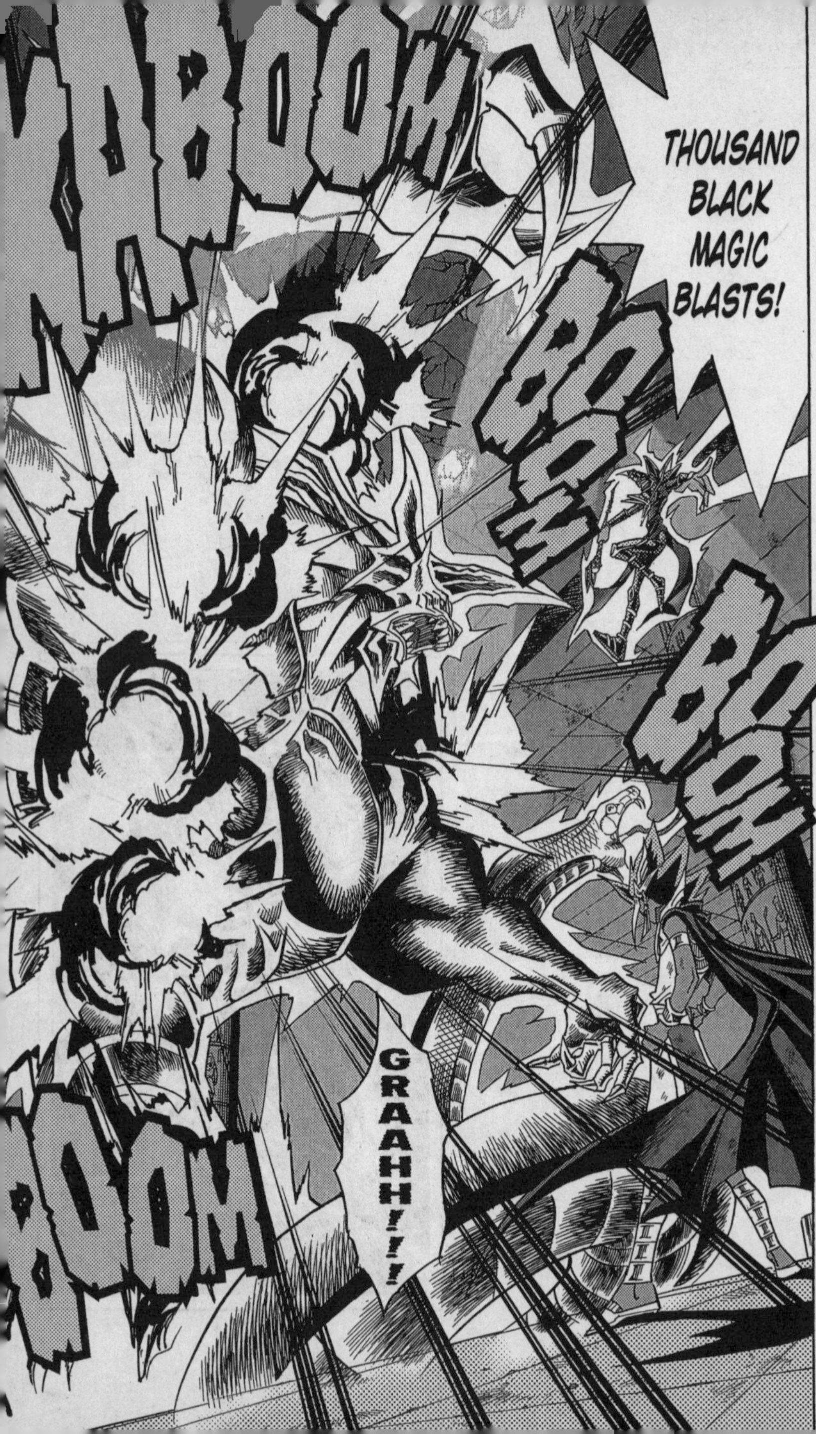
THOUSAND BLACK MAGIC BLASTS!
BOOM
BOOM
ABOOM
GRAAHH!!!
OOM

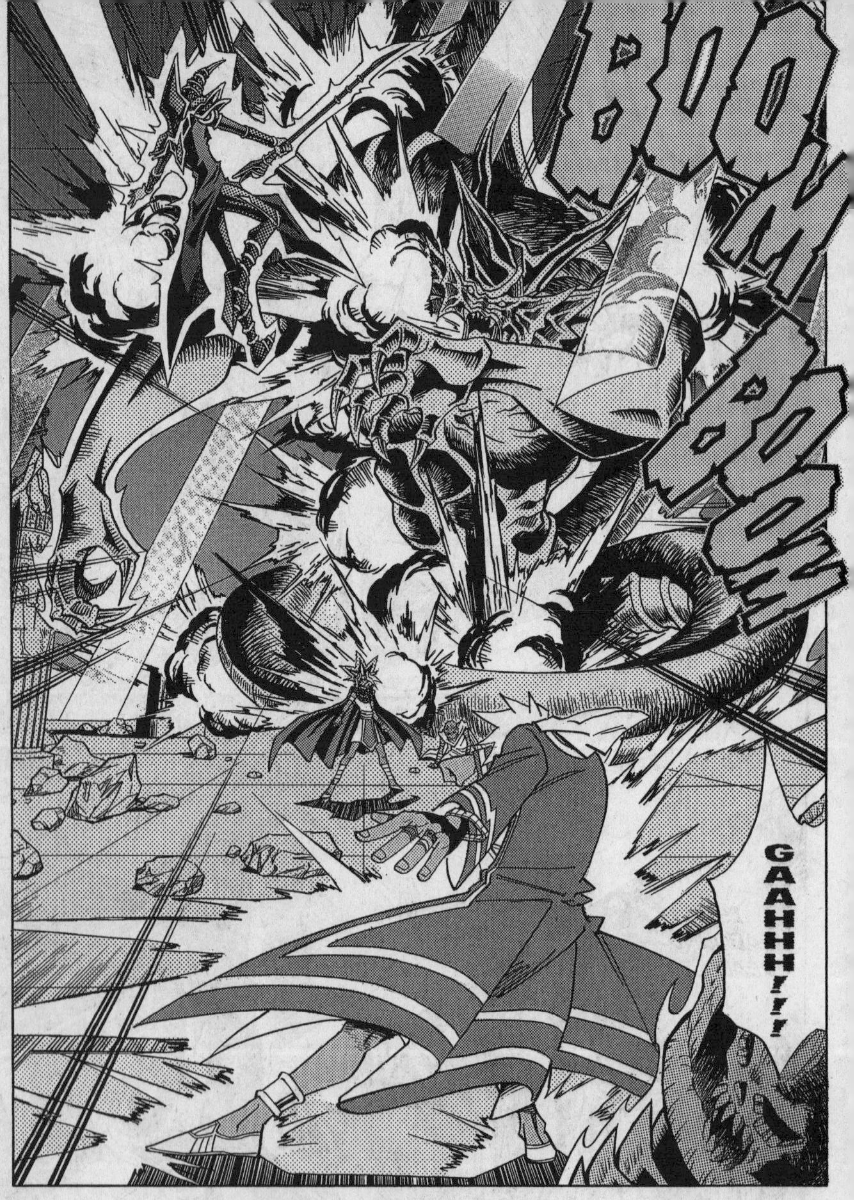
BOOM
BOOM
GAAHHH!!!

Duel 316:
Aura Shield!!

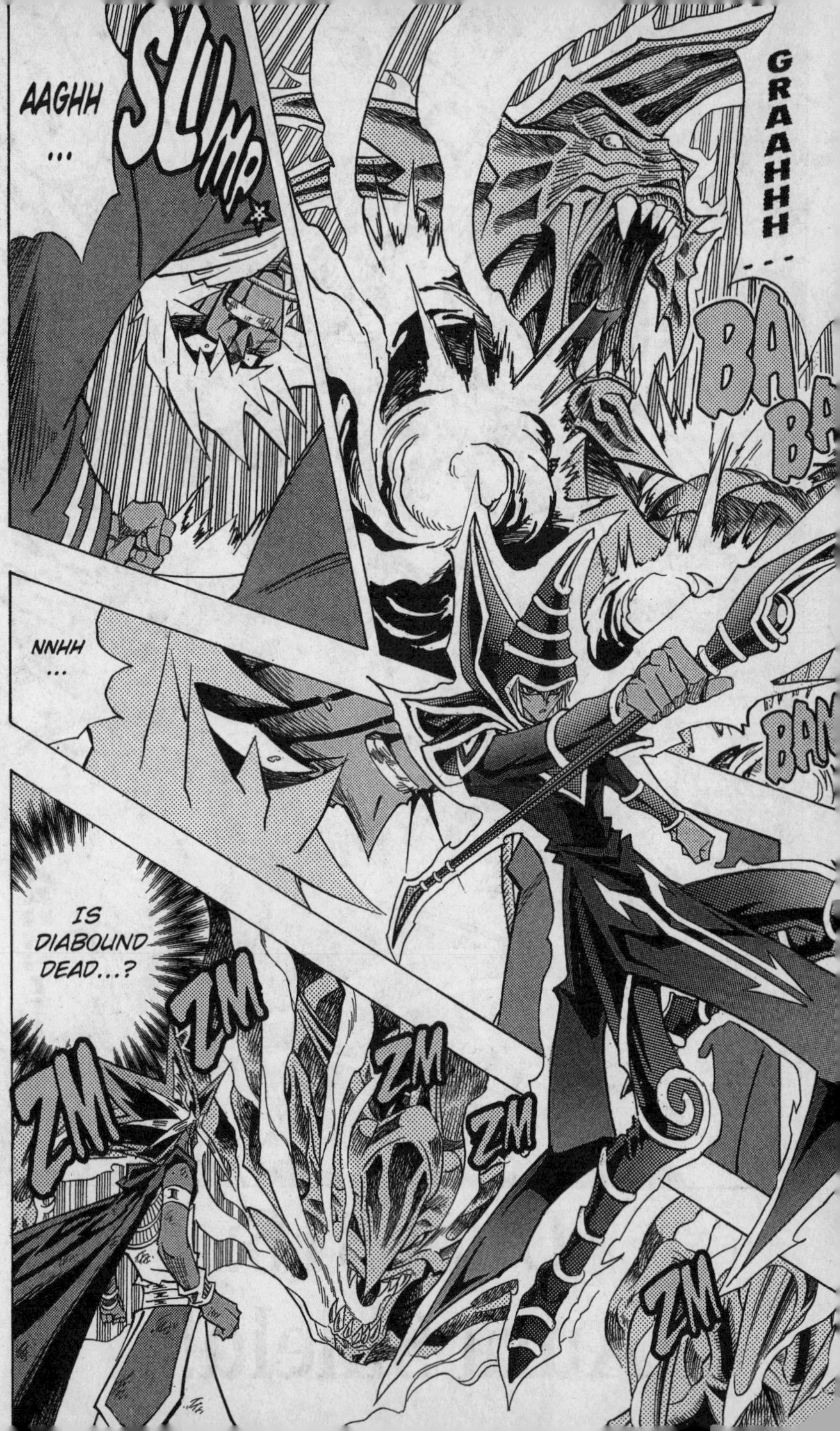
GRAAHHH---
BA
BA
AAGHH...
SLUMP
NNHH...
BAM
IS DIABOUND DEAD...?
ZM
ZM
ZM
ZM
ZM
ZM

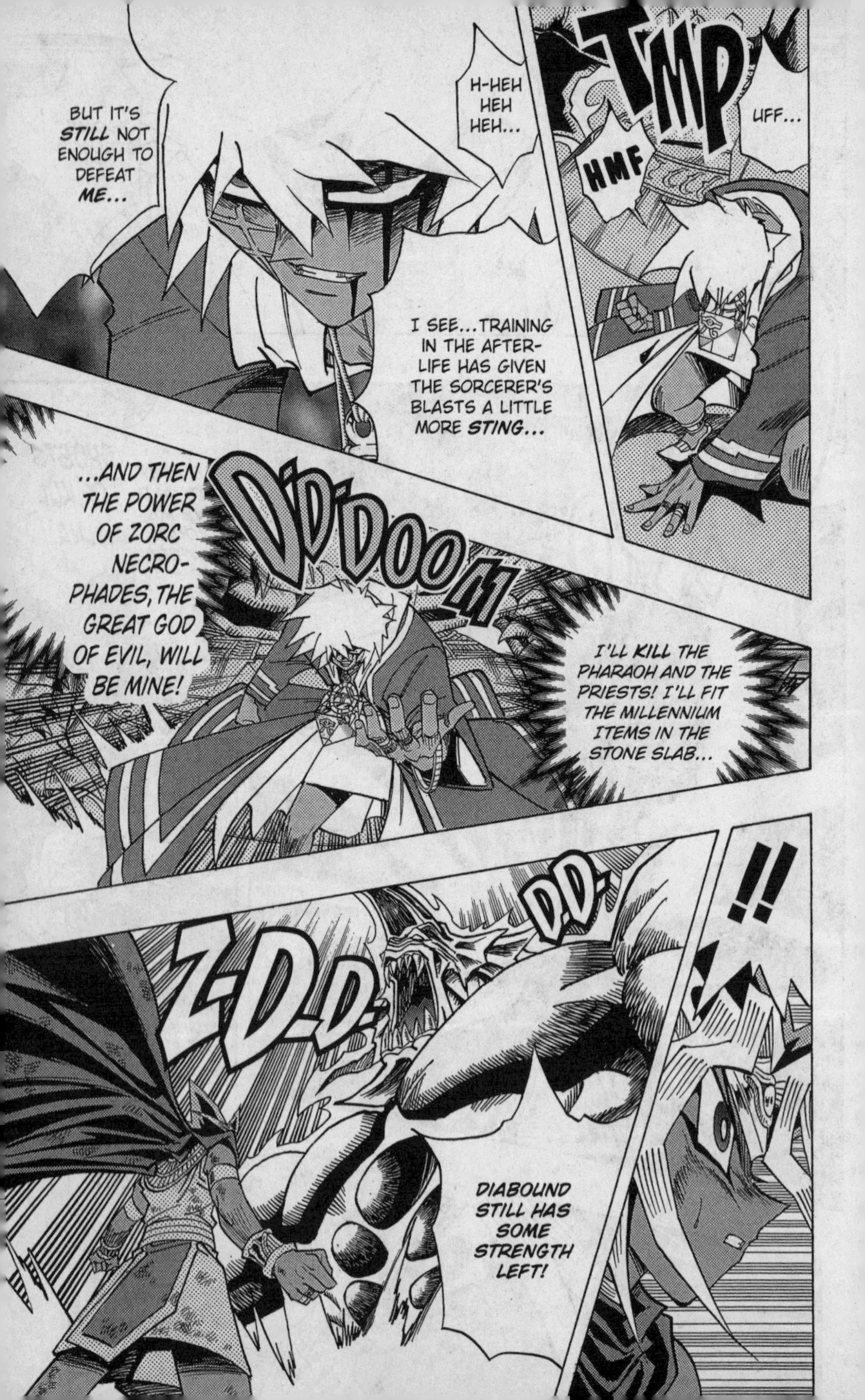
TMP
UFF...
HMF
H-HEH HEH HEH...
I SEE...TRAINING IN THE AFTER-LIFE HAS GIVEN THE SORCERER'S BLASTS A LITTLE MORE STING...
BUT IT'S STILL NOT ENOUGH TO DEFEAT ME...
D-D-DOOM
I'LL KILL THE PHARAOH AND THE PRIESTS! I'LL FIT THE MILLENNIUM ITEMS IN THE STONE SLAB...
...AND THEN THE POWER OF ZORC NECRO-PHADES, THE GREAT GOD OF EVIL, WILL BE MINE!
!!
D-D-
Z-D-D-
DIABOUND STILL HAS SOME STRENGTH LEFT!

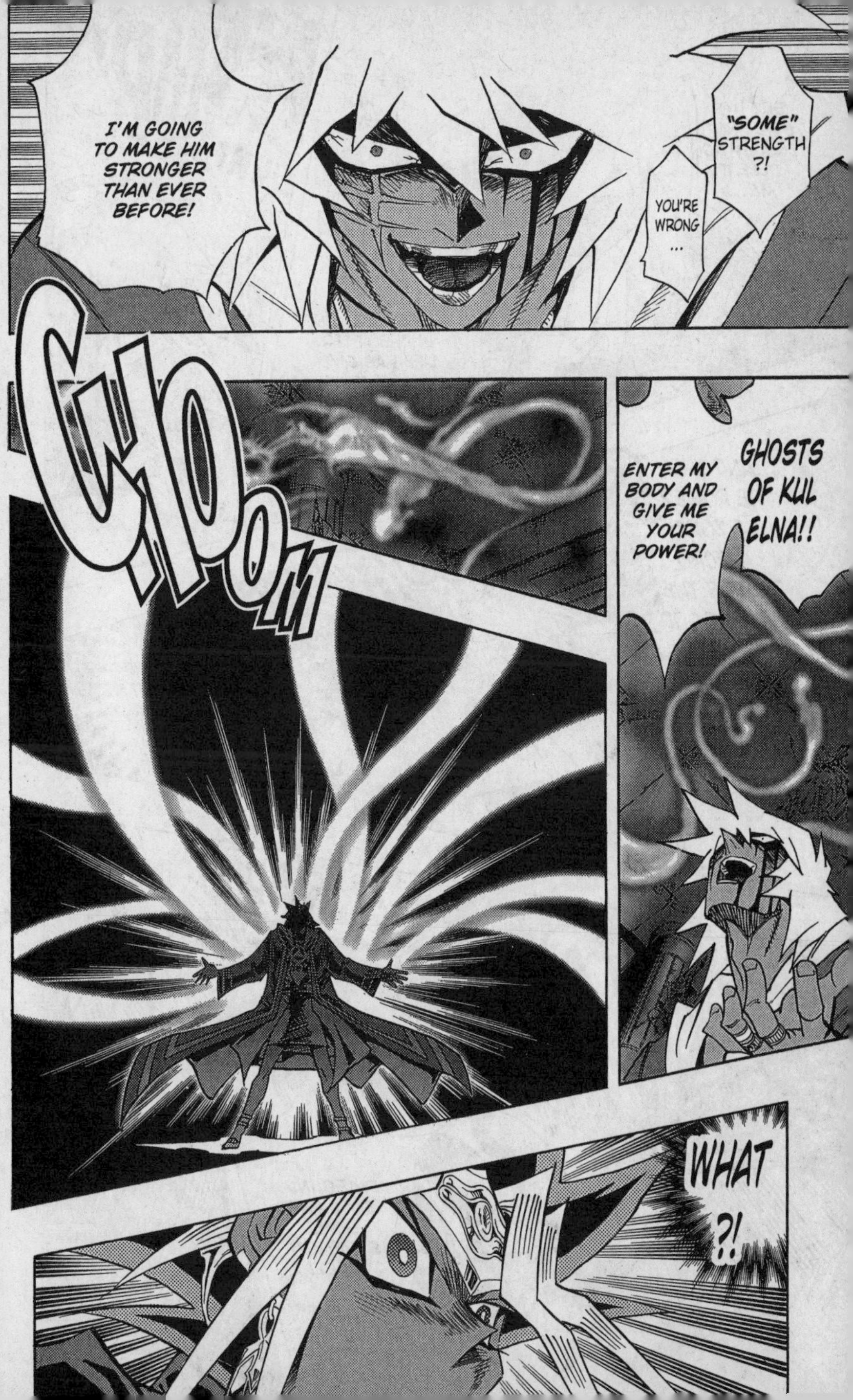
"SOME" STRENGTH ?!
YOU'RE WRONG ...
I'M GOING TO MAKE HIM STRONGER THAN EVER BEFORE!
GHOSTS OF KUL ELNA!!
ENTER MY BODY AND GIVE ME YOUR POWER!
CHOOM
WHAT ?!

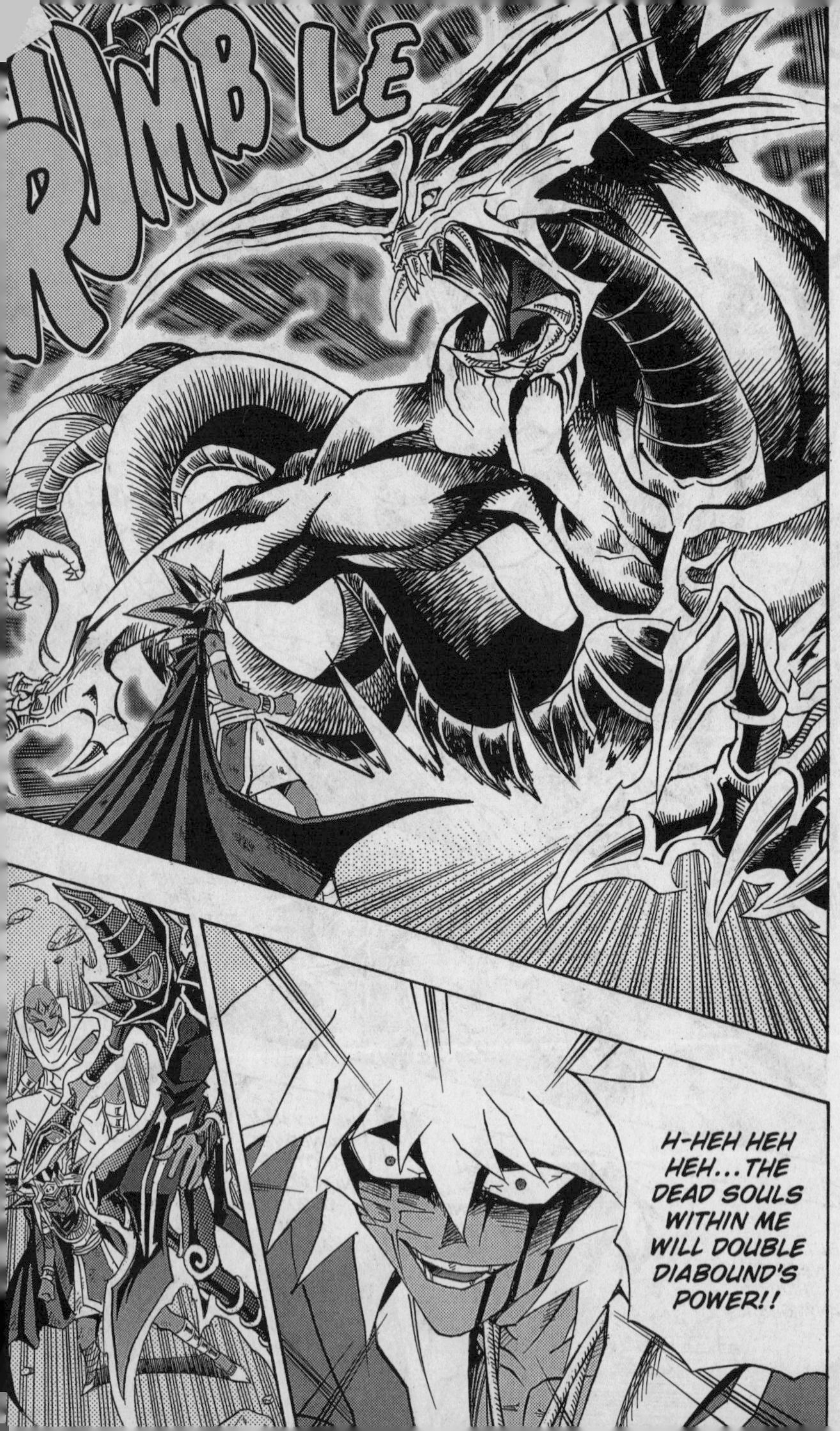
RUMBLE
H-HEH HEH
HEH...THE
DEAD SOULS
WITHIN ME
WILL DOUBLE
DIABOUND'S
POWER!!

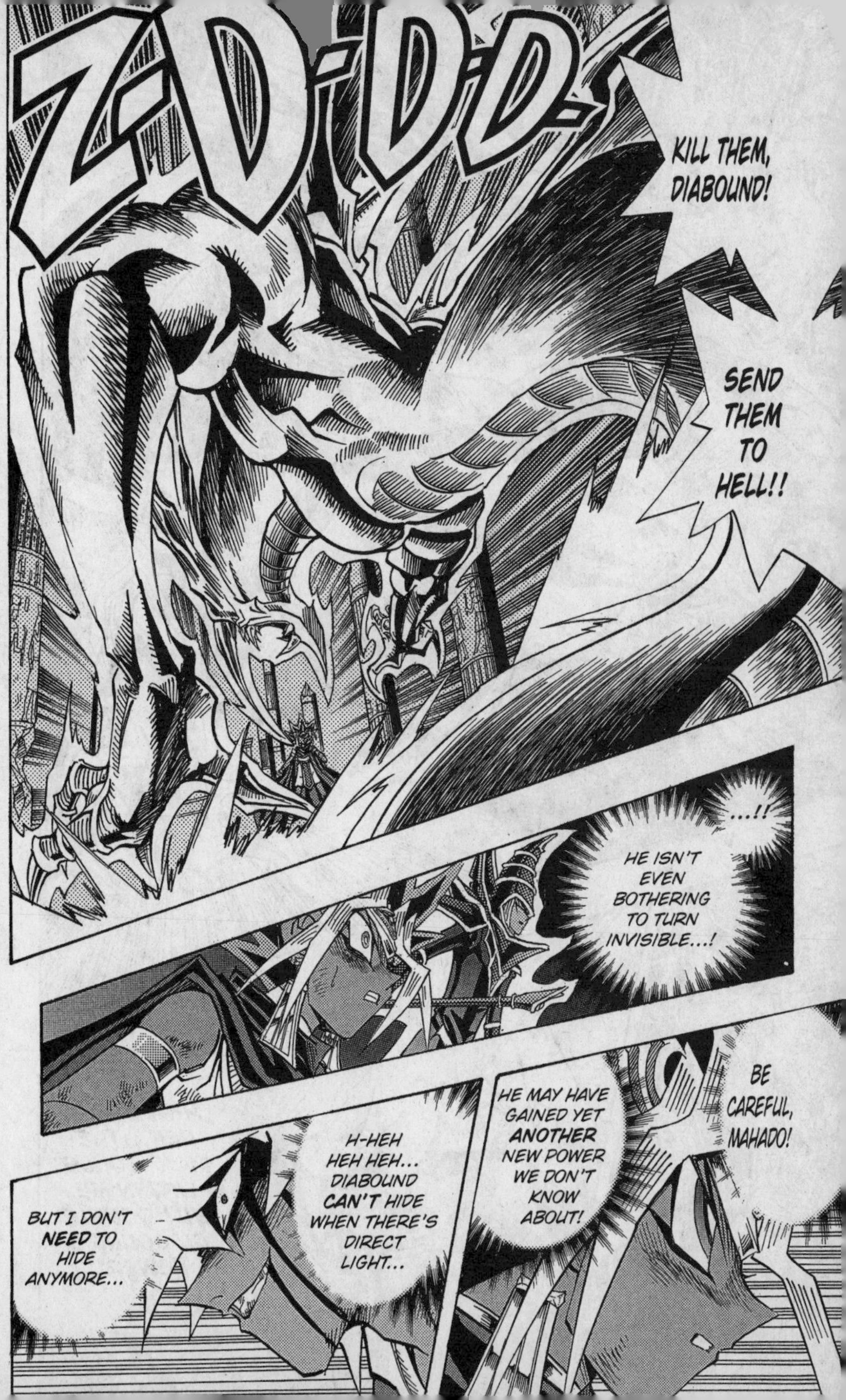

Z-D-D-D
KILL THEM, DIABOUND!
SEND THEM TO HELL!!
...!!
HE ISN'T EVEN BOTHERING TO TURN INVISIBLE...!
BE CAREFUL, MAHADO!
HE MAY HAVE GAINED YET ANOTHER NEW POWER WE DON'T KNOW ABOUT!
H-HEH HEH HEH... DIABOUND CAN'T HIDE WHEN THERE'S DIRECT LIGHT...
BUT I DON'T NEED TO HIDE ANYMORE...

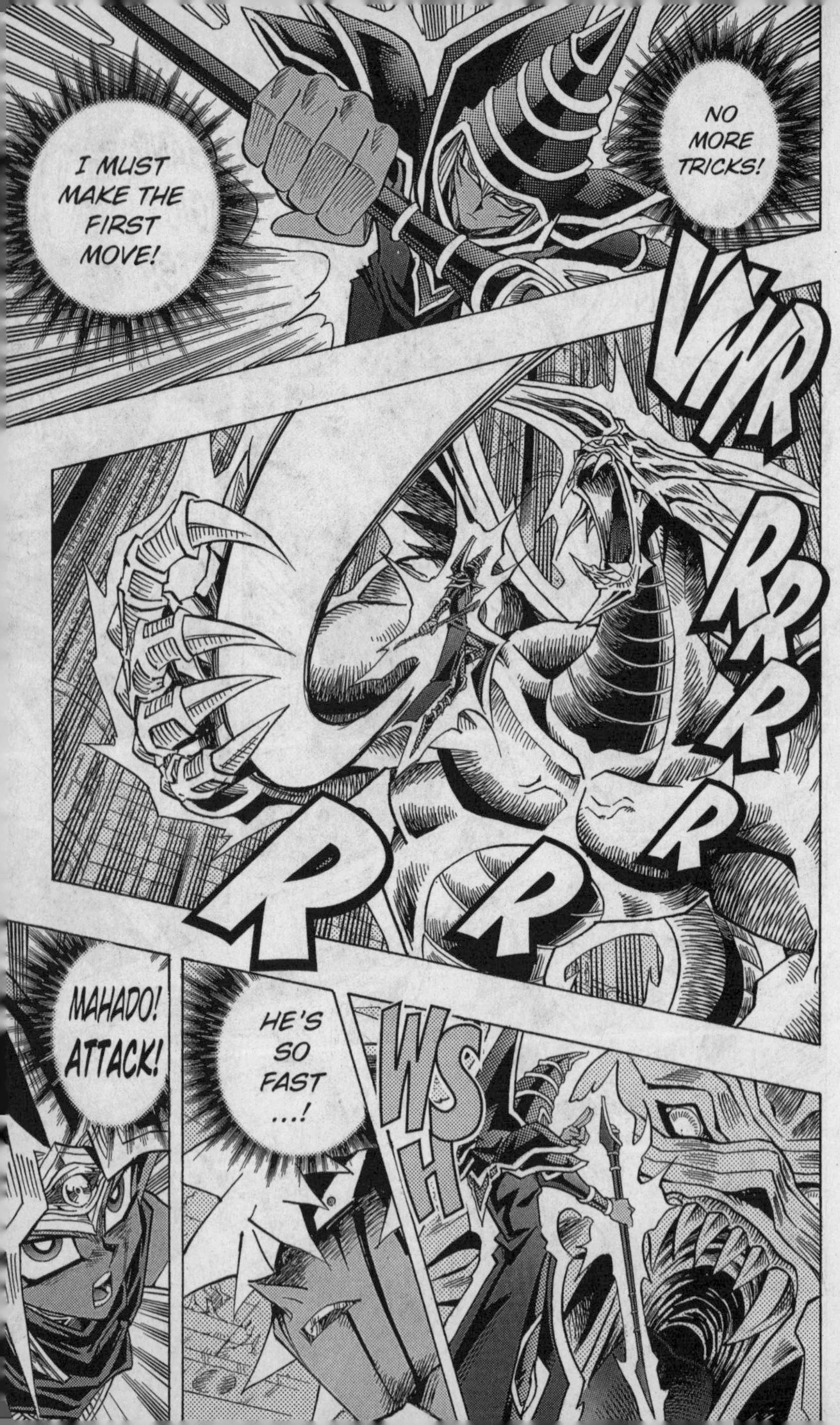
NO MORE TRICKS!
I MUST MAKE THE FIRST MOVE!
VVR
RRRR
RR
WSH
HE'S SO FAST ...!
MAHADO! ATTACK!

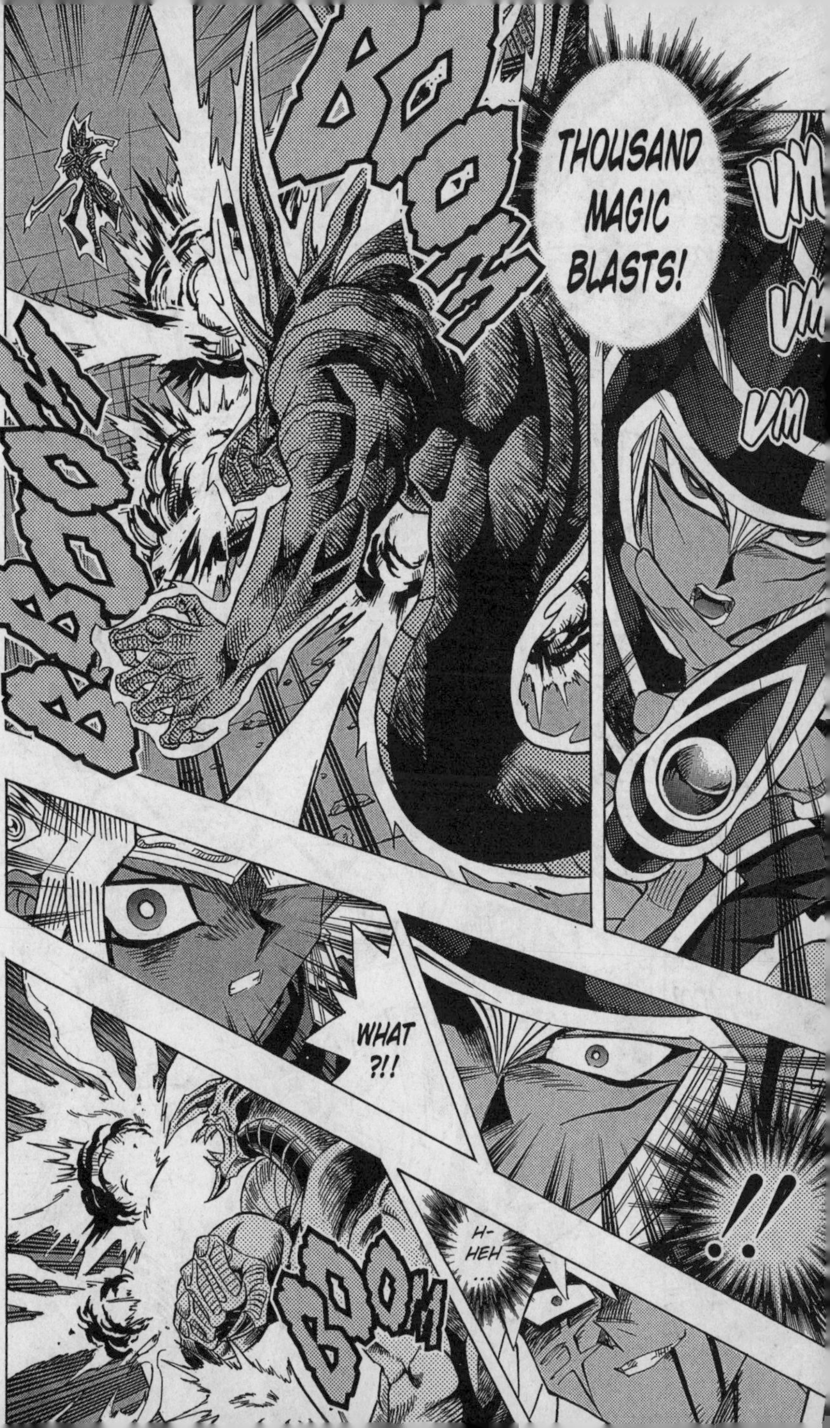

VM
VM
VM
THOUSAND MAGIC BLASTS!
BOOM
BOOM
!!
WHAT ?!!
H-HEH...
BOOM

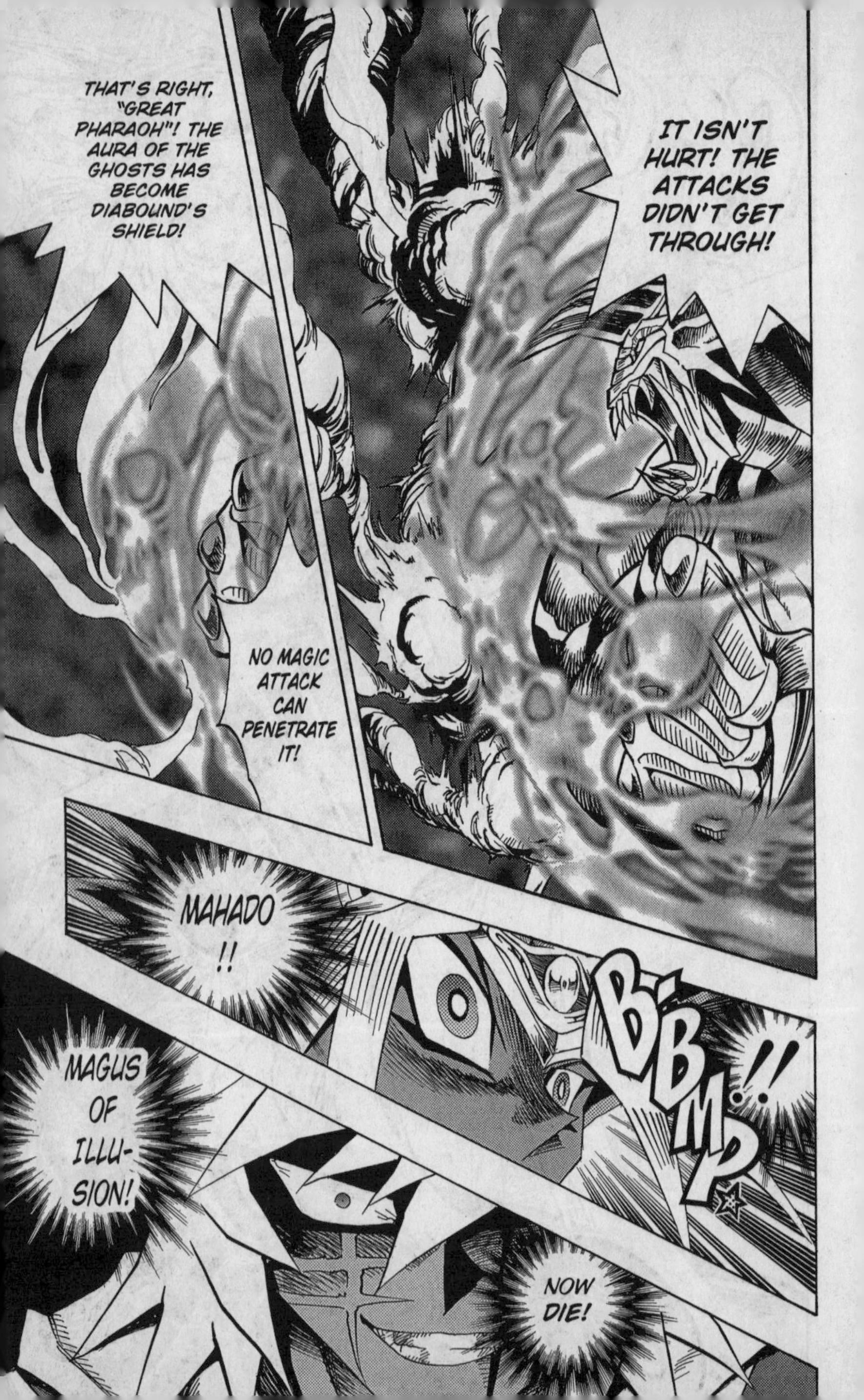
IT ISN'T HURT! THE ATTACKS DIDN'T GET THROUGH!
THAT'S RIGHT, "GREAT PHARAOH"! THE AURA OF THE GHOSTS HAS BECOME DIABOUND'S SHIELD!
NO MAGIC ATTACK CAN PENETRATE IT!
B'BMP!!
MAHADO !!
MAGUS OF ILLU-SION!
NOW DIE!

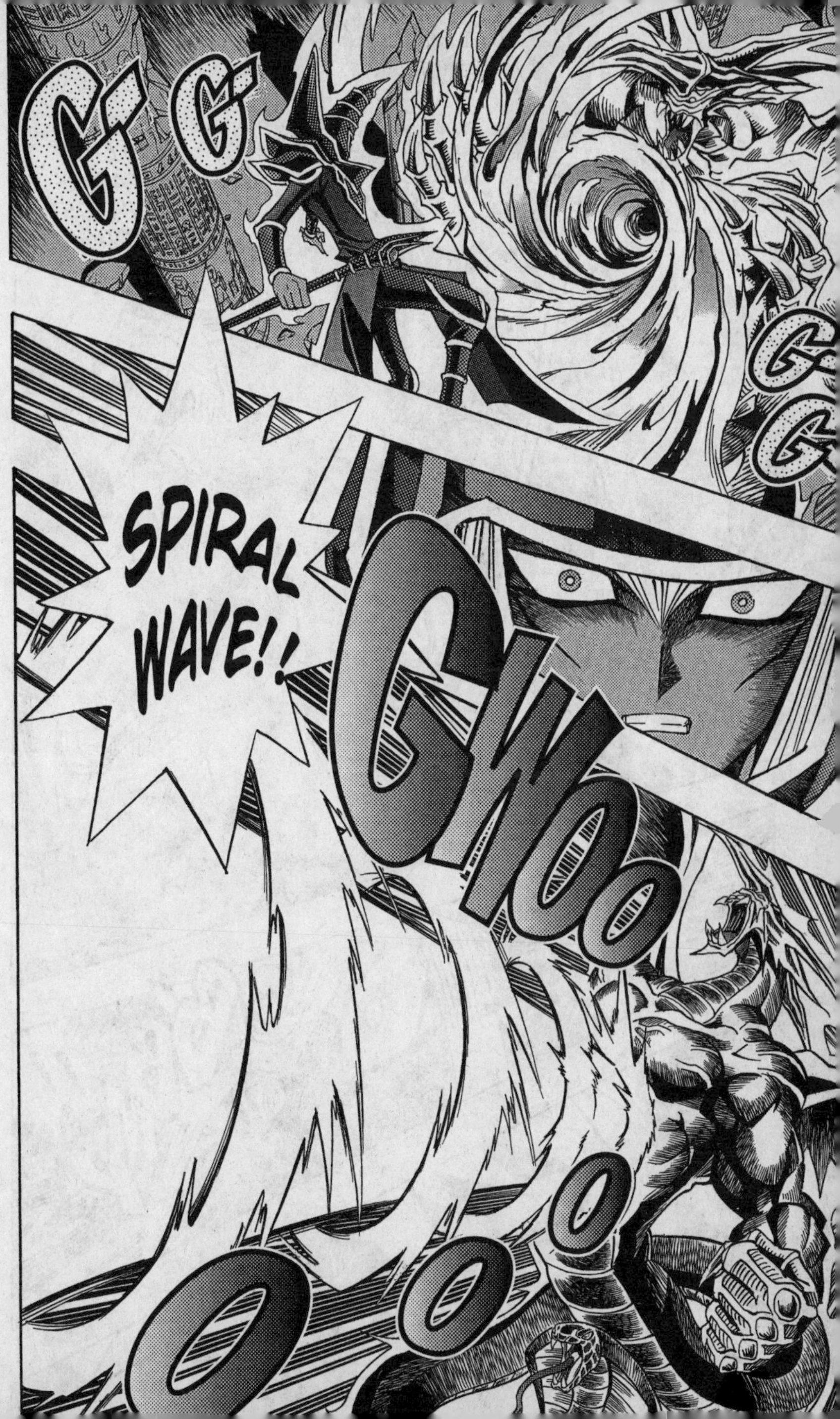
GG
GG
SPIRAL WAVE!!
GHOOOOOO

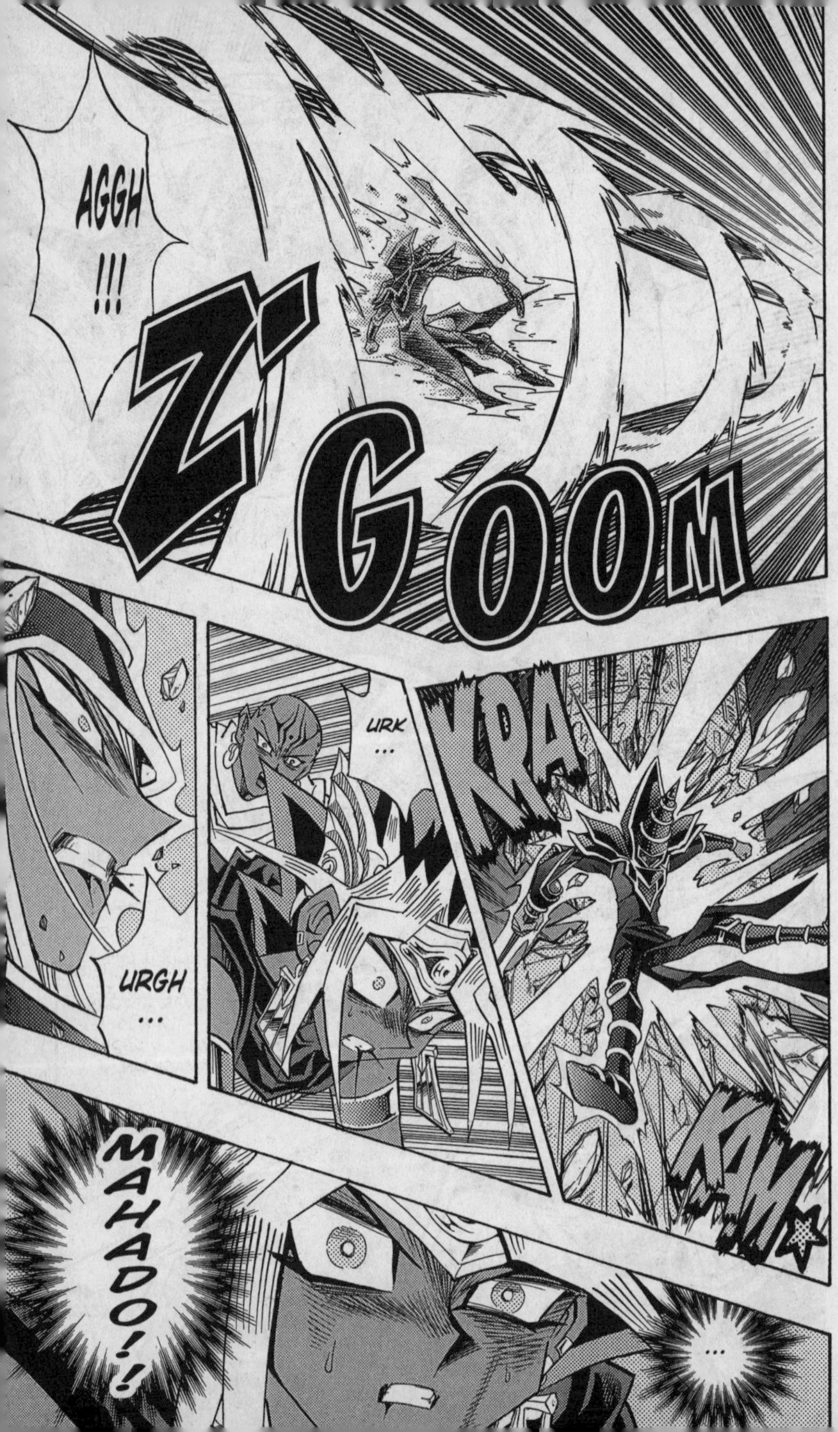
AGGH!!!
ZGOOM
KRA
URK...
URGH...
KAN
...
MAHADO!!

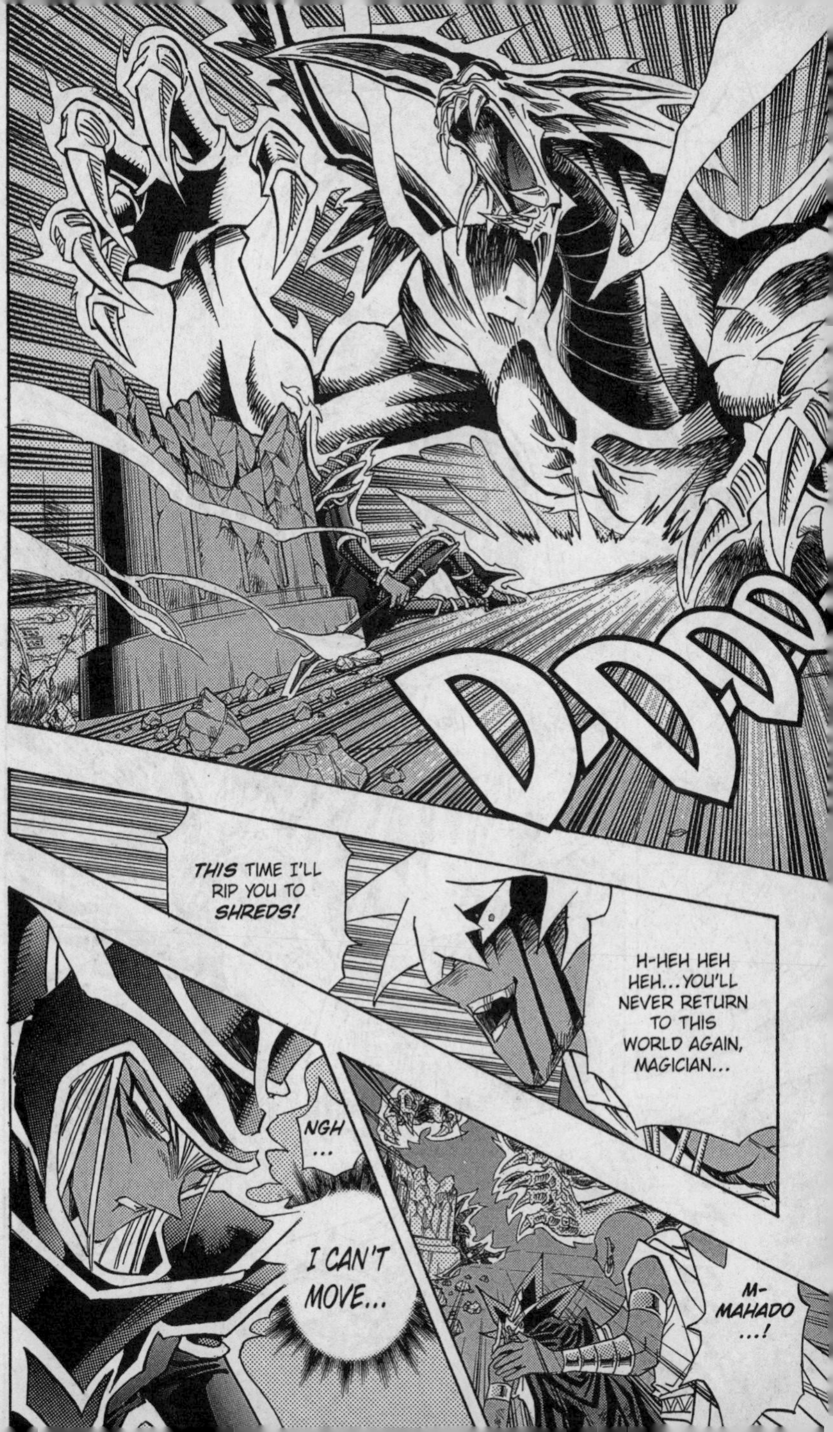
D.D.D
THIS TIME I'LL RIP YOU TO SHREDS!
H-HEH HEH HEH...YOU'LL NEVER RETURN TO THIS WORLD AGAIN, MAGICIAN...
M-MAHADO...!
NGH...
I CAN'T MOVE...

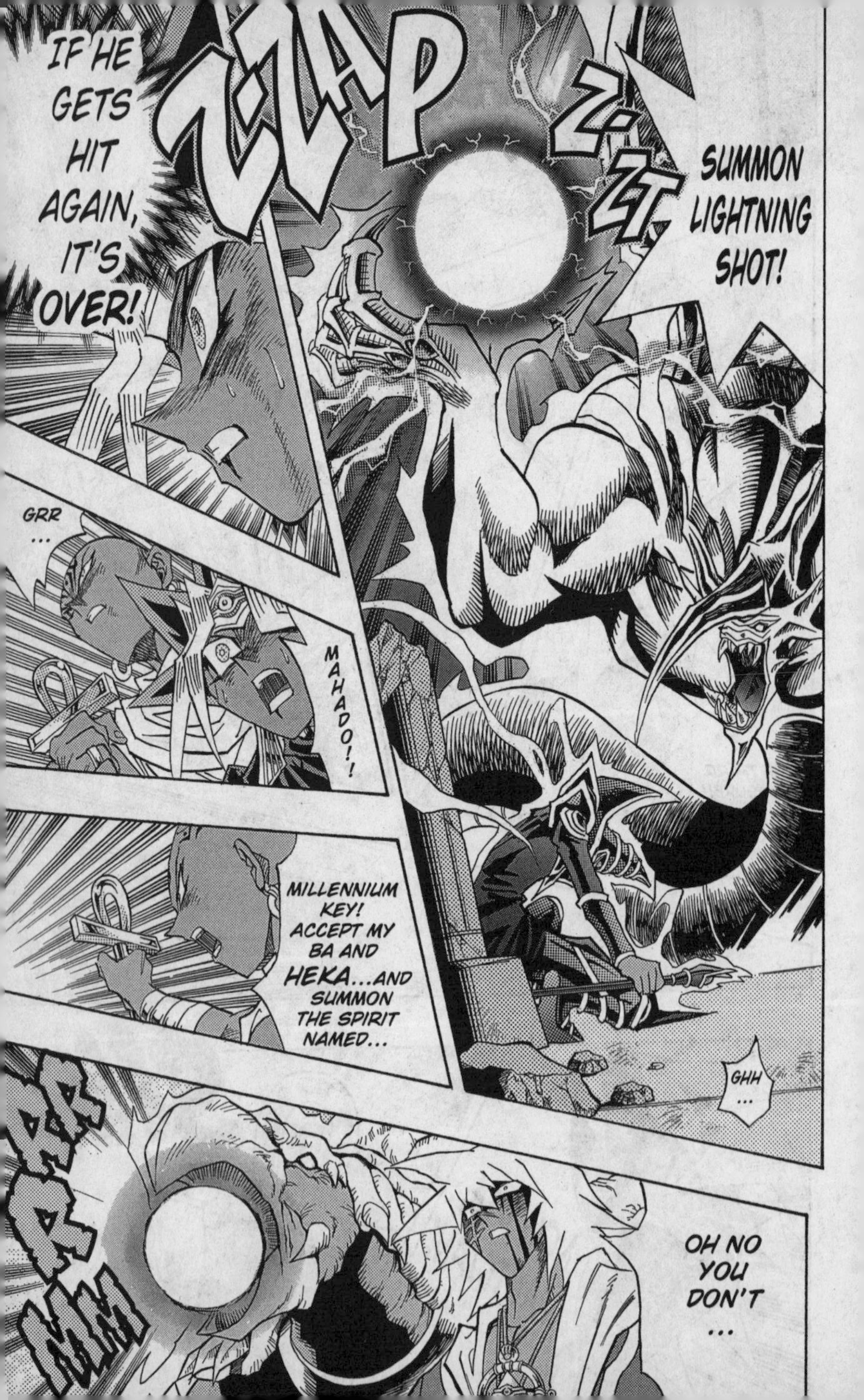
SUMMON LIGHTNING SHOT!
Z-ZT
ZZAP
IF HE GETS HIT AGAIN, IT'S OVER!
GRR...
MAHADO!!
GHH...
MILLENNIUM KEY! ACCEPT MY BA AND HEKA...AND SUMMON THE SPIRIT NAMED...
OH NO YOU DON'T...

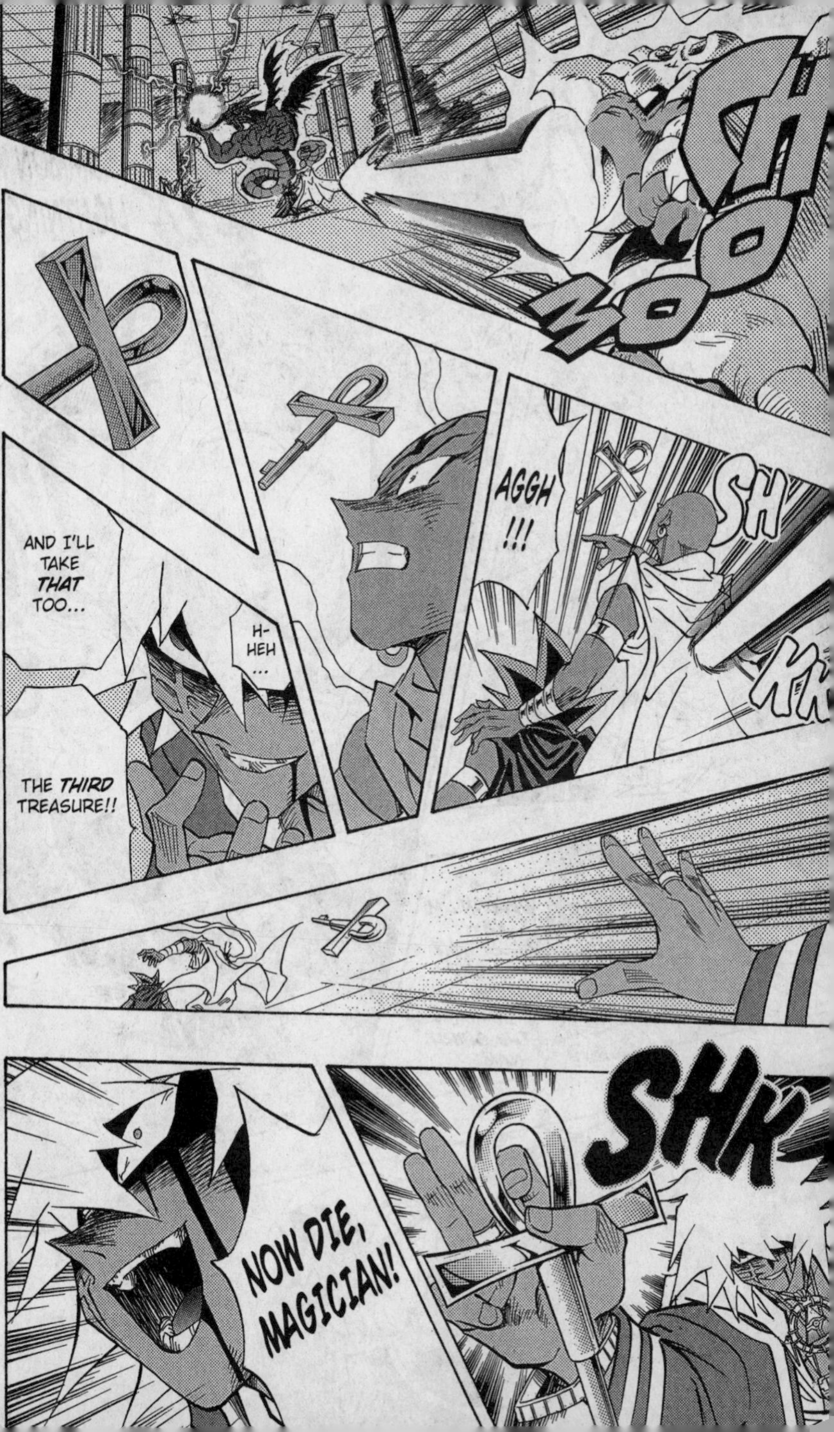
CHOOM
AGGH!!!
SH
KK
H-HEH...
AND I'LL TAKE THAT TOO...
THE THIRD TREASURE!!
SHK
NOW DIE, MAGICIAN!

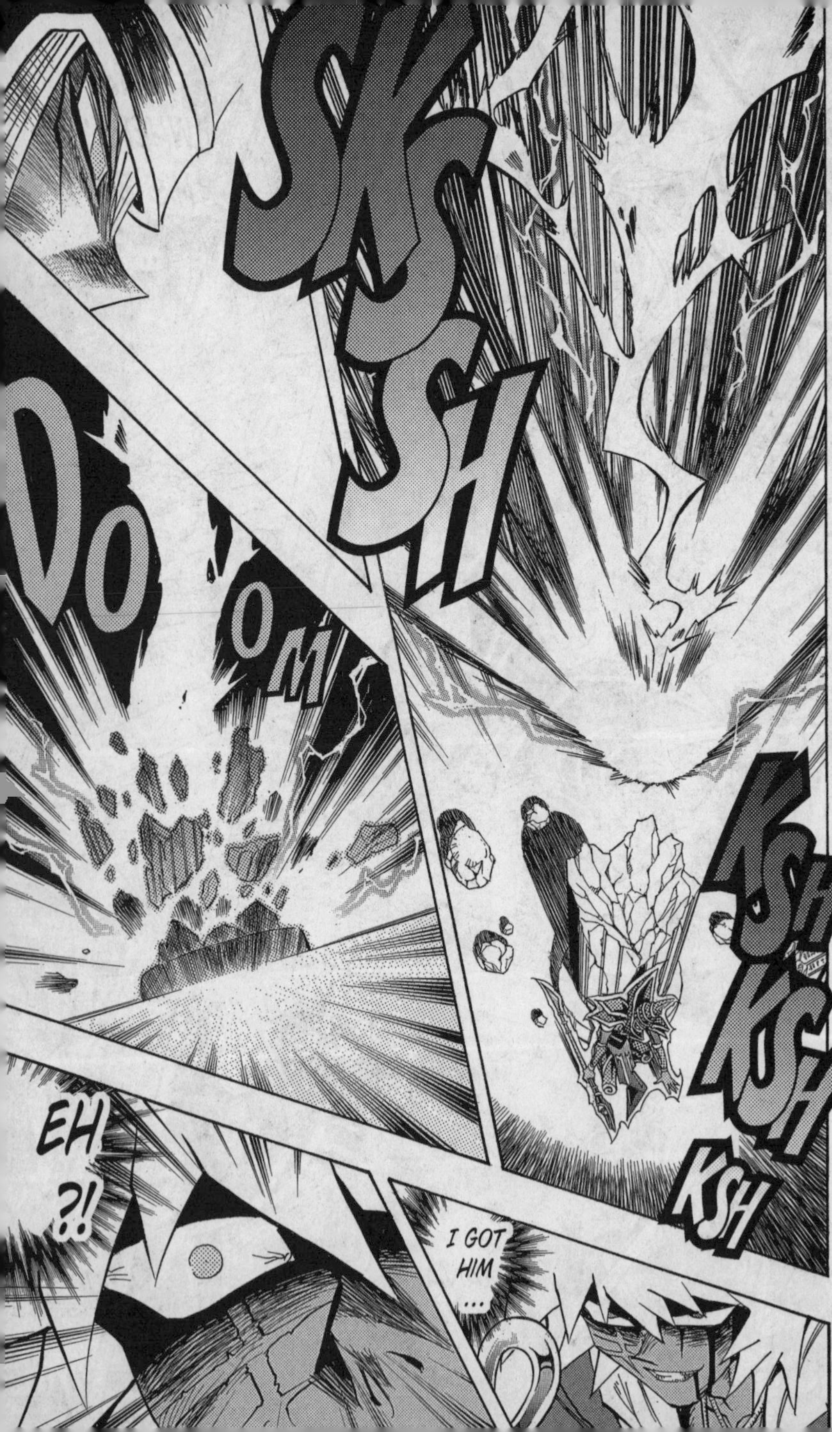
SKSSH
DOOM
KSH KSH KSH
I GOT HIM...
EH ?!

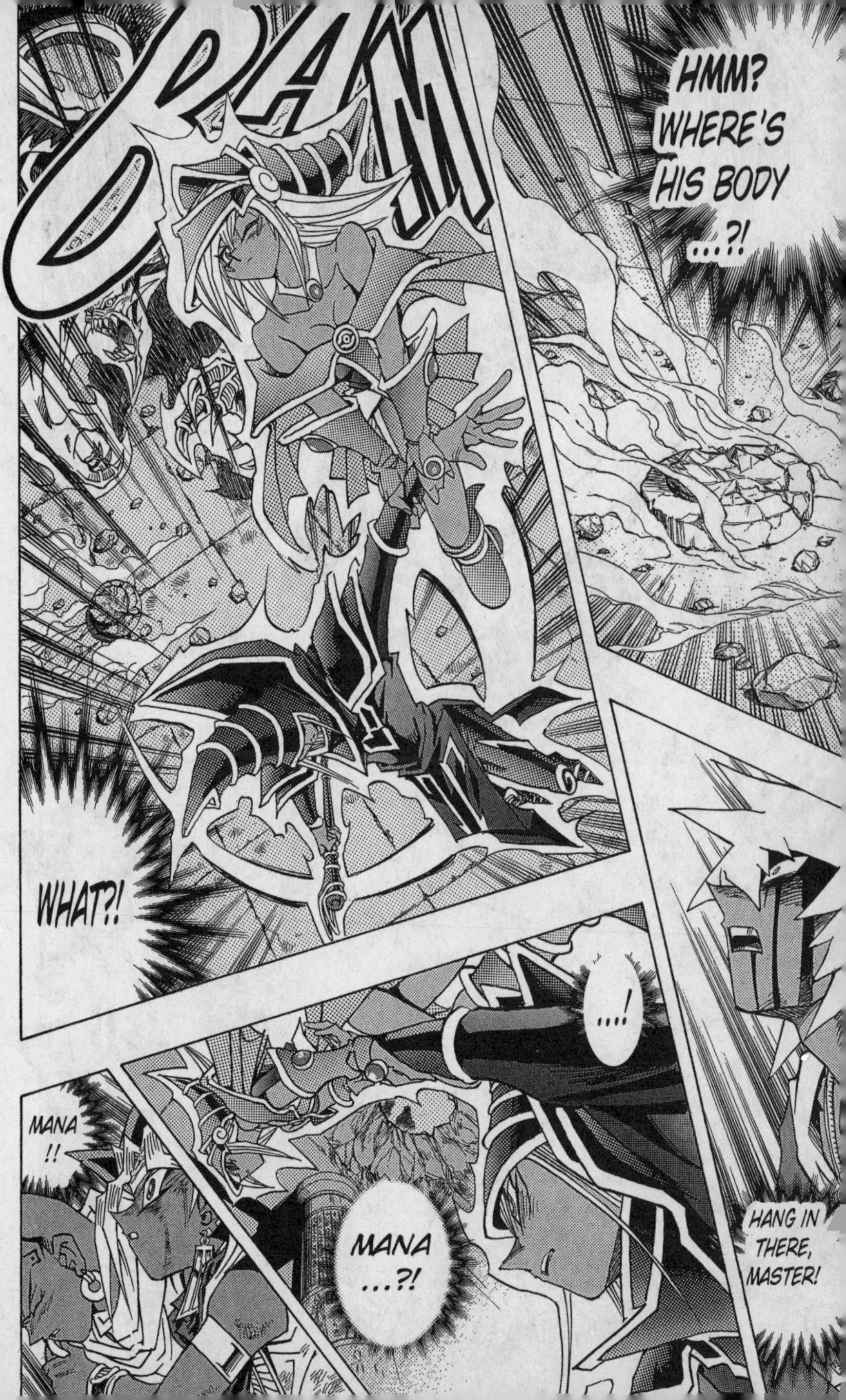
HMM? WHERE'S HIS BODY ...?!
WHAT?!
...!
HANG IN THERE, MASTER!
MANA ...?!
MANA !!

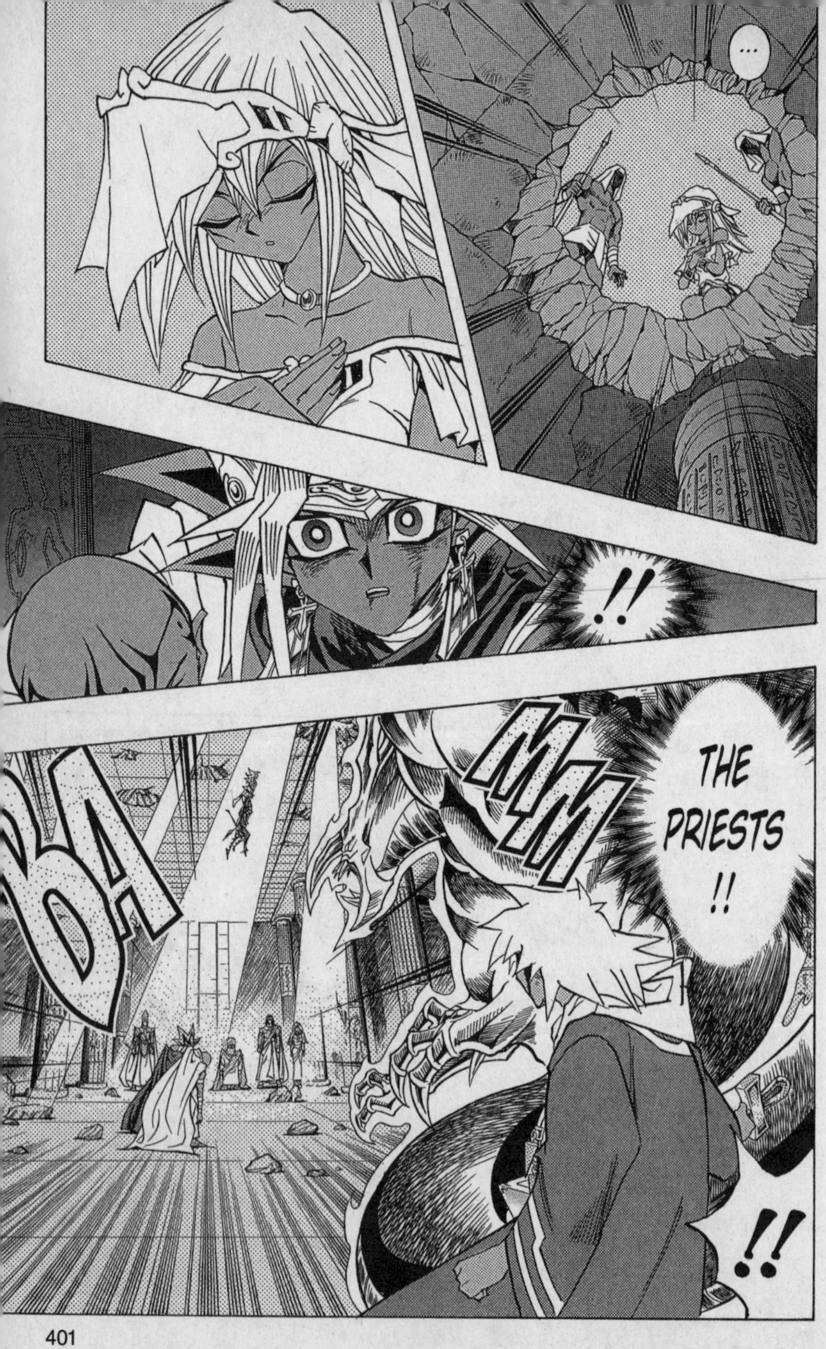
...
!!
THE PRIESTS !!
MM
BA
!!

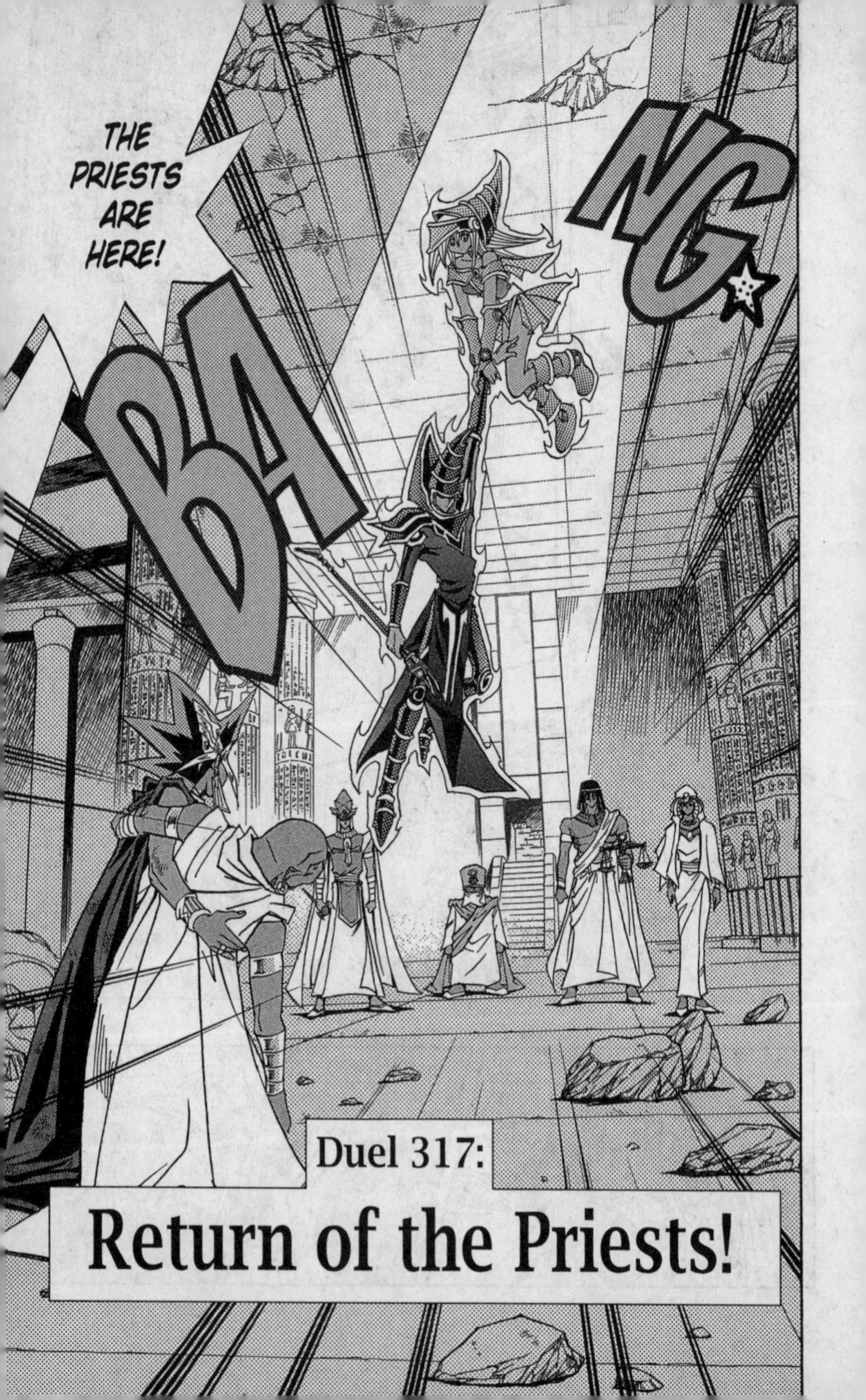
THE PRIESTS ARE HERE!
BANG☆

Duel 317:
Return of the Priests!

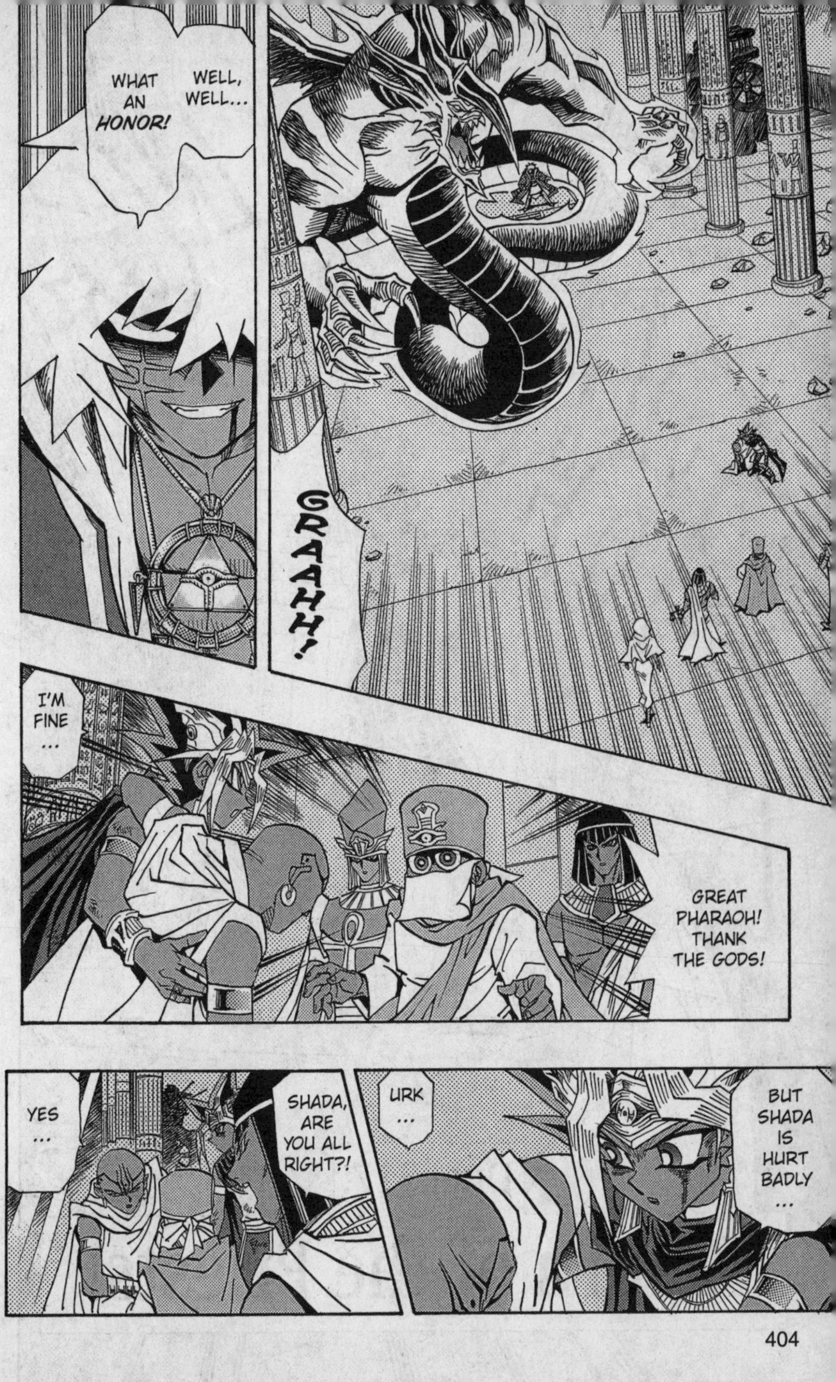
GRAAHH!
WELL, WELL... WHAT AN HONOR!
GREAT PHARAOH! THANK THE GODS!
I'M FINE...
BUT SHADA IS HURT BADLY...
URK...
SHADA, ARE YOU ALL RIGHT?!
YES...

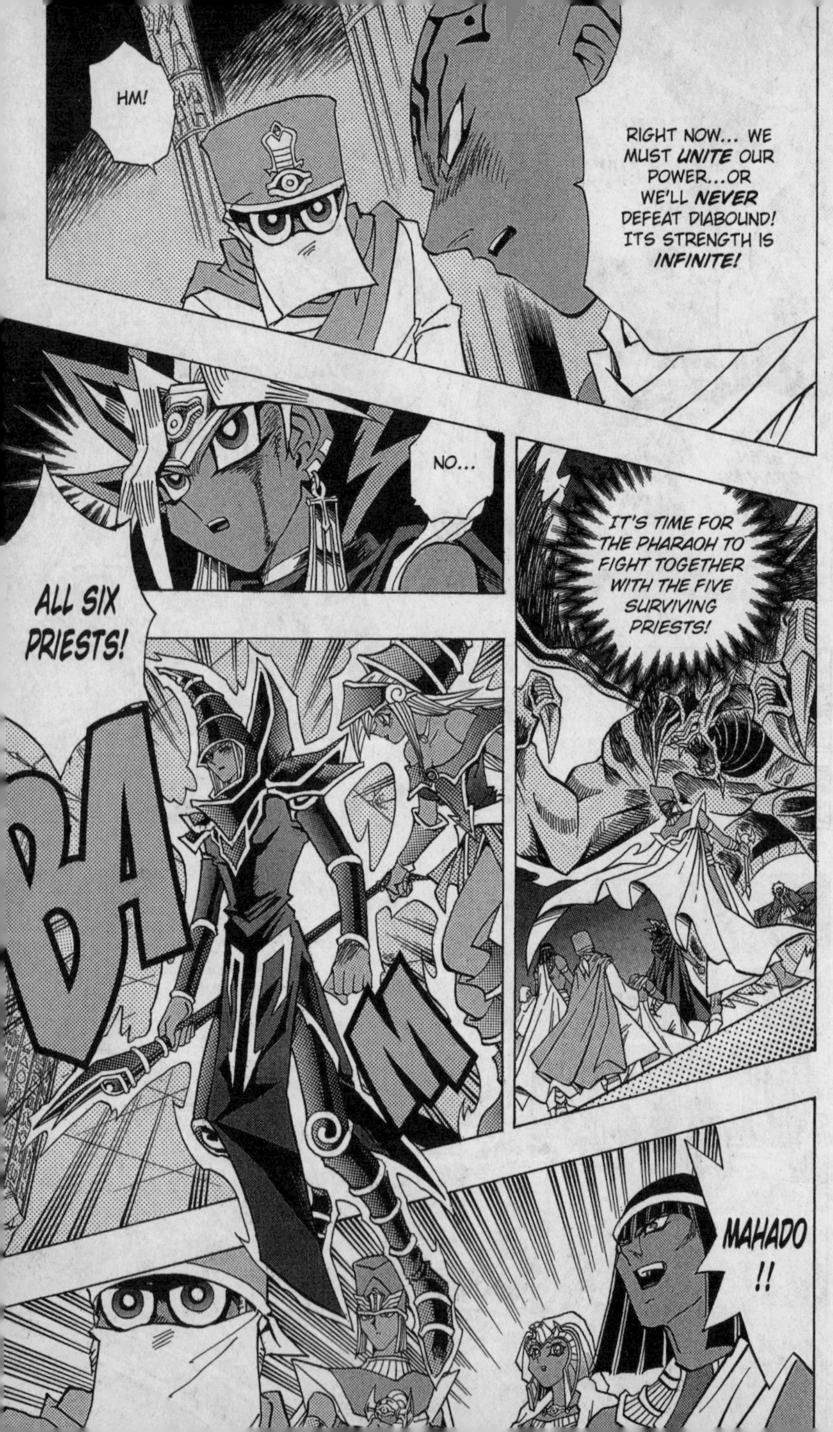
RIGHT NOW... WE MUST *UNITE* OUR POWER...OR WE'LL *NEVER* DEFEAT DIABOUND! ITS STRENGTH IS *INFINITE!*
HM!
NO...
IT'S TIME FOR THE PHARAOH TO FIGHT TOGETHER WITH THE FIVE SURVIVING PRIESTS!
ALL SIX PRIESTS!
BAM
MAHADO !!

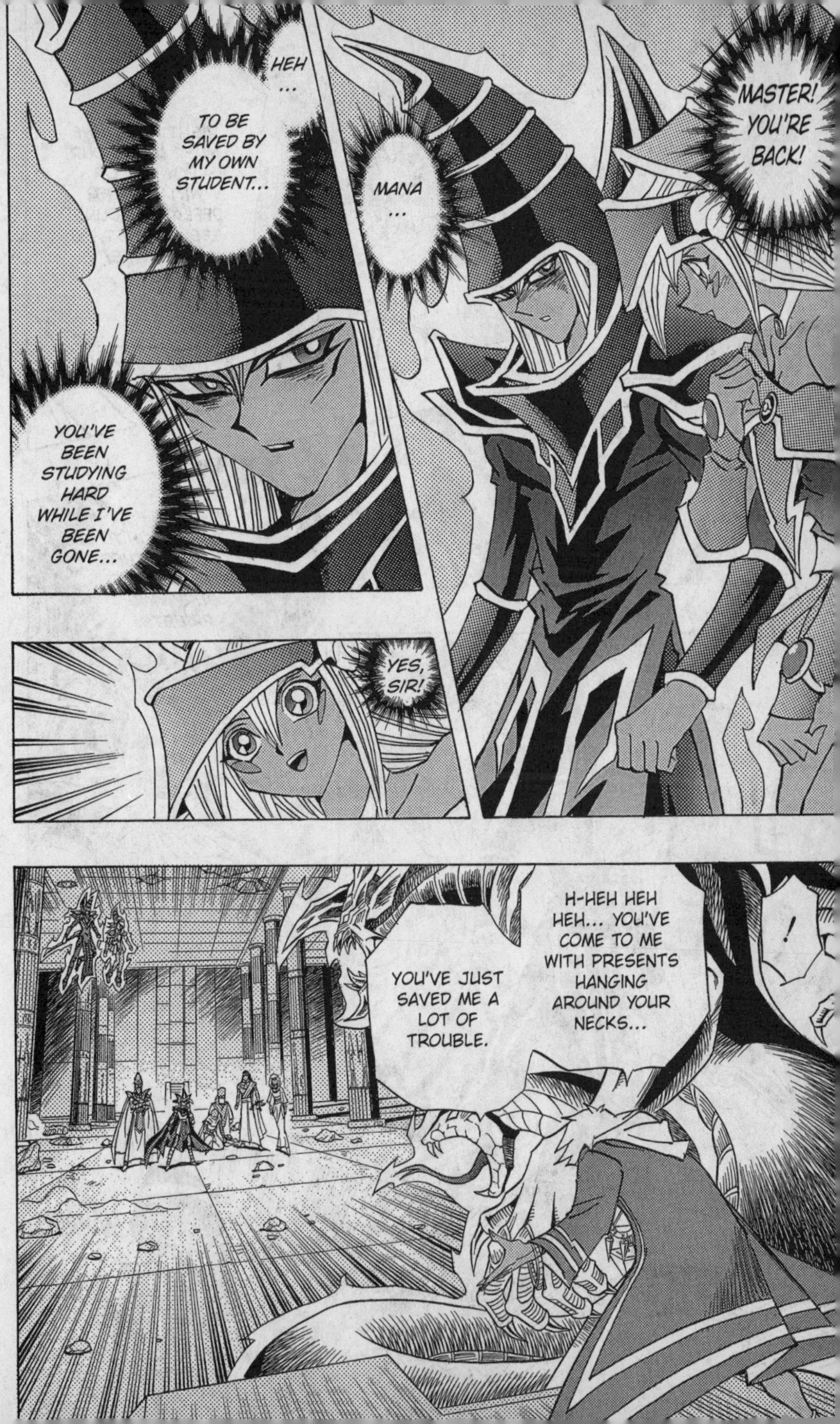
MASTER! YOU'RE BACK!
MANA...
HEH...
TO BE SAVED BY MY OWN STUDENT...
YOU'VE BEEN STUDYING HARD WHILE I'VE BEEN GONE...
YES, SIR!
!
H-HEH HEH HEH... YOU'VE COME TO ME WITH PRESENTS HANGING AROUND YOUR NECKS...
YOU'VE JUST SAVED ME A LOT OF TROUBLE.

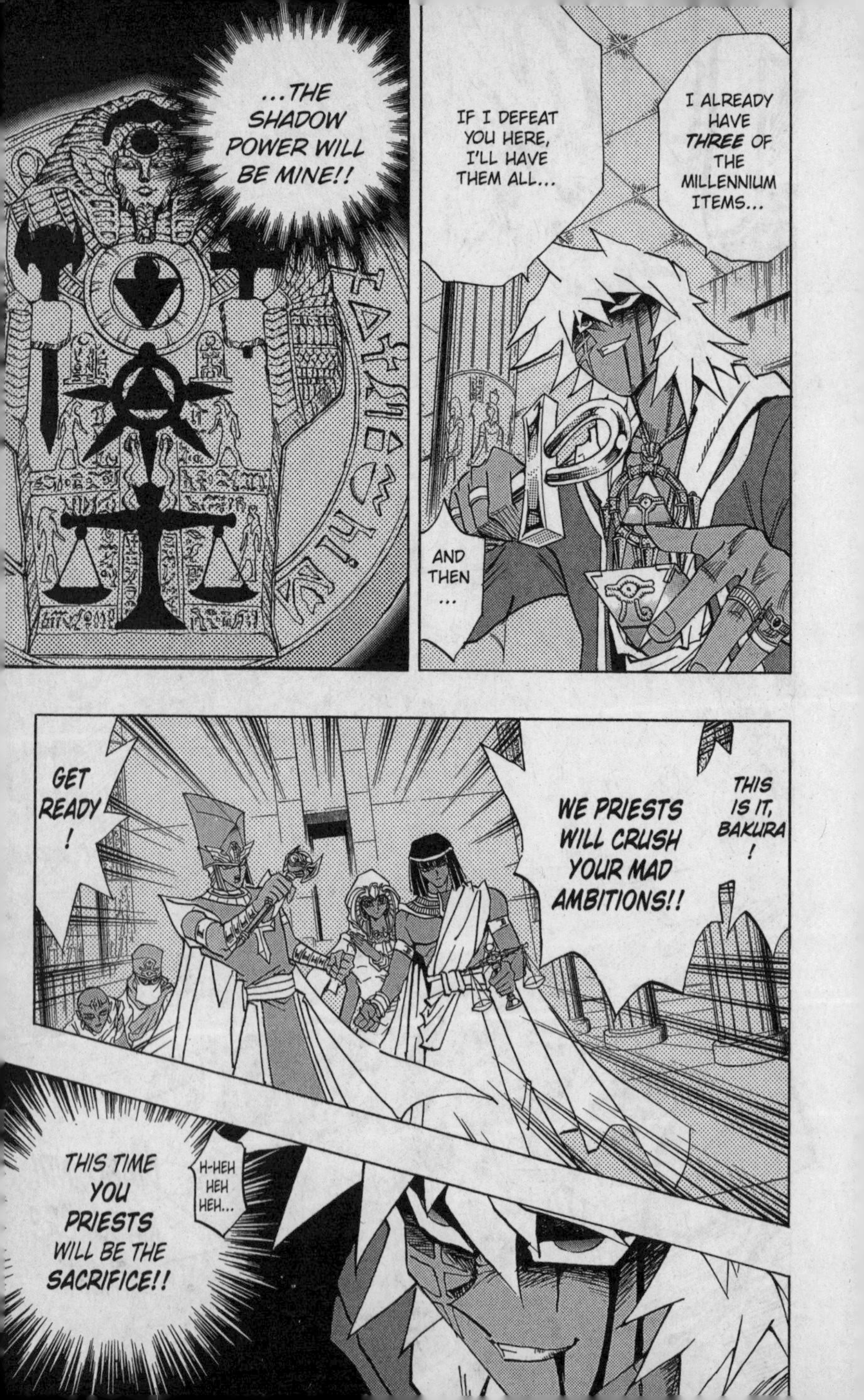
I ALREADY HAVE THREE OF THE MILLENNIUM ITEMS...
IF I DEFEAT YOU HERE, I'LL HAVE THEM ALL...
AND THEN ...
...THE SHADOW POWER WILL BE MINE!!
THIS IS IT, BAKURA!
WE PRIESTS WILL CRUSH YOUR MAD AMBITIONS!!
GET READY!
H-HEH HEH HEH...
THIS TIME YOU PRIESTS WILL BE THE SACRIFICE!!

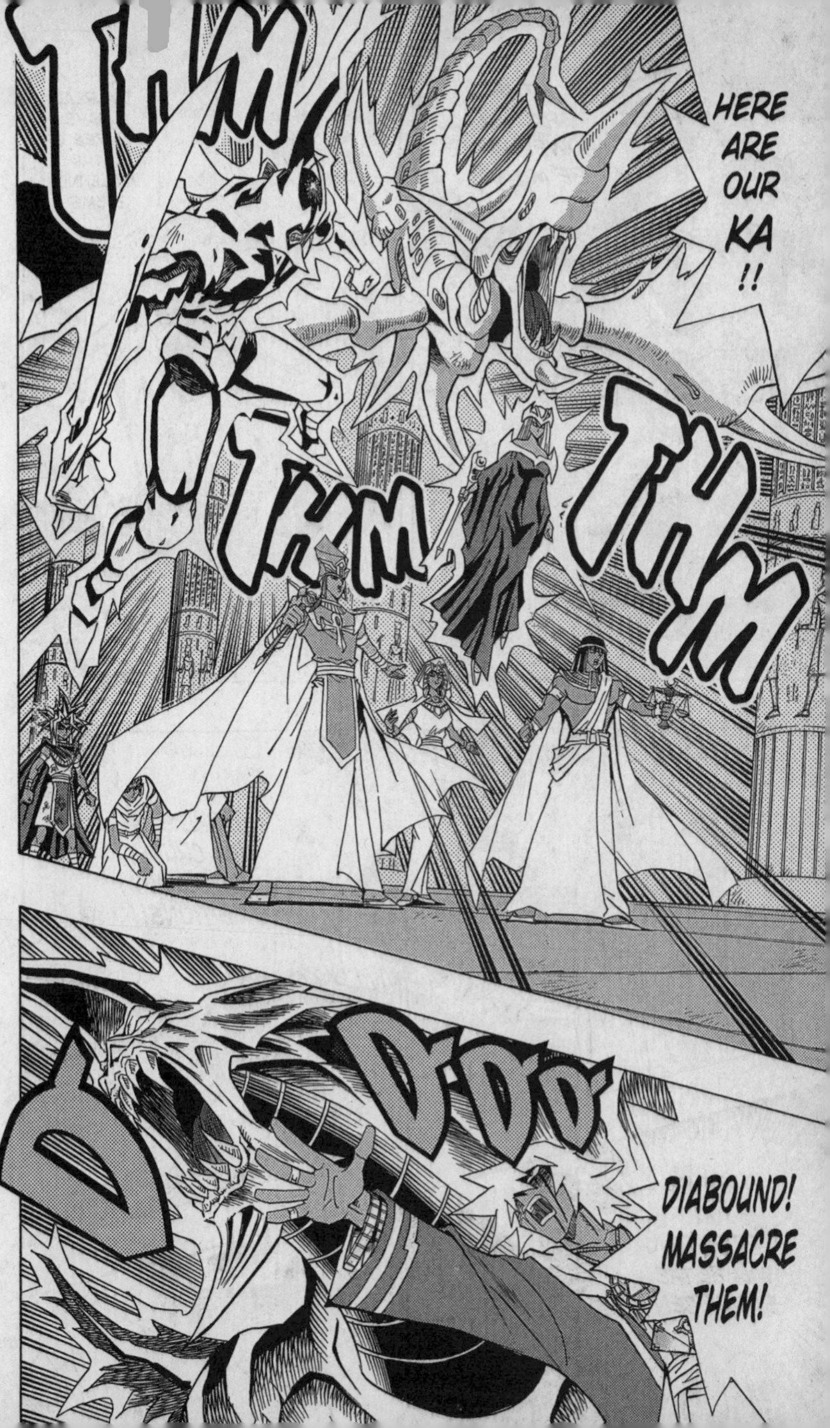
HERE ARE OUR KA!!
THM
THM
THM
DIABOUND! MASSACRE THEM!

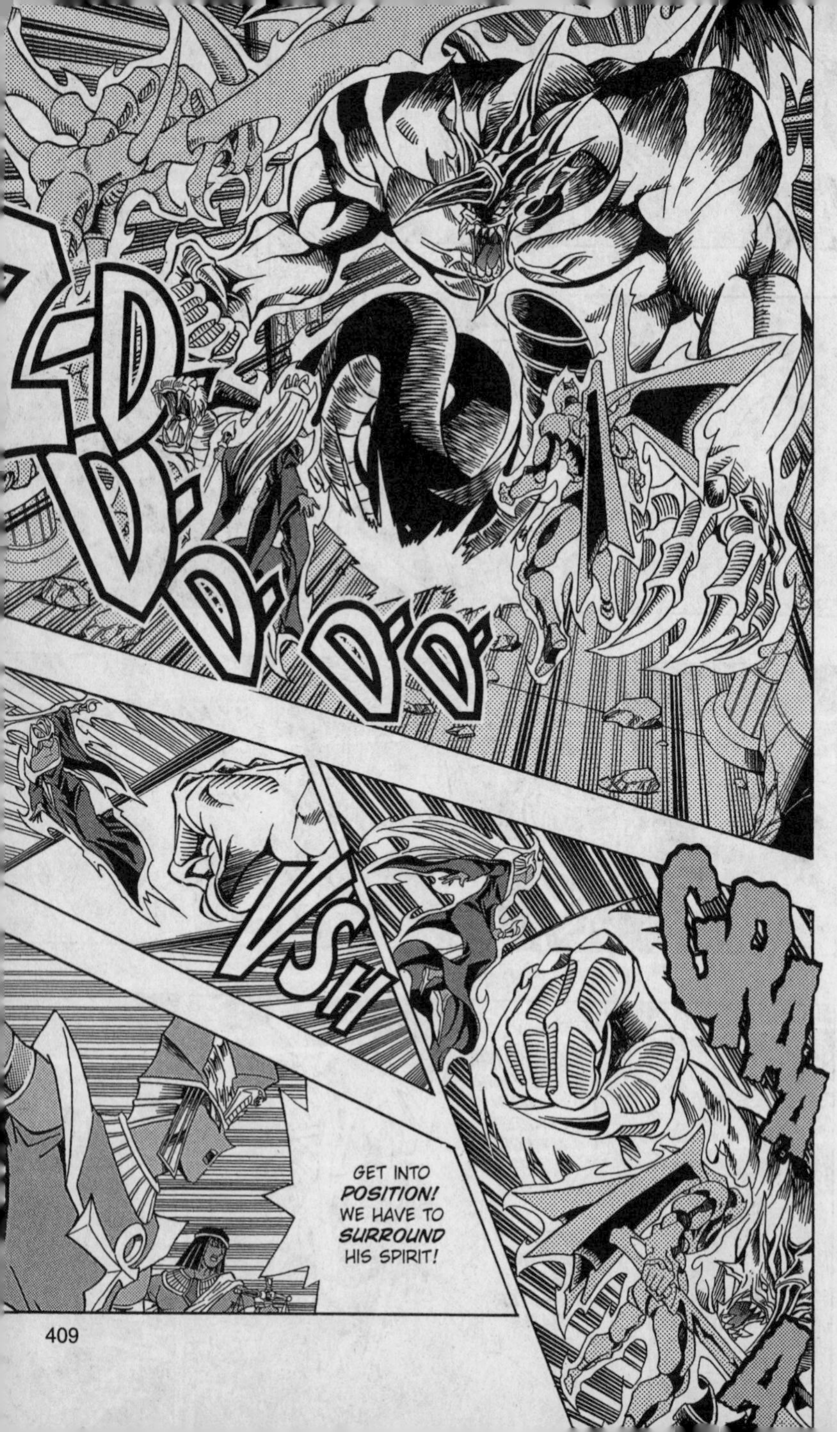
VSH
GET INTO *POSITION!* WE HAVE TO *SURROUND* HIS SPIRIT!

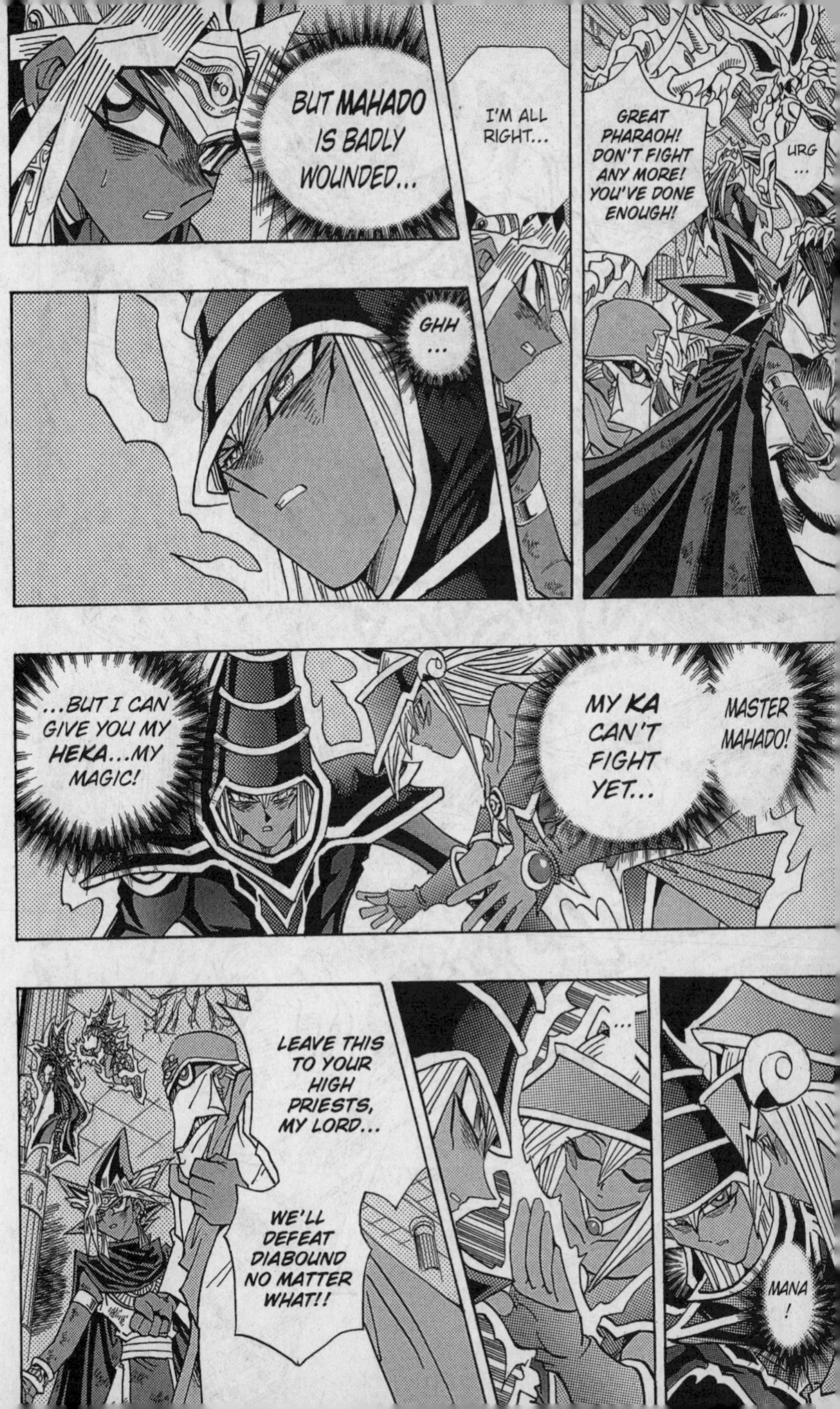
GREAT PHARAOH! DON'T FIGHT ANY MORE! YOU'VE DONE ENOUGH!
URG...
I'M ALL RIGHT...
BUT MAHADO IS BADLY WOUNDED...
GHH...
MASTER MAHADO!
MY KA CAN'T FIGHT YET...
...BUT I CAN GIVE YOU MY HEKA...MY MAGIC!
MANA!
...
LEAVE THIS TO YOUR HIGH PRIESTS, MY LORD...
WE'LL DEFEAT DIABOUND NO MATTER WHAT!!

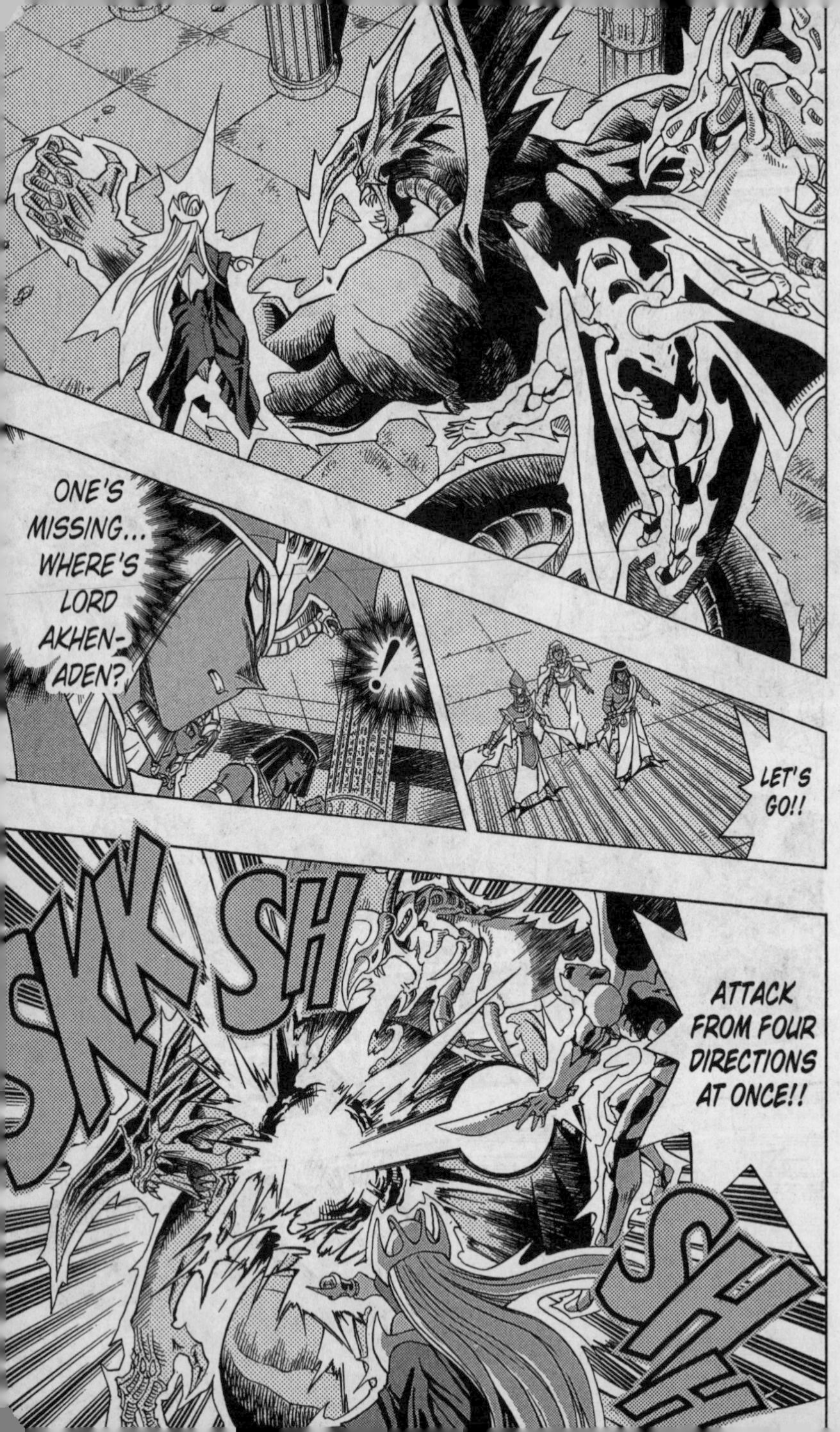
LET'S GO!!
ONE'S MISSING... WHERE'S LORD AKHEN-ADEN?
!
ATTACK FROM FOUR DIRECTIONS AT ONCE!!
SH
SH

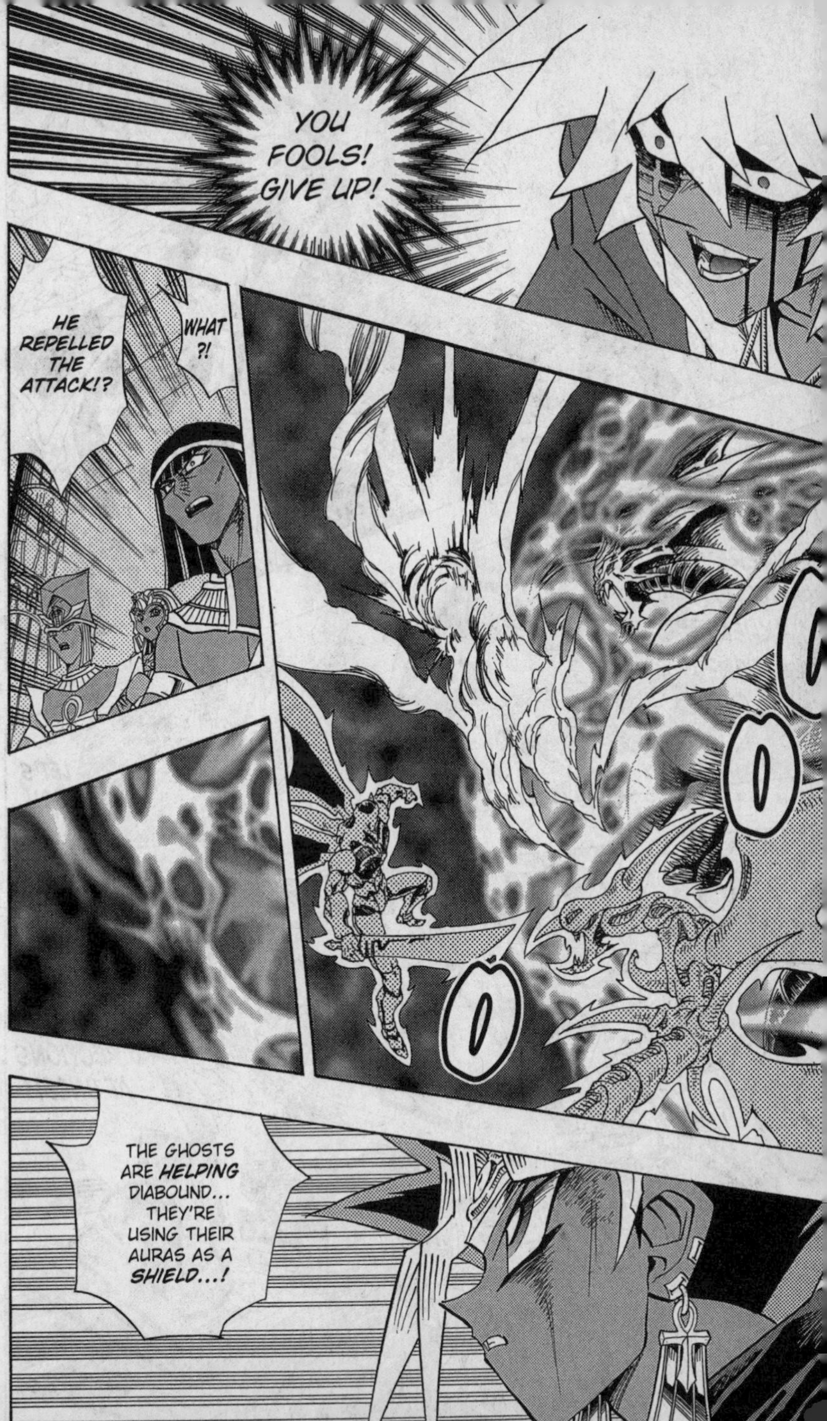
YOU FOOLS! GIVE UP!
WHAT ?!
HE REPELLED THE ATTACK!?
THE GHOSTS ARE HELPING DIABOUND... THEY'RE USING THEIR AURAS AS A SHIELD...!

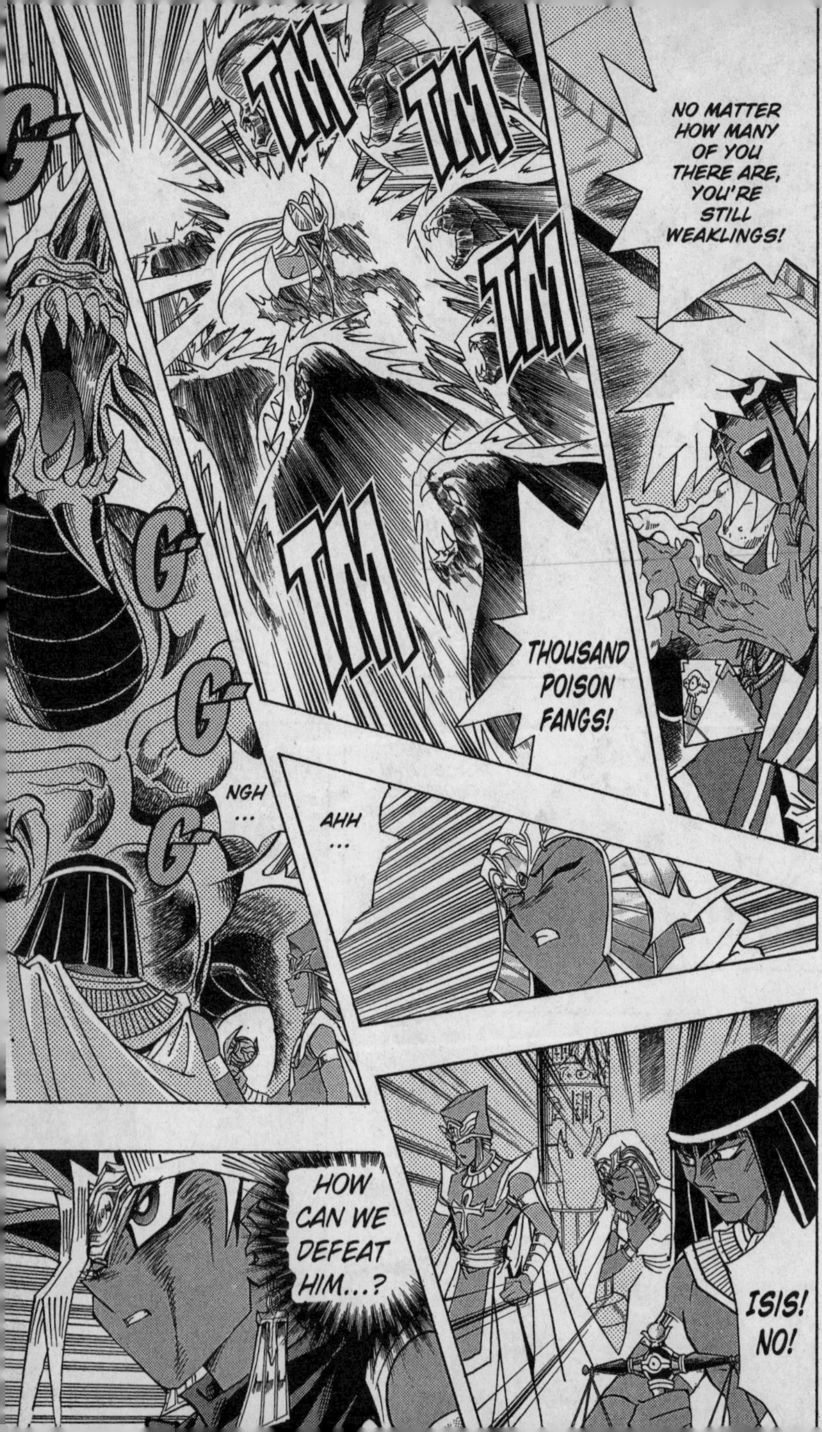
NO MATTER HOW MANY OF YOU THERE ARE, YOU'RE STILL WEAKLINGS!
TM
TM
TM
TM
THOUSAND POISON FANGS!
G
G
G
G
AHH ...
NGH ...
ISIS! NO!
HOW CAN WE DEFEAT HIM...?

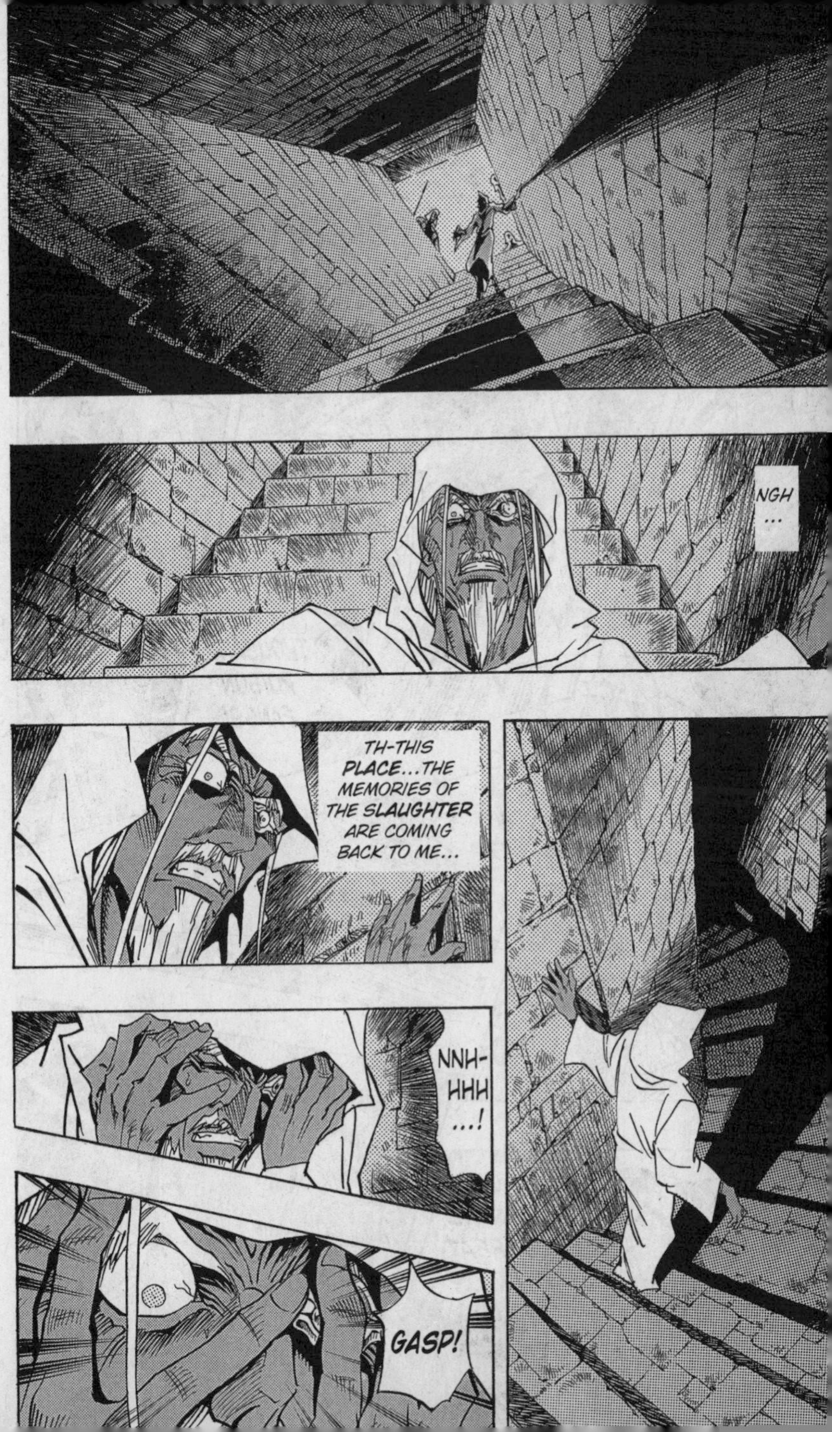
NGH ...
TH-THIS PLACE...THE MEMORIES OF THE SLAUGHTER ARE COMING BACK TO ME...
NNH-HHH ...!
GASP!

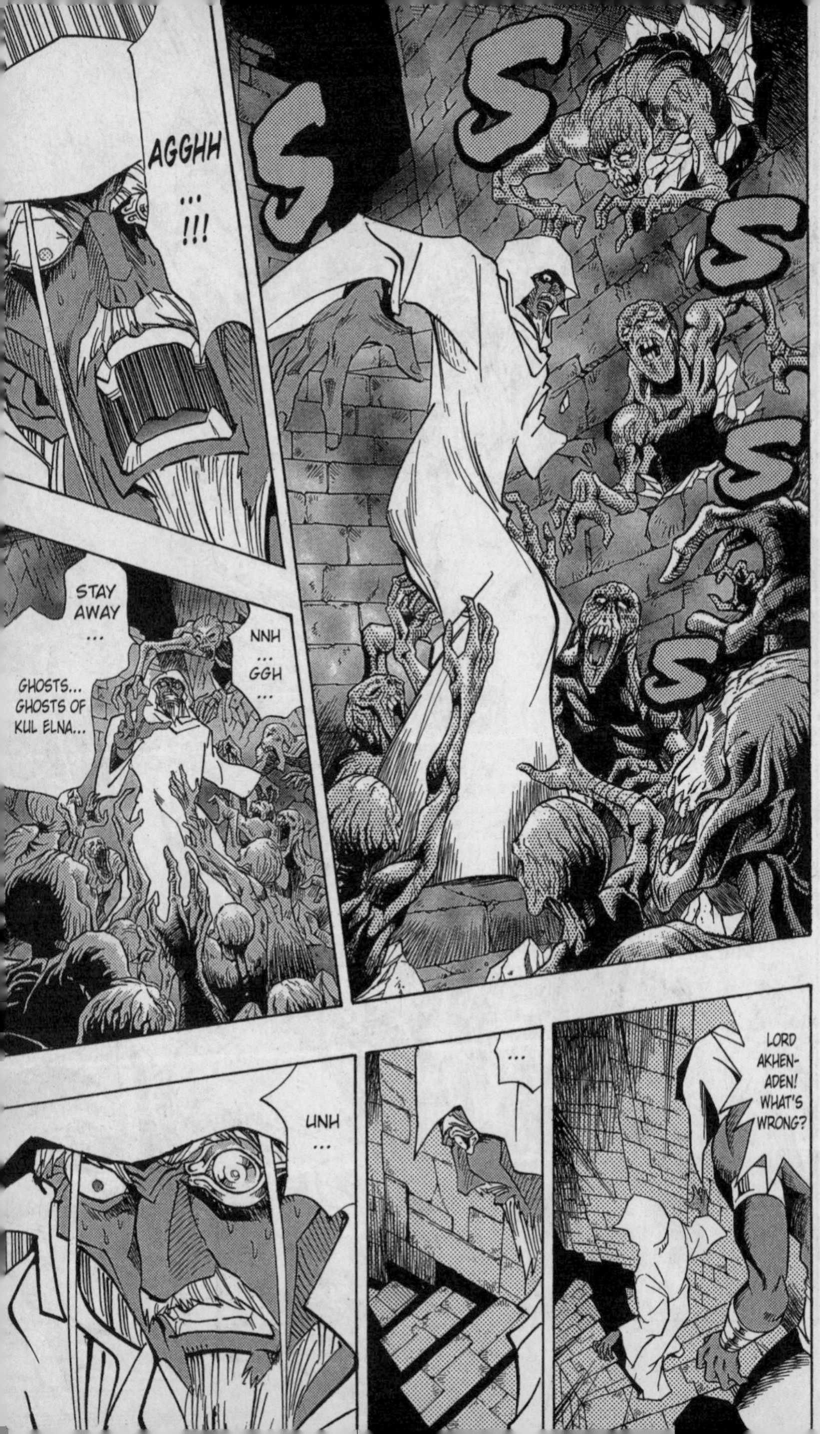
S
S
S
S
S
AGGHH ... !!!
NNH ... GGH ...
STAY AWAY ...
GHOSTS... GHOSTS OF KUL ELNA...
LORD AKHEN-ADEN! WHAT'S WRONG?
...
UNH ...

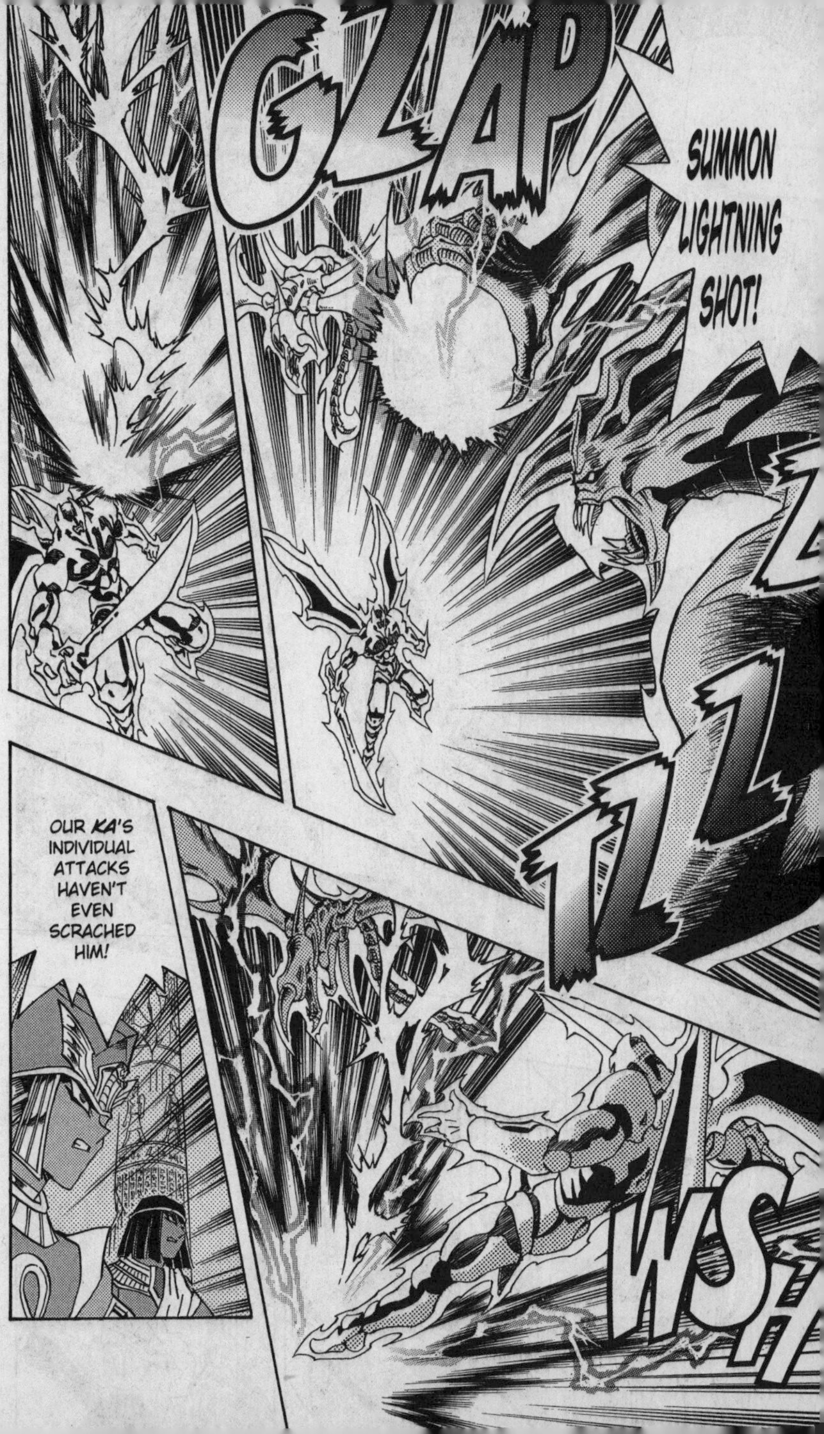
SUMMON LIGHTNING SHOT!
GZAP
ZZZ
OUR KA'S INDIVIDUAL ATTACKS HAVEN'T EVEN SCRACHED HIM!
WSH

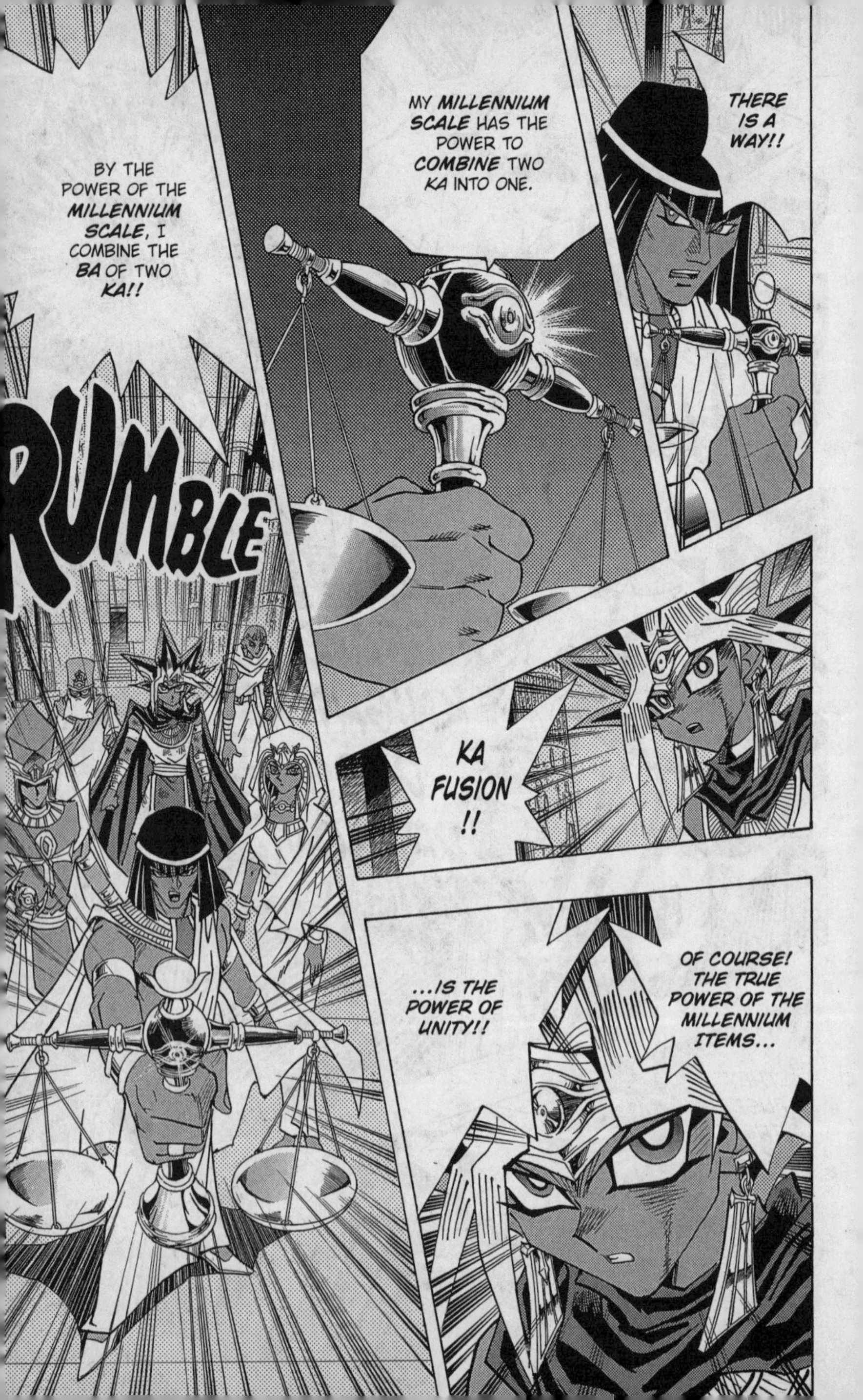
THERE IS A WAY!!
MY MILLENNIUM SCALE HAS THE POWER TO COMBINE TWO KA INTO ONE.
BY THE POWER OF THE MILLENNIUM SCALE, I COMBINE THE BA OF TWO KA!!
RUMBLE
KA FUSION !!
OF COURSE! THE TRUE POWER OF THE MILLENNIUM ITEMS...
...IS THE POWER OF UNITY!!

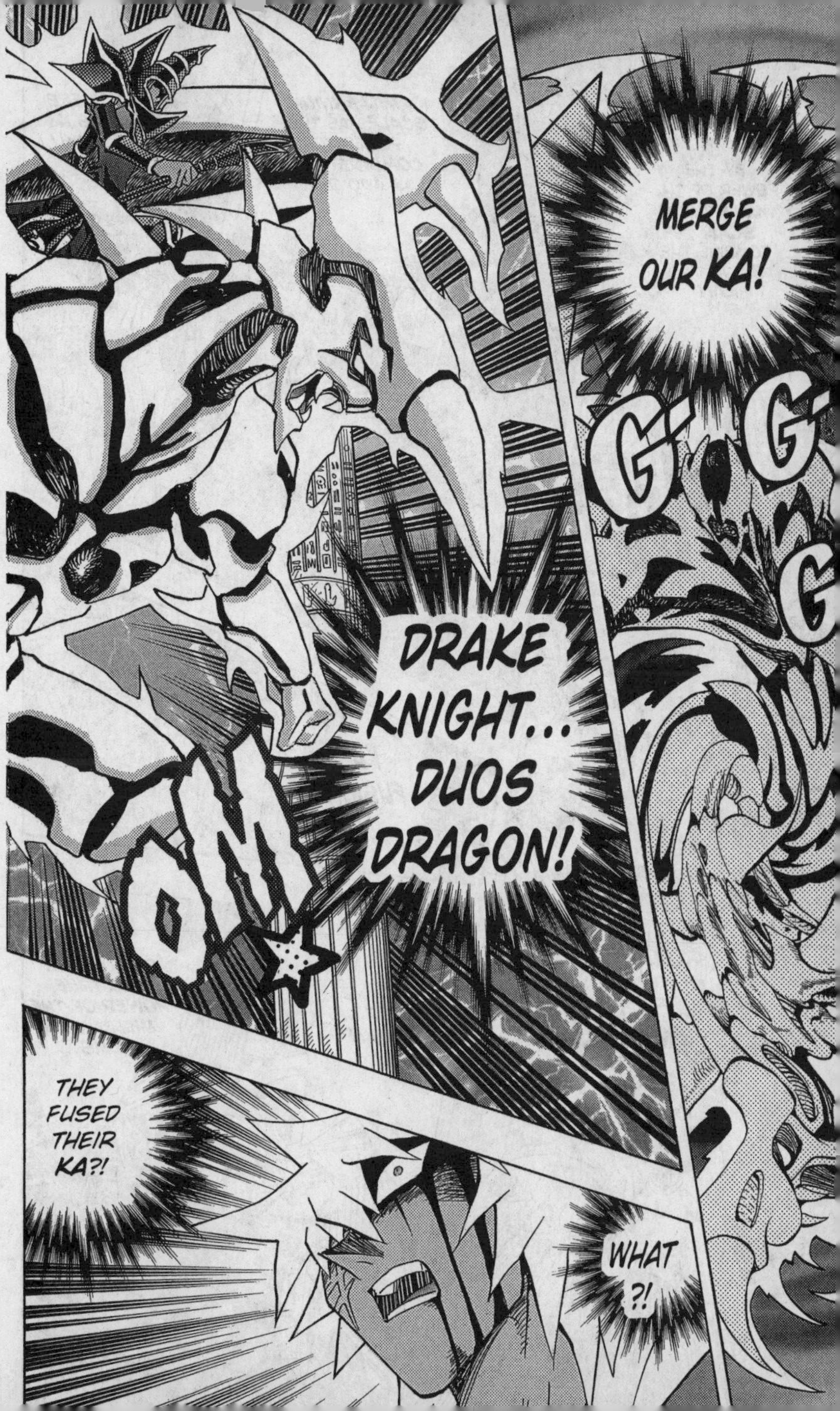
MERGE OUR KA!
G-G-G
DRAKE KNIGHT... DUOS DRAGON!
OM
WHAT ?!
THEY FUSED THEIR KA?!

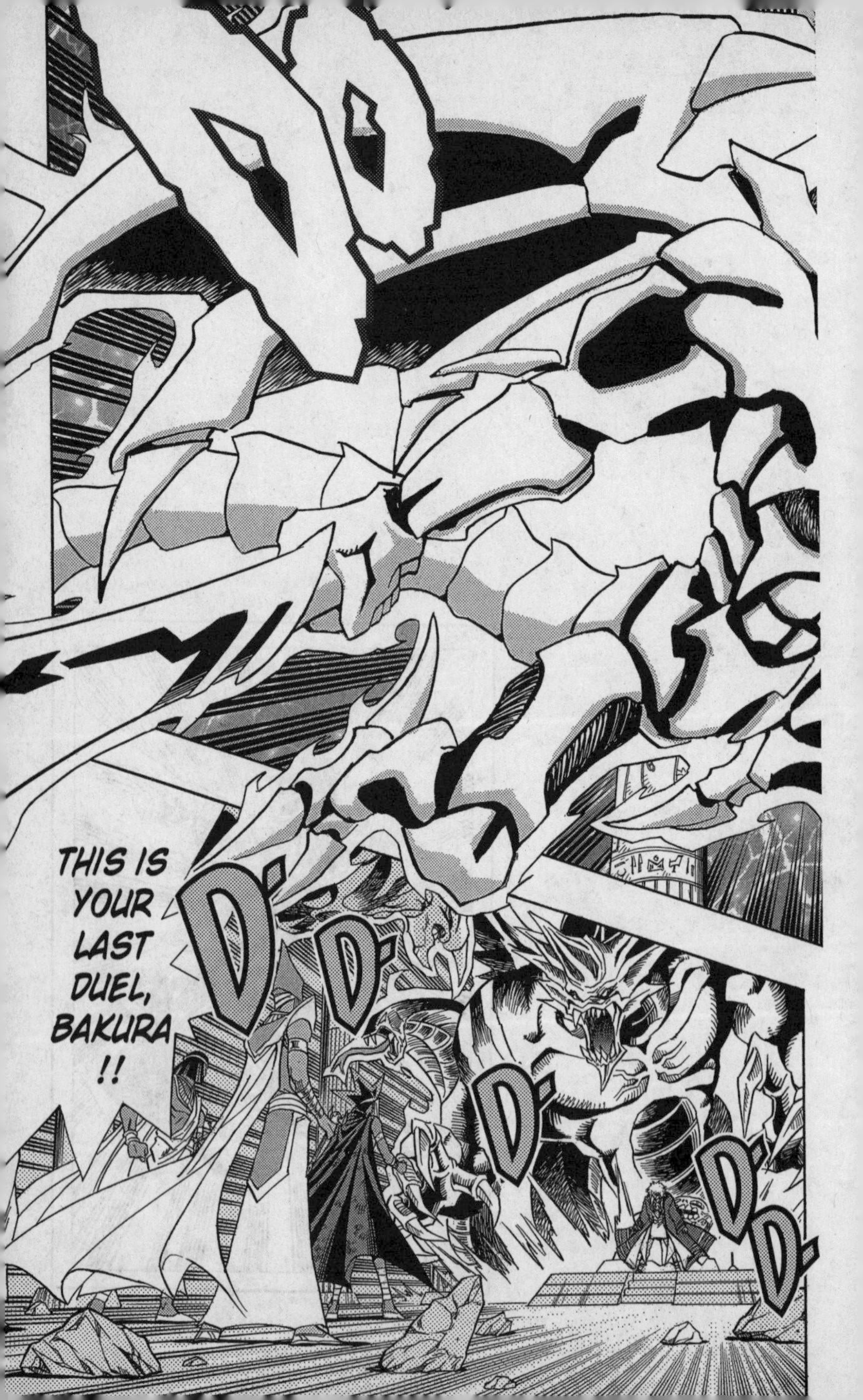
THIS IS YOUR LAST DUEL, BAKURA !!
D
D
D
D
D

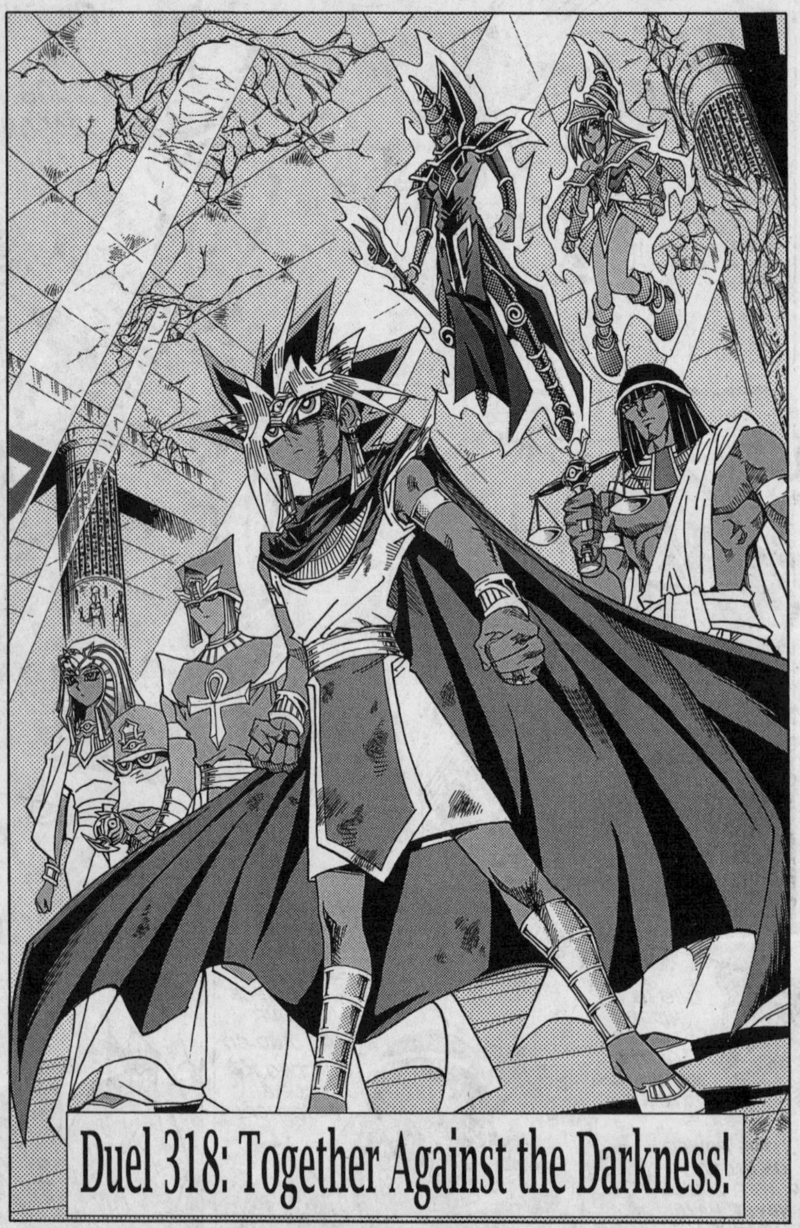
Duel 318: Together Against the Darkness!

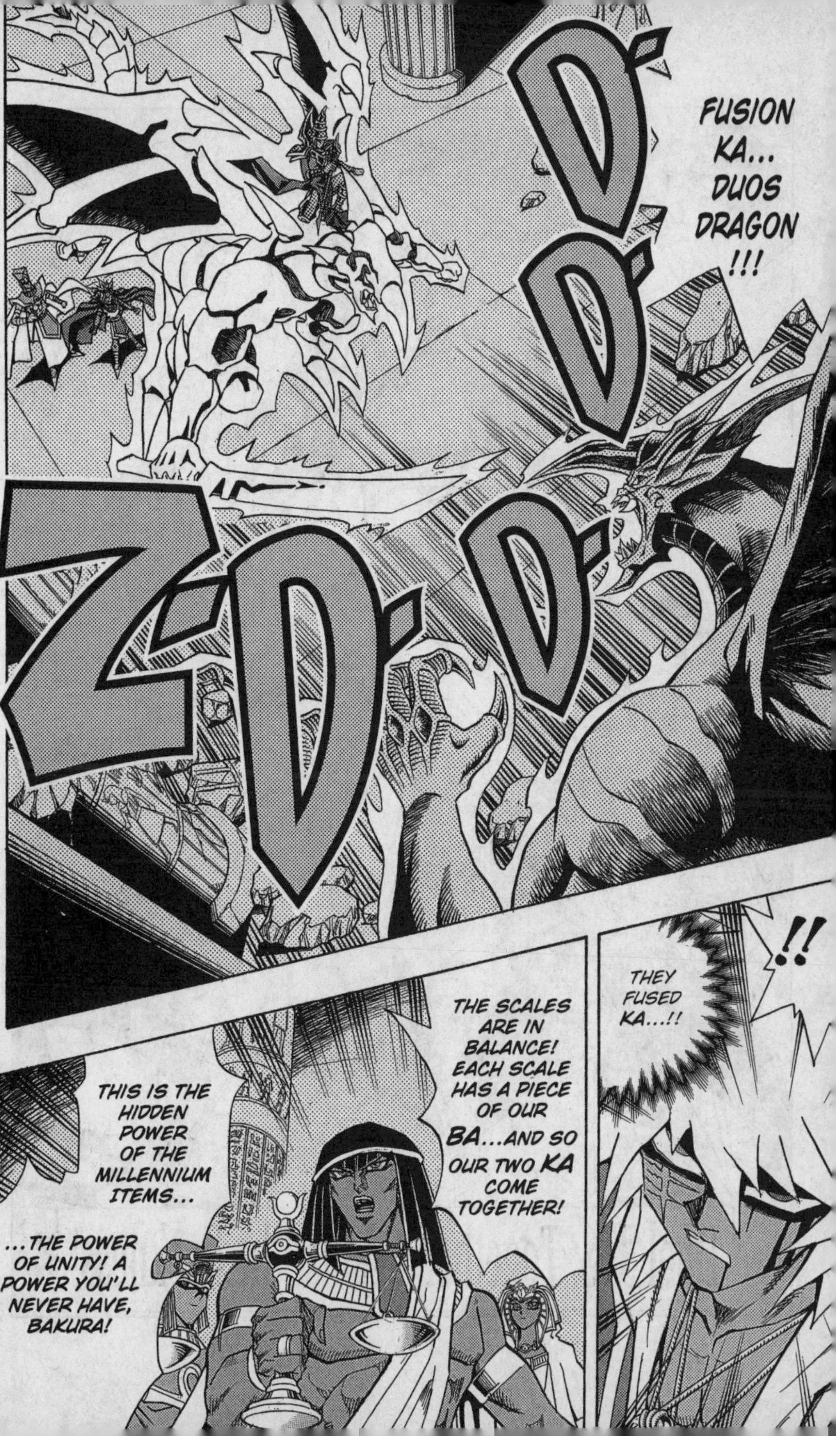
FUSION KA... DUOS DRAGON !!!
ZDDDD
!!
THEY FUSED KA...!!
THE SCALES ARE IN BALANCE! EACH SCALE HAS A PIECE OF OUR BA...AND SO OUR TWO KA COME TOGETHER!
THIS IS THE HIDDEN POWER OF THE MILLENNIUM ITEMS...
...THE POWER OF UNITY! A POWER YOU'LL NEVER HAVE, BAKURA!

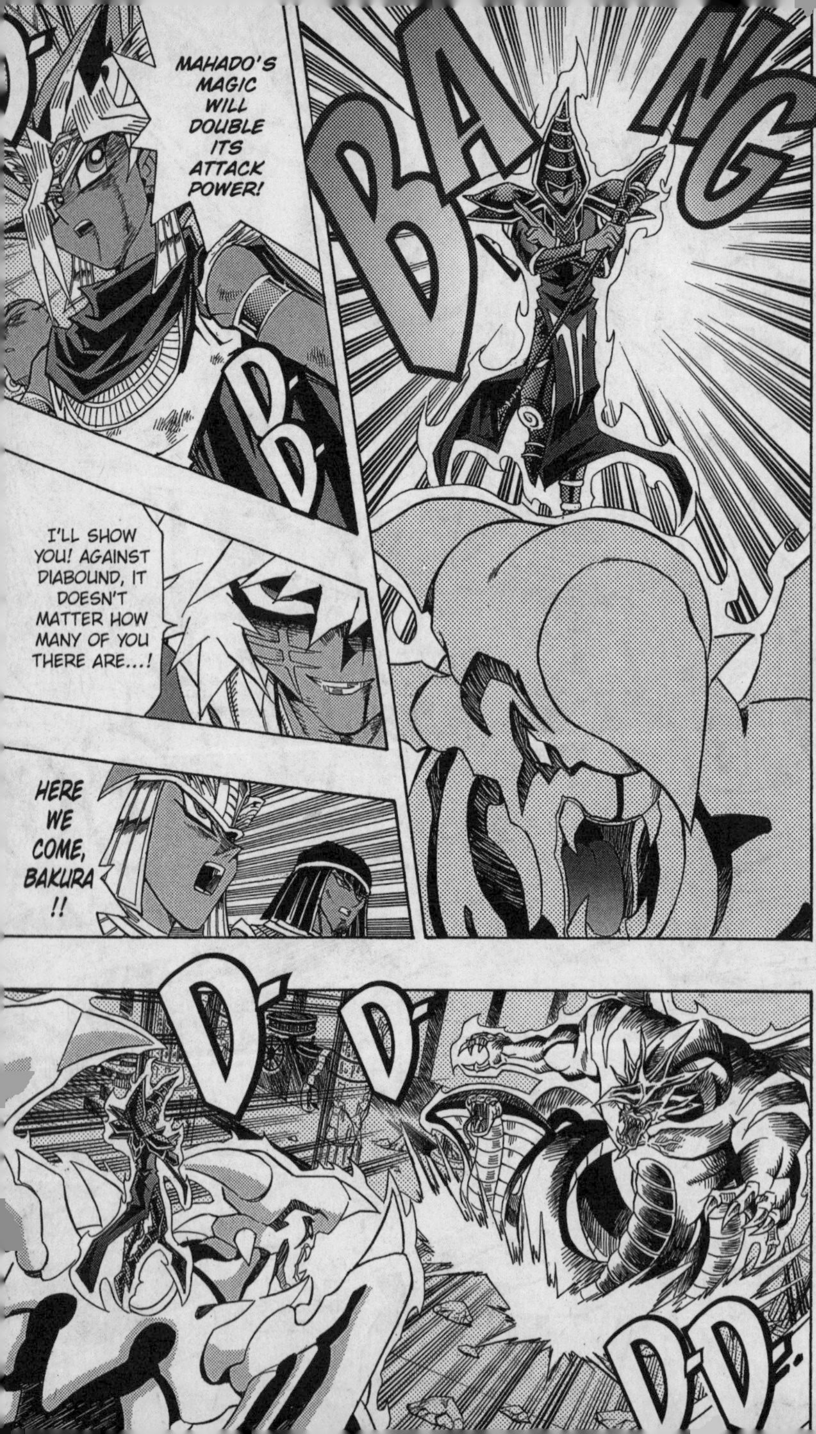
BANG
MAHADO'S MAGIC WILL DOUBLE ITS ATTACK POWER!
DD
I'LL SHOW YOU! AGAINST DIABOUND, IT DOESN'T MATTER HOW MANY OF YOU THERE ARE...!
HERE WE COME, BAKURA!!
D D
D-D

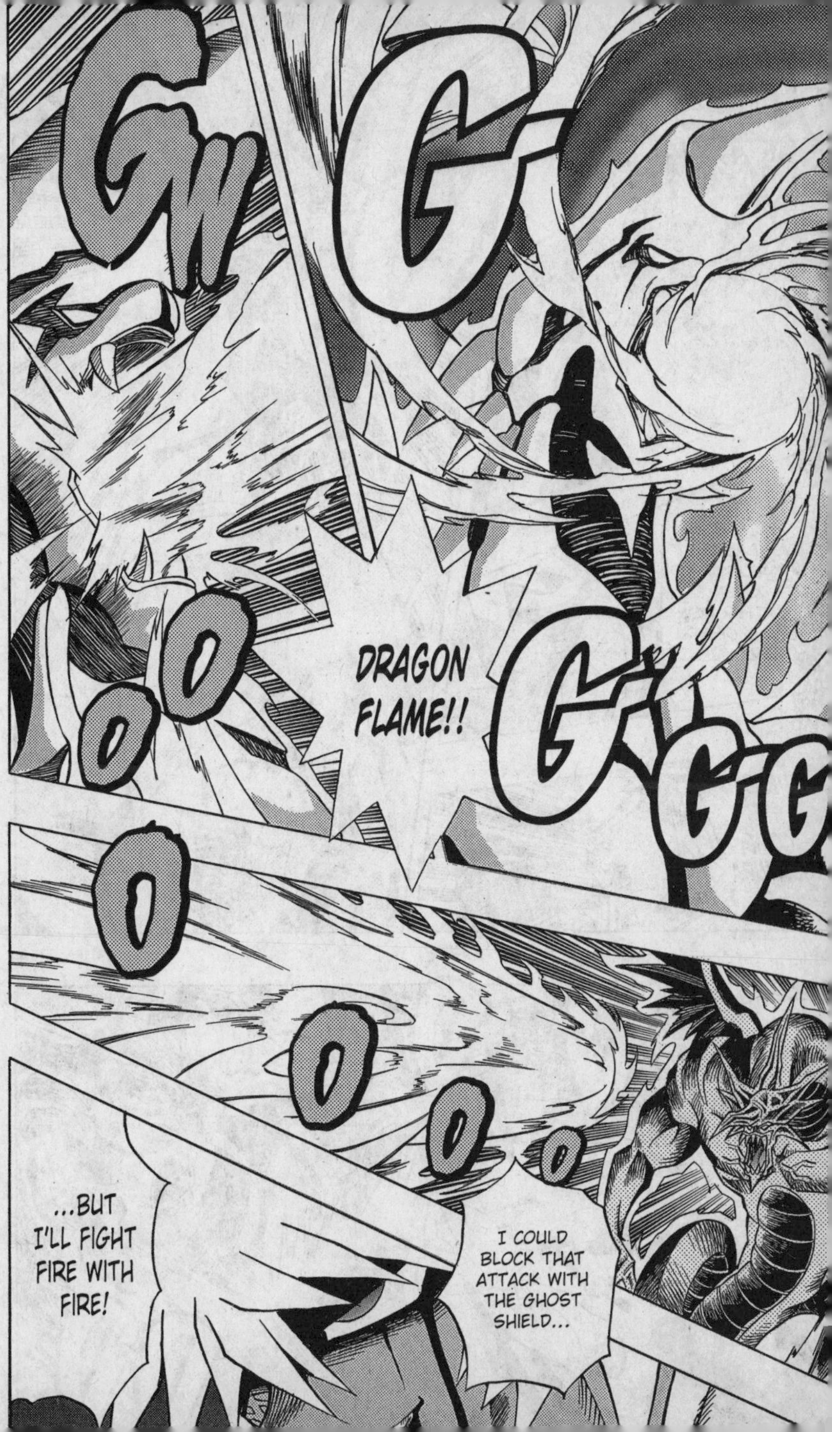

GN G-G
DRAGON FLAME!!
G-GGG
OOOO
OOOO
I COULD BLOCK THAT ATTACK WITH THE GHOST SHIELD...
...BUT I'LL FIGHT FIRE WITH FIRE!

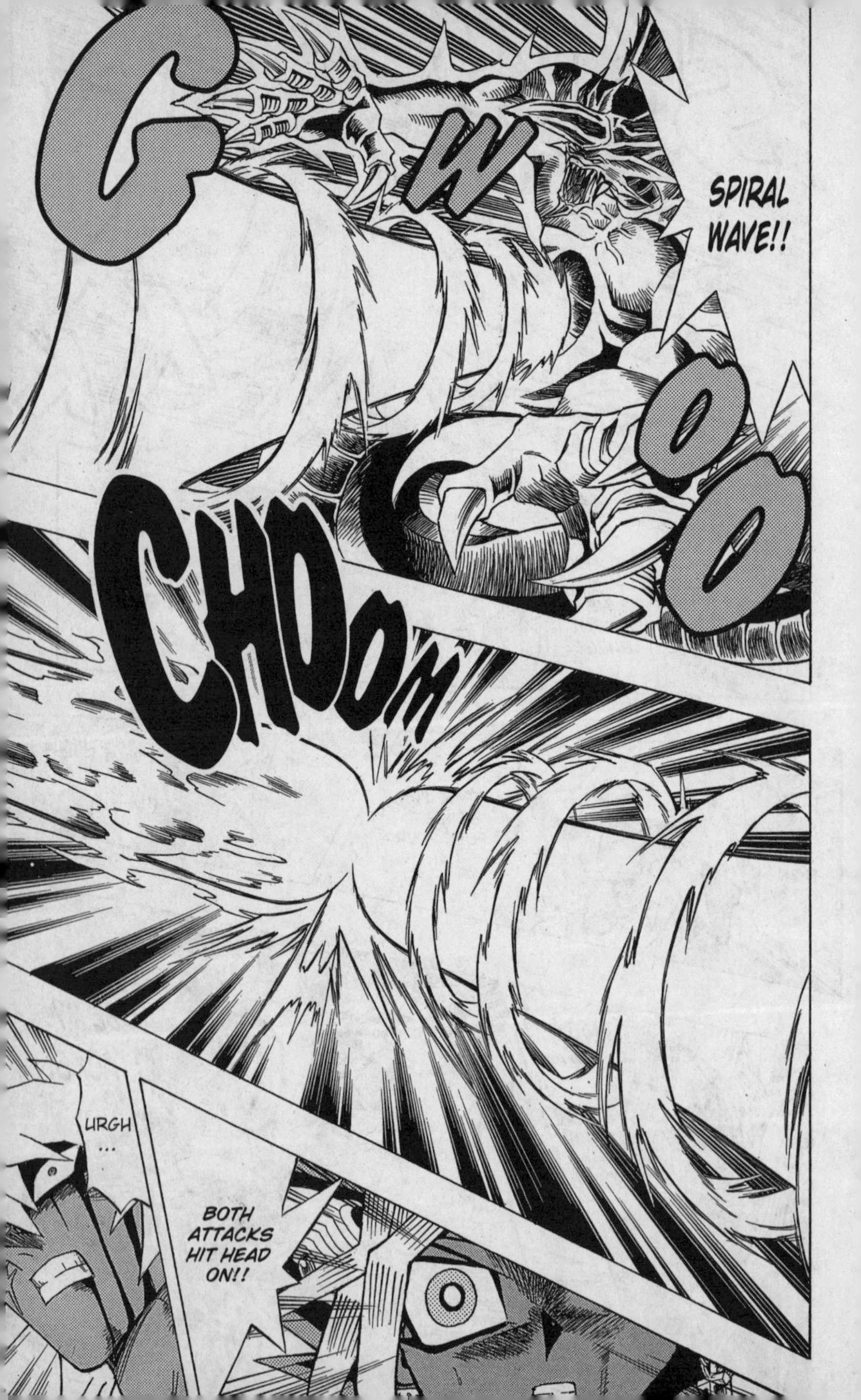
SPIRAL WAVE!!
GWOOO
CHOOM
URGH...
BOTH ATTACKS HIT HEAD ON!!

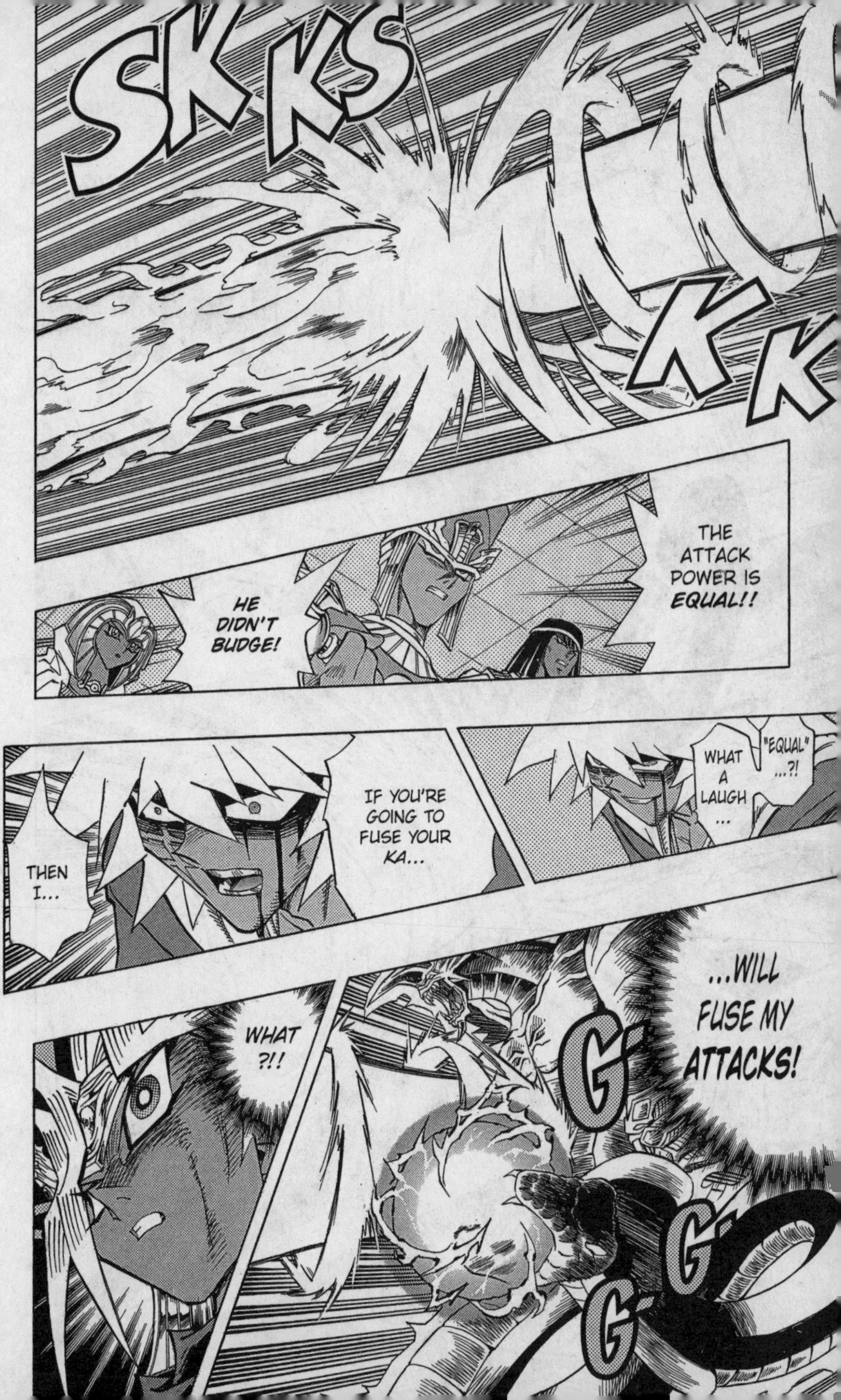
K K
SKKS
THE ATTACK POWER IS EQUAL!!
HE DIDN'T BUDGE!
"EQUAL" ...?!
WHAT A LAUGH ...
IF YOU'RE GOING TO FUSE YOUR KA...
THEN I...
...WILL FUSE MY ATTACKS!
G
WHAT ?!!
G G G

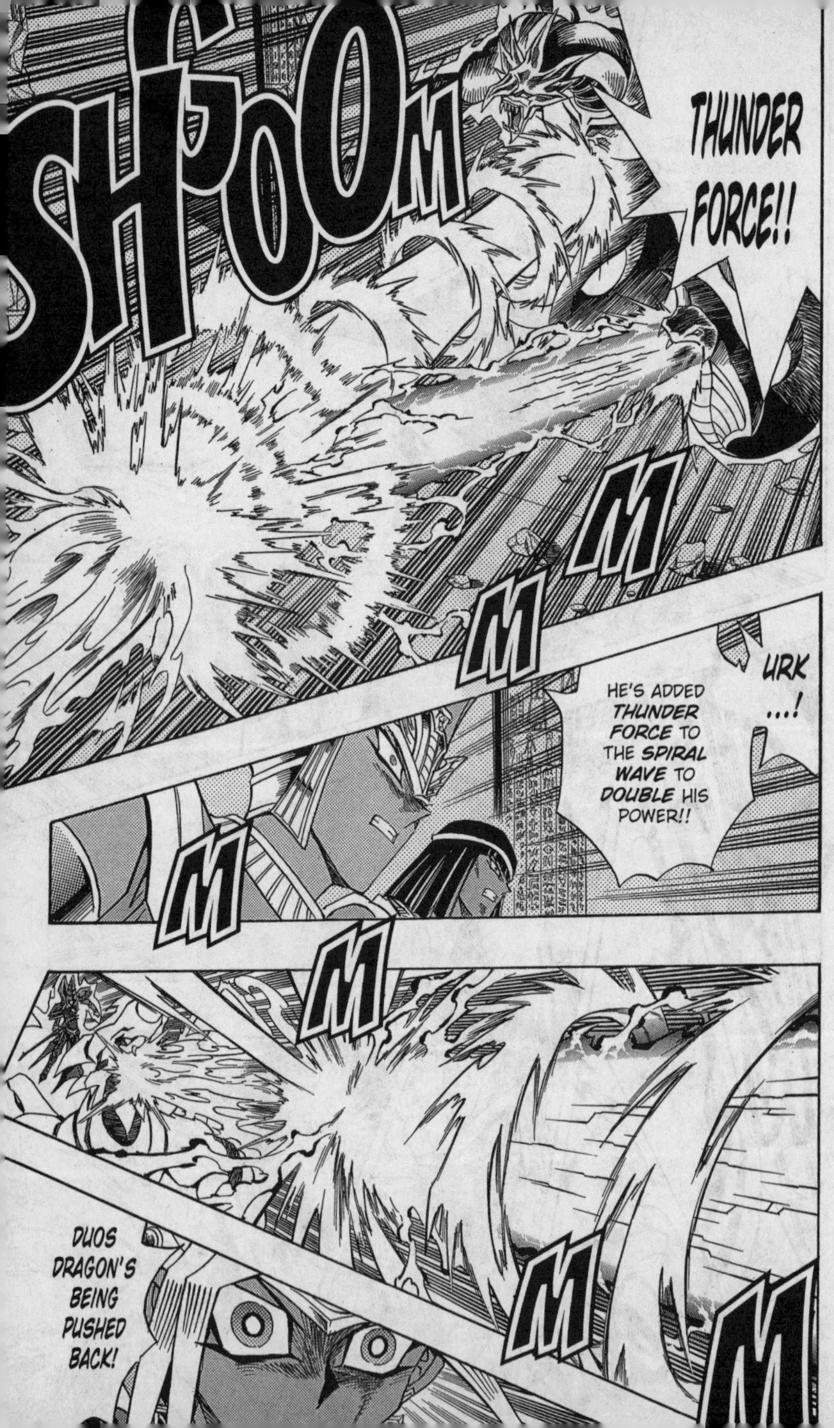
SHOOOM
THUNDER FORCE!!
MMMM
URK ...!
HE'S ADDED THUNDER FORCE TO THE SPIRAL WAVE TO DOUBLE HIS POWER!!
MMM
DUOS DRAGON'S BEING PUSHED BACK!

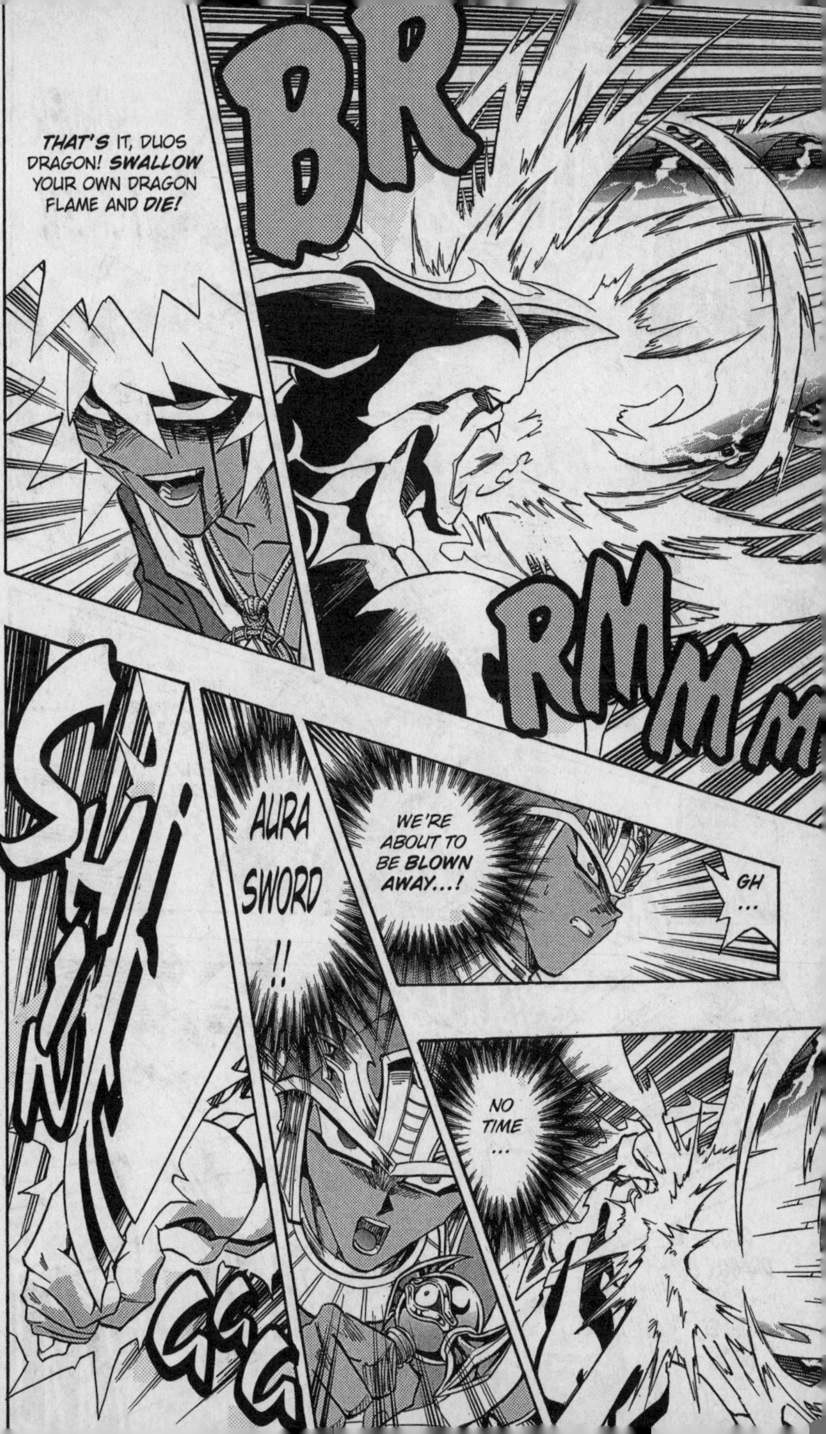
BR
RMMM
THAT'S IT, DUOS DRAGON! SWALLOW YOUR OWN DRAGON FLAME AND DIE!
GH...
WE'RE ABOUT TO BE BLOWN AWAY...!
NO TIME...
AURA SWORD!!

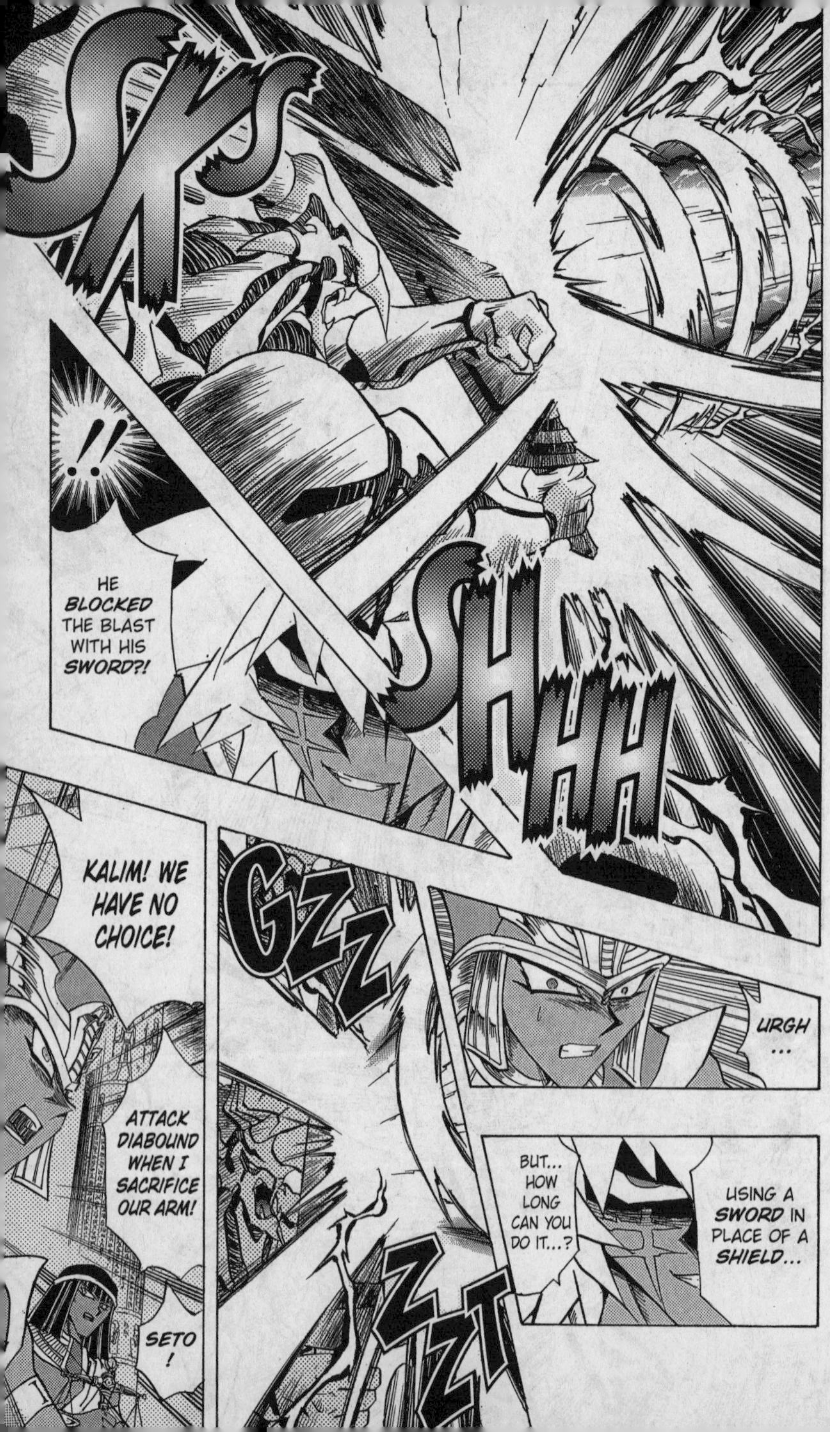
SKS
!!
HE BLOCKED THE BLAST WITH HIS SWORD?!
SHHH
KALIM! WE HAVE NO CHOICE!
ATTACK DIABOUND WHEN I SACRIFICE OUR ARM!
SETO!
GZZ
URGH...
USING A SWORD IN PLACE OF A SHIELD...
BUT... HOW LONG CAN YOU DO IT...?
ZZT

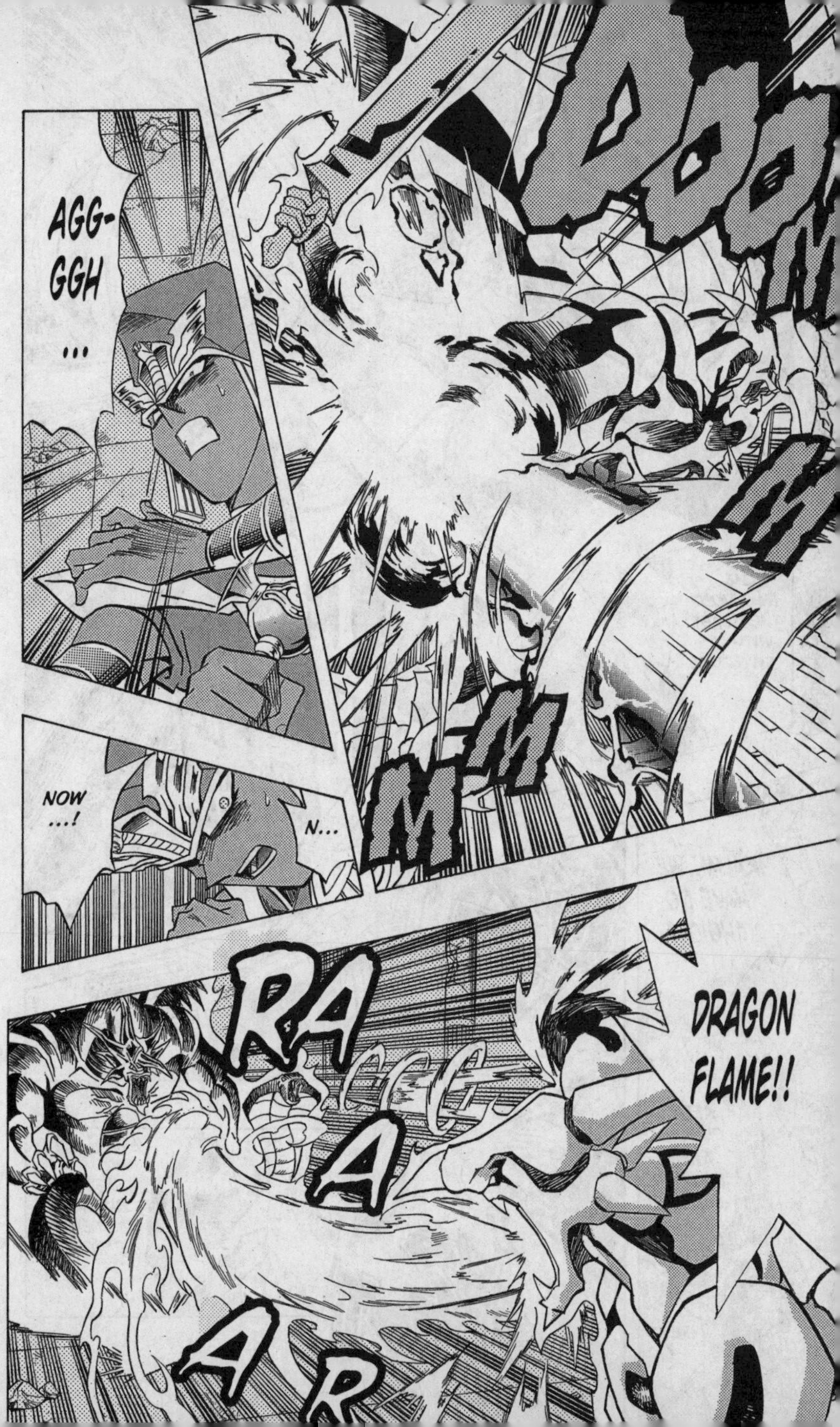

DOOM
AGG-GGH ...
MMM
N...
NOW ...!
DRAGON FLAME!!
RAAAR

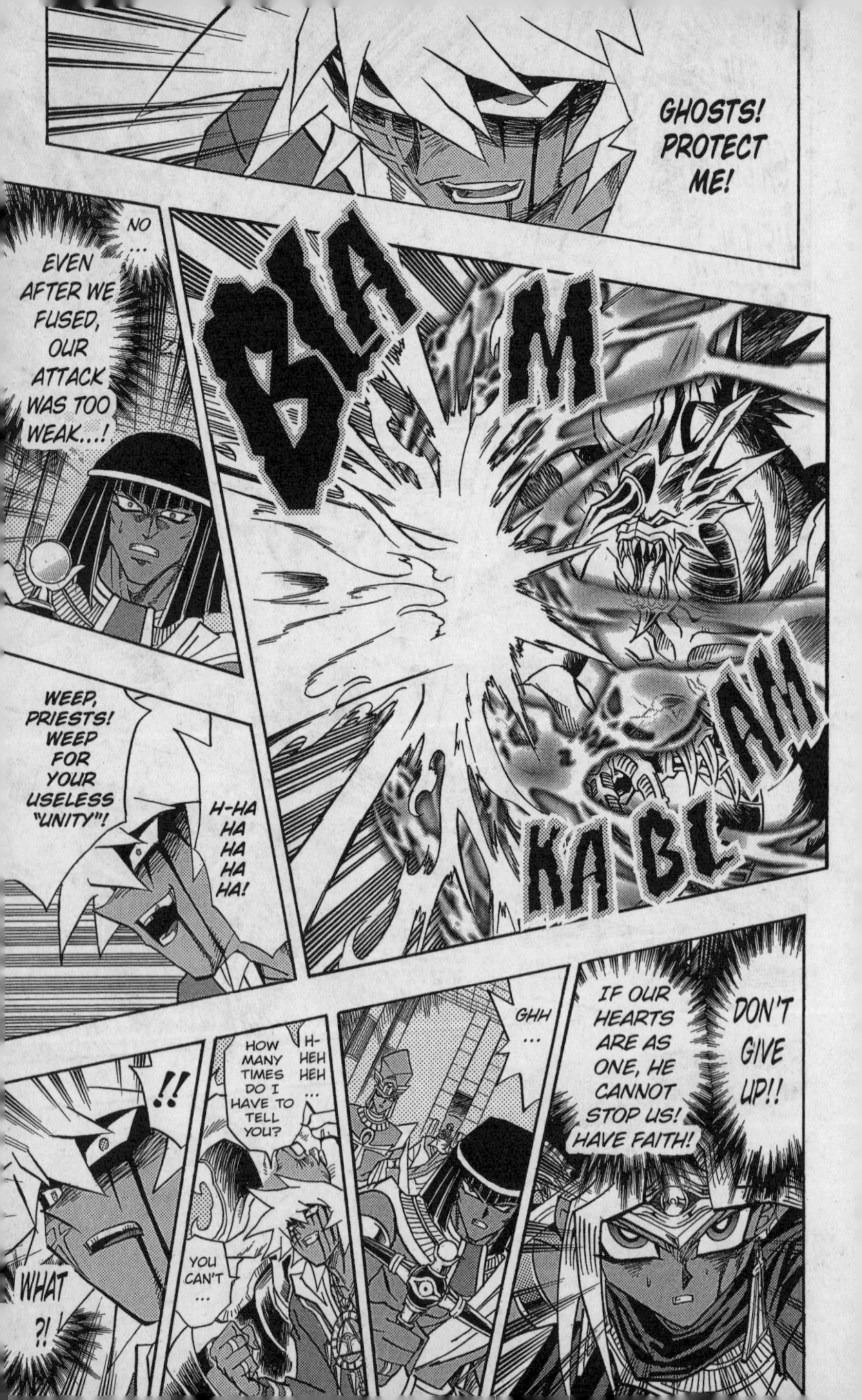
GHOSTS! PROTECT ME!
BLAM
KABLAM
NO ...
EVEN AFTER WE FUSED, OUR ATTACK WAS TOO WEAK...!
WEEP, PRIESTS! WEEP FOR YOUR USELESS "UNITY"!
H-HA HA HA HA HA!
DON'T GIVE UP!!
IF OUR HEARTS ARE AS ONE, HE CANNOT STOP US! HAVE FAITH!
GHH ...
H-HEH HEH ...
HOW MANY TIMES DO I HAVE TO TELL YOU?
YOU CAN'T ...
!!
WHAT ?!

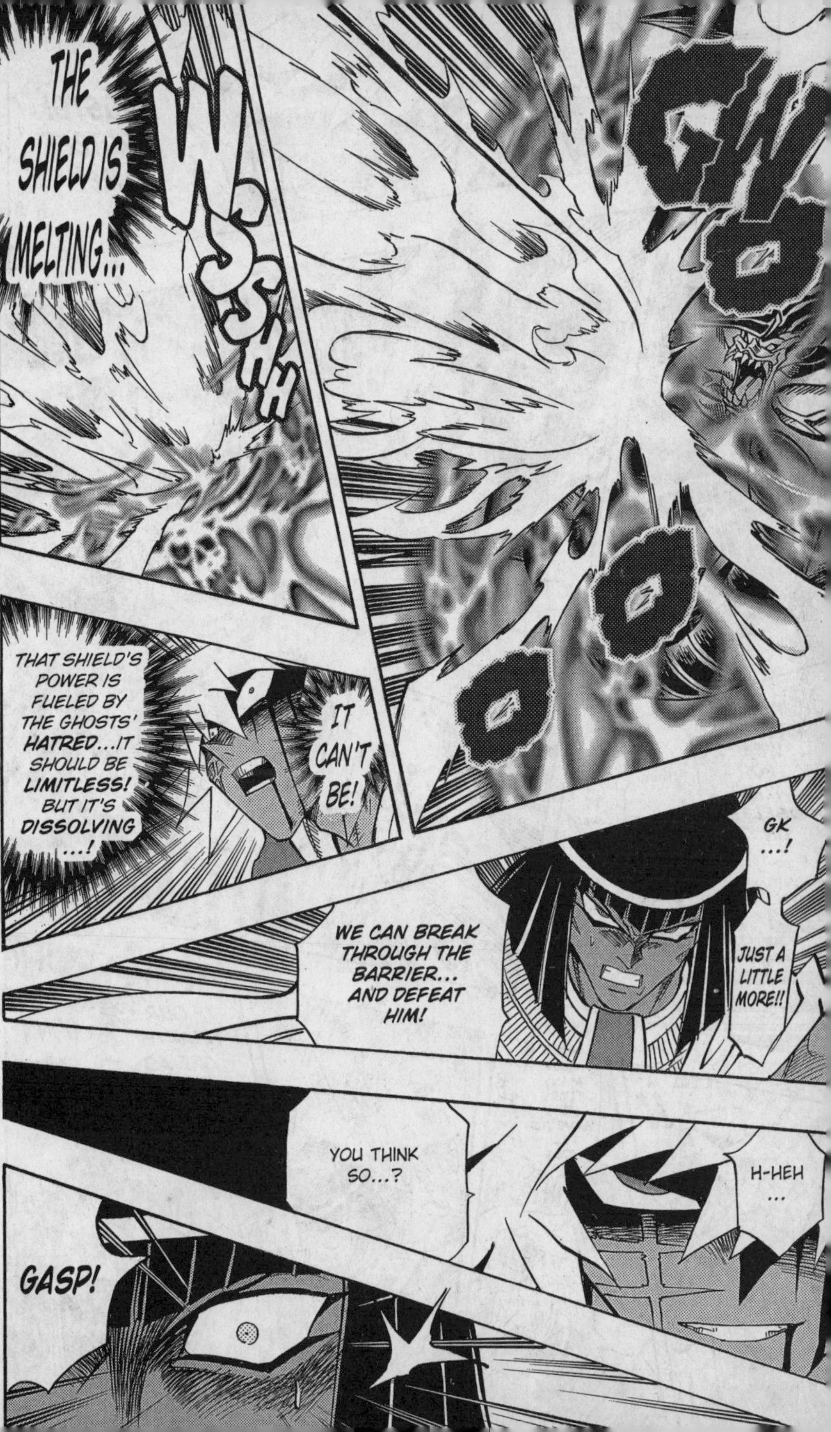
WSHH
THE SHIELD IS MELTING...
IT CAN'T BE!
THAT SHIELD'S POWER IS FUELED BY THE GHOSTS' HATRED...IT SHOULD BE LIMITLESS! BUT IT'S DISSOLVING ...!
GK ...!
JUST A LITTLE MORE!!
WE CAN BREAK THROUGH THE BARRIER... AND DEFEAT HIM!
H-HEH ...
YOU THINK SO...?
GASP!

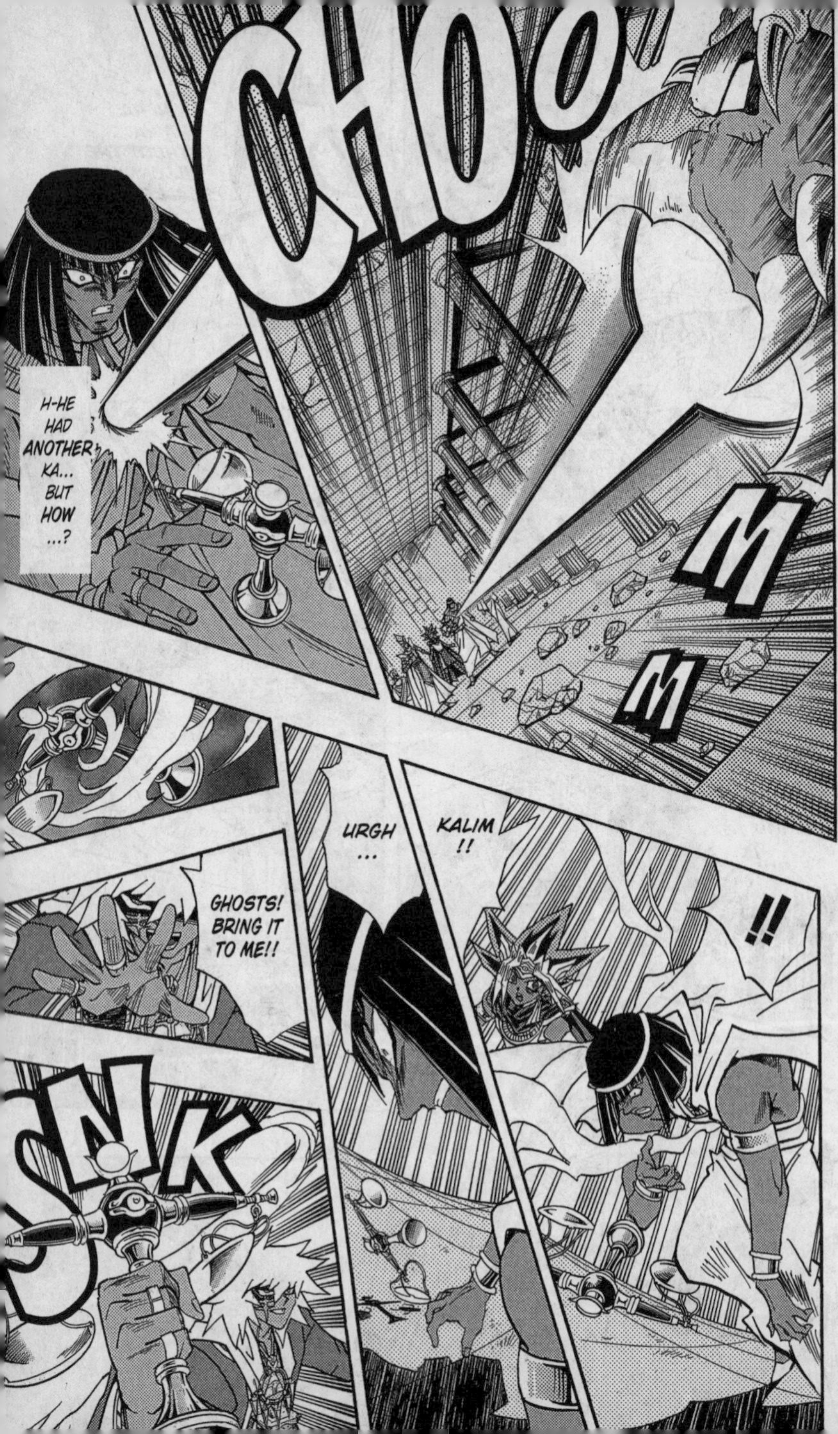
CHOO
H-HE HAD ANOTHER KA... BUT HOW ...?
M
M
KALIM !!
!!
URGH ...
GHOSTS! BRING IT TO ME!!
NK

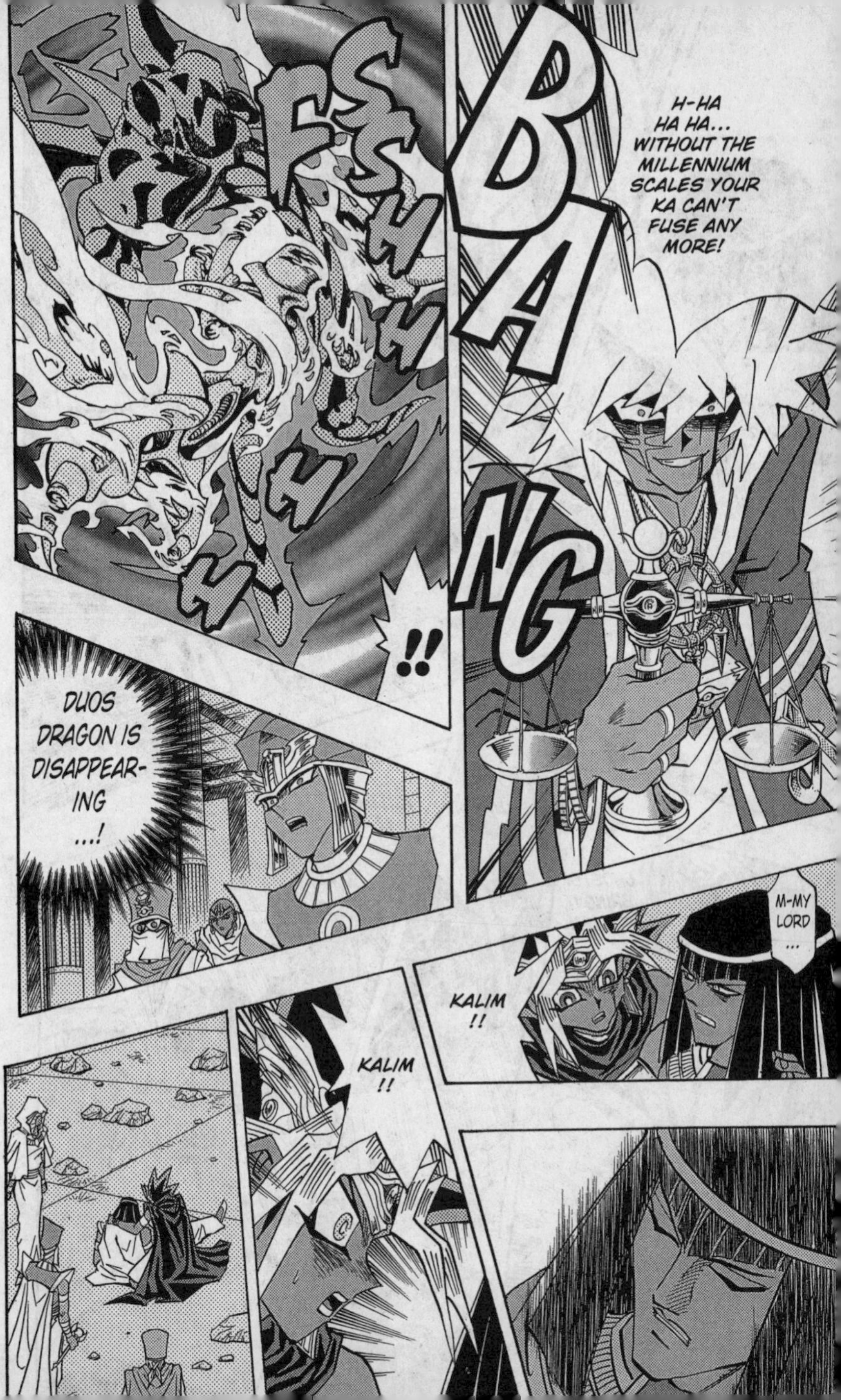
BADANG
H-HA HA HA... WITHOUT THE MILLENNIUM SCALES YOUR KA CAN'T FUSE ANY MORE!
FSHHHHH
!!
DUOS DRAGON IS DISAPPEAR-ING ...!
M-MY LORD ...
KALIM !!
KALIM !!

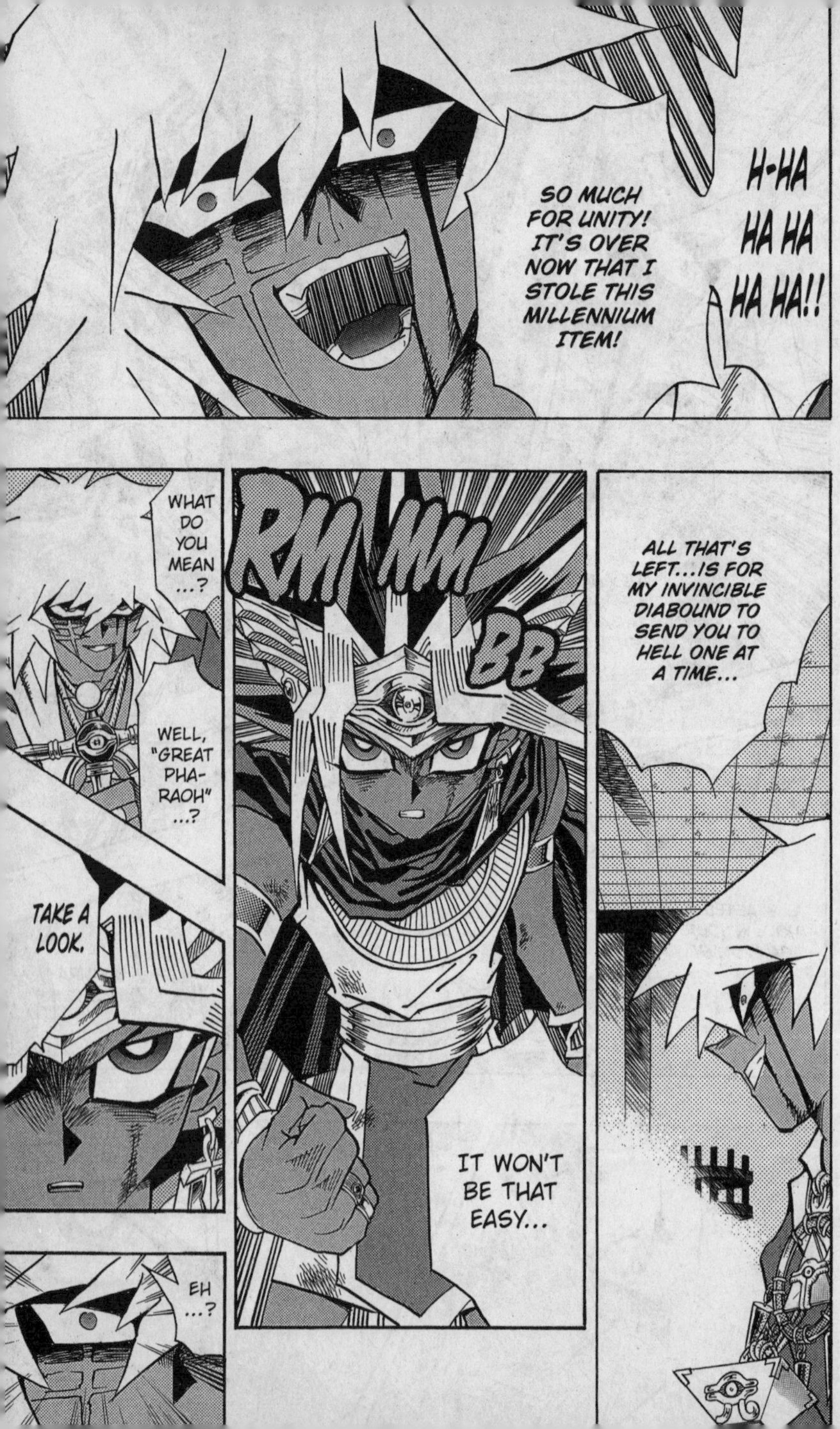
H-HA HA HA HA HA!!
SO MUCH FOR UNITY! IT'S OVER NOW THAT I STOLE THIS MILLENNIUM ITEM!
ALL THAT'S LEFT...IS FOR MY INVINCIBLE DIABOUND TO SEND YOU TO HELL ONE AT A TIME...
RMMMMBB
IT WON'T BE THAT EASY...
WHAT DO YOU MEAN ...?
WELL, "GREAT PHARAOH" ...?
TAKE A LOOK.
EH ...?

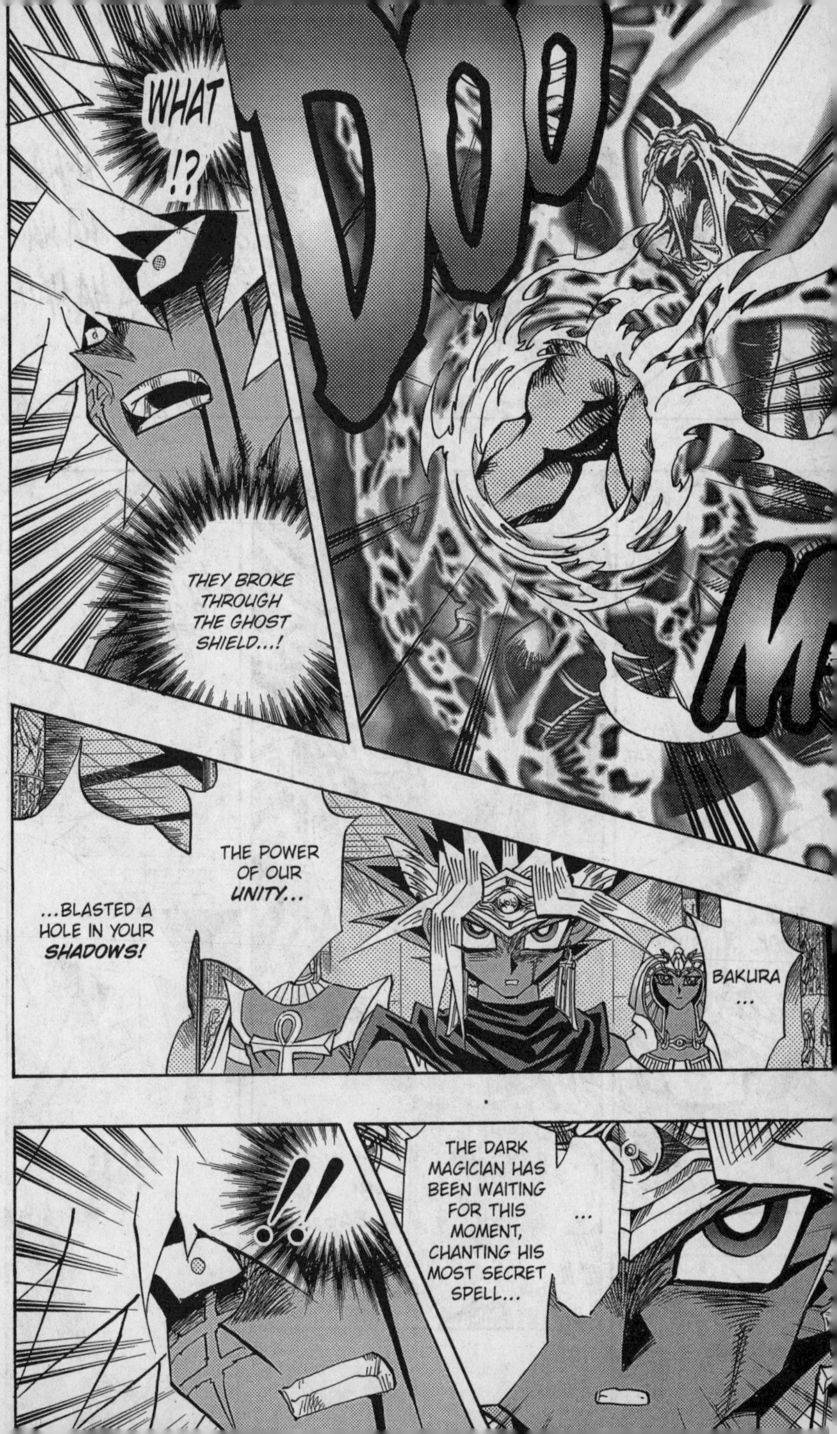

DOO
WHAT !?
THEY BROKE THROUGH THE GHOST SHIELD...!
M
BAKURA ...
THE POWER OF OUR UNITY...
...BLASTED A HOLE IN YOUR SHADOWS!
...
THE DARK MAGICIAN HAS BEEN WAITING FOR THIS MOMENT, CHANTING HIS MOST SECRET SPELL...
!!

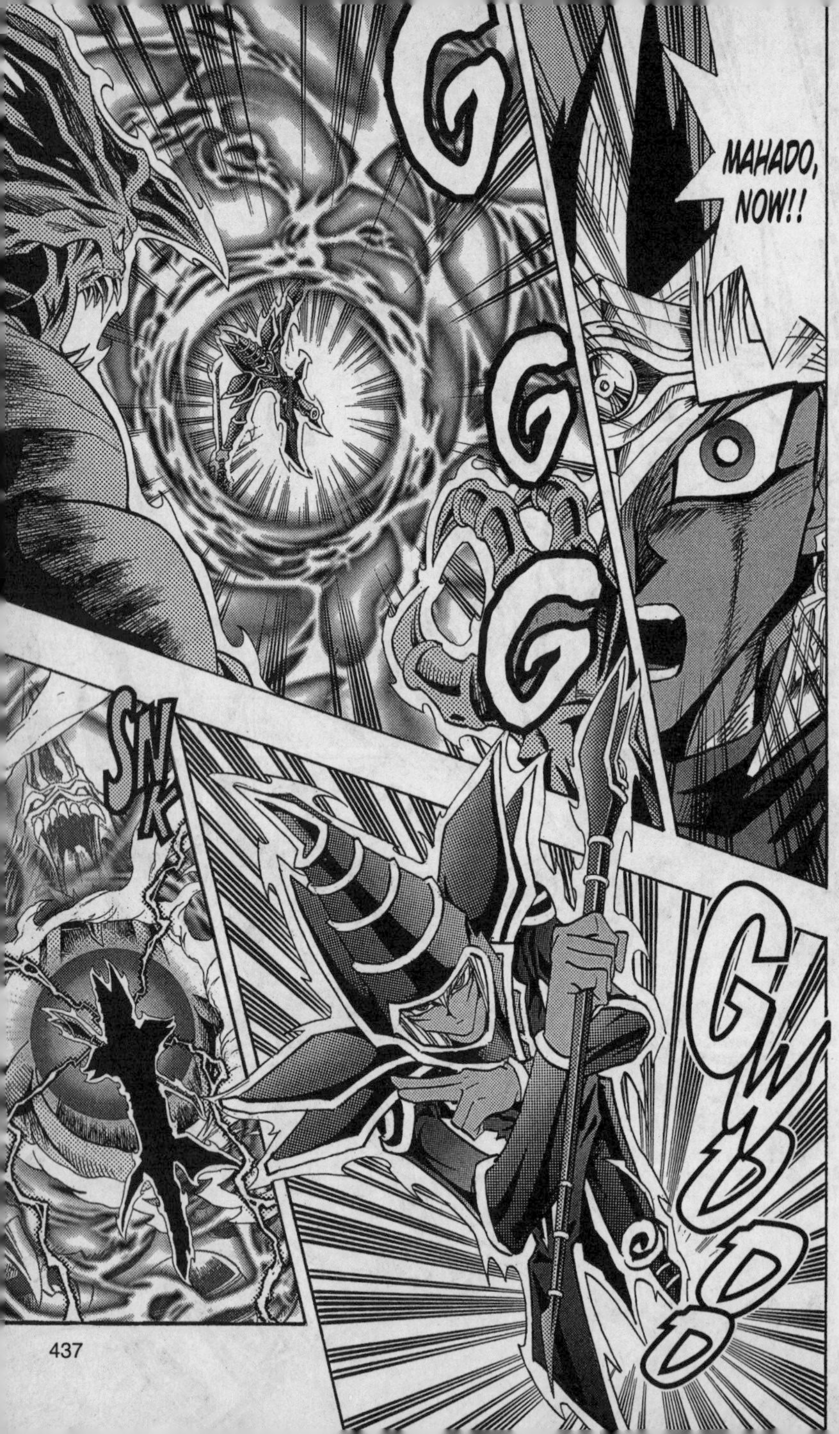
GGGG
MAHADO, NOW!!
SNK
GWDDDD

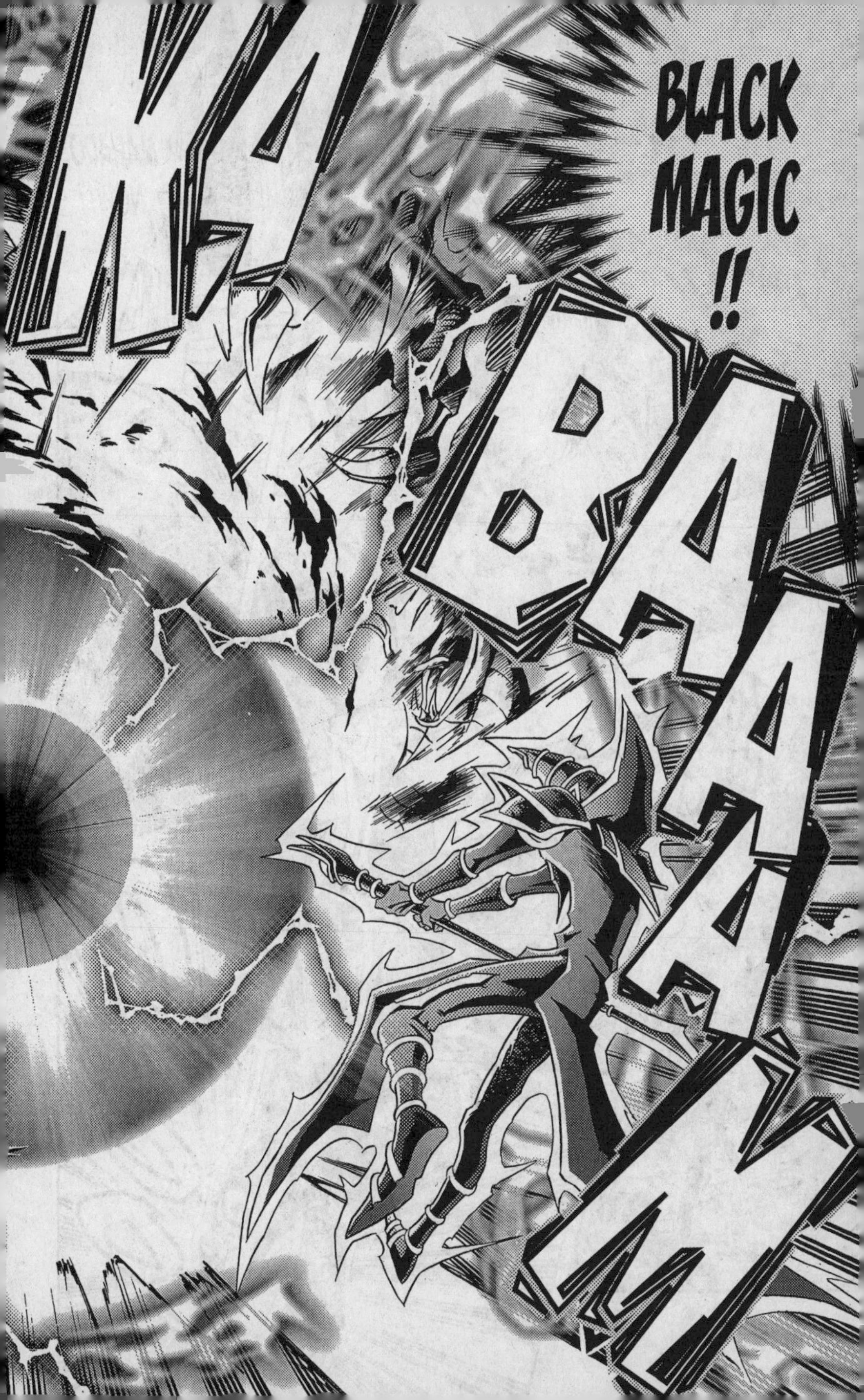
BLACK MAGIC !!
KA BAAAM

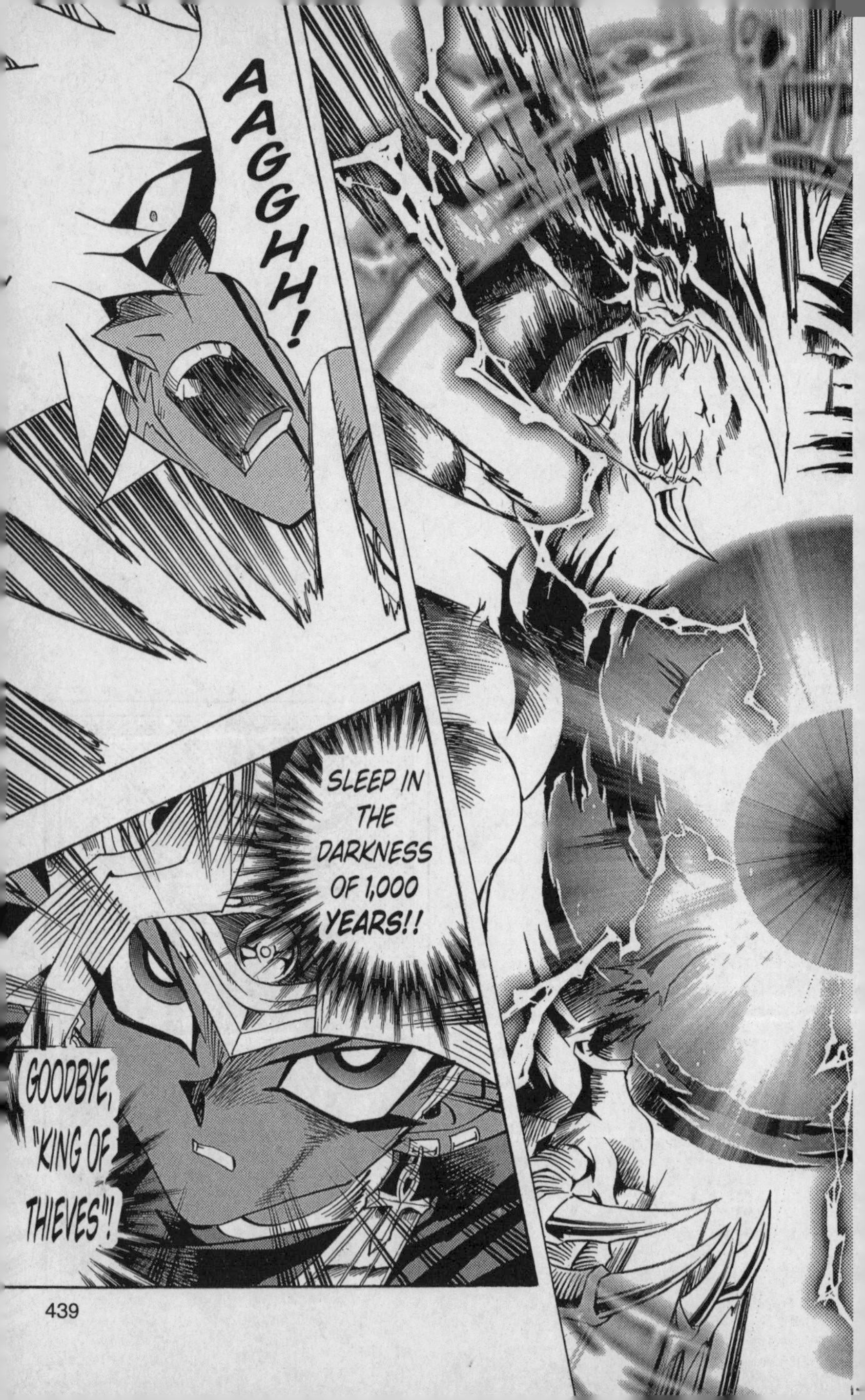
AAGGHH!
SLEEP IN THE DARKNESS OF 1,000 YEARS!!
GOODBYE, "KING OF THIEVES"!

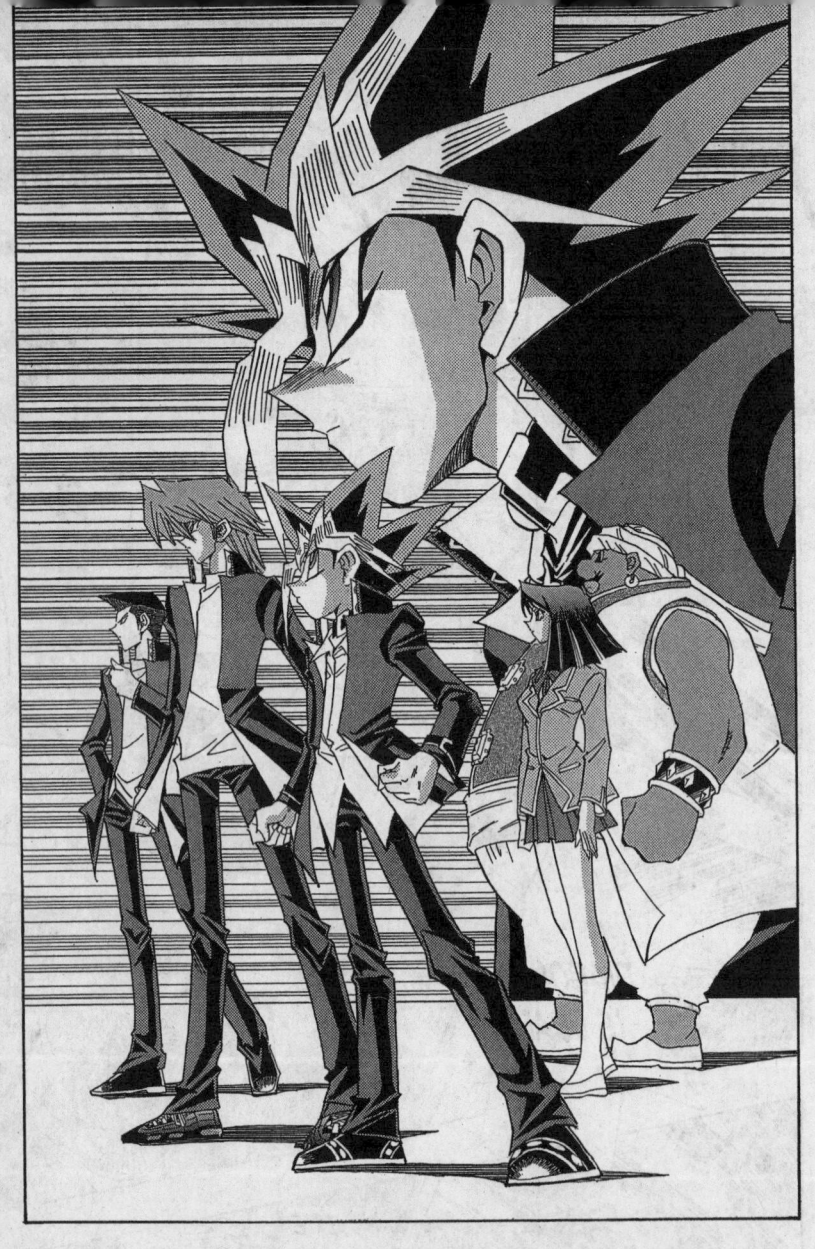

Duel 319: The Pawns of Memory!

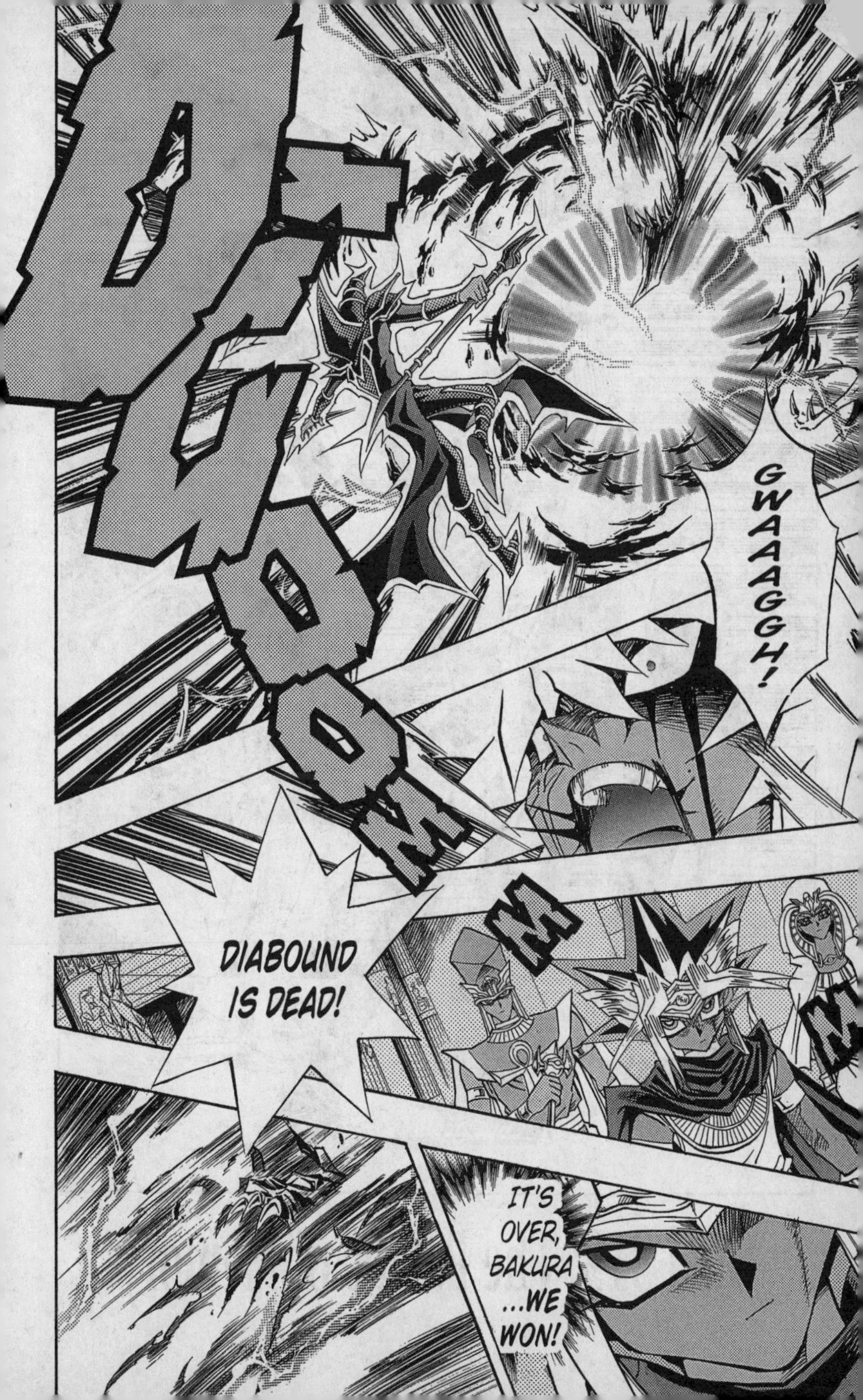
DOOOMMM
GWAAAAGGH!
DIABOUND IS DEAD!
IT'S OVER, BAKURA ...WE WON!

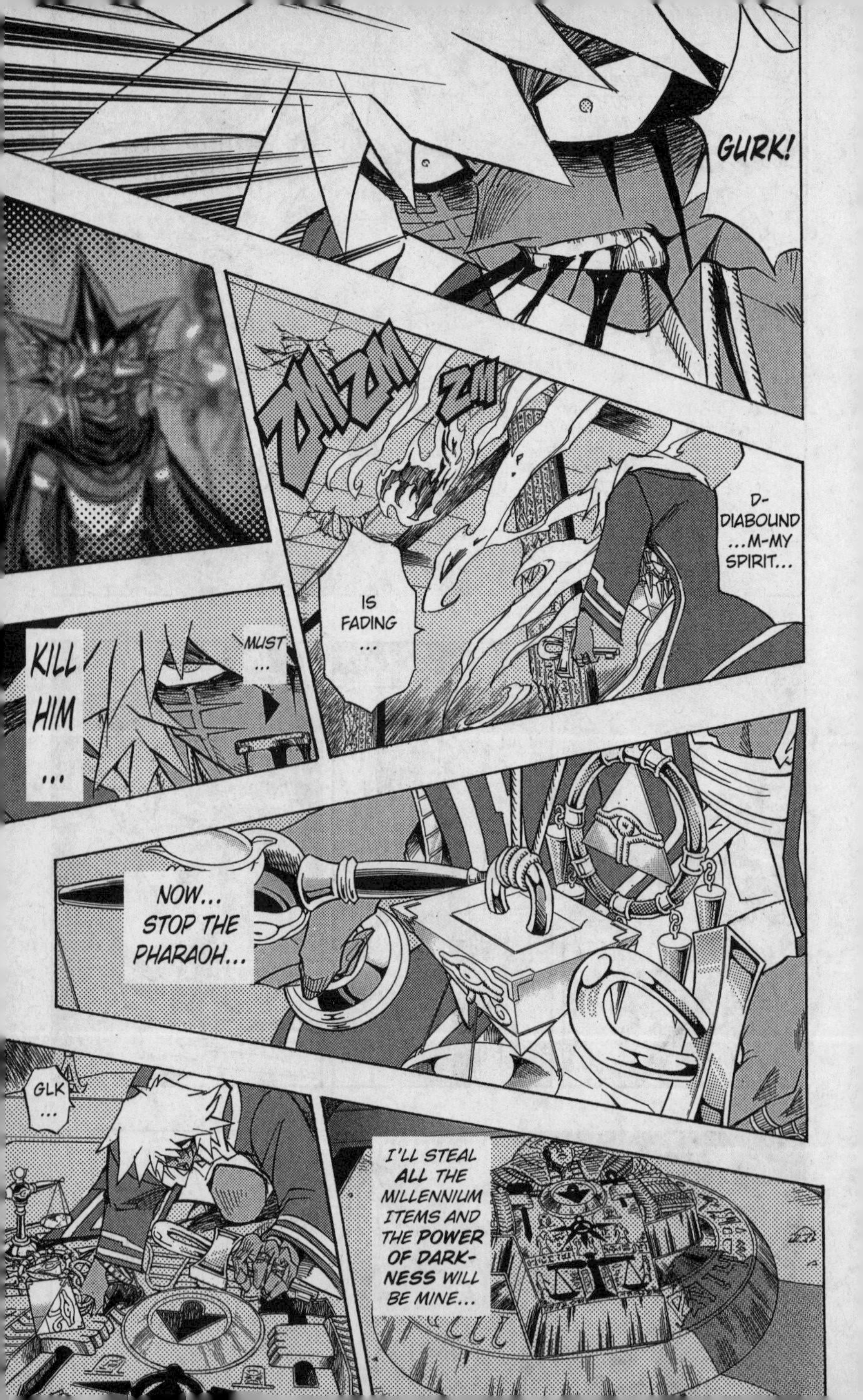

GURK!
D-DIABOUND ...M-MY SPIRIT...
IS FADING ...
ZAH ZAH ZAH
MUST ...
KILL HIM ...
NOW... STOP THE PHARAOH...
I'LL STEAL ALL THE MILLENNIUM ITEMS AND THE POWER OF DARK-NESS WILL BE MINE...
GLK ...

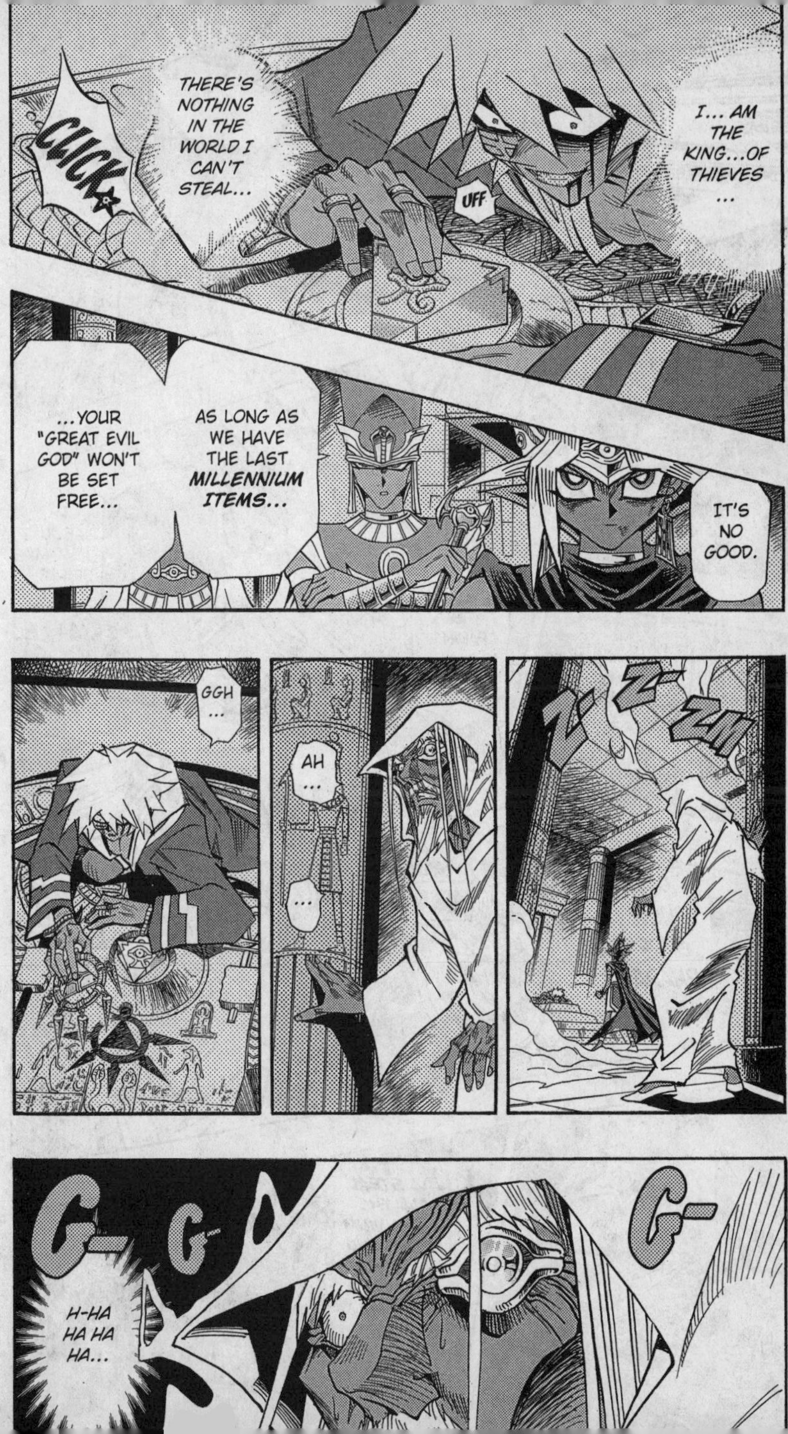
I... AM THE KING...OF THIEVES ...
UFF
THERE'S NOTHING IN THE WORLD I CAN'T STEAL...
CLICK
IT'S NO GOOD.
AS LONG AS WE HAVE THE LAST MILLENNIUM ITEMS...
...YOUR "GREAT EVIL GOD" WON'T BE SET FREE...
Z- Z- ZM
AH ...
...
GGH ...
G-
G
G-
H-HA HA HA HA...

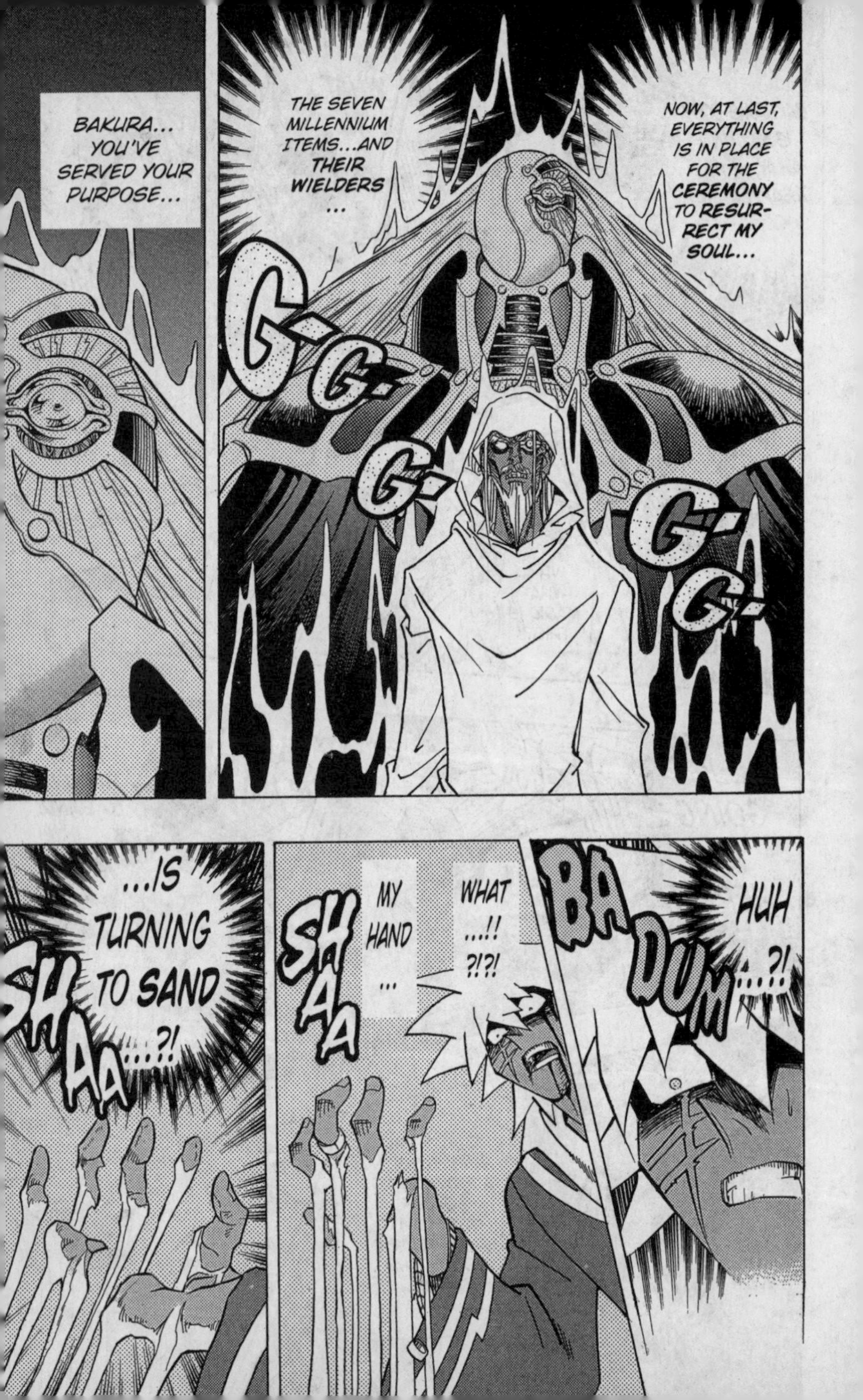
NOW, AT LAST, EVERYTHING IS IN PLACE FOR THE CEREMONY TO RESURRECT MY SOUL...
THE SEVEN MILLENNIUM ITEMS...AND THEIR WIELDERS...
G-G-G-G-G-G-
BAKURA... YOU'VE SERVED YOUR PURPOSE...
HUH...?!
BA DUM
WHAT...!! ?!?!
MY HAND...
SHAA
...IS TURNING TO SAND...?!
SHAA

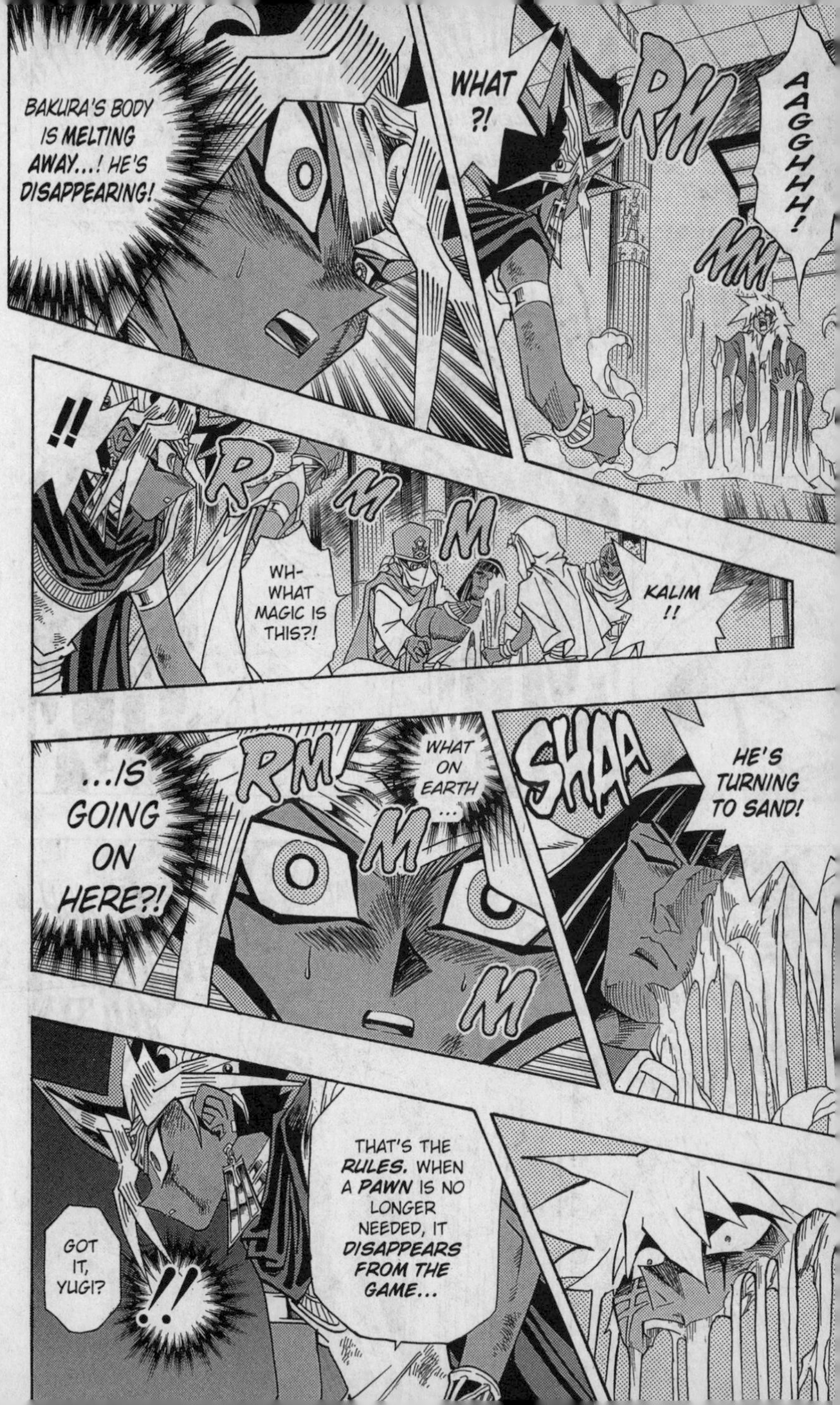

BAKURA'S BODY IS MELTING AWAY...! HE'S DISAPPEARING!
WHAT ?!
RM
MM
AAGGHHH!
!!
RMM
WH-WHAT MAGIC IS THIS?!
KALIM !!
RM
WHAT ON EARTH...
...IS GOING ON HERE?!
MM
SHAA
HE'S TURNING TO SAND!
GOT IT, YUGI?
!!
THAT'S THE RULES. WHEN A PAWN IS NO LONGER NEEDED, IT DISAPPEARS FROM THE GAME...

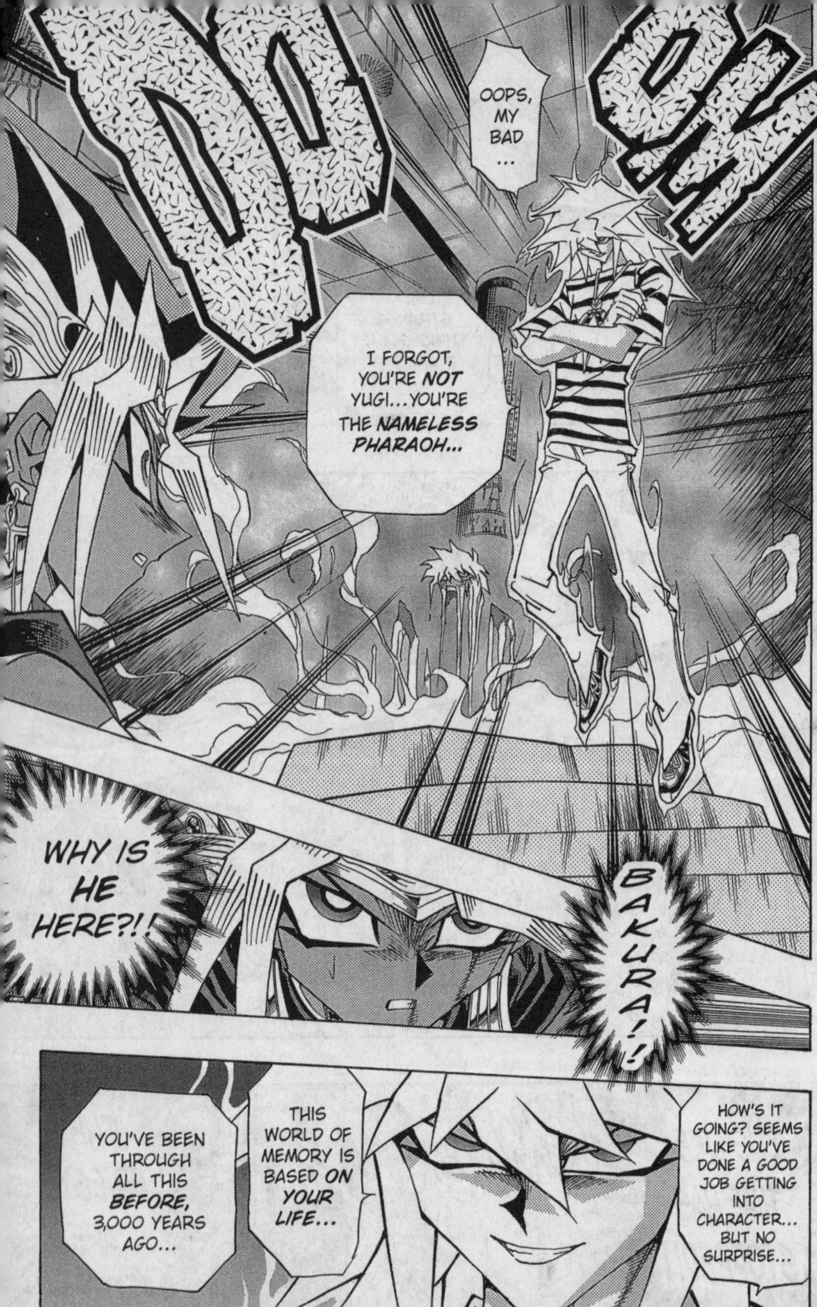

OOPS, MY BAD ...
I FORGOT, YOU'RE NOT YUGI...YOU'RE THE NAMELESS PHARAOH...
BAKURA!!
WHY IS HE HERE?!!
HOW'S IT GOING? SEEMS LIKE YOU'VE DONE A GOOD JOB GETTING INTO CHARACTER... BUT NO SURPRISE...
THIS WORLD OF MEMORY IS BASED ON YOUR LIFE...
YOU'VE BEEN THROUGH ALL THIS BEFORE, 3,000 YEARS AGO...

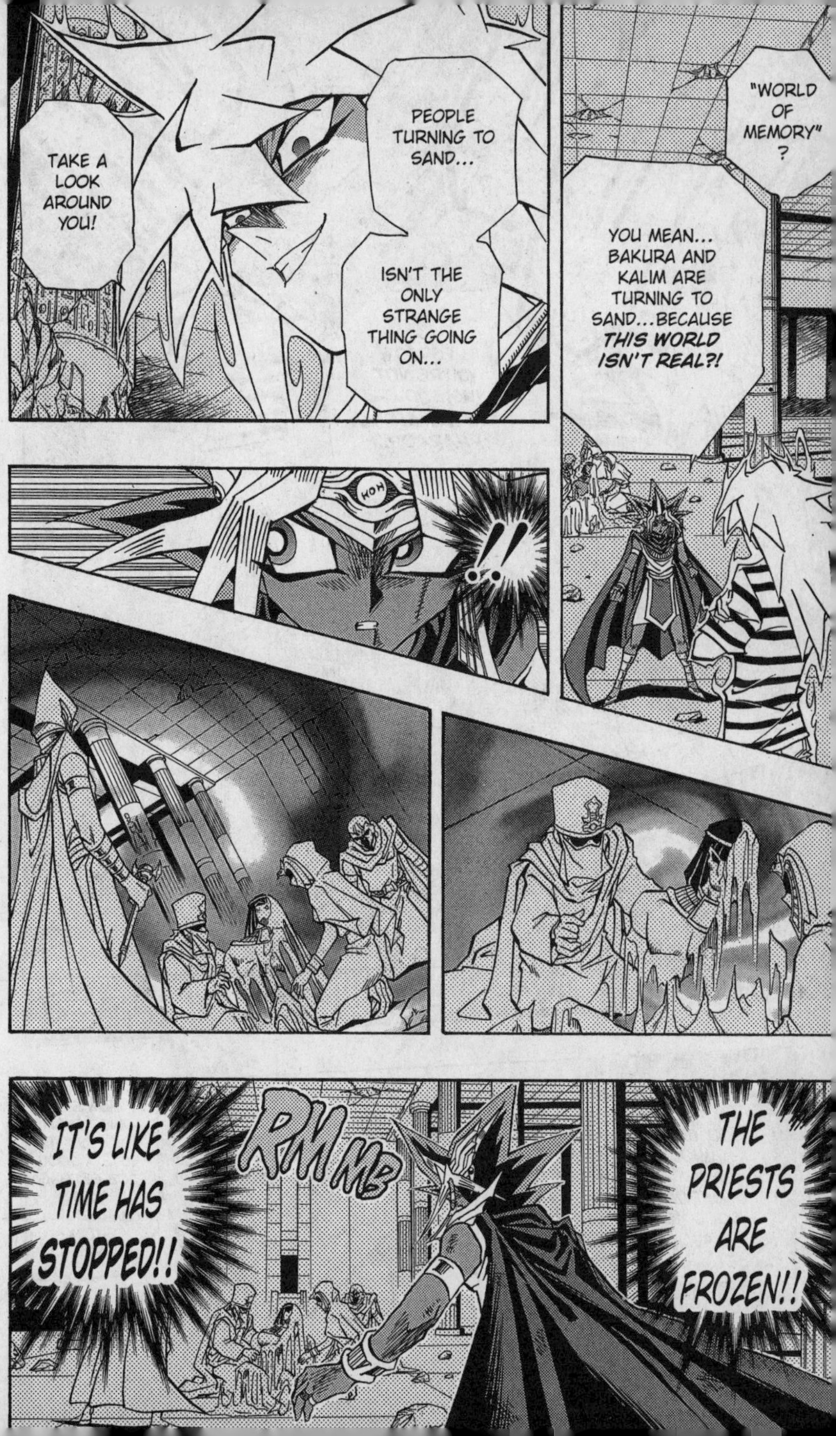
"WORLD OF MEMORY"?
YOU MEAN... BAKURA AND KALIM ARE TURNING TO SAND...BECAUSE *THIS WORLD ISN'T REAL?!*
PEOPLE TURNING TO SAND...
ISN'T THE ONLY STRANGE THING GOING ON...
TAKE A LOOK AROUND YOU!
!!
THE PRIESTS ARE FROZEN!!
RMMB
IT'S LIKE TIME HAS STOPPED!!

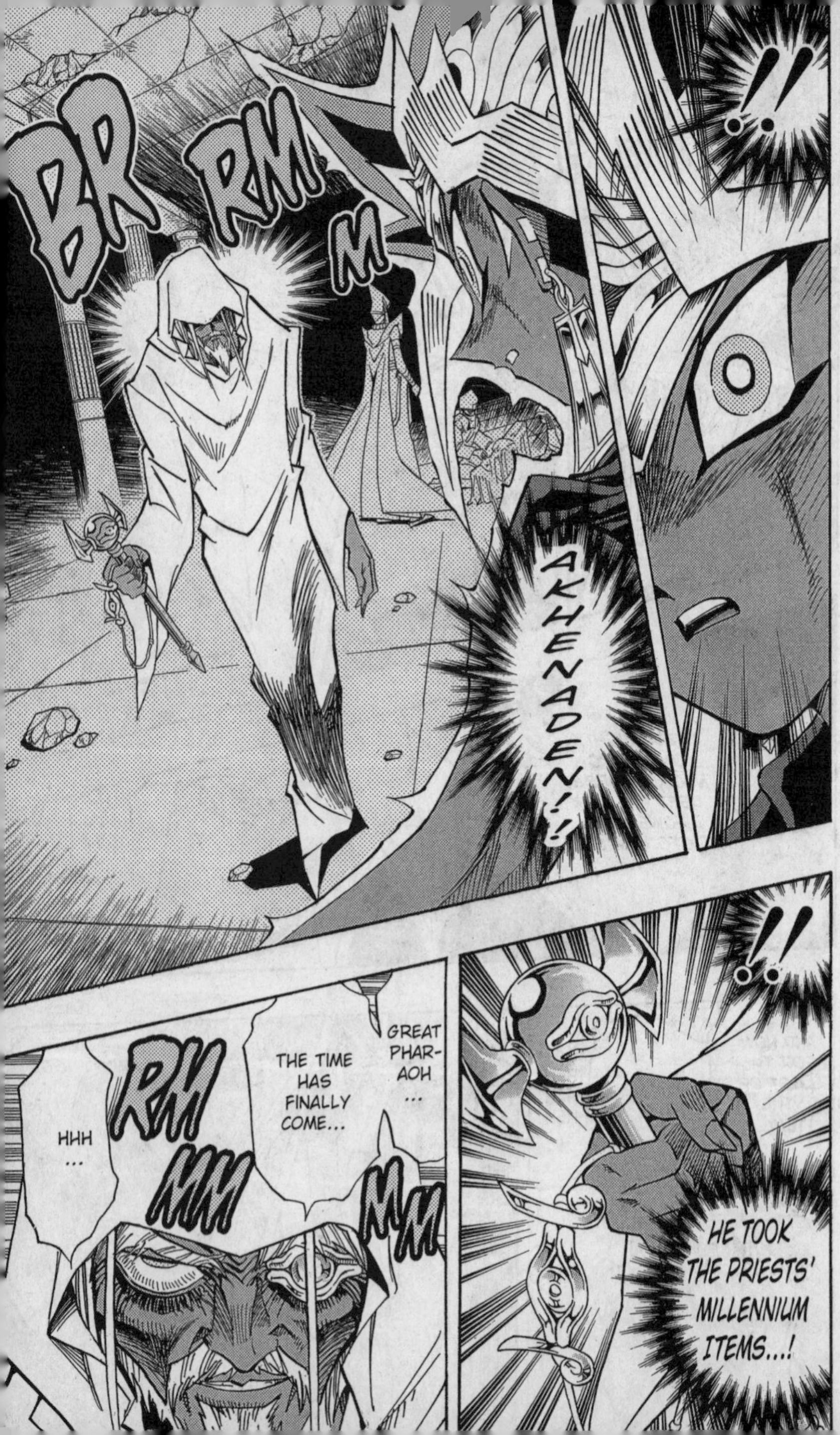

!!
AKHENADEN!!
BR RM M
!!
HE TOOK THE PRIESTS' MILLENNIUM ITEMS...!
GREAT PHARAOH...
THE TIME HAS FINALLY COME...
HHH...
RM MM MM

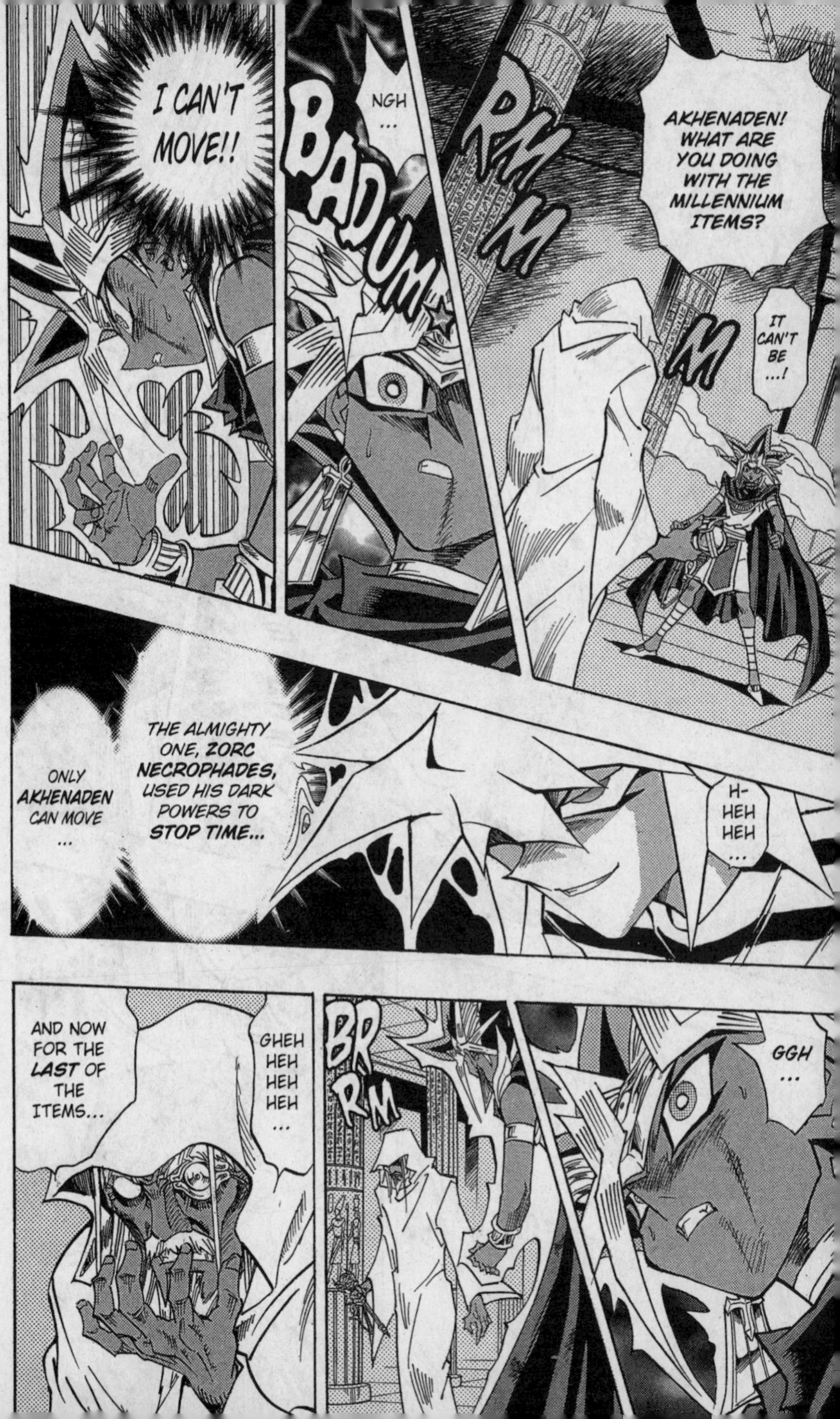

AKHENADEN! WHAT ARE YOU DOING WITH THE MILLENNIUM ITEMS?
RMMM
IT CAN'T BE ...!
NGH ...
BADUM
I CAN'T MOVE!!
H-HEH HEH HEH ...
THE ALMIGHTY ONE, ZORC NECROPHADES, USED HIS DARK POWERS TO STOP TIME...
ONLY AKHENADEN CAN MOVE ...
GGH ...
BRRM
GHEH HEH HEH HEH ...
AND NOW FOR THE LAST OF THE ITEMS...

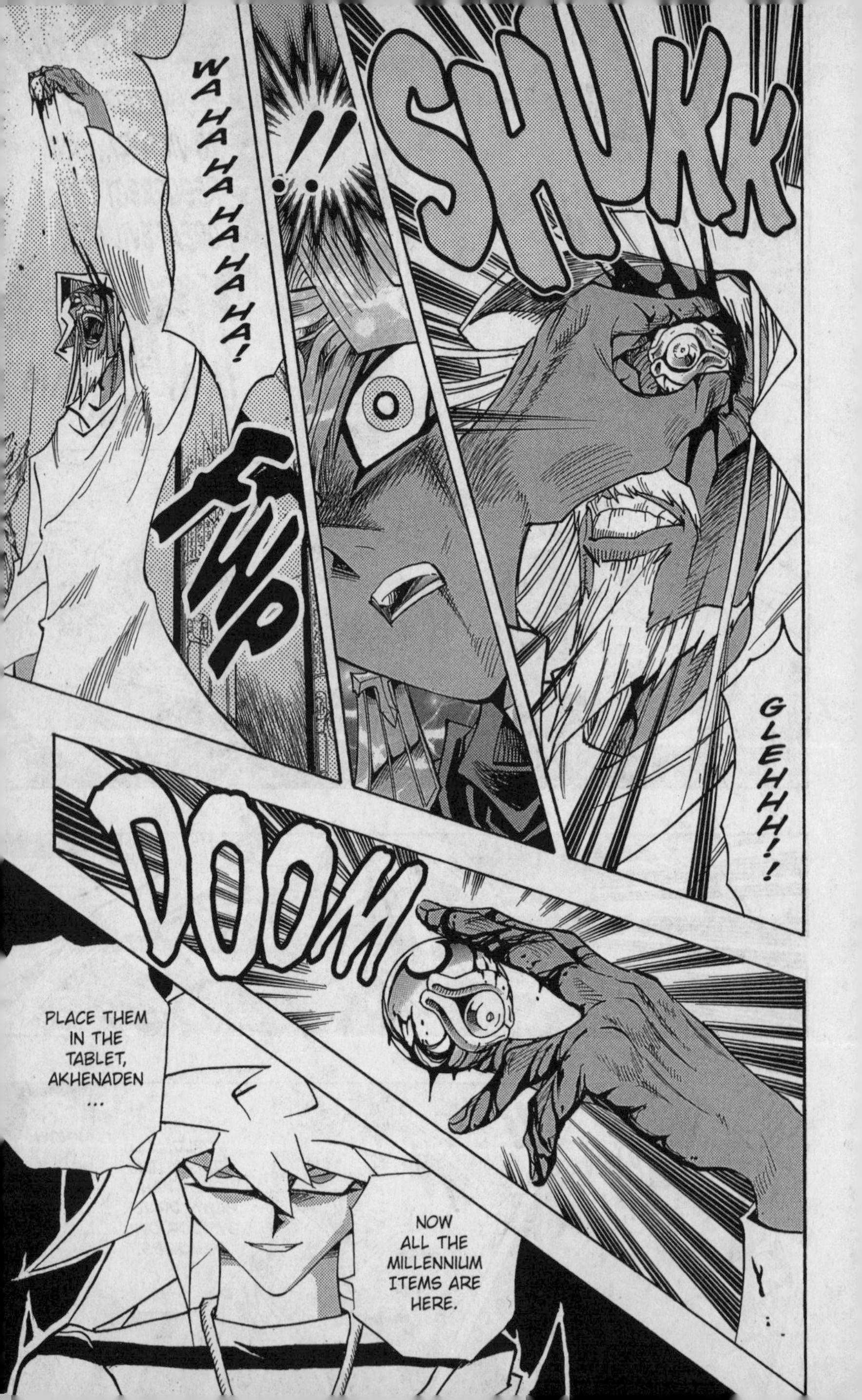
SHUKK
!!
WAHAHAHAHAHAHAHA!
THP
GLEHHHH!!
DOOM
NOW ALL THE MILLENNIUM ITEMS ARE HERE.
PLACE THEM IN THE TABLET, AKHENADEN ...

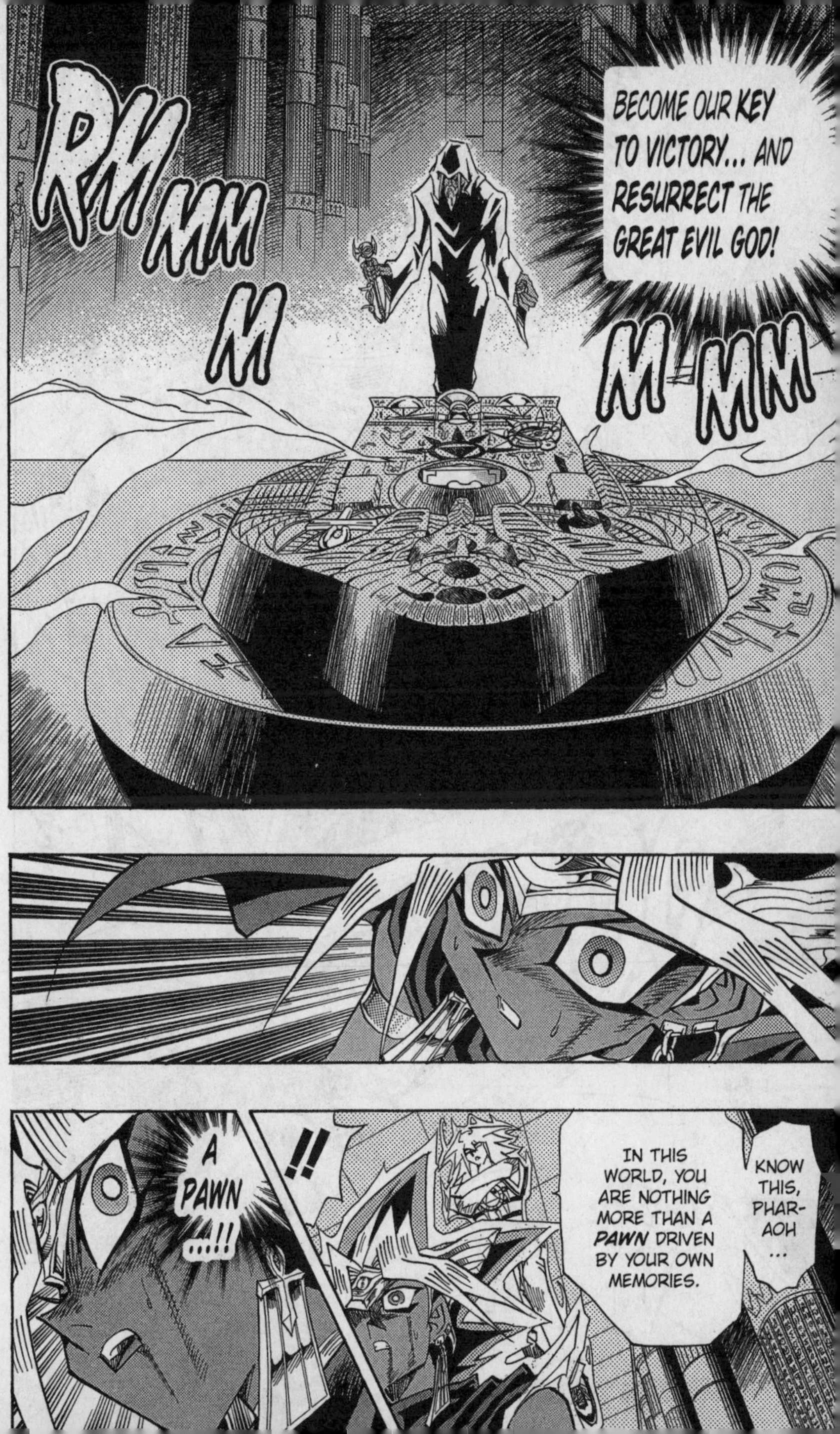

BECOME OUR KEY TO VICTORY... AND RESURRECT THE GREAT EVIL GOD!
M-MM
RHMMM M
KNOW THIS, PHARAOH ...
IN THIS WORLD, YOU ARE NOTHING MORE THAN A PAWN DRIVEN BY YOUR OWN MEMORIES.
!!
A PAWN ...!!

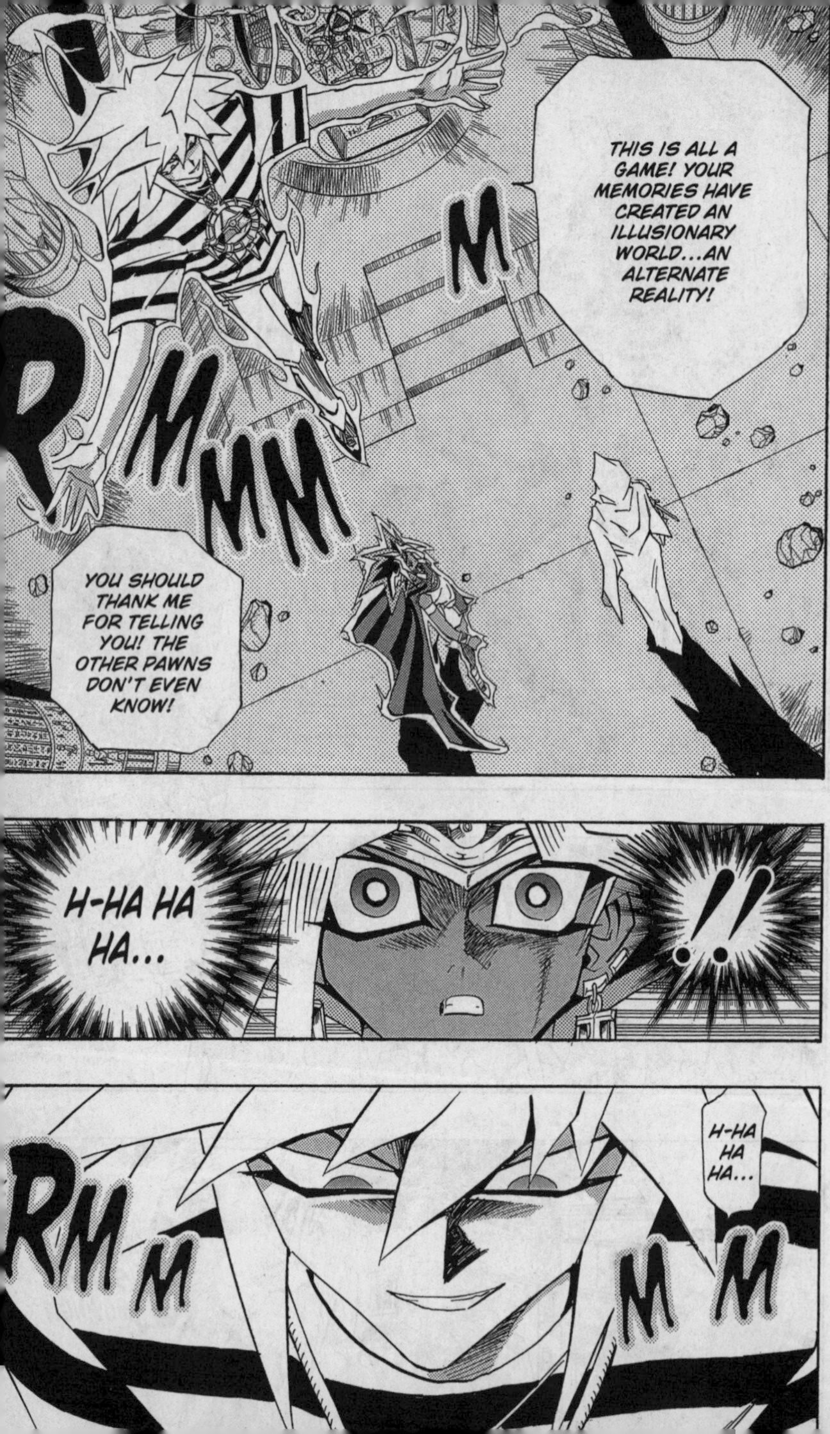
THIS IS ALL A GAME! YOUR MEMORIES HAVE CREATED AN ILLUSIONARY WORLD...AN ALTERNATE REALITY!
RMMMMM
YOU SHOULD THANK ME FOR TELLING YOU! THE OTHER PAWNS DON'T EVEN KNOW!
!!
H-HA HA HA...
H-HA HA HA...
RMMMMM

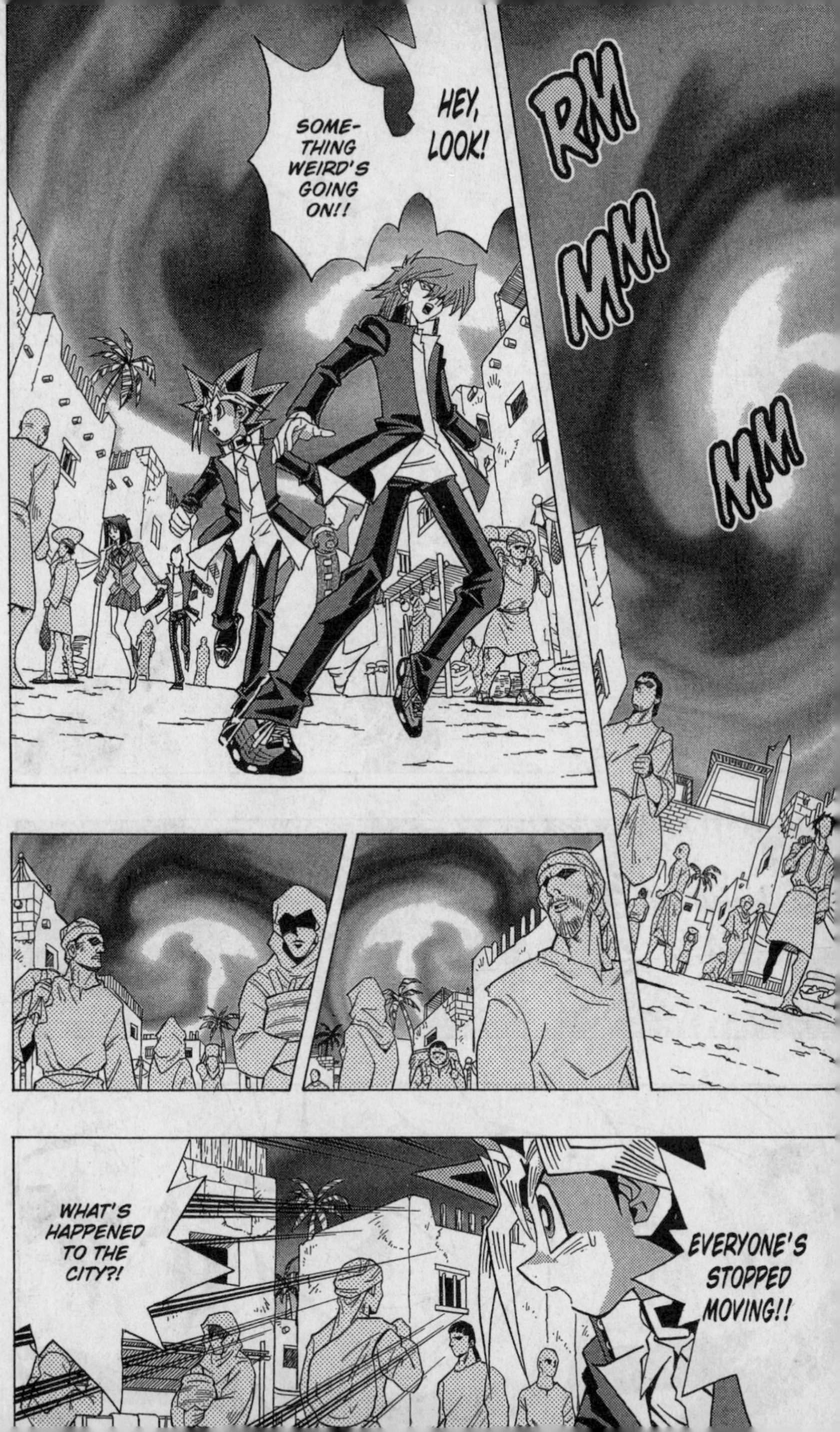
RMMMMM
HEY, LOOK!
SOME-THING WEIRD'S GOING ON!!
EVERYONE'S STOPPED MOVING!!
WHAT'S HAPPENED TO THE CITY?!

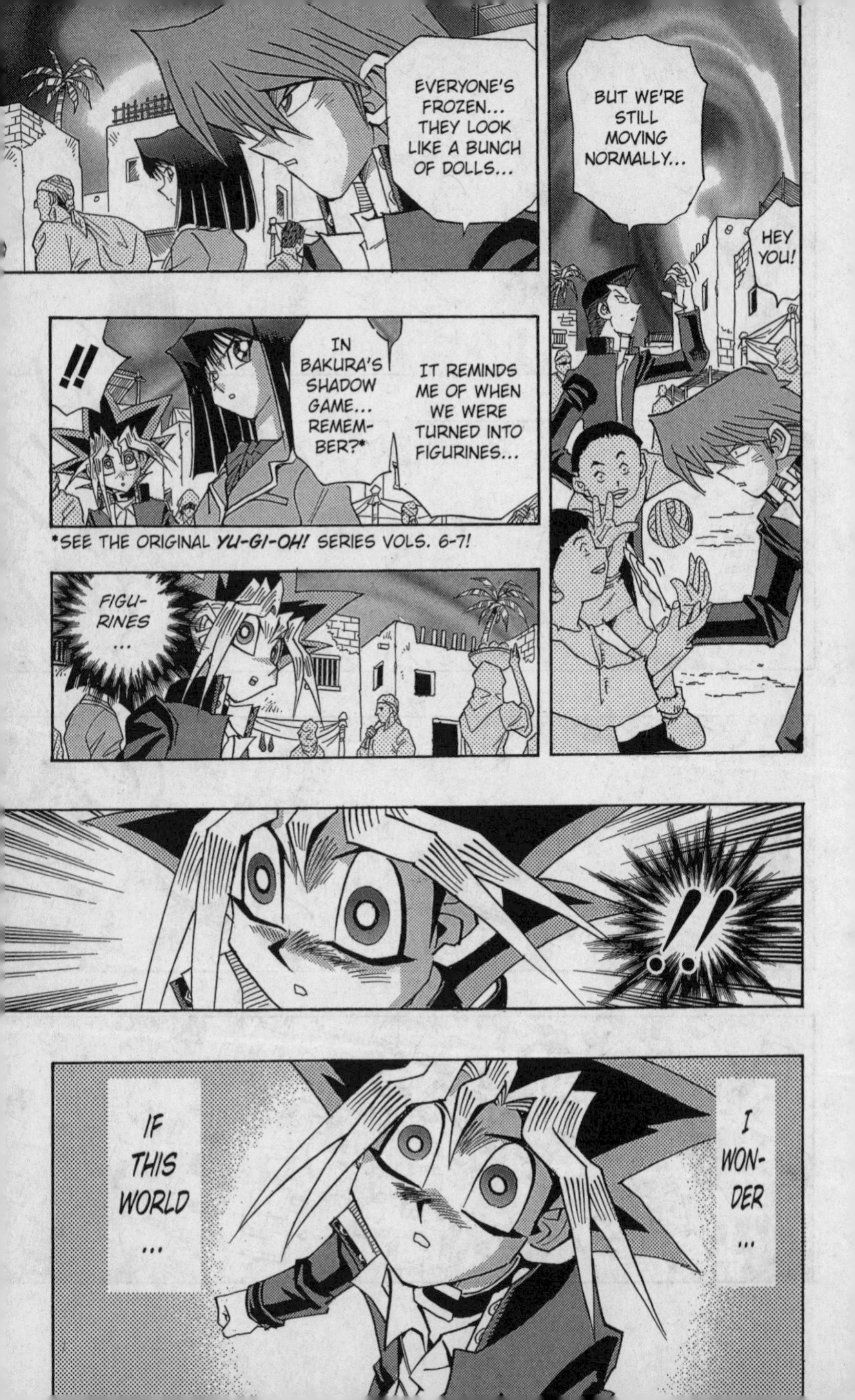
EVERYONE'S FROZEN... THEY LOOK LIKE A BUNCH OF DOLLS...
BUT WE'RE STILL MOVING NORMALLY...
HEY YOU!
!!
IT REMINDS ME OF WHEN WE WERE TURNED INTO FIGURINES...
IN BAKURA'S SHADOW GAME... REMEMBER?*
*SEE THE ORIGINAL YU-GI-OH! SERIES VOLS. 6-7!
FIGURINES...
!!
I WONDER...
IF THIS WORLD...

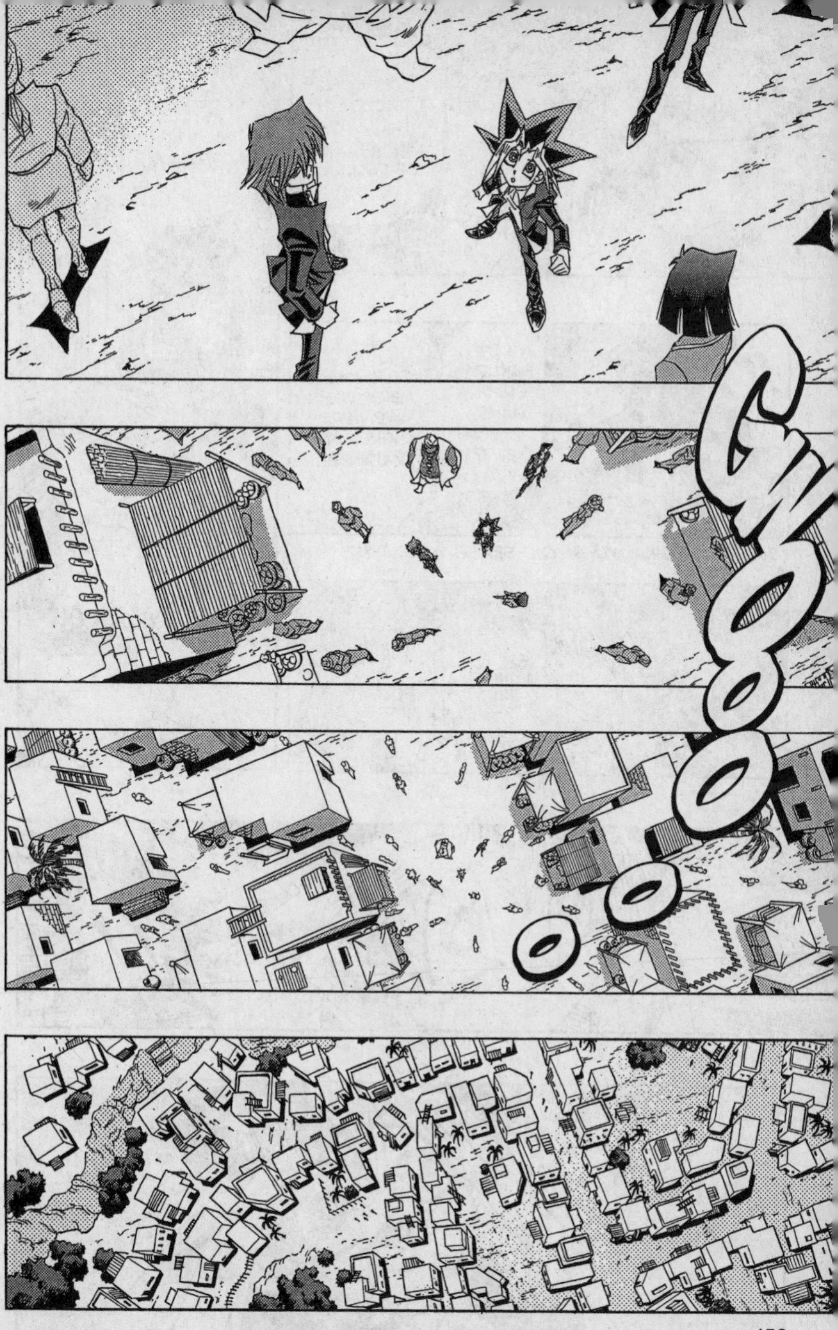
GWOOOOOO

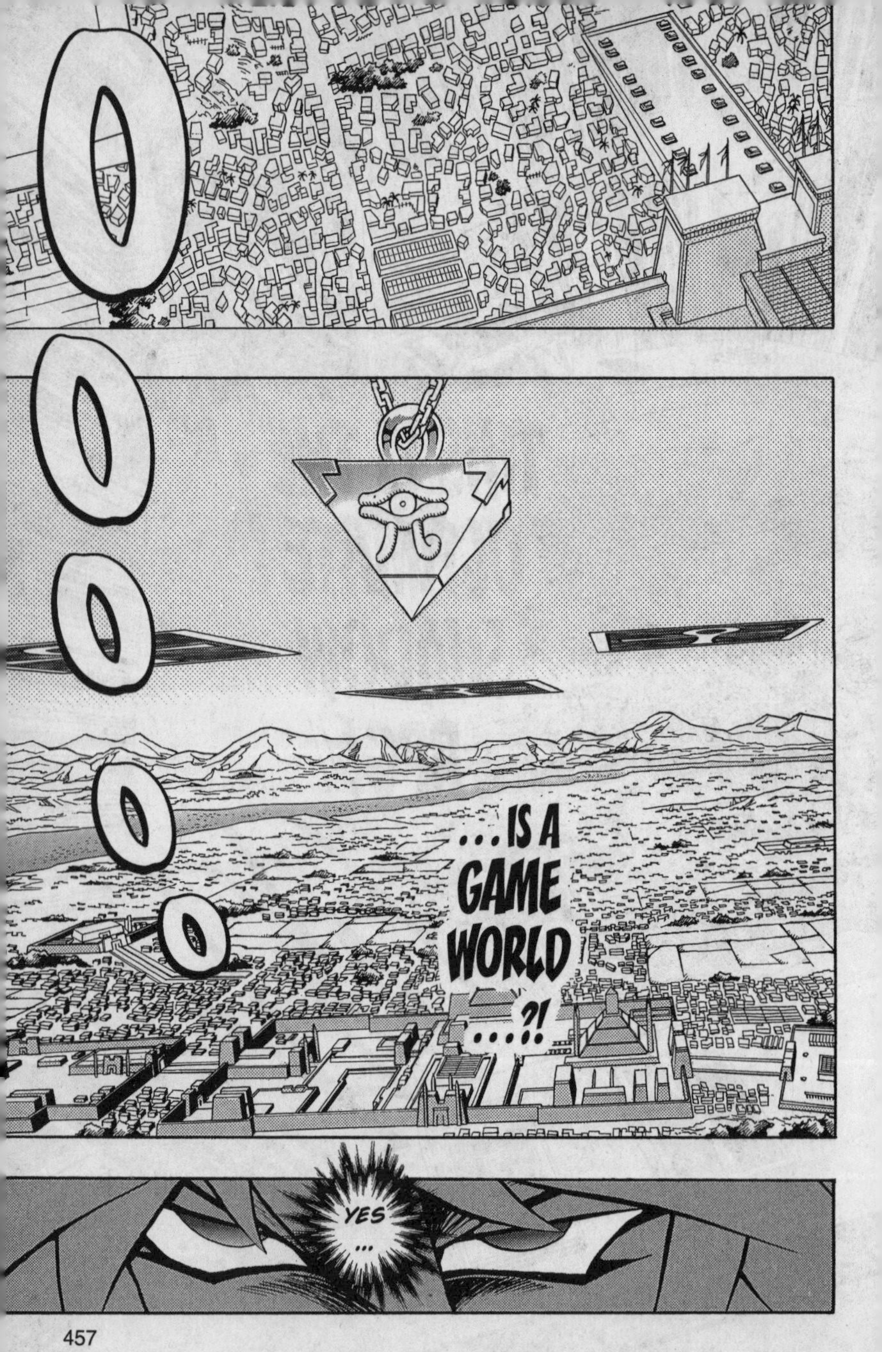
...IS A GAME WORLD
...?!
YES ...

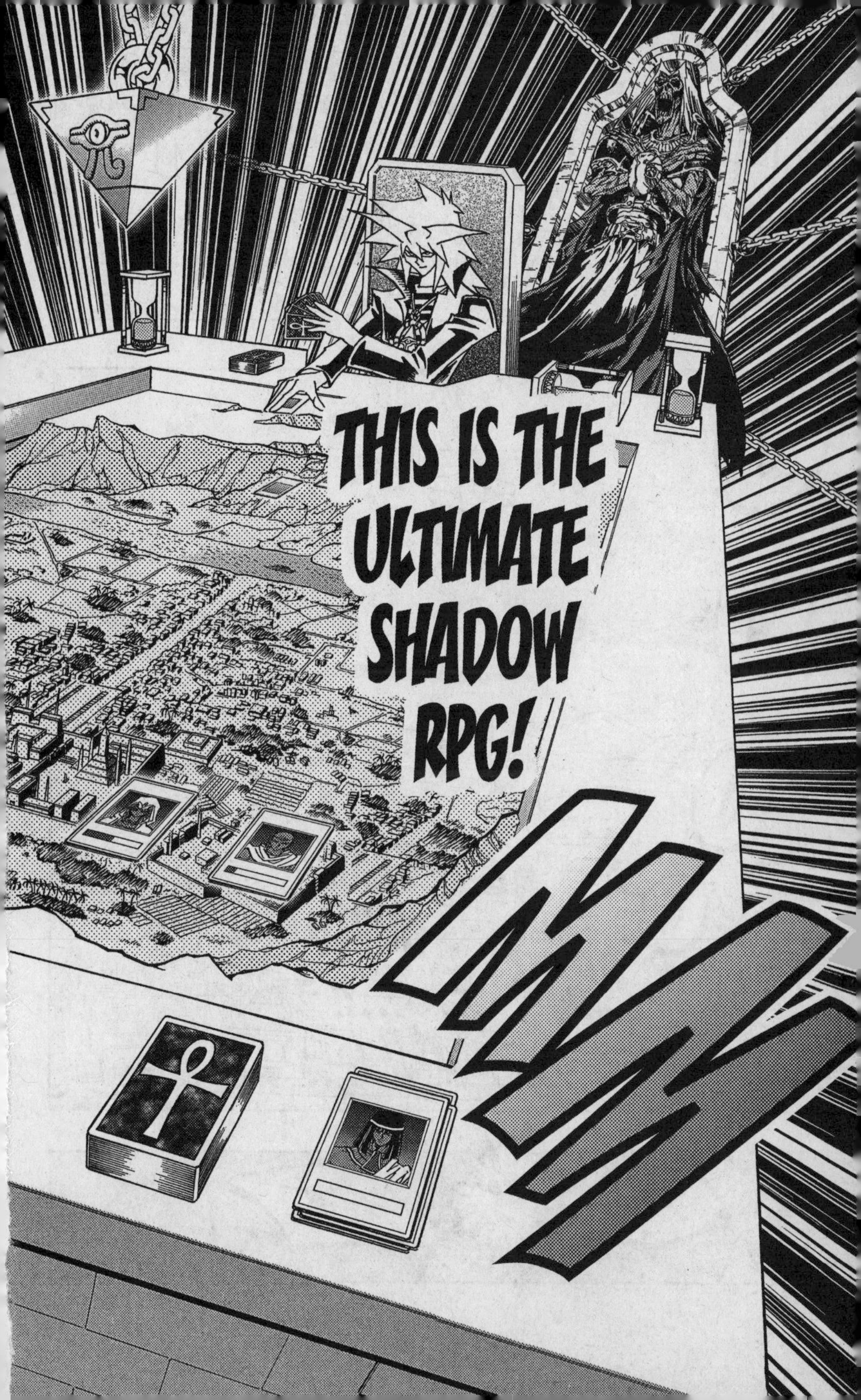
THIS IS THE ULTIMATE SHADOW RPG!

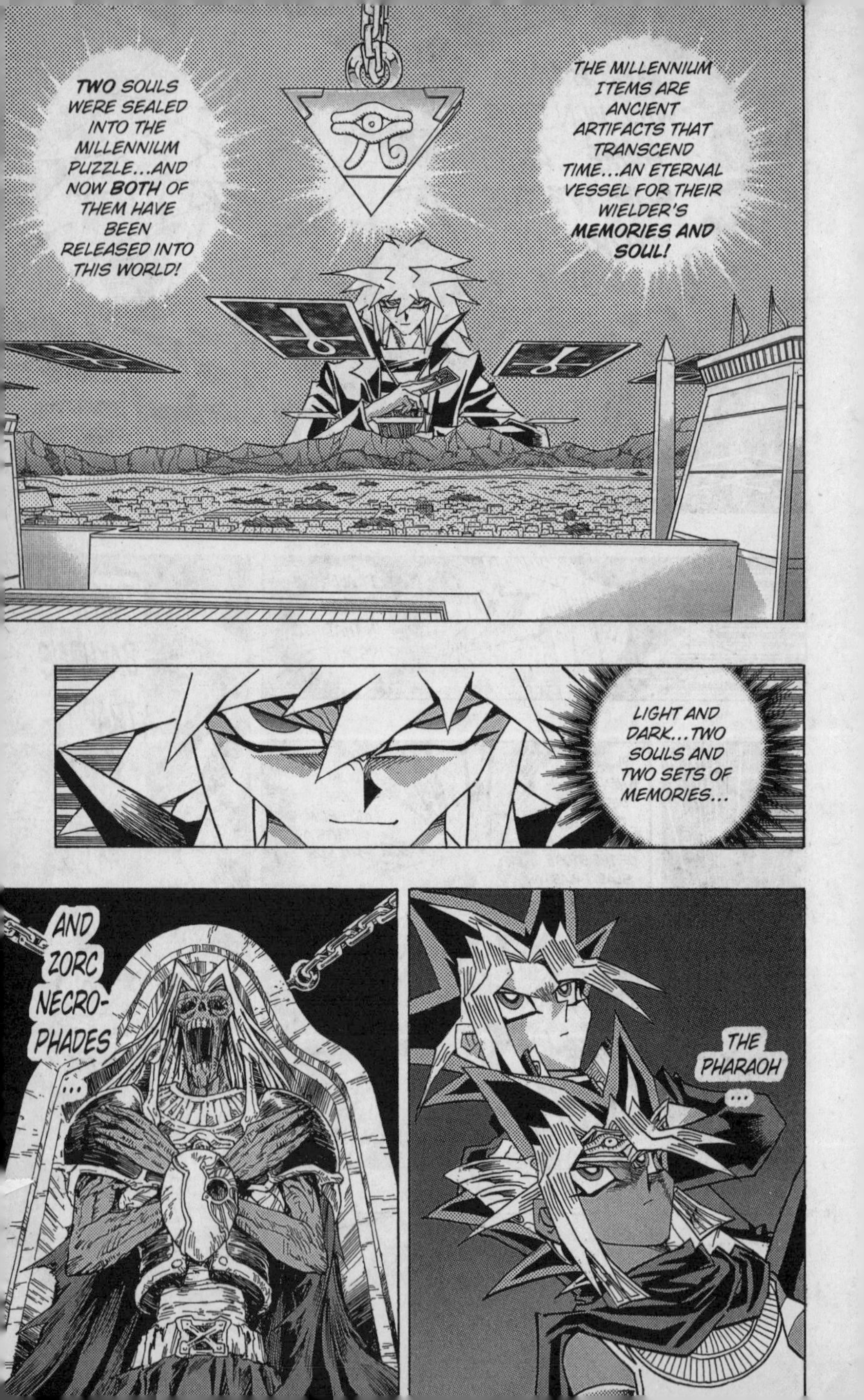
THE MILLENNIUM ITEMS ARE ANCIENT ARTIFACTS THAT TRANSCEND TIME...AN ETERNAL VESSEL FOR THEIR WIELDER'S MEMORIES AND SOUL!
TWO SOULS WERE SEALED INTO THE MILLENNIUM PUZZLE...AND NOW BOTH OF THEM HAVE BEEN RELEASED INTO THIS WORLD!
LIGHT AND DARK...TWO SOULS AND TWO SETS OF MEMORIES...
THE PHARAOH ...
AND ZORC NECRO-PHADES ...

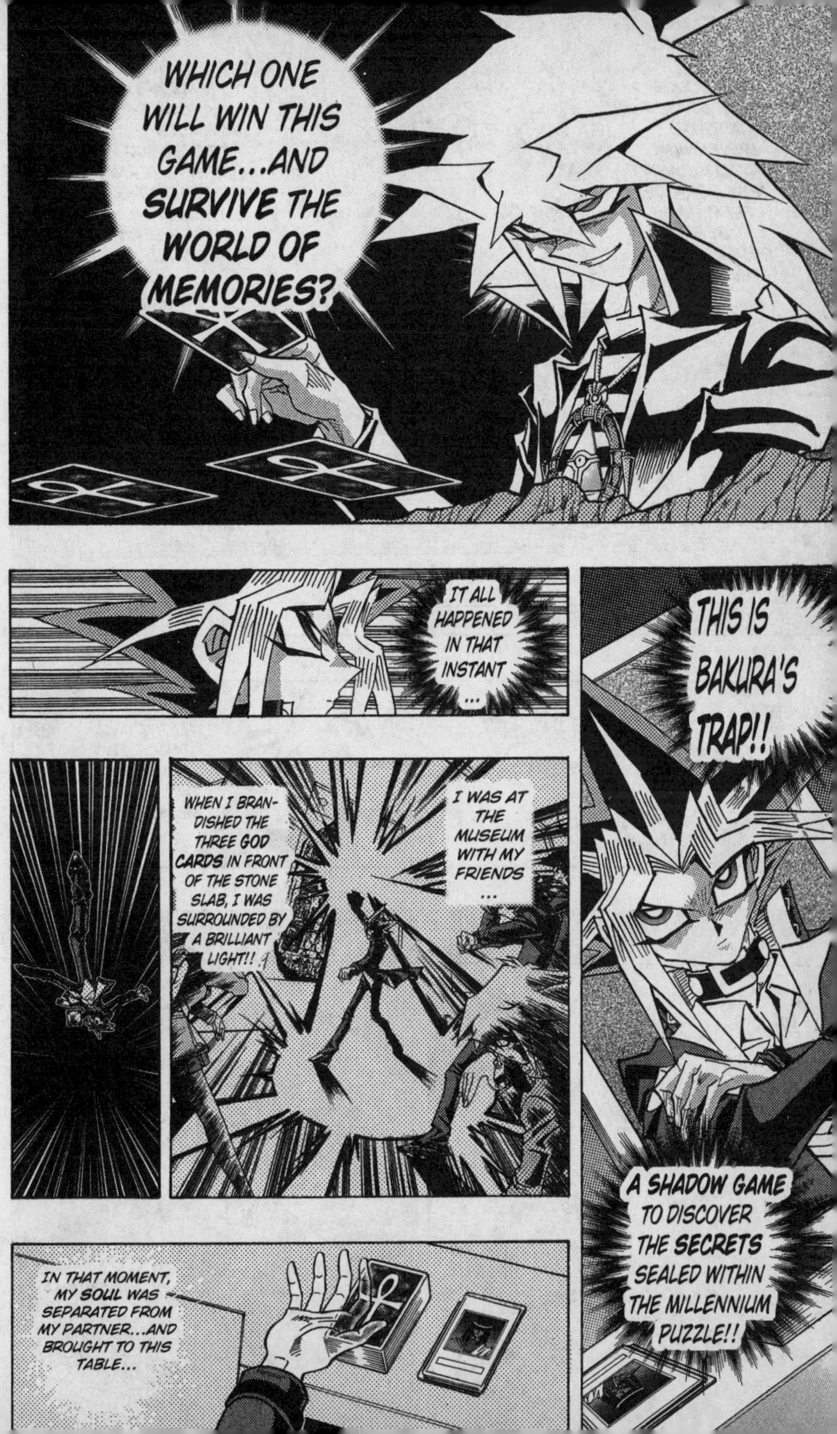
WHICH ONE WILL WIN THIS GAME...AND SURVIVE THE WORLD OF MEMORIES?
THIS IS BAKURA'S TRAP!!
A SHADOW GAME TO DISCOVER THE SECRETS SEALED WITHIN THE MILLENNIUM PUZZLE!!
IT ALL HAPPENED IN THAT INSTANT...
I WAS AT THE MUSEUM WITH MY FRIENDS...
WHEN I BRANDISHED THE THREE GOD CARDS IN FRONT OF THE STONE SLAB, I WAS SURROUNDED BY A BRILLIANT LIGHT!!
IN THAT MOMENT, MY SOUL WAS SEPARATED FROM MY PARTNER...AND BROUGHT TO THIS TABLE...

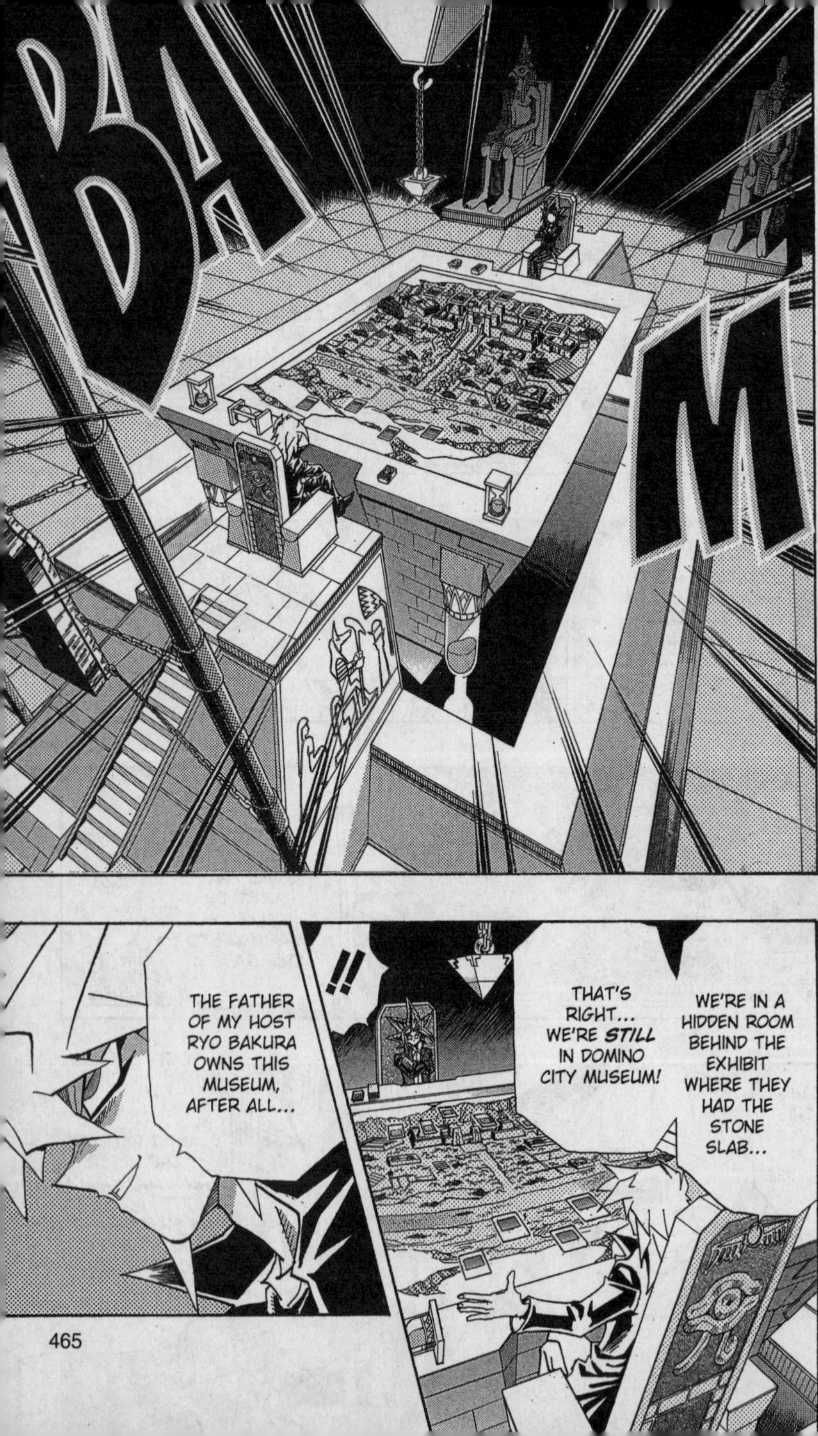
WE'RE IN A HIDDEN ROOM BEHIND THE EXHIBIT WHERE THEY HAD THE STONE SLAB...
THAT'S RIGHT... WE'RE *STILL* IN DOMINO CITY MUSEUM!
!!
THE FATHER OF MY HOST RYO BAKURA OWNS THIS MUSEUM, AFTER ALL...

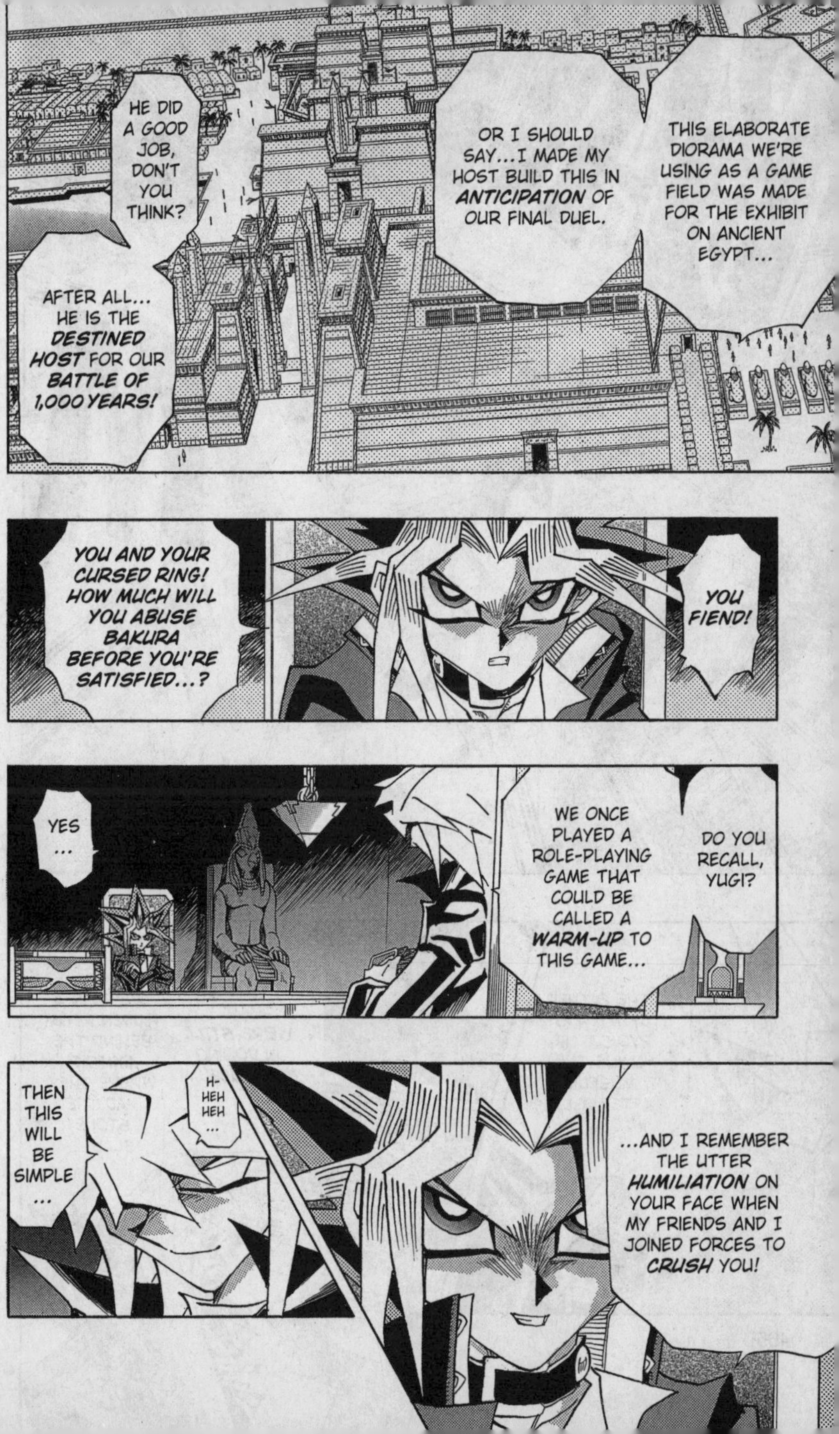
THIS ELABORATE DIORAMA WE'RE USING AS A GAME FIELD WAS MADE FOR THE EXHIBIT ON ANCIENT EGYPT...
OR I SHOULD SAY...I MADE MY HOST BUILD THIS IN *ANTICIPATION* OF OUR FINAL DUEL.
HE DID A GOOD JOB, DON'T YOU THINK?
AFTER ALL... HE IS THE *DESTINED HOST* FOR OUR *BATTLE OF 1,000 YEARS!*
YOU FIEND!
YOU AND YOUR CURSED RING! HOW MUCH WILL YOU ABUSE BAKURA BEFORE YOU'RE SATISFIED...?
DO YOU RECALL, YUGI?
WE ONCE PLAYED A ROLE-PLAYING GAME THAT COULD BE CALLED A *WARM-UP* TO THIS GAME...
YES...
...AND I REMEMBER THE UTTER *HUMILIATION* ON YOUR FACE WHEN MY FRIENDS AND I JOINED FORCES TO *CRUSH* YOU!
H-HEH HEH...
THEN THIS WILL BE SIMPLE...

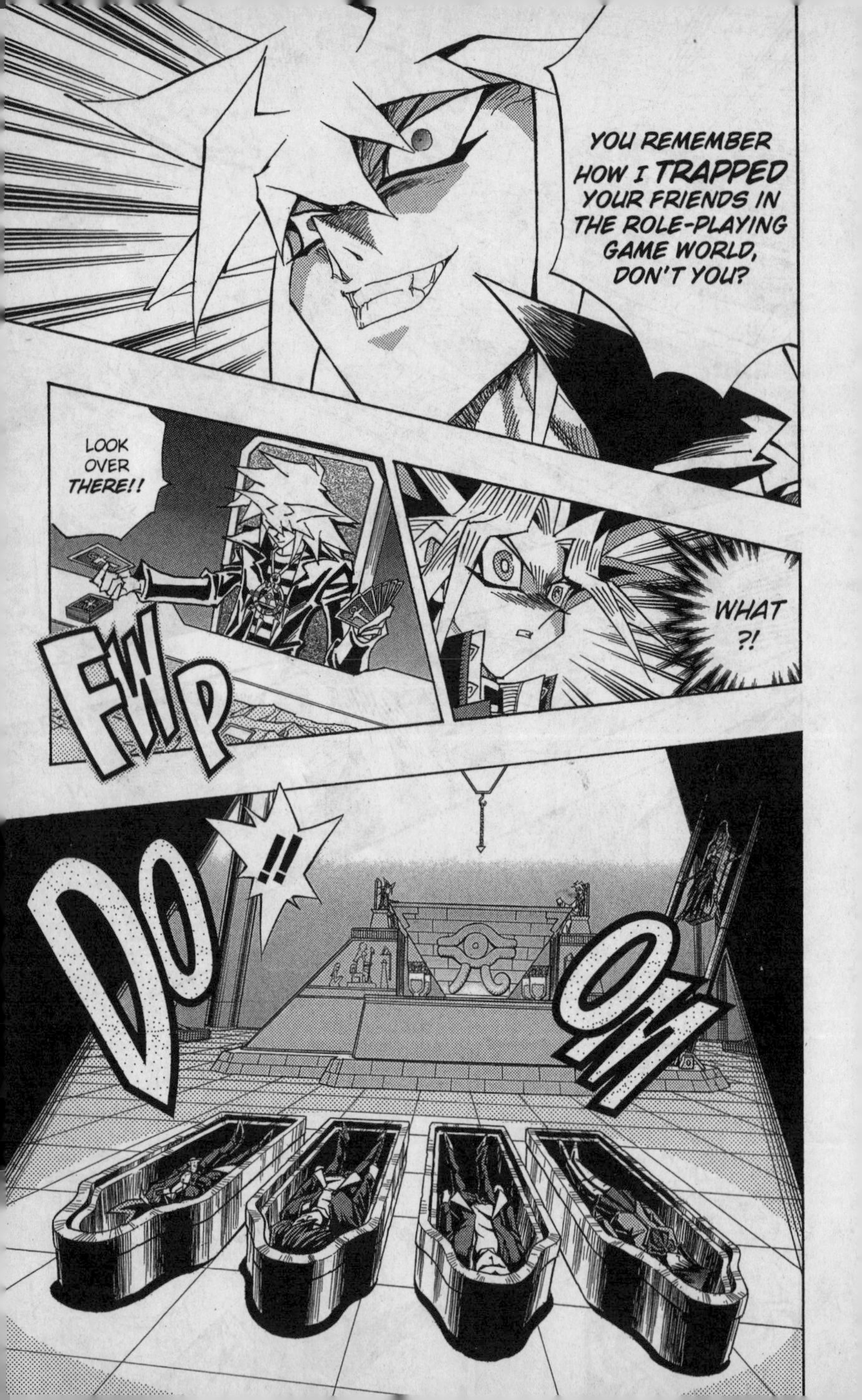
YOU REMEMBER HOW I TRAPPED YOUR FRIENDS IN THE ROLE-PLAYING GAME WORLD, DON'T YOU?
WHAT ?!
LOOK OVER THERE!!
FWP
DOOM
!!

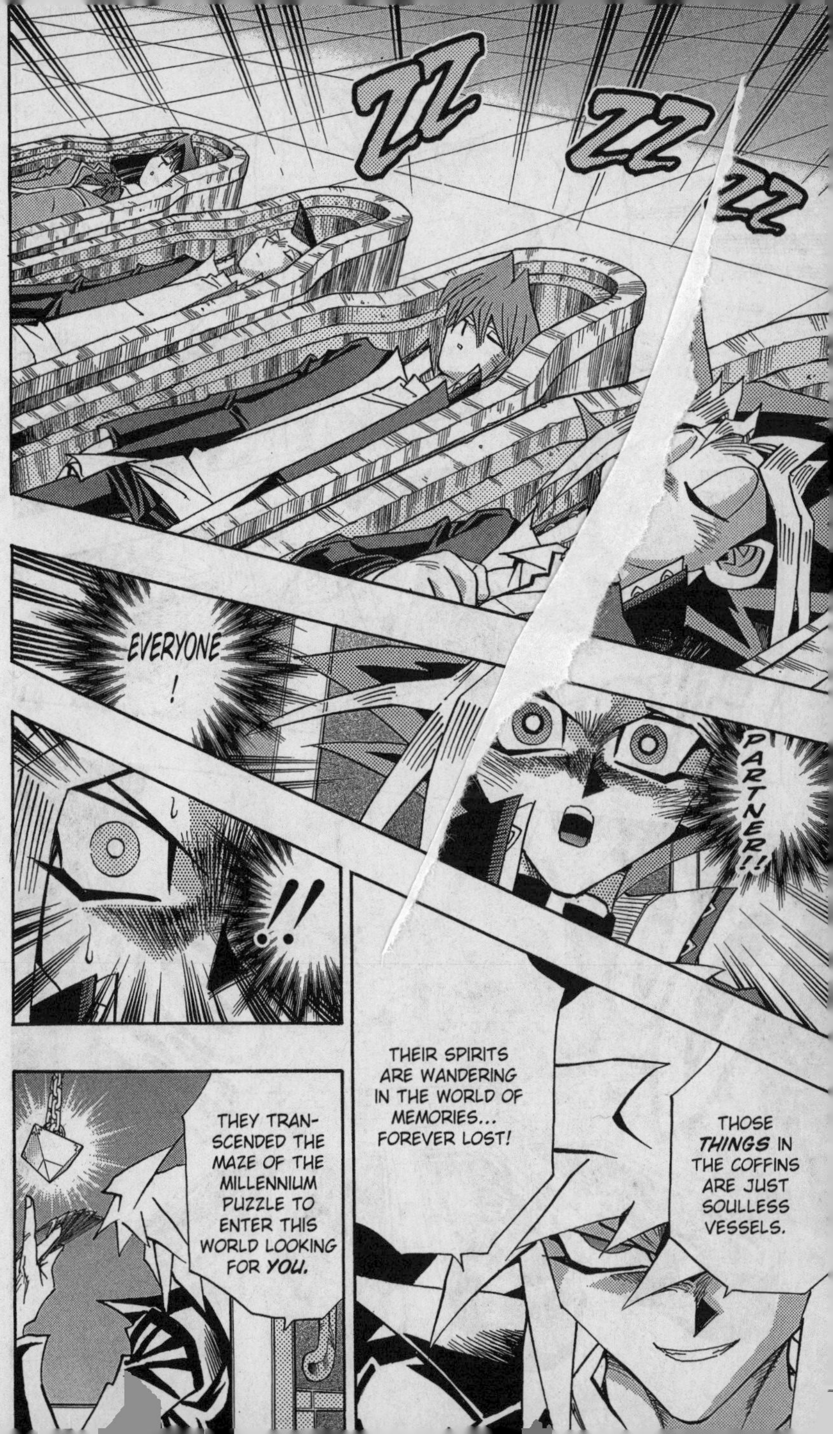

ZZ
ZZ
ZZ
EVERYONE!
PARTNER!!
!!
THOSE THINGS IN THE COFFINS ARE JUST SOULLESS VESSELS.
THEIR SPIRITS ARE WANDERING IN THE WORLD OF MEMORIES... FOREVER LOST!
THEY TRANSCENDED THE MAZE OF THE MILLENNIUM PUZZLE TO ENTER THIS WORLD LOOKING FOR YOU.

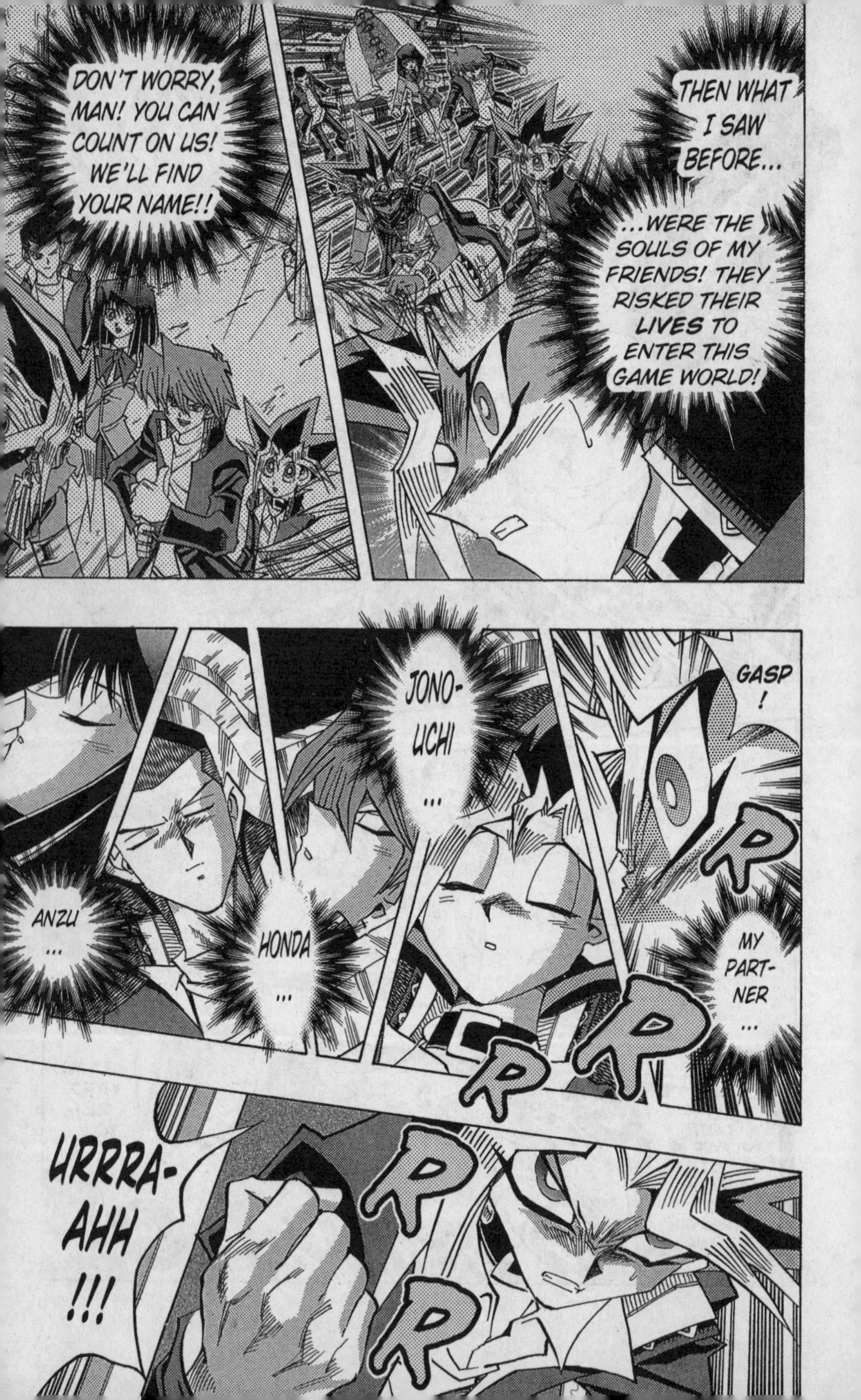
THEN WHAT I SAW BEFORE...
...WERE THE SOULS OF MY FRIENDS! THEY RISKED THEIR LIVES TO ENTER THIS GAME WORLD!
DON'T WORRY, MAN! YOU CAN COUNT ON US! WE'LL FIND YOUR NAME!!
GASP!
MY PARTNER...
JONO-UCHI...
HONDA...
ANZU...
RRRRRR
URRRA-AHH!!!

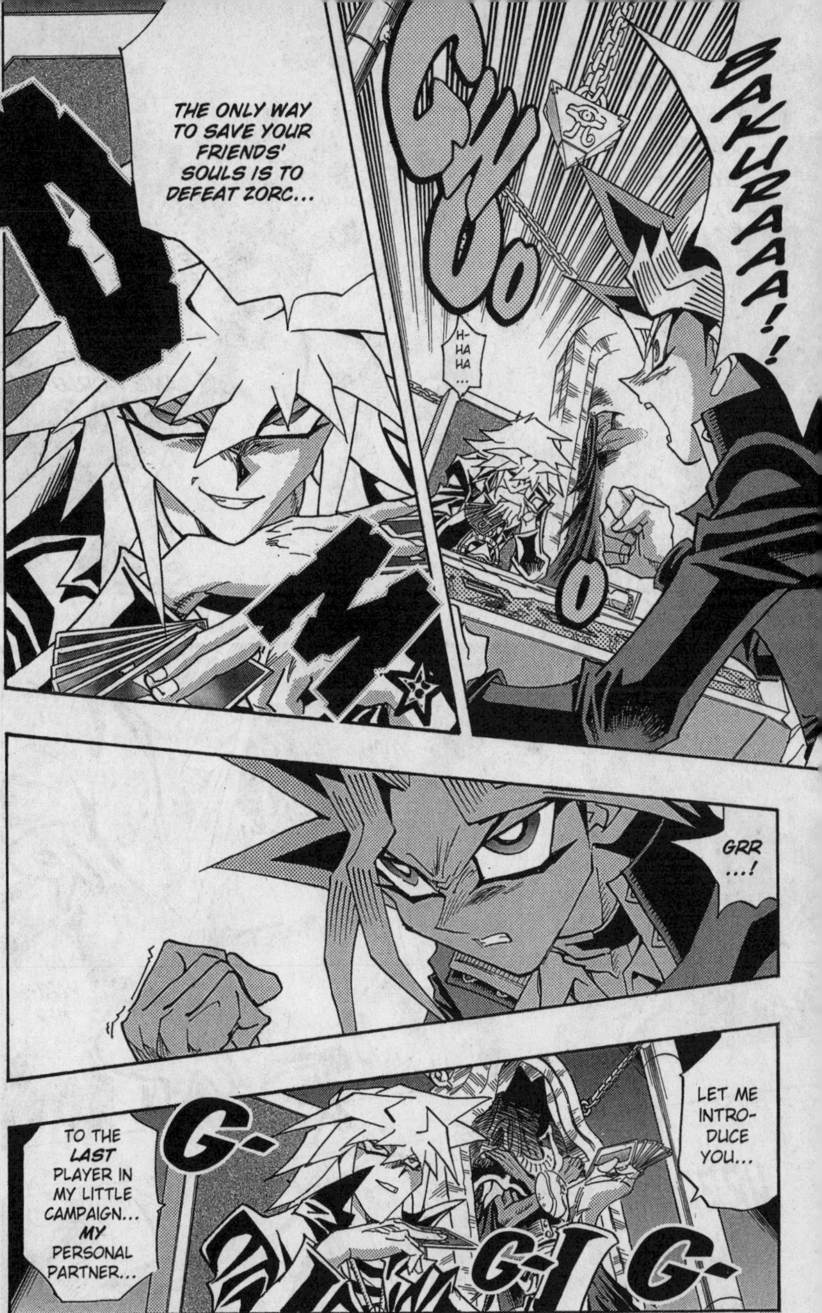
BAKURAAAA!!
H-HA HA...
THE ONLY WAY TO SAVE YOUR FRIENDS' SOULS IS TO DEFEAT ZORC...
GRR...!
LET ME INTRO-DUCE YOU...
TO THE LAST PLAYER IN MY LITTLE CAMPAIGN... MY PERSONAL PARTNER...

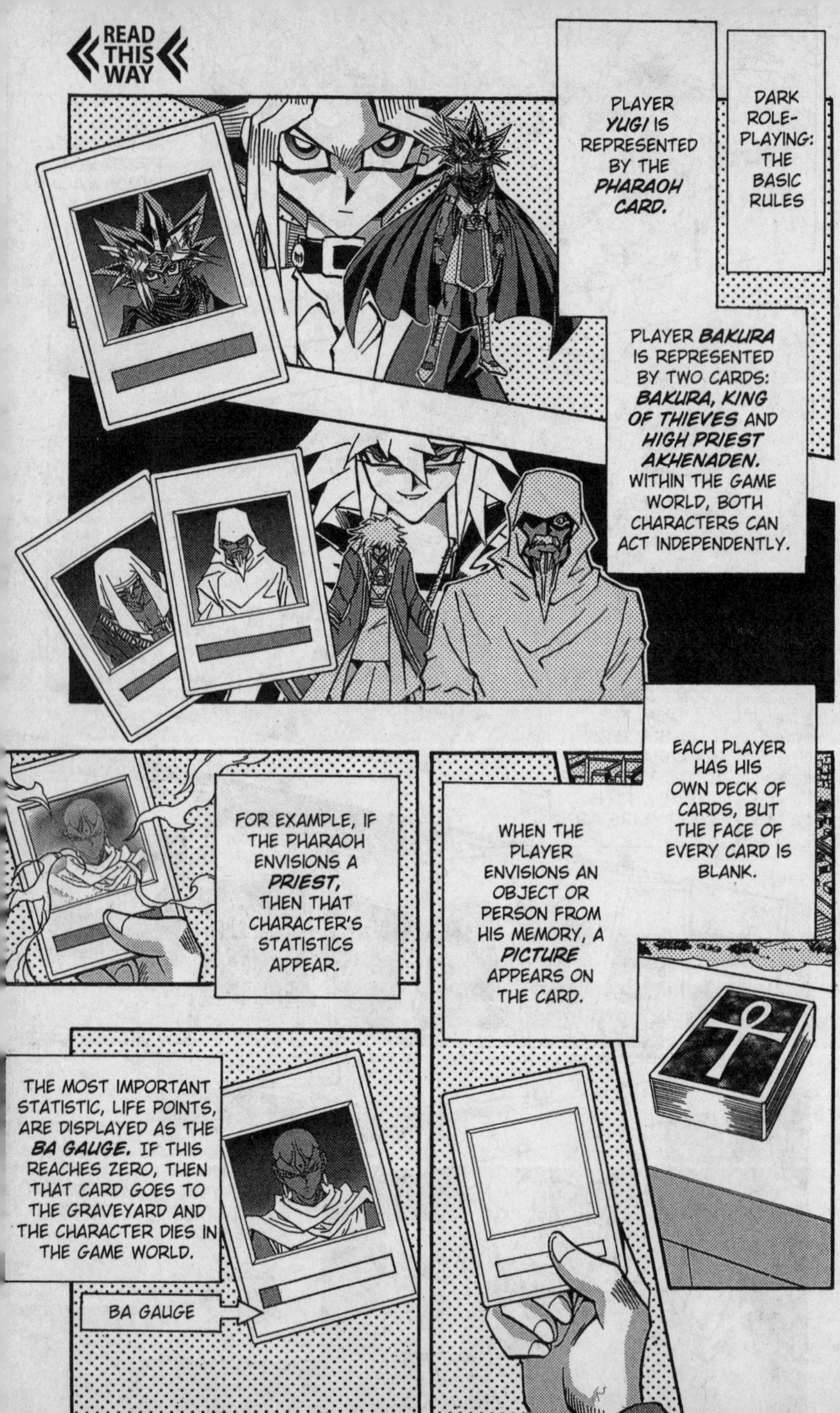
READ THIS WAY
DARK ROLE-PLAYING: THE BASIC RULES
PLAYER *YUGI* IS REPRESENTED BY THE *PHARAOH CARD.*
PLAYER *BAKURA* IS REPRESENTED BY TWO CARDS: *BAKURA, KING OF THIEVES* AND *HIGH PRIEST AKHENADEN.* WITHIN THE GAME WORLD, BOTH CHARACTERS CAN ACT INDEPENDENTLY.
EACH PLAYER HAS HIS OWN DECK OF CARDS, BUT THE FACE OF EVERY CARD IS BLANK.
WHEN THE PLAYER ENVISIONS AN OBJECT OR PERSON FROM HIS MEMORY, A *PICTURE* APPEARS ON THE CARD.
FOR EXAMPLE, IF THE PHARAOH ENVISIONS A *PRIEST,* THEN THAT CHARACTER'S STATISTICS APPEAR.
THE MOST IMPORTANT STATISTIC, LIFE POINTS, ARE DISPLAYED AS THE *BA GAUGE.* IF THIS REACHES ZERO, THEN THAT CARD GOES TO THE GRAVEYARD AND THE CHARACTER DIES IN THE GAME WORLD.
BA GAUGE

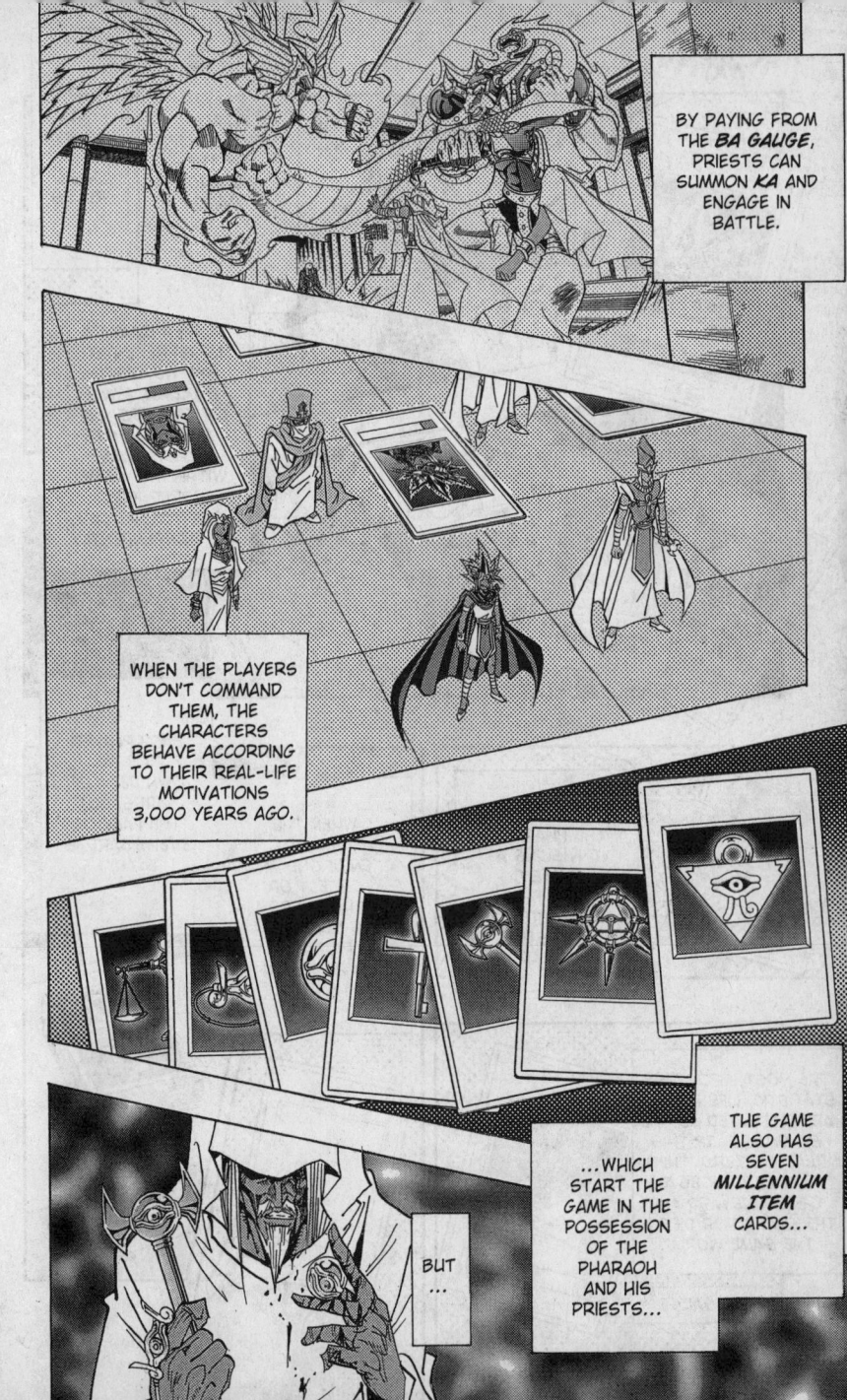

BY PAYING FROM THE *BA GAUGE*, PRIESTS CAN SUMMON *KA* AND ENGAGE IN BATTLE.

WHEN THE PLAYERS DON'T COMMAND THEM, THE CHARACTERS BEHAVE ACCORDING TO THEIR REAL-LIFE MOTIVATIONS 3,000 YEARS AGO.

THE GAME ALSO HAS SEVEN *MILLENNIUM ITEM* CARDS...

...WHICH START THE GAME IN THE POSSESSION OF THE PHARAOH AND HIS PRIESTS...

BUT...

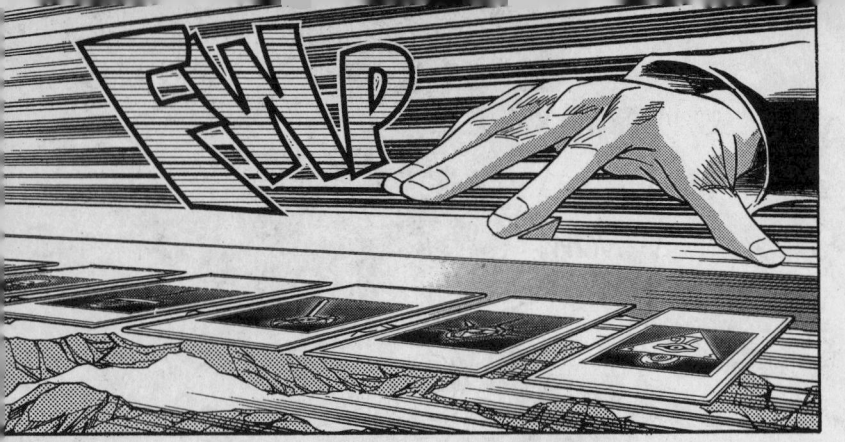

THE SEVEN MILLENNIUM ITEMS HAVE FALLEN INTO AKHENADEN'S HANDS! HE PLACES THEM IN THE STONE TABLET!!

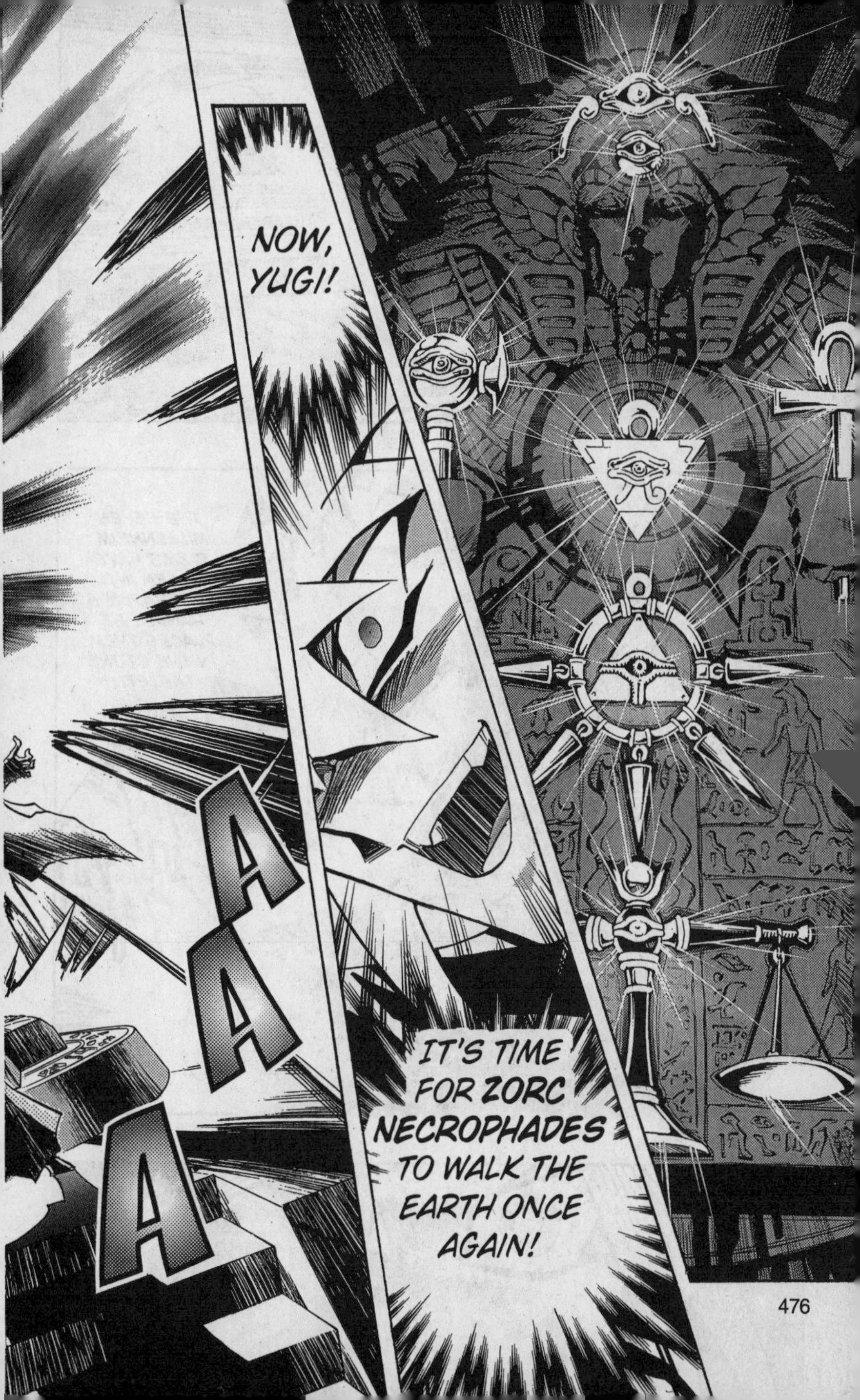
NOW, YUGI!
IT'S TIME FOR ZORC NECROPHADES TO WALK THE EARTH ONCE AGAIN!
AAA

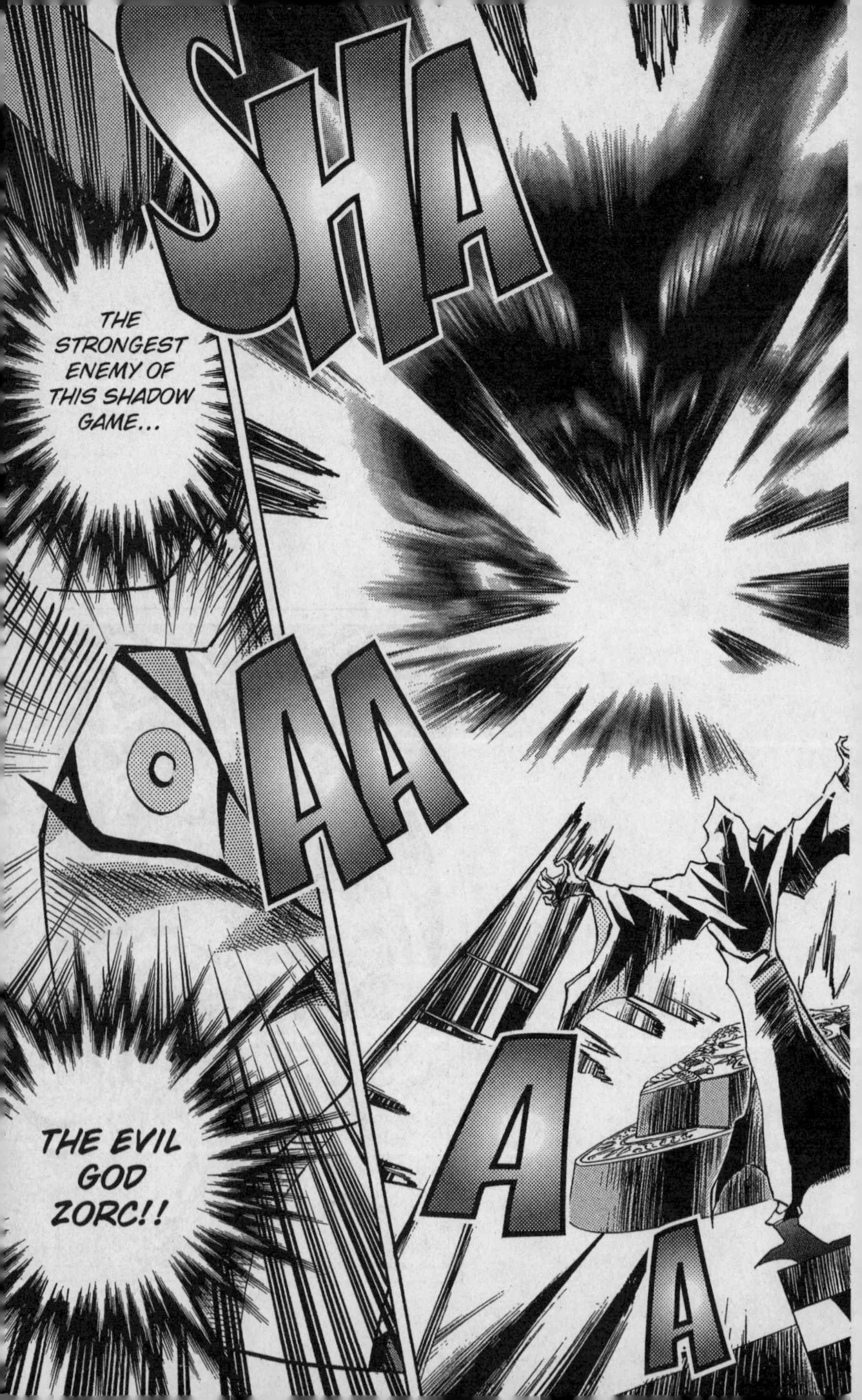
SHAAAAA
THE STRONGEST ENEMY OF THIS SHADOW GAME...
THE EVIL GOD ZORC!!

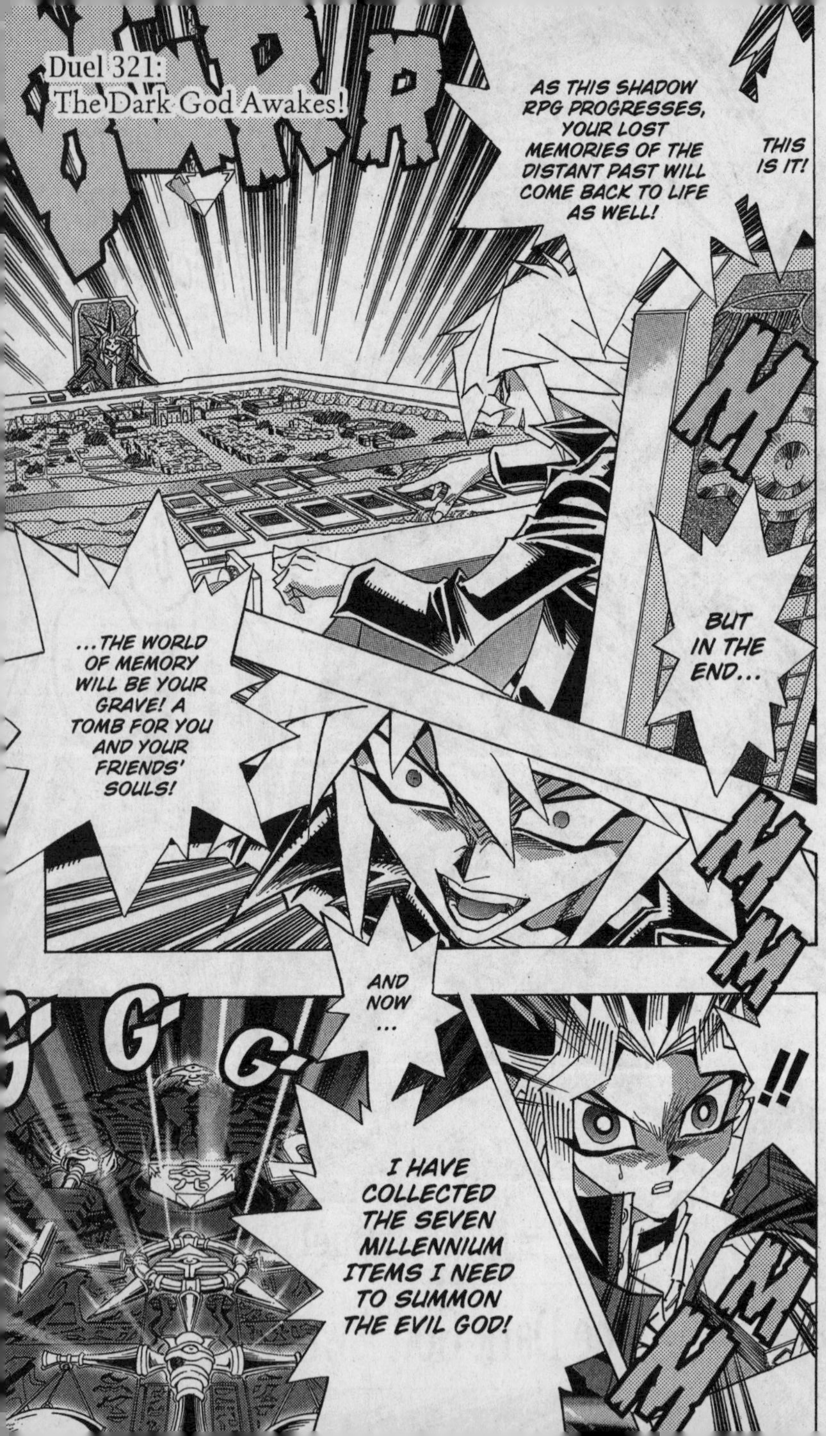
Duel 321:
The Dark God Awakes!
THIS IS IT!
AS THIS SHADOW RPG PROGRESSES, YOUR LOST MEMORIES OF THE DISTANT PAST WILL COME BACK TO LIFE AS WELL!
BUT IN THE END...
...THE WORLD OF MEMORY WILL BE YOUR GRAVE! A TOMB FOR YOU AND YOUR FRIENDS' SOULS!
AND NOW...
I HAVE COLLECTED THE SEVEN MILLENNIUM ITEMS I NEED TO SUMMON THE EVIL GOD!
!!

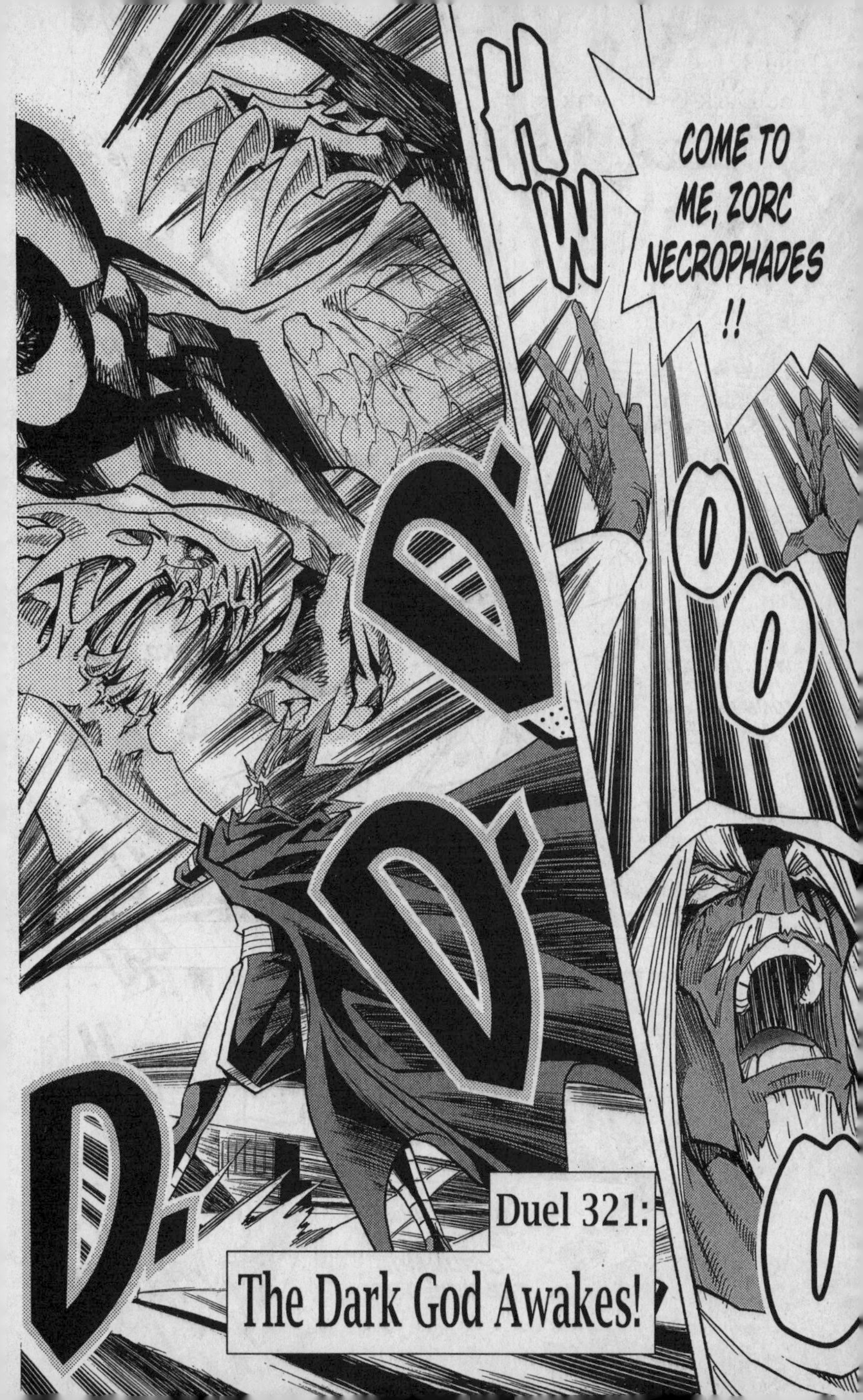
COME TO ME, ZORC NECROPHADES !!
Duel 321:
The Dark God Awakes!

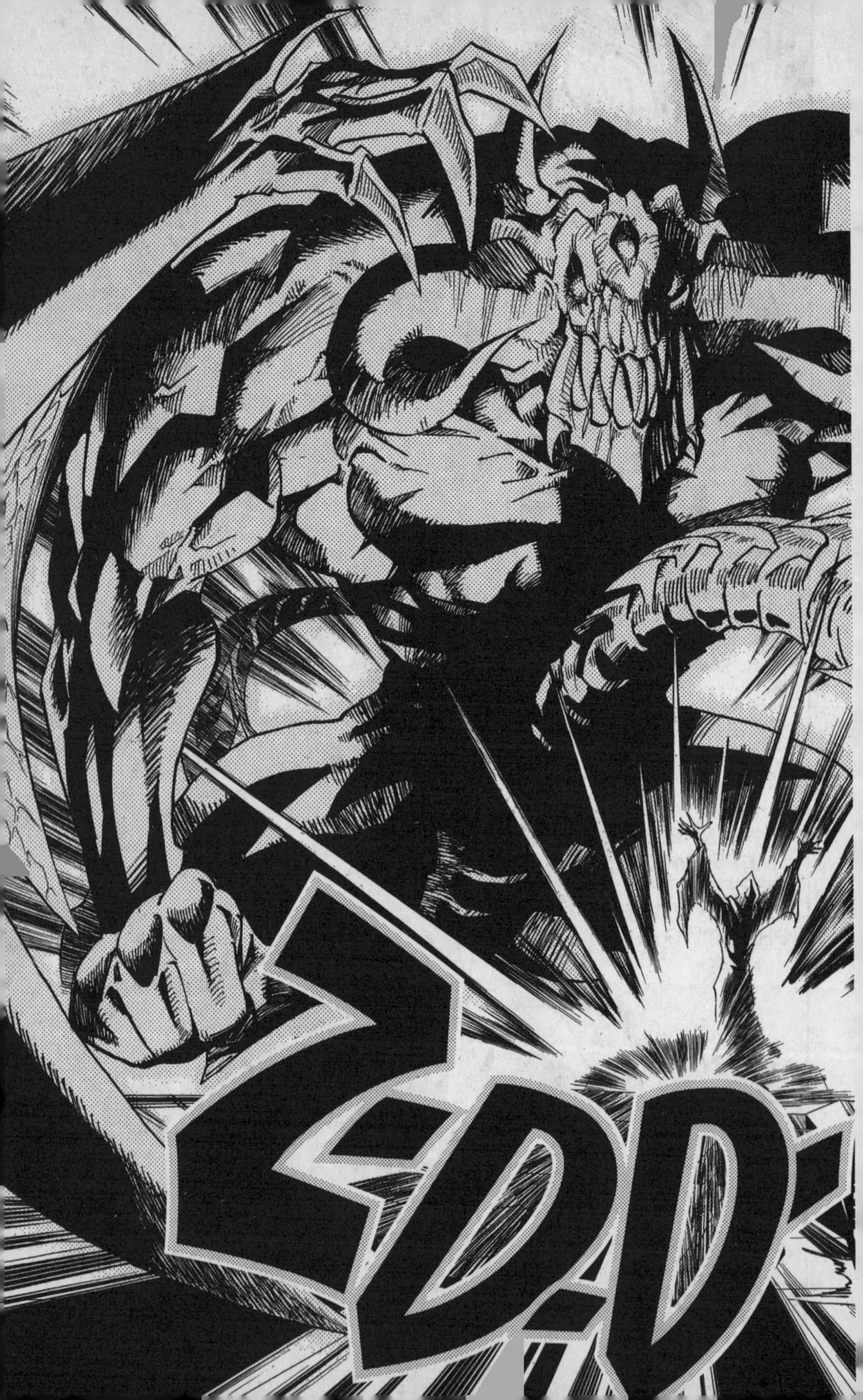
ZDD

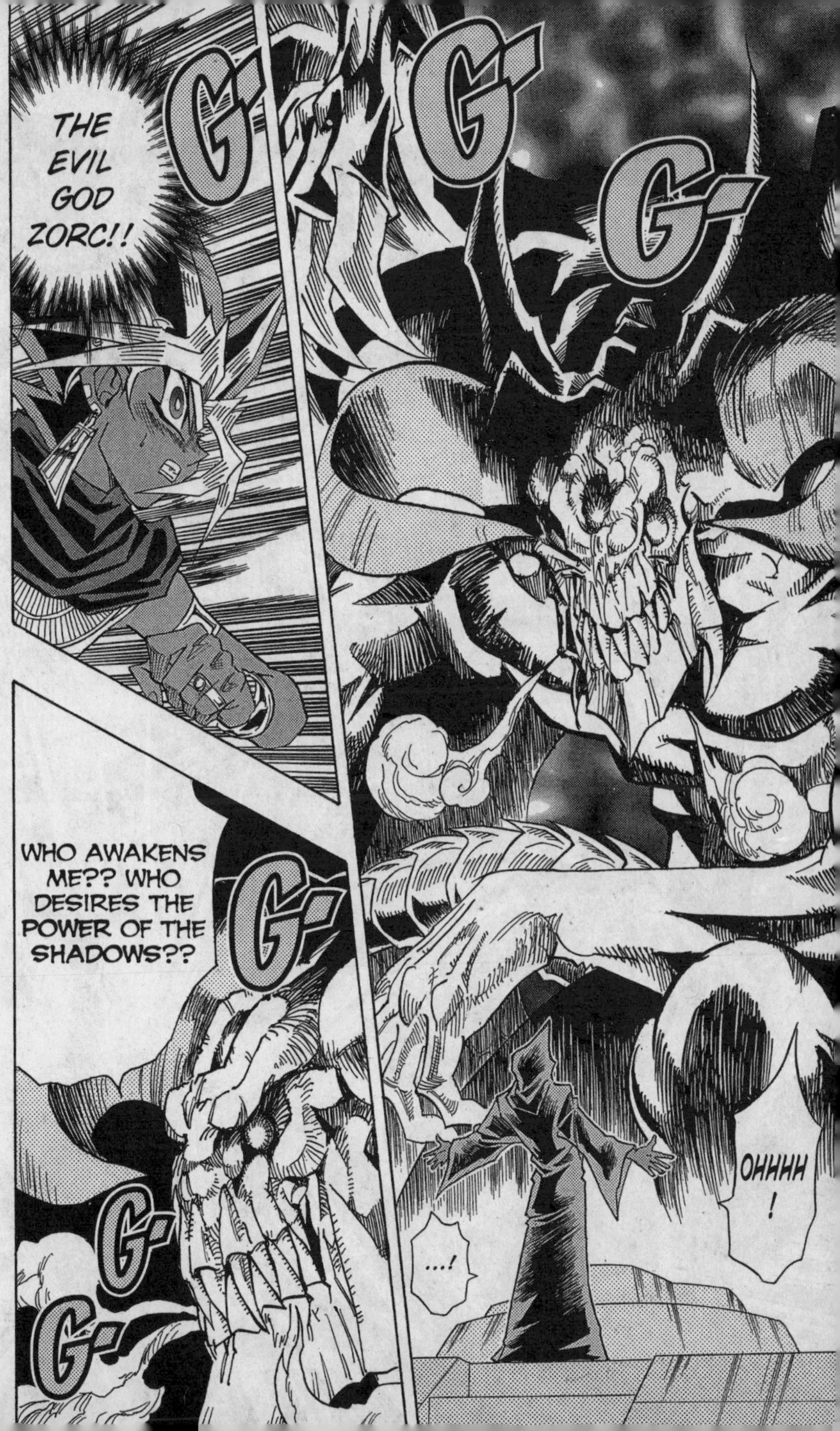
THE EVIL GOD ZORC!!
G-
G-
G-
WHO AWAKENS ME?? WHO DESIRES THE POWER OF THE SHADOWS??
G-
G-
G-
OHHHH!
...!

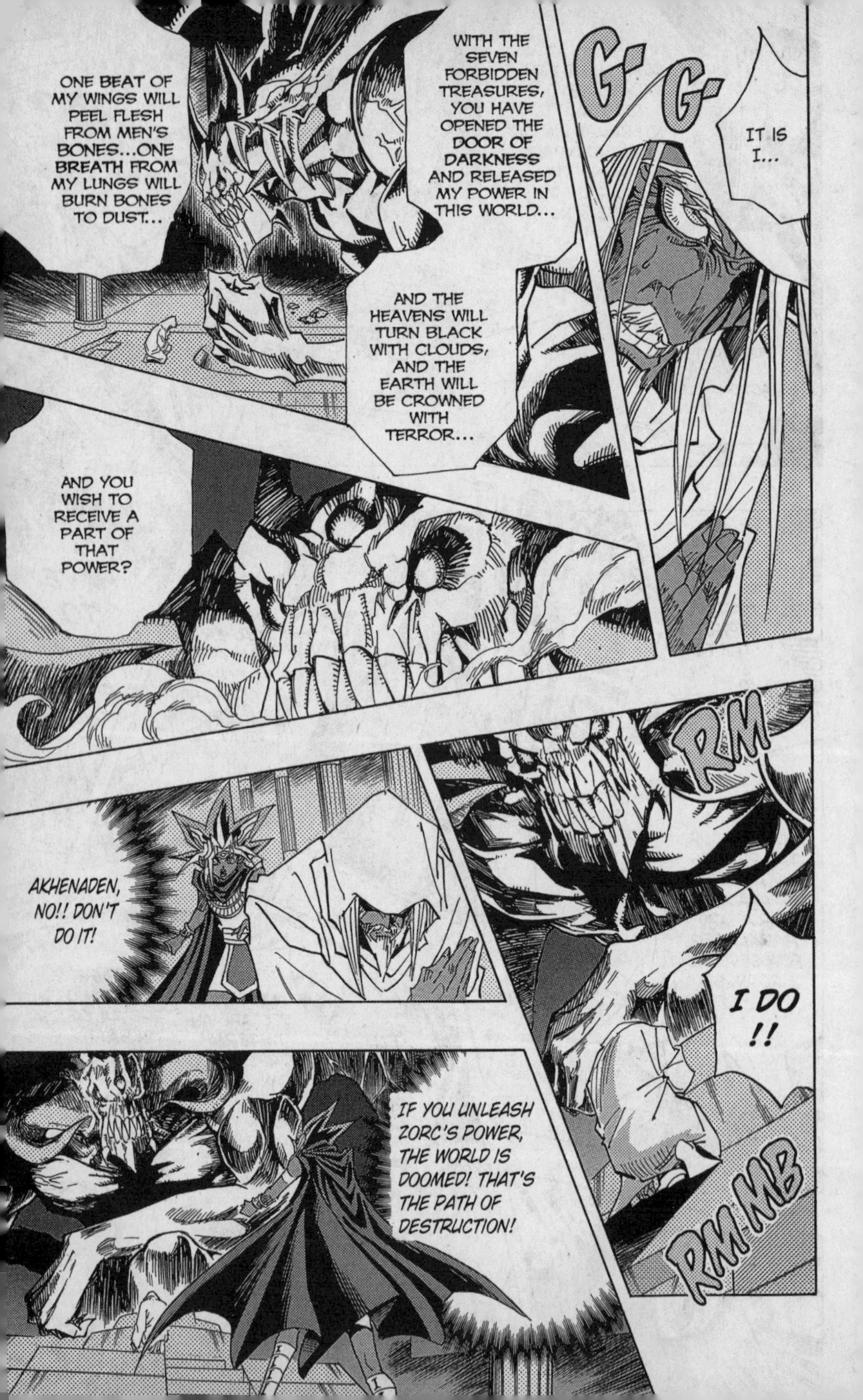
G G
IT IS I...
WITH THE SEVEN FORBIDDEN TREASURES, YOU HAVE OPENED THE DOOR OF DARKNESS AND RELEASED MY POWER IN THIS WORLD...
ONE BEAT OF MY WINGS WILL PEEL FLESH FROM MEN'S BONES...ONE BREATH FROM MY LUNGS WILL BURN BONES TO DUST...
AND THE HEAVENS WILL TURN BLACK WITH CLOUDS, AND THE EARTH WILL BE CROWNED WITH TERROR...
AND YOU WISH TO RECEIVE A PART OF THAT POWER?
RM
I DO !!
RMMB
AKHENADEN, NO!! DON'T DO IT!
IF YOU UNLEASH ZORC'S POWER, THE WORLD IS DOOMED! THAT'S THE PATH OF DESTRUCTION!

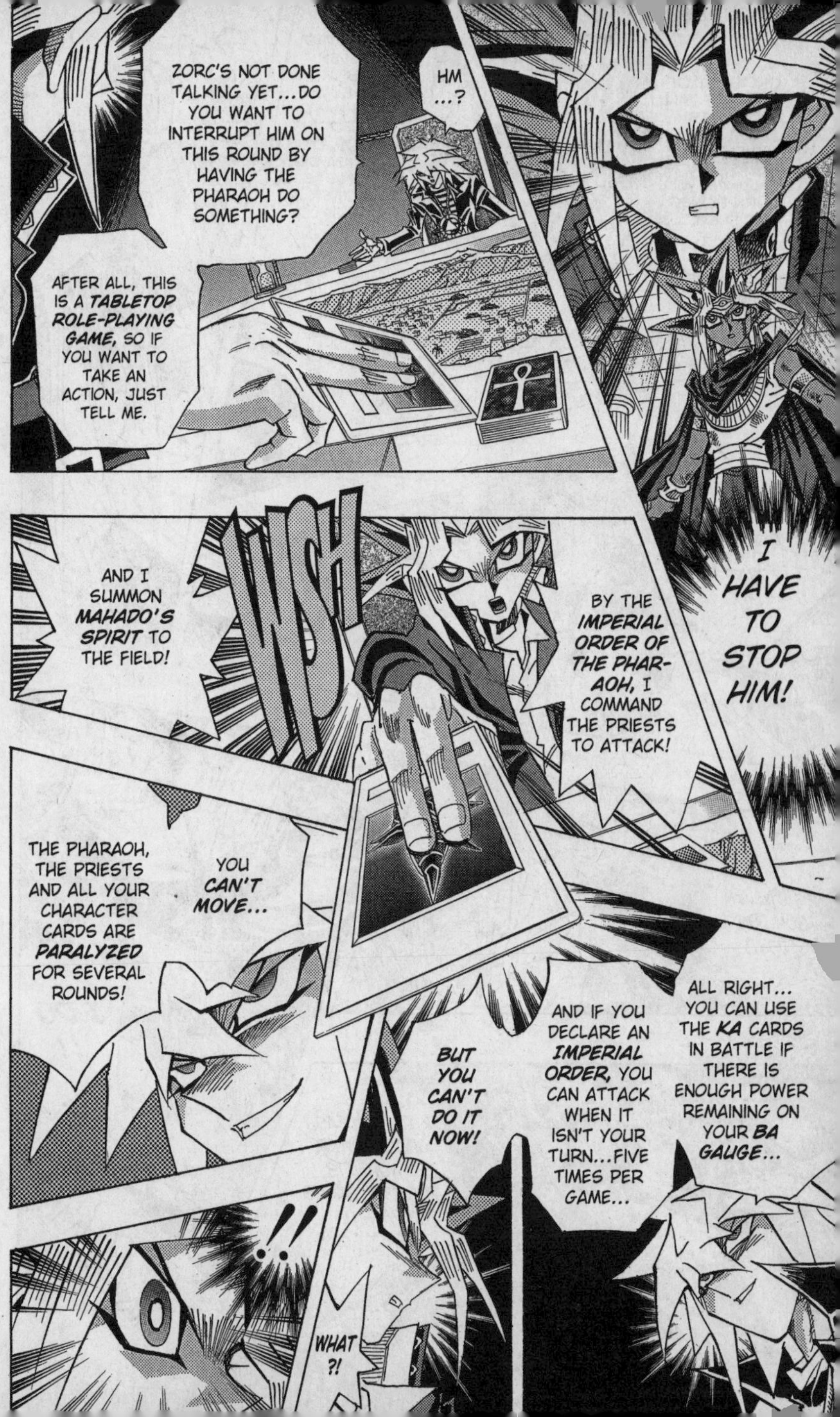
HM ...?
ZORC'S NOT DONE TALKING YET...DO YOU WANT TO INTERRUPT HIM ON THIS ROUND BY HAVING THE PHARAOH DO SOMETHING?
AFTER ALL, THIS IS A *TABLETOP ROLE-PLAYING GAME,* SO IF YOU WANT TO TAKE AN ACTION, JUST TELL ME.
I HAVE TO STOP HIM!
BY THE *IMPERIAL ORDER OF THE PHARAOH,* I COMMAND THE PRIESTS TO ATTACK!
WSH
AND I SUMMON *MAHADO'S SPIRIT* TO THE FIELD!
YOU *CAN'T MOVE...*
THE PHARAOH, THE PRIESTS AND ALL YOUR CHARACTER CARDS ARE *PARALYZED* FOR SEVERAL ROUNDS!
ALL RIGHT... YOU CAN USE THE *KA* CARDS IN BATTLE IF THERE IS ENOUGH POWER REMAINING ON YOUR *BA GAUGE...*
AND IF YOU DECLARE AN *IMPERIAL ORDER,* YOU CAN ATTACK WHEN IT ISN'T YOUR TURN...FIVE TIMES PER GAME...
BUT YOU CAN'T DO IT NOW!
!!
WHAT ?!

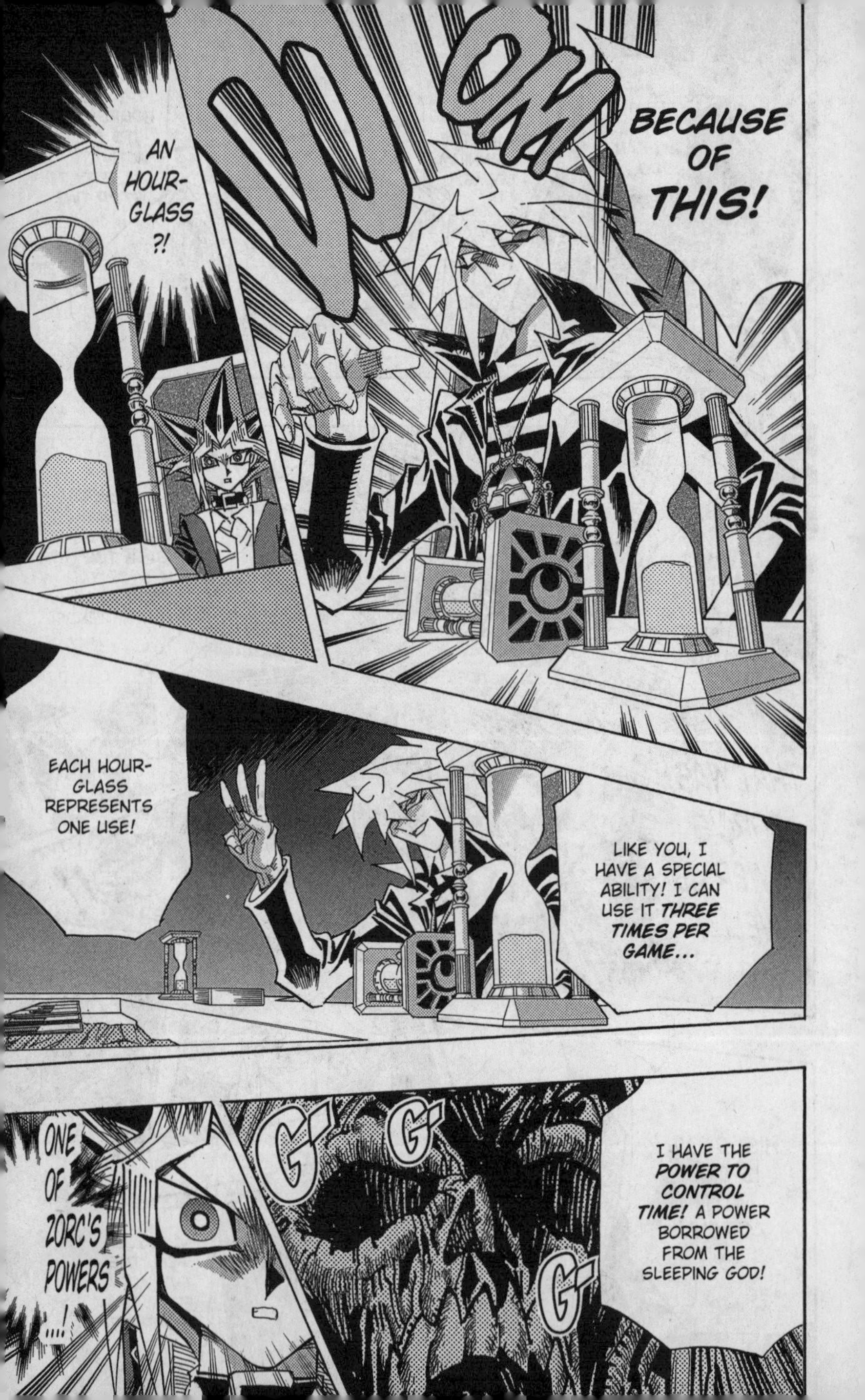
BECAUSE OF THIS!
AN HOUR-GLASS?!
LIKE YOU, I HAVE A SPECIAL ABILITY! I CAN USE IT THREE TIMES PER GAME...
EACH HOUR-GLASS REPRESENTS ONE USE!
I HAVE THE POWER TO CONTROL TIME! A POWER BORROWED FROM THE SLEEPING GOD!
G
G
G
ONE OF ZORC'S POWERS...!

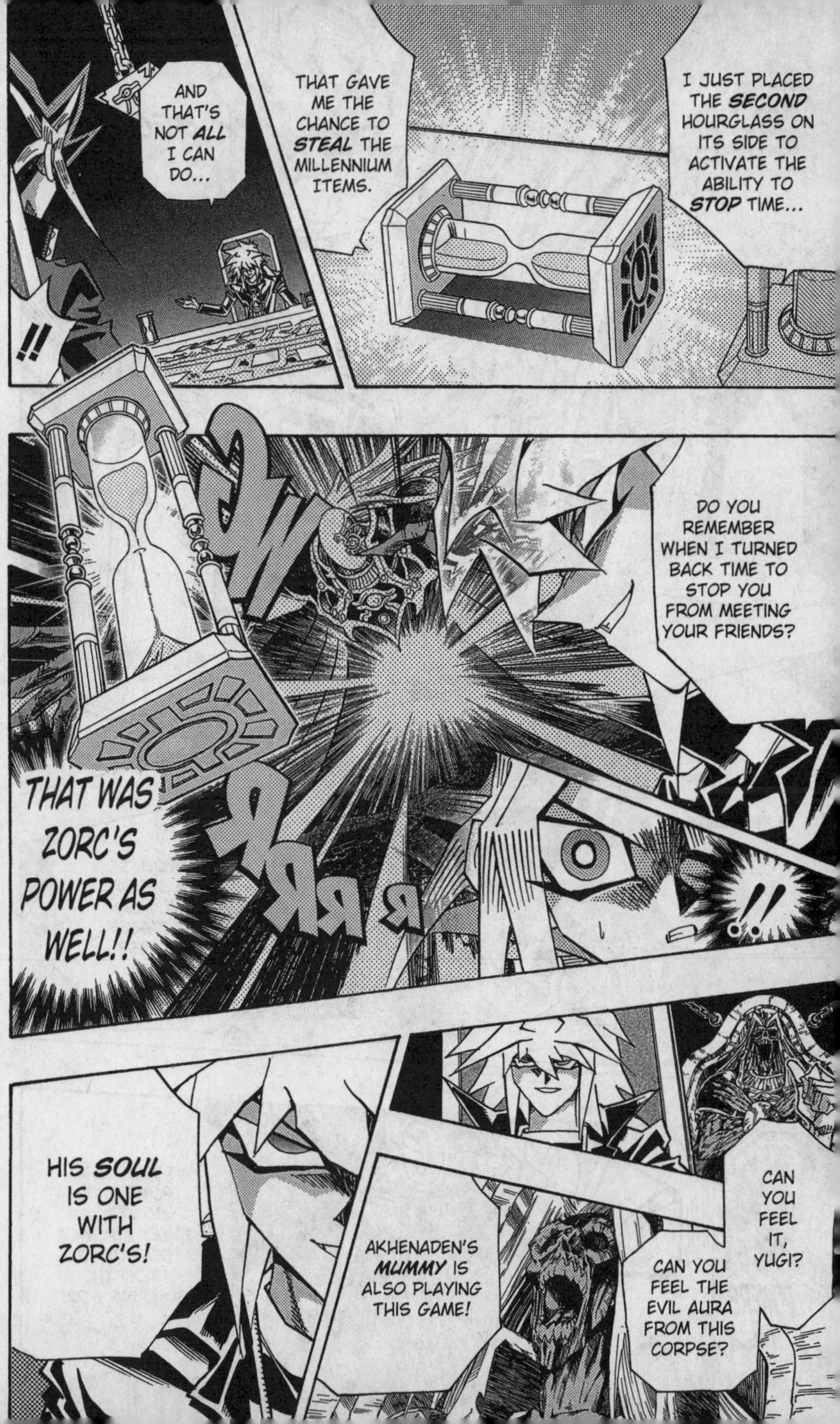
I JUST PLACED THE SECOND HOURGLASS ON ITS SIDE TO ACTIVATE THE ABILITY TO STOP TIME...
THAT GAVE ME THE CHANCE TO STEAL THE MILLENNIUM ITEMS.
AND THAT'S NOT ALL I CAN DO...
!!
DO YOU REMEMBER WHEN I TURNED BACK TIME TO STOP YOU FROM MEETING YOUR FRIENDS?
THAT WAS ZORC'S POWER AS WELL!!
!!
CAN YOU FEEL IT, YUGI?
CAN YOU FEEL THE EVIL AURA FROM THIS CORPSE?
AKHENADEN'S MUMMY IS ALSO PLAYING THIS GAME!
HIS SOUL IS ONE WITH ZORC'S!

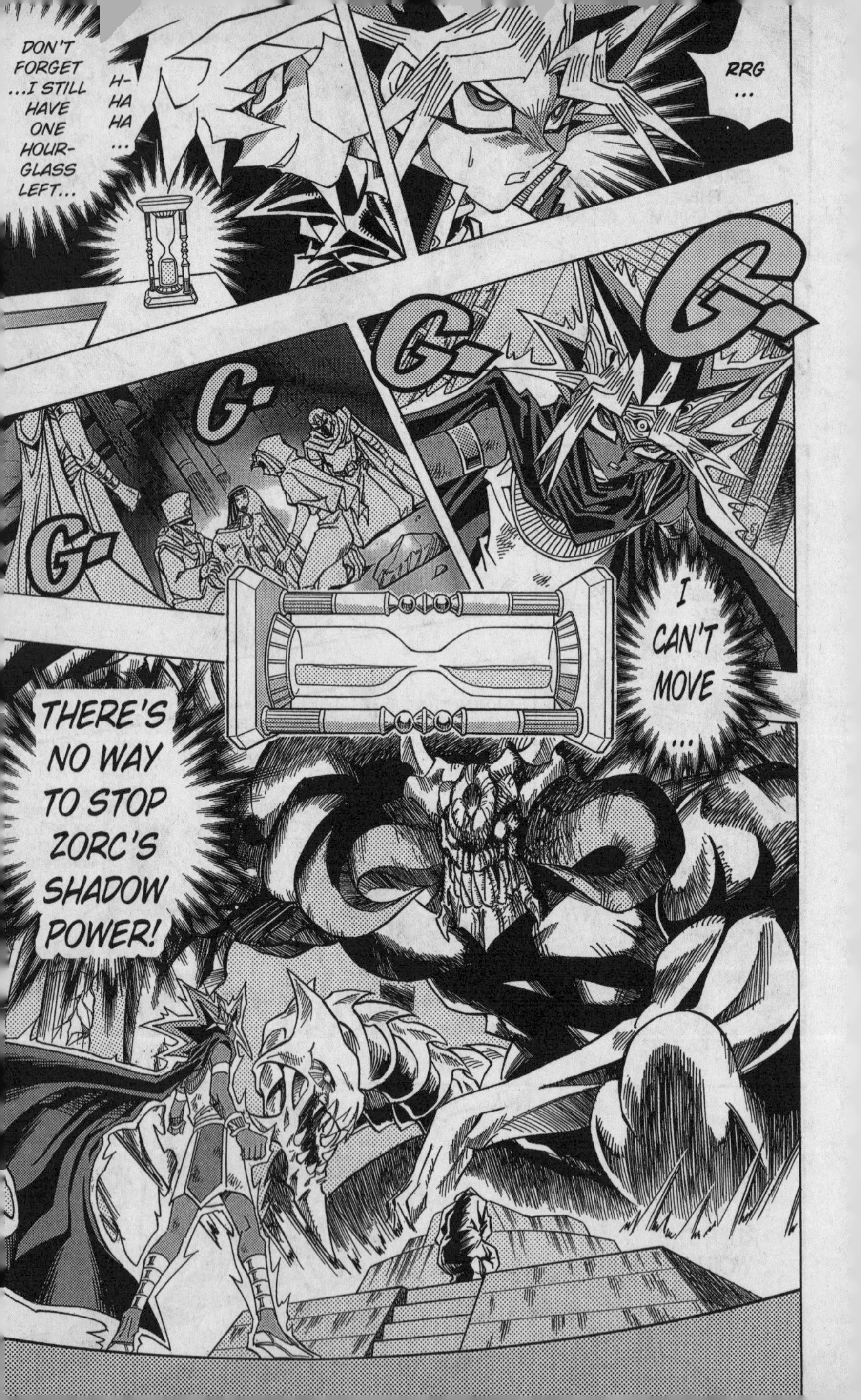
RRG ...
H-HA HA ...
DON'T FORGET ...I STILL HAVE ONE HOURGLASS LEFT...
G-
G-
G-
G-
I CAN'T MOVE ...
THERE'S NO WAY TO STOP ZORC'S SHADOW POWER!

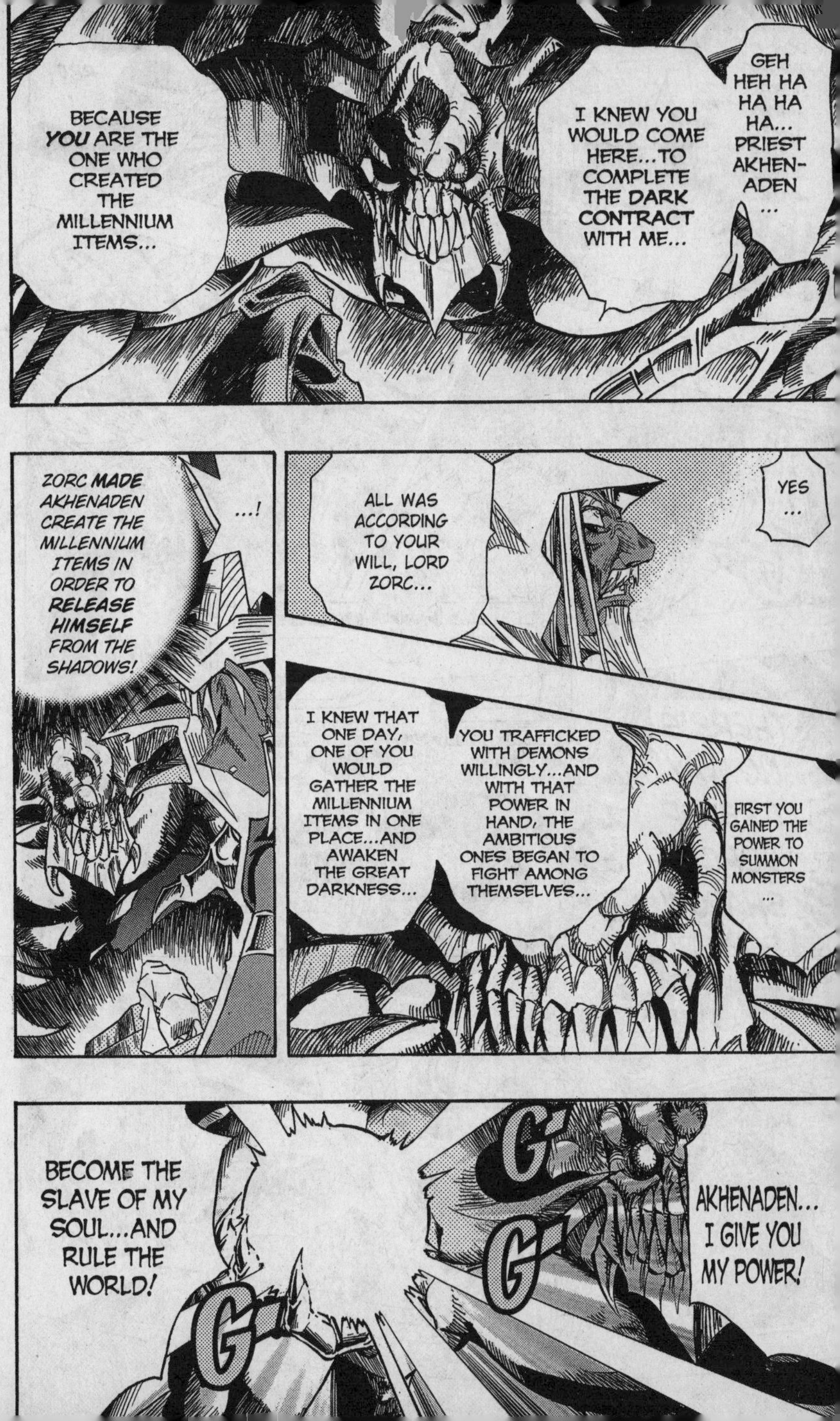
GEH HEH HA HA HA HA... PRIEST AKHENADEN...
I KNEW YOU WOULD COME HERE...TO COMPLETE THE DARK CONTRACT WITH ME...
BECAUSE YOU ARE THE ONE WHO CREATED THE MILLENNIUM ITEMS...
YES...
ALL WAS ACCORDING TO YOUR WILL, LORD ZORC...
FIRST YOU GAINED THE POWER TO SUMMON MONSTERS...
YOU TRAFFICKED WITH DEMONS WILLINGLY...AND WITH THAT POWER IN HAND, THE AMBITIOUS ONES BEGAN TO FIGHT AMONG THEMSELVES...
I KNEW THAT ONE DAY, ONE OF YOU WOULD GATHER THE MILLENNIUM ITEMS IN ONE PLACE...AND AWAKEN THE GREAT DARKNESS...
...!
ZORC MADE AKHENADEN CREATE THE MILLENNIUM ITEMS IN ORDER TO RELEASE HIMSELF FROM THE SHADOWS!
AKHENADEN... I GIVE YOU MY POWER!
BECOME THE SLAVE OF MY SOUL...AND RULE THE WORLD!
G
G
G

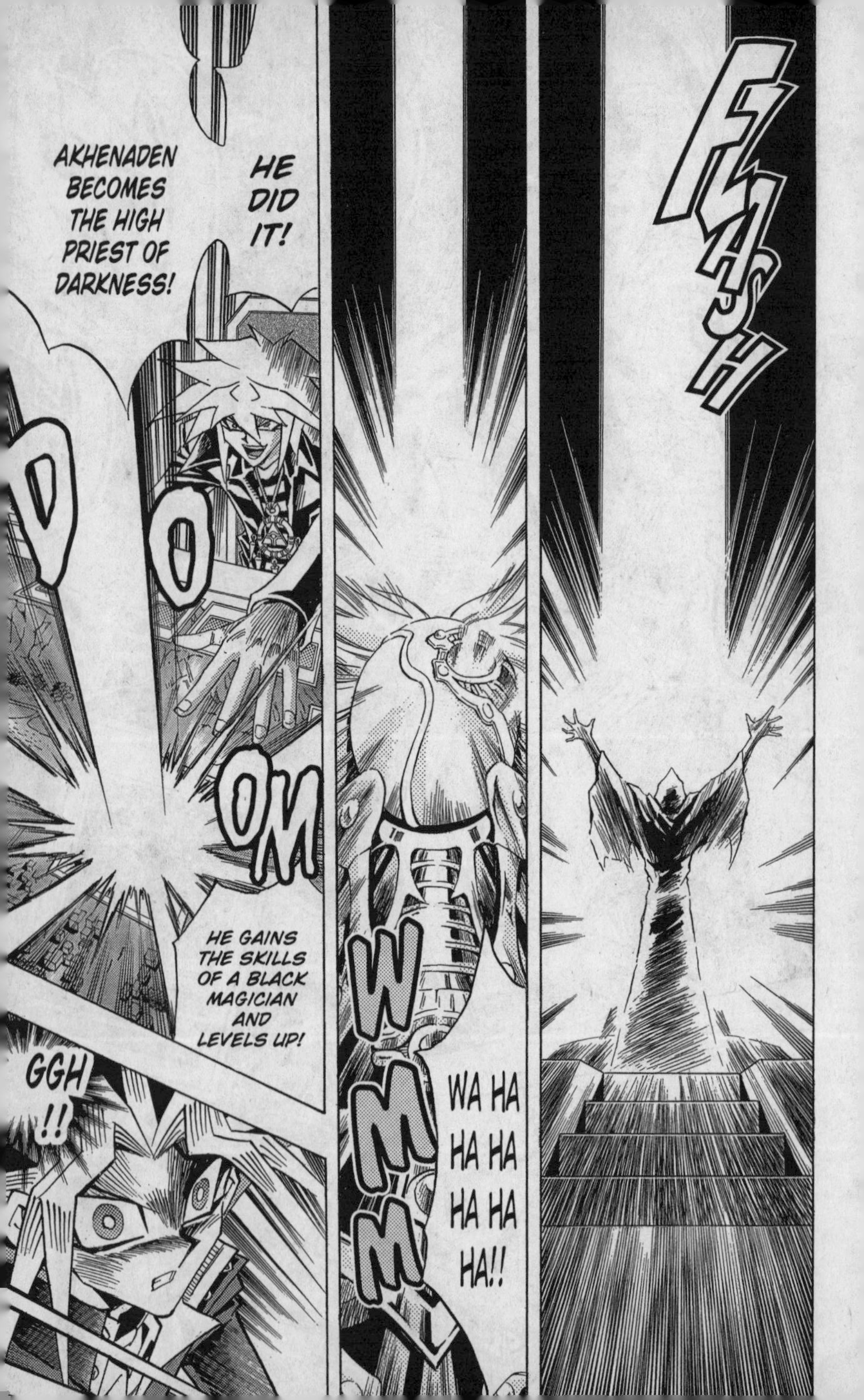
FLASH
WMMM
WA HA HA HA HA HA HA!!
HE DID IT!
AKHENADEN BECOMES THE HIGH PRIEST OF DARKNESS!
DOOM
HE GAINS THE SKILLS OF A BLACK MAGICIAN AND LEVELS UP!
GGH!!

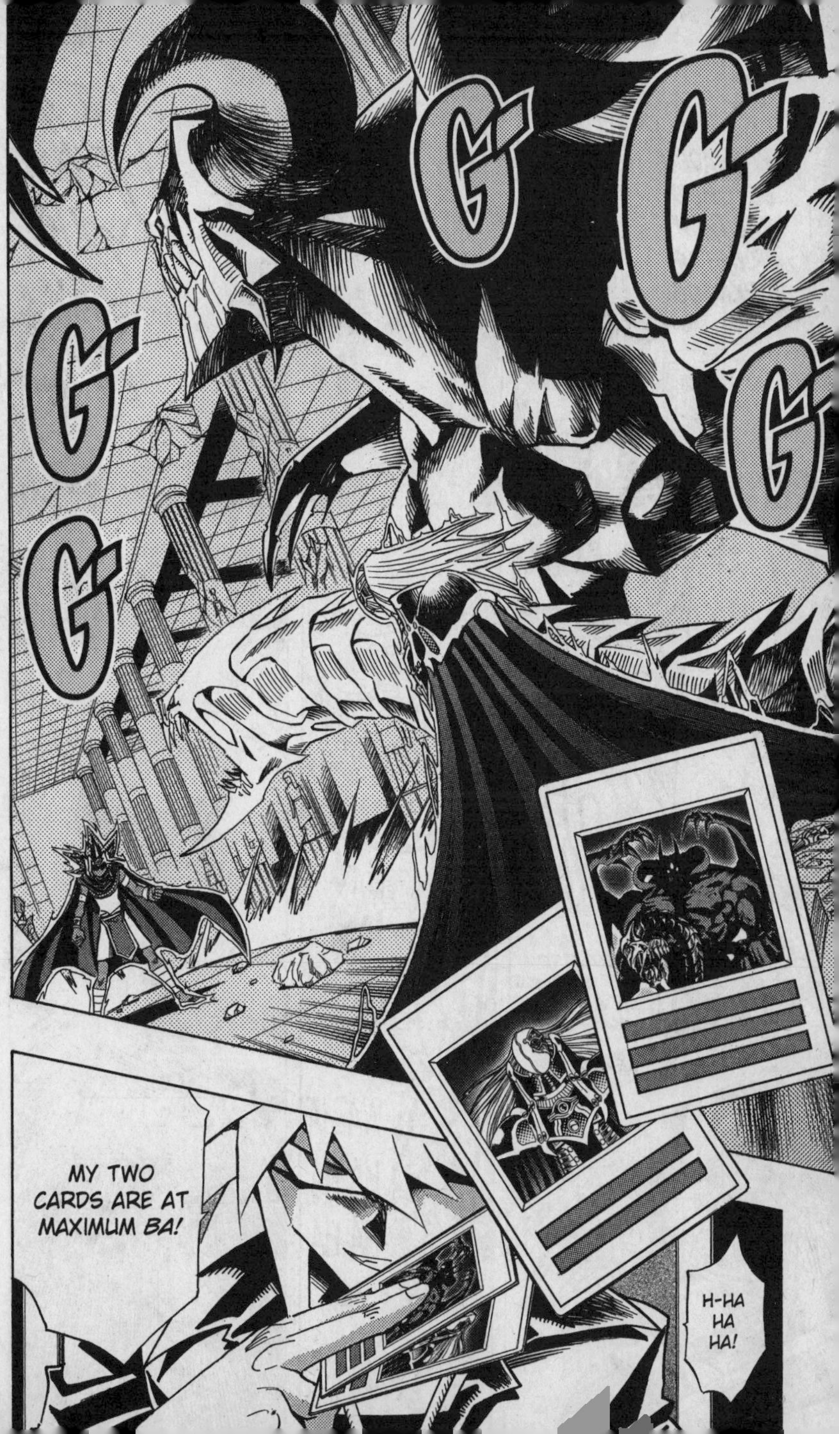
G
G
G
G
G
H-HA
HA
HA
HA!
MY TWO
CARDS ARE AT
MAXIMUM BA!

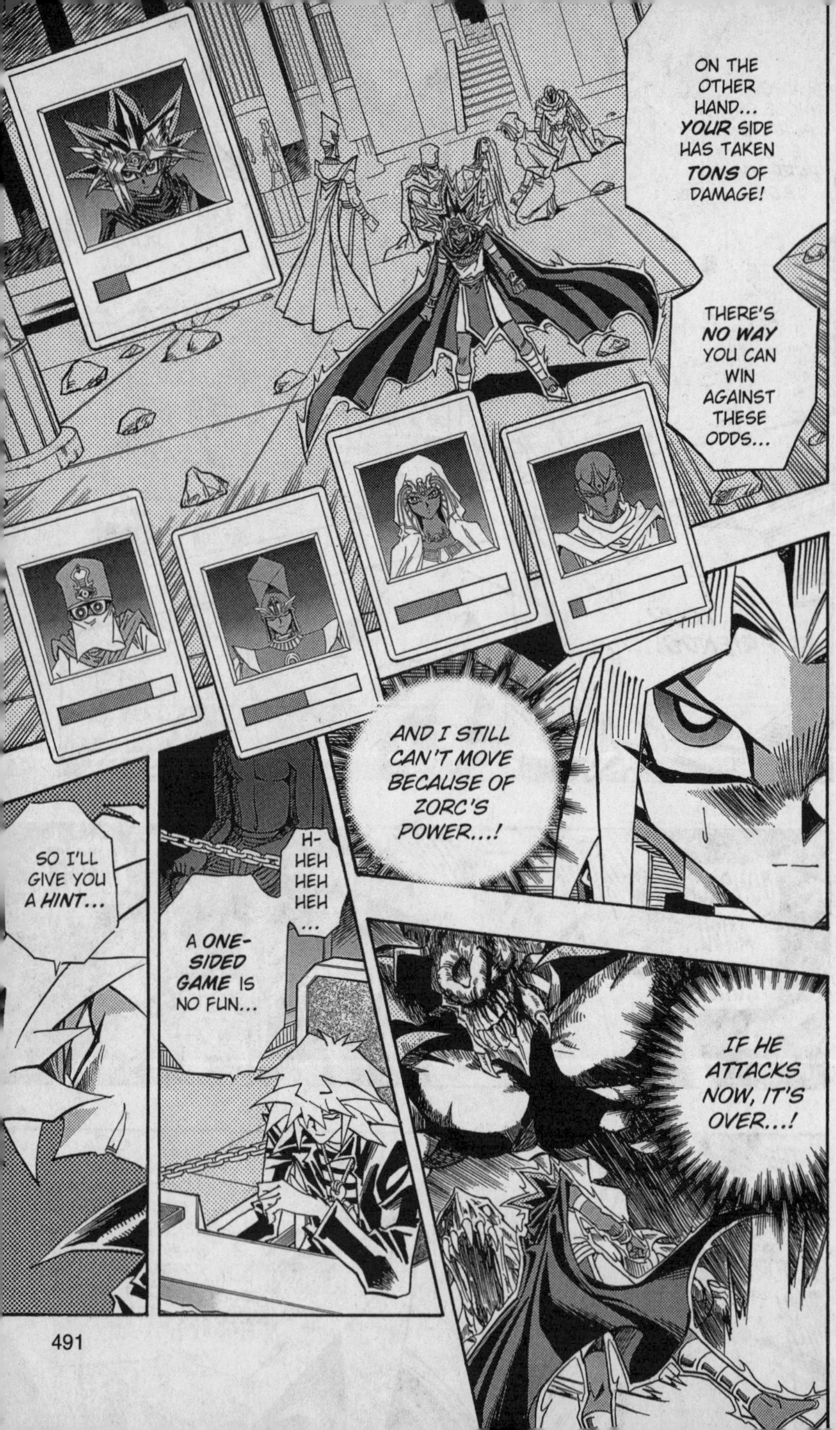
ON THE OTHER HAND... YOUR SIDE HAS TAKEN TONS OF DAMAGE!
THERE'S NO WAY YOU CAN WIN AGAINST THESE ODDS...
AND I STILL CAN'T MOVE BECAUSE OF ZORC'S POWER...!
IF HE ATTACKS NOW, IT'S OVER...!
H-HEH HEH HEH...
A ONE-SIDED GAME IS NO FUN...
SO I'LL GIVE YOU A HINT...

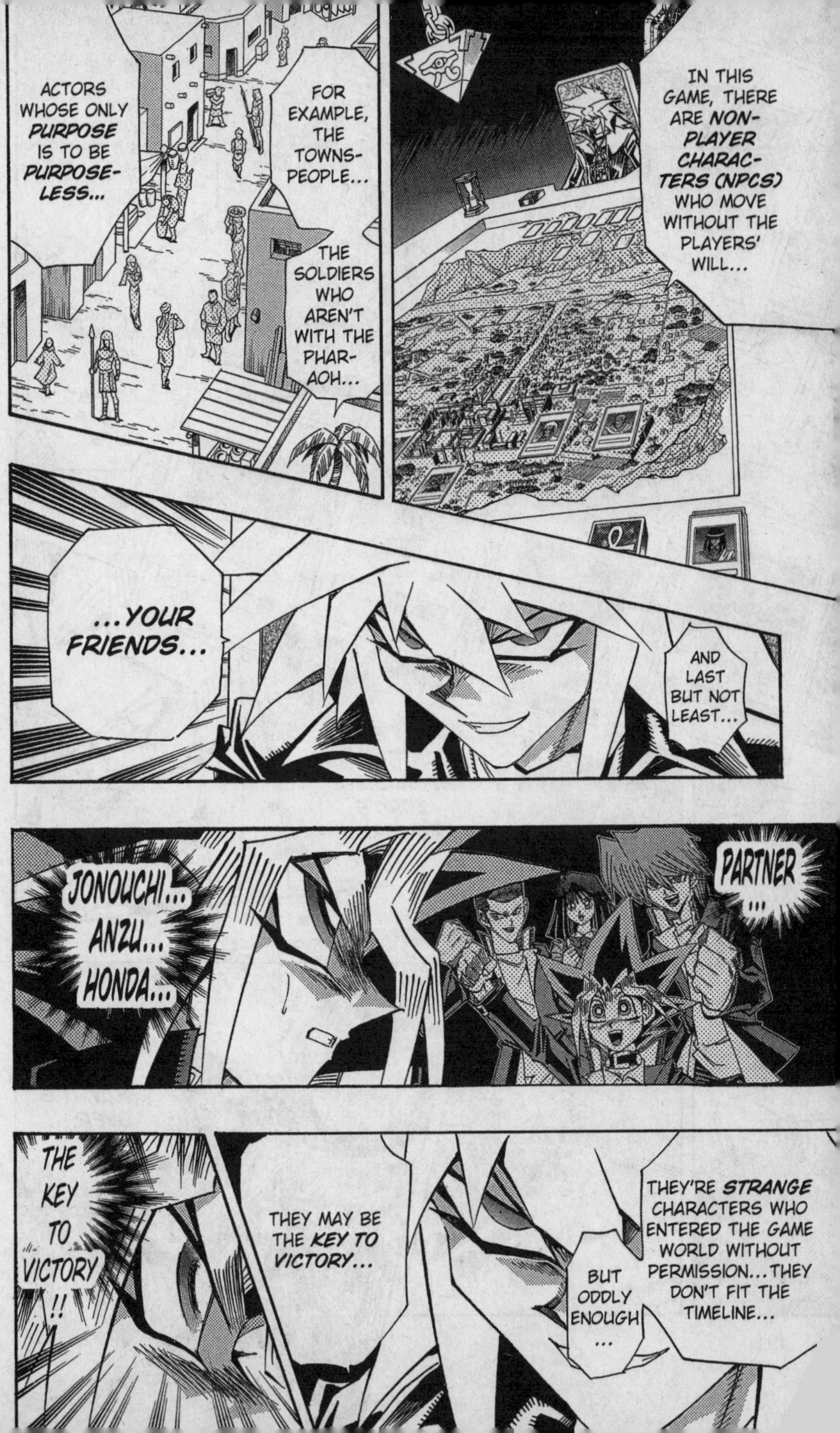
IN THIS GAME, THERE ARE NON-PLAYER CHARACTERS (NPCS) WHO MOVE WITHOUT THE PLAYERS' WILL...
FOR EXAMPLE, THE TOWNS-PEOPLE...
THE SOLDIERS WHO AREN'T WITH THE PHAR-AOH...
ACTORS WHOSE ONLY PURPOSE IS TO BE PURPOSE-LESS...
AND LAST BUT NOT LEAST...
...YOUR FRIENDS...
PARTNER!!!
JONOUCHI... ANZU... HONDA...
THEY'RE STRANGE CHARACTERS WHO ENTERED THE GAME WORLD WITHOUT PERMISSION...THEY DON'T FIT THE TIMELINE...
BUT ODDLY ENOUGH...
THEY MAY BE THE KEY TO VICTORY...
THE KEY TO VICTORY!!

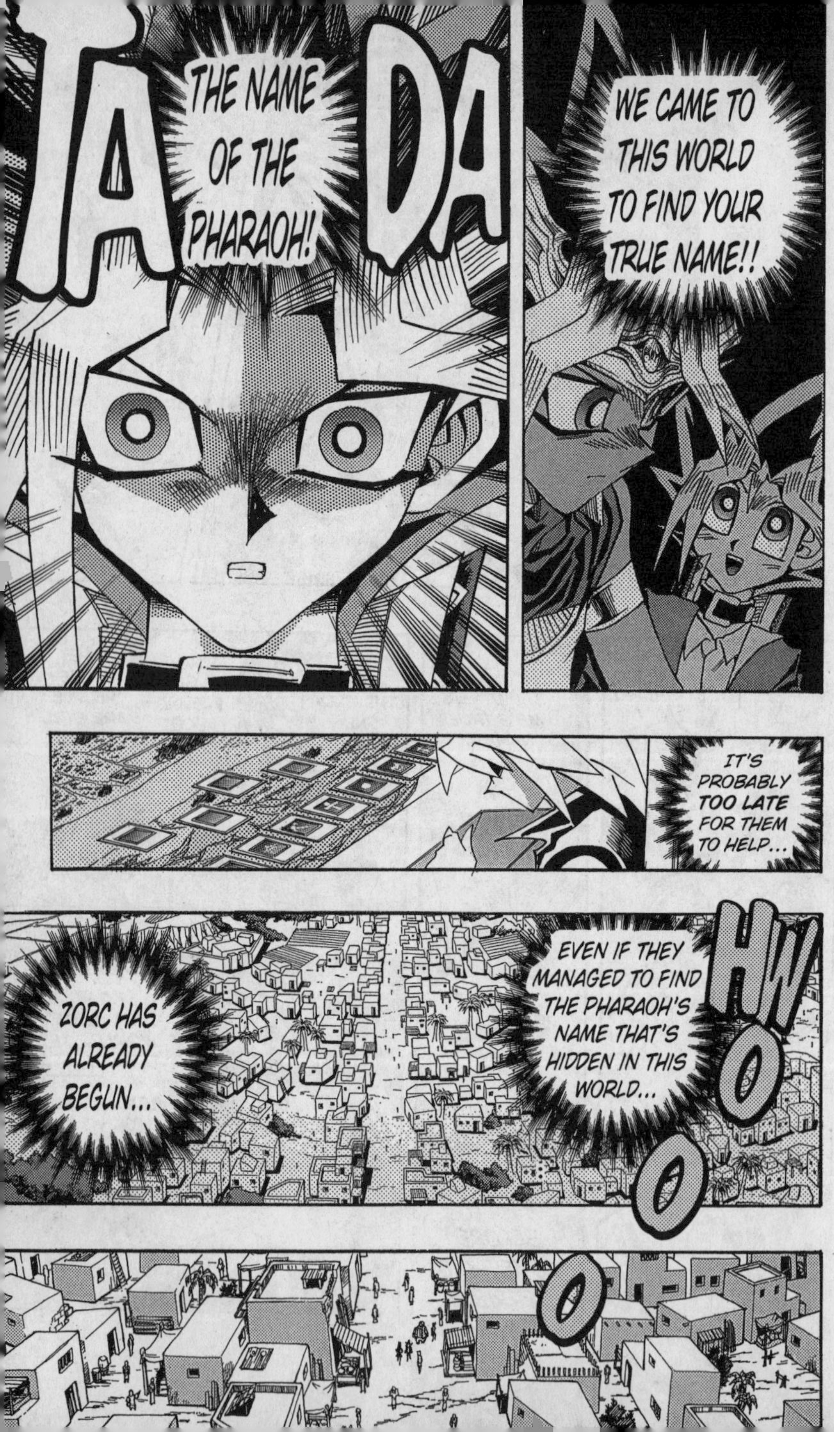
WE CAME TO THIS WORLD TO FIND YOUR TRUE NAME!!
TA
DA
THE NAME OF THE PHARAOH!
IT'S PROBABLY TOO LATE FOR THEM TO HELP...
HW
EVEN IF THEY MANAGED TO FIND THE PHARAOH'S NAME THAT'S HIDDEN IN THIS WORLD...
ZORC HAS ALREADY BEGUN...
OOO

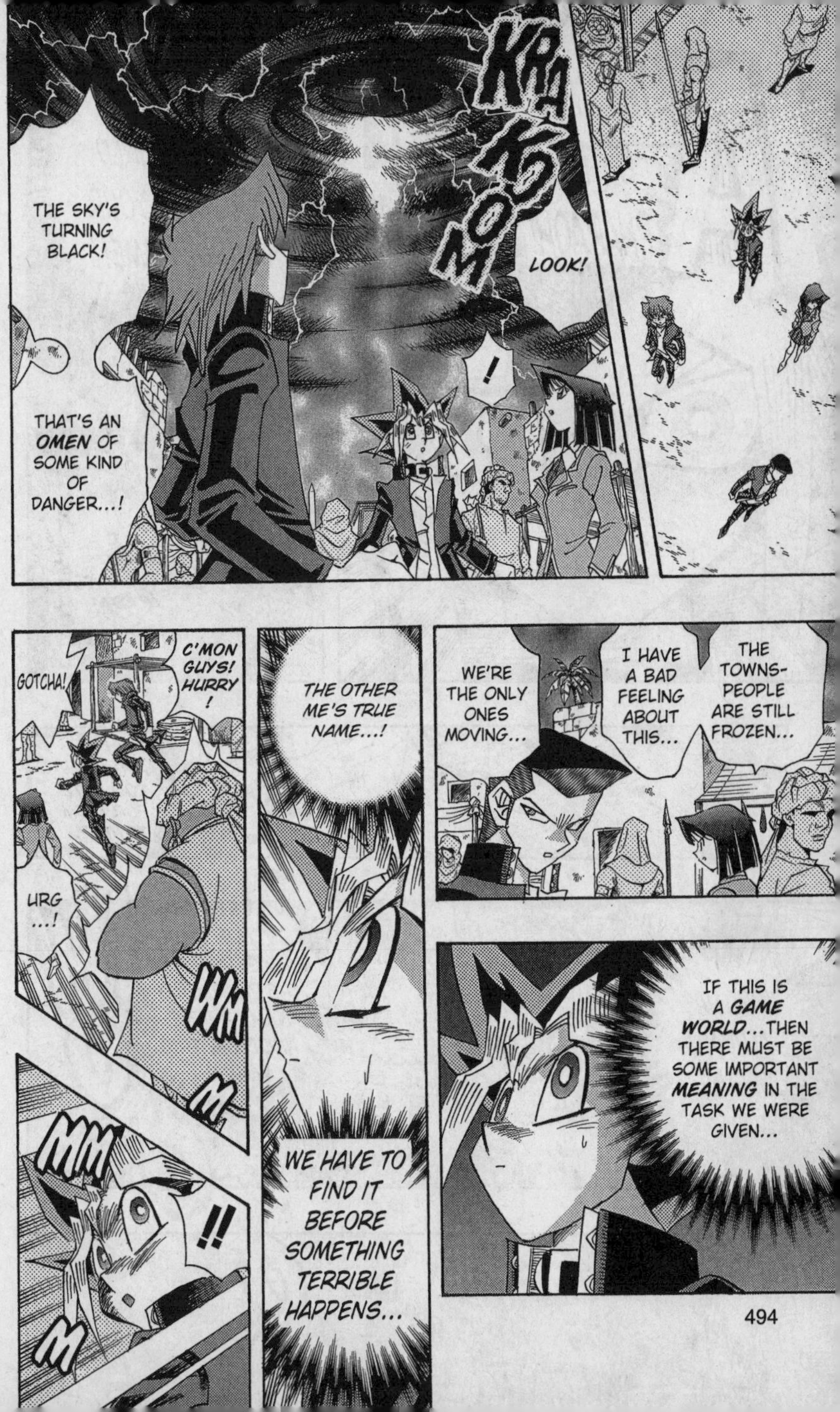

LOOK!
KRA KOOM
!
THE SKY'S TURNING BLACK!
THAT'S AN OMEN OF SOME KIND OF DANGER...!
THE TOWNS-PEOPLE ARE STILL FROZEN...
I HAVE A BAD FEELING ABOUT THIS...
WE'RE THE ONLY ONES MOVING...
IF THIS IS A GAME WORLD...THEN THERE MUST BE SOME IMPORTANT MEANING IN THE TASK WE WERE GIVEN...
THE OTHER ME'S TRUE NAME...!
WE HAVE TO FIND IT BEFORE SOMETHING TERRIBLE HAPPENS...
C'MON GUYS! HURRY!
GOTCHA!
URG...!
WMMMM
!!

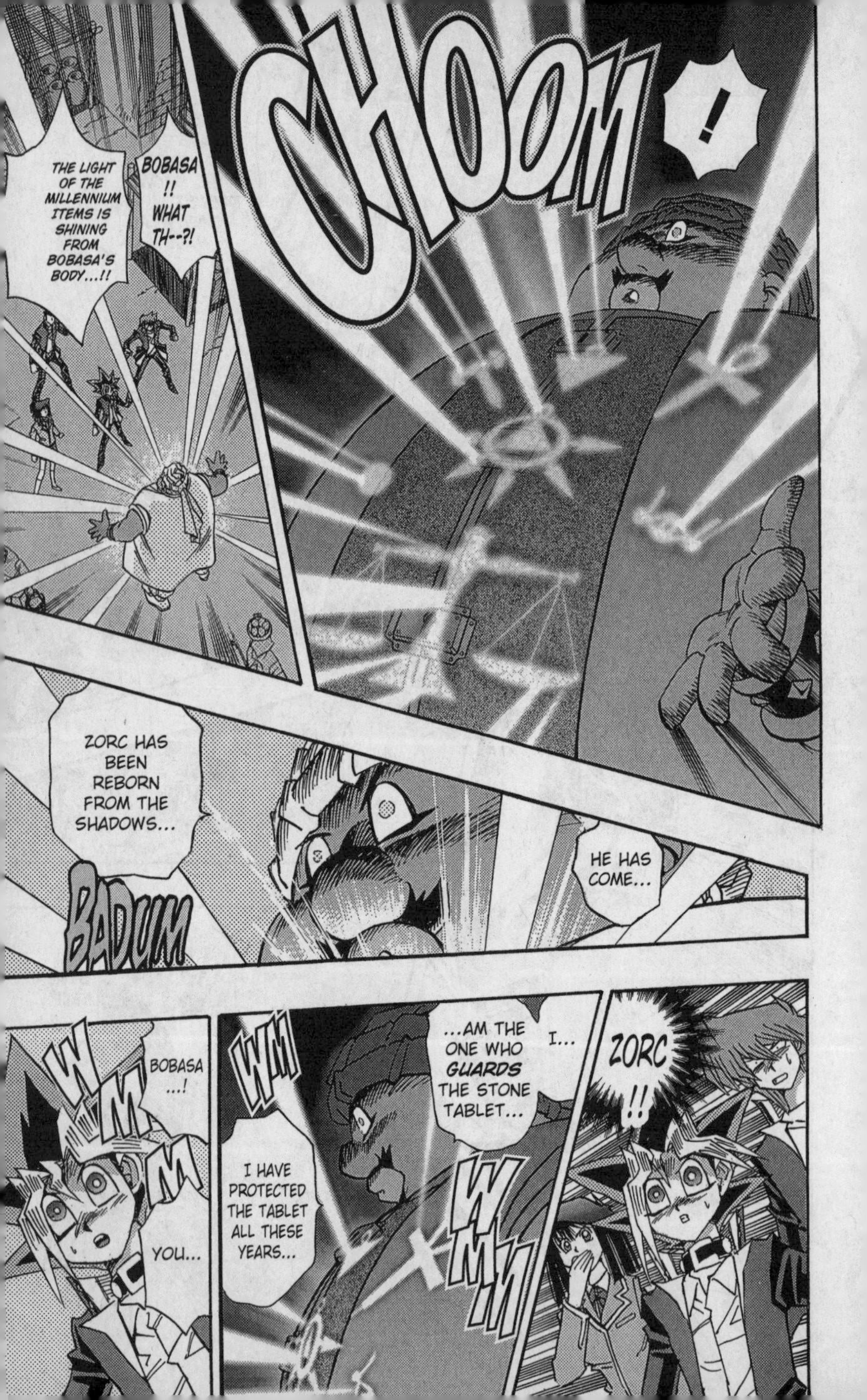
CHOOM
!
BOBASA !! WHAT TH--?!
THE LIGHT OF THE MILLENNIUM ITEMS IS SHINING FROM BOBASA'S BODY...!!
HE HAS COME...
ZORC HAS BEEN REBORN FROM THE SHADOWS...
BADUM
ZORC !!
I...
...AM THE ONE WHO **GUARDS** THE STONE TABLET...
I HAVE PROTECTED THE TABLET ALL THESE YEARS...
WM
WMM
BOBASA ...!
YOU...
WMMM

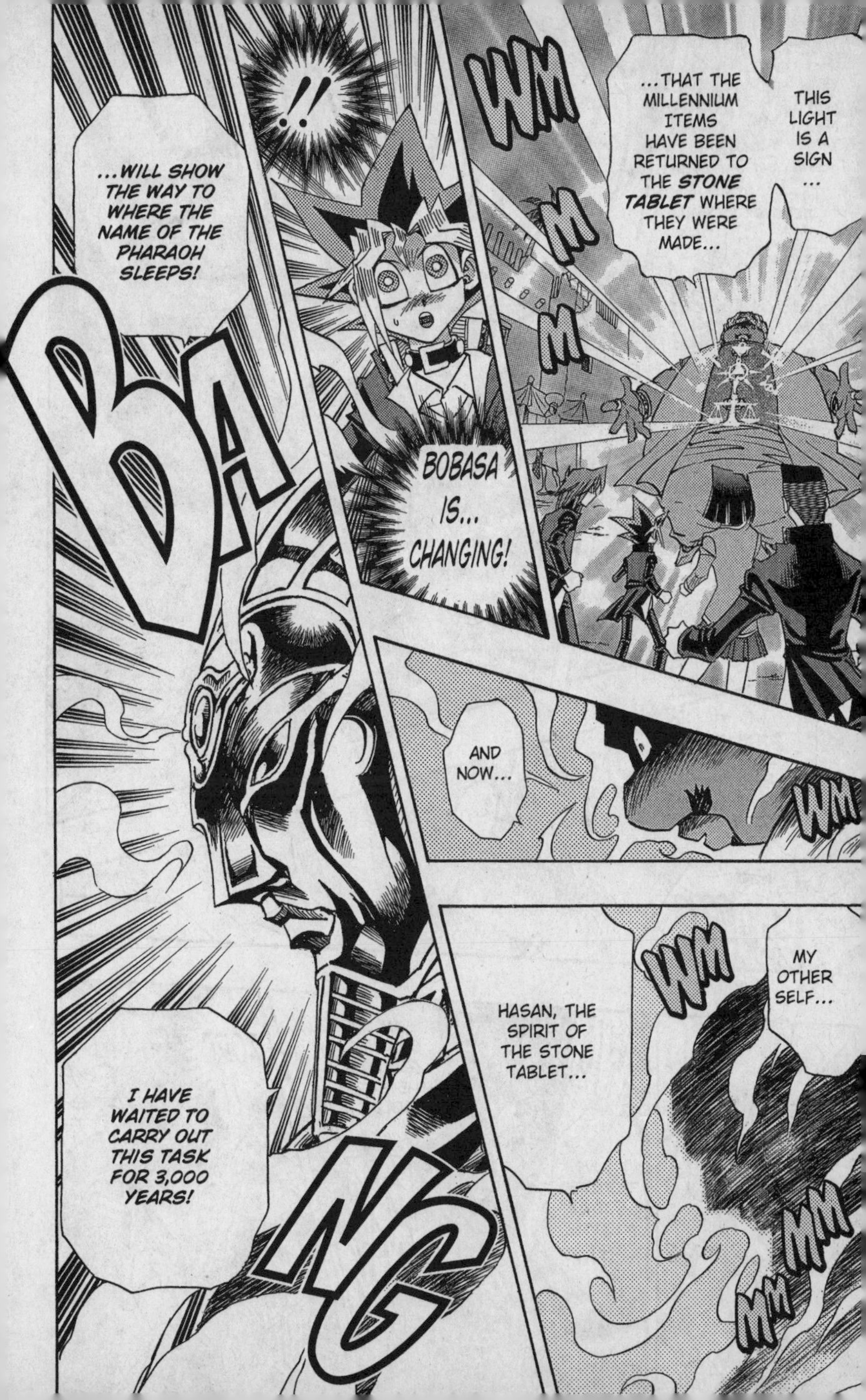
THIS LIGHT IS A SIGN...
...THAT THE MILLENNIUM ITEMS HAVE BEEN RETURNED TO THE STONE TABLET WHERE THEY WERE MADE...
WMMMM
!!
BOBASA IS... CHANGING!
WM
AND NOW...
MY OTHER SELF...
WM
HASAN, THE SPIRIT OF THE STONE TABLET...
MMMMM
...WILL SHOW THE WAY TO WHERE THE NAME OF THE PHARAOH SLEEPS!
BADANG
I HAVE WAITED TO CARRY OUT THIS TASK FOR 3,000 YEARS!

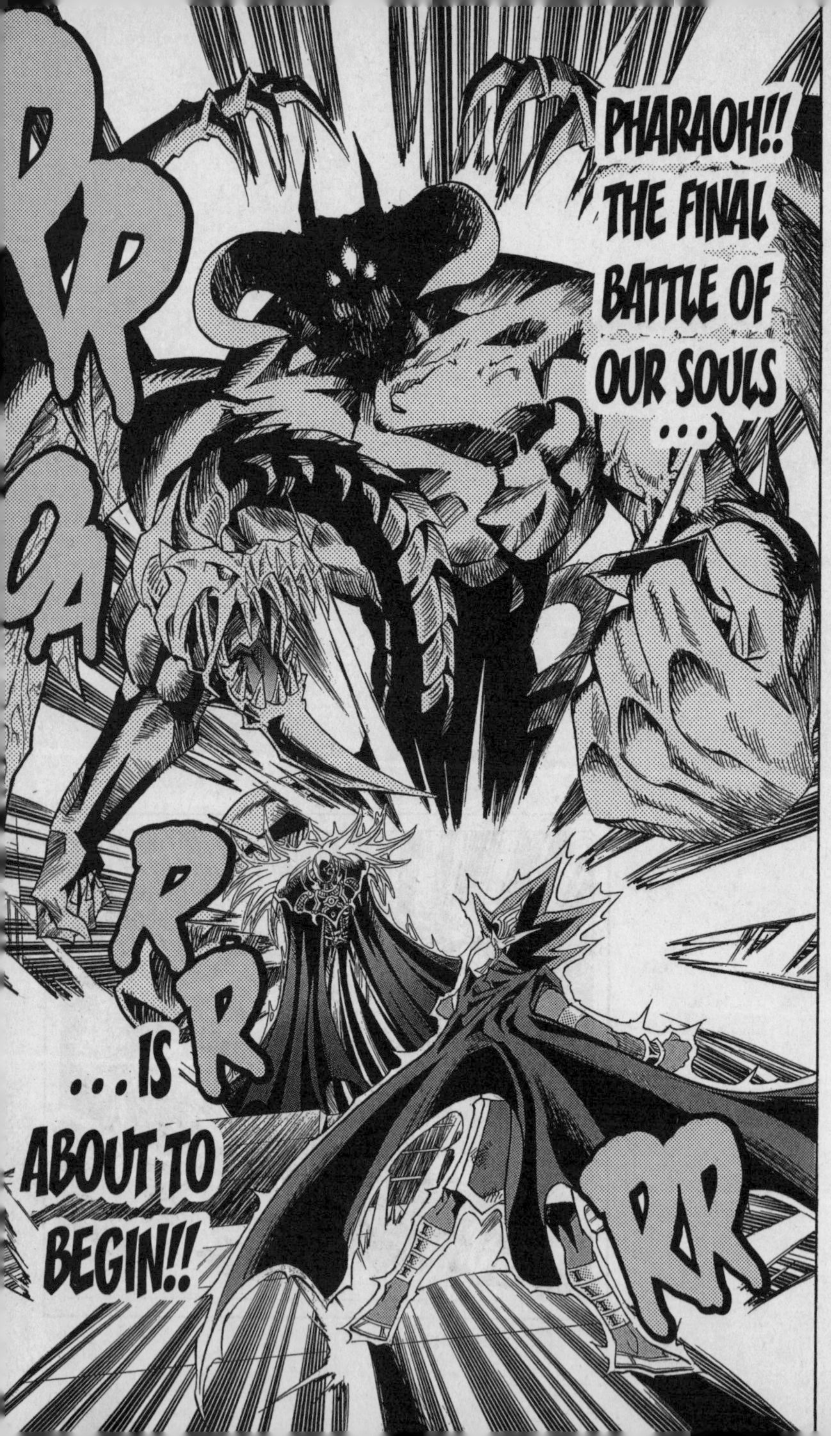
PHARAOH!! THE FINAL BATTLE OF OUR SOULS ...
...IS ABOUT TO BEGIN!!
ROAR

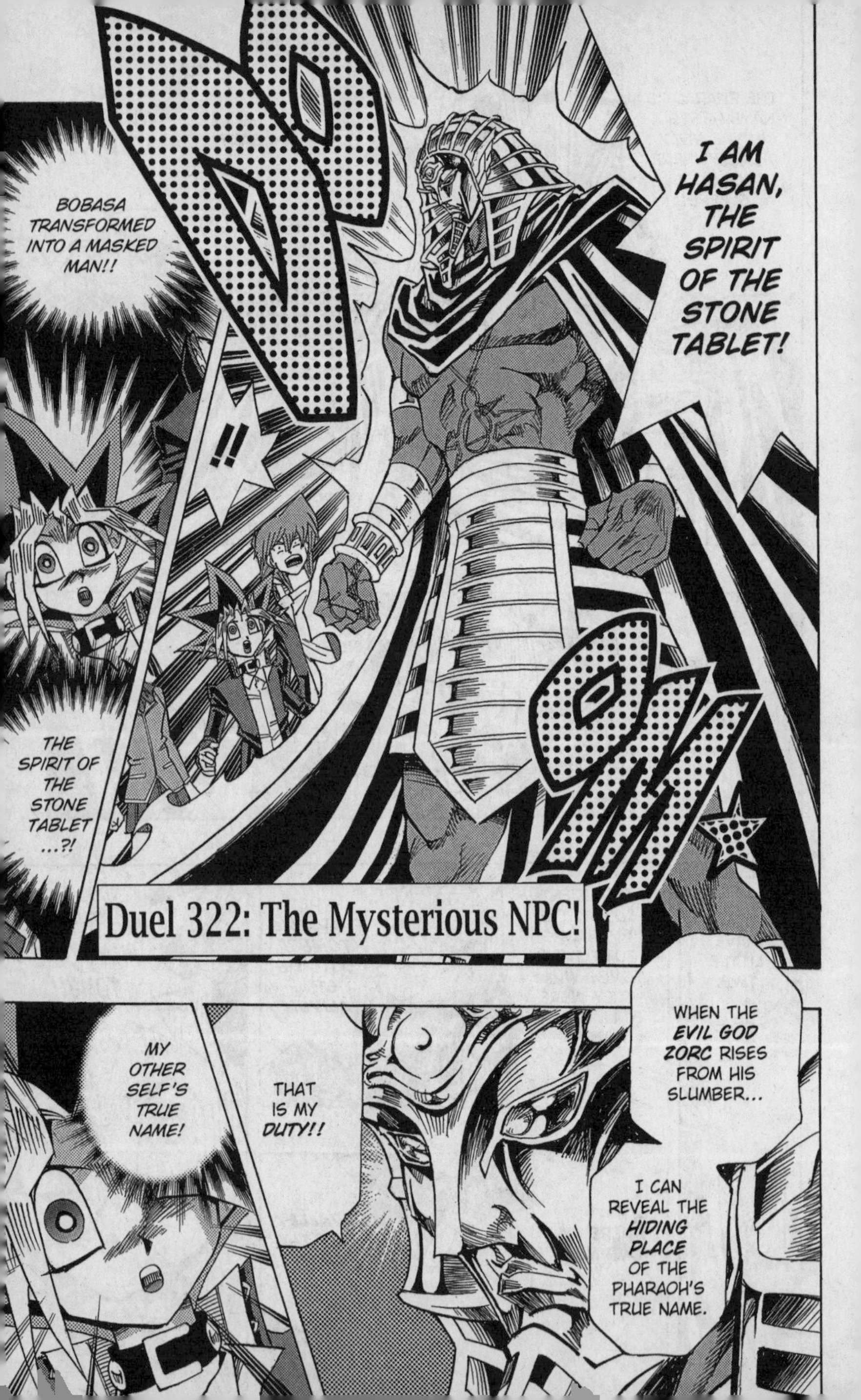
I AM HASAN, THE SPIRIT OF THE STONE TABLET!
BOBASA TRANSFORMED INTO A MASKED MAN!!
!!
THE SPIRIT OF THE STONE TABLET ...?!
Duel 322: The Mysterious NPC!
WHEN THE EVIL GOD ZORC RISES FROM HIS SLUMBER...
I CAN REVEAL THE HIDING PLACE OF THE PHARAOH'S TRUE NAME.
THAT IS MY DUTY!!
MY OTHER SELF'S TRUE NAME!

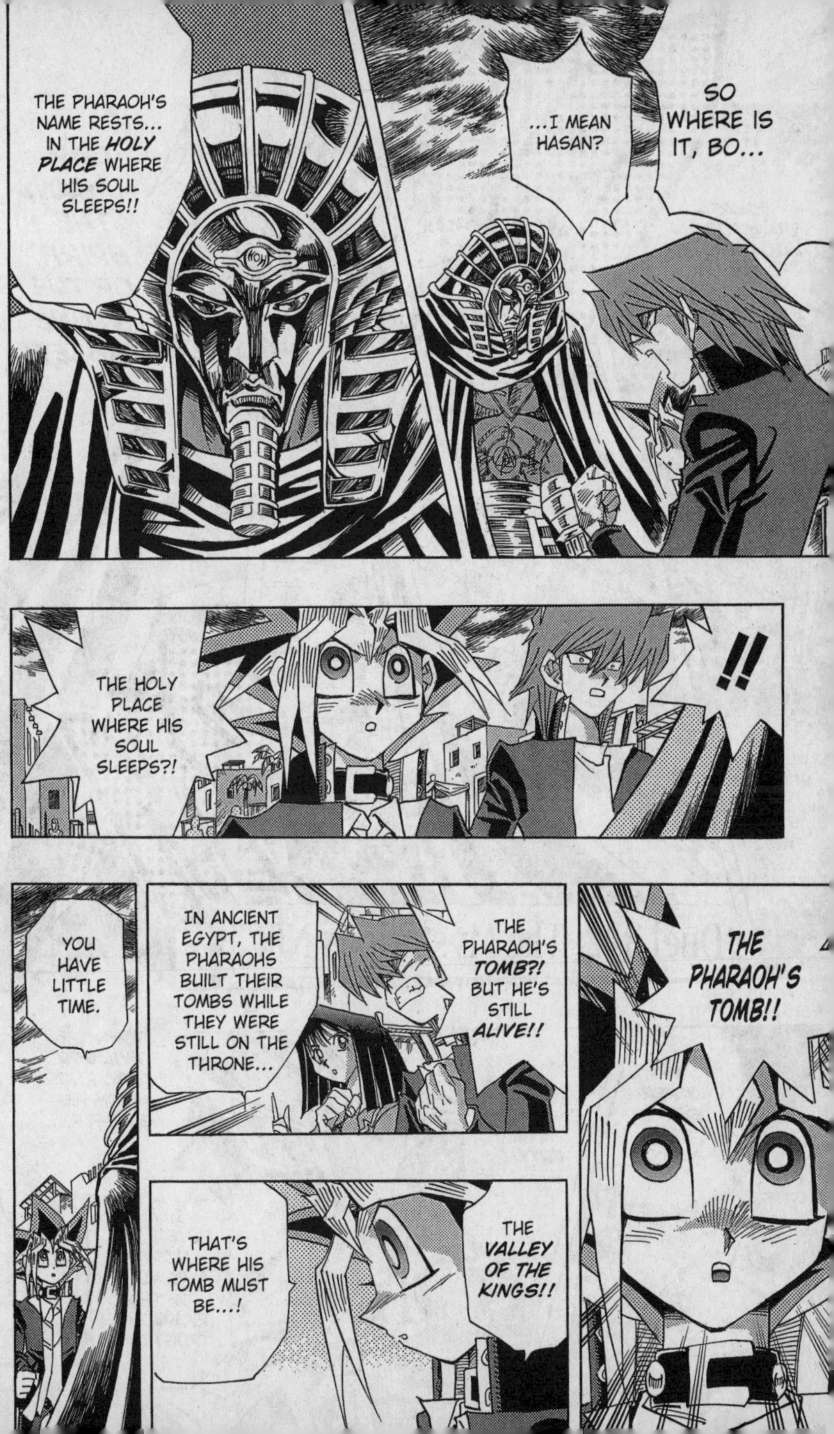
SO WHERE IS IT, BO...
...I MEAN HASAN?
THE PHARAOH'S NAME RESTS... IN THE HOLY PLACE WHERE HIS SOUL SLEEPS!!
!!
THE HOLY PLACE WHERE HIS SOUL SLEEPS?!
THE PHARAOH'S TOMB!!
THE PHARAOH'S TOMB?! BUT HE'S STILL ALIVE!!
IN ANCIENT EGYPT, THE PHARAOHS BUILT THEIR TOMBS WHILE THEY WERE STILL ON THE THRONE...
YOU HAVE LITTLE TIME.
THE VALLEY OF THE KINGS!!
THAT'S WHERE HIS TOMB MUST BE...!

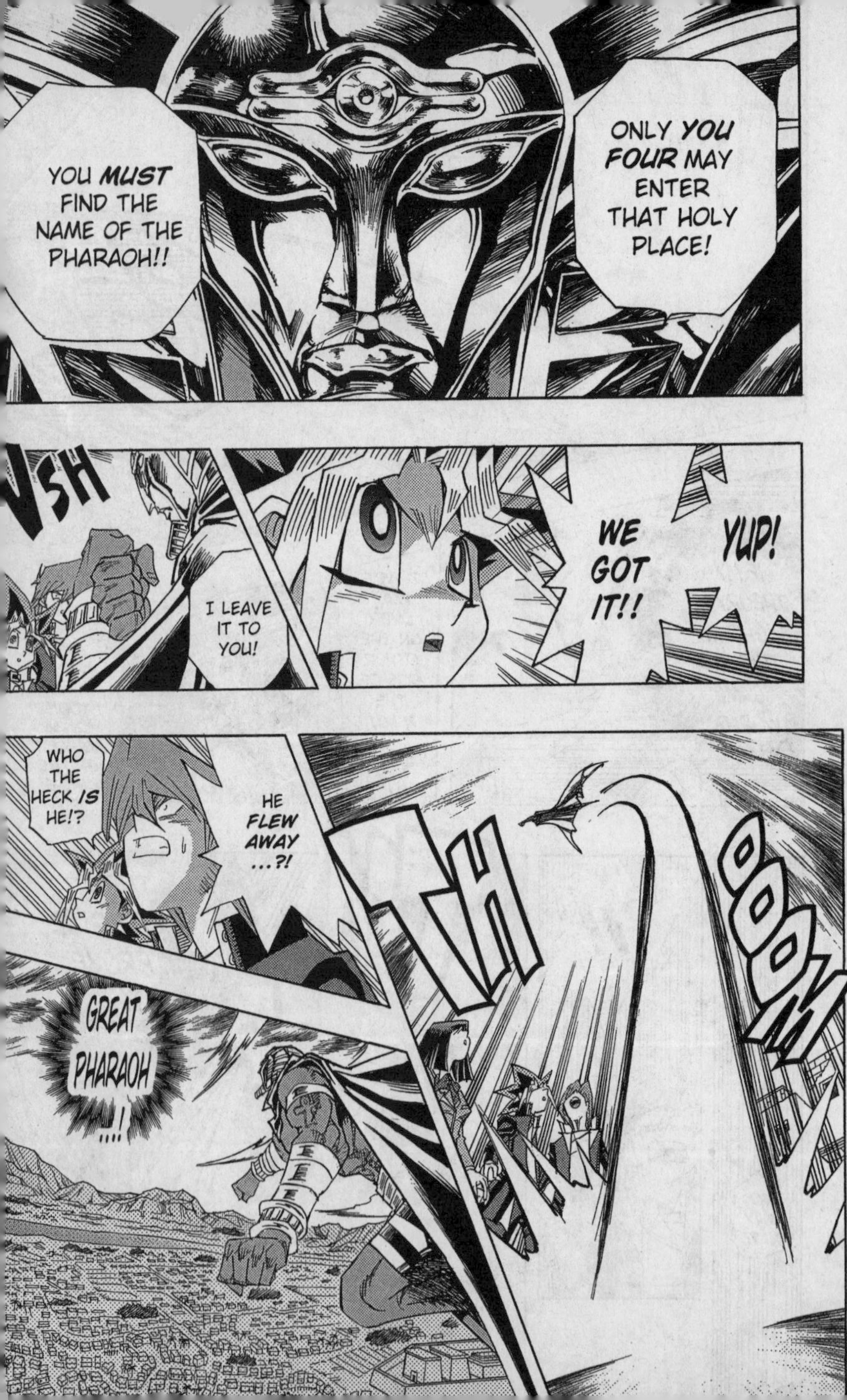
ONLY YOU FOUR MAY ENTER THAT HOLY PLACE!
YOU MUST FIND THE NAME OF THE PHARAOH!!
YUP!
WE GOT IT!!
I LEAVE IT TO YOU!
HE FLEW AWAY ...?!
WHO THE HECK IS HE!?
GREAT PHARAOH ...!

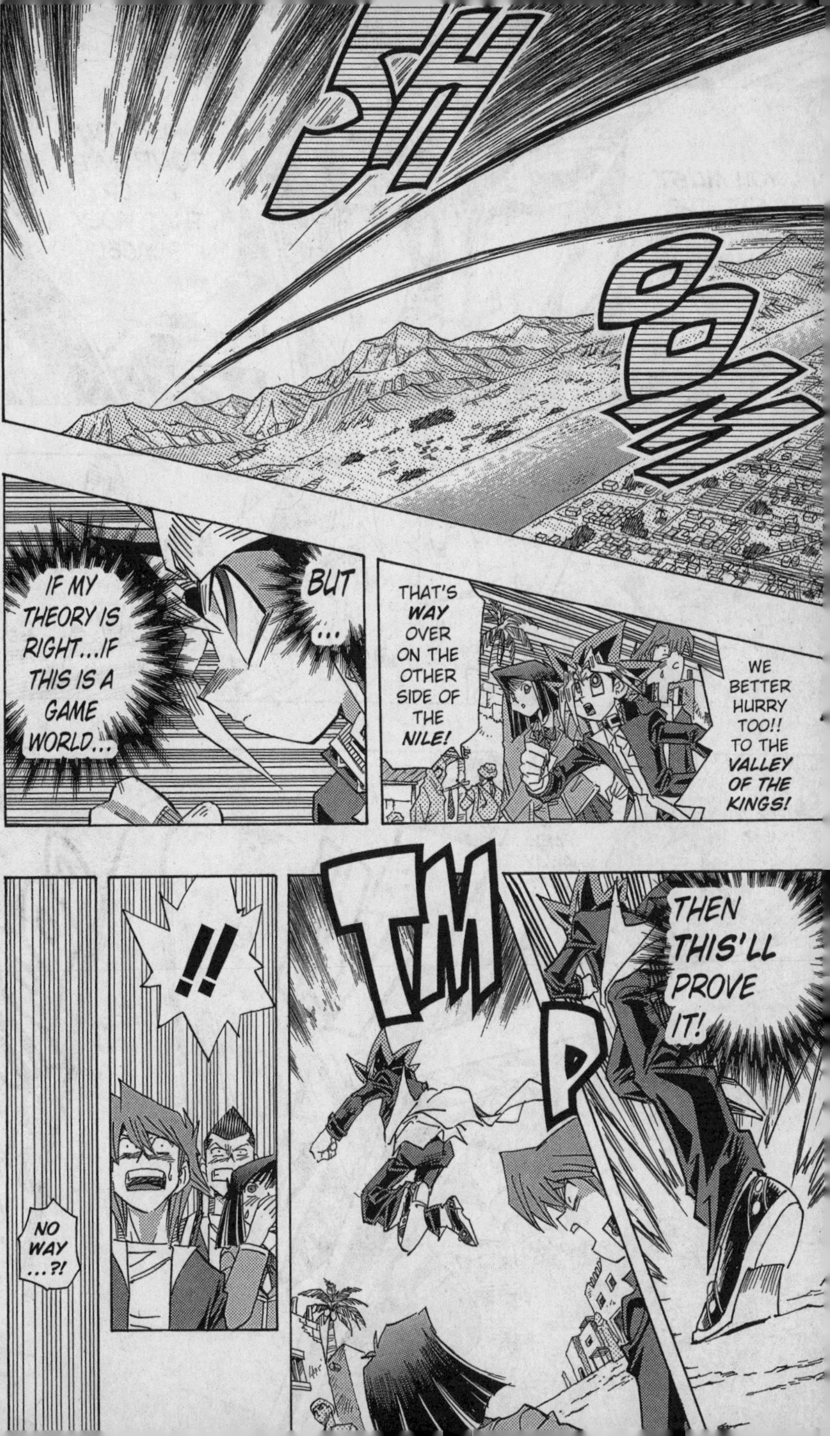
SH
OOM
WE BETTER HURRY TOO!! TO THE VALLEY OF THE KINGS!
THAT'S WAY OVER ON THE OTHER SIDE OF THE NILE!
BUT ...
IF MY THEORY IS RIGHT...IF THIS IS A GAME WORLD...
THEN THIS'LL PROVE IT!
TMP
!!
NO WAY ...?!

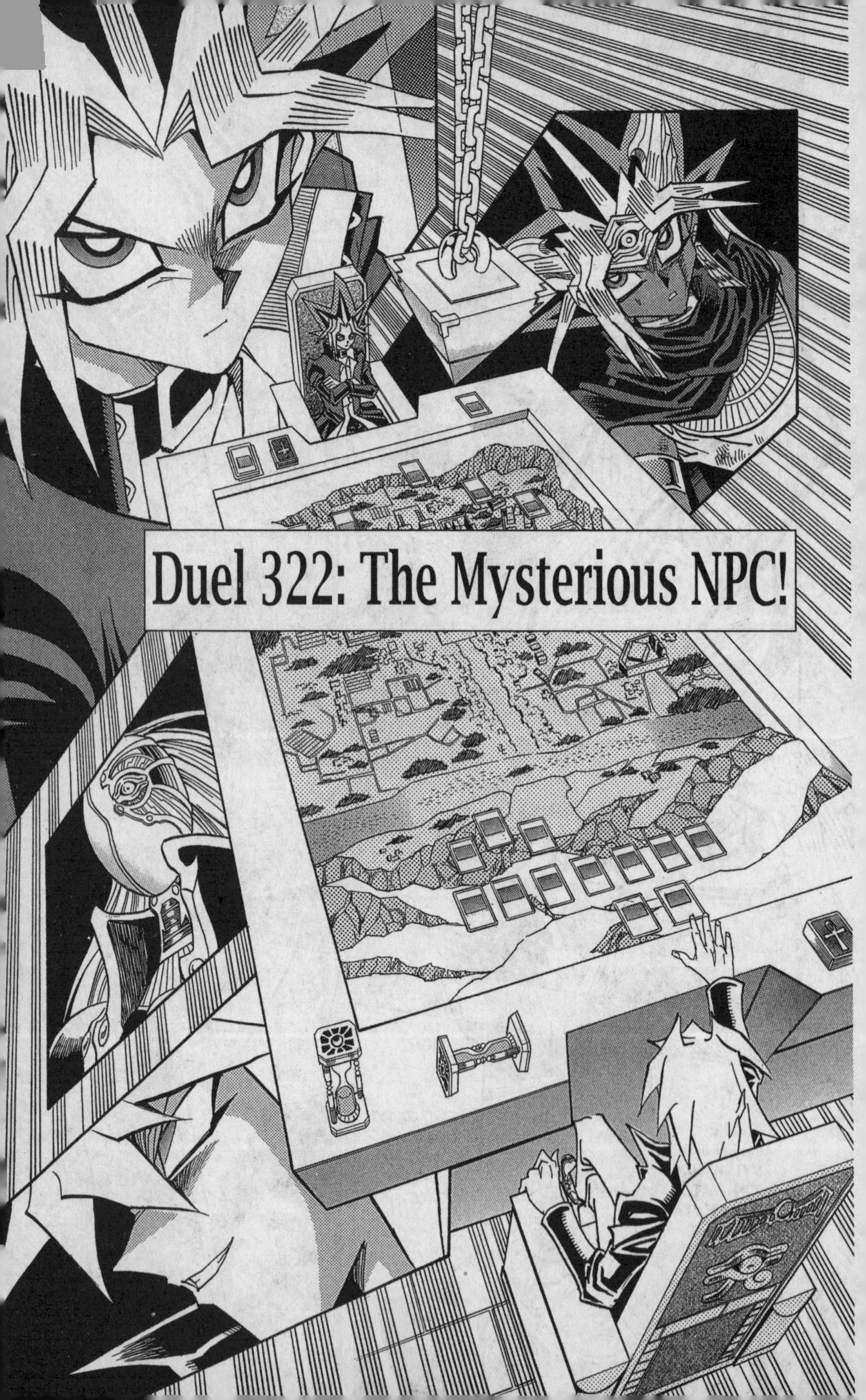
Duel 322: The Mysterious NPC!

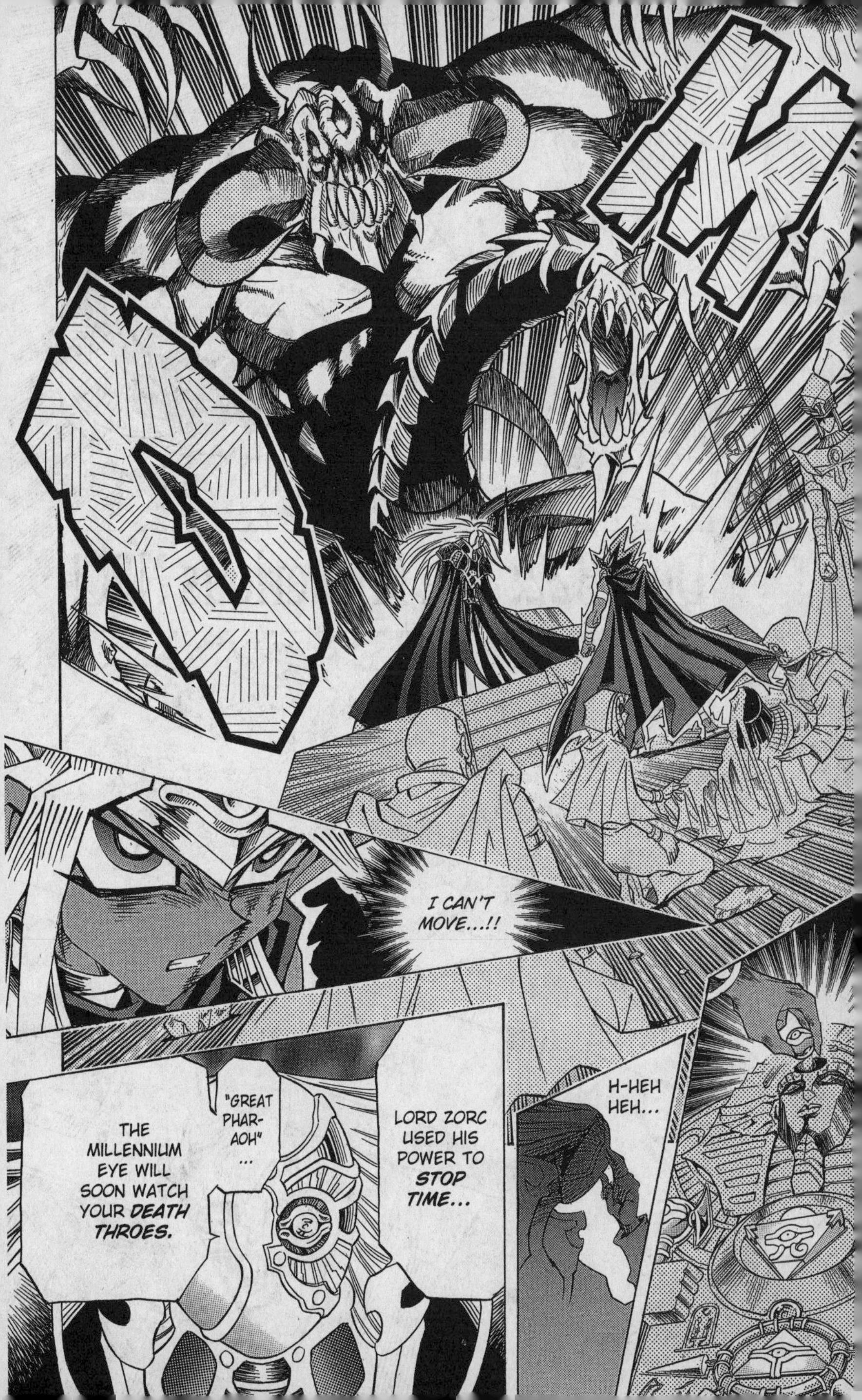
I CAN'T MOVE...!!
H-HEH HEH...
LORD ZORC USED HIS POWER TO STOP TIME...
"GREAT PHARAOH"...
THE MILLENNIUM EYE WILL SOON WATCH YOUR DEATH THROES.

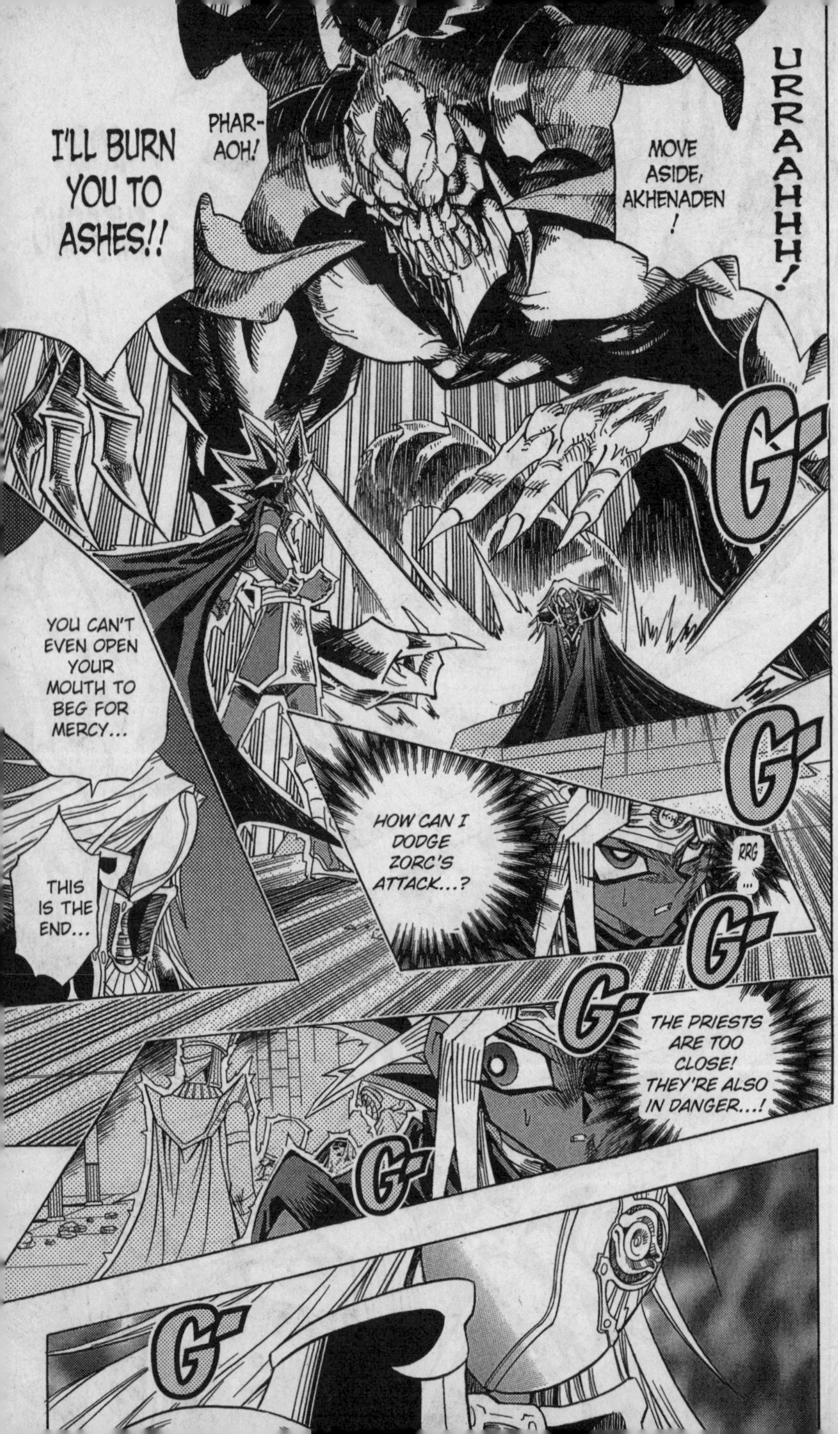
URRAAHHH!
MOVE ASIDE, AKHENADEN!
PHAR-AOH!
I'LL BURN YOU TO ASHES!!
G-
YOU CAN'T EVEN OPEN YOUR MOUTH TO BEG FOR MERCY...
G-
RRG...
HOW CAN I DODGE ZORC'S ATTACK...?
THIS IS THE END...
G-
G-
THE PRIESTS ARE TOO CLOSE! THEY'RE ALSO IN DANGER...!
G-
G-

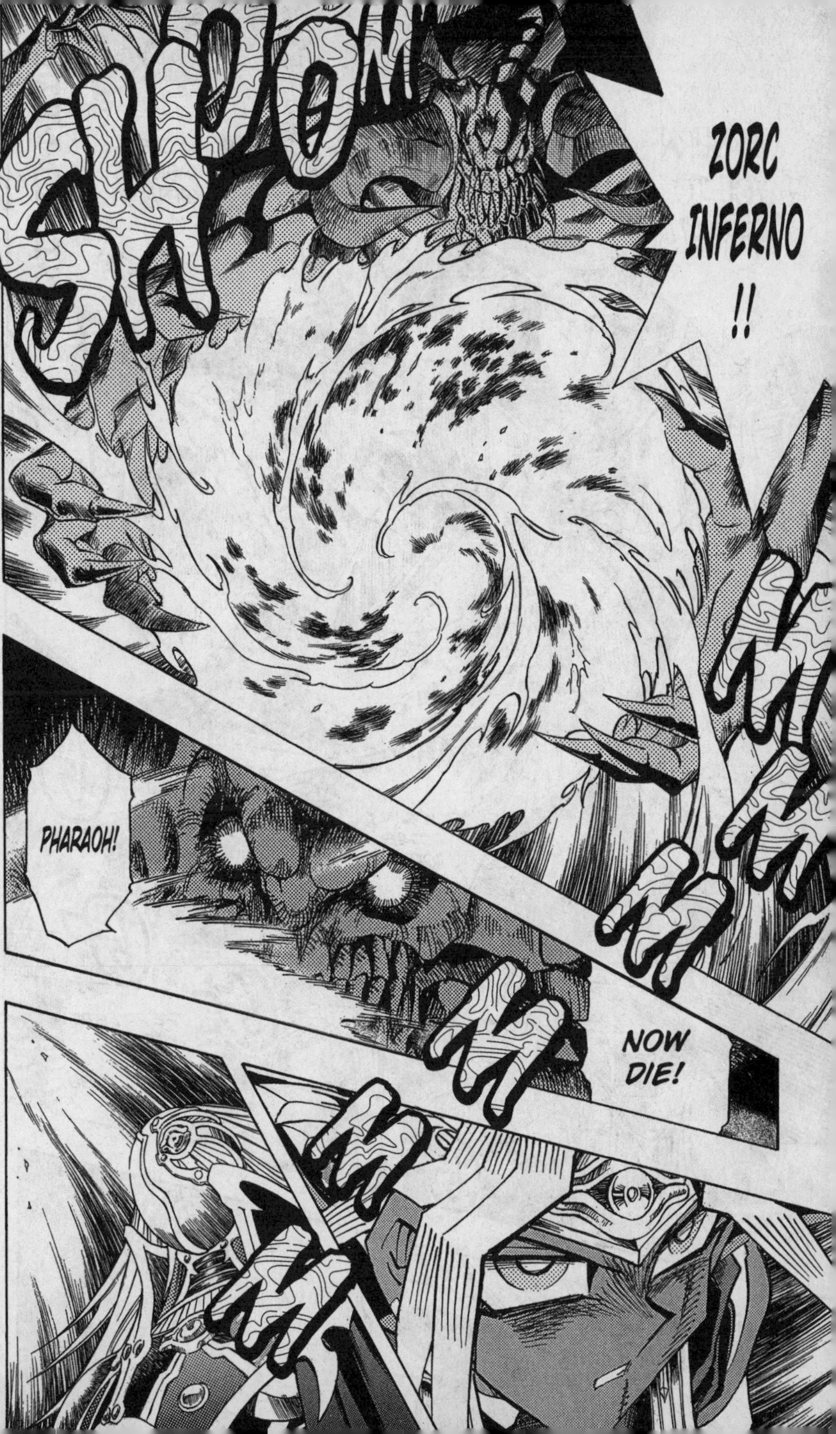
ZORC INFERNO !!
PHARAOH!
NOW DIE!

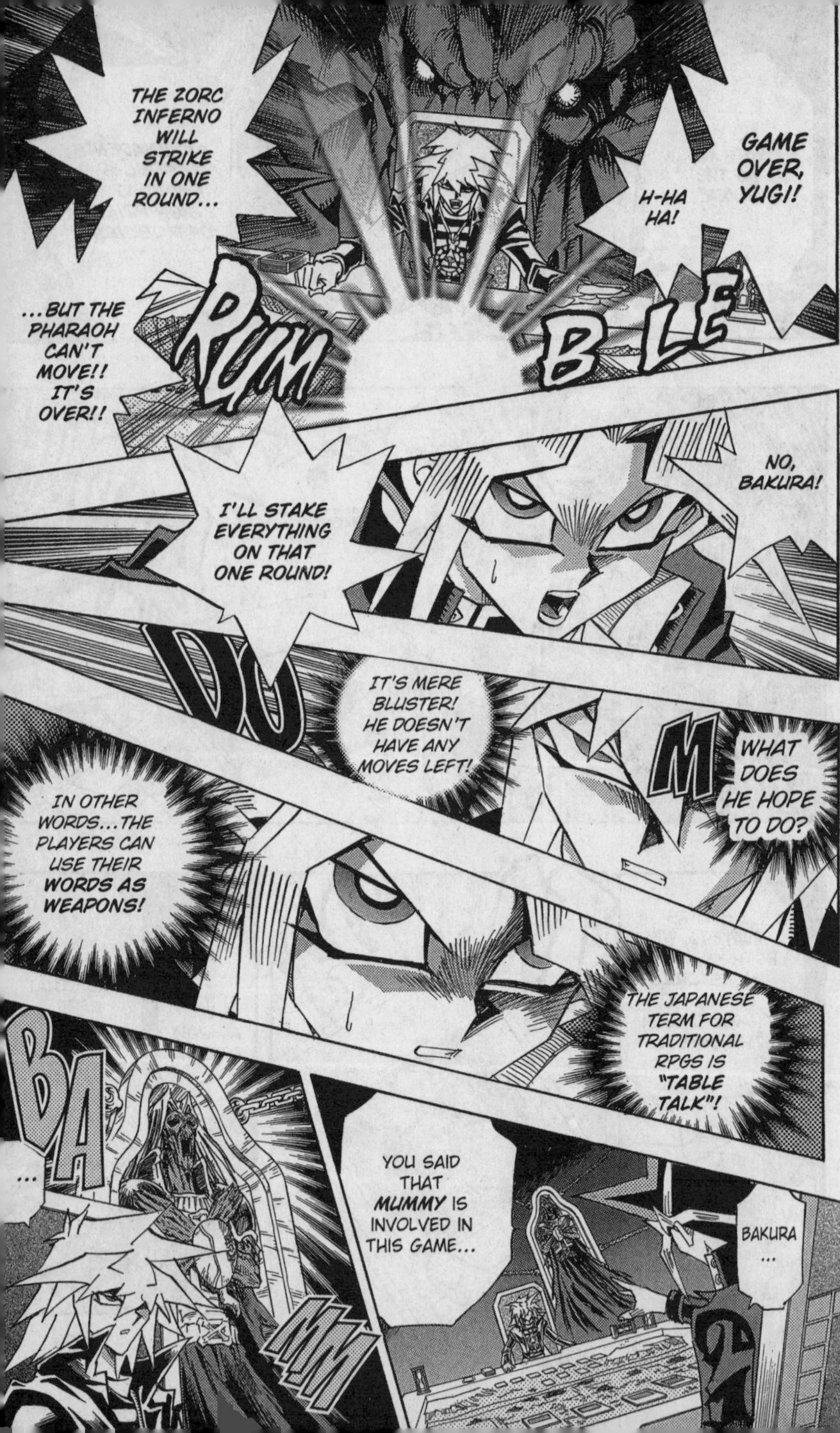
GAME OVER, YUGI!
H-HA HA!
THE ZORC INFERNO WILL STRIKE IN ONE ROUND...
...BUT THE PHARAOH CAN'T MOVE!! IT'S OVER!!
RUM B LE
NO, BAKURA!
I'LL STAKE EVERYTHING ON THAT ONE ROUND!
DO M
WHAT DOES HE HOPE TO DO?
IT'S MERE BLUSTER! HE DOESN'T HAVE ANY MOVES LEFT!
IN OTHER WORDS...THE PLAYERS CAN USE THEIR WORDS AS WEAPONS!
THE JAPANESE TERM FOR TRADITIONAL RPGS IS "TABLE TALK"!
BAKURA ...
YOU SAID THAT MUMMY IS INVOLVED IN THIS GAME...
BA ...
MM

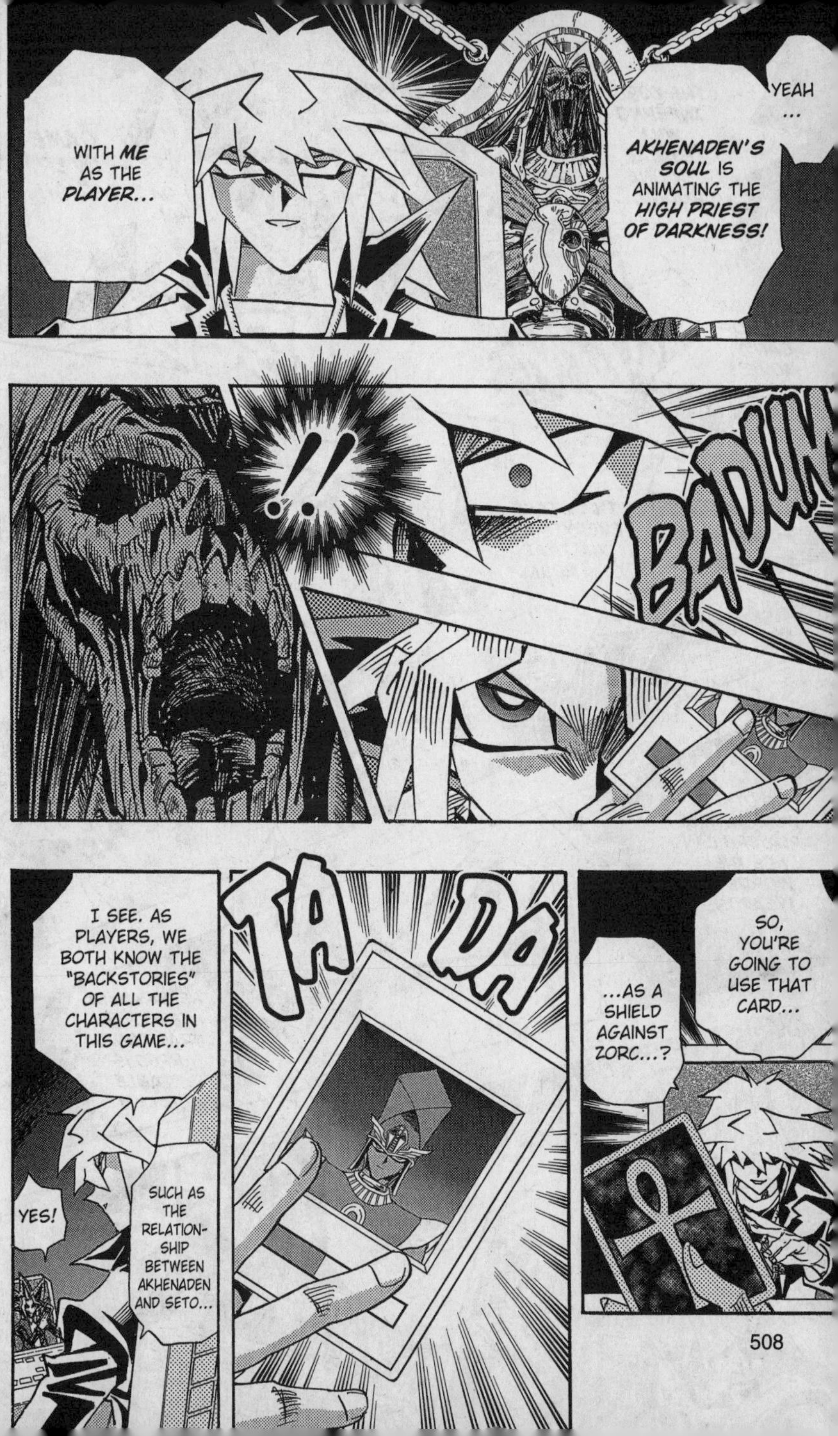
YEAH ...
AKHENADEN'S SOUL IS ANIMATING THE HIGH PRIEST OF DARKNESS!
WITH ME AS THE PLAYER...
BADUM
!!
SO, YOU'RE GOING TO USE THAT CARD...
...AS A SHIELD AGAINST ZORC...?
TA DA
I SEE. AS PLAYERS, WE BOTH KNOW THE "BACKSTORIES" OF ALL THE CHARACTERS IN THIS GAME...
SUCH AS THE RELATION-SHIP BETWEEN AKHENADEN AND SETO...
YES!

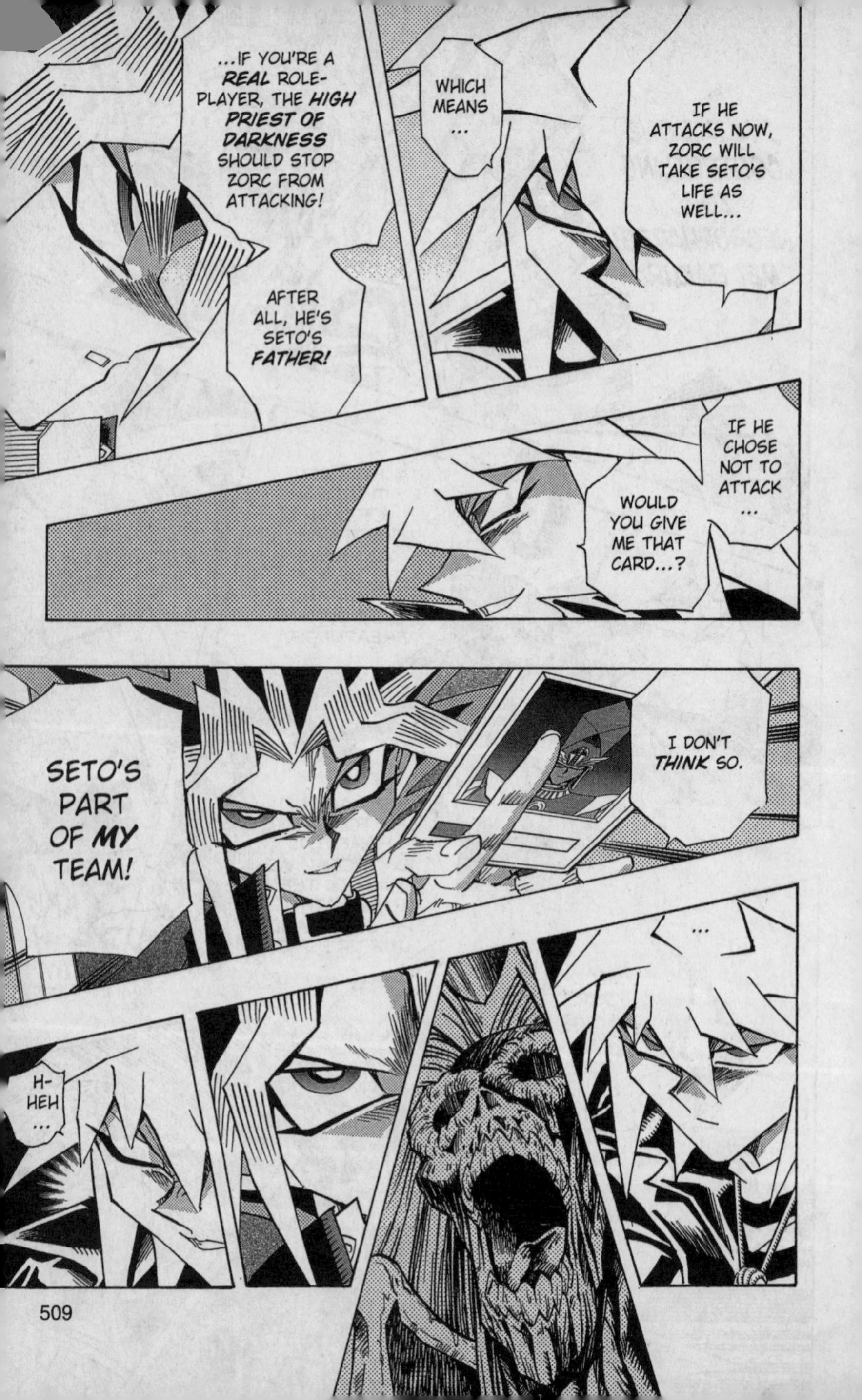
...IF YOU'RE A REAL ROLE-PLAYER, THE HIGH PRIEST OF DARKNESS SHOULD STOP ZORC FROM ATTACKING!
AFTER ALL, HE'S SETO'S FATHER!
WHICH MEANS...
IF HE ATTACKS NOW, ZORC WILL TAKE SETO'S LIFE AS WELL...
IF HE CHOSE NOT TO ATTACK...
WOULD YOU GIVE ME THAT CARD...?
I DON'T THINK SO.
SETO'S PART OF MY TEAM!
H-HEH...
...

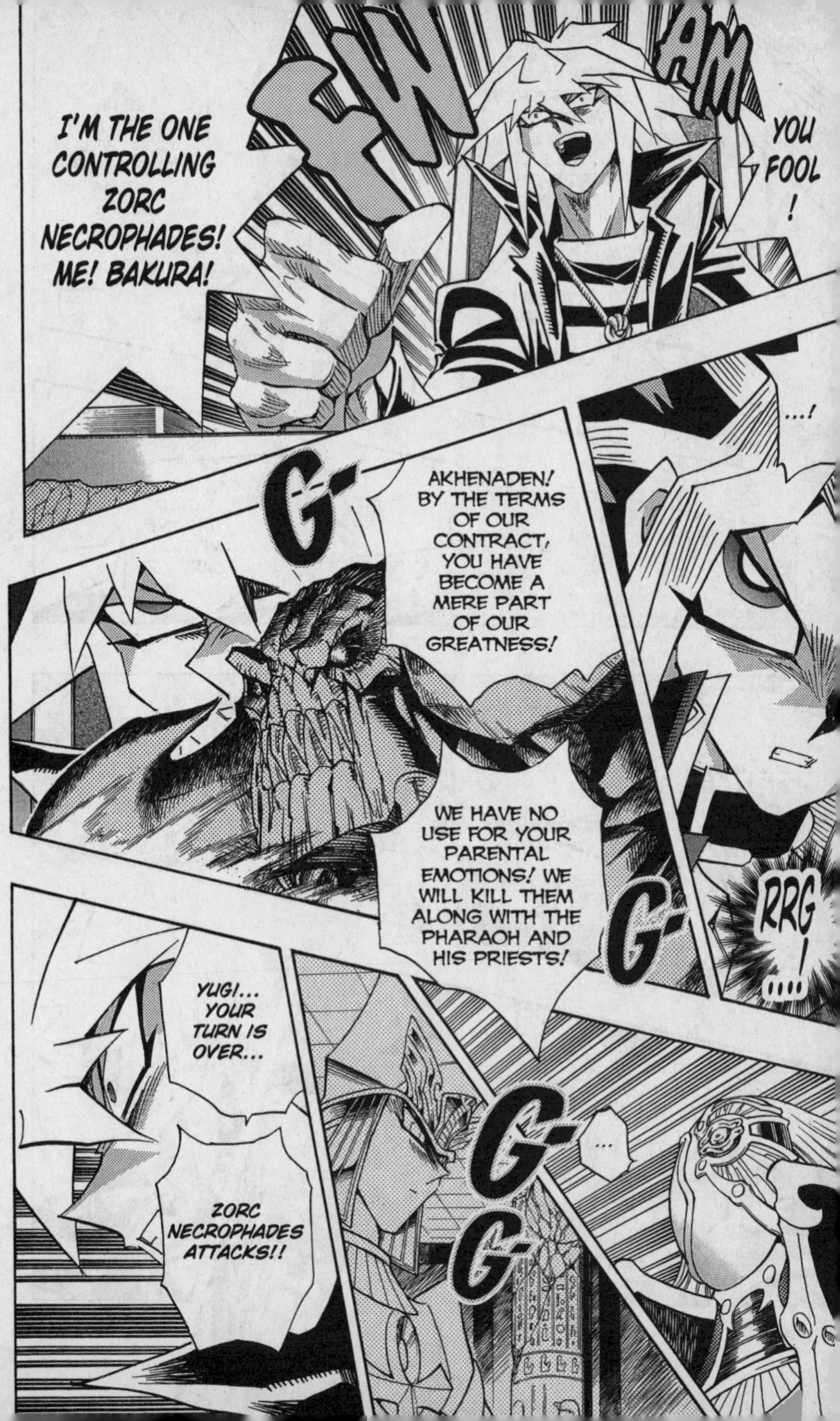
AM
YOU FOOL!
I'M THE ONE CONTROLLING ZORC NECROPHADES! ME! BAKURA!
...!
G-
AKHENADEN! BY THE TERMS OF OUR CONTRACT, YOU HAVE BECOME A MERE PART OF OUR GREATNESS!
WE HAVE NO USE FOR YOUR PARENTAL EMOTIONS! WE WILL KILL THEM ALONG WITH THE PHARAOH AND HIS PRIESTS!
RRG...!
G-
...
G-
G-
YUGI... YOUR TURN IS OVER...
ZORC NECROPHADES ATTACKS!!

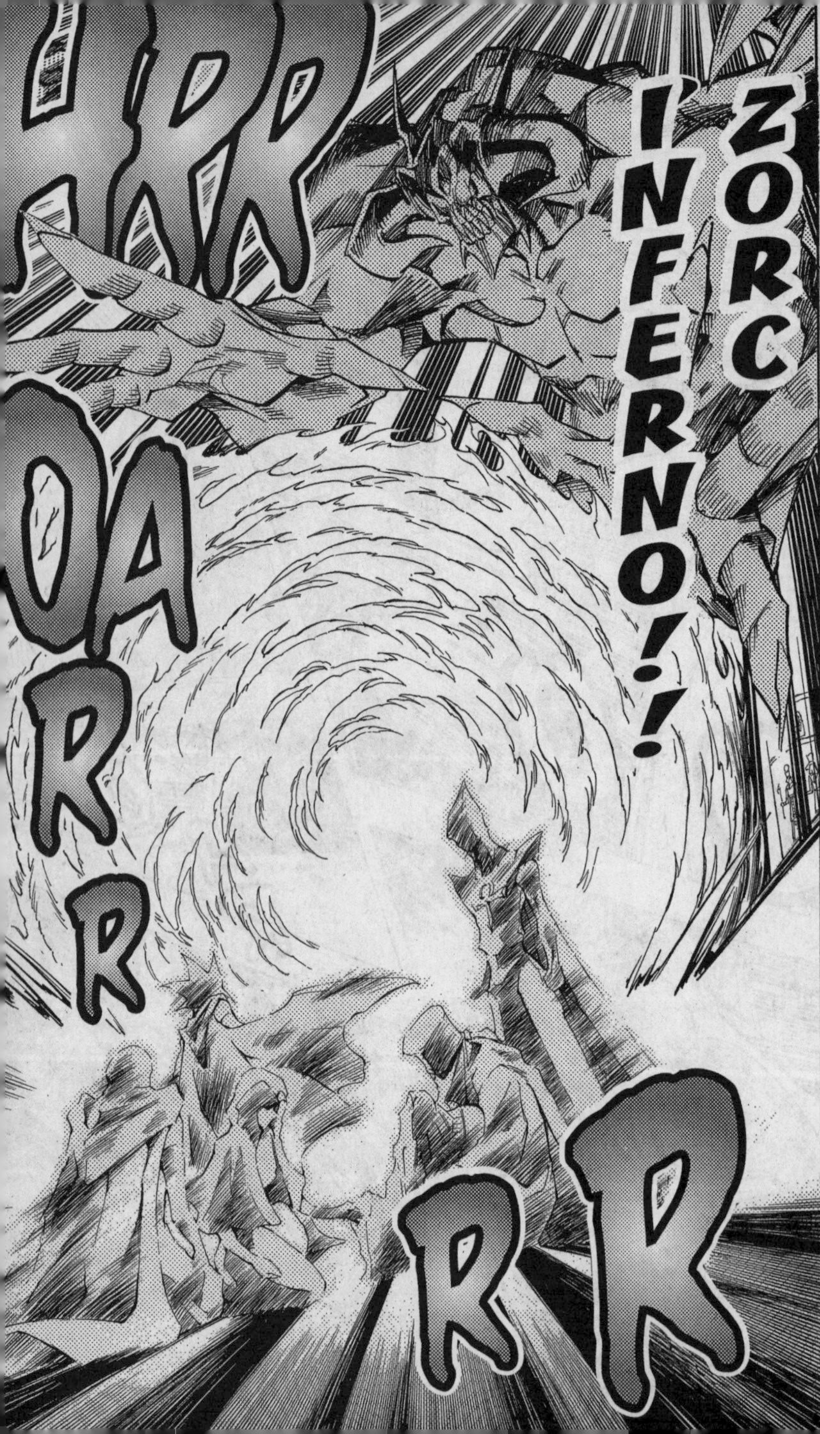
ZORC INFERNO!!
OARRRR

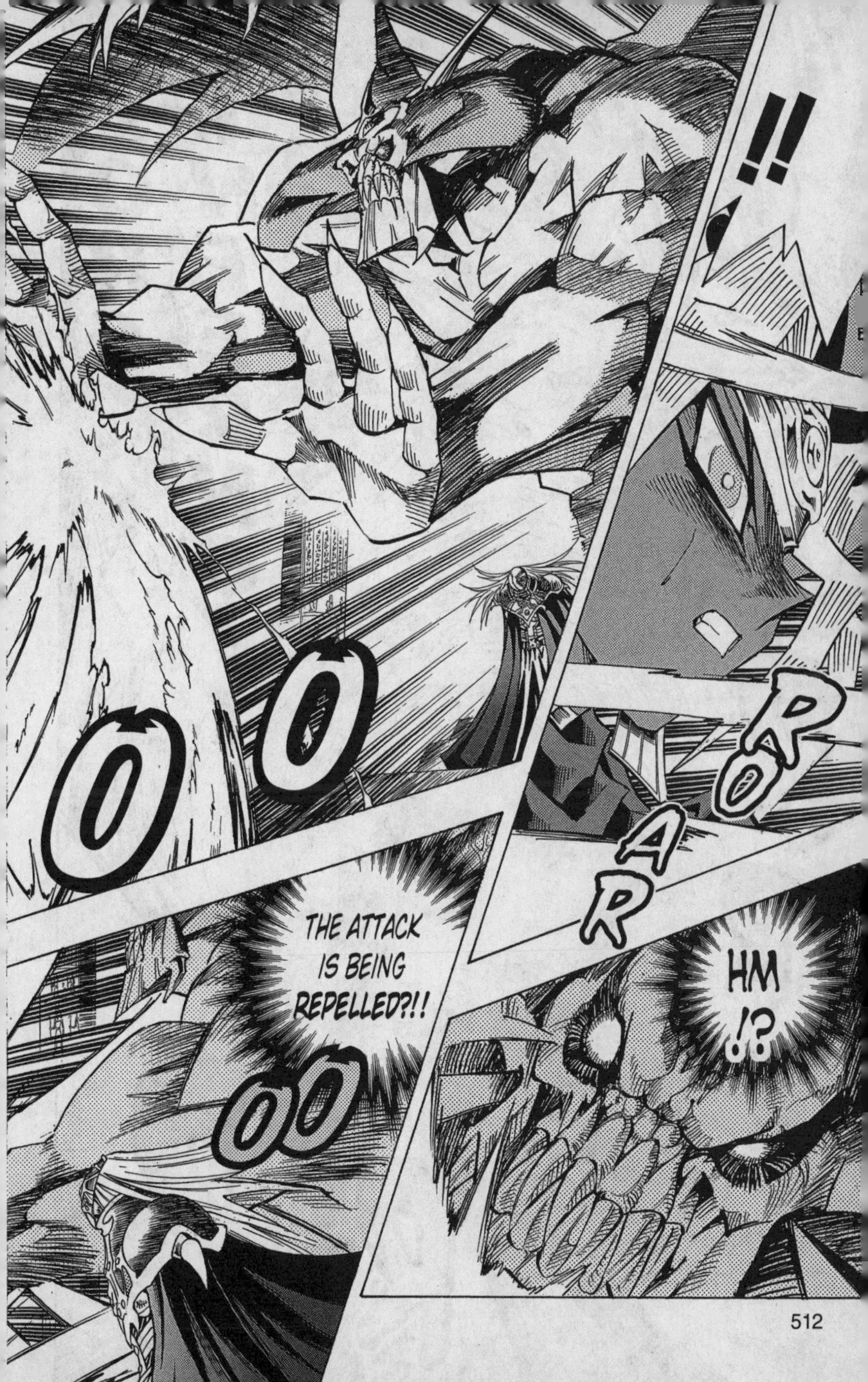
!!
ROAR
OO
HM !?
THE ATTACK IS BEING REPELLED?!!
OO

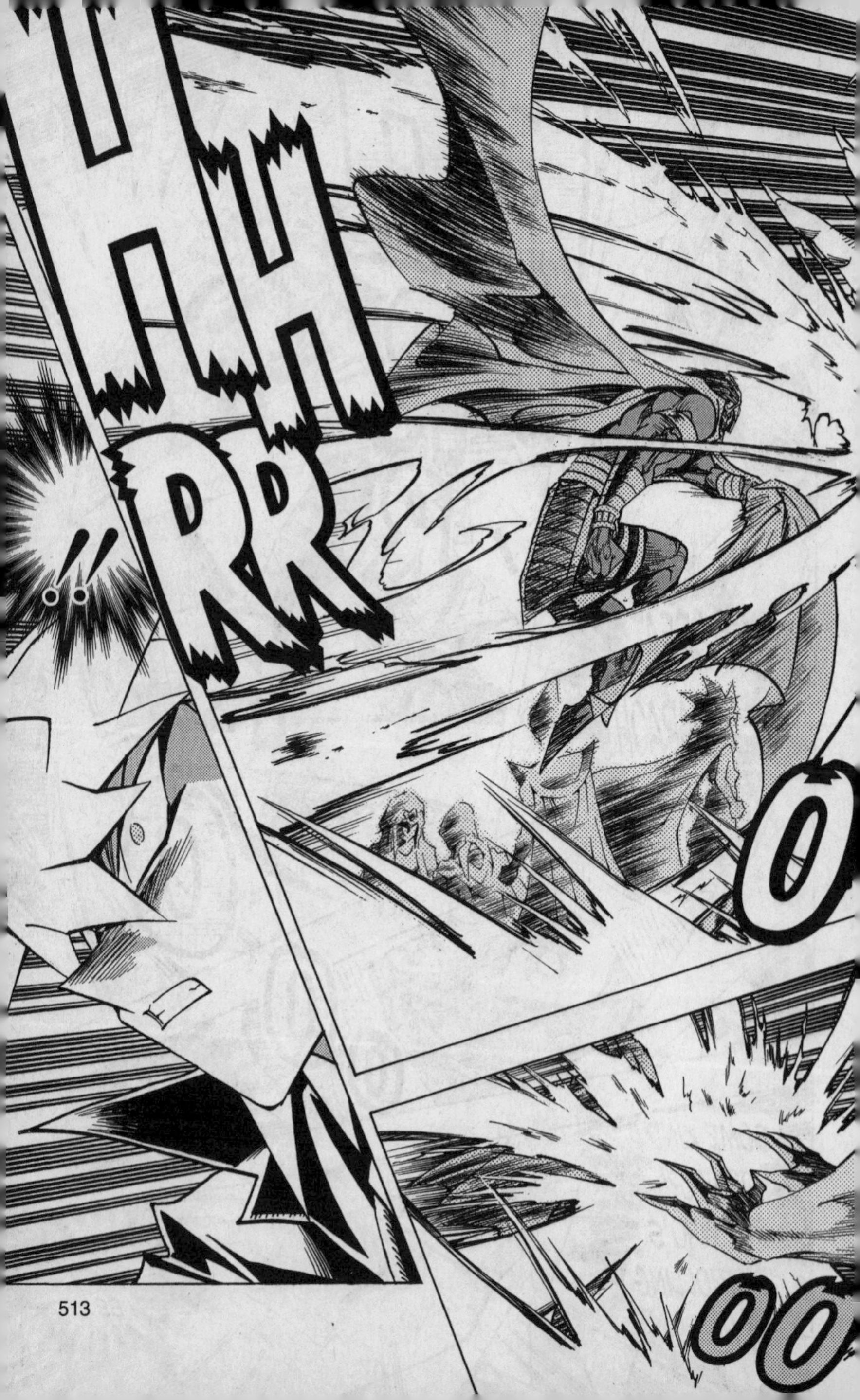

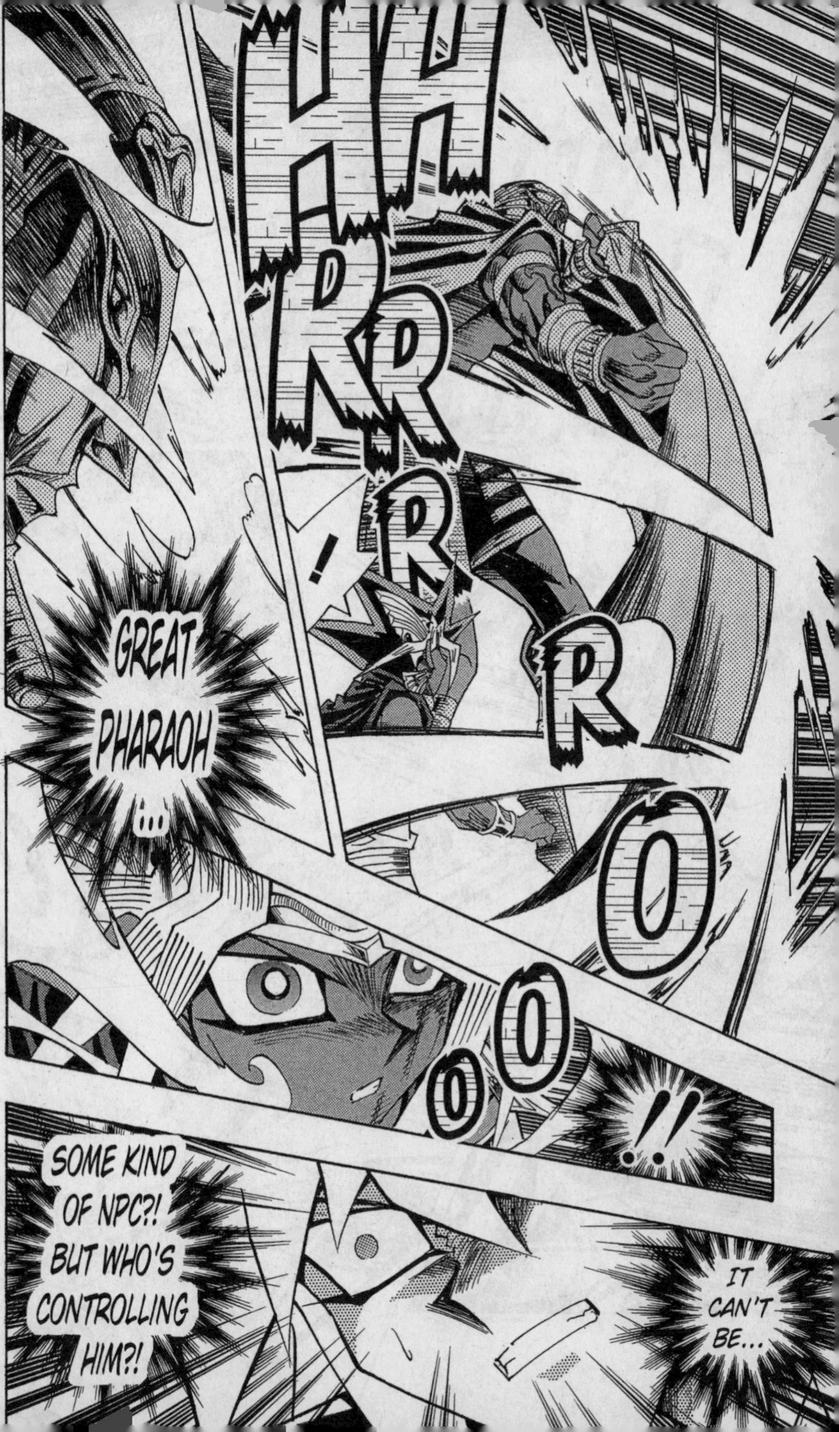

HHH... A... RRRRR... OOOO!!
!
GREAT PHARAOH...
SOME KIND OF NPC?! BUT WHO'S CONTROLLING HIM?!
IT CAN'T BE...

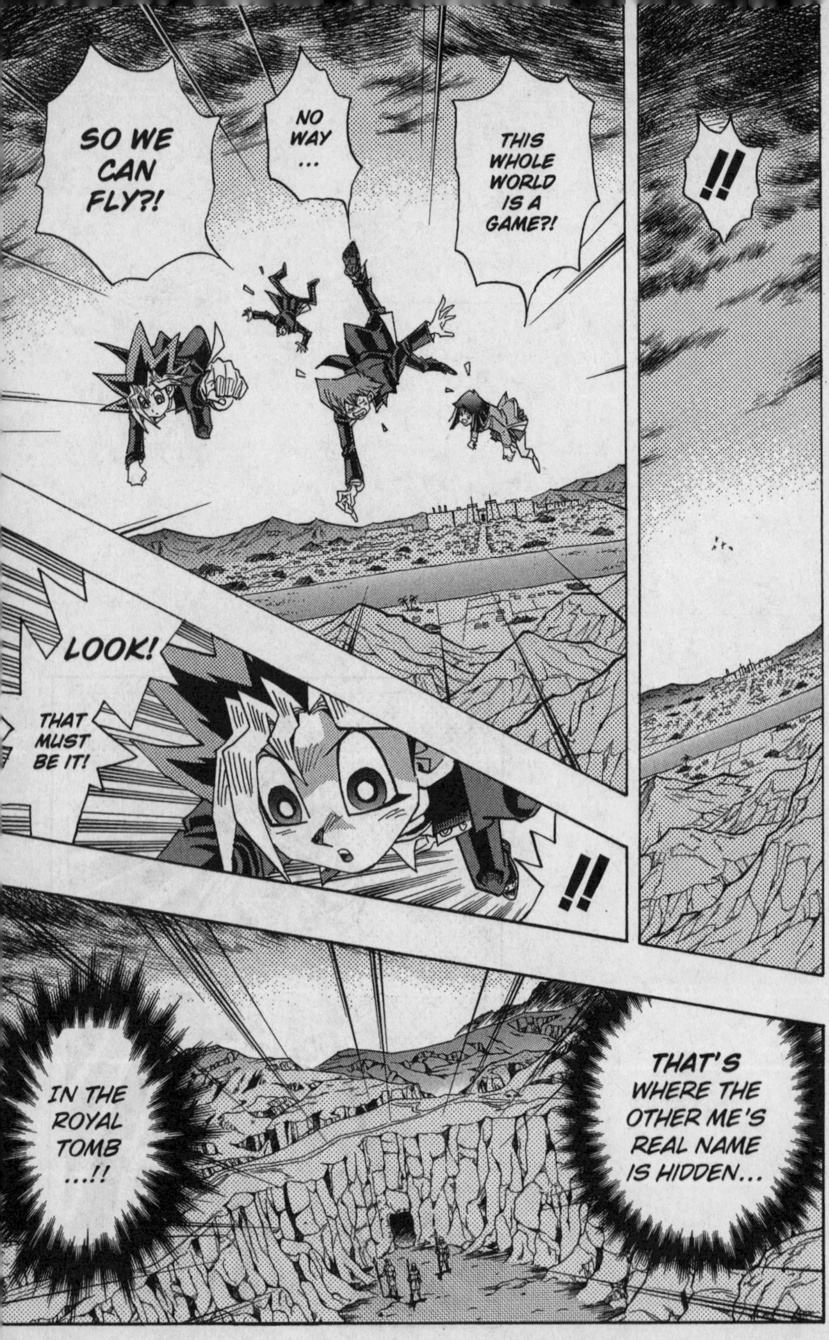
!!
THIS WHOLE WORLD IS A GAME?!
NO WAY ...
SO WE CAN FLY?!
LOOK!
THAT MUST BE IT!
!!
THAT'S WHERE THE OTHER ME'S REAL NAME IS HIDDEN...
IN THE ROYAL TOMB ...!!

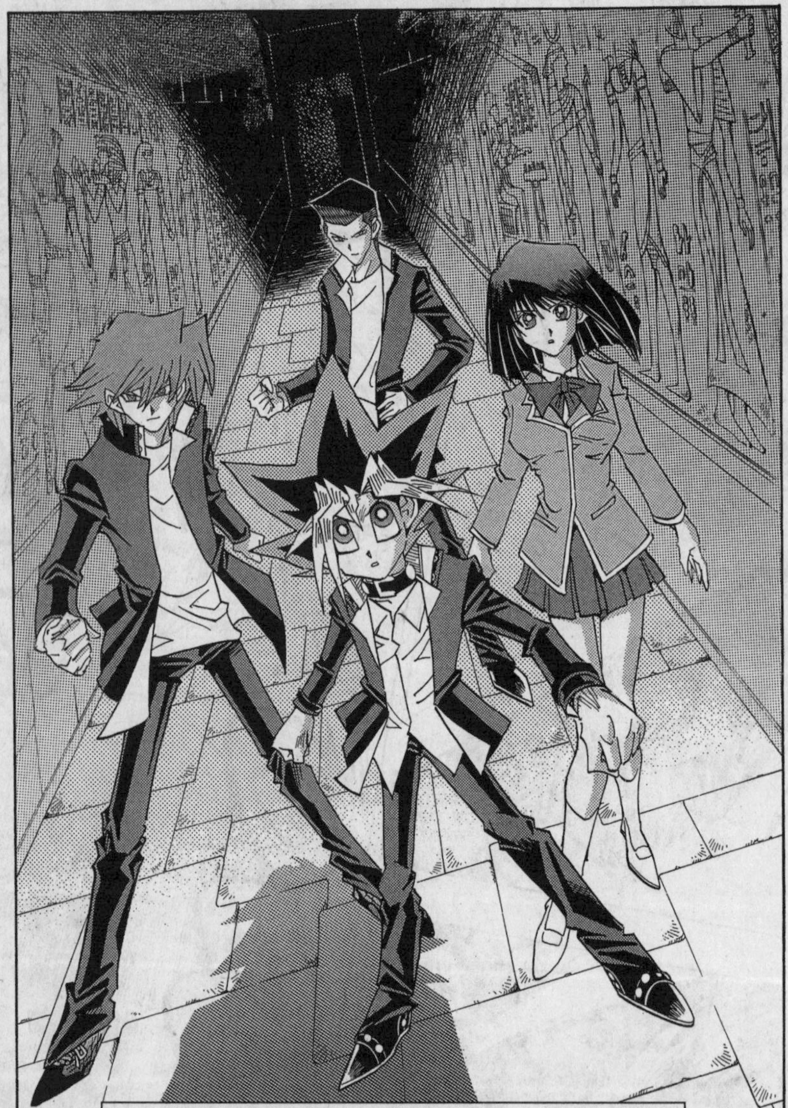
Duel 323: Into the Tomb!

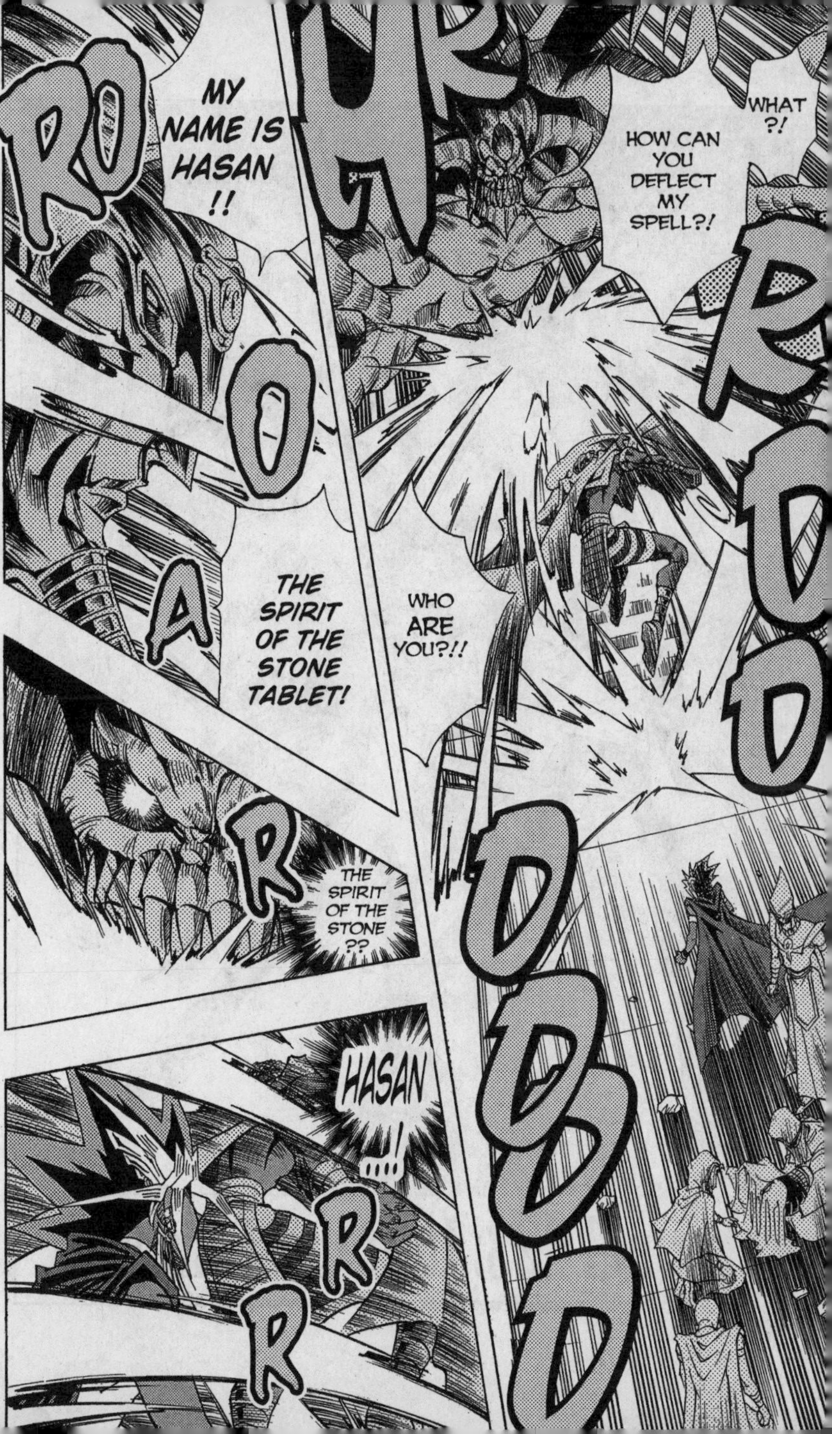
WHAT?!
HOW CAN YOU DEFLECT MY SPELL?!
WHO ARE YOU?!!
MY NAME IS HASAN!!
THE SPIRIT OF THE STONE TABLET!
ROOARRR
THE SPIRIT OF THE STONE??
HASAN...!

READ THIS WAY

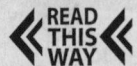

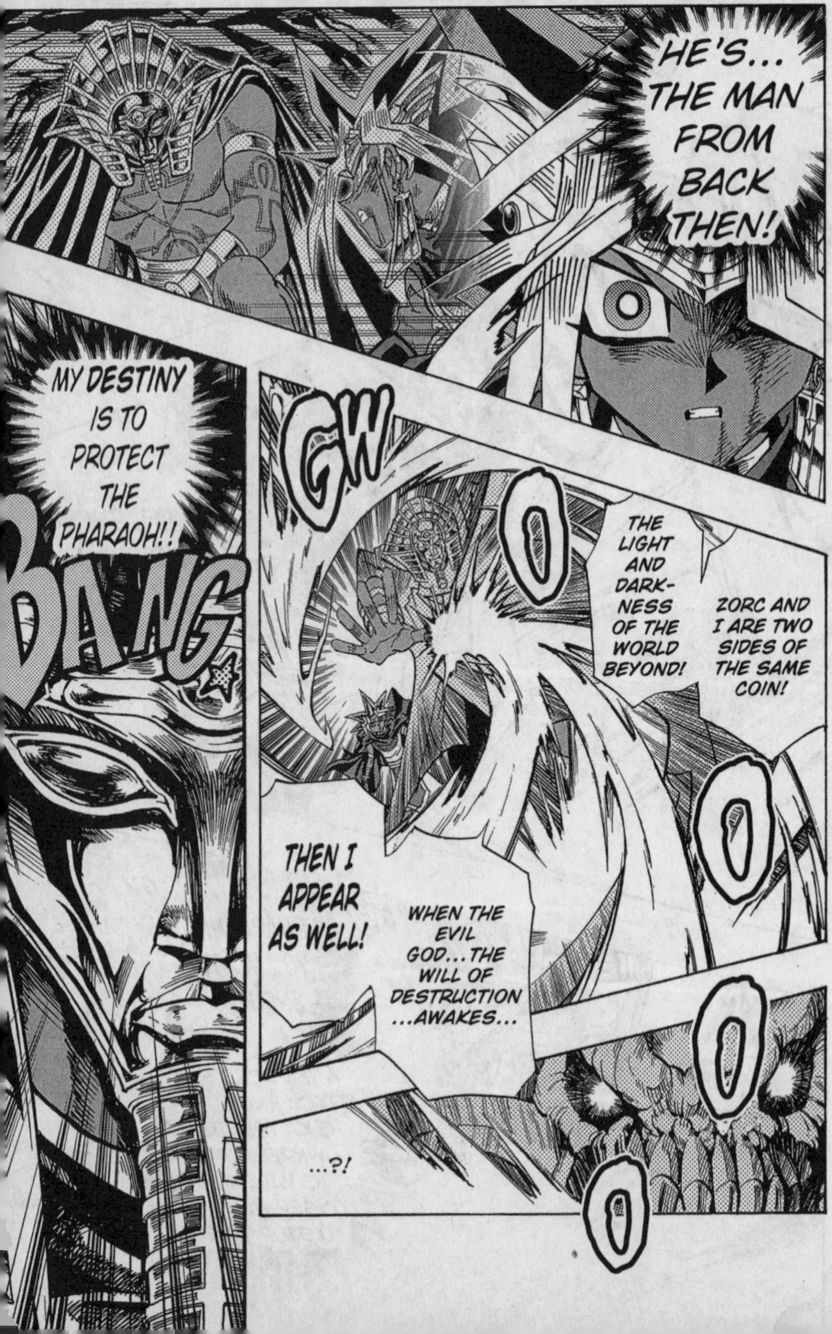
HE'S... THE MAN FROM BACK THEN!
GW
THE LIGHT AND DARKNESS OF THE WORLD BEYOND!
ZORC AND I ARE TWO SIDES OF THE SAME COIN!
WHEN THE EVIL GOD...THE WILL OF DESTRUCTION ...AWAKES...
THEN I APPEAR AS WELL!
...?!
MY DESTINY IS TO PROTECT THE PHARAOH!!
BANG

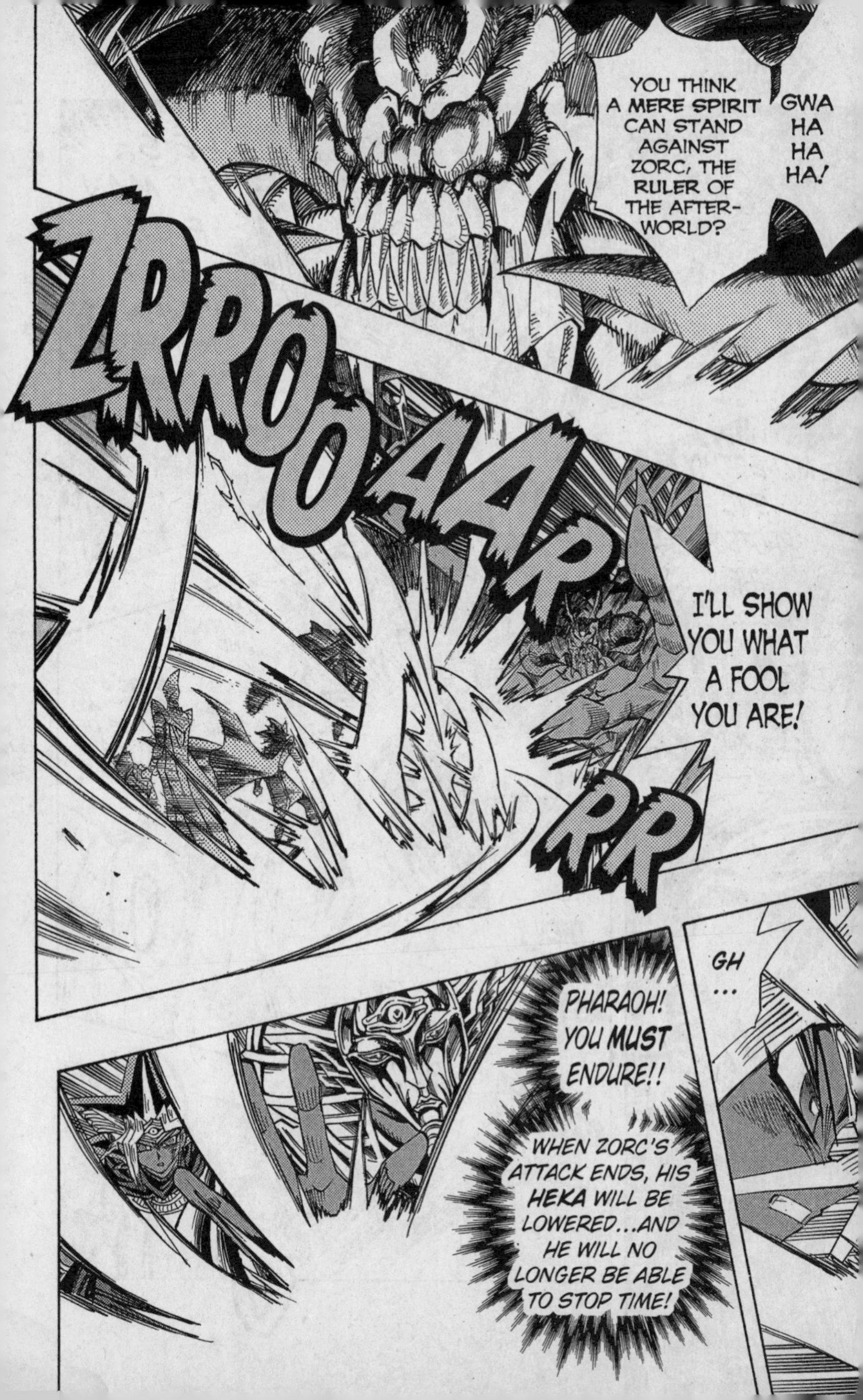
GWA HA HA HA!
YOU THINK A MERE SPIRIT CAN STAND AGAINST ZORC, THE RULER OF THE AFTER-WORLD?
ZRROOAARRR
I'LL SHOW YOU WHAT A FOOL YOU ARE!
GH...
PHARAOH! YOU MUST ENDURE!!
WHEN ZORC'S ATTACK ENDS, HIS HEKA WILL BE LOWERED...AND HE WILL NO LONGER BE ABLE TO STOP TIME!

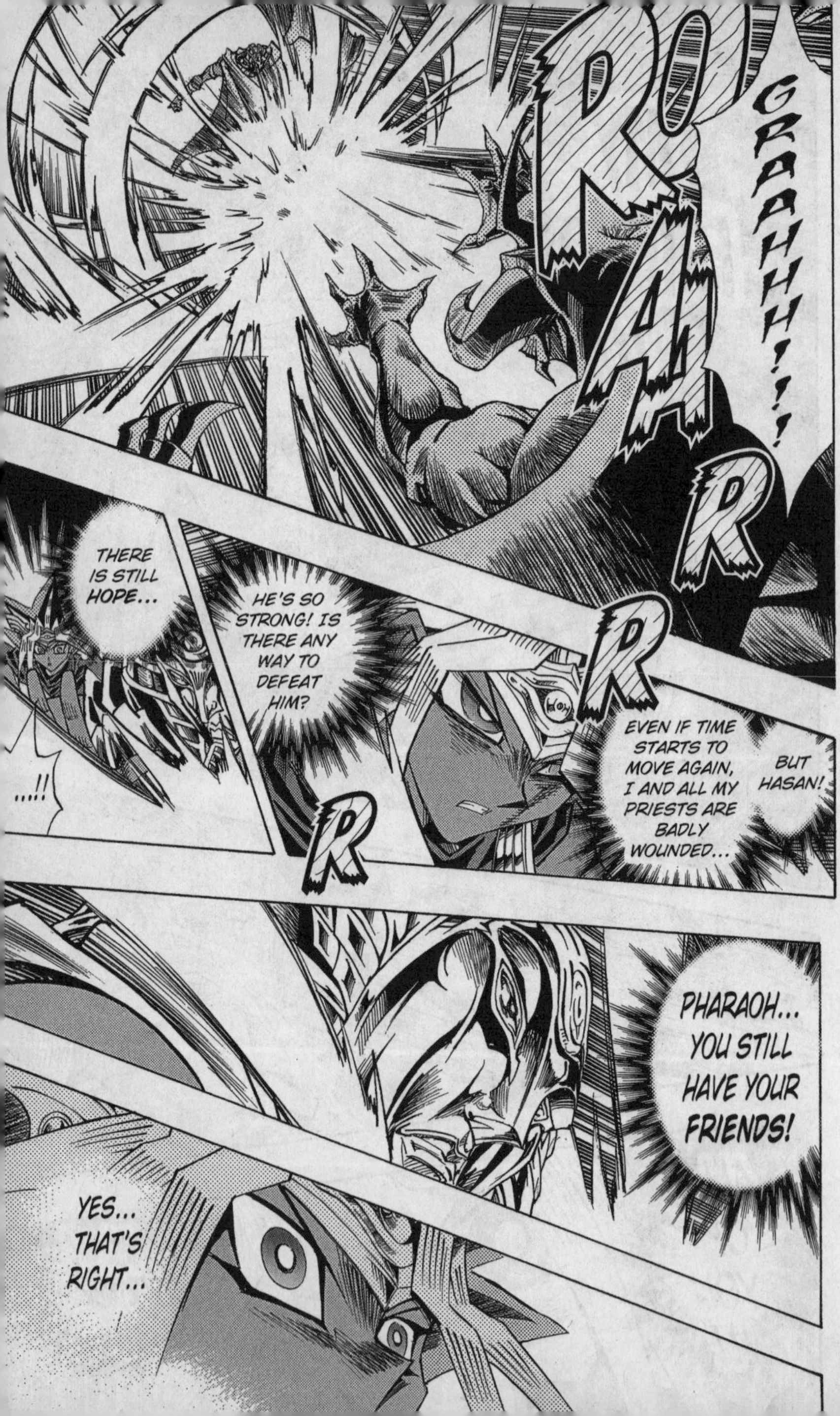
ROARRR
GRAAHHH!!!
BUT HASAN!
EVEN IF TIME STARTS TO MOVE AGAIN, I AND ALL MY PRIESTS ARE BADLY WOUNDED...
HE'S SO STRONG! IS THERE ANY WAY TO DEFEAT HIM?
THERE IS STILL HOPE...
...!!
PHARAOH... YOU STILL HAVE YOUR FRIENDS!
YES... THAT'S RIGHT...

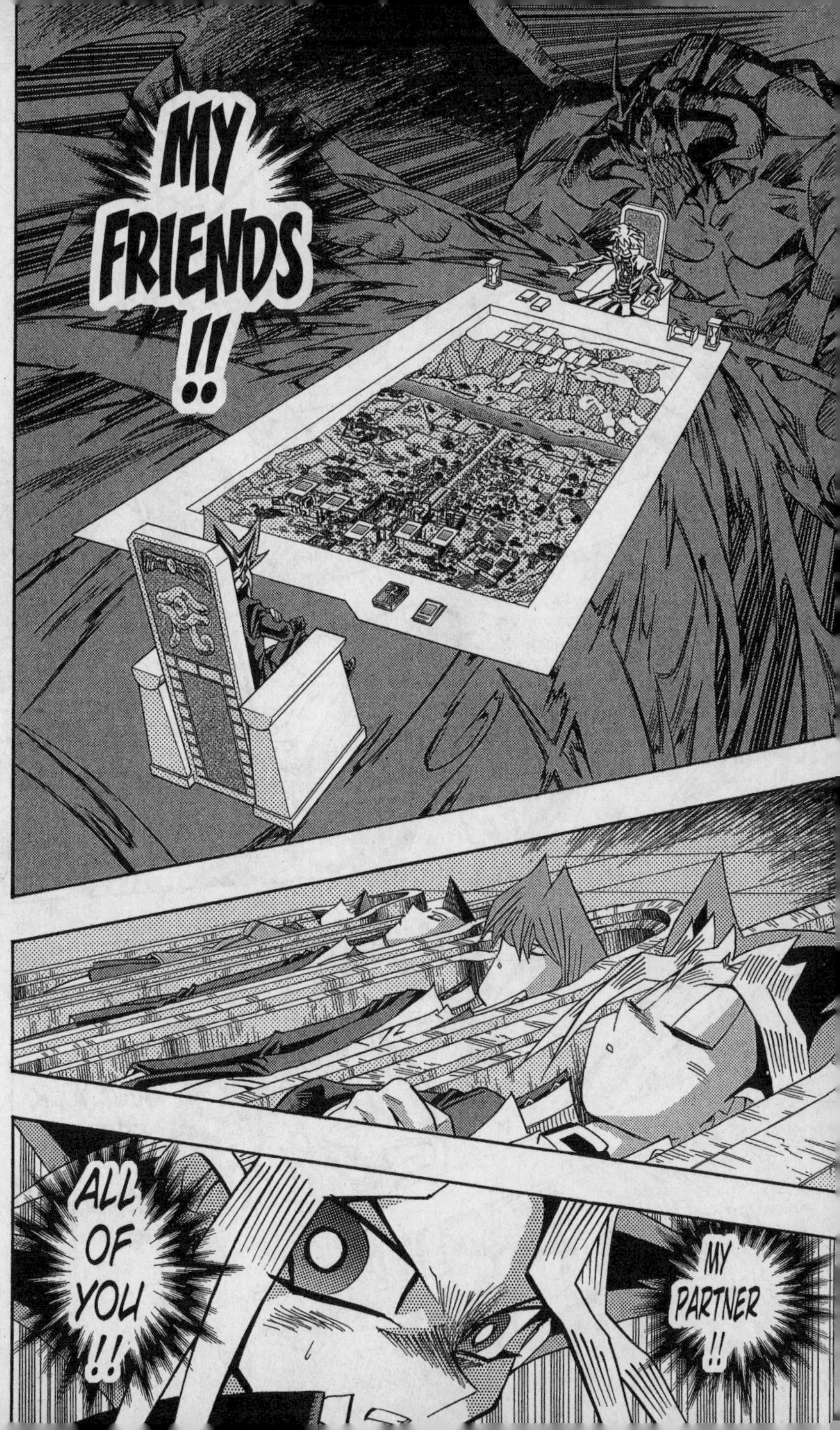
MY FRIENDS!!
MY PARTNER!!
ALL OF YOU!!

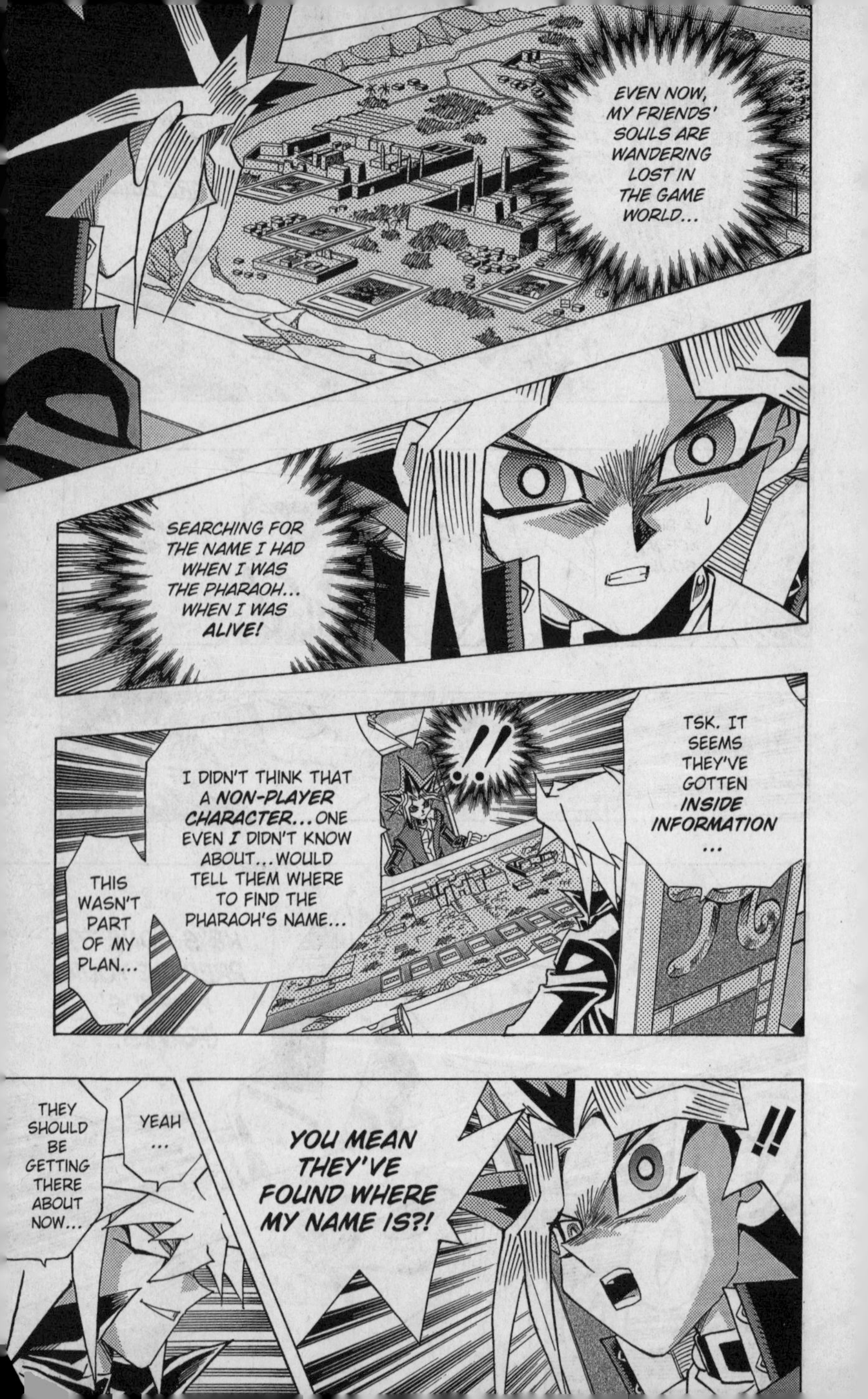

EVEN NOW, MY FRIENDS' SOULS ARE WANDERING LOST IN THE GAME WORLD...
SEARCHING FOR THE NAME I HAD WHEN I WAS THE PHARAOH... WHEN I WAS ALIVE!
TSK. IT SEEMS THEY'VE GOTTEN INSIDE INFORMATION...
!!
I DIDN'T THINK THAT A NON-PLAYER CHARACTER... ONE EVEN I DIDN'T KNOW ABOUT... WOULD TELL THEM WHERE TO FIND THE PHARAOH'S NAME...
THIS WASN'T PART OF MY PLAN...
!!
YOU MEAN THEY'VE FOUND WHERE MY NAME IS?!
YEAH...
THEY SHOULD BE GETTING THERE ABOUT NOW...

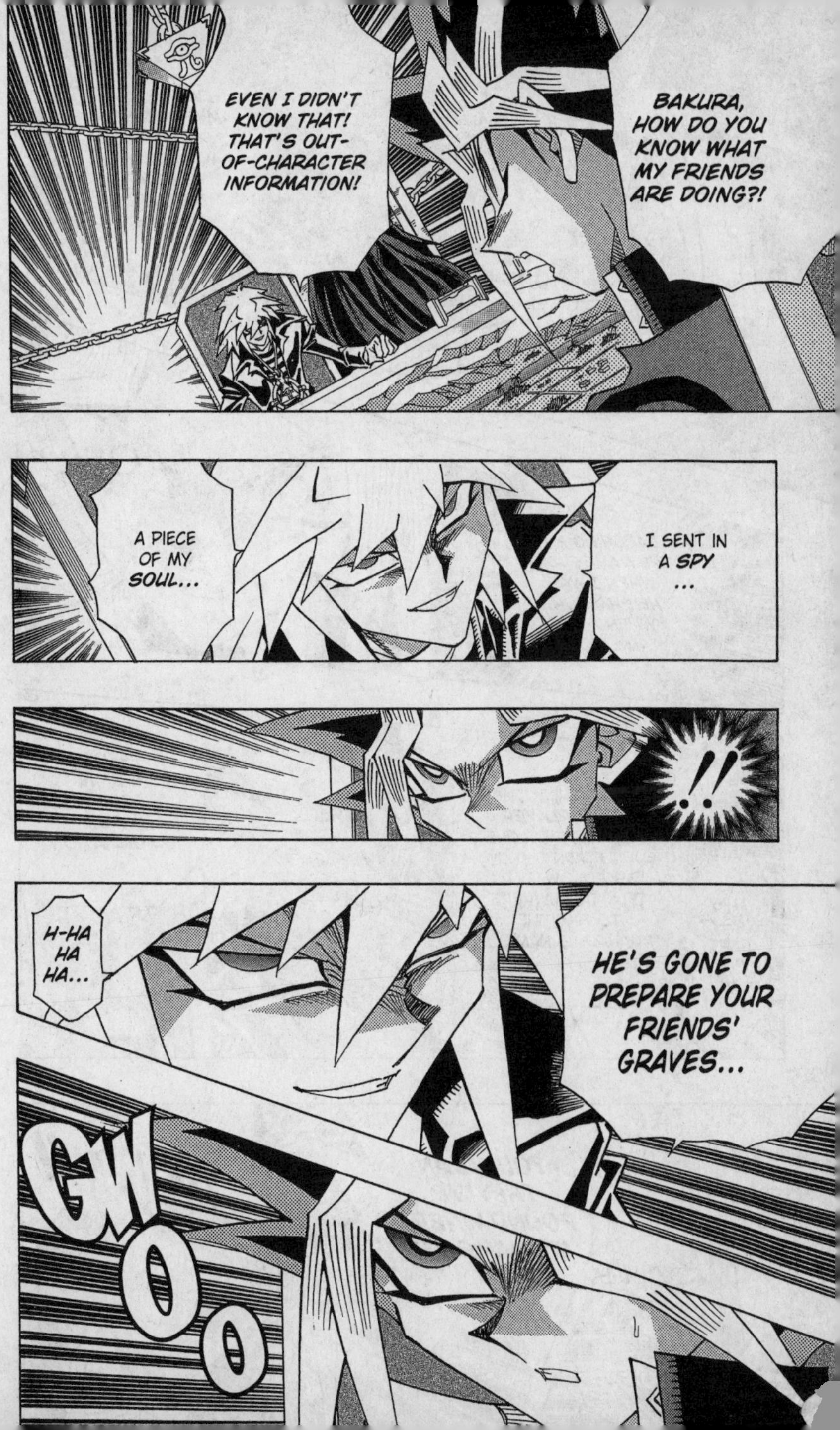
BAKURA, HOW DO YOU KNOW WHAT MY FRIENDS ARE DOING?!
EVEN I DIDN'T KNOW THAT! THAT'S OUT-OF-CHARACTER INFORMATION!
I SENT IN A SPY ...
A PIECE OF MY SOUL...
!!
HE'S GONE TO PREPARE YOUR FRIENDS' GRAVES...
H-HA HA HA...
GWOOO

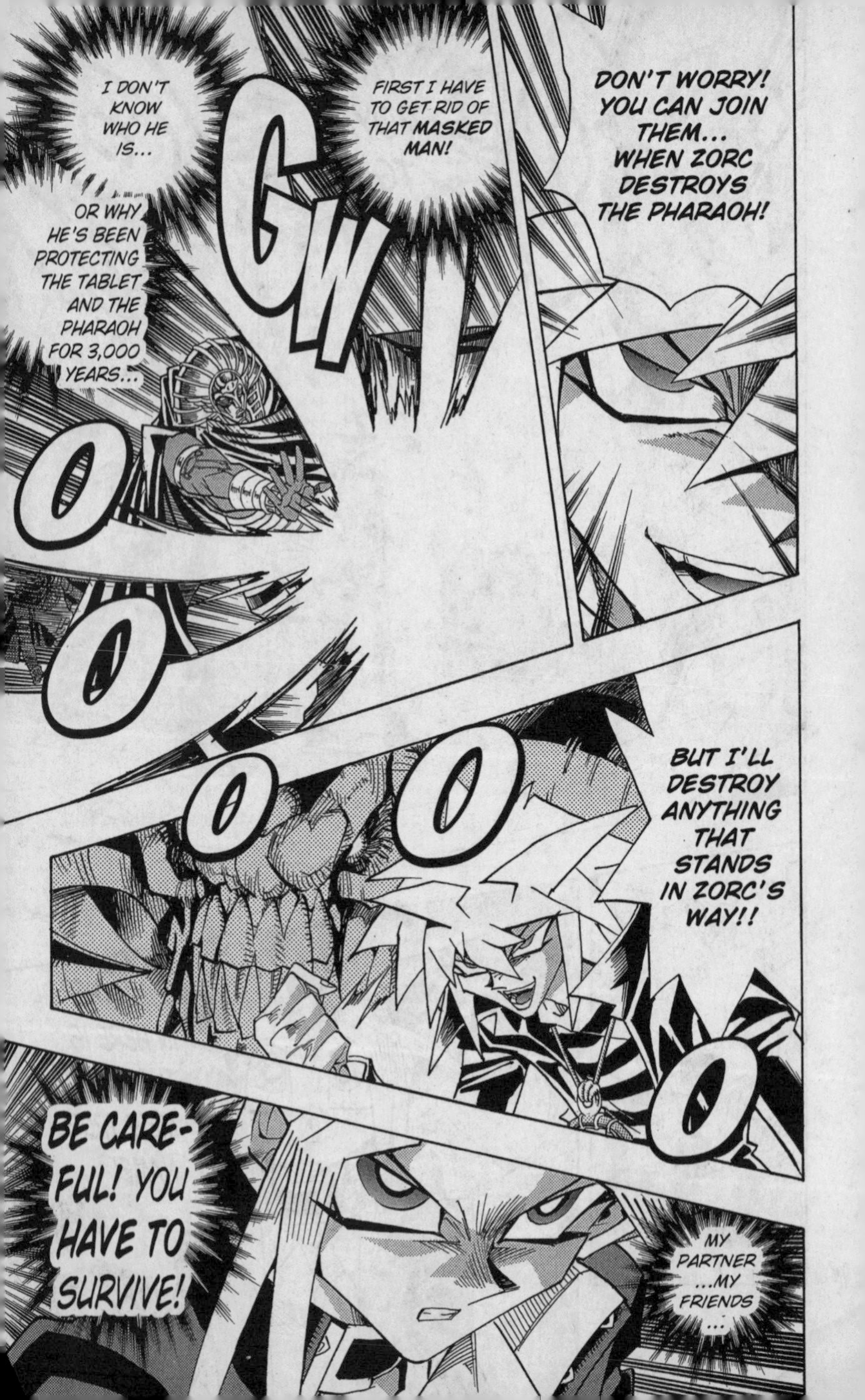
DON'T WORRY! YOU CAN JOIN THEM... WHEN ZORC DESTROYS THE PHARAOH!
FIRST I HAVE TO GET RID OF THAT MASKED MAN!
I DON'T KNOW WHO HE IS...
OR WHY HE'S BEEN PROTECTING THE TABLET AND THE PHARAOH FOR 3,000 YEARS...
GWOOOOOO
BUT I'LL DESTROY ANYTHING THAT STANDS IN ZORC'S WAY!!
MY PARTNER ...MY FRIENDS ...
BE CARE-FUL! YOU HAVE TO SURVIVE!

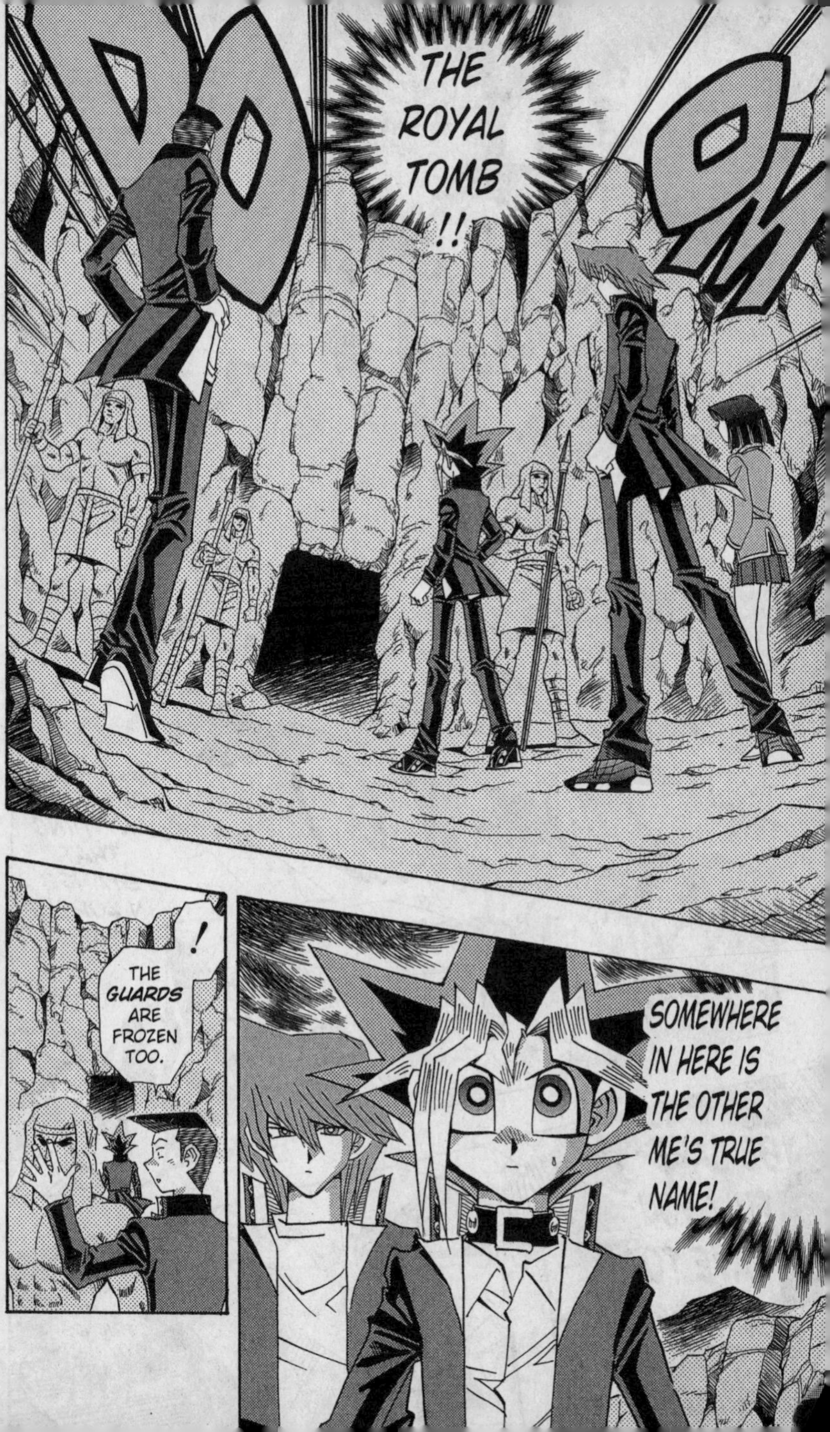
THE ROYAL TOMB!!
THE GUARDS ARE FROZEN TOO.
!
SOMEWHERE IN HERE IS THE OTHER ME'S TRUE NAME!

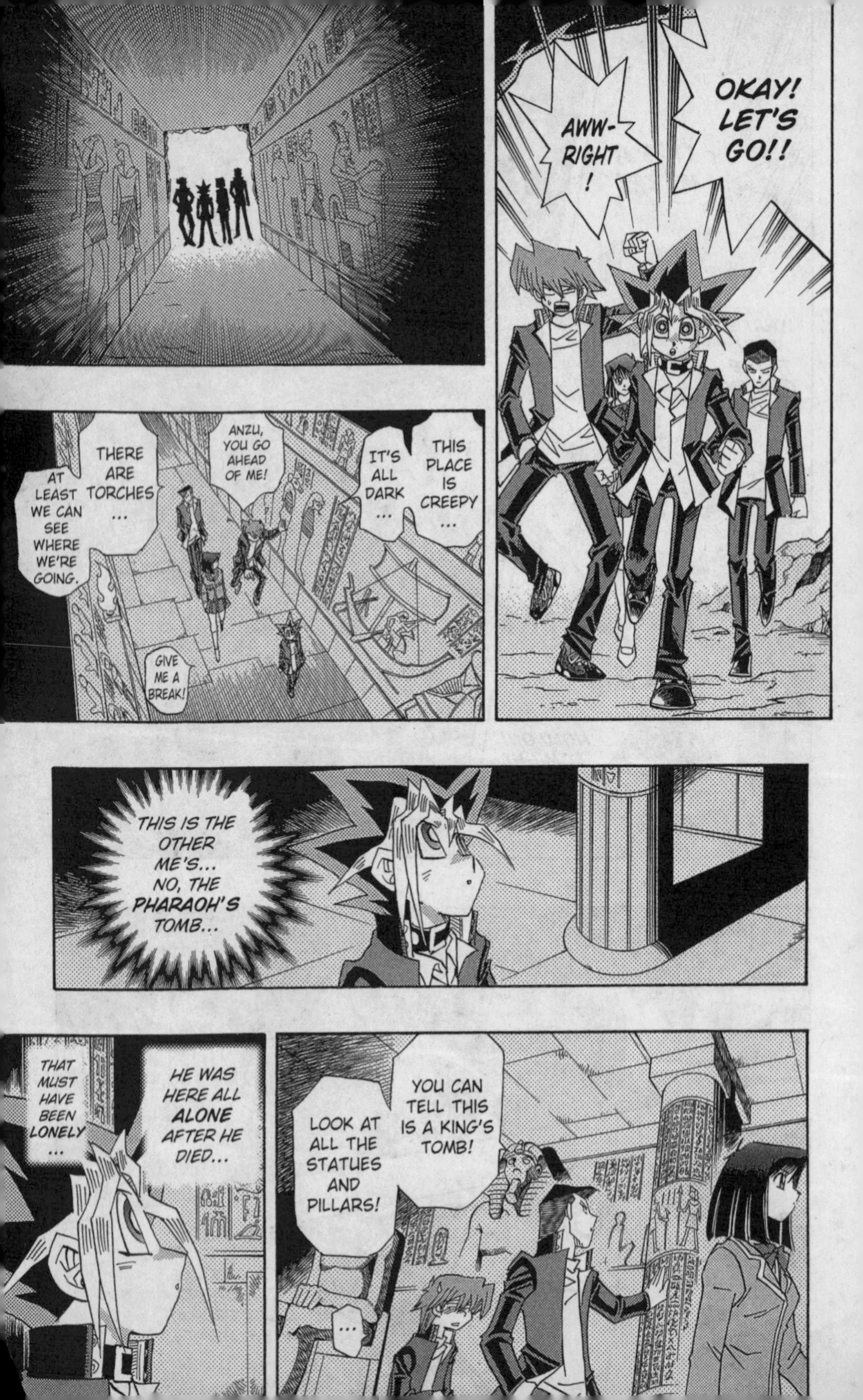
OKAY! LET'S GO!!
AWW-RIGHT!
THIS PLACE IS CREEPY...
IT'S ALL DARK...
ANZU, YOU GO AHEAD OF ME!
THERE ARE TORCHES...
AT LEAST WE CAN SEE WHERE WE'RE GOING.
GIVE ME A BREAK!
THIS IS THE OTHER ME'S... NO, THE PHARAOH'S TOMB...
YOU CAN TELL THIS IS A KING'S TOMB!
LOOK AT ALL THE STATUES AND PILLARS!
...
HE WAS HERE ALL ALONE AFTER HE DIED...
THAT MUST HAVE BEEN LONELY...

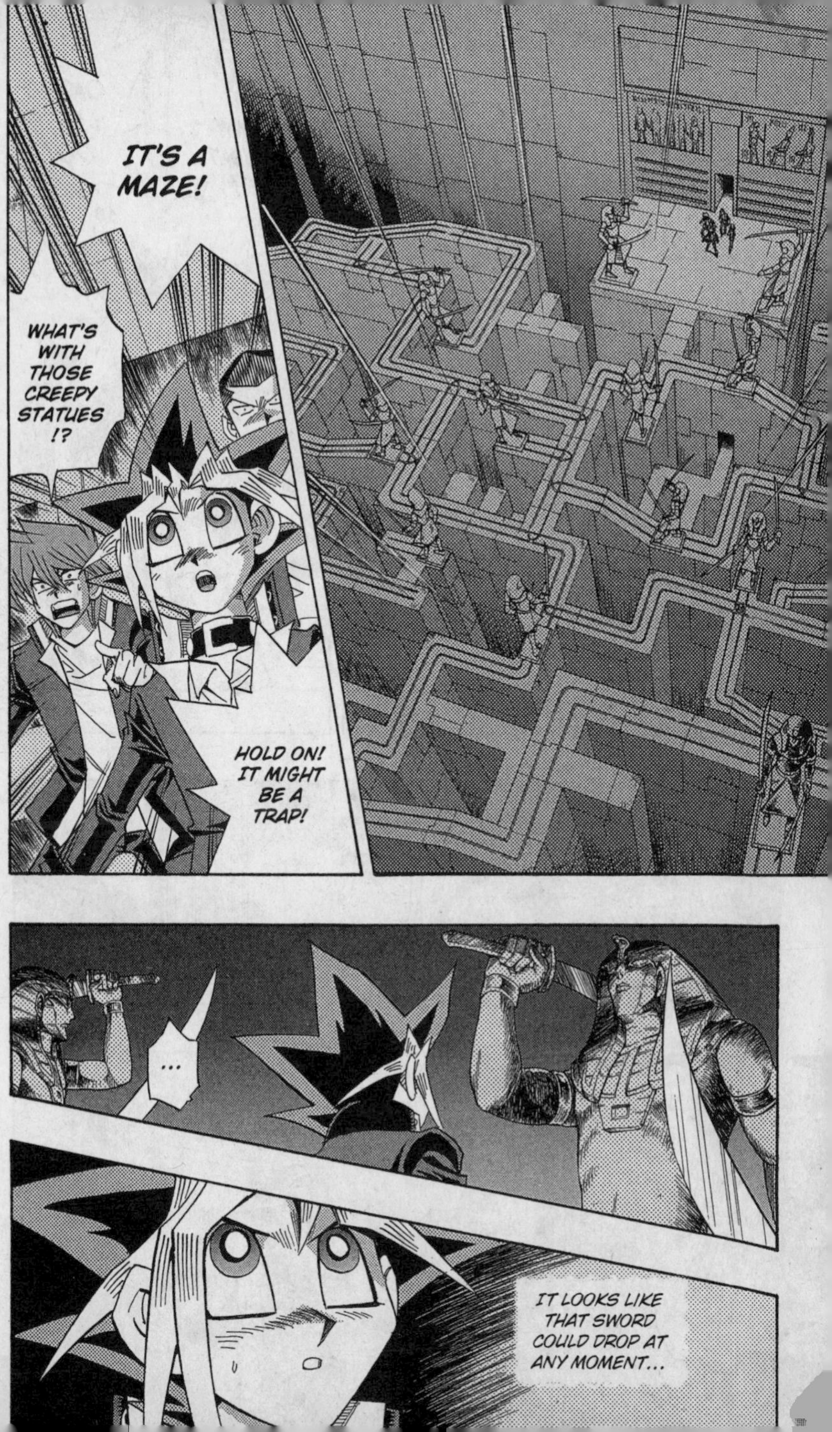
IT'S A MAZE!
WHAT'S WITH THOSE CREEPY STATUES !?
HOLD ON! IT MIGHT BE A TRAP!
...
IT LOOKS LIKE THAT SWORD COULD DROP AT ANY MOMENT...

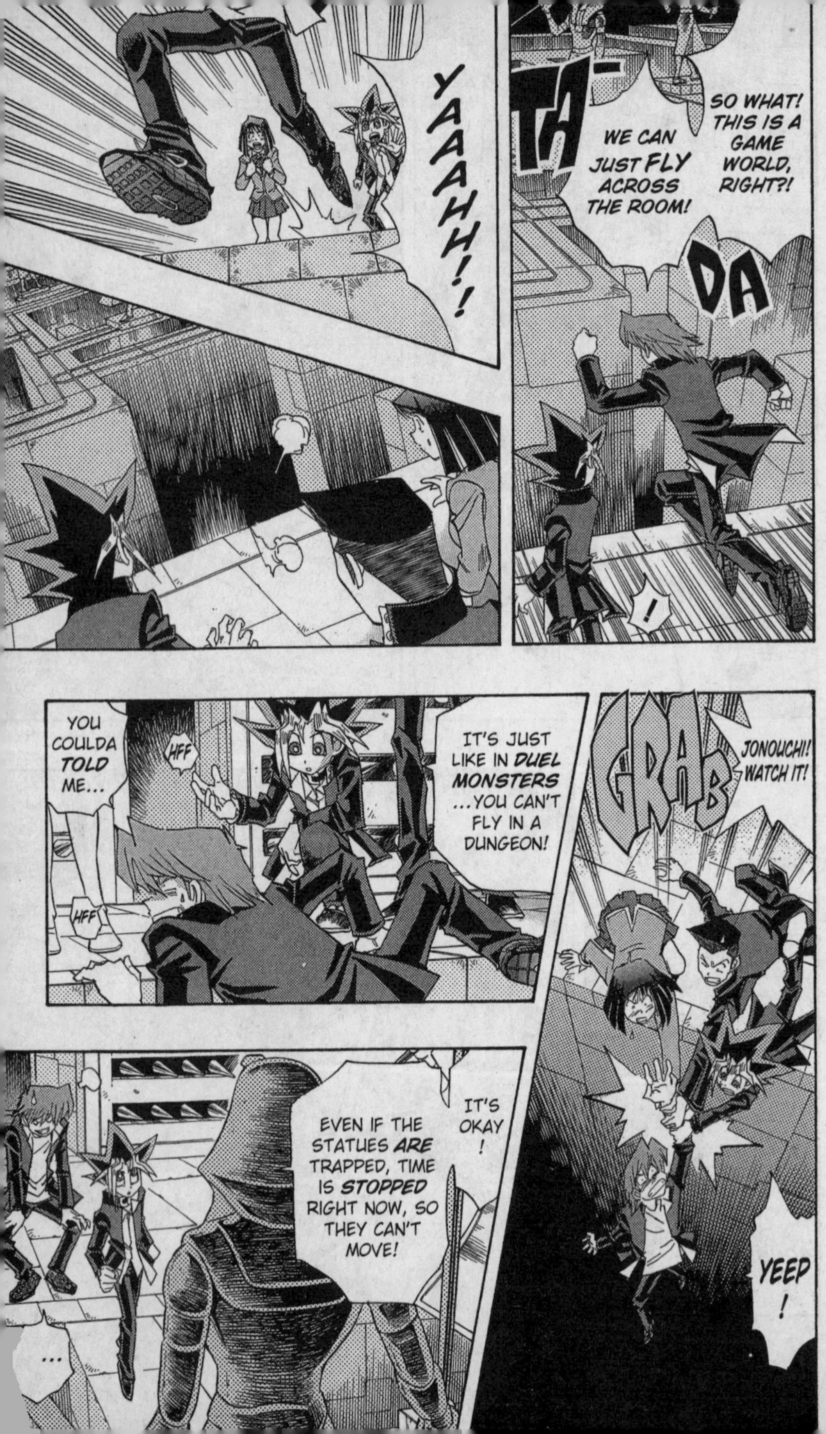
TA-
SO WHAT! THIS IS A GAME WORLD, RIGHT?!
WE CAN JUST FLY ACROSS THE ROOM!
DA
!
YAAAHH!!
GRAB
JONOUCHI! WATCH IT!
YEEP!
IT'S JUST LIKE IN DUEL MONSTERS ...YOU CAN'T FLY IN A DUNGEON!
HFF
YOU COULDA TOLD ME...
HFF
IT'S OKAY!
EVEN IF THE STATUES ARE TRAPPED, TIME IS STOPPED RIGHT NOW, SO THEY CAN'T MOVE!
...

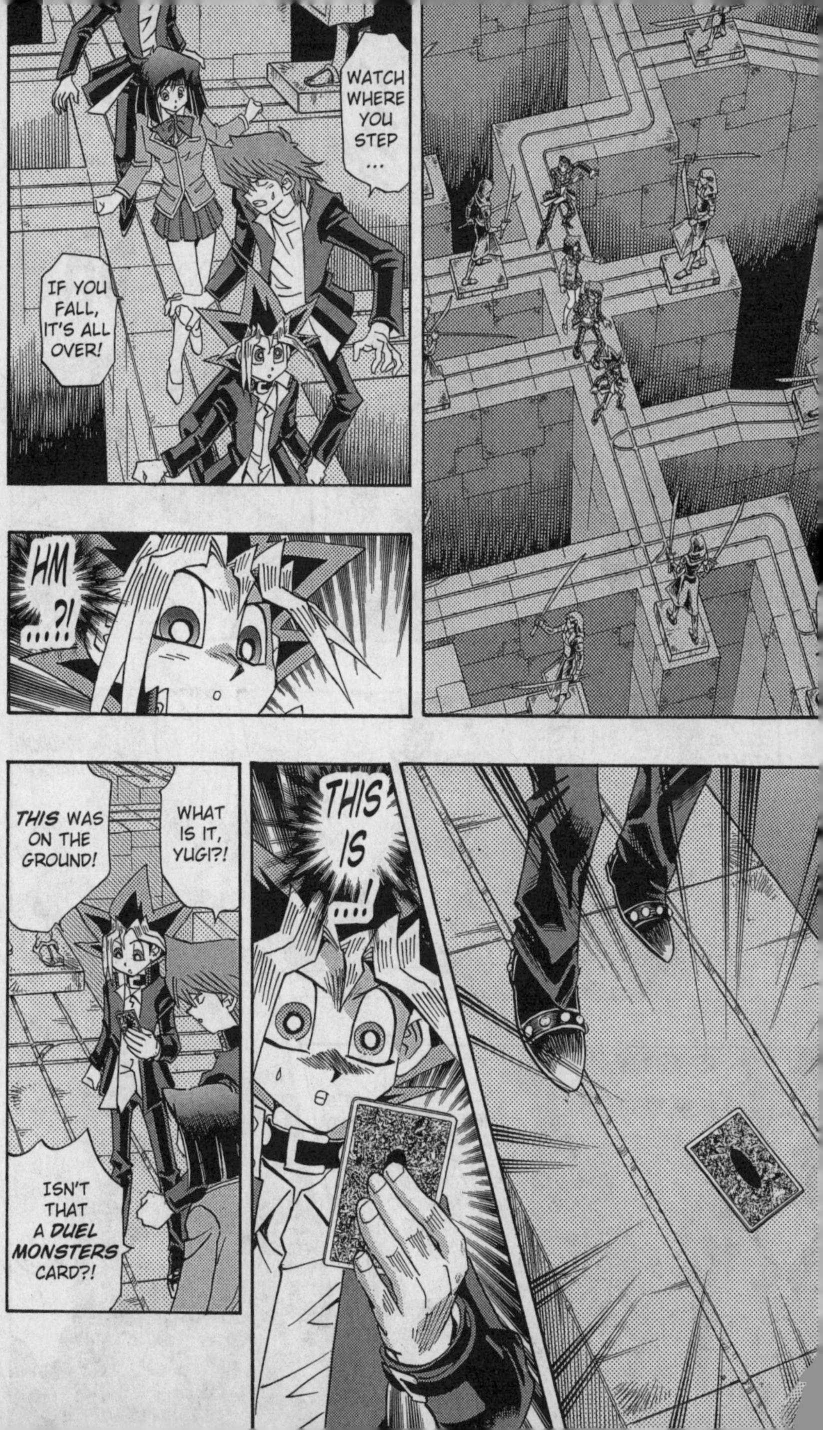
WATCH WHERE YOU STEP ...
IF YOU FALL, IT'S ALL OVER!
HM ...?!
THIS IS ...!!
WHAT IS IT, YUGI?!
THIS WAS ON THE GROUND!
ISN'T THAT A DUEL MONSTERS CARD?!

I WONDER ...!

...

DESTINY BOARD
[PERMANENT
TRAP/SPELL CARD]

This card is activated when "Dark Necrofear" is sent to the graveyard. At the end of each of your opponent's turns, one card of Spirit Message spells the word "DEATH" one by one. If you have all five letters on the field, you win all opposing places.

RMM

RMM

SOME-ONE'S IN HERE ...

RMM

RM

RM

RM

RM

RM

531

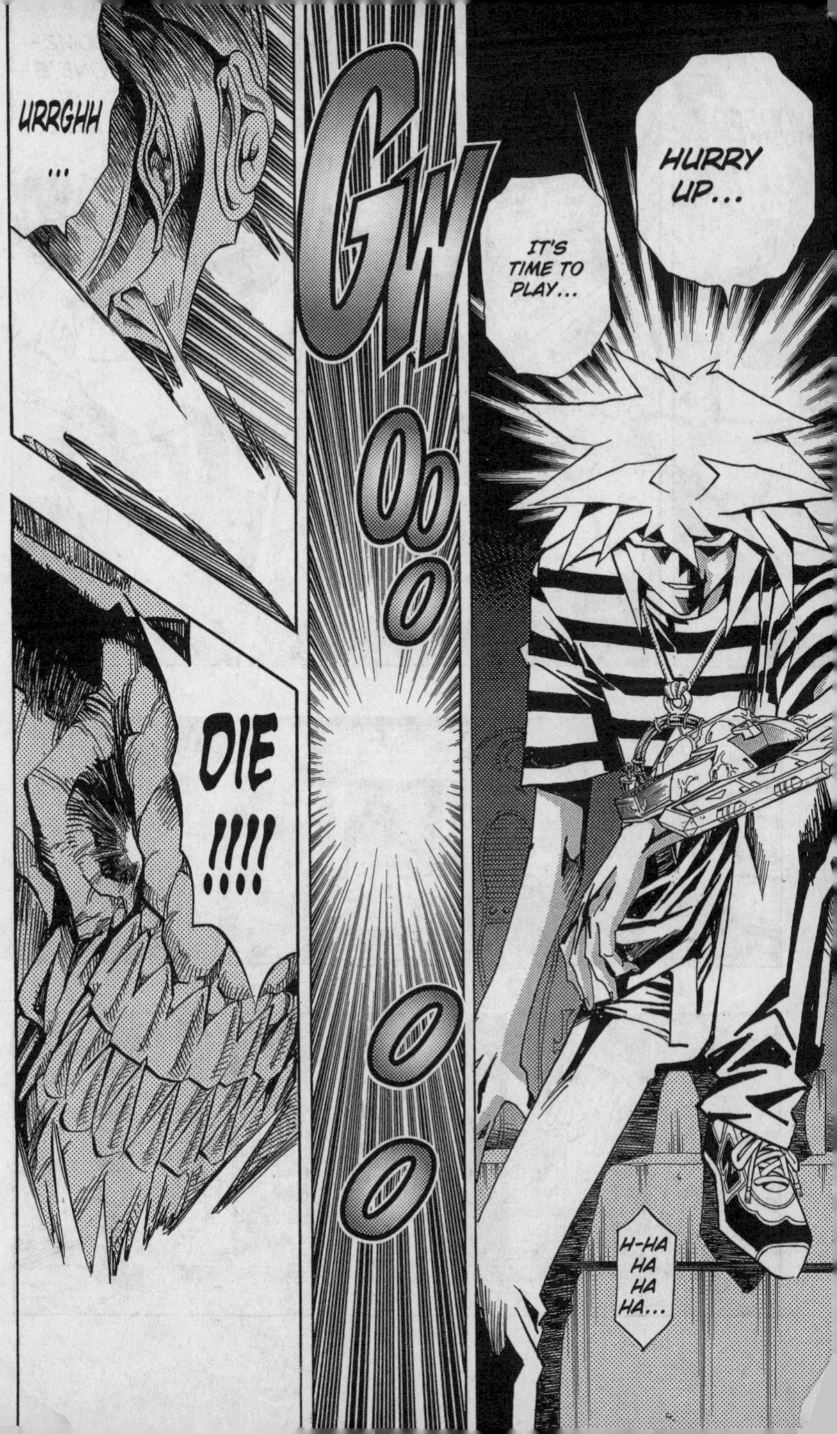
HURRY UP...
IT'S TIME TO PLAY...
H-HA HA HA HA...
GWOOOOOOO
URRGHH ...
DIE !!!!

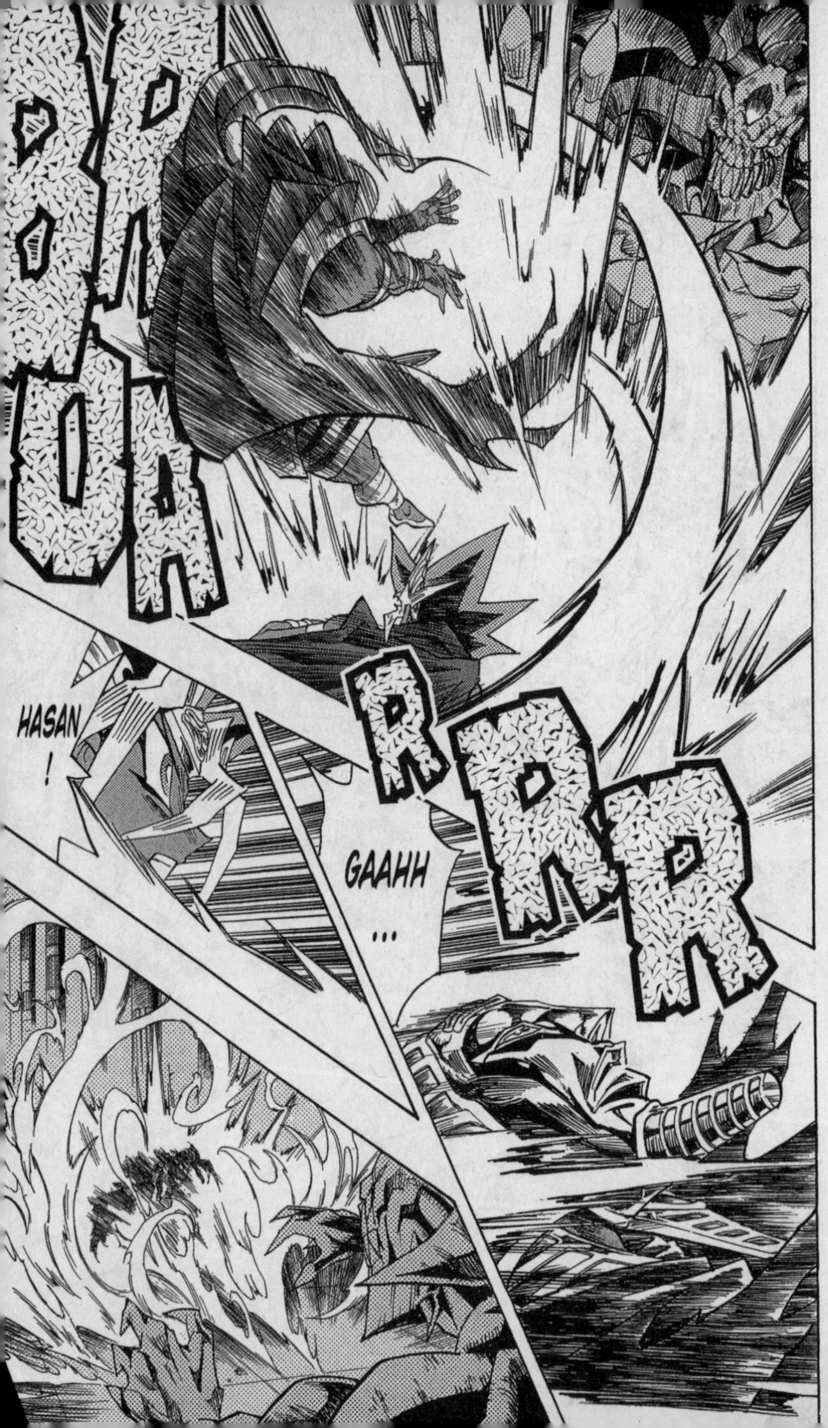
RRR
GAAHH...
HASAN!

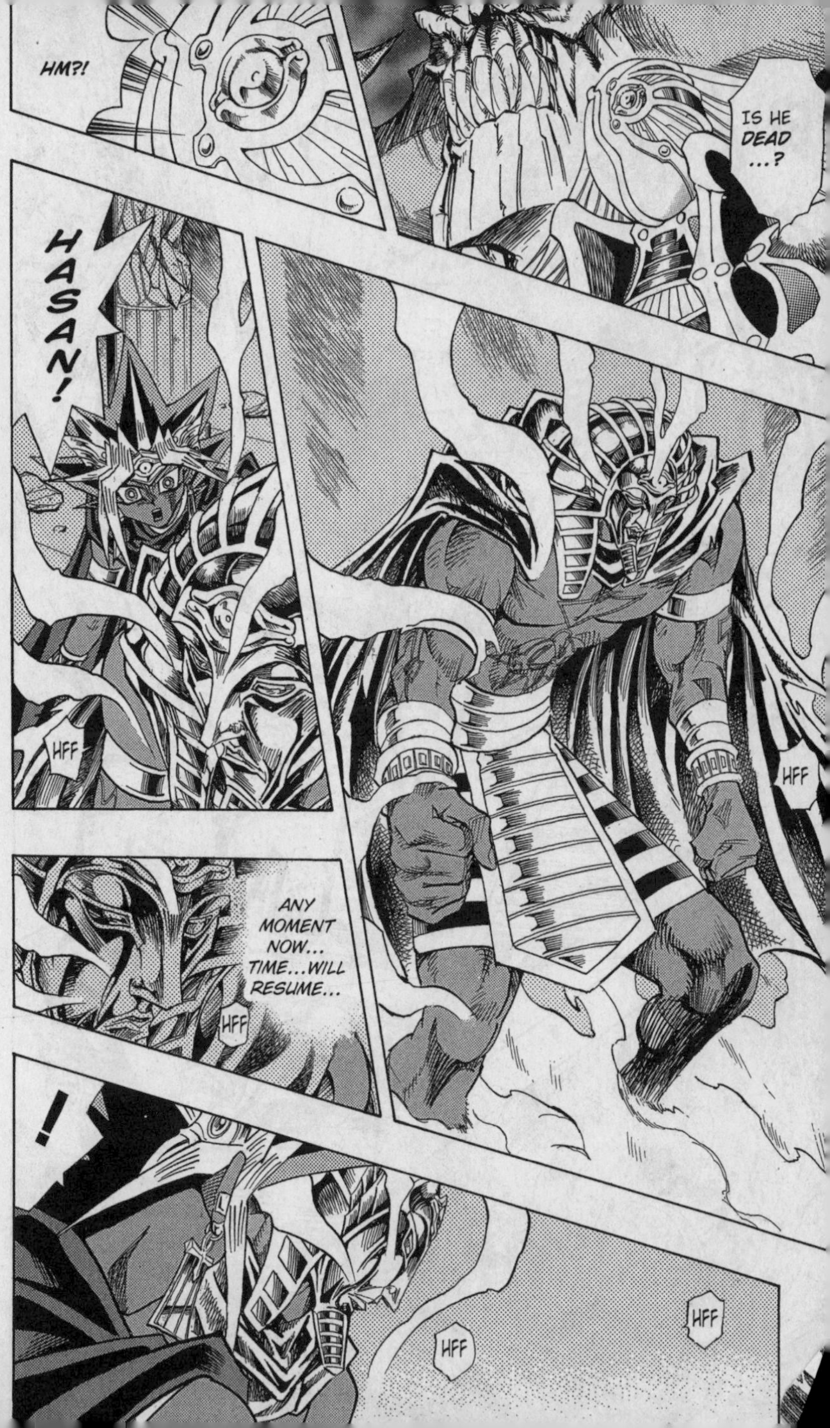
IS HE DEAD ...?
HM?!
HFF
HASAN!
HFF
ANY MOMENT NOW... TIME...WILL RESUME...
HFF
!
HFF
HFF